THE KODANSHA

KANJI SYNONYMS GUIDE

THE KODANSHA
KANJI SYNONYMS GUIDE

EDITOR IN CHIEF

Jack Halpern

Kodansha USA

Published by Kodansha USA, Inc., 451 Park Avenue South, New York, NY 10016

Distributed in the United Kingdom and continental Europe by Kodansha Europe, Ltd.

Printed in Canada through Dai Nippon Printing Co., Ltd.
26 25 24 23 22 21 20 19 18 17   12 11 10 9 8 7 6 5 4 3 2 1

Cover design by Toyoko Kon

Library of Congress Cataloging-in-Publication Data

Names: Halpern, Jack, 1946- author.
Title: The Kodansha Kanji synonyms guide / by Jack Halpern.
Other titles: Kanji synonyms guide
Description: New York, NY : Kodansha USA, Inc., [2017] | Text in English and
    Japanese. | Includes indexes.
Identifiers: LCCN 2017018563 | ISBN 9781568365855
Subjects: LCSH: Japanese language--Synonyms and antonyms--Dictionaries. |
    Japanese language--Writing--Kana. | Chinese
    characters--Dictionaries--Japanese. | Japanese language--Textbooks for
    foreign speakers--English.
Classification: LCC PL667 .H24 2017 | DDC 495.63/12--dc23 LC record available at https://lccn.loc.gov/2017018563

www.kodanshausa.com

CONTENTS
目 次

INDEXES

PREFACE
序 言

The Kodansha Kanji Synonyms Guide (KKSG) is a new type of reference tool that enables intermediate and advanced learners to deepen their understanding of how kanji are used in contemporary Japanese. Based on the author's renowned **The Kodansha Kanji Dictionary: Revised and Expanded** (Kodansha USA), this work serves as the first ever bilingual kanji thesaurus.

The new work offers complete guidance on the precise distinctions between characters of similar meaning, referred to as **kanji synonyms.** Since a proper understanding of the meanings of each character is essential for the effective mastery of the Japanese vocabulary, this is of considerable benefit to the serious student. "Characters" here refers mostly to single characters (one kanji possibly followed by kana) that function mostly as *word elements* (components of compound words), rather than to independent words.

Based on a systematic approach and a firm theoretical foundation, this work enables users to quickly find characters from their meanings, then study those meanings in contrast to other characters that share the same basic concept but differ, often subtly, in meaning. It thus serves as a powerful learning aid because it clearly shows the differences and similarities between closely related kanji. This is achieved in four ways:

1. The alphabetically-arranged **group headwords,** representing the *shared concept* for each **synonym group,** show how the group members *resemble* each other.
2. The **synonym keywords** show at a glance how the group members *differ* from each other.
3. The **character meanings** show in greater detail the distinctive features of each group member.
4. The many **compound words** illustrate how each kanji functions (mostly) as a word element.

It is important to note that the core meanings and character meanings serve as a practical guide to kanji usage because they are based on actual occurrences, and because they are illustrated by many compound words. These are drawn from the author's kanji dictionaries, such as **The Kodansha Kanji Dictionary,** while avoiding the historical and archaic meanings often found in traditional kanji dictionaries.

The new approach to the study of kanji presented here motivates the learner to explore the nuances of closely related characters by studying them together, rather than as isolated units. This helps the learner better understand their distinctive features, while stimulating a desire to learn. It also provides the educator and scholar with a valuable source of reference data for creating learning materials.

It is my sincere hope that this unique work will help Japanese language learners deepen their knowledge of written Japanese in general, and the subtle difference between kanji synonyms in particular.

ACKNOWLEDGMENTS

I wish to extend my heartfelt gratitude to the team of editors, programmers, and consultants for **The Kodansha Kanji Dictionary** upon which this dictionary is based. Special recognition is due to the team of editors and programmers engaged in the editing, proofreading, and automated typesetting of this work, without whose contributions it would not have seen the light of day.

KIYOSHI ITO	Software Engineer, The CJK Dictionary Institute
NICOLA METTIFOGO	Typesetter, The CJK Dictionary Institute
KIMIKO MORISHITA	Senior Editor, The CJK Dictionary Institute
TYLER REID	Software Engineer, The CJK Dictionary Institute

November 2017
Saitama, Japan

JACK HALPERN
Editor in Chief

INTRODUCTION
序 説

1 KANJI SYNONYMS

The words of a language form a closely linked network of interdependent units. The meaning of a word or expression cannot really be understood unless its relationships with other closely related words are taken into account. For example, such words as *kill, murder,* and *execute* share the meaning of 'put to death', but differ considerably in usage and connotation. Similarly, in Japanese there are many kanji that share a common meaning but differ in detail, such as 破 BREAK, 崩 CRUMBLE, 壊 BREAK DOWN and 折 BREAK OFF. Intermediate and advanced learners of Japanese need to distinguish between such similar kanji in order to gain a full understanding of their individual shades of meaning.

2 IN-DEPTH UNDERSTANDING

Let us see how **The Kodansha Kanji Synonyms Guide** helps the learner gain an in-depth understanding of four members of the **synonym group BREAK.**

破 ▷BREAK
　break, smash
　破壊する はかいする break (down), destroy,
　　wreck

壊 ▷BREAK DOWN
　break down, destroy, smash; (of a dam) **burst**
　壊滅 かいめつ destruction, annihilation

崩 ▷CRUMBLE
　crumble, collapse
　崩壊する ほうかいする collapse, crumble, break
　　down, cave in

折 ▷BREAK OFF
　**break off (as a branch), break (a bone), snap
　　(in two), split**
　折半 せっぱん halving

The **synonym keyword** (usually a **core meaning**), preceded by the symbol ▷, is described in more detail by the **character meaning.** In this case 'break, smash' for 破 and 'break down, destroy, smash etc.' for 壊. As can be seen, whereas 破 means 'to break' in general, 壊 refers to destruction, 折 implies the application of a sudden force to such things as branches and bones, 崩 denotes 'breaking into small pieces', and so on. The many compound words (only one for each member is shown above) illustrate how each kanji functions as a word element (as a morpheme on the word formation level) and sometimes as an independent word.

Comparing the character meanings and illustrative compounds of the synonym group members to each other provides a deeper understanding of their (often subtle) differences and similarities.

3 CORE MEANINGS

Most of the synonym keywords are actually the (or one of the) **core meaning(s)** of the kanji synonym in question. This is a concise keyword that provides a clear grasp of the central or most fundamental concept that links the principal senses of a character into a single conceptual unit, as illustrated below.

Consider KEEP, one of the core meanings of 留:

Arbitrary List	Expansion from Core
keep from moving	KEEP in place
detain	KEEP in custody
leave behind	KEEP for future use

By grasping that the central concept represented by 留 is KEEP, one can immediately see that such seemingly unrelated ideas as 'keep in place' and 'detain' are merely variants of the same basic concept. The core meaning thus *integrates* widely differing senses into a single conceptual unit.

The core meaning is one of the salient features of **The Kodansha Kanji Dictionary** (KKD) and **The Kodansha Kanji Learner's Dictionary** (KKLD), and is used here to help show the often fine distinctions between closely related kanji. For a fuller understanding of the kanji in question, refer to the entry in KKLD, the entry number for which can be found to the right of the kanji synonyms entry preceded by the symbol Ⓚ.

4 ENTRY FORMAT

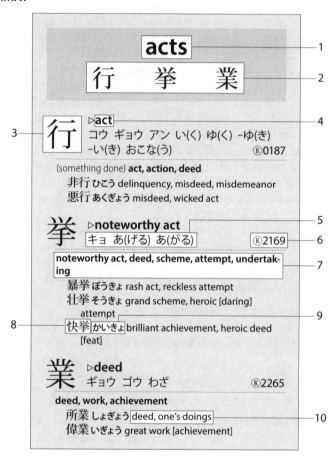

Below is a description of the various components of synonym group entry.

1. The **group headword** is a word or phrase that concisely expresses the semantic relationship, usually the *shared concept*; that is, the meaning shared by the members of a synonym group.

2. The **synonym group** is a collection of two or more kanji synonyms. Closely related synonyms are usually located in close proximity.

3. The **kanji synonym** is a single kanji character (usually a word element) that is a member of a synonym group.

4. The **synonym keyword,** preceded by the symbol ▷, is a concise keyword that aptly represents the sense of a kanji synonym that is relevant to the synonym group (usually identical to one of the **core meanings**).

5. The **character readings,** given in katakana for *on* readings and hiragana for *kun* readings, cover the official readings approved in the Jōyō Kanji list and some important unapproved readings as well. *Okurigana*

(kana endings) conforming to the official rules are shown in parentheses.

6. The **KKLD number,** preceded by the symbol Ⓚ, is the entry number of **The Kodansha Kanji Learner's Dictionary** for characters present in that dictionary.

7. The **character meanings** give the English equivalent for the kanji synonyms in a manner that shows its distinctive feature in relation to the other members of the synonym group.

8. The **compound words** illustrate how each kanji functions as a word or word element.

9. The **compound readings,** given in hiragana, are the readings of the compound words.

10. The **equivalent** is the English translation for each compound word.

5 HOW TO LOCATE AN ENTRY

The kanji synonym groups or individual kanji synonym entries can be located in three ways:

1. The synonym groups in the main body of this book are arranged alphabetically by their **group headwords,** such as **accompany.** If you know the group headword or something close to it you can leaf through the pages to find the desired synonym group for that headword.

2. The **On-Kun Index** lists the characters alphabetically by their *on* (Chinese-derived) and *kun* (native Japanese) readings. It offers a quick way to find a synonym group from the reading of one of its members.

3. The **Group Index** is an alphabetical list of keywords for quickly finding synonym groups from their group headwords, synonym keywords, or their derivatives. For example, if you look up the word "advance" you find the following group headwords, **advance • make progress • move forward,** separated by a middle dot. This means that characters with the synonym keyword **advance** can be found in these three synonym groups.

6 SEMANTIC RELATIONSHIPS

Below is some of the linguistic background related to kanji synonyms. Several categories of semantic relationships exist among the synonym group members and the group headword, as explained below (these categories are not necessarily mutually exclusive).

1. *Class-inclusion,* or *kind of,* is a relationship in which the group headword (*superordinate word*) is a general term that includes the meanings of the specific terms (*hyponyms*) represented by the individual group members:

graves
墓 GRAVE
墳 TUMULUS
陵 IMPERIAL MAUSOLEUM
塚 grave mound

2. *Synonymy,* a relationship in which the group members share a basic meaning or are similar or identical in meaning, is often indicated by a group headword given in the singular form:

matter
質 MATTER
物 substance
材 MATERIAL
料 MATERIALS
資 material resources

3. *Part-whole,* a relationship in which the meanings of the group members are part of each other or of the thing represented by the group headword, is often indicated by a headword in the form "parts of…" or "… parts":

parts of towns
区 WARD
街 CITY QUARTER
町 town section (*cho*)
丁 TOWN SUBSECTION (*chome*)
字 village or town section

4. *Complementarity* is a relationship in which the meanings of the group members contrast with each other and are mutually exclusive:

siblings
妹 YOUNGER SISTER
姉 OLDER SISTER
兄 OLDER BROTHER
弟 YOUNGER BROTHER

7 KANJI INTEGRATED TOOLS

The Kodansha Kanji Synonyms Guide is the latest addition to **Kanji Integrated Tools** (KIT), a series of computer-edited dictionaries and software applications for the effective study of kanji. The use of the latest computational lexicography techniques ensures that all KIT dictionaries and applications are tightly integrated and of consistent quality. To date (November 2017), the following dictionaries have been published:

1.	New Japanese-English Character Dictionary (NJECD)	Kenkyusha, 1990	Japanese market edition
2.	New Japanese-English Character Dictionary (NJECD-NTC)	NTC, 1993	international edition
3.	New Japanese-English Character Dictionary (NJECD-EB)	Nichigai Associates, 1995	electronic book edition
4.	The Kodansha Kanji Learner's Dictionary (KALD)	Kodansha International, 1999	learner's edition
5.	The Kodansha Kanji Learner's Dictionary (KALD-ED)	CASIO, 2007	electronic dictionary edition
6.	Japanese-Romanian Gakushu Kanji Dictionary (KALD-RM)	Polirom, 2008	Romanian edition
7.	The Kodansha Kanji Learner's Dictionary for iOS (iKALD)	The CJK Dictionary Institute, 2012	iOS edition
8.	The Kodansha Kanji Learner's Dictionary (KKLD)	Kodansha USA, 2013	revised and expanded
9.	The Kodansha Kanji Dictionary (KKD)	Kodansha USA, 2013	new edition of NJECD
10.	The Kodansha Kanji Learner's Dictionary for iOS (iKKLD)	The CJK Dictionary Institute, 2013	iOS edition of KKLD
11.	The Kodansha Kanji Learner's Dictionary (aKKLD)	The CJK Dictionary Institute, 2014	Android edition of KKLD
12.	The Kodansha Kanji Usage Guide (KKUG)	Kodansha USA, 2015	first edition
13.	The Kodansha Kanji Usage Guide for iOS (iKKUG)	The CJK Dictionary Institute, 2015	iOS edition of KKUG
14.	The Kodansha Kanji Synonyms Guide (KKSG)	Kodansha USA, 2018	first edition
15.	The Kodansha Kanji Synonyms Guide for iOS (iKKSG)	The CJK Dictionary Institute, 2018	iOS edition of KKSG

THE KODANSHA

KANJI
SYNONYMS
GUIDE

abnormal
変 奇 畸 怪 妖 妙 異 珍

変 ▷**abnormal**
ヘン か(わる) か(わり) か(える)　　Ⓚ1782

abnormal, extraordinary, unusual, irregular, eccentric, odd
変則の へんそくの irregular, abnormal
変態性欲 へんたいせいよく abnormal sexuality, perversion
変人 へんじん eccentric person, crank
変化 へんげ goblin, ghost

奇 ▷**unusual**
キ　　Ⓚ1902

unusual, strange, odd, extraordinary, queer, eccentric
奇異な きいな unusual, strange
奇人 きじん eccentric (person), queer [odd] fellow
奇妙な きみょうな strange, queer, odd
奇跡(=奇蹟) きせき miracle, wonder
奇談 きだん strange story
珍奇な ちんきな novel, curious; rare; strange
怪奇 かいき mystery, wonder
好奇心 こうきしん curiosity
偏奇 へんき eccentricity

畸 ▷**unusual**
キ

unusual, strange, odd, extraordinary, queer, eccentric
畸人 きじん eccentric (person), queer [odd] fellow

怪 ▷**mysterious**
カイ ケ あや(しい) あや(しむ)　　Ⓚ0264

[also prefix] **mysterious, strange, unusual, suspicious, suspicious-looking**
怪奇 かいき mystery, wonder
怪異な かいいな mysterious, marvelous, grotesque
怪盗 かいとう mysterious thief
怪聞 かいぶん strange rumor, scandal
怪事件 かいじけん mystery case
怪文書 かいぶんしょ mysterious document; subversive literature
怪人物 かいじんぶつ mysterious person

妖 ▷**mysterious**
ヨウ あや(しい)　　Ⓚ0212

mysterious, strange, unusual

妖怪 ようかい ghost, apparition, phantom, goblin
妖精 ようせい fairy, elf, sprite
妖婆 ようば witch, hag
妖術 ようじゅつ black magic, witchcraft, sorcery
妖気 ようき ghostly [unearthly, weird] air [atmosphere]

妙 ▷**strange**
ミョウ　　Ⓚ0210

(arousing marvel) **strange, odd, queer, singular**
奇妙な きみょうな strange, queer, odd
珍妙な ちんみょうな queer, odd, fantastic

異 ▷**not ordinary**
イ こと こと(なる)　　Ⓚ2241

not ordinary: **strange, unusual, abnormal, unorthodox, extraordinary, exceptional, peculiar**
異常な いじょうな abnormal, unusual, extraordinary
異端 いたん heresy, paganism, heterodoxy
異心 いしん treasonous intention, betrayal; eccentricity
異例 いれい singular case, exception
異色の いしょくの novel, unique
異才 いさい genius, prodigy
奇異な きいな unusual, strange

珍 ▷**curious**
チン めずら(しい)　　Ⓚ0814

[also prefix] **curious, strange, queer, odd, funny**
珍妙な ちんみょうな queer, odd, fantastic
珍奇な ちんきな novel, curious; rare; strange
珍現象 ちんげんしょう strange phenomenon
珍紛漢紛 ちんぷんかんぷん gibberish, unintelligible speech

abridge
要 抄 約 略

要 ▷**summarize**
ヨウ かなめ い(る)　　Ⓚ2290

summarize (the important points), outline
要旨 ようし gist, point, essentials, summary; purport
要綱 ようこう outline, gist; general plan
要領 ようりょう gist, essentials; outline; procedure

抄 ▷**excerpt**
ショウ　　Ⓚ0226

excerpt, extract, abridge, select
抄出する しょうしゅつする take excerpts

抄録 しょうろく quotation, summary
抄訳 しょうやく abridged translation
抄本 しょうほん extract, abstract

約 ▷contract
ヤク   Ⓚ1177

[original meaning] **contract, abridge, summarize, shorten**
括約筋 かつやくきん sphincter
制約 せいやく restriction, limitation; condition
集約的な しゅうやくてきな intensive
要約 ようやく summary, abridged statement

略 ▷omit
リャク   Ⓚ1081

omit, leave out
省略する しょうりゃくする omit, abbreviate, abridge
中略 ちゅうりゃく ellipsis, omission (of interior parts)

abstain →AVOID AND ABSTAIN

abstract thing
事　　物

事 ▷abstract thing
ジ　ズ　こと   Ⓚ2986

[also suffix] **abstract thing, affair, matter, fact**
事柄 ことがら matter, affair, circumstances
明白な事 めいはくなこと obvious fact
学校の事を話す がっこうのことをはなす speak about the school, talk about school affairs
物事 ものごと things, matter; everything
勝負事 しょうぶごと gambling, competition, game

物 ▷thing
ブツ　モツ　もの   Ⓚ0777

(abstract entity) **thing(s), matter, affair, something**
物情 ぶつじょう public feeling
物騒な ぶっそうな dangerous, insecure, disturbed
禁物 きんもつ taboo, prohibited thing

accompany
伴　添　陪　侍　従　随

伴 ▷accompany
ハン　バン　ともな(う)   Ⓚ0044

(go along with) **accompany, go with, attend on**
伴奏 ばんそう accompaniment

伴食大臣 ばんしょくだいじん nominal [figurehead] minister
お相伴 おしょうばん participation
同伴する どうはんする accompany, go with
随伴する ずいはんする attend, accompany, follow

添 ▷accompany
テン　そ(える)　そ(う)   Ⓚ0485

accompany, go along with, attend on
添乗員 てんじょういん (escort) courier, tour conductor

陪 ▷accompany a superior
バイ   Ⓚ0492

accompany a superior, perform an action in the company of a superior, keep company with a person of rank, attend upon
陪席 ばいせき sitting with one's superior
陪従する ばいじゅうする wait upon, attend on, accompany
陪食 ばいしょく dining with a superior
陪乗する ばいじょうする ride in the same carriage [car] (with a superior), attend on (one's superior) in the same carriage
陪審 ばいしん jury
陪侍 ばいじ attending on the nobility; retainer

侍 ▷attend upon
ジ　さむらい   Ⓚ0066

attend upon, wait upon, serve
侍女 じじょ lady attendant
侍従 じじゅう chamberlain
侍医 じい court physician, personal physician
陪侍 ばいじ attending on the nobility; retainer
近侍 きんじ attendant

従 ▷follow
ジュウ　ショウ　ジュ　したが(う)　したが(える)   Ⓚ0376

(go after) **follow, accompany, attend on**
従軍する じゅうぐんする follow [join] the army, go to the front
随従する ずいじゅうする follow the lead of, play second fiddle to
追従する ついじゅうする follow, be servile to; imitate

随 ▷follow
ズイ   Ⓚ0573

(go after) **follow, attend (on), accompany**
随行する ずいこうする attend on, accompany, follow
随員 ずいいん attendants, retinue
付随の ふずいの accompanying, incidental

accomplish
達 遂 成 徹 破 叶

達 ▷attain
タツ -たち   Ⓚ2706

(succeed in reaching a goal) **attain, achieve, reach, realize**

達成する たっせいする attain, achieve, accomplish
調達 ちょうたつ supply, procurement; execution (of an order); raising (money)
栄達 えいたつ success in life, rise in the world

遂 ▷accomplish
スイ と(げる) つい(に)   Ⓚ2705

(complete successfully) **accomplish, achieve, attain, complete, carry out, execute, commit, perform**

遂行する すいこうする accomplish, execute, perform, carry out
完遂する かんすいする execute successfully, accomplish, bring to completion
未遂の みすいの attempted (suicide, etc.)

成 ▷achieve
セイ ジョウ な(る) な(す)   Ⓚ2964

achieve, attain, accomplish, succeed

成功する せいこうする succeed, be successful
成果 せいか result, fruit, outcome
成績 せいせき results, record, achievement
成就する じょうじゅする accomplish, achieve, attain
成仏する じょうぶつする enter Nirvana, attain Buddhahood; die
成算 せいさん prospects of success

徹 ▷go through
テツ   Ⓚ0659

go through [with], be thorough, be exhaustive

徹底的 てっていてき thorough, exhaustive
貫徹する かんてつする carry through, go through with, accomplish, attain
一徹な いってつな obstinate, stubborn
透徹した とうてつした lucid, clear, penetrating

破 ▷carry through with
ハ やぶ(る) やぶ(れる)   Ⓚ1064

carry through with, perform an action to the end

読破する どくはする read through
走破する そうはする run [cover] the whole distance
描破する びょうはする depict thoroughly

叶 ▷be fulfilled
キョウ ギョウ かな(う) かな(える)   Ⓚ0161

(of a wish) **be fulfilled, be realized, be granted**

叶わない かなわない be unable, be beyond one's power
叶わぬ時の神頼み かなわぬときのかみだのみ Man turns to God in times of trouble
望みが叶う のぞみがかなう have one's wish realized

accomplishment
績 功 勲

績 ▷achievements
セキ   Ⓚ1288

achievements, accomplishments, merit, results, record

成績 せいせき results, record, achievement
実績 じっせき (actual) result, positive achievements
業績 ぎょうせき achievements; business results
功績 こうせき meritorious deed, achievement
戦績 せんせき war record, military achievements; results, score
不成績 ふせいせき poor result, underachievement

功 ▷merit
コウ ク   Ⓚ0165

merit(s), meritorious deed [service]

功績 こうせき meritorious deed, achievement
功労 こうろう meritorious deed, (distinguished) services
功名 こうみょう great exploit; distinction, fame
功罪 こうざい merits and demerits
功徳 くどく virtue, merits of one's pious acts
功力 くりき merits [influence] of one's pious acts or religious practice
年功 ねんこう long service, years' [long] experience
勲功 くんこう distinguished services, merit
戦功 せんこう merit of war

勲 ▷meritorious service
クン   Ⓚ2500

meritorious [distinguished] service, merit, meritorious deed, exploits

勲功 くんこう distinguished services, merit
勲章 くんしょう decoration, order, medal
殊勲 しゅくん meritorious deeds, distinguished service
武勲 ぶくん deeds of arms, distinguished military service

accumulate
積 溜 累 重 盛 堆

積 ▷accumulate
セキ つ(む) -づ(み) つ(もる)
つ(もり)　　　　　　　　Ⓚ1142

[original meaning] **accumulate, pile up, heap up**
積載 せきさい loading, carrying
積極的に せっきょくてきに positively, actively
堆積 たいせき accumulation, pile, heap
蓄積 ちくせき accumulation, stockpiling
山積する さんせきする form a (huge) pile
累積 るいせき accumulation

溜 ▷accumulate
リュウ た(める) -ため た(まる)　Ⓚ0608

accumulate (as of water)
溜飲 りゅういん water brash, sour stomach
溜飲が下がる りゅういんがさがる be cured of water
brash; have one's grudge satisfied

累 ▷cumulate
ルイ　　　　　　　　　　Ⓚ2242

cumulate, accumulate, pile up
累積 るいせき accumulation
累加 るいか cumulation, cumulative rise
累計 るいけい total
累増 るいぞう cumulative increase, progressive
increase
累乗 るいじょう *math* involution, power
累算温度 るいさんおんど cumulative temperature

重 ▷pile up
ジュウ チョウ え おも(い) おも(り)
かさ(ねる) かさ(なる)　　Ⓚ2991

pile up, heap up, stack
重箱 じゅうばこ nest [tier] of boxes
重奏 じゅうそう duet
重合 じゅうごう polymerization
重積する じゅうせきする pile up
重層的 じゅうそうてき multilayered, stratified
重畳たる ちょうじょうたる piled up, placed one
upon another; excellent, splendid

盛 ▷heap up
セイ ジョウ も(る) さか(る)
さか(ん)　　　　　　　　Ⓚ2332

heap up (sand), pile (up)
盛り上がり もりあがり climax (of a story), upsurge

盛り上げる もりあげる pile up, heap up; stir up,
bring to a climax
盆に胡桃を盛る ぼんにくるみをもる heap a tray
with walnuts

堆 ▷piled high
タイ　　　　　　　　　　Ⓚ0425

ⓐ **piled high, accumulated**
ⓑ **be piled up, accumulate**
ⓐ 堆石 たいせき pile of stones; moraine
堆朱 ついしゅ red lacquerware with patterns
carved in relief
ⓑ 堆積 たいせき accumulation, pile, heap
堆肥 たいひ barnyard manure

accuse →BLAME AND ACCUSE

a certain
某 或 一

某 ▷a certain
ボウ　　　　　　　　　　Ⓚ2216

[also prefix] **a certain, one**
某日 ぼうじつ a certain day
某氏 ぼうし a certain person
某国 ぼうこく a certain country
某女 ぼうじょ Ms. So-and-so
某某 ぼうぼう so-and-so
某所 ぼうしょ a certain place
某高校 ぼうこうこう a certain high school
某博士 ぼうはかせ Dr. X

或 ▷a certain
ワク あ(る) ある(いは)　　Ⓚ2763

a certain, some
或る日 あるひ a certain day, one day
或る程度 あるていど a certain extent, some extent
或る種 あるしゅ certain, some kind, some sort
或る人 あるひと someone
と或る とある a certain

一 ▷one
イチ イツ ひと- ひと(つ)　Ⓚ2850

[also prefix] (a certain) **one, a, an, another**
一夜 いちや(=ひとよ) one night, a night
一説 いっせつ another view, another version
[report]
一日本人 いちにほんじん one [a] Japanese
一要素 いちようそ one factor, one element
一員 いちいん member

act →DO AND ACT

acting arbitrarily
横 独 恣 耽 擅 専 逞

横 ▷arbitrary
オウ よこ   Ⓚ0979

arbitrary, perverse, despotic, tyrannical, overbearing

横暴な おうぼうな arbitrary, tyrannical, despotic
横着な おうちゃくな impudent, brazen; idle, lazy
横領 おうりょう seizure, embezzlement, usurpation
横行する おうこうする be rampant, overrun, swagger, strut
横柄な おうへいな overbearing, arrogant
専横 せんおう arbitrariness, despotism

独 ▷act arbitrarily
ドク ひと(り)   Ⓚ0354

act arbitrarily, act without the advice of others

独断 どくだん arbitrary decision, dogmatism
独善 どくぜん self-righteousness

恣 ▷self-indulgent
シ   Ⓚ2304

self-indulgent, selfish, arbitrary

恣意 しい selfishness, arbitrariness
恣意的 しいてき arbitrary, selfish
放恣 ほうし licentiousness, self-indulgence
驕恣 きょうし being proud and self-indulgent

耽 ▷indulge in
タン ふけ(る)   Ⓚ1201

【タン】
indulge in, be absorbed in
耽溺する たんできする indulge in (pleasure)
耽美派 たんびは the aesthetic school

【ふけ(る)】
indulge in, be absorbed in
読み耽る よみふける be absorbed in reading

擅 ▷arrogate to oneself
セン ほしいまま

[now also 専] [original meaning] **arrogate to oneself, claim arbitrarily, do something on one's own authority**

擅断 せんだん arbitrary decision, arbitrariness
独擅場 どくせんじょう one's unrivaled sphere of activity, one's monopoly

専 ▷arrogate to oneself
セン もっぱ(ら)   Ⓚ2297

[formerly also 擅] **arrogate to oneself, claim arbitrarily, do something on one's own authority**

専横 せんおう arbitrariness, despotism
専行 せんこう arbitrary action
専断 せんだん arbitrary decision, arbitrariness

逞 ▷do as one pleases
テイ たくま(しい)   Ⓚ2776

do as one pleases, be self-indulgent

不逞 ふてい recalcitrance, outlawry, insubordination
不逞の輩 ふていのやから lawless people [gang], malcontents, recalcitrants

active
活 動

活 ▷active
カツ い(きる) い(かす)   Ⓚ0345

active, lively, live, energetic, moving

活動 かつどう activity, action; function
活躍する かつやくする be active in, be actively engaged
活発な かっぱつな lively, active
活性 かっせい activity
活気 かっき vigor, spirit, animation
活況 かっきょう activity, briskness, prosperity
活写する かっしゃする describe vividly, paint a lively picture of
活火山 かっかざん active volcano
敏活 びんかつ quickness, alacrity
不活性化 ふかっせいか inactivation

動 ▷dynamic
ドウ うご(く) うご(かす)   Ⓚ1583

[also prefix] **dynamic, moving, kinetic**

動安定 どうあんてい dynamic stability
動摩擦 どうまさつ kinetic friction

acts
行 挙 業

行 ▷act
コウ ギョウ アン い(く) ゆ(く) –ゆ(き)
–い(き) おこな(う)   Ⓚ0187

(something done) **act, action, deed**

非行 ひこう delinquency, misdeed, misdemeanor
悪行 あくぎょう misdeed, wicked act

挙 ▷noteworthy act
キョ あ(げる) あ(がる)　　Ⓚ2169

noteworthy act, deed, scheme, attempt, undertaking

暴挙 ぼうきょ rash act, reckless attempt
壮挙 そうきょ grand scheme, heroic [daring] attempt
快挙 かいきょ brilliant achievement, heroic deed [feat]

業 ▷deed
ギョウ ゴウ わざ　　Ⓚ2265

deed, work, achievement

所業 しょぎょう deed, one's doings
偉業 いぎょう great work [achievement]

---

add

加　足　〆

加 ▷add
カ くわ(える) くわ(わる)　　Ⓚ0024

math **add, sum up**

加算 かさん addition
加減 かげん addition and subtraction; degree, extent; adjustment

足 ▷add
ソク あし た(りる) た(る) た(す)　　Ⓚ1873

add; supplement, make up for; do (one's business)

足し算 たしざん addition
接ぎ足す つぎたす add, extend
用を足す ようをたす do one's business; relieve oneself

〆 ▷sum
しめ(る) しめ

sum, sum [add] up; close the account
〆て しめて in all, all told

---

additional

追　補　副

追 ▷additional
ツイ お(う)　　Ⓚ2667

[also prefix] **additional, supplementary**

追徴金 ついちょうきん additional imposition
追試験 ついしけん supplementary exam

補 ▷supplementary
ホ おぎな(う)　　Ⓚ1103

supplementary, extra

補習 ほしゅう supplementary lessons
補則 ほそく supplementary rules

副 ▷accessory
フク　　Ⓚ1581

(in addition to the main thing) **accessory, side-, extra, supplementary, additional**

副詞 ふくし adverb
副神経 ふくしんけい accessory nerves
副賞 ふくしょう supplementary [extra] prize
副業 ふくぎょう subsidiary business
副収入 ふくしゅうにゅう additional income
副産物 ふくさんぶつ by-product, side line

---

additionally

亦　兼　又　而　及
並　傍　尚　更　且

亦 ▷also
エキ また　　Ⓚ1734

[now usu. 又] [often preceded by も] **also, too, as well**

彼も亦良い人だ かれもまたいいひとだ He is a nice man, too
私も亦 わたしもまた I also, me too

兼 ▷concurrently
ケン か(ねる)　　Ⓚ1979

concurrently, simultaneously, and, cum, in addition

総理大臣兼外務大臣 そうりだいじんけんがいむだいじん Prime Minister and (concurrently) Foreign Minister
居間兼食堂 いまけんしょくどう living-room-cum-dining-room

又 ▷also, and
また また(の)-　　Ⓚ2853

❶ [formerly also 亦] [often preceded by も] **also, too, as well**

私も又 わたくしもまた I also, me too
それも又結構だ それもまたけっこうだ That's also good

❷ **and, besides, further**

勝利又勝利 しょうりまたしょうり victory after victory

而 ▷and
ジ しこ(うして) しか(して) しか(も) Ⓚ1747

and
然り而うして しかりしこうして Aye, and...

及 ▷and
キュウ およ(ぶ) およ(び)
およ(ぼす) Ⓚ2868

and, as well as
太陽及び地球 たいようおよびちきゅう the sun and
the earth

並 ▷and also
ヘイ なみ なら(べる) なら(ぶ)
なら(びに) Ⓚ1936

and also, besides, and, in addition
性別並びに国籍 せいべつならびにこくせき sex and
nationality

傍 ▷besides
ボウ かたわ(ら) そば Ⓚ0127

besides, while; side
傍らに寄る かたわらによる step aside
勉強の傍ら音楽を聞く べんきょうのかたわらおんが
くをきく listen to music while studying

尚 ▷still
ショウ なお Ⓚ1919

(in increasing degree) **still (more), all the more**
尚の事 なおのこと all the more, still more
尚一層悪い事は なおいっそうわるいことは what is
worse still
この方が尚良い このほうがなおよい This is still
better

更 ▷furthermore
コウ さら さら(に) ふ(ける)
ふ(かす) Ⓚ2967

**furthermore, moreover; still more; anew, afresh,
again;** (not) **in the least**
更に一歩を進める さらにいっぽをすすめる go a
step further

且 ▷as well
か(つ) Ⓚ2927

**as well (as), at the same time, besides, moreover,
both...and**
且つ又 かつまた moreover
且つ飲み且つ歌う かつのみかつうたう drink as well
as sing, drink and sing at the same time
彼は英語を話し且つ書く かれはえいごをはなしか
つかく He speaks English and writes it as well

---

add to
付 附 加 追 添

付 ▷attach
フ つ(ける) -づ(ける) つ(け) -づ(け)
つ(く) -づ(く) つ(き) -づ(き) Ⓚ0019

ⓐ attach, append, add to, affix
ⓑ attached, additional, supplementary
ⓐ 付記する ふきする add, write in addition
付加する ふかする add, supplement
添付する てんぷする attach, append, annex
貼付する ちょうふ(=てんぷ)する stick, paste, append
ⓑ 付録 ふろく appendix, supplement
付言 ふげん postscript, additional remarks
付図 ふず attached map, appended figure [graph]
付則 ふそく additional rules, bylaw

附 ▷attach
フ Ⓚ0307

ⓐ [original meaning] attach, append, add to, affix
ⓑ attached, additional, supplementary
ⓐ 添附する てんぷする attach, append, annex
ⓑ 附則 ふそく additional rules, bylaw

加 ▷add
カ くわ(える) くわ(わる) Ⓚ0024

add, append
加速 かそく acceleration
加速度 かそくど acceleration
加味する かみする tinge with, add to

追 ▷add
ツイ お(う) Ⓚ2667

add, perform in addition to
追加 ついか addition, appendix, supplement
追刊 ついかん additional publication

添 ▷add to
テン そ(える) そ(う) Ⓚ0485

add to, append, affix, accompany
添加する てんかする add, annex, append
添削 てんさく correction
添付する てんぷする attach, append, annex
添書 てんしょ accompanying letter

adhere to
執　着

執 ▷**adhere to**
シツ　シュウ　と(る)　　　Ⓚ1501

adhere to, stick fast to, hold fast to, persist in

執念 しゅうねん tenacity of purpose, vindictiveness, spite
執着する しゅうちゃく(=しゅうじゃく)する be attached to; adhere to, hold fast to
執拗な しつような obstinate; tenacious, persistent
固執する こしつ(=こしゅう)する adhere to, persist in
確執 かくしつ(=かくしゅう) discord, strife
偏執狂 へんしつきょう(=へんしゅうきょう) monomaniac

着 ▷**stick to**
チャク　ジャク　き(る)　−ぎ　き(せる)　−き(せ)　つ(く)　つ(ける)　　　Ⓚ2826

(figuratively) **stick to, adhere to, hold fast to**

執着 しゅうちゃく(=しゅうじゃく) attachment; tenacity
愛着 あいちゃく(=あいじゃく) attachment, affection; love
無頓着な むとんちゃくな indifferent, unmindful, careless

advance
進　興　奨　勧

進 ▷**advance**
シン　すす(む)　すす(める)　　　Ⓚ2689

(aid the progress of) **advance, promote, further**

推進する すいしんする propel, drive; promote
促進する そくしんする promote, spur on, facilitate
増進する ぞうしんする promote, improve, advance

興 ▷**cause to rise**
コウ　キョウ　おこ(る)　おこ(す)　　　Ⓚ2525

cause to rise (to prosperity), promote, further, advance, develop

興業 こうぎょう promotion of industry
興国 こうこく making a country prosperous
興信所 こうしんじょ private inquiry agency, credit bureau
振興 しんこう promotion, furtherance, rousing
復興する ふっこうする revive, restore to the original state, reconstruct

再興する さいこうする revive, restore
作興する さっこうする promote; awaken, arouse, enhance

奨 ▷**encourage**
ショウ　　　Ⓚ2474

(stimulate by assistance) **encourage, promote, stimulate**

奨励 しょうれい encouragement, promotion, stimulation, incitement
奨学金 しょうがくきん scholarship (grant)
報奨 ほうしょう reward, compensation

勧 ▷**encourage**
カン　すす(める)　　　Ⓚ1645

encourage, promote

勧業 かんぎょう encouragement of industry
勧奨する かんしょうする encourage, promote, stimulate
勧善懲悪 かんぜんちょうあく rewarding good and punishing evil, political justice
勧銀 かんぎん hypothecary bank

advocate
唱　説

唱 ▷**advocate**
ショウ　とな(える)　　　Ⓚ0418

advocate, preach

唱導 しょうどう advocacy
提唱する ていしょうする advocate, propose

説 ▷**preach**
セツ　ゼイ　と(く)　　　Ⓚ1405

preach, advocate; persuade

説教 せっきょう preaching, scolding
説法 せっぽう (Buddhist) sermon, preaching, moralizing
説得 せっとく persuasion
遊説 ゆうぜい electioneering tour; campaign speech

affair
事　儀　件

事 ▷**affair**
ジ　ズ　こと　　　Ⓚ2986

(something that is done) **affair, something, matter, thing, fact**

事物 じぶつ things, affairs
事実 じじつ fact, reality; as a matter of fact
事項 じこう matters, facts; articles, items
返事 へんじ answer, reply
房事 ぼうじ sex, lovemaking
記事 きじ news, article; account
食事 しょくじ meal, dinner, board

儀 ▷affair
ギ   Ⓚ0147

affair, matter, case
余儀 よぎ another method; another problem
難儀 なんぎ hardship, trouble

件 ▷matter
ケン   Ⓚ0035

matter, affair, case, incident, item
一件 いっけん matter, affair, item
用件 ようけん matter (of business), things to be done
人件費 じんけんひ personnel expenses, labor cost
条件 じょうけん condition; item, proviso
事件 じけん affair, incident, case, event
案件 あんけん matter, case, item
要件 ようけん important matter; necessary condition
別件 べっけん separate case, another matter

affairs
用   事   務

用 ▷things to do
ヨウ もち(いる)   Ⓚ2569

things to do, business, task, errand
用事 ようじ things to do, errand, business, engagement
用件 ようけん matter (of business), things to be done
用談 ようだん business talk
用足し ようたし taking care of business, running an errand; relieving oneself
所用 しょよう things to do, errand, business, engagement
公用 こうよう official business [duty], official mission; public use
私用 しよう private business; private use

事 ▷affairs
ジ ズ こと   Ⓚ2986

(business matters) **affairs, business, work**
事務 じむ business, clerical work, duties of an office

事務室 じむしつ office
事業 じぎょう undertaking, enterprise, business; achievement
用事 ようじ things to do, errand, business, engagement
家事 かじ household affairs, housework
軍事 ぐんじ naval and military affairs
工事 こうじ construction
人事 じんじ human affairs, personnel affairs

務 ▷affairs
ム つと(める) つと(まる)   Ⓚ1085

affairs, business
国務 こくむ duties of state, national affairs
外務 がいむ foreign affairs
事務 じむ business, clerical work, duties of an office
総務 そうむ general affairs; manager, director
公務 こうむ public service, official affairs
専務 せんむ managing [executive] director
法務 ほうむ judicial affairs; clerical duty

after
後   余

後 ▷after
ゴ コウ のち うし(ろ) あと おく(れる)   Ⓚ0321

[sometimes also 后] [also suffix] (subsequent in time)
after, afterwards, later, subsequent
後遺症 こういしょう sequela, aftereffect (of a disease)
後任 こうにん successor, replacement
後天的 こうてんてき acquired (immunity), learned
直後 ちょくご immediately after
生後 せいご after birth
今後 こんご after this, from now on
以後 いご after this, from now on, in future; after that, thereafter
午後 ごご afternoon
老後 ろうご one's old age
十年後 じゅうねんご ten years after [hence]
終戦後の しゅうせんごの postwar

余 ▷after
ヨ あま(る) あま(り) あま(す)   Ⓚ1757

after
余震 よしん aftershock

齢 ▷age
レイ   Ⓚ1675

[also 令] **age, years**
年齢 ねんれい age, years
樹齢 じゅれい age of a tree
高齢 こうれい advanced age
老齢 ろうれい old age
学齢 がくれい school age
月齢 げつれい moon's age

令 ▷age
レイ   Ⓚ1725

[also 齢] **age, years**
年令 ねんれい age, years

年 ▷years
ネン とし   Ⓚ1752

years, one's age
年齢(=年令) ねんれい age, years
年輩(=年配) ねんぱい age, years; elderly age
少年 しょうねん boy
定年 ていねん mandatory retirement age
中年 ちゅうねん middle age
晩年 ばんねん late in life

歳 ▷age suffix
サイ セイ とし   Ⓚ2190

[also 才] **age suffix**
一歳 いっさい one year old
何歳 なんさい how old, what age
万歳 ばんざい Banzai!/Hurrah!/Long live…!

才 ▷age suffix
サイ   Ⓚ2880

[also 歳] **age suffix**
十二才 じゅうにさい 12 years old
何才 なんさい how old, what age

寿 ▷life span
ジュ ス ことぶき   Ⓚ2979

life span, age, natural life
寿命 じゅみょう life span
天寿 てんじゅ one's natural life span

使 ▷envoy
シ つか(う) つか(い) -づか(い)   Ⓚ0072

[also suffix] **envoy, messenger, emissary, ambassador, delegate**
使節 しせつ envoy, ambassador
使者 ししゃ messenger
使命 しめい mission, appointed task
大使 たいし ambassador
公使 こうし minister, attaché
特使 とくし special envoy [messenger]
天使 てんし angel
遣唐使 けんとうし Japanese envoy to Tang China

偵 ▷spy
テイ   Ⓚ0122

[original meaning] **spy**
密偵 みってい spy, emissary
探偵 たんてい detective work; detective, sleuth

agree and approve
賛 可 認 諾 承 肯 容

賛 ▷approve of
サン   Ⓚ2446

approve of, agree with
賛成 さんせい approval, agreement, support
賛否 さんぴ approval or disapproval; yes or no
賛意 さんい approval
賛同 さんどう approval, endorsement

可 ▷approve
カ   Ⓚ2562

[original meaning] **approve, be in favor of, permit**
可決 かけつ approval [adoption] of a bill
可否 かひ right or wrong, propriety
許可する きょかする permit, approve, authorize
認可 にんか approval, authorization, permission

認 ▷recognize
ニン みと(める)   Ⓚ1404

(approve or give permission for) **recognize, acknowledge, approve, admit**
認可する にんかする approve, authorize, give permission

認定 にんてい authorization, recognition, acknowledgment

認知 にんち recognition, acknowledgment

承認 しょうにん approval, recognition

公認 こうにん official recognition [approval], authorization, certification

黙認 もくにん tacit [silent] approval, toleration

諾 ▷consent
ダク ⓚ1418

consent (to), say yes, agree to, assent

受諾 じゅだく acceptance

承諾 しょうだく consent, assent, agreement, acceptation

応諾 おうだく consent, assent

快諾 かいだく ready consent

内諾 ないだく informal [private] consent

承 ▷agree to
ショウ うけたまわ(る) ⓚ0007

agree to, consent, accept

承諾する しょうだくする consent, assent, agree, accept

承知する しょうちする consent [agree] to; permit; forgive; know, understand

承認 しょうにん approval, recognition

承服 しょうふく consent, acceptance

了承 りょうしょう acknowledgment, understanding

肯 ▷assent
コウ ⓚ2142

assent, nod agreement, consent, permit

肯定 こうてい affirmation, affirmative

首肯する しゅこうする assent, nod one's assent, consent

容 ▷tolerate
ヨウ ⓚ1968

tolerate, permit, allow

容赦する ようしゃする pardon, forgive, have mercy on

容疑者 ようぎしゃ suspected person

容共 ようきょう procommunist

容認する ようにんする admit, approve, accept

受容する じゅようする receive, accept

許容する きょようする tolerate, allow, permit

aircraft and spacecraft
機 空 船

機 ▷aircraft
キ はた ⓚ0989

[also suffix] aircraft, airplane

機種 きしゅ type of airplane [machine], model

機首 きしゅ nose (of an airplane)

機体 きたい fuselage, body (of an airplane); machine

機長 きちょう plane captain

日航機 にっこうき JAL airplane

ジェット機 じぇっとき jet airplane

空 ▷aircraft
クウ そら あ(く) あ(き) あ(ける) から むな(しい) ⓚ1913

aircraft, airplane

空港 くうこう airport

空軍 くうぐん air force

空輸 くうゆ air transportation

空路 くうろ air route, airway

船 ▷spaceship
セン ふね ふな- -ぶね ⓚ1229

spaceship, airship

宇宙船 うちゅうせん spaceship

軌道船 きどうせん orbiter

飛行船 ひこうせん ship, airship

all

皆 悉 総 諸 毎 各 都
万 全 渾 一 満 丸 完

皆 ▷all
カイ みな みんな ⓚ2160

[original meaning] **all, whole, everything; everybody, everyone**

皆目 かいもく altogether, wholly; (not) at all

皆無 かいむ nothing

皆勤 かいきん perfect attendance

皆既食 かいきしょく total solar [lunar] eclipse

免許皆伝 めんきょかいでん initiation into all the mysteries of an art

国民皆兵 こくみんかいへい universal conscription

国民皆保険 こくみんかいほけん medical insurance for the whole nation

悉 ▷thoroughly
シツ ことごと(く)　Ⓚ2387

thoroughly, completely, entirely
悉皆 しっかい all, to the last
知悉する ちしつする have thorough knowledge

総 ▷total
ソウ　Ⓚ1261
see also →TOTAL

[also prefix] total, whole, combined, full, complete, gross
総額 そうがく total amount, sum total
総数 そうすう total (number)
総点 そうてん sum total of one's marks
総体 そうたい the whole, all; on the whole, generally
総掛かり そうがかり combined efforts
総二階 そうにかい full two-story house
総予算 そうよさん complete budget
総量 そうりょう gross weight [volume]

諸 ▷various
ショ　Ⓚ1427
see also →VARIOUS

[also prefix] various, all kinds of; many, all
諸説 しょせつ various views [theories]
諸島 しょとう archipelago
諸派 しょは minor parties
諸君 しょくん Ladies and Gentlemen, my friends, you
諸国 しょこく various [all] countries
諸般の しょはんの various, several, all, every
諸問題 しょもんだい various [all] questions [problems]
諸行無常 しょぎょうむじょう All things flow and nothing is permanent (a Buddhist concept)

毎 ▷every
マイ －ごと(に)　Ⓚ1751

[also prefix] every, each
毎日 まいにち every day
毎朝 まいあさ every morning
毎回 まいかい every time
毎年 まいねん(=まいとし) every year
毎号 まいごう each [every] issue
毎度 まいど every [each] time, always
毎週 まいしゅう every week
毎土曜日 まいどようび every Saturday

各 ▷each
カク おのおの　Ⓚ1856

[also prefix] each, every, every one, all, various
各社 かくしゃ each company
各自 かくじ each one, every individual
各国 かっこく every country, each nation, various states
各般 かくはん every, various
各地 かくち every place, various parts [areas] (of the country)
各種の かくしゅの each [every] kind, various
各位 かくい gentlemen, sirs
各団体 かくだんたい each group
各大学 かくだいがく each university, all universities

都 ▷all
ト ツ みやこ　Ⓚ1505

all, every, everything
都度 つど each time, whenever
都合 つごう convenience, circumstances; in all, altogether, totally

万 ▷all
マン バン　Ⓚ2542

all
万国 ばんこく all nations
万病 まんびょう all kinds of diseases
万全の ばんぜんの perfect, infallible, absolutely secure
万能 ばんのう omnipotence
万事 ばんじ all things, everything
万人 ばんにん(=ばんじん) all people

全 ▷whole
ゼン まった(く) すべ(て)　Ⓚ1743
❶ⓐ [also prefix] (including everything) whole, all, complete, total, entire
ⓑ wholly, completely; at the height of
ⓒ in all, a total of
ⓐ 全部 ぜんぶ all, the whole; wholly, entirely
全体の ぜんたいの whole, entire; general
全力 ぜんりょく all one's might, full capacity
全焼 ぜんしょう total destruction by fire
全般の ぜんぱんの whole, general, overall
全集 ぜんしゅう complete works
全員 ぜんいん all members, entire staff
全額 ぜんがく sum total, total amount
全速力 ぜんそくりょく full [top] speed, full steam
ⓑ 全勝する ぜんしょうする win all the games, make a clean sweep
全廃する ぜんぱいする abolish wholly, do away with
全国民 ぜんこくみん the whole nation
ⓒ 全然 ぜんぜん wholly, totally, completely; (not) at all

全六巻 ぜんろっかん complete in six volumes, six volumes in all

❷ (extending over the full range) **whole, all, pan-**

全国 ぜんこく the whole country

全校 ぜんこう the whole school

全米 ぜんべい all America, pan-America

全世界 ぜんせかい the whole world

全アジア会議 ぜんあじあかいぎ Pan-Asiatic Conference

❸ⓐ (free from flaws or damage) **whole, complete, perfect, intact**

　ⓑ (free from impurities) **whole, pure**

ⓐ 完全な かんぜんな perfect, complete, whole

万全の ばんぜんの perfect, infallible, absolutely secure

安全 あんぜん safety, security

健全な けんぜんな healthy, sound

ⓑ 全乳 ぜんにゅう whole milk, pure milk

全麦の ぜんばくの whole-wheat

渾 ▷**entire**
コン

[also 混] (unified in an integrated whole) **entire, whole, complete**

渾身 こんしん whole body

渾然一体となる こんぜんいったいとなる be joined together, form a complete whole

一 ▷**all in one**
イチ イツ ひと- ひと(つ) Ⓚ2850

all in one, everything, the whole

一般の いっぱんの general, universal, widespread

一切の いっさいの all, entire, whole

一掃する いっそうする clean out, wipe out, dispel, eradicate

一同 いちどう all (of us), all persons concerned

一座 いちざ the whole company, all present

一天 いってん the whole sky

満 ▷**full**
マン み(ちる) み(つ) み(たす) Ⓚ0553

(complete) **full, whole, entire, perfect**

満点 まんてん full marks, perfect score

満面 まんめん whole face

満座 まんざ the whole assembly

丸 ▷**complete(ly)**
ガン まる まる(い) まる(める) Ⓚ2883

[also prefix] **complete(ly), total(ly), perfect(ly)**

丸っきり まるっきり just like; completely, perfectly

丸丸 まるまる completely, entirely

丸儲け まるもうけ clear profit

丸二日 まるふつか for a full two days

丸焼けになった まるやけになった completely burned

魚を丸ごと食べる さかなをまるごとたべる eat a fish whole

完 ▷**complete**
カン Ⓚ1883

(having all its parts intact) **complete, perfect, whole, full, intact**

完全な かんぜんな perfect, complete, whole

完璧な かんぺきな perfect, flawless

完備した かんびした fully-equipped, perfect, complete

完投する かんとうする pitch a whole game

完封 かんぷう complete blockade [seal]; baseball shutout

allot

充 当

充 ▷**allot**
ジュウ あ(てる) Ⓚ1737

allot, assign, appropriate

充当する じゅうとうする allot, appropriate, earmark

充用する じゅうようする appropriate, earmark

当 ▷**assign**
トウ あ(たる) あ(たり) あ(てる) あ(て) Ⓚ1865

assign, allot, appropriate

配当 はいとう apportionment, allotment

充当する じゅうとうする allot, appropriate, earmark

日当 にっとう daily allowance

勘当 かんどう disinheritance

almost

殆 瀕 甫 辛

殆 ▷**almost**
タイ ほとん(ど) Ⓚ0811

almost, nearly, mostly

殆どの人 ほとんどのひと most people

瀕 ▷**on the verge of**
ヒン Ⓚ0716

[rarely also 頻] **on the verge of**

瀕死 ひんし on the verge of death

甫 ▷**barely**
ホ フ はじ(めて) ⓚ2972

literary **barely, just**
我齢は甫めて九つなるに わがよわいははじめてここ
のつなるに I was barely nine years old

辛 ▷**bare**
シン から(い) ⓚ1755

[in compounds] **bare, narrow**
辛うじて かろうじて barely, narrowly
辛くも からくも barely, narrowly, with difficulty

alone
独　　孤

独 ▷**alone**
ドク ひと(り) ⓚ0354

alone, by oneself, single, sole, solo
独走 どくそう running alone; easy victory, walkover
独演 どくえん solo recital
独奏する どくそうする play solo, play alone
独立 どくりつ independence, self-reliance
独学 どくがく self-study, self-teaching
独身 どくしん single life; celibacy
独占 どくせん exclusive possession, monopoly
独裁 どくさい dictatorship, autocracy
単独の たんどくの single, independent, sole, lone
孤独の こどくの solitary, lonely, alone

孤 ▷**solitary**
コ ⓚ0317

solitary, lone, isolated
孤独の こどくの solitary, lonely, alone
孤立 こりつ isolation
孤客 こかく lone traveler
孤島 ことう solitary island
孤軍 こぐん lone [isolated] force, forlorn force
孤城 こじょう solitary [isolated] castle

alternate
迭　交　輪

迭 ▷**alternate**
テツ ⓚ2650

[original meaning] **alternate, change, take turns**
更迭する こうてつする reshuffle, change (as of
government officials), exchange places

交 ▷**interchange**
コウ まじ(わる) まじ(える) ま(じる)
ま(ざる) ま(ぜる) -か(う) か(わす) ⓚ1738

(succeed each other) **interchange, alternate, go back
and forth**
交代(=交替)する こうたいする relieve (a person),
take turns, alternate
交番 こうばん police box
交互に こうごに mutually, reciprocally, alternately
交流 こうりゅう alternating current; interchange
交通 こうつう traffic, transport; communications
交通費 こうつうひ transportation expenses, carfare
交通事故 こうつうじこ traffic accident
交渉 こうしょう negotiation, bargaining, discussion

輪 ▷**take turns**
リン わ ⓚ1436

take turns, rotate, alternate
輪転 りんてん rotation
輪番 りんばん turn, rotation
輪唱する りんしょうする troll, sing in a circular
canon
輪読 りんどく reading by turns

amphibians →REPTILES AND AMPHIBIANS

anger
怒　憤　慨

怒 ▷**get angry**
ド いか(る) おこ(る) ⓚ2228

ⓐ [original meaning] **get angry, be enraged**
ⓑ **anger, rage**
a 怒鳴る どなる shout, yell
憤怒 ふんど(=ふんぬ) anger, rage, resentment
b 怒気 どき anger, indignation
怒声 どせい angry voice, harsh words
怒濤 どとう raging billows [waves]
怒号 どごう (angry) roar, outcry, bellow
激怒 げきど wild rage, fury
喜怒哀楽 きどあいらく joy and anger; emotion

憤 ▷**indignation**
フン いきどお(る) ⓚ0662

ⓐ **indignation, resentment, exasperation, rage**
ⓑ **be indignant, resent, be angry**
a 憤怒 ふんど(=ふんぬ) anger, rage, resentment
公憤 こうふん public indignation [resentment]
義憤 ぎふん righteous indignation
b 憤激する ふんげきする be inflamed by anger, flare
up
憤慨 ふんがい resentment, indignation

憤然と ふんぜんと indignantly, in a rage
憤死する ふんしする die in a fit of anger
悲憤 ひふん indignation, resentment

慨 ▷resent
ガイ   Ⓚ0588

resent, be indignant, be angry
憤慨 ふんがい resentment, indignation

angle and angular measure
角   度

角 ▷angle
カク かど つの   Ⓚ1761

ⓐ [also suffix] **angle**
ⓑ [prefix] *phys* **angular**
a 角度 かくど angle, angular measure, degree
　多角的な たかくてきな multilateral, many-sided, diversified
　三角 さんかく triangle
　直角 ちょっかく right angle
　方角 ほうがく direction
　迎え角 むかえかく angle of attack
　前進角 ぜんしんかく angle of advance
b 角速度 かくそくど angular velocity
　角分散 かくぶんさん angular dispersion

度 ▷degree
ド ト タク たび   Ⓚ2670

(unit of angular measure, latitude, longitude, etc.) **degree**
度数 どすう degree
角度 かくど angle, angular measure, degree
緯度 いど latitude
経度 けいど longitude
二度三十分 にどさんじゅっぷん 2°30′

angular measure →ANGLE AND ANGULAR MEASURE

animal
獣 畜 生 物

獣 ▷beast
ジュウ けもの   Ⓚ1673

[original meaning] **beast, animal**
獣医 じゅうい veterinarian
野獣 やじゅう wild animal, wild game
猛獣 もうじゅう fierce [savage] animal [beast]

怪獣 かいじゅう monster; beast
珍獣 ちんじゅう rare animal

畜 ▷livestock
チク   Ⓚ1801

ⓐ **livestock, domestic animals or fowls**
ⓑ **beast, animal**
a 畜類 ちくるい livestock, domestic animals
　畜産業 ちくさんぎょう stockraising
　畜舎 ちくしゃ barns and poultry sheds
　家畜 かちく domestic animal, livestock
　有畜農業 ゆうちくのうぎょう agriculture with livestock raising as a major side line
b 畜力 ちくりょく animal power
　畜生 ちくしょう beast; Damn it!
　人畜無害な じんちくむがいな harmless to man and beast

生 ▷life
セイ ショウ い(きる) い(かす) い(ける)
う(まれる) う(まれ) う(む) お(う) は(える)
は(やす) き なま な(る)   Ⓚ2933

(living organisms) **life, living things**
生物 せいぶつ living thing, life, organism
生理学 せいりがく physiology
生態 せいたい ecology; mode of life
原生動物 げんせいどうぶつ protozoan
幼生 ようせい larva
抗生物質 こうせいぶっしつ antibiotic
殺生 せっしょう destruction of life; cruelty
畜生 ちくしょう beast; Damn it!
写生する しゃせいする sketch [draw] from nature; portray

物 ▷living thing
ブツ モツ もの   Ⓚ0777

(animate entity) **living thing, life**
動物 どうぶつ animal
植物 しょくぶつ plant, vegetation
生物 せいぶつ living thing, life, organism

animals →COUNTERS FOR ANIMALS

answer
答 解 返 応

答 ▷answer
トウ こた(える) こた(え)   Ⓚ2340

ⓐ [original meaning] **answer (a question), reply, respond**
ⓑ **answer (to a question), reply**
ⓒ **answer, solve**

ⓓ answer (to a problem), solution

a 答礼 とうれい return salute
答申 とうしん report, reply (to the jury)
答弁 とうべん reply, answer; defending oneself

b 応答 おうとう answer, response, reply
回答 かいとう reply, answer
確答 かくとう definite answer [reply]
返答 へんとう reply, answer
問答 もんどう questions and answers, catechism

c 答案 とうあん examination paper; answer

d 解答 かいとう solution, answer

解 ▷solve
カイ ゲ と(く) と(かす) と(ける)　Ⓚ1375

ⓐ solve, find a solution, settle
ⓑ solution, answer

a 解決 かいけつ solution, settlement
解答する かいとうする solve, answer
解法 かいほう solution, key to solution
和解 わかい reconciliation, amicable settlement

b 正解 せいかい right answer, correct solution

返 ▷reply
ヘン かえ(す) かえ(る)　Ⓚ2633

reply, answer
返信 へんしん reply, answer
返事 へんじ answer, reply
返電 へんでん reply telegram
返答 へんとう reply, answer

応 ▷respond
オウ こた(える)　Ⓚ2640

(make a reply) **respond, answer, reply**
応答 おうとう answer, response, reply
呼応して こおうして in concert, in response

謝 ▷apologize
シャ あやま(る)　Ⓚ1465

apologize
謝罪 しゃざい apology
陳謝 ちんしゃ apology

詫 ▷apologize
タ わ(びる)　Ⓚ1387

apologize
詫び状 わびじょう letter of apology
詫びを入れる わびをいれる make an apology

お詫び おわび apology

appear
現　　出　　顕

現 ▷appear
ゲン あらわ(れる) あらわ(す)　Ⓚ0879

appear, become visible, come into view, be revealed, materialize
現象 げんしょう phenomenon
出現する しゅつげんする appear, make an appearance, emerge
実現する じつげんする realize, materialize
表現する ひょうげんする express, represent, manifest; give expression to

出 ▷come out
シュツ スイ で(る) -で だ(す)　Ⓚ2934

(come into view or existence) **come out, appear, emerge, occur**
出現 しゅつげん appearance, emergence
出火 しゅっか outbreak of fire
神出鬼没の しんしゅつきぼつの appearing and disappearing unexpectedly, elusive
初出 しょしゅつ first appearance
続出する ぞくしゅつする appear in succession
露出 ろしゅつ exposure, disclosure; (photographic) exposure

顕 ▷manifest
ケン　Ⓚ1605

[original meaning] (show plainly) **manifest, reveal, expose**
顕微鏡 けんびきょう microscope

appearance
容　貌　姿　相　体　色　風

容 ▷appearance
ヨウ　Ⓚ1968

appearance, looks, view, figure, countenance
容姿 ようし face and figure, appearance
容貌 ようぼう looks, personal appearance
容態(=容体) ようだい one's condition, one's state of health
美容 びよう beauty
威容 いよう dignified [majestic] appearance
変容 へんよう transfiguration, transformation

貌 ▷appearance
ボウ   Ⓚ1408

[original meaning] **appearance, looks, figure**
容貌 ようぼう looks, personal appearance
美貌 びぼう good looks, pretty features
体貌 たいぼう appearance
変貌 へんぼう transfiguration, metamorphosis

姿 ▷figure
シ すがた   Ⓚ2291

[original meaning] (outer shape, esp. of the body) **figure, form, shape, appearance, looks, aspect**
容姿 ようし face and figure, appearance
英姿 えいし gallant figure, majestic appearance
雄姿 ゆうし brave [imposing] figure

相 ▷phase
ソウ ショウ あい-   Ⓚ0808

(outer appearance or state, esp. as indication of characteristic essence) **phase, looks, appearance, aspect, state, condition**
様相 ようそう aspect, phase, condition
時代相 じだいそう phases of the times
貧相な ひんそうな poor-looking
寝相 ねぞう one's sleeping posture
色相 しきそう color phase
世相 せそう phases [aspect] of life, social conditions
真相 しんそう truth, facts, real situation
諸相 しょそう various aspects, various phases
実相 じっそう real state of affairs

体 ▷form (outer appearance)
タイ テイ からだ   Ⓚ0055

(outer appearance) **form, appearance**
体貌 たいぼう appearance
体裁 ていさい decency, form, style, appearance
風体 ふうてい(=ふうたい) appearance, looks; posture
世間体 せけんてい appearance (in the eyes of society), decency
職人体の男 しょくにんていのおとこ man of workmanlike appearance

色 ▷color
ショク シキ いろ   Ⓚ1748

(characteristic feature) **color, character, feature**
特色 とくしょく characteristic
地方色 ちほうしょく local color
異色の いしょくの novel, unique
物色する ぶっしょくする look for, pick out

風 ▷air
フウ フ かぜ かざ-   Ⓚ2591

[also suffix] **air, airs, appearance, manner, bearing, atmosphere**
風格 ふうかく (distinctive) character, (admirable) appearance; style, race
風采 ふうさい appearance, air, mien, getup
風体 ふうてい(=ふうたい) appearance, looks; posture
軍人風の ぐんじんふうの of military bearing

---

appoint
任 補 挙

任 ▷appoint
ニン まか(せる) まか(す)   Ⓚ0038

appoint (to an office), nominate, place
任命 にんめい appointment, nomination
任用する にんようする appoint, employ
選任する せんにんする select and appoint, assign [nominate] a person to a post

補 ▷appoint
ホ おぎな(う)   Ⓚ1103

(fill a vacancy) **appoint, assign, select**
補任する ほにんする appoint to office
候補者 こうほしゃ candidate, applicant

挙 ▷nominate
キョ あ(げる) あ(がる)   Ⓚ2169

nominate, appoint, recommend
挙用する きょようする appoint, promote
選挙 せんきょ election
推挙する すいきょする recommend, nominate

---

approach
寄 迫 近 接 捗

寄 ▷draw near
キ よ(る) -よ(り) よ(せる)   Ⓚ1983

draw near, draw up, come near, approach
近寄る ちかよる go near, approach
歩み寄る あゆみよる step up; compromise, meet halfway
最寄りの もよりの nearest, nearby
身寄り みより relative, relation, kinsfolk
思いも寄らない おもいもよらない unexpected, unforeseen, inconceivable

迫 ▷**press**
ハク せま(る)   Ⓚ2647

[original meaning] (close in on) **press on, close in, draw near**
迫撃 はくげき close attack
迫真の はくしんの true to life, realistic
切迫する せっぱくする draw near, press; become acute, grow tense

近 ▷**near**
キン ちか(い)   Ⓚ2634

[original meaning] (come close) **near, approach**
接近する せっきんする approach, draw near, come close

接 ▷**come close to**
セツ つ(ぐ)   Ⓚ0460

come close to, approach
接近する せっきんする approach, draw near, come close
直接に ちょくせつに directly
間接的な かんせつてきな indirect, roundabout

拶 ▷**press**
サツ   Ⓚ0336

press on, draw near; be imminent
挨拶 あいさつ greeting, salutation; speech, address; reply, response
挨拶状 あいさつじょう greeting card

approve →AGREE AND APPROVE

approximately
約 概 大 頃 位 方 程 辺

約 ▷**approximately**
ヤク   Ⓚ1177

approximately, about
約百万円 やくひゃくまんえん approximately one million yen
約三年 やくさんねん about three years

概 ▷**general**
ガイ   Ⓚ0959

general, on the whole, approximate, rough
概論 がいろん outline, general remarks
概算 がいさん approximation, rough estimate [calculation]
概況 がいきょう general condition [situation], outlook
概念 がいねん general idea, concept

大 ▷**in substance**
ダイ タイ おお- おお(きい) おお(いに)   Ⓚ2882

in substance, on the whole, in general, for the most part
大意 たいい substance, gist, general outline
大概 たいがい generally, mostly; probably, maybe
大勢 たいせい general trend [tendency]
大体 だいたい outline, substance; generally, roughly, on the whole
大抵 たいてい generally, mostly, for the most part
大半 たいはん the greater part, majority
大部分 だいぶぶん most, greater part; mostly, for the most part
大分 だいぶ(=だいぶん) very, greatly, considerably
大多数 だいたすう majority, greater part

頃 ▷**about**
ころ -ごろ   Ⓚ0124

[also suffix] **about, around, toward**
十八世紀の終わり頃 じゅうはっせいきのおわりごろ toward the end of the eighteenth century
八時頃 はちじごろ about eight o'clock

位 ▷**about**
イ くらい ぐらい   Ⓚ0045

about, approximately
十分位 じっぷんぐらい about ten minutes
これ位の大きさ これくらいのおおきさ about this size

方 ▷**about**
ホウ かた -がた -なた   Ⓚ1709

about; by
二割方減 にわりがたげん decrease of about 20 percent
利子を二分方引き下げる りしをにぶがたひきさげる lower the rate of interest by 2 percent

程 ▷**...or thereabouts**
テイ -ほど   Ⓚ1100

...or thereabouts, about, approximately
三週間程 さんしゅうかんほど three weeks or thereabouts

辺 ▷**thereabouts**
ヘン あた(り) -べ   Ⓚ2607

[also suffix] (near that place or time) **thereabouts, about**
一昨年辺り いっさくねんあたり the year before last or thereabouts

areas and localities
地方辺域区領帯圏

地 ▷place
チ ジ ⓚ0181

[also suffix] (particular region) **place, locality, region, district**

地元 じもと local end, local area
地名 ちめい place name
産地 さんち place of production; place of birth
辺地 へんち remote place
寒冷地 かんれいち cold [northern] district
遠隔地 えんかくち distant place

方 ▷locality
ホウ かた -がた -なた ⓚ1709

locality, place, district, region, area, countryside

方面 ほうめん direction, district; field, sphere
方言 ほうげん dialect
方々に ほうぼうに in several places; everywhere, all over
遠方 えんぽう great distance; distant place
地方 ちほう locality, district, region

辺 ▷vicinity
ヘン あた(り) -べ ⓚ2607

[also suffix] (nearby area) **vicinity, surroundings, neighborhood, environs, outskirts**

周辺 しゅうへん environs, outskirts; circumference
身辺 しんぺん one's person, one's immediate surroundings
近辺 きんぺん vicinity, neighborhood
官辺 かんぺん government [official] circles, official quarters
東京辺で とうきょうへんで in the vicinity of Tokyo

域 ▷bounded area
イキ ⓚ0421

bounded area, region, limits, zone, district

域内の いきないの within the area
地域 ちいき region, area
水域 すいいき water area, waters
区域 くいき zone, area; limits
海域 かいいき sea area
全域 ぜんいき the whole area, entire region

区 ▷district
ク ⓚ2559

[also suffix] **district, zone, region, area, section**
区域 くいき zone, area; limits

区間 くかん section, territory
地区 ちく district, area, region, lot
管区 かんく district (under jurisdiction); parish
学区 がっく school district [area]
選挙区 せんきょく electoral district, precinct
禁漁区 きんりょうく game preserve, wildlife sanctuary

領 ▷territory
リョウ ⓚ1133

[also suffix] **territory, domain, possession, estate**

領土 りょうど territory, domain
領内 りょうない domains, territory
領海 りょうかい territorial water
領地 りょうち territory, possession, dominion, domain; fief, feud
領空 りょうくう airspace
天領 てんりょう imperial demesne; shogunal demesne
日本領 にほんりょう Japanese territory
カンボジア領 かんぼじありょう Cambodian possession

帯 ▷belt
タイ お(びる) おび ⓚ2237

[also suffix] (geographical area) **belt, zone, region**

帯状の おびじょう(=たいじょう)の belt-shaped
地帯 ちたい zone, area
一帯 いったい belt, zone, tract (of land), area
熱帯 ねったい tropics, torrid zone
緑地帯 りょくちたい green belt
時間帯 じかんたい time belt
バンアレン帯 ばんあれんたい Van Allen Belt

圏 ▷sphere
ケン ⓚ2714

(spherical domain of action) **sphere, realm, circle, domain, zone, radius, range**

対流圏 たいりゅうけん troposphere
生物圏 せいぶつけん biosphere
暴風圏 ぼうふうけん storm zone
通信圏外 つうしんけんがい out of the range of communication
ポンド圏 ぽんどけん sterling zone
北極圏 ほっきょくけん arctic zone; Arctic Circle

area units

坪　歩　畝　反　町

坪 ▷*tsubo* (3.3 sq. m)
つぼ Ⓚ0248

unit of sq. measure equiv. to approx. 3.3 sq. m or 36 sq. *shaku* (尺), used esp. for measuring land area
十坪 とつぼ 10 *tsubo*
建て坪 たてつぼ floor space

歩 ▷*bu* (3.3 sq. m)
ホ ブ フ ある(く) あゆ(む) Ⓚ2141

bu: unit of sq. measure equiv. to approx. 3.3 sq. m or 36 sq. *shaku* (尺), used esp. for measuring fields or farms
三十歩 さんじゅうぶ 30 *bu*

畝 ▷*se* (0.99 ares)
うね せ Ⓚ1332

[original meaning] **ridge, furrow; rib, cord (of textiles)**
畝溝 うねみぞ furrow ridges
畝織 うねおり rep, ribbed fabric

反 ▷*tan* (9.9 ares)
ハン ホン タン そ(る) そ(らす) Ⓚ2549

[formerly also 段] unit of sq. measure equiv. to approx. 9.9 ares or 300 *bu* (歩)
土地四反 とちよんたん a lot of 4 *tan* (approx. 1 acre)

町 ▷*cho* (99.2 ares)
チョウ まち Ⓚ1028

unit of sq. measure equiv. to approx. 99.2 ares or 10 *tan* (反)
町歩 ちょうぶ hectare

argue and discuss

議　争　論　弁　諏

議 ▷discuss
ギ Ⓚ1480

ⓐ [original meaning] (talk together) **discuss, consult**
ⓑ (conduct a formal discussion) **discuss, debate, deliberate, argue, propose**
a 議題 ぎだい topic for discussion
　議決 ぎけつ decision, resolution
　議事 ぎじ proceedings, business
　会議 かいぎ conference, meeting, council
　審議する しんぎする deliberate, consider, discuss

閣議 かくぎ cabinet conference
b 議論 ぎろん argument, discussion
　討議する とうぎする discuss, debate on, deliberate upon
　論議する ろんぎする discuss, argue, debate
　不思議な ふしぎな strange, mysterious, wonderful
　衆議院 しゅうぎいん House of Representatives, Lower House

争 ▷contend
ソウ あらそ(う) Ⓚ1749

(strive in debate) **contend, dispute, argue**
争議 そうぎ dispute, strike
争点 そうてん point of contention, issue
論争 ろんそう dispute, argument

論 ▷argue
ロン Ⓚ1424

ⓐ [original meaning] (put forth reasons) **argue, discuss, discourse, reason**
ⓑ (contend in argument) **argue, dispute**
ⓒ **argument, argumentation, debate**
a 論評 ろんぴょう comment, criticism, review
　論説 ろんせつ discourse, dissertation; editorial
　論理 ろんり logic
　論理的 ろんりてき logical
　評論 ひょうろん comment, criticism, review
　理論 りろん theory
　言論 げんろん speech, discussion
　推論 すいろん reasoning, inference, induction, deduction
b 論議 ろんぎ discussion, argument, debate
　論争する ろんそうする dispute, argue
c 討論 とうろん debate, discussion, argument
　議論 ぎろん argument, discussion
　結論 けつろん conclusion
　反論 はんろん counterargument, refutation
　勿論 もちろん of course, no doubt, naturally

弁 ▷argue (for)
ベン Ⓚ1730

[formerly 辯]
ⓐ **argue, debate, dispute**
ⓑ **argue for [in favor of], speak (up) for, defend, explain, justify**
a 弁論 べんろん discussion, argument; oral proceedings
　弁護士 べんごし lawyer, attorney
　詭弁 きべん sophism, sophistry
　代弁する だいべんする speak [act] for another; pay by proxy
b 弁明 べんめい vindication, explanation, defense
　弁解 べんかい explanation, vindication, justification, excuse

抗弁する こうべんする make a plea, demur, defend oneself

諏 ▷consult
シュ ス   Ⓚ1428

consult
諏訪湖 すわこ Lake Suwa
諮諏 ししゅ [rare] consult, refer (a matter) to

arm →HAND AND ARM

---

armed forces
軍 兵 勢 隊

軍 ▷army
グン   Ⓚ1789

ⓐ [also prefix and suffix] **army, the military, armed forces, troops**
ⓑ **suffix after names of armies**
ⓒ **military**
ⓓ **organization resembling an army**

a   軍隊 ぐんたい army, troops
軍人 ぐんじん soldier, military man
軍事力 ぐんじりょく military force
軍縮 ぐんしゅく reduction of armaments
軍部 ぐんぶ military authorities, the military
軍当局 ぐんとうきょく military authorities
空軍 くうぐん air force
敵軍 てきぐん hostile army force, enemy troops
b   連合軍 れんごうぐん allied forces, the Allies
アメリカ軍 あめりかぐん U.S. Army
c   軍服 ぐんぷく military uniform
軍医 ぐんい military doctor
軍政 ぐんせい military administration
軍国主義 ぐんこくしゅぎ militarism
d   救世軍 きゅうせいぐん Salvation Army

兵 ▷the military
ヘイ ヒョウ   Ⓚ2207

the military, army, soldiery
兵事 へいじ military affairs
兵役 へいえき military service
兵糧 ひょうろう army provisions, food
徴兵 ちょうへい conscription, enlistment, draft

勢 ▷forces
セイ いきお(い)   Ⓚ2487

[also suffix] **forces, army**
勢揃いする せいぞろいする assemble in full force, muster
加勢する かせいする held, aid, assist
軍勢 ぐんぜい army, force; number of soldiers

総勢 そうぜい the whole army
徳川勢 とくがわぜい Tokugawa forces

隊 ▷party
タイ   Ⓚ0570

(organized group of troops) **party, army unit, corps, body of troops**
隊長 たいちょう captain, leader, commander
隊形 たいけい battle formation, disposition of troops
軍隊 ぐんたい army, troops
部隊 ぶたい unit, corps, party, squad
連隊 れんたい regiment
中隊 ちゅうたい company, squadron
兵隊 へいたい soldier; troops
艦隊 かんたい squadron, fleet
自衛隊 じえいたい Self Defense Forces
警官隊 けいかんたい police force [squad]
分遣隊 ぶんけんたい detachment
別動隊 べつどうたい detached party [column]

---

arrange
並 比 列 陳 羅 揃 整 理

並 ▷line up
ヘイ なみ なら(べる) なら(ぶ) なら(びに)   Ⓚ1936

line up, place in a row, place side by side, stand in a row
並立 へいりつ standing abreast
並列 へいれつ arrangement; row, parallel

比 ▷rank
ヒ くら(べる)   Ⓚ0014

[original meaning] **rank, line up**
比翼 ひよく wings abreast; single garment made to look double
比肩する ひけんする equal, rank with, compare favorably

列 ▷arrange in a row
レツ   Ⓚ0729

arrange in a row, line up
列車 れっしゃ (railway) train
列島 れっとう archipelago
列挙 れっきょ enumeration, listing
整列する せいれつする stand in a row, line up
陳列する ちんれつする exhibit, display

陳 ▷lay out (for exhibit)
チン   Ⓚ0493

[original meaning] **lay out (for exhibit), put on display, spread out**

陳列する ちんれつする exhibit, display
出陳 しゅっちん submitting (something) to an exhibition

羅 ▷spread out
ラ   Ⓚ2278

spread out, arrange, line up; lie in a row

羅列する られつする arrange, itemize
羅針盤 らしんばん compass
森羅万象 しんらばんしょう all creation, Nature

揃 ▷arrange properly
セン そろ(える) そろ(う) そろ(い)
－ぞろ(い)   Ⓚ0539

arrange properly, put in order

靴を揃える くつをそろえる arrange the shoes

整 ▷put in order
セイ ととの(える) ととの(う)   Ⓚ2501

[original meaning] **put in order, arrange, adjust properly, make straight**

整理する せいりする put in order, arrange; liquidate, disorganize; retrench; cut, dispose of
整備 せいび maintenance, servicing, preparation
整風 せいふう rectification
整形外科 せいけいげか orthopedic surgery, orthopedics
整列する せいれつする stand in a row, line up
整地 せいち leveling of ground, soil preparation
整頓 せいとん proper arrangement
調整 ちょうせい regulation, adjustment

理 ▷put in order
リ   Ⓚ0881

put in order, arrange

修理する しゅうりする repair, mend
整理する せいりする put in order, arrange; liquidate, disorganize; retrench; cut, dispose of

arrive
着 到 至 及 届 達

着 ▷arrive
チャク ジャク き(る) －ぎ き(せる) －き(せ)
つ(く) つ(ける)   Ⓚ2826

[rarely also 著]

ⓐ **arrive at, reach, come to hand**

ⓑ **land**

ⓒ **suffix indicating time, place or order of arrival**

a 着駅 ちゃくえき destination station
着信 ちゃくしん arrival of mail
着米 ちゃくべい arriving in America
到着 とうちゃく arrival
先着順 せんちゃくじゅん order of arrival
帰着する きちゃくする return, come back; arrive at, result in
発着 はっちゃく departure and arrival

b 着陸 ちゃくりく landing, alighting
着地 ちゃくち landing
着水 ちゃくすい alighting [landing] on the water

c 五時着の列車 ごじちゃくのれっしゃ train due at five o'clock
東京着の時間 とうきょうちゃくのじかん time of arrival in Tokyo
第一着 だいいっちゃく first to arrive

到 ▷arrive
トウ   Ⓚ1163

arrive (at), reach, come to

到着 とうちゃく arrival
到達 とうたつ arrival; attainment
到来 とうらい arrival, advent
殺到する さっとうする rush in, pour in; descend on

至 ▷come to
シ いた(る)   Ⓚ1869

[original meaning] **come to, arrive at, reach**

必至だ ひっしだ be inevitable

及 ▷reach to
キュウ およ(ぶ) およ(び)
およ(ぼす)   Ⓚ2868

[original meaning] (go as far as or arrive at a goal) **reach to, come up to (a standard), attain (successful results)**

及第する きゅうだいする pass an examination
及落 きゅうらく passing or failing an examination
追及する ついきゅうする pursue, seek after, follow, press (a person) hard
企及する ききゅうする try to attain (something)

届 ▷reach
とど(ける) －とど(け) とど(く)   Ⓚ2651

ⓐ (succeed in touching) **reach, get at**

ⓑ (be delivered) **reach (a destination), arrive, be received**

a 手の届く所 てのとどくところ within one's reach
目の届く限り めのとどくかぎり as far as the eye can reach

b 届かない手紙 とどかないてがみ letter that fails to reach its destination

達 ▷attain
タツ -たち   Ⓚ2706

(arrive at) **attain, reach, arrive, come up to, gain**

到達 とうたつ arrival; attainment
先達 せんだつ guide, precursor, pioneer, leader
発達する はったつする develop, grow, make progress

arrogance →BOASTING AND ARROGANCE

art
技　倆　術　芸　道

技 ▷skill
ギ わざ   Ⓚ0221
see also →SKILL

[sometimes also 伎] [original meaning] **skill, ability, craft, art**

技術 ぎじゅつ technique, art, skill; technology
技能 ぎのう skill, ability, capacity
技師 ぎし engineer, technician
技量 ぎりょう skill, ability, capacity
技巧 ぎこう art, craftsmanship, technical skill; trick
競技 きょうぎ match, contest, game; sporting event
演技 えんぎ acting, performance
特技 とくぎ one's special ability [talent], one's special skill [art]
実技 じつぎ practical technique [skill]

倆 ▷skill
リョウ
see also →SKILL

[now usu. 量] **skill**

技倆(=伎倆) ぎりょう skill, ability, capacity

術 ▷practical art
ジュツ   Ⓚ0433

ⓐ **practical art, technique, skill**
ⓑ **technical art, technique, technology**

a 美術 びじゅつ art, fine arts
芸術 げいじゅつ art, the arts
手術 しゅじゅつ surgical operation
戦術 せんじゅつ tactics, strategy
奇術 きじゅつ conjuring tricks, jugglery
医術 いじゅつ art of medicine
催眠術 さいみんじゅつ hypnotism, mesmerism
用兵術 ようへいじゅつ tactics, strategy
b 術語 じゅつご technical term, terminology
技術 ぎじゅつ technique, art, skill; technology
学術 がくじゅつ science, learning; arts and sciences

芸 ▷art
ゲイ   Ⓚ1892

art, craft, skill

芸術 げいじゅつ art, the arts
芸事 げいごと artistic accomplishments
工芸 こうげい technical art, technology
民芸 みんげい folkcraft
手芸 しゅげい handicrafts, manual arts
技芸 ぎげい arts, crafts, accomplishments
文芸 ぶんげい literature, literary art, art and literature
学芸 がくげい arts and sciences; culture
多芸は無芸 たげいはむげい Jack-of-all-trades and master of none

道 ▷the way of an art
ドウ トウ みち   Ⓚ2701

[also suffix] **the way of an art, esp. the principles of training and mental discipline of an art (as a martial art); art, way of life**

道場 どうじょう *dojo*, gymnasium
柔道 じゅうどう judo
武道 ぶどう martial arts
書道 しょどう calligraphy, penmanship
茶道 さどう(=ちゃどう) tea ceremony
武士道 ぶしどう Bushido (samurai code of behavior)
陰陽道 おんみょうどう(=おんようどう) art of divining

ascend
昇　上　騰　登

昇 ▷ascend
ショウ のぼ(る)   Ⓚ2139

[original meaning] **ascend, rise, go up**

昇天 しょうてん the Ascension; death
昇降口 しょうこうぐち entrance, hatchway
上昇する じょうしょうする ascend, rise

上 ▷go up
ジョウ ショウ うえ うわ- かみ あ(げる)
あ(がる) あ(がり) のぼ(る) のぼ(り)
のぼ(せる) のぼ(す)   Ⓚ2876

【ジョウ ショウ】

(proceed to or as if to a higher place) **go up, rise, ascend; board, get on**

上昇する じょうしょうする ascend, rise
上陸する じょうりくする land, disembark
上船する じょうせんする embark
浮上する ふじょうする surface, rise [float] to the surface

溯上する そじょうする go upstream; retroact, retrospect

北上する ほくじょうする go up north

【あ(がる)】

go up, come up, rise, climb

屋根に上がる やねにあがる go up on the roof

風呂から上がる ふろからあがる step out of the bath

騰 ▷rise (esp. in price)

トウ   Ⓚ1024

[original meaning] **rise, jump up, advance**—said esp. of prices

騰貴 とうき rise (in prices)

騰落 とうらく rise and fall, fluctuations

高騰(=昂騰) こうとう steep rise (in prices), jump

暴騰 ぼうとう sudden (price) rise

沸騰 ふっとう boiling, seething, bubbling

登 ▷climb

トウ ト のぼ(る)   Ⓚ2251

climb, ascend, mount, go up

登山 とざん mountain climbing, mountaineering

登頂 とうちょう climbing to the summit

登楼する とうろうする go into a tall building; visit a brothel

登高する とうこうする climb up

Asian countries

日 緬 老 華 蒙 鮮
泰 越 印 竺 比

日 ▷Japan

ニチ ジツ ひ -び -か   Ⓚ2606

see also →**JAPAN**

Japan

日本 にほん(=にっぽん) Japan

日銀 にちぎん Bank of Japan

日米 にちべい Japan and U.S.

日韓 にっかん Japan and (South) Korea

日ソ にっそ Soviet-Japanese, Japanese-Soviet

日本酒 にほんしゅ sake, rice wine

来日する らいにちする come to Japan

緬 ▷Myanmar

メン

[rare] **Burma, Myanmar**

緬甸 めんでん(=びるま) Burma

英緬戦争 えいめんせんそう Anglo-Burmese Wars

老 ▷Laos

ロウ お(いる) ふ(ける)   Ⓚ2754

Laos

老日辞書 ろうにちじしょ Lao-Japanese Dictionary

華 ▷China

カ ケ はな   Ⓚ1973

see also →**CHINA**

China

華僑 かきょう Chinese merchant living abroad

華北 かほく North China

中華料理 ちゅうかりょうり Chinese food

日華 にっか Japan and China

蒙 ▷Mongolia

モウ こうむ(る)   Ⓚ2045

abbrev. of 蒙古 もうこ: **Mongolia**

内蒙 ないもう Inner Mongolia

満蒙 まんもう Manchuria and Mongolia

鮮 ▷Korea

セン あざ(やか)   Ⓚ1656

see also →**KOREA**

Korea

朝鮮 ちょうせん (North) Korea

南鮮 なんせん South Korea

北鮮 ほくせん North Korea

泰 ▷Thailand

タイ   Ⓚ2239

Thailand, Siam

泰国 たいこく Thailand, Siam

泰語 たいご Thai, Siamese

対泰関係 たいたいかんけい relations with Thailand

越 ▷Vietnam

エツ こ(す) -ご(し) こ(える)
-ご(え)   Ⓚ2825

abbrev. of 越南 えつなん: **Vietnam**

中越紛争 ちゅうえつふんそう dispute between China and Vietnam

反越 はんえつ anti-Vietnam

印 ▷India

イン しるし -じるし   Ⓚ0733

India

印綿(=印棉) いんめん Indian raw cotton

日印関係 にちいんかんけい Japan-India relations

竺 ▷India

ジク   Ⓚ2280

India

竺学 じくがく [rare] Indian [Buddhist] studies
天竺 てんじく India

比 ▷Philippines
ヒ くら(べる)　　　　　　　　Ⓚ0014

Philippines
比島 ひとう the Philippines
比日 ひにち the Philippines and Japan

aspect
面　上　柄

面 ▷side
メン おも おもて つら　　　　Ⓚ1796

[also suffix] (distinct aspect) **side, aspect, phase, plane**
局面 きょくめん situation, aspect of an affair; position (in a chess game)
場面 ばめん scene; situation
技術面 ぎじゅつめん technical side
軍事面 ぐんじめん military plane

上 ▷from the viewpoint of
ジョウ ショウ うえ うわ– かみ あ(げる)
あ(がる) あ(がり) のぼ(る) のぼ(り)
のぼ(せる) のぼ(す)　　　　Ⓚ2876

[also suffix] **from the viewpoint of, -ly, by reasons of**
史上 しじょう historically, from the historical point of view
身上 しんじょう one's history; one's merit
身上 しんしょう fortune, property
事実上 じじつじょう actually, as a matter of fact
便宜上 べんぎじょう for convenience' sake

柄 ▷considering the character of
ヘイ がら え　　　　　　　　Ⓚ0799

[suffix] **considering the character of (the matter in question), in view of; in character, appropriate to**
時局柄 じきょくがら in view of the present situation
時節柄の贈り物 じせつがらのおくりもの seasonable gift

assembly
会　集

会 ▷meeting
カイ エ あ(う) あ(わせる)　　Ⓚ1741

[also suffix] **meeting, gathering; assembly, conference**

会合 かいごう meeting, gathering
会館 かいかん hall, assembly hall
会場 かいじょう place of meeting, site
会議 かいぎ conference, meeting, council
集会 しゅうかい gathering, meeting, assembly
総会 そうかい general meeting
開会 かいかい opening a meeting
大会 たいかい mass meeting, rally; meet, tournament
座談会 ざだんかい round-table talk, symposium

集 ▷gathering
シュウ あつ(まる) あつ(める)
つど(う)　　　　　　　　　Ⓚ2413

gathering, meeting, assembly; collection
集会 しゅうかい gathering, meeting, assembly
集団 しゅうだん group, body, mass, crowd
群集 ぐんしゅう crowd, mob; forming a large group (of people)

assistant
補　丞

補 ▷assistant
ホ おぎな(う)　　　　　　　Ⓚ1103

[suffix] **assistant, aid, apprentice**
書記補 しょきほ assistant clerk
警部補 けいぶほ assistant inspector
外交官補 がいこうかんほ probationary diplomat

丞 ▷aide
ジョウ　　　　　　　　　　Ⓚ2198

aide, assistant officer (in ancient China)
丞相 じょうしょう prime minister (in ancient China)

associates →FRIENDS AND ASSOCIATES

assume upright position
立　起

立 ▷stand
リツ リュウ た(つ) た(ち)- た(てる)
た(て)- –だ(て) –だ(てる)　　Ⓚ1723

ⓐ [original meaning] **stand, stand up, stand erect**
ⓑ stand on one's own legs, be independent
a 立像 りつぞう standing image, statue
立腹する りっぷくする get angry, lose one's temper

立身する りっしんする establish oneself in life
立候補 りっこうほ candidacy
起立 きりつ standing up, rising
直立する ちょくりつする stand erect [upright], rise perpendicularly

b 自立する じりつする become independent, establish oneself
独立する どくりつする become independent, stand on one's own legs [feet]

起 ▷rise
キ お(きる) お(こる) お(こす)　　Ⓚ2818

ⓐ [original meaning] (assume a standing position) **rise (to one's feet), stand up**
ⓑ (get out of bed) **rise, get up**

a 起立する きりつする stand up, rise
起居 ききょ one's daily life

b 起床 きしょう getting up, rising
起座する きざする sit up in bed

atmosphere
雰　　気

雰 ▷atmosphere
フン　　Ⓚ2414

atmosphere
雰囲気 ふんいき atmosphere, mood

気 ▷atmosphere
キ ケ　　Ⓚ2751

ⓐ **atmosphere**
ⓑ (psychological environment) **atmosphere, tone**

a 気圧 きあつ atmospheric [air] pressure
気温 きおん (atmospheric) temperature
大気 たいき the atmosphere

b 気運 きうん luck, tendency, opportunity
景気 けいき things, times; business conditions
雰囲気 ふんいき atmosphere, mood
殺気 さっき menace of death, reek of murder
熱気 ねっき hot air, heat; fevered air, enthusiasm

atmospheric discharges
雷　　電

雷 ▷thunder
ライ かみなり　　Ⓚ2432

ⓐ [original meaning] **thunder**

ⓑ **lightning**

a 雷電 らいでん thunder and lightning, thunderbolt
雷雲 らいうん thunder cloud
雷神 らいじん god of thunder

b 落雷 らくらい strike of a thunderbolt
避雷針 ひらいしん lightning rod

電 ▷lightning
デン　　Ⓚ2431

[original meaning] **lightning**
電光 でんこう lightning; electric light
雷電 らいでん thunder and lightning, thunderbolt

atmospheric vapor →KINDS OF ATMOSPHERIC VAPOR

attack
攻　撃　襲　侵　爆

攻 ▷attack
コウ せ(める)　　Ⓚ0215

ⓐ **attack, take the offensive**
ⓑ **attack, offensive, offense**

a 攻撃 こうげき attack, assault; criticism; *baseball* batting
攻勢 こうせい offensive, aggression
攻略 こうりゃく capture, conquest; invasion
正攻法 せいこうほう regular tactics for attack

b 攻守 こうしゅ offense and defense; batting and fielding
速攻 そっこう swift attack
反攻 はんこう counterattack, counteroffensive

撃 ▷strike
ゲキ う(つ)　　Ⓚ2492

strike, make a military attack, destroy
撃破する げきはする defeat, rout; destroy
攻撃 こうげき attack, assault; criticism; *baseball* batting
爆撃 ばくげき bombing, bombardment
反撃する はんげきする counterattack, strike [fight] back
襲撃する しゅうげきする raid, attack, assault

襲 ▷raid
シュウ おそ(う)　　Ⓚ2533

ⓐ **raid, make a surprise attack on, assault, invade**
ⓑ **raid, surprise attack**

ab 襲撃 しゅうげき raid, attack, assault
来襲 らいしゅう attack, invasion, raid
急襲 きゅうしゅう raid, surprise attack
空襲 くうしゅう air raid
奇襲 きしゅう surprise attack

逆襲 ぎゃくしゅう counterattack

侵 ▷invade
シン おか(す)　　　Ⓚ0085

(enter by force) invade, raid

侵略 しんりゃく invasion, aggression
侵入 しんにゅう invasion, raid, trespass, intrusion
侵犯 しんぱん invasion; violation

爆 ▷bomb
バク　　　Ⓚ1020

bomb, raid

空爆 くうばく aerial bombing
被爆者 ひばくしゃ victim of atomic air raid

attain proficiency
達　　熟

達 ▷attain proficiency
タツ −たち　　　Ⓚ2706

attain proficiency or maturity, understand thoroughly, be versed in, be skillful

達観 たっかん philosophic view [ripeness]; farsighted view
達人 たつじん expert, master
達筆 たっぴつ good handwriting
達者な たっしゃな expert, proficient, clever; healthy, well, strong, robust
上達する じょうたつする make progress, attain proficiency
熟達する じゅくたつする attain proficiency, become expert

熟 ▷become skilled
ジュク う(れる)　　　Ⓚ2498

become skilled, attain proficiency

熟練 じゅくれん skill, dexterity
熟達する じゅくたつする attain proficiency, become expert
円熟した えんじゅくした mature, mellow, ripe, fully developed
習熟する しゅうじゅくする get skilled (in), become practiced (in)

attend
臨　登　出

臨 ▷be present at
リン のぞ(む)　　　Ⓚ1470

be present at, be on the spot, attend, come to, visit

臨床医 りんしょうい clinician
臨席 りんせき presence, attendance
臨場 りんじょう presence, attendance; visit
臨検 りんけん spot inspection, raid
臨在 りんざい presence
来臨 らいりん attendance, presence; visit

登 ▷attend
トウ ト のぼ(る)　　　Ⓚ2251

attend, go to, appear

登校 とうこう attending school
登庁する とうちょうする attend a government office
登院 とういん attendance at the House
登城 とじょう attendance at a castle
登場する とうじょうする come on stage; appear

出 ▷appear
シュツ スイ で(る) −で だ(す)　　　Ⓚ2934

appear, attend, be present at

出席 しゅっせき attendance, presence
出勤する しゅっきんする attend one's office, go to work
出頭する しゅっとうする attend, present oneself
出演する しゅつえんする appear on stage, perform, play
出場する しゅつじょうする take part, participate
出願する しゅつがんする make an application

attention
気　　念

気 ▷care
キ ケ　　　Ⓚ2751

care, attention, precaution

気遣う きづかう feel anxious about, worry about, have apprehensions of
気配り きくばり attention to detail
気付 きづけ c/o (care of)
気兼ねする きがねする feel hesitant, be ill at ease, be afraid of giving trouble

念 ▷**attention**
ネン   Ⓚ1773

attention, care, precaution
　念入りな ねんいりな careful, elaborate
　入念に にゅうねんに carefully, scrupulously
　丹念 たんねん application, assiduity, diligence

authority →POWER AND AUTHORITY

avoid and abstain
避 逃 禦 忌 禁

避 ▷**avoid**
ヒ さ(ける)   Ⓚ2742

[original meaning] **avoid, evade, shirk**
　避暑 ひしょ summering
　避妊 ひにん contraception
　避難 ひなん refuge, shelter, evacuation
　逃避 とうひ escape, evasion, flight
　退避 たいひ taking refuge, evacuation
　回避する かいひする evade, dodge, avoid
　不可避な ふかひな inevitable, unavoidable, inescapable

逃 ▷**escape**
トウ に(げる) に(がす) のが(す)
のが(れる)   Ⓚ2666

(succeed in avoiding) **escape, evade, shirk**
　逃避 とうひ escape, evasion, flight

禦 ▷**ward off**
ギョ ふせ(ぐ)

[original meaning] **ward off, resist, keep out**
　防禦する ぼうぎょする defend, protect, safeguard

忌 ▷**shun**
キ い(む) い(み) い(まわしい)   Ⓚ1889

shun, avoid, abstain from
　忌避 きひ evasion, shirking
　忌憚 きたん reserve, scruple
　禁忌 きんき taboo; contraindication

禁 ▷**abstain from**
キン   Ⓚ2435

abstain from, refrain from, give up
　禁酒する きんしゅする abstain from [give up] drinking
　禁欲的な きんよくてきな abstentious, self-denying, ascetic

awake
悟 醒 覚 惺

悟 ▷**awake to**
ゴ さと(る)   Ⓚ0379

❶ **awake to, become aware of, realize, comprehend**
　悟了 ごりょう complete comprehension
　覚悟する かくごする be ready [prepared] for; be resigned; make up one's mind
❷ **awake to the Truth, become enlightened, attain satori**
　悟道 ごどう spiritual enlightenment; philosophy; (Buddhist) enlightenment

醒 ▷**awake**
セイ   Ⓚ1457

ⓐ **awake, wake up**
ⓑ **be disillusioned**
　a 覚醒する かくせいする awake, wake up; be awakened, be disillusioned
　半睡半醒 はんすいはんせい half asleep and half awake
　警醒 けいせい warning; waking up

覚 ▷**awake**
カク おぼ(える) さ(ます) さ(める)   Ⓚ2258

ⓐ **awake, wake up; be disillusioned**
ⓑ **awake to the Truth, become enlightened**
　a 覚醒する かくせいする awake, wake up; be awakened, be disillusioned
　覚醒剤 かくせいざい stimulant
　b 覚者 かくしゃ Buddha, the awakened one

惺 ▷**awake to**
セイ   Ⓚ0533

[original meaning, now rare] **awake to**
　惺悟する せいごする awaken to the Truth, become enlightened

bad
悪 劣 下 弊 粗 駄 廃

悪 ▷**bad**
アク オ わる(い) わる- あ(し)   Ⓚ2393

(inferior in quality) **bad, inferior, poor, unsatisfactory**
　悪質な あくしつな bad, malicious; malignant
　悪筆 あくひつ poor handwriting
　悪日 あくにち(=あくび) unlucky day

悪循環 あくじゅんかん vicious circle
悪条件 あくじょうけん bad terms
最悪 さいあく the worst

劣 ▷inferior
レツ おと(る)　Ⓚ2124

(lower in quality or status) **inferior, poor, subgrade, low-grade; weak**

劣等感 れっとうかん inferiority complex
劣悪な れつあくな inferior, coarse
優劣 ゆうれつ superiority or inferiority, quality
卑劣な ひれつな mean, base, cowardly

下 ▷of low grade
カ ゲ した しも もと さ(げる) さ(がる)
くだ(る) くだ(り) くだ(す) くだ(さる)
お(ろす) お(りる)　Ⓚ2862

of low grade, low-class, humble

下等な かとうな low, lower, inferior, mean
下宿 げしゅく lodging, boarding house
下水 げすい sewerage, drainage; foul water
下品な げひんな vulgar; low; mean; dirty

弊 ▷shabby
ヘイ　Ⓚ2508

shabby, worn-out, ragged, poor, impoverished

弊衣破帽 へいいはぼう shabby clothes and an old hat
弊履 へいり worn-out sandals [shoes]

粗 ▷coarse
ソ あら(い) あら-　Ⓚ1214

(of inferior quality) **coarse, crude, inferior, poor, humble, shabby**—used esp. as a term of humility before items presented as gifts

粗悪な そあくな coarse, crude, bad, inferior
粗品 そしな trifling gift, inferior goods
粗茶 そちゃ coarse tea
粗末な そまつな coarse, crude, inferior, humble
お粗末様 おそまつさま [humble] It was nothing at all/The pleasure was all mine

駄 ▷good for nothing
ダ タ　Ⓚ1617

[also prefix] **good for nothing, no good, poor, shabby, useless, worthless**

駄目 だめ go cross that does not constitute a territory; no good, useless; No!
駄作 ださく poor piece of writing
駄菓子 だがし cheap sweets
駄洒落 だじゃれ poor joke, pun
駄駄を捏ねる だだをこねる be unreasonable
無駄な むだな no good, fruitless, wasteful

廃 ▷waste
ハイ すた(れる) すた(る)　Ⓚ2712

waste, useless, discarded, abandoned, obsolete

廃品 はいひん waste articles, junk
廃ガス はいがす waste gas
廃熱 はいねつ waste heat
廃坑 はいこう abandoned mine
廃語 はいご obsolete word
荒廃 こうはい desolation, waste, ruin

bags
俵 袋 鞄 包 胞

俵 ▷straw sack
ヒョウ たわら　Ⓚ0097

straw sack [bag], sack

土俵 どひょう sumo (wrestling) ring; sandbag

袋 ▷bag
タイ ふくろ　Ⓚ2245

[original meaning] **bag, sack**

郵袋 ゆうたい mailbag
製袋 せいたい bag manufacturing
風袋 ふうたい tare

鞄 ▷bag (for carrying)
ホウ かばん　Ⓚ1594

bag, briefcase, suitcase

鞄持ち かばんもち private secretary; flunky
旅行鞄 りょこうかばん traveling bag, suitcase
通学鞄 つうがくかばん school bag

包 ▷wrapper
ホウ つつ(む)　Ⓚ2560

wrap(per), package, parcel
包帯 ほうたい bandage, dressing

胞 ▷membranous sac
ホウ　Ⓚ0826

any small membranous sac such as a vesicle, theca, sac, sheath, capsule or cell

胞子 ほうし spore
細胞 さいぼう cell
芽胞 がほう spore
小胞 しょうほう vesicle
肺胞 はいほう alveolus

bamboo

竹　笹　篠

竹 ▷bamboo
チク たけ　　　　　　　　Ⓚ0201

bamboo
- 竹馬の友 ちくばのとも childhood friend, old play-mate
- 竹材 ちくざい bamboo
- 竹林 ちくりん bamboo grove

笹 ▷bamboo grass
ささ　　　　　　　　　　Ⓚ2321

[sometimes also 篠] **bamboo grass**
- 笹原 ささはら field of bamboo grass
- 笹舟 ささぶね toy bamboo-leaf boat
- 熊笹 くまざさ *Sasa albo-marginata*, low and striped bamboo

篠 ▷dwarf bamboo
ショウ しの ささ　　　　　Ⓚ2372

thin-culmed dwarf bamboo growing in clusters
- 篠竹 しのだけ thin-culmed dwarf bamboo growing in clusters
- 篠笛 しのぶえ Japanese transverse bamboo flute
- 篠突く雨 しのつくあめ driving rain

bank

銀　　　行

銀 ▷bank
ギン　　　　　　　　　　Ⓚ1534

abbrev. of 銀行 ぎんこう: **bank**
- 日銀 にちぎん Bank of Japan
- 勧銀 かんぎん hypothecary bank
- 開銀 かいぎん development bank

行 ▷bank
コウ ギョウ アン い(く) ゆ(く) -ゆ(き) -い(き) おこな(う)　　Ⓚ0187

abbrev. of 銀行 ぎんこう: **bank**
- 行員 こういん bank clerk
- 行務 こうむ bank business
- 当行 とうこう our bank

barren

荒　　寥

荒 ▷wild
コウ あら(い) あら- あ(れる) あ(らす) -あ(らし)　　　　　Ⓚ1950

(in a primitive or uninhabited state) **wild, barren, desolate, bleak, deserted; devastated, ruined**
- 荒野 こうや wilderness, the wilds, wasteland
- 荒蕪地 こうぶち wild [waste] land, wilderness
- 荒廃 こうはい desolation, waste, ruin
- 荒涼たる こうりょうたる desolate, dreary
- 荒城 こうじょう ruined castle

寥 ▷desolate
リョウ

[now also 涼] **desolate, deserted, empty**
- 荒寥たる こうりょうたる desolate, dreary
- 寂寥たる せきりょうたる lonely, desolate

bases →BOTTOMS AND BASES

basis

基　本　素　礎　底　根　拠

基 ▷base
キ もと もとい　　　　　Ⓚ2330

(nonphysical support) **base, basis, foundation, ground**
- 基本 きほん basis, foundation
- 基準 きじゅん standard, criterion, basis
- 基幹 きかん mainstay, nucleus
- 基金 ききん fund, foundation, endowment
- 基調 きちょう keynote, underlying tone, basis

本 ▷basis
ホン もと　　　　　　　Ⓚ2937

basis, base, foundation
- 本拠 ほんきょ base, stronghold, headquarters
- 本位 ほんい (monetary) standard; standard, basis; original standing
- 基本 きほん basis, foundation
- 国本 こくほん foundation of a country
- 抜本的な ばっぽんてきな radical, drastic
- 根本 こんぽん basis, foundation; origin, source
- 農本主義 のうほんしゅぎ "agriculture-first" principle

素 ▷element
ソス   ⓚ2171

element, basic constituent, component
- 素子 そし *elec* element
- 要素 ようそ (essential) element, constituent, factor
- 酵素 こうそ ferment; enzyme
- 色素 しきそ pigment, coloring matter
- 栄養素 えいようそ nutritive elements [substance]
- 葉緑素 ようりょくそ chlorophyll
- 元素 げんそ element, chemical element

礎 ▷foundation
ソ いしずえ   ⓚ1152

(nonphysical support) **foundation, basis**
- 基礎 きそ basis, foundation
- 国礎 こくそ pillar of state

底 ▷bottom
テイ そこ   ⓚ2656

[formerly also 柢] (fundamental part) **bottom, basis, origin**
- 底本 ていほん original text
- 根底 こんてい root, basis, foundation
- 基底 きてい base, basis, foundation; *math* base
- 徹底 てってい thoroughness, completeness

根 ▷root
コン ね   ⓚ0841

(essential part) **root, basis, foundation**
- 根本 こんぽん basis, foundation; origin, source
- 根底 こんてい root, basis, foundation
- 根拠 こんきょ grounds, basis, authority

拠 ▷grounds
キョ コ   ⓚ0276

grounds, base, basis, foundation; authority
- 拠点 きょてん strongpoint, base
- 根拠 こんきょ grounds, basis, authority
- 本拠 ほんきょ base, stronghold, headquarters
- 論拠 ろんきょ grounds [basis] of an argument
- 典拠 てんきょ authority
- 証拠 しょうこ proof, evidence

baths
浴 湯 泉

浴 ▷bath
ヨク あ(びる) あ(びせる)   ⓚ0404

[suffix] **bath, bathing**
- 海水浴 かいすいよく sea bathing
- 日光浴 にっこうよく sunbath
- 冷水浴 れいすいよく cold-water bath

湯 ▷hot bath
トウ ゆ   ⓚ0561

hot bath, hot spring
- 湯治 とうじ hot spring cure, taking healing baths
- 入湯 にゅうとう taking a hot bath
- 銭湯 せんとう public bath, bathhouse

泉 ▷hot spring
セン いずみ   ⓚ2224

[also suffix] **hot spring**
- 鉱泉 こうせん mineral spring
- 源泉 げんせん fountainhead, source
- 硫黄泉 いおうせん sulfur spring
- アルカリ泉 あるかりせん alkali spring

bays →INLETS AND BAYS

be →EXIST AND BE

bear
負 荷 担 支

負 ▷bear (on the back)
フ ま(ける) ま(かす) お(う)   ⓚ1799

[original meaning] **bear [carry] on the back**
- 負荷 ふか load, burden

荷 ▷carry on shoulder
カ に   ⓚ1972

carry on shoulder, bear a burden
- 荷担(=加担) かたん assistance, support, participation
- 負荷 ふか load, burden

担 ▷bear on shoulder
タン かつ(ぐ) にな(う)   ⓚ0283

[original meaning] **bear [carry] on one's shoulder, shoulder, bear**
- 担架 たんか stretcher

支 ▷support
シ ささ(える)   ⓚ1717

(bear the weight of) **support, prop up, hold up**
- 支柱 しちゅう prop, stay, support
- 支点 してん fulcrum, point of support
- 支索 しさく stay

bear and endure

堪　忍　耐

堪 ▷endure
カン　タン　た(える)　たま(る)　　Ⓚ0514

endure, bear, tolerate
堪忍(=勘忍)する かんにんする have patience, bear with; forgive, pardon

忍 ▷bear
ニン　しの(ぶ)　しの(ばせる)　　Ⓚ1899

bear, endure, tolerate, suffer patiently
忍耐する にんたいする persevere, be patient, endure
忍従 にんじゅう submission, resignation
忍苦 にんく endurance, stoicism

耐 ▷withstand
タイ　た(える)　　Ⓚ1178

❶ (resist physical forces) **withstand, resist**
耐火 たいか fireproof
耐震 たいしん earthquake-proof
耐熱 たいねつ heat-resisting
耐水 たいすい waterproof
耐アルカリ性 たいあるかりせい alkali resistance

❷ endure, bear, last
耐久 たいきゅう endurance, persistence; durability, life
耐乏 たいぼう austerity, voluntary privation
忍耐 にんたい perseverance, patience, endurance

beautiful

美　彪　綺　娃　佳　瑶
麗　艶　妙　華　絢　斐

美 ▷beautiful
ビ　うつく(しい)　　Ⓚ1955

[sometimes also 媚] [original meaning] **beautiful, pretty, lovely**
美人 びじん beautiful woman
美少年 びしょうねん handsome youth
美女 びじょ beautiful woman [girl]
美容院 びよういん beauty shop [parlor]
美術 びじゅつ art, fine arts
美術館 びじゅつかん art museum [gallery]
美観 びかん fine view, beautiful sight
美化 びか beautification

優美 ゆうび grace, elegance
明美な めいびな picturesque, beautiful

彪 ▷magnificent
ヒョウ　ヒュウ　　Ⓚ2831

[archaic] **as magnificent and gorgeous as tiger stripes**

綺 ▷beautiful
キ　　Ⓚ1252

[now also 奇] **beautiful, gorgeous, elegant, decorative**
綺麗な きれいな beautiful, pretty; clean; fair
綺想曲 きそうきょく caprice, capriccio

娃 ▷beautiful
アイ　　Ⓚ0313

ⓐ beautiful
ⓑ beautiful woman
a 娃鬟 あいかん beautiful woman
b 館娃 かんあい name of a palace in China

佳 ▷fine
カ　　Ⓚ0068

[original meaning] (of pleasing appearance) **fine(-looking), beautiful**
佳人 かじん beautiful woman
佳麗 かれい beauty
佳景 かけい fine [beautiful] view
絶佳の ぜっかの superb (landscape)

瑶 ▷exquisite
ヨウ　　Ⓚ0942

[rare] **exquisite, beautiful like a gem, glittering, splendid; ornamented with gems**
瑶台 ようだい beautiful building ornamented with gems; fairyland
瑶顔 ようがん exquisite countenance, beautiful face

麗 ▷of graceful beauty
レイ　うるわ(しい)　　Ⓚ1845

[original meaning] **of graceful beauty, lovely, beautiful and neat [refreshing], resplendent**
麗人 れいじん beauty, belle
麗質 れいしつ beauty, charm
奇麗(=綺麗)な きれいな beautiful, pretty; clean; fair
美麗な びれいな beautiful, gorgeous
華麗な かれいな splendid, magnificent, resplendent, gorgeous
端麗な たんれいな graceful, elegant, handsome
豊麗な ほうれいな rich (design), beautiful, splendid
鮮麗 せんれい resplendent beauty

美辞麗句 びじれいく flowery words

艶 ▷charming
エン つや ⓚ1683

[original meaning] **charming, beautiful, fascinating, voluptuous**
艶容 えんよう fascinating figure, charming look
艶美 えんび beauty, charm
濃艶な のうえんな charming, bewitching, enchanting
妖艶な ようえんな fascinating, voluptuous

妙 ▷of marvelous beauty
ミョウ ⓚ0210

[original meaning] **of marvelous beauty, exquisite, charming, subtle**
妙法蓮華経 みょうほうれんげきょう Lotus Sutra
妙味 みょうみ subtle charm, beauty
美妙な びみょうな elegant, exquisite
微妙な びみょうな subtle, delicate

華 ▷magnificent
カ ケ はな ⓚ1973

magnificent, gorgeous, splendid, brilliant, flowery
華麗な かれいな splendid, magnificent, resplendent, gorgeous
華言 かげん [rare] flowery words, rhetorical flourishes
豪華な ごうかな gorgeous, splendid, pompous

絢 ▷gorgeous
ケン ⓚ1234

gorgeous, resplendent, brilliant, florid
絢爛たる けんらんたる gorgeous, dazzling; flowery (speech)

斐 ▷florid
ヒイ ⓚ2417

[archaic] **florid, embellished, beautiful**
斐然たる ひぜんたる florid, beautiful

become stupefied
酔　麻

酔 ▷become intoxicated
スイ よ(う) よ(い) ⓚ1348

become intoxicated (with alcohol), get drunk
酔態 すいたい drunkenness, intoxication
酔漢 すいかん drunkard, drunken fellow
泥酔した でいすいした dead-drunk
麻酔 ますい anesthesia

麻 ▷become numb
マ マー あさ ⓚ2694

become numb, become palsied
麻酔 ますい anesthesia
麻薬 まやく narcotic, drug
麻痺 まひ paralysis, palsy, numbness, anesthesia

before
前　先　予

前 ▷before
ゼン まえ ⓚ1957

[also suffix] (preceding in time) **before, ago, previous, past**
前日 ぜんじつ the day before
前年 ぜんねん the year before
前年度 ぜんねんど preceding (fiscal) year
午前 ごぜん morning, forenoon
以前 いぜん before, ago, since
寸前に すんぜんに immediately before
三年前 さんねんぜん three years ago

先 ▷ahead
セン さき ま(ず) ⓚ2123

(antecedent in time or order) **ahead of, in advance, first, previous, preceding, prior, beforehand**
先発する せんぱつする start in advance, go ahead, precede
先着 せんちゃく first arrival
先取する せんしゅする take first, score first
先見 せんけん foresight, anticipation
先決 せんけつ previous decision, prior settlement
先入観 せんにゅうかん preconception, bias, prejudice
先番 せんばん one's turn to make the first move
先輩 せんぱい senior, superior, elder
先生 せんせい teacher; doctor
優先 ゆうせん preference, priority

予 ▷in advance
ヨ ⓚ1719

[sometimes also 預] **in advance, pre-, fore-, beforehand, previously, prior to, preliminary**
予言 よげん prediction, forecast
予知 よち premonition, foreknowledge
予報 よほう forecast, prediction
予測 よそく estimate, forecast, prediction
予算 よさん budget; estimate, calculation
予期 よき expectation, anticipation, hope
予価 よか probable [predetermined] price

予約 よやく reservation, preengagement; subscription

予定 よてい schedule, plan, prearrangement; expectation; estimate

予備 よび reserve, spare; preparation, preliminaries

予科 よか preparatory course

予防 よぼう prevention, protection, precaution

予習 よしゅう preparation (of one's lessons)

予感 よかん premonition, hunch

begin

始 出 掛 発 起
就 開 創 肇

始 ▷begin
シ はじ(める) はじ(まる)　Ⓚ0252

begin, start, open

始動 しどう starting (machines)

始業式 しぎょうしき opening ceremony of the school term

開始する かいしする begin, commence, open

創始する そうしする initiate, create, found

出 ▷begin to do
シュツ スイ で(る) −で −だ(す)　Ⓚ2934

begin to do, start doing

勉強し出す べんきょうしだす begin to study

雨が降り出した あめがふりだした It began to rain

逃げ出す にげだす make a break, run off, make off

打ち出す うちだす set out [forth], work out, hammer out; strike out, emboss; announce

掛 ▷start doing
−か(ける) か(け) −が(け) か(かる)
−が(かる) か(かり) −が(かり)　Ⓚ0449

start doing, begin to do; be about to do

走り掛ける はしりかける start running

死に掛ける しにかける be dying

発 ▷start
ハツ ホツ た(つ)　Ⓚ2222

(bring into being) **start, originate, initiate, give rise to, generate, produce**

発端 ほったん origin, beginning, outset

発会 はっかい opening of a meeting; first meeting

発足する ほっそく(=はっそく)する start, be inaugurated

発刊する はっかんする publish, issue

発動する はつどうする exercise, invoke; move, put in motion

発電 はつでん generation of electricity; telegraphing

発熱 はつねつ generation of heat; attack of fever

発癌 はつがん carcinogenesis, production of cancer

発想 はっそう conception; *music* expression

発明 はつめい invention, contrivance

発起人 ほっきにん originator; promoter; proposer

起 ▷start
キ お(きる) お(こる) お(こす)　Ⓚ2818

start, begin, initiate, promote

起訴 きそ prosecution, indictment, litigation

起草する きそうする draft (a bill), draw up

起工 きこう start of construction work

起爆 きばく priming (in explosives)

就 ▷set about
シュウ ジュ つ(く) つ(ける)　Ⓚ1512

set about a task, set out, proceed to do, set to, enter upon, launch into, take up (a position)

就職 しゅうしょく finding employment

就任 しゅうにん assumption of office, inauguration

就学する しゅうがくする enter school

就労する しゅうろうする set to work, find employment

就航 しゅうこう (of ships) going into commission

就業 しゅうぎょう employment, starting work

開 ▷open
カイ ひら(く) ひら(き) −びら(き)
ひら(ける) あ(く) あ(ける)　Ⓚ2835

open, commence, establish

開始する かいしする begin, commence, open

開会 かいかい opening a meeting

開祖 かいそ founder, originator

開運 かいうん beginning of good luck

開催する かいさいする hold an event, open (an exhibition)

開店する かいてんする open a store [shop]; set up a business

再開する さいかいする reopen, resume

創 ▷initiate
ソウ つく(る)　Ⓚ1610

initiate, originate, start

創立する そうりつする establish, organize, start

創始 そうし initiating, creation, foundation

創刊 そうかん launching a magazine; first issue

創業 そうぎょう inauguration of an enterprise

創設 そうせつ establishment, founding

肇 ▷originate
チョウ　Ⓚ2439

[rare] **originate, found, create, begin**

肇国 ちょうこく founding of a state

beginnings
緒 序 端 始 初
元 本 根 源

緒 ▷outset
ショ チョ お   Ⓚ1260

outset, beginning, inception, first step, early stage

緒戦 しょせん(=ちょせん) beginning of hostilities, early stage of a war

緒論 しょろん introduction, preface

緒言 しょげん(=ちょげん) foreword, preface

端緒 たんしょ(=たんちょ) beginning, start, first step; clue

序 ▷introductory part
ジョ   Ⓚ2639

ⓐ introductory part of something: **opening, beginning, inception, first stage**

ⓑ introductory part of a book: **preface, introduction, foreword**

ⓒ introductory [first] part of a traditional Japanese performance

a 序盤 じょばん opening (in the game of go)

序曲 じょきょく prelude, overture

序説 じょせつ introduction

序幕 じょまく opening act, curtain raiser

b 自序 じじょ author's preface

c 序破急 じょはきゅう artistic modulations in traditional Japanese performances; opening, middle and climax [end]

端 ▷start
タン はし は はた –ばた   Ⓚ1131

start, beginning, starting point, origin

端緒 たんしょ(=たんちょ) beginning, start, first step; clue

端午 たんご festival on the 5th of May (of the lunar calendar)

発端 ほったん origin, beginning, outset

戦端を開く せんたんをひらく take up arms (against), open hostilities

途端に とたんに just as, just at the moment

始 ▷beginning
シ はじ(める) はじ(まる)   Ⓚ0252

ⓐ **beginning, inception, start, origin**

ⓑ (source of something) **beginning, origin; first, starting**

a 始末する しまつする manage, deal with, dispose of; put in order

始終 しじゅう from beginning to end, at all times

年始 ねんし beginning of the year; New Year's greetings

終始 しゅうし from beginning to end, always

原始的な げんしてきな primitive, primeval

b 始発 しはつ first departure; starting station

初 ▷beginning
ショ はじ(め) はじ(めて) はつ うい–
–そ(める) –ぞ(め)   Ⓚ1031

ⓐ [also suffix] **beginning, origin, early stages**

ⓑ **beginning stages, first steps**

a 最初 さいしょ first, outset, beginning

当初の とうしょの original, initial, first

b 初期 しょき early days, early stage, beginning; early, initial

初夏 しょか early summer

初歩 しょほ first steps, rudiments, the ABCs (of)

初級 しょきゅう beginner's class, junior course

初心者 しょしんしゃ beginner

元 ▷origin
ゲン ガン もと   Ⓚ1690

origin, beginning, original state

元日 がんじつ New Year's Day

根元 こんげん root; base

還元 かんげん restoration; reduction, deoxidization

本 ▷origin
ホン もと   Ⓚ2937

origin, source, root, beginning

本源 ほんげん source, origin; principle

本初 ほんしょ origin, beginning, start

日本 にほん(=にっぽん) Japan

根 ▷root
コン ね   Ⓚ0841

(primary source) **root, source, origin**

根源 こんげん root, origin, source

語根 ごこん root [origin] of a word

源 ▷source
ゲン みなもと   Ⓚ0600

[also suffix] **source, origin, beginning, root**

源泉 げんせん fountainhead, source

根源 こんげん root, origin, source

起源 きげん origin, beginning

語源 ごげん derivation of a word, etymology

資源 しげん resources

財源 ざいげん revenue source, financial resources

震源 しんげん earthquake [seismic] center

栄養源 えいようげん source of nutrients

behavior
行　挙　動

行 ▷conduct
コウ ギョウ アン い(く) ゆ(く) -ゆ(き) -い(き) おこな(う)　　　Ⓚ0187

(personal behavior) **conduct, behavior**
行儀 ぎょうぎ manners, behavior
品行 ひんこう (moral) conduct, behavior, deport-ment
言行 げんこう speech and conduct
奇行 きこう eccentric conduct

挙 ▷deportment
キョ あ(げる) あ(がる)　　　Ⓚ2169

deportment, behavior, action, conduct, bearing
挙動 きょどう deportment, conduct, behavior, action
挙措 きょそ behavior, manner
挙止 きょし bearing, deportment

動 ▷behavior
ドウ うご(く) うご(かす)　　　Ⓚ1583

behavior, conduct

be late and delay
遅　後　滞　延　猶

遅 ▷be late
チ おく(れる) おく(らす) おそ(い)　Ⓚ2700

be late, be tardy, be delayed
遅刻 ちこく tardiness, lateness
遅参 ちさん lateness, tardiness

後 ▷fall behind
ゴ コウ のち うし(ろ) あと おく(れる)　　　Ⓚ0321

[original meaning] **fall behind, fall back, lag behind, be backwards**
後進国 こうしんこく underdeveloped countries
後配株 こうはいかぶ deferred stock
後家 ごけ widow

滞 ▷fall into arrears
タイ とどこお(る)　　　Ⓚ0609

fall into arrears, leave unpaid

滞納 たいのう nonpayment, delinquency (in payment)
延滞 えんたい arrear, arrearage

延 ▷postpone
エン の(びる) の(べる) の(べ) の(ばす)　　　Ⓚ2646

postpone, delay, defer
延期 えんき postponement, deferment
延納 えんのう delayed [deferred] payment
延着 えんちゃく delayed arrival
延発 えんぱつ postponement of departure, delayed departure
延会 えんかい adjournment [postponement] of a meeting
延滞 えんたい arrear, arrearage
遅延 ちえん delay, retardation

猶 ▷delay
ユウ　　　Ⓚ0566

delay, put off, postpone; waver, dally
猶予する ゆうよする postpone, delay, extend; hesitate
執行猶予 しっこうゆうよ stay of execution, proba-tion, suspended sentence

bells
鈴　鐘

鈴 ▷bell (that jingles or rings)
レイ リン すず　　　Ⓚ1526

[original meaning] **bell (that jingles or rings)**
電鈴 でんれい electric bell
振鈴 しんれい ringing bell, hand bell
予鈴 よれい the first bell
銀鈴 ぎんれい silver bell
風鈴 ふうりん wind-bell
呼び鈴 よびりん (call) bell, doorbell

鐘 ▷bell (that tolls)
ショウ かね　　　Ⓚ1578

ⓐ [original meaning] **bell (that tolls)**
ⓑ **bell or sound of a bell (as for announcing), alarm**
a 鐘楼 しょうろう bell tower, belfry
梵鐘 ぼんしょう temple bell
b 警鐘 けいしょう alarm bell, warning
時鐘 じしょう time bell
半鐘 はんしょう fire bell [alarm]

bend

曲 彎 屈 折 勾 歪

曲 ▷curve
キョク ま(がる) ま(げる)　　Ⓚ2956

ⓐ curve, bend
ⓑ curved, bent
a 曲折する きょくせつする bend, wind; zigzag
　曲率 きょくりつ curvature
　曲度 きょくど curvature
　湾曲 わんきょく curve, crook, bend
　屈曲 くっきょく bending, winding
　婉曲な えんきょくな roundabout, indirect; euphemistic
b 曲線 きょくせん curve, curved line
　曲管 きょくかん curved pipe, siphon

彎 ▷curve (become bow-shaped)
ワン

[now replaced by 湾] [original meaning] **curve**
　彎曲 わんきょく curve, crook, bend
　彎入する わんにゅうする curve in
　彎月 わんげつ crescent moon

▷bend
クツ　　Ⓚ2652

[original meaning] **bend, flex, crouch**
　屈伸 くっしん bending and stretching, extension and contraction
　屈折 くっせつ bending, turn; refraction
　屈曲する くっきょくする bend, wind
　屈指の くっしの leading, foremost
　前屈 ぜんくつ bending forward, anteflexion

折 ▷bend
セツ お(る) おり お(れる)　　Ⓚ0225

【セツ】
　bend
　曲折 きょくせつ bending, winding; zigzags
　屈折 くっせつ bending, turn; refraction
【お(る)】
　bend, turn back
　折り曲げる おりまげる bend, double, turn up [down]
　折り返す おりかえす turn back; turn up
　折り返し おりかえし turn, turning point; return (trip), shuttle (service); lapel

勾 ▷be bent
コウ　　Ⓚ2546

be bent, be hooked, be curved
　勾配 こうばい slope, incline; gradient

歪 ▷distort
ワイ ゆが(める) ゆが(む) ひず(む) いびつ

distort, warp, twist, bend
　歪力 わいりょく stress (intensity)
　歪度 わいど skewness

benefit

利 益 為 用 役

利 ▷advantage
リ き(く)　　Ⓚ1029

ⓐ advantage, benefit, superiority, convenience, expediency
ⓑ be of advantage to, benefit
a 利点 りてん advantage, point in favor
　有利な ゆうりな advantageous, favorable; profitable
　権利 けんり right; authority; privilege
　便利 べんり convenience, handiness, usefulness
b 利用する りようする utilize, make use of, avail oneself of

益 ▷benefit
エキ ヤク ま(す)　　Ⓚ1978

ⓐ benefit, good, advantage
ⓑ beneficial, useful
a 有益な ゆうえきな beneficial; profitable
　公益 こうえき public benefit
　実益 じつえき practical use, benefit, actual profit
　御利益 ごりやく grace of God
b 益友 えきゆう useful friend
　益虫 えきちゅう beneficial insect

為 ▷sake
イ ため な(す)　　Ⓚ2994

sake, benefit, advantage, profit
　人の為を思う ひとのためをおもう wish someone well

用 ▷use(ful)
ヨウ もち(いる)　　Ⓚ2569

ⓐ be useful, be effective, work
ⓑ use, usefulness, utility
a 作用 さよう action, operation, function; effect
　信用 しんよう trust, credit, confidence

効用 こうよう use, usefulness, effect
b 無用の むようの useless; unnecessary; forbidden
有用な ゆうような useful, serviceable

役 ▷service
ヤク エキ   Ⓚ0217

service, serviceability, usefulness, utility
役立つ やくだつ be of use, serve a purpose
役立てる やくだてる put to use, make use of, turn to account

---

be subjected to
被 受

被 ▷be subjected to
ヒ こうむ(る)   Ⓚ1077

be subjected to, undergo, suffer
被害 ひがい damage, harm
被弾 ひだん being bombed
被災 ひさい suffering, affection

受 ▷be subjected to
ジュ う(ける) –う(け) う(かる)   Ⓚ2146

be subjected to, undergo, suffer
受難 じゅなん ordeal, crucifixion
受刑者 じゅけいしゃ prisoner, convict

---

between
中 仲 間 際

中 ▷middle
チュウ ジュウ なか   Ⓚ2902

❶ **middle, Middle, mid-, central, intermediate**
中点 ちゅうてん middle point
中部 ちゅうぶ central [middle] part
中衛 ちゅうえい middle guard
中耳 ちゅうじ middle ear, *auris media*
中欧 ちゅうおう Central Europe
中東 ちゅうとう Middle East
中労委(=中央労働委員会) ちゅうろうい(=ちゅうおうろうどういいんかい) Central Labor Relations Committee
中継する ちゅうけいする relay, rebroadcast
❷ⓐ (of time) **middle, medieval, Middle**
ⓑ **in the middle, halfway**
a 中年 ちゅうねん middle age
中古の ちゅうこの medieval
中世 ちゅうせい Middle [Medieval] Ages

中石器時代 ちゅうせっきじだい Mesolithic period
中期 ちゅうき middle period; metaphase
b 中止する ちゅうしする suspend, stop, discontinue
中断 ちゅうだん interruption, discontinuance, suspension
中退する ちゅうたいする drop out of [quit] school
途中で とちゅうで on the way
❸ⓐ [also prefix] (of intermediate size, quality or extent) **middle, medium, intermediate, average**
ⓑ (being at neither extreme) **middle (course), moderate, neutral, medial**
a 中型 ちゅうがた medium size
中肉中背の ちゅうにくちゅうぜいの of medium build
中ヒール ちゅうひーる medium-high heel
中小企業 ちゅうしょうきぎょう small-to-medium-sized enterprises
中細の ちゅうぼits medium-fine
中古の ちゅうこ(=ちゅうぶる)の secondhand, used
中波 ちゅうは medium waves
中辞典 ちゅうじてん medium-sized dictionary
中産階級 ちゅうさんかいきゅう middle class, bourgeoisie
中学 ちゅうがく junior high school
中学校 ちゅうがっこう junior high school
中学生 ちゅうがくせい junior high school student
中級の ちゅうきゅうの middle-class [grade], intermediate
b 中庸 ちゅうよう the (golden) mean, the middle path
中立 ちゅうりつ neutrality; neutralization
中和する ちゅうわする neutralize; counteract
中道 ちゅうどう middle road, golden mean

仲 ▷intermediate
チュウ なか   Ⓚ0028

occupying an intermediate position:
ⓐ **middle [second month] of a season**
ⓑ **middle [second-born] brother**
a 仲秋(=中秋) ちゅうしゅう mid-autumn, August according to the old calendar
b 仲兄 ちゅうけい second brother
伯仲する はくちゅうする be equal to

間 ▷between
カン ケン あいだ ま   Ⓚ2836

[also suffix] **between, among, midway**
間食 かんしょく eating between meals; snack
中間 ちゅうかん middle, midway
民間の みんかんの private, nongovernmental, civil
世間 せけん world, society; the public, people
人間 にんげん human being, man; people, mankind
三遊間 さんゆうかん *baseball* between third and shortstop
友人間に ゆうじんかんに among one's friends

際 ▷inter-
サイ きわ -ぎわ   Ⓚ0646

inter-, between, among
- 国際的な こくさいてきな international
- 学際的 がくさいてき interdisciplinary
- 州際通商委員会 しゅうさいつうしょういいんかい
  Interstate Commerce Commission

bewildered
迷　惑

迷 ▷perplexed
メイ まよ(う)   Ⓚ2663

(be at a loss at what to do) **be perplexed, be puzzled, be bewildered; hesitate**
- 迷惑 めいわく trouble, annoyance
- 迷信 めいしん superstition
- 混迷 こんめい confusion, bewilderment; [formerly 昏迷] stupor, unconsciousness
- 混迷 こんめい [formerly 昏迷] stupor, unconsciousness
- 低迷する ていめいする hang low; (of the market) be sluggish

惑 ▷bewildered
ワク まど(う)   Ⓚ2427

[original meaning] **bewildered, perplexed, puzzled, confused**
- 惑乱 わくらん bewilderment, confusion
- 迷惑 めいわく trouble, annoyance
- 当惑 とうわく perplexity, confusion, embarrassment
- 困惑 こんわく embarrassment, perplexity, confusion

big and huge
大　太　浩　巨　厖

大 ▷big
ダイ タイ おお- おお(きい)
おお(いに)   Ⓚ2882

[also prefix] (great in size, extent or quantity) **big, large, great, major, grand, vast, numerous**
- 大小 だいしょう large and small; size; long and short swords
- 大会 たいかい mass meeting, rally; meet, tournament
- 大陸 たいりく continent
- 大衆 たいしゅう the masses, populace

- 大量 たいりょう large quantity, great volume, mass
- 大規模 だいきぼ large scale
- 大金 たいきん large sum of money
- 大正 たいしょう Taisho era
- 拡大する かくだいする magnify, enlarge, expand
- 最大の さいだいの biggest, largest, greatest
- 巨大な きょだいな huge, gigantic, enormous
- 莫大な ばくだいな vast, immense, enormous

太 ▷great
タイ タ ふと(い) ふと(る)   Ⓚ1846

(extremely large in size or scale) **great, large, big, enormous**
- 太陽 たいよう sun
- 太鼓 たいこ (big) drum; professional jester; flatterer; big obi bow
- 太陰 たいいん moon
- 太白 たいはく Venus; thick silk thread; kind of sweet potato
- 太古 たいこ ancient times, remote ages
- 太平洋 たいへいよう Pacific Ocean

浩 ▷vast
コウ   Ⓚ0396

vast (amount), huge (quantity); numerous
- 浩瀚な こうかんな bulky, voluminous

巨 ▷huge
キョ   Ⓚ2616

ⓐ (of extraordinary size) **huge, enormous, giant, big, large, great**
ⓑ (of extraordinary quantity) **huge, enormous, great**
- *a* 巨大な きょだいな huge, gigantic, enormous
- 巨人 きょじん giant; great person
- 巨星 きょせい giant star; great person [star], big shot
- 巨象 きょぞう gigantic elephant
- 巨岩 きょがん huge rock, crag
- 巨視的 きょしてき macroscopic, all-inclusive
- *b* 巨額 きょがく enormous sum
- 巨費 きょひ great expenditure

厖 ▷bulky
ボウ

[now replaced by 膨] **bulky, extensive**
- 厖大な ぼうだいな bulky, massive, extensive

bird

鳥　禽　雛

鳥 ▷bird
チョウ とり　　　Ⓚ2822

[also suffix] [original meaning] **bird, fowl**
- 鳥類 ちょうるい birds, fowls
- 野鳥 やちょう wild fowl, wild bird
- 愛鳥週間 あいちょうしゅうかん Bird Week
- 保護鳥 ほごちょう protected bird
- 益鳥 えきちょう beneficial bird
- 害鳥 がいちょう injurious bird
- 白鳥 はくちょう swan
- 七面鳥 しちめんちょう turkey
- 雷鳥 らいちょう snow grouse
- 一石二鳥 いっせきにちょう killing two birds with one stone

禽 ▷bird
キン とり　　　Ⓚ1837

bird, fowl
- 禽類 きんるい birds
- 禽獣 きんじゅう birds and animals
- 禽舎 きんしゃ poultry shed
- 家禽 かきん poultry, domestic fowl
- 猛禽 もうきん bird of prey
- 水禽 すいきん waterfowl, aquatic bird
- 野禽 やきん wild bird

雛 ▷chick
スウ ジュ ひな ひよこ　　　Ⓚ1633

chick(en), fledgling, poultry
- 雛鳥 ひなどり fledgling (esp. chicken)
- 雛げし ひなげし red poppy, corn poppy, ponceau

birds

鷹 鷗 烏 雀 燕 鴻 鳳
凰 鵬 鶏 酉 隼 鳩 鷲
鳶 鶴 鷺 鵜 鴨 雁

鷹 ▷hawk
ヨウ オウ たか　　　Ⓚ2748

[original meaning] **hawk, falcon**
- 放鷹 ほうよう hawking, falconry

鷗 ▷gull
オウ かもめ　　　Ⓚ1666

gull, seagull
- 白鷗 はくおう white gull

烏 ▷crow
ウ オ からす　　　Ⓚ2811

crow, raven
- 烏合の衆 うごうのしゅう disorderly crowd, mob
- 烏鷺 うろ crows and herons; black and white
- 烏滸がましい おこがましい presumptuous, impertinent; ridiculous, absurd

雀 ▷sparrow
ジャク ジャン すずめ　　　Ⓚ2178

sparrow
- 燕雀 えんじゃく small birds
- 孔雀 くじゃく peacock

燕 ▷swallow
エン つばめ　　　Ⓚ2196

swallow, martin
- 燕尾服 えんびふく tailcoat
- 燕麦 えんばく wild oat, *Avena fatua*
- 燕雀 えんじゃく small birds
- 燕窩 えんか edible bird's nest
- 飛燕 ひえん swallow in flight

鴻 ▷large wild bird
コウ グ おおとり ひしくい　　　Ⓚ0710

【コウ グ】
large wild bird such as a goose or swan
- 鴻鵠 こうこく wild swan; symbol of a great man

【おおとり】
[also 大鳥 or 鳳] **large wild bird such as a crane or white stork**

鳳 ▷male phoenix
ホウ ブウ おおとり　　　Ⓚ2601

male phoenix, mythical Chinese phoenix
- 鳳凰 ほうおう male and female Chinese phoenixes
- 白鳳時代 はくほうじだい name of an archaic Japanese era

凰 ▷female phoenix
オウ　　　Ⓚ2595

female phoenix, mythical Chinese phoenix
- 鳳凰 ほうおう male and female Chinese phoenixes
- 鳳凰座 ほうおうざ the Phoenix (constellation)

鵬 ▷**mythical huge bird**
ホウ ボウ おおとり   Ⓚ1021

【ホウ ボウ】
as huge or great as a Chinese mythical bird
【おおとり】
[also 大鳥 or 鳳] huge bird such as a mythical Chinese phoenix

鶏 ▷**chicken**
ケイ にわとり   Ⓚ1577

[original meaning] **chicken, hen, cock; poultry**
鶏肉 けいにく chicken (meat)
鶏卵 けいらん (hen's) egg
鶏舎 けいしゃ henhouse
養鶏 ようけい chicken raising
闘鶏 とうけい cockfight, fighting cock

酉 ▷**Rooster**
ユウ とり   Ⓚ2969

tenth sign of the Oriental zodiac: **the Rooster**—(time) 5-7 p.m., (direction) west, (season) August (of the lunar calendar)
丁酉 ていゆう 34th of the sexagenary cycle

隼 ▷**falcon**
シュン はやぶさ   Ⓚ2404

[original meaning, now archaic] **falcon**
鷹隼 ようしゅん hawk and falcon

鳩 ▷**pigeon**
キュウ はと   Ⓚ0141

pigeon, dove, carrier pigeon
鳩舎 きゅうしゃ pigeon house
鳩信 きゅうしん communication by carrier pigeon

鷲 ▷**eagle**
シュウ ジュ わし   Ⓚ2514

eagle
鷲鼻 わしばな hooked [aquiline] nose
鷲摑みにする わしづかみにする grab
鷲座 わしざ Aquila
大鷲 おおわし Steller's sea eagle
白頭鷲 はくとうわし bald eagle

鳶 ▷**black kite**
エン とび とんび   Ⓚ2727

black kite (kind of bird)
鳶目兎耳 えんもくとじ sharp eyes and ears ("eyes of a black kite and ears of a rabbit")

鶴 ▷**crane**
カク つる   Ⓚ1641

[original meaning, now archaic] **crane, stork**

鷺 ▷**heron**
ロ さぎ   Ⓚ2524

heron
烏鷺 うろ crows and herons; black and white

鵜 ▷**cormorant**
テイ う   Ⓚ1475

cormorant
鵜呑み うのみ accepting (a story) unthinkingly; swallowing whole
鵜飼い うかい cormorant fishing; cormorant fisherman
鵜匠 うしょう cormorant fisherman
鵜の目鷹の目 うのめたかのめ eyes of a predator, keen eyes
川鵜 (=河鵜) かわう great cormorant

鴨 ▷**duck**
オウ かも   Ⓚ1143

wild duck, duck
鴨脚 おうきゃく [rare] ginkgo

雁 ▷**wild goose**
ガン かり かりがね   Ⓚ2597

wild goose
雁行 がんこう flight formation of geese; forming an echelon
雁首 がんくび *colloq* neck, head; bowl of a Japanese smoking pipe
雁擬き がんもどき deep-fried tofu mixed with thinly sliced vegetables
雁木 がんぎ zigzag; steps of a pier; large-toothed saw; rasp
落雁 らくがん wild geese descending on a pond; candy made of rice or other flour mixed with sugar

bite
噛　啄

噛 ▷**bite**
ゴウ か(む) か(ます) か(ませる)

bite
窮鼠噛猫 きゅうそごうびょう A cornered rat will bite the cat

啄 ▷**peck**
タク トク ついば(む)   Ⓚ0363

peck, pick
啄木 たくぼく *literary* woodpecker

black colors

黒　漆　黎

黒 ▷black
コク　くろ　くろ(い)　Ⓚ2388

[also suffix] [original meaning] **black, blackish**
黒海 こっかい Black Sea
黒板 こくばん blackboard
黒点 こくてん black [dark] spot, sunspot
黒人 こくじん black, Negro
黒褐色 こっかっしょく blackish brown
漆黒 しっこく pitch black

漆 ▷pitch-black
シツ　うるし　Ⓚ0637

(as black as lacquer) **pitch-black**
漆黒 しっこく pitch black

黎 ▷black
レイ　ライ　リ　Ⓚ2448

black, dark
黎明 れいめい dawn, daybreak, beginning (of a new age)

blame and accuse

責　叱　詰　難　批　劾　弾

責 ▷blame
セキ　せ(める)　Ⓚ2176

blame, condemn, censure
叱責する しっせきする reproach, scold, reprove
問責 もんせき censure, reproof
自責 じせき self-accusation

叱 ▷scold
シツ　しか(る)　Ⓚ0162

[original meaning] **scold, reprehend, reproach**
叱咤する しったする scold, give a scolding; command
叱責する しっせきする reproach, scold, reprove
叱正 しっせい correction (of errors)

詰 ▷reprimand
キツ　つ(める)　つ(め)　-づ(め)　つ(まる)
つ(む)　Ⓚ1380

[original meaning] **reprimand, reprove, censure, rebuke**

詰責する きっせきする [rare] reproach, reprove, reprimand
面詰する めんきつする reprimand (a person) personally
難詰する なんきつする blame, censure, reproach

難 ▷find fault with
ナン　かた(い)　-がた(い)　むずか(しい)
むつか(しい)　Ⓚ1632

find fault with, criticize, blame, reproach
難色 なんしょく disapproval, reluctance
難詰する なんきつする blame, censure, reproach
非難(=批難) ひなん criticism, blame

批 ▷criticize
ヒ　Ⓚ0223

criticize, comment, review
批評 ひひょう criticism, comment
批難(=非難) ひなん criticism, blame
批評家 ひひょうか critic, reviewer
批判 ひはん criticism, comment
批議する ひぎする blame, criticize

劾 ▷expose crimes
ガイ　Ⓚ1165

expose (a person's) crimes or misdeeds, impeach, accuse; investigate crime
劾奏する がいそうする report an official's offense to the emperor
弾劾する だんがいする impeach, denounce, accuse

弾 ▷impeach
ダン　ひ(く)　-ひ(き)　はず(む)　たま　Ⓚ0524

impeach, censure
弾劾 だんがい impeachment, denunciation, accusation
糾弾 きゅうだん impeachment, censure

bloom →SPROUT AND BLOOM

blow →BREATHE AND BLOW

blue and purple colors

青　碧　瑠　紺　藍　紫　蒼

青 ▷blue
セイ　ショウ　チン　あお　あお(い)　Ⓚ2152

blue
青色 せいしょく blue
青天 せいてん blue sky

青色症 せいしょくしょう cyanosis
紺青 こんじょう Prussian blue, deep blue
緑青 ろくしょう verdigris, copper [green] rust
丹青 たんせい red and blue; painting

碧 ▷deep blue
ヘキ   Ⓚ2469

[original meaning] **deep blue, azure, blue**
碧水 へきすい blue water
碧空 へきくう blue sky
金髪碧眼の外人 きんぱつへきがんのがいじん
     foreigner with golden hair and blue eyes
紺碧 こんぺき deep blue, azure

瑠 ▷lapis lazuli (bright blue)
ル   Ⓚ0972

(variant of blue) **lapis lazuli, lapis lazuli blue**
瑠璃色 るりいろ lapis lazuli blue, bright blue
瑠璃唐草 るりからくさ baby blue-eyes (name of
     plant)
浄瑠璃 じょうるり *joruri*, ballad drama; clear lapis
     lazuli

紺 ▷dark blue
コン   Ⓚ1219

[original meaning] **dark blue, navy blue**
紺色 こんいろ dark blue, navy blue
紺地 こんじ dark blue ground; dark blue cloth
紺青 こんじょう Prussian blue, deep blue
紺屋 こうや(=こんや) dyer; dyer's shop
紫紺 しこん purplish blue
濃紺 のうこん dark blue, navy blue

藍 ▷indigo
ラン あい   Ⓚ2108

[also prefix] **indigo blue, deep blue, blue**
藍綬褒章 らんじゅほうしょう Blue Ribbon Medal
藍晶石 らんしょうせき cyanite
青藍 せいらん indigo blue

紫 ▷purple
シ むらさき   Ⓚ2348

[original meaning] **purple, violet**
紫紺 しこん purplish blue
紫外線 しがいせん ultraviolet rays
紫斑病 しはんびょう purpura

蒼 ▷pale blue
ソウ あお(い)   Ⓚ2050

[usu. 青い] **pale blue; pale; green**
顔が蒼い かおがあおい look pale [green]

board games
局 棋 碁 雀

局 ▷board game
キョク   Ⓚ2636

ⓐ **board game (as chess or shogi)**
ⓑ **counter for board games**
a 対局 たいきょく game of go [shogi]
b 一局 いっきょく a game (of go or shogi)
     チェス十二局 ちぇすじゅうにきょく 12 chess games

棋 ▷shogi
キ   Ⓚ0899

shogi, Japanese chess; chess
棋士 きし professional go [shogi] player
棋界 きかい go circles; shogi circles
棋譜 きふ record of a game of shogi [go]
棋道 きどう art of shogi [go]
将棋 しょうぎ shogi, Japanese chess
西洋将棋 せいようしょうぎ chess

碁 ▷go
ゴ   Ⓚ2354

[original meaning] **go, Japanese checkers**
碁石 ごいし go stone
碁盤 ごばん go board, checkerboard
碁会所 ごかいしょ commercial go playing parlor
囲碁 いご (the game of) go
西洋碁 せいようご checkers

雀 ▷mahjong
ジャク ジャン すずめ   Ⓚ2178

abbrev. of 麻雀 まーじゃん: **mahjong**
雀荘 じゃんそう mahjong club
雀球 じゃんきゅう *jankyu* (combination of Japanese
     pinball and mahjong)
雀卓 じゃんたく mahjong board

boards and plates
板 盤

板 ▷board, plate
ハン バン いた   Ⓚ0762

❶ [original meaning] (sheet of wood) **board, plank**
掲示板 けいじばん notice board
黒板 こくばん blackboard
看板 かんばん signboard, sign

甲板 かんぱん(=こうはん) deck

❷ⓐ [also suffix] (sheet of hard material, esp. metal) **plate, sheet, slab, tablet**

ⓑ [sometimes also 鈑] **sheet metal**

ⓒ abbrev. of 投手板 とうしゅばん: **pitcher's plate**

a 鉄板 てっぱん iron [steel] plate
鋼板 こうはん steel plate
投手板 とうしゅばん pitcher's plate

b 板金 ばんきん sheet metal
ニッケル板 にっけるばん nickel plate

c 登板する とうばんする take the plate

盤 ▷board
バン　　　　　　　　　　Ⓚ2481

[also suffix] (flat surface for specific purpose) **board (as for shogi or chess), panel, plate**

将棋盤 しょうぎばん chessboard
鍵盤 けんばん keyboard
算盤 そろばん Japanese abacus, *soroban*
制御盤 せいぎょばん control panel
配電盤 はいでんばん distributing board [panel], switchboard

boasting and arrogance
誇　慢　傲

誇 ▷boast
コ　ほこ(る)　　　　　　Ⓚ1381

[original meaning] **boast, brag, be proud**

誇称 こしょう boasting, exaggeration
誇示 こじ ostentation, display, showing off
誇色 こしょく proud countenance

慢 ▷arrogant
マン　　　　　　　　　　Ⓚ0625

arrogant, supercilious, haughty, conceited, proud

慢心 まんしん self-conceit; pride
自慢 じまん pride, self-praise, vanity
高慢な こうまんな haughty, arrogant, proud
傲慢な ごうまんな arrogant, haughty, insolent
我慢 がまん patience, endurance; self-restraint

傲 ▷arrogant
ゴウ　　　　　　　　　　Ⓚ0131

arrogant, proud, haughty

傲慢な ごうまんな arrogant, haughty, insolent
傲然と ごうぜんと arrogantly, haughtily
傲岸な ごうがんな arrogant, haughty
倨傲 きょごう arrogance, pride

驕傲 きょうごう arrogance, pride

boats →PARTS OF BOATS AND SHIPS

boats and ships
船 舶 艦 潜 舟 艇 隻

船 ▷ship
セン ふね ふな- -ぶね　　Ⓚ1229

[original meaning] **ship, boat, vessel, seacraft**

船舶 せんぱく ship, vessel; craft
船長 せんちょう (ship) captain
汽船 きせん steamship
風船 ふうせん balloon
造船 ぞうせん shipbuilding
商船 しょうせん merchant ship, trading vessel
貨物船 かもつせん freighter, cargo ship

舶 ▷oceangoing ship
ハク　　　　　　　　　　Ⓚ1228

[original meaning] **oceangoing ship, ship, vessel**

舶用機関 はくようきかん marine engine
船舶 せんぱく ship, vessel; craft

艦 ▷warship
カン　　　　　　　　　　Ⓚ1303

warship, battleship

艦船 かんせん ships and warships
艦隊 かんたい squadron, fleet
艦艇 かんてい war vessels
艦長 かんちょう captain of a warship
軍艦 ぐんかん warship

潜 ▷submarine
セン ひそ(む) もぐ(る)　Ⓚ0680

abbrev. of 潜水艦 せんすいかん: **submarine**

原潜 げんせん nuclear submarine

舟 ▷small boat
シュウ ふね ふな- -ぶね　Ⓚ2965

【シュウ】
[original meaning] (small) **boat, ship**

舟艇 しゅうてい boat, craft
舟行 しゅうこう navigation, going by ship
舟運 しゅううん transportation by water
呉越同舟 ごえつどうしゅう bitter enemies in the same boat

【ふね】
small boat [craft], (row)boat

小舟 こぶね small craft

艇 ▷boat
テイ   Ⓚ1246

[also suffix] [original meaning] **boat, small boat, light craft**

艇長 ていちょう coxswain, captain (of a submarine)
舟艇 しゅうてい boat, craft
短艇 たんてい boat
競艇 きょうてい boat race
艦艇 かんてい war vessels
警備艇 けいびてい guardship
救命艇 きゅうめいてい lifeboat

隻 ▷counter for ships
セキ   Ⓚ2403

counter for ships

一隻 いっせき one ship
数隻 すうせき several ships

bodies
体 塊 球

体 ▷body
タイ テイ からだ   Ⓚ0055

geometry **body, solid body, figure**

六面体 ろくめんたい hexahedron

塊 ▷lump
カイ かたまり   Ⓚ0579

lump, mass; ingot; nugget

塊土 かいど lump of earth
塊鉱 かいこう lump ore
地塊 ちかい block, landmass
金塊 きんかい nugget, gold ingot

球 ▷ball
キュウ たま   Ⓚ0880

[original meaning] (spherical body) **ball, globe, sphere**

球体 きゅうたい sphere, globe
球形 きゅうけい globular shape
球根 きゅうこん bulb
地球 ちきゅう the Earth
眼球 がんきゅう eyeball

bodily secretions
乳 精 汗 涙 唾

乳 ▷milk
ニュウ ちち ち   Ⓚ1306

(mammalian secretion) **milk**

母乳 ぼにゅう mother's milk
牛乳 ぎゅうにゅう (cow's) milk

精 ▷sperm
セイ ショウ   Ⓚ1248

(essential substance of life) **sperm, semen**

精子 せいし sperm
精液 せいえき semen, sperm
受精 じゅせい fertilization, impregnation; pollination
夢精 むせい nocturnal emission, wet dream

汗 ▷sweat
カン あせ   Ⓚ0194

sweat, perspiration

汗腺 かんせん sweat gland
汗顔 かんがん sweating from shame
汗血 かんけつ sweat and blood
発汗する はっかんする perspire, sweat
冷汗 れいかん cold sweat

涙 ▷tear
ルイ なみだ   Ⓚ0399

[original meaning] **tear, tears**

涙腺 るいせん lachrymal gland
涙嚢 るいのう lachrymal sac, dacryocyst
落涙する らくるいする shed tears
催涙ガス さいるいがす tear gas
暗涙に咽ぶ あんるいにむせぶ shed silent tears

唾 ▷saliva
ダ つば つばき   Ⓚ0416

saliva, spit, sputum

唾液 だえき saliva, sputum
唾壺 だこ spittoon

body

体 身 肉 屍 尸 骸

体 ▷body
タイ テイ からだ   Ⓚ0055

ⓐ [also suffix] (physical organism) **body, corpse**
ⓑ **counter for dead bodies [corpses]**

a 体力 たいりょく physical strength, strength of one's body
体質 たいしつ physical constitution
体内 たいない interior of the body
体操 たいそう gymnastics, physical exercise
体重 たいじゅう body weight
体育 たいいく physical training [education]
体温 たいおん body temperature
体温計 たいおんけい (clinical) thermometer
体長 たいちょう body length (of animals)
身体 しんたい body
人体 じんたい human body
一体 いったい one body; a style, a form; (why, what) on earth, (what, why) in the world
自体 じたい one's own body; itself
全体 ぜんたい whole (body), whole span
肉体 にくたい body, flesh
焼死体 しょうしたい charred body
遺体 いたい remains, body, corpse
脂肪体 しぼうたい corpus adiposum
b 死体三体 したいさんたい three corpses

身 ▷body (esp. vs. mind)
シン み   Ⓚ2977

(material) **body, human body (esp. vs. mind), one's person, the flesh**

身体 しんたい body
身長 しんちょう stature, height
身障者 しんしょうしゃ physically handicapped person, disabled person
全身 ぜんしん the whole body
心身 しんしん mind and body
焼身 しょうしん burning oneself (to death), self-immolation
変身 へんしん transformation, metamorphosis

肉 ▷flesh
ニク   Ⓚ2756

the flesh (versus the spirit)

肉体 にくたい body, flesh
肉欲 にくよく lusts of the flesh, animal passions

屍 ▷corpse
シ しかばね

[now also 死] [original meaning] **corpse, dead body**

屍体 したい corpse
屍蠟 しろう adipocere
屍姦 しかん necrophilia, necrophilism
死屍 しし corpse

尸 ▷corpse
シ しかばね

[original meaning] **corpse**

尸諌(=屍諌)する しかんする admonish (one's master) at the cost of one's life

骸 ▷dead body
ガイ   Ⓚ1625

dead body, corpse

死骸(=屍骸) しがい corpse, body, remains
遺骸 いがい remains, corpse, body
残骸 ざんがい ruins, wreckage
形骸化する けいがいかする become a mere shell [dead letter]

body projections

角   尾

角 ▷horn
カク かど つの   Ⓚ1761

[original meaning] **horn, antler, antenna**
牛角 ぎゅうかく horns
触角 しょっかく feeler, antenna

尾 ▷tail
ビ お   Ⓚ2635

[original meaning] **tail**
有尾類 ゆうびるい tailed amphibians

bombs →PROJECTILES AND BOMBS

bone

骨 髄 椎 脊 肋 骼 骸

骨 ▷bone
コツ ほね   Ⓚ2310

[also suffix] [original meaning] **bone**

骨折 こっせつ bone fracture
骨格 こっかく frame, physique; framework, skeletal structure

人骨 じんこつ human bone
肋骨 ろっこつ rib, costa
遺骨 いこつ (skeletal) remains; ashes
白骨 はっこつ bleached bone, skeleton
大腿骨 だいたいこつ thighbone, femur
骸骨 がいこつ skeleton

髄 ▷marrow
ズイ （K)1634

[original meaning] **marrow, pith**
髄液 ずいえき spinal fluid
髄虫 ずいむし rice borer, pearl moth
骨髄 こつずい bone marrow
脊髄 せきずい spinal cord

椎 ▷spine
ツイ しい （K)0905

spine, backbone
椎骨 ついこつ vertebra
脊椎 せきつい spine, backbone

脊 ▷spine
セキ （K)2317

spine, backbone
脊髄 せきずい spinal cord
脊椎 せきつい spine, backbone
脊柱 せきちゅう spinal column
脊梁 せきりょう backbone, spine
脊索 せきさく notochord

肋 ▷rib
ロク あばら ばら （K)0732

[original meaning] **rib, costa**
肋骨 ろっこつ rib, costa
肋膜 ろくまく pleura
肋間神経痛 ろっかんしんけいつう intercostal
   neuralgia
肋木 ろくぼく wall bars
中肋 ちゅうろく midrib, rachis (of a leaf)

骼 ▷skeletal frame
カク

[now replaced by 格] **skeletal frame, skeleton, build**
骨骼 こっかく frame, physique; framework, skeletal
   structure

骸 ▷skeleton
ガイ （K)1625

bones, skeleton
骸骨 がいこつ skeleton

books

本 典 経 書 冊 籍
著 巻 編 篇 鑑

本 ▷book
ホン もと （K)2937

[also suffix] (source of knowledge) **book, volume, work,
magazine**
本屋 ほんや bookstore; bookseller
読本 とくほん reader, reading book
絵本 えほん picture book
ビニ本 びにぼん vinyl-covered porno magazine
単行本 たんこうぼん separate volume, independent
   volume

典 ▷standard work
テン （K)2283

[original meaning] standard work of reference or scholarship:
❶ reference book, dictionary, encyclopedia
❷ classics, scriptures
a 辞典 じてん dictionary
   事典 じてん cyclopedia
   字典 じてん Chinese character dictionary
b 原典 げんてん original text
   古典 こてん classics; old book
   聖典 せいてん sacred book, scriptures

経 ▷religious classic
ケイ キョウ へ(る) た(つ) （K)1218

religious classic, Buddhist scriptures, sutra
経典 きょうてん sacred books, scripture, sutras;
   Bible
経文 きょうもん sutras
阿弥陀経 あみだきょう the Sukhavati sutra
仏経 ぶっきょう sutras

書 ▷book
ショ か(く) -が(き) （K)2314

[also suffix] **book, literary work**
書物 しょもつ book, volume
書店 しょてん bookstore
書籍 しょせき books, publications
辞書 じしょ dictionary
図書 としょ books
図書館 としょかん library
読書 どくしょ reading a book, reading
良書 りょうしょ good book, valuable work
教科書 きょうかしょ textbook, schoolbook

冊 ▷bound book
サツ サク   Ⓚ2925

bound book, volume, copy
小冊子 しょうさっし booklet, pamphlet
分冊 ぶんさつ separate volume
大冊 たいさつ great volume, bulky book
各冊 かくさつ each book [volume, copy]
別冊 べっさつ separate volume, extra issue

籍 ▷books
セキ   Ⓚ2381

books, written works, records
書籍 しょせき books, publications
史籍 しせき history books
漢籍 かんせき Chinese books, Chinese classics
典籍 てんせき classical books, books

著 ▷literary work
チョ あらわ(す) いちじる(しい)   Ⓚ1993

literary work, book, writing
著書 ちょしょ literary work, book
新著 しんちょ new book
拙著 せっちょ my humble work
名著 めいちょ famous book, masterpiece

巻 ▷volume
カン ま(く) まき   Ⓚ2298

volume, book
巻末 かんまつ end of a book
全巻 ぜんかん the whole volume [reel]
上中下巻 じょうちゅうげかん set of three volumes
別巻 べっかん separate volume, extra issue

編 ▷piece of writing
ヘン あ(む) -あ(み)   Ⓚ1270

[also suffix] **piece of writing, literary work; film**
巨編 きょへん great literary work
長編 ちょうへん long piece, full-length work (as of a novel or a film)
予告編 よこくへん preview, trailer
詩編 しへん book of poetry; Psalms

篇 ▷piece of writing
ヘン   Ⓚ2365

[also suffix] **piece of writing, literary work; film**
巨篇 きょへん great literary work
短篇 たんぺん short piece
予告篇 よこくへん preview, trailer
詩篇 しへん book of poetry; Psalms

鑑 ▷reference volume
カン かんが(みる)   Ⓚ1580

reference volume, directory, handbook, book
図鑑 ずかん picture [illustrated] book
年鑑 ねんかん yearbook
名鑑 めいかん list, directory
宝鑑 ほうかん handbook, thesaurus

books →COUNTERS FOR BOOKS

borrow →LEND AND BORROW

bottoms and bases
底 柢 下 基 礎
麓 磐 盤 床

底 ▷bottom
テイ そこ   Ⓚ2656

bottom, base
底流 ていりゅう bottom current, undercurrent
海底 かいてい sea bottom
心底 しんてい bottom of one's heart, inmost thoughts

柢 ▷bottom
テイ

[now replaced by 底] **bottom, basis, origin**
根柢 こんてい root, basis, foundation

下 ▷lower part
カ ゲ した しも もと さ(げる) さ(がる) くだ(る) くだ(り) くだ(す) くだ(さる) お(ろす) お(りる)   Ⓚ2862

【カ ゲ】
[also suffix] **down, under, below; lower part**
下線 かせん underline
下記の かきの following, undermentioned
上下 じょうげ upper and lower parts [sides], high and low; going up and down, rise and fall; first and second volumes
地下 ちか underground
投下する とうかする throw down, drop, airdrop; invest
廊下 ろうか corridor, gallery, passage
以下 いか or less than, not more than, under; and downward; the following
氷点下 ひょうてんか below the freezing point
【した】
lower part, bottom, foot
坂の下に さかのしたに at the foot of a slope

基 ▷base
キ もと もとい   Ⓚ2330

(physical support) **base, basis, foundation**
基礎 きそ basis, foundation
基盤 きばん bedrock, base, foundation
基底 きてい base, basis, foundation; *math* base
基石 きせき foundation stone
基地 きち base
開基 かいき foundation of a temple

礎 ▷foundation stone
ソ いしずえ   Ⓚ1152

foundation stone, cornerstone, foundation
礎石 そせき foundation stone, cornerstone
礎材 そざい foundation materials
柱礎 ちゅうそ plinth
定礎 ていそ laying of a foundation stone

麓 ▷foot of mountain
ロク ふもと   Ⓚ2453

foot [base] of a mountain
山麓 さんろく foot [base] of a mountain
岳麓 がくろく foot of Mt. Fuji

磐 ▷bedrock
バン いわ   Ⓚ2482

[now usu. 盤] **bedrock, base rock, base, foundation**
磐石 ばんじゃく huge rock; firmness
落磐 らくばん cave-in
大磐石である だいばんじゃくである be as firm as rock

盤 ▷bedrock
バン   Ⓚ2481

[formerly also 磐] **bedrock, base rock, base, foundation**
盤石 ばんじゃく huge rock; firmness
基盤 きばん bedrock, base, foundation
岩盤 がんばん bedrock, base rock
地盤 じばん ground, foundation, base
落盤 らくばん cave-in

床 ▷bed
ショウ とこ ゆか   Ⓚ2641

(bed-shaped support or underlying part) **bed, foundation or ore deposit**
温床 おんしょう hotbed
岩床 がんしょう bedrock
視床 ししょう thalamus
銃床 じゅうしょう gunstock
鉱床 こうしょう ore deposit

boundaries →EDGES AND BOUNDARIES

---

bow
礼   拝

礼 ▷courtesy bow
レイ ライ   Ⓚ0724

[also suffix] **courtesy bow, salutation**
礼砲 れいほう salute gun
一礼 いちれい bow, greeting; courtesy
敬礼 けいれい salutation, salute, bow
栄誉礼 えいよれい salute of guards of honor

拝 ▷bow in veneration
ハイ おが(む)   Ⓚ0268

bow in veneration, make a bow
拝礼 はいれい worship
遥拝する ようはいする worship from afar
三拝九拝する さんぱいきゅうはいする kowtow, bow many times

---

bowed
凹   凸   嵯

凹 ▷concave
オウ ぼこ   Ⓚ2924

[original meaning] **concave, hollow, indented**
凹面鏡 おうめんきょう concave mirror
凹地 おうち hollow, pit
凹凸 おうとつ unevenness, irregularities
凹レンズ おうれんず concave lens
凹版印刷 おうはんいんさつ intaglio printing
凸凹紙 とつおうし embossed paper

凸 ▷convex
トツ でこ   Ⓚ2928

[original meaning] **convex, gibbous, protruding**
凸レンズ とつれんず convex lens
凸面 とつめん convex surface
凸角 とっかく convex angle
凸版 とっぱん letterpress, relief printing
凹凸 おうとつ unevenness, irregularities

嵯 ▷rugged
サ ザ シ   Ⓚ0585

[rare] (of mountains) **rugged, uneven; steep**
嵯峨たる さがたる (of mountains) steep and high

branch
支　分

支 ▷branch
シ ささ(える)　　　Ⓚ1717

[sometimes also 枝] (something structurally analogous to a branch) **branch, offshoot**

支店 してん branch (office), branch (store)
支局 しきょく branch office
支部 しぶ branch office
支社 ししゃ branch office

分 ▷branch
ブン フン ブ わ(ける) わ(け) わ(かれる)
わ(かる) わ(かつ)　　　Ⓚ1713

[also prefix] **branch, offshoot**

分家 ぶんけ branch family, offshoot; setting up a branch family
分派 ぶんぱ branch, sect, denomination
分工場 ぶんこうじょう branch factory

branches and twigs
枝　梢

枝 ▷branch
シ えだ　　　Ⓚ0767

[original meaning] **branch, twig**

枝葉 しよう branches and leaves; minor details
枝垂れ桜 しだれざくら weeping cherry
楊枝 ようじ tooth pick
樹枝状の じゅしじょうの arborescent

梢 ▷tip of a twig
ショウ こずえ　　　Ⓚ0874

[original meaning] **tip of a twig or branch**

末梢 まっしょう tip, end; tip of a twig; *anat* periphery

branch of study
科　学　門

科 ▷subject of study
カ　　　Ⓚ1053

[also suffix] **subject of study, branch of academic study, subdivision of a discipline**

科目 かもく school subject; subdivision, items
教科 きょうか school subject; course of study, curriculum
学科 がっか school subject; course of study
理科 りか science; science department
分科会 ぶんかかい sectional subcommittee
百科事典 ひゃっかじてん encyclopedia
社会科 しゃかいか social studies

学 ▷branch of study
ガク まな(ぶ)　　　Ⓚ2211

[also suffix] **branch of study, -ology**

文学 ぶんがく literature, letters
医学 いがく medical science, medicine
数学 すうがく mathematics
化学 かがく chemistry
物理学 ぶつりがく physics, physical science

門 ▷field
モン かど　　　Ⓚ0789

field, branch, division

門外漢 もんがいかん layman, outsider
専門 せんもん specialty, profession
部門 ぶもん class, group, division, department, section; genus
仏門 ぶつもん Buddhism; priesthood

brave
勇　侠　赳　驍　敢
豪　雄　壮　義　凜

勇 ▷brave
ユウ いさ(む)　　　Ⓚ1798

[original meaning] **brave, courageous, bold, valiant**

勇敢な ゆうかんな brave, courageous, daring, heroic
勇気 ゆうき courage, valor, bravery, nerve
勇将 ゆうしょう brave general
勇猛 ゆうもう daring, bravery, valor
勇士 ゆうし brave warrior
勇退する ゆうたいする retire voluntarily

侠 ▷chivalrous
キョウ きゃん　　　Ⓚ0080

chivalrous, gallant

侠客 きょうかく chivalrous person, self-styled humanitarian

赳 ▷**valiant**
キュウ   Ⓚ2819

[rare] **valiant, brave and strong, gallant**
   赳赳たる武夫 きゅうきゅうたるぶふ soldier of dauntless courage

驍 ▷**valiant**
ギョウ   Ⓚ1642

valiant, brave and strong, gallant
   驍将 ぎょうしょう valiant general [leader]
   驍勇 ぎょうゆう bravery, courage, gallantry

敢 ▷**bold**
カン あ(えて) あ(えず)   Ⓚ1522

bold, daring, brave, fearless, resolute
   敢行 かんこう decisive [daring] action
   果敢な かかんな bold, daring; resolute
   勇敢な ゆうかんな brave, courageous, daring, heroic

豪 ▷**bold and unrestrained**
ゴウ   Ⓚ1838

bold and unrestrained, heroic, chivalrous
   豪快な ごうかいな exciting, heroic, largehearted
   豪放な ごうほうな largehearted, openhearted
   豪語する ごうごする talk big, boast, brag
   豪遊 ごうゆう wild merrymaking

雄 ▷**heroic**
ユウ お- おす   Ⓚ0920

heroic, manly, brave, bold
   雄壮な ゆうそうな brave, heroic, gallant
   雄姿 ゆうし brave [imposing] figure
   雄武 ゆうぶ bravery
   雄断 ゆうだん manly decision

壮 ▷**heroic**
ソウ   Ⓚ0198

heroic, ambitious, brave, dauntless
   壮烈な そうれつな heroic, brave
   壮挙 そうきょ grand scheme, heroic [daring] attempt
   壮士 そうし desperado, brave, swashbuckler
   壮途 そうと ambitious embarkment
   勇壮な ゆうそうな brave, heroic
   悲壮な ひそうな pathetic, tragic

義 ▷**chivalrous**
ギ   Ⓚ2052

chivalrous, heroic, self-sacrificing, public-spirited
   義侠 ぎきょう chivalry, generosity
   義気 ぎき chivalry, heroism

   義兵 ぎへい army in the cause of justice, volunteer corps
   義捐金(=義援金) ぎえんきん donation, contribution

凛 ▷**gallant**
リン   Ⓚ0151

gallant; brave
   凛凛しい りりしい gallant, brave, manly, dignified
   勇気凛凛 ゆうきりんりん full of spirit, in high spirit

break

破 拉 崩 挫 壊 毀
折 割 裂 砕 摧 潰

破 ▷**break**
ハ やぶ(る) やぶ(れる)   Ⓚ1064

[original meaning] **break, smash**
   破壊する はかいする break (down), destroy, wreck
   破片 はへん fragment, broken piece, scrap
   破損 はそん damage, breakdown
   破砕する はさいする crush, smash, crack to pieces
   破滅 はめつ ruin, destruction, wreck, collapse, downfall
   爆破 ばくは blasting, blowing up, explosion
   難破 なんぱ shipwreck
   打破する だはする break down, overthrow, abolish

拉 ▷**crush**
ラ ひし(ぐ)   Ⓚ0279

ⓐ **crush, squash**
ⓑ **discourage**
 ⓐ 取り拉ぐ とりひしぐ crush
 ⓑ 打ち拉がれる うちひしがれる be stricken [overcome, overwhelmed] (with grief, etc.); be utterly defeated

崩 ▷**crumble**
ホウ くず(れる) -くず(れ) くず(す) Ⓚ1989

crumble, collapse
   崩壊する ほうかいする collapse, crumble, break down, cave in
   崩落 ほうらく collapse, cave-in; crash; (of the market) decline

挫 ▷**sprain**
ザ   Ⓚ0392

ⓐ **sprain, twist**
ⓑ **bruise, injure**
 ⓐ 捻挫 ねんざ sprain

b 挫傷 ざしょう contusion

壊 ▷break down
カイ こわ(す) こわ(れる) Ⓚ0684

[sometimes also 潰] **break down, destroy, smash;** (of a dam) **burst**

壊滅 かいめつ destruction, annihilation
破壊する はかいする break (down), destroy, wreck
崩壊 ほうかい collapse, crumbling, breakdown, cave-in
全壊 ぜんかい complete collapse
決壊 けっかい rip, break
倒壊する とうかいする collapse, be destroyed, crumble

毀 ▷break down
キ こわ(す) Ⓚ1592

[usu. 壊す] *vt* **break (down), destroy, smash, take apart; spoil, mar, upset**

取り毀す とりこわす demolish, pull down

折 ▷break off
セツ お(る) おり お(れる) Ⓚ0225

(separate through the application of a sudden bending force) **break off (as a branch), break (a bone), snap (in two), split**

折半 せっぱん halving
折衷 せっちゅう compromise, eclecticism
骨折 こっせつ bone fracture

割 ▷crack
カツ わ(る) わり わ(れる) さ(く) Ⓚ1611

ⓐ **crack, break**
ⓑ **split, chop (wood)**
a コップを割る こっぷをわる crack [break] a glass
b 割り印 わりいん tally impression
割り箸 わりばし half-split (disposable) chopsticks
二つ割り ふたつわり cutting in two; one half

裂 ▷split
レツ さ(く) さ(ける) Ⓚ2347

ⓐ [original meaning] (separate or become separated into pieces) **split, tear, crack**
ⓑ **crack, fissure**
a 破裂 はれつ explosion, bursting
核分裂 かくぶんれつ nuclear fission
b 裂傷 れっしょう lacerated wound
亀裂 きれつ crack, fissure

砕 ▷crush up
サイ くだ(く) くだ(ける) Ⓚ1048

[formerly also 摧] [original meaning] **crush up, break into pieces, smash**

砕岩機 さいがんき rock crusher

砕氷船 さいひょうせん ice breaker
砕石 さいせき quarrying
破砕する はさいする crush, smash, crack to pieces
粉砕する ふんさいする pulverize, shatter, smash, crush
爆砕する ばくさいする blast, blow to pieces
玉砕 ぎょくさい death for honor

摧 ▷crush up
サイ くだ(く) くだ(ける)

[now replaced by 砕] **crush up, break into pieces, smash**

破摧する はさいする crush, smash, crack to pieces
玉摧する ぎょくさいする die but never surrender

潰 ▷crush
カイ つぶ(す) つぶ(れる) Ⓚ0677

crush, smash, batter, squash; scrap, junk
缶を潰す かんをつぶす crush a can

break into small pieces
砕　　抹

砕 ▷crush up
サイ くだ(く) くだ(ける) Ⓚ1048

[formerly also 摧] [original meaning] **crush up, break into pieces, smash**

砕岩機 さいがんき rock crusher
砕氷船 さいひょうせん ice breaker
砕石 さいせき quarrying
破砕する はさいする crush, smash, crack to pieces
粉砕する ふんさいする pulverize, shatter, smash, crush
爆砕する ばくさいする blast, blow to pieces
玉砕 ぎょくさい death for honor

抹 ▷pulverize
マツ Ⓚ0277

pulverize, powder
抹茶 まっちゃ powdered tea
抹香 まっこう incense powder, incense
抹香臭い まっこうくさい sound religious, smack of religion

breathe and blow
息 気 吸 呼 吹

息 ▷**breath**
ソク いき   Ⓚ2301

[original meaning] **breath, respiration**
嘆息 たんそく sigh
喘息 ぜんそく asthma
窒息 ちっそく suffocation, asphyxia

気 ▷**breath**
キ ケ   Ⓚ2751

breath
気管 きかん trachea, windpipe
気息 きそく breathing; breath
一気に いっきに at a breath, in one breath; on [at] a
   stretch [stroke]

吸 ▷**breathe in**
キュウ す(う)   Ⓚ0179

breathe in, inhale
吸入する きゅうにゅうする inhale, breath in; suck
   (in); imbibe
吸気 きゅうき inhalation of air; air breathed in
呼吸 こきゅう breathing, respiration

呼 ▷**breathe out**
コ よ(ぶ)   Ⓚ0246

[original meaning] **breathe out, exhale**
呼吸する こきゅうする breathe, respire
呼気 こき exhalation

吹 ▷**blow**
スイ ふ(く)   Ⓚ0204

[original meaning] **blow, breathe out**
吹鳴する すいめいする blow (a whistle)

brew and ferment
醸 醱 酵

醸 ▷**brew**
ジョウ かも(す)   Ⓚ1483

brew, make alcoholic beverages
醸造 じょうぞう brewing; distilling
醸母 じょうぼ yeast, leaven
醸成する じょうせいする brew; bring about

醱 ▷**brew**
ハツ

[now usu. 発] **brew, ferment**
醱酵 はっこう fermentation, zymosis

酵 ▷**ferment**
コウ   Ⓚ1413

(undergo fermentation) **ferment**
発酵 はっこう fermentation, zymosis

bridges
橋 桟

橋 ▷**bridge**
キョウ はし   Ⓚ0991

[also suffix] [original meaning] **bridge**
橋梁 きょうりょう bridge
橋脚 きょうきゃく bridge pier
架橋 かきょう bridge building
鉄橋 てっきょう iron bridge
歩道橋 ほどうきょう pedestrian bridge

桟 ▷**plank bridge**
サン   Ⓚ0843

**plank bridge, suspension bridge, plank passage-
way**
桟道 さんどう plank road, plank bridge, suspension
   bridge
桟橋 さんばし (landing) pier, jetty, wharf
桟梯子 さんばしご gangway ladder

bright
明 昭 蛍 晃 燦
赫 暉 熙 晟

明 ▷**bright**
メイ
ミョウ あ(かり) あか(るい) あか(るむ)
あか(らむ) あき(らか) あ(ける) -あ(け)
あ(く) あ(くる) あ(かす)   Ⓚ0756

[original meaning] **bright, brilliant, light**
明月 めいげつ bright moon, full moon; harvest
   moon
明星 みょうじょう Venus
明暗 めいあん light and dark; contrast
照明 しょうめい illumination, lighting
鮮明な せんめいな vivid, clear

昭 ▷luminous
ショウ   Ⓚ0796

ⓐ [original meaning, now rare] (emitting light) **luminous, bright, shining**
ⓑ (enjoying the glory of enlightened rule) **enlightened, glorious, illustrious**
a 昭昭たる しょうしょうたる [rare] bright, clear; obvious, plain
b 昭代 しょうだい enlightened era, glorious reign
昭和 しょうわ Showa era

蛍 ▷fluorescent
ケイ ほたる   Ⓚ2248

(luminous as a firefly) **fluorescent**
蛍光 けいこう fluorescence
蛍光灯 けいこうとう fluorescent lamp [light]
蛍石 けいせき fluorite

晃 ▷dazzling
コウ   Ⓚ2165

[archaic] **dazzling, brilliant**
晃晃たる こうこうたる dazzling, brilliant
晃朗たる こうろうたる bright and brilliant
晃曜 こうよう dazzling brightness

燦 ▷brilliant
サン   Ⓚ1007

brilliant, bright, glittering, shining
燦然たる さんぜんたる brilliant, glorious
燦燦と降り注ぐ さんさんとふりそそぐ (of the sun) shine brilliantly

赫 ▷blazing
カク かがや(く)

ⓐ (shining intensely) **blazing, resplendent, brilliant**
ⓑ (magnificent) **blazing, resplendent, brilliant, glorious**
ab 赫赫たる かっかくたる(=かくかくたる) splendid, brilliant, glorious
赫奕たる かくえき(=かくやく)たる bright, brilliant, glowing; vigorous, energetic, thriving

暉 ▷radiant
キ   Ⓚ0924

[archaic] **as bright as sunlight, radiant, luminous**

熙 ▷bright
キ   Ⓚ2499

bright, prosperous; glorious, peaceful
熙熙たる ききたる *literary* in a delightful manner; extensive, vast; (of traffic) busy

晟 ▷sunny
セイ ジョウ   Ⓚ2167

[archaic] **sunny, bright, full of sunshine**

brown colors
褐   茶

褐 ▷brown
カツ   Ⓚ1118

brown, dirty brown
褐色 かっしょく brown
褐炭 かったん brown coal, lignite
褐藻 かっそう brown algae
茶褐色 ちゃかっしょく brown, liver brown

茶 ▷light brown
チャ サ   Ⓚ1948

light brown
茶色 ちゃいろ light brown
焦げ茶 こげちゃ dark brown

Buddha
仏   釈

仏 ▷Buddha
ブツ フツ ほとけ   Ⓚ0010

Buddha, Sakyamuni
仏陀 ぶっだ Buddha
神仏 しんぶつ gods and Buddha; Shinto and Buddhism

釈 ▷Sakyamuni
シャク   Ⓚ1349

Śākyamuni, **Buddha**
釈迦 しゃか *Śākyamuni, Gautama*
釈典 しゃくてん Buddhist literature, Buddhist sutras

build
建   造   築   設

建 ▷build (a building)
ケン コン た(てる) た(て) -だ(て) た(つ)   Ⓚ2661

build (a building), construct, erect, put up
建築 けんちく construction, building, architecture

建設する けんせつする construct, build, erect
建造 けんぞう building, construction
建碑 けんぴ erection of a monument
建立 こんりゅう erection, building (as a temple)
再建 さいけん reconstruction, rehabilitation

造 ▷build (various structures)
ゾウ つく(る) つく(り) -づく(り)　　Ⓚ2679

build (various structures as building or ships), construct
造船 ぞうせん shipbuilding
造成する ぞうせいする create, clear, reclaim
築造 ちくぞう building, construction

築 ▷construct
チク きず(く)　　Ⓚ2369

[original meaning] construct, erect, build
築港 ちっこう harbor construction
築城 ちくじょう castle construction
建築 けんちく construction, building, architecture
建築家 けんちくか architect
構築 こうちく construction, building
新築 しんちく new building [construction]
増築 ぞうちく enlargement of a building

設 ▷set up
セツ もう(ける)　　Ⓚ1338

(assemble and/or erect) set up, install, erect, construct
設備 せつび equipment, facilities
建設 けんせつ construction, building, erection
埋設する まいせつする put [lay] underground
施設 しせつ equipment, facilities; institution, establishment

buildings
閣 宇 殿 堂 館 舎 棟 厩

閣 ▷tall magnificent building
カク　　Ⓚ2841

tall magnificent building, tower, pavilion, stately mansion, palace
閣下 かっか Your [His] Excellency
楼閣 ろうかく multistoried building
天守閣 てんしゅかく castle-tower; dungeon, keep
仏閣 ぶっかく Buddhist temple
銀閣寺 ぎんかくじ Ginkaku Temple

宇 ▷large building
ウ　　Ⓚ1863

large building, building with large roof
堂宇 どうう edifice, temple, hall

殿 ▷palace
デン テン との -どの　　Ⓚ1593

(large stately building) palace, hall, mansion
殿堂 でんどう hall, palace, shrine; sanctuary
寝殿 しんでん main house

堂 ▷hall
ドウ　　Ⓚ2246

[also suffix] (building for public gatherings) hall, public building
公会堂 こうかいどう town [public] hall
議事堂 ぎじどう assembly hall; Diet Building

館 ▷public building
カン やかた　　Ⓚ1562

ⓐ [also suffix] public building (esp. a large building for cultural activities), hall, edifice, pavilion
ⓑ building
a 館長 かんちょう director, superintendent
会館 かいかん hall, assembly hall
図書館 としょかん library
大使館 たいしかん embassy
公民館 こうみんかん public hall, citizen's hall
体育館 たいいくかん gymnasium, gym
映画館 えいがかん cinema house, movie theater
文明館 ぶんめいかん The Bunmeikan Theater
カナダ館 かなだかん The Canada Pavilion
b 館内 かんない in the building
本館 ほんかん this building; main building
別館 べっかん annex, extension, outbuilding

舎 ▷building
シャ　　Ⓚ1774

building, house, quarter, hut
駅舎 えきしゃ station building
校舎 こうしゃ school building
庁舎 ちょうしゃ government building
鶏舎 けいしゃ henhouse

棟 ▷block
トウ むね むな-　　Ⓚ0904

ⓐ [also suffix] (long building or part thereof) block, building, ward
ⓑ counter for blocks of flats or buildings
a 病棟 びょうとう (hospital) ward
翼棟 よくとう wing (of a building)
研究室棟 けんきゅうしつとう research laboratory building, laboratory block
b 第三棟 だいさんとう Block No. 3

厩 ▷horse stable
キュウ うまや　　Ⓚ2598

horse stable, horse barn

厩舎 きゅうしゃ barn, stable
厩務員 きゅうむいん stable hand, groom

bundles and clusters
束　房

束 ▷bundle
ソク たば たば(ねる) つか　Ⓚ2978

technical term for various bundlelike clusters:
- ⓐ [also suffix] anat, biol **bundle**
- ⓑ chem, math **lattice**
- ⓒ [also suffix] phys, biol **flux**
- a 繊維束 せんいそく fiber bundle, fascicle
  維管束 いかんそく vascular bundle
- b 束群 そくぐん lattice group
- c 磁束 じそく magnetic flux
  中性子束 ちゅうせいしそく neutron flux

房 ▷tuft
ボウ ふさ　Ⓚ1702

tuft, tassel
乳房 にゅうぼう(=ちぶさ) breast, nipple

burden
荷　貨

荷 ▷load
カ に　Ⓚ1972

- ⓐ load, burden; cargo, goods
- ⓑ counter for loads or burdens
- ⓒ elec **load**
- a 荷重 かじゅう load
  出荷する しゅっかする forward, ship, consign
  入荷 にゅうか arrival of goods (at a shop), receipt of
    goods
  集荷 しゅうか collection of cargo, cargo booking
  在荷 ざいか stock, goods on hand
- b 一荷 いっか one load
- c 電荷 でんか electric charge
  装荷 そうか loading

貨 ▷freight
カ　Ⓚ2175

freight, cargo
貨物 かもつ freight, cargo, goods
貨車 かしゃ freight car
貨客 かきゃく freight and passengers

burn
焼 燃 焚 焦 灼 炮 燎

焼 ▷burn
ショウ や(く) や(き) や(ける)　Ⓚ0909

- ⓐ [original meaning] (set or be set on fire) **burn, incinerate**
- ⓑ be burnt (down), be destroyed by fire
- a 焼却する しょうきゃくする destroy by fire, incinerate
  焼身自殺 しょうしんじさつ suicide by fire, burning
    oneself to death
  焼香する しょうこうする burn [offer] incense
  焼夷弾 しょういだん incendiary bomb
  焼死 しょうし death by fire
  焼酎 しょうちゅう shochu
- b 全焼する ぜんしょうする be burnt down
  半焼 はんしょう partial destruction by fire
  類焼する るいしょうする catch fire from next door

燃 ▷burn (undergo combustion)
ネン も(える) も(やす) も(す)　Ⓚ0995

burn, undergo combustion
燃焼 ねんしょう combustion, burning
燃料 ねんりょう fuel
燃費 ねんぴ mileage
可燃性 かねんせい combustibility
内燃機関 ないねんきかん internal combustion
  engine
再燃する さいねんする revive, come to the fore
  again

焚 ▷burn (build a fire)
フン た(く)　Ⓚ2418

burn, kindle, build a fire
焚き火 たきび bonfire
焚き付け たきつけ kindling, fire lighter
焚き付ける たきつける kindle, build a fire; instigate,
  stir up
空焚き からだき heating a pan or bathtub without
  water in it
追い焚き おいだき reheating (of bath)

焦 ▷scorch
ショウ こ(げる) こ(がす) こ(がれる)
あせ(る)　Ⓚ2412

- ⓐ [original meaning] **scorch, burn**
- ⓑ [also prefix] **pyro-**
- a 焦点 しょうてん focus, focal point; (photographic)
    focus
  焦土 しょうど scorched earth
  焦熱 しょうねつ scorching heat

焦眉 しょうび emergency, urgency, imminence
b 焦性硫酸 しょうせいりゅうさん pyrosulfuric acid
焦電気 しょうでんき pyroelectricity

灼 ▷scorch
シャク や(く) あらた(か)　　Ⓚ0741

ⓐ scorch, burn
ⓑ cauterize
a 灼熱 しゃくねつ heat
b 焼灼 しょうしゃく cautery, cauterization

炮 ▷roast
ホウ

[original meaning] **roast, bake**
炮烙(=焙烙) ほうろく parching pan, baking pan

燎 ▷set on fire
リョウ　　Ⓚ0996

set on fire, burn
燎原の火 りょうげんのひ prairie fire, wild fire; fast-spreading disaster [rumor]

bury

埋　　葬

埋 ▷bury
マイ う(める) う(まる) う(もれる)　Ⓚ0364

[original meaning] **bury, embed**
埋葬 まいそう burial, interment
埋蔵物 まいぞうぶつ buried treasure
埋没する まいぼつする be buried; fall into oblivion
埋線 まいせん underground cable
埋設する まいせつする put [lay] underground

葬 ▷bury (a corpse)
ソウ ほうむ(る)　　Ⓚ2022

[original meaning] **bury (a corpse), entomb, inter**
埋葬する まいそうする bury, inter
火葬 かそう cremation
水葬 すいそう burial at sea

business →INDUSTRY AND BUSINESS

busy

忙　繁　慌

忙 ▷busy
ボウ いそが(しい)　　Ⓚ0188

busy, occupied
忙殺される ぼうさつされる be very busily occupied, be worked to death
多忙な たぼうな busy
繁忙である はんぼうである be busy, be fully occupied

繁 ▷bustling
ハン　　Ⓚ2484

bustling, busy
繁忙 はんぼう pressure of business, business
繁閑 はんかん press and slack of business
農繁期 のうはんき busy farming season

慌 ▷flurried
コウ あわ(てる) あわ(ただしい)　Ⓚ0532

be flurried [fluttered], be confused, be in a hurry
慌てふためく あわてふためく be all in a flurry, hurry-scurry, act helter-skelter
慌てて あわてて in confusion, in hot haste
慌て者 あわてもの flutterer, scatterbrain, bustling fellow
大慌て おおあわて total fluster, hot haste

buttocks

尻　　肛

尻 ▷buttocks
しり　　Ⓚ2610

buttocks, hips, the rear, ass
お尻 おしり buttocks; backside (of a kettle)
尻に帆掛けて逃げる しりにほかけてにげる take to one's heels ("stick a sail in one's ass and take off like the devil")
尻の軽い女 しりのかるいおんな wanton girl
尻尾 しっぽ tail; one's true colors

肛 ▷anus
コウ

[original meaning] **anus**
肛門 こうもん anus
肛門科 こうもんか proctology; proctology clinic
脱肛 だっこう prolapse of the anus

buy

買　購

買 ▷buy
バイ か(う)　　　Ⓚ2252

[original meaning] **buy, purchase**
買収 ばいしゅう buying up, purchasing; bribing
購買 こうばい purchase, buying
売買 ばいばい buying and selling, trade

購 ▷purchase
コウ　　　Ⓚ1467

[original meaning] **purchase, buy**
購買 こうばい purchase, buying
購読 こうどく subscription
購入 こうにゅう purchase, buying
購書 こうしょ purchasing books; purchased books

calculate and count

算　計　数

算 ▷calculate
サン　　　Ⓚ2359

ⓐ **calculate, compute reckon, count**
ⓑ [also suffix] **calculation, arithmetical operation**

a　算出する さんしゅつする compute, calculate
算数 さんすう arithmetic; calculation
算術 さんじゅつ arithmetic
計算 けいさん computation, calculation
換算表 かんさんひょう conversion table

b　採算 さいさん (commercial) profit
概算 がいさん approximation, rough estimate [calculation]
清算 せいさん settlement, liquidation; clearing (off)
暗算 あんざん mental arithmetic [calculation]
予算 よさん budget; estimate, calculation
電算機 でんさんき electronic computer
足し算 たしざん addition
読み上げ算 よみあげざん calculation by abacus, having the figures read aloud by another person

計 ▷compute
ケイ はか(る) はか(らう)　　　Ⓚ1309

compute, calculate, reckon, count, estimate
計算 けいさん computation, calculation
計上する けいじょうする sum up, appropriate (a sum for some purpose)

計量 けいりょう measuring, weighing
推計する すいけいする estimate
統計 とうけい statistics
会計 かいけい account, finance; bill
集計 しゅうけい totalization, classified total

数 ▷count
スウ ス かず かぞ(える)　　　Ⓚ1591

count, enumerate, reckon
数詞 すうし *gram* numeral
算数 さんすう arithmetic; calculation

calendars

暦　新　旧

暦 ▷calendar
レキ こよみ　　　Ⓚ2599

[also suffix] **calendar**
暦年 れきねん calendar year
太陽暦 たいようれき solar calendar
旧暦 きゅうれき old [lunar] calendar
西暦 せいれき Christian Era, A.D.
陰暦 いんれき lunar calendar

新 ▷new calendar
シン あたら(しい) あら(た) あら– にい–　　　Ⓚ1587

abbrev. of 新暦 しんれき: **new [Gregorian] calendar**
新正月 しんしょうがつ January (according to the new calendar)

旧 ▷old calendar
キュウ　　　Ⓚ0005

old calendar, lunar calendar
旧暦 きゅうれき old [lunar] calendar
旧正月 きゅうしょうがつ New Year's Day in the lunar calendar

calendar signs

戊　庚　壬

戊 ▷fifth calendar sign
ボ つちのえ　　　Ⓚ2943

fifth calendar sign
戊辰 ぼしん fifth of the sexagenary cycle
戊戌 ぼじゅつ 35th of the sexagenary cycle
戊夜 ぼや fifth division of the night (around four o'clock in the morning)

庚 ▷seventh calendar sign
コウ かのえ Ⓚ2655

seventh calendar sign
庚申 こうしん 57th of the sexagenary cycle

壬 ▷ninth calendar sign
ジン みずのえ Ⓚ2899

ninth calendar sign
壬申 じんしん ninth of the sexagenary cycle

call and invite
呼　喚　召　招

呼 ▷call
コ よ(ぶ) Ⓚ0246

(summon) **call, send for, invite**
呼び出し よびだし call, calling out, summons
呼び寄せる よびよせる call, summon, send for, call together
医者を呼ぶ いしゃをよぶ call the doctor

喚 ▷call
カン Ⓚ0503

call, call to, summon
喚問 かんもん summons
召喚する しょうかんする summon, cite, subpoena

召 ▷summon
ショウ め(す) Ⓚ1727

[original meaning] **summon (esp. one's inferior), call together, convene**
召集する しょうしゅうする call together
召還する しょうかんする recall, call back
召喚 しょうかん summons, citation
応召者 おうしょうしゃ draftee

招 ▷invite
ショウ まね(く) Ⓚ0281

ⓐ **invite**
ⓑ [original meaning] **beckon (with the hand), call**
ⓐ 招待 しょうたい invitation
招宴 しょうえん invitation to a party; party
招請国 しょうせいこく inviting country, host nation
ⓑ 招集する しょうしゅうする call, summon, convene
招致 しょうち summons, invitation
招聘 しょうへい invitation; engagement

calm and peaceful
安康寧泰静平穏

安 ▷peaceful
アン やす(い) やす やす(らか) Ⓚ1859

peaceful, tranquil, calm, quiet, gentle
安住する あんじゅうする live peacefully
安泰 あんたい peace, security, tranquility
安眠 あんみん quiet sleep, peaceful slumber
安定 あんてい stability; composure
安静 あんせい rest, quiet, repose

康 ▷peaceful
コウ Ⓚ2693

(free from danger or hardship) **peaceful, secure, safe**
康寧 こうねい [rare] peacefulness, tranquility
小康 しょうこう lull, respite, breathing spell (of peace)

寧 ▷peaceful
ネイ Ⓚ2061

peaceful, quiet, tranquil
寧日 ねいじつ peaceful day
安寧 あんねい public peace, tranquility
康寧 こうねい [rare] peacefulness, tranquility

泰 ▷tranquil
タイ Ⓚ2239

tranquil, peaceful, composed, calm
泰平 たいへい tranquility, perfect peace
泰然たる たいぜんたる calm, composed; firm
安泰 あんたい peace, security, tranquility

静 ▷quiet
セイ ジョウ しず- しず(か) しず(まる) しず(める) Ⓚ1539

(free of agitation) **quiet, calm, serene, tranquil**
沈静 ちんせい stillness, tranquility, slackness
平静な へいせいな calm, serene
冷静な れいせいな cool, calm, cool-headed, dispassionate

平 ▷calm
ヘイ ビョウ たい(ら) -だいら ひら Ⓚ2921

calm, peaceful, quiet
平和 へいわ peace, harmony
平気 へいき nonchalance, unconcern; composure
平穏 へいおん calmness, quiet, tranquility
平静な へいせいな calm, serene

平安 へいあん calmness, peace, quietness, tranquility; Heian period
平成 へいせい Heisei era
和平 わへい peace
太平 (=泰平) たいへい tranquility, perfect peace

穏 ▷calm
オン おだ(やか) Ⓚ1141

calm, peaceful, quiet, tranquil, placid
平穏な へいおんな calm, quiet, tranquil
安穏 あんのん peace, quiet, tranquility
不穏な ふおんな disquieting, restless

camps
陣　　営

陣 ▷camp
ジン Ⓚ0411

army camp, encampment, position
陣営 じんえい camp, quarters
陣地 じんち encampment, position
退陣する たいじんする decamp, withdraw
論陣を張る ろんじんをはる argue about, take a firm stand

営 ▷barracks
エイ いとな(む) Ⓚ2257

barracks, camp, encampment; fort
兵営 へいえい barracks
陣営 じんえい camp, quarters
野営 やえい camping, campground

capacity units
勺　合　立　升　斗　石

勺 ▷shaku (0.018 liters)
シャク Ⓚ2540

former unit of capacity equiv. to approx. 0.018 liters or 1/10 of a go (合)
一勺 いっしゃく 1 shaku

合 ▷go (0.18 liters)
ゴウ ガッ- カッ- あ(う) あ(い) あ(わす) あ(わせる) Ⓚ1740

unit of capacity equiv. to approx. 0.18 liters or 1/10 of a sho (升)
五合升 ごごうます 5-go measure

立 ▷liter
リツ リュウ りっとる た(つ) た(ち)- た(てる) た(て)- -だ(て) -だ(てる) Ⓚ1723

liter
五十立 ごじゅうりっとる 50 liters

升 ▷sho (1.8 liters)
ショウ ます Ⓚ2906

sho: unit of capacity equiv. to approx. 1.8 liters or 10 go (合), used esp. for sake or rice
一升瓶 いっしょうびん 1-sho bottle

斗 ▷to (18 liters)
ト Ⓚ2554

to: unit of capacity equiv. to approx. 18 liters or 10 sho (升), used esp. for sake or rice
斗酒 としゅ a to of sake, big supply of sake
二斗 にと 2 to

石 ▷koku (180 liters)
セキ シャク コク いし Ⓚ2564

former unit of capacity equiv. to approx. 180 liters or 10 to (斗), used esp. as unit of rice stipends in feudal Japan
石高 こくだか yield, fief, stipend
二千石 にせんごく stipend of 2000 koku in rice
一石 いっこく 1 koku

cardinal points
東　西　北　南　巽　艮

東 ▷east
トウ ひがし Ⓚ2987

east, eastern
東方 とうほう east, eastward
東南 とうなん southeast
東亜 とうあ East Asia
東洋 とうよう Orient
東部 とうぶ eastern part; the East (of the United States)
東西南北 とうざいなんぼく north, south, east and west
関東 かんとう Kanto district
中東 ちゅうとう Middle East
遼東の豕 りょうとうのいのこ being self-complacent

西 ▷west
セイ サイ にし Ⓚ2951

west, western
西部 せいぶ western part; the West

西経 せいけい west longitude
西洋人 せいようじん Westerner
関西 かんさい Kansai district
東西 とうざい east and west
北西 ほくせい northwest

北 ▷north
ホク きた Ⓚ0176

north
北部 ほくぶ north, northern part
北欧 ほくおう Northern Europe, Scandinavia
北爆 ほくばく bombing the North (Vietnam)
北東 ほくとう northeast
北極 ほっきょく North Pole
北緯 ほくい north latitude
北方 ほっぽう north, northward; northern district

南 ▷south
ナン ナ みなみ Ⓚ1791

【ナン ナ】
south, southern
南北 なんぼく north and south
南西 なんせい southwest
南阿 なんあ Republic of South Africa
南海 なんかい southern sea; South Seas
南極 なんきょく South Pole
南下する なんかする go down south
南蛮人 なんばんじん early Europeans (in Japan);
　southern barbarians
南東 なんとう southeast
南部 なんぶ south(ern) part; South
東南 とうなん southeast

【みなみ】
[also prefix] **south**
南アメリカ みなみあめりか South America
南風 みなみかぜ south wind
南口 みなみぐち south exit

巽 ▷southeast
ソン たつみ Ⓚ2346

southeast
巽の方角 たつみのほうがく southeast direction

艮 ▷northeast
コン ゴン うしとら

[rare] one of the four supplementary signs of the Oriental zodiac: **northeast**

慎 ▷prudent
シン つつし(む) Ⓚ0590

prudent, discreet, careful
慎重 しんちょう prudence, discretion, circumspection
謹慎 きんしん house arrest, domiciliary confinement; penitence
戒慎する かいしんする be cautious, be discreet

謹 ▷carefully
キン つつし(む) Ⓚ1462

carefully, attentively, cautiously
謹製 きんせい careful production
謹聴する きんちょうする listen attentively
謹慎 きんしん house arrest, domiciliary confinement; penitence

精 ▷meticulous
セイ ショウ Ⓚ1248

meticulous, careful, elaborate, precise, exact, detailed, fine
精査 せいさ minute investigation, close inspection, careful examination
精選 せいせん careful selection
精緻な せいちな minute, subtle, delicate, exquisite
精巧な せいこうな elaborate, exquisite, ingenious
精密 せいみつ precision, accuracy, minuteness
精度 せいど precision, accuracy
精算 せいさん exact calculation; settlement of accounts
精通する せいつうする be well versed in, have thorough knowledge of

運 ▷carry
ウン はこ(ぶ) Ⓚ2707

ⓐ (move something from one place to another in one's hands or in a vehicle) **carry, transport, ship**
ⓑ **carriage, transport, transportation**
a 運輸 うんゆ transport(ation), conveyance
運送 うんそう shipping, transportation
運搬する うんぱんする carry, transport, convey, deliver

海運 かいうん marine transportation, merchant shipping

陸運 りくうん land transportation [carriage]

舟運 しゅううん transportation by water

b 運賃 うんちん freight [shipping] expense, passenger fare

運河 うんが canal

搬 ▷carry
ハン   Ⓚ0592

[original meaning] **carry, transport, convey**

搬送 はんそう conveyance

搬出する はんしゅつする carry out

搬入する はんにゅうする carry in

搬送波 はんそうは carrier wave

可搬式 かはんしき portable

運搬する うんぱんする carry, transport, convey, deliver

輸 ▷transport
ユ   Ⓚ1454

[original meaning] (transfer by vehicle) **transport, ship, carry, convey**

輸送する ゆそうする transport, convey

運輸 うんゆ transport(ation), conveyance

空輸 くうゆ air transportation

carve →FORM AND CARVE

catch a criminal

捕　逮　拘　勾

捕 ▷catch
ホ と(らえる) と(らわれる) と(る)
つか(まえる) つか(まる)   Ⓚ0387

(capture by force) **catch, capture, arrest**

捕鯨 ほげい whaling

捕虜 ほりょ prisoner of war, captive

逮 ▷catch a criminal
タイ   Ⓚ2691

[original meaning] (chase after and reach out to capture) **catch a criminal, capture**

逮捕 たいほ arrest, capture

逮捕状 たいほじょう warrant of arrest

拘 ▷arrest
コウ かか(わる)   Ⓚ0274

[sometimes also 勾] [original meaning] **arrest, detain, confine**

拘留 こうりゅう penal detention up to 30 days

拘禁する こうきんする detain, confine, imprison

拘置 こうち detention, confinement, arrest

拘束 こうそく restriction, restraint, binding

拘引 こういん arrest, custody

勾 ▷arrest
コウ   Ⓚ2546

[now also 拘] **arrest, detain, confine**

勾引 こういん arrest, custody

勾留 こうりゅう detention for investigation

cattle

牛　丑

牛 ▷cattle
ギュウ うし   Ⓚ2903

[original meaning] (any bovine animal) **cattle, cow, bull, ox**

牛乳 ぎゅうにゅう (cow's) milk

牛肉 ぎゅうにく beef

牛皮(=牛革) ぎゅうかわ cowhide, oxhide

牛飲馬食する ぎゅういんばしょくする gorge and swill, drink like a cow and eat like a horse

牛歩戦術 ぎゅうほせんじゅつ cow's-pace tactics

乳牛 にゅうぎゅう(=ちちうし) milch cow, dairy cattle

闘牛 とうぎゅう bullfight, fighting bull

丑 ▷the Ox
チュウ うし   Ⓚ2889

second sign of the Oriental zodiac: **the Ox**—(time) 1-3 a.m., (direction) NNE, (season) December (of the lunar calendar)

癸丑 きちゅう 50th of the sexagenary cycle

cause

致　誘

致 ▷bring about
チ いた(す)   Ⓚ1202

bring about, cause to, lead to, incur

致死の ちしの lethal, fatal

致命的 ちめいてき fatal

一致 いっち accord, agreement

合致 がっち agreement, concurrence

誘 ▷induce
ユウ さそ(う)   Ⓚ1407

(stimulate the occurrence of) **induce, bring about, cause**

誘発する ゆうはつする cause, induce, lead up to
誘起する ゆうきする give rise to, lead to
誘因 ゆういん immediate cause, incentive

cause and reason
因 由 為 故 訳

因 ▷cause
イン よ(る)   Ⓚ2629

cause, reason, origin, factor
因果 いんが cause and effect; karma
因子 いんし *math* factor
因数 いんすう *math* factor
死因 しいん cause of death
原因 げんいん cause, origin
要因 よういん primary factor, main cause

由 ▷reason
ユ ユウ ユイ よし   Ⓚ2935

reason (for what has happened), cause, origin, derivation
由来 ゆらい origin, source, cause; history
由緒 ゆいしょ history, lineage
理由 りゆう reason, cause, ground
事由 じゆう reason, cause, ground
来由 らいゆ(=らいゆう) cause, origin

為 ▷because
イ ため な(す)   Ⓚ2994

[often followed by に] **because (of), owing to, as a result of**
雨の為に あめのために because of the rain

故 ▷reason
コ ゆえ   Ⓚ1056

reason, cause, grounds
故に ゆえに therefore, accordingly
．．．の故に …のゆえに on account of…, by reason of…
故有って ゆえあって for a certain reason; owing to unavoidable circumstances

訳 ▷reason
ヤク わけ   Ⓚ1340

reason, cause, ground(s)
訳も無く わけもなく without reason, without cause
言い訳 いいわけ apology, excuse, explanation
申し訳 もうしわけ excuse, apology, explanation

cavities →HOLES AND CAVITIES

celebrating and congratulating
祝 慶 賀 寿

祝 ▷celebrate
シュク シュウ いわ(う)   Ⓚ0822

ⓐ celebrate
ⓑ congratulate, felicitate
a 祝賀 しゅくが celebration; congratulation
  祝日 しゅくじつ holiday, festival day
  慶祝 けいしゅく celebration, congratulation
b 祝言 しゅうげん wedding
  祝儀 しゅうぎ celebration; congratulatory gift; tip
  祝電 しゅくでん congratulatory telegram

慶 ▷felicitation
ケイ   Ⓚ2739

felicitation, congratulation; celebration, rejoicing
慶祝 けいしゅく celebration, congratulation
慶弔 けいちょう congratulations and condolences
慶事 けいじ happy [auspicious] event
同慶 どうけい (matter of) mutual congratulations
国慶 こっけい National day (of China)

賀 ▷congratulate
ガ   Ⓚ2253

ⓐ congratulate, greet
ⓑ celebrate
a 賀状 がじょう greeting card
  賀詞 がし greetings, congratulations
  賀正 がしょう New Year's congratulations, Happy New Year
  慶賀 けいが congratulation, felicitation
  年賀 ねんが New Year's greetings; New Year's card
b 祝賀会 しゅくがかい celebration, party of congratulation

寿 ▷congratulations
ジュ ス ことぶき   Ⓚ2979

congratulations, felicitation, celebration, greetings; longevity
寿教室 ことぶききょうしつ culture courses for the aged
新年の寿 しんねんのことぶき New Year's greetings

central parts
核 仁 心 芯

 ▷**nucleus**
カク   Ⓚ0836

ⓐ (central part) **nucleus, core**
ⓑ *biol, chem* **nucleus**
ⓒ [original meaning] **kernel (of a fruit), putamen**

 a 核仁 かくじん nucleus
    核家族 かくかぞく nucleus family
    中核 ちゅうかく core, nucleus; kernel
 b 核崩壊 かくほうかい disintegration of a cell nucleus
    核酸 かくさん nucleic acid
    細胞核 さいぼうかく nucleus (of a cell)
    神経核 しんけいかく neuron
    結核 けっかく tuberculosis
    痔核 じかく hemorrhoids
 c 果核 かかく putamen

 ▷**kernel**
ジン ニ   Ⓚ0011

kernel, core; karyosome
    杏仁 きょうにん apricot stone
    核仁 かくじん nucleus

心 ▷**core**
シン こころ -ごころ   Ⓚ0004

[usu. 芯] **core (of fruit); wick; lead (of a pencil); padding**
    心抜き器 しんぬきき corer
    花心 かしん center of a flower
    灯心 とうしん (lamp) wick
    替え心 かえしん spare lead
    帯心 おびしん sash padding

 ▷**core**
シン   Ⓚ1898

[sometimes also 心] **core (of fruit); wick; lead (of a pencil); padding**
    芯地 しんじ padding, lining
    花芯 かしん center of a flower
    空芯菜 くうしんさい water morning glory
    摘芯 てきしん thinning (of buds)
    灯芯 とうしん (lamp) wick
    替え芯 かえしん spare lead

ceramics ware
陶 窯 磁

陶 ▷**pottery**
トウ   Ⓚ0499

pottery, ceramics, earthenware
    陶器 とうき pottery, porcelain, chinaware
    陶芸 とうげい ceramic art
    陶磁器 とうじき porcelain, pottery, ceramics
    陶工 とうこう potter, ceramist

窯 ▷**ceramics**
ヨウ かま   Ⓚ2081

ceramics
    窯業 ようぎょう ceramics, ceramic industry

磁 ▷**porcelain**
ジ   Ⓚ1123

porcelain, chinaware
    陶磁器 とうじき porcelain, pottery, ceramics
    青磁 せいじ celadon porcelain
    白磁 はくじ white porcelain

cereal
穀 禾 粉

穀 ▷**cereal**
コク   Ⓚ1620

cereal, grain, corn
    穀物 こくもつ grain, cereals
    穀類 こくるい grains
    穀粒 こくりゅう grain
    穀倉 こくそう granary, grain elevator
    穀粉 こくふん grain [rice] flour
    穀食 こくしょく cereal diet, grain-eating
    五穀 ごこく the five cereals, (staple) grains

禾 ▷**cereal**
カ   Ⓚ2938

ⓐ **cereal, grain**
ⓑ [archaic] **rice; foxtail millet**

 a 禾本科 かほんか *Gramineae*
    禾穀類 かこくるい cereal crops

粉 ▷**flour**
フン こ こな   Ⓚ1186

(powdered meal) **flour, meal**

穀粉 こくふん grain [rice] flour
澱粉 でんぷん starch
米粉 べいふん rice flour
製粉 せいふん flour milling

cereals
米麦豆粟黍蕎蒋

米 ▷rice
ベイ マイ こめ   Ⓚ2958
see also →RICE

[also suffix] **rice**
米穀 べいこく rice
米価 べいか price of rice
米作 べいさく rice crop
米飯 べいはん cooked rice
玄米 げんまい unpolished rice
精米 せいまい rice polishing; polished [white] rice
外米 がいまい foreign [imported] rice
配給米 はいきゅうまい rationed rice
新潟米 にいがたまい Niigata rice

麦 ▷wheat
バク むぎ   Ⓚ2133

wheat, barley, oats, rye
麦秋 ばくしゅう wheat harvest [season]; early summer
麦価 ばくか price of wheat
麦芽 ばくが wheat germ, malt
麦酒 ばくしゅ(=びーる) beer
米麦 べいばく rice and barley; corn
精麦 せいばく cleaning barley or wheat; polished barley or wheat

豆 ▷bean
トウ ズ まめ   Ⓚ1700

ⓐ **bean, pea**
ⓑ **soybean**
a 豆腐 とうふ tofu (Japanese bean curd)
　大豆 だいず soybean
b 豆乳 とうにゅう soybean milk
　納豆 なっとう fermented soybeans

粟 ▷foxtail millet
ゾク あわ   Ⓚ2343

foxtail millet
粟粒 ぞくりゅう millet grain

黍 ▷proso millet
ショ きび

[original meaning] **proso millet, common millet**

蜀黍 しょくしょ(=もろこし) sorghum, Indian millet

蕎 ▷buckwheat
キョウ   Ⓚ2086

buckwheat
蕎麦 きょうばく(=そば) common buckwheat

蒋 ▷wild rice
ショウ   Ⓚ2075

[original meaning, now obsolete] **wild rice**
蒋介石 しょうかいせき Chiang Kai-shek

ceremonies and festivities
式儀典礼斎会祭

式 ▷ceremony
シキ   Ⓚ2623

[also suffix] **ceremony, rite, rituals, celebration, exercises**
式典 しきてん ceremony
儀式 ぎしき ceremony, rite, ritual
挙式 きょしき holding a ceremony
葬式 そうしき funeral ceremony
結婚式 けっこんしき wedding ceremony
卒業式 そつぎょうしき graduation ceremony

儀 ▷ceremony
ギ   Ⓚ0147

ceremony, rite, ritual
儀式 ぎしき ceremony, rite, ritual
婚儀 こんぎ wedding ceremony
葬儀 そうぎ funeral service [rites]

典 ▷formal ceremony
テン   Ⓚ2283

formal ceremony, celebration
典礼 てんれい formal ceremony
式典 しきてん ceremony
祭典 さいてん festival
祝典 しゅくてん celebration, festival

礼 ▷rite
レイ ライ   Ⓚ0724

[also suffix] [original meaning] **rite, ceremony, ritual, religious service**
礼典 れいてん ceremony, ritual, rite
礼服 れいふく ceremonial dress
婚礼 こんれい wedding ceremony

洗礼 せんれい baptism
朝礼 ちょうれい morning gathering
立太子礼 りったいしれい ceremonial of instituting the Crown Prince

斎 ▷religious ritual
サイ   Ⓚ1817

ⓐ religious ritual [service], Shinto ritual (esp. at Ise Shrine)
ⓑ Buddhist ritual [service]
a 斎主 さいしゅ Chief Priest of the Great Shrine of Ise
b 斎場 さいじょう funeral hall; site of a religious service

会 ▷Buddhist ceremony
カイ エ あ(う) あ(わせる)   Ⓚ1741

Buddhist ceremony
法会 ほうえ Buddhist mass
放生会 ほうじょうえ ceremony of releasing captive animals

祭 ▷festival
サイ まつ(る) まつ(り)   Ⓚ2329

ⓐ [also suffix] festival, feast, celebration, holiday
ⓑ religious festival, rite
a 祭日 さいじつ national holiday, festival [feast] day
祝祭日 しゅくさいじつ national holiday, festival [feast] day
文化祭 ぶんかさい cultural festival
芸術祭 げいじゅつさい art festival
前夜祭 ぜんやさい eve
b 祭礼 さいれい festival, feast, rituals
祭祀 さいし religious service; festival

certain →A CERTAIN

certain
必 確 筈

必 ▷without fail
ヒツ かなら(ず)   Ⓚ0006

[original meaning] **without fail, certainly, surely; inevitable**
必須の ひっすの indispensable, essential
必要 ひつよう need, necessity
必死 ひっし inevitable death; desperation
必需 ひつじゅ necessary
必然の ひつぜんの inevitable, necessary
必然的 ひつぜんてき inevitable
必至の ひっしの inevitable, necessary
必勝 ひっしょう certain victory

確 ▷certain
カク たし(か) たし(かめる)   Ⓚ1135

certain, definite, positive, sure, reliable, accurate
確認 かくにん confirmation, ascertainment
確実な かくじつな certain, sure, reliable; sound, solid
確証 かくしょう certain [definite] proof, positive evidence, corroboration
確率 かくりつ probability
確答 かくとう definite answer [reply]
正確な せいかくな accurate, precise, exact
明確な めいかくな clear, precise, distinct
的確な てきかくな precise, accurate, exact

筈 ▷ought to
カツ はず   Ⓚ2336

ⓐ (be a matter of course) **ought to, sure to, bound to, should, must**
ⓑ (be scheduled) **ought to, expected to, due to, supposed to, should**
a 出来る筈 できるはず should be able to
b 手筈 てはず arrangements, plan
今夜届く筈 こんやとどくはず expected to arrive tonight

certificates
証 券 状 免

証 ▷certificate
ショウ   Ⓚ1365

[also suffix] **certificate, card, license**
免許証 めんきょしょう license
会員証 かいいんしょう membership card

券 ▷certificate
ケン   Ⓚ2286

[also suffix] **certificate, voucher, bond**
旅券 りょけん passport
証券 しょうけん bill, bond, securities
債券 さいけん bond, debenture
株券 かぶけん share [stock] certificate
日銀券 にちぎんけん Bank of Japan bond

状 ▷official document
ジョウ   Ⓚ0244

official document [paper], official letter, certificate, warrant
信任状 しんにんじょう credentials, letter of credence
免状 めんじょう license, diploma
令状 れいじょう warrant, writ

遺言状 ゆいごんじょう will, testament

免 ▷license
メン まぬか(れる) まぬが(れる)　Ⓚ1779

abbrev. of 免許 めんきょ: license

特免 とくめん special exemption; special license

change and replace
変 替 代 迭 更 改
易 化 遷 転 換 交

変 ▷change
ヘン か(わる) か(わり) か(える)　Ⓚ1782

ⓐ [original meaning] **change, alter, transform, vary, shift**
ⓑ **change, variation, mutation**

a 変化 へんか change, transformation, variety; declension
変質 へんしつ change in quality, degeneration
変更 へんこう alteration, change, modification
変動 へんどう change, fluctuation
変形 へんけい transformation
変電所 へんでんしょ transformer substation
変革 へんかく change, reform, revolution
変貌 へんぼう transfiguration, metamorphosis
b 一変する いっぺんする change completely
激変(=劇変) げきへん sudden change, upheaval

替 ▷replace
タイ か(える) か(え)- か(わる)　Ⓚ2424

[original meaning] **replace (one thing or person by another), change places, substitute, change**

代替 だいたい substitution
交替(=交代) こうたい alternation, shift, change

代 ▷substitute
ダイ タイ か(わる) か(わり) -が(わり)
か(える) よ しろ　Ⓚ0018
see also →SUBSTITUTE

[original meaning] **substitute, replace, represent, act for another, alternate**

代用する だいようする substitute, use for another
代行する だいこうする act for another, execute (business) for another
代表する だいひょうする represent, stand for; typify
代理人 だいりにん representative, deputy, proxy
代議 だいぎ popular representation
代議士 だいぎし member of the Diet [House of Representatives]
代打 だいだ pinch-hitting; pinch hitter

代替エネルギー だいたいえねるぎー alternative [substitute] energy
代謝(=新陳代謝) たいしゃ(=しんちんたいしゃ) metabolism; renewal, regeneration
代名詞 だいめいし pronoun
交代する こうたいする relieve (a person), take turns, alternate

迭 ▷alternate
テツ　Ⓚ2650
see also →ALTERNATE

[original meaning] **alternate, change, take turns**

更迭する こうてつする reshuffle, change (as of government officials), exchange places

更 ▷change
コウ さら さら(に) ふ(ける)
ふ(かす)　Ⓚ2967

change, exchange, alternate

更迭 こうてつ reshuffle, change, exchanging places

改 ▷change
カイ あらた(める) あらた(まる)　Ⓚ0216

change, convert, modify

改名 かいめい changing a name
改行する かいぎょうする change lines [paragraphs]

易 ▷change
エキ イ やさ(しい) やす(い)　Ⓚ2135

change, be transformed; be reformed

不易の ふえきの immutable, unchangeable
改易 かいえき change of rank

化 ▷change into, -ize
カ ケ ば(ける) ば(かす)　Ⓚ0012

❶ⓐ **change into, transform into, turn into, convert**
ⓑ **change (a person) for the better, convert, influence**

a 化石 かせき fossil, fossil remains; petrifaction
化成 かせい chemical synthesis, transformation
化合 かごう chemical combination
消化 しょうか digestion; assimilation; consumption
同化 どうか assimilation
変化 へんか change, transformation, variety; declension
b 文化 ぶんか culture
感化する かんかする influence, exert influence, inspire
教化する きょうかする enlighten, educate, civilize

❷ [also suffix]
ⓐ (cause to become) **-ize, -ify, make into**
ⓑ (become) **-ize, become transformed, turn into**

a 強化 きょうか strengthening, intensification, build-up, reinforcement

液化 えきか liquefaction
浄化する じょうかする purify, cleanse
近代化 きんだいか modernization
コンピュータ化 こんぴゅーたか computerization
b 酸化 さんか oxidation
激化する げきかする(=げっか)する intensify, become
aggravated
悪化する あっかする worsen, aggravate, deteriorate
軟化 なんか softening; weakening (of the market)

遷 ▷undergo transition
セン   Ⓚ2735

undergo transition, change, elapse, pass by
遷移 せんい transition, change
遷延 せんえん delay, procrastination
変遷 へんせん changes, vicissitudes

転 ▷turn into
テン ころ(がる) ころ(げる) ころ(がす)
ころ(ぶ)   Ⓚ1346

(undergo change) turn into, turn, change, convert
転化 てんか change, transformation, inversion
転換 てんかん conversion, switchover, turnabout
転向 てんこう turn, conversion, about-face
転義 てんぎ figurative meaning
変転 へんてん change, transition
好転 こうてん take a turn for the better
一転 いってん complete change; turn
逆転 ぎゃくてん reversal, turnabout, inversion;
reverse rotation

換 ▷exchange
カン か(える) か(わる)   Ⓚ0537

exchange, interchange, change, turn, convert; take
the place of, replace
換気 かんき ventilation
換金する かんきんする cash (a check), turn into
money
換算する かんざんする convert, change, exchange
変換 へんかん change, conversion, transformation
転換 てんかん conversion, switchover, turnabout
互換性 ごかんせい interchangeability, compatibility
交換する こうかんする exchange, interchange,
barter, substitute

交 ▷interchange
コウ まじ(わる) まじ(える) ま(じる)
ま(ざる) ま(ぜる) -か(う) か(わす) Ⓚ1738

(give and receive mutually) interchange, exchange
交換する こうかんする exchange, interchange,
barter, substitute
交易 こうえき trade, commerce

文化交流 ぶんかこうりゅう cultural exchange

character →NATURE AND CHARACTER

characters
字 文 漢 旁

字 ▷character
ジ あざ   Ⓚ1860

ⓐ character, letter; type; word
ⓑ Chinese character, kanji, ideograph, logograph
ⓒ counter for (Chinese) characters
a 字体 じたい character form, type
字義 じぎ character definition, meaning of a word
[term]
字引 じびき dictionary
文字 もじ(=もんじ) character, letter
大文字 おおもじ capital letter
文字 もんじ character, letter; writings
ローマ字 ろーまじ Roman letters
漢字 かんじ Chinese characters, kanji
活字 かつじ movable type, printing type
数字 すうじ figure, numeral
習字 しゅうじ penmanship
赤字 あかじ deficit, red figures
b 字画 じかく stroke-count
字音 じおん Chinese-derived pronunciation of
kanji, on reading
c 五百字 ごひゃくじ 500 (Chinese) characters

文 ▷letter
ブン モン ふみ   Ⓚ1708

ⓐ (written symbol) letter, character, script, inscription
ⓑ style of writing, calligraphic style
a 文字 もじ(=もんじ) character, letter
文字通り もじどおり literally
文字 もんじ character, letter; writings
文盲 もんもう illiteracy
金石文 きんせきぶん ancient inscriptions on monuments
b 古文 こぶん classics, ancient writings, paleography

漢 ▷kanji
カン   Ⓚ0602

kanji, Chinese character, logograph
漢和辞典 かんわじてん Chinese-Japanese character
dictionary
漢英辞典(=漢英字典) かんえいじてん Japanese-
English character dictionary, kanji dictionary
漢プリ かんぷり kanji printer
単漢選択キー たんかんせんたくきー single character selector button (in kanji word processors)

旁
ボウ つくり かたがた
▷right radical

right radical of a Chinese characters
偏旁 へんぼう left and right radicals

charm

魅　幻　媚

魅
ミ
▷charm
Ⓚ2844

charm, bewitch, enchant, fascinate
魅力 みりょく charm, glamour, appeal
魅惑 みわく fascination, enchantment, charm
魅了する みりょうする charm, fascinate

幻
ゲン まぼろし
▷bewitch
Ⓚ0159

bewitch, bewilder, create an illusion
幻術 げんじゅつ magic, witchcraft
幻惑 げんわく bewitching, fascination
夢幻 むげん dream; vision; fantasy

媚
ビ こ(びる) こび
▷fawn upon

fawn upon; curry favor with
媚態 びたい coquetry
媚薬 びやく aphrodisiac, love potion

chastity

貞　操

貞
テイ
▷chaste
Ⓚ1792

chaste, faithful
貞女 ていじょ chaste woman, faithful wife
貞操 ていそう chastity, virginity
貞節 ていせつ chastity, virtue; constancy, principle
貞淑 ていしゅく chastity, female virtue
貞潔な ていけつな chaste and pure
不貞な ふていな unchaste
童貞 どうてい male virgin, virginity

操
ソウ みさお あやつ(る)
▷chastity
Ⓚ0693

chastity
操守 そうしゅ preserving one's chastity, adhering to moral principles

貞操 ていそう chastity, virginity

chest

胸　乳

胸
キョウ むね むな-
▷chest
Ⓚ0858

[original meaning] **chest, breast, thorax**
胸囲 きょうい chest measurement
胸部 きょうぶ breast, chest
胸骨 きょうこつ breastbone
胸郭 きょうかく thorax, chest
気胸 ききょう pneumothorax

乳
ニュウ ちち ち
▷breast
Ⓚ1306

breast, breasts
乳房 にゅうぼう(=ちぶさ) breast, nipple
乳癌 にゅうがん breast cancer
乳頭 にゅうとう nipple

child

児　子　童　幼　坊

児
ジ ニ
▷child (of any age)
Ⓚ2203

ⓐ [also suffix] **child (of any age), youngster, youth**
ⓑ [original meaning] **small child, infant**
ⓒ (offspring of man) **child, son, daughter**

a 児童 じどう child, juvenile
　園児 えんじ kindergarten child
　小児科 しょうにか (department of) pediatrics
　健康児 けんこうじ healthy child
　幼児 ようじ young child, infant
　男児 だんじ boy, son; man
　二歳児 にさいじ two-year old child
b 乳児 にゅうじ infant, baby, suckling
　育児 いくじ infant rearing, nursing of children
　胎児 たいじ embryo, fetus
c 児孫 じそん children and grandchildren; descendants
　愛児 あいじ one's beloved [favorite] child

子
シ ス こ -(っ)こ
▷child
Ⓚ2872

[sometimes also 児] (boy or girl) **child, kid, youngster**
男の子 おとこのこ boy, baby boy
迷子 まいご lost child

童 ▷child (young person)
ドウ わらべ   Ⓚ1828

(young person) **child, youngster**
- 童心 どうしん child's mind [heart]
- 童顔 どうがん boyish face, baby face
- 童謡 どうよう children's song, nursery rhyme
- 童話 どうわ nursery tale, fairy tale
- 児童 じどう child, juvenile
- 学童 がくどう schoolchild

幼 ▷young child
ヨウ おさな(い)   Ⓚ0168

[original meaning] **young child, child**
- 長幼 ちょうよう young and old
- 老幼 ろうよう old people and children

坊 ▷sonny
ボウ ボッ-   Ⓚ0205

sonny, boy, sonny boy
- 坊や ぼうや sonny, sonny boy, boy
- 坊ちゃん ぼっちゃん sonny, boy; Master Daring; greenhorn, baby
- 凸坊 でこぼう mischievous boy, imp

China
華 漢 支 中 胡 台 唐 呉

華 ▷China
カ ケ はな   Ⓚ1973

China
- 華僑 かきょう Chinese merchant living abroad
- 華北 かほく North China
- 中華料理 ちゅうかりょうり Chinese food
- 日華 にっか Japan and China

漢 ▷Chinese
カン   Ⓚ0602

(of ancient China or its people) **Chinese; old name for China, ancient China**
- 漢土 かんど China
- 漢方薬 かんぽうやく Chinese (herbal) medicine
- 漢民族 かんみんぞく Chinese people, Han race

支 ▷China
シ ささ(える)   Ⓚ1717

China
- 支那 しな China
- 南支 なんし South China
- 駐支の ちゅうしの resident in China

中 ▷People's Republic of China
チュウ ジュウ なか   Ⓚ2902

People's Republic of China, China
- 中華 ちゅうか Middle Kingdom, China; Chinese food
- 中共 ちゅうきょう Communist China
- 訪中 ほうちゅう visit to China
- 日中友好協会 にっちゅうゆうこうきょうかい Japan-China Amity Association

胡 ▷natives of ancient China
コ ゴ ウ   Ⓚ1057

natives living in the north or west of ancient China
- 胡国 ここく ancient countries in the north or west of China; barbarous country
- 胡服 こふく Mongol [Tatar] dress
- 胡弓 こきゅう Chinese fiddle

台 ▷Taiwan
ダイ タイ   Ⓚ1731

Taiwan, Formosa
- 台湾 たいわん Taiwan
- 台中関係 たいちゅうかんけい relations between Taiwan and China
- 台北 たいほく Taipei

唐 ▷Cathay
トウ から   Ⓚ2685

Cathay, China; foreign countries in general
- 唐人 とうじん Chinese; foreigner
- 唐音 とうおん Tang reading of Chinese characters
- 唐辛子 とうがらし red pepper
- 毛唐 けとう *slang* foreigner, Westerner

呉 ▷**Kingdom of Wu**
ゴ   Ⓚ2206

Kingdom of Wu, name of an ancient Chinese state in the Three Kingdom period (220-280 A.D.)
- 呉国 ごこく Kingdom of Wu
- 呉音 ごおん Wu reading of Chinese characters
- 呉越 ごえつ Wu and Yue, two rival states in ancient China
- 呉越同舟 ごえつどうしゅう bitter enemies in the same boat

Chinese
漢   中

漢 ▷**Chinese (language)**
カン   Ⓚ0602

Chinese (language), classical Chinese

漢語 かんご Chinese-derived word, Chinese expression
漢文 かんぶん Chinese classics, Chinese writing
漢字 かんじ Chinese characters, kanji
漢詩 かんし classical Chinese poetry [poem]

中 ▷Modern Chinese
チュウ ジュウ なか Ⓚ2902

Modern Chinese, Mandarin
中日辞典 ちゅうにちじてん Chinese-Japanese dictionary

choose
選 撰 択 採 摘 擢 抜 汰

選 ▷choose
セン えら(ぶ) Ⓚ2734

[sometimes also 撰 せん *TPLACEHOLD*] [original meaning]
choose, select, elect
選択する せんたくする select, choose
選抜 せんばつ selection, choice
選民 せんみん chosen people
選者 せんじゃ judge, selector
選考(=銓衡)する せんこうする select, screen
選挙 せんきょ election
選出する せんしゅつする elect
選手 せんしゅ representative athlete [player]
選任 せんにん assignment, nomination
選定する せんていする select, choose
予選 よせん preliminary match; primary election

撰 ▷choose
セン サン えら(ぶ) Ⓚ0672

[usu. 選] **choose, select, elect**
特撰 とくせん special, select

択 ▷select
タク Ⓚ0227

[original meaning] **select, choose, pick out**
選択する せんたくする select, choose
採択する さいたくする adopt, select
二者択一 にしゃたくいつ choosing an alternative

採 ▷pick
サイ と(る) Ⓚ0459

pick (out), select, adopt
採用 さいよう adoption, acceptance; employment, appointment
採択する さいたくする adopt, select
採決 さいけつ ballot taking, vote, roll call

摘 ▷pick out
テキ つ(む) Ⓚ0629

(choose the best part) **pick out, select, make an extract**
摘要 てきよう summary
摘記する てっきする summarize, epitomize

擢 ▷single out
テキ ぬき(んでる) Ⓚ0708

single out, select
抜擢 ばってき selection, choice

抜 ▷single out
バツ ぬ(く) ぬ(き) ぬ(ける) ぬ(かす) ぬ(かる) Ⓚ0219

single out, select, pick out, extract, excerpt
抜擢 ばってき selection, choice
抜粋 ばっすい extract, excerpt, selection
選抜する せんばつする select, choose, pick out

汰 ▷sift out
タ Ⓚ0237

sift out
淘汰する とうたする select, weed out, screen, sift; dismiss, cashier
自然淘汰 しぜんとうた natural selection
沙汰 さた instructions; notice, tidings, rumor; affair

circle
円 圏 丸 椿

円 ▷circle
エン まる(い) まる Ⓚ2555

circle
円周 えんしゅう circumference
楕円形 だえんけい ellipse
同心円 どうしんえん concentric circles

圏 ▷circle
ケン Ⓚ2714

circle
圏点 けんてん circle (for emphasis)
大圏コース たいけんこーす great circle route

丸 ▷round or spherical shape
ガン まる まる(い) まる(める) Ⓚ2883

ⓐ **round or spherical shape**
ⓑ [sometimes also 円] **circle**
a 日の丸 ひのまる Rising Sun Flag

楕 ▷ellipse
ダ   Ⓚ0926

ellipse, oval

楕円 だえん ellipse, oval
楕円体 だえんたい ellipsoid

---

circles
界 壇

界 ▷world
カイ   Ⓚ2220

[also suffix] (segment of society engaged in same activity)

world, circles

業界 ぎょうかい industry, business world
政界 せいかい political world
各界 かっかい every sphere of life, various circles
学界 がっかい academic circles [world]
経済界 けいざいかい economic world, financial circles
芸能界 げいのうかい entertainment world, world of show business

壇 ▷circles
ダン タン   Ⓚ0682

circles, world

文壇 ぶんだん literary circles, world of literature
俳壇 はいだん haiku world
画壇 がだん artists' world, painting circles
詩壇 しだん poetical circles, world of poetry
劇壇 げきだん stage, theatrical world
土壇場 どたんば the last moment

---

circular objects
環 輪 車 盤 釧

環 ▷ring
カン   Ⓚ1011

ring, circle, loop

環状の かんじょうの ring-shaped, circular
環状線 かんじょうせん belt line
環指 かんし ring finger
環礁 かんしょう atoll
一環 いっかん link; part
金環食 きんかんしょく annular eclipse

輪 ▷wheel, ring
リン わ   Ⓚ1436

❶ⓐ [original meaning] **wheel**

ⓑ counter for wheels

a 車輪 しゃりん wheel
前輪 ぜんりん front wheel
b 二輪車 にりんしゃ two-wheeled vehicle, bicycle
一輪車 いちりんしゃ unicycle; wheelbarrow

❷ ring, circle

輪状の りんじょうの ring-shaped, annular
輪形の りんけいの ring-shaped, circular
年輪 ねんりん annual ring, growth ring
五輪のマーク ごりんのまーく the five-ring Olympic emblem

車 ▷wheel
シャ くるま   Ⓚ2976

wheel

車輪 しゃりん wheel
水車 すいしゃ water wheel
拍車 はくしゃ spur, rowel spur

盤 ▷disk
バン   Ⓚ2481

disk, round plate

円盤 えんばん disk; flying saucer
吸盤 きゅうばん sucker, sucking disk
羅針盤 らしんばん compass
胎盤 たいばん placenta

釧 ▷armlet
セン くしろ   Ⓚ1497

[archaic] **armlet worn around the elbow**

---

cities and towns
都 京 畿 市 町

都 ▷metropolis
ト ツ みやこ   Ⓚ1505

metropolis, capital

都会 とかい city, town
都市 とし cities, urban communities
都市ガス としがす town gas
都心 としん heart [center] of a city
東京都 とうきょうと Metropolis of Tokyo
首都 しゅと capital (city)
遷都 せんと transfer of the capital

京 ▷capital
キョウ ケイ キン   Ⓚ1766

capital, metropolis

京洛 けいらく(=きょうらく) capital; Kyoto
京都 きょうと Kyoto

英京 えいきょう capital of England, London
東京 とうきょう Tokyo
北京 ぺきん Beijing, Peking

畿 ▷capital
キ   Ⓚ3002

ⓐ capital
ⓑ suburbs of a capital
a 畿内 きない territories near the capital [imperial palace]; the Five Home Provinces
b 近畿(=近畿地方) きんき(=きんきちほう) Kinki region

市 ▷city
シ いち   Ⓚ1724

ⓐ city, town
ⓑ [also prefix] (unit of local administration) city, municipality
ⓒ suffix after names of cities
a 市井の出来事 しせいのできごと events on the street
市内 しない city
市民 しみん citizens, townsmen
市外 しがい city outskirts, suburbs
b 市長 しちょう mayor
市営 しえい municipal management
市役所 しやくしょ municipal office, city hall
都市 とし cities, urban communities
同市 どうし same city
c 大阪市 おおさかし Osaka city
高松市 たかまつし Takamatsu city

町 ▷town
チョウ まち   Ⓚ1028

ⓐ town, city
ⓑ (unit of local administration) town
ⓒ suffix after names of towns
a 町人 ちょうにん tradesman (in Edo period), townsman, townsfolk
町家 ちょうか town house; tradesman's house
町長 ちょうちょう town headman [manager]
町名 ちょうめい town name
b 町立の ちょうりつの established by the town
市町村 しちょうそん cities, towns and villages; municipalities
c 小山町 おやまちょう town of Oyama

class
級 段 位 階 身
格 等 流 層

級 ▷grade
キュウ   Ⓚ1175

[also suffix] [original meaning] grade, class, rank, degree, rating, level
等級 とうきゅう class, grade, rank, magnitude
特級品 とっきゅうひん special grade article
階級 かいきゅう class, estate; rank, grade

段 ▷grade
ダン   Ⓚ1059

(step in a ranking system) grade, degree or rank in go, karate, judo or various martial arts (higher than 級 きゅう)
段違い だんちがい different class, different level; widely apart
初段 しょだん first degree black belt (as in karate)
有段者 ゆうだんしゃ grade holder
五段 ごだん fifth grade (as in karate)

位 ▷rank
イ くらい ぐらい   Ⓚ0045

[also suffix] rank, place, grade, position, station
地位 ちい position, status, post, social standing
順位 じゅんい order, rank, precedence
上位 じょうい higher rank, precedence
優位 ゆうい superiority, predominant position
首位 しゅい first place, leading position
学位 がくい academic degree
第一位 だいいちい first place, foremost rank
正二位 しょうにい senior grade of second rank
従三位 じゅさんみ second grade of the third rank of honor

階 ▷rank
カイ   Ⓚ0569

rank, order, grade, class
階級 かいきゅう class, estate; rank, grade
階層 かいそう social stratum, class; tier
位階 いかい court rank
段階 だんかい grade, rank, step, stage

身 ▷social status
シン み   Ⓚ2977

social status, social standing
身代 しんだい fortune, one's property

class

立身する りっしんする establish oneself in life
小身 しょうしん humble position

格 ▷status
カク コウ ⓚ0835

status, rank, capacity, standing, class, grade
格上げする かくあげする raise to higher status, promote to a higher rank
格式 かくしき status, social standing
格付けする かくづけする grade, rate, classify
昇格 しょうかく promotion in status
同格 どうかく same status, equality; apposition
寺格 じかく status of a Buddhist temple
リーダー格 りーだーかく capacity as a leader
価格 かかく price, cost

等 ▷class
トウ ひと(しい) –ら ⓚ2339

[also suffix] **class, grade, rank, degree, place, magnitude (of a star)**
等級 とうきゅう class, grade, rank, magnitude
高等な こうとうな higher, high-grade, advanced
上等の じょうとうの first-class, superior
劣等 れっとう inferiority
中等 ちゅうとう middle-class, secondary grade
一等 いっとう first class; first place
三等星 さんとうせい third magnitude star

流 ▷class
リュウ ル なが(れる) なが(れ)
なが(す) ⓚ0400

class, order, rate, grade
中流 ちゅうりゅう middle class
一流大学 いちりゅうだいがく first-rate university
二流 にりゅう second-rate

層 ▷stratum
ソウ ⓚ2728

[also suffix] **social stratum, class, bracket**
階層 かいそう social stratum, class; tier
下層 かそう lower classes
社会層 しゃかいそう stratum of society
知識層 ちしきそう the intellectual class
読者層 どくしゃそう class of readers [subscribers]

classical particles
耶　也　哉

耶 ▷interrogative particle
ヤ か や ⓚ1179

[formerly also 乎; now always か] **interrogative particle**

女子有り問うて曰く誰耶と じょしありとうていわく
たれかと A woman asked, "Who art thou?"

也 ▷rhetorical particle
ヤ なり や ⓚ2878

[also 哉 or 耶] *classical particle* **rhetorical or interrogative particle like modern か**
これは何ぞ也 これはなんぞや What can this be?

哉 ▷exclamatory particle
サイ かな や ⓚ2807

exclamatory particle
快哉を叫ぶ かいさいをさけぶ shout for joy, shout with exultation
善哉 ぜんざい Well done!/That's it!; thick bean-meal soup (with sugar and rice cake)

class in school
組　　級

組 ▷class
ソ く(む) くみ –ぐみ ⓚ1224

[also suffix] (school) **class**
会話の組 かいわのくみ conversation class
一年三組 いちねんさんくみ first-grade, class three

級 ▷grade
キュウ ⓚ1175

(school) **grade, class, school year**
級友 きゅうゆう classmate
級長 きゅうちょう class president
学級 がっきゅう class, grade
進級する しんきゅうする be promoted (to a higher grade)
同級 どうきゅう same class [grade]
三年級 さんねんきゅう third year class

clean and purified
浄 清 純 潔 粋 精 楚

浄 ▷clean
ジョウ ⓚ0342

clean, pure, unstained
清浄な せいじょうな pure, clean

清 ▷clean
セイ ショウ きよ(い) きよ(まる)
きよ(める)　　　　　　　　　　Ⓚ0479

(free from dirt or impurities) **clean, pure, neat**
清潔 せいけつ cleanliness, neatness, purity
清浄 せいじょう purity, cleanness
清書 せいしょ fair [clean] copy
清純な せいじゅんな pure (and innocent)
清楚な せいそな neat and clean, tidy, trim

純 ▷pure
ジュン　　　　　　　　　　Ⓚ1192

[also prefix] **pure, genuine, unalloyed**
純粋な じゅんすいな pure, genuine; unalloyed,
　unmixed
純良な じゅんりょうな pure (and good), genuine
純金 じゅんきん pure gold, solid gold
純毛 じゅんもう pure wool, all wool
純正な じゅんせいな pure, genuine
純文学 じゅんぶんがく pure literature
単純な たんじゅんな simple, uncomplicated, plain

潔 ▷immaculate
ケツ いさぎよ(い)　　　　　　Ⓚ0678

(free from stain) **immaculate, clean, pure, spotless**
潔癖 けっぺき love of cleanliness, fastidiousness
清潔な せいけつな clean, neat, pure
不潔な ふけつな unclean, dirty, impure, maculate

粋 ▷refined (free from impurities)
スイ いき　　　　　　　　　　Ⓚ1188

(free from impurities) **refined, pure, unmixed**
純粋な じゅんすいな pure, genuine; unalloyed,
　unmixed
生粋の きっすいの trueborn, pure, genuine

精 ▷refined (purified)
セイ ショウ　　　　　　　　Ⓚ1248

(purified) **refined, fine**
精糖 せいとう refined sugar, sugar refining
精油 せいゆ refined oil; essential oil, essence

楚 ▷neat and trim
ソ しもと　　　　　　　　　　Ⓚ2436

neat and trim
楚楚 そそ graceful, neat
清楚 せいそ neat and clean

---

clean and wash
洗 漱 拭 滌 濯 浴
浄 粛 清 払 掃

洗 ▷wash
セン あら(う)　　　　　　　　Ⓚ0350

[original meaning] **wash, clean**
洗浄 せんじょう washing, irrigation
洗顔 せんがん washing one's face
洗剤 せんざい detergent, cleanser
洗礼 せんれい baptism
洗面所 せんめんじょ washroom; bathroom
洗面器 せんめんき washbowl, sink
洗濯 せんたく laundering, washing
洗練 せんれん refinement, polishing, elegance
水洗 すいせん flushing, washing

漱 ▷rinse
ソウ すす(ぐ) くちすす(ぐ)　　Ⓚ0639

rinse (one's mouth), wash, gargle
漱石枕流 そうせきちんりゅう bad loser

拭 ▷wipe
ショク ふ(く) ぬぐ(う)　　　Ⓚ0338

wipe (off, away), wipe clean, mop up
払拭する ふっしょくする wipe out [away], dispel,
　cast aside (worries, etc.)

滌 ▷wash
デキ テキ ジョウ

[now replaced by 浄] **wash, cleanse**
洗滌する せんでき(=せんじょう)する wash, irrigate

濯 ▷rinse
タク　　　　　　　　　　　　Ⓚ0711

[original meaning] **rinse, wash, wash out**
洗濯する せんたくする launder, wash
洗濯機 せんたくき washing machine

浴 ▷bathe
ヨク あ(びる) あ(びせる)　　Ⓚ0404

[original meaning] **bathe**
浴場 よくじょう bath, bathhouse
浴槽 よくそう bathtub
浴室 よくしつ bathroom
入浴する にゅうよくする bathe, take a bath

浄 ▷cleanse
ジョウ   Ⓚ0342

ⓐ cleanse, purify
ⓑ [formerly 淨] wash, cleanse
a 浄化 じょうか purification, cleansing
　浄書 じょうしょ clean copy
　浄水場 じょうすいじょう water purification plant
b 洗浄 せんじょう washing, irrigation

粛 ▷purge
シュク   Ⓚ2996

purge (a political party), clean up, reform
　粛清する しゅくせいする purge (a political party), clean up, liquidate
　粛正する しゅくせいする regulate, enforce (discipline)
　粛党 しゅくとう purging disloyal elements from a party
　粛学 しゅくがく purge of disloyal elements from a school

清 ▷clear
セイ ショウ きよ(い) きよ(まる)
きよ(める)   Ⓚ0479

ⓐ (rid of impurities) **clear, clean**
ⓑ **clear up, settle (a debt)**
a 清掃 せいそう cleaning
　六根清浄 ろっこんしょうじょう purification of one's self through detachment from the senses
b 清算 せいさん settlement, liquidation; clearing (off)
　粛清 しゅくせい purge, purging, liquidation

払 ▷clear away
フツ はら(う) -はら(い) -ばら(い) Ⓚ0171

[original meaning] **clear away, sweep away, wipe away**
　払拭する ふっしょくする wipe out [away], dispel, cast aside (worries, etc.)
　払底 ふってい shortage

掃 ▷sweep
ソウ は(く)   Ⓚ0464

[original meaning] **sweep, sweep away, brush, clean up**
　掃除 そうじ cleaning
　掃除機 そうじき vacuum cleaner
　掃射する そうしゃする sweep with fire, mow down
　掃海 そうかい mine sweeping
　清掃 せいそう cleaning

---

clear
透 澄 清 明 朗 冴

透 ▷transparent
トウ す(く) す(かす) す(ける)   Ⓚ2677

ⓐ (allow light to pass through) **be transparent, be seen through**
ⓑ **see through**
a 透明な とうめいな transparent
　透視図 とうしず perspective drawing, transparent view
　透徹した とうてつした lucid, clear, penetrating
b 透視 とうし seeing through; clairvoyance
　透察 とうさつ insight

澄 ▷limpid
チョウ す(む) す(ます)   Ⓚ0674

limpid, clear, transparent, lucid, serene
　清澄な せいちょうな clear, lucid; serene
　明澄な めいちょうな unclouded, clear, limpid

清 ▷clear (liquid)
セイ ショウ きよ(い) きよ(まる)
きよ(める)   Ⓚ0479

(of liquids) **clear, unmixed**
　清水 せいすい pure [clear] water
　清流 せいりゅう clear [limpid] stream
　清酒 せいしゅ (refined) sake
　血清 けっせい serum
　河清 かせい clearing of the river water

明 ▷clear (unclouded)
メイ
ミョウ あ(かり) あか(るい) あか(るむ)
あか(らむ) あき(らか) あ(ける) -あ(け)
あ(く) あ(くる) あ(かす)   Ⓚ0756

(unclouded) **clear, transparent, translucent**
　明澄な めいちょうな unclouded, clear, limpid
　透明度 とうめいど transparency, degree of clearness

朗 ▷clear (sky)
ロウ ほが(らか)   Ⓚ1210

[original meaning] **clear (sky), bright (moon)**
　晴朗な せいろうな clear, fair, serene

冴 ▷crisp and clear
ゴ さ(える)   Ⓚ0060

be crisp and clear, be crystal-clear (as on an ice-cold winter night), be bright, be vivid

冴え返る さえかえる be exceedingly clear; be keenly cold
冴えた色 さえたいろ bright color

clergymen
僧　坊　尼　父

僧 ▷**bonze**
ソウ　　　　　　　　　　　Ⓚ0138

[also suffix] [original meaning] **bonze, Buddhist monk,
priest**

僧侶 そうりょ bonze, Buddhist priest
僧職 そうしょく priesthood
僧院 そういん monastery, temple
禅僧 ぜんそう Zen priest [monk]
尼僧 にそう nun, sister; (Buddhist) priestess
小僧 こぞう priestling; servant boy; kid, brat
破戒僧 はかいそう sinful priest, depraved monk

坊 ▷**Buddhist priest**
ボウ　ボッ−　　　　　　　Ⓚ0205

Buddhist priest [monk], bonze

坊主 ぼうず Buddhist priest [monk], bonze; shaven
head; sonny, sonny boy, boy
坊さん ぼうさん Buddhist priest
御坊 ごぼう Reverend

尼 ▷**Buddhist nun**
ニ　あま　　　　　　　　　Ⓚ2611

Buddhist nun [priestess], sister

尼僧 にそう nun, sister; (Buddhist) priestess
僧尼 そうに monks and nuns
禅尼 ぜんに Zen nun
修道尼 しゅうどうに nun

父 ▷**Father**
フ　ちち　　　　　　　　　Ⓚ1714

(title of respect for priests) **Father**

神父 しんぷ priest, Father
教父 きょうふ Father (of the Church); godfather

close
閉　鎖　封　梗　塞

閉 ▷**close**
ヘイ　と(じる)　と(ざす)　し(める)
し(まる)　　　　　　　　Ⓚ2832

[original meaning] (move into closed position) **close,
shut, confine**

閉鎖 へいさ closing, closure, shutdown
閉口する へいこうする be dumbfounded
[stumped], be silenced
開閉する かいへいする open and shut [close]; make
and break (circuits)
密閉する みっぺいする close up tightly, seal
hermetically

鎖 ▷**lock up**
サ　くさり　　　　　　　　Ⓚ1573

(from the idea of binding with a chain) **lock up, shut,
confine**

鎖国 さこく national isolation, exclusion of foreigners
閉鎖する へいさする lock, close, shut
封鎖 ふうさ blockade

封 ▷**seal**
フウ　ホウ　　　　　　　　Ⓚ1182

seal, seal off, block, enclose

封印 ふういん (stamped) seal
封鎖 ふうさ blockade
封書 ふうしょ sealed letter
封殺 ふうさつ *baseball* force-out
密封する みっぷうする seal hermetically, seal up
同封する どうふうする enclose (in a letter)

梗 ▷**stop up**
コウ　キョウ　　　　　　　Ⓚ0871

stop up, close up, clog

梗塞 こうそく stoppage; tightness; infarction
脳梗塞 のうこうそく stroke, cerebral infarction

塞 ▷**stop up**
サイ　ソク　ふさ(ぐ)　ふさ(がる)　Ⓚ2033

[original meaning] **stop up, fill in**

塞栓 そくせん embolus
閉塞 へいそく blockade, stoppage
梗塞 こうそく stoppage; tightness; infarction

clothing

服 袴 蓑 着 衣 装 裳 襤 袈 裟 襖

服

▷**clothes**
フク ⓚ0782

[also suffix] **clothes, clothing, dress, costume**

服装 ふくそう dress, garments, attire
服飾 ふくしょく dress and its ornaments
洋服 ようふく (Western) clothes
呉服 ごふく dry goods; drapery
制服 せいふく uniform, regulation uniform
衣服 いふく clothes, dress, clothing
紳士服 しんしふく men's suit
宇宙服 うちゅうふく spacesuit

袴

▷**formal divided skirt**
コ はかま ⓚ1088

Japanese formal divided skirt

着袴の儀 ちゃっこのぎ ceremony of fitting a child with a *hakama*

蓑

▷**straw raincoat**
サ みの ⓚ2048

straw raincoat

蓑虫 みのむし bagworm
蓑笠子 みのかさご luna lionfish, *Pterois lunulata*
隠れ蓑 かくれみの invisibility cloak; pretext

着

▷**wear**
チャク ジャク き(る) -ぎ き(せる) -き(せ) つ(く) つ(ける) ⓚ2826

[sometimes also -衣] [also suffix] **wear, clothes, dress, suit**

晴れ着 はれぎ one's best (clothes), gala [holiday] dress
肌着 はだぎ underwear
上着 うわぎ outer garment, coat, jacket
水着 みずぎ bathing [swimming] suit
不断着(=普段着) ふだんぎ everyday wear [clothes], home wear
訪問着 ほうもんぎ visiting [gala] dress

衣

▷**garment**
イ ころも ⓚ1736

ⓐ **garment, garments, clothing, clothes**
ⓑ **outer garment, gown, (priestly) robe, surplice**

a 衣装(=衣裳) いしょう clothes, garment, dress, costume
衣類 いるい clothes, garments
衣服 いふく clothes, dress, clothing
衣料 いりょう clothing, garments
衣食住 いしょくじゅう food, clothing and shelter, the necessities of life
着衣 ちゃくい one's clothes [clothing]
b 衣鉢 いはつ(=えはつ) mysteries (of Buddhism or an art)
白衣 はくい(=びゃくえ) white robe [dress]; white coat
法衣 ほうい(=ほうえ) sacerdotal robe
僧衣 そうい priestly robe
天衣無縫 てんいむほう perfect beauty with no trace of artifice
胴衣 どうい jacket, vest
外衣 がいい outer garment

装

▷**dress**
ソウ ショウ よそお(う) ⓚ2344

dress, outfit, attire, ornaments

装束 しょうぞく costume, attire
服装 ふくそう dress, garments, attire
旅装 りょそう traveling outfit
和装 わそう Japanese dress, kimono
衣装(=衣裳) いしょう clothes, garment, dress, costume

裳

▷**dress**
ショウ も ⓚ2269

[now usu. 装] **dress, clothing**

裳階 しょうかい(=もこし) decorative pent roof
衣裳 いしょう clothes, garment, dress, costume

襤

▷**rags**
ラン

[rarely also 藍] [original meaning] **rags, tattered clothes**

襤褸 らんる(=ぼろ) rags, tattered clothes

袈

▷**Buddhist surplice**
ケ カ ⓚ2244

Buddhist surplice

袈裟 けさ Buddhist surplice
大袈裟な おおげさな exaggerated, hyperbolical

裟

▷**Buddhist cassock**
サ シャ ⓚ2398

Buddhist cassock

袈裟 けさ Buddhist surplice
大袈裟な おおげさな exaggerated, hyperbolical

襖

▷**overgarment**
オウ ふすま あお ⓚ1157

overgarment

素襖 すおう *hist* ceremonial dress of lower-class samurai

clusters →BUNDLES AND CLUSTERS

coagulate →SOLIDIFY AND COAGULATE

cold

冷 寒 涼 凜

冷 ▷**cold**
レイ つめ(たい) ひ(える) ひ(や)
ひ(ややか) ひ(やす) ひ(やかす) さ(める)
さ(ます)　　　　　　　　　　Ⓚ0061

cold, chilled
冷気 れいき cold air; cold, chill
冷害 れいがい damage from cold weather
冷水 れいすい cold water
冷戦 れいせん Cold War
寒冷 かんれい cold, coldness, chilliness

寒 ▷**cold (weather)**
カン さむ(い)　　　　　　　　Ⓚ2011

(of weather) **cold, chilly**
寒気 かんき cold, cold weather
寒暑 かんしょ hot and cold
寒流 かんりゅう cold current
寒冷 かんれい cold, coldness, chilliness
寒波 かんぱ cold wave
寒暖計 かんだんけい thermometer

涼 ▷**cool**
リョウ すず(しい) すず(む)　　Ⓚ0477

cool, refreshing
涼気 りょうき cool air
涼風 りょうふう cool breeze
涼味 りょうみ coolness, cool
清涼な せいりょうな cool, refreshing

凜 ▷**severely cold**
リン　　　　　　　　　　　　Ⓚ0151

severely cold
凜冽たる りんれつたる piercing cold

cold seasons

冬 寒 秋

冬 ▷**winter**
トウ ふゆ　　　　　　　　　　Ⓚ1851

[original meaning] **winter**
冬季 とうき winter season

冬期 とうき winter, wintertime
冬至 とうじ winter solstice
冬眠 とうみん hibernation ("winter sleep")
越冬 えっとう passing the winter, wintering
初冬 しょとう early winter
立冬 りっとう first day of winter
春夏秋冬 しゅんかしゅうとう four seasons, all (the)
　　year round

寒 ▷**coldest season**
カン さむ(い)　　　　　　　　Ⓚ2011

coldest season, cold season, midwinter
寒鮒 かんぶな crucian caught in midwinter
大寒 だいかん coldest season, midwinter

秋 ▷**autumn**
シュウ あき　　　　　　　　　Ⓚ1054

[original meaning] **autumn, fall**
秋分 しゅうぶん autumnal equinox
秋思 しゅうし lonely feeling of fall
晩秋 ばんしゅう late fall
今秋 こんしゅう this [next] autumn
春秋 しゅんじゅう spring and autumn; years, age;
　　Chronicles of Lu
春夏秋冬 しゅんかしゅうとう four seasons, all (the)
　　year round

collapse

陥 落 崩 没

陥 ▷**fall in**
カン おちい(る) おとしい(れる)　Ⓚ0413

[original meaning] **fall in, cave in, collapse, sink**
陥没する かんぼつする sink, fall, cave in
陥入する かんにゅうする subside, fall [cave] in,
　　collapse
陥落する かんらくする fall in, cave in; surrender

落 ▷**fall**
ラク お(ちる) お(ち) お(とす)　Ⓚ2019

fall in, collapse, crumble
陥落する かんらくする fall in, cave in; surrender

崩 ▷**crumble**
ホウ くず(れる) –くず(れ) くず(す) Ⓚ1989

crumble, collapse
崩壊する ほうかいする collapse, crumble, break
　　down, cave in
崩落 ほうらく collapse, cave-in; crash; (of the market)
　　decline

没 ▷**sink**
ボツ　　　　　　　　　　　　Ⓚ0230

sink into the ground, subside, fall in
　埋没する まいぼつする be buried; fall into oblivion
　陥没する かんぼつする sink, fall, cave in

collection

集　　選　　彙

集 ▷**collection**
シュウ あつ(まる) あつ(める)
つど(う)　　　　　　　　　Ⓚ2413

[also suffix] **collection of literary works, anthology, series**
　詩集 ししゅう anthology of poems
　川端全集 かわばたぜんしゅう the complete works of Kawabata
　万葉集 まんようしゅう(=まんにょうしゅう) Japan's oldest anthology of poems
　書簡集 しょかんしゅう collection of letters

選 ▷**selection**
セン えら(ぶ)　　　　　　　Ⓚ2734

[also suffix] **selection, anthology**
　名作選 めいさくせん selection of masterpieces

彙 ▷**assemblage**
イ　　　　　　　　　　　　Ⓚ2036

(things of the same kind) **assemblage, collection**
　彙類 いるい same kind [class]; classification
　語彙 ごい vocabulary
　辞彙 じい dictionary

collide

衝　　牴　　觝　　突　　当

衝 ▷**collide**
ショウ　　　　　　　　　　Ⓚ0658

collide, dash [run] against, crash
　衝突する しょうとつする collide (with), crash (into); conflict [clash] (with)
　衝撃 しょうげき impact, shock, impulse
　衝動 しょうどう impulse, urge
　衝心 しょうしん heart failure
　衝天 しょうてん high spirits
　緩衝 かんしょう buffer

牴 ▷**collide with**
テイ

[now replaced by 抵] **collide with, touch**
　牴触 ていしょく conflict; contradiction; incompatibility

觝 ▷**collide with**
テイ

[now replaced by 抵] [original meaning] **collide with, touch**
　觝触する ていしょくする conflict with; be contrary to; be incompatible with

突 ▷**dash**
トツ つ(く)　　　　　　　　Ⓚ1918

(strike with violence) **dash against, collide, crash against**
　衝突する しょうとつする collide (with), crash (into); conflict [clash] (with)
　追突する ついとつする collide with from behind
　激突 げきとつ crash, collision

当 ▷**hit**
トウ あ(たる) あ(たり) あ(てる)
あ(て)　　　　　　　　　　Ⓚ1865

hit, strike
　突き当たる つきあたる hit against, run into; come to the end of (a street)
　体当たりする たいあたりする hurl oneself (at), dash oneself (against)

color¹

色　　彩

色 ▷**color**
ショク シキ いろ　　　　　Ⓚ1748

ⓐ [also suffix] **color, coloring**
ⓑ **counter for colors**
a　色彩 しきさい color, coloring, hue, tinge
　色素 しきそ pigment, coloring matter
　青色 せいしょく(=あおいろ) blue
　原色 げんしょく primary color
　天然色 てんねんしょく natural color; technicolor
b　三色写真 さんしょくしゃしん three color photography

彩 ▷**beautiful coloring**
サイ いろど(る)　　　　　　Ⓚ1502

beautiful [brilliant] coloring, coloration, color, variegated colors
　色彩 しきさい color, coloring, hue, tinge

多彩な たさいな colorful, varicolored; variegated, diversified
五彩 ごさい five beautiful colors
虹彩 こうさい iris
光彩 こうさい luster, brilliancy

color²

彩 ▷**color**
　サイ いろど(る)　　　　　Ⓚ1502

[original meaning] **color, paint**
　彩色 さいしょく coloring, painting
　彩画 さいが painting, colored picture
　彩管 さいかん paintbrush

染 ▷**dye**
　セン そ(める) −ぞ(め) そ(まる) し(みる)
　−じ(みる) し(み)　　　　Ⓚ2229

dye, color
　染色 せんしょく dyeing
　染髪 せんぱつ hair dyeing
　染織 せんしょく dyeing and weaving
　染料 せんりょう dyes, dyestuffs
　媒染剤 ばいせんざい mordant

comb

櫛　梳

櫛 ▷**comb**
　シツ くし　　　　　　　Ⓚ1019

comb
　櫛鱗 しつりん ctenoid scales
　櫛比する しっぴする line up in a closely packed row
　櫛風沐雨 しっぷうもくう struggling through wind and rain, undergoing hardships

梳 ▷**comb**
　ソ と(く) と(かす) す(く) けず(る)
　くしけず(る)

[original meaning] **comb (one's hair)**
　梳毛 そもう combed wool [yarn]
　梳綿機 そめんき carding machine

combine

合 結 統 括 総 併 綜 纏

合 ▷**combine**
　ゴウ ガッ− カッ− あ(う) あ(い) あ(わす)
　あ(わせる)　　　　　　Ⓚ1740

[original meaning] **combine, unite, join together, meet**
　合同の ごうどうの combined, united, joint; congruent
　合計する ごうけいする add up, total
　合成 ごうせい composition, synthesis
　合弁 ごうべん joint management [venture]
　合併する がっぺいする combine, unite, merge
　合衆国 がっしゅうこく the United States (of America)
　合唱 がっしょう chorus
　合宿する がっしゅくする lodge together, stay in a camp for training
　合戦 かっせん battle, encounter
　合点 がってん(=がてん) understand, comprehend, grasp
　集合する しゅうごうする gather, meet, assemble; summon, call together
　都合 つごう convenience, circumstances; in all, altogether, totally
　総合 そうごう synthesis, integration
　結合する けつごうする unite, combine, join together
　連合 れんごう combination, union, alliance; association
　統合する とうごうする integrate, combine, unify
　化合物 かごうぶつ (chemical) compound
　混合する こんごうする mix, mingle

結 ▷**tie**
　ケツ むす(ぶ) ゆ(う) ゆ(わえる)　Ⓚ1235

(bring or come together closely) **tie, unite, join**
　結合する けつごうする unite, combine, join together
　結婚 けっこん marriage
　結縁 けちえん making a connection (with Buddha)
　締結する ていけつする conclude, contract
　妥結 だけつ compromise, agreement, understanding

統 ▷**unite**
　トウ す(べる)　　　　　Ⓚ1239

unite, unify, gather into one
　統一 とういつ unity, coordination, standardization
　統合する とうごうする integrate, combine, unify
　統計 とうけい statistics

統轄 とうかつ general control, control and jurisdiction

括 ▷lump together
カツ   Ⓚ0334

lump together, lump, sum up, draw together
括弧 かっこ parentheses, brackets
括約筋 かつやくきん sphincter
一括する いっかつする lump together, sum up
総括的 そうかつてき all-inclusive, all-embracing
概括する がいかつする summarize, sum up, generalize
包括する ほうかつする include, comprehend, comprise
統括する とうかつする generalize

総 ▷integrate
ソウ   Ⓚ1261

[sometimes also 綜] **integrate, unify, total**
総計する そうけいする total, sum up
総合する そうごうする synthesize, integrate, put together
総括する そうかつする generalize, summarize
総論 そうろん introduction, outline

併 ▷join together
ヘイ あわ(せる)   Ⓚ0064

[original meaning] **join together, combine, unite**
合併する がっぺいする combine, unite, merge
兼併する けんぺいする join together, unite

綜 ▷integrate
ソウ   Ⓚ1262

[now usu. 総] **integrate, unify, total**
綜合する そうごうする synthesize, integrate, put together
綜覧 そうらん general survey; comprehensive bibliography

纏 ▷put together
テン まと(める) まと(う) まと(まる)
まつ(わる)   Ⓚ1302

put together, bring together, collect
纏め買い まとめがい bulk buying, stocking up
纏め役 まとめやく mediator, facilitator, organizer
一纏め ひとまとめ one bundle [pack, bunch]

come →GO AND COME

脱 ▷get out of place
ダツ ぬ(ぐ) ぬ(げる)   Ⓚ0886

get out of place, come off
脱線 だっせん derailment; deviation, aberration
脱肛 だっこう prolapse of the anus
脱臼 だっきゅう dislocation

外 ▷come off
ガイ ゲ そと ほか はず(す)
はず(れる)   Ⓚ0163

come off, get out of place, slip out, be separated
ボタンが外れている ぼたんがはずれている be unbuttoned

剥 ▷peel off
ハク は(がす) は(ぐ) は(がれる)
は(げる)   Ⓚ1494

peel off (as of skin), tear [rip] off, strip (off), flay
剥製 はくせい stuffing, mounting; stuffed animal

尽 ▷be exhausted
ジン つ(くす) -づ(くし) つ(きる)
つ(かす)   Ⓚ2624

be exhausted, come to an end
無尽 むじん inexhaustibility; mutual financing association
無尽蔵 むじんぞう inexhaustible supply

絶 ▷come to an end
ゼツ た(える) た(やす) た(つ)   Ⓚ1240

come to an end, cease to exist
絶望 ぜつぼう despair, hopelessness
絶滅 ぜつめつ extermination, eradication; extinction
絶息する ぜっそくする expire, die
気絶する きぜつする faint
杜絶(=途絶) とぜつ stoppage, interruption, cessation

comfortable
楽　安

楽 ▷**comfortable**
ガク ラク たの(しい) たの(しむ)　Ⓚ2460

comfortable, easy
楽観する らっかんする be optimistic, take a hopeful view
楽観的な らっかんてきな optimistic
楽隠居 らくいんきょ comfortable life in retirement
楽楽と らくらくと comfortably; very easily
楽勝 らくしょう easy victory, walkaway
楽天的 らくてんてき optimistic
安楽な あんらくな comfortable, carefree, cozy

安 ▷**easy (without effort)**
アン やす(い) やす やす(らか)　Ⓚ1859

(without effort) **easy, comfortable**
安易な あんいな easy, easygoing
安産 あんざん easy [smooth] delivery (of a baby)
安楽な あんらくな comfortable, carefree, cozy

comic
漫　戯

漫 ▷**comic**
マン　Ⓚ0633

comic, idle
漫画 まんが cartoon, comic strip
漫才 まんざい comic dialogue, comic backchat, *manzai*
漫談 まんだん idle talk, comic chat
漫楽 まんがく *manzai* accompanied by music
漫研(=漫画研究会) まんけん(=まんがけんきゅうかい) comic book [cartoon] research group

戯 ▷**sportive**
ギ たわむ(れる)　Ⓚ1654

sportive, frolicsome, humorous
戯評 ぎひょう humorous [sarcastic] comments, cartoon, caricature
戯画 ぎが cartoon, comics
戯文 ぎぶん nonsense literature, burlesque, literary parody
戯作者 げさくしゃ fiction writer, author of popular stories

command
令　麾　命

令 ▷**command**
レイ　Ⓚ1725

[also suffix] [original meaning] **command, order, decree**
命令 めいれい command, orders; edict, decree
司令 しれい commanding; commander, commandant
軍令 ぐんれい military command
辞令 じれい written appointment; wording, phraseology
指令 しれい order, instruction
訓令 くんれい instructions, (official) orders, directive
号令する ごうれいする give an order, command
動員令 どういんれい mobilization order(s)

麾 ▷**command**
キ

[now also 旗] **command**
麾下の きかの under one's command, under the banner (of)

命 ▷**order**
メイ ミョウ いのち　Ⓚ1772

[original meaning] **order, command, instruction**
命令 めいれい command, orders; edict, decree
使命 しめい mission, appointed task
勅命 ちょくめい Imperial order [command]

comment upon
批　評

批 ▷**criticize**
ヒ　Ⓚ0223

criticize, comment, review
批評 ひひょう criticism, comment
批難(=非難) ひなん criticism, blame
批評家 ひひょうか critic, reviewer
批判 ひはん criticism, comment
批議する ひぎする blame, criticize

評 ▷**comment**
ヒョウ　Ⓚ1361

comment, criticize, review
評論 ひょうろん comment, criticism, review
評判 ひょうばん fame, reputation

評釈 ひょうしゃく annotation, commentary
評者 ひょうしゃ critic, reviewer
論評 ろんぴょう comment, criticism, review
批評する ひひょうする criticize, comment

commit

託 托 預 委 任 嘱

託 ▷entrust
タク   Ⓚ1323

[also 托] [original meaning] **entrust (a person with a thing), place (a thing) in someone's charge, commit, ask**

託児所 たくじしょ day nursery
委託する いたくする entrust with, charge with, consign
嘱託 しょくたく part-time employee
寄託する きたくする deposit, entrust
信託 しんたく trust
結託する けったくする conspire with, be in collusion with
供託金 きょうたくきん deposit money
屈託の無い くったくのない free from worry, carefree

托 ▷entrust
タク   Ⓚ0190

[also 託] **entrust (a person with a thing), place (a thing) in someone's charge, commit, ask**

托卵 たくらん brood parasitism
委托する いたくする entrust with, charge with, consign
一蓮托生 いちれんたくしょう sharing the same fate

預 ▷deposit
ヨ あず(ける) あず(かる)   Ⓚ0954

deposit

預金 よきん deposit, bank account
預託する よたくする deposit
預貸率 よたいりつ loan-deposit ratio
預貯金 よちょきん deposits and savings, bank account
預血する よけつする deposit blood (in a blood bank)

委 ▷commit
イ ゆだ(ねる)   Ⓚ2209

[original meaning] **commit, entrust, leave to, delegate**

委員会 いいんかい committee
委託する いたくする entrust with, charge with, consign
委任する いにんする entrust, delegate, commit

委嘱する いしょくする charge, commission [entrust] with

任 ▷leave to
ニン まか(せる) まか(す)   Ⓚ0038

leave (up) to, entrust to, entrust with

任意の にんいの optional, voluntary, discretionary; arbitrary
委任する いにんする entrust, delegate, commit
信任 しんにん confidence, trust, credence
一任する いちにんする leave (a matter) to (a person), entrust (a person) with the task (of)

嘱 ▷charge with
ショク   Ⓚ0650

[original meaning] **charge (a person) with (a job), ask someone to do something; entrust**

嘱託する しょくたくする entrust with
委嘱する いしょくする charge, commission [entrust] with

communicate →INFORM AND COMMUNICATE

Communism

共 左 赤

共 ▷Communism
キョウ とも とも(に) –ども   Ⓚ2122

❶ abbrev. of 共産主義 きょうさんしゅぎ or 共産党 きょうとう: **Communism, Communist Party**
反共 はんきょう anticommunist
容共 ようきょう procommunist
❷ **Communist Party**
社・共 しゃきょう Social and Communist Parties

左 ▷the Left
サ ひだり   Ⓚ2567

the Left, leftist

左派 さは left wing, left faction
左翼 さよく left wing [flank]; left wing [faction]; left field

赤 ▷Red
セキ シャク あか あか(い) あか(らむ) あか(らめる)   Ⓚ1876

Red, Communist

赤軍 せきぐん Red Army

compare

比 較 譬 校 照 対 参

比 ▷**compare**
ヒ くら(べる)　　　　　Ⓚ0014

compare (with), contrast
比較 ひかく comparison
比較的 ひかくてき comparatively, relatively
対比する たいひする contrast, compare

較 ▷**compare**
カク　　　　　Ⓚ1397

compare
較量 こうりょう [rare] comparison
較差 かくさ(=こうさ) range
比較する ひかくする compare with, draw a
　　comparison

譬 ▷**compare to**
ヒ たと(える)

[now also 比] **compare to, liken**
譬喩 ひゆ simile, metaphor, allegory

校 ▷**collate**
コウ　　　　　Ⓚ0840

collate, proofread, check, examine, revise
校合する きょうごう(=こうごう)する collate, examine
　　and compare
校正 こうせい proofreading
校訂 こうてい revision
校正刷り こうせいずり galley proofs
校閲 こうえつ revision, reviewing, editing
校了 こうりょう final proof

照 ▷**check against**
ショウ て(る) て(らす) て(れる)　Ⓚ2461

**check (one thing) against (another), collate, exam-
ine by comparison, refer**
照査する しょうさする check against [up], examine
　　by reference, verify
照合する しょうごうする verify, compare, collate
照会する しょうかいする inquire, apply for informa-
　　tion
対照 たいしょう contrast, comparison; control

対 ▷**oppose (contrast)**
タイ ツイ　　　　　Ⓚ0735

(place in opposition and compare) **oppose, contrast**
対象 たいしょう object (of study), subject, target
対照 たいしょう contrast, comparison; control

対比する たいひする contrast, compare
対等 たいとう equality, parity
対称的な たいしょうてきな symmetrical
絶対の ぜったいの absolute
相対性理論 そうたいせいりろん theory of relativity

参 ▷**refer**
サン シン まい(る)　　　　Ⓚ1778

refer, consult, collate
参考 さんこう reference, consultation
参考書 さんこうしょ reference book [work]
参照 さんしょう reference, comparison

compel and press

圧 迫 強 押

圧 ▷**pressure**
アツ　　　　　Ⓚ2563

pressure, bring pressure to bear on, press, suppress
圧迫する あっぱくする press, oppress, pressure
圧制 あっせい oppression, coercion
抑圧する よくあつする oppress, repress, suppress
弾圧する だんあつする oppress, suppress

迫 ▷**press**
ハク せま(る)　　　　Ⓚ2647

(force to action) **press upon, press for, urge, force,
compel**
迫力 はくりょく power, force, punch, appeal
脅迫する きょうはくする threaten, intimidate,
　　menace
強迫 きょうはく coercion, compulsion
圧迫する あっぱくする press, oppress, pressure

強 ▷**force**
キョウ ゴウ つよ(い) つよ(まる)
つよ(める) し(いる)　　　　Ⓚ0432

force, compel, coerce
強制する きょうせいする compel, force
強行 きょうこう forcing, enforcement
強要 きょうよう coercion, extortion
強引な ごういんな overbearing, coercive
強訴 ごうそ direct petition
強姦 ごうかん rape
強盗 ごうとう robbery
勉強 べんきょう study; selling cheap; [rare] diligence

87　　　　　　　　compel and press

押 ▷push
オウ お(す) お(し)- お(つ)-
お(さえる) Ⓚ0278

(force to act) **push [force] oneself; push a person (to do something)**

押して おして forcibly, by compulsion; importunately

押し売り おしうり coercive touting, importunate peddling [peddler]

押し問答 おしもんどう bandying words, haggling, argument

中押し ちゅうおし one-sided game, victory by a wide margin (in go)

病気を押して行く びょうきをおしていく go in spite of illness

compensate
償　賠　酬　報

償 ▷recompense
ショウ つぐな(う) Ⓚ0155

[original meaning] (award compensation) **recompense, compensate, indemnify, repay**

償却 しょうきゃく repayment, refundment

報償 ほうしょう recompense, compensation

補償 ほしょう compensation, indemnity

賠償 ばいしょう indemnity, compensation, recompense

弁償 べんしょう compensation, indemnification

代償 だいしょう vicarious compensation

賠 ▷compensate
バイ Ⓚ1431

[original meaning] **compensate, indemnify**

賠償する ばいしょうする indemnify, compensate, recompense

賠償金 ばいしょうきん indemnity, reparation

賠責 ばいせき liability insurance

自賠法 じばいほう Automobile Accident Compensation Act

酬 ▷reciprocate
シュウ Ⓚ1399

reciprocate, requite, recompense; respond

応酬 おうしゅう response, reply; exchange

報 ▷requite
ホウ むく(いる) むく(う) Ⓚ1515

(make return for) **requite, return, repay; reward, recompense**

報奨 ほうしょう reward, compensation

報恩 ほうおん repaying a kindness, gratitude

報酬 ほうしゅう remuneration, reward; pay

返報 へんぽう requital, retaliation, revenge

compete
競　戦　闘　争

競 ▷compete
キョウ ケイ きそ(う) せ(る) Ⓚ1639

[original meaning] **compete, contend, vie**

競争する きょうそうする compete, contend, vie

競技 きょうぎ match, contest, game; sporting event

競泳 きょうえい swimming race

競演 きょうえん recital contest

競走 きょうそう race, sprint

競輪 けいりん bicycle race

競馬 けいば horse racing

戦 ▷contest
セン いくさ たたか(う) Ⓚ1590

contest, contend, play a match [game]

正正堂堂と戦おう せいせいどうどうとたたかおう Let's play the game fairly

闘 ▷fight
トウ たたか(う) Ⓚ2847

(struggle with) **fight (against), contend with, compete with**

闘争 とうそう fight, conflict

闘士 とうし fighter, boxer

闘技 とうぎ competition, contest

健闘 けんとう good fight; strenuous efforts

春闘 しゅんとう spring labor offensive

争 ▷contend
ソウ あらそ(う) Ⓚ1749

[original meaning] (struggle in opposition) **contend, contest, compete, struggle for**

争奪 そうだつ scramble, contest, struggle

戦争 せんそう war, battle

競争する きょうそうする compete, contend, vie

紛争 ふんそう conflict, strife

闘争 とうそう fight, conflict

compile

編 纂 撰 集 輯 著

編 ▷compile
ヘン あ(む) -あ(み)　　　Ⓚ1270

ⓐ compile, edit, compose
ⓑ compiled by, edited by
- a 編集 へんしゅう editing, compilation
  編纂 へんさん compilation, editing
  編者 へんしゃ(=へんじゃ) editor, compiler
  編成する へんせいする form, compose, compile
- b 浅田先生編 あさだせんせいへん edited by Prof. Asada

纂 ▷compile
サン　　　Ⓚ2380

compile, edit
編纂 へんさん compilation, editing
雑纂 ざっさん miscellaneous collection
類纂 るいさん collection of similar objects, classification by similarity

撰 ▷compile
セン サン えら(ぶ)　　　Ⓚ0672

ⓐ compile, edit
ⓑ compilation, selection, anthology
- a 撰者 せんじゃ author, compiler, editor
  新撰 しんせん newly compiled [selected, edited]
  修撰する しゅうせんする edit, compile
- b 官撰 かんせん government compilation
  勅撰集 ちょくせんしゅう imperial-commissioned poetry anthology

集 ▷edit
シュウ あつ(まる) あつ(める) つど(う)　　　Ⓚ2413

(collect written materials) edit, compile
集録 しゅうろく compilation, editing
編集する へんしゅうする edit, compile

輯 ▷edit
シュウ　　　Ⓚ1453

ⓐ (collect written materials) edit, compile
ⓑ edition, series
- a 輯録 しゅうろく compilation, editing
  編輯する へんしゅうする edit, compile
  集輯 しゅうしゅう gather together and compile
- b 特輯 とくしゅう special edition
  第一輯 だいいっしゅう first series

著 ▷author
チョ あらわ(す) いちじる(しい)　　　Ⓚ1993

ⓐ author, write, publish
ⓑ [suffix] authored by, by
- a 著作する ちょさくする write, author
  著述家 ちょじゅつか writer, author
  著者 ちょしゃ author, writer
  著作権 ちょさくけん copyright
  共著 きょうちょ joint authorship, coauthorship
- b 三島由紀夫著 みしまゆきおちょ authored by Mishima Yukio

complex

繁 煩

繁 ▷complicated
ハン　　　Ⓚ2484

complicated, complex, intricate
繁雑な はんざつな complicated, intricate, confused
繁簡 はんかん complexity and simplicity

煩 ▷vexatious
ハン ボン わずら(う) わずら(わす)Ⓚ0937

vexatious, intricate, confused, entangled
煩雑な はんざつな vexatious, troublesome, intricate
煩瑣な はんさな vexatious, troublesome, complicated
煩労 はんろう trouble, pains

compose

著 作 書 筆

著 ▷author
チョ あらわ(す) いちじる(しい)　　　Ⓚ1993

ⓐ author, write, publish
ⓑ [suffix] authored by, by
- a 著作する ちょさくする write, author
  著述家 ちょじゅつか writer, author
  著者 ちょしゃ author, writer
  著作権 ちょさくけん copyright
  共著 きょうちょ joint authorship, coauthorship
- b 三島由紀夫著 みしまゆきおちょ authored by Mishima Yukio

作 ▷compose
サク サ つく(る) つく(り) -づく(り)Ⓚ0052

compose (a literary or musical work), create, write

作品 さくひん (piece of) work, performance, product
作家 さっか writer, novelist, author
作曲する さっきょくする compose, write music
作者 さくしゃ author, writer, playwright
作文 さくぶん composition, essay; writing

書 ▷write
ショ か(く) -が(き)　　　Ⓚ2314

(compose written texts) **write, compose**
小説を書く しょうせつをかく write a novel

筆 ▷write
ヒツ ふで　　　Ⓚ2335
see also →WRITE

write
筆者 ひっしゃ writer
筆記する ひっきする take notes of, write down
筆記試験 ひっきしけん written examination
筆記用具 ひっきようぐ writing materials, pens and pencils
執筆 しっぴつ writing
特筆する とくひつする mention specially

compound
複　倍　重

複 ▷compound
フク　　　Ⓚ1132

compound, double, multiple, complex, composite
複合 ふくごう compound, composite, complex
複利 ふくり compound interest
複視 ふくし polyopia
複葉機 ふくようき biplane
複星 ふくせい multiple star
複数 ふくすう plural
複雑な ふくざつな complicated, complex, involved, intricate

倍 ▷double
バイ　　　Ⓚ0090

double
倍増 ばいぞう redoubling
倍額 ばいがく double amount
倍加 ばいか doubling
人一倍働く ひといちばいはたらく work twice as hard as others

重 ▷duplicate
ジュウ チョウ え おも(い) おも(り) かさ(ねる) かさ(なる)　　　Ⓚ2991

duplicate, double, multiple
重盗 じゅうとう double steal
重訳 じゅうやく retranslation
重版 じゅうはん second printing, reprint; second edition
重婚 じゅうこん bigamy

compromise
妥　譲　嫌

妥 ▷come to terms
ダ　　　Ⓚ2128

come to terms, compromise, arrive at an understanding, agree
妥協 だきょう compromise, agreement, understanding
妥結 だけつ compromise, agreement, understanding

譲 ▷concede
ジョウ ゆず(る)　　　Ⓚ1482

concede, yield to, relinquish
譲歩 じょうほ concession, compromise
互譲 ごじょう mutual concessions, compromise

嫌 ▷make peace
コウ

[now replaced by 講] **make peace, come to terms**
嫌和 こうわ peace, reconciliation

conceive
妊　娠

妊 ▷become pregnant
ニン　　　Ⓚ0211

ⓐ [original meaning] **become pregnant, conceive**
ⓑ **pregnant, expectant**
a 妊娠する にんしんする become pregnant, conceive
避妊 ひにん contraception
懐妊 かいにん pregnancy, conception
不妊 ふにん sterility
b 妊婦 にんぷ pregnant woman
妊産婦 にんさんぷ pregnant women and nursing mothers

娠 ▷**conceive**
シン ⓚ0369

[original meaning] **conceive, become pregnant**
妊娠 にんしん pregnancy, conception

concentrate on
注　　傾

注 ▷**concentrate**
チュウ そそ(ぐ) ⓚ0287

concentrate (on), pay attention to
注意 ちゅうい attention, care, advice
注意深い ちゅういぶかい careful, cautious; discreet
注目 ちゅうもく attention, notice
注視 ちゅうし steady gaze, close observation
傾注 けいちゅう devotion, concentration

傾 ▷**devote oneself to**
ケイ かたむ(く) かたむ(ける)
かし(げる) ⓚ0132

devote oneself to, concentrate on
傾倒する けいとうする devote oneself to, set one's
mind toward; admire
傾聴 けいちょう listening closely
傾注 けいちゅう devotion, concentration

conditional
conjunctions
但　　然

但 ▷**provided that**
ただ(し) ⓚ0056

provided that, on condition that, however, but,
only
但し書き ただしがき proviso, conditional clause
但し付き ただしつき conditional
但し...に就いてはこの限りではない ただし…
についてはこのかぎりではない Provided that the
same shall not apply to…
彼は約束はする、但し履行はせぬ かれはやくそく
はする、ただしりこうはせぬ He makes promises, but
he does not keep them

然 ▷**however**
ゼン ネン しか(し) ⓚ2423

[also 併し] **however, but, nevertheless**
然しながら しかしながら however, nevertheless

confectionery
菓　　飴

菓 ▷**confectionery**
カ ⓚ1997

confectionery, confection, cake, sweets, candy
菓子 かし confectionery, cake, sweets
和菓子 わがし Japanese-style confection
糖菓 とうか sweetmeats, sweets, confection
氷菓 ひょうか ice cream, sherbet
製菓 せいか confectionery (making of confections)
茶菓 さか(=ちゃか) tea and cakes, refreshments
銘菓 めいか excellent cake, cake of an established
name
冷菓 れいか ices, ice cream

飴 ▷**candy**
あめ

candy, sweets; syrup
飴玉 あめだま candy
飴色 あめいろ translucent amber (color)
飴煮 あめに sweet boiled food
飴と鞭 あめとむち carrot and stick (policy)
喉飴 のどあめ throat lozenge, cough drop
水飴 みずあめ starch syrup
綿飴 わたあめ cotton candy
林檎飴 りんごあめ candied apple, toffee apple

confine →IMPRISON AND CONFINE

Confucianists →CONFUCIUS AND CONFUCIANISTS

Confucius and
Confucianists
孔　子　孟

孔 ▷**Confucius**
コウ ⓚ0158

Confucius, Confucianism, Confucian
孔子 こうし Confucius
孔門 こうもん Confucian school

子 ▷**the Master (Confucius)**
シ ス こ -(っ)こ ⓚ2872

the Master, esp. Confucius
孔子 こうし Confucius

孟 ▷Mencius
モウ Ⓚ1906

Mencius
孟子 もうし Mencius; the works of Mencius
孔孟の教え こうもうのおしえ the teachings of
　Confucius and Mencius

congratulating →CELEBRATING AND
　　　　　　　　CONGRATULATING

conjecture
推　憶　測　察

推 ▷infer
スイ お(す) Ⓚ0465

infer, deduce, conjecture, surmise, guess
推定する すいていする presume, infer
推理 すいり reasoning, inference
推測 すいそく conjecture, supposition
推察する すいさつする guess, conjecture, infer,
　imagine
推論 すいろん reasoning, inference, induction,
　deduction
類推 るいすい analogy
邪推する じゃすいする suspect without reason,
　mistrust

憶 ▷speculate
オク Ⓚ0691

[formerly 臆] (engage in conjectural thought) **speculate,
conjecture, guess, infer**
憶説 おくせつ hypothesis, speculation
憶測 おくそく conjecture, speculation, guess
憶断 おくだん jumping to hasty conclusions

測 ▷conjecture
ソク はか(る) Ⓚ0558

**conjecture, surmise, suppose, presume, presup-
pose; expect; estimate**
推測 すいそく conjecture, supposition
予測 よそく estimate, forecast, prediction
不測の ふそくの unexpected, unforeseen
憶測 おくそく conjecture, speculation, guess

察 ▷guess
サツ Ⓚ2062

guess, conjecture, infer, surmise, gather, judge
察知する さっちする infer, gather
推察する すいさつする guess, conjecture, infer,
　imagine
予察する よさつする [rare] guess beforehand,
　conjecture in advance

考察する こうさつする consider, contemplate,
　study

conquer and
suppress
征　討　伐　鎮　靖

征 ▷conquer
セイ Ⓚ0262

**conquer, subjugate (the enemy), attack, assault,
invade**
征服 せいふく conquest, subjugation
征伐 せいばつ subjugation, conquest
征討 せいとう subjugation, conquest

討 ▷suppress by armed force
トウ う(つ) Ⓚ1324

**suppress by armed force, put down [attack] the
enemy, send a punitive expedition**
討伐 とうばつ suppression (of a rebellion), punitive
　expedition
討幕する とうばくする attack the shogunate
討匪 とうひ suppression of bandits
掃討する そうとうする wipe out (the enemy), clear
追討する ついとうする hunt down and kill
征討 せいとう subjugation, conquest

伐 ▷cut down
バツ き(る) Ⓚ0027

**cut down (one's enemies), strike down, send a
punitive expedition against, attack**
殺伐な さつばつな bloody, savage, warlike
征伐 せいばつ subjugation, conquest
討伐 とうばつ suppression (of a rebellion), punitive
　expedition

鎮 ▷quell
チン しず(める) しず(まる) Ⓚ1570

ⓐ (put down by force) **quell, pacify, suppress, subdue,
put down**
ⓑ (make calm) **quell, pacify, appease, soothe**
a 鎮圧する ちんあつする quell, suppress
　鎮定 ちんてい suppression, subdual
　鎮火する ちんかする be extinguished
b 鎮守の神 ちんじゅのかみ guardian god, local deity
　鎮痛剤 ちんつうざい anodyne, painkiller
　鎮静する ちんせいする calm down, be tranquilized,
　　subside; calm, tranquilize
　鎮魂曲 ちんこんきょく requiem

靖 ▷pacify
セイ ⓚ1117

[archaic] **pacify, quell, put down**
靖国 せいこく pacifying the nation

consider →THINK AND CONSIDER

console
慰　弔

慰 ▷console
イ なぐさ(める) なぐさ(む) ⓚ2497

[original meaning] **console, comfort; show sympathy to**
慰問 いもん inquiring after a person's health; consolation
慰霊 いれい comforting the spirits of the dead
慰謝料 いしゃりょう consolation money
慰労 いろう recognition of services

弔 ▷condole
チョウ とむら(う) ⓚ2888

condole, offer one's condolences to a bereaved person, console, mourn
弔辞 ちょうじ message of condolence
弔電 ちょうでん telegram of condolence
弔問 ちょうもん condolence call
弔慰 ちょうい condolence, sympathy

conspicuous
著　顕　卓　傑

著 ▷conspicuous
チョ あらわ(す) いちじる(しい) ⓚ1993

(since writing makes things clearly visible) (attracting attention) **conspicuous, remarkable, prominent, well-known**
著大な ちょだいな exceptionally large
著名 ちょめい prominence, eminence, distinction
顕著な けんちょな notable, conspicuous; clear, obvious

顕 ▷manifest
ケン ⓚ1605

(readily perceived) **manifest, apparent, noticeable, obvious**
顕著な けんちょな notable, conspicuous; clear, obvious
顕示する けんじする reveal

顕在化する けんざいかする be actualized
顕現 けんげん manifestation
露顕(=露見) ろけん discovery, detection, exposure

卓 ▷prominent
タク ⓚ1777

[original meaning] **prominent, eminent, outstanding, unexcelled, superior**
卓効 たっこう remarkable efficacy
卓見 たっけん farsightedness, penetration, excellent views
卓越 たくえつ excellence, superiority
卓説 たくせつ excellent opinion
卓立する たくりつする be prominent, stand out
卓抜 たくばつ prominence, excellence, superiority

傑 ▷outstanding
ケツ ⓚ0133

outstanding, remarkable, extraordinary
傑作 けっさく masterpiece, magnum opus; blunder
傑出する けっしゅつする excel, stand out
傑人 けつじん outstanding person

constant
定　恒　常　例

定 ▷fixed
テイ ジョウ さだ(める) さだ(まる) さだ(か) ⓚ1916

[also prefix] [original meaning] (unchanging) **fixed, definite, regular, constant**
定価 ていか fixed [set] price
定員 ていいん fixed number of regular personnel; capacity
定期 ていき fixed term; fixed deposit; commuter's pass; regular, periodic
定期券 ていきけん commuter's pass
定休 ていきゅう regular holiday
定休日 ていきゅうび regular holiday
定数 ていすう fixed number, constant
定則 ていそく established rule
定刻 ていこく regular [appointed] time
定形 ていけい fixed form
定食 ていしょく day's special, table d'hôte
安定した あんていした stable, steady, firm; calm

恒 ▷constant
コウ ⓚ0327

ⓐ [original meaning] **constant, unchanging, fixed**
ⓑ **regular, established**
a 恒常 こうじょう constancy

恒産 こうさん fixed property
b 恒数 こうすう constant (in science)
恒星 こうせい fixed star
恒例 こうれい regular ceremony, established custom

常 ▷regular
ジョウ つね とこ-　　　　　　Ⓚ2247

regular, habitual, standing
常務 じょうむ managing [executive] director
常連 じょうれん regular visitors [customers], frequenters
常緑樹 じょうりょくじゅ evergreen tree
常食 じょうしょく daily food, staple food
常用 じょうよう common use, daily use
常用漢字 じょうようかんじ Chinese characters designated for daily use
常時の じょうじの regular, standing
常任委員 じょうにんいいん standing committee
日常の にちじょうの daily, everyday

例 ▷regular
レイ たと(える)　　　　　　Ⓚ0071

regular, usual, established
例会 れいかい regular meeting
例年 れいねん normal year, average year
例日 れいじつ regular day
例刻 れいこく regular time

constellation
奎　彗　昴

奎 ▷Andromeda
ケイ キ　　　　　　Ⓚ1938

[original meaning, now obsolete] **Andromeda; zodiac sign symbolizing literature**

彗 ▷comet
スイ ズイ エイ エ　　　　　　Ⓚ2410

comet
彗星 すいせい comet

昴 ▷Pleiades
ボウ すばる　　　　　　Ⓚ2158

the Pleiades
昴宿 ぼうしゅく *literary* the Pleiades

consume
消　費　尽　耗　銷

消 ▷spend
ショウ き(える) け(す)　　　　　　Ⓚ0402

spend, use up, consume; become spent out
消費する しょうひする consume, spend
消費者 しょうひしゃ consumer
消耗する しょうもうする consume, exhaust, use up

費 ▷expend
ヒ つい(やす) つい(える)　　　　　　Ⓚ2261

[original meaning] **expend, spend, consume, use up**
消費 しょうひ consumption, spending
浪費 ろうひ waste, extravagance
空費 くうひ waste

尽 ▷exhaust
ジン つ(くす) -づ(くし) つ(きる) つ(かす)　　　　　　Ⓚ2624

exhaust, use up completely, finish
蕩尽する とうじんする squander, dissipate
理不尽な りふじんな unreasonable, unjust, absurd
大尽 だいじん millionaire, magnate; seeker of riotous pleasures; last day of 31-day month

耗 ▷wear away
モウ コウ　　　　　　Ⓚ1199

wear away, wear out, use up, consume
摩耗する まもうする wear away, wear out
減耗する げんもう natural decrease
消耗する しょうもうする consume, exhaust, use up
損耗する そんもう(=そんこう)する wear out, be wasted, be worn out

銷 ▷use up
ショウ

use up, consume, spend
銷夏 しょうか summering
意気銷沈する いきしょうちんする be dispirited, be disheartened

contain and include
含 容 包 挟

 ▷**contain (have as a part)**
ガン ふく(む) ふく(める) Ⓚ1756

(have as a part) **contain, include, comprise**
含有する がんゆうする contain, have, hold
含糖量 がんとうりょう sugar content
含水炭素 がんすいたんそ carbohydrate
包含する ほうがんする include, encompass, cover; imply

容 ▷**contain (have within)**
ヨウ Ⓚ1968

(have within) **contain, hold, accommodate**
容器 ようき receptacle, container, vessel
容量 ようりょう capacity, volume
収容する しゅうようする accommodate, receive (guests)
包容する ほうようする encompass, comprehend; imply; tolerate

 ▷**encompass**
ホウ つつ(む) Ⓚ2560

(hold within) **encompass, include, envelop, contain; include hidden meanings, imply**
包含する ほうがんする include, encompass, cover; imply
包容する ほうようする encompass, comprehend; imply; tolerate
包蔵する ほうぞうする contain, comprehend; imply; cherish
内包 ないほう connotation, intention, comprehension

挟 ▷**hold between**
キョウ はさ(む) はさ(まる) Ⓚ0335

hold between, pinch
挟瞼器 きょうけんき entropion forceps
挟撃 きょうげき attack on both sides, pincer movement
挟殺 きょうさつ *baseball* rundown

containers
箱 壺 槽 樽 棺 桶
笈 鞘 簞 函 籠 袋
鞄 器 瓶 缶 缶

箱 ▷**box**
はこ Ⓚ2366

ⓐ [sometimes also 函] [also suffix] **box, case, chest, bin**
ⓑ **counter for boxes**
ₐ 箱入りの はこいりの cased, boxed
箱入り娘 はこいりむすめ innocent [naive] girl of a good family
小箱 こばこ small box; casket
郵便箱 ゆうびんばこ mailbox
巣箱 すばこ bird box, bird house
本箱 ほんばこ bookcase
救急箱 きゅうきゅうばこ first-aid kit
ᵦ 二箱 ふたはこ two boxes

壺 ▷**jar**
コ つぼ

globular vessel: **jar, pot, crock, vase; jug**
壺中 こちゅう inside a pot
唾壺 だこ spittoon
酒壺 しゅこ(=さかつぼ) wine jar, liquor jar

槽 ▷**tank**
ソウ Ⓚ0981

[also suffix] **tank, vat, tub**
油槽 ゆそう oil tank
浴槽 よくそう bathtub
貯水槽 ちょすいそう water tank
水槽 すいそう water tank
浄化槽 じょうかそう tank for purifying water

樽 ▷**barrel**
ソン たる Ⓚ0992

barrel, cask, keg
樽俎 そんそ party (with food and drink)
樽酒 そんしゅ(=たるざけ) barreled sake

棺 ▷**coffin**
カン Ⓚ0897

[original meaning] **coffin, casket**
棺桶 かんおけ coffin, casket
石棺 せっかん sarcophagus
納棺する のうかんする place a body in a coffin
出棺 しゅっかん carrying the coffin out of the house

桶 ▷bucket
トウ おけ   Ⓚ0876

bucket, tub, pail; wooden vessel
湯桶読み ゆとうよみ reading of a compound in which *kun* and *on* are mixed (in that order)

笈 ▷box carried on the back
キュウ おい   Ⓚ2299

box carried on the back to store one's belongings
笈摺 おいずり(=おいずる) sleeveless overgarment worn by pilgrims

鞘 ▷sheath
ショウ さや   Ⓚ1598

sheath, scabbard, casing
鞘翅類 しょうしるい beetles
腱鞘 けんしょう sheath of tendon
髄鞘 ずいしょう myelin sheath

簞 ▷bamboo box
タン   Ⓚ2375

[original meaning] **bamboo box [basket]**
簞笥 たんす chest of drawers, cabinet, dresser
瓢簞 ひょうたん bottle gourd, calabash

函 ▷box
カン はこ   Ⓚ2587

[original meaning] **box, case, mailbox**
函蓋 かんがい box and cover
書函 しょかん letterbox; book chest
投函する とうかんする mail (a letter), put in the post
潜函病 せんかんびょう caisson disease

籠 ▷basket
ロウ かご こ(もる)   Ⓚ2383

【ロウ】
[original meaning] **basket, cage, coop, case**
籠球 ろうきゅう basketball
灯籠 とうろう garden lantern; hanging lantern
薬籠 やくろう medicine chest [container]

【かご】
[also suffix] **basket, hamper, crate, cage, case**
屑籠 くずかご wastebasket
鳥籠 とりかご bird cage
果物籠 くだものかご fruit basket

袋 ▷bag
タイ ふくろ   Ⓚ2245

[original meaning] **bag, sack**
郵袋 ゆうたい mailbag
製袋 せいたい bag manufacturing

風袋 ふうたい tare

鞄 ▷bag (for carrying)
ホウ かばん   Ⓚ1594

bag, briefcase, suitcase
鞄持ち かばんもち private secretary; flunky
旅行鞄 りょこうかばん traveling bag, suitcase
通学鞄 つうがくかばん school bag

器 ▷vessel
キ うつわ   Ⓚ2368

[original meaning] **vessel, receptacle, container**
容器 ようき receptacle, container, vessel
陶器 とうき pottery, porcelain, chinaware
便器 べんき toilet bowl, urinal
食器 しょっき tableware, dinner set
花器 かき flower vase [bowl]

瓶 ▷bottle
ビン   Ⓚ1231

[also suffix] **bottle, flask, decanter, vase, jar**
瓶詰め びんづめ bottling
広口瓶 ひろくちびん widemouthed bottle, jar
花瓶 かびん flower vase
魔法瓶 まほうびん thermos bottle
徳用瓶 とくようびん economy bottle

缶 ▷can
カン   Ⓚ1750

ⓐ **can, tin**
ⓑ [suffix] **canned [tinned] food**
ⓐ 缶切り かんきり can opener
缶詰め かんづめ canned goods, canning; cooping-up, confining
ⓑ ビスケット缶 びすけっとかん can of biscuits
蟹缶 かにかん canned crab

缶 ▷earthenware jar
フ

[original meaning, now rare] **earthenware jar**
撃缶 げきふ beating the vase for marking time

continents
亜 阿 欧 米 豪

亜 ▷Asia
ア   Ⓚ2966

Asia
東亜 とうあ East Asia
興亜 こうあ development of Asia

継起する けいきする occur in succession

阿 ▷Africa
ア お- おもね(る)   Ⓚ0305

Africa
南阿共和国 なんあきょうわこく Republic of South Africa

欧 ▷Europe
オウ   Ⓚ0787

Europe
欧州 おうしゅう Europe
欧米 おうべい Europe and America
欧亜 おうあ Europe and Asia
欧文 おうぶん foreign text
全欧 ぜんおう the whole of Europe
西欧 せいおう West Europe, the Occident
東欧 とうおう East Europe

米 ▷America
ベイ マイ こめ   Ⓚ2958

continent of America
渡米 とべい going to America
欧米 おうべい Europe and America
南米 なんべい South America

豪 ▷Australia
ゴウ   Ⓚ1838

[formerly also 濠] **Australia**
豪州 ごうしゅう Australia
日豪の にちごうの Japanese-Australian

---

continue

続 ▷continue
ゾク つづ(く) つづ(ける)   Ⓚ1244

[original meaning] **continue, follow, ensue, be adjacent**
続行 ぞっこう continuation
続出する ぞくしゅつする appear in succession
続落 ぞくらく continuous drop (of stocks)
続続 ぞくぞく in rapid succession, one after another
継続する けいぞくする continue, last, maintain
連続 れんぞく continuation, succession, series
接続する せつぞくする connect, join
持続力 じぞくりょく tenacity

継 ▷succeed
ケイ つ(ぐ)   Ⓚ1242

(come next or after) **succeed, continue, follow**
継続する けいぞくする continue, last, maintain

連 ▷in succession
レン つら(なる) つら(ねる) つ(れる) -づ(れ)   Ⓚ2672
see also →IN SUCCESSION

ⓐ in succession, in series, continually, repeatedly
ⓑ [also prefix] successive, in a row, consecutive, continued
a 連発する れんぱつする fire in rapid succession, fire in volleys
連載する れんさいする serialize, publish serially
連続する れんぞくする continue, occur in succession
連戦 れんせん series of battles [games], every battle [game]
五連敗 ごれんぱい five-game losing streak
b 連休 れんきゅう consecutive holidays
連日 れんじつ day after day, everyday
連山 れんざん mountain range
連分数 れんぶんすう continued fraction

持 ▷hold
ジ も(つ) -も(ち) も(てる)   Ⓚ0333

hold out, hold up, last, endure
持続する じぞくする continue, last; maintain
持久 じきゅう endurance, sustenance, persistence
持病 じびょう chronic illness
保持する ほじする maintain, preserve, retain
維持 いじ maintenance, upkeep, preservation
護持する ごじする defend, protect; uphold

---

contract and shrink
縮 約 攣

縮 ▷shrink
シュク ちぢ(む) ちぢ(まる) ちぢ(める) ちぢ(れる) ちぢ(らす)   Ⓚ1290

[original meaning] (draw together) **shrink, contract**
収縮 しゅうしゅく contraction, shrinking
伸縮 しんしゅく expansion and contraction
短縮 たんしゅく shortening, contraction, reduction

約 ▷contract
ヤク   Ⓚ1177

[original meaning] **contract, abridge, summarize, shorten**
括約筋 かつやくきん sphincter
制約 せいやく restriction, limitation; condition
集約的な しゅうやくてきな intensive
要約 ようやく summary, abridged statement

攣 ▷cramp
レン つ(る)

[original meaning] **cramp, have a cramp**
攣縮 れんしゅく spasm
痙攣 けいれん convulsions, cramp

cook
煮 沸 炊 蒸 焼 揚 煎

煮 ▷boil (cook by boiling)
シャ に(る) -に に(える) に(やす) Ⓚ2426

[original meaning] (cook by boiling) **boil, cook**
煮沸 しゃふつ boiling

沸 ▷boil (undergo boiling)
フツ わ(く) わ(かす) Ⓚ0291

(undergo boiling) **boil**
沸騰する ふっとうする boil, seethe, bubble
沸点 ふってん boiling point
煮沸 しゃふつ boiling

炊 ▷cook
スイ た(く) -だ(き) Ⓚ0773

[original meaning] **cook, boil**
炊事 すいじ cooking
炊婦 すいふ cook, kitchen maid
自炊 じすい cooking food for oneself

蒸 ▷steam
ジョウ む(す) む(れる) む(らす) Ⓚ2043

steam, heat with steam
蒸籠 せいろう steaming basket
薫蒸する くんじょうする fumigate, smoke

焼 ▷cook by fire
ショウ や(く) や(き) や(ける) Ⓚ0909

cook by fire: **bake, roast, broil, grill, toast**
焼き網 やきあみ toasting grill, broiling grill

揚 ▷fry in deep fat
ヨウ あ(げる) -あ(げ) あ(がる) Ⓚ0542

fry in deep fat
揚げ あげ fried bean curd
揚げ物 あげもの fried food, a fry
魚を揚げる さかなをあげる fry fish

煎 ▷roast, decoct
セン い(る) Ⓚ2054

❶ **roast, parch**

煎餅 せんべい rice cracker, wafer
焙煎 ばいせん roasting (of coffee, etc.)
❷ **decoct, boil, brew**
煎茶 せんちゃ green tea
湯煎 ゆせん warming something by immersion in
hot water

cooked dishes
焼 揚 煮

焼 ▷roasted, baked or fried food
ショウ や(く) -や(き) や(ける) Ⓚ0909

roasted, baked or fried food
鋤焼き すきやき sukiyaki
鉄板焼き てっぱんやき meat and vegetables roasted on hot plate
目玉焼き めだまやき fried eggs, sunny side up
カルメ焼き かるめやき brittle

揚 ▷fried food
ヨウ あ(げる) -あ(げ) あ(がる) Ⓚ0542

[also suffix] **fried food, fry**
精進揚げ しょうじんあげ fried vegetables

煮 ▷boiled food
シャ に(る) -に に(える) に(やす) Ⓚ2426

[suffix] **boiled food, boiling**
甘露煮 かんろに sweet boiled food

cooperate
協 携 調

協 ▷cooperate
キョウ Ⓚ0074

[original meaning] **cooperate, collaborate, work
together; be in harmony**
協力する きょうりょくする cooperate, collaborate,
work together
協同 きょうどう cooperation, collaboration, association
協調 きょうちょう cooperation, harmony
協賛 きょうさん support, cooperation
協奏曲 きょうそうきょく concerto

携 ▷join hands
ケイ たずさ(える) たずさ(わる) Ⓚ0593

join hands, work together, act in concert

提携する ていけいする cooperate with, act in concert with, tie up with
連携 れんけい cooperation, league, concert

調 ▷harmonize
チョウ しら(べる) しら(べ) ととの(う) ととの(える)　Ⓚ1417

ⓐ [original meaning] **harmonize, bring into accord [harmony], mediate**
ⓑ **act in harmony, cooperate**
a 調印 ちょういん signing, sealing; signature
　調停する ちょうていする mediate, arbitrate, make peace
　調和 ちょうわ harmony, accord, agreement, symmetry
b 協調する きょうちょうする cooperate, act harmoniously
　同調する どうちょうする align oneself, act in concert with

copy
写　謄　複　拓

写 ▷copy
シャ うつ(す) うつ(る)　Ⓚ1726

(reproduce an original, esp. by writing) **copy, make a copy, transcribe, reproduce, imitate**
写経 しゃきょう copying of a sutra, copied sutra
写生 しゃせい sketching [drawing] from nature; portrayal
写本 しゃほん manuscript, written copy
謄写 とうしゃ copy, reproduction, mimeograph
複写 ふくしゃ copy, duplication
書写 しょしゃ transcription, copying, handwriting
模写(=摸写) もしゃ copying, tracing, reproduction

謄 ▷transcribe
トウ　Ⓚ1013

[original meaning] (make an exact copy of an original text) **transcribe, copy, duplicate (a document)**
謄本 とうほん certified copy, transcript; copy of the domiciliary register
謄写 とうしゃ copy, reproduction, mimeograph
謄写版 とうしゃばん mimeograph

複 ▷duplicate
フク　Ⓚ1132

duplicate, copy
複本(=副本) ふくほん duplicate, copy
複製 ふくせい duplication, reproduction
複写 ふくしゃ copy, duplication

拓 ▷copy by rubbing
タク　Ⓚ0282

copy by rubbing, make rubbings from inscriptions on stone
拓本 たくほん rubbed copy
魚拓 ぎょたく fish print

corners
角　圭　隅　隈

角 ▷corner
カク かど つの　Ⓚ1761

ⓐ **corner, angle, edge**
ⓑ *baseball* **corner**
a 天の一角 てんのいっかく corner of the sky, point of heaven
　折角 せっかく with much trouble; specially
b 内角 ないかく inside corner; inner angle

圭 ▷sharp corner
ケイ ケ　Ⓚ1854

sharp corner (of ancient ceremonial jade tablet), point
圭角の有る けいかくのある angular, harsh-mannered, rough
尖圭コンジローム せんけいこんじろーむ pointed condyloma

隅 ▷nook
グウ すみ　Ⓚ0568

[original meaning] **nook, corner**
一隅 いちぐう corner, nook

隈 ▷recess
ワイ くま　Ⓚ0571

recess, nook, corner
界隈 かいわい neighborhood, vicinity

correct
正　直　訂　改　矯　匡

正 ▷right
セイ ショウ ただ(しい) ただ(す) まさ まさ(に)　Ⓚ2926

(set right) **right, correct, rectify**
改正する かいせいする revise, amend
訂正する ていせいする correct, amend, revise

修正する しゅうせいする amend, revise, correct; retouch
是正する ぜせいする correct
校正 こうせい proofreading
綱紀粛正 こうきしゅくせい enforcing discipline (among government officials)

直 ▷correct
チョク ジキ ジカ ただ(ちに) なお(す)
なお(る) なお(き) す(ぐ)　　Ⓚ2539

correct, rectify, remedy, reform, cure (a bad habit)
誤りを直す あやまりをなおす correct an error
行儀を直す ぎょうぎをなおす mend one's manners

訂 ▷revise
テイ　　Ⓚ1310
see also →REVISE

revise, correct, edit
訂正する ていせいする correct, amend, revise
改訂する かいていする revise, edit
校訂する こうていする revise

改 ▷reform
カイ あらた(める) あらた(まる)　　Ⓚ0216
see also →REFORM

reform, renew, rectify, correct, revise, amend
改善する かいぜんする improve, ameliorate
改新 かいしん renovation, reformation
改革 かいかく reform, reformation
改正 かいせい revision, amendment
改築 かいちく remodeling, rebuilding

矯 ▷rectify
キョウ た(める)　　Ⓚ1146

rectify, reform, correct, straighten out
矯正 きょうせい correction, rectification
矯風 きょうふう moral reform

匡 ▷rectify
キョウ　　Ⓚ2580

rectify, correct, reform
匡正する きょうせいする reform (bad customs)

correspond to
該　準　当

該 ▷correspond to
ガイ　　Ⓚ1377

correspond to, conform to, apply to, fall under

該当する がいとうする come under, be applicable to
当該 とうがい the said, the concerned

準 ▷apply correspondingly
ジュン　　Ⓚ2486

apply correspondingly, conform to, be proportionate
準拠 じゅんきょ conformity
準用する じゅんようする apply correspondingly

当 ▷be equivalent
トウ あ(たる) あ(たり) あ(てる)
あ(て)　　Ⓚ1865

[original meaning] **be equivalent, correspond to, equal**
相当する そうとうする correspond to, be proportionate; be suitable for, become
グラム当量 ぐらむとうりょう gram equivalent

cosmetics
紅　粉　黛

紅 ▷rouge
コウ ク べに くれない　　Ⓚ1174

rouge, lipstick; crimson, red
紅花 べにばな safflower
紅色 べにいろ red, crimson
口紅 くちべに lipstick, rouge
頬紅 ほおべに blusher

粉 ▷face powder
フン こ こな　　Ⓚ1186

face powder, cosmetics
脂粉 しふん cosmetics, rouge and powder
紅粉 こうふん rouge and powder

黛 ▷eyebrow ink
タイ ダイ まゆずみ　　Ⓚ2275

eyebrow ink
黛眉 たいび black eyebrows

count →CALCULATE AND COUNT

counters for animals
匹　頭　羽　疋

匹 ▷**counter for animals**
ヒツ ひき　　　　　　　　　Ⓚ2558

[formerly also 疋] counter for animals
犬五匹 いぬごひき five dogs
数匹 すうひき several animals

頭 ▷**counter for large animals**
トウ ズト あたま かしら -がしら Ⓚ1450

counter for large animals, esp. cattle; head (of cattle)
頭数 とうすう number of heads
牛五頭 うしごとう five head of cattle

羽 ▷**counter for birds**
ウ は わ はね　　　　　　Ⓚ0200

counter for birds or rabbits
一羽 いちわ one bird [rabbit]
三羽 さんば three birds [rabbits]

疋 ▷**counter for animals**
ヒキ　　　　　　　　　　Ⓚ2922

[now usu. 匹] counter for animals
猫三疋 ねこさんびき three cats

counters for books
冊　　巻　　部

冊 ▷**counter for books**
サツ サク　　　　　　　　Ⓚ2925

counter for books, volumes or copies
冊数 さっすう number of books
四冊 よんさつ four volumes

巻 ▷**counter for volumes**
カン ま(く) まき　　　　Ⓚ2298

counter for volumes
全六巻の著作 ぜんろっかんのちょさく work in six volumes
第一巻 だいいっかん first volume, Vol. 1

部 ▷**counter for copies**
ブ　　　　　　　　　　　Ⓚ1498

counter for copies of printed matter
部数 ぶすう number of copies, circulation

一部二百円 いちぶにひゃくえん 200 yen per copy

counters for flat things
枚　葉　丁　頁　通　竿

枚 ▷**counter for flat things**
マイ　　　　　　　　　　Ⓚ0764

counter for thin flat things, as sheets (of paper), boards, leaves (of a book), pages, articles of clothing, panes, etc.
枚数 まいすう number of flat things
紙五枚 かみごまい five sheets of paper
十円切手五枚 じゅうえんきってごまい five 10-yen stamps

葉 ▷**counter for leaves**
ヨウ は　　　　　　　　Ⓚ2024

counter for leaves or sheets
紙二葉 かみによう two sheets of paper
三葉虫 さんようちゅう trilobite

丁 ▷**counter for sheets**
チョウ テイ　　　　　　Ⓚ2851

counter for such sheets (1 丁 = 2 pages)
五丁 ごちょう five sheets

頁 ▷**counter for pages**
ケツ ぺーじ　　　　　　Ⓚ1795

counter for pages; page no.
九十頁 きゅうじゅっぺーじ page 90
五百頁の本 ごひゃくぺーじのほん book of 500 pages

通 ▷**counter for letters**
ツウ ツ とお(る) とお(り)
-どお(り) とお(す) とお(し) -どお(し)
かよ(う)　　　　　　　Ⓚ2678

counter for letters or documents
手紙二通 てがみについう two letters

竿 ▷**counter for flags**
カン さお　　　　　　　Ⓚ2288

flags (on poles)

counters for houses
軒　戸　棟

軒　▷counter for houses
ケン　のき　　　　　　　　Ⓚ1328

counter for houses
四軒 よんけん four houses
一軒家 いっけんや solitary house; private home
数軒 すうけん several houses

戸　▷counter for households
コ　と　　　　　　　　　Ⓚ1691

counter for households or houses
五戸 ごこ five houses

棟　▷counter for buildings
トウ　むね　むな-　　　　Ⓚ0904

counter for buildings or houses
一棟四戸建て ひとむねよんこだて tenement house
　divided into four apartments
三棟 みむね three buildings [houses]

counters for long objects
本　筋　竿　挺

本　▷counter for cylindrical objects
ホン　もと　　　　　　　Ⓚ2937

cylindrical objects, as bottles, pencils, etc.
八本の鉛筆 はっぽんのえんぴつ eight pencils
ビール二本 びーるにほん two bottles of beer

筋　▷counter for slender objects
キン　すじ　　　　　　　Ⓚ2337

counter for long, slender objects
一筋の涙 ひとすじのなみだ a trickle of tears

竿　▷counter for poles or rods
カン　さお　　　　　　　Ⓚ2288

counter for poles or rods
一竿 いっかん one pole, one rod

挺　▷counter for long solid objects
チョウ　テイ　　　　　　Ⓚ0385

[now also 丁]

ⓐ counter for long solid objects such as guns, oars,
　guitars or candles
ⓑ counter for human-powered vehicles such as
　palanquins or rickshaws
ⓐ ピストル五挺 ぴすとるごちょう five pistols
　ギター三挺 ぎたーさんちょう three guitars

counters for persons
人　名

人　▷counter for people
ジン　ニン　ひと　-り　-と　Ⓚ2857

counter for people
人数 にんずう number of people
二十人 にじゅうにん 20 people

名　▷counter for persons
メイ　ミョウ　な　　　　Ⓚ1857

counter for persons
会員五名 かいいんごめい five members

country →THE COUNTRY

country
国　邦　土

国　▷country
コク　くに　　　　　　　Ⓚ2659

[also suffix] **country, nation, state**
国家 こっか state, country, nation
国会 こっかい National Diet; national assembly,
　congress
国際 こくさい international
国際的な こくさいてきな international
国旗 こっき national flag
国防 こくぼう national defense
国民 こくみん people, nation; the people
国境 こっきょう (national) boundary [border]
国外の こくがいの foreign, external
国際化 こくさいか internationalization
国名 こくめい country name
全国 ぜんこく the whole country
外国 がいこく foreign country
傾国 けいこく beautiful woman; courtesan
先進国 せんしんこく advanced [developed] nation
　[country]

邦 ▷state
ホウ   ⓚ0750

state, country, nation
邦家 ほうか one's country, the state
隣邦 りんぽう neighboring country
盟邦 めいほう ally, allied powers
東邦 とうほう eastern country, Oriental nation; the Orient
友邦 ゆうほう friendly nation, ally
連邦 れんぽう federation, confederation, union
本邦 ほんぽう this [our] country
異邦人 いほうじん foreigner, alien

土 ▷land
ド ト つち   ⓚ2875

land, ground, territory, country
土地 とち land
国土 こくど country, territory, realm
領土 りょうど territory, domain
本土 ほんど mainland; the country proper
風土 ふうど natural features (of a region), climate
郷土 きょうど one's birthplace

courage
勇   胆

勇 ▷bravery
ユウ いさ(む)   ⓚ1798

bravery, courage, valor, heroism
武勇 ぶゆう bravery, valor
豪勇 ごうゆう bravery, valor, daring
蛮勇 ばんゆう brute courage, reckless valor

胆 ▷pluck
タン   ⓚ0828

pluck, guts, courage, nerve, gall
胆力 たんりょく pluck, courage, nerve
大胆 だいたん boldness, daring
豪胆 ごうたん boldness, iron nerves
落胆 らくたん disappointment, discouragement

court
廷   裁

廷 ▷court
テイ   ⓚ2631

[also suffix] **court of law**

廷内で ていないで in the court
法廷 ほうてい law court
開廷 かいてい opening of a court, trial
出廷 しゅってい appearance in court
公判廷 こうはんてい court, public trial court

裁 ▷court
サイ た(つ) さば(く)   ⓚ2813

abbrev. of 裁判所 さいばんしょ: **court**
最高裁 さいこうさい Supreme Court
家裁 かさい family court

courteous
寧   鄭   叮   嚀   丁

寧 ▷courteous
ネイ   ⓚ2061

[formerly 嚀] **courteous, polite**
丁寧(=叮嚀)な ていねいな polite, courteous

鄭 ▷courteous
テイ ジョウ   ⓚ1670

[now replaced by 丁] **courteous**
鄭重な ていちょうな polite, courteous

叮 ▷courteous
テイ

[now replaced by 丁] **courteous**
叮嚀(=丁寧)な ていねいな polite, courteous

嚀 ▷courteous
ネイ

[now replaced by 寧] **courteous, polite**
叮嚀(=丁寧)な ていねいな polite, courteous

丁 ▷courteous
チョウ テイ   ⓚ2851

[formerly 叮 or 鄭] **courteous**
丁寧(=叮嚀)な ていねいな polite, courteous
丁重(=鄭重)に ていちょうに politely, courteously

cover and wrap
覆 掩 被 包 蓋 蔽 葺

覆 ▷cover
フク おお(う) くつがえ(す) くつがえ(る)　Ⓚ2376

[original meaning] **cover**
覆面 ふくめん mask, veil
覆土 ふくど covering up seeds with soil
被覆 ひふく covering, coating

掩 ▷cover
エン おお(う)

❶ [original meaning] **cover, hide, conceal**
掩蔽 えんぺい cover, obscuration
掩蓋 えんがい cover; gun apron
❷ [now also 援] **cover, protect**
掩護する えんごする cover, protect, shelter
掩壕 えんごう cover trench

被 ▷cover
ヒ こうむ(る)　Ⓚ1077

cover, envelope; wear
被覆 ひふく covering, coating
被膜 ひまく tunic, capsule

包 ▷wrap
ホウ つつ(む)　Ⓚ2560

[formerly also 繃] **wrap, pack, envelop, cover**
包装 ほうそう wrapping, packing
梱包 こんぽう packing, packaging; package

蓋 ▷cover
ガイ おお(う) ふた　Ⓚ2040

cover, veil
空を蓋う そらをおおう cover up the sky

蔽 ▷cover
ヘイ　Ⓚ2084

[original meaning] **cover, screen, shield, hide**
遮蔽 しゃへい shield, cover, screen; *elec* shielding
隠蔽する いんぺいする conceal, cover up, hide
掩蔽 えんぺい cover, obscuration
建蔽率 けんぺいりつ coverage, building coverage ratio

葺 ▷thatch
シュウ ふ(く) -ぶき　Ⓚ2021

thatch, cover (a roof)

葺き替える ふきかえる rethatch, reroof, retile
葺き板 ふきいた shingles

create
創 作 綴 生 発 起

創 ▷create
ソウ つく(る)　Ⓚ1610

create, bring into being, invent
創造 そうぞう creation
創作する そうさくする create, produce; write a story
創意 そうい original idea, ingenuity
創世記 そうせいき Genesis
独創的 どくそうてき original, creative

作 ▷compose
サク サ つく(る) つく(り) -づく(り)　Ⓚ0052
see also →COMPOSE

compose (a literary or musical work), create, write
作品 さくひん (piece of) work, performance, product
作家 さっか writer, novelist, author
作曲する さっきょくする compose, write music
作者 さくしゃ author, writer, playwright
作文 さくぶん composition, essay; writing

綴 ▷compose
テイ テツ つづ(る) と(じる)　Ⓚ1264

(put words together correctly) **compose, write**
綴文 ていぶん(=てつぶん) compose, write

生 ▷produce
セイ ショウ い(きる) い(かす) い(ける) う(まれる) う(まれ) う(む) お(う) は(える) は(やす) き なま な(る)　Ⓚ2933

(bring into existence) **produce, give rise to**
生産 せいさん production
生成する せいせいする create, generate; be created

発 ▷start
ハツ ホツ た(つ)　Ⓚ2222

(bring into being) **start, originate, initiate, give rise to, generate, produce**
発端 ほったん origin, beginning, outset
発会 はっかい opening of a meeting; first meeting
発足する ほっそく(=はっそく)する start, be inaugurated
発刊する はっかんする publish, issue
発動する はつどうする exercise, invoke; move, put in motion

発電 はつでん generation of electricity; telegraphing
発熱 はつねつ generation of heat; attack of fever
発癌 はつがん carcinogenesis, production of cancer
発想 はっそう conception; *music* expression
発明 はつめい invention, contrivance
発起人 ほっきにん originator; promoter; proposer

起 ▷generate
キ お(きる) お(こる) お(こす)   Ⓚ2818

generate, produce
起電 きでん generation of electricity
起磁力 きじりょく magnetomotive force
励起 れいき excitation

crimes and offenses
犯　　罪　　凶

犯 ▷offense
ハン おか(す)   Ⓚ0175

ⓐ [also suffix] **offense, crime**
ⓑ **counter for offenses**
a 犯罪 はんざい offense, crime
　犯行 はんこう criminal act, crime, offense
　防犯 ぼうはん crime prevention
　初犯 しょはん first offense
　過失犯 かしつはん careless offense
b 前科三犯 ぜんかさんぱん previously convicted
　　three times

罪 ▷crime
ザイ つみ   Ⓚ2264

ⓐ [also suffix] **crime, offense**
ⓑ **guilt**
a 罪状 ざいじょう offense, charges
　罪人 ざいにん criminal, offender; sinner
　犯罪 はんざい offense, crime
　余罪 よざい other crimes [charges]
　微罪 びざい minor offense, misdemeanor
　破廉恥罪 はれんちざい infamous offense
b 有罪 ゆうざい guiltiness, guilt
　無罪の むざいの not guilty, innocent

凶 ▷atrocious crime
キョウ   Ⓚ2557

atrocious [lethal] crime, murder, wicked deed
凶器 きょうき murder [dangerous] weapon
凶刃 きょうじん assassin's dagger [knife]

cross
渡　　渉　　越

渡 ▷cross
ト わた(る) わた(す)   Ⓚ0560

[original meaning] **cross (a body of water), ford, cross over, go overseas, go across**
渡航 とこう crossing, passage, voyage
渡米 とべい going to America
渡河 とか wading [fording] a river
渡来 とらい importation, influx

渉 ▷wade
ショウ   Ⓚ0482

[original meaning] **wade (across water), ford**
渉禽類 しょうきんるい wading birds
徒渉 としょう wading, fording

越 ▷go beyond
エツ こ(す) -ご(し) こ(える)
-ご(え)   Ⓚ2825

go beyond or over a physical or abstract boundary: **go over, skip over, jump over**
飛越する ひえつする jump over (a hurdle), clear (a fence)

crowd
群　　衆　　叢　　簇

群 ▷group
グン む(れる) む(れ) むら
むら(がる)   Ⓚ1400

[also suffix] **group (of any kind), crowd, flock, cluster, swarm**
群衆 ぐんしゅう crowd of people, multitude
群像 ぐんぞう *art* group
魚群 ぎょぐん school of fish
一群の羊 いちぐんのひつじ flock of sheep
抜群の ばつぐんの preeminent, outstanding
層群 そうぐん *geol* group
子音群 しいんぐん consonant cluster
流星群 りゅうせいぐん meteoric swarm

衆 ▷multitude
シュウ シュ   Ⓚ2342

(large crowd) **multitude, crowd**
群衆 ぐんしゅう crowd of people, multitude
観衆 かんしゅう audience

アメリカ合衆国 あめりかがっしゅうこく United States of America

叢 ▷crowd together
ソウ むら むら(がる) くさむら　Ⓚ2277

grassy place, thicket, bush
叢林 そうりん Buddhist monastery

簇 ▷form a cluster
ゾク ソウ

[now also 族] [original meaning] **form a cluster**
簇生する ぞくせい(=そうせい)する (of plants) grow in clusters
簇出する ぞくしゅつ(=そうしゅつ)する spring up in clusters

---

cruel
虐 惨 酷 辣 残 凶 苛

虐 ▷cruel
ギャク しいた(げる)　Ⓚ2769

cruel, savage, tyrannical, oppressive
虐待 ぎゃくたい maltreatment, abuse, cruelty
残虐な ざんぎゃくな cruel, atrocious, brutal, inhuman
悪虐無道の あくぎゃくむどうの treacherous, heinous
暴虐な ぼうぎゃくな tyrannical, cruel, atrocious

惨 ▷cruel
サン ザン みじ(め)　Ⓚ0441

[usu. 残] cruel, ruthless, atrocious
惨殺する ざんさつする murder cruelly, slaughter, butcher
惨酷 ざんこく cruelty, atrocity, brutality
無惨な むざんな cruel, atrocious; pitiful, tragic, miserable

酷 ▷severe
コク　Ⓚ1414

severe, harsh, cruel, brutal, merciless
酷刑 こっけい severe punishment
酷評 こくひょう severe criticism
酷薄(=刻薄)な こくはくな cruel, inhumane
酷使する こくしする drive (a person) hard, abuse, sweat (one's workers), overwork
残酷な ざんこくな cruel, ruthless, atrocious
苛酷(=過酷)な かこくな severe, harsh, cruel

辣 ▷severe
ラツ　Ⓚ1412

(cruel) severe, harsh, brutal
悪辣 あくらつ unscrupulous, crafty, wily, foul

残 ▷ruthless
ザン のこ(る) のこ(す)　Ⓚ0851

[sometimes also 惨] ruthless, cruel, brutal
残酷な ざんこくな cruel, ruthless, atrocious
残虐な ざんぎゃくな cruel, atrocious, brutal, inhuman
残忍 ざんにん cruelty, atrocity, brutality
無残な むざんな cruel, atrocious; pitiful, tragic, miserable

凶 ▷atrocious
キョウ　Ⓚ2557

atrocious, ferocious, wicked, brutal, cruel
凶悪な きょうあくな atrocious, villainous, fiendish
凶暴な きょうぼうな atrocious, ferocious, brutal
凶漢 きょうかん villain, ruffian, assailant
凶行 きょうこう violence, murder, crime

苛 ▷harsh
カ　Ⓚ1929

harsh, severe, cruel
苛酷 かこく severe, cruel, harsh
苛烈 かれつ severe, stern
苛政 かせい tyranny, despotism

---

crustaceans
蝦 蟹

蝦 ▷shrimp
カ えび　Ⓚ1279

shrimp, prawn, lobster, crayfish
蝦蟹 えびがに crayfish
蝦尾 えびお goldfish with a shrimp-like tail; head of a shamisen or lute
小蝦 こえび small shrimp

蟹 ▷crab
カイ かに　Ⓚ2520

crab
蟹行する かいこうする walk sideways

cry and sigh
泣　嘆　歎

泣 ▷cry
キュウ な(く)　　　Ⓚ0300

[original meaning] **cry, weep, sob**

泣訴する きゅうそする implore with tears in one's eyes
号泣する ごうきゅうする wail, lament
感泣する かんきゅうする weep with emotion, be moved to tears

嘆 ▷sigh
タン なげ(く) なげ(かわしい)　　　Ⓚ0577

[original meaning] **sigh (in grief or despair), grieve, lament**

嘆息 たんそく sigh
嘆願 たんがん entreaty, appeal
悲嘆 ひたん grief, sorrow, lamentation
慨嘆 がいたん deploring, regret

歎 ▷sigh
タン なげ(く)　　　Ⓚ1652

[original meaning] **sigh (in grief or despair), grieve, lament; deplore**

歎声 たんせい sigh, lamentation; sigh of admiration
歎息する たんそくする sigh; sigh in grief
歎願する たんがんする entreat, petition, appeal
悲歎 ひたん grief, sorrow, lamentation
慨歎する がいたんする deplore, lament, regret
嗟歎 さたん lamentation, deploration; admiration

cultivate
修　養　練　錬　鍛　磨　琢

修 ▷cultivate
シュウ シュ おさ(める) おさ(まる)　Ⓚ0105

cultivate (one's intellect or character), improve oneself, foster, pursue, study, train, practice

修養する しゅうようする cultivate one's mind, improve oneself
修道院 しゅうどういん monastery, convent
修了 しゅうりょう completion (of a course)
修行 しゅぎょう training, study; ascetic practices
修験者 しゅげんじゃ ascetic (living in the mountains)
修学旅行 しゅうがくりょこう school excursion
修士 しゅうし Master, master's degree

研修 けんしゅう study and training
履修 りしゅう completion (of a course), taking (a course)
必修の ひっしゅうの required, compulsory

養 ▷foster (one's intellect)
ヨウ やしな(う)　　　Ⓚ2089

foster one's intellect, cultivate one's mind, train

養成する ようせいする train, educate, bring up
教養 きょうよう culture, education, cultivation
修養 しゅうよう mental culture, cultivation of the mind, character-building

練 ▷train
レン ね(る) ね(り)-　　　Ⓚ1256

[sometimes also 錬] **train, practice, exercise, drill, discipline; refine**

練成 れんせい training, drilling
練習 れんしゅう practice, training
習練する しゅうれんする train, discipline

錬 ▷refine
レン　　　Ⓚ1553

[usu. 練] **refine one's mental and physical skills, train, cultivate, improve one's character**

錬成 れんせい training, drilling
錬磨する れんまする train, practice, cultivate
修錬する しゅうれんする train, discipline

鍛 ▷train
タン きた(える)　　　Ⓚ1567

train, cultivate one's physical and mental skills, attain proficiency

鍛成 たんせい training, cultivation

磨 ▷polish
マ みが(く)　　　Ⓚ2744

polish [improve] (one's skill), cultivate, train

錬磨 れんま training, practice, cultivation

琢 ▷polish
タク　　　Ⓚ0883

polish [improve] one's skills, cultivate one's mind

切磋琢磨 せっさたくま working hard together, assiduity in friendly rivalry

cultivated fields
畑 畠 牧 園 田 佃 圃

畑 ▷field
はた　はたけ　-ばたけ　　　Ⓚ0812

【はた】
[formerly also 畠] (plowed or cultivated) field, farm, vegetable garden, plantation
畑地 はたち farmland
畑作 はたさく dry field farming, dry field crop
田畑 たはた(=でんぱた) fields and rice paddies

【はたけ】
(plowed or cultivated) field, farm, vegetable garden, plantation
畑を作る はたけをつくる cultivate a field, farm

畠 ▷field
はた　はたけ　-ばたけ　　　Ⓚ2234

【はた】
[now usu. 畑] (plowed or cultivated) field, farm, vegetable garden, plantation
田畠 たはた(=でんぱた) fields (of rice and other crops)

【はたけ】
(plowed or cultivated) field, farm, vegetable garden, plantation
畠を耕す はたけをたがやす plow a field

牧 ▷pasture
ボク　まき　　　Ⓚ0776

pasture, grazing land, meadow
牧場 ぼくじょう stock farm, pasture
牧草 ぼくそう pasture, grass
牧野 ぼくや pasture land, ranch
放牧地 ほうぼくち grazing land, pasture

園 ▷garden
エン　その　　　Ⓚ2722

[sometimes also 苑] [also suffix] [original meaning] garden, park, plantation, farm
園芸 えんげい gardening, horticulture
田園 でんえん fields and gardens, rural districts
庭園 ていえん garden, park
公園 こうえん park, public garden
楽園 らくえん paradise
果樹園 かじゅえん fruit garden, orchard

田 ▷rice field
デン　た　　　Ⓚ2617

ⓐ rice field, paddy field

ⓑ [original meaning] field, farmland
ⓐ 田畑 でんぱた(=たはた) fields and rice paddies
田地 でんち land, farm, rice fields
田作 でんさく rice-field tilling
乾田 かんでん dry rice field
水田 すいでん paddy field, rice field
ⓑ 田園 でんえん fields and gardens, rural districts

佃 ▷cultivated rice field
デン　つくだ　　　Ⓚ0042

cultivated rice field
佃煮 つくだに preserved food boiled in soy

圃 ▷vegetable garden
ホ　　　Ⓚ2687

[sometimes also 甫] [original meaning] vegetable garden; rice nursery
圃場 ほじょう cultivated land [field]
田圃 でんぼ fields and rice paddies
苗圃 びょうほ seedbed

cure and recover
療 治 医 癒 快

療 ▷treat
リョウ　　　Ⓚ2803

ⓐ [original meaning] treat, care for
ⓑ medical treatment
ⓐ 治療する ちりょうする treat, cure
診療 しんりょう diagnosis and treatment
ⓑ 療法 りょうほう method of treatment, cure, remedy
療養中 りょうようちゅう under medical care, in recuperation
医療 いりょう medical treatment [care]
施療 せりょう gratuitous treatment, free medical treatment
物療 ぶつりょう physiotherapy, physical treatment

治 ▷cure
ジ　チ　おさ(める)　おさ(まる)　なお(る)
なお(す)　　　Ⓚ0297

ⓐ cure, treat, heal
ⓑ cure, recovery
ⓐ 治療 ちりょう medical treatment [cure]
治癒 ちゆ healing, cure, recovery
主治医 しゅじい physician in charge
不治の ふじの incurable, fatal
ⓑ 根治 こんじ(=こんち) complete [radical] cure
湯治 とうじ hot spring cure, taking healing baths

医 ▷cure
イ   Ⓚ2583

cure
- 医学 いがく medical science, medicine
- 医療 いりょう medical treatment [care]
- 医者 いしゃ doctor
- 医薬 いやく medicine, drug; medical practice and dispensary
- 医薬品 いやくひん pharmaceuticals, medicines
- 医院 いいん clinic

癒 ▷heal
ユ い(える) い(やす)   Ⓚ2806

ⓐ [original meaning] **heal, recover**
ⓑ **heal (a wound), cure**

a
- 治癒 ちゆ healing, cure, recovery
- 平癒 へいゆ recovery, restoration to health

b
- 癒着 ゆちゃく adhesion, conglutination; connection, collusion
- 癒傷組織 ゆしょうそしき wound-healing tissue

快 ▷recover
カイ こころよ(い)   Ⓚ0218

recover, convalesce
- 快方 かいほう convalescence
- 快復 かいふく recovery (from illness)
- 全快 ぜんかい complete recovery

curtain
幕 簾 帳

幕 ▷curtain
マク バク   Ⓚ2044

[original meaning] **curtain, screen**
- 幕屋 まくや tent, tabernacle; Makuya (Original Gospel Movement of Japan)
- 天幕 てんまく tent
- 垂れ幕 たれまく hanging screen, curtain
- 内幕 うちまく inside facts, inner workings; [original meaning] inner curtain
- 除幕式 じょまくしき unveiling ceremony
- 煙幕 えんまく smoke screen

簾 ▷bamboo screen
レン すだれ す   Ⓚ2378

bamboo screen [blind], reed screen
- 暖簾 のれん shop curtain, *noren*; credit, reputation
- 珠暖簾 たまのれん bead curtain
- 鋤簾 じょれん long-handled winnow used to sift earth [sand]

帳 ▷drapery
チョウ   Ⓚ0430

[original meaning] **drapery, drop curtain, curtain**
- 几帳 きちょう screen
- 几帳面な きちょうめんな exact, precise, punctual
- 緞帳 どんちょう thick curtain, drop curtain
- 几帳 きちょう screen
- 開帳する かいちょうする unveil a Buddhist image; gamble

custom
慣 例 習 風 俗 癖 弊

慣 ▷habitual practice
カン な(れる) な(らす)   Ⓚ0624

habitual [usual, established] practice, custom, habit, usual way, convention
- 慣行 かんこう habitual [usual] practice
- 慣例 かんれい custom, usage, precedent
- 習慣 しゅうかん custom, habit

例 ▷established practice
レイ たと(える)   Ⓚ0071

established practice, custom, usage
- 恒例 こうれい regular ceremony, established custom
- 慣例 かんれい custom, usage, precedent
- 家例 かれい family usage [practice, custom]
- 常例 じょうれい usual practice, common usage, established custom

習 ▷custom
シュウ なら(う) なら(い)   Ⓚ2324

custom, habit, practice, tradition
- 習慣 しゅうかん custom, habit
- 慣習 かんしゅう custom, usage, tradition
- 風習 ふうしゅう manners and customs
- 悪習 あくしゅう bad habit
- 奇習 きしゅう strange custom

風 ▷manners
フウ フ かぜ かざ-   Ⓚ2591

(prevailing customs) **manners, customs, tradition**
- 風俗 ふうぞく manners, customs; popular [public] morals
- 風習 ふうしゅう manners and customs
- 家風 かふう family traditions [customs]

俗 ▷popular custom
ゾク   Ⓚ0088

[original meaning] **popular custom, folk custom, folkways, convention**
- 風俗 ふうぞく manners, customs; popular [public] morals
- 習俗 しゅうぞく manners and customs, folkways
- 民俗 みんぞく folk customs, folkways
- 良俗 りょうぞく good custom

癖 ▷habit
ヘキ くせ くせ(に)   Ⓚ2805

[also suffix] **habit, habitual practice, propensity, peculiarity, weakness**
- 悪癖 あくへき bad habit, vice
- 性癖 せいへき one's natural disposition, propensity, mental habit
- 習癖 しゅうへき (bad) habit, habitual practice
- 病癖 びょうへき peculiarity, weakness, morbid habit
- 潔癖 けっぺき love of cleanliness, fastidiousness
- 飲酒癖 いんしゅへき inebriety, drinking habit
- 放浪癖 ほうろうへき vagrant habits, vagabondism

弊 ▷evil practice
ヘイ   Ⓚ2508

evil [corrupt] practice, bad habit, defect
- 弊習 へいしゅう corrupt custom, bad habit
- 弊政 へいせい misgovernment, maladministration
- 積弊 せきへい deep-rooted evil

cut
切 薙 剪 削 挽 断 截
裁 斬 割 剖 刈 伐

切 ▷cut
セツ サイ き(る) き(り) –ぎ(り) き(れる) き(れ) –ぎ(れ)   Ⓚ0015

[formerly also 截] [original meaning] **cut, sever**
- 切断する せつだんする cut (off), sever
- 切開 せっかい incision, section
- 切除する せつじょする cut off, excise
- 切腹 せっぷく harakiri, suicide by disembowelment
- 半切 はんせつ half size

薙 ▷mow down
テイ チ な(ぐ)   Ⓚ2099

mow down
- 薙ぎ払う なぎはらう mow down
- 薙ぎ倒す なぎたおす mow down, knock down; defeat one after another

草薙の剣 くさなぎのつるぎ sword of the Imperial regalia
水薙鳥 みずなぎどり Procellariidae, Procellariiformes

剪 ▷prune
セン き(る) つ(む)

[original meaning] **prune, trim, shear**
- 剪定する せんていする prune, trim
- 剪断 せんだん shearing, shear

削 ▷cut by chipping
サク けず(る)   Ⓚ1316

cut by chipping, whittle, cut metal (with a cutting tool), machine
- 切削 せっさく cutting, machining
- 研削 けんさく grinding
- 旋削 せんさく turning (on a lathe)

挽 ▷grind, saw
バン ひ(く)   Ⓚ0384

❶ **grind (meat or coffee)**
- 挽き肉 ひきにく ground [minced] meat
- 挽き立てのコーヒー ひきたてのこーひー freshly ground coffee
- 粗挽き あらびき coarsely ground (coffee, grain), coarsely minced (meat)
- 合い挽き あいびき beef and pork ground together

❷ **saw, cut with a saw**
- 木挽き歌 こびきうた sawyer's song
- 縦挽き鋸 たてびきのこ ripsaw

断 ▷cut off
ダン た(つ) ことわ(る)   Ⓚ1355

[original meaning] (detach by severing) **cut off, sever, cut apart**
- 断片 だんぺん fragment, piece
- 断面 だんめん (cross) section, profile
- 断頭台 だんとうだい guillotine
- 断裁機 だんさいき paper cutter
- 切断する せつだんする cut (off), sever

截 ▷cut off
セツ サイ き(る)

[now also 切] [original meaning] **cut off, sever**
- 截断 せつだん cutting
- 截然たる せつぜんたる distinct, clear-cut, sharp
- 直截な ちょくせつ(=ちょくさい)な direct, plain, straightforward

裁 ▷cut out
サイ た(つ) さば(く)   Ⓚ2813

[original meaning] **cut out (a garment)**
- 裁縫 さいほう sewing, needlework, dressmaking

裁断師 さいだんし (tailor's) cutter

斬 ▷**cut with a sword**
ザン き(る) Ⓚ1347

cut (a person) with a sword, cut down, kill

斬首 ざんしゅ decapitation
斬罪 ざんざい decapitation

割 ▷**cut with a knife**
カツ わ(る) わり わ(れる) さ(く) Ⓚ1611

[original meaning] **cut with a knife, cut in two**

割腹 かっぷく disembowelment, harakiri
割礼 かつれい circumcision
割線 かっせん secant

剖 ▷**dissect**
ボウ Ⓚ1492

[original meaning] **dissect, cut open, split in two**

剖検 ぼうけん autopsy, necropsy
解剖する かいぼうする dissect, anatomize, hold an
  autopsy; analyze
解剖学 かいぼうがく anatomy

刈 ▷**clip**
か(る) Ⓚ0017

(cut grass, hair or the like by sharp instrument) **clip, crop,
cut, shear, mow, prune, trim**

刈り込む かりこむ prune
刈り取る かりとる mow, cut down, reap, harvest
刈り立ての かりたての newly mown, newly
  cropped (head), just clipped
草刈り くさかり mowing, mower
羊毛を刈る ようもうをかる shear sheep

伐 ▷**cut down**
バツ き(る) Ⓚ0027

cut down (trees), fell, chop down

伐採する ばっさいする lumber, fell, deforest
伐木 ばつぼく felling, cutting, logging
濫伐(=乱伐)する らんばつする deforest indiscrimi-
  nately, cut down [fell] trees recklessly
盗伐 とうばつ secret felling of trees

cutting instruments

刀 鎌 刃 鋏 鋸
斧 鍬 錐 鑿

刀 ▷**cutting tool**
トウ かたな Ⓚ2534

cutting tool, knife, blade, -tome

彫刻刀 ちょうこくとう graver, chisel

鎌 ▷**sickle**
かま Ⓚ1572

[original meaning] **sickle, scythe**

刃 ▷**blade**
ジン は Ⓚ2537

❶ [original meaning] (part for cutting) **blade, edge**
❷ (weapon for cutting) **blade, sword, dagger, knife**

a 白刃 はくじん drawn sword
  凶刃 きょうじん assassin's dagger [knife]
  利刃 りじん sharp sword
  兵刃 へいじん sword

鋏 ▷**scissors**
キョウ はさみ はさ(む)

scissors, shears

鋸 ▷**saw**
キョ のこぎり のこ Ⓚ1552

saw

鋸歯 きょし saw tooth

斧 ▷**axe**
フ おの Ⓚ1775

[original meaning] **axe, hatchet**

斧斤 ふきん axe
斧鑿 ふさく [archaic] elaboration; lucubration; chisel
  and axe
斧正 ふせい forthright correction [revision]
石斧 せきふ stone axe

鍬 ▷**hoe**
シュウ くわ Ⓚ1566

hoe

鍬入れ くわいれ ground breaking
鍬形虫 くわがたむし stag beetle
馬鍬 まぐわ(=まんが) harrow, rake

錐 ▷**drill**
スイ きり Ⓚ1558

drill, auger, awl

錐刀 すいとう stiletto, dagger
試錐 しすい (test) boring
立錐の余地もない りっすいのよちもない tightly
  packed (with people) ("no space to set a drill")

鑿 ▷**chisel**
サク のみ

[original meaning] **chisel**

斧鑿 ふさく [archaic] elaboration; lucubration; chisel
  and axe

cutting weapons
刀 剣 矛 戟 鉾 戈

刀 ▷**sword (single-edged)**
トウ かたな　　　　　　　　Ⓚ2534

[original meaning] (single-edged) **sword**
刀剣 とうけん sword
刀身 とうしん sword blade
名刀 めいとう excellent blade, famous sword
日本刀 にほんとう Japanese sword
短刀 たんとう dagger

剣 ▷**sword (double-edged)**
ケン つるぎ　　　　　　　　Ⓚ1493

[original meaning] (double-edged) **sword, sword, blade**
刀剣 とうけん sword
銃剣 じゅうけん bayonet
真剣 しんけん real sword; seriousness
手裏剣 しゅりけん throwing knife

矛 ▷**halberd**
ム ほこ　　　　　　　　　　Ⓚ1732

[original meaning] **ancient Chinese weapon resembling a halberd or spear**
矛盾 むじゅん contradiction

戟 ▷**halberd**
ゲキ ほこ　　　　　　　　　Ⓚ1514

[original meaning] **halberd, two-pronged lance**
剣戟 けんげき weapons, arms

鉾 ▷**decorative halberd**
ボウ ほこ

decorative halberd
山鉾 やまぼこ festival float mounted with a decorative halberd
蒲鉾 かまぼこ steamed fish paste

戈 ▷**dagger-ax**
カ ほこ

[original meaning] **ancient Chinese dagger-ax (consisting of a long shaft with a double-edged blade attached crosswise to its end)**
干戈 かんか arms, weapons
兵戈 へいか swords and halberds, arms; warfare

dairy products
酪 乳 醍 醐

酪 ▷**dairy products**
ラク　　　　　　　　　　　Ⓚ1398

dairy products
酪農 らくのう dairy farming
酪農家 らくのうか dairy farmer, dairyman
酪製品 らくせいひん dairy products
酪酸 らくさん butyric acid
乳酪 にゅうらく dairy products
牛酪 ぎゅうらく butter
乾酪 かんらく cheese

乳 ▷**milk**
ニュウ ちち ち　　　　　　Ⓚ1306

(food product) **milk**
乳業 にゅうぎょう dairy industry
乳価 にゅうか price of milk
粉乳 ふんにゅう powdered milk
脱脂乳 だっしにゅう nonfat milk

醍 ▷**cream**
ダイ　　　　　　　　　　　Ⓚ1455

[archaic] **cream made from butter**—now used only in 醍醐 だいご
醍醐 だいご cream made from butter; *Buddhism* the best taste, the finest thing in this world
醍醐味 だいごみ the best, the epitome

醐 ▷**cream**
ゴ　　　　　　　　　　　　Ⓚ1456

[archaic] **cream made from butter**—now used only in 醍醐 だいご
醍醐 だいご cream made from butter; *Buddhism* the best taste, the finest thing in this world
醍醐味 だいごみ the best, the epitome

damage →HARM AND DAMAGE

dance
踊 舞

踊 ▷**dance (energetically)**
ヨウ おど(る) おど(り)　　Ⓚ1410

【ヨウ】
dance
舞踊 ぶよう dancing, dance

民踊 みんよう folk dance

【おど(る)】
dance (energetically)
　踊り手 おどりて dancer

舞 ▷dance (gracefully)
ブ ま(う) まい　　　　　Ⓚ1844

【ブ】
[original meaning]
ⓐ dance, dancing
ⓑ to dance
a 舞曲 ぶきょく dance music, music and dancing
　剣舞 けんぶ sword dance
　日舞 にちぶ Japanese dancing
　歌舞伎 かぶき kabuki
b 舞踏 ぶとう dancing
　舞台 ぶたい stage, the boards
　舞踏会 ぶとうかい ball, dance

【ま(う)】
dance (gracefully, esp. traditional dances); flutter, fly, circle (in the sky)
　舞を舞う まいをまう perform a dance, dance
　舞い上がる まいあがる soar, fly high

danger
危　殆　険

危 ▷dangerous
キ あぶ(ない) あや(うい)
あや(ぶむ)　　　　　Ⓚ2755

[original meaning] **dangerous, precarious**
　危険な きけんな dangerous
　危機 きき crisis, emergency
　危害 きがい injury, harm; danger, risk
　危難 きなん danger, distress, hazard
　危篤 きとく on the verge of death, critical condition
　安危 あんき safety or danger, fate, welfare

殆 ▷dangerous
タイ ほとん(ど)　　　　Ⓚ0811

dangerous, precarious
　危殆 きたい danger, jeopardy, peril

険 ▷danger
ケン けわ(しい)　　　　Ⓚ0495

ⓐ danger, risk, hazard
ⓑ dangerous, risky, hazardous
a 危険な きけんな dangerous
　保険 ほけん insurance
b 険悪な けんあくな dangerous, threatening, serious
　冒険 ぼうけん adventure, risk

探険(=探検) たんけん exploration, expedition

dark
暗　黒　陰　闇　晦
昏　昧　冥　曖

暗 ▷dark
アン くら(い)　　　　　Ⓚ0921

[formerly also 闇] [original meaning] **dark, dim**
　暗黒 あんこく darkness
　暗室 あんしつ dark room
　暗雲 あんうん dark clouds
　暗夜 あんや dark night

黒 ▷black
コク くろ くろ(い)　　　Ⓚ2388

(lacking light) **black, dark**
　暗黒 あんこく darkness

陰 ▷shaded
イン かげ かげ(る)　　　Ⓚ0494

shaded, dark
　陰湿な いんしつな dark and damp, dampish
　夜陰 やいん darkness of the night, shades of night

闇 ▷dark
アン やみ　　　　　　　Ⓚ2846

ⓐ [original meaning] **dark, dim**
ⓑ darkness
a 闇夜 あんや dark night
　闇黒 あんこく darkness
　闇然とした あんぜんとした dark, black, unclear;
　　doleful, dispirited
b 諒闇 りょうあん court [national] mourning

晦 ▷dark
カイ くら(ます) つごもり　Ⓚ0864

dark, obscure
　晦冥 かいめい darkness
　晦渋な かいじゅうな ambiguous, obscure, equivocal

昏 ▷dark
コン くら(い)　　　　　Ⓚ2143

ⓐ [original meaning] **dark**
ⓑ dusk, twilight
a 昏冥 こんめい darkness, gloom
b 黄昏 こうこん(=たそがれ) dusk, twilight

昧 ▷dark
マイ   Ⓚ0794

dark, dim
　曖昧 あいまい vague, unclear, ambiguous, fuzzy

冥 ▷dark
メイ ミョウ   Ⓚ1810

ⓐ [original meaning] **dark, dim**
ⓑ **darkness**
　a 冥冥 めいめい dark, invisible, obscure
　　冥闇 (=冥暗) めいあん gloom, shade
　b 晦冥 かいめい darkness

曖 ▷shady
アイ   Ⓚ1001

shady, indistinct, unclear
　曖昧 あいまい vague, unclear, ambiguous, fuzzy

dark-colored
暗 濃 深

暗 ▷dark
アン くら(い)   Ⓚ0921

[also prefix] **dark-colored**
　暗色 あんしょく dark color
　暗赤色 あんせきしょく dark red

濃 ▷dark
ノウ こ(い)   Ⓚ0697

[also prefix] **dark-colored, deep, rich**
　濃紺 のうこん dark blue, navy blue
　濃グレー のうぐれー dark gray
　濃淡 のうたん light and shade
　濃緑色 のうりょくしょく dark green

深 ▷deep
シン ふか(い) -ぶか(い) ふか(まる)
ふか(める)   Ⓚ0480

[also prefix] **deep-colored, dark**
　深緑 しんりょく dark [deep] green
　深紅色 しんこうしょく deep crimson, scarlet

date
日 忌

日 ▷date
ニチ ジツ ひ -び -か   Ⓚ2606

(day on which something occurs) **date, day, anniversary**
　日時 にちじ date, time
　期日 きじつ (fixed) date, due date
　生年月日 せいねんがっぴ date of birth
　命日 めいにち anniversary of death

忌 ▷death anniversary
キ い(む) い(み) い(まわしい)   Ⓚ1889

[also suffix] **death anniversary**
　忌日 きにち death anniversary
　一周忌 いっしゅうき first anniversary of death
　桜桃忌 おうとうき Death Anniversary of Dazai
　　Osamu

dawn →MORNING AND DAWN

days
日 曜 昼 旦 朔 晦

日 ▷day
ニチ ジツ ひ -び -か   Ⓚ2606

ⓐ (period of light) **day**
ⓑ [also suffix] (24-hour period) **day, daily**
ⓒ **counter for days**
ⓓ **suffix for days of the month**
　a 日夜 にちや day and night
　　日中 にっちゅう during the day
　b 日給 にっきゅう daily wage
　　日数 にっすう number of days
　　日運動 にちうんどう daily motion
　　日用品 にちようひん daily necessities
　　日刊の にっかんの published daily
　　毎日 まいにち every day
　　今日 こんにち today, these days
　　一日 いちにち a day; all day
　　本日 ほんじつ today
　　平日 へいじつ weekday
　　太陽日 たいようじつ solar day
　c 五十日 ごじゅうにち 50 days
　d 十一月三十日 じゅういちがつさんじゅうにち November 30

曜 ▷day of the week
ヨウ   Ⓚ1014

day of the week, -day
- 曜日 ようび day of the week
- 七曜 しちよう seven days of the week; [archaic] sun, moon and five planets
- 日曜日 にちようび Sunday
- 木曜日 もくようび Thursday
- 水曜日 すいようび Wednesday
- 七曜表 しちようひょう calendar

昼 ▷daytime
チュウ ひる   Ⓚ2668

[original meaning] **daytime**
- 昼間 ちゅうかん daytime, day
- 昼夜 ちゅうや day and night

旦 ▷first day
タン ダン   Ⓚ2119

first day, day
- 元旦 がんたん New Year's Day
- 月旦 げったん criticism, comment; [rare] first day of the month

朔 ▷first day of the lunar month
サク ついたち   Ⓚ1209

first day of the lunar month
- 朔日 さくじつ(=ついたち) [usu. 一日] first day of the lunar month

晦 ▷last day of the lunar month
カイ くら(ます) つごもり   Ⓚ0864

[also 晦日] **last day of the lunar month**

days of the week
日 月 火 水 木 金 土

日 ▷Sunday
ニチ ジツ ひ -び -か   Ⓚ2606

Sunday
- 日曜(日) にちよう(び) Sunday
- 土日 どにち Saturday and Sunday, weekend

月 ▷Monday
ゲツ ガツ つき   Ⓚ2556

Monday
- 月曜(日) げつよう(び) Monday
- 月水金 げっすいきん Mondays, Wednesdays and Fridays

火 ▷Tuesday
カ ひ -び ほ-   Ⓚ2911

Tuesday
- 火曜(日) かよう(び) Tuesday

水 ▷Wednesday
スイ みず   Ⓚ0003

Wednesday
- 水曜(日) すいよう(び) Wednesday
- 月水金 げっすいきん Mondays, Wednesdays and Fridays

木 ▷Thursday
ボク モク き こ-   Ⓚ2901

Thursday
- 木曜(日) もくよう(び) Thursday
- 火木 かもく Tuesdays and Thursdays

金 ▷Friday
キン コン かね かな- -がね   Ⓚ1771

Friday
- 金曜(日) きんよう(び) Friday
- 月金 げつきん(=げっきん) Mondays and Fridays

土 ▷Saturday
ド ト つち   Ⓚ2875

Saturday
- 土曜(日) どよう(び) Saturday
- 土日 どにち Saturday and Sunday, weekend

dead
故 亡

故 ▷the late
コ ゆえ   Ⓚ1056

[prefix] **the late, deceased**
- 故川田氏 こかわだし the late Mr. Kawada
- 故人 こじん the deceased

亡 ▷deceased
ボウ モウ な(い) な(き)-   Ⓚ2874

[also prefix] **deceased, one's late**
- 亡父 ぼうふ deceased father
- 亡妻 ぼうさい deceased wife
- 亡者 もうじゃ the dead
- 亡祖父 ぼうそふ deceased [one's late] grandfather

deal with
扱　処　辦　措　置

扱 ▷handle
あつか(う) あつか(い)   Ⓚ0189

(deal with) **handle (a matter), deal with, treat, manage**
- 問題を扱う もんだいをあつかう deal with [handle] a matter
- 取り扱う とりあつかう handle, deal with, treat; deal in; handle, manipulate, operate; conduct; accept, take in
- 薬を扱う くすりをあつかう deal in medicines

処 ▷deal with
ショ   Ⓚ2609

deal with, dispose of, manage, cope with, treat
- 処理する しょりする manage, deal with, dispose of; process, treat
- 処置 しょち disposal, measure, treatment
- 処方箋 しょほうせん prescription
- 処分 しょぶん disposal, measure; punishment
- 対処する たいしょする cope [deal] with, meet
- 善処する ぜんしょする make the best of

辦 ▷dispose of
ベン

[now replaced by 弁] [original meaning] **dispose of, manage, attend to**
- 合辦 ごうべん joint management [venture]

措 ▷dispose of
ソ   Ⓚ0463

(deal with) **dispose of, take steps, manage**
- 措置 そち measure, step, action

置 ▷take proper steps
チ お(く) -お(き)   Ⓚ2262

take proper steps, adopt measures, deal with
- 処置する しょちする dispose of, deal with
- 措置 そち measure, step, action

decay
朽　腐　枯　萎　錆

朽 ▷decay
キュウ く(ちる)   Ⓚ0727

[original meaning] **decay, rot**

朽廃する きゅうはいする decay, be dilapidated [ruined]
- 腐朽 ふきゅう deterioration, decay
- 老朽 ろうきゅう superannuation, decrepitude
- 不朽の ふきゅうの immortal, undecaying, eternal

腐 ▷rot
フ くさ(る) くさ(れる) くさ(れ) くさ(らす)   Ⓚ2729

[original meaning] **rot, decay, decompose; corrode**
- 腐敗する ふはいする rot, decay; become corrupt
- 腐朽 ふきゅう deterioration, decay
- 腐食 ふしょく corrosion; erosion
- 防腐 ぼうふ preservation from decay
- 豆腐 とうふ tofu (Japanese bean curd)

枯 ▷wither
コ か(れる) か(らす)   Ⓚ0801

(of plants) (dry up and die) **wither, die**
- 枯死 こし withering, dying

萎 ▷wither
イ な(える)   Ⓚ1996

[now also 委] [original meaning] **wither, weaken, decline**
- 萎縮 いしゅく withering, atrophy; being crestfallen
- 萎黄病 いおうびょう greensickness, chlorosis
- 陰萎 いんい impotence

錆 ▷rust
セイ さび さ(びる)   Ⓚ1556

rust; patina
- 防錆 ぼうせい anti-rust
- 不錆鋼 ふせいこう stainless steel

deceive
欺　騙　詐　惑　拐　偽　詭

欺 ▷deceive
ギ あざむ(く)   Ⓚ1519

[original meaning] **deceive, cheat, swindle**
- 欺瞞 ぎまん deception, imposition
- 詐欺 さぎ swindle, fraud

騙 ▷deceive
ヘン だま(す) かた(る)

deceive, cheat, swindle, defraud
- 騙取 へんしゅ swindling
- 欺騙 ぎへん deception

詐 ▷swindle
サ   Ⓚ1362

swindle, defraud, falsify, deceive; feign, pretend
- 詐欺 さぎ swindle, fraud
- 詐取 さしゅ fraud, swindle
- 詐称 さしょう misrepresentation, false statement

惑 ▷mislead
ワク まど(う)   Ⓚ2427

mislead, lead astray, entice
- 魅惑 みわく fascination, enchantment, charm
- 誘惑 ゆうわく temptation, seduction
- 眩惑 げんわく dazzle, daze, bewilderment

拐 ▷defraud
カイ   Ⓚ0272

defraud, swindle, abscond
- 拐帯 かいたい abscondence with money

偽 ▷falsify
ギ いつわ(る) にせ   Ⓚ0114

[original meaning] **falsify, forge, deceive**
- 偽造 ぎぞう forgery, fabrication
- 偽証 ぎしょう perjury

詭 ▷trick
キ

[now also 奇] [original meaning] **trick, cheat, deceive, defraud**
- 詭計 きけい artifice, trick
- 詭弁 きべん sophism, sophistry

decide
決   断   定

決 ▷decide
ケツ き(める) -ぎ(め) き(まる)   Ⓚ0233

(make up one's mind) **decide, determine, fix**
- 決定 けってい decision, settlement, conclusion
- 決意 けつい resolution, determination
- 決心 けっしん determination, resolution, decision
- 解決 かいけつ solution, settlement

断 ▷resolve
ダン た(つ) ことわ(る)   Ⓚ1355

(make a firm decision or judgment) **resolve, decide, conclude**
- 断定 だんてい decision, conclusion
- 断言 だんげん (positive) assertion, declaration
- 断罪 だんざい judgment of a crime

- 決断 けつだん decision, determination, resolution
- 判断 はんだん judgment, decision
- 診断 しんだん diagnosis
- 予断 よだん prediction, foregone conclusion

定 ▷fix
テイ ジョウ さだ(める) さだ(まる) さだ(か)   Ⓚ1916

fix, determine, decide, set, settle
- 決定 けってい decision, settlement, conclusion
- 断定 だんてい decision, conclusion
- 一定する いっていする fix, define, unify
- 確定する かくていする make a definite decision, decide upon; be decided
- 予定 よてい schedule, plan, prearrangement; expectation; estimate
- 否定 ひてい denial, negation
- 指定 してい designation, appointment
- 勘定 かんじょう calculation; account, settlement of accounts

decorate
飾   粧   粉   装

飾 ▷decorate
ショク かざ(る) かざ(り)   Ⓚ1530

ⓐ [original meaning] **decorate, adorn, ornament, embellish**
ⓑ **decoration, ornament**
- a 装飾する そうしょくする ornament, adorn, decorate
- 修飾する しゅうしょくする decorate, ornament; *gram* modify
- 電飾 でんしょく decorative illumination
- 満艦飾の船 まんかんしょくのふね full dress ship
- b 服飾 ふくしょく dress and its ornaments

粧 ▷apply makeup
ショウ   Ⓚ1232

[original meaning] **apply makeup [cosmetics], make up, adorn oneself**
- 化粧する けしょうする make up, put on makeup
- 美粧院 びしょういん beauty shop

粉 ▷apply face powder
フン こ こな   Ⓚ1186

apply face powder, make up
- 粉飾 ふんしょく embellishment, makeup

装 ▷dress
ソウ ショウ よそお(う)   Ⓚ2344

(decorate) **dress (up), ornament, trim**

装飾する そうしょくする ornament, adorn, decorate
新装 しんそう refurbishment, redecoration
改装 かいそう remodeling, refurbishing

decrease

減 耗 削 縮 落 蝕

減 ▷decrease
ゲン へ(る) へ(らす)   Ⓚ0548

ⓐ [original meaning] (grow or cause to grow less) **decrease, reduce, lessen**
ⓑ [also suffix] **decrease, reduction, fall**

a 減少する げんしょうする decrease, reduce, lessen
減税 げんぜい reduction of taxes, tax cut
減速 げんそく speed reduction
減配 げんぱい reduction in a dividend; smaller ration
減点 げんてん demerit mark
b 削減 さくげん curtailment, reduction
10%減 じゅっぱーせんとげん decrease of 10 percent

耗 ▷wear away
モウ コウ   Ⓚ1199

wear away, wear out, use up, consume
摩耗する まもうする wear away, wear out
減耗 げんもう natural decrease
消耗する しょうもうする consume, exhaust, use up
損耗する そんもう(=そんこう)する wear out, be wasted, be worn out

削 ▷cut down
サク けず(る)   Ⓚ1316

cut down, whittle down, curtail
削減 さくげん curtailment, reduction

縮 ▷shrink
シュク ちぢ(む) ちぢ(まる) ちぢ(める)
ちぢ(れる) ちぢ(らす)   Ⓚ1290

(make or become smaller) **shrink, reduce, shorten**
縮小 しゅくしょう reduction, curtailment, cut
縮減する しゅくげんする reduce, diminish
軍縮 ぐんしゅく reduction of armaments
濃縮する のうしゅくする concentrate

落 ▷fall
ラク お(ちる) お(ち) お(とす)   Ⓚ2019

ⓐ (esp. of stock prices)
ⓑ (become less) **fall, drop, decline**
ⓒ (reduction in value) **fall, drop**

a 低落する ていらくする fall, depreciate, go down

下落 げらく fall, drop, decline; deterioration
ab 急落 きゅうらく sudden drop [fall], steep decline
暴落 ぼうらく slump, crash, heavy decline (in prices)

蝕 ▷erode
ショク むしば(む)

[original meaning] (be eaten as if by worms) **erode, corrode**
浸蝕 しんしょく erosion, corrosion
腐蝕 ふしょく corrosion
侵蝕 しんしょく infringement, violation

degenerate

落 衰 頽 堕 綻 破

落 ▷fall
ラク お(ちる) お(ち) お(とす)   Ⓚ2019

(decline in status) **fall, decline, decay**
落魄 らくはく straitened [reduced] circumstances
堕落 だらく degeneration, corruption, decadence
没落 ぼつらく ruin, fall, collapse

衰 ▷decline
スイ おとろ(える)   Ⓚ1806

decline, fall into decay, degenerate, weaken, emaciate
衰退 すいたい decline, decay, degeneration
衰弱する すいじゃくする weaken, lose vigor
減衰する げんすいする damp, be attenuated
老衰 ろうすい senility
盛衰 せいすい ups and downs, rise and fall, prosperity and decline

頽 ▷decline
タイ

[now also 退] **decline, decay**
頽勢 たいせい one's declining fortunes, decay
頽廃 たいはい degeneration, decadence, deterioration
頽唐 たいとう decadence, decline
頽齢 たいれい declining years
衰頽 すいたい decline, decay, degeneration

堕 ▷degenerate
ダ   Ⓚ2456

degenerate, become degraded into, sink into evil ways, descend to
堕落 だらく degeneration, corruption, decadence
堕罪 だざい sinking into sin

綻 ▷unravel
タン ほころ(びる) ほころ(ぶ) Ⓚ1263

unravel, come apart, fall apart
破綻 はたん failure, rupture; bankruptcy

破 ▷break down
ハ やぶ(る) やぶ(れる) Ⓚ1064

break down, go to pieces, go broke
破局 はきょく collapse, catastrophe
破綻 はたん failure, rupture; bankruptcy
破産する はさんする go bankrupt, go broke

degree
程　度　分

程 ▷extent
テイ ほど Ⓚ1100

extent, degree, range, limit
程度 ていど degree, extent, standard

度 ▷degree
ド ト タク たび Ⓚ2670

[also suffix] **degree, extent**
度合 どあい degree, extent, rate
程度 ていど degree, extent, standard
高度 こうど altitude, height; high degree
震度 しんど seismic intensity
限度 げんど limit, bounds
速度 そくど speed, velocity
精度 せいど precision, accuracy
透明度 とうめいど transparency, degree of clearness
知名度 ちめいど publicity

分 ▷relative degree
ブン フン ブ わ(ける) わ(け) わ(かれる)
わ(かる) わ(かつ) Ⓚ1713

relative degree, extent, rate
十分(=充分)な じゅうぶんな full, enough, sufficient; plentiful
多分 たぶん probably, perhaps, maybe
幾分 いくぶん partially, somewhat, in a way
随分 ずいぶん extremely, considerably ("as much as one pleases")
存分に ぞんぶんに to one's heart's content, freely

delay →BE LATE AND DELAY

deliver →TRANSMIT AND DELIVER

dense
濃　密

濃 ▷thick (concentrated)
ノウ こ(い) Ⓚ0697

[also prefix] **thick, concentrated, dense, heavy**
濃厚な のうこうな thick, dense, heavy, rich
濃度 のうど density
濃縮 のうしゅく concentration
濃霧 のうむ dense [thick] fog
濃密な のうみつな thick; crowded
濃硫酸 のうりゅうさん concentrated sulfuric acid

密 ▷close
ミツ Ⓚ1984

(closely crowded) **close, dense, thick, compact, tight**
密集する みっしゅうする crowd, swarm, aggregate densely
密林 みつりん close thicket, dense forest, jungle
密度 みつど density
密室 みっしつ secret room [chamber]; locked room
過密な かみつな overcrowded

depressed →SAD AND DEPRESSED

descend and fall
落　墜　降　下　倒

落 ▷fall
ラク お(ちる) お(ち) お(とす) Ⓚ2019

ⓐ [original meaning] fall, fall off, drop, sink
ⓑ let fall, drop
a 落下 らっか fall, drop, descent
落馬する らくばする fall from a horse
落日 らくじつ setting sun
墜落する ついらくする fall, drop; crash
b 落球する らっきゅうする fail to catch a ball
落涙する らくるいする shed tears
落盤 らくばん cave-in

墜 ▷drop down
ツイ Ⓚ2506

ⓐ [original meaning] (fall suddenly from a great height)
drop down, drop, fall down, crash down
ⓑ cause to drop down, drop
a 墜落 ついらく fall, crash
墜死する ついしする fall to one's death (as from a cliff)
b 撃墜する げきついする shoot down

降 ▷descend
コウ お(りる) お(ろす) ふ(る)
ふ(り)　　　　　　　　　　Ⓚ0414

[original meaning] **descend, fall, come down, drop**
降下する こうかする descend, fall, drop
滑降 かっこう descent (in skiing)
昇降する しょうこうする ascend and descend, go up and down
沈降する ちんこうする precipitate, subside

下 ▷go down
カ ゲ した しも もと さ(げる) さ(がる)
くだ(る) くだ(り) くだ(す) くだ(さる)
お(ろす) お(りる)　　　　　　Ⓚ2862

(proceed to or as if to a lower place) **go down, descend, drop, sink**
下降する かこうする descend, go down; subside
下山する げざんする descend a mountain; leave a temple
落下する らっかする fall, drop, descend
低下する ていかする fall, sink, lower, go down
南下する なんかする go down south

倒 ▷topple
トウ たお(れる) -だお(れ)
たお(す)　　　　　　　　　　Ⓚ0106

ⓐ **topple, tumble down, fall over, fall, collapse**
ⓑ **cause to topple, overturn, overthrow, knock down**
a 倒木 とうぼく fallen tree
倒壊する とうかいする collapse, be destroyed, crumble
卒倒する そっとうする faint, fall unconscious, swoon
転倒する てんとうする tumble, fall down; invert, reverse; upset
b 倒産 とうさん insolvency, bankruptcy; breech birth
倒閣する とうかくする overthrow the cabinet
倒幕 とうばく overthrowing the shogunate
打倒する だとうする overthrow, knock down, defeat

descendant
孫　　胤　　末

孫 ▷grandchild, descendant
ソン まご　　　　　　　　　　Ⓚ0370

❶ [original meaning] **grandchild**
皇孫 こうそん Imperial grandchild
嫡孫 ちゃくそん heir of the eldest son
王孫 おうそん royal grandson

❷ **descendant**
子孫 しそん descendant, offspring
天孫 てんそん descendant of a god

胤 ▷progeny
イン たね　　　　　　　　　　Ⓚ0008

progeny, descendant, posterity
落胤 らくいん illegitimate child, love child
後胤 こういん descendant, scion
皇胤 こういん [archaic] Imperial descendant [posterity]

末 ▷posterity
マツ バツ すえ　　　　　　　Ⓚ2940

posterity, descendants
末裔 まつえい descendant, offspring
末代 まつだい all generations, all ages to come

describe
叙　　抒　　描　　写

叙 ▷describe
ジョ　　　　　　　　　　　　Ⓚ1314

[formerly also 抒] **describe, narrate, depict, explain**
叙述 じょじゅつ description, depiction
叙説 じょせつ explanation, interpretation
叙情詩 じょじょうし lyric poem [poetry]
叙事 じょじ narration, description
自叙伝 じじょでん autobiography
平叙文 へいじょぶん declarative sentence

抒 ▷describe
ジョ

[now usu. 叙] **describe, narrate, depict, explain**
抒情 じょじょう description of feelings, lyricism
抒情詩 じょじょうし lyric poem [poetry]

描 ▷depict
ビョウ えが(く) か(く)　　　Ⓚ0445

(represent in words) **depict, describe**
描写 びょうしゃ depiction, description; portrayal; drawing
描出 びょうしゅつ depiction, description; portrayal; drawing

写 ▷portray
シャ うつ(す) うつ(る)　　　Ⓚ1726

(depict in pictures or words) **portray, picture, depict, describe**
写真 しゃしん photograph

写実 しゃじつ objective description; realism
描写 びょうしゃ depiction, description; portrayal; drawing

desire →WISH AND DESIRE

destroy

滅 毀 亡 消 剿

 滅 ▷**destroy**
メツ ほろ(びる) ほろ(ぶ)
ほろ(ぼす) Ⓚ0606

ⓐ **destroy, ruin, annihilate, wipe out**
ⓑ **meet with destruction, go to ruin, cease to exist**

ⓐ 滅菌 めっきん sterilization
撃滅する げきめつする destroy, exterminate
絶滅 ぜつめつ extermination, eradication; extinction

ⓑ 滅亡 めつぼう ruin, downfall
消滅 しょうめつ extinction, disappearance
不滅 ふめつ immortality, indestructibility, imperishability
全滅 ぜんめつ annihilation, total destruction
潰滅(=壊滅) かいめつ destruction, annihilation
死滅 しめつ extinction, annihilation, destruction
自滅 じめつ natural decay; self-destruction, self-ruin
破滅 はめつ ruin, destruction, wreck, collapse, downfall

毀 ▷**destroy**
キ Ⓚ1592

[now also 棄] [original meaning] **destroy, ruin, damage**
毀棄する ききする destroy, demolish, damage
毀傷 きしょう injury, damage
名誉毀損 めいよきそん libel, defamation, slander
破毀する はきする reverse (the original judgment)

亡 ▷**perish**
ボウ モウ な(い) な(き)- Ⓚ2874

[original meaning] (become destroyed) **perish, go to ruin, cease to exist**
亡国 ぼうこく ruined country, national ruin
滅亡する めつぼうする go to ruin, fall
衰亡 すいぼう ruin, fall, collapse

消 ▷**extinguish**
ショウ き(える) け(す) Ⓚ0402

(wipe out of existence) **extinguish, eliminate, remove from, obliterate**
消化 しょうか digestion; assimilation; consumption
消毒 しょうどく disinfection, sterilization

消音 しょうおん silencing (a machine)
消臭剤 しょうしゅうざい deodorant
消却する しょうきゃくする efface; erase
消磁 しょうじ demagnetization
解消する かいしょうする liquidate, annul, solve; be liquidated, be solved
抹消する まっしょうする erase, strike out

剿 ▷**exterminate**
ソウ ショウ

[now replaced by 掃] **exterminate, wipe out**
剿滅する そうめつする wipe out, annihilate

detailed

詳 細 緻 密 精

 詳 ▷**detailed**
ショウ くわ(しい) Ⓚ1386

detailed, minute, full
詳細 しょうさい details, particulars
詳密な しょうみつな minute, detailed, elaborate
詳察 しょうさつ careful observation

細 ▷**minute**
サイ ほそ(い) ほそ(る) こま(か)
こま(かい) Ⓚ1220

(detailed) **minute, detailed, close, elaborate**
細部 さいぶ details, particulars
細心 さいしん carefulness, discretion
細工 さいく work, craftsmanship; artifice, tactics
詳細 しょうさい details, particulars
明細 めいさい particulars, details, specifics
精細な せいさいな detailed, minute, exact

緻 ▷**minute**
チ Ⓚ1283

minute, detailed, elaborate, careful, fine
緻密な ちみつな minute, close, elaborate, exact
精緻な せいちな minute, subtle, delicate, exquisite
細緻な さいちな minute, delicate, meticulous
巧緻な こうちな elaborate, exquisite, detailed

 密 ▷**close**
ミツ Ⓚ1984

(characterized by exacting minuteness) **close, minute, elaborate, careful**
精密 せいみつ precision, accuracy, minuteness
厳密な げんみつな strict, precise, rigid, exact
綿密な めんみつな close, minute, detailed
緻密な ちみつな minute, close, elaborate, exact

detailed

精 ▷meticulous
セイ ショウ   Ⓚ1248

meticulous, careful, elaborate, precise, exact, detailed, fine

精査 せいさ minute investigation, close inspection, careful examination
精選 せいせん careful selection
精緻な せいちな minute, subtle, delicate, exquisite
精巧な せいこうな elaborate, exquisite, ingenious
精密 せいみつ precision, accuracy, minuteness
精度 せいど precision, accuracy
精算 せいさん exact calculation; settlement of accounts
精通する せいつうする be well versed in, have thorough knowledge of

detect
検   感   嗅

検 ▷detect
ケン   Ⓚ0898

detect, search, measure

検索する けんさくする look up (a word in a dictionary), search for, refer to
検出する けんしゅつする detect, find
検温 けんおん thermometry
検波 けんぱ detection, demodulation
検流計 けんりゅうけい galvanometer

感 ▷sense
カン   Ⓚ2468

(detect) **sense, be sensitive to**

感光板 かんこうばん sensitive plate
感熱剤 かんねつざい heat sensitizer

嗅 ▷smell
キュウ か(ぐ)   Ⓚ0576

smell, scent, sniff

嗅覚 きゅうかく sense of smell
嗅神経 きゅうしんけい olfactory nerve

deviate
逸   外

逸 ▷deviate
イツ   Ⓚ2688

deviate from the norm, swerve from a course

逸脱 いつだつ deviation, departure from the norm

放逸 ほういつ self-indulgence, looseness, dissoluteness

外 ▷miss
ガイ ゲ そと ほか はず(す) はず(れる)   Ⓚ0163

miss, go wide, fail

外れ はずれ end, verge; miss, failure
並外れの なみはずれの out of the ordinary, far above the average

diagram
表   図

表 ▷table
ヒョウ おもて あらわ(す) あらわ(れる)   Ⓚ2151

table, chart, diagram, schedule, tabular form

図表 ずひょう chart, diagram
年表 ねんぴょう chronological table
時刻表 じこくひょう timetable, schedule
予定表 よていひょう schedule

図 ▷drawing
ズ ト はか(る)   Ⓚ2645

drawing, plan, diagram, figure, illustration, picture

図面 ずめん drawing, plan, map, sketch
図形 ずけい figure, diagram
図表 ずひょう chart, diagram
図鑑 ずかん picture [illustrated] book
図書 としょ books
図書室 としょしつ library
図示 ずし illustration, graphic(al) representation
設計図 せっけいず plan, blueprint

die
死   萎   没   亡   殉
歿   去   逝   斃   枯

死 ▷die
シ し(ぬ) し(に)-   Ⓚ2952

ⓐ [original meaning] **die, perish, come to an end**
ⓑ [also suffix] **death, demise**

ⓐ 死亡 しぼう death
死刑 しけい capital punishment, death penalty
死後 しご after one's death
死去 しきょ death, passing away

b 戦死する せんしする die in battle
即死 そくし instant death, death on the spot
焼死 しょうし death by fire
中毒死 ちゅうどくし death from poisoning

萎 ▷**wither**
イ な(える)   ⓚ1996

[now also 委] [original meaning] **wither, weaken, decline**
萎縮 いしゅく withering, atrophy; being crestfallen
萎黄病 いおうびょう greensickness, chlorosis
陰萎 いんい impotence

没 ▷**die**
ボツ   ⓚ0230

[formerly also 歿] **die, perish**
没後 ぼつご after one's death
没年 ぼつねん year of death
戦没する せんぼつする be killed in action

亡 ▷**decease**
ボウ モウ な(い) な(き)-   ⓚ2874

decease, die, pass away, perish
亡霊 ぼうれい departed spirit, ghost
死亡する しぼうする die
存亡 そんぼう destiny; life or death
未亡人 みぼうじん widow, widowed lady

殉 ▷**die a martyr**
ジュン   ⓚ0849

die a martyr, sacrifice oneself, die for a cause
殉教 じゅんきょう martyrdom
殉職 じゅんしょく dying at one's post
殉国 じゅんこく dying for one's country
殉難者 じゅんなんしゃ martyr, victim

歿 ▷**die**
ボツ

[now replaced by 没] [original meaning] **die, perish**
歿後 ぼつご after one's death
戦歿する せんぼつする be killed in action
死歿 しぼつ death, demise
病歿 びょうぼつ death from sickness

去 ▷**pass away**
キョ コ さ(る)   ⓚ1850

(go away from this world) **pass away, die**
逝去 せいきょ death
死去する しきょする die, pass away

逝 ▷**depart this life**
セイ ゆ(く) い(く)   ⓚ2673

depart this life, pass away, die suddenly

逝去する せいきょする pass away, die
急逝する きゅうせいする die suddenly
長逝 ちょうせい death, passing

斃 ▷**fall down dead**
ヘイ たお(す) たお(れる)

[original meaning] **fall down dead, perish, die**
斃死する へいしする fall dead, perish

枯 ▷**wither**
コ か(れる) か(らす)   ⓚ0801

(of plants) (dry up and die) **wither, die**
枯死 こし withering, dying

difference →DIFFERING AND DIFFERENCE

differing and difference
違 異 差

違 ▷**differ**
イ ちが(う) ちが(い) ちが(える)   ⓚ2716

differ, be different
違和感 いわかん feeling of being out of place, incongruity
相違 そうい difference, disparity

異 ▷**different**
イ こと こと(なる)   ⓚ2241

[original meaning] (not alike) **different, unlike; opposite**
異議 いぎ objection, complaint
異性 いせい opposite sex
異動 いどう shifting, reshuffle
異文化 いぶんか different cultures
差異 さい difference, disparity

差 ▷**difference**
サ さ(す) さ(し)   ⓚ2821

[also suffix]
❶ [original meaning] **difference, discrepancy, inequality, differential**
❷ (quantitative) **difference;** *math* **remainder**
a 差異 さい difference, disparity
差別 さべつ discrimination
大差 たいさ big difference
格差 かくさ difference in quality [price]
個人差 こじんさ individual differences
b 差額 さがく difference (in prices), balance
時差 じさ time difference

dig

掘 鑿 削 穿

掘 ▷dig
クツ ほ(る) -ほ(り)   Ⓚ0454

ⓐ [original meaning] **dig, excavate**
ⓑ **dig out, dig up, excavate**
  ₐ 掘削する くっさくする dig out, excavate
    採掘 さいくつ mining
    試掘 しくつ prospecting, trial digging
  ᵦ 掘進する くっしんする excavate, tunnel
    発掘する はっくつする dig, excavate

鑿 ▷excavate
サク のみ

[now also 削] **excavate, drill, bore, dig**
  鑿岩機 さくがんき rock drill
  鑿井 さくせい well drilling
  開鑿 かいさく excavation, cutting, digging
  掘鑿する くっさくする dig out, excavate
  穿鑿する せんさくする scrutinize, dig into

削 ▷excavate
サク けず(る)   Ⓚ1316

[formerly 鑿] (cut a hole in) **excavate, drill**
  削岩機 さくがんき rock drill
  削井 さくせい well drilling
  掘削する くっさくする dig out, excavate
  開削 かいさく excavation, cutting, digging

穿 ▷drill
セン は(く) うが(つ) ほじく(る)
ほじ(る)   Ⓚ1941

[original meaning] **drill, bore, pierce**
  穿孔 せんこう perforation, punching; rupture
  穿鑿する せんさくする scrutinize, dig into
  穿刺 せんし puncture, stab
  穿通 せんつう penetration
  穿山甲 せんざんこう pangolin

dignified

荘 威 儼 厳 粛

荘 ▷dignified
ソウ   Ⓚ1954

dignified, solemn, grave, sublime
  荘厳な そうごんな solemn, sublime
  荘重な そうちょうな solemn, grave, impressive

威 ▷dignified
イ   Ⓚ2993

dignified, majestic, imposing
  威厳 いげん solemn dignity
  威風 いふう majesty, dignity
  威容 いよう dignified [majestic] appearance
  威儀 いぎ dignity, dignified manner
  威信 いしん prestige, dignity, authority

儼 ▷solemn
ゲン

[now replaced by 厳] **solemn, majestic, dignified-looking**
  儼然たる げんぜんたる solemn, grave, majestic, stern

厳 ▷solemn
ゲン ゴン おごそ(か) きび(しい)   Ⓚ2804

[formerly also 儼] **solemn, grave, awe-inspiring, dignified**
  厳然たる げんぜんたる solemn, grave, majestic, stern
  厳粛な げんしゅくな grave, solemn, austere
  威厳 いげん solemn dignity
  謹厳な きんげんな stern, grave, solemn
  荘厳な そうごんな solemn, sublime

粛 ▷solemnly
シュク   Ⓚ2996

solemnly, with profound awe; reverently, respectfully
  粛然と しゅくぜんと quietly, silently; solemnly; reverently
  厳粛な げんしゅくな grave, solemn, austere

direct and supervise

制 理 経 管 轄 掌
監 督 司 宰 営

制 ▷control
セイ   Ⓚ1170

(exercise authority) **control, regulate, dominate, command**
  制海権 せいかいけん command of the sea, naval supremacy
  管制塔 かんせいとう control tower
  統制する とうせいする control, regulate
  規制する きせいする regulate, control

理 ▷manage
リ   Ⓚ0881

manage, run
- 理事 りじ director, trustee
- 管理する かんりする administer, supervise, manage, exercise control [jurisdiction] over
- 処理する しょりする manage, deal with, dispose of; process, treat
- 総理大臣 そうりだいじん prime minister
- 代理 だいり representation; agency; proxy, deputy
- 料理する りょうりする cook; handle, manage
- 受理する じゅりする accept (a report)

経 ▷manage
ケイ キョウ へ(る) た(つ)   Ⓚ1218

manage (the affairs of an organization or a state), administer
- 経世 けいせい administration, government, conduct of state affairs
- 経理 けいり accounting
- 経済 けいざい economy, economics
- 経済的 けいざいてき economical, economic
- 経営 けいえい management

管 ▷exercise control
カン くだ   Ⓚ2357

exercise control [jurisdiction] over, control, manage, administer, take charge of
- 管理する かんりする administer, supervise, manage, exercise control [jurisdiction] over
- 管轄 かんかつ jurisdiction, control
- 管制 かんせい control
- 保管する ほかんする take custody [charge] of, keep
- 移管 いかん transfer of control [jurisdiction]
- 選管 せんかん Election Administration Commission

轄 ▷exercise jurisdiction over
カツ   Ⓚ1468

exercise [have] jurisdiction over, control, supervise, administer
- 統轄 とうかつ general control, control and jurisdiction
- 管轄 かんかつ jurisdiction, control
- 直轄 ちょっかつ direct jurisdiction [control], immediate supervision
- 分轄 ぶんかつ separate control [jurisdiction]
- 所轄 しょかつ jurisdiction

掌 ▷take charge of
ショウ   Ⓚ2256

 take charge of, be in charge of, supervise
 charge, duties
- a 掌理する しょうりする take charge of, preside over, manage

- 職掌 しょくしょう office, function
- 車掌 しゃしょう conductor
- b 分掌 ぶんしょう division of duties
- 管掌 かんしょう taking charge, management

監 ▷oversee
カン   Ⓚ2483

oversee, supervise, overlook, watch over, superintend, inspect
- 監督する かんとくする supervise, superintend; direct (a film)
- 監視する かんしする watch, keep under observation, exercise surveillance
- 監査 かんさ inspection; inspector, supervisor
- 監修 かんしゅう (editorial) supervision

督 ▷supervise
トク   Ⓚ2437

[original meaning] **supervise, oversee, superintend**
- 督学官 とくがくかん school inspector
- 監督 かんとく supervision, superintendence; supervisor; film director

司 ▷officiate
シ   Ⓚ2538

[original meaning] **officiate, administer, take charge of, manage**
- 司法 しほう administration of justice
- 司書 ししょ librarian
- 司祭 しさい Catholic priest, rabbi
- 司直 しちょく administration of justice; judicial authorities
- 司令官 しれいかん commander
- 司会する しかいする preside at, take the chair, officiate; emcee (a show)

宰 ▷preside
サイ   Ⓚ1965

preside (over), superintend, supervise, manage
- 宰領 さいりょう supervision, management; supervisor, superintendent
- 主宰する しゅさいする preside (over), superintend, supervise

営 ▷manage
エイ いとな(む)   Ⓚ2257

 manage (the affairs of an organization), conduct, administer, operate, run, engage in
ⓑ [also suffix] **managed by, operated by**
- a 営業する えいぎょうする conduct [do] business, trade in
- 営林 えいりん forest management
- 経営する けいえいする manage (a firm), conduct (a business)

       direct and supervise

運営する うんえいする operate, manage

b 公営 こうえい public management
名古屋市営 なごやしえい managed by the Nagoya Municipality

direction
方　　　向

方 ▷**direction**
ホウ かた -がた -なた　　　Ⓚ1709

[original meaning] **direction, bearing, orientation**
方向 ほうこう direction, bearing; course
方位 ほうい direction, bearing
四方 しほう all directions, cardinal points
前方 ぜんぽう front
左方に さほうに to the left, on the left side
北方 ほっぽう north, northward; northern district
快方に向かう かいほうにむかう get better, improve, convalesce
途方に暮れる とほうにくれる be at a loss, be puzzled

向 ▷**direction**
コウ む(く) む(き) む(ける) -む(け)
む(かう) む(こう)　　　Ⓚ2627

direction, orientation
方向 ほうこう direction, bearing; course
転向 てんこう turn, conversion, about-face
指向する しこうする point to
風向 ふうこう direction of the wind
偏向 へんこう deviation, deflection

direction indicators
至行向迄以自来而

至 ▷**to**
シ いた(る)　　　Ⓚ1869

to, as far as
至徳島 しとくしま to Tokushima
乃至 ないし from…to…, between…and…; or

行 ▷**bound for**
コウ ギョウ アン い(く) ゆ(く) -ゆ(き)
-い(き) おこな(う)　　　Ⓚ0187

[suffix] **bound for, for**
東京行きの列車 とうきょうゆきのれっしゃ train (bound) for Tokyo

向 ▷**(bound) for**
コウ む(く) む(き) む(ける) -む(け)
む(かう) む(こう)　　　Ⓚ2627

[suffix] **(bound) for, meant for**
国内向けの こくないむけの for domestic use

迄 ▷**up to**
キツ まで　　　Ⓚ2757

ⓐ (as far as a designated place) **up to, as far as**
ⓑ (as far as a designated time) **up to, till, until, to**
a 京都迄の切符 きょうとまでのきっぷ ticket to Kyoto
b 今迄 いままで till now, so far, up to the present
百歳迄生きる ひゃくさいまでいきる live to be a hundred

以 ▷**to the…of**
イ もっ(て)　　　Ⓚ0026

[formerly also 已] directional preposition placed before localizers to indicate the point of reference in compounds related to direction, time or range: **to the…of, -ward**
以東 いとう to the east of, eastward
以上 いじょう or more than, not less than; beyond; the above-mentioned; now that; that's all
以来 いらい as of, since then, from that time on
以下 いか or less than, not more than, under; and downward; the following
以外に いがいに except for, excluding
以内 いない within, less than
以前 いぜん before, ago, since
以降 いこう on and after, hereafter
以後 いご after this, from now on, in future; after that, thereafter

自 ▷**from**
ジ シ みずか(ら) おの(ずから)　　　Ⓚ2954

[also prefix] **from, as of, since**
自今 じこん hereafter
自東京 じとうきょう from Tokyo

来 ▷**since**
ライ く(る) きた(る) きた(す)　　　Ⓚ2975

[also suffix] **since, as of, from**
以来 いらい as of, since then, from that time on
従来は じゅうらいは hitherto, so far
本来 ほんらい originally, essentially, naturally
古来 こらい from ancient times
昨年来 さくねんらい since last year

而 ▷**direction word**
ジ しこ(うして) しか(して) しか(も)　　　Ⓚ1747

direction word indicating direction in space or time
而来 じらい since then, after that
而後 じご from now on, hereafter

而立 じりつ age 30
形而上学 けいじじょうがく metaphysics
形而下 けいじか physical, material

dirty[1]

汚　染

汚 ▷dirty
オ けが(す) けが(れる) けが(らわしい)
よご(す) よご(れる) きたな(い)　Ⓚ0196

【オ】
(make or become unclean) **dirty, soil, defile; become
dirty, become defiled**
　汚染 おせん pollution, contamination

【よご(す)】
(make unclean) **make dirty, soil, defile;** (bring dishonor
upon) **defile, corrupt, dishonor**
　服を汚す ふくをよごす soil one's clothes
　面汚し つらよごし disgrace, shame

染 ▷contaminate
セン そ(める) −ぞ(め) そ(まる) し(みる)
−じ(みる) し(み)　Ⓚ2229

contaminate
　汚染 おせん pollution, contamination

dirty[2]

汚　濁

汚 ▷dirty
オ けが(す) けが(れる) けが(らわしい)
よご(す) よご(れる) きたな(い)　Ⓚ0196

dirty, contaminated, defiled
　汚水 おすい dirty [filthy] water, sewage
　汚物 おぶつ dirt, filth, impurities

濁 ▷turbid
ダク にご(る) にご(す)　Ⓚ0695

turbid, muddy, cloudy, impure
　濁流 だくりゅう muddy stream
　濁度 だくど turbidity
　濁酒 だくしゅ unrefined sake
　混濁した こんだくした turbid, thick, muddy, cloudy
　清濁 せいだく purity and impurity; good and evil
　水質汚濁 すいしつおだく water pollution

disappear

消　没

消 ▷disappear
ショウ き(える) け(す)　Ⓚ0402

disappear, vanish
　消息 しょうそく (personal) news, movements; letter
　消失する しょうしつする disappear, vanish; die away
　消滅する しょうめつする become extinct, disappear

没 ▷disappear
ボツ　Ⓚ0230

disappear, vanish, go out of sight, hide
　出没する しゅつぼつする make frequent appear-
　　ances; haunt

disaster →MISFORTUNE AND DISASTER

discard and abandon

捨　棄　諦

捨 ▷discard
シャ す(てる)　Ⓚ0461

ⓐ **discard, reject, cast away**
ⓑ **give up, abandon**
ⓐ 取捨 しゅしゃ adoption or rejection, choice
　用捨 ようしゃ adoption or rejection, choice
　四捨五入 ししゃごにゅう rounding (to the nearest
　　integer)
ⓑ 捨身 しゃしん becoming a priest; risking one's life
　　for others

棄 ▷abandon
キ　Ⓚ1835

ⓐ **abandon, forsake, desert, discard**
ⓑ [original meaning] **throw away; give up, abandon**
ⓐ 棄権する きけんする abstain from voting, abandon
　　one's right
　棄却する ききゃくする turn down, reject, renounce
　放棄する ほうきする abandon, resign
　破棄する はきする break (a treaty), annul
ⓐⓑ 廃棄 はいき discarding, abolition, annulment
ⓑ 投棄する とうきする abandon, give up, throw away

諦 ▷give up
テイ あきら(める)   Ⓚ1444

give up, abandon, resign oneself
　諦念 ていねん feeling of resignation; a heart that understands truth

discernment
識　　眼

識 ▷power of discrimination
シキ   Ⓚ1477

power of discrimination, discernment
　意識する いしきする be conscious of, be aware of

眼 ▷eye
ガン ゲン まなこ め   Ⓚ1084

[also suffix] (power of discrimination) **eye, discernment, insight**
　眼力 がんりき insight, power of observation
　眼識 がんしき insight, discrimination
　審美眼 しんびがん an eye for the beautiful, aesthetic sense

discharge from mouth
吐　　吹

吐 ▷spew
ト は(く)   Ⓚ0180

[original meaning] **spew, vomit**
　吐出 としゅつ spew, vomit, disgorge
　吐血 とけつ vomiting blood
　吐息 といき sigh, long breath
　嘔吐 おうと vomiting
　音吐朗朗と おんとろうろうと in a clear voice

吹 ▷blow
スイ ふ(く)   Ⓚ0204

[original meaning] **blow, breathe out**
　吹鳴する すいめいする blow (a whistle)

discolor
褪　　晒

褪 ▷fade
タイ トン あ(せる)

[now usu. 退] **fade, discolor**
　褪色する たいしょくする fade, grow dull in color
　褪紅色 たいこうしょく pink

晒 ▷bleach
サイ さら(す)   Ⓚ0831

bleach, refine
　晒し さらし bleaching; bleached cotton
　晒木綿 さらしもめん bleached cotton cloth
　洗い晒し あらいざらし faded from washing

discontinue
絶　廃　断　止　休　停　已

絶 ▷break off
ゼツ た(える) た(やす) た(つ)   Ⓚ1240

break off, discontinue, cut off, sever
　絶交 ぜっこう breaking off friendship [diplomatic relations]
　絶縁 ぜつえん breaking off relations; insulation, isolation
　絶版になる ぜっぱんになる go out of print
　絶食 ぜっしょく fasting
　断絶 だんぜつ severance, rupture; discontinuation
　中絶 ちゅうぜつ interruption, discontinuance; abortion
　根絶する こんぜつする eradicate, exterminate, root out

廃 ▷abolish
ハイ すた(れる) すた(る)   Ⓚ2712

abolish, abandon, discontinue, give up
　廃止する はいしする abolish, abandon, discontinue
　廃案 はいあん rejected bill [project]
　廃刊 はいかん discontinuance of publication
　廃棄 はいき discarding, abolition, annulment
　廃藩 はいはん abolition of the *han* system
　廃絶 はいぜつ extinction
　全廃 ぜんぱい (total) abolition
　撤廃 てっぱい abolition, removal

▷cut off
ダン た(つ) ことわ(る) Ⓚ1355

(cause to discontinue) **cut off (the water supply), sever (a connection), break off (relations), discontinue**

断絶 だんぜつ severance, rupture; discontinuation
断交 だんこう severing [breaking off] relations
断続的に だんぞくてきに intermittently, off and on
断水 だんすい suspension of water supply
中断する ちゅうだんする interrupt, discontinue, suspend
遮断 しゃだん interception, interruption, blockade, isolation
油断 ゆだん negligence, carelessness, inattentiveness

 ▷stop
シ と(まる) –ど(まり) と(める) –ど(め)
や(める) や(む) Ⓚ2545

ⓐ (cease acting) **stop, cease, discontinue**
ⓑ **cause to stop, arrest, discontinue, suspend**

a 終止 しゅうし termination, cessation
　休止 きゅうし pause, standstill, dormancy; rest
b 止血する しけつする stop [arrest] bleeding
　中止する ちゅうしする suspend, stop, discontinue
　廃止する はいしする abolish, abandon, discontinue

 ▷suspend
キュウ やす(む) やす(まる)
やす(める) Ⓚ0037

suspend, discontinue; cancel

休演する きゅうえんする suspend performance
休会 きゅうかい adjournment, recess (of the Diet)
休戦 きゅうせん truce, armistice
休講 きゅうこう cancellation of lecture (for the day)
休校 きゅうこう temporary closure of school
休学 きゅうがく leave of absence (from school)
運休 うんきゅう suspension of (bus) service
閑話休題 かんわきゅうだい to return to the subject

停 **▷suspend**
テイ と(める) と(まる) Ⓚ0121

suspend, discontinue

停学 ていがく suspension from school
停職 ていしょく suspension from office
停戦 ていせん cease-fire, armistice
停電 ていでん stoppage of electric power, power failure
調停する ちょうていする mediate, arbitrate, make peace

 ▷cease
イ や(む) や(める) すで(に) Ⓚ2861

[also 止む] (bring to an end) **cease, discontinue; not do**

已むを得ない やむをえない unavoidable, cannot be helped
已む無く やむなく unavoidably, out of necessity
已むに已まれぬ事情 やむにやまれぬじじょう circumstances beyond one's control

discriminate
識　弁　分

 ▷discriminate
シキ Ⓚ1477

discriminate, discern, recognize

識別する しきべつする discriminate, discern, recognize
認識 にんしき cognition, perception; understanding
鑑識する かんしきする identify, judge; discern
眼識 がんしき insight, discrimination

弁 **▷distinguish**
ベン Ⓚ1730

[formerly 辨 or 辯] **distinguish, discriminate, differentiate, discern**

弁別する べんべつする discriminate, distinguish
弁証法 べんしょうほう dialectic
思弁 しべん speculation
勘弁する かんべんする pardon, forgive; tolerate

分 **▷tell apart**
ブン フン ブ わ(ける) わ(け) わ(かれる)
わ(かる) わ(かつ) Ⓚ1713

tell apart, distinguish

分別 ふんべつ discretion, prudence, judgment, good sense
不分明な ふぶんめいな obscure, vague
検分する けんぶんする inspect, examine, survey

discuss →ARGUE AND DISCUSS

disdain
侮　軽　蔑　嘲

 ▷despise
ブ あなど(る) Ⓚ0063

despise, disdain, hold in contempt, make light of

侮蔑 ぶべつ contempt, scorn
軽侮する けいぶする look down upon, despise, disdain

軽 ▷make light of
ケイ かる(い) かろ(やか)　　Ⓚ1372

make light of, think little of
軽視する けいしする make light of, despise; neglect
軽蔑 けいべつ contempt, disdain

蔑 ▷despise
ベツ さげす(む)　　Ⓚ2068

despise, disdain, scorn, look down on
蔑視する べっしする regard with contempt, scorn, look down on
蔑称 べっしょう disparaging [derogatory] name [term]
軽蔑 けいべつ contempt, disdain
侮蔑 ぶべつ contempt, scorn

嘲 ▷scoff at
チョウ あざけ(る)　　Ⓚ0648

scoff at, jeer at, ridicule, scorn, mock
嘲笑する ちょうしょうする laugh at, deride
嘲罵する ちょうばする taunt, insult, abuse
嘲弄 ちょうろう taunting, mockery, ridicule
自嘲 じちょう self-derision

disease
病 疾 風 症 患 疫 罹 臥

病 ▷illness
ビョウ ヘイ や(む) -や(み)
やまい　　Ⓚ2791

[also suffix] [original meaning] illness, sickness, disease
病気 びょうき illness, sickness, disease
病院 びょういん hospital
病室 びょうしつ patient [sick] room
病死 びょうし death of sickness
疾病 しっぺい sickness, disease
看病 かんびょう nursing, nursing care
難病 なんびょう incurable [intractable] disease
肺病 はいびょう lung disease; pulmonary tuberculosis
精神病 せいしんびょう mental disease
高山病 こうざんびょう altitude sickness
臆病 おくびょう cowardice, timidity

疾 ▷disease
シツ　　Ⓚ2793

[original meaning] disease, illness
疾患 しっかん disease, ailment, trouble, disorder
疾病 しっぺい sickness, disease
悪疾 あくしつ malignant disease

痼疾 こしつ chronic disease
廃疾 はいしつ disablement

風 ▷(infectious) disease
フウ フ かぜ かざ-　　Ⓚ2591

(infectious) disease, serious disease
風疹 ふうしん German measles, rubella
中風 ちゅうぶ(=ちゅうぶう, ちゅうふう) palsy, paralysis
破傷風 はしょうふう tetanus

症 ▷pathological condition
ショウ　　Ⓚ2794

pathological condition, illness, disease, -osis, -ia
神経症 しんけいしょう neurosis, nervous disease
既往症 きおうしょう previous illness, medical history
不眠症 ふみんしょう insomnia
尿毒症 にょうどくしょう uremia
重症 じゅうしょう serious illness

患 ▷affected by disease
カン わずら(う)　　Ⓚ2395

ⓐ affected by disease, diseased, sick
ⓑ affection, disease
a 患者 かんじゃ patient
　 患部 かんぶ diseased part, affected area
b 罹患 りかん contraction of a disease
　 疾患 しっかん disease, ailment, trouble, disorder

疫 ▷epidemic
エキ ヤク　　Ⓚ2790

[original meaning] epidemic, disease
疫病 えきびょう epidemic, plague
疫学 えきがく epidemiology
疫病神 やくびょうがみ God of the plagues; abominable person, pest
免疫 めんえき immunity (from a disease)
検疫 けんえき quarantine, medical inspection
防疫 ぼうえき prevention of epidemics

罹 ▷fall ill
リ かか(る)

fall ill, contract (a disease)
罹患 りかん contraction of a disease

臥 ▷be sick in bed
ガ ふ(せる) ふ(す)　　Ⓚ1307

be confined to one's bed, be sick in bed
臥床 がしょう being confined to bed
病臥 びょうが being sick in bed

虫垂炎 ちゅうすいえん appendicitis

diseases and disease symptoms
痘 淋 癌 熱 炎 痢 下

痘 ▷smallpox
トウ   Ⓚ2798

❶ [original meaning] **smallpox**
痘瘡 とうそう smallpox
痘苗 とうびょう vaccine, vaccine virus; smallpox vaccine
天然痘 てんねんとう smallpox
種痘 しゅとう vaccination against smallpox

❷ pox
牛痘 ぎゅうとう cow pox, vaccinia
水痘 すいとう chicken pox, varicella

淋 ▷gonorrhea
リン さび(しい) さみ(しい)   Ⓚ0476

gonorrhea
淋病 りんびょう gonorrhea
淋菌 りんきん gonococcus

癌 ▷cancer
ガン

[also suffix] [original meaning] **cancer; cancerous**
癌腫 がんしゅ carcinoma
癌細胞 がんさいぼう cancer cell
癌遺伝子 がんいでんし oncogene, cancer gene
抗癌剤 こうがんざい anticancer drug
肺癌 はいがん lung cancer
乳癌 にゅうがん breast cancer
発癌 はつがん carcinogenesis, production of cancer
末期癌 まっきがん terminal cancer

熱 ▷fever
ネツ あつ(い)   Ⓚ2495

[also suffix] (abnormal bodily heat) **fever, temperature**
熱病 ねつびょう fever
発熱 はつねつ generation of heat; attack of fever
微熱 びねつ slight fever
産褥熱 さんじょくねつ puerperal fever

炎 ▷inflammation
エン ほのお   Ⓚ2145

[also suffix] **inflammation, -itis**
炎症 えんしょう inflammation
脳炎 のうえん brain inflammation, encephalitis
肺炎 はいえん pneumonia, inflammation of the lungs

痢 ▷diarrhea
リ   Ⓚ2796

diarrhea
下痢 げり diarrhea
赤痢 せきり dysentery
疫痢 えきり children's dysentery

下 ▷diarrhea
カ ゲ した しも もと さ(げる) さ(がる)
くだ(る) くだ(り) くだ(す) くだ(さる)
お(ろす) お(りる)   Ⓚ2862

diarrhea
下痢 げり diarrhea
下剤 げざい purgative, laxative
下血 げけつ bloody bowel discharge

disease symptoms →DISEASES AND DISEASE SYMPTOMS

disgrace
恥 羞 辱 侮 罵 汚 誹 譏

恥 ▷shame
チ は(じる) はじ は(じらう)
は(ずかしい)   Ⓚ1200

ⓐ shame, disgrace, dishonor, humiliation
ⓑ feel [be] ashamed
a 恥辱 ちじょく disgrace, dishonor, shame
  羞恥 しゅうち shyness; sense of shame
b 厚顔無恥な こうがんむちな shameless, unscrupulous
  破廉恥 はれんち shamelessness, infamy, impudence

羞 ▷shame
シュウ   Ⓚ2823

put to shame, disgrace
閉月羞花 へいげつしゅうか Such beauty as to make the moon hide and shame flowers (as of a woman)

辱 ▷humiliate
ジョク はずかし(める)   Ⓚ2384

humiliate, disgrace, dishonor, insult
侮辱する ぶじょくする insult, treat with contempt
屈辱 くつじょく humiliation, disgrace, insult
恥辱 ちじょく disgrace, dishonor, shame
雪辱する せつじょくする vindicate one's honor, get revenge for one's defeat
凌辱する りょうじょくする insult, disgrace; rape

disgrace

侮 ▷**insult**
ブ あなど(る) Ⓚ0063

[original meaning] **insult, humiliate, make a fool of**
侮辱する ぶじょくする insult, treat with contempt
侮言 ぶげん words of insult

罵 ▷**abuse**
バ ののし(る) Ⓚ2271

[original meaning] **abuse, revile, speak ill of, swear at, call names**
罵倒 ばとう abuse, denunciation, calling names
罵詈雑言 ばりぞうごん vituperation, all manner of abuse
罵声 ばせい boos, jeers
面罵 めんば abusing someone to his [her] face
痛罵 つうば castigation, invective, severe abuse

汚 ▷**defile**
オ けが(す) けが(れる) けが(らわしい)
よご(す) よご(れる) きたな(い) Ⓚ0196

(bring dishonor upon) **defile, disgrace, corrupt, dishonor**
汚職 おしょく (official) corruption, bribery
汚名 おめい bad name, ill fame, disgrace
汚点 おてん disgrace, flaw; stain, blot
汚濁 おだく(=おじょく) corruption

誹 ▷**slander**
ヒ ハイ そし(る) Ⓚ

[now also 非] [original meaning] **slander, calumniate, defame**
誹諧(=俳諧) はいかい haikai, (humorous) haiku
誹謗 ひぼう slander, abuse
誹議する ひぎする criticize, censure

譏 ▷**slander**
キ そし(る)

[original meaning] **slander, censure, criticize**
譏誹 きひ [archaic] slander, abuse
譏嫌 きげん [now usu. 機嫌] mood, temper, disposition; health

disguise
装　　化

装 ▷**dress up**
ソウ ショウ よそお(う) Ⓚ2344

dress up, disguise, play the part
装身具 そうしんぐ personal ornaments [outfit]

男装する だんそうする disguise oneself as a man, wear men's clothes
変装する へんそうする disguise oneself
仮装する かそうする disguise oneself, dress up (as)

化 ▷**change oneself into**
カ ケ ば(ける) ば(かす) Ⓚ0012

change [transform] oneself into, take the form of; disguise oneself
化粧品 けしょうひん cosmetics
化身 けしん Buddhist incarnation, reincarnation
権化 ごんげ incarnation, embodiment
変化 へんげ goblin, ghost

dislike →HATE AND DISLIKE

dismiss
罷　　免　　解

罷 ▷**dismiss**
ヒ Ⓚ2272

dismiss, remove from office
罷免 ひめん dismissal, discharge
罷官 ひかん [archaic] removal from office

免 ▷**discharge**
メン まぬか(れる) まぬが(れる) Ⓚ1779

discharge, dismiss, remove from office
免職 めんしょく dismissal, discharge
懲戒免職 ちょうかいめんしょく disciplinary discharge
罷免 ひめん dismissal, discharge
任免 にんめん appointment and dismissal [removal]

解 ▷**release from office**
カイ ゲ と(く) と(かす) と(ける) Ⓚ1375

release from office, discharge, dismiss
解任する かいにんする release from office, dismiss, discharge
解雇する かいこする discharge, dismiss, fire

disordered
紛 乱 錯 混 雑 沌

紛 ▷**confused**
フン まぎ(れる) −まぎ(れ) まぎ(らす)
まぎ(らわす) まぎ(らわしい)　　Ⓚ1191

[original meaning] (in a jumbled state) **confused, tangled, disorderly**

紛争 ふんそう conflict, strife
紛失 ふんしつ loss
紛紛と ふんぷんと confusedly; in profusion
紛乱 ふんらん confusion, disorder
紛糾 ふんきゅう complication, disorder, entanglement

乱 ▷**disordered**
ラン みだ(れる) みだ(る) みだ(す)　Ⓚ1161

disordered, confused, chaotic, boisterous, abusive, reckless

乱雑 らんざつ disorder, confusion
乱暴 らんぼう violence, roughness; rape
乱闘 らんとう free-for-all [confused] fight, melee
乱気流 らんきりゅう turbulent air, turbulence
波乱(=波瀾) はらん disturbance, troubles; fluctuation
混乱 こんらん disorder, confusion, chaos

錯 ▷**mixed up**
サク　　　　　　　　　　　　　Ⓚ1555

mixed up, intricate, confused, disordered, complicated

錯雑 さくざつ complication, intricacy
錯綜 さくそう complication, intricacy
交錯した こうさくした mingled, entangled, complicated, intricate

混 ▷**mixed up**
コン ま(じる) −ま(じり) ま(ざる) ま(ぜる)
こ(む)　　　　　　　　　　　　Ⓚ0475

mixed up, confused, disorderly, chaotic

混雑 こんざつ confusion, disorder, congestion
混乱 こんらん disorder, confusion, chaos
混同 こんどう confusion; mixing
混迷 こんめい confusion, bewilderment; [formerly 昏迷] stupor, unconsciousness
混沌 こんとん [sometimes also 渾沌] chaos

雑 ▷**mixed up**
ザツ ゾウ　　　　　　　　　　Ⓚ1267

mixed up, disorderly, confused, intricate

雑然とした ざつぜんとした promiscuous, disorderly

複雑な ふくざつな complicated, complex, involved, intricate
混雑した こんざつした confused, disorderly; congested
乱雑な らんざつな disorderly, confused
繁雑な はんざつな complicated, intricate, confused
煩雑な はんざつな vexatious, troublesome, intricate
錯雑 さくざつ complication, intricacy

沌 ▷**primeval chaos**
トン　　　　　　　　　　　　　Ⓚ0239

primeval chaos

混沌 こんとん [sometimes also 渾沌] chaos

disperse
解 散

解 ▷**dissolve**
カイ ゲ と(く) と(かす) と(ける)　Ⓚ1375

(cause to disperse) **dissolve (a meeting), break up (an organization), dispel**

解散 かいさん breakup, dispersion; dissolution
解組する かいそする break up an organization
解放する かいほうする release, set free
解消 かいしょう liquidation, annulment, solution

散 ▷**scatter**
サン ち(る) ち(らす) ち(らかす)
ち(らかる) ち(らばる)　　　　Ⓚ1518

[formerly also 撒] [original meaning] (cause to) **scatter, sprinkle, adjourn (a meeting), disperse**

散髪 さんぱつ haircut
散布 さんぷ(=さっぷ) scattering, sprinkling, spraying
散水 さんすい water sprinkling
散会する さんかいする break up, adjourn, disperse

display
展 陳 掲

展 ▷**display**
テン　　　　　　　　　　　　　Ⓚ2681

(spread out before the view of the public) **display, exhibit, put on display**

展示する てんじする put on display, exhibit
展覧会 てんらんかい exhibition
展観する てんかんする exhibit

陳 ▷**lay out (for exhibit)**
チン ⓚ0493

[original meaning] **lay out (for exhibit), put on display, spread out**
　陳列する ちんれつする exhibit, display
　出陳 しゅっちん submitting (something) to an exhibition

掲 ▷**put up**
ケイ かか(げる) ⓚ0450

put up, display, hoist, raise
　掲揚する けいようする hoist, put up, fly (a flag)
　掲示する けいじする put up a notice [bulletin]

distance and interval

距　間　程　隙

距 ▷**distance**
キョ ⓚ1370

distance, range, spacing
　角距 かっきょ angular distance
　測距儀 そっきょぎ range finder
　輪距 りんきょ wheel track
　高距 こうきょ elevation (above sea level)

間 ▷**interval**
カン ケン あいだ ま ⓚ2836

[also suffix] (space between) **interval, space, opening, distance**
　間隔 かんかく interval, space
　間接 かんせつ indirect
　空間 くうかん space, room
　区間 くかん section, territory
　東京大阪間 とうきょうおおさかかん between Tokyo and Osaka

程 ▷**extent**
テイ ほど ⓚ1100

(range of distance) **extent, distance, range, mileage, journey**
　射程 しゃてい shooting range
　旅程 りょてい distance to be covered; plan of one's trip
　航程 こうてい run (of a ship), sail; flight
　マイル程 まいるてい mileage
　音程 おんてい (musical) interval, distance (between tones)

隙 ▷**gap**
ゲキ すき ⓚ0614

[original meaning] **gap, interval, opening, space**
　間隙 かんげき gap, interval
　空隙 くうげき opening, crevice, gap, void
　填隙 てんげき caulking

distant

遠　遥　悠　遼　隔　離　迂

遠 ▷**distant**
エン オン とお(い) ⓚ2715

ⓐ distant (in space), far, remote
ⓑ distant (in time), far-off, remote
ⓒ become distant
　a 遠隔の えんかくの distant, remote, far
　遠景 えんけい distant view, perspective
　遠方 えんぽう great distance; distant place
　遠足 えんそく excursion, hike, long walk
　遠征 えんせい (punitive) expedition, invasion; tour
　遠視 えんし farsightedness
　遠距離 えんきょり long distance
　望遠鏡 ぼうえんきょう telescope
　b 永遠 えいえん eternity
　久遠 くおん eternity
　c 遠心力 えんしんりょく centrifugal force

遥 ▷**far**
ヨウ はる(か) ⓚ2708

far, faraway, far-off, distant, remote
　遥拝 ようはい worshiping from afar
　遥遠な ようえんな [rare] very far-off, remote

悠 ▷**far-off**
ユウ ⓚ2389

[original meaning] (remote in space or time) **far-off, faraway, remote, distant**
　悠遠 ゆうえん remoteness
　悠久な ゆうきゅうな eternal, everlasting, permanent

遼 ▷**faraway**
リョウ ⓚ2733

faraway, remote, distant, stretching a great distance
　遼遠な りょうえんな remote, far-off

隔 ▷**apart**
カク へだ(てる) へだ(たる) ⓚ0615

apart, separated, distant

隔世 かくせい distant age
隔絶する かくぜつする be separated, be isolated
遠隔の えんかくの distant, remote, far

離 ▷separated
リ はな(れる) はな(す) Ⓚ1663

(be apart) **separated, distant**
離島 りとう outlying island
離心率 りしんりつ eccentricity
距離 きょり distance, range; interval

迂 ▷roundabout
ウ Ⓚ2759

roundabout, circuitous
迂回 うかい detour
迂闊 うかつ careless, absentminded
迂遠な うえんな roundabout, devious
迂曲する うきょくする meander

distribute
配　頒　分

配 ▷distribute
ハイ くば(る) Ⓚ1330

distribute, apportion, allot, allocate
配達 はいたつ delivery
配給 はいきゅう distribution, supply; rationing
配本 はいほん distribution of books
配付 はいふ distribution, apportionment
配当する はいとうする allot
配役 はいやく cast (of a play)
分配 ぶんぱい division, distribution, allotment
勾配 こうばい slope, incline; gradient

頒 ▷distribute widely
ハン Ⓚ0955

distribute widely, circulate, promulgate
頒布 はんぷ distribution, circulation
頒価 はんか distribution price
頒行 はんこう [rare] distribution, circulation, promulgation

分 ▷divide
ブン フン ブ わ(ける) わ(け) わ(かれる)
わ(かる) わ(かつ) Ⓚ1713

(parcel out) **divide (up), distribute, apportion, share**
分配する ぶんぱいする divide, distribute, allot
配分 はいぶん distribution, division, allocation
按分(=案分)する あんぶんする divide [distribute] proportionally

diverge
岐　分

岐 ▷diverge
キ ギ Ⓚ0214

diverge, branch off, ramify, fork
分岐 ぶんき divergence, ramification, forking
分岐点 ぶんきてん junction
多岐 たき many branches, many divergences

分 ▷branch off
ブン フン ブ わ(ける) わ(け) わ(かれる)
わ(かる) わ(かつ) Ⓚ1713

branch off, branch out, diverge
分岐する ぶんきする diverge, branch off
分身 ぶんしん the other self, one's alter ego; branch, offshoot

divide
除　割

除 ▷divide
ジョ ジ のぞ(く) Ⓚ0412

math **divide**
除数 じょすう divisor
乗除 じょうじょ multiplication and division

割 ▷divide
カツ わ(る) わり わ(れる) さ(く) Ⓚ1611

math **divide**
割り算 わりざん division
割り切る わりきる divide; give a clear-cut solution

dividend →INTEREST AND DIVIDEND

divine
占　卜　易

占 ▷divine
セン し(める) うらな(う) Ⓚ1729

[original meaning] **divine, tell fortune, augur**
占星術 せんせいじゅつ astrology

卜 ▷divine
ボク うらな(う) うらない   Ⓚ2856

[original meaning] **divine, tell (a person's) fortune, augur**

卜者 ぼくしゃ fortuneteller, diviner
卜占 ぼくせん augury
卜筮 ぼくぜい fortunetelling, divination
卜居 ぼっきょ choosing a homesite by divination
亀卜 きぼく divination by tortoiseshells
売卜 ばいぼく fortunetelling (as an occupation)

易 ▷divination
エキ イ やさ(しい) やす(い)   Ⓚ2135

divination, fortunetelling

易者 えきしゃ fortuneteller, diviner
易学 えきがく science of divination

divisions of organizations
課　部　局

課 ▷section
カ   Ⓚ1423

[also suffix] **section, department (of a company or government office)**

課長 かちょう section chief [head]
分課 ぶんか section, subdivision; dividing into sections
人事課 じんじか personnel section
会計課 かいけいか accounts [accounting] section

部 ▷department
ブ   Ⓚ1498

[also suffix] section or major subdivision of an organization: **department, division, section, faculty; military unit**

部属 ぶぞく section, division
部長 ぶちょう section chief, department head
部会 ぶかい section meeting
部下 ぶか subordinate
部隊 ぶたい unit, corps, party, squad
幹部 かんぶ executive, (managing) staff
学部 がくぶ faculty, department
編集部 へんしゅうぶ editorial department [staff]
文学部 ぶんがくぶ department [faculty] of literature
営業部 えいぎょうぶ business department, sales department
文化事業部 ぶんかじぎょうぶ Cultural Affairs Department

局 ▷bureau
キョク   Ⓚ263(

[also suffix] **bureau, department (esp. of a government office)**

局長 きょくちょう bureau chief, director, postmaster
部局 ぶきょく department, bureau
水道局 すいどうきょく Water Works Bureau
法制局 ほうせいきょく Legislative Bureau
総務局 そうむきょく General Affairs Bureau
薬局 やっきょく drugstore, pharmacy
事務局 じむきょく secretariat
当局 とうきょく the authorities concerned

do and act
為　仕　致　行　作

為 ▷do
イ ため な(す)   Ⓚ2994

do, make; act, behave

為政家 いせいか politician
行為 こうい act, deed, conduct, transaction
無為 むい inactivity; *Buddhism* that which is not created
作為 さくい artificiality, intention; commission (of a crime)

仕 ▷do
シ ジ つか(える)   Ⓚ0021

used for し as the second (continuative) base of the verb する: do

仕事 しごと work, employment, business
仕立て したて tailoring, dressmaking
仕方 しかた way, method, means
仕方が無い しかたがない have no choice; it is no use; cannot bear
仕手 して doer; protagonist in a noh drama; operator, speculator
仕組み しくみ construction; arrangement; plan, plot
仕上げ しあげ finish, elaboration, completion
仕返し しかえし doing over, tit for tat, revenge
仕合わせ しあわせ [also 幸せ, formerly also 倖せ] happiness, blessing; good fortune
仕入れる しいれる lay in, stock
仕入れ しいれ purchasing, stocking
仕送りする しおくりする supply, provide; send money to
仕舞い しまい end, conclusion, close
給仕 きゅうじ office boy, page (boy), waiter; service at table

致 ▷do humbly
チ いた(す)　　　　　　Ⓚ1202

do humbly, perform an action (with humility)

致し方 いたしかた way, method
これは如何致しましょうか これはいかがいたしましょうか What shall I do with this?
どう致しまして どういたしまして You are welcome

行 ▷act
コウ ギョウ アン い(く) ゆ(く) -ゆ(き)
-い(き) おこな(う)　　　Ⓚ0187

(perform an action) **act, do, carry out, perform, conduct**

行動 こうどう action, conduct, behavior
行為 こうい act, deed, conduct, transaction
行政 ぎょうせい administration
行事 ぎょうじ event, function
実行 じっこう practice, action; execution

作 ▷work
サク サ つく(る) つく(り) -づく(り) Ⓚ0052

work, do, perform, function

作業 さぎょう work, operation
作用 さよう action, operation, function; effect
作動する さどうする operate, function, work; run, go
操作する そうさする operate, manipulate, handle

dog
犬　　狗　　戌

犬 ▷dog
ケン いぬ　　　　　　　Ⓚ2912

[also suffix] [original meaning] **dog, hound**

忠犬 ちゅうけん faithful dog
番犬 ばんけん watchdog
猟犬 りょうけん hound, hunting dog
野犬 やけん stray dog
コリー犬 こりーけん collie
盲導犬 もうどうけん guide dog, Seeing Eye dog

狗 ▷dog
ク いぬ

[original meaning] **dog (esp. of small variety)**

走狗 そうく running dog; dupe, tool, cat's paw
羊頭狗肉 ようとうくにく using a better name to sell inferior goods, crying wine and selling vinegar
天狗 てんぐ tengu, long-nosed goblin; braggart

戌 ▷the Dog
ジュツ いぬ

11th sign of the Oriental zodiac: **the Dog**—(time) 7-9 p.m., (direction) WNW, (season) September (of the lunar calendar)

戌戌 ぼじゅつ 35th of the sexagenary cycle

domesticated mammals
牛 馬 豚 羊 犬 猫 兎

牛 ▷cattle
ギュウ うし　　　　　　Ⓚ2903
see also →CATTLE

[original meaning] (any bovine animal) **cattle, cow, bull, ox**

牛乳 ぎゅうにゅう (cow's) milk
牛肉 ぎゅうにく beef
牛皮(=牛革) ぎゅうかわ cowhide, oxhide
牛飲馬食する ぎゅういんばしょくする gorge and swill, drink like a cow and eat like a horse
牛歩戦術 ぎゅうほせんじゅつ cow's-pace tactics
乳牛 にゅうぎゅう(=ちちうし) milch cow, dairy cattle
闘牛 とうぎゅう bullfight, fighting bull

馬 ▷horse
バ うま　　　　　　　　Ⓚ2809
see also →HORSE

[also suffix] [original meaning] **horse**

馬車 ばしゃ horse-drawn carriage, coach, wagon
馬力 ばりき horsepower; energy, effort; cart, wagon
馬身 ばしん horse's length
馬肉 ばにく horsemeat
乗馬 じょうば horse riding
競馬 けいば horse racing
竹馬の友 ちくばのとも childhood friend, old play-mate
関西馬 かんさいば Kansai horse

豚 ▷pig
トン ぶた　　　　　　　Ⓚ0889

[original meaning] **pig, hog, swine**

豚舎 とんしゃ pigsty, pigpen
養豚 ようとん swine keeping

羊 ▷sheep
ヨウ ひつじ　　　　　　Ⓚ1870
see also →SHEEP

[original meaning] **sheep, ram, ewe**

羊肉 ようにく mutton
羊毛 ようもう wool
羊頭狗肉 ようとうくにく using a better name to sell inferior goods, crying wine and selling vinegar
羊羹 ようかん sweet jelly of beans
牧羊 ぼくよう sheep farming

犬 ▷dog
ケン いぬ   Ⓚ2912
see also →DOG

[also suffix] [original meaning] **dog, hound**
忠犬 ちゅうけん faithful dog
番犬 ばんけん watchdog
猟犬 りょうけん hound, hunting dog
野犬 やけん stray dog
コリー犬 こりーけん collie
盲導犬 もうどうけん guide dog, Seeing Eye dog

猫 ▷cat
ビョウ ねこ   Ⓚ0488

[original meaning] **cat**
猫額大の土地 びょうがくだいのとち narrow strip of land
愛猫家 あいびょうか cat lover

兎 ▷rabbit
ト うさぎ   Ⓚ2981

rabbit, hare
兎耳 うさぎみみ long ears; (figuratively) someone with long [big] ears
兎跳び うさぎとび hopping forward from a squatting position
野兎 のうさぎ hare
雪兎 ゆきうさぎ mountain hare

donate
施 恵 寄 醵 献

施 ▷give alms
シ セ ほどこ(す)   Ⓚ0792

give alms, give charity, dispense gratis, render services (to the needy)
施薬 せやく free medicine
施行する せぎょうする give alms
施主 せしゅ chief mourner; donor, benefactor
施餓鬼 せがき service for the unmourned dead
布施 ふせ alms

恵 ▷give charity
ケイ エ めぐ(む)   Ⓚ2315

give charity [alms]

乞食に金を恵む こじきにかねをめぐむ give money to a beggar

寄 ▷contribute
キ よ(る) -よ(り) よ(せる)   Ⓚ198.

(give money or goods) **contribute, donate**
寄付 きふ contribution, donation
寄金 ききん contribution, donation
寄贈する きぞう(=きそう)する donate, present as a gift
寄与 きよ contribution, services

醵 ▷contribute money
キョ

[now also 拠] **contribute money to a common purpose**
醵出 きょしゅつ donation, contribution
醵金 きょきん contribution, subscription

献 ▷donate
ケン コン   Ⓚ1588

donate, contribute
献木 けんぼく donating lumber to a shrine
献金する けんきんする donate [contribute] money
献血 けんけつ blood donation
貢献 こうけん contribution, services

doors
戸 扉 門 口 襖

戸 ▷door
コ と   Ⓚ1691

[original meaning] **door**
戸外 こがい open-air, outdoors
門戸 もんこ door, entrance; school

扉 ▷hinged door
ヒ とびら   Ⓚ1705

[also suffix] [original meaning] **hinged door, door, door leaf**
開扉する かいひする open the door
門扉 もんぴ leaves [doors] of a gate
鉄扉 てっぴ iron door
防水扉 ぼうすいひ watertight door

門 ▷gate
モン かど   Ⓚ0789

[also suffix] [original meaning] **gate, gateway, entrance, door**
門戸 もんこ door, entrance; school
門番 もんばん gatekeeper, janitor

正門 せいもん main gate, main entrance
校門 こうもん school gate
通用門 つうようもん side door

口 ▷entrance (or exit)
コウ ク くち Ⓚ2865

[also suffix] **entrance, exit, entranceway, doorway, gateway, door**
口金 くちがね metal clasp, snap; metal cap
窓口 まどぐち window, wicket; clerk at a window
間口 まぐち frontage, front; width
入り口 いりぐち entrance
西口 にしぐち westside entrance [exit]
非常口 ひじょうぐち emergency exit
改札口 かいさつぐち ticket barrier [gate], wicket

襖 ▷opaque sliding door
オウ ふすま あお Ⓚ1157

opaque sliding door
襖絵 ふすまえ images drawn or painted on fusuma

doubt
疑　怪

疑 ▷doubt
ギ うたが(う) Ⓚ1416

doubt, suspect
疑惑 ぎわく doubt, suspicion
疑問 ぎもん question, problem, doubt
疑心 ぎしん doubt, suspicion, fear
半信半疑の はんしんはんぎの dubious, incredulous
懐疑 かいぎ doubt, skepticism, disbelief
容疑 ようぎ suspicion

怪 ▷suspect
カイ ケ あや(しい) あや(しむ) Ⓚ0264

suspect, be suspicious; doubt; wonder, marvel
怪しむに足りない あやしむにたりない It is no
wonder (that)

dragon
竜　辰

竜 ▷dragon
リュウ たつ Ⓚ1805

dragon
竜神 りゅうじん dragon god, dragon king
竜宮 りゅうぐう Palace of the Dragon King

竜虎 りゅうこ(=りょうこ) dragon and tiger; hero

辰 ▷the Dragon
シン たつ Ⓚ2582

fifth sign of the Oriental zodiac: **the Dragon**—(time) 7-9 a.m., (direction) ESE, (season) March (of the lunar calendar)
戊辰 ぼしん fifth of the sexagenary cycle

draw
描　画

描 ▷depict
ビョウ えが(く) か(く) Ⓚ0445

[original meaning] (represent in a picture) **depict, draw, paint**
描画する びょうがする draw a picture, paint
素描 そびょう (rough) sketch
点描 てんびょう sketch
実物描写 じつぶつびょうしゃ model drawing

画 ▷draw
ガ カク Ⓚ2586

draw, paint
画家 がか artist, painter

drinks
汁　乳　酒　茶　珈　醇　酎

汁 ▷juice, soup
ジュウ しる Ⓚ0173

ⓐ juice, sap
ⓑ soup, broth
a 汁液 じゅうえき juice
果汁 かじゅう fruit juice
b 一汁一菜 いちじゅういっさい simple meal
肉汁 にくじゅう meat juice, gravy

乳 ▷milk
ニュウ ちち ち Ⓚ1306

(food product) **milk**
乳業 にゅうぎょう dairy industry
乳価 にゅうか price of milk
粉乳 ふんにゅう powdered milk
脱脂乳 だっしにゅう nonfat milk

酒 ▷alcoholic drink
シュ さけ さか– Ⓚ0403

ⓐ [also suffix] [original meaning] **alcoholic drink, wine, liquor, beer**
ⓑ **sake, rice wine**

a 酒造 しゅぞう sake brewing; distilling
酒家 しゅか wine shop, pub; heavy drinker
酒宴 しゅえん banquet, drinking bout
飲酒 いんしゅ drinking (alcoholic drinks)
洋酒 ようしゅ foreign wine [liquors]
醸造酒 じょうぞうしゅ brewage, liquor
b 清酒 せいしゅ (refined) sake

茶 ▷tea
チャ サ Ⓚ1948

tea (the beverage), tea leaves
茶菓 さか(=ちゃか) tea and cakes, refreshments
茶話会 さわかい tea party
茶碗 ちゃわん teacup; rice bowl
茶の間 ちゃのま living room
茶の湯 ちゃのゆ tea ceremony
新茶 しんちゃ new season's tea
紅茶 こうちゃ black tea
番茶 ばんちゃ coarse tea
喫茶店 きっさてん coffee shop, tea house

珈 ▷coffee
カ Ⓚ0817

used phonetically for ka, kō or ko, esp. in the sense of coffee
珈琲 こーひー coffee

醇 ▷undiluted wine
ジュン シュン Ⓚ1437

undiluted wine [liquor]
醇酒 じゅんしゅ mellow wine
醇味 じゅんみ (of liquor) rich [mellow] taste
芳醇(=芳純)な ほうじゅんな (of liquor) mellow, rich

酎 ▷shochu
チュウ Ⓚ1329

(low-class distilled spirits) *shochu*
酎ハイ ちゅうはい *shochu* with tonic water
焼酎 しょうちゅう *shochu*

drip →FLOW AND DRIP

---

drive out
斥 排 追 退 駆 逐 払

斥 ▷expel
セキ Ⓚ2565

expel, repel, reject, exclude
斥力 せきりょく repulsion, repulsive force
排斥する はいせきする expel, reject, exclude, ostracize
擯斥 ひんせき rejection, ostracism

排 ▷exclude
ハイ Ⓚ0446

[original meaning] **exclude, expel, reject, drive out**
排除 はいじょ exclusion, removal, elimination
排斥する はいせきする expel, reject, exclude, ostracize
排他的な はいたてきな exclusive, clannish
排他主義 はいたしゅぎ exclusivism

追 ▷chase away
ツイ お(う) Ⓚ2667

chase away, drive out, expel
追放する ついほうする banish, purge, exile
追儺 ついな ceremony of driving out the devils

退 ▷cause to retreat
タイ しりぞ(く) しりぞ(ける) Ⓚ2665

cause to retreat, drive back, repulse
退学 たいがく leave school; be expelled from school
撃退する げきたいする repulse, drive back; reject, repulse

駆 ▷drive away
ク か(ける) か(る) Ⓚ1619

drive away, drive out, expel
駆除する くじょする exterminate, destroy, drive away
駆逐する くちくする drive away, drive out, expel
駆虫剤 くちゅうざい insecticide, vermicide

逐 ▷drive out
チク Ⓚ2671

ⓐ **drive out, expel**
ⓑ [original meaning] **pursue, chase after**
a 放逐する ほうちくする expel, banish, expatriate
駆逐する くちくする drive away, drive out, expel

払 ▷clear out
フツ はら(う) -はら(い) -ばら(い) Ⓚ0171

[also verbal suffix] (drive off) **clear out, drive away, expel, exorcise**
- 追い払う(=追っ払う) おいはらう(=おっぱらう) drive away, expel, exorcise
- 露払い つゆはらい herald; heralding, ushering
- 厄払い やくばらい exorcism
- 焼き払う やきはらう clear away by burning, reduce to ashes

dry

乾　干　燥　涸　渇　旱

乾 ▷dry
カン かわ(く) かわ(かす) Ⓚ1500

ⓐ [original meaning] **dry, dry up, desiccate**
ⓑ **dry, dried**
- *a* 乾燥する かんそうする dry up, desiccate, become parched [dry]
- 乾杯する かんぱいする drink a toast, toast
- 乾季 かんき dry season
- *b* 乾枯する かんこする completely dry up
- 乾物 かんぶつ dry provisions, groceries
- 乾パン かんぱん cracker, hard biscuit
- 乾電池 かんでんち dry cell
- 乾溜(=乾留) かんりゅう dry distillation

干 ▷dry
カン ほ(す) ほ(し)- -ぼ(し) ひ(る) Ⓚ2863

dry, dry up, desiccate
- 干拓する かんたくする reclaim by drainage
- 干魚(=乾魚) かんぎょ dried fish

燥 ▷dry up (desiccate)
ソウ Ⓚ1009

[original meaning] (become very dry, esp. by the action of heat) **dry up, parch, desiccate**
- 乾燥する かんそうする dry up, desiccate, become parched [dry]
- 枯燥する こそうする dry up, parch
- 高燥地 こうそうち high and dry ground
- 無味乾燥な むみかんそうな dry as dust, insipid

涸 ▷dry up (run dry)
コ か(れる) か(らす)

[now also 枯] [original meaning] **dry up, run dry**
- 涸渇する こかつする dry up, run dry; be exhausted, be depleted

渇 ▷run dry
カツ かわ(く) Ⓚ0473

[original meaning] **run dry, dry up**
- 渇水 かっすい water shortage
- 枯渇する こかつする dry up, run dry; be exhausted, be depleted

旱 ▷drought
カン

[now replaced by 干] **drought, dry weather**
- 旱魃 かんばつ drought
- 旱害 かんがい drought damage
- 旱天 かんてん drought, dry weather

during

間　中　内

間 ▷for an interval of
カン ケン あいだ ま Ⓚ2836

for an interval of, during
- 十年間 じゅうねんかん for ten years

中 ▷in (the course of)
チュウ ジュウ なか Ⓚ2902

[also suffix] within the confines of a given period:
ⓐ **in, in the course of, during, while**
ⓑ **in the process of, in progress, under**
- *a* 午前中 ごぜんちゅう in the morning
- 今週中に こんしゅうちゅうに in the course of the week, before the week is over
- 授業中 じゅぎょうちゅう while in class
- *b* 建築中 けんちくちゅう under construction
- 修繕中 しゅうぜんちゅう during repairs, in the process of being repaired

内 ▷within (a given period)
ナイ ダイ うち Ⓚ2914

[sometimes also 中] **within (a given period), in the course of, while, during**
- 一週間の内に いっしゅうかんのうちに within a week
- 若い内 わかいうち while young
- その内 そのうち before long, one of these days, sooner or later; in the meantime

eager
懇 切 摯 篤 熱

懇 ▷**earnest**
コン ねんご(ろ)
Ⓚ2517

earnest, fervent, sincere
懇願する こんがんする beg earnestly, implore, entreat
懇望 こんもう entreaty, solicitation, earnest request
懇請する こんせいする request earnestly, solicit, entreat
懇懇と こんこんと earnestly, repeatedly

切 ▷**eager**
セツ サイ き(る) き(り) -ぎ(り) き(れる) き(れ) -ぎ(れ)
Ⓚ0015

eager, earnest, ardent
切望 せつぼう earnest desire, eager wish
切切と せつせつと eagerly, earnestly, with emotion

摯 ▷**serious**
シ
Ⓚ2496

serious, sincere
真摯 しんし sincerity, earnestness

篤 ▷**devoted**
トク
Ⓚ2370

devoted, fervent, sincere
篤信 とくしん devoutness
篤学 とくがく love of learning, devotion to one's studies
篤農家 とくのうか exemplary good farmer
篤実 とくじつ sincerity, faithfulness

熱 ▷**hot**
ネツ あつ(い)
Ⓚ2495

(showing intense feeling) **hot (with excitement), fervent, passionate, ardent, enthusiastic, earnest**
熱意 ねつい zeal, ardor, enthusiasm
熱心に ねっしんに enthusiastically, zealously, fervently, earnestly
熱戦 ねっせん hot contest, hard fight
熱中する ねっちゅうする be absorbed in, become enthusiastic
熱望 ねつぼう fervent hope, earnest desire
熱烈な ねつれつな ardent, fervent, vehement
熱血漢 ねっけつかん hot-blooded man
情熱 じょうねつ passion, enthusiasm

earlier Chinese dynasties
夏 商 周 漢 晋 秦

夏 ▷**Xia Dynasty**
カ ゲ なつ
Ⓚ1815

Xia Dynasty (c. 2205-c. 1782 B.C.) (the first Chinese dynasty)
夏朝 かちょう Xia Dynasty

商 ▷**Shang Dynasty**
ショウ あきな(う)
Ⓚ1818

Shang [Yin] Dynasty (16th-11th centuries B.C.)
商王朝 しょうおうちょう Shang Dynasty

周 ▷**Zhou Dynasty**
シュウ まわ(り)
Ⓚ2585

Zhou Dynasty (approx. 1100-256 B.C.)
周王朝 しゅうおうちょう Zhou Dynasty

漢 ▷**Han Dynasty**
カン
Ⓚ0602

Han Dynasty (206 B.C.-220 A.D.)
漢朝 かんちょう Han Dynasty
前漢 ぜんかん Former Han

晋 ▷**Jin Dynasty**
シン
Ⓚ2312

Jin Dynasty (265-420 A.D.)
晋書 しんじょ History of the Jin Dynasty

秦 ▷**Qin Dynasty**
シン ジン はた
Ⓚ2238

Qin Dynasty (221-206 B.C.)
秦の始皇帝 しんのしこうてい first emperor of Qin Dynasty

early states of animal life
胎 卵

胎 ▷**fetus**
タイ
Ⓚ0827

[original meaning] **fetus, embryo**
胎児 たいじ embryo, fetus

胎動 たいどう quickening, fetal movement; indication

堕胎 だたい abortion

卵 ▷egg
ラン たまご   Ⓚ0751

[original meaning] egg; spawn, roe

卵殻 らんかく eggshell

卵黄 らんおう yolk

鶏卵 けいらん (hen's) egg

産卵 さんらん egg-laying, spawning

early states of plant life
芽 蕾 苗 種

芽 ▷bud
ガ め   Ⓚ1927

[original meaning] bud, sprout

芽胞 がほう spore

発芽する はつがする bud, sprout, germinate

麦芽 ばくが wheat germ, malt

萌芽 ほうが germination, beginning; sprout

胚芽 はいが embryo bud, germ

蕾 ▷bud (of a flower)
ライ つぼみ つぼ(む)   Ⓚ2095

bud (of a flower)

味蕾 みらい taste buds

苗 ▷seedling
ビョウ ミョウ なえ なわ-   Ⓚ1924

[original meaning] seedling, sapling, young plant

苗圃 びょうほ seedbed

苗字(=名字) みょうじ surname, family name

種苗 しゅびょう seedlings, seeds and saplings

育苗 いくびょう seedling culture

種 ▷seed
シュ たね   Ⓚ1128

seed

種子 しゅし seed, pit, stone

種皮 しゅひ seed coat, testa

earnings →PAY AND EARNINGS

easy
易 安 簡 軽

易 ▷easy (without difficulty)
エキ イ やさ(しい) やす(い)   Ⓚ2135

[also prefix] (without difficulty) easy, simple

易損品 いそんひん fragile article

容易な よういな easy, simple

安易な あんいな easy, easygoing

簡易な かんいな simple, simplified; easy

平易な へいいな plain, simple, easy

安 ▷easy (without effort)
アン やす(い) やす やす(らか)   Ⓚ1859

(without effort) easy, comfortable

安易な あんいな easy, easygoing

安産 あんざん easy [smooth] delivery (of a baby)

安楽な あんらくな comfortable, carefree, cozy

簡 ▷simple
カン   Ⓚ2374

simple, easy, light

簡単な かんたんな simple, easy, light

簡素な かんそな plain, simple

簡易な かんいな simple, simplified; easy

軽 ▷light
ケイ かる(い) かろ(やか)   Ⓚ1372

[also prefix] (not difficult or serious) light, easy, simple

軽易な けいいな easy, light, simple

軽労働 けいろうどう light labor

軽犯罪 けいはんざい minor offense

軽音楽 けいおんがく light music

economizing and economy
省 節 倹

省 ▷save
セイ ショウ かえり(みる) はぶ(く)   Ⓚ2164

save, conserve

省力 しょうりょく labor saving

省エネルギー しょうえねるぎー energy conservation

省資源 しょうしげん saving resources

節 ▷economize
セツ セチ ふし -ぶし   Ⓚ2349

a economize, save, be frugal
b be moderate, be temperate

a 節約する せつやくする economize, save
　節減 せつげん curtailment, economy
　節水 せっすい water economy
　節電 せつでん economy of electric power
　節炭器 せったんき coal [fuel] economizer
b 節制 せっせい temperance, moderation, self-restraint
　節度 せつど standard; moderation
　節煙 せつえん moderation in smoking
　節食 せっしょく moderation in eating, spare diet
　お節介な おせっかいな meddlesome, nosy
　調節 ちょうせつ regulation, adjustment; modulation, tuning

倹 ▷frugal
ケン   Ⓚ0098

frugal, thrifty, economical, sparing
　倹約 けんやく economy, frugality, thrift
　勤倹 きんけん diligence and thrift
　節倹 せっけん economy, frugality, thrift

economy →ECONOMIZING AND ECONOMY

edges and boundaries
縁 端 辺 境 疆 界 際 涯

縁 ▷edge
エン ふち   Ⓚ1269

edge, margin
　縁辺 えんぺん border, edge; relations

端 ▷edge
タン はし は はた -ばた   Ⓚ1131

【はし】
edge, margin, brink, border; side
　端端に はしばしに here and there, in some parts
　道の端 みちのはし edge of a street
　右端 みぎはし right side, right margin

【はた】
[also suffix] **edge, side**
　池の端で いけのはたで near [by] the pond
　道端 みちばた roadside, wayside
　海岸端 かいがんばた seaside

辺 ▷border
ヘン あた(り) -べ   Ⓚ260?

[original meaning] **border, edge, periphery, fringe**
　広大無辺な こうだいむへんな boundless, infinite
　縁辺 えんぺん border, edge; relations

境 ▷boundary
キョウ ケイ さかい   Ⓚ0618

[formerly also 疆] [original meaning] **boundary, border, frontier**
　境界 きょうかい boundary, border
　境域 きょういき boundary; precincts, grounds
　境内 けいだい grounds [premises] (of a shrine or temple)
　国境 こっきょう (national) boundary [border]
　越境 えっきょう border transgression, violation of the border
　辺境 へんきょう frontier (district), remote region, border(land)
　県境 けんきょう prefectural border

疆 ▷boundary
キョウ

[now usu. 境] [original meaning] **boundary, border, frontier**
　辺疆 へんきょう frontier (district), remote region, border(land)
　新疆 しんきょう Xinjiang

界 ▷bounds
カイ   Ⓚ2220

[original meaning] **bounds, boundary, border**
　界面 かいめん interface
　限界 げんかい boundary, limit, bounds
　境界 きょうかい boundary, border
　臨界点 りんかいてん critical point [temperature]

際 ▷verge
サイ きわ -ぎわ   Ⓚ0646

verge, brink, edge
　際限 さいげん limits, end, bounds
　際涯 さいがい limits, end, extremity
　金輪際 こんりんざい never; *Buddhism* deepest bottom of the earth
　天際 てんさい horizon

涯 ▷outer limits
ガイ   Ⓚ0469

outer limits, end, bound
　生涯 しょうがい life, lifetime, career; for life
　際涯 さいがい limits, end, extremity
　天涯 てんがい far-off land (as remote as the horizon)

editions

版 刊 訂 刷

版 ▷edition
ハン   Ⓚ0775

ⓐ [also suffix] **edition, impression, printing**
ⓑ **counter for editions**
ⓐ 初版 しょはん first edition
重版 じゅうはん second printing, reprint; second edition
地方版 ちほうばん local edition
決定版 けっていばん authoritative edition; last word
ⓑ 第二版 だいにはん second edition

刊 ▷publication
カン   Ⓚ0167

publication, edition, issue
週刊 しゅうかん weekly publication, weekly
朝刊 ちょうかん morning edition [paper]
夕刊 ゆうかん evening edition [paper]

訂 ▷revision
テイ   Ⓚ1310

revision, edition
新訂 しんてい new revision

刷 ▷printing
サツ す(る) -ず(り)   Ⓚ1169

counter for printings
第四版三刷 だいよんはんさんさつ fourth edition, third printing

elapse

過 経 歴 去

過 ▷pass by
カ す(ぎる) -す(ぎ) す(ごす) あやま(つ) あやま(ち)   Ⓚ2704

(of time) **pass by [away], elapse**
過去 かこ the past, bygone days
過日 かじつ the other day, some days ago

経 ▷pass
ケイ キョウ へ(る) た(つ)   Ⓚ1218

(of time) **pass, elapse**
経過する けいかする pass, elapse

歴 ▷pass
レキ   Ⓚ2600

pass, elapse, pass through, experience
歴史 れきし history
歴戦 れきせん long record of active service
遍歴 へんれき travels, pilgrimage

去 ▷pass away
キョ コ さ(る)   Ⓚ1850

pass away, elapse, go by
過去 かこ the past, bygone days

elated

亢 高 昂 奮

亢 ▷high-spirited
コウ

[now replaced by 興 or 高] **high-spirited, excited, elated**
亢奮(=興奮)する こうふんする get excited, be agitated, be aroused
亢進(=高進、昂進)する こうしんする rise, exasperate, accelerate

高 ▷high-spirited
コウ たか(い) たか -だか たか(まる) たか(める)   Ⓚ1803

[formerly also 昂 or 亢] **high-spirited, excited, elated**
高揚(=昂揚)する こうようする exalt, enhance, uplift; surge up
意気軒高(=意気軒昂)として いきけんこうとして in high spirits

昂 ▷high-spirited
コウ   Ⓚ2136

ⓐ [now usu. 高 or 興] **high-spirited, excited, elated**
ⓑ [now replaced by 高] (showing pride) **high, proud, haughty**
ⓐ 昂奮(=興奮) こうふん excitement, agitation, stimulation
昂進(=高進、亢進)する こうしんする rise, exasperate, accelerate
昂揚(=高揚)する こうようする exalt, enhance, uplift; surge up
激昂(=激高)する げっこう(=げきこう)する get excited, be exasperated, become indignant
意気軒昂(=意気軒高)として いきけんこうとして in high spirits
ⓑ 昂然(=高然)たる こうぜんたる elated, triumphant, proud

揚 ▷**exalted**
ヨウ あ(げる) -あ(げ) あ(がる)　Ⓚ0542

(raise one's spirits) **be exalted, be in high spirits**
意気揚揚と いきようようと exultantly, in exalted
spirits, proudly

奮 ▷**roused up**
フン ふる(う)　Ⓚ2090

be roused up, get excited, be angered
興奮(=昂奮) こうふん excitement, agitation, stimulation

election →VOTE AND ELECTION

electricity and magnetism
電　流　磁

電 ▷**electricity**
デン　Ⓚ2431

electricity
電気 でんき electricity; electric light
電子 でんし electron
電力 でんりょく electric power, electricity
電車 でんしゃ train, electric train, trolley
電波 でんぱ electromagnetic waves, radio waves
電話 でんわ telephone; phone call
電話帳 でんわちょう telephone book [directory]
電報 でんぽう telegram
電算機 でんさんき electronic computer
電源 でんげん power source [supply]
発電する はつでんする generate electricity; telegraph
停電 ていでん stoppage of electric power, power
failure

流 ▷**electric current**
リュウ ル なが(れる) なが(れ)
なが(す)　Ⓚ0400

electric current
電流 でんりゅう electric current
交流 こうりゅう alternating current; interchange
整流 せいりゅう rectification

磁 ▷**magnetism**
ジ　Ⓚ1123

ⓐ **magnetism**
ⓑ [also prefix] **magnetic**
a 磁気 じき magnetism
磁力線 じりょくせん line of magnetic force

磁場 じば magnetic field
磁極 じきょく magnetic pole
電磁波 でんじは electromagnetic waves
b 磁方位 じほうい magnetic bearing

elegance →FLAVOR AND ELEGANCE

elegant
雅　淑　優　粋　彬

雅 ▷**elegant**
ガ　Ⓚ1106

ⓐ **elegant, refined, graceful, artistic, sophisticated**
ⓑ **proper and elegant, standard, classical**
a 雅趣 がしゅ elegance, artistry, taste
雅号 がごう pen name, pseudonym
優雅な ゆうがな elegant, graceful, refined
風雅 ふうが elegance, refinement, daintiness
b 雅楽 ががく ceremonial court music
高雅な こうがな refined, elegant, chaste

淑 ▷**graceful**
シュク　Ⓚ0483

(of women) **graceful, gentle and kind, refined, fair**
淑徳 しゅくとく feminine grace, womanly virtues
淑女 しゅくじょ lady, gentlewoman
貞淑 ていしゅく chastity, female virtue

優 ▷**graceful**
ユウ やさ(しい) すぐ(れる)　Ⓚ0156

graceful, elegant, delicate
優美な ゆうびな graceful, elegant, refined
優雅 ゆうが elegance, grace
優艶な ゆうえんな beautiful, charming

粋 ▷**refined**
スイ いき　Ⓚ1188

(free from coarseness) **refined, sophisticated, polished, elegant, cultivated, tasteful**
粋人 すいじん refined [romantic] man
粋狂(=酔狂) すいきょう vagary, whim
無粋(=不粋)な ぶすいな lacking in polish, inele-
gant; unromantic

彬 ▷**refined and gentle**
ヒン　Ⓚ0868

[rare] (having both appearance and substance) **refined
and gentle, handsome and solid in character, having a due combination of plainness and ornament**
彬蔚 ひんうつ handsome, erudite and refined
文質彬彬 ぶんしつひんぴん refined, handsome and
solid in character

element
素　元　単

素 ▷**element**
ソス　　　　　　　　　Ⓚ2171

[also suffix]
ⓐ **element, basic constituent, component**
ⓑ **chemical element**
ⓒ (structural element of language) **-eme**
ⓓ (pertaining to an element) **elementary, elemental**

a 素子 そし *elec* element
　要素 ようそ (essential) element, constituent, factor
　酵素 こうそ ferment; enzyme
　色素 しきそ pigment, coloring matter
　栄養素 えいようそ nutritive elements [substance]
　葉緑素 ようりょくそ chlorophyll
　元素 げんそ element, chemical element
b 酸素 さんそ oxygen
　炭素 たんそ carbon
c 音素 おんそ phoneme
　形態素 けいたいそ morpheme
d 素反応 そはんのう elementary reaction

元 ▷**element**
ゲン ガン もと　　　　　Ⓚ1690

ⓐ **element, unit, basic element, essence, entity**
ⓑ *math* **element, dimension**

a 元素 げんそ element, chemical element
　二元論 にげんろん dualism
　単元制度 たんげんせいど unit credit system
b 単位元 たんいげん unit element
　三次元 さんじげん three dimensions

単 ▷**unit**
タン　　　　　　　　　Ⓚ1946

unit
　単位 たんい unit
　単価 たんか unit cost, unit price
　単語 たんご word
　単元 たんげん unit

elevations in water
島　州　礁　洲

島 ▷**island**
トウ しま　　　　　　　Ⓚ2820

ⓐ [also suffix] [original meaning] **island**
ⓑ **suffix after names of islands**

a 島嶼 とうしょ islands
　島民 とうみん islanders
　諸島 しょとう archipelago
　半島 はんとう peninsula
　列島 れっとう archipelago
　無人島 むじんとう uninhabited island
b 色丹島 しこたんとう Shikotan Island

州 ▷**sandbar**
シュウ す　　　　　　　Ⓚ0040

[formerly also 洲] **sandbar, shallows, shoal**
　三角州 さんかくす delta
　砂州 さす sandbar, sandbank
　座州する ざすする strand, run aground

礁 ▷**reef**
ショウ　　　　　　　　Ⓚ1148

[original meaning] **reef, sunken rock**
　岩礁 がんしょう reef
　珊瑚礁 さんごしょう coral reef
　座礁(=坐礁)する ざしょうする run aground, be
　　stranded
　環礁 かんしょう atoll
　暗礁 あんしょう sunken rock, unknown reef; dead-
　　lock

洲 ▷**sandbar**
シュウ す　　　　　　　Ⓚ0352

【シュウ】
[original meaning] **sandbar, shallows, shoal**
【す】
[now usu. 州] **sandbar, shallows, shoal**
　砂洲 さす sandbar, sandbank
　座洲する ざすする strand, run aground

eliminate
却 排 払 剥 耘 削 抹
省 脱 去 外 除 撤

却 ▷**eliminate**
キャク　　　　　　　　Ⓚ1034

eliminate, exclude, remove, get rid of—used as the
second element in verbal compounds similar to *off* in *kill off*
　除却する じょきゃくする exclude, eliminate
　脱却する だっきゃくする get rid of; slough off
　消却する しょうきゃくする efface; erase
　忘却する ぼうきゃくする forget
　焼却する しょうきゃくする destroy by fire, incinerate
　売却する ばいきゃくする sell off, dispose of by sale
　償却する しょうきゃくする repay, refund

排 ▷exclude
ハイ   Ⓚ0446

[original meaning] **exclude, expel, reject, drive out**
排除 はいじょ exclusion, removal, elimination
排斥する はいせきする expel, reject, exclude, ostracize
排他的な はいたてきな exclusive, clannish
排他主義 はいたしゅぎ exclusivism

払 ▷clear away
フツ はら(う) -はら(い) -ばら(い) Ⓚ0171

(remove something undesirable) **clear away, sweep away, brush off, prune**
払い除ける はらいのける brush off, sweep away
払い落とす はらいおとす shake off, brush off
足払い あしばらい tripping up
取り払う とりはらう clear away, remove

剝 ▷peel off
ハク は(がす) は(ぐ) は(がれる) は(げる)   Ⓚ1494

(come off of a surface) **peel off, wear off**
剝離 はくり exfoliation, peeling off
剝落 はくらく coming off, peeling off
剝片 はくへん flake, chip

耘 ▷weed
ウン

[now also 耘] [original meaning] **weed, remove weeds**
耕耘機 こううんき cultivator, tiller

削 ▷cross out
サク けず(る)   Ⓚ1316

cross out, strike off, delete, cancel
削除 さくじょ deletion, elimination, cancellation
添削する てんさくする correct, touch up ("add and delete")

抹 ▷wipe off
マツ   Ⓚ0277

(remove by rubbing) **wipe off, wipe out, erase, strike out**
抹殺する まっさつする erase, strike out; deny, ignore; do away with, liquidate
抹消する まっしょうする erase, strike out

省 ▷leave out
セイ ショウ かえり(みる) はぶ(く) Ⓚ2164

leave out, omit
省略 しょうりゃく omission, abbreviation, abridgment

脱 ▷remove
ダツ ぬ(ぐ) ぬ(げる)   Ⓚ0886

[also prefix] **remove, eliminate, de- (as in *decarbonate*)**
脱脂 だっし fat removal
脱毛 だつもう removal of hair; falling out of hair
脱色 だっしょく decolorization
脱水 だっすい dehydration
脱炭酸 だつたんさん decarbonation

去 ▷take away
キョ コ さ(る)   Ⓚ1850

take away, remove, get rid of, eliminate
去勢 きょせい castration; enervation
除去する じょきょする rid of, remove, eliminate
撤去する てっきょする remove, dismantle (a building); evacuate (an army)

外 ▷take off
ガイ ゲ そと ほか はず(す) はず(れる)   Ⓚ0163

take off, remove, undo, detach; miss, let go, fail; avoid, dodge, slip away; leave out, exclude
眼鏡を外す めがねをはずす take off one's glasses
取り外す とりはずす remove, dismantle
機会を外す きかいをはずす miss a chance
席を外している せきをはずしている be not at one's desk
予定から外す よていからはずす exclude from the schedule

除 ▷rid of
ジョ ジ のぞ(く)   Ⓚ0412

rid of, clear away, remove, eliminate
除去する じょきょする rid of, remove, eliminate
除雪する じょせつする get rid of snow, remove snow
除外 じょがい exclusion, exception
解除する かいじょする remove [lift] (a ban), cancel; release, acquit
掃除 そうじ cleaning
排除 はいじょ exclusion, removal, elimination
削除する さくじょする delete, eliminate, cancel
控除 こうじょ (tax) deduction, subtraction

撤 ▷withdraw
テツ   Ⓚ0673

[original meaning] (take back) **withdraw, remove, take away**
撤去 てっきょ removal, dismantlement (of a building); evacuation (of an army)
撤回 てっかい withdrawal, retraction
撤廃 てっぱい abolition, removal

embankment
堤　防　堰

堤 ▷**embankment**
テイ つつみ ⓚ0515

[also suffix] [original meaning] **embankment, dike, bank**
堤防 ていぼう bank, embankment, dike
突堤 とってい pier, breakwater
築堤 ちくてい embankment, bank; building an
embankment
防潮堤 ぼうちょうてい tide embankment, seawall
防波堤 ぼうはてい breakwater

防 ▷**dike**
ボウ ふせ(ぐ) ⓚ0242

[original meaning] **dike**
堤防 ていぼう bank, embankment, dike

堰 ▷**dam**
エン せき せ(く) ⓚ0510

dam, sluice, weir
堰堤 えんてい dike, weir

embrace
抱　擁

抱 ▷**hug**
ホウ だ(く) いだ(く) かか(える) ⓚ0271

[formerly also 捧] [original meaning] **hug, embrace, hold
in one's arms, enfold**
抱擁する ほうようする embrace, hug, hold in one's
arms
抱卵 ほうらん incubation
抱腹絶倒する ほうふくぜっとうする double up with
laughter
介抱する かいほうする nurse, care for

擁 ▷**embrace**
ヨウ ⓚ0694

[original meaning] **embrace, hold in one's arms, hug**
抱擁する ほうようする embrace, hug, hold in one's
arms

emit
出発放排射噴吐湧

出 ▷**put out**
シュツ スイ で(る) -で だ(す) ⓚ2934

put out, give out, discharge, send out, take out
出荷する しゅっかする forward, ship, consign
出超 しゅっちょう excess of exports over imports
放出する ほうしゅつする release, discharge, emit
検出する けんしゅつする detect, find
選出する せんしゅつする elect
救出する きゅうしゅつする rescue, relieve, deliver
輸出 ゆしゅつ export
提出する ていしゅつする present, submit, turn in

発 ▷**emit**
ハツ ホツ た(つ) ⓚ2222

(give off) **emit, send out, issue, discharge, dispatch,
transmit**
発光 はっこう radiation, luminescence
発汗 はっかん perspiring, sweating
発音 はつおん pronunciation
発火 はっか ignition; combustion
発散 はっさん emission; radiation; evaporation
発病する はつびょうする fall ill, get sick
蒸発 じょうはつ evaporation, volatilization; mysterious disappearance

放 ▷**radiate**
ホウ はな(す) -(っ)ぱな(し) はな(つ)
はな(れる) ほう(る) ⓚ0754

ⓐ (give off in all directions) **radiate, emit, emanate,
broadcast**
ⓑ **let out, discharge, excrete**
a 放射する ほうしゃする radiate, emit, emanate
放光 ほうこう emission of light
放映 ほうえい telecasting
放送 ほうそう broadcasting
民放 みんぽう commercial broadcast
b 放水 ほうすい discharge, drainage
放屁 ほうひ breaking wind

排 ▷**discharge**
ハイ ⓚ0446

(put out, esp. undesirable substances) **discharge, exhaust, drain, excrete**
排出 はいしゅつ discharge, exhaust, evacuation
排水 はいすい drainage, draining; (of ships) displacement
排気 はいき exhaust, used steam; exhaustion,
evacuation

排気ガス はいきがす exhaust gas
排尿 はいにょう urination

射 ▷shoot
シャ い(る) さ(す)   Ⓚ1327

(emit forcefully) **shoot (out) (radiation or liquids), emit, radiate, discharge, eject**
射精 しゃせい ejaculation, seminal emission
放射する ほうしゃする radiate, emit, emanate
日射 にっしゃ insolation, solar radiation
反射 はんしゃ reflection
直射日光 ちょくしゃにっこう direct rays of the sun
注射 ちゅうしゃ injection, shot

噴 ▷spout
フン ふ(く)   Ⓚ0649

[original meaning] **spout, emit, spurt, gush out**
噴出 ふんしゅつ spouting, gushing
噴水 ふんすい jet (of water), fountain
噴火 ふんか eruption, volcanic activity
噴火山 ふんかざん volcano
噴霧器 ふんむき sprayer, vaporizer, atomizer
噴射 ふんしゃ jet, jet propulsion
噴飯する ふんぱんする burst out laughing

吐 ▷spew
ト は(く)   Ⓚ0180

[original meaning] **spew, vomit**
吐出 としゅつ spew, vomit, disgorge
吐血 とけつ vomiting blood
吐息 といき sigh, long breath
嘔吐 おうと vomiting
音吐朗朗と おんとろうろうと in a clear voice

湧 ▷well up
ユウ わ(く)   Ⓚ0563

【ユウ】
[original meaning] **well up, spring forth, gush out**
湧出 ゆうしゅつ welling, gushing
湧水 ゆうすい welling of water
【わ(く)】
well up, spring forth, gush out
湧き水 わきみず spring water
湧き出る わきでる well up, spring forth

employ
雇 用 使 傭 役

雇 ▷employ
コ やと(う)   Ⓚ170⬛

employ, engage
雇用(=雇傭)する こようする employ, hire
雇主 こしゅ employer
雇員 こいん employee
解雇 かいこ discharge, dismissal

用 ▷employ
ヨウ もち(いる)   Ⓚ2569

[formerly also 傭 or 庸] **employ (a person), engage**
用人 ようにん steward, manager
雇用(=雇傭) こよう employment, hire

使 ▷employ
シ つか(う) つか(い) -づか(い)   Ⓚ0072

employ, keep (in one's employ)
人を使う ひとをつかう employ, take a person in one's service

傭 ▷hire
ヨウ やと(う)   Ⓚ0139

[now usu. 用] **hire, employ**
傭兵 ようへい mercenary soldier, hireling
傭人 ようにん employee
雇傭する こようする employ, hire
被傭者 ひようしゃ employee

役 ▷press into service
ヤク エキ   Ⓚ0217

press into service, enlist one's service, employ
使役 しえき employment, service; *gram* causative
労役 ろうえき labor, work, toil
雑役 ざつえき miscellaneous services, odd jobs
懲役 ちょうえき penal servitude, imprisonment with hard labor

employment →WORK AND EMPLOYMENT

emptiness and nothing

空 白 虚 無

空 ▷empty
クウ そら あ(く) あ(き) あ(ける) から　むな(しい)　Ⓚ1913

[original meaning] **empty, vacant, unoccupied, blank**

空車 くうしゃ vacant taxi, empty car
空砲 くうほう blank shot [cartridge]
空白 くうはく blank, empty space; void, vacuum
空席 くうせき vacant seat; vacancy
真空 しんくう vacuum

白 ▷white (blank)
ハク ビャク しろ しら- しろ(い)　Ⓚ2929

(not written or printed upon) **white, blank**

白紙 はくし blank sheet, flyleaf; clean slate
白票 はくひょう blank ballot
白痴 はくち idiocy, idiot
白文 はくぶん unpunctuated Chinese text
空白 くうはく blank, empty space; void, vacuum

虚 ▷void
キョ コ　Ⓚ2778

(containing nothing) **void, empty, vacant, hollow**

虚無 きょむ nothingness; nihility
虚無僧 こむそう flute-playing Zen mendicant priest
虚脱 きょだつ (physical) collapse, prostration; absentmindedness
虚空 こくう empty space, sky
空虚な くうきょな empty, void; inane

無 ▷nothing
ム ブ な(い)　Ⓚ1832

nothing, nothingness, nonexistence

皆無 かいむ nothing
有無 うむ existence, presence; yes or no
絶無 ぜつむ nothing, nil, naught

end

終 絶 閉 了 済
上 完 結 竣

終 ▷end
シュウ お(わる) お(える)　Ⓚ1223

ⓐ end, come to an end, finish, terminate
ⓑ bring to an end, finish, complete
ⓒ end one's life, die

a 終了する しゅうりょうする end, conclude, complete; expire
終結 しゅうけつ end, conclusion, termination
終戦 しゅうせん end of the war
終極の しゅうきょくの ultimate, final
b 終業時間 しゅうぎょうじかん closing hour
c 臨終 りんじゅう hour of death, one's last moment

絶 ▷come to an end
ゼツ た(える) た(やす) た(つ)　Ⓚ1240
see also →COME TO AN END

come to an end, cease to exist

絶望 ぜつぼう despair, hopelessness
絶滅 ぜつめつ extermination, eradication; extinction
絶息する ぜっそくする expire, die
気絶する きぜつする faint
杜絶(=途絶) とぜつ stoppage, interruption, cessation

閉 ▷close
ヘイ と(じる) と(ざす) し(める)　し(まる)　Ⓚ2832

(bring to an end) **close (a shop), adjourn, end**

閉会 へいかい closing (of a meeting), adjournment
閉店 へいてん closing the shop
閉幕となる へいまくとなる come to a close [end]
閉校 へいこう closing a school

了 ▷finish
リョウ　Ⓚ2852

finish, complete, conclude

議了する ぎりょうする finish discussion, close a debate
未了 みりょう unfinished, incomplete
完了する かんりょうする complete, finish; be completed, be finished
終了する しゅうりょうする end, conclude, complete; expire
修了 しゅうりょう completion (of a course)
満了する まんりょうする expire, become due

済 ▷settle
サイ す(む) –ず(み) す(まない) す(ます)
す(ませる)   Ⓚ0478

settle, conclude, finish
完済 かんさい full payment, liquidation
未済の みさいの unsettled, unpaid, outstanding;
   unfinished

上 ▷completion suffix
ジョウ ショウ うえ うわ– かみ –あ(げる)
あ(がる) あ(がり) のぼ(る) のぼ(り)
のぼ(せる) のぼ(す)   Ⓚ2876

verbal suffix indicating completion of an action
作り上げる つくりあげる make up, build up,
   complete
仕上げる しあげる finish, complete, perfect
書き上げる かきあげる finish writing

完 ▷complete
カン   Ⓚ1883

ⓐ (bring to a final stage) **complete, conclude, finish,
end**
ⓑ **be completed, come to an end**
a 完成する かんせいする complete, finish; be
   completed, be finished
完結 かんけつ completion, conclusion, finish
完遂する かんすいする execute successfully,
   accomplish, bring to completion
b 完了する かんりょうする complete, finish; be
   completed, be finished
未完の みかんの incomplete, unfinished

結 ▷conclude
ケツ むす(ぶ) ゆ(う) ゆ(わえる)   Ⓚ1235

(bring to an end) **conclude, close, finish, settle**
結論 けつろん conclusion
結局 けっきょく after all, finally, in conclusion
結末 けつまつ termination, end, close, conclusion
結語 けつご conclusion, concluding remarks
結願 けちがん expiration of one's vow term
終結する しゅうけつする end, close, terminate
完結する かんけつする complete, conclude, finish;
   be complete, be concluded, be finished

竣 ▷complete
シュン   Ⓚ1102

complete, finish (a project or task)
竣工する しゅんこうする (of construction work) be
   completed

ends
末 終 畢 尾 局

末 ▷last part
マツ バツ すえ   Ⓚ2940

last part, last stage, termination, end
末尾 まつび end, close
年末 ねんまつ end of year
期末 きまつ end of term
週末 しゅうまつ weekend
結末 けつまつ termination, end, close, conclusion
始末 しまつ management, dealing, disposal;
   circumstances; result, outcome

終 ▷end
シュウ お(わる) お(える)   Ⓚ1223

end, ending, finish
最終 さいしゅう last, the end; final

畢 ▷end
ヒツ おわ(る)   Ⓚ2240

ⓐ **end, come to an end, finish, terminate**
ⓑ **bring to an end, finish, complete**
ab 畢生 ひっせい lifetime

尾 ▷end
ビ お   Ⓚ2635

end
首尾 しゅび beginning and end; result, issue
竜頭蛇尾 りゅうとうだび bright start, dull finish
巻尾 かんび end of a book
末尾 まつび end, close
語尾 ごび ending of a word

局 ▷close
キョク   Ⓚ2636

close, end, conclusion
終局 しゅうきょく end, conclusion, termination; end
   of a game
結局 けっきょく after all, finally, in conclusion

endure →BEAR AND ENDURE

enemy

敵　　仇

敵 ▷enemy
テキ かたき　　Ⓚ1648

ⓐ [also prefix] **enemy, foe**
ⓑ **opponent, rival**

a 敵国 てきこく enemy country
　敵意 てきい hostility, enmity
　強敵 きょうてき powerful enemy [rival]
b 敵王 てきおう opponent's king (in shogi)
　敵艦隊 てきかんたい enemy fleet

仇 ▷foe
キュウ あだ あだ(する) かたき

foe, enemy
　仇敵 きゅうてき bitter enemy
　仇怨 きゅうえん foe, enemy; grudge, hatred

energy and force

力　勢　気　圧　鋒

力 ▷power, force
リョク リキ ちから　　Ⓚ2860

ⓐ (source of energy) **power, energy; motive power**
ⓑ *phys* **force**

a 力織機 りきしょっき power loom
　電力 でんりょく electric power, electricity
　原子力 げんしりょく atomic energy, nuclear power
　馬力 ばりき horsepower; energy, effort; cart,
　　wagon
　動力源 どうりょくげん power source
　出力 しゅつりょく generating power, output
b 重力 じゅうりょく gravity, force of gravity
　圧力 あつりょく pressure
　表面張力 ひょうめんちょうりょく surface tension

勢 ▷physical power
セイ いきお(い)　　Ⓚ2487

physical power, force; momentum; energy
　火勢 かせい force of the fire, flames
　強勢 きょうせい emphasis, stress, accent
　筆勢 ひっせい stroke [dash] of the pen
　余勢 よせい surplus power, reserve energy

気 ▷energy
キ ケ　　Ⓚ2751

energy, force

電気 でんき electricity; electric light
磁気 じき magnetism

圧 ▷pressure
アツ　　Ⓚ2563

pressure
　水圧 すいあつ water pressure
　気圧 きあつ atmospheric [air] pressure
　血圧 けつあつ blood pressure
　電圧 でんあつ voltage, electric pressure

鋒 ▷brunt
ホウ きっさき ほこ ほこさき　　Ⓚ1545

brunt, sharp force
　鋭鋒 えいほう brunt (of an attack); incisive reason-
　　ing
　舌鋒 ぜっぽう (sharp) tongue
　筆鋒 ひっぽう power of the pen, sharp pen; tip of a
　　writing brush

enlist

徴　　募

徴 ▷levy
チョウ　　Ⓚ0622

ⓐ (enlist troops) **levy, conscript, recruit**
ⓑ (collect by force) **requisition, commandeer**

a 徴兵 ちょうへい conscription, enlistment, draft
　徴募 ちょうぼ recruitment
　徴集する ちょうしゅうする levy, recruit
b 徴発 ちょうはつ commandeering, requisition

募 ▷raise
ボ つの(る)　　Ⓚ2013

[original meaning] (gather persons or money by appealing
to the public) **raise (troops or funds), collect, recruit,
enlist**
　募集する ぼしゅうする recruit, enlist; raise, collect
　募金 ぼきん fund-raising, collection of subscrip-
　　tions
　募債 ぼさい raising of a loan, loan flotation
　応募する おうぼする apply for, subscribe for [to],
　　enlist for
　公募 こうぼ appeal for public subscription
　徴募 ちょうぼ recruitment

enter

入　込

入 ▷enter
ニュウ い(る) −い(り) い(れる) −い(れ)
はい(る)　　　　　　　　　　　　Ⓚ2859

[original meaning] **enter, come in, go in**
入場 にゅうじょう entrance, admission
入国 にゅうこく entry [entrance] into a country
入室する にゅうしつする enter a room; join (a laboratory)
収入 しゅうにゅう income, earnings, receipts
侵入する しんにゅうする invade, raid, trespass, intrude
介入 かいにゅう intervention

込 ▷move inward
−こ(む) こ(み) こ(める)　　　　Ⓚ2608

[original meaning] **move inward, get in, come in**
乗り込む のりこむ board, go on board; march into
迷い込む まよいこむ stray [wander] into
割り込み わりこみ breaking into a queue, wedging oneself in

envious →JEALOUS AND ENVIOUS

equip and install

据　敷　架　装　設　備

据 ▷install
す(える) す(わる)　　　　　　　Ⓚ0455

(set in position) **install, place in position, fix, mount, set up; set (a table); lay (a foundation)**
据え付ける すえつける install, equip, fit
据え置き すえおき leaving (a thing) as it stands; deferred savings
据え膳 すえぜん meal set before one; women's advances
見据える みすえる fix one's eyes, look hard

敷 ▷lay
フ し(く) −し(き)　　　　　　　Ⓚ1653

[also 布] [original meaning] (dispose over a surface) **lay (as a railroad track), spread**
敷設 ふせつ construction, laying
敷衍 ふえん expatiation, amplification, elaboration

架 ▷lay across
カ か(ける) か(かる)　　　　　　Ⓚ2226

lay (a bridge or wire) across, build across, span (a river) with (a bridge), bridge
架設する かせつする construct, erect, build, install
架線 かせん aerial wiring
架橋 かきょう bridge building
架空の かくうの overhead, aerial; fanciful, fictitious
高架橋 こうかきょう elevated bridge

装 ▷fit out
ソウ ショウ よそお(う)　　　　Ⓚ2344

fit out, equip, outfit, furnish, install
装備する そうびする equip, fit out, furnish
装置 そうち equipment, device, installation
艤装する ぎそうする fit out (a ship), equip
武装 ぶそう armament, equipment

設 ▷set up
セツ もう(ける)　　　　　　　Ⓚ1338

(assemble and/or erect) **set up, install, erect, construct**
設備 せつび equipment, facilities
建設 けんせつ construction, building, erection
埋設する まいせつする put [lay] underground
施設 しせつ equipment, facilities; institution, establishment

備 ▷provide
ビ そな(える) そな(わる)　　　Ⓚ0126

ⓐ **provide (with), equip, fit**
ⓑ **be provided with, be equipped with**
a 備品 びひん fixtures, furnishings
　設備する せつびする equip [provide] (with)
　整備 せいび maintenance, servicing, preparation
　装備 そうび equipment, outfit
b 完備した かんびした fully-equipped, perfect, complete
　具備する ぐびする be endowed [equipped] with, possess

escape

逃　遁　亡　走　脱

逃 ▷escape
トウ に(げる) に(がす) のが(す)
のが(れる)　　　　　　　　　　Ⓚ2666

[original meaning] **escape, run away, flee**
逃亡する とうぼうする escape, abscond, desert
逃走 とうそう flight, escape

遁 ▷flee
トン のが(れる)   Ⓚ2782

flee, escape, evade; shirk away
- 遁走 とんそう fleeing, escape
- 遁世 とんせい seclusion from the world
- 遁術 とんじゅつ ninja art of escape
- 隠遁 いんとん retirement (from the world), seclusion
- 水遁 すいとん ninja art of water-escape

亡 ▷flee
ボウ モウ な(い) な(き)-   Ⓚ2874

flee, escape
- 亡命 ぼうめい exile
- 逃亡 とうぼう escape, abscondence, desertion

走 ▷run away
ソウ はし(る)   Ⓚ1877

run away, flee
- 逃走 とうそう flight, escape
- 脱走する だっそうする desert, escape

脱 ▷escape from
ダツ ぬ(ぐ) ぬ(げる)   Ⓚ0886

[also prefix] **escape from (an undesirable situation), get away from, extricate oneself from, withdraw from**
- 脱税 だつぜい tax evasion
- 脱退 だったい withdrawal, secession
- 脱出 だっしゅつ escape, extrication
- 脱走 だっそう desertion, escape
- 脱獄 だつごく prison break, jailbreak
- 脱却する だっきゃくする get rid of; slough off
- 脱会 だっかい withdrawal (from an organization)
- 脱石油 だつせきゆ extrication from dependence on oil
- 離脱 りだつ breakaway, separation, secession

escort →LEAD AND ESCORT

essential content
実 体 味

実 ▷substance
ジツ み みの(る)   Ⓚ1911

substance, contents
- 充実した じゅうじつした full, complete, rich
- 情実 じょうじつ private circumstances, personal consideration; favoritism
- 口実 こうじつ excuse, pretext, pretense

体 ▷substance
タイ テイ からだ   Ⓚ0055

(main or essential part) **substance, reality, real thing**
- 体言 たいげん indeclinable parts of speech in Japanese, substantive
- 主体 しゅたい main part; subject
- 実体 じったい substance, essence
- 本体 ほんたい substance, thing itself; object of worship; main part
- 大体 だいたい outline, substance; generally, roughly, on the whole

味 ▷contents
ミ あじ あじ(わう)   Ⓚ0247

contents, substance; meaning
- 正味の しょうみの net, full, clear
- 意味 いみ meaning, intention, significance, purport

essential part
精 粋 髄 枢 幹 綱 旨 要

精 ▷essence (essential part)
セイ ショウ   Ⓚ1248

(essential part) **essence, quintessence, spirit**
- 精髄 せいずい essence, soul, spirit, pith
- 精華 せいか flower, essence, glory

粋 ▷essence (best part)
スイ いき   Ⓚ1188

(best part) **essence, quintessence**
- 精粋 せいすい essence, purity
- 国粋 こくすい national characteristics

髄 ▷essence (vital part)
ズイ   Ⓚ1634

(vital part) **essence, core, heart**
- 真髄(=神髄) しんずい essence, quintessence, soul
- 精髄 せいずい essence, soul, spirit, pith

枢 ▷pivot
スウ   Ⓚ0770

(central part) **pivot, center**
- 枢要な すうような pivotal, cardinal
- 枢軸国 すうじくこく the Axis Powers
- 枢機 すうき most important affairs (of state)
- 枢密 すうみつ secret government affairs
- 中枢 ちゅうすう pivot, center

幹 ▷trunk
カン みき   Ⓚ1531

(main part of something) **trunk, main part**
- 幹線 かんせん trunk line, main line
- 幹部 かんぶ executive, (managing) staff
- 幹事 かんじ manager, secretary; organizer
- 基幹 きかん mainstay, nucleus
- 主幹 しゅかん editor in chief

綱 ▷essential points
コウ つな   Ⓚ1253

essential [main] points, essence, gist, outline
- 綱領 こうりょう essential [main] points, gist, outline; summary
- 綱要 こうよう elements, essentials; outline
- 要綱 ようこう outline, gist; general plan
- 大綱 たいこう outline, general features

旨 ▷purport
シ むね   Ⓚ1744

(main idea) **purport, meaning, tenet, substance, gist, point**
- 要旨 ようし gist, point, essentials, summary; purport
- 主旨 しゅし gist, main point, substance
- 論旨 ろんし point of an argument

要 ▷summary
ヨウ かなめ い(る)   Ⓚ2290

[also suffix] **summary (of important points), gist, essence**
- 概要 がいよう outline, summary, synopsis
- 紀要 きよう bulletin, proceedings
- 提要 ていよう summary, outline
- 哲学史要 てつがくしよう Concise History of Philosophy

estrange

疎   離   遠

疎 ▷estrange
ソ うと(い) うと(む)   Ⓚ1091

ⓐ **estrange, alienate, neglect**
ⓑ **estranged, alienated, distant**
- ₐ 疎外 そがい estrangement, alienation
- 疎隔 そかく estrangement, alienation
- ᵦ 疎水性の そすいせいの hydrophobic
- 疎遠 そえん estrangement, alienation, neglect

離 ▷separate from
リ はな(れる) はな(す)   Ⓚ1663

(sever relations) **separate from, withdraw, be estranged, be alienated**
- 離婚 りこん divorce
- 離縁する りえんする divorce; cancel adoption
- 離反 りはん estrangement, alienation, desertion
- 背離する はいりする be estranged, be alienated
- 乖離 かいり estrangement, alienation; detachment

遠 ▷distant
エン オン とお(い)   Ⓚ271

distant (in relationship), estranged
- 遠慮 えんりょ reserve; hesitation; forethought, prudence
- 敬遠する けいえんする keep at a respectful distance; avoid
- 疎遠 そえん estrangement, alienation, neglect

etiquette
礼   儀

礼 ▷etiquette
レイ ライ   Ⓚ0724

etiquette, courtesy, propriety, manners, ceremony
- 礼儀 れいぎ etiquette, courtesy, propriety, manners
- 礼節 れいせつ courtesy, etiquette
- 礼式 れいしき etiquette, manner
- 失礼 しつれい impoliteness, rudeness; bad manners; I beg your pardon/Goodbye

儀 ▷ceremony
ギ   Ⓚ0147

[original meaning] (polite behavior) **ceremony**
- 儀礼 ぎれい etiquette, courtesy
- 礼儀 れいぎ etiquette, courtesy, propriety, manners
- 行儀 ぎょうぎ manners, behavior

European countries
英 独 仏 伊 葡
西 蘭 希 露 白

英 ▷England
エイ   Ⓚ1925

England, United Kingdom; English, British
- 英国 えいこく England, Great Britain, the U.K.

英米 えいべい England and America, Anglo-American
英領 えいりょう British territory [possession]
英文学 えいぶんがく English literature

独 ▷Germany
ドク ひと(り)   Ⓚ0354

Germany
西独 せいどく West Germany

仏 ▷France
ブツ フツ ほとけ   Ⓚ0010

France
仏印 ふついん French Indochina
日仏 にちふつ Japan and France

伊 ▷Italy
イ   Ⓚ0033

Italy
日独伊 にちどくい Japan, Germany and Italy
駐伊 ちゅうい stationed in Italy

葡 ▷Portugal
ブ ホ ポ   Ⓚ2014

Portugal
日葡関係 にっぽかんけい Japan-Portugal relations

西 ▷Spain
セイ サイ にし   Ⓚ2951

Spain
米西戦争 べいせいせんそう Spanish-American War

蘭 ▷the Netherlands
ラン   Ⓚ2114

Holland, the Netherlands
蘭人 らんじん Dutch people

希 ▷Greece
キ まれ   Ⓚ1763

Greece, Greek
希臘 ぎりしゃ Greece

露 ▷Russia
ロ ロウ つゆ   Ⓚ2454

[sometimes also 魯] **Russia**
露帝 ろてい Czar, Russian emperor
日露戦争 にちろせんそう Russo-Japanese war (of 1904-05)

白 ▷Belgium
ハク ビャク しろ しら- しろ(い)   Ⓚ2929

Belgium

日白 にっぱく Japan and Belgium

evening and night
夜　晩　夕　宵　暮

夜 ▷night
ヤ よる   Ⓚ1770

[original meaning] **night, evening**
夜間 やかん night, nighttime
夜分 やぶん nighttime, night, evening
夜半 やはん midnight
夜学 やがく evening class, night school
夜具 やぐ bedclothes, bedding; quilt
昼夜 ちゅうや day and night
今夜 こんや tonight, this evening
徹夜 てつや all night vigil [sitting]
深夜 しんや dead of night, midnight
前夜 ぜんや previous night; eve

晩 ▷evening
バン   Ⓚ0891

evening, night
晩方 ばんがた toward evening
晩鐘 ばんしょう evening bell, curfew (bell)
晩御飯 ばんごはん supper
毎晩 まいばん every evening [night]
今晩 こんばん this evening, tonight
今晩は こんばんは good evening

夕 ▷evening
セキ ゆう   Ⓚ2871

[original meaning] **evening, dusk, night**
今夕 こんせき this evening, tonight
一朝一夕に いっちょういっせきに in one day, in a short time
旦夕 たんせき morning and evening, day and night

宵 ▷early evening
ショウ よい   Ⓚ1967

ⓐ [original meaning] **early evening, evening, nightfall**
ⓑ night
a 春宵 しゅんしょう spring evening
b 徹宵 てっしょう all night long, throughout the night

暮 ▷dusk
ボ く(れる) く(らす)   Ⓚ2070

[original meaning] **dusk, nightfall**
暮色 ぼしょく dusk, twilight scene
暮夜 ぼや night
薄暮 はくぼ nightfall, dusk, twilight

evident
明 鮮 亮 顕 瞭

明 ▷**clear**
メイ
ミョウ あ(かり) あか(るい) あか(るむ)
あか(らむ) あき(らか) あ(ける) -あ(け)
あ(く) あ(くる) あ(かす) Ⓚ0756

(free from doubt) **clear, lucid, distinct, evident, obvious, explicit, manifest**

明確な めいかくな clear, precise, distinct
明治 めいじ Meiji era
明記する めいきする write clearly, specify
表明 ひょうめい manifestation, demonstration
不明な ふめいな obscure, unknown
自明の じめいの self-evident, obvious
公明正大な こうめいせいだいな fair, just
文明 ぶんめい civilization, culture

鮮 ▷**vivid**
セン あざ(やか) Ⓚ1656

vivid, brilliant, clean

鮮麗な せんれいな vivid, gorgeous
鮮烈な せんれつな glaringly vivid, striking
鮮明な せんめいな vivid, clear

亮 ▷**lucid**
リョウ Ⓚ1784

[now always 瞭] (easily understood) **lucid, clear**

亮然たる りょうぜんたる obvious, clear
明亮な めいりょうな lucid, clear, plain

顕 ▷**manifest**
ケン Ⓚ1605

(readily perceived) **manifest, apparent, noticeable, obvious**

顕著な けんちょな notable, conspicuous; clear, obvious
顕示する けんじする reveal
顕在化する けんざいかする be actualized
顕現 けんげん manifestation
露顕(=露見) ろけん discovery, detection, exposure

瞭 ▷**clear**
リョウ Ⓚ1145

[rarely also 亮] **clear, obvious**

明瞭な めいりょうな clear, plain, lucid

evil →**WRONGDOING AND EVIL**

evil
邪 兇 凶 悪

邪 ▷**evil**
ジャ Ⓚ1039

(morally bad) **evil, wicked, bad, unjust, heretical, wrong**

邪悪 じゃあく wickedness, vice
邪心 じゃしん wicked heart, evil design
邪道 じゃどう evil course; heresy

兇 ▷**atrocious**
キョウ

 atrocious, ferocious, wicked, brutal, cruel
 atrocious [lethal] crime, murder, wicked deed

a 兇悪な きょうあくな atrocious, villainous, fiendish
兇暴な きょうぼうな atrocious, ferocious, brutal
兇漢 きょうかん villain, ruffian, assailant
兇行 きょうこう violence, murder, crime
b 兇器 きょうき murder [dangerous] weapon
兇刃 きょうじん assassin's dagger [knife]

凶 ▷**atrocious**
キョウ Ⓚ2557

atrocious, ferocious, wicked, brutal, cruel

凶悪な きょうあくな atrocious, villainous, fiendish
凶暴な きょうぼうな atrocious, ferocious, brutal
凶漢 きょうかん villain, ruffian, assailant
凶行 きょうこう violence, murder, crime

悪 ▷**bad**
アク オ わる(い) わる- あ(し) Ⓚ2393

(morally evil) **bad, evil, wicked, immoral**

悪魔 あくま devil, demon, satan
悪徳 あくとく vice, corruption, immorality
悪事 あくじ evil deed
悪化する あっかする worsen, aggravate, deteriorate
悪用 あくよう abuse, misuse, improper use
悪人 あくにん wicked person, scoundrel
悪女 あくじょ wicked woman; ugly woman

evil beings →**SUPERNATURAL AND EVIL BEINGS**

exact
確　正　真　恰

確 ▷certain
カク たし(か) たし(かめる)　Ⓚ1135
see also →CERTAIN

certain, definite, positive, sure, reliable, accurate

確認 かくにん confirmation, ascertainment
確実な かくじつな certain, sure, reliable; sound, solid
確証 かくしょう certain [definite] proof, positive evidence, corroboration
確率 かくりつ probability
確答 かくとう definite answer [reply]
正確な せいかくな accurate, precise, exact
明確な めいかくな clear, precise, distinct
的確な てきかくな precise, accurate, exact

正 ▷right
セイ ショウ ただ(しい) ただ(す) まさ まさ(に)　Ⓚ2926

[also prefix] (in a precise manner) **right, accurate, exact(ly), just, due (north)**

正確な せいかくな accurate, precise, exact
正午 しょうご noon, noontime
正北 せいほく due north
正反対 せいはんたい exactly opposite
正六時に しょうろくじに at six sharp

真 ▷right
シン ま-　Ⓚ1813

right, just, exactly, due (north)

真上 まうえ right above
真北 まきた due north
真正面 ましょうめん right in front
真弓 まゆみ [also 檀] spindle tree, Euonymus sieboldiana

恰 ▷just
カッ- コウ あたか(も)　Ⓚ0326

[original meaning] **just, exactly**

恰好(=格好) かっこう suitability, moderateness (in price); shape, form; appearance, manner
恰幅 かっぷく physique, bodily build
不恰好 ぶかっこう unshapely, misshapen; awkward, clumsy

examination
検　試

検 ▷examination
ケン　Ⓚ0898

examination, inspection, test, -opsy

車検 しゃけん automobile inspection
三等検 さんとうけん test for third-grade articles
生検 せいけん biopsy

試 ▷examination (school test)
シ こころ(みる) ため(す)　Ⓚ1385

abbrev. of 試験 しけん: **examination, school test**

入試 にゅうし entrance examination
追試 ついし supplementary examination
模試 もし sham examination

examine →INVESTIGATE AND EXAMINE

example
例　型

例 ▷example
レイ たと(える)　Ⓚ0071

ⓐ [also suffix] (something representative) **example, instance, case**
ⓑ **previous example, precedent**

a 例題 れいだい example, exercise
例文 れいぶん illustrative sentence, example (sentence)
一例 いちれい example, instance, case, illustration
範例 はんれい example
実例 じつれい example, instance, concrete case
用例 ようれい example, illustration (of the use of a word)
特例 とくれい special case [example]; exception
具体例 ぐたいれい concrete example
b 例外 れいがい exception
類例 るいれい similar example, parallel
先例 せんれい precedent, former example
前例 ぜんれい precedent; above example
判例 はんれい (judicial) precedent

型 ▷type
ケイ かた -がた　Ⓚ2292

(representative specimen) **type, model**
典型 てんけい type, pattern, model, exemplar

余剰 よじょう surplus, remainder, residue
余裕 よゆう surplus, margin, room; composure
余分 よぶん excess, extra, surplus
余計な よけいな excess, surplus; needless
余程 よほど very, greatly, highly, considerably; by far
残余 ざんよ remainder, residue, remnant

過 ▷exceed
カ す(ぎる) -す(ぎ) す(ごす) あやま(つ) あやま(ち)　　　　　　Ⓚ2704

ⓐ exceed, be above, be over
ⓑ [prefix] excessive, over-, too much, super-

- a 過剰 かじょう surplus, excess
  過密 かみつ overcrowding
  過当な かとうな excessive, undue, unreasonable
  過熱する かねつする overheat, superheat
  過労 かろう overwork
  超過する ちょうかする exceed, be in excess, be above
- b 過半数 かはんすう majority, more than half
  過保護 かほご overprotectiveness

超 ▷surpass
チョウ こ(える) こ(す)　　　　　　Ⓚ2824

(go beyond in quantity or degree) **surpass, exceed, be over**

超過 ちょうか excess
入超 にゅうちょう excess of imports over exports

越 ▷go beyond
エツ こ(す) -ご(し) こ(える) -ご(え)　　　　　　Ⓚ2825

go or be beyond in degree: **be more than, exceed, surpass**

激越な げきえつな violent, vehement
超越する ちょうえつする transcend, surpass

濫 ▷excessive
ラン　　　　　　Ⓚ0713

[also 乱] **excessive, indiscriminate, extravagant, inordinate, haphazard, reckless**

濫造 らんぞう excessive production, careless manufacture
濫伐 らんばつ indiscriminate deforestation, overcutting of forests
濫費 らんぴ extravagance, money wasting
濫用する らんようする abuse, use to excess
紙幣の濫発 しへいのらんぱつ excessive [reckless] issue of bank notes

余 ▷excess
ヨ あま(る) あま(り) あま(す)　　　　　　Ⓚ1757

excess, surplus, remainder, overplus

剰 ▷surplus
ジョウ　　　　　　Ⓚ1584

[original meaning] **surplus, excessive, redundant**

剰余 じょうよ surplus, remainder, balance
剰員 じょういん superfluous member
過剰 かじょう surplus, excess
余剰 よじょう surplus, remainder, residue

冗 ▷redundant
ジョウ　　　　　　Ⓚ1716

(exceeding what is necessary) **redundant, superfluous, useless, unnecessary**

冗長な じょうちょうな verbose, redundant, prolix
冗費 じょうひ unnecessary expenses
冗員 じょういん useless member of the staff
冗談 じょうだん joke

勝 ▷excel
ショウ か(つ) -が(ち) まさ(る)　　　　　　Ⓚ0918

excel, surpass, outdo
殊勝な しゅしょうな laudable, praiseworthy

抜 ▷stand out
バツ ぬ(く) ぬ(き) ぬ(ける) ぬ(かす) ぬ(かる)　　　　　　Ⓚ0219

stand out [above], rise above, surpass, excel
抜群の ばつぐんの preeminent, outstanding
奇抜な きばつな novel, unconventional, extraordinary
卓抜する たくばつする excel, surpass, stand high, be distinguished
海抜 かいばつ above sea level

擢 ▷stand out
テキ ぬき(んでる)　　　　　　Ⓚ0708

[usu. 抜きん出る] **stand out, excel, surpass**

超 ▷surpass
チョウ こ(える) こ(す)　　　　　　Ⓚ2824

(go beyond the limit) **surpass, transcend, excel**

超越する ちょうえつする transcend, surpass
超絶 ちょうぜつ transcendence; excellence, superiority
超然たる ちょうぜんたる transcendental, standing aloof

 ▷go beyond
エツ こ(す) －ご(し) こ(える)
－ご(え)　　　　　　　　　Ⓚ2825

go beyond the bounds of the ordinary: **be better than, transcend, surpass, excel**

優越 ゆうえつ superiority, supremacy
卓越する たくえつする excel, surpass

凌 **▷surpass**
リョウ しの(ぐ)　　　　　　Ⓚ0109

【リョウ】
[now also 陵] **surpass, outdo, outshine**
凌駕する りょうがする surpass, exceed, outshine, outdo

【しの(ぐ)】
surpass, outdo, outshine
壮者を凌ぐ そうしゃをしのぐ put young men to shame

駕 **▷outdo**
ガ　　　　　　　　　　　Ⓚ2273

outdo, surpass
凌駕(=陵駕) りょうが excelling, surpassing

excellent and superior

優 絶 卓 快 妙 秀 英
尤 傑 穎 逸 名 上

 ▷superior
ユウ やさ(しい) すぐ(れる)　Ⓚ0156

(far above average) **superior, excellent, dominant, predominant**
優秀な ゆうしゅうな excellent, superior, best
優良品 ゆうりょうひん excellent articles
優等生 ゆうとうせい honor student, prize pupil
優越 ゆうえつ superiority, supremacy
優越感 ゆうえつかん superiority complex
優勝する ゆうしょうする win the victory [championship]
優先 ゆうせん preference, priority
優勢 ゆうせい superiority, lead, predominance
優性形質 ゆうせいけいしつ dominant character

絶 **▷without match**
ゼツ た(える) た(やす) た(つ)　　Ⓚ1240

without match, peerless, unparalleled
絶対 ぜったい absoluteness; absolute; absolutely, unconditionally
絶対に ぜったいに absolutely, unconditionally
絶賛 ぜっさん great admiration
絶好の ぜっこうの splendid, grand, best, golden
絶妙な ぜつみょうな miraculous, exquisite, superb
絶世の ぜっせいの peerless, unequaled
絶景 ぜっけい superb view, picturesque scenery
絶唱 ぜっしょう superb song [poem]
空前絶後 くうぜんぜつご the first and probably the last

卓 **▷prominent**
タク　　　　　　　　　　Ⓚ1777

[original meaning] **prominent, eminent, outstanding, unexcelled, superior**
卓効 たっこう remarkable efficacy
卓見 たっけん farsightedness, penetration, excellent views
卓越 たくえつ excellence, superiority
卓説 たくせつ excellent opinion
卓立する たくりつする be prominent, stand out
卓抜 たくばつ prominence, excellence, superiority

快 **▷splendid**
カイ こころよ(い)　　　　Ⓚ0218

[also prefix] **splendid, fine, good**
快挙 かいきょ brilliant achievement, heroic deed [feat]
快晴 かいせい fine weather, fair and clear weather
快男児 かいだんじ fine fellow, spirited fellow

妙 **▷marvelous**
ミョウ　　　　　　　　　Ⓚ0210

(of incredible excellence) **marvelous, superb, excellent; adroit, ingenious**
妙案 みょうあん bright idea, excellent plan
妙技 みょうぎ wonderful skill; stunt
巧妙な こうみょうな skillful, ingenious, clever

秀 **▷excellent**
シュウ ひい(でる)　　　　Ⓚ2202

excellent, supreme
秀逸 しゅういつ supreme excellence
秀歌 しゅうか excellent [superb] tanka, gem of tankas
秀麗な しゅうれいな graceful, beautiful, handsome
優秀な ゆうしゅうな excellent, superior, best

英 ▷distinguished
エイ   Ⓚ1925

[rarely also 穎] **distinguished, outstanding, excellent, talented; wise**
- 英雄 えいゆう hero
- 英武 えいぶ distinguished [surpassing] valor
- 英才 えいさい [formerly also 穎才] talent, genius; gifted person, talented person
- 英断 えいだん prompt decision; resolute step
- 英知 えいち [sometimes also 叡智] sagacity, wisdom
- 英姿 えいし gallant figure, majestic appearance
- 英気 えいき spirit, energy; vigor

尤 ▷outstanding
ユウ もっと(も)   Ⓚ2604

outstanding, excellent
- 尤物 ゆうぶつ superfine thing; beauty, belle

傑 ▷outstanding
ケツ   Ⓚ0133

outstanding, remarkable, extraordinary
- 傑作 けっさく masterpiece, magnum opus; blunder
- 傑出する けっしゅつする excel, stand out
- 傑人 けつじん outstanding person

穎 ▷talented
エイ

talented, intelligent, distinguished, outstanding
- 穎才 えいさい [now usu. 英才] talent, genius; gifted person, talented person
- 穎悟 えいご intelligent, shrewd

逸 ▷exceptional
イツ   Ⓚ2688

exceptional, superb, outstanding, excellent
- 逸品 いっぴん superb article
- 逸材 いつざい person of (exceptional) talent
- 秀逸 しゅういつ supreme excellence

名 ▷first-rate
メイ ミョウ な   Ⓚ1857

first-rate, master, excellent, fine, great
- 名人 めいじん (past) master, master hand, expert
- 名作 めいさく masterpiece, fine work
- 名画 めいが famous picture, masterpiece; noted film
- 名曲 めいきょく excellent [exquisite] piece of music, famous tune
- 名月 めいげつ full moon, harvest moon
- 名投手 めいとうしゅ star pitcher
- 名探偵 めいたんてい great detective

上 ▷of upper grade
ジョウ ショウ うえ うわ– かみ あ(げる) あ(がる) あ(がり) のぼ(る) のぼ(り) のぼ(せる) のぼ(す)   Ⓚ287◌

[also prefix] **of upper grade, top-quality, first-class, excellent, best, good**
- 上水 じょうすい water supply; tap water
- 上手な じょうずな skilled, dexterous, good at
- 上等の じょうとうの first-class, superior
- 上製 じょうせい superior make; superior (book) binding
- 上白 じょうはく first-class rice; first-class sugar
- 上出来 じょうでき good performance, master stroke
- 上天気 じょうてんき fine weather, splendid weather

excess →EXCEEDING AND EXCESS

excreta
便 尿 汗

便 ▷excreta
ベン ビン たよ(り)   Ⓚ007◌

(feces or urine) **excreta, excrement, feces, urine**
- 便所 べんじょ lavatory, bathroom
- 便秘 べんぴ constipation
- 便器 べんき toilet bowl, urinal
- 大便 だいべん feces, excrement
- 小便 しょうべん urine

尿 ▷urine
ニョウ   Ⓚ263◌

[original meaning] **urine**
- 尿素 にょうそ urea
- 尿酸 にょうさん uric acid
- 排尿 はいにょう urination
- 検尿 けんにょう urinalysis
- 糖尿病 とうにょうびょう diabetes
- 夜尿症 やにょうしょう bed wetting, nocturia

汗 ▷sweat
カン あせ   Ⓚ0194

sweat, perspiration
- 汗腺 かんせん sweat gland
- 汗顔 かんがん sweating from shame
- 汗血 かんけつ sweat and blood
- 発汗する はっかんする perspire, sweat
- 冷汗 れいかん cold sweat

execute
執 行 履 施 践 果 遂

実践する じっせんする put in practice, implement

果 ▷**effect**
カ は(たす) は(てる) は(て)　　Ⓚ2982

vt **effect, carry out, discharge, accomplish; realize (one's wishes); kill**
- 果たして はたして as was expected, sure enough; really
- 果たし合い はたしあい duel, fight to death
- 使命を果たす しめいをはたす carry out one's mission

遂 ▷**accomplish**
スイ と(げる) つい(に)　　Ⓚ2705
see also →ACCOMPLISH

執 ▷**execute**
シツ シュウ と(る)　　Ⓚ1501

(perform a specific task with care) **execute, carry out, perform, conduct**
- 執行する しっこうする execute, perform, carry out
- 執務 しつむ performance of one's official duties
- 執事 しつじ steward, butler
- 中執(=中央執行委員会) ちゅうしつ(=ちゅうおうしつこういいんかい) Central Executive Committee

(complete successfully) **accomplish, achieve, attain, complete, carry out, execute, commit, perform**
- 遂行する すいこうする accomplish, execute, perform, carry out
- 完遂する かんすいする execute successfully, accomplish, bring to completion
- 未遂の みすいの attempted (suicide, etc.)

行 ▷**act**
コウ ギョウ アン い(く) ゆ(く) -ゆ(き) -い(き) おこな(う)　　Ⓚ0187

(perform an action) **act, do, carry out, perform, conduct**
- 行動 こうどう action, conduct, behavior
- 行為 こうい act, deed, conduct, transaction
- 行政 ぎょうせい administration
- 行事 ぎょうじ event, function
- 実行 じっこう practice, action; execution

exert oneself
努 勉 励 勤 尽 精 孜

努 ▷**exert**
ド つと(める)　　Ⓚ2204

[original meaning] **exert (oneself), make efforts, endeavor**
- 努力 どりょく endeavor, effort, exertion
- 努力家 どりょくか hard worker
- 努力賞 どりょくしょう prize awarded for a person's effort

履 ▷**fulfill**
リ は(く)　　Ⓚ2736

(carry out an obligation) **fulfill, carry out, execute, perform, complete**
- 履行する りこうする fulfill, perform, carry out
- 履歴 りれき personal history, career
- 履歴書 りれきしょ résumé, personal history
- 履修 りしゅう completion (of a course), taking (a course)

勉 ▷**endeavor**
ベン　　Ⓚ2829

[original meaning] **endeavor, make efforts, work diligently, exert oneself**
- 勉励 べんれい diligence, industry
- 勉強 べんきょう study; selling cheap; [rare] diligence
- 勉学 べんがく study
- 勤勉な きんべんな diligent, assiduous, industrious, hardworking

施 ▷**carry out**
シ セ ほどこ(す)　　Ⓚ0792

carry out, put into practice, enforce, execute, conduct
- 施行する しこうする enforce, execute, carry out
- 施工する せこう(=しこう)する execute (a building contract), carry out
- 施術 しじゅつ surgical operation
- 施策 しさく enforcement of a policy
- 施政 しせい administration, government
- 実施する じっしする carry out, enforce, execute

励 ▷**make efforts**
レイ はげ(む) はげ(ます)　　Ⓚ1035

[original meaning] **make efforts, work hard at, be diligent**
- 励行する れいこうする observe strictly, carry out
- 励声 れいせい straining one's voice
- 精励 せいれい diligence, industry

践 ▷**implement**
セン　　Ⓚ1396

(give practical effect to and ensure actual fulfillment) **implement, carry through, put in practice, carry out**
- 践言する せんげんする keep one's word

勉励 べんれい diligence, industry
奮励 ふんれい strenuous efforts [exertions]

勤 ▷work diligently
キン ゴン つと(める) -づと(め)
つと(まる)　　　　　　　　Ⓚ1613

work diligently [hard], labor, strive; work faithfully
勤勉 きんべん diligence, assiduity, industry
勤務する きんむする do duty, serve, be on duty, work
勤労 きんろう labor, work, service
勤倹 きんけん diligence and thrift
勤行 ごんぎょう Buddhistic service, sutra chanting
忠勤 ちゅうきん loyal [faithful] service

尽 ▷use all one's strength
ジン つ(くす) -づ(くし) つ(きる)
つ(かす)　　　　　　　　　Ⓚ2624

【ジン】
use [exhaust] all one's strength (in the performance of one's duties), make utmost efforts, exert oneself
尽力 じんりょく efforts, assistance
尽忠報国 じんちゅうほうこく loyalty and patriotism
不尽 ふじん Yours sincerely

【つ(くす)】
use [exhaust] all one's strength (in the performance of one's duties), make utmost efforts, exert oneself
心尽くし こころづくし kindness, consideration, solicitude
最善を尽くす さいぜんをつくす do something to the best of one's ability, do one's best
手段を尽くす しゅだんをつくす leave no stone unturned, try everything
人類の為に尽くす じんるいのためにつくす render a service to humanity

精 ▷put one's heart into
セイ ショウ　　　　　　　Ⓚ1248

put one's heart into, be diligent
精励 せいれい diligence, industry
精勤 せいきん diligence, good attendance
精進 しょうじん diligence, concentration, devotion; religious purification; abstinence from (eating) fish and meat
丹精(=丹誠) たんせい efforts, pains
無精 ぶしょう indolence, laziness

孜 ▷make diligent efforts
シ　　　　　　　　　　　　Ⓚ0213

make diligent efforts
孜孜 しし assiduously, diligently

在 ▷be
ザイ あ(る)　　　　　　　Ⓚ257

❶ [also prefix] [original meaning] (exist in a specified place) **be at [in], be situated in, be sited**
在庫 ざいこ stock, stockpile
在学する ざいがくする be in school
在校する ざいこうする be in school
在宅する ざいたくする be in, be at home
在東京 ざいとうきょう situated in Tokyo
不在 ふざい absence
所在 しょざい whereabouts, position, situation
❷ (exist in actuality) **be, exist**
現在の げんざいの present time, now; present tense; actually
存在する そんざいする exist, be
自在に じざいに freely, unrestrictedly, at will
実在 じつざい real [actual] existence, entity

存 ▷exist
ソン ゾン　　　　　　　　Ⓚ257

(have actuality) **exist, be**
存在 そんざい existence, being
存否 そんぴ existence; life or death
存続 そんぞく continuation, maintenance
存亡 そんぼう destiny; life or death
共存 きょうぞん coexistence
依存 いぞん(=いそん) dependence, reliance
既存の きそんの existing
現存の げんぞんの(=げんそん)の existing, living
残存する ざんそん(=ざんぞん)する survive, subsist, be extant
実存 じつぞん existence

有 ▷exist
ユウ ウ あ(る)　　　　　Ⓚ257

exist, be, be present
有無 うむ existence, presence; yes or no
現有の げんゆうの present, existing

居 ▷be present
キョ い(る) -い お(る)　　Ⓚ265

(of living beings) **be present, be, be found, stay**
家居する かきょする stay at home

臨 ▷be present at
リン のぞ(む)　　　　　　Ⓚ147

be present at, be on the spot, attend, come to, visit

臨床医 りんしょうい clinician
臨席 りんせき presence, attendance
臨場 りんじょう presence, attendance; visit
臨検 りんけん spot inspection, raid
臨在 りんざい presence
来臨 らいりん attendance, presence; visit

也 ▷classical copula
ヤ なり や   Ⓚ2878

classical copula equiv. to である: be
金十円也 きんじゅうえんなり ten yen

expand
脹 膨 張 氾 広 拡 伸 延

張 ▷swell
チョウ は(れる) ふく(らむ)
ふく(れる)   Ⓚ0916

swell, expand, bulge
膨脹(=膨張) ぼうちょう expansion, swelling;
  growth, increase
腫脹 しゅちょう swelling, puffiness

膨 ▷expand
ボウ ふく(らむ) ふく(れる)   Ⓚ0999

[original meaning] expand, swell, bulge, inflate
膨大 ぼうだい swelling, expansion
膨脹(=膨張) ぼうちょう expansion, swelling;
  growth, increase
膨隆する ぼうりゅうする swell up
膨満する ぼうまんする be inflated

張 ▷spread
チョウ は(る) −は(り) −ば(り)   Ⓚ0431

(open to the full extent) spread (out), extend (over),
stretch
拡張 かくちょう expansion, extension, enlargement
膨張(=膨脹) ぼうちょう expansion, swelling;
  growth, increase
伸張 しんちょう expansion, elongation
出張する しゅっちょうする travel on official business

氾 ▷spread out
ハン   Ⓚ0172

spread out, overflow
氾濫 はんらん flooding, overflowing, inundation

広 ▷spread (out)
コウ ひろ(い) ひろ(まる) ひろ(める)
ひろ(がる) ひろ(げる)   Ⓚ2613

spread (out), outstretch
地図を広げる ちずをひろげる spread a map

拡 ▷enlarge
カク   Ⓚ0273

[original meaning] enlarge, expand, magnify, widen,
extend
拡大する かくだいする magnify, enlarge, expand
拡張する かくちょうする expand, extend, enlarge
拡散 かくさん scattering, diffusion
拡声器 かくせいき (loud)speaker, megaphone
拡充 かくじゅう expansion, amplification
軍拡 ぐんかく expansion of armaments

伸 ▷stretch
シン の(びる) の(びやか) の(ばす)
の(べる)   Ⓚ0054

[original meaning] stretch, elongate, extend, spread
伸縮 しんしゅく expansion and contraction
伸張 しんちょう expansion, elongation

延 ▷extend
エン の(びる) の(べる) の(べ)
の(ばす)   Ⓚ2646

ⓐ [original meaning] extend (in space or time), prolong, spread
ⓑ metallurgy (cause to extend) flatten out, roll
a 延長 えんちょう extension, prolongation, continuation
延焼 えんしょう spread of a fire
延延たる えんえんたる lengthy
延髄 えんずい medulla oblongata
b 熱延 ねつえん hot rolling
圧延鋼 あつえんこう rolled steel

expect
期 　 待

期 ▷expect
キ ゴ   Ⓚ1520

expect, look forward to, anticipate, hope for
期待する きたいする expect, look forward to, anticipate, hope for
予期する よきする expect, anticipate, hope for
所期の しょきの expected, anticipated, hoped-for

待 ▷wait for
タイ ま(つ) -ま(ち) Ⓚ0323

wait for, await, expect, look forward to
待命 たいめい waiting for orders
待望の たいぼうの hoped-for, long-awaited
期待 きたい expectation, anticipation, hope

expensive
貴　高

貴 ▷precious
キ たっと(い) とうと(い) たっと(ぶ)
とうと(ぶ) Ⓚ2260

precious, valuable, costly
貴重な きちょうな precious, valuable
物価騰貴 ぶっかとうき rise in prices

高 ▷high-priced
コウ たか(い) たか -だか たか(まる)
たか(める) Ⓚ1803

high-priced, expensive
高価な こうかな expensive, high-priced
高騰(=昂騰) こうとう steep rise (in prices), jump

explain
説 明 釈 詮 講 解 注

説 ▷explain
セツ ゼイ と(く) Ⓚ1405

ⓐ [original meaning] **explain**
ⓑ **explanation, statement**
a 説明 せつめい explanation, description
　解説 かいせつ explanation, commentary
　演説 えんぜつ (public) speech, address, oration
　論説 ろんせつ discourse, dissertation; editorial
　力説する りきせつする emphasize, lay stress on,
　　insist upon
b 概説 がいせつ general statement, outline
　序説 じょせつ introduction
　言説 げんせつ remark, statement

明 ▷make clear
メイ
ミョウ あ(かり) あか(るい) あか(るむ)
あか(らむ) あき(らか) あ(ける) -あ(け)
あ(く) あ(くる) あ(かす) Ⓚ0756

**make clear, clarify, throw light on, prove, demon-
strate**

証明 しょうめい proof, evidence, verification
説明する せつめいする explain, illustrate

釈 ▷elucidate
シャク Ⓚ1349

elucidate, explain, interpret, explicate
解釈 かいしゃく interpretation, explanation
注釈 ちゅうしゃく annotation, note, comment
会釈する えしゃくする salute, greet, bow slightly

詮 ▷expound
セン Ⓚ1383

expound, elucidate, explain
詮議 せんぎ discussion, examination; interrogation
詮索 せんさく scrutiny, prying, inquiry
所詮 しょせん after all

講 ▷expound
コウ Ⓚ1463

ⓐ **expound, explain, interpret**
ⓑ **speak, tell**
a 講義 こうぎ lecture
　講話 こうわ lecture, discourse
b 講談 こうだん storytelling, narration; historical
　　narrative

解 ▷clarify
カイ ゲ と(く) と(かす) と(ける) Ⓚ1375

ⓐ **clarify, explain, elucidate, interpret**
ⓑ **explanation, commentary**
a 解説 かいせつ explanation, commentary
　解釈 かいしゃく interpretation, explanation
　解明する かいめいする explain, elucidate
　弁解 べんかい explanation, vindication, justifica-
　　tion, excuse
　図解 ずかい explanatory diagram, illustration
b 詳解 しょうかい detailed [minute] explanation, full
　　commentary
　注解 ちゅうかい annotation, explanatory notes

注 ▷annotate
チュウ そそ(ぐ) Ⓚ0287

annotate, explain with notes
注釈 ちゅうしゃく annotation, note, comment
注解 ちゅうかい annotation, explanatory notes
注記 ちゅうき annotation, commentary

explanatory remarks
注 評

注 ▷**annotation**
チュウ そそ(ぐ)　　　　　Ⓚ0287

annotation, explanatory notes, comment
- 頭注 とうちゅう headnote
- 脚注 きゃくちゅう footnote
- 評注 ひょうちゅう commentary, notes and comments

評 ▷**comment**
ヒョウ　　　　　Ⓚ1361

[also suffix] **comment, criticism**
- 好評 こうひょう favorable criticism [comment], public favor
- 定評 ていひょう established reputation
- 書評 しょひょう book reviews
- 下馬評 げばひょう gossip, advance rumor
- 映画評 えいがひょう film review

explode
爆 発

爆 ▷**explode**
バク　　　　　Ⓚ1020

[original meaning] **explode, detonate, burst**
- 爆発 ばくはつ explosion, blast; eruption
- 爆弾 ばくだん bomb
- 爆破する ばくはする blast, blow up, explode
- 爆風 ばくふう (bomb or explosion) blast
- 爆笑する ばくしょうする roar with laughter, burst into laughter
- 爆撃 ばくげき bombing, bombardment

発 ▷**discharge**
ハツ ホツ た(つ)　　　　　Ⓚ2222

(be discharged) **discharge, explode**
- 不発 ふはつ misfire
- 爆発する ばくはつする explode, burst; erupt
- 一触即発 いっしょくそくはつ touch-and-go situation, hair-trigger crisis

express
表 揮 寓

表 ▷**express**
ヒョウ おもて あらわ(す)
あらわ(れる)　　　　　Ⓚ2151

express, manifest, show
- 表明する ひょうめいする express, state, show, demonstrate
- 表現する ひょうげんする express, represent, manifest; give expression to
- 表示する ひょうじする indicate, show, express, manifest
- 表彰 ひょうしょう commendation, awarding
- 表彰状 ひょうしょうじょう certificate of commendation
- 表決 ひょうけつ decision, resolution
- 表意文字 ひょういもじ ideograph, ideographic character
- 発表する はっぴょうする announce, make public, publish
- 公表する こうひょうする announce officially [in public], proclaim

揮 ▷**wield**
キ　　　　　Ⓚ0538

wield (one's power), display (one's abilities)
- 発揮する はっきする display, exhibit, demonstrate

寓 ▷**imply**
グウ　　　　　Ⓚ2010

imply, suggest
- 寓話 ぐうわ fable, allegory
- 寓意 ぐうい hidden meaning, allegory; moral (of a story)

expression
顔 色

顔 ▷**face**
ガン かお　　　　　Ⓚ1608

(facial expression) **face, looks, features**
- 顔色 がんしょく(=かおいろ) complexion, countenance, expression
- 童顔の どうがんの boyish looking, baby-faced
- 厚顔な こうがんな impudent, shameless, brazen
- 破顔 はがん broad smile

色 ▷**color**
　ショク　シキ　いろ　　　　　Ⓚ1748

(facial expression) **color, complexion, countenance, look**

　顔色 がんしょく(=かおいろ) complexion, countenance, expression
　血色 けっしょく complexion
　気色 きしょく(=けしき) mood, feeling; looks, countenance

expressions →WORDS AND EXPRESSIONS

extend over
亘　及　跨

亘 ▷**extend over**
　コウ　わた(る)　　　　　Ⓚ1697

[archaic] **extend over, extend across, extend for, range**

　亘古 こうこ from ancient times, for ever
　連亘 れんこう extending in a row

及 ▷**reach to**
　キュウ　および(ぶ)　および(び)
　および(ぼす)　　　　　Ⓚ2868

(extend as far as) **reach to, extend over, range over**

　普及 ふきゅう diffusion, spread, propagation
　波及する はきゅうする be propagated; extend, spread; affect
　遡及的な そきゅうてき(=さっきゅうてき)な retroactive

跨 ▷**straddle**
　コ　また(ぐ)　また(がる)　　　　　Ⓚ1393

ⓐ (be astride) **straddle, sit [stand] astride**
ⓑ (extend across) **straddle, stretch across [over]**
　a 跨座式鉄道 こざしきてつどう straddle-beam monorail
　b 跨線橋 こせんきょう overpass

extensive →WIDE AND EXTENSIVE

extinguish
消　熄　滅

消 ▷**extinguish**
　ショウ　き(える)　け(す)　　　　　Ⓚ0402

(put out a light or fire) **extinguish, put out; switch off**

　消防 しょうぼう fire fighting, prevention and extinction of fires

　消防車 しょうぼうしゃ fire engine
　消火 しょうか fire fighting
　消灯する しょうとうする turn off the lights

熄 ▷**go out**
　ソク

[now replaced by 息] [original meaning] **go out, die out**

　終熄する しゅうそくする cease, come to an end

滅 ▷**go out**
　メツ　ほろ(びる)　ほろ(ぶ)
　ほろ(ぼす)　　　　　Ⓚ060◦

go out, be extinguished

　点滅する てんめつする (of light) go [come] on and off; turn [switch] on and off
　明滅する めいめつする flicker, blink

extreme
極　窮　限　涯　果

極 ▷**extreme**
　キョク　ゴク　きわ(める)　きわ(まる)
　きわ(まり)　きわ(み)　　　　　Ⓚ090◦

extreme, utmost point, extremity, limit

　極右 きょくう extreme right
　極東 きょくとう Far East
　極度 きょくど highest degree, extreme

窮 ▷**extremity**
　キュウ　きわ(める)　きわ(まる)　きわ(まり)
　きわ(み)　　　　　Ⓚ207◦

extremity, limit, end

　無窮 むきゅう eternity, infinitude, immortality

限 ▷**limit**
　ゲン　かぎ(る)　かぎ(り)　　　　　Ⓚ035◦

[also suffix] **limit, bounds**

　限度 げんど limit, bounds
　限界 げんかい boundary, limit, bounds
　期限 きげん time limit, term
　上限 じょうげん upper limit, maximum
　権限 けんげん power, authority; competence (of law)
　門限 もんげん closing-time, lockup
　無限の むげんの infinite, endless, unfathomable
　最小限 さいしょうげん minimum

涯 ▷**outer limits**
　ガイ　　　　　Ⓚ046◦

outer limits, end, bound

生涯 しょうがい life, lifetime, career; for life
際涯 さいがい limits, end, extremity
天涯 てんがい far-off land (as remote as the horizon)

果 ▷end
カ は(たす) は(てる) は(て)　　Ⓚ2982

end, extremity, limit; result
果てしない はてしない endless, boundless, everlasting
世界の果て せかいのはて end of the world
挙げ句の果てに あげくのはてに in the end, on top of all this

extreme in degree

酷 強 凄 重 高 深 大 厳
激 極 痛 切 甚 祁 超 頻

酷 ▷severe
コク　　Ⓚ1414

(of great intensity) **severe, intense**
酷寒 こっかん severe [intense] cold; depth of winter
酷暑 こくしょ severe heat
酷似 こくじ close resemblance

強 ▷strong
キョウ ゴウ つよ(い) つよ(まる)
つよ(める) し(いる)　　Ⓚ0432

(of great intensity) **strong, severe, intense**
強度 きょうど intensity; strength
強風 きょうふう strong [high] wind
強震 きょうしん severe earthquake
強打 きょうだ heavy blow, slug; hitting (the ball) hard
強烈な きょうれつな intense, severe

凄 ▷tremendous
セイ すご(い)　　Ⓚ0110

(great in degree) **tremendous, terrific, extreme**
凄く すごく very, extremely, tremendously

重 ▷heavy
ジュウ チョウ え おも(い) おも(り)
かさ(ねる) かさ(なる)　　Ⓚ2991

(great in degree) **heavy, serious, severe**
重傷 じゅうしょう heavy [serious] wound, severe injury
重態(=重体) じゅうたい serious condition, critical state
重税 じゅうぜい heavy taxation

重労働 じゅうろうどう heavy labor
厳重に げんじゅうに strictly, severely, closely; securely, firmly

高 ▷high
コウ たか(い) たか -だか たか(まる)
たか(める)　　Ⓚ1803

[also prefix] (of great degree or quantity) **high**
高速 こうそく high speed, high gear
高熱 こうねつ intense heat; high fever
高級 こうきゅう high rank, high class [grade]
高等な こうとうな higher, high-grade, advanced
高等学校 こうとうがっこう senior high school
高校 こうこう senior high school
高裁 こうさい high court
高齢 こうれい advanced age
高給 こうきゅう high salary
高血圧 こうけつあつ high blood pressure
高温 こうおん high temperature
高音 こうおん high-pitched sound [tone], high key
高気圧 こうきあつ high (atmospheric) pressure
高速道路 こうそくどうろ freeway, expressway; highway, turnpike
高炭素鋼 こうたんそこう high-carbon steel
最高の さいこうの maximum, supreme, highest

深 ▷deep
シン ふか(い) -ぶか(い) ふか(まる)
ふか(める)　　Ⓚ0480

(of great intensity) **deep, intense, extreme, profound**
深刻な しんこくな serious, grave, keen, poignant
深甚なる しんじんなる deep, extreme
深謝 しんしゃ deep gratitude, sincere apology

大 ▷big
ダイ タイ おお- おお(きい)
おお(いに)　　Ⓚ2882

[also prefix] (of great intensity or degree) **big, great, extreme, intense, severe, loud**
大変な たいへんな awful, terrible; serious, grave
大病 たいびょう serious illness, dangerous disease
大切な たいせつな important, weighty; valuable
大丈夫 だいじょうぶ safe, sure, all right
大地震 だいじしん big earthquake
大歓迎 だいかんげい warm welcome
大層 たいそう very, greatly, highly, very much
大嫌いだ だいきらいだ hate, detest
大好きだ だいすきだ like very much, be very fond of
大戦 たいせん world war; great war

厳 ▷severe
ゲン ゴン おごそ(か) きび(しい)　　Ⓚ2804

(of great intensity) **severe, intense, extreme**

厳寒 げんかん severe [intense] cold
厳冬 げんとう severe winter

激 ▷intense
ゲキ はげ(しい)　　　Ⓚ0696

[sometimes also 劇] (of great intensity) **intense, violent, severe, strong**
激化 げきか(=げっか) intensification, aggravation
激賞 げきしょう high praise, unbounded admiration
激痛(=劇痛) げきつう violent [intense] pain
過激派 かげきは extreme radicals

極 ▷extreme
キョク ゴク きわ(める) きわ(まる)
きわ(まり) きわ(み)　　　Ⓚ0900

[also suffix] (utmost or exceedingly great) **extreme, utmost, maximum, ultimate, highest, ultra-, hyper-**
極端な きょくたんな extreme; radical
極限 きょくげん utmost limits, limit
極楽 ごくらく *Buddhism* paradise

痛 ▷bitter(ly)
ツウ いた(い) いた(む) いた(ましい)
いた(める)　　　Ⓚ2799

bitter(ly), severe(ly), vehement(ly), keen(ly)
痛言 つうげん bitter criticism, harsh words
痛烈な つうれつな sharp, biting, scathing, cutting
痛感する つうかんする feel strongly, take to heart
痛快 つうかい thrill, keen pleasure
痛切に つうせつに keenly, acutely
痛打 つうだ hard blow, severe attack
痛恨 つうこん deep regret, great sorrow

切 ▷keen
セツ サイ き(る) き(り) -ぎ(り) き(れる)
き(れ) -ぎ(れ)　　　Ⓚ0015

keen, acute, intense
切実に せつじつに acutely, keenly, earnestly; sincerely, heartily
痛切な つうせつな keen, acute, poignant

甚 ▷extremely
ジン はなは(だ) はなは(だしい)　　　Ⓚ2296

ⓐ **extremely, very, exceedingly**
ⓑ **extreme, excessive**
ₐ 甚大な じんだいな extremely big, very great; serious; heavy
幸甚である こうじんである be very glad, deem a favor
♭ 深甚な しんじんな profound; careful, mature
蝕甚(=食尽) しょくじん maximum eclipse

祁 ▷extremely
キ　　　Ⓚ104.

extremely, intensely, exceedingly
祁寒 きかん severe cold

超 ▷super-
チョウ こ(える) こ(す)　　　Ⓚ282.

[also prefix] **super-, ultra-**
超人 ちょうじん superman
超自然的な ちょうしぜんてきな supernatural
超国家的な ちょうこっかてきな ultranationalistic
超音速 ちょうおんそく supersonic speed
超大型 ちょうおおがた extra-large
超特急 ちょうとっきゅう superexpress (train)

頗 ▷exceedingly
ハ すこぶ(る)　　　Ⓚ112

exceedingly, extremely, very much

extreme in power
激 荒 狂 烈 猛

激 ▷violent
ゲキ はげ(しい)　　　Ⓚ069.

(acting with extreme force) **violent, fierce, vehement**
激烈な げきれつな vehement, furious, violent, severe
激戦 げきせん fierce [hard-fought] battle; hot contest
激突 げきとつ crash, collision
激情 げきじょう violent emotion, passion

荒 ▷wild
コウ あら(い) あら- あ(れる) あ(らす)
-あ(らし)　　　Ⓚ195.

【コウ】
(of natural phenomena) **wild, stormy, fierce**
荒天 こうてん stormy weather
【あら(い)】
(of natural phenomena) **wild, violent, rough**
荒さ あらさ wildness, roughness; extravagance
荒い波 あらいなみ wild [raging] waves, stormy seas

狂 ▷raging
キョウ くる(う) くる(おしい) くる(わす)
くる(わせる)　　　Ⓚ0241

raging, wild, furious
狂奔する きょうほんする rush around, run madly about, run wild; make frantic efforts, be very busy (in)

狂喜 きょうき wild joy, ecstasy

烈 ▷vehement
レツ   Ⓚ2308

vehement, violent, strong, furious, fierce, intense
   烈風 れっぷう violent [strong] wind
   烈震 れっしん violent [disastrous] earthquake
   強烈な きょうれつな intense, severe
   痛烈な つうれつな sharp, biting, scathing, cutting
   猛烈な もうれつな violent, vehement, fierce
   激烈な げきれつな vehement, furious, violent,
     severe
   熱烈な ねつれつな ardent, fervent, vehement

猛 ▷fierce
モウ   Ⓚ0490

[also prefix] (extremely severe) **fierce, violent; heavy,
hard, intensive**
   猛烈な もうれつな violent, vehement, fierce
   猛然と もうぜんと fiercely
   猛毒 もうどく deadly poison
   猛爆 もうばく heavy bombing
   猛襲 もうしゅう fierce attack
   猛練習 もうれんしゅう hard training

extremity
端 末 梢 先 尖 鋒

端 ▷end
タン はし は はた -ばた   Ⓚ1131

【タン】
end, extremity, tip
   端子 たんし terminal
   突端 とったん tip, point
   両端 りょうたん both ends
   先端(=尖端) せんたん pointed end, tip; spearhead;
     vanguard
   末端 まったん end, tip, termination
   一端 いったん one end, edge, side; a part
   極端 きょくたん extreme, extremity, pole
   異端 いたん heresy, paganism, heterodoxy
【はし】
end, extremity, tip
   紐の端 ひものはし end of a string
   両端 りょうはし both ends

末 ▷end
マツ バツ すえ   Ⓚ2940

end, tip
   末端 まったん end, tip, termination

末梢 まっしょう tip, end; tip of a twig; *anat* periphery
端末 たんまつ terminal

梢 ▷tip
ショウ こずえ   Ⓚ0874

tip, end
   末梢神経 まっしょうしんけい peripheral nerve

先 ▷point
セン さき ま(ず)   Ⓚ2123

(pointed end) **point, end, tip**
   先端 せんたん pointed end, tip; spearhead;
     vanguard
   先兵 せんぺい advance-guard point; advance
     detachment

尖 ▷point
セン とが(る) とんが(る)   Ⓚ1864

(pointed end) **point, end, tip**
   尖端 せんたん pointed end, tip; spearhead;
     vanguard
   尖兵 せんぺい advance-guard point; advance
     detachment
   肺尖 はいせん apex of a lung

鋒 ▷point of a blade
ホウ きっさき ほこ ほこさき   Ⓚ1545

[original meaning] **point of a blade [sword]; spearhead**
   鋒鋩 ほうぼう point of a blade; sharp words, vicious
     character
   機鋒 きほう sword point, spearhead; brunt

eye
目 眼 眸 瞳

目 ▷eye
モク ボク め ま-   Ⓚ2619

[original meaning] **eye**
   目前の もくぜんの before one's eyes, imminent
   盲目 もうもく blindness
   耳目 じもく eyes and ears; one's attention

眼 ▷eye
ガン ゲン まなこ め   Ⓚ1084

ⓐ [original meaning] **eye**
ⓑ (small hole) **eye, eyelet, loop**
 ⓐ 眼球 がんきゅう eyeball
   眼科 がんか ophthalmology
   碧眼 へきがん blue eyes

近眼 きんがん nearsightedness
双眼鏡 そうがんきょう binoculars
開眼 かいげん opening one's eyes to the truth, enlightenment
b 銃眼 じゅうがん loophole, eyelet

眸 ▷eye
ボウ ひとみ ⓚ1082

ⓐ [original meaning] eye, eyes
ⓑ pupil (of the eye)
a 眸子 ぼうし eye; pupil
双眸 そうぼう both eyes
明眸 めいぼう bright eyes, beautiful eyes
一眸(=一望) いちぼう sweep of the eye

瞳 ▷pupil
ドウ ひとみ ⓚ1144

[original meaning] pupil (of the eye)
瞳孔 どうこう pupil
瞳子 どうし pupil

fabric
布　　地　　巾

布 ▷cloth
フ ぬの ⓚ2566

[original meaning] cloth, textile
布巾 ふきん dishcloth, napkin
毛布 もうふ blanket
綿布 めんぷ cotton cloth
財布 さいふ purse, wallet

地 ▷fabric
チ ジ ⓚ0181

[also suffix] fabric, texture, cloth, material
服地 ふくじ cloth, dress material, clothing fabric
裏地 うらじ lining (cloth), material for lining
厚地 あつじ thick cloth
織地 おりじ fabric, texture
タオル地 たおるじ toweling
プリント地 ぷりんとじ printed cloth

巾 ▷cloth
キン はば ⓚ2879

[original meaning] cloth, napkin
巾着 きんちゃく purse
雑巾 ぞうきん rag; mop
布巾 ふきん dishcloth, napkin
茶巾 ちゃきん tea cloth [napkin]
三角巾 さんかくきん triangle bandage

fabrics
織　紬　紗　絹　綾
綿　棉　麻　毛　錦

織 ▷woven fabric
ショク シキ お(る) お(り) ⓚ1295

woven fabric, textile
織布 しょくふ woven fabric

紬 ▷pongee
チュウ つむぎ ⓚ1215

pongee, coarse silk [cotton] cloth
紬糸 つむぎいと silk thread spun from either waste cocoons or cotton

紗 ▷gauze
サ シャ ⓚ1196

[original meaning] gauze, silk gauze, gossamer, thin silk [cloth]
薄紗 はくさ gossamer, delicate gauze
羅紗 らしゃ woolen cloth
袱紗 ふくさ (small) crepe wrapper

絹 ▷silk
ケン きぬ ⓚ1243

[original meaning] silk
絹布 けんぷ silk, silk cloth
絹糸 けんし(=きぬいと) silk thread
人絹 じんけん artificial silk; rayon
正絹 しょうけん (pure) silk

綾 ▷twill
リョウ あや ⓚ1258

[in compounds] twill, twilled fabric
綾織り あやおり twill
綾錦 あやにしき twill damask and brocade

綿 ▷cotton
メン わた ⓚ125

cotton fiber, cotton cloth, cotton wool
綿糸 めんし cotton yarn [thread]
綿羊(=緬羊) めんよう sheep
綿紡 めんぼう cotton spinning
綿織物 めんおりもの cotton goods
原綿 げんめん raw cotton
木綿 もめん cotton, cotton cloth
梳綿機 そめんき carding machine
印綿 いんめん Indian raw cotton

棉 ▷cotton
メン わた

cotton fiber, cotton cloth, cotton wool
　印棉 いんめん Indian raw cotton

麻 ▷hemp
マ マー あさ　　　　　　Ⓚ2694

【マ マー】
hemp fiber, flax fiber
【あさ】
hemp, flax, jute; hemp fiber, flax fiber
　麻布 あさぬの hemp cloth, linen
　麻袋 あさぶくろ jute bag
　マニラ麻 まにらあさ Manila hemp

毛 ▷wool
モウ け　　　　　　　　Ⓚ2904

wool
　毛製品 もうせいひん woolen goods
　毛布 もうふ blanket
　純毛 じゅんもう pure wool, all wool
　原毛 げんもう raw wool

錦 ▷brocade
キン にしき　　　　　　Ⓚ1549

[original meaning] **brocade**
　錦旗 きんき gold-brocade flag; pennant

---

face
向　　面　　対

向 ▷turn toward
コウ む(く) む(き) む(ける) -む(け)
む(かう) む(こう)　　Ⓚ2627

ⓐ **turn toward, face, look toward**
ⓑ **turn (one's heart or mind) to**
ⓒ **(meet face to face) face, confront**

a 向日性 こうじつせい disposition (in flowers) to turn toward the sun, heliotropism
b 向上心 こうじょうしん ambition, aspiration
　向学心 こうがくしん desire for learning, intellectual appetite
c 向寒 こうかん facing the winter
　対向車 たいこうしゃ car (running) on the opposite lane

面 ▷face
メン おも おもて つら　Ⓚ1796

ⓐ **(have the front toward) face, front on, look toward**
ⓑ **meet face to face, confront in person**

a 面壁 めんぺき meditation facing the wall
　直面する ちょくめんする face, confront
　当面の とうめんの present, immediate; urgent, pressing
b 面会する めんかいする see, have an interview
　面接 めんせつ interview
　面罵 めんば abusing someone to his [her] face
　面識 めんしき acquaintance
　面談 めんだん interview

対 ▷face (each other)
タイ ツイ　　　　　　　Ⓚ0735

[original meaning] **face (each other), confront**
　対面する たいめんする meet, face
　相対 そうたい relativity

---

face orifices
口　鼻　耳　目

口 ▷mouth
コウ ク くち　　　　　Ⓚ2865

[original meaning] **(oral cavity) mouth**
　口腔 こうくう(=こうこう) mouth, oral cavity
　口内 こうない in the mouth
　口角 こうかく corners of one's mouth
　経口の けいこうの oral
　閉口する へいこうする be dumbfounded [stumped], be silenced

鼻 ▷nose
ビ はな　　　　　　　　Ⓚ2362

nose
　鼻音 びおん nasal sound
　鼻孔 びこう nostrils
　鼻炎 びえん nasal inflammation
　鼻下長 びかちょう amorous man, spoony
　耳鼻 じび nose and ears

耳 ▷ear
ジ みみ　　　　　　　　Ⓚ2948

[original meaning] **ear**
　耳目 じもく eyes and ears; one's attention
　耳鼻咽喉 じびいんこう nose, ear and throat
　耳鼻科 じびか otorhinology
　中耳炎 ちゅうじえん otitis media; tympanitis
　外耳 がいじ external ear, concha

目 ▷eye
モク ボク め まー　　　Ⓚ2619
see also →EYE

[original meaning] **eye**

目前の もくぜんの before one's eyes, imminent
盲目 もうもく blindness
耳目 じもく eyes and ears; one's attention

fail
敗　落　損

敗 ▷fail
ハイ やぶ(れる)　Ⓚ1342

fail
失敗 しっぱい failure, mistake
成敗 せいはい success or failure
成敗 せいばい punishment

落 ▷fall through
ラク お(ちる) お(ち) お(とす)　Ⓚ2019

fall through, fail (an examination)
落選 らくせん election defeat; rejection
落第 らくだい failure in an examination
落伍者 らくごしゃ straggler

損 ▷fail to (do)
ソン -そこ(なう) そこ(ねる)　Ⓚ0596

fail to (do), fail in (doing)
見損なう みそこなう fail to see; make a mistake, misjudge

fall →DESCEND AND FALL

false
虚　仮　偽　擬　義

虚 ▷false
キョ コ　Ⓚ2778

false, sham, untrue, feigned
虚偽 きょぎ falsehood, lie, fallacy
虚言 きょげん falsehood
虚報 きょほう false alarm
虚構 きょこう fabrication, fiction
虚虚実実の戦い きょきょじつじつのたたかい match between persons equal in shrewdness

仮 ▷fake
カ ケ かり　Ⓚ0034

fake, false, sham, feigned, pseudo
仮面 かめん mask, disguise
仮装 かそう disguise, fancy dress
仮名 かめい pseudonym, alias

仮病 けびょう feigned illness

偽 ▷sham
ギ いつわ(る) にせ　Ⓚ011

[also prefix] **sham, imitation, fake, forgery**
偽物 にせもの sham, imitation, fake, forgery
偽札 にせさつ counterfeit paper money
偽君子 にせくんし sham gentleman

擬 ▷imitation
ギ　Ⓚ070

[also prefix] **imitation, dummy, pseudo**
擬毛 ぎもう imitation wool
擬古典的な ぎこてんてきな pseudoclassic
擬爆弾 ぎばくだん dummy bomb

義 ▷artificial
ギ　Ⓚ205

artificial
義足 ぎそく artificial leg
義眼 ぎがん artificial eye

falsehood
偽　嘘

偽 ▷falsehood
ギ いつわ(る) にせ　Ⓚ011

falsehood, lie
真偽 しんぎ truth or falsehood; authenticity
虚偽 きょぎ falsehood, lie, fallacy

嘘 ▷lie
キョ うそ

lie, falsehood
嘘言 きょげん lie

familiar and friendly
親　密　近　睦　懇　和

親 ▷intimate
シン おや した(しい) した(しむ)　Ⓚ159

intimate, familiar, close, friendly
親友 しんゆう close [intimate] friend
親密な しんみつな intimate, close
親愛 しんあい love, affection
親切な しんせつな kind, friendly, obliging

日イ親善 にちいしんぜん friendly relations between Japan and Israel

密 ▷close
ミツ   ⓚ1984

(very near in relationship) **close, intimate**

密接な みっせつな close, intimate
緊密な きんみつな close, tight
親密な しんみつな intimate, close

近 ▷near
キン ちか(い)   ⓚ2634

(close in relationship) **near, close, personal; intimate**

近親 きんしん near relative
近衛 このえ Imperial Guards
親近感 しんきんかん feeling of intimacy
側近 そっきん close associate, aide

睦 ▷friendly
ボク むつ(まじい) むつ(む)   ⓚ1107

friendly, harmonious, peaceful

親睦 しんぼく friendliness, amity, intimacy
和睦 わぼく reconciliation, peace
敦睦な とんぼくな [archaic] cordial and friendly, affectionate

懇 ▷familiar
コン ねんご(ろ)   ⓚ2517

familiar, friendly, intimate

懇談 こんだん familiar talk [chat]
懇談会 こんだんかい social gathering; round table conference
懇意 こんい intimacy, friendship; kindness
懇親 こんしん friendship, intimacy
懇話 こんわ friendly [familiar] chat [talk]
別懇 べっこん intimacy

和 ▷harmonious
ワ オ やわ(らぐ) やわ(らげる) なご(む) なご(やか)   ⓚ1044

harmonious, in accord, peaceful, friendly

和気 わき harmonious atmosphere
和合 わごう harmony, concord; union
調和 ちょうわ harmony, accord, agreement, symmetry
共和制 きょうわせい republicanism

family and relations
族 家 門 氏 縁
姻 親 戚 曽

族 ▷family
ゾク   ⓚ0863

family, kinsman; relatives

家族 かぞく family, household
遺族 いぞく bereaved family
親族 しんぞく relative
一族 いちぞく kinsman, relative, one's (whole) family; race
血族 けつぞく blood relative

家 ▷family
カ ケ いえ や うち   ⓚ1963

ⓐ **family, house, household**
ⓑ [suffix] **family, House**

a 家族 かぞく family, household
家庭 かてい home, family, household
家計 かけい household economy, family finances
家内 かない family, household; wife
家事 かじ household affairs, housework
家裁 かさい family court
実家 じっか family in which one was born; one's parents' home
良家 りょうけ good family
一家 いっか family, household; one's family; style (of established reputation)
b 将軍家 しょうぐんけ family to inherit the shogunate
徳川家 とくがわけ the Tokugawas, the House of Tokugawa
宮田家 みやたけ the Miyata family

門 ▷family
モン かど   ⓚ0789

family, clan

門閥 もんばつ (renowned) lineage, pedigree
名門 めいもん distinguished [noted] family; prestigious establishment
一門 いちもん family, the whole clan

氏 ▷clan
シ うじ   ⓚ2552

ⓐ **clan, family**
ⓑ **suffix after names of clans or families**

a 氏族 しぞく clan, family
b 源氏 げんじ the Genji family, the Minamotos
平氏 へいし the Heike [Taira] clan [family], the Heikes

縁 ▷**relation**
エン ふち　　　　　　　　Ⓚ1269

family relation, relations, relative, kinsman
　血縁 けつえん blood relation
　遠縁 とおえん distant relation

姻 ▷**relative by marriage**
イン　　　　　　　　　　Ⓚ0315

relative by marriage
　姻族 いんぞく relatives by marriage
　姻戚 いんせき relatives by marriage, in-laws

親 ▷**relatives**
シン おや した(しい) した(しむ)　Ⓚ1599

relatives, kin, relations (by marriage)
　親族 しんぞく relative
　親類 しんるい relatives, relations
　親戚 しんせき relative
　三親等 さんしんとう kinsman of the third degree
　　(of consanguinity)
　肉親 にくしん blood relation

戚 ▷**relatives**
セキ　　　　　　　　　　Ⓚ2997

relatives, kin, relations (by marriage)
　親戚 しんせき relative
　姻戚 いんせき relatives by marriage, in-laws
　遠戚 えんせき distant relative
　外戚 がいせき maternal relative

曽 ▷**great-**
ソウ ゾ ひ ひい　　　　　Ⓚ1823

(three generations removed) **great-**
　曽孫 そうそん great-grandchild
　曽祖父母 そうそふぼ great-grandparents

farm and plant
植 栽 培 耕 作 農 蒔 播

植 ▷**plant**
ショク う(える) う(わる)　Ⓚ0903

[original meaning] **plant**
　植樹 しょくじゅ tree planting
　植栽 しょくさい raising trees and plants
　移植 いしょく transplanting

栽 ▷**plant (saplings)**
サイ　　　　　　　　　　Ⓚ2810

plant (saplings), transplant, grow, raise
　栽培 さいばい cultivation, raising, growing
　植栽 しょくさい raising trees and plants
　輪栽 りんさい rotation of crops
　果樹栽培 かじゅさいばい fruit culture, pomiculture

培 ▷**cultivate**
バイ つちか(う)　　　　Ⓚ042

[original meaning] (work the earth to grow vegetation)
cultivate, raise, grow
　栽培 さいばい cultivation, raising, growing

耕 ▷**till**
コウ たがや(す)　　　　Ⓚ119

[original meaning] **till, plow**
　耕作する こうさくする cultivate, plow, till
　耕地 こうち arable land, farm land
　耕具 こうぐ farm implements
　耕運機 こううんき cultivator, tiller
　農耕 のうこう farming
　深耕 しんこう deep plowing
　晴耕雨読 せいこううどく working in the field in fine
　　weather and reading at home in rainy weather

作 ▷**raise crops**
サク サ つく(る) つく(り) -づく(り)　Ⓚ005

raise crops, cultivate, farm
　作物 さくもつ crops
　作付 さくづけ planting
　耕作 こうさく cultivation, farming
　連作 れんさく repeated cultivation; story made up
　　by several writers working on it in turn
　輪作 りんさく rotation of crops
　畑作 はたさく dry field farming, dry field crop

農 ▷**farm, farming**
ノウ　　　　　　　　　　Ⓚ235

ⓐ **farming, agriculture**
ⓑ [original meaning] **farm, till**
a 　農業 のうぎょう agriculture
　農家 のうか farmhouse, farmer
　農村 のうそん farm village, agricultural community
　農地 のうち farmland, farming land
　農場 のうじょう farm
　農協 のうきょう agricultural cooperative
　農政 のうせい agricultural administration
　農閑期 のうかんき leisure season for farmers
　農具 のうぐ farming implements
　離農 りのう giving up farming
　酪農 らくのう dairy farming
b 　農作 のうさく land cultivation
　農婦 のうふ farmerette
　農民 のうみん peasants, farmers

蒔 ▷sow
ジ シ ま(く)　　　　　　Ⓚ2042

[also 播く] sow
種を蒔く たねをまく sow seed

播 ▷sow
ハ バン ま(く)　　　　　　Ⓚ0669

[original meaning] sow
播種 はしゅ sowing, planting
点播 てんぱ sowing seeds at regular intervals

fast

速 早 疾 快 急
迅 敏 即 捷

速 ▷quick
ソク はや(い) はや– はや(める)
はや(まる) すみ(やか)　　　Ⓚ2674

🅐 [original meaning] **quick, speedy, fast, rapid, swift, prompt, hasty**
🅑 **quickly, swiftly**

a 速球 そっきゅう fast ball
速射 そくしゃ quick firing
速達便 そくたつびん special delivery, express mail
速報 そくほう prompt report, news flash
快速 かいそく high speed; fast (local) train
急速な きゅうそくな rapid, swift, prompt
迅速な じんそくな swift, rapid
b 速記 そっき shorthand, stenography
速断 そくだん hasty conclusion; prompt decision
早速 さっそく immediately

早 ▷quick
ソウ サッ– はや(い) はや はや(まる)
はや(める) さ–　　　　　Ⓚ2120

🅐 **quick, fast**
🅑 **hasty, rash**

a 早早 そうそう quickly, without delay, immediately; early
早速 さっそく immediately
早急に さっきゅう(=そうきゅう)に urgently, pressingly, in a hurry
b 早計 そうけい rashness

疾 ▷fast
シツ　　　　　　　　　Ⓚ2793

fast, swift, at full speed
疾走 しっそう sprint, dash
疾駆する しっくする ride fast, drive a horse fast
疾風 しっぷう gale, strong wind

快 ▷fast
カイ こころよ(い)　　　　　Ⓚ0218

fast, speedy, rapid, quick
快速 かいそく high speed; fast (local) train
快走 かいそう fast running, fast sailing
快足の かいそくの quick of foot, fast
特快 とっかい special fast (local) train
軽快な けいかいな light, nimble, quick; cheerful

急 ▷rapid
キュウ いそ(ぐ) いそ(ぎ)　　Ⓚ1800

rapid, fast, swift, speedy, express
急速な きゅうそくな rapid, swift, prompt
急ピッチ きゅうぴっち quick [fast] pace
急性の きゅうせいの acute
急進する きゅうしんする advance rapidly, make rapid progress
急流 きゅうりゅう rapid stream, swift current; swift-running river; rapids
急遽 きゅうきょ in a hurry, in haste
緩急 かんきゅう fast and slow motion, high and low speed; emergency

迅 ▷swift
ジン　　　　　　　　　Ⓚ2621

[original meaning] swift, fast, rapid
迅速な じんそくな swift, rapid

敏 ▷nimble
ビン　　　　　　　　　Ⓚ1206

(physically agile) nimble, agile, quick, alert
敏速 びんそく quickness, agility, activity
敏捷な びんしょうな agile, nimble, quick; shrewd, smart
機敏 きびん smartness, shrewdness, sharpness; quickness, promptness

即 ▷immediate
ソク すなわ(ち)　　　　　Ⓚ1036
see also →IMMEDIATE

immediate, prompt, instant, on the spot
即死 そくし instant death, death on the spot
即売 そくばい sale on the spot, spot sale
即時 そくじ immediately, promptly
即刻 そっこく immediately, instantly
即座に そくざに immediately, promptly, at once
即効 そっこう immediate effect
即答 そくとう prompt answer
即金 そっきん immediate cash, ready cash
一触即発 いっしょくそくはつ touch-and-go situation, hair-trigger crisis

捷 ▷agile
ショウ ジョウ   Ⓚ0462

agile, nimble, quick, alert; shrewd, keen
敏捷な びんしょうな agile, nimble, quick; shrewd, smart

fate and fortune
運 命 業 縁 籤

運 ▷fortune
ウン はこ(ぶ)   Ⓚ2707

fortune, luck, fate, destiny, chance
運命 うんめい fate, fortune, destiny
運良く うんよく fortunately, luckily
好運 こううん good luck
不運 ふうん misfortune, bad luck
社運 しゃうん fortune of the company

命 ▷fate
メイ ミョウ いのち   Ⓚ1772

fate, god's will, destiny, luck
命運 めいうん one's fate [doom]
革命 かくめい revolution
運命 うんめい fate, fortune, destiny
宿命 しゅくめい fate, destiny
本命 ほんめい probable [prospective] winner, most likely candidate

業 ▷karma
ギョウ ゴウ わざ   Ⓚ2265

(one's deeds as a determinant factor in one's future life)
karma
業報 ごうほう karmic effects, fate, inevitable retribution
悪業 あくごう evil doings in one's former existence, evil karma
自業自得 じごうじとく natural consequence of one's own deeds
罪業 ざいごう sin, iniquity
非業の死 ひごうのし unnatural death

縁 ▷karma relation
エン ふち   Ⓚ1269

karma relation, predestination, fate, destiny
宿縁 しゅくえん karma, destiny, fate
縁起 えんぎ origin, history; omen, luck

籤 ▷lot
セン くじ

[now also 選] **lot, lottery**

抽籤 ちゅうせん drawing of lots
当籤する とうせんする win a prize, draw a lucky number

fats and oils
油 脂 肪 膏 蠟

油 ▷oil
ユ あぶら   Ⓚ0303

oil, animal oil, vegetable oil
油脂 ゆし fats and oils
油断 ゆだん negligence, carelessness, inattentiveness
醬油 しょうゆ soy sauce
サラダ油 さらだゆ(=さらだあぶら) salad oil
オリーブ油 おりーぶゆ olive oil

脂 ▷fat
シ あぶら   Ⓚ0861

[original meaning] **fat, grease, animal fat**
脂肪 しぼう fat, grease
脂質 ししつ lipid, fats
油脂 ゆし fats and oils
脱脂粉乳 だっしふんにゅう skim milk

肪 ▷animal fat
ボウ   Ⓚ078

[original meaning] **animal fat, fat**
脂肪 しぼう fat, grease

膏 ▷fat
コウ あぶら   Ⓚ183

[original meaning] **fat, grease; greasy substance**
膏肓 こうこう(=こうもう) inmost part (of the body)
膏血 こうけつ sweat and blood

蠟 ▷wax
ロウ   Ⓚ130

[original meaning] **wax, beeswax**
蠟燭 ろうそく candle
蠟人形 ろうにんぎょう wax figure
蠟石 ろうせき agalmatolite
蜜蠟 みつろう beeswax
封蠟 ふうろう sealing wax
屍蠟 しろう adipocere
生蠟 きろう crude Japan wax

fatten

肥　　太

肥 ▷**fatten**
ヒ こ(える) こえ こ(やす) こ(やし) Ⓚ0783

fatten, fat up, grow fat, make fat
肥大した ひだいした fat, enlarged
肥満する ひまんする become obese
肥馬 ひば fat horse
肥育 ひいく fattening

太 ▷**grow fat**
タイ タ ふと(い) ふと(る) Ⓚ1846

[sometimes also 肥る] **grow fat, fatten, gain weight**
太った ふとった fat, stout, plump

faults and flaws

難　短　疵　陥　欠

難 ▷**fault**
ナン かた(い) -がた(い) むずか(しい)
むつか(しい) Ⓚ1632

fault, defect, blemish
難点 なんてん weakness, fault, flaw; difficult point
無難 ぶなん safety, security; faultlessness

短 ▷**shortcoming**
タン みじか(い) Ⓚ1093

shortcoming, defect
短所 たんしょ shortcoming, defect
一長一短 いっちょういったん merits and demerits,
　　strong and weak points

疵 ▷**defect**
シ きず

defect, flaw, crack, fault, weak point
疵瑕 しか flaw, blemish, defect
瑕疵 かし defect, flaw

陥 ▷**defect**
カン おちい(る) おとしい(れる) Ⓚ0413

defect, fault
欠陥 けっかん defect, fault, deficiency

欠 ▷**incompleteness**
ケツ か(ける) か(く) か(かす) Ⓚ1721

incompleteness, imperfection, defect

欠点 けってん weak point, defect
完全無欠 かんぜんむけつ absolute perfection

favor

恵　　徳　　恩

恵 ▷**favor**
ケイ エ めぐ(む) Ⓚ2315

ⓐ **favor, grace, kindness**
ⓑ [original meaning] **favor, bestow with a favor, show
kindness to**
a 恵沢 けいたく blessing, pity, favor, benefit
　恩恵 おんけい benefit, grace, favor, blessing
　互恵 ごけい reciprocity, mutual benefits
　特恵 とっけい special favor [benefit], preference,
　　preferentialism
b 恵方 えほう lucky direction

徳 ▷**act of kindness**
トク Ⓚ0623

act of kindness, favor
徳沢 とくたく grace, blessing
徳政 とくせい benevolent administration
報徳 ほうとく requital of a person's kindness

恩 ▷**grace**
オン Ⓚ2311

[original meaning] **grace, favor, kindness, benevolence, blessing**
恩恵 おんけい benefit, grace, favor, blessing
恩返し おんがえし repaying another's kindness
恩人 おんじん benefactor, patron
恩寵 おんちょう grace (of God), favor

fear

怖　凄　恐　惧　慄
兢　惶　畏　臆　怯

怖 ▷**fearful**
フ こわ(い) こわ(がる) Ⓚ0263

【フ】
[original meaning] **fear, be afraid of**
畏怖 いふ awe, fear, dread, fright
恐怖 きょうふ fear
【こわ(い)】
[also 恐い] **fearful, scary, uncanny; be afraid**
怖さ こわさ fear, dreadfulness

怖怖 こわごわ timidly, gingerly
怖い顔 こわいかお angry look, grim face
犬が怖い いぬがこわい be afraid of dogs

凄 ▷uncanny
セイ すご(い)   Ⓚ0110

uncanny, dreadful, terrible, fierce
凄惨 せいさん ghastliness, gruesomeness
凄絶な せいぜつな fierce, violent

恐 ▷fear
キョウ おそ(れる) おそ(る)
おそ(ろしい)   Ⓚ2306

ⓐ [formerly also 恟] [original meaning] **fear, be afraid of, dread**
ⓑ **fearful, frightening**
a 恐怖 きょうふ fear
恐慌 きょうこう panic, scare, alarm
恐懼 きょうく dread, fear, awe
恐妻家 きょうさいか henpecked husband, man bossed by his wife
恐水病 きょうすいびょう hydrophobia
閉所恐怖症 へいしょきょうふしょう claustrophobia
戦戦恐恐として せんせんきょうきょうとして with fear and trembling
b 恐竜 きょうりゅう dinosaur, titanosaur

惧 ▷fear
グ   Ⓚ0437

fear, be afraid of, dread
危惧 きぐ fear, misgivings
絶滅危惧種 ぜつめつきぐしゅ endangered species
疑惧 ぎく apprehension, misgivings

慄 ▷tremble with fear
リツ   Ⓚ0589

[rarely also 栗] [original meaning] **tremble with fear, shudder**
慄然として りつぜんとして with horror
戦慄する せんりつする shudder, shiver

兢 ▷be in fear
キョウ

[now replaced by 恐] **be in fear, tremble**
戦戦兢兢として せんせんきょうきょうとして with fear and trembling

惶 ▷be afraid
コウ

[now usu. 皇] **be afraid, be anxious; be flurried**
蒼惶(=倉皇)として そうこうとして in great haste
恐惶敬白 きょうこうけいはく Very truly yours

畏 ▷be overawed
イ おそ(れる)   Ⓚ221

[original meaning] **be overawed, stand in awe, fear**
畏怖 いふ awe, fear, dread, fright
畏縮する いしゅくする shrink, flinch, wince
畏懼 いく reverence, awe, fear
畏服 いふく awed submission

臆 ▷feel timid
オク   Ⓚ101

[sometimes also 憶] **feel timid, fear**
臆病 おくびょう cowardice, timidity
臆面もなく おくめんもなく audaciously, impudently, unabashedly

怯 ▷be frightened
キョウ おび(える) ひる(む)

be frightened (by), be terrified (by), be scared (of)
怯え上がる おびえあがる be frightened to death, tremble in fear
怯えた顔で おびえたかおで with a scared look
その光景に怯える そのこうけいにおびえる be frightened at the sight

fee and price
料 代 賃 銭 費 価 値

料 ▷fee
リョウ   Ⓚ118

(charge for services) **fee, charge, rate, allowance**
料金 りょうきん charge, rate, fee, fare
無料 むりょう no charge, free
送料 そうりょう postage, carriage
手数料 てすうりょう commission, (handling) fee, charge
使用料 しようりょう rental fee
入場料 にゅうじょうりょう admission fee

代 ▷charge
ダイ タイ か(わる) か(わり) -が(わり)
か(える) よ しろ   Ⓚ001

[also suffix] (price charged) **charge, fare, rate, fee, price, rent**
代金 だいきん charge, fee, price
ホテル代 ほてるだい charge for staying at a hotel
無代 むだい free of charge
タクシー代 たくしーだい taxi fare
地代 じだい land rent, rental
部屋代 へやだい room rent

賃 ▷charges
チン   Ⓚ2350

[also suffix] **charges (for rental or transportation), fare, rent, hire, fee**
- 賃貸し ちんがし lease, hire
- 家賃 やちん (house) rent
- 運賃 うんちん freight [shipping] expense, passenger fare
- 船賃 ふなちん boat fare, passage; shipping charges
- 無賃の むちんの charge-free
- 借り賃 かりちん rent, hire

銭 ▷money paid
セン ぜに   Ⓚ1537

money paid, charges, fee
- 銭湯 せんとう public bath, bathhouse
- 木戸銭 きどせん gate money, admission fee
- 煙草銭 たばこせん tobacco money

費 ▷expense
ヒ つい(やす) つい(える)   Ⓚ2261

[also suffix] **expense, expenses, expenditure, cost**
- 費用 ひよう expenses, outlay
- 費目 ひもく item of expenditure
- 会費 かいひ fee, membership fee
- 学費 がくひ school [educational] expenses
- 食費 しょくひ food expenses; (charge for) board
- 出費 しゅっぴ expenses, expenditure, outlay
- 経費 けいひ expense(s), cost(s), expenditure, upkeep
- 生活費 せいかつひ living expenses, cost of living

価 ▷price
カ あたい   Ⓚ0067

[original meaning] (monetary value) **price, cost**
- 価格 かかく price, cost
- 物価 ぶっか prices (of commodities)
- 高価な こうかな expensive, high-priced
- 米価 べいか price of rice
- 定価 ていか fixed [set] price

値 ▷price
チ ね あたい   Ⓚ0091

[also suffix] **price, cost**
- 値が張る ねがはる be expensive
- 値段 ねだん price
- 値上げ ねあげ price hike
- 値打ち ねうち value, worth
- 値切る ねぎる beat down the price, bargain
- 値引き ねびき reduction in price, discount
- 高値 たかね high price
- 仕入れ値 しいれね cost price

---

feel deeply
感   動   嘆

感 ▷feel deeply
カン   Ⓚ2468

[original meaning] **feel deeply, feel admiration, be moved, be affected, be impressed**
- 感動する かんどうする be moved, be impressed
- 感銘 かんめい deep impression
- 感激 かんげき deep emotion
- 感心 かんしん admiration

動 ▷be moved
ドウ うご(く) うご(かす)   Ⓚ1583

be moved with emotion, be excited, be startled
- 動転する どうてんする be frightened, be stunned
- 感動する かんどうする be moved, be impressed

嘆 ▷sigh in admiration
タン なげ(く) なげ(かわしい)   Ⓚ0577

sigh in admiration, exclaim, admire, praise
- 嘆声 たんせい sigh, lamentation; sigh of admiration
- 詠嘆 えいたん exclamation, admiration
- 賛嘆 さんたん praise, admiration
- 驚嘆 きょうたん admiration, wonder
- 感嘆する かんたんする admire, be struck with admiration

---

feeling
感   情   心   気

感 ▷sense (feeling)
カン   Ⓚ2468

[also suffix] **sense, feeling, sensation, sentiment, emotion**
- 感情 かんじょう feelings, emotion, sentiment
- 感想 かんそう thoughts, impressions
- 同感 どうかん same sentiment, sympathy
- 劣等感 れっとうかん inferiority complex
- 責任感 せきにんかん sense of responsibility
- 親近感 しんきんかん feeling of intimacy

情 ▷emotion
ジョウ セイ なさ(け)   Ⓚ0439

[original meaning] **emotion, feeling, sentiment, passion**
- 情緒 じょうちょ(=じょうしょ) emotion, feeling
- 情操 じょうそう sentiment

激情 げきじょう violent emotion, passion
感情 かんじょう feelings, emotion, sentiment
友情 ゆうじょう friendship, fellowship
表情 ひょうじょう expression, look

心 ▷heart
シン こころ -ごころ   Ⓚ0004

(emotional state) **heart, feelings, emotion**

心を動かす こころをうごかす move one's heart; impress, touch (a person's heart)
心残りだ こころのこりだ feel sorry, regret
心細い こころぼそい helpless, forlorn; lonely
心安い こころやすい intimate, familiar
心持ち こころもち feeling, mood; slightly
心行く迄 こころゆくまで to one's heart's content
心強い こころづよい reassuring, heartening
気心 きごころ temper, disposition
恋心 こいごころ one's love

気 ▷spirits
キ ケ   Ⓚ2751

(emotional state) **spirits, one's feelings, mood, frame of mind**

気持 きもち feeling, sensation, mood
気分 きぶん feeling, mood; atmosphere
気前 きまえ generosity
気軽な きがるな lighthearted, cheerful; ready
人気 にんき popularity; temperament of the people; business conditions
平気 へいき nonchalance, unconcern; composure
本気 ほんき seriousness, earnestness
呆気に取られる あっけにとられる be astonished, be amazed

fellow
奴 漢 輩 徒 棒 坊 屋 物

奴 ▷guy
ド やつ   Ⓚ0164

guy, fellow, chap

奴等 やつら those guys, they
黒い奴 くろいやつ *derogatory* nigger; black one

漢 ▷fellow
カン   Ⓚ0602

[also suffix] **fellow, man**

好漢 こうかん nice fellow
痴漢 ちかん molester of women, masher
熱血漢 ねっけつかん hot-blooded man
大食漢 たいしょくかん great eater, glutton

輩 ▷fellow (*belittling*)
ハイ   Ⓚ2444

[also suffix] [belittling] **fellow, guy**

鼠輩 そはい insignificant fellow, small fry
徒輩 とはい set, company, fellows
我が輩(=吾輩) わがはい I
中野輩 なかのはい the likes of Nakano

徒 ▷fellows
ト   Ⓚ0377

ⓐ **fellows, companions, gang, party**
ⓑ **fellow, person**

ⓐ 徒党 ととう clique, faction, conspirators
暴徒 ぼうと rioters, mobsters, insurgents
ⓑ 博徒 ばくと gambler

棒 ▷tough guy
ボウ   Ⓚ0894

tough guy, fellow, chum

泥棒 どろぼう thief, crook
用心棒 ようじんぼう bodyguard, bouncer; bar, bolt
相棒 あいぼう pal, mate, companion

坊 ▷colloquial person suffix
ボウ ボッ-   Ⓚ0205

colloquial person suffix: **indicates endearment, intimacy or derision,** as the English "Jimmy boy" for James or such nicknames as "fatso" for a fat person

赤ん坊 あかんぼう baby
春坊 はるぼう nickname for such names as Haruo or Haruko
朝寝坊 あさねぼう late riser, sleepy head
けちん坊 けちんぼう miser, niggard, stingy fellow
食いしん坊 くいしんぼう glutton
風来坊 ふうらいぼう wanderer, vagabond, hobo
見栄坊 みえぼう fop, swell, dude, coxcomb

屋 ▷colloquial person suffix
オク や   Ⓚ2669

colloquial suffix indicating the peculiarity or idiosyncrasy of a person

気取り屋 きどりや affected person, snob
分からず屋 わからずや obstinate person, hardhead
恥ずかしがり屋 はずかしがりや shy person

物 ▷character
ブツ モツ もの   Ⓚ0777

(person distinguished by some characteristic) **character, person, man**

人物 じんぶつ character; person, figure
難物 なんぶつ hard character, person hard to please; hard nut to crack, difficulty
俗物 ぞくぶつ vulgar person, snob, Philistine

傑物 けつぶつ great man, outstanding figure

fences and walls
壁 塀 垣 牆 柵 堵 囲 欄

壁 ▷**wall**
ヘキ　かべ　　　　　　　　　Ⓚ2515

[original meaning] **wall, partition, fence, barrier**
　壁画 へきが wall painting, fresco
　障壁 しょうへき [formerly also 牆壁] fence, wall;
　　barrier
　防火壁 ぼうかへき fire wall

塀 ▷**fence (for screening)**
ヘイ　　　　　　　　　　　Ⓚ0511

[also suffix] [original meaning] **fence (for screening),
wall, board fence, enclosure**
　土塀 どべい mud wall, plaster wall
　板塀 いたべい board fence, wooden wall
　煉瓦塀 れんがべい brick wall
　ブロック塀 ぶろっくべい concrete (block) wall

垣 ▷**fence (for partitioning)**
かき　　　　　　　　　　　Ⓚ0311

[original meaning, now archaic] **fence, wall**
　垣牆 えんしょう fence, hedge

牆 ▷**fence (for partitioning)**
ショウ　かき

[now replaced by 牆] [original meaning] **fence, wall**
　牆壁 しょうへき fence, wall; barrier

柵 ▷**fence (with spaced pickets)**
サク　　　　　　　　　　　Ⓚ0804

fence, palisade, stockade, paling
　柵状組織 さくじょうそしき palisade layer
　鉄柵 てっさく iron fence

堵 ▷**fence (made of earth)**
ト　　　　　　　　　　　　Ⓚ0516

[original meaning] **fence (made of earth), enclosure**
　安堵する あんどする feel relieved, feel a sense of
　　peace [security]
　本領安堵 ほんりょうあんど recognition by the
　　shogunate of ownership of the inherited estate
　　of a samurai in medieval Japan

囲 ▷**enclosure**
イ　かこ(む)　かこ(う)　かこ(い)　Ⓚ2643

enclosure, fence

囲いに入れる かこいにいれる place in an enclosure

欄 ▷**railing**
ラン　　　　　　　　　　　Ⓚ1023

railing, balustrade, handrail
　欄干 らんかん railing, handrail, balustrade
　高欄 こうらん balustrade, handrail

ferment →BREW AND FERMENT

festivities →CEREMONIES AND FESTIVITIES

feudal territorial divisions
藩 国 領 封 荘

藩 ▷**feudal domain**
ハン　　　　　　　　　　　Ⓚ2106

❶ *han*: feudal domain (governed by a daimyo in
　Edo Japan), fief; feudal clan
❷ suffix after names of feudal domains
　a 藩校 はんこう *han* school
　　藩内 はんない within the *han*
　　藩閥 はんばつ clan favoritism, clanship
　　廃藩 はいはん abolition of the *han* system
　b 薩摩藩 さつまはん Satsuma Han

国 ▷**province (in former Japan)**
コク　くに　　　　　　　　Ⓚ2659

(unit of administration in former Japan equiv. to modern
prefecture) **province**
　国司 こくし provincial governor
　国府 こくふ National Government (of China);
　　provincial capital

領 ▷**fief**
リョウ　　　　　　　　　　Ⓚ1133

fief, feudal estate, feudal manor
　領主 りょうしゅ lord of a fief [manor]
　領民 りょうみん population of a fief

封 ▷**daimiate**
フウ　ホウ　　　　　　　　Ⓚ1182

(territory of a daimyo) **daimiate, fief**
　封地 ほうち daimiate, fief
　封土 ほうど daimiate, fief

荘 ▷**manor (in feudal Japan)**
ソウ　　　　　　　　　　　Ⓚ1954

❶ [sometimes also 庄] **manor (in feudal Japan),
village**

ⓑ used in the formation of the names of former feudal villages (farm villages that were formerly manors)

- a 荘園 しょうえん manor
  荘司 しょうじ administrator of a manor
- b 五家荘 ごかのしょう Gokanosho (place name)

few

少寡乏薄微寸僅些

 ▷**little**
ショウ すく(ない) すこ(し) Ⓚ2915

(of small quantity or number) **little, few, small**
少少 しょうしょう a little, a few, slightly
少数 しょうすう small number, minority
少量(=小量) しょうりょう small quantity [amount]
少額 しょうがく small sum
多少 たしょう a little, somewhat
軽少の けいしょうの little, slight, trifling
僅少差 きんしょうさ narrow [slim] margin

寡 ▷**few**
カ Ⓚ2059

few, little
寡少の かしょうの few, little, scanty
寡占 かせん oligopoly
寡黙な かもくな silent, taciturn, reticent
寡聞 かぶん having little knowledge (of), being ill-informed
多寡 たか quantity, number, amount

 ▷**scanty**
ボウ とぼ(しい) Ⓚ1693

(insufficient) **scanty, scarce, lacking, deficient**
欠乏 けつぼう lack, shortage, scarcity

薄 ▷**meager**
ハク うす(い) うす- うす(める) うす(まる)
うす(らぐ) うす(ら)- うす(れる) Ⓚ2093

meager, scanty, little, small (amount)
薄給 はっきゅう meager [scanty, small] salary
薄利 はくり small profits, low interest
薄謝 はくしゃ small remuneration, small token of gratitude
薄弱な はくじゃくな weak, feeble, frail

微 ▷**slight**
ビ かす(か) Ⓚ0587

(of very small quantity) **slight, very little**
微微たる びびたる slight, small, insignificant

微量 びりょう slight amount, extremely small quantity
微少 びしょう minute quantity

寸 ▷**a bit of**
スン Ⓚ254

(of small amount) **a bit of, very little, small, brief**
寸前に すんぜんに immediately before
寸時 すんじ a moment, a minute

僅 ▷**a little**
キン わず(か) Ⓚ013◄

a little, a few
僅少 きんしょう a few, a little, trifling

些 ▷**a bit**
サ いささ(か) Ⓚ2282

a bit, a little, somewhat, slightly
些細な ささいな trifling, slight, insignificant
些末な さまつな trivial, trifling
些事 さじ trivial matter, trifle
些少 さしょう a trivial amount [degree]

fiber-producing plants

麻　　綿

麻 ▷**hemp**
マ マー あさ Ⓚ2694

[original meaning] **hemp, flax or other similar plants**
亜麻 あま flax
黄麻 こうま(=おうま) jute
製麻 せいま hemp dressing, flax [hemp] spinning
大麻 たいま hemp; paper amulet used in Shinto rites

綿 ▷**cotton**
メン わた Ⓚ1254

cotton plant
綿花 めんか raw cotton, cotton wool

fibers →THREADS AND FIBERS

fidelity

忠 義 孝 悌 誠
実 信 操 節

忠 ▷loyalty
チュウ   Ⓚ2154

loyalty, devotion, faithfulness, fidelity
忠実 ちゅうじつ faithfulness, devotion, honesty
忠孝 ちゅうこう loyalty and filial piety
忠義 ちゅうぎ loyalty, fidelity, devotion

義 ▷faith
ギ   Ⓚ2052

faith, loyalty, duty
義務 ぎむ duty, obligation
義理 ぎり sense of duty [honor], obligation, debt of
    gratitude; justice; courtesy
忠義 ちゅうぎ loyalty, fidelity, devotion
信義 しんぎ fidelity, faith, loyalty
恩義 おんぎ obligation, debt of gratitude

孝 ▷filial piety
コウ   Ⓚ2761

filial piety, filial devotion
孝行 こうこう filial piety
孝心 こうしん filial devotion [affection]
孝養 こうよう discharge of filial duties
孝子 こうし filial child, good son
忠孝 ちゅうこう loyalty and filial piety
不孝 ふこう(=ふきょう) lack of filial piety, undutiful-
    ness

悌 ▷brotherly love
テイ ダイ   Ⓚ0381

[original meaning] **brotherly love, obedience to one's
older brother**
孝悌 こうてい filial piety and brotherly love

誠 ▷sincerity
セイ まこと   Ⓚ1382

sincerity, true heart, honesty, fidelity
誠実 せいじつ sincerity, honesty, faith
誠意 せいい sincerity, good faith
忠誠 ちゅうせい faithfulness, fidelity
至誠 しせい sincerity, devotion

実 ▷faithfulness
ジツ み みの(る)   Ⓚ1911

faithfulness, sincerity, fidelity

実直な じっちょくな upright, honest, steady
切実な せつじつな acute, keen, earnest; urgent
誠実な せいじつな sincere, honest, faithful
忠実な ちゅうじつな faithful, devoted, honest

信 ▷fidelity
シン   Ⓚ0084

[original meaning] **fidelity, faith, sincerity**
信義 しんぎ fidelity, faith, loyalty
威信 いしん prestige, dignity, authority
背信 はいしん breach of faith [trust], betrayal

操 ▷constancy
ソウ みさお あやつ(る)   Ⓚ0693

constancy, integrity, fidelity, moral principles
情操 じょうそう sentiment
節操 せっそう constancy, fidelity, integrity, honor

節 ▷moral integrity
セツ セチ ふし -ぶし   Ⓚ2349

moral integrity, principle, fidelity, loyalty
節操 せっそう constancy, fidelity, integrity, honor
貞節 ていせつ chastity, virtue; constancy, principle
忠節 ちゅうせつ loyalty, allegiance, fidelity

fight and war

闘 戦 征

闘 ▷fight
トウ たたか(う)   Ⓚ2847

fight (with)
闘牛 とうぎゅう bullfight, fighting bull
奮闘 ふんとう hard fighting
乱闘 らんとう free-for-all [confused] fight, melee
戦闘 せんとう battle, fight, combat
決闘 けっとう duel

戦 ▷war
セン いくさ たたか(う)   Ⓚ1590

[original meaning] **war, wage war, fight**
戦争 せんそう war, battle
戦闘 せんとう battle, fight, combat
戦場 せんじょう battlefield, front

征 ▷go on a military expedition
セイ   Ⓚ0262

**go on a military expedition, go to war, go to the
front, lead a punitive force, invade**

征夷大将軍 せいいたいしょうぐん Commander in Chief of the Expeditionary Force Against the Barbarians

遠征 えんせい (punitive) expedition, invasion; tour

出征する しゅっせいする go to war

fill

充 湛 塡 満 詰

充 ▷fill
ジュウ あ(てる) Ⓚ1737

ⓐ **fill, become full**
ⓑ **fill, fill up, stop up**

ⓐ 充塡する じゅうてんする fill, fill up, plug; replenish
　充満する じゅうまんする be full, be filled with, overflow
　充分(=十分)な じゅうぶんな full, enough, sufficient; plentiful
　拡充 かくじゅう expansion, amplification
ⓑ 充足 じゅうそく sufficiency
　充実した じゅうじつした full, complete, rich

湛 ▷be full of
タン たた(える) Ⓚ0559

be full of (liquid), fill with (liquid)

湛水 たんすい filling (a paddy field) with water

塡 ▷fill
テン Ⓚ0581

fill (in), stuff, load

塡料 てんりょう filler (for making paper)
充塡する じゅうてんする fill, fill up, plug; replenish
装塡する そうてんする load, charge

満 ▷fill
マン み(ちる) み(つ) み(たす) Ⓚ0553

ⓐ [original meaning] **fill, fill up, be filled**
ⓑ **reach the full extent, expire**

ⓐ 充満する じゅうまんする be full, be filled with, overflow
　金満家 きんまんか man of wealth, millionaire
ⓑ 満期 まんき expiration (of a term)
　満了 まんりょう expiration, due

詰 ▷stuff
キツ つ(める) つ(め) -づ(め) つ(まる) つ(む) Ⓚ1380

ⓐ (fill by packing closely) **stuff, fill, pack into, cram; charge**
ⓑ (fill an aperture) **stuff (up), stop up, block up**

ⓐ 瓶に詰める びんにつめる fill a bottle

ⓑ 詰め合わせ つめあわせ combination, assortment
詰め込む つめこむ cram, stuff, pack
詰め物 つめもの stuffing
息を詰める いきをつめる hold one's breath

fire

火 炎 焰

火 ▷fire
カ ひ -び ほ- Ⓚ2911

[original meaning] **fire**

火災 かさい fire, conflagration
火事 かじ fire
火炎 かえん flames, blaze
火力 かりょく caloric force; firepower
点火 てんか ignition, lighting
出火 しゅっか outbreak of fire
大火 たいか great fire, conflagration
消火 しょうか fire fighting

炎 ▷flame
エン ほのお Ⓚ2145

[original meaning] **flame, blaze**

火炎 かえん flames, blaze
紅炎 こうえん red blazes of flame

焰 ▷flame
エン ほのお Ⓚ0908

[original meaning] **flame, blaze**

焰硝(=煙硝) えんしょう gunpowder
火焰 かえん flames, blaze
光焰 こうえん light and flame

firm and obstinate

堅 固 確 毅 剛 頑 硬

堅 ▷firm
ケン かた(い) -がた(い) Ⓚ2457

ⓐ (of a person's character) **firm, steadfast, trustworthy**
ⓑ (unfluctuating) **firm, steady, stable**
ⓒ **firmly, resolutely**

ⓐ 堅固な けんごな strong, secure, firm, steadfast
　堅実な けんじつな steady, sound, reliable
　堅志 けんし iron purpose
　中堅 ちゅうけん the mainstay, nucleus (of a company)
ⓑ 堅調 けんちょう bullish, firm (market)
ⓒ 堅持する けんじする maintain firmly, hold fast to

固 ▷firm, stiff
コ かた(める) かた(まる) かた(まり) かた(い) ⓚ2658

❶ (having determination) **firm, resolute, determined**
固辞する こじする decline positively, decline firmly
堅固な けんごな strong, secure, firm, steadfast
強固な きょうこな firm, stable, solid, strong

❷ **firmly persistent, stiff, unyielding, stubborn**
固執する こしつ(=こしゅう)する adhere to, persist in
頑固な がんこな stubborn, obstinate, bigoted

確 ▷firm
カク たし(か) たし(かめる) ⓚ1135

(not easily moved) **firm, solid, steadfast, sound**
確保する かくほする secure, make sure of, ensure
確立する かくりつする establish, build up
確信する かくしんする believe firmly, be convinced
確執 かくしつ(=かくしゅう) discord, strife
確定 かくてい decision, settlement; confirmation
確固たる かっこたる firm, sure, resolute

毅 ▷resolute
キ ⓚ1649

resolute, determined, firm, dauntless
毅然として きぜんとして resolutely, firmly, bravely
剛毅な ごうきな hardy, sturdy

剛 ▷tough
ゴウ ⓚ1495

(of strong spirit) **tough, stout, resolute, brave**
剛毅な ごうきな hardy, sturdy
剛健 ごうけん fortitude and vigor, sturdiness, virility; manliness
剛直 ごうちょく moral courage, integrity
剛勇 ごうゆう bravery, prowess

頑 ▷stubborn
ガン ⓚ0953

ⓐ **stubborn, obstinate; hardheaded, thickheaded**
ⓑ (unyielding) **stubborn, firm, tenacious**
ⓐ 頑固な がんこな stubborn, obstinate, bigoted
頑強な がんきょうな stubborn, unyielding
頑丈な がんじょうな solid, firm; strong
頑健 がんけん robust health
ⓑ 頑張る がんばる persist, be tenacious, hold out

硬 ▷hard-line
コウ かた(い) ⓚ1095

[formerly also 鞕] **hard-line, stiff, unyielding, obdurate**
硬派 こうは hard-line elements, stalwart
硬軟両派 こうなんりょうは stalwart and insurgent factions

強硬な きょうこうな firm (attitude), unbending; drastic (measure)

first

甲　初

甲 ▷first
コウ カン カ ⓚ2923

the first, A; first class, grade A; the former
甲乙 こうおつ first and second, former and latter
甲種 こうしゅ grade A, first grade

初 ▷first
ショ はじ(め) はじ(めて) はつ うい– –そ(める) –ぞ(め) ⓚ1031

ⓐ **first, initial, original**
ⓑ [prefix] **first**
ⓐ 初回 しょかい first time; first inning
初日 しょにち first day, opening day
初版 しょはん first edition
初代 しょだい first generation, founder
初任給 しょにんきゅう initial salary
初志 しょし original aim [intention]
ⓑ 初対面 しょたいめん first meeting

first person pronouns

私　我　己　身　僕　俺
吾　予　余　麿　朕　自

私 ▷I (polite)
シ わたくし わたし ⓚ1030

I, myself—polite first person pronoun
私達 わたくしたち we
私小説 わたくししょうせつ(=ししょうせつ) first person novel, private [real] life novel

我 ▷self
ガ われ わ わ(が)- ⓚ2971

ⓐ **self, one's own self**
ⓑ **ego, self**
ⓐ 我慢 がまん patience, endurance; self-restraint
我流 がりゅう self-taught method, one's own way
ⓑ 自我 じが self, ego
無我 むが self-effacement; *Buddhism* nonself, nonego

己 ▷oneself
コ キ おのれ   Ⓚ2864

oneself, self
自己 じこ oneself, self, ego
利己主義 りこしゅぎ egoism
克己 こっき self-denial, self-control
知己 ちき acquaintance; intimate friend

身 ▷one's person
シン み   Ⓚ2977

【シン】
one's person, one's own person, oneself, self
身辺 しんぺん one's person, one's immediate
  surroundings
自身 じしん self, oneself; itself
出身地 しゅっしんち one's native place
独身 どくしん single life; celibacy
単身 たんしん alone, by oneself, unaccompanied
前身 ぜんしん one's former self, one's past life;
  predecessor
保身 ほしん self-protection
献身 けんしん self-sacrifice, devotion

【み】
one's person, one's own person, oneself, self
身の上 みのうえ one's career, one's condition, one's
  fortune
身近な みぢかな near oneself, close to one, familiar
身元(=身許) みもと one's birth, one's identity,
  one's background
身寄り みより relative, relation, kinsfolk
身投げ みなげ suicide by drowning or jumping
  from a high place
身柄 みがら one's person; social standing
身勝手 みがって selfishness, egoism, egotism

僕 ▷I (*familiar*)
ボク   Ⓚ0142

I, myself—familiar first person pronoun used by men in
addressing inferiors or peers
僕達 ぼくたち we

俺 ▷I (*intimate*)
おれ   Ⓚ0092

I—intimate first person pronoun used by men; though
usu. expressing intimacy, it sometimes has vulgar overtones
俺達 おれたち we
俺が俺がの連中 おれがおれがのれんちゅう ego-
  driven men

吾 ▷I (*elegant*)
ゴ われ わが- あ-   Ⓚ2132

elegant **I; we**
吾等 われら we, I; you

予 ▷I (*pompous*)
ヨ   Ⓚ1719

[also 余] **I, myself, the present writer**—historically
used as a formal first person pronoun but now only used
pompously
予の辞書に不可能の文字は無い よのじしょにふ
  かのうのもじはない In my dictionary, there's no
  such word as impossible

余 ▷I (*pompous*)
ヨ あま(る) あま(り) あま(す)   Ⓚ1752

[also 予] **I, myself, the present writer**—historically
used as a formal first person pronoun but now only used
pompously
余の辞書に不可能の文字は無い よのじしょにふ
  かのうのもじはない In my dictionary, there's no
  such word as impossible

麿 ▷I (*archaic*)
まろ   Ⓚ2746

[archaic] **I**—used esp. by noblemen mainly in the Heian
period

朕 ▷imperial we
チン   Ⓚ0856

Imperial We—formal first person pronoun used chiefly
by the emperor of Japan
朕の ちんの Our
朕が意 ちんがい Our will

自 ▷self
ジ シ みずか(ら) おの(ずから)   Ⓚ2954

ⓐ [also prefix] **self, oneself**
ⓑ one's own, one's
a 自分 じぶん self, oneself
自己 じこ oneself, self, ego
自身 じしん self, oneself; itself
自信 じしん self-confidence
自殺 じさつ suicide
自供 じきょう (voluntary) confession
自衛 じえい self-defense, self-protection
自慢 じまん pride, self-praise, vanity
自習 じしゅう self-study, self-teaching
自営の じえいの independent, self-employed
自問する じもんする question oneself
自営業 じえいぎょう self-employment
独自の どくじの original; personal, individual
b 自宅 じたく one's house, one's home
自国 じこく one's own country

fish

魚　貝

魚
▷**fish**
ギョ うお さかな -ざかな　　　Ⓚ1825

[also suffix] [original meaning] **fish**
魚類 ぎょるい fishes
魚介類 ぎょかいるい marine products
金魚 きんぎょ goldfish
鮮魚 せんぎょ fresh fish
人魚 にんぎょ mermaid, merman
深海魚 しんかいぎょ deep-sea fish
熱帯魚 ねったいぎょ tropical fish

貝
▷**shellfish**
バイ かい　　　Ⓚ2200

【バイ】
shellfish
魚貝 ぎょばい fish and shellfish

【かい】
[sometimes also 介] **shellfish**
貝類 かいるい shellfish
貝柱 かいばしら adductor muscle
赤貝 あかがい arc shell
巻き貝 まきがい roll-shell; snail
魚貝類(=魚介類) ぎょかいるい marine products

fish →HUNT AND FISH

fishes

鯉　鮎　鯛　鰯　鱒　鮫

鯉
▷**carp**
リ こい　　　Ⓚ1658

[original meaning, now rare] **carp**
養鯉 ようり carp breeding

鮎
▷**ayu**
デン ネン あゆ　　　Ⓚ1655

ayu, sweetfish
鮎並 あいなめ rock trout
稚鮎 ちあゆ young ayu

鯛
▷**tai**
チョウ たい　　　Ⓚ1660

tai, sea bream, porgy
鯛飯 たいめし rice and minced tai

鯛焼き たいやき fish-shaped pancake filled with
　　bean jam
真鯛 まだい red tai, red sea bream

鰯
▷**sardine**
いわし　　　Ⓚ1665

sardine
鰯雲 いわしぐも cirrocumulus
鰯鯨 いわしくじら sei whale
真鰯 まいわし Japanese pilchard, Japanese sardine
片口鰯 かたくちいわし Japanese anchovy
畳鰯 たたみいわし sheet of dried sardines
鯛の尾より鰯の頭 たいのおよりいわしのかしら
　　Better be the head of a dog than the tail of a
　　lion

鱒
▷**trout**
ソン ます　　　Ⓚ1667

trout
鮭鱒 けいそん salmon and trout
養鱒 ようそん trout farming

鮫
▷**shark**
コウ さめ

shark
鮫人 こうじん Chinese mermaid [merman]

fit

合　塡　適　揃

合
▷**fit**
ゴウ ガッ- カッ- あ(う) あ(い) あ(わす)
あ(わせる)　　　Ⓚ1740

fit, suit, agree, accord, coincide
合格 ごうかく passing an examination, eligibility
合理 ごうり rationality
合理化 ごうりか rationalization, streamlining
合法 ごうほう legality, legitimacy
合意 ごうい mutual agreement [consent]
合致 がっち agreement, concurrence
適合する てきごうする suit, be fit, conform (to)

塡
▷**fit**
テン は(まる)　　　Ⓚ0581

fit, be fit for, suit

適
▷**suit**
テキ　　　Ⓚ2726

suit, fit
適用する てきようする apply
適法 てきほう legality, lawfulness

適応 てきおう adaptation, adjustment
適合する てきごうする suit, be fit, conform (to)
適性 てきせい aptitude

揃 ▷make uniform
セン そろ(える) そろ(う) そろ(い)
－ぞろ(い)　　　　　　Ⓚ0539

make uniform [even], act in line [concert]

高さを揃える たかさをそろえる make all of uniform
height
歩調を揃える ほちょうをそろえる keep step with
口を揃えて くちをそろえて unanimously, in chorus

five
五　　伍

五 ▷five
ゴ いつ いつ(つ)　　　　　Ⓚ2892

[original meaning] **five, fifth**

五百 ごひゃく 500
五十音 ごじゅうおん Japanese syllabary
五感 ごかん the five senses
五指 ごし the five fingers
五分 ごぶ half, 50 percent
五分五分 ごぶごぶ evenly matched; tie
五輪旗 ごりんき five-ringed Olympic flag
五目飯 ごもくめし Japanese pilaf
五月 ごがつ May
五階 ごかい fifth floor

伍 ▷five (in legal documents)
ゴ　　　　　　　　　　Ⓚ0031

five—used in legal documents and checks
金伍千円也 きんごせんえんなり 5000 yen

flag
旗　幡　旒

旗 ▷flag
キ はた　　　　　　　　Ⓚ0958

❶ flag, banner, standard, ensign
❷ [suffix] flag, emblem
a 旗艦 きかん flagship
旗手 きしゅ standard bearer
国旗 こっき national flag
反旗を翻す はんきをひるがえす rise the standard of
revolt, raise in revolt
b 星条旗 せいじょうき the Stars and Stripes

国連旗 こくれんき United Nations Emblem
日章旗 にっしょうき Rising Sun flag

幡 ▷long flag
ハン バン マン はた　　　　Ⓚ065●

long flag, streamer, flag (esp. in Buddhism)
幢幡 どうばん hanging banner used as ornament in
Buddhist temples
八幡船 ばはんせん Japanese pirate ship
八幡 はちまん God of War, *Hachiman*

旒 ▷counter for flags
リュウ

[now also 流] **counter for flags**
旗二旒 はたにりゅう two flags

flat
平　扁　坦

平 ▷flat
ヘイ ビョウ たい(ら) －だいら
ひら　　　　　　　　　Ⓚ2921

[original meaning] **flat, level, even**
平方 へいほう square (measure); square (of a
number)
平野 へいや plain(s), open field
平面 へいめん level surface, plain
平坦な へいたんな flat, level, even
水平の すいへいの horizontal, level, even

扁 ▷flat
ヘン

flat
扁平な へんぺいな flat
扁桃 へんとう almond; tonsils

坦 ▷level
タン　　　　　　　　　Ⓚ0249

[original meaning] **level, flat, even**
坦坦 たんたん level, flat; uneventful
平坦 へいたん flat, level, even

flat supports
台　座　壇　棚　架　床

台 ▷stand
ダイ タイ　　　　　　　Ⓚ1731

[also suffix]

ⓐ (structure for placing on) **stand, pedestal, rack, table, support, mount**
ⓑ (elevated structure) **stand, platform**

a 台座 だいざ pedestal, base, stand
　燭台 しょくだい candlestick, candlestand
　楽譜台 がくふだい music stand
　鏡台 きょうだい dressing table
　荷台 にだい carrier, bed (of a truck)
　寝台 しんだい bed, sleeping berth
　流し台 ながしだい sink, washstand
　実験台 じっけんだい testing bench; subject of an
　　experiment
b 閲兵台 えっぺいだい reviewing stand
　証人台 しょうにんだい witness stand
　滑り台 すべりだい (playground) slide; launching
　　platform

座 ▷seat
ザ すわ(る)　　　　　Ⓚ2686

(supporting base) **seat, mount, base, platform, stand**
　座金 ざがね (metal) washer
　台座 だいざ pedestal, base, stand
　弁座 べんざ valve seat
　機関座 きかんざ seat of an engine

壇 ▷platform
ダン タン　　　　　Ⓚ0682

ⓐ **platform, raised floor, stage, dais**
ⓑ [original meaning] **platform for religious rites, altar**

a 壇上 だんじょう on the platform, on the stage
　壇場 だんじょう stage
　演壇 えんだん platform, rostrum
　花壇 かだん flower bed
　教壇 きょうだん teacher's platform, rostrum
b 戒壇 かいだん ordination platform (in temples)
　仏壇 ぶつだん family Buddhist altar
　祭壇 さいだん altar

棚 ▷shelf
たな -だな　　　　　Ⓚ0895

[original meaning] **shelf**
　陸棚 りくほう continental shelf

架 ▷rack
カ か(ける) か(かる)　　　　　Ⓚ2226

rack, shelf, stand, mount, support, frame
　銃架 じゅうか arm rack, rifle stand
　画架 がか easel
　担架 たんか stretcher
　十字架 じゅうじか cross, crucifix
　書架 しょか bookshelf, bookstack
　開架 かいか open access, open shelves

床 ▷bed
ショウ とこ ゆか　　　　　Ⓚ2641

ⓐ **bed, sickbed**
ⓑ **counter for beds**

a 起床する きしょうする get up, rise
　臨床医 りんしょうい clinician
b 百床病院 ひゃくしょうびょういん hospital with 100
　　beds

flat things →COUNTERS FOR FLAT THINGS

flavor and elegance
趣 味 風 品

趣 ▷flavor
シュ おもむき　　　　　Ⓚ2827

ⓐ **flavor, distinctive charm, elegance, taste, beauty, sentiment**
ⓑ **interest, taste, hobby**

a 情趣 じょうしゅ mood, sentiment, artistic effects,
　　charms
　野趣 やしゅ charms of the countryside, rural beau-
　　ty
　興趣 きょうしゅ taste, elegance, flavor
b 趣味 しゅみ hobby, interest, taste
　俗趣 ぞくしゅ vulgar taste

味 ▷taste
ミ あじ あじ(わう)　　　　　Ⓚ0247

(quality of attracting interest) **taste, interest, flavor, charm, beauty**
　趣味 しゅみ hobby, interest, taste
　興味 きょうみ interest
　妙味 みょうみ subtle charm, beauty

風 ▷elegance
フウ フ かぜ かざ-　　　　　Ⓚ2591

elegance, charm, taste
　風味 ふうみ flavor, taste
　風雅 ふうが elegance, refinement, daintiness
　風流 ふうりゅう refined elegance, taste
　風情 ふぜい appearance, air, taste, elegance

品 ▷refinement
ヒン しな　　　　　Ⓚ1937

refinement, grace, elegance, good character
　上品 じょうひん elegance, refinement
　気品 きひん dignity, grace, nobility

flaws →FAULTS AND FLAWS

flesh

肉　筋

肉 ▷**flesh**
ニク   Ⓚ2756

[original meaning] **flesh (of humans or animals)**
- 肉腫 にくしゅ sarcoma
- 肉離れ にくばなれ torn muscle
- 筋肉 きんにく muscle, sinews
- 皮肉 ひにく cynicism, sarcasm; irony

筋 ▷**muscle**
キン すじ   Ⓚ2337

[also suffix] [original meaning] **muscle**
- 筋肉 きんにく muscle, sinews
- 筋骨 きんこつ sinews and bones
- 筋炎 きんえん myositis, inflammation of a muscle
- 心筋 しんきん myocardium, heart muscle
- 腹筋 ふっきん abdominal muscle
- 上腕筋 じょうわんきん brachial muscle

float

漂　浮

漂 ▷**drift**
ヒョウ ただよ(う)   Ⓚ0632

[original meaning] **drift, float**
- 漂流する ひょうりゅうする drift, be adrift
- 漂着 ひょうちゃく drifting ashore
- 浮漂 ふひょう floating

浮 ▷**float**
フ う(く) う(かれる) う(かぶ)
う(かべる)   Ⓚ0393

[original meaning] **float, rise to the surface**
- 浮沈 ふちん rise and fall, ebb and flow; ups and downs
- 浮上する ふじょうする surface, rise [float] to the surface
- 浮揚 ふよう floating
- 浮力 ふりょく buoyancy, lift
- 浮標 ふひょう (marker) buoy
- 浮遊 ふゆう floating, suspension

floor

階　層

階 ▷**floor**
カイ   Ⓚ0569

- *a* **floor, story**
- *b* **counter for floors**
- a 地階 ちかい basement, cellar
- 各階 かくかい every floor
- b 三階 さんがい third floor

層 ▷**story**
ソウ   Ⓚ2728

- *a* **story (of a building)**
- *b* **counter for stories**
- a 高層 こうそう high altitude; tall (building)
- b 三層楼 さんそうろう three-storied house [building]

flourish

茂　繁

茂 ▷**grow thick**
モ しげ(る)   Ⓚ1934

grow thick, grow luxuriantly, be overgrown
- 茂林 もりん [rare] luxuriant [dense] forest
- 繁茂する はんもする grow thick, luxuriate

繁 ▷**thrive**
ハン   Ⓚ2484

[formerly also 蕃] (grow vigorously) **thrive, luxuriate, grow thick**
- 繁殖する はんしょくする breed, propagate, increase, multiply
- 繁茂 はんも luxuriant growth

flow and drip

流 注 濫 溢 漏 滴 泌 瀝

流 ▷**flow**
リュウ ル なが(れる) なが(れ)
なが(す)   Ⓚ0400

- *a* [original meaning] **flow, stream, run**
- *b* **let flow, spill out, discharge, shed**
- *c* **be swept away by the flow, drift**
- a 流動する りゅうどうする flow, circulate, be liquid

流出 りゅうしゅつ outflow, effusion
漂流する ひょうりゅうする drift, be adrift
合流する ごうりゅうする flow together; join, unite
b 流血 りゅうけつ bloodshed
放流 ほうりゅう discharge; stocking (a river) with
(fish)
c 流失する りゅうしつする be washed away
流木 りゅうぼく driftwood
浮流 ふりゅう floating, drifting

注 ▷pour
チュウ そそ(ぐ)　　　　　Ⓚ0287

pour, pour into, pour on, inject
注入する ちゅうにゅうする pour into, inject
注水 ちゅうすい flooding; douche
注射 ちゅうしゃ injection, shot
注油 ちゅうゆ oiling, lubrication

濫 ▷overflow
ラン　　　　　Ⓚ0713

[original meaning] **overflow, flow over, inundate**
氾濫する はんらんする overflow, flood

溢 ▷overflow
イツ あふ(れる) こぼ(す)
こぼ(れる)　　　　　Ⓚ0601

overflow, inundate, spill
溢流する いつりゅうする overflow, spill
横溢する おういつする be filled with (vitality),
overflow with
脳溢血 のういっけつ intracranial hemorrhage
充溢する じゅういつする overflow with, brim with

漏 ▷leak
ロウ も(る) も(れる) も(らす)　　Ⓚ0635

[original meaning] **leak**
漏出 ろうしゅつ leak
漏水 ろうすい water leakage
漏電 ろうでん short circuit, leakage
歯槽膿漏 しそうのうろう pyorrhea alveolaris

滴 ▷drop
テキ しずく したた(る)　　Ⓚ0640

drop, drip, trickle
滴下する てきかする drip, trickle
滴水 てきすい water dripping
点滴 てんてき falling drops of water; intravenous
infusion

泌 ▷secrete
ヒツ ヒ　　　　　Ⓚ0294

[original meaning] **secrete**
泌尿器 ひにょうき urinary organs

分泌 ぶんぴつ(=ぶんぴ) secretion
内分泌腺 ないぶんぴせん endocrine gland

瀝 ▷drip
レキ

[original meaning] **drip, trickle**
瀝青炭 れきせいたん bituminous coal

flower
花　　　　華

花 ▷flower
カ はな　　　　　Ⓚ1894

[original meaning] **flower, blossom**
花壇 かだん flower bed
花弁 かべん(=はなびら) petal
花瓶 かびん flower vase
花粉 かふん pollen
国花 こっか national flower
造花 ぞうか artificial flower; artificial flower making
開花する かいかする flower, blossom, come into
bloom
沈丁花 じんちょうげ(=ちんちょうげ) (sweet-smelling)
daphne

華 ▷flower
カ ケ はな　　　　　Ⓚ1973

[original meaning] **flower, blossom**
華道 かどう flower arrangement
法華経 ほけきょう the Lotus Sutra
香華 こうげ incense and flowers
散華する さんげする fall as flowers do, die a glorious death

flowering plants
菊 菖 菫 蓮 葛 蓬 葵
蓉 芙 蘭 萩 藤 桜 梅

菊 ▷chrysanthemum
キク　　　　　Ⓚ1999

[also suffix] [original meaning] **chrysanthemum**
菊花 きっか chrysanthemum
菊人形 きくにんぎょう chrysanthemum figure [doll]
野菊 のぎく wild chrysanthemum; aster
白菊 しらぎく white chrysanthemum
除虫菊 じょちゅうぎく pyrethrum

菖 ▷iris
ショウ   Ⓚ2005

iris, sweet flag
菖蒲 しょうぶ sweet flag; Japanese water iris, *Iris ensata* var. *ensata*

菫 ▷violet
キン コン すみれ   Ⓚ2001

【キン コン】
violet
【すみれ】
violet (the flower)
菫色 すみれいろ violet (the color)
三色菫 さんしょくすみれ(=さんしきすみれ) pansy, heartsease

蓮 ▷lotus
レン はす はちす   Ⓚ2047

【レン】
lotus
蓮華 れんげ lotus flower; Chinese milk vetch; Chinese (porcelain) spoon
木蓮 もくれん lily magnolia; cucumber tree; *Magnolia liliflora*
【はす】
lotus
蓮池 はすいけ lotus pond

葛 ▷kudzu
カツ くず   Ⓚ2017

【カツ】
kudzu, Japanese arrowroot
葛藤 かっとう complication, troubles, discord
葛根湯 かっこんとう antifebrile infusion
【くず】
kudzu, Japanese arrowroot
葛布 くずふ cloth made from kudzu fiber
葛粉 くずこ arrowroot starch [flour]
葛餅 くずもち kudzu starch cake
葛餡 くずあん kudzu sauce

蓬 ▷Japanese mugwort
ホウ よもぎ   Ⓚ2072

ⓐ Japanese mugwort
ⓑ tumbleweed
ⓐ 蓬矢 ほうし arrow made of mugwort
ⓑ 転蓬 てんぽう tumbleweed

葵 ▷mallow
キ あおい   Ⓚ2018

mallow, hollyhock
戎葵 じゅうき hollyhock

蓉 ▷cotton rose
ヨウ   Ⓚ2051

cotton rose, hibiscus
芙蓉 ふよう cotton rose; lotus

芙 ▷lotus
フ   Ⓚ1891

lotus
芙蓉 ふよう cotton rose; lotus
芙蓉峰 ふようほう Mt. Fuji ("lotus-shaped mountain")

蘭 ▷orchid
ラン   Ⓚ2114

orchid
蘭栽培法 らんさいばいほう orchidology

萩 ▷*hagi*
シュウ はぎ   Ⓚ2020

hagi*, Japanese bush clover, *Lespedeza bicolor
萩属 はぎぞく *Lespedeza*

藤 ▷wisteria
トウ ふじ   Ⓚ2109

wisteria
葛藤 かっとう complication, troubles, discord

桜 ▷cherry blossom
オウ さくら   Ⓚ0842

cherry blossom
観桜 かんおう cherry-blossom viewing

梅 ▷*ume* blossom
バイ うめ   Ⓚ0833

***ume* blossom**
紅梅 こうばい red-blossomed Japanese apricot
観梅 かんばい *ume* blossom viewing
塩梅 あんばい seasoning, flavoring; taste, flavor; condition, state

fly

飛   蜚   翔   航

飛 ▷fly
ヒ と(ぶ) と(ばす)   Ⓚ2990

[formerly also 蜚] **fly**
飛行 ひこう flight, aviation
飛行機 ひこうき airplane
飛行場 ひこうじょう airport, airfield

飛来する ひらいする come flying, come by air
飛鳥 ひちょう flying bird
雄飛する ゆうひする launch out, embark upon (a career)

蜚 ▷fly
ヒ

[now replaced by 飛]

fly; flying
蜚鳥 ひちょう flying bird
蜚語 ひご false report, flying rumor

翔 ▷soar
ショウ かけ(る) と(ぶ) Ⓚ1241

soar, fly
翔破する しょうはする complete a flight
飛翔 ひしょう flight, soaring
滑翔機 かっしょうき sailplane, glider
競翔 きょうしょう flying race (between pigeons)

航 ▷navigate
コウ Ⓚ1204

(travel through the air) **navigate, fly**
航空 こうくう aviation, aerial navigation
航空機 こうくうき aircraft, airplane
航空券 こうくうけん plane ticket
航宙 こうちゅう space flight

-fold
倍　　重

倍 ▷times
バイ Ⓚ0090

times, -fold
倍数 ばいすう multiple
倍率 ばいりつ magnification, magnifying power; rate of competition (in examinations)
三倍 さんばい three times, triple
数倍 すうばい several times (as large)

重 ▷-fold
ジュウ チョウ え おも(い) おも(り)
かさ(ねる) かさ(なる) Ⓚ2991

-fold, layer, story (of a building)
多重の たじゅうの multiple, multiplex
三重の さんじゅうの threefold, triple

fold
折　　畳

折 ▷fold
セツ お(る) おり お(れる) Ⓚ0225

【セツ】
fold
折角 せっかく with much trouble; specially

【お(る)】
fold
折り重ねる おりかさねる fold back [up]
折り紙 おりがみ folded paper; the art of paper folding

畳 ▷fold up
ジョウ たた(む) たた(み)- Ⓚ2249

fold up, fold; shut; bear in mind; do away with
畳まる たたまる be folded (up)
畳んでしまえ たたんでしまえ Down with him!
折り畳みの おりたたみの collapsible
家を畳む いえをたたむ shut up one's house
胸に畳む むねにたたむ bear in mind

follow and pursue
従　随　辿　追

従 ▷follow
ジュウ ショウ ジュ したが(う)
したが(える) Ⓚ0376

(go after) **follow, accompany, attend on**
従軍する じゅうぐんする follow [join] the army, go to the front
随従する ずいじゅうする follow the lead of, play second fiddle to
追従する ついじゅうする follow, be servile to; imitate

随 ▷follow
ズイ Ⓚ0573

(go after) **follow, attend (on), accompany**
随行する ずいこうする attend on, accompany, follow
随員 ずいいん attendants, retinue
付随の ふずいの accompanying, incidental

辿 ▷follow (a path)
テン たど(る) Ⓚ2758

follow (a path), pursue (a course)

辿り着く たどりつく work one's way (to), arrive somewhere

追 ▷chase
ツイ お(う)　　　Ⓚ2667

chase, pursue, follow, seek
追跡する ついせきする pursue, chase, follow up
追突 ついとつ rear-end collision
追求する ついきゅうする pursue
追及する ついきゅうする pursue, seek after, follow, press (a person) hard
追究 ついきゅう thorough investigation, close inquiry
追随する ついずいする follow (in the wake of)
追従 ついしょう flattery, sycophancy
猛追 もうつい hot chase [pursuit]

followers →STUDENTS AND FOLLOWERS

food
飯 膳 食 糧 餌 肴

飯 ▷meal
ハン めし　　　Ⓚ1509

ⓐ **meal**
ⓑ **food**

a 飯店 はんてん (high-class) Chinese restaurant; hotel (in Chinese)
飯場 はんば bunkhouse, workers' living quarters
夕飯 ゆうはん evening meal, supper
b 飯台 はんだい dining table
残飯 ざんぱん leftover food [rice]

膳 ▷meal
ゼン　　　Ⓚ1000

meal, meal served on a tray, cooked food
据え膳 すえぜん meal set before one; women's advances

食 ▷food, meal
ショク ジキ く(う) く(らう)
た(べる)　　　Ⓚ1787

❶ [also prefix and suffix] **food, dish**
食糧 しょくりょう provisions, food, foodstuffs
食中毒 しょくちゅうどく food poisoning
食パン しょくぱん plain bread
食物 しょくもつ food, provisions
主食 しゅしょく staple food
和食 わしょく Japanese-style food
乞食 こじき beggar
流動食 りゅうどうしょく liquid food [diet]
❷ **meal**

食後に しょくごに after meals
朝食 ちょうしょく breakfast
給食 きゅうしょく (provision of) meals

糧 ▷food provisions
リョウ ロウ かて　　　Ⓚ1294

food provisions, food, foodstuffs
糧食 りょうしょく provisions, food, rations
糧道 りょうどう supply of provisions
食糧 しょくりょう provisions, food, foodstuffs
衣糧 いりょう clothing and food
兵糧 ひょうろう army provisions, food

餌 ▷animal feed
ジ えさ え　　　Ⓚ1597

animal feed
給餌 きゅうじ feeding (animals)
食餌療法 しょくじりょうほう dietary cure

肴 ▷accompaniment for drinks
コウ さかな　　　Ⓚ1780

side dish to go with drinks
酒肴 しゅこう(=さけさかな) food and drink
佳肴(=嘉肴) かこう delicacy, rare treat

foolish
愚 暗 痴 鈍 呆 魯 闇 蒙

愚 ▷foolish
グ おろ(か)　　　Ⓚ2467

[original meaning] **foolish, stupid, ignorant**
愚劣な ぐれつな stupid, silly, foolish
愚痴 ぐち idle complaint, grumble; querulousness
愚人 ぐじん fool
愚鈍な ぐどんな stupid, silly
愚問 ぐもん silly question

暗 ▷dark
アン くら(い)　　　Ⓚ0921

[formerly also 闇] (lacking wisdom) **dark, ignorant, foolish**
暗愚な人人 あんぐなひとびと dark souls
暗黒時代 あんこくじだい the Dark Ages
暗君 あんくん foolish ruler

痴 ▷stupid
チ　　　Ⓚ2800

ⓐ [original meaning] **stupid, foolish, silly**
ⓑ **lacking ability, slow**
a 痴呆 ちほう imbecility, dementia

痴人 ちじん fool, simpleton, idiot, dunce
白痴 はくち idiocy, idiot
愚痴 ぐち idle complaint, grumble; querulousness
b 音痴 おんち tone deafness
運痴 うんち *colloq* slow in one's movements

鈍 ▷dull
ドン にぶ(い) にぶ(る) にぶ- Ⓚ1507

(not agile) **dull, dull-witted, slow, stupid**
鈍才 どんさい dullness, stupidity
鈍感 どんかん thickheadedness
鈍重な どんじゅうな dull-witted, phlegmatic
愚鈍 ぐどん stupidity, silliness

呆 ▷dim-witted
ホウ ボウ あき(れる) ほう(ける) ぼ(ける)

[original meaning] **dim-witted, foolish, stupid**
痴呆 ちほう imbecility, dementia
阿呆 あほう(=あほ) fool, idiot
阿呆らしい あほらしい ridiculous, absurd

魯 ▷dull
ロ Ⓚ1843

[original meaning] **dull, stupid, foolish**
魯鈍 ろどん imbecility, stupidity
烏焉魯魚 うえんろぎょ miswriting a word

闇 ▷dark
アン やみ Ⓚ2846

(lacking wisdom) **dark, ignorant, foolish**
闇愚 あんぐ imbecility, feeblemindedness

蒙 ▷ignorance
モウ こうむ(る) Ⓚ2045

ignorance
蒙昧 もうまい ignorance
啓蒙 けいもう enlightenment, instruction

footwear
靴 沓 駄 履 足

靴 ▷shoes
カ くつ Ⓚ1586

[original meaning] **shoes, boots**
製靴 せいか shoemaking
軍靴 ぐんか military shoes, combat boots
隔靴掻痒 かっかそうよう having an itch that one
  cannot scratch

沓 ▷footwear
トウ くつ Ⓚ2144

[usu. 靴] **footwear, sandals, clogs**
沓脱ぎ くつぬぎ stepstone, doorstone
沓下 くつした socks
沓摺り くつずり doorsill
雪沓 ゆきぐつ straw snow boots [shoes]

駄 ▷clogs
ダ タ Ⓚ1617

clogs, sandals
下駄 げた geta, wooden clogs
足駄 あしだ high clogs, rain clogs
雪駄 せった leather-soled sandals

履 ▷footwear
リ は(く) Ⓚ2736

footwear, footgear; sandals, shoes, clogs
草履 ぞうり Japanese sandals, *zori*
弊履 へいり worn-out sandals [shoes]

足 ▷counter for footwear
ソク あし た(りる) た(る) た(す) Ⓚ1873

**counter for pairs of footwear, as shoes, slippers or
socks**
靴一足 くついっそく a pair of shoes

force →ENERGY AND FORCE

force to move
推 駆 押

推 ▷propel
スイ お(す) Ⓚ0465

propel, drive, push
推進する すいしんする propel, drive; promote
推力 すいりょく thrust, driving force
推薬 すいやく propellant
推敲する すいこうする polish (a draft), refine

駆 ▷drive
ク か(ける) か(る) Ⓚ1619

drive (a machine), set in motion, handle
駆動 くどう drive (of a machine)
駆使する くしする use freely, have good command
  of

押 ▷push
オウ お(す) お(し)- お(つ)-
お(さえる)   Ⓚ0278

(force to move) **push, press, thrust, shove**
押し おし pushing, push; self-confidence, impudence; fall (in prices)
押す おす PUSH (marking on doors)
押し上げる おしあげる push up, boost
押し返す おしかえす push back, force back
押し釦 おしぼたん push-button
押し屋 おしや commuter train packer
押しも押されもせぬ おしもおされもせぬ of established reputation
後押し あとおし pushing; support, backing

foreign
外   異

外 ▷foreign
ガイ ゲ そと ほか はず(す)
はず(れる)   Ⓚ0163

foreign, external
外国 がいこく foreign country
外人 がいじん foreigner, alien
外車 がいしゃ imported car
外為 がいため foreign exchange
外交 がいこう diplomacy, foreign relations
外務 がいむ foreign affairs
外貨 がいか foreign currency [money]; foreign [imported] goods
外来語 がいらいご loanword, foreign word
在外の ざいがいの overseas

異 ▷foreign
イ こと こと(なる)   Ⓚ2241

(of a different place) **foreign**
異境 いきょう foreign country, strange land
異邦人 いほうじん foreigner, alien

forest
林   森   杜

林 ▷forest, small woods
リン はやし   Ⓚ0765

【リン】
[also suffix] [original meaning] **forest, woods, grove**
林業 りんぎょう forestry

林道 りんどう path through a forest, trail through the woods
林檎 りんご apple
森林 しんりん forest, woodland
山林 さんりん mountains and forests; forest on a mountain
杏林 きょうりん doctor
密林 みつりん close thicket, dense forest, jungle
営林 えいりん forest management
造林 ぞうりん afforestation, reforestation
原始林 げんしりん primeval forest

【はやし】
[also suffix] **small woods, grove, thicket**
松林 まつばやし pine forest
雑木林 ぞうきばやし thicket of assorted trees

森 ▷thick woods
シン もり   Ⓚ2184

[original meaning] **thick woods, forest**
森林 しんりん forest, woodland

杜 ▷grove
ト トウ ズ もり   Ⓚ0739

[usu. 森] **grove, small woods (esp. surrounding temples or shrines)**
鎮守の杜 ちんじゅのもり grove of the village shrine

forget
忘   遺

忘 ▷forget
ボウ わす(れる)   Ⓚ1753

[original meaning] **forget**
忘却する ぼうきゃくする forget
忘恩 ぼうおん ingratitude
忘年会 ぼうねんかい year-end party ("forget the year party")
健忘 けんぼう forgetfulness, short memory
備忘 びぼう reminder

遺 ▷leave behind
イ ユイ   Ⓚ2731

[original meaning] **leave (a thing) behind, forget**
遺失物 いしつぶつ lost article

forgive

赦 免 許 恕 宥

赦 ▷amnesty
シャ Ⓚ1344

ⓐ (forgive a crime or error) **amnesty, pardon, forgive, excuse**
ⓑ **amnesty, general pardon**

a 赦免 しゃめん pardon, amnesty, clemency
　容赦 ようしゃ pardon, forgiveness, mercy
b 恩赦 おんしゃ amnesty, general pardon
　特赦 とくしゃ amnesty, special pardon
　大赦 たいしゃ amnesty, general amnesty

免 ▷exempt
メン まぬか(れる) まぬが(れる) Ⓚ1779

ⓐ **exempt from, free from, release, excuse, forgive**
ⓑ **be exempted, be immune**
ⓒ **exemption, remission**

a 免除 めんじょ exemption, exoneration, dismissal
　免税 めんぜい tax exemption
　御免 ごめん (your) pardon; decline, refusal; permission
　御免なさい ごめんなさい I'm sorry/Excuse me
　御免下さい ごめんください Excuse me/Pardon me
　赦免 しゃめん pardon, amnesty, clemency
b 免疫 めんえき immunity (from a disease)
c 減免 げんめん reduction and exemption

許 ▷forgive
キョ ゆる(す) Ⓚ1337

forgive, pardon, excuse
　過失を許す かしつをゆるす forgive (a person) for his [her] fault

恕 ▷forgive with compassion
ジョ ショ Ⓚ2305

forgive with compassion, pardon, tolerate
　寛恕する かんじょする forgive, pardon, tolerate

宥 ▷pardon
ユウ ウ なだ(める) Ⓚ1944

pardon, excuse, forgive
　宥免する ゆうめんする pardon (a crime), excuse
　宥和する ゆうわする forgive and make peace

form

形 状 体 姿

形 ▷shape
ケイ ギョウ かた -がた かたち Ⓚ0749

[also suffix] [original meaning] **shape, material form, figure**
　形状 けいじょう shape, form, configuration
　形態(=形体) けいたい shape, form, structure, morphology
　形式 けいしき form, model, formality
　形式的 けいしきてき formal
　図形 ずけい figure, diagram
　体形 たいけい form, figure
　球形 きゅうけい globular shape
　変形する へんけいする change shape, transform
　人形 にんぎょう doll
　長方形 ちょうほうけい rectangle
　半月形の はんげつけいの semicircular, crescent-shaped

状 ▷form (external)
ジョウ Ⓚ0244

ⓐ [original meaning] (external) **form, shape, appearance**
ⓑ [also suffix] **-form, in the form of, -shaped, -like**

a 形状 けいじょう shape, form, configuration
　環状の かんじょうの ring-shaped, circular
　波状 はじょう wave, undulation
　球状 きゅうじょう shape of a globe, globular shape
b 帯状の おびじょう(=たいじょう)の belt-shaped
　ガス状の がすじょうの gaseous, gasiform
　液状の えきじょうの liquefied

体 ▷form (characteristic)
タイ テイ からだ Ⓚ0055

(characteristic) **form, shape**
　体系 たいけい system, organization
　字体 じたい character form, type
　具体的な ぐたいてきな concrete, definite, specific
　正体 しょうたい one's natural [true] shape; consciousness

姿 ▷figure
シ すがた Ⓚ2291

[original meaning] (outer shape, esp. of the body) **figure, form, shape, appearance, looks, aspect**
　容姿 ようし face and figure, appearance
　英姿 えいし gallant figure, majestic appearance
　雄姿 ゆうし brave [imposing] figure

form and carve
刻 彫 塑 鋳

刻 ▷engrave
コク きざ(む) きざ(み)   Ⓚ1166

[original meaning] (cut letters or designs on a surface)
engrave, carve, chisel
刻印 こくいん carved seal, stamp
刻字 こくじ carving characters; carved characters
彫刻する ちょうこくする sculpt, carve, engrave
陰刻 いんこく white line

彫 ▷carve
チョウ ほ(る) –ぼ(り)   Ⓚ1503

[original meaning] (cut so as to form a desired shape or design) **carve, sculpt, engrave**
彫刻 ちょうこく sculpture, carving, engraving
彫像 ちょうぞう carved statue
彫金 ちょうきん metal carving, chasing
彫塑 ちょうそ carving and modeling, plastic arts; clay model

塑 ▷model
ソ   Ⓚ2475

[original meaning] (make by shaping a plastic material, esp. clay) **model, mold, sculpt**
塑造 そぞう modeling, molding
彫塑 ちょうそ carving and modeling, plastic arts; clay model

鋳 ▷cast
チュウ い(る)   Ⓚ1543

[original meaning] **cast, mint, coin**
鋳鉄 ちゅうてつ iron casting
鋳造 ちゅうぞう casting, minting, coining
鋳金 ちゅうきん casting
鋳鋼 ちゅうこう cast steel
改鋳 かいちゅう recoinage, recasting

former
旧 元 故 前 嘗 曽 先 既

旧 ▷former
キュウ   Ⓚ0005

[also prefix] **former, ex-, old-time, old**
旧夫 きゅうふ former husband
旧居 きゅうきょ former residence
旧軍人 きゅうぐんじん ex-soldier

旧制 きゅうせい old system, old style

元 ▷former
ゲン ガン もと   Ⓚ1690

[also prefix] **former, ex-, one-time, past**
元首相 もとしゅしょう ex-Prime Minister
元の通り もとのとおり as it was before

故 ▷old (earlier time)
コ ゆえ   Ⓚ1056

(of an earlier time) **old, former**
故郷 こきょう hometown, birthplace
故国 ここく one's native land [country]
故旧 こきゅう old acquaintance

前 ▷previous
ゼン まえ   Ⓚ1957

[also prefix] (immediately preceding in order of time) **previous, former, ex-, onetime**
前夫 ぜんぷ former husband, ex-husband
前大統領 ぜんだいとうりょう former president
前住所 ぜんじゅうしょ one's former address

嘗 ▷previously
ショウ ジョウ な(める) な(めずる) かつ(て)   Ⓚ2268

previously, formerly, once, before
嘗ての友 かつてのとも former friend

曽 ▷previously
ソウ ゾ ひ ひい   Ⓚ1823

previously, formerly, once, before
曽遊 そうゆう previous visit
未曽有 みぞう unprecedented, unheard of

先 ▷former
セン さき ま(ず)   Ⓚ2123

former, previous
先夫 せんぷ former husband
先主 せんしゅ former master
先君 せんくん previous ruler

既 ▷already
キ すで(に)   Ⓚ1079

[also prefix] **already, previous**
既刊の きかんの already published
既婚の きこんの already married
既存の きそんの existing
既定の きていの fixed, prearranged
既往症 きおうしょう previous illness, medical history
既知数 きちすう known quantity
既報 きほう previous report

既製の きせいの ready-made, ready-to-wear
既製品 きせいひん ready-made goods
既発表の きはっぴょうの already published

fortune →FATE AND FORTUNE

found
立　設　置

立 ▷establish
リツ　リュウ　た(つ)　た(ち)-　た(てる)
た(て)-　-だ(て)　-だ(てる)　Ⓚ1723

ⓐ establish, set up, erect, found, institute
ⓑ established by (the nation, municipality, etc.)
a 設立 せつりつ establishment, foundation, setting
　up
　樹立する じゅりつする establish, found
　創立する そうりつする establish, organize, start
　確立 かくりつ establishment
　建立 こんりゅう erection, building (as a temple)
b 市立の しりつ(=いちりつ)の municipal, city
　私立の しりつ(=わたくしりつ)の private, nongovern-
　　mental
　会社立の かいしゃりつの established by the compa-
　　ny

設 ▷set up
セツ　もう(ける)　Ⓚ1338

(found) set up (as an institution), establish, found
　設立する せつりつする establish, found, set up
　設置する せっちする establish, found, set up
　設定 せってい establishment, creation, fixation,
　　setting up
　開設 かいせつ establishment, inauguration
　創設 そうせつ establishment, founding
　特設する とくせつする set up specially
　私設の しせつの private

置 ▷found
チ　お(く)　-お(き)　Ⓚ2262

found, establish, set up
　設置する せっちする establish, found, set up
　増置する ぞうちする establish more (offices)
　常置の じょうちの permanent; standing

fragrance →SMELL AND FRAGRANCE

frames
枠　骼　格　額

枠 ▷frame
わく　Ⓚ0771

ⓐ frame, framework
ⓑ [original meaning] spool, reel
a 枠を付ける わくをつける frame, set a frame
　枠組み わくぐみ framework, frame
　窓枠 まどわく window frame, sash
b 糸枠 いとわく spool

骼 ▷skeletal frame
カク

[now replaced by 格] **skeletal frame, skeleton, build**
　骨骼 こっかく frame, physique; framework, skeletal
　　structure

格 ▷framework
カク　コウ　Ⓚ0835

framework, latticework, grid
　格子 こうし latticework, lattice, grid
　格天井 ごうてんじょう coffered ceiling

額 ▷picture frame
ガク　ひたい　Ⓚ1604

picture frame, frame, framed picture
　額縁 がくぶち (picture) frame
　扁額 へんがく tablet, framed picture

friendly →FAMILIAR AND FRIENDLY

friends and
associates
僚　輩　朋　友　侶

僚 ▷colleague
リョウ　Ⓚ0143

[original meaning] **colleague, associate, co-worker,**
companion
　僚友 りょうゆう comrade, colleague, fellow worker
　僚機 りょうき consort plane
　同僚 どうりょう colleague, associate, comrade,
　　fellow official

輩 ▷fellow
ハイ　　　　　　　　Ⓚ2444

fellow(s), companion, comrade
- 先輩 せんぱい senior, superior, elder
- 後輩 こうはい one's junior, younger generation, peer
- 同輩 どうはい fellow, comrade, colleague
- 朋輩 ほうばい comrade, friend, associate
- 若輩 じゃくはい young people; greenhorn

朋 ▷comrade
ホウ とも　　　　　　Ⓚ0784

comrade, friend, companion, mate, fellow
- 朋友 ほうゆう friend, companion
- 朋輩 ほうばい comrade, friend, associate

友 ▷friend
ユウ とも　　　　　　Ⓚ2553

friend, comrade
- 友人 ゆうじん friend
- 友情 ゆうじょう friendship, fellowship
- 親友 しんゆう close [intimate] friend
- 朋友 ほうゆう friend, companion
- 僚友 りょうゆう comrade, colleague, fellow worker
- 戦友 せんゆう comrade-in-arms

侶 ▷companion
リョ　　　　　　　　Ⓚ0083

companion, mate
- 伴侶 はんりょ companion
- 僧侶 そうりょ bonze, Buddhist priest
- 学侶 がくりょ scholar-monk

---

front
前　面　首

前 ▷front
ゼン まえ　　　　　　Ⓚ1957

front, fore part
- 前に まえに ahead, before
- 前足 まえあし forelegs
- 前置き まえおき introductory remark
- 前書き まえがき preface, foreword

面 ▷face
メン おも おもて つら　Ⓚ1796

(front or significant surface) **face, front**
- 表面 ひょうめん surface, face, outside; appearance
- 全面 ぜんめん front, facade

- 正面衝突 しょうめんしょうとつ head-on collision, front crash
- 画面 がめん picture; television field; screen
- 印面 いんめん face of a seal
- 額面 がくめん face value; denomination
- 書面 しょめん letter, document
- 図面 ずめん drawing, plan, map, sketch

首 ▷head
シュ くび　　　　　　Ⓚ1956

(forepart of a vessel) **head**
- 機首 きしゅ nose (of an airplane)
- 艦首 かんしゅ bow (of a war vessel)

---

front parts of head
顔　面　額　顎　頬　吻

顔 ▷face
ガン かお　　　　　　Ⓚ1608

face, countenance
- 顔面 がんめん face
- 洗顔 せんがん washing one's face
- 紅顔 こうがん rosy face, peachy cheeks

面 ▷face
メン おも おもて つら　Ⓚ1796

[original meaning] (front of head) **face, countenance**
- 面相 めんそう countenance, features, looks
- 面通し めんとおし identification parade
- 面食い めんくい person who puts much store by good looks (in choosing his [her] lover)
- 面面 めんめん everyone, all
- 顔面 がんめん face
- 洗面 せんめん washing one's face
- 七面鳥 しちめんちょう turkey

額 ▷forehead
ガク ひたい　　　　　Ⓚ1604

[original meaning] **forehead, brow**
- 前額部 ぜんがくぶ forehead; frontlet

顎 ▷chin
ガク あご　　　　　　Ⓚ1607

chin
- 顎鬚 あごひげ beard
- 顎で使う あごでつかう order someone about
- 二重顎 にじゅうあご double chin

頰 ▷cheek
キョウ ほお ほほ   Ⓚ1460

cheek
頰骨 きょうこつ cheekbone, zygomatic bone
頰筋 きょうきん buccinator (muscle)

吻 ▷proboscis
フン   Ⓚ0202

proboscis, nose, snout, muzzle, trunk, beak
口吻 こうふん proboscis, muzzle, snout; way of speaking, intimation
黄吻 こうふん young and inexperienced person ("yellow beak")

frozen water →KINDS OF FROZEN WATER

fruit
果   実

果 ▷fruit
カ は(たす) は(てる) は(て)   Ⓚ2982

ⓐ [original meaning] **fruit**
ⓑ **counter for fruits, jewels or seals**
a 果実 かじつ fruit, berry
果汁 かじゅう fruit juice
青果 せいか vegetables and fruits
摘果 てきか thinning out superfluous fruit
b 林檎一果 りんごいっか one apple

実 ▷fruit
ジツ み みの(る)   Ⓚ1911

fruit
果実 かじつ fruit, berry
結実する けつじつする bear fruit; be successful, achieve success
綿実 めんじつ cottonseed

fruits and fruit trees

桃 榛 椎 柚 椰 柑 橙 葡
萄 柿 檎 李 枇 杷 苺 菱
杏 梅 橘 栗 栃 梨 蕉

桃 ▷peach
トウ もも   Ⓚ0848

[original meaning] **peach tree; peach**
桃花 とうか [rare] peach blossom

桃李 とうり peach and plum
桜桃 おうとう cherry
黄桃 おうとう yellow peach
扁桃腺 へんとうせん tonsils

榛 ▷hazel
シン はしばみ はり はん-   Ⓚ0965

hazel, *Corylus heterophylla var. Thunbergii*

椎 ▷chinquapin
ツイ しい   Ⓚ0905

chinquapin
椎茸 しいたけ shiitake (mushroom), *Lentinula edodes*
椎の実 しいのみ sweet acorn

柚 ▷yuzu
ユウ ユ ゆず   Ⓚ0810

【ユウ ユ】
(aromatic Japanese citron) **yuzu**
柚子 ゆず [also 柚] yuzu
柚餅子 ゆべし sweet yuzu dumpling
晩白柚 ばんぺいゆ pomelo

【ゆず】
[also 柚子] (aromatic Japanese citron) **yuzu**
柚湯 ゆずゆ yuzu hot bath

椰 ▷coconut
ヤ   Ⓚ0932

coconut tree; coconut
椰子 やし coconut tree; coconut

柑 ▷citrus
カン   Ⓚ0800

citrus, orange
柑橘類 かんきつるい citrus fruits, oranges
金柑 きんかん kumquat
伊予柑 いよかん Iyo orange, *Citrus iyo*

橙 ▷bitter orange
トウ だいだい   Ⓚ0993

bitter orange, *Citrus aurantium*
橙皮油 とうひゆ orange-peel oil

葡 ▷grape
ブ ホ ポ   Ⓚ2014

grape, grapevine
葡萄 ぶどう grape
葡萄酒 ぶどうしゅ (grape) wine
山葡萄 やまぶどう crimson glory vine

萄 ▷grape
ドウ   Ⓚ1994

grape, grapevine
  葡萄 ぶどう grape
  葡萄酒 ぶどうしゅ (grape) wine
  山葡萄 やまぶどう crimson glory vine

柿 ▷persimmon
シ かき   Ⓚ0806

persimmon
  熟柿 じゅくし ripe persimmon

檎 ▷apple
ゴ   Ⓚ1004

apple
  林檎 りんご apple
  林檎病 りんごびょう fifth disease, *Erythema infectiosum*

李 ▷plum
リ すもも   Ⓚ2126

plum tree; plum
  李花 りか plum blossoms
  李下に冠を正さず りかにかんむりをたださず Refrain from doing anything that may incur suspicion

枇 ▷loquat
ビ   Ⓚ0758

loquat
  枇杷 びわ loquat

杷 ▷loquat
ハ ワ   Ⓚ0760

loquat
  枇杷 びわ loquat

苺 ▷strawberry
ボウ バイ いちご   Ⓚ1923

strawberry
  木苺 きいちご bramble, *Rubus*
  草苺 くさいちご *Rubus hirsutus*
  蛇苺 へびいちご false strawberry, *Duchesnea chrysantha*
  海老殻苺 えびがらいちご wineberry

菱 ▷water chestnut
リョウ ひし   Ⓚ2003

[original meaning] **water chestnut**
  菱花 りょうか water chestnut flower

杏 ▷apricot
キョウ アン あんず   Ⓚ212

[original meaning] **apricot tree; apricot**
  杏子 あんず apricot; apricot tree
  杏仁 きょうにん apricot stone
  杏林 きょうりん doctor
  銀杏 ぎんなん(=いちょう) ginkgo nut, ginkgo tree

梅 ▷Japanese apricot
バイ うめ   Ⓚ083

Japanese apricot tree, *ume* tree; Japanese apricot, *ume*
  梅林 ばいりん *ume* grove
  梅花 ばいか *ume* blossoms
  梅雨(=黴雨) ばいう rainy season (of early summer)

橘 ▷mandarin
キツ たちばな   Ⓚ0990

mandarin orange, tangerine; citrus fruit; mandarin tree
  柑橘類 かんきつるい citrus fruits, oranges

栗 ▷chestnut
リツ リ くり   Ⓚ2303

【リツ リ】
[original meaning] **chestnut tree, Japanese chestnut tree; chestnut**
  栗鼠 りす squirrel

【くり】
chestnut tree, Japanese chestnut tree; chestnut
  栗石 くりいし cobblestone
  栗毛 くりげ chestnut (horse)
  勝ち栗 かちぐり dried chestnut

栃 ▷Japanese horse chestnut
とち   Ⓚ0809

Japanese horse chestnut
  栃の木 とちのき Japanese horse chestnut
  栃木県 とちぎけん Tochigi Prefecture
  栃栗毛 とちくりげ dark chestnut color (said of horses)

梨 ▷pear
リ なし   Ⓚ2392

pear tree; pear
  梨花 りか pear blossoms
  梨果 りか pome

蕉 ▷plantain
ショウ   Ⓚ2087

plantain
  芭蕉 ばしょう Japanese banana plant, *Musa basjoo*; plantain

fruit trees →FRUITS AND FRUIT TREES

fuel →KINDS OF FUEL

full

満　飽

満 ▷full
マン み(ちる) み(つ) み(たす)　　Ⓚ0553

ⓐ (filled to capacity) **full**
ⓑ (to the maximum extent) **full**

a 満員 まんいん full to capacity
　満塁 まんるい full bases
　満満の まんまんの full of, brimming with
　満腹の まんぷくの full, satiated
　満場 まんじょう the whole house [assembly]
　肥満した ひまんした fat, obese, corpulent
b 満月 まんげつ full moon
　満開 まんかい full bloom
　満潮 まんちょう high tide, high water
　満載 まんさい full load
　未満の みまんの less than

飽 ▷satiated
ホウ あ(きる) あ(かす) あ(く)　　Ⓚ1528

[original meaning] (have a full stomach) **satiated, sated, satisfied, surfeited**

　飽食する ほうしょくする satiate oneself, surfeit, eat one's fill
　飽満 ほうまん satiety, surfeit
　飽食暖衣 ほうしょくだんい being well fed and well clad
　飽和 ほうわ saturation

fungus

黴　茸　菌

黴 ▷mold
バイ かび か(びる)

[now also 梅] **mold, mildew, fungus**
　黴毒 ばいどく syphilis
　黴雨 ばいう rainy season (of early summer)
　黴菌 ばいきん bacterium, germ

茸 ▷mushroom
ジョウ きのこ たけ　　Ⓚ1949

【ジョウ】
mushroom, fungus
　茸状乳頭 じじょうにゅうとう fungiform papilla

【きのこ】
mushroom, fungus
　茸狩り きのこがり mushroom gathering
　茸雲 きのこぐも mushroom cloud
　毒茸 どくきのこ toadstool, poisonous mushroom

菌 ▷fungus
キン　　Ⓚ2000

fungus, mushroom
　菌類 きんるい fungi
　菌毒 きんどく mushroom poison
　菌糸 きんし hypha, mycelium

furcation

叉　俣　股　岐

叉 ▷fork
サ シャ また　　Ⓚ2870

(place of furcation) **fork (as of a road), crotch (as of a tree)**
　音叉 おんさ tuning fork
　蹄叉 ていさ fourchette
　轍叉 てっさ *railway* frog

俣 ▷bifurcation
また　　Ⓚ0081

[usu. 股, sometimes also 叉] [in compounds] **bifurcation, fork (as of a body of water)**
　二俣 ふたまた bifurcation; *slang* two-timing
　水俣病 みなまたびょう Minamata disease

股 ▷crotch
コ また もも　　Ⓚ0785

[sometimes also 叉 or 俣] (place of furcation) **crotch (of a tree), fork (of a road)**
　二股 ふたまた bifurcation; *slang* two-timing
　三股 さんまた forked stick

岐 ▷forked road
キ ギ　　Ⓚ0214

[original meaning] **forked road, branch road**
　岐路 きろ forked road, crossroad

future

来　　　後

来 ▷coming generations
ライ く(る) きた(る) きた(す)　　Ⓚ2975

coming generations, the future
未来 みらい future
将来 しょうらい future; in the future

後 ▷afteryears
ゴ コウ のち うし(ろ) あと
おく(れる)　　Ⓚ0321

afteryears, future generations, posterity
後世 こうせい future life, life to come
後事 こうじ future affairs, affairs after one's death
後裔 こうえい descendant, scion, offspring
後継者 こうけいしゃ successor, inheritor, heir
後続 こうぞく succession

game

技　　　戦

技 ▷game
ギ わざ　　Ⓚ0221

game, sport, pastime
球技 きゅうぎ ball game
国技 こくぎ national sport game

戦 ▷match
セン いくさ たたか(う)　　Ⓚ1590

[also suffix] **match, game, contest**
観戦する かんせんする watch (a ball game); observe
(military operations)
早明戦 そうめいせん Waseda-Meiji (baseball) game
決勝戦 けっしょうせん final round match, finals

gardens

園　庭　苑

園 ▷garden
エン その　　Ⓚ2722

[sometimes also 苑] [also suffix] [original meaning] **garden, park, plantation, farm**
園芸 えんげい gardening, horticulture
田園 でんえん fields and gardens, rural districts

庭園 ていえん garden, park
公園 こうえん park, public garden
楽園 らくえん paradise
果樹園 かじゅえん fruit garden, orchard

庭 ▷garden
テイ にわ　　Ⓚ2684

garden, ornamental garden
庭園 ていえん garden, park
庭前 ていぜん garden
石庭 せきてい rock garden

苑 ▷imperial garden
エン オン その　　Ⓚ1926

[sometimes also 園] **imperial garden, garden, park**
御苑 ぎょえん Imperial garden
内苑 ないえん inner garden of the Imperial Palace
神宮外苑 じんぐうがいえん Outer Gardens of Meiji
Shrine
鹿野苑 ろくやおん The Deer Park, *Mṛgadāva* (where
Buddha delivered his first sermon)

garment parts

襟　袖　懐　衿　裾

襟 ▷collar
キン えり　　Ⓚ1156

collar, lapel
開襟シャツ かいきんしゃつ wing-collared [open-
neck] shirt

袖 ▷sleeve
シュウ そで　　Ⓚ1078

[original meaning] **sleeve**
袖手傍観する しゅうしゅぼうかんする look on with
folded arms [with one's hands in one's sleeves],
remain a passive onlooker
袖珍本 しゅうちんぼん pocket-size book
袖状移植片 しゅうじょういしょくへん sleeve graft
領袖 りょうしゅう leader, chief

懐 ▷bosom
カイ ふところ なつ(かしい) なつ(かしむ)
なつ(く) なつ(ける)　　Ⓚ0689

(underside of garment covering chest) **bosom, pocket**
懐中 かいちゅう one's pocket

衿 ▷collar
キン えり　　Ⓚ1055

【キン】
collar, lapel, neck

開衿(=開襟)シャツ かいきんしゃつ wing-collared [open-neck] shirt

【えり】

[original meaning] **collar, lapel, neck**

衿裏 えりうら lining of the collar
半衿 はんえり neckpiece (on a kimono)

裾 ▷**hem**
すそ　　　　　　　　　　　Ⓚ1119

a **hem, cuff, skirt, train**
b **edge, fringe**
a 裾礁 きょしょう fringing reef

gas and vapor
気　空　汽

気 ▷**gas**
キ ケ　　　　　　　　　　Ⓚ2751

a [original meaning] **gas, vapor**
b **air**
a 気体 きたい gas, vapor, gaseous body
気化 きか gasification, evaporation
空気 くうき air; atmosphere
排気 はいき exhaust, used steam; exhaustion, evacuation
b 気流 きりゅう air [atmospheric] current, air stream
気団 きだん air mass
冷気 れいき cold air; cold, chill
換気 かんき ventilation

空 ▷**air**
クウ そら あ(く) あ(き) あ(ける) から
むな(しい)　　　　　　　　Ⓚ1913

air
空気 くうき air; atmosphere
空調 くうちょう air conditioning
空圧 くうあつ air [pneumatic] pressure

汽 ▷**steam**
キ　　　　　　　　　　　　Ⓚ0234

steam, vapor
汽車 きしゃ (steam) train
汽船 きせん steamship
汽圧 きあつ steam pressure
汽缶 きかん boiler
汽笛 きてき steam whistle
汽水 きすい brackish water

gather
集 蒐 聚 収 採 采 萃 湊

集 ▷**collect**
シュウ あつ(まる) あつ(める)
つど(う)　　　　　　　　　Ⓚ2413

a (bring together) **collect, gather, concentrate, assemble, recruit**
b [original meaning] (come together) **collect, gather, congregate**
a 集金 しゅうきん collecting money
集配 しゅうはい collection and delivery
集貨 しゅうか collection of freight
採集する さいしゅうする collect, gather
収集(=蒐集)する しゅうしゅうする collect, gather, accumulate
招集する しょうしゅうする call, summon, convene
募集する ぼしゅうする recruit, enlist; raise, collect
徴集する ちょうしゅうする levy, recruit
b 集中する しゅうちゅうする concentrate, focus; converge
集合する しゅうごうする gather, meet, assemble; summon, call together
集落 しゅうらく community, settlement, town, village; colony
結集する けっしゅうする concentrate, marshal

蒐 ▷**collect**
シュウ　　　　　　　　　　Ⓚ2049

[now replaced by 収 or 集] **collect, gather**
蒐集(=収集)する しゅうしゅうする collect, gather, accumulate
蒐荷(=集荷) しゅうか collection of cargo, cargo booking

聚 ▷**collect**
シュウ ジュ

collect, gather
聚散 しゅうさん collection and distribution
類聚 るいじゅ(=るいじゅう) collection of similar objects

収 ▷**collect**
シュウ おさ(める) おさ(まる)　Ⓚ0016

a **collect materials and record [write down]**
b [formerly also 蒐] **collect**
a 収録する しゅうろくする collect, record, write down
収集する しゅうしゅうする collect, gather, accumulate
b 徴収する ちょうしゅうする collect taxes [payment]

採 ▷gather
サイ と(る)   Ⓚ0459

gather (something useful), collect, mine, extract
採集 さいしゅう collecting, gathering
採掘 さいくつ mining
採炭 さいたん coal mining
採油 さいゆ drilling for oil, oil extraction
採血 さいけつ blood collecting [gathering]
採算 さいさん (commercial) profit
採点 さいてん marking, grading, rating
採録する さいろくする transcribe, record

采 ▷gather
サイ   Ⓚ2147

gather; pick; select
采詩 さいし gathering folk poetry and music in ancient China
采配を振る さいはいをふる direct, command
拍手喝采する はくしゅかっさいする applaud with hand clapping

萃 ▷gather
スイ

[original meaning] **gather, assemble**

湊 ▷come together
ソウ みなと   Ⓚ0557

come together, gather, collect
輻湊 ふくそう congestion, overcrowding; convergence

general
総   惣   汎

総 ▷general
ソウ   Ⓚ1261

[formerly also 惣] [also suffix] (applicable to the whole)
general, overall; ordinary
総会 そうかい general meeting
総務 そうむ general affairs; manager, director
総選挙 そうせんきょ general election
総辞職 そうじしょく resignation en masse
総評(=日本労働組合総評議会) そうひょう(=にほんろうどうくみあいそうひょうぎかい) General Council of Trade Unions of Japan
総菜 そうざい daily [household] dish, side dish
総社 そうじゃ shrine enshrining several gods
総嫁 そうか streetwalker (in the Edo period)

惣 ▷general
ソウ   Ⓚ2419

(applicable to the whole or the usual) **general, overall; ordinary**
惣菜 そうざい daily [household] dish, side dish
惣社 そうじゃ shrine enshrining several gods
惣嫁 そうか streetwalker (in the Edo period)

汎 ▷overall
ハン   Ⓚ019

ⓐ **overall, general, universal, versatile**
ⓑ [prefix] **pan-**
a 汎論 はんろん general remarks; outline
汎愛 はんあい philanthropy
汎用 はんよう generic, general-purpose, all-purpose, universal, versatile
汎用型コンピュータ はんようがたこんぴゅーた mainframe computer
b 汎神論 はんしんろん pantheism
汎アメリカ主義 はんあめりかしゅぎ Pan-Americanism

general counters
丁   個   箇   点   件

丁 ▷miscellaneous counter
チョウ テイ   Ⓚ285

counter for miscellaneous things, as:
ⓐ **cakes (of bean curd)**
ⓑ **servings (as of cutlet, noodles, etc.)**
ⓒ **carpenter's tools**
ⓓ [also 挺] **guns**
a 豆腐一丁 とうふいっちょう one cake of bean curd
b ラーメン三丁 らーめんさんちょう three bowls of Chinese noodles
c 鋸二丁 のこぎりにちょう two saws
d ピストル五丁 ぴすとるごちょう five pistols

個 ▷general counter
コ カ   Ⓚ010

general counter for things or articles
個数 こすう number of articles
一個 いっこ one, a piece
林檎三個 りんごさんこ three apples
十個 じっこ ten articles

箇 ▷counter for items
カ   Ⓚ235

counter for items, places or units of time
二箇所 にかしょ two places
一箇月 いっかげつ one month

点 ▷counter for articles
テン   Ⓚ1793

counter for various articles
三点セット さんてんせっと set of three pieces (of furniture)

件 ▷counter for cases
ケン   Ⓚ0035

counter for cases or affairs
件数 けんすう number of cases or items
五十件 ごじっけん 50 cases, 50 items

generation
代   世

代 ▷generation
ダイ タイ か(わる) か(わり) −が(わり)
か(える) よ しろ   Ⓚ0018

generation, lifetime
代代 だいだい generation after generation
世代 せだい generation

世 ▷generation
セイ セ よ   Ⓚ2932

ⓐ generation, family line
ⓑ of previous generations, hereditary
ⓒ counter for generations or reign periods

a 世代 せだい generation
b 世襲 せしゅう heredity, descent
c 二世 にせい second-generation [American-born] Japanese, nisei
　ナポレオン三世 なぽれおんさんせい Napoleon III

genitals
陰   胎   恥

陰 ▷sex organ
イン かげ かげ(る)   Ⓚ0494

sex [reproductive] organ, esp. the female genital organ
陰部 いんぶ private parts, sex organ
陰唇 いんしん labium
陰茎 いんけい penis

胎 ▷womb
タイ   Ⓚ0827

womb, uterus
胎内 たいない interior of the womb

胎生 たいせい viviparity
胎教 たいきょう prenatal care
母胎 ぼたい mother's womb

恥 ▷private parts
チ は(じる) はじ は(じらう)
は(ずかしい)   Ⓚ1200

private parts, pubic region
恥骨 ちこつ pubic bone, pubis
恥丘 ちきゅう mons pubis, mons veneris
恥部 ちぶ private parts; something to be ashamed of

gentle
優   穏   柔

優 ▷gentle
ユウ やさ(しい) すぐ(れる)   Ⓚ0156

gentle, tender, sweet
優男 やさおとこ man of gentle manners
優しい声 やさしいこえ soft voice

穏 ▷mild
オン おだ(やか)   Ⓚ1141

mild, gentle, moderate, temperate
穏健な おんけんな moderate, temperate, sound
穏和(=温和)な おんわな gentle, mild, genial
穏当な おんとうな proper, reasonable, moderate
穏便な おんびんな gentle, quiet, peaceable; private

柔 ▷soft
ジュウ ニュウ やわ(らか)
やわ(らかい)   Ⓚ1797

(of gentle disposition) **soft, softhearted, gentle, mild**
柔順な じゅうじゅんな obedient, gentle
柔和 にゅうわ gentleness, mildness, tenderness, meekness

gentleman
紳   子   士

紳 ▷gentleman
シン   Ⓚ1221

gentleman, gentry; men of rank
紳士 しんし gentleman
紳商 しんしょう merchant prince, rich merchant
貴紳 きしん men of rank, notables

子 ▷gentleman
シ ス こ -(っ)こ Ⓚ2872

gentleman, man of learning—sometimes used as
familiar second person pronoun

君子 くんし man of virtue, wise man
遊子 ゆうし wanderer, traveler

士 ▷man of learning and virtue
シ Ⓚ2877

man of learning and virtue, gentleman, scholar,
man of good breeding

士君子 しくんし man of learning and virtue, gentleman
博士 はくし doctor, Ph.D.
紳士 しんし gentleman
名士 めいし man of distinction, big name
国士 こくし distinguished citizen; patriot
同士 どうし fellow (as in 学生同士 がくせいどうし
"fellow students")

get
得 拾 獲 収 取

得 ▷acquire
トク え(る) う(る) Ⓚ0435

(obtain possession of) acquire, obtain, gain

獲得する かくとくする get, acquire, obtain
取得する しゅとくする acquire, gain; purchase

拾 ▷pick up
シュウ ジュウ ひろ(う) Ⓚ0339

[original meaning] pick up, gather

拾得する しゅうとくする pick up, find
拾遺 しゅうい gleaning
収拾する しゅうしゅうする get under control, save
(the situation)

獲 ▷obtain
カク え(る) Ⓚ0699

obtain, get, acquire

獲得する かくとくする get, acquire, obtain

収 ▷take in
シュウ おさ(める) おさ(まる) Ⓚ0016

(take possession of, esp. in payment) take in, receive,
accept

収入 しゅうにゅう income, earnings, receipts
収益 しゅうえき profit, earnings, proceeds, returns
収賄 しゅうわい acceptance of a bribe, corruption
収得する しゅうとくする take possession of

領収 りょうしゅう receipt

取 ▷take
シュ と(る) と(り) -ど(り) Ⓚ1162

(bring into one's possession) take, obtain, acquire, get,
gather

取材する しゅざいする collect data [materials],
gather news
取得する しゅとくする acquire, gain; purchase
摂取する せっしゅする take (in), ingest, absorb
二点先取する にてんせんしゅする take [score] the
first two points of the game
聴取する ちょうしゅする listen to, give a hearing to

get off
降　　下

降 ▷alight
コウ お(りる) お(ろす) ふ(る)
ふ(り) Ⓚ0414

alight, get off

降車する こうしゃする alight, get off, get down
乗降 じょうこう boarding and alighting, getting on
and off

下 ▷get down
カ ゲ した しも もと さ(げる) さ(がる)
くだ(る) くだ(り) くだ(す) くだ(さる)
お(ろす) お(りる) Ⓚ2862

get down from (a horse or vehicle), dismount, alight

下車する げしゃする alight, get off
下馬 げば dismounting

get on
乗　　搭

乗 ▷get on
ジョウ の(る) -の(り) の(せる) Ⓚ2992

[original meaning] (take a place on a vehicle or animal) get
on, board, go aboard, mount

乗車する じょうしゃする take a train, get aboard,
get on
乗船する じょうせんする embark, go on board
乗降 じょうこう boarding and alighting, getting on
and off

搭 ▷board
トウ   Ⓚ0541

board, get on, embark
  搭乗する とうじょうする board, get on a plane, embark

---

give

与 呈 進 上 下 呉
授 賜 贈 賄 賂

与 ▷give
ヨ あた(える)   Ⓚ2887

give, present, grant
  与件 よけん postulate, given conditions
  供与する きょうよする offer, present, submit
  給与する きゅうよする allow, grant; pay (a salary)
  授与する じゅよする grant, give, confer
  寄与する きよする contribute, render services to
  贈与する ぞうよする donate, present

呈 ▷present
テイ   Ⓚ1874

[also suffix] **present (a gift), give**
  呈上 ていじょう presentation
  進呈する しんていする proffer, present
  謹呈する きんていする present, make a present
  贈呈 ぞうてい presentation
  案内書呈 あんないしょてい presentation of a guide-book

進 ▷present to a superior
シン すす(む) すす(める)   Ⓚ2689

present to a superior, proffer, offer
  進呈する しんていする proffer, present
  進物 しんもつ gift
  寄進 きしん contribution, donation

上 ▷give (to superior or others)
ジョウ ショウ うえ うわ- かみ あ(げる)
あ(がる) あ(がり) のぼ(る) のぼ(り)
のぼ(せる) のぼ(す)   Ⓚ2876

【ジョウ ショウ】
present something before a superior or higher authority; perform an action for a superior
  上納 じょうのう payment (to the authorities)
  上奏する じょうそうする report to the Throne
  献上する けんじょうする present (a gift to a superior)
  参上する さんじょうする go to see, call on, pay one's respects

【あ(げる)】
give, offer, present, hand (to a superior, equal or others, not the speaker)
  彼に本を上げた かれにほんをあげた I gave him a book

下 ▷give (to inferior or speaker)
カ ゲ した しも もと さ(げる) さ(がる)
くだ(る) くだ(り) くだ(す) くだ(さる)
お(ろす) お(りる)   Ⓚ2862

【カ ゲ】
give to an inferior, grant
  下賜 かし imperial grant
  下付する かふする grant, issue

【くだ(さる)】
[honorific] **give, confer (to the speaker or speaker's group)**
  それを私に下さい それをわたしにください Give it to me

呉 ▷give (to speaker)
ゴ く(れる)   Ⓚ2206

give (to the speaker); give (to an inferior, animal or plant); [following the TE-form of verbs] do something for (the benefit of the speaker)
  呉れ呉れも宣しく くれぐれもよろしく Give my best regards to (her)
  それを呉れ それをくれ Give it to me
  乞食に金を呉れてやる こじきにかねをくれてやる give money to a beggar
  彼が仕事をして呉れた かれがしごとをしてくれた He did the work for me

授 ▷confer
ジュ さず(ける) さず(かる)   Ⓚ0448

confer, grant, award; give, hand over
  授与する じゅよする grant, give, confer
  授賞 じゅしょう awarding a prize
  授産 じゅさん providing with work, giving employment
  授受 じゅじゅ giving and receiving
  授乳 じゅにゅう breast-feeding

賜 ▷deign to give
シ たまわ(る)   Ⓚ1433

[original meaning] **deign to give, bestow, grant, award; be awarded, have the honor to receive**
  賜金 しきん money grant
  賜杯 しはい trophy given by the emperor [prince]
  賜暇 しか leave of absence, furlough
  下賜する かしする grant, deign to give

贈 ▷present a gift
ゾウ ソウ おく(る)   Ⓚ1472

present a gift, give a present
贈答品 ぞうとうひん present, gift
贈呈 ぞうてい presentation
贈与 ぞうよ donation, presentation
贈賄 ぞうわい bribery, corruption
寄贈 きぞう(=きそう) donation, presentation

賄 ▷bribe
ワイ まかな(う)   Ⓚ1390

bribe
賄賂 わいろ bribe, bribery
収賄 しゅうわい acceptance of a bribe, corruption
贈賄する ぞうわいする bribe, corrupt
贈収賄 ぞうしゅうわい corruption, bribery

賂 ▷bribe
ロ   Ⓚ1389

bribe; bribery
賄賂 わいろ bribe, bribery

give birth
生 誕 産 娩 殖

生 ▷be born
セイ ショウ い(きる) い(かす) い(ける)
う(まれる) う(まれ) う(む) お(う) は(える)
は(やす) き なま な(る)   Ⓚ2933

ⓐ be born
ⓑ bear, give birth to
ⓒ birth

ₐ 生家 せいか house where one was born
生年月日 せいねんがっぴ date of birth
誕生する たんじょうする be born, come into the
   world
更生する こうせいする be born again, start one's
   life all over; recycle
再生 さいせい reclamation; regeneration, resuscitation; playback
双生児 そうせいじ twins
往生する おうじょうする pass away; be at a loss
ᵦ 生母 せいぼ one's (biological) mother
生殖 せいしょく reproduction, procreation, generation
卵生の らんせいの oviparous
꜀ 生後二週間 せいごにしゅうかん two weeks after
   one's birth
生滅 しょうめつ birth and death

誕 ▷be born
タン   Ⓚ143○

ⓐ be born
ⓑ birth
ₐ 誕生 たんじょう birth, nativity
誕生日 たんじょうび birthday
ᵦ 誕辰 たんしん birthday
生誕 せいたん birth, nativity
キリストの降誕 きりすとのこうたん the Nativity, the
   Advent

産 ▷give birth
サン う(む) う(まれる) うぶ-   Ⓚ281▢

ⓐ give birth (to), deliver, bear, breed
ⓑ be born
ⓒ childbirth, delivery
ₐ 産婦 さんぷ woman in childbirth
産卵 さんらん egg-laying, spawning
産婦人科 さんふじんか obstetrics and gynecology
出産する しゅっさんする give birth (to), deliver, bea▢
   (a child)
ᵦ 産制 さんせい birth control
꜀ 安産 あんざん easy [smooth] delivery (of a baby)
死産 しざん stillbirth

娩 ▷give birth
ベン   Ⓚ036

give birth (to), deliver, bear
娩出する べんしゅつする give birth, deliver
分娩 ぶんべん delivery, childbirth
擬娩 ぎべん couvade

殖 ▷multiply
ショク ふ(える) ふ(やす)   Ⓚ090

[original meaning] (produce offspring) **multiply, propa-**
gate, breed
増殖する ぞうしょくする multiply, propagate,
   increase
繁殖する はんしょくする breed, propagate,
   increase, multiply
生殖 せいしょく reproduction, procreation, generation

give out a call
叫 号 喝 喚 呼 鳴 吠

叫 ▷shout
キョウ さけ(ぶ)   Ⓚ017

[original meaning] **shout, cry (out), shriek, scream, ye▢**
叫喚 きょうかん shout, cry, scream
叫号する きょうごうする [rare] cry aloud

絶叫する ぜっきょうする exclaim, ejaculate, scream, shout

号 ▷holler
ゴウ ⑥1847

[original meaning] **holler, call out, shout, cry, wail**
号泣 ごうきゅう wailing, lamentation
怒号 どごう (angry) roar, outcry, bellow

喝 ▷shout at
カツ ⑥0417

shout at, roar, bark, bellow, bawl, bawl out
喝采 かっさい applause, cheers
喝破する かっぱする shout someone down, declare, pronounce
一喝 いっかつ thundering cry, roar
大喝する だいかつする shout in a thunderous voice

喚 ▷call out
カン ⑥0503

[original meaning] **call out, scream, shout, yell**
喚声 かんせい shout, yell, scream, clamor
叫喚 きょうかん shout, cry, scream

呼 ▷call
コ よ(ぶ) ⑥0246

(cry out in a loud voice) **call, call out to**
呼応する こおうする hail to each other, act in concert
呼号する こごうする cry out, proclaim
指呼する しこする beckon
点呼 てんこ roll call
歓呼する かんこする cheer, cry out

鳴 ▷cry
メイ な(く) な(る) な(らす) ⑥0616

ⓐ [original meaning] (of birds and animals) **cry, howl**
ⓑ cry out, shout
a 鶏鳴 けいめい cockcrowing
b 悲鳴 ひめい shriek, scream

吠 ▷bark
バイ ハイ ベイ ほ(える)

bark, bay, howl, roar, cry
犬吠 けんばい barking (of a dog)
狗吠 くはい barking (of a dog)

---

go and come

| 行 | 徠 | 往 | 出 | 参 |
| 来 | 通 | 向 | 赴 | 嚮 |

行 ▷go
コウ ギョウ アン い(く) ゆ(く) -ゆ(き) -い(き) おこな(う) ⑥0187

go, walk, travel
行進する こうしんする march, parade
行列 ぎょうれつ procession, queue; matrix
徐行 じょこう going slowly
旅行 りょこう travel, trip
歩行 ほこう walk, walking
流行 りゅうこう fashion; prevalence
平行 へいこう parallelism, parallel; going side by side; occurring together

徠 ▷come
ライ ⑥0434

come, come to
徂徠 そらい coming and going

往 ▷go on
オウ ⑥0261

go on, proceed, move ahead, go by
往復 おうふく going and returning; round trip
往来 おうらい come-and-go, traffic; road, street
往診 おうしん doctor's visit to a patient, house call
右往左往する うおうさおうする go this way and that
一往(=一応) いちおう once; in outline; tentatively; for the time being

出 ▷go to
シュツ スイ で(る) -で だ(す) ⑥2934

go to, proceed to, come to
出漁する しゅつりょうする go (off) fishing
出馬する しゅつばする come forward as a candidate; go in person
出世する しゅっせする succeed in life; be promoted
進出する しんしゅつする advance, go [march] into; debouch

参 ▷go somewhere
サン シン まい(る) ⑥1778

go somewhere, go (to), come
参観 さんかん visit, inspection
参集する さんしゅうする gather, meet, congregate
持参する じさんする bring [take] with one, carry

古参 こさん senior, old-timer, veteran; seniority
新参 しんざん newcomer, greenhorn

来 ▷come
ライ く(る) きた(る) きた(す)　　Ⓚ2975

come, come to
来訪 らいほう visit, call
来日 らいにち coming to Japan
来客 らいきゃく visitor, guest
到来する とうらいする come, arrive
伝来する でんらいする be transmitted, be imported
舶来の はくらいの imported, foreign-made
在来の ざいらいの ordinary, common, usual
往来 おうらい come-and-go, traffic; road, street

通 ▷go to and from
ツウ ツ とお(る) とお(り)
-どお(り) とお(す) とお(し) -どお(し)
かよ(う)　　Ⓚ2678

go to and from, go back and forth, commute
通勤 つうきん commuting, commutation, attending office
通学 つうがく attending school, going to school
通商 つうしょう commerce, trade, commercial relation [intercourse]

向 ▷head toward
コウ む(く) む(き) む(ける) -む(け)
む(かう) む(こう)　　Ⓚ2627

head toward, go toward, proceed to
向心力 こうしんりょく central force, centripetal force
出向する しゅっこうする proceed to, leave for, be temporarily transferred to
下向する げこうする go away from the capital, go down (to a province)

赴 ▷proceed to
フ おもむ(く)　　Ⓚ2816

proceed to (as a new appointment), go to, head for, attend
赴任 ふにん proceeding to a new post

嚮 ▷go toward
コウ キョウ

[original meaning] **go toward, head toward**
嚮導する きょうどうする guide, conduct, lead

god
神 帝 天 主 祇

神 ▷god
シン ジン かみ かん- こう-　　Ⓚ0821

❶ god, God, deity, spirit
❷ Shinto deity, *kami*
a 神学 しんがく theology
神父 しんぷ priest, Father
神仏 しんぶつ gods and Buddha; Shinto and Buddhism
多神教 たしんきょう polytheism
b 神宮 じんぐう Shinto shrine; Grand Shrine at Ise
神道 しんとう Shinto, the Way of the Gods
神社 じんじゃ Shinto shrine

帝 ▷the Supreme Being
テイ　　Ⓚ1786

[original meaning] **the Supreme Being, Lord of Heaven**
天帝 てんてい Lord of Heaven, the Creator
上帝 じょうてい God, the Lord

天 ▷Heaven
テン あめ あま-　　Ⓚ2898

Heaven, the Creator, Ruler of the Universe, God
天帝 てんてい Lord of Heaven, the Creator
天主 てんしゅ Lord of Heaven, God

主 ▷Lord
シュ ス ぬし おも あるじ　　Ⓚ1696

[also suffix] **Lord, our Lord, Jesus Christ**
天主 てんしゅ Lord of Heaven, God
救世主 きゅうせいしゅ the Savior, the Messiah
造物主 ぞうぶつしゅ Creator, Maker

祇 ▷earthly god
ギ シ　　Ⓚ1049

earthly god, local god, god
神祇 じんぎ gods of heaven and earth
地祇 ちぎ earthly deities

good

良 善 好 順 佳 美

良 ▷good
リョウ よ(い) い(い) Ⓚ2980

(having positive qualities) **good, fine, favorable, excellent**

良好な りょうこうな good, fine, excellent, favorable
良質の りょうしつの of fine quality, superior
良否 りょうひ good or bad, quality
良導体 りょうどうたい good conductor
最良の さいりょうの best, superfine, most excellent
優良な ゆうりょうな superior, excellent
改良する かいりょうする improve, reform, make better
純良品 じゅんりょうひん genuine article
不良 ふりょう badness, inferiority; delinquency; juvenile delinquent

善 ▷good
ゼン よ(い) Ⓚ2030

(having positive qualities) **good**

善意 ぜんい good intention; favorable sense
善良な ぜんりょうな good, virtuous
善政 ぜんせい good government [administration]
改善 かいぜん improvement, amelioration
最善 さいぜん best

好 ▷favorable
コウ この(む) す(く) よ(い) い(い) Ⓚ0184

[also prefix] **favorable, good, fine**

好調 こうちょう favorable [good] condition
好機 こうき favorable opportunity, good chance
好況 こうきょう brisk market, prosperity
好意 こうい goodwill, favor, kindness
好感 こうかん good feeling, good impression
好評 こうひょう favorable criticism [comment], public favor
好影響 こうえいきょう favorable influence
好都合な こうつごうな favorable, fortunate
絶好の ぜっこうの splendid, grand, best, golden

順 ▷favorable
ジュン Ⓚ0009

favorable, satisfactory, right

順調 じゅんちょう favorable condition, smooth progress
順風 じゅんぷう favorable wind
順当な じゅんとうな proper, right, reasonable
順境 じゅんきょう favorable circumstances [condition]

佳 ▷fine
カ Ⓚ0068

(of superior quality) **fine, good, excellent**

佳作 かさく fine work
佳境 かきょう most interesting part, climax
佳品 かひん choice [excellent] article
佳味 かみ fine [good] taste; delicious food

美 ▷beautiful
ビ うつく(しい) Ⓚ1955

(very satisfactory) **beautiful, good, superior**

美風 びふう beautiful [laudable] custom
美点 びてん point of beauty, good point
美味 びみ good flavor, delicacy
美名 びめい good name, high reputation
美徳 びとく virtue, good deed

good fortune

吉 嘉 祥 瑞 禎 幸 福 倖

吉 ▷lucky
キチ キツ Ⓚ1855

[original meaning] **lucky, propitious, auspicious, favorable, good**

吉兆 きっちょう good omen, lucky sign
吉日 きちじつ(=きつじつ) lucky day
吉凶 きっきょう good or ill luck, fortune
吉事 きちじ auspicious event
大吉 だいきち excellent [good] luck
不吉 ふきつ ill omen, inauspiciousness

嘉 ▷happy
カ よみ(する) Ⓚ2056

[also 佳] **happy, auspicious, lucky, good**

嘉節 かせつ happy [auspicious] occasion
嘉例 かれい happy precedent, festive annual custom
嘉日 かじつ auspicious day, good day

祥 ▷auspicious
ショウ Ⓚ0855

ⓐ auspicious, propitious, favorable
ⓑ auspicious omen, lucky sign

a 不祥事 ふしょうじ scandal, inauspicious event
b 吉祥 きちじょう(=きっしょう) auspicious omen
発祥 はっしょう origin; appearance of auspicious omen
瑞祥 ずいしょう auspicious sign, good omen

瑞 ▷auspicious omen
ズイ スイ みず- ⓀＫ0943

ⓐ auspicious [good] omen, luck sign
ⓑ auspicious, propitious, good

a 奇瑞 きずい auspicious [good] omen
b 瑞祥 ずいしょう auspicious sign, good omen
瑞兆 ずいちょう auspicious sign, good omen
瑞雲 ずいうん auspicious clouds

禎 ▷propitious omen
テイ Ⓚ0946

propitious omen
禎祥 ていしょう good omen

幸 ▷good fortune
コウ さいわ(い) さち しあわ(せ) Ⓚ1901

[original meaning] good fortune, good luck
幸運 こううん good fortune, good luck
射幸心 しゃこうしん speculative spirit

福 ▷fortune
フク Ⓚ0944

(good) fortune, blessing, good luck, prosperity, happiness

福徳 ふくとく fortune, happiness and prosperity
福利 ふくり public welfare, well-being, prosperity
福祉 ふくし welfare
福音 ふくいん gospel, good news
祝福 しゅくふく blessing
大福 だいふく great fortune, good luck; rice cake stuffed with bean jam
禍福 かふく fortune and misfortune
幸福な こうふくな happy; blessed, fortunate

倖 ▷good fortune
コウ しあわ(せ) Ⓚ0102

【コウ】
[original meaning] good fortune, good luck
射倖心 しゃこうしん speculative spirit
僥倖 ぎょうこう good fortune, luck, lucky chance
薄倖 はっこう unhappiness; sad fate, misfortune
【しあわ(せ)】
[now usu. 幸せ or 仕合わせ] happiness, blessing; good fortune

govern
治　統

治 ▷govern
ジ チ おさ(める) おさ(まる) なお(る) なお(す) Ⓚ0297

govern, administer, rule over, reign over
治国 ちこく government
治世 ちせい reign, rule, regime, dynasty
自治 じち self-government, autonomy
統治 とうち rule, government, reign
明治 めいじ Meiji era

統 ▷rule
トウ す(べる) Ⓚ1239

(unite under one rule) rule, govern, command
統治する とうちする rule, govern, reign over
統制 とうせい control, regulation
統率 とうそつ leadership, command
総統 そうとう sovereign, highest post of the government
大統領 だいとうりょう president

government
政　治

政 ▷political administration
セイ ショウ まつりごと Ⓚ1058

[also suffix] political administration, government
政府 せいふ government, administration
政治 せいじ government, administration, politics
政権 せいけん political power, administrative power
政策 せいさく policy, political measures
政令 せいれい government ordinance, cabinet order
行政 ぎょうせい administration
内政 ないせい domestic administration, internal affairs
郵政 ゆうせい postal system
国政 こくせい (national) administration, government
施政 しせい administration, government
民政 みんせい civil administration [government]
摂政 せっしょう regency; regent
東京都政 とうきょうとせい government of Tokyo Metropolis

治 ▷government
ジ　チ　おさ(める)　おさ(まる)　なお(る)
なお(す)　　　　　　　　　　　　　　Ⓚ0297

government, rule, administration
治下の ちかの under the rule of
政治 せいじ government, administration, politics
内治 ないじ(=ないじ) home administration
法治 ほうち constitutional government
文治 ぶんち civil administration

governments →PARTS OF GOVERNMENTS

governments
官　幕　廷　朝　宮

官 ▷government
カン　　　　　　　　　　　　　　　Ⓚ1912

[original meaning] **government, court**
官房 かんぼう secretariat
官邸 かんてい official residence
官庁 かんちょう government office [agency]
官僚 かんりょう government official(s); bureaucracy, officialdom
官製の かんせいの government manufactured
官吏 かんり government official
官女 かんじょ court lady

幕 ▷shogunate
マク　バク　　　　　　　　　　　　Ⓚ2044

shogunate, feudal government of Japan
幕僚 ばくりょう staff, staff officer
幕府 ばくふ shogunate
幕末 ばくまつ closing days of the Tokugawa shogunate
佐幕 さばく adherence to the shogunate

廷 ▷court
テイ　　　　　　　　　　　　　　　Ⓚ2631

[rarely also 庭] **court, Imperial Court**
廷臣 ていしん court official
朝廷 ちょうてい Imperial Court
宮廷 きゅうてい the Court, the Palace

朝 ▷court
チョウ　あさ　　　　　　　　　　　Ⓚ1513

court, government
朝廷 ちょうてい Imperial Court
朝野 ちょうや government and people
朝貢する ちょうこうする bring tribute

宮 ▷Imperial Court
キュウ　グウ　ク　みや　　　　　　Ⓚ1964

Imperial Court, court
宮廷 きゅうてい the Court, the Palace
宮中 きゅうちゅう Imperial Court
宮内庁 くないちょう Imperial Household Agency
皇宮警察 こうぐうけいさつ Imperial Guard

grasses →KINDS OF GRASSES

gratitude →THANKING AND GRATITUDE

graves
墓　墳　陵　廟　祢　塚

墓 ▷grave
ボ　はか　　　　　　　　　　　　　Ⓚ2037

[original meaning] **grave, tomb**
墓碑 ぼひ tombstone, gravestone
墓地 ぼち graveyard, cemetery, burial grounds
墓標 ぼひょう grave post, grave marker, gravestone
墓参 ぼさん visit to a grave

墳 ▷tumulus
フン　　　　　　　　　　　　　　　Ⓚ0653

tumulus, grave mound, tomb
墳墓 ふんぼ grave, tomb
古墳 こふん tumulus, ancient tomb, old mound
円墳 えんぷん burial mound

陵 ▷imperial mausoleum
リョウ　みささぎ　　　　　　　　　Ⓚ0497

[also suffix] **imperial mausoleum, imperial tomb**
陵墓 りょうぼ imperial tomb
御陵 ごりょう imperial mausoleum
皇陵 こうりょう imperial mausoleum
仁徳陵 にんとくりょう Mausoleum of Emperor Nintoku

廟 ▷mausoleum
ビョウ　　　　　　　　　　　　　　Ⓚ2738

[original meaning] **mausoleum, ancestral mausoleum [shrine]**
霊廟 れいびょう mausoleum
帝廟 ていびょう imperial mausoleum
宗廟 そうびょう ancestral shrine [temple]

祢 ▷father's mausoleum
デイ　ネ　　　　　　　　　　　　　Ⓚ0820

[original meaning, now rare] **father's mausoleum**
祢廟 でいびょう father's mausoleum

祢祖 でいそ mausoleums of one's father and grandfather; one's late father and late grandfather

塚 ▷grave mound
つか -づか ⓚ0509

grave mound, tumulus; grave
塚穴 つかあな grave

---

great
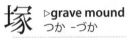
偉 大 宏 壮 豪 雄 碩

偉 ▷great (of superior character)
イ えら(い) ⓚ0128

(of superior character) **great, grand**
偉大な いだいな great, mighty, grand
偉人 いじん great man
偉業 いぎょう great work [achievement]
偉勲 いくん great achievement
偉観 いかん grand sight
魁偉な かいいな gigantic, large-boned and impressive

大 ▷big
ダイ タイ おお- おお(きい)
おお(いに) ⓚ2882

(characterized by greatness) **big, great, grand, important, chief, prominent, excellent**
大使 たいし ambassador
大統領 だいとうりょう president
大臣 だいじん minister (of state)
大学 だいがく university, college
大学生 だいがくせい university student; undergraduate
大国 たいこく world power, great country; large country
大事 だいじ great thing, serious affair; importance
大家 たいか great master, authority
大前提 だいぜんてい major premise
偉大な いだいな great, mighty, grand
重大な じゅうだいな important, serious, grave

宏 ▷grand (large in scale)
コウ ⓚ1884

(large in scale) **grand, great, magnificent**
宏壮な こうそうな grand, magnificent, imposing
宏弁 こうべん [rare] eloquence, fluency

壮 ▷grand (having grandeur)
ソウ ⓚ0198

(having grandeur) **grand, magnificent, splendid**

壮観 そうかん grand sight, magnificent view
壮大な そうだいな grand, magnificent, grandiose
壮麗な そうれいな grand, magnificent, splendid, imposing
豪壮な ごうそうな grand, magnificent, splendid
宏壮な こうそうな grand, magnificent, imposing

豪 ▷magnificent
ゴウ ⓚ183▪

magnificent, grand, grandiose, great, splendid
豪華な ごうかな gorgeous, splendid, pompous
豪壮な ごうそうな grand, magnificent, splendid
豪勢な ごうせいな great, grand, magnificent

雄 ▷heroic
ユウ お- おす ⓚ092▪

(impressive in scale) **heroic, grand, magnificent**
雄弁な ゆうべんな eloquent, fluent
雄渾な ゆうこんな magnificent, sublime; vigorous, bold
雄図 ゆうと ambitious enterprise, grand project
雄飛する ゆうひする launch out, embark upon (a career)
雄大な ゆうだいな grand, magnificent, heroic

碩 ▷eminent
セキ ジャク ⓚ112▪

eminent, great
碩学 せきがく literary eminent scholar, man of erudition

---

great persons

豪 傑 雄 匠 聖

豪 ▷great man
ゴウ ⓚ183▪

great man, person of extraordinary powers, champion, hero
豪傑 ごうけつ hero, great [extraordinary] man
文豪 ぶんごう great man of letters, literary master
酒豪 しゅごう great [heavy] drinker
剣豪 けんごう great swordsman, master fencer
強豪(=強剛) きょうごう veteran, champion
富豪 ふごう wealthy man, millionaire

傑 ▷outstanding person
ケツ ⓚ013▪

[original meaning] **outstanding person, hero, great man, master**
傑物 けつぶつ great man, outstanding figure
豪傑 ごうけつ hero, great [extraordinary] man

女傑 じょけつ heroine, lady of character
怪傑 かいけつ man of extraordinary talent, wonder man
英傑 えいけつ great man, hero, master mind

雄 ▷hero
ユウ お- おす   Ⓚ0920

hero, great man, great leader, master
英雄 えいゆう hero
両雄 りょうゆう two great men
群雄 ぐんゆう rival leaders [barons]

匠 ▷craftsman
ショウ   Ⓚ2581

(master of an art) **craftsman, master, artist**
師匠 ししょう master, teacher
巨匠 きょしょう great master, maestro

聖 ▷great master
セイ   Ⓚ2464

great master
楽聖ベートーベン がくせいべーとーべん Beethoven, the great musician
棋聖 きせい great master of go [shogi]

great respect
栄 誉 光

栄 ▷glory
エイ さか(える) は(え) -ば(え) は(える)   Ⓚ2231

glory, honor, splendor, fame, distinction
栄誉 えいよ honor, glory, distinction
栄光 えいこう glory
栄華 えいが prosperity, splendor, glory
栄達 えいたつ success in life, rise in the world
栄冠 えいかん honor, glory; garland, laurels
栄転 えいてん promotion

誉 ▷honor
ヨ ほま(れ)   Ⓚ2193

honor, good reputation, fame, glory
名誉 めいよ honor, glory; dignity
栄誉 えいよ honor, glory, distinction
声誉 せいよ fame, reputation, honor and distinction, credit

光 ▷honor
コウ ひか(る) ひかり   Ⓚ2121

honor, glory

光明 こうみょう glory, hope, right future
光栄 こうえい honor, glory; privilege
栄光 えいこう glory

green colors
緑 青 翠

緑 ▷green
リョク ロク みどり   Ⓚ1259

ⓐ [original meaning] **green, emerald**
ⓑ [prefix] **greenish**
a 緑色 りょくしょく green, verdure
緑茶 りょくちゃ green tea, Japanese tea
緑青 ろくしょう verdigris, copper [green] rust
葉緑素 ようりょくそ chlorophyll
b 緑白色 りょくはくしょく greenish white

青 ▷green
セイ ショウ チン あお あお(い)   Ⓚ2152

green, greenish
青松 せいしょう green pine
青椒肉絲 ちんじゃおろーす stir-fried shredded meat and green pepper
青梗菜 ちんげんさい bok choy

翠 ▷jade green
スイ みどり   Ⓚ2361

jade green, emerald green, verdure, yellowish green
翠色 すいしょく verdure, emerald green
翠玉 すいぎょく emerald, jade
翡翠色 ひすいいろ jade green

grieve
慨 嘆 悼 傷 悲 悄

慨 ▷deplore
ガイ   Ⓚ0588

deplore, lament, regret, grieve
慨歎する がいたんする deplore, lament, regret
慨然と がいぜんと deploringly; indignantly
慨世 がいせい concern for the public welfare
感慨 かんがい deep [profound] emotion
慷慨 こうがい patriotic lamentation, deploration; righteous indignation

grieve

嘆 ▷**sigh**
タン なげ(く) なげ(かわしい) Ⓚ0577

[original meaning] **sigh (in grief or despair), grieve, lament**
嘆息 たんそく sigh
嘆願 たんがん entreaty, appeal
悲嘆 ひたん grief, sorrow, lamentation
慨嘆 がいたん deploring, regret

悼 ▷**mourn**
トウ いた(む) Ⓚ0443

mourn, grieve, lament
悼辞 とうじ message of condolence
哀悼する あいとうする condole, mourn, grieve
追悼 ついとう mourning

傷 ▷**grieve**
ショウ きず いた(む) いた(める) Ⓚ0137

be grieved at heart, be wounded, be pained
傷心 しょうしん heartbreak, grief
感傷 かんしょう sentiment, sentimentality
愁傷 しゅうしょう grief, lamentation, condolence

悲 ▷**feel sad**
ヒ かな(しい) かな(しむ) Ⓚ2416

[original meaning] **feel sad, feel sorrow**
悲嘆 ひたん grief, sorrow, lamentation
悲哀 ひあい sorrow, sadness

悄 ▷**become dispirited**
ショウ

[now usu. 消] **become dispirited, become disheartened; be worried**
悄然たる しょうぜんたる dejected, dispirited
悄悄と しょうしょうと dejectedly, dispiritedly

groups

群 班 軍 組 陣 連
族 党 隊 団 伍

群 ▷**group (of any kind)**
グン む(れる) む(れ) むら
むら(がる) Ⓚ1400

ⓐ [also suffix] **group (of any kind), crowd, flock, cluster, swarm**
ⓑ **group (in U.S. Army or Air Force)**
ⓒ *chem* **group**
a 群衆 ぐんしゅう crowd of people, multitude
群像 ぐんぞう *art* group

魚群 ぎょぐん school of fish
一群の羊 いちぐんのひつじ flock of sheep
抜群の ばつぐんの preeminent, outstanding
層群 そうぐん *geol* group
子音群 しいんぐん consonant cluster
流星群 りゅうせいぐん meteoric swarm

班 ▷**squad**
ハン Ⓚ085⸱

squad, group, party, team, crew
班長 はんちょう squad [group] leader
班員 はんいん member of a group
取材班 しゅざいはん data collecting party
三班 さんぱん group 3
救護班 きゅうごはん relief squad [party]
作業班 さぎょうはん work party

軍 ▷**team**
グン Ⓚ178⸱

[also suffix] **team**
巨人軍 きょじんぐん Giants (Japanese baseball team)
一軍 いちぐん major league team
女性軍 じょせいぐん women's team

組 ▷**group (of people)**
ソ く(む) くみ -ぐみ Ⓚ122⸱

ⓐ **group (of people), team, company, party, gang**
ⓑ **set (of tea cups), suit**
a 組合 くみあい union, guild, association
組合頭 くみあいがしら group leader
組を作る くみをつくる make up a party
赤組 あかぐみ red team
b 茶器組 ちゃきぐみ tea set

陣 ▷**lineup**
ジン Ⓚ041⸱

[suffix] (group of persons performing a common action)
lineup, corps, camp, group
報道陣 ほうどうじん reportorial camp, press corps
教授陣 きょうじゅじん professorate, faculty, group of professors

連 ▷**set**
レン つら(なる) つら(ねる) つ(れる)
-づ(れ) Ⓚ267⸱

[also suffix] **set, party, company, gang, clique**
連中 れんちゅう(=れんじゅう) party, company, clique those fellows [guys]
常連 じょうれん regular visitors [customers], frequenters
愚連隊 ぐれんたい hooligans, hoodlums
文士連 ぶんしれん the literary set
ハイカラ連 はいかられん the smart set

族 ▷common-interest group (*slang*)
ゾク   Ⓚ0863

[also suffix] *slang* **(group of persons who share a common interest or engage in a common activity) tribe, herd, clan, gang, set, clique**

- 雷族 かみなりぞく Thunder Herd, hot-rodders
- 暴走族 ぼうそうぞく motorcycle gang, hot-rodders
- 深夜族 しんやぞく the night owls
- 社用族 しゃようぞく expense-account spenders
- ながら族 ながらぞく persons who do two things at the same time (as studying while watching TV)
- 団地族 だんちぞく housing project dwellers

党 ▷party
トウ   Ⓚ2236

(group of persons) **party, companions, clique, fellows, fellow**

- 一党 いっとう party, league, clique; a political party
- 徒党 ととう clique, faction, conspirators
- 残党 ざんとう remnants (of a defeated party), refugees
- 悪党 あくとう scoundrel, rogue

隊 ▷party (organized group)
タイ   Ⓚ0570

[also suffix] (organized group of people) **party, group, troop, company, band**

- 隊員 たいいん member of the group
- 一隊 いったい party (of mountaineers), company (of soldiers), gang, troop, squad
- 楽隊 がくたい musical band
- デモ隊 でもたい demonstrators
- 捜索隊 そうさくたい search party
- 親衛隊 しんえいたい bodyguards; groupies

団 ▷body
ダン トン   Ⓚ2628

[also suffix] (collective group) **body, corps, group, party**

- 団体 だんたい group, party, body, corps; corporation, organization
- 団長 だんちょう leader [head] of a body [party]
- 団交 だんこう collective bargaining
- 集団 しゅうだん group, body, mass, crowd
- 一団 いちだん body, group, party, troupe
- 星団 せいだん star cluster
- 観光団 かんこうだん sightseeing party
- 外交団 がいこうだん diplomatic corps [body]
- 顧問団 こもんだん advisory body

伍 ▷ranks
ゴ   Ⓚ0031

(members of the same group) **ranks, rank and file, squad, group**

- 伍長 ごちょう corporal; foreman

---

grow
成 長 生 育 発 伸 展

 ▷grow up
セイ ジョウ な(る) な(す)   Ⓚ2964

grow up, mature

- 成長する せいちょうする grow up
- 成熟 せいじゅく maturity, ripeness, full growth
- 成育する せいいくする grow (up), be brought up
- 養成する ようせいする train, educate, bring up
- 促成栽培の野菜 そくせいさいばいのやさい forced vegetables

長 ▷grow (up)
チョウ なが(い)   Ⓚ2212

grow (up), develop, prolong

- 成長 せいちょう growth
- 延長 えんちょう extension, prolongation, continuation

生 ▷grow
セイ ショウ い(きる) い(かす) い(ける) う(まれる) う(まれ) う(む) お(う) は(える) は(やす) き なま な(る)   Ⓚ2933

[original meaning] (of plants) **grow**

- 生育する せいいくする grow, vegetate
- 生長(=成長) せいちょう (physical) growth
- 自生する じせいする grow wild [naturally]
- 群生する ぐんせいする grow gregariously [in crowds]
- 実生 みしょう seedling, plant raised from the seed
- 晩生植物 ばんせいしょくぶつ slow grower
- 対生葉 たいせいよう opposite leaves

 ▷grow
イク そだ(つ) そだ(ち) そだ(てる) はぐく(む)   Ⓚ1764

[original meaning] **grow, grow up, be brought up**

- 発育する はついくする grow, develop
- 成育する せいいくする grow (up), be brought up

 ▷develop
ハツ ホツ た(つ)   Ⓚ2222

develop, grow

- 発達 はったつ development, growth, progress
- 発育する はついくする grow, develop
- 発展する はってんする expand, grow, develop; prosper
- 開発する かいはつする develop, open out; enlighten

伸 ▷expand
シン の(びる) の(びやか) の(ばす)
の(べる) Ⓚ0054

expand, grow, develop
伸展する しんてんする expand, extend

展 ▷unfold
テン Ⓚ2681

unfold, develop, expand, evolve
展開 てんかい unfolding, development, evolution;
deployment
発展 はってん expansion, growth, development;
prosperity
進展 しんてん development, progress
伸展する しんてんする expand, extend

guard
哨 衛 守 警

哨 ▷sentry
ショウ Ⓚ0362

sentry, watch, guard
哨戒 しょうかい patrol, patrolling
哨戒機 しょうかいき patrol aircraft
哨兵 しょうへい sentry
哨舎 しょうしゃ sentry box
前哨 ぜんしょう outpost
前哨戦 ぜんしょうせん preliminary skirmish;
prelude, run-up
歩哨 ほしょう sentry

衛 ▷guard
エイ Ⓚ0686

guard, keeper
守衛 しゅえい guard, doorkeeper
前衛 ぜんえい advance guard, vanguard; forward
player
警衛 けいえい guard, patrol, escort

守 ▷guard
シュ ス まも(る) まも(り) もり Ⓚ1861

guard, keeper
看守 かんしゅ jailer, prison guard

警 ▷guard
ケイ Ⓚ2512

guard, watchman, police officer
夜警 やけい night watch; night watchman
婦警 ふけい policewoman

hair
毛 髪 辮 羽 眉 鬚

毛 ▷hair (of any kind)
モウ け Ⓚ290◀

ⓐ [original meaning] **hair (of humans or animals), fur,
feather**
ⓑ **hair (of plants)**
a 毛髪 もうはつ hair
毛筆 もうひつ (writing or painting) brush
羊毛 ようもう wool
羽毛 うもう feathers, plumage, down
b 毛茸 もうじょう trichome

髪 ▷hair (on the head)
ハツ かみ Ⓚ247▪

hair (on the head)
頭髪 とうはつ hair, head hair
毛髪 もうはつ hair
散髪 さんぱつ haircut
白髪 はくはつ white [gray] hair

辮 ▷plait
ベン

[now usu. 弁] **plait, braid**
辮髪 べんぱつ pigtail, queue

羽 ▷feather
ウ は わ はね Ⓚ020◀

[original meaning] **feather, plumage**
羽毛 うもう feathers, plumage, down

眉 ▷eyebrow
ビ ミ まゆ Ⓚ277◀

eyebrow
焦眉の急 しょうびのきゅう urgent need

鬚 ▷beard
シュ ひげ

[rarely also 須] [original meaning] **beard**
鬚髯 しゅぜん beard

hand and arm
手 腕 肘 掌 指 拇 拳

手 ▷hand
シュ ズ て た- Ⓚ2907

[original meaning] **hand, palm, arm**
手中に しゅちゅうに in the hands
握手 あくしゅ handshake, handshaking
拍手 はくしゅ applause, clapping
義手 ぎしゅ artificial arm [hand]
入手する にゅうしゅする obtain, get, come by,
  procure

腕 ▷arm
ワン うで Ⓚ0919

arm
腕章 わんしょう armband, arm badge
腕力 わんりょく muscular strength
上腕 じょうわん upper arm
左腕投手 さわんとうしゅ left-handed pitcher

肘 ▷elbow
チュウ ひじ Ⓚ0746

elbow, area of arm around the elbow joint
肘内障 ちゅうないしょう nursemaid's elbow, pulled
  elbow
掣肘 せいちゅう restraint (by another person)

掌 ▷palm
ショウ Ⓚ2256

[original meaning] **palm of the hand**
掌中本 しょうちゅうぼん pocket edition
掌握する しょうあくする hold, seize, grasp,
  command
合掌する がっしょうする join one's hands (in prayer)
指掌紋 ししょうもん hand print

指 ▷finger
シ ゆび さ(す) -さ(し) Ⓚ0337

ⓐ [original meaning] **finger**
ⓑ **counter for fingers**
a 指紋 しもん fingerprint
  指圧 しあつ *shiatsu*, acupressure
b 五指 ごし the five fingers

拇 ▷thumb
ボ

[now also 母] [original meaning] **thumb**
拇指 ぼし thumb
拇印 ぼいん thumbprint

拳 ▷fist
ケン こぶし Ⓚ2316

fist
拳銃 けんじゅう pistol, handgun
拳骨 げんこつ fist
鉄拳 てっけん clenched fist

handle
扱 馭 操 揮 運

扱 ▷handle
あつか(う) あつか(い) Ⓚ0189

[original meaning] (manipulate with the hands) **handle,
manipulate, work**
粗末に扱う そまつにあつかう handle (a thing)
  roughly
機械を扱う きかいをあつかう work a machine,
  handle a tool
上手に扱う じょうずにあつかう handle skillfully

馭 ▷handle
ギョ

handle, control, manage
制馭する せいぎょする control, govern, suppress

操 ▷manipulate
ソウ みさお あやつ(る) Ⓚ0693

manipulate, handle, operate (a machine)
操作 そうさ operation, manipulation, handling
操縦する そうじゅうする manage, control; steer;
  pilot, fly
操業 そうぎょう operation, work
操車 そうしゃ marshaling (in a classification yard)

揮 ▷wield
キ Ⓚ0538

ⓐ [original meaning] **wield, brandish, wave**
ⓑ **wield the writing brush, write**
a 指揮者 しきしゃ conductor; commander
b 揮毫する きごうする write, draw, paint

運 ▷control movement skillfully
ウン はこ(ぶ) Ⓚ2707

control movement skillfully, handle, set in motion
運転する うんてんする operate, drive, run
運転士 うんてんし officer, mate; driver
運営する うんえいする operate, manage
運用する うんようする make use of; invest in; apply
  to
運筆 うんぴつ handling the brush

handles
柄　手　把

柄 ▷**handle**
ヘイ がら え　　　Ⓚ0799

【ヘイ】

[original meaning] **handle, handhold, grip**

柄杓 ひしゃく ladle, dipper, scoop
葉柄 ようへい leafstalk, stipe

【え】

handle, crank, grip, haft; shaft

柄の長い柄杓 えのながいひしゃく long-handled ladle
長柄 ながえ long handle, long shaft
取り柄 とりえ merit, worth, recommendable feature

手 ▷**handle**
シュ ズ て た-　　　Ⓚ2907

handle, knob

取っ手(=把っ手) とって handle, knob

把 ▷**grip**
ハ ワ　　　Ⓚ0222

a grip, a handle

把手 はしゅ(=とって) handle, knob

hang
掛　垂　懸　吊　釣

掛 ▷**hang**
か(ける) か(け) -が(け) か(かる)
-が(かる) か(かり) -が(かり)　　　Ⓚ0449

hang, hang up, suspend

掛け物 かけもの hanging scroll
掛け看板 かけかんばん hanging sign
カーテンを掛ける かーてんをかける hang up a curtain

垂 ▷**hang down**
スイ た(れる) たらす) た(れ)　　　Ⓚ2985

hang down, hang, droop, dangle

懸垂 けんすい suspension, pendency; chinning exercises
口蓋垂 こうがいすい uvula

懸 ▷**suspend**
ケン ケ か(ける) か(かる)　　　Ⓚ252

suspend, be suspended (in midair), hang (over), overhang

懸垂 けんすい suspension, pendency; chinning exercises
懸架 けんが suspension (of an automobile)
懸吊 けんちょう suspension
懸濁 けんだく *chem* suspension
懸崖 けんがい overhanging cliff

吊 ▷**suspend**
チョウ つ(る) つ(り) つ(るす)

[original meaning] **suspend, hang, sling**

懸吊 けんちょう suspension

釣 ▷**suspended**
チョウ つ(る) つ(り)-　　　Ⓚ149

[also 吊り] **suspended, hanging**

釣り橋 つりばし suspension bridge
釣鐘 つりがね hanging bell, temple bell
釣り合う つりあう balance; match, be in harmony
釣り合い つりあい balance, equilibrium; proportion
釣り下げる つりさげる suspend from

happiness
幸　祉　福

幸 ▷**happiness**
コウ さいわ(い) さち しあわ(せ)　Ⓚ190

happiness, well-being, felicity

幸福 こうふく happiness; good fortune
薄幸 はっこう unhappiness; sad fate, misfortune
不幸 ふこう unhappiness; misfortune; bereavemen
多幸 たこう great happiness; great fortune

祉 ▷**blessedness**
シ　　　Ⓚ078

[original meaning] **blessedness, happiness**

祉福 しふく [archaic] happiness, prosperity; blessed ness and joy
福祉 ふくし welfare

福 ▷**fortune**
フク　　　Ⓚ094

(good) **fortune, blessing, good luck, prosperity, happiness**

福徳 ふくとく fortune, happiness and prosperity
福利 ふくり public welfare, well-being, prosperity

福祉 ふくし welfare
福音 ふくいん gospel, good news
祝福 しゅくふく blessing
大福 だいふく great fortune, good luck; rice cake stuffed with bean jam
禍福 かふく fortune and misfortune
幸福な こうふくな happy; blessed, fortunate

hard

硬 堅 鞏 固 剛 強 勁

硬
▷**hard**
コウ かた(い)　　　Ⓚ1095

[original meaning] **hard, firm, tough, solid**
硬度 こうど hardness
硬化する こうかする harden, stiffen
硬貨 こうか coin, metallic currency
硬式 こうしき hardball (baseball)
硬直 こうちょく stiffness, rigidity
硬骨 こうこつ hard bone; firmness

堅
▷**firm**
ケン かた(い) –がた(い)　　Ⓚ2457

[original meaning] (resisting deformation) **firm, hard, solid, sturdy**
堅材 けんざい hard wood
堅牢な けんろうな solid, durable, fast
堅果 けんか nut (hard fruit)

鞏
▷**tough**
キョウ

[now also 強] **tough, firm, solid, strong, hard**
鞏固な きょうこな firm, stable, solid, strong
鞏膜 きょうまく sclera

固
▷**solid**
コ かた(める) かた(まる) かた(まり) かた(い)　　Ⓚ2658

solid
固体 こたい solid, solid matter
固溶体 こようたい solid solution
固形の こけいの solid

剛
▷**tough**
ゴウ　　　Ⓚ1495

[original meaning] (hard and strong) **tough, strong, rigid, hard**
剛性 ごうせい rigidity
剛体 ごうたい rigid body
剛力(=強力) ごうりき Herculean strength; mountain carrier [guide]

剛球 ごうきゅう baseball fast ball
金剛石 こんごうせき diamond

強
▷**strong**
キョウ ゴウ つよ(い) つよ(まる) つよ(める) し(いる)　　Ⓚ0432

[formerly also 彊] (capable of enduring) **strong, hard, solid, tough**
強壮な きょうそうな robust, strong, vigorous
強固な きょうこな firm, stable, solid, strong
強硬な きょうこうな firm (attitude), unbending; drastic (measure)
強情な ごうじょうな obstinate, headstrong
強膜 きょうまく sclera

勁
▷**strong**
ケイ キョウ　　　Ⓚ1313

strong, stiff, hard
勁草 けいそう strong man with sense of fidelity
勁弓 けいきゅう stiff bow

harm and damage

害 損 傷

害
▷**harm, damage**
ガイ　　　Ⓚ1962

❶ⓐ **harm, evil, ill effect**
　ⓑ **harm, injure, damage**
ⓐ 害毒 がいどく harm, evil, evil influence
　被害 ひがい damage, harm
　弊害 へいがい evil, abuse, vice
　有害な ゆうがいな harmful, pernicious, noxious
ⓑ 害虫 がいちゅう harmful insect
　傷害 しょうがい injury, bodily harm
　侵害 しんがい infringement, violation
❷ **damage; pollution**
　公害 こうがい environmental pollution
　災害 さいがい calamity, disaster, accident
　損害 そんがい damage, harm
　冷害 れいがい damage from cold weather
　水害 すいがい flood damage

損
▷**damage**
ソン そこ(なう) そこ(ねる)　　Ⓚ0596

damage, harm
損害 そんがい damage, harm
損傷 そんしょう damage, injury
破損 はそん damage, breakdown
毀損(=棄損) きそん damage, injury, waste

傷 ▷wound
ショウ きず いた(む) いた(める)　Ⓚ0137

wound, injure, hurt; damage
傷害 しょうがい injury, bodily harm
殺傷 さっしょう killing and wounding
損傷 そんしょう damage, injury

harvest
採 摘 穫 刈

採 ▷pick
サイ と(る)　Ⓚ0459

[original meaning] **pick, pluck, gather**
採取 さいしゅ picking, collecting, harvesting
採綿器 さいめんき cotton picker
伐採 ばっさい lumbering, lumber-felling, deforestation

摘 ▷pick
テキ つ(む)　Ⓚ0629

[original meaning] **pick (flowers), pluck, gather**
摘果 てきか thinning out superfluous fruit
摘出する てきしゅつする extract, excise, remove; point out

穫 ▷harvest
カク　Ⓚ1155

[original meaning] **harvest, reap, gather**
収穫する しゅうかくする harvest, gather in, reap

刈 ▷reap
か(る)　Ⓚ0017

reap, crop, harvest
刈り入れ かりいれ harvest, reap
稲刈り いねかり rice reaping

hate and dislike
憎 悪 忌 嫌 恨 怨 厭

憎 ▷hate
ゾウ にく(む) にく(い) にく(らしい) にく(しみ)　Ⓚ0626

❶ [original meaning] **hate, detest**
❷ **hate, hatred**
a 憎悪 ぞうお abhorrence, hatred
b 愛憎 あいぞう love and hate

悪 ▷hate
アク オ わる(い) わる- あ(し)　Ⓚ239?

hate, bear ill will, despise
悪意 あくい malicious intent
憎悪 ぞうお abhorrence, hatred
嫌悪 けんお hatred, dislike, repugnance

忌 ▷abhor
キ い(む) い(み) い(まわしい)　Ⓚ188?

(regard with horror) **abhor, loathe, detest, hate**
忌み嫌う いみきらう abhor, detest
忌むべき いむべき detestable, abominable

嫌 ▷dislike
ケン ゲン きら(う) きら(い) いや　Ⓚ058?

dislike, hate, detest
嫌悪 けんお hatred, dislike, repugnance
嫌忌 けんき dislike, aversion
機嫌 きげん [sometimes also 譏嫌] mood, temper, disposition; health

恨 ▷hold a grudge
コン うら(む) うら(めしい)　Ⓚ032?

❶ **hold a grudge, hate, feel bitter against**
❷ **grudge, hatred**
a 遺恨 いこん grudge, rancor, ill will
怨恨 えんこん grudge, enmity
b 多情多恨 たじょうたこん sensibility

怨 ▷hold a grudge
エン オン　Ⓚ222?

❶ [original meaning] **hold a grudge, feel resentment, feel bitter against**
❷ **grudge, hatred, malice**
a 怨恨 えんこん grudge, enmity
怨声 えんせい complaint, resentful voice
怨念 おんねん grudge
怨霊 おんりょう revengeful ghost [specter]
怨敵 おんてき sworn enemy
b 私怨 しえん personal grudge [enmity]
宿怨 しゅくえん old grudge

厭 ▷disagreeable
エン オン いや あ(きる) いと(う)

[now usu. 嫌] **disagreeable, unpleasant, detestable**
厭な いやな disagreeable, repulsive
厭厭 いやいや grudgingly, unwillingly; (of children) shaking of the head in refusal
厭がる いやがる dislike, hate
厭がらせ いやがらせ harassment

head →FRONT PARTS OF HEAD

head
頭　首　脳

頭 ▷head
トウ ズ ト あたま かしら -がしら Ⓚ1450

[original meaning] **head**

頭骨 とうこつ skull
頭部 とうぶ head
頭囲 とうい head measurement
頭痛 ずつう headache
頭脳 ずのう brain; brains, head
羊頭狗肉 ようとうくにく using a better name to sell inferior goods, crying wine and selling vinegar
没頭する ぼっとうする be absorbed in
出頭する しゅっとうする attend, present oneself

首 ▷head
シュ くび Ⓚ1956

[original meaning] **head**

首肯する しゅこうする assent, nod one's assent, consent
首級 しゅきゅう decapitated head
斬首 ざんしゅ decapitation

脳 ▷brain
ノウ Ⓚ0888

[also prefix] [original meaning] **brain**

脳髄 のうずい brain
脳炎 のうえん brain inflammation, encephalitis
脳細胞 のうさいぼう brain cells
脳死 のうし brain death
大脳 だいのう cerebrum

headgear
帽　冠　笠　兜

帽 ▷headgear
ボウ Ⓚ0522

[also suffix] [original meaning] **headgear, hat, cap**

帽子 ぼうし cap, hat
帽章 ぼうしょう badge on a cap
学帽 がくぼう school cap
制帽 せいぼう regulation [school] cap
脱帽 だつぼう taking off one's cap [hat]; submission
ベレー帽 べれーぼう beret (cap)
無帽の むぼうの hatless
登山帽 とざんぼう climber's hat

冠 ▷crown
カン かんむり Ⓚ1790

[original meaning] **crown, coronet; cap, headgear**

王冠 おうかん crown, diadem, cap
戴冠式 たいかんしき coronation (ceremony)

笠 ▷sedge hat
リュウ かさ Ⓚ2320

sedge hat, bamboo hat, conical hat

笠雲 かさぐも cap cloud
笠の台が飛ぶ かさのだいがとぶ be decapitated; be fired
編み笠 あみがさ braided hat
陣笠 じんがさ ancient soldier's hat; party rank and file

兜 ▷headpiece
トトウ かぶと Ⓚ2455

headpiece, headgear

兜巾(=頭巾、頭襟) ときん headgear worn by mountain ascetics

healthy
康　健　生

康 ▷healthy
コウ Ⓚ2693

healthy, robust

健康 けんこう health
健康な けんこうな healthy, sound, well

健 ▷robust
ケン すこ(やか) Ⓚ0117

(strong and in good health) **robust, healthy, sound, strong**

健康な けんこうな healthy, sound, well
健保(=健康保険) けんぽ(=けんこうほけん) health insurance
健在だ けんざいだ be well, be in good health
健全 けんぜん health, soundness
健脚の けんきゃくの strong in walking
強健な きょうけんな robust, healthy, strong
保健 ほけん (preservation of) health, sanitation
穏健な おんけんな moderate, temperate, sound
剛健な ごうけんな strong and sturdy, virile; manly

生 ▷**health**
セイ ショウ い(きる) い(かす) い(ける)
う(まれる) う(まれ) う(む) お(う) は(える)
は(やす) き なま な(る)　　　Ⓚ2933

health, welfare
衛生 えいせい hygiene, sanitation, preservation of health
摂生 せっせい preservation of one's health
厚生 こうせい public welfare, health promotion
民生 みんせい public welfare, people's livelihood

hear
聞　　聴

聞 ▷**hear**
ブン モン き(く) き(こえる)　　　Ⓚ2840

ⓐ (perceive by ear) **hear**
ⓑ (learn by being told) **hear of, be told**
a 見聞 けんぶん experience, observation, knowledge
b 上聞 じょうぶん imperial hearing
聴聞会 ちょうもんかい hearing
前代未聞の ぜんだいみもんの unheard-of, unprecedented

聴 ▷**listen**
チョウ き(く)　　　Ⓚ1292

[original meaning] **listen, hear**
聴取する ちょうしゅする listen to, give a hearing to
聴衆 ちょうしゅう audience
聴講 ちょうこう lecture attendance
聴聞会 ちょうもんかい hearing
聴覚 ちょうかく sense of hearing
傍聴する ぼうちょうする hear, listen to; attend
視聴者 しちょうしゃ viewer, audience
公聴会 こうちょうかい public [open] hearing
傾聴 けいちょう listening closely

heat
熱　　暑

熱 ▷**heat**
ネツ あつ(い)　　　Ⓚ2495

(source of warmth) **heat**
高熱 こうねつ intense heat; high fever
加熱 かねつ heating
光熱費 こうねつひ fuel and electricity expenses
地熱 じねつ(=ちねつ) terrestrial heat
耐熱性 たいねつせい heat-resisting property

暑 ▷**summer heat**
ショ あつ(い)　　　Ⓚ2182

[original meaning] **summer heat, hot weather, hottest day of summer, summer**
暑気 しょき hot weather
暑中 しょちゅう midsummer
暑中見舞 しょちゅうみまい best wishes for the hot season
暑熱 しょねつ heat of summer
避暑 ひしょ summering
炎暑 えんしょ scorching heat of summer
残暑 ざんしょ lingering summer
猛暑 もうしょ fierce heat
酷暑 こくしょ severe heat
大暑 たいしょ Japanese midsummer day

heating devices
炉　窯　缶

炉 ▷**furnace**
ロ　　　Ⓚ077

furnace, kiln
高炉 こうろ blast furnace
転炉 てんろ rotary kiln
溶鉱炉 ようこうろ smelting [blast] furnace
電気炉 でんきろ electric furnace
反射炉 はんしゃろ reverberatory furnace
乾燥炉 かんそうろ drying kiln
燃焼炉 ねんしょうろ combustion furnace

窯 ▷**kiln**
ヨウ かま　　　Ⓚ208

kiln, furnace
官窯 かんよう governmental porcelain furnace

缶 ▷**steam boiler**
カン　　　Ⓚ175

[usu. 罐] **steam boiler**
汽缶室 きかんしつ boiler room; stokehold, fire room

height
高　丈　背

高 ▷**height**
コウ たか(い) たか -だか たか(まる)
たか(める)　　　Ⓚ180

height; high place
標高 ひょうこう elevation, (height) above the sea

座高 ざこう one's sitting height
登高 とうこう climbing a height

丈 ▷stature
ジョウ たけ   Ⓚ2885

stature, height
偉丈夫 いじょうふ towering [great] man; hero
大丈夫 だいじょうぶ safe, sure, all right

背 ▷stature
ハイ せ せい そむ(く) そむ(ける) Ⓚ2230

[sometimes also 脊] **stature, height**
背の順 せのじゅん order of height

help

助 佑 祐 援 佐 補 輔 済

助 ▷help
ジョ たす(ける) たす(かる) すけ Ⓚ1037

ⓐ [original meaning] **help, aid, assist**
ⓑ (act of helping) **help, aid**
ⓒ **save, rescue, relieve**

a 助手 じょしゅ assistant, helper
助成 じょせい fostering; aid, assistance
助言 じょげん advice
援助 えんじょ aid, assistance, help
補助 ほじょ assistance, support, aid
b 一助 いちじょ help, aid
天助 てんじょ Heaven's help
c 助命 じょめい sparing a person's life
救助 きゅうじょ rescue, relief

佑 ▷help (said esp. of God)
ユウ ウ   Ⓚ0058

ⓐ [original meaning] **help, succor, protect**—said esp.
of God
ⓑ [also 祐] **divine help, heavenly assistance [pro-
tection]**
a 佑助 ゆうじょ help, divine help
b 天佑 てんゆう grace of Heaven, providential help

祐 ▷divine help
ユウ ウ   Ⓚ0824

ⓐ [also 佑] [original meaning] **divine help, heavenly
assistance [protection]**
ⓑ [also 右] **help, assist**
a 天祐 てんゆう grace of Heaven, providential help
神祐 しんゆう [rare] divine help, heavenly protection
b 祐筆 ゆうひつ amanuensis, private secretary

援 ▷aid
エン   Ⓚ0536

[original meaning] **aid, help out, give a hand, give
support**
援助 えんじょ aid, assistance, help
援軍 えんぐん relieving force, reinforcements
支援 しえん support, backing, aid
応援 おうえん aid, reinforcement; support; cheering
後援する こうえんする give support [backing]

佐 ▷assist
サ   Ⓚ0051

assist, aid, second
佐幕派 さばくは supporters of the shogun
補佐(=輔佐)する ほさする assist, help

補 ▷assist
ホ おぎな(う)   Ⓚ1103

[formerly also 輔] **assist, aid; give guidance**
補佐(=輔佐)する ほさする assist, help
補助する ほじょする assist, support, aid
補導する ほどうする guide, direct, lead; take into
custody

輔 ▷assist
ホ フ   Ⓚ1411

[now usu. 補] **assist, aid; give guidance**
輔佐 ほさ assistance, aid; assistant; counselor,
adviser
輔弼 ほひつ assistance, council
輔導 ほどう guidance; custody

済 ▷relieve
サイ す(む) -ず(み) す(まない) す(ます)
す(ませる)   Ⓚ0478

relieve, aid, save, redeem
済民 さいみん relieving the sufferings of the people
済度 さいど *Buddhism* salvation
経済 けいざい economy, economics
救済する きゅうさいする relieve, help, save, deliver
共済 きょうさい mutual aid

hide

隠 蔽 伏 潜 匿 忍

隠 ▷hide
イン かく(す) かく(し)- かく(れる) Ⓚ0645

[original meaning] (conceal from sight) **hide, conceal**
隠蔽する いんぺいする conceal, cover up, hide

隠匿 いんとく concealment; misprision

蔽 ▷cover
ヘイ　　　　　　　　　　　Ⓚ2084

[original meaning] **cover, screen, shield, hide**
遮蔽 しゃへい shield, cover, screen; *elec* shielding
隠蔽する いんぺいする conceal, cover up, hide
掩蔽 えんぺい cover, obscuration
建蔽率 けんぺいりつ coverage, building coverage ratio

伏 ▷lie in concealment
フク ふ(せる) ふ(す)　　　　Ⓚ0030

lie in concealment, hide
伏兵 ふくへい ambush, troops in ambush
伏線 ふくせん preparation, foreshadow
雌伏 しふく remaining in obscurity, lying low, biding one's time
潜伏 せんぷく concealment, hiding; latency
埋伏歯 まいふくし impacted tooth

潜 ▷lurk
セン ひそ(む) もぐ(る)　　Ⓚ0680

lurk, hide, lie concealed; be latent
潜伏 せんぷく concealment, hiding; latency
潜入 せんにゅう infiltration
潜行する せんこうする travel in disguise; move [travel] under water
潜在の せんざいの latent, potential

匿 ▷conceal
トク　　　　　　　　　　　Ⓚ2594

[original meaning] **conceal, hide**
匿名 とくめい anonymity, incognito, pseudonym
隠匿 いんとく concealment; misprision
秘匿する ひとくする hide, conceal
蔵匿する ぞうとくする [rare] conceal, shelter, harbor

忍 ▷perform by stealth
ニン しの(ぶ) しの(ばせる)　Ⓚ1899

perform by stealth, practice the art of making oneself invisible
忍術 にんじゅつ art of making oneself invisible
忍法 にんぽう art of making oneself invisible
忍者 にんじゃ ancient spy who mastered *ninjutsu*

high[1]
高　喬　峻　峨

高 ▷high
コウ たか(い) たか -だか たか(まる) たか(める)　　　　　　　　　　Ⓚ180

(extending upward) **high, tall, lofty**
高度 こうど altitude, height; high degree
高山 こうざん high mountain, lofty peak
高地 こうち high ground, plateau, heights
高原 こうげん plateau, tableland, heights
高架線 こうかせん elevated railway; overhead wire
最高峰 さいこうほう highest peak; highest authority

喬 ▷tall
キョウ　　　　　　　　　　Ⓚ218

tall—said esp. of trees
喬木 きょうぼく tall tree, forest tree

峻 ▷high and steep
シュン　　　　　　　　　　Ⓚ037

(esp. of mountains) **high and steep, rising sharply, precipitous, towering, lofty**
峻険な しゅんけんな steep, precipitous
峻嶺 しゅんれい steep peak, high rugged mountain
急峻な きゅうしゅんな steep, sharp

峨 ▷high and rugged
ガ　　　　　　　　　　　　Ⓚ0371

high and rugged, precipitous
峨峨たる ががたる rugged, precipitous

high[2]
高　上　嵳

高 ▷high
コウ たか(い) たか -だか たか(まる) たか(める)　　　　　　　　　　Ⓚ1803

(extending upward) **high, tall, lofty**
高度 こうど altitude, height; high degree
高山 こうざん high mountain, lofty peak
高地 こうち high ground, plateau, heights
高原 こうげん plateau, tableland, heights
高架線 こうかせん elevated railway; overhead wires
最高峰 さいこうほう highest peak; highest authority

上 ▷upper
ジョウ ショウ うえ うわ- かみ あ(げる)
あ(がる) あ(がり) のぼ(る) のぼ(り)
のぼ(せる) のぼ(す)　　　Ⓚ2876

[also prefix] **upper, higher, outer**

上部 じょうぶ upper part [section], top; surface
上空 じょうくう skies, upper air
上記の じょうきの above-mentioned
上流 じょうりゅう upper stream (of a river); upper class
上皮 じょうひ outer skin, epidermis
上甲板 じょうかんぱん upper deck
上半身 じょうはんしん upper part of the body
以上 いじょう or more than, not less than; beyond; the above-mentioned; now that; that's all

崚 ▷lofty
リョウ　　　Ⓚ0429

[archaic] **as lofty as a steep mountain range**
崚層 りょうそう (of mountains) lofty, soaring

相 ▷minister
ソウ ショウ あい-　　　Ⓚ0808

[also suffix] **minister (of state), councilor**

首相 しゅしょう prime minister
蔵相 ぞうしょう Minister of Finance
文相 ぶんしょう Minister of Education, Science and Culture
外相 がいしょう Minister of Foreign Affairs
労働相 ろうどうしょう Minister of Labor

宰 ▷chief minister
サイ　　　Ⓚ1965

chief minister
宰相 さいしょう prime minister, chancellor

卿 ▷state minister
キョウ ケイ　　　Ⓚ0574

ⓐ [also suffix] **state minister, minister, peer, noble**
ⓑ courtesy title for noblemen and knighted persons of Britain: **Lord, Sir**

a 卿相 けいしょう top members of the imperial court
公卿 くぎょう(=こうけい、くげ) *hist* high-ranking court nobles
枢機卿 すうききょう(=すうきけい) (Catholic) cardinal
b ウィンストン卿 うぃんすとんきょう Sir Winston

貴 ▷noble
キ たっと(い) とうと(い) たっと(ぶ)
とうと(ぶ)　　　Ⓚ2260

ⓐ (of noble rank) **noble, high-ranking**
ⓑ (lofty in character) **noble, exalted, honorable, dignified**

a 貴族 きぞく nobility, noble
貴婦人 きふじん lady of rank, gentlewoman
b 富貴な ふうきな(=ふっきな) wealthy and noble
高貴な こうきな high and noble

上 ▷upper
ジョウ ショウ うえ うわ- かみ あ(げる)
あ(がる) あ(がり) のぼ(る) のぼ(り)
のぼ(せる) のぼ(す)　　　Ⓚ2876

(of higher rank or position) **upper, higher, superior, advanced**

上位 じょうい higher rank, precedence
上級 じょうきゅう higher grade, advanced class, high class
上官 じょうかん higher officer, senior
上院 じょういん Upper House
上人 しょうにん Buddhist saint

高 ▷high
コウ たか(い) たか -だか たか(まる)
たか(める)　　　Ⓚ1803

(elevated in rank or character) **high, noble, eminent, lofty**

高位 こうい high rank, honors
高官 こうかん high office, high official, dignitary
高貴な こうきな high and noble
高名 こうめい fame, high reputation; your name
高尚な こうしょうな high, noble, elegant
高潔な こうけつな noble, high-minded, upright

総 ▷general
ソウ　　　Ⓚ1261

[also prefix] (of highest or supreme rank) **general, -general, supreme, head, -in-chief**

総長 そうちょう president of a university, chancellor
総監 そうかん governor-general, inspector general
総裁 そうさい president, governor
総理 そうり president, prime minister
総統 そうとう sovereign, highest post of the government
総監督 そうかんとく general manager

総本山 そうほんざん sectarian headquarters temple
総領息子 そうりょうむすこ eldest son

太 ▷of highest rank
タイ タ ふと(い) ふと(る)   Ⓚial846

of highest rank, grand, great
太子 たいし crown prince
太閤 たいこう father of the imperial adviser; Toyotomi Hideyoshi
太守 たいしゅ governor general, viceroy
太夫 たゆう chief actor in a noh play; entertainer, courtesan
太祖 たいそ founder; first emperor (of a Chinese dynasty)

hills

丘 畝 岡 台 坂
阪 塚 阜 陵 稜

丘 ▷hill
キュウ おか   Ⓚ2931

[original meaning] hill
丘陵 きゅうりょう hill, hillock
砂丘 さきゅう sand dune, sand hill
段丘 だんきゅう terrace, bench (in geography)
円丘 えんきゅう knoll
火口丘 かこうきゅう volcanic cone

畝 ▷ridge
うね せ   Ⓚ1332

[original meaning] ridge, furrow; rib, cord (of textiles)
畝溝 うねみぞ furrow ridges
畝織 うねおり rep, ribbed fabric

岡 ▷hill
おか   Ⓚ2584

[archaic] hill
岡陵 こうりょう hill

台 ▷heights
ダイ タイ   Ⓚ1731

(elevated land structure) heights, hill, terrace, table-land
台地 だいち plateau, tableland
高台 たかだい high ground, hill, height

坂 ▷slope
ハン さか   Ⓚ0206

[original meaning] slope, incline, hill

急坂 きゅうはん steep hill [slope]
登坂 とはん climbing a slope [hill]

阪 ▷slope
ハン さか   Ⓚ024

[original meaning] slope, incline, hill

塚 ▷mound
つか -づか   Ⓚ050

mound, hillock, heap
塚を築く つかをきずく pile up a mound
蟻塚 ありづか anthill
貝塚 かいづか shell heap, shell mound; kitchen midden
一里塚 いちりづか milepost, milestone

阜 ▷mound
フ   Ⓚ228

[original meaning] mound
岐阜県 ぎふけん Gifu Prefecture
陰阜 いんふ mons pubis, mons veneris

陵 ▷high mound
リョウ みささぎ   Ⓚ049

[original meaning] high mound, hillock
丘陵 きゅうりょう hill, hillock
高陵土 こうりょうど kaolin, porcelain clay

稜 ▷ridge
リョウ ロウ   Ⓚ111()

ridge
稜線 りょうせん ridgeline

hinder →OBSTRUCT AND HINDER

history

史 伝 歴

史 ▷history
シ   Ⓚ294()

[also suffix] history, chronicles; history book
史料 しりょう historical materials [records]
史書 ししょ history book
史跡 しせき historic spot [remains]
史学者 しがくしゃ historian
史上に例を見ない しじょうにれいをみない be unparalleled in history
歴史 れきし history
青史 せいし history, history book
世界史 せかいし world history
日本史 にほんし Japanese history

伝 ▷**biography**
デン つた(わる) つた(える) つた(う)
-づた(い)   Ⓚ0029

[also suffix] **biography**
伝記 でんき biography
列伝 れつでん series of biographies
ナポレオン伝 なぽれおんでん life of Napoleon

歴 ▷**personal history**
レキ   Ⓚ2600

[also suffix] **personal history, one's career, experience, personal record**
履歴 りれき personal history, career
学歴 がくれき academic career
経歴 けいれき personal history
病歴 びょうれき case history
逮捕歴 たいほれき criminal record
一輪車歴 いちりんしゃれき one's experience as a
unicyclist

hold
持　提　携　捧

持 ▷**hold**
ジ も(つ) -も(ち) も(てる)   Ⓚ0333

[original meaning] **hold, grasp, have; have with one**
持参する じさんする bring [take] with one, carry
把持 はじ grasp, hold, grip
棒持する ほうじする hold up, bear, present
支持する しじする support, maintain, back up
所持する しょじする have (money) about one;
possess

提 ▷**carry in hand**
テイ チョウ さ(げる)   Ⓚ0540

carry in hand
提琴 ていきん violin
提灯 ちょうちん paper lantern

携 ▷**carry in hand**
ケイ たずさ(える) たずさ(わる)   Ⓚ0593

carry in hand, carry (along) on one's person
携帯する けいたいする carry, bring with one, equip
oneself with
携行する けいこうする carry along, bring
携帯カメラ けいたいかめら hand camera
必携 ひっけい indispensableness; handbook,
manual

捧 ▷**hold up in both hands**
ホウ ささ(げる) ささ(ぐ)   Ⓚ0447

offer respectfully
捧呈する ほうていする dedicate, present, offer (to a
high personage)

hold an event
催　挙

催 ▷**hold an event**
サイ もよお(す)   Ⓚ0136

hold an event [a meeting], give (a dinner), sponsor
催事場 さいじじょう event hall
開催する かいさいする hold an event, open (an
exhibition)
共催 きょうさい joint auspices, cosponsorship
主催 しゅさい sponsorship, promotion

挙 ▷**hold a function**
キョ あ(げる) あ(がる)   Ⓚ2169

hold a function, perform (a ceremony)
挙式 きょしき holding a ceremony
挙行する きょこうする hold, perform, celebrate

hold in the mind
持　抱　懐

持 ▷**hold**
ジ も(つ) -も(ち) も(てる)   Ⓚ0333

hold on to one's opinion, adhere to
持論 じろん pet theory
堅持する けんじする maintain firmly, hold fast to
固持する こじする persist in, adhere to

抱 ▷**hug**
ホウ だ(く) いだ(く) かか(える)   Ⓚ0271

(harbor a thought or feeling) **hug, cherish, entertain**
抱懐する ほうかいする harbor, cherish, entertain
抱負 ほうふ aspiration, ambition
辛抱 しんぼう patience, endurance, forbearance

懐 ▷**embosom**
カイ ふところ なつ(かしい) なつ(かしむ)
なつ(く) なつ(ける)   Ⓚ0689

(harbor a thought) **embosom, cherish, harbor**
懐疑 かいぎ doubt, skepticism, disbelief
抱懐する ほうかいする harbor, cherish, entertain

holes and cavities

穴 洞 窟 窪 腔 孔 口
坑 堀 溝 壕 濠 凹

穴 ▷hole
ケツ あな   Ⓚ1852

ⓐ hole, cavity
ⓑ counter for holes
ⓒ [original meaning] **cave, den**

  ₐ 穴隙 けつげき aperture, crevice
    墓穴 ぼけつ grave
  ᵦ 二穴 にけつ two holes
  ᵪ 穴居 けっきょ cave dwelling, troglodytism
    虎穴 こけつ tiger's den; dangerous place

洞 ▷cave
ドウ ほら   Ⓚ0340

[also suffix] [original meaning] **cave, cavern, grotto; cavity, tunnel**

  洞窟 どうくつ cavern, cave
  洞穴 どうけつ cave, den, excavation
  空洞 くうどう cave, cavern, hollow
  風洞 ふうどう wind tunnel
  鐘乳洞 しょうにゅうどう limestone cave [grotto]

窟 ▷cave
クツ   Ⓚ2032

[now also 屈] [original meaning] **cave, cavern, hole**

  洞窟 どうくつ cavern, cave
  岩窟王 がんくつおう The Count of Monte Cristo
  理窟 りくつ reason, logic; argument; pretext; theory

窪 ▷hollow
ワ くぼ くぼ(む) くぼ(まる)   Ⓚ2063

[original meaning] (of the ground) **become hollow, become depressed, cave in**

  窪下 わか [rare] depressed place, hollow; low and depressed

腔 ▷body cavity
コウ クウ   Ⓚ0917

ⓐ body cavity
ⓑ body

  ₐ 腔腸動物 こうちょうどうぶつ coelenterate
    口腔 こうくう(=こうこう) mouth, oral cavity
    腹腔 ふくくう(=ふくこう, ふっこう) abdominal cavity
    腹腔鏡 ふくくうきょう laparoscope
    滑腔砲 かっこうほう smoothbore
  ᵦ 満腔 まんこう heartfelt, wholehearted

孔 ▷open hole
コウ   Ⓚ015

[also suffix] **open or bottomless hole, opening, aperture**

  鼻孔 びこう nostrils
  気孔 きこう pore, stoma
  瞳孔 どうこう pupil
  穿孔 せんこう perforation, punching; rupture
  排水孔 はいすいこう scupper (hole); osculum

口 ▷mouth
コウ ク くち   Ⓚ286

[also suffix] (mouthlike opening) **mouth, opening, hole, aperture**

  口径 こうけい caliber, bore; diameter
  河口 かこう river mouth, estuary
  火口 かこう crater
  銃口 じゅうこう muzzle (of a rifle)
  排気口 はいきこう exhaust port
  突破口 とっぱこう breach, breakthrough

坑 ▷pit
コウ   Ⓚ0208

[original meaning] **pit, shaft**
  坑道 こうどう tunnel, pit; (mine) level; shaft

堀 ▷ditch
ほり   Ⓚ042

ditch, canal
  堀川 ほりかわ canal
  堀割り ほりわり canal, ditch
  用水堀 ようすいぼり irrigation ditch
  釣り堀 つりぼり fishing pond, fishpond

溝 ▷channel
コウ みぞ   Ⓚ0604

[original meaning] **channel, ditch, gutter, canal, trench**

  溝渠 こうきょ ditch, sewer, canal
  側溝 そっこう channel, ditch, gutter
  排水溝 はいすいこう waterway, drainage, canal
  下水溝 げすいこう ditch
  海溝 かいこう sea trench

壕 ▷trench
ゴウ ほり   Ⓚ0703

trench, dugout
  塹壕 ざんごう trench, dugout
  掩壕 えんごう cover trench
  防空壕 ぼうくうごう air-raid shelter

濠 ▷moat
ゴウ ほり

[original meaning] **moat**
環濠集落 かんごうしゅうらく moated settlement

凹 ▷concavity
オウ ぼこ   Ⓚ2924

[in compounds] **concavity**
凸凹 でこぼこ unevenness, roughness; imbalance
穴凹 あなぼこ hole, hollow

---

holiday
休   暇

休 ▷holiday
キュウ やす(む) やす(まる)
やす(める)   Ⓚ0037

abbrev. of 休暇 きゅうか or 休業 きゅうぎょう: **holiday, vacation, suspension of business, day off**
連休 れんきゅう consecutive holidays
週休 しゅうきゅう weekly holiday
定休 ていきゅう regular holiday
臨休 りんきゅう extra [special] holiday
産休 さんきゅう maternity leave

暇 ▷leave of absence
カ ひま   Ⓚ0923

leave of absence, vacation
賜暇 しか leave of absence, furlough
請暇 せいか request for leave of absence; leave of absence

---

holy
聖   神   霊

聖 ▷holy
セイ   Ⓚ2464

holy, sacred, divine
聖書 せいしょ Bible
聖霊 せいれい Holy Ghost, Holy Spirit
聖歌 せいか sacred song, hymn
聖域 せいいき holy [sacred] precincts, sanctuary
聖火 せいか sacred fire [torch]
神聖な しんせいな holy, sacred, divine

神 ▷divine
シン ジン かみ かん- こう-   Ⓚ0821

divine, sacred, godly, supernatural, mysterious
神聖な しんせいな holy, sacred, divine
神話 しんわ myth, mythology
神木 しんぼく sacred tree
神童 しんどう child prodigy
神秘的な しんぴてきな mysterious

霊 ▷miraculous
レイ リョウ たま   Ⓚ2442

miraculous, sacred, divine
霊場 れいじょう holy ground, sacred place
霊峰 れいほう sacred mountain
霊験 れいげん(=れいけん) miracle, miraculous virtue
霊感 れいかん inspiration, extrasensory perception
霊水 れいすい miracle-working water
霊妙な れいみょうな miraculous, wonderful

---

honorific prefixes
御   貴   尊   令

御 ▷general honorific term
ギョ ゴ おん- お-   Ⓚ0529

[also prefix] **general honorific term for conveying respect**
御用 ごよう your order, your business
御飯 ごはん boiled rice; meal
御存じの方 ごぞんじのかた your acquaintance
御意 ぎょい your will, your pleasure
御馳走 ごちそう feast, treat
御成功 ごせいこう your success
御両親 ごりょうしん your (honorable) parents
御自身 ごじしん yourself; himself, herself

貴 ▷your honorable
キ たっと(い) とうと(い) たっと(ぶ)
とうと(ぶ)   Ⓚ2260

[also prefix] [honorific] **your honorable, your, your esteemed**
貴社 きしゃ your company
貴翰 きかん your letter

尊 ▷your honorable
ソン たっと(い) とうと(い) たっと(ぶ)
とうと(ぶ)   Ⓚ2029

[honorific] **your honorable, your**
尊顔 そんがん your countenance
尊父 そんぷ your father
尊宅 そんたく your house

令 ▷your honorable
レイ ⓚ1725

[also prefix] [honorific] **your honorable**
令嬢 れいじょう daughter; young lady
令夫人 れいふじん Mrs., madam, your wife

honorific suffixes
翁 老

翁 ▷honorific suffix
オウ ⓚ1809

honorific suffix after names of venerable old men
吉田翁 よしだおう the venerable Mr. Yoshida, old
Mr. Yoshida

老 ▷honorific suffix
ロウ お(いる) ふ(ける) ⓚ2754

honorific suffix after names of old men
野村老 のむらろう old Mr. Nomura

horse
馬 駒 駿 午

馬 ▷horse
バ うま ⓚ2809

[also suffix] [original meaning] **horse**
馬車 ばしゃ horse-drawn carriage, coach, wagon
馬力 ばりき horsepower; energy, effort; cart,
wagon
馬身 ばしん horse's length
馬肉 ばにく horsemeat
乗馬 じょうば horse riding
競馬 けいば horse racing
竹馬の友 ちくばのとも childhood friend, old play-
mate
関西馬 かんさいば Kansai horse

駒 ▷horse (*elegant*)
こま ⓚ1623

ⓐ *elegant* **horse, colt**
ⓑ [original meaning] **pony, small horse**
ⓐ 駒座 こまざ Equuleus
駒鳥 こまどり robin
当歳駒 とうさいごま one year-old colt, yearling

駿 ▷fleet steed
シュン スン ⓚ1627

[original meaning] **fleet steed, swift horse, fine horse**

駿馬 しゅんば(=しゅんめ) fleet steed, fine horse

午 ▷the Horse
ゴ ⓚ1720

seventh sign of the Oriental zodiac: **the Horse**—(time)
11 a.m.-1 p.m., (direction) south, (season) May (of the lunar
calendar)
子午線 しごせん meridian
端午 たんご festival on the 5th of May (of the lunar
calendar)

hot
熱 暑 炎 温 暖

熱 ▷hot
ネツ あつ(い) ⓚ2495

[original meaning] **hot, boiling**
熱湯 ねっとう boiling water
熱帯 ねったい tropics, torrid zone
熱気 ねっき hot air, heat; fevered air, enthusiasm
灼熱 しゃくねつ heat

暑 ▷hot (weather)
ショ あつ(い) ⓚ2182

hot (weather), warm, sultry
暑さ あつさ heat, summer heat, hot weather
真夏の暑さ まなつのあつさ heat of high summer
蒸し暑い むしあつい sultry, sweltering

炎 ▷scorching
エン ほのお ⓚ2145

(hot like a flame) **scorching, sweltering, burning hot**
炎暑 えんしょ scorching heat of summer
炎天下で えんてんかで under the blazing sun
炎熱 えんねつ scorching weather, extreme heat

温 ▷warm
オン あたた(か) あたた(かい)
あたた(まる) あたた(める) ⓚ0554

[also prefix] **warm, hot, temperate**
温暖な おんだんな warm, mild
温泉 おんせん hot spring
温水プール おんすいぷーる heated swimming pool
温室 おんしつ greenhouse
温度 おんど temperature
温和な おんわな (of the weather) mild, temperate
温湿布 おんしっぷ hot compress
温帯 おんたい temperate zone

暖 ▷warm (esp. weather)
ダン ノン あたた(か) あたた(かい)
あたた(まる) あたた(める) Ⓚ0922

warm (esp. weather), mild, genial, temperate
- 暖流 だんりゅう warm current
- 暖地 だんち warm district, region of mild climate
- 暖冬 だんとう mild winter
- 暖衣飽食 だんいほうしょく warm clothes and plenty to eat
- 温暖な おんだんな warm, mild

ⱶouses →COUNTERS FOR HOUSES

houses
家 屋 軒 戸 宅
居 邸 住 庵

家 ▷house

カ ケ いえ や うち Ⓚ1963

[original meaning] **house, home, dwelling**
- 家屋 かおく house, building
- 家具 かぐ furniture
- 人家 じんか dwelling (house), human habitation
- 民家 みんか private house

屋 ▷house
オク や Ⓚ2669

house, building
- 屋外 おくがい outdoors, open air, exterior of a house
- 屋内 おくない indoors
- 家屋 かおく house, building
- 社屋 しゃおく office building
- 廃屋 はいおく deserted house

軒 ▷house

ケン のき Ⓚ1328

house
- 軒別に けんべつに house to house

戸 ▷household

コ と Ⓚ1691

(house as a social unit) **household, house, family**
- 戸別に こべつに from house to house
- 戸戸 ここ every [each] house
- 戸籍 こせき family register
- 戸主 こしゅ head of a family, master of a house
- 戸数 こすう number of households [houses]

宅 ▷dwelling house
タク Ⓚ1862

[also suffix] (house where one lives) **dwelling house, home, abode, house, residence**
- 宅地 たくち land for housing, residential land
- お宅 おたく your home, your house; you
- 帰宅 きたく homecoming
- 自宅 じたく one's house, one's home
- 拙宅 せったく my home, my humble abode
- 住宅 じゅうたく housing, dwelling house, residence
- 社宅 しゃたく company house
- 邸宅 ていたく residence, mansion
- 横江氏宅 よこえしたく residence of Mr. Yokoe

居 ▷residence
キョ い(る) -い お(る) Ⓚ2653

residence, dwelling, address
- 住居 じゅうきょ house, dwelling, residence
- 皇居 こうきょ Imperial Palace
- 入居する にゅうきょする move into (a flat)
- 転居する てんきょする move, change one's residence

邸 ▷stately residence
テイ Ⓚ1045

ⓐ **stately residence, mansion, official residence, villa, house**
ⓑ **suffix for forming names of residences or mansions**
ⓒ [original meaning, now obsolete] **residence where feudal lords used to lodge when in the capital**

a
- 邸宅 ていたく residence, mansion
- 公邸 こうてい official residence
- 官邸 かんてい official residence
- 私邸 してい one's private residence
- 別邸 べってい villa, country residence

b
- 徳川公爵邸 とくがわこうしゃくてい mansion of Prince Tokugawa
- 山本氏邸 やまもとしてい Mr. Yamamoto's residence

住 ▷housing
ジュウ す(む) す(まう) -ず(まい) Ⓚ0047

housing, residence, house, dwelling
- 住宅 じゅうたく housing, dwelling house, residence
- 住宅地 じゅうたくち residential district
- 公住 こうじゅう apartment house built by the Japan Housing Corporation
- 衣食住 いしょくじゅう food, clothing and shelter, the necessities of life

庵 ▷hermitage

アン いおり Ⓚ2692

hermitage, retreat

庵主 あんしゅ owner of a hermitage; abbess, prioress, nun in charge of a Buddhist convent
庵室 あんしつ hermit's cell, retreat
沢庵(=沢庵漬け) たくあん(=たくあんづけ) pickled daikon [Japanese radish]
草庵 そうあん thatched hut
僧庵 そうあん priest's hermitage

how many
幾　　　何

幾 ▷**how many**
キ いく- いく(つ) いく(ら)　　Ⓚ2999

how many, how much
幾何(学) きか(がく) geometry

何 ▷**how many**
カ なに- なん-　　Ⓚ0048

how many
何度 なんど how many degrees; how many times
何人 なんにん how many people

huge →BIG AND HUGE

humble
謙　　遜　　　拝

謙 ▷**humble**
ケン　　Ⓚ1461

humble, modest
謙遜 けんそん humility, modesty
謙虚な けんきょな humble, modest
謙譲 けんじょう modesty, humility

遜 ▷**humble**
ソン　　Ⓚ2786

humble, modest
謙遜 けんそん humility, modesty
不遜 ふそん arrogance, insolence

拝 ▷**humbly**
ハイ おが(む)　　Ⓚ0268

humbly, respectfully, reverentially—honorific term expressing humility in reference to an action of the speaker
拝見する はいけんする have the honor of seeing, see, look at, inspect
拝借する はいしゃくする borrow
拝聴する はいちょうする listen attentively [respectfully]

拝受する はいじゅする receive [accept] (humbly)

humble prefixes
小　弊　拙　愚

小 ▷**my little (humble)**
ショウ ちい(さい) こ- お-　　Ⓚ000

[humble] **my little, my humble, our humble**
小生 しょうせいⅠ
小社 しょうしゃ my company; little shrine
小店 しょうてん my little shop

弊 ▷**our [my] humble**
ヘイ　　Ⓚ250

[humble] **our [my] humble**
弊社 へいしゃ our firm
弊店 へいてん our shop

拙 ▷**my humble**
セツ つたな(い)　　Ⓚ028

[humble] **my humble, my poor**
拙者 せっしゃⅠ
拙宅 せったく my home, my humble abode

愚 ▷**my foolish**
グ おろ(か)　　Ⓚ246

[humble] **my foolish, my humble**
愚息 ぐそく my (foolish) son
愚妻 ぐさい my (foolish) wife
愚案 ぐあん my humble opinion, my (foolish) plan

hunger and thirst
渇　餓　飢　饉

渇 ▷**thirst**
カツ かわ(く)　　Ⓚ047

thirst, be thirsty; thirst
渇死する かっしする [archaic] die of thirst
飢渇 きかつ hunger and thirst

餓 ▷**starved**
ガ　　Ⓚ154

[original meaning] **starved, hungry**
餓死 がし death from starvation
餓鬼 がき hungry ghost; *slang* kid
飢餓 きが starvation, hunger, famine

飢 ▷**starve**
キ う(える)　Ⓚ1490

[original meaning] **starve, be hungry, famish**
飢餓 きが starvation, hunger, famine
飢民 きみん starving people
飢渇 きかつ hunger and thirst

饑 ▷**starve**
キ

[original meaning] **starve, be hungry, famish**
饑餓 きが starvation, hunger, famine
饑渇 きかつ hunger and thirst

hunt and fish
猟　狩　獲　漁　釣　弋

猟 ▷**hunting**
リョウ　Ⓚ0491

[original meaning] **hunting, shooting**
猟季 りょうき hunting season
猟銃 りょうじゅう hunting gun
猟犬 りょうけん hound, hunting dog
狩猟 しゅりょう hunting, hunt
銃猟 じゅうりょう shooting, hunting
禁猟 きんりょう prohibition of shooting [hunting]

狩 ▷**hunt**
シュ か(る) か(り) -が(り)　Ⓚ0356

[original meaning] **hunt**
狩猟 しゅりょう hunting, hunt
狩猟期 しゅりょうき hunting season

獲 ▷**catch game**
カク え(る)　Ⓚ0699

[original meaning] **catch game, fish, hunt, capture**
漁獲 ぎょかく fishing; haul [catch] (of fish)
捕獲する ほかくする catch (fish); capture (a ship), seize
乱獲 らんかく reckless fishing, excessive hunting
収獲 しゅうかく game; (good) result
鹵獲する ろかくする capture, seize, plunder

漁 ▷**fish**
ギョ リョウ　Ⓚ0631

ⓐ [original meaning] **fish, angle**
ⓑ [also suffix] **fishing, fishery**
ⓐ 漁業 ぎょぎょう fishing industry
漁船 ぎょせん fishing boat
漁獲 ぎょかく fishing; haul [catch] (of fish)
漁場 ぎょじょう fishing ground, fishery

漁師 りょうし fisherman
ⓑ 禁漁 きんりょう prohibition of fishing
出漁する しゅつりょうする go (off) fishing
鮭漁 さけりょう salmon fishing
延縄漁 はえなわりょう longline fishing

釣 ▷**angle**
チョウ つ(る) つ(り)　Ⓚ1496

【チョウ】
[original meaning] **angle, fish**
釣魚 ちょうぎょ fishing, angling
釣果 ちょうか catch, haul
【つ(る)】
angle, fish
釣り上げる つりあげる fish up, land

弋 ▷**catch**
ヨク

catch, capture
遊弋する ゆうよくする cruise, patrol

hurry
急　　促

急 ▷**hurry**
キュウ いそ(ぐ) いそ(ぎ)　Ⓚ1800

hurry, hasten
急造 きゅうぞう hurried construction
急派する きゅうはする dispatch, expedite, rush
急行 きゅうこう express train [bus]; going in a hurry

促 ▷**hasten**
ソク うなが(す)　Ⓚ0087

(cause to act with haste) **hasten, urge, hurry, press (for)**
促進する そくしんする promote, spur on, facilitate
促成 そくせい growth promotion
催促する さいそくする press for, urge, demand
督促状 とくそくじょう demand note, dunning letter [note]

husband
夫　　主

夫 ▷**husband**
フ フウ ブ おっと　Ⓚ2909

husband
夫婦 ふうふ husband and wife, married couple

夫妻 ふさい husband and wife, Mr. and Mrs., married couple
夫人 ふじん wife, married lady, Mrs.
前夫 ぜんぷ former husband, ex-husband

主 ▷master of the house
シュ ス ぬし おも あるじ Ⓚ1696

master of the house, head of a family, husband

主客 しゅきゃく host and guest; principal and auxiliary; main guest
主婦 しゅふ housewife
戸主 こしゅ head of a family, master of a house
亭主 ていしゅ husband; master, host

illusory mental images
夢　　幻

夢 ▷dream
ム ゆめ Ⓚ2046

[original meaning] **dream**

夢想 むそう dream, vision; daydream
夢想家 むそうか dreamer
夢幻 むげん dream; vision; fantasy
夢中で むちゅうで like one in a dream; like one dazed; frantically
悪夢 あくむ nightmare, bad dream
白昼夢 はくちゅうむ waking dream
迷夢 めいむ illusion, delusion, fallacy

幻 ▷phantom
ゲン まぼろし Ⓚ0159

phantom, phantasm, fantasy, illusion, hallucination, vision

幻像 げんぞう phantom, vision, illusion
幻肢 げんし phantom limb
幻影 げんえい vision, phantom, illusion
幻想 げんそう fantasy, illusion
幻覚 げんかく illusion, hallucination
幻聴 げんちょう auditory hallucination
幻滅 げんめつ disillusionment
変幻自在の へんげんじざいの ever-changing, phantasmagoric

image
像　　影

像 ▷image
ゾウ Ⓚ0144

optical image

影像 えいぞう image; shadow, phantom
映像 えいぞう (TV) picture, image; reflection
画像 がぞう portrait, likeness
現像する げんぞうする develop (film)
実像 じつぞう real image
虚像 きょぞう virtual image

影 ▷shadow
エイ かげ Ⓚ1671

(reflected image) **shadow, image, reflection**

影像 えいぞう image; shadow, phantom
人影 じんえい human figure; shadow of a person
投影 とうえい cast shadow; projection
倒影 とうえい inverted image
撮影 さつえい photographing, shooting (of a movie)

images
像　仏　偶

像 ▷image
ゾウ Ⓚ0144

[also suffix] (sculptured or painted likeness) **image, likeness, figure, statue; picture, portrait**

仏像 ぶつぞう image of Buddha; Buddhist statue
肖像 しょうぞう portrait, likeness
マリア像 まりあぞう image of the Virgin Mary
銅像 どうぞう bronze statue [image]
自画像 じがぞう self-portrait

仏 ▷Buddhist image
ブツ フツ ほとけ Ⓚ0010

[also suffix] **Buddhist image**

仏像 ぶつぞう image of Buddha; Buddhist statue
仏壇 ぶつだん family Buddhist altar
石仏 せきぶつ stone Buddhist image
三尊仏 さんぞんぶつ image of the three honorable ones
大仏 だいぶつ great statue of Buddha

偶 ▷**figure**
グウ Ⓚ0115

[original meaning] (wooden) **figure, idol, image**
偶像 ぐうぞう idol, image
土偶 どぐう earthen [clay] figure

象 ▷**represent**
ショウ ゾウ Ⓚ1831

represent, symbolize
象徴する しょうちょうする symbolize
象形文字 しょうけいもじ hieroglyph, pictograph

imitate
擬 倣 摸 模 肖 象

immediate
即　直　忽

擬 ▷**imitate**
ギ Ⓚ0706

[original meaning] **imitate, copy, mimic, model after**
擬装 ぎそう camouflage, disguise
擬似 ぎじ false, dummy, pseudo
擬声語 ぎせいご onomatopoeic word
擬人 ぎじん personification, impersonation
擬製 ぎせい imitation, forgery
模擬の もぎの imitation, sham, mock, simulated

倣 ▷**copy after**
ホウ なら(う) Ⓚ0095

copy after, copy from, imitate
模倣(=摸倣)する もほうする imitate, copy

摸 ▷**pattern after**
モ モウ

[now replaced by 模] **pattern after, imitate, copy, model upon**
摸写する もしゃする copy, trace, reproduce
摸倣する もほうする imitate, copy
摸造 もぞう imitation, counterfeit
摸擬試験 もぎしけん sham [trial] examination

模 ▷**pattern after**
モ ボ Ⓚ0963

[formerly also 摸] **pattern after, imitate, copy, model upon**
模造 もぞう imitation, counterfeit
模擬の もぎの imitation, sham, mock, simulated
模擬試験 もぎしけん mock examination
模倣する もほうする imitate, copy
模写する もしゃする copy, trace, reproduce

肖 ▷**model**
ショウ Ⓚ1887

[original meaning] (make a model of) **model, imitate**
肖像 しょうぞう portrait, likeness

即 ▷**immediate**
ソク すなわ(ち) Ⓚ1036

immediate, prompt, instant, on the spot
即死 そくし instant death, death on the spot
即売 そくばい sale on the spot, spot sale
即時 そくじ immediately, promptly
即刻 そっこく immediately, instantly
即座に そくざに immediately, promptly, at once
即効 そっこう immediate effect
即答 そくとう prompt answer
即金 そっきん immediate cash, ready cash
一触即発 いっしょくそくはつ touch-and-go situation, hair-trigger crisis

直 ▷**straight away**
チョク ジキ ジカ ただ(ちに) なお(す)
なお(る) なお(き) す(ぐ) Ⓚ2539

straight away, immediately
直後 ちょくご immediately after
直答 ちょくとう prompt answer; direct answer
直答 じきとう direct answer
直流 ちょくりゅう direct current
直通 ちょくつう direct communication [service]; through service [traffic]
直感 ちょっかん intuition
直前に ちょくぜんに just [immediately] before
直列 ちょくれつ *elec* (in) series
直観 ちょっかん intuition

忽 ▷**in an instant**
コツ たちま(ち) ゆるが(せ) Ⓚ2149

in an instant, immediately, all of a sudden
忽然と こつぜん(=こつねん)と suddenly; unexpectedly

impartial
公　平

公 ▷impartial
コウ おおやけ　　　　　　　　Ⓚ1715

impartial, fair, unbiased, just
公明 こうめい fairness, justice
公正 こうせい justice, fairness, impartiality
公平 こうへい impartiality, fairness

平 ▷equal
ヘイ ビョウ たい(ら) -だいら
ひら　　　　　　　　　　　　Ⓚ2921

equal, impartial, fair
平均 へいきん average, (arithmetical) mean; equilib-
　rium, balance
平行 へいこう parallelism, parallel; going side by
　side; occurring together
平等 びょうどう equality, impartiality
公平 こうへい impartiality, fairness

impatient
焦　躁　燥

焦 ▷be impatient
ショウ こ(げる) こ(がす) こ(がれる)
あせ(る)　　　　　　　　　　Ⓚ2412

be impatient, be too eager, burn to do something
焦燥 しょうそう fretfulness, impatience
焦慮 しょうりょ impatience; worry
焦心 しょうしん impatience

躁 ▷restless
ソウ

[now also 燥] [original meaning] **restless, impatient,
rash, impetuous**
躁病 そうびょう mania
躁鬱病 そううつびょう manic-depressive psychosis
狂躁(=狂騒) きょうそう wild excitement
焦躁 しょうそう fretfulness, impatience

燥 ▷restless
ソウ　　　　　　　　　　　　Ⓚ1009

[formerly 躁] **restless, impatient, rash, impetuous**
焦燥 しょうそう fretfulness, impatience

imperial decree
勅　詔　宣

勅 ▷imperial decree
チョク　　　　　　　　　　　Ⓚ1319

imperial [royal] decree, imperial order [edict]
勅宣 ちょくせん imperial decree
勅語 ちょくご imperial rescript
詔勅 しょうちょく imperial edict
神勅 しんちょく oracle

詔 ▷imperial edict
ショウ みことのり　　　　　　Ⓚ1366

[original meaning] **imperial edict, imperial rescript**
詔令 しょうれい imperial edict
詔勅 しょうちょく imperial edict
詔書 しょうしょ imperial edict
大詔 たいしょう imperial rescript [mandate]

宣 ▷imperial proclamation
セン　　　　　　　　　　　　Ⓚ1940

imperial proclamation, imperial edict
宣下 せんげ imperial proclamation
院宣 いんぜん imperial command [decree]

important
要　重

要 ▷important
ヨウ かなめ い(る)　　　　　Ⓚ2290

important, essential, principal, leading
要約 ようやく summary, abridged statement
要素 ようそ (essential) element, constituent, factor
要因 よういん primary factor, main cause
要件 ようけん important matter; necessary condi-
　tion
要点 ようてん main [essential] point, gist
要談 ようだん important talk
要所 ようしょ important point; strategic position
重要な じゅうような important, essential, principal
主要な しゅような main, principal, essential
枢要な すうような pivotal, cardinal
肝要な かんような important, vital, essential, neces-
　sary
不要(=不用)な ふような unnecessary, useless;
　disused, waste

重 ▷heavy
ジュウ チョウ え おも(い) おも(り)
かさ(ねる) かさ(なる) Ⓚ2991

(great in importance) **heavy, weighty, important, grave**

重要な じゅうような important, essential, principal
重点 じゅうてん important point; importance, emphasis, stress; priority
重大な じゅうだいな important, serious, grave
重視する じゅうしする attach importance to, think much of
重任 じゅうにん heavy responsibility, important duty; reappointment
重宝 ちょうほう convenience, usefulness, handiness
重文(=重要文化財) じゅうぶん(=じゅうようぶんかざい) important cultural property; compound sentence
貴重な きちょうな precious, valuable

impose
徴 課

徴 ▷levy
チョウ Ⓚ0622

(collect taxes or payment) **levy, collect, impose**

徴収する ちょうしゅうする collect taxes [payment]
徴税 ちょうぜい tax collection
追徴する ついちょうする collect in addition
課徴金 かちょうきん surcharge (on imports)

課 ▷impose
カ Ⓚ1423

impose, levy

課題 かだい task, assignment; problem
課税 かぜい taxation
課徴金 かちょうきん surcharge (on imports)
賦課 ふか levy, imposition, assessment

imprison and confine
拘 禁 留 置 錮

拘 ▷arrest
コウ かか(わる) Ⓚ0274

[sometimes also 勾] [original meaning] **arrest, detain, confine**

拘留 こうりゅう penal detention up to 30 days
拘禁する こうきんする detain, confine, imprison
拘置 こうち detention, confinement, arrest
拘束 こうそく restriction, restraint, binding
拘引 こういん arrest, custody

禁 ▷confine
キン Ⓚ2435

confine, imprison

禁固 きんこ imprisonment
監禁する かんきんする imprison, confine
拘禁 こうきん detention, confinement, imprisonment

留 ▷keep in custody
リュウ ル と(める) -ど(め) と(まる)
とど(まる) Ⓚ2235

keep in custody, detain

留置 りゅうち detention, custody, retention
抑留する よくりゅうする detain, intern, seize, arrest

置 ▷place in custody
チ お(く) -お(き) Ⓚ2262

place in custody, detain

留置 りゅうち detention, custody, retention
拘置する こうちする detain, confine, arrest

錮 ▷imprison
コ Ⓚ1550

[now also 固] **imprison, hold in custody**

禁錮 きんこ imprisonment

incident
事 故 変

事 ▷affair
ジ ズ こと Ⓚ2986

【ジ ズ】
(something that occurs) **affair, something, event, occurrence, incident, unexpected event, accident**

事件 じけん affair, incident, case, event
事故 じこ accident, incident, trouble
事情 じじょう circumstances, conditions, situation
事態 じたい situation, state of affairs
無事に ぶじに safely, without accident, successfully; peacefully, amicably
火事 かじ fire
好事家 こうずか dilettante, person of fantastic taste
関心事 かんしんじ matter of concern and interest

【こと】

(event of special import) **affair, something, incident, case, occurrence; trouble**

事を起こす ことをおこす cause trouble [a disturbance]

事勿れ主義 ことなかれしゅぎ peace-at-any-price principle

どんな事にも準備が出来ている どんなことにもじゅんびができている be ready for any contingency

大変な事が起こった たいへんなことがおこった A terrible accident occurred

出来事 できごと occurrence, happening; affair, incident; accident

故 ▷incident
コ ゆえ ⓚ1056

incident, affair, event, occurrence

故障 こしょう malfunction, breakdown; physical disorder; hindrance, obstacle, accident; objection, protest

事故 じこ accident, incident, trouble

世故 せこ worldly affairs

変 ▷unexpected event
ヘン か(わる) か(わり) か(える) ⓚ1782

unexpected event [incident], extraordinary phenomenon, accident, disaster, emergency

変事 へんじ accident, emergency

変死 へんし accidental [unnatural] death

異変 いへん accident, extraordinary event

天変地異 てんぺんちい extraordinary natural phenomenon

大変な たいへんな awful, terrible; serious, grave

---

incite

挑　唆　扇　煽　激
奮　振　動　起

挑 ▷provoke
チョウ いど(む) ⓚ0331

[original meaning] **provoke, arouse, instigate, stir up, challenge**

挑戦 ちょうせん challenge, defiance

挑発する ちょうはつする provoke, incite, excite, stimulate

唆 ▷instigate
サ そそのか(す) ⓚ0361

[original meaning] **instigate, incite, abet**

教唆 きょうさ instigation, incitement

示唆する しさする suggest, hint

扇 ▷fan
セン おうぎ ⓚ170◦

[formerly also 煽] (move to action) **fan, stir up, instigate**

扇動する せんどうする instigate, agitate

扇情的な せんじょうてきな inflammatory, lasciviou◦

煽 ▷fan
セン あお(る) おだ(てる) あお(ぐ)

[now usu. 扇] (move to action) **fan, stir up, instigate**

煽動する せんどうする instigate, agitate

煽情的な せんじょうてきな inflammatory, lasciviou◦

激 ▷excite
ゲキ はげ(しい) ⓚ069◦

[formerly also 戟] **excite, stimulate, stir up**

激励 げきれい encouragement

感激する かんげきする be deeply moved

憤激する ふんげきする be inflamed by anger, flare up

刺激する しげきする stimulate, excite

奮 ▷rouse up
フン ふる(う) ⓚ209◦

rouse up, rouse oneself (to action), be stirred up, be stimulated, be enlivened

奮起する ふんきする rouse [bestir] oneself, rise (to the occasion)

発奮(=発憤)する はっぷんする be stimulated, be inspired, be roused

感奮する かんぷんする be inspired, be moved to action

振 ▷arouse to action
シン ふ(る) ぶ(る) ふ(り) -ぶ(り) ふ(るう) ふ(れる) ⓚ038◦

arouse to action, rouse up

振作する しんさくする promote, enhance, stimulate

動 ▷move
ドウ うご(く) うご(かす) ⓚ1583

move to action, arouse, stir

動員する どういんする mobilize (an army)

動機 どうき motive, incentive

出動する しゅつどうする take the field, be dispatched, turn out

扇動する せんどうする instigate, agitate

発動する はつどうする exercise, invoke; move, put in motion

起 ▷rise to action
キ　お(きる)　お(こる)　お(こす)　　　Ⓚ2818

rise [rouse oneself] to action, spring up, be stirred up
- 奮起する　ふんきする　rouse [bestir] oneself, rise (to the occasion)
- 決起する　けっきする　rise to action, spring up
- 再起　さいき　comeback, recovery, restoration

inclining →OBLIQUENESS AND INCLINING

inclining toward
偏　傾

偏 ▷one-sided
ヘン　かたよ(る)　　　Ⓚ0116

(favoring one side) one-sided, biased, partial, unfair, prejudiced
- 偏執狂　へんしつきょう(=へんしゅうきょう)　monomaniac
- 偏見　へんけん　prejudice, biased view, narrow view
- 偏重する　へんちょうする　attach too much importance, overemphasize
- 偏愛　へんあい　partiality, favoritism

傾 ▷incline toward
ケイ　かたむ(く)　かたむ(ける)
かし(げる)　　　Ⓚ0132

incline toward, be inclined to, tend to, lean to
- 傾向　けいこう　tendency, trend; disposition
- 左傾　さけい　tendency [inclination] to the left
- 右傾する　うけいする　lean to the right

include →CONTAIN AND INCLUDE

increase
加　増　殖　倍

加 ▷add to
カ　くわ(える)　くわ(わる)　　　Ⓚ0024

add to, increase
- 追加する　ついかする　add, append, supplement
- 増加　ぞうか　increase, gain, rise

増 ▷increase
ゾウ　ま(す)　ま(し)　ふ(える)
ふ(やす)　　　Ⓚ0619

ⓐ [original meaning] (grow or cause to grow in quantity or number) increase, multiply, augment

ⓑ [also suffix] increase, rise
- ⓐ 増加する　ぞうかする　increase, multiply, rise
  - 増産　ぞうさん　production increase
  - 増税　ぞうぜい　tax increase
  - 増員する　ぞういんする　increase the staff [personnel]
  - 増進する　ぞうしんする　promote, improve, advance
  - 増幅　ぞうふく　amplification
  - 増大する　ぞうだいする　increase, enlarge, enhance
- ⓑ 増減　ぞうげん　increase and decrease, rise and fall
  - 急増　きゅうぞう　sudden [rapid] increase
  - 自然増　しぜんぞう　natural increase

殖 ▷multiply
ショク　ふ(える)　ふ(やす)　　　Ⓚ0907

(increase the quantity of, esp. wealth) multiply, increase, make (money)
- 殖産　しょくさん　increase of production; enhancement of one's fortune
- 利殖　りしょく　moneymaking

倍 ▷double
バイ　　　Ⓚ0090

double, multiply, increase
- 倍大　ばいだい　double size

indicate
指　示　標　宛

指 ▷point
シ　ゆび　さ(す)　-さ(し)　　　Ⓚ0337

point (to), point out, indicate, show
- 指定する　していする　designate, appoint
- 指示する　しじする　instruct, point out; indicate, point to
- 指摘する　してきする　point out
- 指数　しすう　index (number); exponent
- 指名する　しめいする　nominate, designate, name

示 ▷show
ジ　シ　しめ(す)　　　Ⓚ1694

(point out) show, indicate, suggest, instruct
- 示唆　しさ　suggestion, hint
- 示談　じだん　out-of-court [private] settlement
- 示威　じい　show of force
- 示達　じたつ(=したつ)　instructions, directions
- 指示　しじ　instruction; indication
- 暗示　あんじ　hint, suggestion
- 誇示する　こじする　make a display of, show off
- 啓示　けいじ　revelation
- 訓示　くんじ　instruction

教示 きょうじ instruction, teaching

標 ▷mark
ヒョウ   Ⓚ0976

mark, indicate, designate
標示する ひょうじする post up, declare, demonstrate
標語 ひょうご slogan, motto, catch word
標本 ひょうほん specimen, sample
標高 ひょうこう elevation, (height) above the sea
標記する ひょうきする mark; write a title
標題 ひょうだい title, headline, caption

宛 ▷address
エン あ(てる) –あ(て)   Ⓚ1908

address (a letter), direct
宛て先 あてさき destination, address
宛名 あてな address
手紙を宛てる てがみをあてる address [direct] a letter to a person

industry and business
業 商 産 工

業 ▷business, industry
ギョウ ゴウ わざ   Ⓚ2265

❶ [also suffix] **business, trade, enterprise**
業務 ぎょうむ business, affairs, work, service
業者 ぎょうしゃ the trade, businessman
開業する かいぎょうする start a business, open a practice
商業 しょうぎょう commerce, trade, business
営業 えいぎょう business, trade
兼業 けんぎょう side business
事業 じぎょう undertaking, enterprise, business; achievement
企業 きぎょう undertaking, enterprise; business enterprise, company
印刷業 いんさつぎょう printing business
❷ [also suffix] **industry**
業界 ぎょうかい industry, business world
業種 ぎょうしゅ type of industry, category of business
産業 さんぎょう industry
工業 こうぎょう industry, manufacturing industry
農業 のうぎょう agriculture
鉱業 こうぎょう mining (industry)
興業 こうぎょう promotion of industry
製造業 せいぞうぎょう manufacturing industry

商 ▷trade
ショウ あきな(う)   Ⓚ1818

trade, commerce, business; sales
商談 しょうだん business talk; negotiations
通商 つうしょう commerce, trade, commercial relation [intercourse]
行商 ぎょうしょう itinerant trade, peddling
月商 げっしょう monthly sales

産 ▷industry
サン う(む) う(まれる) うぶ-   Ⓚ2812

abbrev. of 産業 さんぎょう: **industry**
産別会議 さんべつかいぎ Congress of Industrial Organizations (CIO)
通産省 つうさんしょう Ministry of International Trade and Industry

工 ▷manufacturing industry
コウ ク   Ⓚ2866

abbrev. of 工業 こうぎょう: **manufacturing industry**
商工 しょうこう commerce and industry
重工 じゅうこう heavy industry

inexpensive
安 廉 低

安 ▷inexpensive
アン やす(い) やす やす(らか)   Ⓚ1859

inexpensive, cheap
安価 あんか low price
安直な あんちょくな cheap, inexpensive; easy, simple

廉 ▷cheap
レン   Ⓚ2720

cheap, low-priced, bargain-priced, inexpensive
廉価な れんかな cheap, low-priced
廉売 れんばい bargain sale
低廉な ていれんな cheap, inexpensive

低 ▷low-priced
テイ ひく(い) ひく(める) ひく(まる)   Ⓚ0057

low-priced, inexpensive
低価 ていか low price
低廉な ていれんな cheap, inexpensive
低賃金 ていちんぎん low wages

inflorescences
穂　穎

穂 ▷spike
スイ ほ　　　　　Ⓚ1139

[original meaning] **spike, ear [head] of grain**
　穂状の すいじょうの shaped like an ear of grain
　出穂期 しゅっすいき sprouting season (of ears of grain)
　花穂 かすい spike

穎 ▷glume
エイ

ⓐ [original meaning] **glume, awn**
ⓑ **tip of a pointed object**
a 穎果 えいか caryopsis
b 穎脱する えいだつする gain recognition, rise above one's fellows

inform and communicate
報　通　告　届　達
知　申　稟　宣

報 ▷inform
ホウ むく(いる) むく(う)　　　Ⓚ1515

inform, report, announce, convey
　報道 ほうどう news, report, information
　報告する ほうこくする report, inform
　通報する つうほうする report, send information

通 ▷communicate
ツウ ツ とお(る) とお(り)
-どお(り) とお(す) とお(し) -どお(し)
かよ(う)　　　　　Ⓚ2678

(transmit or interchange information) **communicate, exchange information, let know**
　通信 つうしん correspondence, communication, information
　通達する つうたつする communicate, notify; attain proficiency
　通告 つうこく notice, notification, announcement
　通話 つうわ telephone call
　文通 ぶんつう correspondence, exchange of letters

告 ▷notify
コク つ(げる)　　　　　Ⓚ2134

ⓐ (let know, esp. in writing) **notify, inform, announce, advise, tell, report**
ⓑ (make widely known) **notify, announce, proclaim**
a 告知する こくちする notify, announce
　通告する つうこくする notify, announce
　報告 ほうこく report, information
　申告 しんこく report, statement, notification
　予告 よこく advance notice, preliminary announcement
　公告 こうこく public notice
　広告 こうこく public notice; advertisement
b 告示 こくじ notification, bulletin

届 ▷give notice
とど(ける) -とど(け) とど(く)　　Ⓚ2651

give notice (to the authorities), report, notify, file notice
　届け とどけ report, notice; delivery, forwarding
　届け出る とどけでる report, notify
　無届けの むとどけの without notice

達 ▷issue a notice
タツ -たち　　　　　Ⓚ2706

issue a notice, issue [deliver] orders, notify
　通達 つうたつ communication, notification; proficiency
　示達 じたつ(=したつ) instructions, directions
　上意下達する じょういかたつする convey the will of the governing to the governed
　執達吏 しったつり bailiff

知 ▷let know
チ し(る) し(らせる) し(れる)　　Ⓚ1041

let know, inform
　通知する つうちする notify, inform, let know
　告知する こくちする notify, announce

申 ▷report
シン もう(す) もう(し)-　　　Ⓚ2942

report (to a superior), state, submit a report
　申告 しんこく report, statement, notification
　上申する じょうしんする report (to a superior official)
　答申する とうしんする submit a report [reply]
　内申 ないしん unofficial report
　追申 ついしん [usu. 追伸] postscript

稟 ▷report to
ヒン リン　　　　　Ⓚ1833

report to (a superior), petition
　稟議 りんぎ(=ひんぎ) reaching a decision via circular

稟告 りんこく petition, application

宣 ▷proclaim
セン   Ⓚ1940

ⓐ (make widely known) **proclaim, declare, announce, publicize**
ⓑ (declare in public) **proclaim, pronounce, declare**

a 宣伝 せんでん publicity, propaganda; advertisement
  宣教 せんきょう missionary work
b 宣言 せんげん declaration, proclamation
  宣戦 せんせん proclamation [declaration] of war
  宣布 せんぷ proclamation, promulgation
  宣告 せんこく sentence, verdict, pronouncement
  宣誓 せんせい oath, swearing, vowing

information
報 信 訃

報 ▷information
ホウ むく(いる) むく(う)   Ⓚ1515

information, report, news
  一報 いっぽう information, notification
  予報 よほう forecast, prediction
  情報 じょうほう information, intelligence, report, news
  電報 でんぽう telegram
  広報(=弘報) こうほう (public) information, public relations
  公報 こうほう public [official] report [bulletin]
  日報 にっぽう daily report, daily news
  速報 そくほう prompt report, news flash

信 ▷message
シン   Ⓚ0084

message, signal, news, tidings
  信号 しんごう signal; traffic light
  受信 じゅしん reception (of radio waves); receipt of a message
  混信 こんしん jamming, interference, cross talk
  交信 こうしん exchange of messages, communications
  花信 かしん tidings of flowers, information about flowers for viewing
  通信 つうしん correspondence, communication, information

訃 ▷news of death
フ   Ⓚ1308

news of a person's death
  訃報 ふほう news of a person's death, obituary
  訃音 ふいん(=ふおん) news of a person's death

in front
前 先

前 ▷before
ゼン まえ   Ⓚ195⁞

[also prefix] (in front) **before, ahead, front, fore**
  前後 ぜんご before and after; order, sequence
  前方 ぜんぽう front
  前進 ぜんしん advance, going ahead
  前面 ぜんめん front, frontage, facade
  前線 ぜんせん front line, fighting front; *meteorology* front
  前途 ぜんと one's future, prospects; distance yet to cover
  前車輪 ぜんしゃりん front wheel

先 ▷ahead
セン さき ま(ず)   Ⓚ212⁞

[original meaning] (at the head or front) **ahead, fore, before, forward**
  先頭 せんとう forefront, head, top
  先駆者 せんくしゃ pioneer, forerunner
  先陣 せんじん advance guard, vanguard
  先遣する せんけんする send ahead [in advance]
  率先する そっせんする take the lead [initiative]

ingest
喫 服 食 喰 飲 呑 啄

喫 ▷ingest
キツ   Ⓚ050⁞

(introduce into one's body) **ingest, eat, drink, inhale, swallow**
  喫飯 きっぱん [rare] eating, taking a meal
  喫茶店 きっさてん coffee shop, tea house
  喫煙 きつえん smoking
  満喫する まんきつする have enough, enjoy fully

服 ▷take
フク   Ⓚ0782

take (medicine or tea)
  服用する ふくようする take (medicine)
  服毒する ふくどくする take poison
  内服薬 ないふくやく medicine for internal use

食 ▷eat
ショク ジキ く(う) く(らう)
た(べる)   Ⓚ1787

[original meaning] **eat**

食事 しょくじ meal, dinner, board
食欲 しょくよく appetite (for food)
食卓 しょくたく dining table
食堂 しょくどう dining hall [room]; restaurant
飲食 いんしょく eating and drinking
寝食 しんしょく eating and sleeping
断食 だんじき fasting
蚕食する さんしょくする encroach on, make an
    inroad into
菜食主義者 さいしょくしゅぎしゃ vegetarian

喰 ▷eat

サン く(う) く(らう)   Ⓚ0507

eat (greedily), devour

虫喰い むしくい worm-eaten; vermiculation, worm-
    hole, moth hole; leaf warbler
一口喰う ひとくちくう take a bite, have a munch
飯を喰う めしをくう devour a meal

飲 ▷drink
イン の(む) -の(み)   Ⓚ1510

ⓐ drink
ⓑ [original meaning] **drink alcoholic beverages**
ⓒ drink, beverage

a 飲食 いんしょく eating and drinking
    飲食店 いんしょくてん eating place, restaurant
    飲酒 いんしゅ drinking (alcoholic drinks)
b 愛飲する あいいんする be fond of drinking
c 飲料 いんりょう drink, beverage
    飲料水 いんりょうすい drinking [potable] water
    溜飲 りゅういん water brash, sour stomach

呑 ▷swallow

ドン の(む)   Ⓚ2131

[original meaning] **swallow, gulp**

呑吐 どんと swallowing and vomiting
呑舟の魚 どんしゅうのうお great fish; great man;
    notorious man
併呑 へいどん annexation, merger

啄 ▷peck

タク トク ついば(む)   Ⓚ0363

【タク トク】
peck, pick
啄木 たくぼく *literary* woodpecker

【ついば(む)】
peck, pick
虫を啄む むしをついばむ (of a bird) pick at a worm

嫡 ▷legitimate child
チャク   Ⓚ0620

legitimate child, heir, successor

嫡子 ちゃくし legitimate child
廃嫡 はいちゃく disinheritance

嗣 ▷heir
シ   Ⓚ1532

heir, successor

嗣子 しし heir, successor
後嗣 こうし heir, successor
令嗣 れいし your [his] heir
皇嗣 こうし Imperial Heir, Crown Prince

---

injury
傷   創   擦

傷 ▷wound
ショウ きず いた(む) いた(める)   Ⓚ0137

[also suffix] **wound, injury, bruise, scar**

傷病 しょうびょう injuries and sickness
負傷する ふしょうする be injured [wounded], get
    hurt
重傷 じゅうしょう heavy [serious] wound, severe
    injury
打撲傷 だぼくしょう bruise, contusion

創 ▷wound (cut)
ソウ つく(る)   Ⓚ1610

[original meaning] **wound, cut, laceration**

創傷 そうしょう wound
銃創 じゅうそう gunshot wound
絆創膏 ばんそうこう adhesive plaster [tape]

擦 ▷sore
サツ す(る) す(れる) -ず(れ)   Ⓚ0707

sore

靴擦れ くつずれ shoe sore
床擦れ とこずれ bedsores

---

in-laws
婿　嫁　姑

婿 ▷son-in-law
セイ　むこ   Ⓚ0520

[original meaning] **son-in-law**
女婿 じょせい son-in-law
令婿 れいせい your son-in-law

嫁 ▷daughter-in-law
カ　よめ　とつ(ぐ)   Ⓚ0582

daughter-in-law
嫁いびり よめいびり bullying a young wife

姑 ▷mother-in-law
コ　しゅうとめ　しゅうと   Ⓚ0318

[original meaning] **mother-in-law**
舅姑 きゅうこ parents-in-law

inlets and bays
江　浦　湾　峡

江 ▷inlet
コウ　え   Ⓚ0195

inlet, cove
入り江 いりえ inlet, cove, creek

浦 ▷coastal indentation
ホ　うら   Ⓚ0395

coastal indentation, inlet, small bay
浦曲 うらわ coastal indentations

湾 ▷bay
ワン   Ⓚ0562

ⓐ [original meaning] **bay, gulf, inlet**
ⓑ **suffix after names of bays and gulfs**
a 湾口 わんこう bay entrance
湾内 わんない inside the bay
港湾局 こうわんきょく Port and Harbor Authority
b 東京湾 とうきょうわん Tokyo Bay
メキシコ湾 めきしこわん Gulf of Mexico

峡 ▷narrows
キョウ   Ⓚ0318

narrows, strait
峡湾 きょうわん fjord
海峡 かいきょう straits, narrows, channel, sound

地峡 ちきょう isthmus

inner
奥　深　幽

奥 ▷inner
オウ　おく   Ⓚ2458

[in compounds] **inner, interior**
奥庭 おくにわ inner garden, backyard
奥歯 おくば molars, back teeth
奥日光 おくにっこう the secluded spots [recesses] of
Nikko
奥座敷 おくざしき inner room [chamber]

深 ▷deep
シン　ふか(い)　-ぶか(い)　ふか(まる)
ふか(める)   Ⓚ0480

(extending inward) **deep, distant, inmost, secluded**
深山幽谷に しんざんゆうこくに deep in the moun-
tains
深窓 しんそう secluded inner room

幽 ▷quiet and secluded
ユウ   Ⓚ2592

quiet and secluded, deep and remote
幽棲(=幽栖)する ゆうせいする live a quiet life in
seclusion away from the masses
幽谷 ゆうこく deep ravine, secluded valley
幽寂な ゆうじゃくな quiet, sequestered

inquire
問　詰　聞　質　尋
訊　伺　諮　詢

問 ▷question
モン　と(う)　と(い)　とん   Ⓚ2833

[original meaning] **question, ask, inquire**
質問 しつもん question
尋問する じんもんする question, examine, interrogate
詰問する きつもんする cross-examine, cross-
question, question closely
顧問 こもん adviser, consultant

詰
▷question closely
キツ　つ(める)　つ(め)　−づ(め)　つ(まる)
つ(む)　　　　　　　　　　　　　Ⓚ1380

question closely, press a person hard with questions, interrogate
　詰問する きつもんする cross-examine, cross-question, question closely

聞
▷ask
ブン　モン　き(く)　き(こえる)　Ⓚ2840

[formerly also 訊く] **ask, inquire**
　聞き返す ききかえす inquire again
　道を聞く みちをきく ask the way

質
▷query
シツ　シチ　チ　　　　　　　　Ⓚ2445

query, question, verify, confront
　質問 しつもん question
　質疑 しつぎ question, interrogation
　対質する たいしつする confront, cross-examine

尋
▷inquire
ジン　たず(ねる)　　　　　　　Ⓚ2027

[sometimes also 訊ねる] **inquire (about, after), ask, question**
　理由を尋ねる りゆうをたずねる ask the reason

訊
▷inquire
ジン　き(く)　たず(ねる)　　　Ⓚ1320

[now usu. 聞く] **ask, inquire**
　訊き返す ききかえす ask again; ask in return
　道を訊く みちをきく ask the way

伺
▷inquire (*humble*)
シ　うかが(う)　　　　　　　　Ⓚ0053

(put a question) **inquire (about), ask**
　伺い うかがい question, inquiry; consulting the oracle; call, visit
　御意見を伺う ごいけんをうかがう ask the opinion of (a superior)

諮
▷consult
シ　はか(る)　　　　　　　　　Ⓚ1443

consult, confer, ask for advice, inquire
　諮問する しもんする consult, inquire
　諮議する しぎする consult, confer

詢
▷ask for advice
ジュン　シュン　　　　　　　　Ⓚ1378

[rare] **ask for advice, consult, inquire**
　諮詢(=咨詢)する しじゅんする consult, inquire

insect
虫　昆　繭

虫
▷insect
チュウ　むし　　　　　　　　　Ⓚ2959

[also suffix] **insect, worm, bug**
　虫類 ちゅうるい insects and worms
　虫害 ちゅうがい insect damage
　虫垂 ちゅうすい appendix
　昆虫 こんちゅう insect
　防虫加工の ぼうちゅうかこうの mothproof
　殺虫剤 さっちゅうざい insecticide, vermicide
　寄生虫 きせいちゅう parasite

昆
▷insect
コン　　　　　　　　　　　　　Ⓚ2138

insect; swarm of insects
　昆虫 こんちゅう insect
　昆布 こんぶ(=こぶ) sea tangle, kelp

繭
▷cocoon
ケン　まゆ　　　　　　　　　　Ⓚ2107

[original meaning] **cocoon**
　繭糸 けんし cocoon and silk-thread, silk-thread
　繭価 けんか price of cocoons

insects
蚊　蛍　蝶　蚕　蟬　蜂　蚓

蚊
▷mosquito
か　　　　　　　　　　　　　　Ⓚ1205

[original meaning] **mosquito**
　飛蚊症 ひぶんしょう myodesopsia

蛍
▷firefly
ケイ　ほたる　　　　　　　　　Ⓚ2248

[original meaning] **firefly, glowfly**
　蛍火 けいか light of a firefly
　蛍雪 けいせつ diligent study

蝶
▷butterfly
チョウ　　　　　　　　　　　　Ⓚ1278

[also suffix] [original meaning] **butterfly**
　蝶蝶 ちょうちょう butterfly
　胡蝶 こちょう butterfly
　高山蝶 こうざんちょう alpine butterfly
　紋白蝶 もんしろちょう cabbage butterfly

蚕 ▷silkworm
サン かいこ   Ⓚ2170

[original meaning] **silkworm**

蚕糸 さんし silk raising and reeling, sericulture
蚕室 さんしつ silkworm-raising room
蚕食する さんしょくする encroach on, make an inroad into
養蚕 ようさん sericulture, silkworm culture

蟬 ▷cicada
セン せみ   Ⓚ1298

cicada

蛙鳴蟬噪 あめいせんそう annoying noise, loud buzz; fruitless argument

蜂 ▷bee
ホウ はち   Ⓚ1247

bee, wasp, hornet

蜂巣 ほうそう beehive, hive
養蜂 ようほう beekeeping, apiculture

蛔 ▷roundworm
カイ

[now replaced by 回] [original meaning] **roundworm, ascarid**

蛔虫 かいちゅう roundworm, ascarid

---

inside
内 裏 奥 中

内 ▷inside
ナイ ダイ うち   Ⓚ2914

ⓐ [also prefix] [original meaning] (inner side or part) **inside, interior, within, internal, inner**
ⓑ [also suffix] (inside a given range) **within, within the scope of, in**

a 内容 ないよう contents, import, substance
内部 ないぶ interior, inner parts
内外 ないがい inside and outside; approximately
内科 ないか (department of) internal medicine
内出血 ないしゅっけつ internal hemorrhage
内分泌 ないぶんぴつ internal secretion
内心 ないしん one's inmost heart; one's real intention; *math* inner center
内陸 ないりく inland, interior
内向 ないこう introversion
内向的 ないこうてき introversive
内面 ないめん inside, interior
案内する あんないする guide, show; inform, notify
b 国内の こくないの domestic, internal, inland

境内 けいだい grounds [premises] (of a shrine or temple)
以内 いない within, less than
権限内に けんげんないに within the scope of authority
都内で とないで in Tokyo Metropolis

裏 ▷inside
リ うら   Ⓚ1836

inside, within, in

脳裏 のうり brain, mind, memory
胸裏 きょうり one's bosom, one's heart, one's feelings
手裏剣 しゅりけん throwing knife
禁裏 きんり the Imperial Palace

奥 ▷inner part
オウ おく   Ⓚ2458

inner part, interior, the back, the heart, the depths, the recesses

奥まる おくまる extend far back, lie deep in
奥行き おくゆき depth, length
山奥 やまおく deep in the mountains, in the recesses of a mountain
森の奥 もりのおく deep in the forest

中 ▷in
チュウ ジュウ なか   Ⓚ2902

in, within, inside, interior

空中で くうちゅうで in the air [sky]
水中眼鏡 すいちゅうめがね swimming goggles
市中銀行 しちゅうぎんこう city bank
暗中模索 あんちゅうもさく groping in the dark
意中の人 いちゅうのひと person one is thinking of; man of one's heart
一酸化炭素中で いっさんかたんそちゅうで in an atmosphere of carbon monoxide

---

insignia
紋 章

紋 ▷crest
モン   Ⓚ1194

[also suffix] **crest, family crest, coat of arms**

紋章 もんしょう crest, family insignia, coat of arms
紋付き もんつき crested kimono
紋様 もんよう crest pattern
家紋 かもん family crest [badge]

章 ▷badge
ショウ   Ⓚ1819

ⓐ [also suffix] (device serving as insignia) **badge, emblem, medal, insignia**
ⓑ (distinctive mark) **badge, emblem**

- *a* 帽章 ぼうしょう badge on a cap
  腕章 わんしょう armband, arm badge
  会員章 かいいんしょう membership badge
  紋章 もんしょう crest, family insignia, coat of arms
  校章 こうしょう school emblem
- *b* 印章 いんしょう seal, stamp

install →EQUIP AND INSTALL

instruct
訓   指

訓 ▷instruct
クン   Ⓚ1322

(give orders) **instruct, advise, order**
    訓示 くんじ instruction
    訓令 くんれい instructions, (official) orders, directive

指 ▷direct
シ ゆび さ(す) -さ(し)   Ⓚ0337

direct, instruct
    指南 しなん instruction, teaching; instructor, teacher
    指導する しどうする guide, lead, instruct
    指揮 しき command
    指揮者 しきしゃ conductor; commander
    指令 しれい order, instruction

instruments for beating or pounding
槌   杵   砧

槌 ▷hammer
ツイ つち   Ⓚ0968

hammer, mallet
    槌骨 ついこつ malleus
    鉄槌 てつつい (iron) hammer

杵 ▷wooden pestle
ショ きね   Ⓚ0768

wooden pestle [mallet, pounder]

金剛杵 こんごうしょ *vajra* (mystical weapon in Hinduism and Buddhism)

砧 ▷block for beating cloth
チン きぬた   Ⓚ1063

stone block for beating cloth
    鉄砧 てっちん anvil

in succession
連   歴   逐   遞   漸

連 ▷in succession
レン つら(なる) つら(ねる) つ(れる) -づ(れ)   Ⓚ2672

ⓐ in succession, in series, continually, repeatedly
ⓑ [also prefix] successive, in a row, consecutive, continued

- *a* 連発する れんぱつする fire in rapid succession, fire in volleys
  連載する れんさいする serialize, publish serially
  連続する れんぞくする continue, occur in succession
  連戦 れんせん series of battles [games], every battle [game]
  五連敗 ごれんぱい five-game losing streak
- *b* 連休 れんきゅう consecutive holidays
  連日 れんじつ day after day, everyday
  連山 れんざん mountain range
  連分数 れんぶんすう continued fraction

歴 ▷successive
レキ   Ⓚ2600

successive, successively, one by one
    歴任 れきにん successive service in various posts
    歴訪する れきほうする make a round of calls
    歴代 れきだい successive reigns

逐 ▷one by one
チク   Ⓚ2671

one by one, successively, one after another
    逐一 ちくいち one by one, in detail
    逐次 ちくじ one by one, successively
    逐条審議 ちくじょうしんぎ article-by-article discussion
    逐語訳 ちくごやく word for word translation
    逐日 ちくじつ day after day, every day
    逐年 ちくねん annually, year by year

遞 ▷progressively
テイ   Ⓚ2675

progressively, successively, gradually, in order

逓増する ていぞうする increase progressively [gradually]
逓減する ていげんする diminish successively, decrease in order
逓次 ていじ in order, successively
逓降変圧器 ていこうへんあつき step-down transformer

漸
▷**gradually**
ゼン
Ⓚ0641

gradually, gradual
漸次 ぜんじ gradually
漸進 ぜんしん gradual advance
漸減 ぜんげん gradual decrease

intelligent and wise

賢 俊 鋭 敏 叡 智 慧
怜 悧 俐 哲 明 聡

賢
▷**wise**
ケン かしこ(い)
Ⓚ2472

wise, intelligent, sagacious, bright
賢明な けんめいな wise, intelligent; sensible
賢者 けんじゃ wise man
賢母 けんぼ wise mother

俊
▷**brilliant**
シュン
Ⓚ0086

[sometimes also 駿] **brilliant, talented, bright**
俊傑 しゅんけつ genius, hero
俊童 しゅんどう brilliant boy, infant prodigy
俊敏な しゅんびんな keen, quick-witted

鋭
▷**sharp**
エイ するど(い)
Ⓚ1544

sharp-witted, quick, trenchant
鋭敏な えいびんな sharp, keen, sensitive

敏
▷**nimble**
ビン
Ⓚ1206

(mentally agile) **nimble, clever, shrewd; keen, sharp**
敏感な びんかんな sensitive
敏腕 びんわん ability, capability
鋭敏な えいびんな sharp, keen, sensitive

叡
▷**profoundly wise**
エイ
Ⓚ1684

[now usu. 英] [original meaning] **profoundly wise, intelligent, farsighted, wise**
叡智 えいち sagacity, wisdom

智
▷**wise**
チ
Ⓚ2425

[original meaning] **wise, clever, resourceful**
智慮 ちりょ foresight
智者 ちしゃ wise man; learned priest
智将 ちしょう resourceful general

慧
▷**intelligent**
ケイ エ
Ⓚ2447

[original meaning] **intelligent, wise, bright, clever, cunning**
慧眼 けいがん discerning [quick] eye, keen insight
慧敏な けいびんな [rare] clever, of quick intellect

怜
▷**clever**
レイ レン
Ⓚ0265

[rarely also 伶] **clever, quick-witted, bright, nimble**
怜悧(=伶俐) れいり cleverness, sagacity

悧
▷**clever**
リ

[now also 利] **sharp, keen, clever**
悧巧(=利口)な りこうな clever, bright, sharp, shrewd
怜悧(=伶俐) れいり cleverness, sagacity

俐
▷**clever**
リ
Ⓚ0082

clever, bright, sharp-witted
俐巧(=利口)な りこうな clever, bright, sharp, shrewd
伶俐(=怜悧) れいり cleverness, sagacity

哲
▷**sagacious**
テツ
Ⓚ2386

[original meaning] **sagacious, wise, intelligent**
明哲 めいてつ wisdom, sagacity; wise man
賢哲 けんてつ sage, wise man

明
▷**clear-sighted**
メイ
ミョウ あ(かり) あか(るい) あか(るむ) あか(らむ) あき(らか) あ(ける) -あ(け) あ(く) あ(くる) あ(かす)
Ⓚ0756

clear-sighted, bright, discerning, intelligent, wise
明哲 めいてつ wisdom, sagacity; wise man
明察 めいさつ discernment, insight
賢明な けんめいな wise, intelligent; sensible
聡明な そうめいな sagacious, wise, sharp, mentally acute
不明 ふめい lack of sagacity [foresight], ignorance; missing persons
発明する はつめいする invent, devise

聡 ▷sharp-witted
ソウ さと(い)   Ⓚ1266

sharp-witted, quick-witted, clever, bright, astute, perceptive
聡明な そうめいな sagacious, wise, sharp, mentally acute

intention →WILL AND INTENTION

intercross
交 差

交 ▷intercross
コウ まじ(わる) まじ(える) まじ(る) ま(ざる) ま(ぜる) –か(う) か(わす) Ⓚ1738

[original meaning] **intercross, intersect, cross**
交差する こうさする cross, intersect (each other)
交差点 こうさてん crossing, intersection, crossroads; junction
交戦 こうせん war, battle

差 ▷cross
サ さ(す) さ(し)   Ⓚ2821

[formerly 乂] **cross, intersect**
交差 こうさ crossing, intersection
三差路 さんさろ three-forked road

interest and dividend
利 子 配

利 ▷interest
リ き(く)   Ⓚ1029

[also suffix] **interest (on money)**
利子 りし interest
利息 りそく interest
複利 ふくり compound interest
六分半利 ろくぶはんり 6.5% bonds

子 ▷interest
シ ス こ -(つ)こ   Ⓚ2872

("offspring" of money) **interest**
利子 りし interest
金子 きんす money, funds

配 ▷dividend
ハイ くば(る)   Ⓚ1330

abbrev. of 配当 はいとう: **dividend**
減配 げんぱい reduction in a dividend; smaller ration
無配の むはいの without dividend

internal organs
心 肺 胃 腸 肝 胆 腎

心 ▷heart
シン こころ –ごころ   Ⓚ0004

[also suffix] [original meaning] **heart (the organ)**
心臓 しんぞう heart
心電図 しんでんず electrocardiogram
心不全 しんふぜん heart failure
狭心症 きょうしんしょう angina pectoris
衝心 しょうしん heart failure
脂肪心 しぼうしん fatty heart

肺 ▷lung
ハイ   Ⓚ0825

a [original meaning] **lung, lungs**
b [also prefix] **pulmonary**
a 肺臓 はいぞう lungs
肺活量 はいかつりょう lung breathing capacity
肺癌 はいがん lung cancer
肺炎 はいえん pneumonia, inflammation of the lungs
b 肺結核 はいけっかく pulmonary tuberculosis

胃 ▷stomach
イ   Ⓚ2219

a [original meaning] **stomach**
b [prefix] **gastric**
a 胃腸 いちょう stomach and intestines [bowels]
胃腸病学 いちょうびょうがく gastroenterology
胃弱 いじゃく dyspepsia, indigestion
ab 胃袋 いぶくろ stomach
胃下垂 いかすい gastric ptosis
胃炎 いえん gastritis
胃潰瘍 いかいよう stomach ulcer
胃癌 いがん gastric cancer
胃カタル いかたる gastric catarrh

腸 ▷intestines
チョウ   Ⓚ0948

a [original meaning] **intestines, entrails, bowels**
b [prefix] **intestinal, enteric**
a 腸炎 ちょうえん enteritis
胃腸 いちょう stomach and intestines [bowels]

小腸 しょうちょう small intestine
脱腸 だっちょう enterocele
盲腸 もうちょう cecum, appendix
灌腸(=浣腸)する かんちょうする give an enema
b 腸結核 ちょうけっかく intestinal tuberculosis
腸チフス ちょうちふす typhoid fever

肝 ▷**liver**
カン きも   Ⓚ0747

[original meaning] **liver**
肝臓 かんぞう liver
肝油 かんゆ liver oil
肝炎 かんえん hepatitis

胆 ▷**gallbladder**
タン   Ⓚ0828

gallbladder, gall
胆嚢 たんのう gall, gallbladder
胆汁 たんじゅう bile, gall
胆石 たんせき gallstone

腎 ▷**kidney**
ジン   Ⓚ2465

[original meaning] **kidney**
腎臓 じんぞう kidneys
腎炎 じんえん nephritis
腎盂 じんう renal pelvis
副腎 ふくじん adrenal glands

interrogatives
奈 那 何 誰

奈 ▷**interrogative forming element**
ナ   Ⓚ1905

[also 那] element for forming interrogative words
奈辺 なへん where?

那 ▷**interrogative forming element**
ナ   Ⓚ0748

[also 奈] element for forming interrogative words
那辺 なへん where?

何 ▷**what**
カ なに なん   Ⓚ0048

what, which
幾何学 きかがく geometry
誰何する すいかする challenge (an unknown
person), ask a person's identity

誰 ▷**who**
だれ   Ⓚ1429

[original meaning] **who**
誰何する すいかする challenge (an unknown
person), ask a person's identity

interval →DISTANCE AND INTERVAL

investigate and examine
閲 審 験 勘 糾 究 察
討 探 検 診 調 査

閲 ▷**review**
エツ   Ⓚ2845

[original meaning] **review (troops), inspect, examine**
閲兵 えっぺい inspection [review] of troops
観閲 かんえつ inspection of troops

審 ▷**examine carefully**
シン   Ⓚ2080

examine carefully, investigate
審議 しんぎ deliberation, consideration, careful
discussion
審査する しんさする examine, investigate, judge
審判 しんぱん(=しんばん) refereeing, judgment;
referee, umpire

験 ▷**test**
ケン ゲン   Ⓚ1628

[original meaning] **test, try, attempt, examine, verify**
験算(=検算) けんざん verification of accounts,
checking figures
試験する しけんする test, examine
実験 じっけん experiment
体験する たいけんする experience, go through,
(actually) feel
受験する じゅけんする take an examination

勘 ▷**check**
カン   Ⓚ1582

check, examine, collate, compare
勘定 かんじょう calculation; account, settlement of
accounts
勘校する かんこうする examine and correct, collate
勘合 かんごう [rare] checking and verifying

糾 ▷inquire into
キュウ   Ⓚ1176

inquire into (esp. a crime), investigate into, examine
糾明 きゅうめい searching examination
糾弾 きゅうだん impeachment, censure
糾問 きゅうもん cross-examination, arraignment

究 ▷study exhaustively
キュウ きわ(める)   Ⓚ1885

study exhaustively, investigate thoroughly, delve into, go to the bottom of
究明する きゅうめいする investigate, study
究理 きゅうり study of natural laws
研究 けんきゅう research, study
追究する ついきゅうする investigate thoroughly, inquire into
学究 がっきゅう scholar, student
探究 たんきゅう investigation, search, inquiry

察 ▷inspect
サツ   Ⓚ2062

(examine officially) inspect, investigate, examine
警察 けいさつ police, police station
視察 しさつ inspection, observation
巡察 じゅんさつ round of inspection, patrol
検察 けんさつ criminal investigation; prosecution
査察 ささつ inspection, investigation
診察 しんさつ medical examination

討 ▷study
トウ う(つ)   Ⓚ1324

(inquire into and examine closely) study, scrutinize, examine, discuss
討議 とうぎ discussion, debate, deliberation
討論 とうろん debate, discussion, argument
討究 とうきゅう investigation, study
検討する けんとうする examine, study, investigate

探 ▷probe
タン さぐ(る) さが(す)   Ⓚ0466

probe, search into, explore, inquire
探求 たんきゅう quest, search, pursuit
探究 たんきゅう investigation, search, inquiry
探査 たんさ inquiry, investigation
探測 たんそく sounding, probing
探訪 たんぼう (private) inquiry
探検(=探険) たんけん exploration, expedition

検 ▷examine
ケン   Ⓚ0898

examine, inspect, investigate, verify, test, check
検査 けんさ inspection, examination, test
検討する けんとうする examine, study, investigate

検診 けんしん medical examination
検証 けんしょう verification, identification; inspection
検察 けんさつ criminal investigation; prosecution
検事 けんじ public prosecutor
検閲 けんえつ censorship; inspection, review
検便 けんべん stool examination
検定 けんてい examination; official approval
探検(=探険) たんけん exploration, expedition
点検 てんけん inspection, examination

診 ▷examine a patient
シン み(る)   Ⓚ1364

examine a patient, diagnose
診察する しんさつする examine (a patient)
診療 しんりょう diagnosis and treatment
診療所 しんりょうじょ clinic
診断 しんだん diagnosis
聴診器 ちょうしんき stethoscope
検診 けんしん medical examination
往診 おうしん doctor's visit to a patient, house call
本日休診 ほんじつきゅうしん Office Closed Today (sign at doctor's office)
打診する だしんする sound out, tap (a person's views); examine by percussion

調 ▷investigate
チョウ しら(べる) しら(べ) ととの(う) ととの(える)   Ⓚ1417

investigate, look into, examine, inquire, check
調査 ちょうさ investigation, examination, inquiry, survey
調書 ちょうしょ protocol, written evidence, record
再調する さいちょうする reexamine, reinvestigate

査 ▷look into
サ   Ⓚ2159

look into, investigate, examine, check, inspect, find out, inquire into
査察 ささつ inspection, investigation
査閲 さえつ inspection, examination
査問 さもん inquiry, hearing
調査 ちょうさ investigation, examination, inquiry, survey
捜査 そうさ criminal investigation, search
検査 けんさ inspection, examination, test
審査する しんさする examine, investigate, judge
鑑査 かんさ inspection, audit

invite →CALL AND INVITE

iron and steel
鉄　銑　鋼

鉄 ▷iron
テツ　　　　　　　　　　　　Ⓚ1527

[original meaning] **iron**
- 鉄鋼 てっこう iron and steel
- 鉄板 てっぱん iron [steel] plate
- 鉄筋 てっきん ferro-(concrete)
- 鉄砲 てっぽう gun, firearm
- 鉄道 てつどう railway
- 鉄骨 てっこつ steel [iron] frame
- 製鉄 せいてつ iron manufacture
- 非鉄金属 ひてつきんぞく nonferrous metals

銑 ▷pig iron
セン　　　　　　　　　　　　Ⓚ1538

pig iron
- 銑鉄 せんてつ pig iron
- 溶銑 ようせん molten iron
- 白銑 はくせん white pig iron

鋼 ▷steel
コウ　はがね　　　　　　　　Ⓚ1551

[also suffix] [original meaning] **steel**
- 鋼材 こうざい steel materials, structural steel
- 鋼板 こうはん steel plate
- 鋼管 こうかん steel pipe [tubing]
- 鋼線 こうせん steel wire
- 製鋼 せいこう steel manufacture
- 鉄鋼 てっこう iron and steel
- ステンレス鋼 すてんれすこう stainless steel

Japan
日　和　邦　国　倭

日 ▷Japan
ニチ　ジツ　ひ　-び　-か　　Ⓚ2606

Japan
- 日本 にほん(=にっぽん) Japan
- 日銀 にちぎん Bank of Japan
- 日米 にちべい Japan and U.S.
- 日韓 にっかん Japan and (South) Korea
- 日ソ にっそ Soviet-Japanese, Japanese-Soviet
- 日本酒 にほんしゅ sake, rice wine
- 来日する らいにちする come to Japan

和 ▷Japan
ワ　オ　やわ(らぐ)　やわ(らげる)　なご(む)　なご(やか)　　Ⓚ104４

Japan, Japanese
- 和服 わふく Japanese clothes, kimono
- 和歌 わか Japanese poem, tanka
- 和食 わしょく Japanese-style food
- 和風 わふう Japanese style; gentle breeze
- 和語 わご native Japanese word (not derived from Chinese)

邦 ▷Japan
ホウ　　　　　　　　　　　　Ⓚ075０

Japan, our country
- 邦人 ほうじん Japanese, fellow countryman
- 邦楽 ほうがく Japanese music

国 ▷Japanese
コク　くに　　　　　　　　　Ⓚ265９

(of Japan) **Japanese**
- 国語 こくご national language; Japanese
- 国文学 こくぶんがく Japanese literature
- 国史 こくし Japanese history

倭 ▷ancient name for Japan
ワイ　カ　やまと　　　　　　Ⓚ010１

【ワイ　カ】
ancient name for Japan
- 倭人 わじん ancient name for Japanese
- 倭寇 わこう Japanese corsairs

【やまと】
[also 大和] *elegant* **ancient name for Japan**
- 倭建命 やまとたけるのみこと name of a mythical hero

Japanese money denominations
文　両　厘　銭　円

文 ▷mon
ブン　モン　ふみ　　　　　　Ⓚ170８

former monetary unit equiv. to 1/1000 of a *kan* (貫)
- 文無しの もんなしの penniless

両 ▷ryo
リョウ　　　　　　　　　　　Ⓚ294９

former monetary unit equiv. to 4 *kan* (貫)
- 両替 りょうがえ money changing, exchange of money

千両箱 せんりょうばこ chest containing a thousand pieces of gold
銀五両 ぎんごりょう 5 *ryo* of silver
十両 じゅうりょう 10 *ryo*

厘 ▷*rin*
リン   ⓚ2589

former monetary unit equiv. to 1/1000 of a yen (円)
一厘 いちりん 1 *rin*

銭 ▷sen
セン ぜに   ⓚ1537

sen:
ⓐ **monetary unit equiv. to 1/100 of a yen (円)**
ⓑ **former monetary unit equiv. to 1/1000 of a *kan* (貫)**
a 二円五十銭 にえんごじゅっせん 2 yen 50 sen

円 ▷yen
エン まる(い) まる   ⓚ2555

[also prefix and suffix] **yen,**
円貨 えんか yen currency
円高 えんだか appreciation of the yen
円安 えんやす low yen rate, depreciation of the yen
円相場 えんそうば yen exchange rate
五百円 ごひゃくえん 500 yen

jealous and envious
嫉 妬 羨

嫉 ▷jealous
シツ   ⓚ0584

ⓐ **be jealous, be envious**
ⓑ **jealousy, envy**
a 嫉視する しっしする regard with jealousy
b 嫉妬 しっと jealousy

妬 ▷jealous
ト ねた(む) ねた(ましい)   ⓚ0254

be jealous, be envious
妬心 としん jealousy
嫉妬 しっと jealousy

羨 ▷envious
セン うらや(む) うらや(ましい)   ⓚ2055

be envious, be jealous
羨望 せんぼう envy, jealousy

bin →PARTICIPATE AND JOIN

join
結 繋 縛 綴 繃
束 梱 連 係 接

結 ▷tie
ケツ むす(ぶ) ゆ(う) ゆ(わえる)   ⓚ1235

[original meaning] **tie (up), bind, knot**
結髪 けっぱつ hairdressing, hairdo
結縄 けつじょう knotting a rope
結束 けっそく unity, union
連結する れんけつする connect, couple, link
直結する ちょっけつする connect directly with

繋 ▷connect
ケイ つな(ぐ) つな(がる) つな(げる)
かか(る)   ⓚ2521

[original meaning] **connect, link, bind, fasten, anchor, moor**
繋船 けいせん mooring a ship
繋留 けいりゅう mooring, anchorage

縛 ▷bind
バク しば(る)   ⓚ1282

[original meaning] **bind, tie up**
緊縛 きんばく tight binding
就縛する しゅうばくする be put in bonds, come under arrest

綴 ▷bind
テイ テツ つづ(る) と(じる)   ⓚ1264

bind, file
点綴する てんてい(=てんてつ)する intersperse; dot
補綴 ほてい(=ほてつ) mending; composing (poetry)

繃 ▷bind up
ホウ

[now replaced by 包] **bind up, strap up**
繃帯 ほうたい bandage, dressing

束 ▷tie up
ソク たば たば(ねる) つか   ⓚ2978

[original meaning] **tie up (in a bundle), bundle, bind**
束髪 そくはつ bundled hair, hair done up in a bun
束帯 そくたい old ceremonial court dress
装束 しょうぞく costume, attire

梱 ▷pack
コン こり

pack, (tie in a) bundle

梱包 こんぽう packing, packaging; package
同梱する どうこんする include (something) in a package
開梱する かいこんする open (a pack), unpack

連 ▷link
レン つら(なる) つら(ねる) つ(れる) -づ(れ)　　　Ⓚ2672

(join together) **link, join**
連結 れんけつ connection, coupling, linking
連辞 れんじ copula
連鎖 れんさ chain (as of reasoning), link, series; connection
連星 れんせい binary star

係 ▷connect
ケイ かか(る) かかり -がかり かか(わる)　　　Ⓚ0078

connect, tie up, fasten, moor
係留 けいりゅう mooring, anchorage
係船 けいせん mooring a ship

接 ▷join
セツ つ(ぐ)　　　Ⓚ0460

bring into contact:
ⓐ **join, connect**
ⓑ **weld, welding**
a 接合 せつごう joining, union
接続 せつぞく connection, joining
接着 せっちゃく adhesion, gluing
b 溶接 ようせつ welding
融接 ゆうせつ fusion welding
鍛接 たんせつ forge welding

joint
節　　　関

節 ▷joint
セツ セチ ふし -ぶし　　　Ⓚ2349

ⓐ [also suffix] *anat* **joint, knuckle, node**
ⓑ [original meaning] *bot* **joint (as in a bamboo), node, knot**
a 節足動物 せっそくどうぶつ arthropod
関節 かんせつ joint
結節 けっせつ node, knotting, knot
リンパ節 りんぱせつ lymph node
神経節 しんけいせつ ganglion
b 末節 まっせつ minor details, nonessentials

関 ▷connection
カン せき -ぜき かか(わる)　　　Ⓚ2842

connection, link; turning point
関節 かんせつ joint
機関 きかん engine, machine; agency, facilities, institution

journey
旅　　行　　遊　　巡

旅 ▷travel
リョ たび　　　Ⓚ0829

ⓐ **travel, traveling, journey, trip**
ⓑ **travel, take a trip**
a 旅行 りょこう travel, trip
旅券 りょけん passport
b 旅装 りょそう traveling outfit
旅費 りょひ traveling expenses
旅客 りょかく traveler, passenger, tourist
旅客機 りょかっき passenger plane

行 ▷trip
コウ ギョウ アン い(く) ゆ(く) -ゆ(き) -い(き) おこな(う)　　　Ⓚ0187

[also suffix] **trip, journey**
行幸 ぎょうこう imperial visit
行脚 あんぎゃ pilgrimage; walking tour; tour
箱根行 はこねこう trip to Hakone

遊 ▷tour
ユウ ユ あそ(ぶ) あそ(ばす)　　　Ⓚ2709

tour, take a pleasure trip or excursion, make a study tour
遊学 ゆうがく traveling to study
遊山 ゆさん excursion, outing, picnic
遊説 ゆうぜい electioneering tour; campaign speech
外遊 がいゆう foreign tour, trip abroad
歴遊 れきゆう traveling, tour, pleasure trip

巡 ▷tour around
ジュン めぐ(る) めぐ(り)　　　Ⓚ2622

tour around, visit, make a pilgrimage
巡業 じゅんぎょう provincial tour
巡歴 じゅんれき tour, trip
巡礼 じゅんれい pilgrimage; pilgrim
巡行 じゅんこう round, patrol, tour
巡拝 じゅんぱい circuit pilgrimage

judge

判 裁 鑑 評 審 決 視

判 ▷judge
ハン バン   Ⓚ1038

ⓐ (pass legal judgment) **judge, hand down a decision, pronounce sentence**
ⓑ (decide upon critically) **judge, decide, distinguish, differentiate**

a 判決 はんけつ judicial decision, judgment, sentence
判事 はんじ judge
判例 はんれい (judicial) precedent
裁判 さいばん trial, judgment, decision
公判 こうはん (public) trial [hearing]
b 判断する はんだんする judge, decide; interpret, foretell, read
判定する はんていする judge, decide
批判する ひはんする criticize, comment
評判 ひょうばん fame, reputation
審判 しんぱん(=しんばん) refereeing, judgment; referee, umpire

裁 ▷judge
サイ た(つ) さば(く)   Ⓚ2813

(pass judgment) **judge, decide, try, arbitrate**
裁判 さいばん trial, judgment, decision
裁定 さいてい decision, ruling, arbitration
裁決 さいけつ decision, ruling
裁量 さいりょう discretion
制裁 せいさい sanction, punishment, discipline
仲裁 ちゅうさい arbitration, mediation

鑑 ▷appraise
カン かんが(みる)   Ⓚ1580

appraise, judge, appreciate, discern, identify
鑑賞 かんしょう appreciation
鑑定する かんていする appraise, judge, estimate, identify
鑑識する かんしきする identify, judge; discern
鑑別 かんべつ discrimination, judgment
無鑑査の むかんさの not submitted to the selecting committee

評 ▷evaluate
ヒョウ   Ⓚ1361

evaluate, appraise, judge, decide by consultation
評価 ひょうか evaluation, appraisal
評点 ひょうてん examination marks, rating
評定 ひょうてい rating, evaluation
評議 ひょうぎ conference, consultation
評定 ひょうじょう conference, consultation
評決 ひょうけつ decision, verdict

審 ▷try
シン   Ⓚ2080

try, hold a court trial, hear, judge
審理する しんりする try, examine, inquire into
審問 しんもん trial, hearing, formal interrogation

決 ▷decide
ケツ き(める) -ぎ(め) き(まる)   Ⓚ0233

(pronounce judgment) **decide, resolve, settle**
決算 けっさん settlement of accounts
決勝 けっしょう decision (of a contest)
決議 けつぎ resolution, decision

視 ▷regard
シ み(る)   Ⓚ0884

[also suffix] **regard as, consider**
軽視する けいしする make light of, despise; neglect
敵視する てきしする regard as an enemy
無視する むしする ignore, disregard
重要視する じゅうようしする regard as important, think much of

jump

跳 躍 蹴

跳 ▷jump
チョウ は(ねる) と(ぶ) -と(び)   Ⓚ1392

[original meaning] **jump, leap, spring**
跳躍する ちょうやくする jump, leap, spring
跳馬 ちょうば long horse (vault)
反跳 はんちょう *phys* recoil

躍 ▷leap
ヤク おど(る)   Ⓚ1484

[original meaning] **leap, jump up, spring**
躍進する やくしんする make rapid progress, advance by leaps and bounds
飛躍 ひやく leap, jump
一躍 いちやく at a bound, with a jump
跳躍する ちょうやくする jump, leap, spring

蹶 ▷spring to one's feet
ケツ

[now also 決] **spring to one's feet, rouse oneself**
蹶起する けっきする rise to action
蹶然と けつぜんと with a spring; resolutely

Kansai cities

阪 神 京 洛

阪 ▷Osaka
ハン さか   Ⓚ0243

Osaka

阪神 はんしん Hanshin, Osaka and Kobe
阪大 はんだい Osaka University
阪急デパート はんきゅうでぱーと Hankyu Department Store
来阪する らいはんする come to Osaka

神 ▷Kobe
シン ジン かみ かん- こう-   Ⓚ0821

Kobe

阪神 はんしん Hanshin, Osaka and Kobe

京 ▷Kyoto
キョウ ケイ キン   Ⓚ1766

Kyoto

京女 きょうおんな Kyoto woman
京人形 きょうにんぎょう Kyoto doll
京阪神 けいはんしん Kyoto-Osaka-Kobe
京大 きょうだい University of Kyoto

洛 ▷Kyoto
ラク   Ⓚ0348

Kyoto; capital

洛中 らくちゅう inside Kyoto; inside the capital
洛外 らくがい outside Kyoto; outside the capital
京洛 けいらく(=きょうらく) capital; Kyoto
上洛する じょうらくする go to Kyoto
入洛する じゅらく(=にゅうらく)する enter Kyoto

Kanto region

京 東 都 浜 埼 湘

京 ▷Tokyo
キョウ ケイ キン   Ⓚ1766

Tokyo

京浜 けいひん Tokyo and Yokohama
上京する じょうきょうする go to Tokyo
帰京する ききょうする return to Tokyo
滞京する たいきょうする stay in Tokyo [the capital]
在京中 ざいきょうちゅう during one's stay in Tokyo

東 ▷Tokyo
トウ ひがし   Ⓚ2987

Tokyo

東京 とうきょう Tokyo
東上 とうじょう going up to Tokyo
東名高速道路 とうめいこうそくどうろ Tokyo-Nagoya Expressway

都 ▷Metropolis of Tokyo
ト ツ みやこ   Ⓚ1505

ⓐ **Metropolis of Tokyo, Tokyo**
ⓑ (of the Metropolis of Tokyo) **Metropolitan, Tokyo**

a 都立の とりつの metropolitan, under control of the Tokyo Metropolitan government
都内で とないで in Tokyo Metropolis
都営 とえい run by the metropolitan government
東都 とうと Tokyo Metropolis
b 都庁 とちょう Tokyo Metropolitan Government Office
都電 とでん Metropolitan Electric Railway
都議選 とぎせん Tokyo Assembly elections

浜 ▷Yokohama
ヒン はま   Ⓚ039

Yokohama

京浜 けいひん Tokyo and Yokohama

埼 ▷Saitama
さい さき   Ⓚ0422

Saitama Prefecture

埼玉県 さいたまけん Saitama Prefecture
埼京線 さいきょうせん Saikyo Line
埼北 さいほく Saihoku (northern Saitama)

湘 ▷Shonan
ショウ   Ⓚ0556

abbrev. of 湘南 しょうなん Shonan
西湘 せいしょう west Shonan

keys →LOCKS AND KEYS

kill

殺 劉 刺 絞 窒

殺 ▷kill
サツ サイ セツ ころ(す) -ごろ(し) Ⓚ1208

kill, murder

殺人 さつじん murder, homicide
殺生する せっしょうする destroy life, kill animals
殺害 さつがい(=せつがい) murder, killing, assassination

殺菌 さっきん sterilization, pasteurization
暗殺 あんさつ assassination
自殺 じさつ suicide
謀殺 ぼうさつ premeditated murder
射殺する しゃさつする shoot to death
銃殺する じゅうさつする shoot to death, execute by
firing squad

劉 ▷kill
リュウ   Ⓚ1680

[original meaning, now obsolete] **kill**—now used only in
names

刺 ▷stab to death
シ さ(す) さ(さる) さ(し)   Ⓚ1171

stab to death, assassinate
刺客 しかく assassin

絞 ▷strangle
コウ しぼ(る) し(める) し(まる)   Ⓚ1236

strangle, strangulate, hang
絞殺する こうさつする strangle, hang
絞首刑 こうしゅけい death [execution] by hanging
絞罪 こうざい hanging, execution by hanging

窒 ▷choke
チツ   Ⓚ1980

choke, suffocate
窒息 ちっそく suffocation, asphyxia
窒死 ちっし [rare] death from suffocation

kind
厚 篤 懇 慈 温 渥 優

厚 ▷kind
コウ あつ(い)   Ⓚ2588

kind, cordial, hearty, heartfelt, kindhearted, warm
厚意 こうい kindness, favor
厚情 こうじょう kindness, favor, hospitality
厚志 こうし kindness, kind thought [intention]
厚遇 こうぐう cordial welcome, kind treatment
温厚な おんこうな gentle, courteous

篤 ▷cordial
トク   Ⓚ2370

cordial, warmhearted, affectionate
篤志家 とくしか benevolent person; volunteer,
supporter
篤行 とっこう good deed
懇篤な こんとくな cordial, kind

懇 ▷cordial
コン ねんご(ろ)   Ⓚ2517

cordial, kindly, kind
懇切な こんせつな kind, cordial; exhaustive
懇篤 こんとく cordiality, kindness
懇書 こんしょ your kind letter
懇情 こんじょう kindliness

慈 ▷affectionate
ジ いつく(しむ)   Ⓚ2053

[original meaning] **affectionate (towards one's child),
tender, gentle and loving, kind**
慈愛 じあい affection, love, benevolence
慈母 じぼ affectionate [loving] mother

温 ▷warmhearted
オン あたた(か) あたた(かい)
あたた(まる) あたた(める)   Ⓚ0554

warmhearted, kindly, gentle
温和(=穏和)な おんわな gentle, mild, genial
温厚な おんこうな gentle, courteous
温情 おんじょう warm feeling, kindliness, warm-
heartedness

渥 ▷gracious
アク   Ⓚ0546

gracious, cordial, benevolent
優渥な ゆうあくな gracious (words of the emperor)

優 ▷kindly
ユウ やさ(しい) すぐ(れる)   Ⓚ0156

kindly, gracious, gentle, kind, cordial
優遇 ゆうぐう favorable treatment, warm reception
優待する ゆうたいする treat kindly, receive hospitably, give special consideration

kinds and types
型 類 色 般 属 品 種 様

型 ▷type
ケイ かた -がた   Ⓚ2292

(general form characterizing a class) **type, kind, pattern,
form**
型式 けいしき model
類型 るいけい similar type, prototype, pattern
同型 どうけい same type [pattern]
定型 ていけい type, definite form
体型 たいけい form, figure

類 ▷kind
ルイ たぐ(い)　　　Ⓚ1606

kind, class, sort, category, genus, species
　種類 しゅるい kind, sort, species, type
　人類 じんるい mankind, humankind
　同類 どうるい same kind, same class
　衣類 いるい clothes, garments

色 ▷kind
ショク シキ いろ　　　Ⓚ1748

ⓐ **kind, sort**
ⓑ **counter for kinds**
a 色んな いろんな various kinds of
　色色な いろいろな various kinds of
　十人十色 じゅうにんといろ So many men, so many
　　minds
b 二色 ふたいろ two kinds

般 ▷sort
ハン　　　Ⓚ1203

(things of the same category) **sort, kind, way**
　一般の いっぱんの general, universal, widespread
　全般の ぜんぱんの whole, general, overall
　万般 ばんぱん all things, all affairs, all sorts of
　　matters
　百般の ひゃっぱんの all, every, all sorts of
　諸般の しょはんの various, several, all, every

属 ▷genus
ゾク　　　Ⓚ2711

genus, kind, sort, family; category
　金属 きんぞく metal
　尊属 そんぞく ascendant

品 ▷category
ヒン しな　　　Ⓚ1937

category, classification, type
　品目 ひんもく list of articles [items]
　品種 ひんしゅ kind, variety, description, brand
　品詞 ひんし part of speech

種 ▷variety
シュ たね　　　Ⓚ1128

variety, kind, type, sort, breed, race
　種目 しゅもく item; event (as a race)
　種種の しゅじゅの various, diverse
　各種の かくしゅの each [every] kind, various
　一種の いっしゅの a kind of, of a sort
　機種 きしゅ type of airplane [machine], model
　業種 ぎょうしゅ type of industry, category of busi-
　　ness
　職種 しょくしゅ type of occupation, occupational
　　category

　品種 ひんしゅ kind, variety, description, brand
　人種 じんしゅ (human) race

様 ▷variety
ヨウ さま　　　Ⓚ096▮

variety, sort, kind
　一様 いちよう uniformity, equality
　多様な たような various, manifold
　左様 さよう such; yes; let me see

kinds of atmospheric vapor
霧　霞　雲

霧 ▷fog
ム きり　　　Ⓚ245▮

[original meaning] **fog, mist**
　霧笛 むてき foghorn
　霧氷 むひょう rime, hoarfrost, silver frost
　濃霧 のうむ dense [thick] fog
　煙霧 えんむ smog
　雲散霧消する うんさんむしょうする scatter and
　　vanish, vanish like mist

霞 ▷mist
カ かすみ かす(む)　　　Ⓚ245▮

mist, haze
　煙霞 えんか mist [haze] and smoke; beauties of
　　nature
　雲霞の如く うんかのごとく in swarms
　朝霞 ちょうか morning mist [haze]; [archaic] morn-
　　ing glow

雲 ▷cloud
ウン くも -ぐも　　　Ⓚ241▮

ⓐ [original meaning] **cloud**
ⓑ **something resembling a cloud**
a 雲海 うんかい sea of clouds
　雲霧 うんむ clouds and fog
　雲泥の差 うんでいのさ great difference (as
　　between clouds and mud)
　積乱雲 せきらんうん cumulonimbus
b 風雲 ふううん state of affairs, situation
　星雲 せいうん nebula

kinds of frozen water
氷　雪

氷
▷ice
ヒョウ こおり ひ　　　Ⓚ0025

ice
氷晶 ひょうしょう ice crystal
氷河 ひょうが glacier
氷山 ひょうざん iceberg
氷雪 ひょうせつ ice and snow
樹氷 じゅひょう trees covered with ice
製氷 せいひょう ice making

雪
▷snow
セツ ゆき　　　Ⓚ2406

snow, snowfall
雪上車 せつじょうしゃ snowmobile
豪雪 ごうせつ tremendous snowfall
降雪 こうせつ snowfall, snow
積雪 せきせつ (fallen) snow
新雪 しんせつ fresh snow
蛍雪 けいせつ diligent study

kinds of fuel
炭　薪　油

炭
▷coal, charcoal
タン すみ　　　Ⓚ1947

❶ [also suffix] [original meaning] **coal**
炭抗 たんこう coal mine, coal pit
炭鉱 たんこう coal mine
石炭 せきたん coal
無煙炭 むえんたん anthracite, smokeless coal
❷ **charcoal**
木炭 もくたん charcoal
薪炭 しんたん firewood and charcoal
塗炭 とたん misery, distress

薪
▷firewood
シン たきぎ　　　Ⓚ2098

firewood, wood for fuel
薪炭 しんたん firewood and charcoal
薪水 しんすい cooking

油
▷oil
ユ あぶら　　　Ⓚ0303

(petroleum or petroleum derivative) **oil, petroleum**
石油 せきゆ petroleum, oil
重油 じゅうゆ fuel oil
灯油 とうゆ kerosene, lamp oil
原油 げんゆ crude oil
潤滑油 じゅんかつゆ lubricant, lubricating oil

kinds of grasses
草　荻　蒲　莱　蕨　叢　芝
笹　茅　萱　藁　芦　葦　菅

草
▷grass
ソウ くさ -ぐさ　　　Ⓚ1953

[also suffix] **grass, weed**
草原 そうげん grassland, prairie, savannah, pampas, steppe
草木 そうもく trees and plants, vegetation
草食の そうしょくの herbivorous
野草 やそう wild grass
雑草 ざっそう weed
海草 かいそう seaweed
除草剤 じょそうざい herbicide
一年草 いちねんそう annual plant, therophyte

荻
▷**Amur silvergrass**
テキ おぎ　　　Ⓚ1976

Amur silvergrass
荻花 てきか flower of Amur silvergrass

蒲
▷cattail
フ ホ かば かま がま　　　Ⓚ2039

cattail, reed mace
蒲団 ふとん [now usu. 布団] futon, bedquilt
蒲柳の質 ほりゅうのしつ delicate [fragile] health

莱
▷goosefoot
ライ　　　Ⓚ2002

goosefoot
蓬莱 ほうらい Mt. Penglai, a mystical land in Chinese mythology

蕨
▷bracken
ケツ わらび　　　Ⓚ2085

bracken, brake
蕨粉 わらびこ bracken starch
蕨餅 わらびもち bracken-starch dumpling

蕨糊 わらびのり glue produced from bracken starch

叢 ▷grassy place
ソウ むら むら(がる) くさむら   Ⓚ2277

[sometimes also 双] **crowd together, meet in large numbers**
  叢生する そうせいする grow in clusters
  叢書(=双書) そうしょ series, library
  叢談 そうだん collection of stories
  叢氷 そうひょう ice pack
  論叢 ろんそう collection of treatises

芝 ▷lawn grass
しば   Ⓚ1867

ⓐ **lawn grass, zoysia**
ⓑ **lawn, turf, sod**
 a 芝草 しばくさ lawn
  芝地 しばち grass plot
  高麗芝 こうらいしば Korean lawn grass
 b 芝生 しばふ lawn, turf
  芝刈り機 しばかりき lawn mower
  芝居 しばい play, drama

笹 ▷bamboo grass
ささ   Ⓚ2321

[sometimes also 篠] **bamboo grass**
  笹原 ささはら field of bamboo grass
  笹舟 ささぶね toy bamboo-leaf boat
  熊笹 くまざさ *Sasa albo-marginata*, low and striped bamboo

茅 ▷cogongrass
ボウ ミョウ かや ちがや   Ⓚ1922

【ボウ ミョウ】
thatch grass such as cogongrass, eulalias and other gramineous plants
  茅屋 ぼうおく thatched cottage, hovel; my humble abode

【かや】
[also 萱] **thatch grass such as cogongrass, eulalias and other gramineous plants**
  茅葺 かやぶき roofing with thatch grass
  茅戸 かやと hilly place with a thick cogongrass bush

萱 ▷thatch grass
カン ケン かや   Ⓚ2016

[also 茅] **thatch grass such as cogongrass, eulalias and other gramineous plants**
  萱葺き かやぶき roofing with thatch grass
  萱鼠 かやねずみ harvest mouse
  茅萱 ちがや cogongrass

藁 ▷straw
コウ わら   Ⓚ2103

straw
  藁葺き わらぶき straw thatching; straw roof
  藁人形 わらにんぎょう straw effigy [doll]
  麦藁 むぎわら (wheat) straw
  稲藁 いねわら(=いなわら) rice [paddy] straw
  敷き藁 しきわら bed of straw, litter
  溺れる者は藁をも摑む おぼれるものはわらをもつかむ A drowning man will catch at a straw

芦 ▷reed
ロ あし よし   Ⓚ1897

common reed, reed
  芦花 ろか reed flower

葦 ▷common reed
イ あし よし   Ⓚ2041

common reed, reed
  葦岸 いがん reedy shore
  一葦 いちい a boat

菅 ▷sedge
カン ケン すげ すが   Ⓚ1998

sedge
  菅蓋 かんがい large sedge parasol

kinds of numbers
数 員 号 番 第 目 次 桁

数 ▷number (mathematical unit)
スウ ス かず かぞ(える)   Ⓚ1591

[also suffix] (abstract mathematical unit) **number, numbers**
  数字 すうじ figure, numeral
  対数 たいすう logarithm
  指数 しすう index (number); exponent
  関数(=函数) かんすう *math* function
  自然数 しぜんすう natural number
  無理数 むりすう irrational number

員 ▷fixed number
イン   Ⓚ195

fixed number, capacity
  員数 いんずう(=いんすう) number, total
  定員 ていいん fixed number of regular personnel; capacity
  満員 まんいん full to capacity

号 ▷number (numerical designation)
ゴウ Ⓚ1847

[also suffix]
- **ⓐ** (numerical designation or label) **number**, as: **room No., house No., type size No., railroad car No., route No., item [subsection] No.,** etc.
- **ⓑ** (single copy of a periodical) **number, issue**

- a 号数 ごうすう number or size of periodicals or pictures, type size
- 番号 ばんごう number, serial number
- 百号室 ひゃくごうしつ room No. 100
- 一丁目二番地九号 いっちょうめにばんちきゅうごう 2-9, 1-chome (part of an address)
- 五号活字 ごごうかつじ No. 5 type, small pica
- 十五号車 じゅうごごうしゃ (railway) car No. 15
- 二号線 にごうせん Route No. 2
- 第二項第四号 だいにこうだいよんごう Subsection 2, Paragraph 4
- b 号外 ごうがい newspaper extra
- 第二号 だいにごう second issue; number two
- 創刊号 そうかんごう inaugural number, first issue

番 ▷No.
バン Ⓚ2396

suffix for expressing numerical order or forming ordinal numbers: **No., number**

- 一番 いちばん first, first place; first verse; most, best; a game, a round, a bout; a number, a piece
- 三番線 さんばんせん Track No. 3

第 ▷ordinal number prefix
ダイ Ⓚ2318

prefix for forming ordinal numbers

- 第五 だいご the fifth, No. 5
- 第一印象 だいいちいんしょう first impression
- 第一 だいいち the first, number one; the best; to begin with, above everything else
- 第三者 だいさんしゃ third party
- 第六感 だいろっかん the sixth sense, intuition

目 ▷ordinal number suffix
モク ボク -め ま- Ⓚ2619

suffix indicating ordinal numbers or order

- 五十年目 ごじゅうねんめ 50th year
- 二番目 にばんめ second

次 ▷numerical order suffix
ジ シ つ(ぐ) つぎ Ⓚ0039

suffix indicating numerical order or number of times

- 一次の いちじの first, primary; *math* linear, of the first degree
- 第二次世界大戦 だいにじせかいたいせん World War II

桁 ▷digit
けた Ⓚ0839

digit, figure, unit, place, order of magnitude

- 桁違い けたちがい different order of magnitude; exceptional, incomparable, in a different league
- 桁外れ けたはずれ exceptional, incomparable, in a different league
- 桁数 けたすう number of digits [places]
- 一桁 ひとけた one digit; single-digit
- 下二桁 しもふたけた last two figures of a number

kinds of precipitation
雨　露　霜　雪

雨 ▷rain
ウ あめ あま- -さめ Ⓚ2983

[original meaning] **rain, rainfall**

- 雨量 うりょう rain, rainfall
- 雨期(=雨季) うき rainy season
- 降雨 こうう rainfall, rain
- 豪雨 ごうう heavy rain, downpour
- 梅雨(=黴雨) ばいう rainy season (of early summer)
- 風雨 ふうう wind and rain, storm

露 ▷dew
ロ ロウ つゆ Ⓚ2454

[original meaning] **dew, dewdrop**

- 露滴 ろてき dewdrop
- 露点 ろてん dew point
- 雨露 うろ rain and dew

霜 ▷frost
ソウ しも Ⓚ2451

[original meaning] **frost, hoarfrost**

- 霜害 そうがい frost damage
- 霜雪 そうせつ frost and snow
- 降霜 こうそう (fall of) frost

雪 ▷snow
セツ ゆき Ⓚ2406

snow, snowfall

- 雪上車 せつじょうしゃ snowmobile
- 豪雪 ごうせつ tremendous snowfall
- 降雪 こうせつ snowfall, snow
- 積雪 せきせつ (fallen) snow
- 新雪 しんせつ fresh snow
- 蛍雪 けいせつ diligent study

kinds of railway

鉄 電 車 両 輌

鉄 ▷railway
テツ   Ⓚ1527

abbrev. of 鉄道 てつどう: **railway, railroad line**
- 国鉄 こくてつ Japanese National Railways (defunct)
- 地下鉄 ちかてつ subway
- 私鉄 してつ nongovernmental [private] railroad line
- 電鉄 でんてつ electric railway

電 ▷electric railway
デン   Ⓚ2431

abbrev. of 電車 でんしゃ: **electric railway, train**
- 終電 しゅうでん last train
- 国電 こくでん National Railway

車 ▷railway car
シャ くるま   Ⓚ2976

railway car, train
- 電車 でんしゃ train, electric train, trolley
- 列車 れっしゃ (railway) train
- 客車 きゃくしゃ passenger car
- 機関車 きかんしゃ locomotive

両 ▷counter for railway cars
リョウ   Ⓚ2949

counter for railway cars
- 三両 さんりょう three cars, three coaches

輌 ▷counter for railway cars
リョウ

counter for railway cars
- 三輌 さんりょう three cars, three coaches

kinds of skin

皮 膚 肌 革 韋 鱗

皮 ▷skin (of any kind)
ヒ かわ   Ⓚ2615

- ⓐ [original meaning] **skin (of human beings or animals), hide, pelt; fur; leather**
- ⓑ **skin (of plants), bark, peel, husk, shell**
- ⓐ 皮膚 ひふ skin
- 皮革 ひかく leather, hides
- 皮下注射 ひかちゅうしゃ hypodermic injection

- 皮肉 ひにく cynicism, sarcasm; irony
- 脱皮 だっぴ ecdysis; self-renewal
- ⓑ 樹皮 じゅひ bark

膚 ▷skin (of the human body)
フ   Ⓚ278■

skin (of the human body)
- 皮膚 ひふ skin
- 完膚無き迄 かんぷなきまで thoroughly, beyond recognition; scathingly

肌 ▷skin (of the human body)
はだ   Ⓚ073

[original meaning] **skin (of the human body)**
- 肌膚 きふ skin
- 肌骨 きこつ skin and bones

革 ▷leather
カク かわ   Ⓚ216■

leather, tanned skin
- 革質の かくしつの coriaceous, leathery
- 皮革 ひかく leather, hides

韋 ▷tanned leather
イ

tanned [dressed] leather [skin], leather
- 韋編 いへん leather cord

鱗 ▷scales
リン うろこ   Ⓚ1668

scales (of animals or plants)
- 鱗粉 りんぷん scales (of an insect)
- 鱗状 りんじょう scaly, scale-like
- 鱗片葉 りんぺんよう scale leaf
- 片鱗 へんりん a scale; part, glimpse, hint
- 逆鱗 げきりん wrath of one's superior, imperial wrath
- 銀鱗 ぎんりん silvery scales; fish

kinds of sound

音 声 響 韻 玲

音 ▷sound
オン イン おと ね   Ⓚ178■

[also suffix]
- ⓐ (vibratory disturbance) **sound, noise, roar**
- ⓑ (auditory sensation) **sound**
- ⓒ [original meaning] **speech sound, voice, pronunciation**
- ⓐ 音響 おんきょう sound
- 騒音 そうおん noise

録音 ろくおん sound recording
b 音質 おんしつ sound [tone] quality
音声 おんせい voice, sound
c 音韻論 おんいんろん phonology
音節 おんせつ syllable
発音 はつおん pronunciation
英音 えいおん English pronunciation
子音 しいん(=しおん) consonant ("child sound")
母音 ぼいん vowel ("mother sound")
五十音 ごじゅうおん Japanese syllabary
破裂音 はれつおん plosive, stop

声 ▷voice
セイ ショウ こえ こわ-　　　　Ⓚ1880

ⓐ [original meaning] **voice, sound**
ⓑ (tone produced in singing) **voice**
ⓒ *phonetics* **voice**

a 声調 せいちょう tone of voice, style; tone (in
　　Chinese phonetics)
声帯 せいたい vocal cords
音声 おんせい voice, sound
発声 はっせい vocalization, utterance
銃声 じゅうせい sound of gunfire
擬声語 ぎせいご onomatopoeic word
大音声 だいおんじょう very loud voice
b 声楽 せいがく vocal music
混声合唱 こんせいがっしょう mixed chorus
c 有声音 ゆうせいおん voiced sound

響 ▷reverberation
キョウ ひび(く)　　　　Ⓚ2504

reverberation, echo, sound
音響 おんきょう sound
交響 こうきょう reverberation
無響室 むきょうしつ anechoic room
交響曲 こうきょうきょく symphony

韻 ▷melodious tone
イン　　　　Ⓚ1609

melodious tone, agreeable sound, resonance
余韻 よいん lingering tone, resonance, reverbera-
　　tion; aftertaste, impregnated elegance
松韻 しょういん music of the pines

玲 ▷tinkling of jades
レイ　　　　Ⓚ0818

[archaic] **tinkling of jades, sound of jewels**
玲玲 れいれい tinkling of jades

---

kinds of stone
硯　　砥

硯 ▷inkstone
ケン すずり　　　　Ⓚ1094

inkstone
　硯石 けんせき(=すずりいし) material out of which
　　inkstones are made

砥 ▷whetstone
シ と(ぐ)　　　　Ⓚ1066

whetstone, grindstone
　砥礪 しれい whetstone; diligent study, self-
　　disciplinary efforts

---

kinds of water
水　湯　汽　氷　淵

水 ▷water
スイ みず　　　　Ⓚ0003

[original meaning] **water, cold water**
　水道 すいどう water service [supply]; channel
　水準 すいじゅん level, standard; water level
　水中 すいちゅう in the water
　水面 すいめん surface of the water
　水力 すいりょく waterpower, hydraulic power
　水蒸気 すいじょうき steam, water vapor
　海水 かいすい seawater
　地下水 ちかすい underground water

湯 ▷hot water
トウ ゆ　　　　Ⓚ0561

[original meaning] **hot water, boiling water**
　給湯 きゅうとう hot water supply
　熱湯 ねっとう boiling water

汽 ▷steam
キ　　　　Ⓚ0234

steam, vapor
　汽車 きしゃ (steam) train
　汽船 きせん steamship
　汽圧 きあつ steam pressure
　汽缶 きかん boiler
　汽笛 きてき steam whistle
　汽水 きすい brackish water

氷 ▷ice
ヒョウ こおり ひ   Ⓚ0025

ice
- 氷晶 ひょうしょう ice crystal
- 氷河 ひょうが glacier
- 氷山 ひょうざん iceberg
- 氷雪 ひょうせつ ice and snow
- 樹氷 じゅひょう trees covered with ice
- 製氷 せいひょう ice making

淵 ▷deep water
エン ふち   Ⓚ0547

【エン】
deep water [pool], depths, abyss
- 淵源 えんげん origin
- 海淵 かいえん ocean depths, deep
- 深淵 しんえん abyss, depths

【ふち】
deep water [pool], depths, abyss
- 川の淵 かわのふち pool in a stream
- 絶望の淵 ぜつぼうのふち depths of despair

kinds of wood
木 材 薪 柴

木 ▷wood
ボク モク き こ-   Ⓚ2901

ⓐ wood, timber
ⓑ wooden
- a 木材 もくざい wood, timber, lumber
- 木目 もくめ wood grain
- 木工 もっこう woodworking, woodworker
- 原木 げんぼく material wood; pulpwood
- 土木 どぼく engineering works
- b 木刀 ぼくとう wooden sword
- 木製の もくせいの wooden, made of wood
- 木造の もくぞうの wooden

材 ▷timber
ザイ   Ⓚ0740

[original meaning] **timber, lumber, wood**
- 材木 ざいもく timber, lumber, wood, logs
- 木材 もくざい wood, timber, lumber
- 良材 りょうざい good timber
- 製材業 せいざいぎょう lumbering [sawing] industry

薪 ▷firewood
シン たきぎ   Ⓚ2098

firewood, wood for fuel
- 薪炭 しんたん firewood and charcoal

- 薪水 しんすい cooking

柴 ▷brushwood
サイ しば   Ⓚ2309

[original meaning] **brushwood, firewood**
- 柴戸 さいこ brushwood door; crude dwelling
- 柴門 さいもん gate made of woven brushwood; humble home

kitchen
厨 庖

厨 ▷kitchen
チュウ ズ くりや   Ⓚ2596

kitchen
- 厨房 ちゅうぼう kitchen, galley
- 庖厨 ほうちゅう kitchen

庖 ▷kitchen
ホウ

[now also 包] [original meaning] **kitchen**
- 庖厨 ほうちゅう kitchen
- 庖丁 ほうちょう kitchen knife, carving knife

know and understand
知 通 得 分 解
諒 了 悟 惺

知 ▷know
チ し(る) し(らせる) し(れる)   Ⓚ1041

know, be aware of, understand; perceive, recognize
- 知識 ちしき knowledge
- 知覚 ちかく perception, sensation
- 周知の しゅうちの known to all, universally known
- 承知する しょうちする consent [agree] to; permit; forgive; know, understand
- 探知 たんち detection

通 ▷know thoroughly
ツウ ツ とお(る) とお(り)
-どお(り) とお(す) とお(し) -どお(し)
かよ(う)   Ⓚ267

know [understand] thoroughly, be thoroughly familiar with, master

通人 つうじん man of the world, man about town; dilettante
精通する せいつうする be well versed in, have thorough knowledge of

得 ▷gain understanding of
トク え(る) う(る)   Ⓚ0435

gain understanding of, comprehend, realize
習得する しゅうとくする learn, master, acquire (an art)
体得する たいとくする realize, learn (from experience), comprehend, master
納得 なっとく assent, consent, understanding

分 ▷understand
ブン フン ブ わ(ける) わ(け) わ(かれる) わ(かる) わ(かつ)   Ⓚ1713

ⓐ (grasp the meaning of) **understand, comprehend, see**
ⓑ (be sympathetic toward) **understand, show understanding for (another's feelings)**
ａ 分かり わかり understanding
  分かり難い わかりにくい hard to understand, incomprehensible, unintelligible
ｂ 分からず屋 わからずや obstinate person, hardhead
  物分かりの良い ものわかりのよい understanding, sensible

解 ▷understand
カイ ゲ と(く) と(かす) と(ける)   Ⓚ1375

understand, comprehend
理解する りかいする understand, comprehend
見解 けんかい opinion, view
了解 りょうかい understanding, comprehension; consent
誤解 ごかい misunderstanding, misconception
難解な なんかいな difficult, hard to understand
不可解な ふかかいな incomprehensible, inexplicable, baffling

諒 ▷understand
リョウ   Ⓚ1425

[now usu. 了]
ⓐ **understand, comprehend, know clearly**
ⓑ [rarely also 亮] **show understanding, be sympathetic, acknowledge, forgive**
ａ 諒解 りょうかい understanding, comprehension; consent
  諒承する りょうしょうする acknowledge, understand, note
ｂ 諒察する りょうさつする consider, take into account, sympathize with

了 ▷comprehend
リョウ   Ⓚ2852

[sometimes also 諒 or 領]
ⓐ **comprehend, know clearly, understand**
ⓑ **show understanding, be sympathetic, acknowledge**
ａ 了解 りょうかい understanding, comprehension; consent
  了承する りょうしょうする acknowledge, understand, note
  了知する りょうちする know, understand, appreciate
ｂ 了察する りょうさつする consider, take into account, sympathize with

悟 ▷awake to
ゴ さと(る)   Ⓚ0379

awake to, become aware of, realize, comprehend
悟了 ごりょう complete comprehension
覚悟する かくごする be ready [prepared] for; be resigned; make up one's mind

惺 ▷awake to
セイ   Ⓚ0533

[original meaning, now rare] **awake to**
惺悟する せいごする awaken to the Truth, become enlightened

knowledge →LEARNING AND KNOWLEDGE

Korea
鮮   朝   韓

鮮 ▷Korea
セン あざ(やか)   Ⓚ1656

Korea
朝鮮 ちょうせん (North) Korea
南鮮 なんせん South Korea
北鮮 ほくせん North Korea

朝 ▷North Korea
チョウ あさ   Ⓚ1513

North Korea, Korea
朝鮮 ちょうせん (North) Korea

韓 ▷South Korea
カン   Ⓚ1575

ⓐ **South Korea, Republic of Korea**
ⓑ **name of state in late Zhou Dynasty**
ⓒ **southern part of Korean Peninsula in ancient times**
ａ 韓国 かんこく South Korea

大韓民国 だいかんみんこく Republic of Korea
日韓 にっかん Japan and (South) Korea
訪韓 ほうかん visit to Korea
bc 三韓 さんかん the Three Han States; the Three Countries of Korea

labels and slips
札 券 票 符 節

札 ▷tag
サツ ふだ   Ⓚ0723

ⓐ tag, plate, placard
ⓑ ticket
ⓒ [original meaning] thin wooden tablet used for writing in ancient China

a 標札(=表札) ひょうさつ nameplate, doorplate
  門札 もんさつ doorplate, nameplate
  鑑札 かんさつ license, certificate
b 検札 けんさつ examination of tickets
  改札口 かいさつぐち ticket barrier [gate], wicket

券 ▷ticket
ケン   Ⓚ2286

[also suffix] ticket, coupon
食券 しょっけん food ticket
乗車券 じょうしゃけん railway [passenger] ticket
入場券 にゅうじょうけん entrance [admission] ticket
定期券 ていきけん commuter's pass

票 ▷slip
ヒョウ   Ⓚ2326

[also suffix] slip, chit, voucher, card
伝票 でんぴょう slip, chit, ticket
証票 しょうひょう voucher, chit
軍票 ぐんぴょう military scrip, army note
入金票 にゅうきんひょう deposit slip
住民票 じゅうみんひょう resident card
調査票 ちょうさひょう questionnaire

符 ▷tally
フ   Ⓚ2319

[original meaning] tally (of wood or bamboo) split in half used for identification (esp. in ancient China); tag
符節 ふせつ tally, check
割符 わりふ tally, check
切符 きっぷ ticket

節 ▷token
セツ セチ ふし ‐ぶし   Ⓚ234

token or bamboo tally used in ancient times as credentials
使節 しせつ envoy, ambassador
符節 ふせつ tally, check

lakes and marshes
沢 沼 湖 池 潟

沢 ▷marsh
タク さわ   Ⓚ023

[original meaning] marsh, swamp
沼沢 しょうたく marsh, swamp

沼 ▷muddy pond
ショウ ぬま   Ⓚ030

[original meaning] muddy pond, low-lying lake, swamp, marsh, bog
沼沢 しょうたく marsh, swamp
沼気 しょうき marsh gas, methane
湖沼 こしょう lakes and marshes

湖 ▷lake
コ みずうみ   Ⓚ055

ⓐ [also suffix] [original meaning] lake
ⓑ suffix after names of lakes
a 湖上 こじょう on the lake
  湖畔 こはん lake shore, lakeside
  湖沼 こしょう lakes and marshes
  淡水湖 たんすいこ freshwater lake
b 琵琶湖 びわこ Lake Biwa

池 ▷pond
チ いけ   Ⓚ019

[also suffix] [original meaning] pond, pool
池畔 ちはん edge of a pond
池沼 ちしょう ponds and swamps
養殖池 ようしょくち fish pond

潟 ▷lagoon
かた ‐がた   Ⓚ067

ⓐ lagoon
ⓑ suffix after names of lagoons
a 八郎潟 はちろうがた Lagoon Hachiro

land and soil
土 地 壌 泥 陸 埴

土 ▷soil
ド ト つち   Ⓚ2875

ⓐ [also suffix] [original meaning] **soil, earth, mud, sand, clay**
ⓑ **earthen**

- a 土砂 どしゃ earth and sand
  土壌 どじょう soil, earth
  土俵 どひょう sumo (wrestling) ring; sandbag
  土台 どだい foundation, base, basis; utterly
  土木 どぼく engineering works
  土砂降り どしゃぶり pouring rain, downpour
  土壇場 どたんば the last moment
  土足で どそくで with one's shoes on
  土手 どて bank, embankment
  土間 どま earth floor, dirt floor; pit
  粘土 ねんど clay
  耕土 こうど arable soil
  珪藻土 けいそうど diatomite, silicious marl
  アルカリ土類 あるかりどるい alkaline earths
- b 土器 どき earthenware
  土瓶 どびん earthen teapot, pipkin
  土用 どよう midsummer

地 ▷ground
チ ジ   Ⓚ0181

[also suffix]
ⓐ (solid surface of the earth) **ground, earth, land**
ⓑ (functionally distinguished tract) **land, ground, soil**

- a 地面 じめん surface, ground, land
  地下の ちかの underground, subterranean
  地震 じしん earthquake
  地上に ちじょうに on the ground; on earth
  地階 ちかい basement, cellar
  地図 ちず map, atlas
  地理 ちり geographical features, topography; geography
  地盤 じばん ground, foundation, base
  地形 ちけい geographical features, topography
  地質 ちしつ geological features; nature of the soil
  土地 とち land
  高地 こうち high ground, plateau, heights
  湿地 しっち damp ground, swamp
  耕地 こうち arable land, farm land
  扇状地 せんじょうち alluvial delta
- b 地主 じぬし landlord, landowner
  地目 ちもく classification of land category
  地価 ちか price [value] of land
  宅地 たくち land for housing, residential land

敷地 しきち (building) site, (plot of) ground, lot
空き地 あきち unoccupied ground, vacant lot
分譲地 ぶんじょうち (building) lots for sale

壌 ▷arable soil
ジョウ   Ⓚ0683

ⓐ [original meaning] **arable soil, (loose or loamy) soil, fertile soil, earth, loam**
ⓑ **earth, land**

- a 土壌 どじょう soil, earth
- b 天壌 てんじょう heaven and earth

泥 ▷mud
デイ どろ   Ⓚ0288

[original meaning] **mud, mire**
泥土 でいど mud, mire
泥水 でいすい(=どろみず) muddy water, liquid mud
泥濘 でいねい mud, slush, mire; muddy road
雲泥の差 うんでいのさ great difference (as between clouds and mud)

陸 ▷land
リク   Ⓚ0496

(solid ground of the earth, as distinguished from the sea)
land, shore
陸地 りくち land
陸上 りくじょう land, ground; shore; track and field
陸橋 りっきょう overland bridge
陸兵 りくへい land troops
陸岸 りくがん shore, land
陸軍 りくぐん army
陸上自衛隊 りくじょうじえいたい Ground Self Defense Forces
大陸 たいりく continent
上陸 じょうりく landing, disembarkation
着陸 ちゃくりく landing, alighting

埴 ▷clay
ショク はに   Ⓚ0424

clay
埴土 しょくど soil with clay content of 50 percent or more

language
語 弁

語 ▷language
ゴ かた(る) かた(らう)   Ⓚ1402

ⓐ [also suffix] **language, speech**
ⓑ **suffix for forming names of languages**

- a 語学 ごがく language study, linguistics

言語 げんご language, speech, words
国語 こくご national language; Japanese
文語 ぶんご literary [written] language
敬語 けいご honorific language, polite speech
標準語 ひょうじゅんご standard language [speech]
外国語 がいこくご foreign language
b 英語 えいご English
日本語 にほんご Japanese

弁 ▷dialect
ベン   Ⓚ1730

[suffix] (regional speech) **dialect, accent**
東北弁 とうほくべん Tohoku dialect [accent]
関西弁 かんさいべん Kansai dialect [accent]

large numbers
百 千 万 億 兆 京

百 ▷hundred
ヒャク   Ⓚ1746

hundred
百円 ひゃくえん 100 yen
百分率 ひゃくぶんりつ percentage
百倍 ひゃくばい hundredfold, hundred times
五百七十 ごひゃくななじゅう 570

千 ▷thousand
セン ち   Ⓚ2881

thousand
千円 せんえん 1000 yen
五千 ごせん 5000

万 ▷ten thousand
マン バン   Ⓚ2542

ten thousand
万年 まんねん 10,000 years, eternity
万一 まんいち(=まんいつ) if by any chance
一万 いちまん 10,000

億 ▷hundred million
オク   Ⓚ0148

hundred million (10^8)
億万長者 おくまんちょうじゃ billionaire
一億 いちおく 100,000,000

兆 ▷trillion
チョウ きざ(す) きざ(し)   Ⓚ0199

trillion (10^{12})
八兆円 はっちょうえん eight trillion yen

京 ▷ten quadrillion
キョウ ケイ キン   Ⓚ176

ten quadrillion (10^{16})
二京 にけい 20 quadrillion

last
末 終

末 ▷last in time
マツ バツ すえ   Ⓚ294

last in time, terminal, final
末日 まつじつ last day
末期 まっき closing years, final stage
末期的 まっきてき decadent; terminal (patient)
末葉 まつよう end [close] of an epoch; descendant
末期 まつご hour of death, one's last moments
末路 まつろ last days; fate

終 ▷last
シュウ お(わる) お(える)   Ⓚ122

[also prefix] **last, final, terminal**
終始 しゅうし from beginning to end, always
終点 しゅうてん last stop, terminus
終盤戦 しゅうばんせん end game
終列車 しゅうれっしゃ last train
終刊号 しゅうかんごう final issue
終着駅 しゅうちゃくえき terminal station, railroad
   terminal

late →BE LATE AND DELAY

late
遅 晩 晏

遅 ▷late (delayed)
チ おく(れる) おく(らす) おそ(い) Ⓚ270

(delayed) **late, tardy**
遅延 ちえん delay, retardation
遅配 ちはい delay in rationing

晩 ▷late (advanced)
バン   Ⓚ089

ⓐ (advanced) **late, drawing toward the end, in the
latter part**
ⓑ **late in life**
a 晩春 ばんしゅん late spring
   早晩 そうばん sooner or later
b 晩学 ばんがく late education

晩年 ばんねん late in life
晩婚 ばんこん late marriage

晏 ▷late
アン エン Ⓚ2166

[original meaning, now rare] **late (hours of the day)**
晏起 あんき getting up late in the morning, late rising

later Chinese dynasties
唐 宋 元 明 清

唐 ▷Tang Dynasty
トウ から Ⓚ2685

Tang Dynasty (618-907 A.D.)
唐朝 とうちょう Tang Dynasty
唐詩 とうし Tang poetry

宋 ▷Song Dynasty
ソウ Ⓚ1886

Song Dynasty (960-1279 A.D.)
宋詞 そうし Song poetry
宋学 そうがく Song-period neo-Confucianism
南宋 なんそう Southern Song Dynasty
北宋 ほくそう Northern Song Dynasty

元 ▷Yuan Dynasty
ゲン ガン もと Ⓚ1690

Yuan Dynasty (1271-1368 A.D.) (Chinese dynasty ruled by the Mongols)
元寇 げんこう the Mongolian Invasions

明 ▷Ming Dynasty
メイ
ミョウ あ(かり) あか(るい) あか(るむ)
あか(らむ) あき(らか) あ(ける) -あ(け)
あ(く) あ(くる) あ(かす) Ⓚ0756

Ming Dynasty (1368-1644 A.D.)
明朝 みんちょう Ming Dynasty
明朝体 みんちょうたい Ming-style typeface

清 ▷Qing Dynasty
セイ ショウ きよ(い) きよ(まる)
きよ(める) Ⓚ0479

Qing Dynasty, Manchu Dynasty (1644-1912 A.D.)
清国 しんこく China under the Manchus
日清戦争 にっしんせんそう the Sino-Japanese War (of 1894-95)

latitude and longitude
緯 経

緯 ▷latitude
イ Ⓚ1285

latitude, lines of latitude
緯度 いど latitude
緯線 いせん parallels of latitude
経緯 けいい latitude and longitude
北緯 ほくい north latitude

経 ▷longitude
ケイ キョウ へ(る) た(つ) Ⓚ1218

longitude
経度 けいど longitude
西経 せいけい west longitude

laugh
笑 莞

笑 ▷laugh
ショウ わら(う) え(む) Ⓚ2300

【ショウ】
❶ **laugh, smile**
一笑する いっしょうする laugh a laugh, smile a smile
爆笑する ばくしょうする roar with laughter, burst into laughter
❷ **laughter, smile**
微笑 びしょう smile
苦笑 くしょう forced [strained] smile
【わら(う)】
laugh, smile; laugh at, ridicule, deride; bloom beautifully
笑い わらい laughter, smile; sneer
笑い声 わらいごえ laughter
笑い話 わらいばなし funny [humorous] story
笑い物 わらいもの object of ridicule, subject of derision
笑い草(=笑い種) わらいぐさ laughingstock

莞 ▷smile sweetly
カン ガン Ⓚ1974

smile sweetly
莞爾たる かんじたる with a (sweet) smile

laws and rules
法 律 典 憲 令 則 矩 規 紀

刑典 けいてん penal code

憲 ▷constitution
ケン ⑥209

constitution, code of laws

憲法 けんぽう constitution, constitutional law
憲政 けんせい constitutional government
憲章 けんしょう constitution, charter
制憲する せいけんする establish a constitution
合憲的 ごうけんてき constitutional
立憲 りっけん constitutionalism

令 ▷ordinance
レイ ⑥172

[also suffix] **ordinance, law, act**

政令 せいれい government ordinance, cabinet order
法令 ほうれい laws and ordinances, statute
戒厳令 かいげんれい martial law

則 ▷rule
ソク ⑥131

[also suffix] **rule, regulation, principle, law**

規則 きそく rule, regulation
法則 ほうそく law, rule
鉄則 てっそく ironclad rule, immutable law
原則 げんそく principle, general rule
学則 がくそく school regulations
教則 きょうそく rules for teaching
反則 はんそく violation of rules, infringement, fou
罰則 ばっそく penal regulations, punitive provisions
付則 ふそく additional rules, bylaw
自民党則 じみんとうそく rules of the Liberal Democratic Party

矩 ▷rule
ク かね ⑥106

(established standard) **rule, standard, criterion**
矩則 くそく rule, standard

規 ▷regulation
キ ⑥089

regulation, rule, standard

規定 きてい regulations, rules; provisions
規則 きそく rule, regulation
規約 きやく agreement, rules, bylaws
規律 きりつ order, discipline; regulation, law
規範 きはん standard, norm, criterion
規格 きかく standard, norm
規準 きじゅん standard, criterion
法規 ほうき laws and regulations
内規 ないき private rules [regulations], bylaws

法 ▷law
ホウ ハツ‐ ホツ‐ ⑥0295

ⓐ [also suffix] **law, rule, act, code of laws**
ⓑ **law(s) (as of an art), principle, rule**

ａ 法律 ほうりつ law
法令 ほうれい laws and ordinances, statute
法学 ほうがく law, jurisprudence
法学部 ほうがくぶ law department [school]
法廷 ほうてい law court
法的 ほうてき legal, legalistic
法規 ほうき laws and regulations
法案 ほうあん bill, legislative proposal
法人 ほうじん legal person, corporation
法典 ほうてん code of laws, statute
法度 はっと law, ordinance, prohibition
憲法 けんぽう constitution, constitutional law
違法の いほうの illegal, unlawful
刑法 けいほう criminal law, penal code
国際法 こくさいほう international laws
農地法 のうちほう Agricultural Land Law
騒音防止法 そうおんぼうしほう Noise Abatement Act
ｂ 法則 ほうそく law, rule
画法 がほう laws [canons] of painting

律 ▷law
リツ リチ ⑥0322

[also suffix] **law, rule, statute, regulation; commandment**

律令 りつりょう ancient laws
律儀 りちぎ honesty, faithfulness, loyalty
法律 ほうりつ law
規律 きりつ order, discipline; regulation, law
不文律 ふぶんりつ unwritten law [rule]
道徳律 どうとくりつ moral law
戒律 かいりつ commandments, precepts
黄金律 おうごんりつ golden rule
因果律 いんがりつ law of cause and effect, principle of causality

典 ▷canon
テン ⑥2283

(standard code of laws) **canon, code, law, rule, principle**

典則 てんそく regulations
法典 ほうてん code of laws, statute

校規 こうき school regulations

紀 ▷discipline
キ　⟨K⟩1173

discipline, morals, order, code of behavior
校紀 こうき school discipline
風紀 ふうき public morals
綱紀 こうき law and order, official discipline
軍紀 ぐんき military discipline, troop morals
党紀 とうき party discipline

lazy
惰　怠　慢

惰 ▷lazy
ダ　⟨K⟩0531

[original meaning] **lazy, indolent, idle**
惰気 だき indolence, inactivity, laziness
惰眠 だみん indolence, idle slumber, inactivity
怠惰 たいだ laziness, idleness

怠 ▷remiss
タイ　おこた(る)　なま(ける)　⟨K⟩1794

ⓐ [original meaning] (inclined to idleness) **remiss, idle, lazy, sluggish**
ⓑ (neglectful) **remiss, negligent, careless**
a 怠惰な たいだな lazy, idle
　倦怠 けんたい fatigue, languor, weariness
b 怠慢な たいまんな negligent, inattentive, remiss
　怠業 たいぎょう slowdown strike, deliberate idleness

慢 ▷sluggish
マン　⟨K⟩0625

[original meaning] (lacking in vigor) **sluggish, lazy, idle**
怠慢な たいまんな negligent, inattentive, remiss

lead and escort
率　引　導　連

率 ▷lead
ソツ　リツ　ひき(いる)　⟨K⟩1820

lead, head, command (troops)
率先 そっせん taking the lead [initiative]
統率する とうそつする lead, command
引率者 いんそつしゃ leader, commander

引 ▷lead
イン　ひ(く)　ひ(き)　-び(き)
ひ(ける)　⟨K⟩0160

lead, guide, take along
引率する いんそつする lead, command
引導 いんどう guidance; address to a departed soul
引致 いんち arrest, custody

導 ▷guide
ドウ　みちび(く)　⟨K⟩2509

(show the way) **guide, lead, conduct**
導入する どうにゅうする lead into, bring into
導因 どういん inducement, incentive
主導権 しゅどうけん leadership, initiative
誘導する ゆうどうする induce, incite; guide, lead
盲導犬 もうどうけん guide dog, Seeing Eye dog

連 ▷take along
レン　つら(なる)　つら(ねる)　つ(れる)
-づ(れ)　⟨K⟩2672

take along, bring along, accompany
連行する れんこうする take a suspect to the police

leaders
主　王　長　頭　首　領　魁

主 ▷master
シュ　ス　ぬし　おも　あるじ　⟨K⟩1696

[also suffix] **master, lord, chief, host, head, owner, proprietor, employer**
主人 しゅじん master, head, host, proprietor; husband
主将 しゅしょう captain
主従 しゅじゅう(=しゅうじゅう) master and servant, lord and vassal
喪主 もしゅ chief mourner
船主 せんしゅ shipowner
商店主 しょうてんしゅ proprietor of a shop, storekeeper

王 ▷king
オウ　⟨K⟩2895

[also suffix] (the most powerful of a group) **king, magnate, baron**
王者 おうじゃ king, monarch, champion
法王 ほうおう pope
海賊王 かいぞくおう pirate king
石油王 せきゆおう oil magnate

長 ▷chief
チョウ なが(い)　Ⓚ2212

[also suffix] **chief, head, president, director, chairman**
長官 ちょうかん director, administrator, chief
課長 かちょう section chief [head]
市長 しちょう mayor
船長 せんちょう (ship) captain
社長 しゃちょう president (of a company)
会長 かいちょう president (of a society)
議長 ぎちょう chairman, president (of the senate)
酋長 しゅうちょう chieftain
裁判長 さいばんちょう presiding [chief] judge

頭 ▷head
トウ ズ ト あたま かしら −がしら Ⓚ1450

(person in a leading position) **head, chief, leader**
頭目 とうもく chief, head, boss
頭取 とうどり (bank) president; greenroom manager
頭領 とうりょう head, chief, boss
教頭 きょうとう head teacher, vice principal

首 ▷leader
シュ くび　Ⓚ1956

(person occupying a head position) **leader, head, chief**
首長 しゅちょう leader, chief, head
首脳 しゅのう head, leader
首相 しゅしょう prime minister
首謀者 しゅぼうしゃ ringleader, mastermind
党首 とうしゅ party chief [leader]
元首 げんしゅ ruler, sovereign

領 ▷leader
リョウ　Ⓚ1133

leader, chief, head, administrator
領事 りょうじ consul, consular representative
領事館 りょうじかん consulate
大統領 だいとうりょう president
首領 しゅりょう leader, head, chief

魁 ▷leader
カイ さきがけ　Ⓚ2838

leader, chief, head, the highest
魁首 かいしゅ leader; top candidate for the classical examinations in ancient China
首魁 しゅかい leader; forerunner, pioneer

learn and study
学 考 習 研 究 攻

学 ▷study
ガク まな(ぶ)　Ⓚ2211

study, learn
学習する がくしゅうする study, learn
学力 がくりょく scholarship, scholastic ability
独学 どくがく self-study, self-teaching
留学 りゅうがく studying abroad
見学 けんがく tour [field trip] for study and observation

考 ▷study
コウ かんが(える) かんが(え)　Ⓚ2753

study, investigate, research
考査 こうさ consideration, test, quiz
考証 こうしょう investigation, research
考古学 こうこがく archaeology
参考 さんこう reference, consultation
選考(=銓衡)する せんこうする select, screen

習 ▷learn
シュウ なら(う) なら(い)　Ⓚ2324

learn, acquire, be taught, study
習得 しゅうとく learning, acquirement
学習 がくしゅう study, learning
練習 れんしゅう practice, training
講習 こうしゅう short training course
独習 どくしゅう self-study, self-teaching
実習 じっしゅう practice, training
演習 えんしゅう exercise, practice; military maneuvers; seminar
補習 ほしゅう supplementary lessons

研 ▷research
ケン と(ぐ)　Ⓚ1046

research, study (hard), investigate
研究 けんきゅう research, study
研修 けんしゅう study and training
研鑽 けんさん study

究 ▷study exhaustively
キュウ きわ(める)　Ⓚ1885

study exhaustively, investigate thoroughly, delve into, go to the bottom of
究明する きゅうめいする investigate, study
究理 きゅうり study of natural laws
研究 けんきゅう research, study

追究する ついきゅうする investigate thoroughly, inquire into
学究 がっきゅう scholar, student
探究 たんきゅう investigation, search, inquiry

攻 ▷specialize
コウ せ(める)　　Ⓚ0215

specialize, study
攻究 こうきゅう investigation, research
専攻する せんこうする major in, specialize in

learning and knowledge
業 学 文 識 知

業 ▷studies
ギョウ ゴウ わざ　　Ⓚ2265

studies, course of study, schoolwork
学業 がくぎょう studies; scholastic attainments
授業 じゅぎょう teaching, instruction; lesson
卒業 そつぎょう graduation
修業する しゅうぎょう(=しゅぎょう)する pursue one's studies, study, complete a course

学 ▷learning
ガク まな(ぶ)　　Ⓚ2211

learning, study, education, scholarship, knowledge, science
学問 がくもん learning, study
学会 がっかい institute, academy, learned society; meeting of a research organization
学識 がくしき learning, scholarship
学芸 がくげい arts and sciences; culture
学術 がくじゅつ science, learning; arts and sciences

文 ▷culture
ブン モン ふみ　　Ⓚ1708

culture, learning, the arts
文化 ぶんか culture
文明 ぶんめい civilization, culture
文教 ぶんきょう education, culture
文部省 もんぶしょう Ministry of Education, Science and Culture
人文科学 じんぶんかがく cultural sciences, humanities

識 ▷knowledge
シキ　　Ⓚ1477

(acquired) knowledge, sense, wisdom, learning
識見 しきけん knowledge, judgment, discernment

知識 ちしき knowledge
常識 じょうしき common sense, common knowledge
良識 りょうしき good sense
有識者 ゆうしきしゃ learned [informed, intellectual] people, the wise
学識 がくしき learning, scholarship

知 ▷knowledge
チ し(る) し(らせる) し(れる)　　Ⓚ1041

[formerly also 智] knowledge, wisdom, intelligence, intellect
知恵 ちえ wisdom, intelligence, sagacity
知能 ちのう intelligence, mental capacity
知性 ちせい intellect, intelligence
知覚知 ちかくち knowledge by acquaintance
知情意 ちじょうい intellect, emotion and volition

leave
遺 残

遺 ▷leave behind
イ ユイ　　Ⓚ2731

leave behind (at one's death), bequeath, bestow; be left behind, remain
遺産 いさん inheritance, bequest
遺族 いぞく bereaved family
遺骨 いこつ (skeletal) remains; ashes
遺憾な いかんな regrettable
遺伝 いでん hereditary transmission
遺体 いたい remains, body, corpse
遺品 いひん article left by the deceased, article left behind
遺賢 いけん able men left out of office
遺言 ゆいごん(=いごん) will, testament
後遺症 こういしょう sequela, aftereffect (of a disease)

残 ▷leave
ザン のこ(る) のこ(す)　　Ⓚ0851

leave (behind), keep back; reserve, save; bequeath, hand down (to posterity); *sumo* remain in competition, stay in the ring; [in compounds] leave undone
食べ残し たべのこし leftover food
取り残す とりのこす leave (behind)
言い残す いいのこす leave word with, state in one's will; leave (something) unsaid, forget to mention

leave and set forth
去 離 発 出 退 撤

去 ▷go away
キョ さ(る)　　　Ⓚ1850

go away, leave, retire, depart from
去来 きょらい coming and going; recurrence
辞去する じきょする leave, quit, retire
退去する たいきょする retreat, withdraw, evacuate

離 ▷leave
リ はな(れる) はな(す)　　　Ⓚ1663

leave, depart, go away, quit, secede
離合 りごう meeting and parting
離脱する りだつする break away, leave, secede
離陸 りりく takeoff
離日 りにち departure from Japan
離村する りそんする desert one's village
離党 りとう secession from a party
離農 りのう giving up farming

発 ▷start
ハツ ホツ た(つ)　　　Ⓚ2222

(begin forward movement) **start, depart, set out, leave**
発着 はっちゃく departure and arrival
発車する はっしゃする start, leave, depart
出発 しゅっぱつ departure, starting
先発する せんぱつする start in advance, go ahead, precede

出 ▷go out
シュツ スイ で(る) -で だ(す)　　　Ⓚ2934

【シュツ スイ】
ⓐ [original meaning] (of persons) **go out, come out; depart, leave**
ⓑ **cause to go out (on a military expedition), dispatch (troops)**
ⓒ (of things) **come out, issue, flow out**
a 出国する しゅっこくする go out of a country
出発 しゅっぱつ departure, starting
出港する しゅっこうする leave port, set sail
出張する しゅっちょうする travel on official business
出動する しゅつどうする take the field, be dispatched, turn out
脱出する だっしゅつする escape, extricate
外出する がいしゅつする go out
b 出兵する しゅっぺいする dispatch troops
派出所 はしゅつじょ branch office; police box
c 出血する しゅっけつする bleed; hemorrhage
流出する りゅうしゅつする flow out, effuse

【で(る)】
ⓐ **go out, come out; leave, go away**
ⓑ **depart, start**
ⓒ (of things) **come out, issue, flow out**
a 出で coming [going] out; outflow; rising (of the sun or moon); graduate (of); one's turn to appear on stage
出入り でいり going in and out; frequentation, usual visit (as by a merchant); indentations; incomings and outgoings; trouble, fight
出入口 でいりぐち doorway, gateway
出迎え でむかえ meeting (someone at the station); receiving
出会う であう (happen to) meet; transact
出口 でぐち exit; exit ramp
出前 でまえ delivering dishes to order
b 出掛ける でかける go out, set off; be about to go out
良い出足 よいであし good start; good turnout of people
c 水の出が悪い みずのでがわるい The water does not come out well

退 ▷retreat
タイ しりぞ(く) しりぞ(ける)　　　Ⓚ266●

[original meaning] **retreat, move back, withdraw, leave**
退場する たいじょうする leave, exit
退去 たいきょ retreat, withdrawal, evacuation
退出 たいしゅつ leaving, withdrawal
退院 たいいん discharge from a hospital
撤退する てったいする withdraw, evacuate, pull ou●
後退する こうたいする retreat, recede
脱退 だったい withdrawal, secession

撤 ▷withdraw
テツ　　　Ⓚ067●

(move back) **withdraw, retreat, evacuate**
撤退 てったい withdrawal, evacuation, pullout
撤兵する てっぺいする withdraw troops
撤収する てっしゅうする withdraw, pull out

left and right
右　左

右 ▷right
ウ ユウ みぎ　　　Ⓚ256●

[original meaning] **right**
右折 うせつ right turn
右往左往する うおうさおうする go this way and that
右岸 うがん right bank

左右 さゆう right and left
座右に ざゆうに at one's (right) hand; by one's side

左 ▷**left**
サ ひだり   Ⓚ2567

[original meaning] **left**
左方 さほう left side
左折する させつする turn to the left
左記 さき undermentioned (statement), following
左表 さひょう chart at the left
左右 さゆう right and left
左右する さゆうする command, dominate, control

leg
足   脚   膝

足 ▷**foot**
ソク あし た(りる) た(る) た(す)   Ⓚ1873

[original meaning] **foot, leg**
足跡 そくせき footprint, footmark; the course of
  one's life, one's achievements
義足 ぎそく artificial leg
蛇足 だそく superfluity, redundancy

脚 ▷**leg**
キャク キャ あし   Ⓚ0887

[original meaning] **leg, foot**
脚力 きゃくりょく strength of one's legs; walking
  ability
脚線美 きゃくせんび beauty of leg lines
馬脚 ばきゃく horse's legs; one's true character
健脚の けんきゃくの strong in walking

膝 ▷**knee**
シツ ひざ   Ⓚ0985

[original meaning] **knee**
膝下 しっか near one's knee; near a parent [guard-
  ian]
膝関節 しつかんせつ knee joint
膝蓋骨 しつがいこつ kneecap, patella
膝行 しっこう moving forward [backward] by
  sliding on one's knees (in the presence of high-
  ranking individuals)

legislature
議   会   院

議 ▷**legislative body**
ギ   Ⓚ1480

[also suffix] **legislative body, legislature**
議会 ぎかい assembly, national assembly
議員 ぎいん member of an assembly, assemblyman
議長 ぎちょう chairman, president (of the senate)
議場 ぎじょう assembly hall; the House
議院 ぎいん House, Diet Chamber

会 ▷**assembly**
カイ エ あ(う) あ(わせる)   Ⓚ1741

(legislative) **assembly, council**
議会 ぎかい assembly, national assembly
国会 こっかい National Diet; national assembly,
  congress
県会 けんかい prefectural assembly

院 ▷**House**
イン   Ⓚ0410

[also suffix] legislative institution or body: **House, Diet,
Congress, Parliament**
院内 いんない inside the House [Diet]
上院 じょういん Upper House
議院 ぎいん House, Diet Chamber
両院 りょういん both Houses
参議院 さんぎいん House of Councilors, Upper
  House
衆議院 しゅうぎいん House of Representatives,
  Lower House

leisure
暇   閑

暇 ▷**free time**
カ ひま   Ⓚ0923

free time, spare time, leisure
余暇 よか leisure, spare time
寸暇 すんか moment's leisure
休暇 きゅうか holiday, vacation

閑 ▷**leisure**
カン   Ⓚ2837

leisure, idleness, spare time
閑暇 かんか leisure
閑散 かんさん leisure, inactivity

leisurely
悠　閑

悠 ▷leisurely
ユウ ⓚ2389

leisurely, at ease, relaxed, composed, serene
悠悠と ゆうゆうと calmly, leisurely; easily, without difficulty; boundlessly
悠長な ゆうちょうな leisurely, easygoing; tedious
悠然として ゆうぜんとして with an air of perfect composure

閑 ▷idle
カン ⓚ2837

idle, leisurely, idly
閑居 かんきょ [sometimes also 間居] idle life, quiet retreat
閑職 かんしょく leisurely post, do-nothing job
安閑と あんかんと idly, in idleness

lend and borrow
借　債　貸　融

借 ▷borrow
シャク か(りる) ⓚ0104

borrow, get a loan
借金する しゃっきんする borrow money, run into debt
借用 しゃくよう borrowing, loan
借家 しゃくや house for rent, rented house
借款 しゃっかん loan
貸借 たいしゃく lending and borrowing, debt and credit, loan
拝借する はいしゃくする borrow
賃借する ちんしゃくする hire, lease

債 ▷debt
サイ ⓚ0135

debt, liability
債権 さいけん credit, claim
債務 さいむ debt, obligation, liabilities
負債 ふさい debt, liabilities
減債 げんさい partial payment of a debt

貸 ▷lend
タイ か(す) か(し)- ⓚ225

[original meaning] lend, loan; rent, hire out
貸借 たいしゃく lending and borrowing, debt and credit, loan
貸与 たいよ loan, lending
賃貸 ちんたい lease, hiring out, charter

融 ▷finance
ユウ ⓚ162

(from the idea of passing smoothly) finance, accommodate with a loan
融資 ゆうし financing, advance of funds, loan
融通 ゆうずう financing, accommodation; flexibilit
金融 きんゆう circulation of money, money marke finance
特融 とくゆう special loan [finance]

length units
寸 浬 反 尺 米 尋
間 丈 町 里 哩

寸 ▷*sun* (3.03 cm)
スン ⓚ254

***sun*, (Japanese) inch: unit of length equiv. to approx. 3.03 cm or 1/10 of a *shaku* (尺)**
二寸 にすん 2 *sun*

浬 ▷*nautical mile* (1852m)
リ かいり のっと ⓚ039

[also 海里] nautical mile

反 ▷*tan* (10.6 m)
ハン ホン タン そ(る) そ(らす) ⓚ254

unit for measuring cloth equiv. to approx. 10.6 m in length and 34 cm in width
反物 たんもの cloth, textiles, dry goods
木綿三反 もめんさんたん three *tan* of cotton cloth

尺 ▷*shaku* (30.3 cm)
シャク ⓚ289

***shaku*: unit of length equiv. to approx. 30.3 cm or 10 *sun* (寸)**
尺貫法 しゃっかんほう Japanese system of weights and measures
尺八 しゃくはち bamboo flute
一尺 いっしゃく 1 *shaku*

米 ▷**meter**
ベイ マイ こめ   Ⓚ2958

meter

尋 ▷**fathom (1.8 m)**
ジン たず(ねる)   Ⓚ2027

hiro, fathom: unit of length equiv. to approx. 1.8 m
or 6 *shaku* (尺), used esp. for measuring the depth
of water
   千尋の谷 せんじんのたに abysmal valley

間 ▷***ken* (1.8 m)**
カン ケン あいだ ま   Ⓚ2836

ken: unit of length equiv. to approx. 1.8 m or 6
shaku (尺)
   間数 けんすう length in *ken*
   三間 さんげん 3 *ken*

丈 ▷***jo* (3.03 m)**
ジョウ たけ   Ⓚ2885

[original meaning] *jo*: unit of length equiv. to approx.
3.03 m or 10 *shaku* (尺)
   一丈一尺 いちじょういっしゃく 1 *jo* 1 *shaku*
   方丈 ほうじょう 10 sq. feet; abbot's chamber; chief
     priest
   万丈 ばんじょう unfathomable height

町 ▷***cho* (109 m)**
チョウ まち   Ⓚ1028

[sometimes also 丁] former unit of length equiv. to
approx. 109 m or 60 *ken* (間)
   二町 にちょう two *cho*

里 ▷**league, *ri* (3.9 km)**
リ さと   Ⓚ2968

ⓐ (former unit of distance) league, mile, *ri*
ⓑ *ri*, Japanese league: unit of length equiv. to
approx. 3.9 km or 36 *cho* (町)
a 里程 りてい mileage
   海里 かいり [also 浬] nautical mile
   一里塚 いちりづか milepost, milestone
   万里の長城 ばんりのちょうじょう Great Wall of
     China
b 千里の道も一歩から せんりのみちもいっぽから A
   journey of a thousand miles starts with but a
   single step

哩 ▷**mile (1609m)**
リ まいる   Ⓚ0360

mile
   海底二万哩 かいていにまんまいる 20000 Leagues
     Under the Sea

---

less in degree
弱 軽 微 低 薄 浅 仄

弱 ▷**weak**
ジャク よわ(い) よわ(る) よわ(まる)
よわ(める)   Ⓚ1080

[also prefix] (lacking force) **weak**
   弱震 じゃくしん weak earthquake, minor tremor
   弱毒 じゃくどく weak poison
   弱電器 じゃくでんき light electrical appliance
   弱酸性 じゃくさんせい slight acidity

軽 ▷**light**
ケイ かる(い) かろ(やか)   Ⓚ1372

(not intense) **light, slight**
   軽震 けいしん weak earthquake
   軽傷 けいしょう slight injury
   軽減する けいげんする reduce, lighten, mitigate
   軽便 けいべん convenience, simplicity
   軽食 けいしょく light meal, snack

微 ▷**slight**
ビ かす(か)   Ⓚ0587

(of low intensity) **slight, weak, faint**
   微笑 びしょう smile
   微震 びしん slight earthquake
   微温 びおん lukewarmness, tepidity
   微光 びこう faint light
   微弱な びじゃくな feeble, weak; faint, slight
   微妙な びみょうな subtle, delicate

低 ▷**low**
テイ ひく(い) ひく(める)
ひく(まる)   Ⓚ0057

(below average in degree) **low**
   低音 ていおん low-pitched sound, bass
   低温 ていおん low temperature
   低能 ていのう low intelligence
   低気圧 ていきあつ low pressure, atmospheric
     depression
   最低の さいていの lowest

薄 ▷**thin**
ハク うす(い) うす- うす(める) うす(まる)
うす(らぐ) うす(ら)- うす(れる)   Ⓚ2093

(lacking intensity) **thin, weak**
   薄光 はっこう pale light, faint light
   薄力粉 はくりきこ wheat flour of low viscosity
   希薄な きはくな dilute, thin, rare, sparse

浅 ▷shallow
セン あさ(い)　　　　　　　　Ⓚ0349

(lacking profundity) **shallow, superficial**

浅薄 せんぱく shallowness, superficiality, flimsiness
浅学 せんがく superficial knowledge
浅慮 せんりょ indiscretion, imprudence, thought-
　lessness
浅才 せんさい lack of ability, incompetence

仄 ▷faint
ソク ほの(か) ほの- ほの(めかす)
ほの(めく)

faint, vague, indistinct

---

let do
放　　　随

放 ▷let go
ホウ はな(す) -(っ)ぱな(し) はな(つ)
はな(れる) ほう(る)　　　　Ⓚ0754

ⓐ **let things go, let alone, leave as it is**
ⓑ **let oneself go, do as one pleases**

a 放任する ほうにんする leave (a matter) to take its
　own course, leave (a person) to himself
　放置する ほうちする leave alone, neglect, leave as
　it is
　放心 ほうしん absence of mind, abstraction
　開放する かいほうする open, leave open
b 放談 ほうだん random [irresponsible] talk
　放蕩する ほうとうする live fast, throw one's money
　away
　放浪 ほうろう wandering, roaming
　奔放な ほんぽうな wild, extravagant; free-spirited
　したい放題 したいほうだい as one pleases, at will
　野放図な のほうずな unrestrained, unruly

随 ▷let do
ズイ　　　　　　　　　　　　Ⓚ0573

**let (oneself) do (as one pleases), let things take their
natural course**

随筆 ずいひつ essay; stray notes
随意に ずいいに voluntarily, at will
随想 ずいそう occasional thoughts
随分 ずいぶん extremely, considerably ("as much as
　one pleases")

---

lie down
伏　　臥　　寝

伏 ▷prostrate
フク ふ(せる) ふ(す)　　　　Ⓚ003

[original meaning] **prostrate (oneself), fall prostrate,
lie down, bend down**

平伏する へいふくする prostrate oneself (before),
　kiss the ground
起伏 きふく ups and downs, undulations
倒伏 とうふく falling down

臥 ▷lie down
ガ ふ(せる) ふ(す)　　　　　Ⓚ130

[original meaning] **lie down**

臥薪嘗胆 がしんしょうたん perseverance; endurin
　hardships for the sake of vengeance
仰臥 ぎょうが lying face up
行住坐臥(=行住座臥) ぎょうじゅうざが the four
　cardinal behaviors (walking, stopping [stand-
　ing], sitting and lying); daily life

寝 ▷lie down
シン ね(る) ね(かす) ね(かせる)　Ⓚ203

lie down

寝転ぶ ねころぶ lie down

---

life
生　　命　　寿

生 ▷life
セイ ショウ い(きる) い(かす) い(ける)
う(まれる) う(まれ) う(む) お(う) は(える)
は(やす) き なま な(る)　　　Ⓚ293

ⓐ (act of being alive) **life, existence**
ⓑ (interval between birth and death) **lifetime, life**

a 生命 せいめい life
　生保(=生命保険) せいほ(=せいめいほけん) life insur
　ance
　生死 せいし life and death
　生涯 しょうがい life, lifetime, career; for life
　人生 じんせい human life, life
b 生前 せいぜん during one's lifetime
　一生 いっしょう a lifetime
　終生 しゅうせい all one's life
　余生 よせい one's remaining years
　平生は へいぜいは in ordinary days

命 ▷life
メイ ミョウ いのち   Ⓚ1772

life
生命 せいめい life
一生懸命(=一所懸命)に いっしょうけんめいに(=いっ
しょけんめいに) for life, with all one's might
寿命 じゅみょう life span
長命 ちょうめい long life
人命 じんめい (human) life
亡命 ぼうめい exile
致命傷 ちめいしょう fatal wound

寿 ▷longevity
ジュ ス ことぶき   Ⓚ2979

[original meaning] **longevity, long life, old age**
寿老人 じゅろうじん God of Longevity
長寿 ちょうじゅ long life, longevity

life energy
精 気

精 ▷spirit
セイ ショウ   Ⓚ1248

(source of vital energy) **spirit, energy, vitality, vigor**
精力 せいりょく energy, vitality, vigor
精気 せいき spirit, energy, essence
精根 せいこん energy, vitality
精精 せいぜい with all one's might; at most, at best
精一杯 せいいっぱい with all one's might

気 ▷vital energy
キ ケ   Ⓚ2751

vital energy, spirit, breath of life, vitality
気力 きりょく energy, spirit, vitality, pluck, guts
気勢 きせい spirit, ardor
病気 びょうき illness, sickness, disease
元気 げんき vigor, energy; spirits; health
意気盛んだ いきさかんだ be in high spirits
勇気 ゆうき courage, valor, bravery, nerve
活気 かっき vigor, spirit, animation
精気 せいき spirit, energy, essence

light
光 明 灯 燭 照 虹

光 ▷light
コウ ひか(る) ひかり   Ⓚ2121

[also suffix] **light, glow**

光線 こうせん ray (of light), beam
光熱 こうねつ light and heat
光化学 こうかがく photochemistry
日光 にっこう sunshine, sunlight
月光 げっこう moonlight, moonshine
発光する はっこうする radiate, emit light
太陽光 たいようこう sunlight

明 ▷light
メイ
ミョウ あ(かり) あか(るい) あか(るむ)
あか(らむ) あき(らか) あ(ける) -あ(け)
あ(く) あ(くる) あ(かす)   Ⓚ0756

light
灯明 とうみょう votive light offered (as to a god);
stand for votive light; candlestand

灯 ▷lamp
トウ ひ   Ⓚ0730

[also suffix] [original meaning] **lamp, light, lantern**
灯台 とうだい lighthouse; oil-lamp stand
灯火 とうか light, lamplight
灯油 とうゆ kerosene, lamp oil
電灯 でんとう lamp, electric light
街灯 がいとう street lamp
尾灯 びとう taillight
蛍光灯 けいこうとう fluorescent lamp [light]

燭 ▷candle
ショク ソク ともしび   Ⓚ1008

ⓐ **candle**
ⓑ **lamp, light, lantern, flame**
ⓐ 燭台 しょくだい candlestick, candlestand
燭光 しょっこう candlepower
手燭 しゅしょく(=てしょく) portable candlestick
国際燭 こくさいしょく international candlepower
メートル燭 めーとるしょく meter candle
ⓑ 蝋燭 ろうそく candle
華燭 かしょく bright light

照 ▷sunlight
ショウ て(る) て(らす) て(れる)   Ⓚ2461

sunlight, light
返照 へんしょう reflection of light [sunlight]
晩照 ばんしょう sunset, setting sun

虹 ▷rainbow
コウ にじ   Ⓚ1180

rainbow
虹蜺 こうげい *literary* rainbow
虹彩 こうさい iris
白虹 はっこう [rare] white rainbow

light-colored
淡 浅 薄 鈍

淡 ▷light
タン あわ(い)   Ⓚ0484

[also prefix] **light-colored, faint, pale**
淡色 たんしょく light color
淡彩 たんさい light color
淡紅色 たんこうしょく pink, rose pink
濃淡 のうたん light and shade

浅 ▷light
セン あさ(い)   Ⓚ0349

light-colored, pale
浅紅 せんこう light red
浅緑 せんりょく(=あさみどり) light green

薄 ▷pale
ハク うす(い) うす- うす(める) うす(まる)
うす(らぐ) うす(ら)- うす(れる)   Ⓚ2093

(of colors) **pale, thin, light**
薄い色 うすいいろ light color

鈍 ▷dull
ドン にぶ(い) にぶ(る) にぶ-   Ⓚ1507

[prefix] (of colors) **dull**
鈍黄色 にぶきいろ dull yellow

lighter elements
水 酸 窒 塩 臭 硫 炭

水 ▷hydrogen
スイ みず   Ⓚ0003

hydrogen
水素 すいそ hydrogen
水爆 すいばく hydrogen bomb
炭水化物 たんすいかぶつ carbohydrates

酸 ▷oxygen
サン す(い)   Ⓚ1415

oxygen
酸素 さんそ oxygen
酸化 さんか oxidation

窒 ▷nitrogen
チツ   Ⓚ1980
see also →NITROGEN

nitrogen
窒素 ちっそ nitrogen
窒化物 ちっかぶつ nitride

塩 ▷chlorine
エン しお   Ⓚ0578

[also suffix] **chlorine, chloride compound**
塩酸 えんさん hydrochloric acid
塩素 えんそ chlorine
塩化 えんか chloridation, salification

臭 ▷bromine
シュウ くさ(い) にお(う) にお(い)   Ⓚ2289

bromine
臭素 しゅうそ bromine

硫 ▷sulfur
リュウ   Ⓚ1096

[original meaning] **sulfur**
硫酸 りゅうさん sulfuric acid
硫安 りゅうあん ammonium sulfate
硫化する りゅうかする sulfurize
加硫 かりゅう vulcanization
脱硫 だつりゅう desulfurization

炭 ▷carbon
タン すみ   Ⓚ1947

carbon
炭素 たんそ carbon
炭水化物 たんすいかぶつ carbohydrates
炭酸 たんさん carbonic acid; seltzer
炭化 たんか carbonization

like →LOVE AND LIKE

limbs
肢 腕 脚

肢 ▷limb
シ   Ⓚ0780

[original meaning] (human or animal appendage) **limb,
member, arm or leg**
肢体 したい limbs, members
下肢 かし lower limbs, legs
四肢 しし limbs, legs and arms
前肢 ぜんし forelimb, front leg

腕 ▷arm
ワン うで   Ⓚ0919

arm
腕章 わんしょう armband, arm badge
腕力 わんりょく muscular strength
上腕 じょうわん upper arm
左腕投手 さわんとうしゅ left-handed pitcher

脚 ▷leg
キャク キャ あし   Ⓚ0887
see also →LEG

[original meaning] **leg, foot**
脚力 きゃくりょく strength of one's legs; walking ability
脚線美 きゃくせんび beauty of leg lines
馬脚 ばきゃく horse's legs; one's true character
健脚の けんきゃくの strong in walking

line
線 筋 条 脈 棒 縞 軸

線 ▷line
セン   Ⓚ1273

Ⓐ (continuous lengthwise mark) **line**
Ⓑ (border, esp. between two surfaces) **line**
a 線画 せんが line drawing
　線審 せんしん linesman
　直線 ちょくせん straight line
　下線 かせん underline
　戦線 せんせん (war) front, battle line
　前線 ぜんせん front line, fighting front; *meteorology* front
b 水平線 すいへいせん horizon

筋 ▷threadlike structure
キン すじ   Ⓚ2337

line, stripe, strip, streak
背筋 せすじ spinal column, spine; seam in the back
金筋 きんすじ gold stripes

条 ▷strip
ジョウ   Ⓚ1882

strip, stripe, streak, vein, line, groove, thread
条痕 じょうこん streak
条虫 じょうちゅう tapeworm
星条旗 せいじょうき the Stars and Stripes

脈 ▷vein
ミャク   Ⓚ0860

Ⓐ something resembling a vein in shape or structure
Ⓑ *geol* **vein, seam**
a 脈脈たる みゃくみゃくたる continuous, unbroken; pulsating forcefully
　山脈 さんみゃく mountain range
　葉脈 ようみゃく veins of a leaf
b 鉱脈 こうみゃく (mineral) vein, deposit, lode
　水脈 すいみゃく water vein; waterway

棒 ▷straight line
ボウ   Ⓚ0894

straight line, thick straight line
棒グラフ ぼうぐらふ bar graph

縞 ▷stripe
コウ しま   Ⓚ1287

stripe, streak
氷縞粘土 ひょうこうねんど varve

軸 ▷axis
ジク   Ⓚ1371

[also suffix]
Ⓐ (line about which rotation occurs) **axis**
Ⓑ *math* **axis**
Ⓒ *optics* **axis**
Ⓓ *anat* **axis**
a 軸線 じくせん axis, shaft line
　地軸 ちじく axis of the earth
　回転軸 かいてんじく axis of revolution
　左右軸 さゆうじく lateral axis
　主軸 しゅじく principal axis; main spindle [shaft]
b 座標軸 ざひょうじく coordinate axis
c 屈折軸 くっせつじく axis of refraction
d 軸索 じくさく axon, axis cylinder

lineage
系   血

系 ▷lineage
ケイ   Ⓚ1701

[also suffix] **lineage, family line, descent, ancestry**
系図 けいず genealogy, pedigree
直系 ちょっけい direct descent line
家系 かけい family line, lineage, ancestry
日系米人 にっけいべいじん American of Japanese descent, Japanese-American

血 ▷blood
ケツ ち Ⓚ2955

blood (relation), lineage
血族 けつぞく blood relative
血統 けっとう lineage, blood, bloodline
混血 こんけつ mixed-blood, racial mixture

linear arrangements
伍 列 行 欄

伍 ▷rank
ゴ Ⓚ0031

rank, file, line
隊伍 たいご ranks, line array, formation
落伍(=落後)する らくごする straggle, drop out of
  line, fall out of the ranks
先頭伍 せんとうご leading file

列 ▷row
レツ Ⓚ0729

[also suffix] **row, line, file, rank; series**
行列 ぎょうれつ procession, queue; matrix
系列 けいれつ order, succession; series
戦列 せんれつ line of battle
序列 じょれつ rank, grade, order
等差数列 とうさすうれつ arithmetical progression
  [series]
パラフィン列 ぱらふぃんれつ paraffin series

行 ▷line (esp. of print)
コウ ギョウ アン い(く) ゆ(く) −ゆ(き)
−い(き) おこな(う) Ⓚ0187

line (esp. of print), row
行間 ぎょうかん between the lines
行数 ぎょうすう linage, number of lines
行中 ぎょうちゅう in the middle of a line
別行 べつぎょう separate line, another row

欄 ▷column
ラン Ⓚ1023

(section of written material) **column, blank column,
blank, space**
欄外 らんがい margin
空欄 くうらん blank column, blank
登記番号欄 とうきばんごうらん registry number
  column

lines →ROPES AND LINES

lines and line segments
線 弧 弦 径 辺

線 ▷line
セン Ⓚ1273

geometry **line**
放物線 ほうぶつせん parabola

弧 ▷arc
コ Ⓚ0320

ⓐ arc
ⓑ *math* arc
a 弧状の こじょうの arc-shaped
  括弧 かっこ parentheses, brackets
b 弧線 こせん arc (of a circle)
  弧形 こけい arc
  円弧 えんこ circular arc; arc of a circle
  劣弧 れっこ minor arc

弦 ▷chord
ゲン つる Ⓚ0257

geometry **chord; hypotenuse**
弦材 げんざい *civil engineering* chord member
補弦 ほげん supplementary chord
正弦 せいげん sine (of an angle)

径 ▷diameter
ケイ Ⓚ0260

diameter
直径 ちょっけい diameter
半径 はんけい radius, semidiameter
口径 こうけい caliber, bore; diameter

辺 ▷side
ヘン あた(り) −べ Ⓚ2607

side
一辺 いっぺん a side (of a triangle)
二等辺三角形 にとうへんさんかっけい equilateral
  [isosceles] triangle

line segments →LINES AND LINE SEGMENTS

liquefy

溶 熔 鎔 解 融

溶 ▷dissolve, melt
ヨウ と(ける) と(かす) と(く)　　Ⓚ0610

❶ (pass or cause to pass into solution) **dissolve**
溶解 ようかい dissolution, liquefaction; melting, fusion
溶液 ようえき solution, solvent
溶媒 ようばい solvent
溶血 ようけつ hemolysis
水溶性の すいようせいの water soluble

❷ [formerly 熔 or 鎔] (change or cause to change from solid to liquid, esp. by heat) **melt**
溶融 ようゆう melting, fusion
溶接 ようせつ welding
溶岩 ようがん lava
溶鉱炉 ようこうろ smelting [blast] furnace

熔 ▷melt (metals)
ヨウ と(ける) と(かす)

[now replaced by 溶] (change or cause to change from solid to liquid, esp. by heat) **melt**
熔解する ようかいする melt, fuse
熔融 ようゆう melting, fusion
熔接する ようせつする weld
熔鉱炉 ようこうろ smelting [blast] furnace
熔銑 ようせん molten iron
熔岩 ようがん lava

鎔 ▷melt (metals)
ヨウ と(ける) と(かす)

[now replaced by 溶] [original meaning] **melt (up) metals, fuse, smelt**
鎔解する ようかいする melt, fuse
鎔接する ようせつする weld
鎔鉱炉 ようこうろ smelting [blast] furnace
鎔銑 ようせん molten iron

解 ▷dissolve
カイ ゲ と(く) と(かす) と(ける)　　Ⓚ1375

dissolve, melt, liquefy
解凍 かいとう thawing, defrosting
溶解する ようかいする dissolve, liquefy; melt, fuse
潮解 ちょうかい deliquescence
融解 ゆうかい fusion, melting
氷解する ひょうかいする melt away, be cleared [dispelled]

融 ▷fuse
ユウ　　Ⓚ1626

(become liquefied by heat, esp. in the joining of metals) **fuse**
融解 ゆうかい fusion, melting
融点 ゆうてん fusion point
融熱 ゆうねつ heat of fusion
融接 ゆうせつ fusion welding
溶融 ようゆう melting, fusion
核融合 かくゆうごう nuclear fusion

liquid

液 汁 水

液 ▷liquid
エキ　　Ⓚ0468

[original meaning] **liquid, fluid**
液体 えきたい liquid, fluid
廃液 はいえき waste fluid
血液 けつえき blood
乳液 にゅうえき milky lotion; latex

汁 ▷fluid
ジュウ しる　　Ⓚ0173

[original meaning] **fluid, body fluid, liquid**
胆汁 たんじゅう bile, gall
墨汁 ぼくじゅう India ink, black writing fluid

水 ▷water
スイ みず　　Ⓚ0003

[also suffix] (liquid or water solution) **water, lotion, liquid, fluid; soda**
水銀 すいぎん mercury, quicksilver
石灰水 せっかいすい lime water
化粧水 けしょうすい toilet water [lotion]

live

活 暮 生

活 ▷live
カツ い(きる) い(かす)　　Ⓚ0345

❶ⓐ live, be alive
　ⓑ let live, keep alive
ⓐ 活路 かつろ means of escape, way out
　復活する ふっかつする revive, come to life again, be resurrected
ⓑ 活用する かつようする utilize, apply; conjugate, inflect

活殺 かっさつ life and death

❷ (pass one's life) **live, lead one's life**
生活 せいかつ life, existence; livelihood
自活 じかつ self-support

暮 ▷**live (pass one's life)**
ボ く(れる) く(らす) Ⓚ2070

(pass one's life) **live, lead one's life, spend one's day;**
(make a living) **live, earn one's livelihood**
暮らし くらし living, livelihood, subsistence; circumstances
暮らし向き くらしむき circumstances
一人暮らしをする ひとりぐらしをする live alone
その日暮らし そのひぐらし hand-to-mouth life

生 ▷**live (be alive)**
セイ ショウ い(きる) い(かす) い(ける)
う(まれる) う(まれ) う(む) お(う) は(える)
は(やす) き なま な(る) Ⓚ2933

ⓐ (be alive) **live, exist**
ⓑ **living, alive**
ⓒ **lively, vivid, fresh**
ₐ 生存する せいぞんする exist, live, survive
生別 せいべつ separation, parting
寄生 きせい parasitism
蘇生 そせい revival, resuscitation
野生の やせいの wild, feral
♭ 生還する せいかんする return alive; *baseball* reach the home plate
生体 せいたい living body, organism
生者 しょうじゃ living things, animate nature
ₑ 生鮮な せいせんな fresh
生彩 せいさい life, vividness
生気 せいき animation, vitality, spirit

load
載 積 搭

載 ▷**load**
サイ の(せる) の(る) Ⓚ2814

[original meaning] **load (a vehicle or ship with cargo), lade, carry**
満載する まんさいする be loaded to capacity (with)
積載する せきさいする load (a vehicle or ship with cargo), carry
搭載 とうさい loading, embarkation
混載 こんさい mixed loading

積 ▷**load**
セキ つ(む) -づ(み) つ(もる)
つ(もり) Ⓚ1142

load, ship, stow aboard
積み込む つみこむ load (up), put on board, stow aboard
船積み ふなづみ shipment, shipping

搭 ▷**load on board**
トウ Ⓚ0541

load on board (a ship or vehicle)
搭載する とうさいする load, embark

localities →AREAS AND LOCALITIES

locks and keys
鍵 錠

鍵 ▷**key**
ケン かぎ Ⓚ1565

【ケン】
[original meaning, now rare] (implement for opening) **key**
関鍵 かんけん [rare] lock and key; locking doors; vital point

【かぎ】
key; lock; (vital information) **key, solution**
鍵穴 かぎあな keyhole
勝敗の鍵を握る しょうはいのかぎをにぎる hold the key to victory, have the game in one's hands

錠 ▷**lock**
ジョウ Ⓚ1548

[also suffix] **lock, padlock**
錠前 じょうまえ lock
手錠 てじょう handcuffs
文字合わせ錠 もじあわせじょう combination lock

longitude →LATITUDE AND LONGITUDE

long objects →COUNTERS FOR LONG OBJECTS

long slender objects
棒 箸 桟 軸 錘
竿 杖 錫 軛

棒 ▷**rod**
ボウ Ⓚ0894

ⓐ [original meaning] **rod, stick, bar, pole, staff, club**

b rodlike, rod-shaped; bar of, stick of

a 棒状 ぼうじょう cylinder or rod-shaped
棒高跳び ぼうたかとび pole vault [jump]
棒術 ぼうじゅつ *bojutsu* (art of using a stick as a weapon), cudgels
警棒 けいぼう policeman's club, nightstick
編み棒 あみぼう knitting needle
棍棒 こんぼう cudgel, club
鉄棒 てつぼう iron rod; horizontal bars
心棒 しんぼう axle, shaft, arbor
延べ棒 のべぼう ingot

b 棒温度計 ぼうおんどけい bar thermometer

箸 ▷chopsticks
はし   Ⓚ2363

[original meaning] **chopsticks**
匕箸 ひちょ spoon and chopsticks

桟 ▷crosspiece
サン   Ⓚ0843

crosspiece; frame; bolt (of a door)
桟を打ち付ける さんをうちつける nail a crosspiece (to)
障子の桟 しょうじのさん frame of a *shoji* (paper sliding door)
戸の桟を外す とのさんをはずす unbolt the door

軸 ▷axle
ジク   Ⓚ1371

a [original meaning] axle, shaft, spindle
b something resembling an axle in shape or function, as a scroll roller or penholder

a 軸箱 じくばこ axle box
車軸 しゃじく wheel axle, axle
動軸 どうじく driving axle
死軸 しじく dead axle

b 軸木 じくぎ splint; scroll roller
巻軸 まきじく scroll; scroll roller
ペン軸 ぺんじく penholder

錘 ▷spindle
スイ つむ おもり   Ⓚ1559

a spindle (for spinning)
b counter for spindles

a 紡錘 ぼうすい spindle
休錘 きゅうすい idle spindles

b 十万錘 じゅうまんすい 100,000 spindles

竿 ▷pole
カン さお   Ⓚ2288

pole, rod
竿頭 かんとう top [end] of a pole
三竿 さんかん (of the sun or moon) being high in the sky

杖 ▷staff
ジョウ つえ   Ⓚ0736

staff, cane, walking stick
杖術 じょうじゅつ form of martial art using a cane staff
錫杖 しゃくじょう *khakkhara*, Buddhist priest's staff
金剛杖 こんごうじょう (=こんごうづえ) pilgrim's staff

錫 ▷Buddhist priest's staff
シャク すず   Ⓚ1557

khakkhara, Buddhist priest's staff
錫杖 しゃくじょう *khakkhara*, Buddhist priest's staff
巡錫 じゅんしゃく preaching tour

軛 ▷yoke
ヤク くびき

[now also 役] [original meaning] **yoke**
共軛 きょうやく *math* conjugation

long time periods

時 代 紀 世 朝 期 劫

時 ▷time
ジ とき -どき   Ⓚ0830

time(s), age, period, season
時代 じだい age, era, period; antiquity
時勢 じせい trend of the times, spirit of the age
時期 じき time, season
当時 とうじ at that time, in those days; at the present time

代 ▷age
ダイ タイ か(わる) か(わり) -が(わり) か(える) よ しろ   Ⓚ0018

age, era, times
時代 じだい age, era, period; antiquity
現代 げんだい present age, modern times, today
古代 こだい ancient times, antiquity, remote ages
年代 ねんだい age, era, period; date

紀 ▷era
キ   Ⓚ1173

era, epoch, period of years, age
紀元 きげん era
世紀 せいき century
西紀 せいき Christian era
皇紀 こうき Imperial era
千年紀 せんねんき millennium

世 ▷age
セイ セ よ   Ⓚ2932

age, period, century, era, the times
世紀 せいき century
中世 ちゅうせい Middle [Medieval] Ages
近世 きんせい modern ages
乱世 らんせい turbulent times

朝 ▷dynastic period
チョウ あさ   Ⓚ1513

dynastic period, age
清朝 しんちょう Qing Dynasty, Manchu Dynasty
平安朝 へいあんちょう Heian Period

期 ▷period
キ ゴ   Ⓚ1520

[also suffix] **period, age, time, occasion**
青年期 せいねんき adolescence
幼児期 ようじき babyhood
平安後期 へいあんこうき late Heian period
画期的な かっきてきな epoch-making, epochal

劫 ▷kalpa
コウ ゴウ おびや(かす)   Ⓚ1033

[original meaning] **threaten, menace, endanger**
劫火 ごうか world-destroying conflagration
劫掠 ごうりゃく(=きょうりゃく) pillage, plunder

look →SEE AND LOOK

loosen
弛 緩

弛 ▷slacken
シ ゆる(む) ゆる(める) たる(む)
たゆ(む)   Ⓚ0186

slacken, slack, loosen, relax
弛緩 しかん relaxation; atony
弛張熱 しちょうねつ remittent fever
一張一弛 いっちょういっし tension and relaxation

緩 ▷slack
カン ゆる(い) ゆる(やか) ゆる(む)
ゆる(める)   Ⓚ1272

(reduce tension) **slack, slacken, loosen**
緩和 かんわ easing, relief, alleviation
緩衝弁 かんしょうべん cushion valve
弛緩 しかん relaxation; atony

lose
負 敗

負 ▷lose
フ ま(ける) ま(かす) お(う)   Ⓚ1799

lose, be defeated
勝負 しょうぶ victory or defeat; match, game

敗 ▷be defeated
ハイ やぶ(れる)   Ⓚ1342

ⓐ be defeated, lose
ⓑ defeat
ⓒ counter for number of defeats
a 敗北 はいぼく defeat, setback
　敗軍 はいぐん defeated army
　敗戦 はいせん lost battle, defeat
　勝敗 しょうはい victory or defeat
b 連敗 れんぱい successive defeats
　完敗 かんぱい crushing defeat; complete failure
c 一勝二敗 いっしょうにはい one victory and two
　　defeats

losing and loss
失 喪 逸 損 佚

失 ▷lose
シツ うしな(う)   Ⓚ2947

ⓐ lose, miss
ⓑ lose one's memory, forget
a 失業する しつぎょうする be out of work, lose one's
　　job
　失礼 しつれい impoliteness, rudeness; bad
　　manners; I beg your pardon/Goodbye
　失望する しつぼうする be disappointed, lose hope
　紛失 ふんしつ loss
　喪失 そうしつ loss, forfeit
　遺失する いしつする lose, leave behind
b 失念 しつねん lapse of memory, oblivion

喪 ▷lose
ソウ も   Ⓚ2459

lose, be deprived of
喪失 そうしつ loss, forfeit
喪神する そうしんする lose consciousness
阻喪(=沮喪) そそう loss of spirit, dejection

逸 ▷let slip
イツ   Ⓚ2688

let slip, miss, lose, let go, let pass
  逸球 いっきゅう muffed ball, missed ball
  逸機する いっきする miss a chance, lose an opportunity
  後逸する こういつする let (a ball) pass, miss (a grounder)

損 ▷loss, lose
ソン そこ(なう) そこ(ねる)   Ⓚ0596

ⓐ loss
ⓑ *elec* **loss**
ⓒ lose, suffer loss
a 損失 そんしつ loss
  損益 そんえき profit and loss; advantage and disadvantage
  損率 そんりつ loss factor
  全損 ぜんそん total loss
  駒損 こまそん(=こまぞん) loss of material (in shogi)
b 損流 そんりゅう loss current
c 欠損 けっそん deficit, deficiency; loss

佚 ▷lost
イツ

lost, missing
  佚書 いっしょ lost book
  散佚する さんいつする be lost and scattered

oss →LOSING AND LOSS

loud
高 朗 騒 喧 嘩

高 ▷loud
コウ たか(い) たか -だか たか(まる)
たか(める)   Ⓚ1803

loud (voice)
  高らかな たからかな loud, sonorous, ringing
  高笑い たかわらい loud laughter

朗 ▷clear (voice)
ロウ ほが(らか)   Ⓚ1210

clear (voice), loud and clear, sonorous, loud, resonant
  朗詠 ろうえい reciting, chanting
  朗吟する ろうぎんする recite, sing
  朗読 ろうどく reading aloud
  朗朗たる ろうろうたる clear (and ringing), sonorous, resonant; bright (moon)

騒 ▷clamorous
ソウ さわ(ぐ)   Ⓚ1630

clamorous, uproarious, noisy

喧 ▷boisterous
ケン やかま(しい) かまびす(しい)
かしま(しい)   Ⓚ0504

boisterous, noisy, clamorous, vociferous
  喧嘩 けんか quarrel, fight, squabble
  喧騒 けんそう clamor, din, noise
  喧伝 けんでん widely talked about
  喧喧囂囂 けんけんごうごう state of uproar, pandemonium

嘩 ▷boisterous
カ   Ⓚ0575

boisterous, noisy, clamorous
  喧嘩 けんか quarrel, fight, squabble
  喧嘩腰 けんかごし belligerent
  口喧嘩 くちげんか quarrel

love
愛 情 恋 艶 寵

愛 ▷love
アイ いと(しい)   Ⓚ2191

ⓐ [also suffix] **love, affection**
ⓑ *Buddhism* **love**
a 愛情 あいじょう love, affection
  愛憎 あいぞう love and hate
  博愛 はくあい philanthropy
  母性愛 ぼせいあい maternal love
  同性愛 どうせいあい homosexual love, lesbianism
b 慈愛 じあい affection, love, benevolence

情 ▷love
ジョウ セイ なさ(け)   Ⓚ0439

love, affection
  愛情 あいじょう love, affection

恋 ▷love (for the opposite sex)
レン こ(う) こい こい(しい)   Ⓚ1804

love (for the opposite sex)
  失恋 しつれん unrequited love
  悲恋 ひれん blighted love

艶 ▷romance
エン つや   Ⓚ1683

romance, love, love affair
  艶聞 えんぶん love affair, romance, one's love story

艶書 えんしょ love letter
艶福 えんぷく good fortune in love

寵 ▷affection
チョウ   Ⓚ2113

affection, love; favor, grace
  寵愛 ちょうあい affection, favor
  寵幸 ちょうこう grace, favor
  君寵 くんちょう favor of one's ruler [lord]
  恩寵 おんちょう grace (of God), favor

love and like
愛 恋 好 慕 惣 玩

愛 ▷love
アイ いと(しい)   Ⓚ2191

❶ⓐ love, have affection for
 ⓑ love (a person of the opposite sex), care deeply for
 ⓐ 愛児 あいじ one's beloved [favorite] child
  愛犬家 あいけんか lover of dogs
  愛国心 あいこくしん patriotism, nationalism
  愛車 あいしゃ one's own car [bicycle]
  愛妻 あいさい one's beloved wife
 ⓑ 愛人 あいじん lover
  愛欲 あいよく love and lust, sexual passion
  恋愛 れんあい love (for the opposite sex)
❷ (have a strong liking for) **love, like, be fond of**
  愛好する あいこうする love, be fond of
  愛用する あいようする use habitually
  愛読する あいどくする read with pleasure
  愛唱する あいしょうする love to sing

恋 ▷love (the opposite sex)
レン こ(う) こい こい(しい)   Ⓚ1804

[original meaning] **love (the opposite sex)**
  恋愛 れんあい love (for the opposite sex)
  恋情 れんじょう love, attachment
  恋慕する れんぼする love, fall in love with

好 ▷like
コウ この(む) す(く) よ(い) い(い) Ⓚ0184

[original meaning] **like, be fond of, love**
  好学 こうがく love of learning
  好物 こうぶつ favorite dish
  好角家 こうかくか sumo fan, wrestling enthusiast
  愛好者 あいこうしゃ lover (of music), fan
  同好会 どうこうかい association of like-minded persons; club

慕 ▷adore
ボ した(う)   Ⓚ2069

adore, love deeply, be attached to
  敬慕する けいぼする adore, love and respect, admire
  恋慕 れんぼ love, attachment

惣 ▷fall in love
コツ ほ(れる) ぼ(ける) ほう(ける) Ⓚ0440

fall in love
  惣れ薬 ほれぐすり love potion
  一目惣れ ひとめぼれ love at first sight

玩 ▷cherish
ガン もてあそ(ぶ)   Ⓚ0778

(appreciate) **take pleasure in, relish, cherish**
  玩味 がんみ relishing, appreciation
  愛玩動物 あいがんどうぶつ pet animal

low
低 下

低 ▷low
テイ ひく(い) ひく(める) ひく(まる)   Ⓚ0057

[original meaning] (having little height) **low**
  低地 ていち low ground, lowlands
  低空 ていくう low altitude
  高低 こうてい high and low

下 ▷lower
カ ゲ した しも もと さ(げる) さ(がる) くだ(る) くだ(り) くだ(す) くだ(さる) お(ろす) お(りる)   Ⓚ2862

[also prefix] (in a lower position) **lower, under-, sub-**
  下流 かりゅう downstream, lower reaches of a stream
  下部 かぶ lower part
  下段 げだん lowest step; lower berth
  下駄 げた geta, wooden clogs
  下半身 かはんしん lower half of one's body
  下意識 かいしき subconsciousness

lower
低　下

低 ▷**lower**
テイ　ひく(い)　ひく(める)
ひく(まる)　　　　　　Ⓚ0057

lower, bring down
低下する ていかする fall, sink, lower, go down
低頭 ていとう bowing low

下 ▷**bring down**
カ ゲ した しも もと さ(げる) さ(がる)
くだ(る) くだ(り) くだ(す) くだ(さる)
お(ろす) お(りる)　　　　　Ⓚ2862

【カ ゲ】
(cause to go down) **bring down, lower**
却下する きゃっかする reject, dismiss, turn down

【さ(げる)】
(move downward) **lower, bring down, drop**
頭を下げる あたまをさげる bow one's head
掘り下げる ほりさげる dig down; investigate,
probe, delve into

lowly
卑　下　低

卑 ▷**mean**
ヒ いや(しい) いや(しむ)
いや(しめる)　　　　　Ⓚ2295

(low in social status) **mean, lowly, humble**
卑賤 ひせん lowly position, humble condition
尊卑 そんぴ upper and lower classes, high and low

下 ▷**of low rank**
カ ゲ した しも もと さ(げる) さ(がる)
くだ(る) くだ(り) くだ(す) くだ(さる)
お(ろす) お(りる)　　　　　Ⓚ2862

of low rank, inferior
下位 かい lower rank [grade], subordinate position
下院 かいん Lower House
下級 かきゅう lower grade [class]

低 ▷**low**
テイ ひく(い) ひく(める)
ひく(まる)　　　　　Ⓚ0057

(of inferior social standing) **low, humble, vulgar**
低級 ていきゅう low grade, low class, vulgar

luster
艶　沢

艶 ▷**gloss**
エン つや　　　　　Ⓚ1683

gloss, luster, glaze
艶艶した つやつやした glossy, bright
艶消し つやけし grinding, frosting; disillusionment

沢 ▷**luster**
タク さわ　　　　　Ⓚ0238

luster, gloss, brightness
光沢 こうたく luster, gloss, polish
色沢 しきたく [rare] luster and color

machines and tools
機 械 具 器 儀 鏡 菫

機 ▷**machine**
キ はた　　　　　Ⓚ0989

ⓐ [also suffix] **machine, machinery, apparatus**
ⓑ **counter for heavy machinery**
ⓒ [also suffix] (electronic device for processing data)
machine, computer

a 機械 きかい machine, mechanism
機器 きき machinery and tools, apparatus
機構 きこう mechanism, structure; system, organization; frame, framework
機関 きかん engine, machine; agency, facilities,
institution
機動性 きどうせい mobility, maneuverability
機動隊 きどうたい riot police
電機 でんき electrical machinery and appliances
洗濯機 せんたくき washing machine
電算機 でんさんき electronic computer
原動機 げんどうき motor, prime mover
b 発電機三機 はつでんきさんき three dynamos
8ビット機 はちびっとき 8-bit machine
IBM互換機 あいびーえむごかんき IBM compatible
computer

械 ▷**mechanical contrivance**
カイ　　　　　Ⓚ0870

mechanical contrivance, device, instrument, tool
機械 きかい machine, mechanism
器械 きかい instrument, apparatus, appliance

具 ▷implement
グ ⓚ2208

[also suffix]
ⓐ (utensil for work) **implement, tool, utensil**
ⓑ (article serving to equip) **implement, equipment, gear, fittings, fixtures, outfit**

a 道具 どうぐ tool, utensil, implement; furniture; theatrical appurtenances; tool, means; ingredient
器具 きぐ utensil, implement, appliance
用具 ようぐ tool, instrument, appliance; outfit
工具 こうぐ tool, implement
治具 じぐ jig
絵の具 えのぐ coloring materials, colors, oils, paint
文房具 ぶんぼうぐ stationery, writing materials
b 家具 かぐ furniture
寝具 しんぐ bedclothes, bedding
仏具 ぶつぐ Buddhist altar fittings
筆記具 ひっきぐ writing materials
装身具 そうしんぐ personal ornaments [outfit]

器 ▷instrument
キ うつわ ⓚ2368

[also suffix] **instrument, device, appliance, implement, utensil**

器具 きぐ utensil, implement, appliance
器械 きかい instrument, apparatus, appliance
楽器 がっき musical instrument
機器 きき machinery and tools, apparatus
計器 けいき meter, gauge; instrument
兵器 へいき arms, weapon, ordnance
注射器 ちゅうしゃき syringe
消火器 しょうかき fire extinguisher
電熱器 でんねつき electric heater, electric cooker

儀 ▷measuring instrument
ギ ⓚ0147

[suffix] **measuring instrument, apparatus (esp. for astronomical applications)**

経緯儀 けいいぎ theodolite
水準儀 すいじゅんぎ leveling instrument, surveyor's level

鏡 ▷optical instrument
キョウ かがみ ⓚ1576

[also suffix] **optical instrument, viewing instrument, -scope, lens**

検鏡 けんきょう microscopic examination, microscopy
望遠鏡 ぼうえんきょう telescope
顕微鏡 けんびきょう microscope
潜望鏡 せんぼうきょう periscope
老眼鏡 ろうがんきょう spectacles for the aged, reading glasses

董 ▷old tool
トウ ⓚ202.

old tool, used article
骨董 こっとう antique, curio

magnetism →ELECTRICITY AND MAGNETISM

mail
郵 便

郵 ▷mail
ユウ ⓚ150.

(postal delivery system) **mail, post**

郵便 ゆうびん mail service, mail, postal matter
郵便局 ゆうびんきょく post office
郵便屋さん ゆうびんやさん mailman
郵政 ゆうせい postal system
郵送 ゆうそう mailing
郵税 ゆうぜい postage, postal rates
郵船 ゆうせん mail steamer
郵貯(=郵便貯金) ゆうちょ(=ゆうびんちょきん) posta [post-office] savings [deposit]
郵袋 ゆうたい mailbag

便 ▷post
ベン ビン たよ(り) ⓚ007.

ⓐ (postal material) **post, mail, letter**
ⓑ [also suffix] **postal service, postal delivery, mail**
a 便箋 びんせん letter paper, stationery, writing paper
郵便 ゆうびん mail service, mail, postal matter
別便 べつびん separate post
b 航空便 こうくうびん airmail
第一便 だいいちびん first delivery

main
主 正 本 親 首

主 ▷main
シュ ス ぬし おも あるじ ⓚ169.

[also prefix] **main, principal, head, leading, chief**

主要な しゅような main, principal, essential
主義 しゅぎ principle, -ism
主力 しゅりょく main force, main body
主流 しゅりゅう main current, mainstream
主演する しゅえんする play the leading part
主役 しゅやく leading part, starring role
主翼 しゅよく wing (of an aircraft)

主成分 しゅせいぶん principal ingredient, main component

正 ▷chief
セイ ショウ ただ(しい) ただ(す) まさ まさ(に)　Ⓚ2926

[also prefix] **chief, main, principal**

正使 せいし senior envoy, chief
正犯 せいはん principal offender
正副議長 せいふくぎちょう chairman and vice-chairman
正門 せいもん main gate, main entrance
正編 せいへん main part of a book
正弦 せいげん sine (of an angle)
正三位 しょうさんみ senior grade of the third court rank

本 ▷head
ホン もと　Ⓚ2937

[also prefix] **head, main, principal**

本部 ほんぶ head office, headquarters, administrative building
本店 ほんてん head [main] office [store]
本社 ほんしゃ head office, this office; head shrine, this shrine
本土 ほんど mainland; the country proper
本予算 ほんよさん main budget
本文 ほんぶん(=ほんもん) (main part of a text) text, body; this sentence [passage, article]
本線 ほんせん main line, trunk line

親 ▷parent
シン おや- した(しい) した(しむ)　Ⓚ1599

[also prefix] **parent, mother; master**

親船 おやぶね mother ship
親会社 おやがいしゃ parent company

首 ▷leading
シュ くび　Ⓚ1956

(occupying a head position) **leading, top, first**

首席 しゅせき top seat [place]; chief, head

make
作 造 成 工 製
産 調 組 構

作 ▷make
サク サ つく(る) つく(り) -づく(り) Ⓚ0052

make, produce, manufacture

作成する さくせいする make, produce, draw up, frame, prepare
作製 さくせい manufacture, production
製作 せいさく manufacture, production
工作 こうさく handicraft; construction, building; maneuvering
試作 しさく trial manufacture

造 ▷make
ゾウ つく(る) つく(り) -づく(り)　Ⓚ2679

make, produce, manufacture, shape, coin

造血 ぞうけつ blood making, hematosis
造花 ぞうか artificial flower; artificial flower making
造形(=造型) ぞうけい molding, modeling
造幣 ぞうへい coinage, mintage
製造 せいぞう production, manufacture
改造 かいぞう remodeling; reorganization
構造 こうぞう structure, construction, framework
創造 そうぞう creation
酒造 しゅぞう sake brewing; distilling

成 ▷form
セイ ジョウ な(る) な(す)　Ⓚ2964

(give form to) **form, make, create, bring to completion**

完成する かんせいする complete, finish; be completed, be finished
合成する ごうせいする compose, compound, synthesize
編成する へんせいする form, compose, compile
結成する けっせいする form, organize
構成 こうせい composition, construction, formation, organization

工 ▷manufacture
コウ ク　Ⓚ2866

(make by tools or machinery) **manufacture, process, fabricate, construct**

工作する こうさくする make; construct, build; maneuver, scheme
工場 こうじょう(=こうば) factory, plant, workshop
工具 こうぐ tool, implement
工芸 こうげい technical art, technology
工学 こうがく engineering
工学部 こうがくぶ department of engineering
工業 こうぎょう industry, manufacturing industry
工員 こういん industrial worker
加工 かこう processing, manufacturing

製 ▷manufacture
セイ　Ⓚ2441

ⓐ manufacture, make, produce, fabricate; bind (books); refine (oil)
ⓑ [also suffix] indicates place or agent of manufacture

a 製造業 せいぞうぎょう manufacturing industry
製作 せいさく manufacture, production
製品 せいひん manufactured goods [articles], product; refined petroleum products
製薬 せいやく pharmaceutical manufacture
製本 せいほん bookbinding
製図 せいず drafting, drawing
精製 せいせい refining; careful manufacture
特製の とくせいの specially made [manufactured]
手製の てせいの handmade
b 官製の かんせいの government manufactured
日本製の にほんせいの made in Japan

産 ▷produce
サン う(む) う(まれる) うぶ- Ⓚ2812

produce, yield
産出する さんしゅつする produce, yield
産業 さんぎょう industry
産地 さんち place of production; place of birth
産物 さんぶつ product, produce

調 ▷prepare
チョウ しら(べる) しら(べ) ととの(う)
ととの(える) Ⓚ1417

ⓐ prepare, make ready, make to order
ⓑ prepare (medicines or food), compound, mix,
blend
a 調製 ちょうせい preparation, manufacture, execution (of an order)
調達 ちょうたつ supply, procurement; execution (of
an order); raising (money)
調度 ちょうど personal effects, furnishings, supplies
新調する しんちょうする make (a new suit), have
(new shoes) made
b 調理する ちょうりする cook, prepare (food)
調味 ちょうみ seasoning, flavoring
調合 ちょうごう compounding, mixing, preparation
調剤 ちょうざい preparation [compounding] of
medicines
調色 ちょうしょく mixing colors

組 ▷assemble
ソ く(む) くみ -ぐみ Ⓚ1224

assemble, construct, put together, fit together
組み立てる くみたてる assemble, construct, erect
組み込む くみこむ incorporate, integrate, put in
組み合わせる くみあわせる combine, assort, join
together, match
組み合わせ くみあわせ combination; assortment
仕組み しくみ construction; arrangement; plan,
plot
番組 ばんぐみ (TV) program
団体を組む だんたいをくむ form an organization

構 ▷construct
コウ かま(える) かま(う) Ⓚ0962

[original meaning] (build by assembling parts) **construct,
frame, assemble, form, compose**
構成 こうせい composition, construction, formation, organization
構造 こうぞう structure, construction, framework
構築する こうちくする construct, build
構文 こうぶん sentence construction, syntax

make progress
進　亨　捗

進 ▷advance
シン すす(む) すす(める) Ⓚ2689

(make progress) **advance, make progress, improve**
進歩 しんぽ progress, advancement, improvement
進展 しんてん development, progress
進化 しんか evolution, progress
先進国 せんしんこく advanced [developed] nation
[country]
躍進 やくしん rapid advance [progress]

亨 ▷go smoothly
コウ キョウ Ⓚ1754

[archaic] **go smoothly, proceed well**
亨通 こうつう prosperous, doing well
亨運 こううん prosperity

捗 ▷make progress
チョク Ⓚ0386

make progress
進捗する しんちょくする progress, be under way

make sound or noise
鳴　響　騒　轟

鳴 ▷sound
メイ な(く) な(る) な(らす) Ⓚ0616

sound, ring, roar
鳴動 めいどう rumbling
共鳴 きょうめい resonance
雷鳴 らいめい thunderclap
吹鳴 すいめい blowing (a whistle)
奏鳴曲 そうめいきょく sonata

響 ▷reverberate
キョウ ひび(く)   Ⓚ2504

[original meaning] **reverberate, resound, echo, ring**
反響する はんきょうする echo, reverberate
反響 はんきょう echo, reverberation; response, repercussions
影響 えいきょう influence, effect

騒 ▷clamor
ソウ さわ(ぐ)   Ⓚ1630

[original meaning] **clamor, raise a clamor, be uproarious, make a noise, bustle**
騒音 そうおん noise
騒騒しい そうぞうしい clamorous, uproarious, noisy, boisterous
騒動 そうどう disturbance, uproar; strife; confusion
騒然たる そうぜんたる noisy, confused
騒乱 そうらん commotion, riot
喧騒 けんそう clamor, din, noise
物騒な ぶっそうな dangerous, insecure, disturbed

轟 ▷resound
ゴウ とどろ(く)   Ⓚ2402

resound, reverberate, boom; roar, rumble, roll
轟音 ごうおん thundering noise, roar, rumble
轟轟 ごうごう thunderous, rumbling
轟沈 ごうちん sinking (a ship) instantly

make widely known
布 流 伝 広 弘 及

布 ▷spread
フ ぬの   Ⓚ2566

(become or cause to become widely known) **spread, disseminate, distribute**
布告する ふこくする proclaim, declare
布教 ふきょう propagation, missionary work
布令 ふれい official notice, proclamation, announcement
公布する こうふする promulgate, proclaim
流布する るふする circulate, disseminate, spread

流 ▷spread
リュウ ル なが(れる) なが(れ) なが(す)   Ⓚ0400

spread, be disseminated, be circulated, pervade
流通 りゅうつう circulation of money or goods; flow of water; ventilation
流布 るふ circulation, dissemination, spread
流行する(=流行る) りゅうこうする(=はやる) be fashionable, be in vogue; prevail

伝 ▷spread
デン つた(わる) つた(える) つた(う) -づた(い)   Ⓚ0029

(disseminate information or religious teachings) **spread, propagate, transmit, teach**
伝道 でんどう gospel preaching, missionary work, evangelism
宣伝 せんでん publicity, propaganda; advertisement

広 ▷spread
コウ ひろ(い) ひろ(まる) ひろ(める) ひろ(がる) ひろ(げる)   Ⓚ2613

spread, disseminate
広告 こうこく public notice; advertisement
広報(=弘報) こうほう (public) information, public relations

弘 ▷disseminate (esp. Buddhism)
コウ グ ひろ(まる) ひろ(める)   Ⓚ0169

disseminate, spread, teach (esp. Buddhism)
弘報(=広報) こうほう (public) information, public relations
弘法 ぐほう spreading Buddhist teachings

及 ▷reach to
キュウ およ(ぶ) およ(び) およ(ぼす)   Ⓚ2868

(extend as far as) **reach to, extend over, range over**
普及 ふきゅう diffusion, spread, propagation
波及する はきゅうする be propagated; extend, spread; affect
遡及的な そきゅうてき(=さっきゅうてき)な retroactive

man
男 郎 雄 牡 夫 翁 爺

男 ▷man
ダン ナン おとこ   Ⓚ2199

[original meaning] **man, male**
男子 だんし boy, young man, man
男性 だんせい male, man
男性的 だんせいてき masculine, manly
男女 だんじょ men and women, both sexes
男尊女卑 だんそんじょひ predominance of men over women, sexism
男児 だんじ boy, son; man
美男子 びだんし(=びなんし) handsome man
下男 げなん male servant, manservant

郎 ▷young man
ロウ   Ⓚ1184

elegant **young man, man; husband**
- 郎君 ろうくん [rare] young nobleman, young lord
- 野郎 やろう guy, fellow, man, rascal
- 遊冶郎 ゆうやろう man of pleasure, libertine
- 新郎新婦 しんろうしんぷ bride and bridegroom

雄 ▷male
ユウ お- おす   Ⓚ0920

[original meaning] (of plants or animals) **male**
- 雄性 ゆうせい male characteristics, manliness
- 雄蕊 ゆうずい(=おしべ) stamen
- 雌雄 しゆう male and female; victory or defeat

牡 ▷male
ボ おす お- おん   Ⓚ0743

[original meaning] (of animals) **male**
- 牡丹 ぼたん peony, *Paeonia suffruticosa*
- 種牡馬 しゅぼば stallion, studhorse

夫 ▷male adult
フ フウ ブ おっと   Ⓚ2909

male adult, man
- 凡夫 ぼんぷ(=ぼんぶ) ordinary man; *Buddhism* common mortal
- 大丈夫 だいじょうぶ safe, sure, all right

翁 ▷old man
オウ   Ⓚ1809

old man, aged man, elder
- 老翁 ろうおう old man
- 村翁 そんおう village elder
- 白頭翁 はくとうおう white-haired old man; windflower

爺 ▷old man
ヤ じじ じじい じい

old man
- 老爺 ろうや old man
- 好好爺 こうこうや good-natured old man

mania and maniacs
痴 狂 魔 熱

痴 ▷infatuated
チ   Ⓚ2800

infatuated, crazy about, blindly in love, amorous
- 痴漢 ちかん molester of women, masher
- 痴情 ちじょう blind love, infatuation, amorous passion; jealousy
- 痴話 ちわ lover's talk, sweet nothings
- 情痴 じょうち love foolery

狂 ▷maniac
キョウ くる(う) くる(おしい) くる(わす) くる(わせる)   Ⓚ0241

[suffix] (enthusiastic fan) **maniac, fanatic, fan, enthusiast**
- 殺人狂 さつじんきょう homicidal maniac
- 映画狂 えいがきょう cinema enthusiast, movie fan
- 窃盗狂 せっとうきょう kleptomaniac
- 偏執狂 へんしつきょう(=へんしゅうきょう) monomaniac

魔 ▷maniac
マ   Ⓚ2747

[also suffix] (person with excessive passion for something) **maniac**
- 放火魔 ほうかま pyromaniac
- 収集魔 しゅうしゅうま collecting maniac
- 通り魔 とおりま phantom killer [robber]

熱 ▷fever
ネツ あつ(い)   Ⓚ2495

[suffix] **fever, craze, enthusiasm, mania**
- 野球熱 やきゅうねつ baseball fever, enthusiasm for baseball
- 海外留学熱 かいがいりゅうがくねつ craze for studying abroad
- 投機熱 とうきねつ speculation fever

maniacs →MANIA AND MANIACS

mansions
邸 館 荘

邸 ▷stately residence
テイ   Ⓚ1045

ⓐ stately residence, mansion, official residence, villa, house
ⓑ suffix for forming names of residences or mansions
ⓒ [original meaning, now obsolete] residence where feudal lords used to lodge when in the capital

a
- 邸宅 ていたく residence, mansion
- 公邸 こうてい official residence
- 官邸 かんてい official residence
- 私邸 してい one's private residence
- 別邸 べってい villa, country residence

b 徳川公爵邸 とくがわこうしゃくてい mansion of
Prince Tokugawa
山本氏邸 やまもとしてい Mr. Yamamoto's residence

館 ▷stately mansion
カン やかた　　　　　　　　　　Ⓚ1562

stately mansion, palace, manor house

荘 ▷villa
ソウ　　　　　　　　　　　　Ⓚ1954

ⓐ villa, cottage
ⓑ suffix after names of villas, inns or apartment
houses
a 別荘 べっそう villa, country cottage
山荘 さんそう mountain villa
b 山水荘 さんすいそう The Sansui Inn

manuscript
稿　草　案

稿 ▷manuscript
コウ　　　　　　　　　　　　Ⓚ1138

[also suffix] manuscript, draft, copy
稿料 こうりょう payment for a manuscript
原稿 げんこう manuscript, draft, copy
寄稿 きこう contribution (to a newspaper)
草稿 そうこう outline, draft
遺稿 いこう posthumous work [manuscript]
投稿する とうこうする contribute (an article)
脱稿する だっこうする finish writing, complete (a
novel)
決定稿 けっていこう final manuscript

草 ▷draft
ソウ くさ -ぐさ　　　　　　　Ⓚ1953

draft, manuscript, outline
草稿 そうこう outline, draft
草案 そうあん (rough) draft
起草する きそうする draft (a bill), draw up

案 ▷draft
アン　　　　　　　　　　　　Ⓚ1960

draft
案内する あんないする guide, show; inform, notify
草案 そうあん (rough) draft

mark
印　押　劃　画　捺

印 ▷imprint
イン しるし -じるし　　　　Ⓚ0733

ⓐ [original meaning] imprint, impress, make a mark
ⓑ imprint on the mind, make an impression
a 印字 いんじ printing, typing
印刻 いんこく engraving
b 印象 いんしょう impression

押 ▷seal
オウ お(す) お(し) お(つ)-
お(さえる)　　　　　　　　Ⓚ0278

(fix a seal) seal, stamp
押印する おういんする seal, affix a seal
押捺 おうなつ sealing (a document)

劃 ▷mark off
カク

[original meaning] mark off, draw a line, demarcate,
partition
劃期的 かっきてき epoch-making, epochal
劃一化 かくいつか standardization
劃定する かくていする demarcate
劃然と かくぜんと distinctly, clearly
区劃 くかく division, section; boundary

画 ▷mark off
ガ カク　　　　　　　　　　Ⓚ2586

[formerly also 劃] [original meaning] mark off, draw a
line, demarcate, partition
画期的な かっきてきな epoch-making, epochal
画一的な かくいつてきな uniform, standardized
画定 かくてい demarcation
区画する くかくする divide, draw a line, mark off

捺 ▷affix a seal
ナツ ダツ ナチ ナ お(す)　　Ⓚ0456

press heavily downwards; stamp
捺印する なついんする affix a seal, stamp
指紋押捺 しもんおうなつ affixing one's fingerprint

market
市　場

市 ▷market
シ いち　　　Ⓚ1724

ⓐ [original meaning] **market, fair**
ⓑ economics **market**
a 市場 しじょう market, mart
　市販 しはん marketing
b 市況 しきょう market conditions, tone of the market
　市価 しか market price

場 ▷market
ジョウ ば　　　Ⓚ0512

market, exchange
市場 しじょう market, mart
上場する じょうじょうする list (stocks)

marks and signs
標　徽　痕　印　跡　蹟
踪　紋　符　号　栞

標 ▷mark (identifying sign)
ヒョウ　　　Ⓚ0976

(identifying sign) **mark, sign, symbol, label, inscription**
標章 ひょうしょう ensign, emblem, mark
標札 (=表札) ひょうさつ nameplate, doorplate
商標 しょうひょう trademark
墓標 ぼひょう grave post, grave marker, gravestone
音標 おんぴょう phonetic sign

徽 ▷emblem
キ　　　Ⓚ0705

[now replaced by 記] **emblem, badge**
徽章 きしょう emblem, insignia

痕 ▷scar
コン あと　　　Ⓚ2795

ⓐ **scar**
ⓑ **trace(s), mark, trail**
a 瘢痕組織 はんこんそしき scar tissue
　聖痕 せいこん stigmata (in Christianity)
b 痕跡 こんせき trace, vestige
　弾痕 だんこん bullet hole [mark]
　墨痕 ぼっこん handwriting; ink marks

印 ▷mark (visible sign)
イン しるし -じるし　　　Ⓚ0733

(visible sign) **mark, imprint, sign**
烙印 らくいん brand

跡 ▷trace
セキ あと　　　Ⓚ1395
see also →TRACE

(mark left by something) **trace(s), track, mark, footprint, trail**
足跡 そくせき footprint, footmark; the course of one's life, one's achievements
追跡 ついせき pursuit, chase, follow-up
軌跡 きせき locus; tracks
航跡 こうせき wake, track; flight path, vapor trail
人跡 じんせき human traces
筆跡 ひっせき handwriting, holograph

蹟 ▷trace
セキ あと　　　Ⓚ1473

[original meaning] (mark left by something) **trace(s), track, mark, footprint, trail**
筆蹟 ひっせき handwriting, holograph
手蹟 しゅせき holograph, calligraphic specimen
真蹟 しんせき genuine handwriting

踪 ▷footprints
ソウ　　　Ⓚ1434

[original meaning] **footprints; traces, remains; whereabouts**
踪跡 そうせき traces, tracks; whereabouts
失踪 しっそう absconding, disappearance

紋 ▷print
モン　　　Ⓚ1194

print
指紋 しもん fingerprint
声紋 せいもん voiceprint
掌紋 しょうもん palm print

符 ▷symbol
フ　　　Ⓚ2319

(arbitrary sign other than a letter representing meaning)
symbol, sign, mark
符号 ふごう sign, mark, symbol
符牒 ふちょう sign; secret price tag; password
疑問符 ぎもんふ question mark
終止符 しゅうしふ period
音符 おんぷ note; phonetic element of kanji
二分音符 にぶおんぷ half note

号 ▷sign
ゴウ   Ⓚ1847

(arbitrary sign, esp. in mathematics) **sign, symbol, mark**
- 等号 とうごう equal sign [mark]
- 負号 ふごう negative sign
- 符号 ふごう sign, mark, symbol
- 記号 きごう symbol, mark, sign
- 暗号 あんごう code, password

栞 ▷bookmark
カン しおり   Ⓚ2307

【カン】
[original meaning, now archaic] **twig or branch used as a waymark in a mountain path**

【しおり】
[sometimes also 枝折り] **bookmark; guidebook**
- 旅の栞 たびのしおり travel guidebook

marriage →MARRYING AND MARRIAGE

marrying and marriage

嫁　婚　姻　縁

嫁 ▷wed a man
カ よめ とつ(ぐ)   Ⓚ0582

wed a man, marry into a family
- 降嫁 こうか marriage of an Imperial princess to a subject
- 再嫁 さいか second marriage

婚 ▷marry
コン   Ⓚ0427

ⓐ **marry, wed**
ⓑ [original meaning] **marriage, wedding**
- ⓐ 婚姻 こんいん marriage, matrimony
- 婚礼 こんれい wedding ceremony
- 婚約 こんやく engagement, betrothal
- 結婚 けっこん marriage
- 求婚 きゅうこん proposal of marriage
- 再婚 さいこん remarriage, second marriage
- 離婚 りこん divorce
- 新婚の しんこんの newly wedded
- ⓑ 婚儀 こんぎ wedding ceremony
- 金婚 きんこん golden wedding
- 近親婚 きんしんこん consanguineous marriage

姻 ▷marriage
イン   Ⓚ0315

marriage

- 婚姻 こんいん marriage, matrimony

縁 ▷marriage relation
エン ふち   Ⓚ1269

marriage relation, marriage
- 縁談 えんだん marriage proposal
- 縁組 えんぐみ marriage, (conjugal) union
- 内縁の妻 ないえんのつま common-law wife

marshes →LAKES AND MARSHES

mathematical power

乗　方　平

乗 ▷power
ジョウ の(る) -の(り) の(せる)   Ⓚ2992

power
- 自乗(=二乗) じじょう square, second power
- 二乗する にじょうする raise to the second power

方 ▷square
ホウ かた -がた -なた   Ⓚ1709

(second power) **square**
- 方丈 ほうじょう 10 sq. feet; abbot's chamber; chief priest
- 平方 へいほう square (measure); square (of a number)
- 立方 りっぽう cube

平 ▷square (measure)
ヘイ ビョウ たい(ら) -だいら
ひら   Ⓚ2921

abbrev. of 平方 へいほう: **square (measure)**
- 平米 へいべい sq. meter

mats

畳　薦　敷

畳 ▷tatami
ジョウ たた(む) たたみ   Ⓚ2249

【ジョウ】
[sometimes also 帖] **counter for tatami or (straw) mats**
- 畳数 じょうすう number of tatami [mats]
- 四畳半の部屋 よじょうはんのへや four-and-a-half-mat room

【たたみ】
tatami, mat, straw mat
- 畳表 たたみおもて mat facing

畳替え たたみがえ refacing [renewing] mats
畳敷きの部屋 たたみじきのへや straw-matted room
青畳 あおだたみ new mat

薦 ▷straw mat
セン すす(める)　　　　　　　Ⓚ2097

[rare] **straw mat**
蒲薦 ほせん bulrush mat

敷 ▷underlay
フ し(く) -し(き)　　　　　　Ⓚ1653

[also suffix] **underlay, mat**
下敷き したじき underlay; being buried; model
土瓶敷き どびんしき teapot mat [rest], tea cloth

matter
質　物　材　料　資

質 ▷matter
シツ シチ チ　　　　　　　　Ⓚ2445

ⓐ **matter, substance, material**
ⓑ [suffix] (specific substance or constituent) **matter**
a 質量 しつりょう phys mass; quality and quantity
　物質 ぶっしつ matter, substance
b 植物質 しょくぶつしつ vegetable matter
　蛋白質 たんぱくしつ protein, albuminous substance

物 ▷substance
ブツ モツ もの　　　　　　　Ⓚ0777

[also suffix] **substance, matter, material**
　物質 ぶっしつ matter, substance
　鉱物 こうぶつ mineral substance
　毒物 どくぶつ poisonous substance, toxin
　薬物 やくぶつ drugs, medicinal substances
　化合物 かごうぶつ (chemical) compound
　有機物 ゆうきぶつ organic matter
　塩化物 えんかぶつ chloride

材 ▷material
ザイ　　　　　　　　　　　　Ⓚ0740

[also suffix] **material, raw material**
　材質 ざいしつ material properties; lumber quality
　材料 ざいりょう material, matter, stuff; factor, element
　素材 そざい material; subject matter
　鋼材 こうざい steel materials, structural steel
　資材 しざい materials

料 ▷materials
リョウ　　　　　　　　　　　Ⓚ1187

ⓐ **materials, material, stuff, matter**
ⓑ [also suffix] materials for cooking: **ingredients, food-stuff, cuisine**
ⓒ (written) **materials, data**
a 材料 ざいりょう material, matter, stuff; factor, element
　原料 げんりょう raw material
　燃料 ねんりょう fuel
　食料 しょくりょう food, foodstuffs
　清涼飲料水 せいりょういんりょうすい cooling drink
b 料理 りょうり cooking, cuisine; handling
　料亭 りょうてい high-class restaurant, Japanese restaurant
　調味料 ちょうみりょう seasoning, flavoring
c 資料 しりょう materials, data
　史料 しりょう historical materials [records]

資 ▷material resources
シ　　　　　　　　　　　　　Ⓚ2351

material resources, materials, means
　資料 しりょう materials, data
　資源 しげん resources
　資材 しざい materials
　物資 ぶっし commodities, goods, resources
　師資 しし relying on someone as one's teacher

mature
熟　成　稔　爛　実

熟 ▷mature
ジュク う(れる)　　　　　　Ⓚ2498

❶ (become ripe, as of fruit) **mature, ripen**
　熟柿 じゅくし ripe persimmon
　未熟な みじゅくな unripe, immature; unskilled, poor
❷ (become fully developed) **mature, ripen, attain full growth**
　熟成 じゅくせい aging, ripening, maturation
　成熟する せいじゅくする mature, ripen, attain full growth
　早熟な そうじゅくな precocious, forward

成 ▷grow up
セイ ジョウ な(る) な(す)　Ⓚ296

grow up, mature
　成長する せいちょうする grow up
　成熟 せいじゅく maturity, ripeness, full growth
　成育する せいいくする grow (up), be brought up
　養成する ようせいする train, educate, bring up

促成栽培の野菜 そくせいさいばいのやさい forced
vegetables

稔 ▷ripen
ネン ジン みの(る)   Ⓚ1115

[original meaning] **ripen**—said esp. of rice
稔実不良 ねんじつふりょう poor crop (of rice)
豊稔 ほうねん(=ほうじん) [archaic] bumper harvest

爛 ▷overripe
ラン ただ(れる)

[now also 乱] **overripe, rotten**
爛熟する らんじゅくする become overripe; attain
full maturity
腐爛する ふらんする ulcerate, decompose

実 ▷bear fruit
ジツ み みの(る)   Ⓚ1911

[sometimes also 稔る] **bear fruit, ripen**
実り みのり crop, ripening
実っている みのっている be in bearing
実らなかった努力 みのらなかったどりょく fruitless
[resultless] efforts

meaning
義 意 訳 旨 趣

義 ▷meaning
ギ   Ⓚ2052

meaning, sense, signification, significance
意義 いぎ meaning, sense, signification, significance
講義 こうぎ lecture
定義 ていぎ definition
字義 じぎ character definition, meaning of a word
[term]
疑義 ぎぎ doubt, doubtful points

意 ▷meaning
イ   Ⓚ1834

meaning, sense, intent
意味 いみ meaning, intention, significance, purport
意義 いぎ meaning, sense, signification, significance
意訳 いやく free translation
真意 しんい true meaning [signification]; real intention
文意 ぶんい meaning (of a passage), purport
表意文字 ひょういもじ ideograph, ideographic
character

訳 ▷sense
ヤク わけ   Ⓚ1340

sense, meaning
訳の分からない言葉 わけのわからないことば
words that make no sense, meaningless words

旨 ▷purport
シ むね   Ⓚ1744

(reason for an action) **purport, purpose, aim**
趣旨 しゅし purpose, aim; purport, meaning
宗旨 しゅうし tenets of a religious sect; (religious)
sect
本旨 ほんし main object, true aim

趣 ▷purpose
シュ おもむき   Ⓚ2827

purpose, aim, motive, object, meaning, purport
趣旨 しゅし purpose, aim; purport, meaning
趣意 しゅい purpose, motive, aim; purport, meaning, point
趣向 しゅこう idea, contrivance, plan
意趣 いしゅ spite, grudge, enmity; [original meaning]
purpose, meaning

means
策 段 手

策 ▷measure
サク   Ⓚ2338

[also suffix] **measure, means, step, resource**
対策 たいさく countermeasure, counterplan
施策 しさく enforcement of a policy
万策 ばんさく all means [measures]
失策 しっさく blunder, slip, error
善後策 ぜんごさく remedial [relief] measure,
countermeasure

段 ▷step
ダン   Ⓚ1059

(means to an end) **step, measure**
段取り だんどり program, plan, step, course of
action
手段 しゅだん means, way, step
算段 さんだん contrivance, management

手 ▷means
シュ ズ て た-   Ⓚ2907

means, method
手段 しゅだん means, way, step
手法 しゅほう technique, mechanism, style

measure
測　量

測 ▷**measure**
ソク はか(る)　　　Ⓚ0558

[original meaning] **measure, gauge, survey, fathom**
測定する そくていする measure, gauge
測量 そくりょう measurement, surveying
測深 そくしん sounding

量 ▷**measure**
リョウ はか(る)　　　Ⓚ2180

[original meaning] (determine the volume, area or weight
of) **measure, gauge, weigh**
測量する そくりょうする measure, survey
計量する けいりょうする measure, weigh

measuring devices
枡　尺　計　衡　秤

枡 ▷**measure**
ます

measure, measuring box
枡目 ますめ measure; square (of graph paper)
五升枡 ごしょうます 5-*sho* measure

尺 ▷**rule**
シャク　　　Ⓚ2896

[also suffix] **rule, measure, scale**
尺度 しゃくど linear measure; standard
巻き尺 まきじゃく measuring tape
計算尺 けいさんじゃく slide rule

計 ▷**meter**
ケイ はか(る) はか(らう)　　　Ⓚ1309

[also suffix] **meter, gauge, measuring instrument**
計器 けいき meter, gauge; instrument
時計 とけい clock, watch
速度計 そくどけい speedometer
地震計 じしんけい seismometer
温度計 おんどけい thermometer

衡 ▷**scales**
コウ　　　Ⓚ0687

❶ **scales, weighing machine**
❷ **beam [arm] of a scale**
a 度量衡 どりょうこう weights and measures

秤 ▷**balance**
ビン ショウ ヒョウ はかり　　　Ⓚ1072

balance, scale(s)
秤量(=称量) しょうりょう weighing on a balance
秤量 ひょうりょう weighing on a balance; maximum
  weight capacity
秤動 ひょうどう libration (of a heavenly body)
天秤 てんびん balance, scale(s)
天秤座 てんびんざ Libra, the Scales

meat
肉　身　脩

肉 ▷**flesh**
ニク　　　Ⓚ2756

(article of food) **flesh, meat**
肉食 にくしょく meat diet
牛肉 ぎゅうにく beef
食肉 しょくにく meat
挽き肉 ひきにく ground [minced] meat
羊頭狗肉 ようとうくにく using a better name to sell
  inferior goods, crying wine and selling vinegar

身 ▷**meat**
シン み　　　Ⓚ2977

meat, flesh
脂身 あぶらみ fat, fatty meat
刺身 さしみ *sashimi*, sliced raw flesh (esp. of fish)

脩 ▷**dried meat**
シュウ　　　Ⓚ0119

❶ [original meaning] **dried meat**
❷ **dried meat or ham as gift to teacher in lieu of
salary in ancient times**
a 束脩 そくしゅう tuition; ham as gift to teacher in
  lieu of tuition

mediating and
mediators
紹　介　媒　仲

紹 ▷**introduce**
ショウ　　　Ⓚ122

introduce, bring together
紹介する しょうかいする introduce, present

紹介状 しょうかいじょう letter of introduction

介 ▷mediate
カイ　　　　Ⓚ1711

mediate, intervene, go between; lie between

介入 かいにゅう intervention
介在する かいざいする lie between
媒介 ばいかい mediation, intervention, intermediation
紹介 しょうかい introduction, presentation
仲介 ちゅうかい mediation

媒 ▷intermediate
バイ　　　　Ⓚ0518

intermediate, mediate, act as a go-between; act as a medium

媒介 ばいかい mediation, intervention, intermediation
媒質 ばいしつ medium
媒体 ばいたい medium
媒染剤 ばいせんざい mordant
触媒 しょくばい catalyst, catalyzer
霊媒 れいばい (spiritualistic) medium

仲 ▷intermediary
チュウ なか　　　　Ⓚ0028

intermediary, middleman, mediator

仲介者 ちゅうかいしゃ intermediary, mediator, agent
仲裁人 ちゅうさいにん arbitrator, mediator

mediators →MEDIATING AND MEDIATORS

medicines
薬 剤 錠 丸 鍼 灸

薬 ▷drug
ヤク くすり　　　　Ⓚ2100

[also suffix] [original meaning] **drug, medicine, remedy, pharmaceutical**

薬剤 やくざい medicine, drugs
薬品 やくひん medicine, drug; chemicals
薬局 やっきょく drugstore, pharmacy
薬効 やっこう effect of a medicine
麻薬 まやく narcotic, drug
医薬 いやく medicine, drug; medical practice and dispensary
製薬 せいやく pharmaceutical manufacture
妙薬 みょうやく miracle drug, golden remedy
胃腸薬 いちょうやく medicine for the stomach and bowels

剤 ▷preparation
ザイ　　　　Ⓚ1491

[also suffix] [original meaning] **pharmaceutical preparation, drug, medicine**

薬剤 やくざい medicine, drugs
調剤する ちょうざいする prepare [compound] medicines
錠剤 じょうざい pill, tablet
ビタミン剤 びたみんざい vitamin preparation
調合剤 ちょうごうざい preparation, mixture
消化剤 しょうかざい digestive, peptic
鎮痛剤 ちんつうざい anodyne, painkiller

錠 ▷pill
ジョウ　　　　Ⓚ1548

ⓐ [also suffix] **pill, tablet**
ⓑ **counter for pills**

a 錠剤 じょうざい pill, tablet
糖衣錠 とういじょう sugar-coated pill
ビタミン錠 びたみんじょう vitamin tablet [pill]
モヒ錠 もひじょう tablet of morphine
b 二錠 にじょう two pills

丸 ▷pill suffix
ガン まる まる(い) まる(める)　　　　Ⓚ2883

suffix after names of pills

救命丸 きゅうめいがん Kyumeigan (name of pill)

鍼 ▷acupuncture
シン はり

[now also 針] **acupuncture**

鍼術 しんじゅつ acupuncture
鍼灸 しんきゅう acupuncture and moxibustion

灸 ▷moxibustion
キュウ やいと　　　　Ⓚ1900

moxibustion

灸点 きゅうてん moxa treatment points
灸治 きゅうじ treatment with moxa
鍼灸(=針灸) しんきゅう acupuncture and moxibustion
温灸 おんきゅう moxibustion

meet
会 遇 遭 見 謁 逢

会 ▷meet
カイ エ あ(う) あ(わせる)　　　　Ⓚ1741

[original meaning] (encounter by chance or arrangement)
meet, see, encounter, interview

会話 かいわ conversation
会談 かいだん conversation, talk, conference
会見 かいけん interview, audience
会食する かいしょくする dine together, have [take]
   a meal together
再会する さいかいする meet again
密会する みっかいする meet secretly
面会 めんかい seeing, interview

遇 ▷encounter
グウ   Ⓚ2702

(meet by chance) **encounter, happen to meet, come across, meet with**

遭遇する そうぐうする encounter, come across
奇遇 きぐう unexpected meeting, chance encounter
千載一遇の せんざいいちぐうの experienced once in a thousand years, very rare

遭 ▷meet with
ソウ あ(う) あ(わせる)   Ⓚ2725

[original meaning] (come upon, esp. by accident) **meet with (disaster)**

遭難する そうなんする meet with disaster
遭遇する そうぐうする encounter, come across

見 ▷see
ケン み(る) み(える) み(せる)   Ⓚ2201

(grant or be granted an audience) **see (someone), interview, give [be given] an audience**

会見 かいけん interview, audience
接見する せっけんする receive, give an interview
朝見 ちょうけん audience with the emperor

謁 ▷be granted an audience
エツ   Ⓚ1420

be granted [have] an audience with a superior, esp. a ruler or the emperor

謁見 えっけん audience
拝謁 はいえつ audience with the emperor

逢 ▷meet
ホウ あ(う)   Ⓚ2774

(encounter by chance) **meet, see, encounter**

逢着する ほうちゃくする encounter, face

---

merchant

産 品 貨 物

産 ▷product
サン う(む) う(まれる) うぶ-   Ⓚ2812

product, produce

水産 すいさん marine products, fisheries
物産 ぶっさん product, produce
名産 めいさん noted product

品 ▷article (of merchandise)
ヒン しな   Ⓚ1937

article of merchandise, goods, commodity, product

商品 しょうひん goods, commodities
製品 せいひん manufactured goods [articles], product; refined petroleum products
納品 のうひん delivery of goods; delivered goods
返品 へんぴん returning goods; returned goods, article sent back
舶来品 はくらいひん imported goods

貨 ▷goods
カ   Ⓚ2175

goods, commodity

百貨店 ひゃっかてん department store
雑貨 ざっか sundries, general cargo; miscellaneous goods
奇貨 きか curiosity, rarity; good opportunity

物 ▷commodity
ブツ モツ もの   Ⓚ0777

[also suffix] **commodity, goods, product**

物価 ぶっか prices (of commodities)
物資 ぶっし commodities, goods, resources
物産 ぶっさん product, produce
名物 めいぶつ specialty, noted product
産物 さんぶつ product, produce
貨物 かもつ freight, cargo, goods
穀物 こくもつ grain, cereals
出版物 しゅっぱんぶつ publication

---

merchant

屋 商

屋 ▷shopkeeper
オク や   Ⓚ266⦙

[suffix] **shopkeeper, dealer**

商 ▷merchant
ショウ あきな(う) ⓚ1818

[also suffix] **merchant, trader, dealer, businessman, shopkeeper**

画商 がしょう picture dealer
豪商 ごうしょう wealthy merchant
貿易商 ぼうえきしょう trading merchant, importer, exporter
士農工商 しのうこうしょう warriors, farmers, artisans and tradesmen (the four classes of Tokugawa Japan)

metal
金　鉱　礦　鈑

金 ▷metal
キン コン かね かな- -がね ⓚ1771

[original meaning] **metal**

金属 きんぞく metal
金鉄 きんてつ metal; firmness
合金 ごうきん alloy, compound metal
冶金 やきん metallurgy
白金 はっきん platinum, platina

鉱 ▷ore
コウ ⓚ1525

[formerly also 礦] [also suffix] [original meaning] **ore**

鉱石 こうせき ore, mineral
鉱床 こうしょう ore deposit
鉱山 こうざん mine
鉱坑 こうこう mine, shaft, pit
金鉱 きんこう gold ore; gold mine
鉄鉱 てっこう iron ore
磁鉄鉱 じてっこう magnetite, loadstone

礦 ▷ore
コウ

[original meaning] **ore**

礦石 こうせき ore, mineral
礦業 こうぎょう mining (industry)

鈑 ▷sheet metal
バン

[now usu. 板] **sheet metal**

鈑金 ばんきん sheet metal

metals
金　銀　銅　鉄　鉛　錫

金 ▷gold
キン コン かね かな- -がね ⓚ1771

[also prefix] **gold**

金貨 きんか gold coin
金鉱 きんこう gold ore; gold mine
金時計 きんどけい gold watch
純金 じゅんきん pure gold, solid gold
黄金 おうごん gold; money

銀 ▷silver
ギン ⓚ1534

silver

銀貨 ぎんか silver coin
水銀 すいぎん mercury, quicksilver
純銀 じゅんぎん pure silver
硝酸銀 しょうさんぎん silver nitrate
金銀 きんぎん gold and silver; money

銅 ▷copper
ドウ ⓚ1533

[also prefix] [original meaning] **copper**

銅鉱 どうこう copper ore
銅線 どうせん copper wire
銅山 どうざん copper mine
銅貨 どうか copper coin, copper
銅相場 どうそうば market price of copper
青銅 せいどう bronze

鉄 ▷iron
テツ ⓚ1527

[original meaning] **iron**

鉄鋼 てっこう iron and steel
鉄板 てっぱん iron [steel] plate
鉄筋 てっきん ferro-(concrete)
鉄砲 てっぽう gun, firearm
鉄道 てつどう railway
鉄骨 てっこつ steel [iron] frame
製鉄 せいてつ iron manufacture
非鉄金属 ひてつきんぞく nonferrous metals

鉛 ▷lead
エン なまり ⓚ1523

[original meaning] **lead**

鉛毒 えんどく lead poisoning
鉛筆 えんぴつ pencil
鉛管 えんかん lead pipe
加鉛ガソリン かえんガソリン leaded gasoline

亜鉛 あえん zinc

錫 ▷tin
シャク すず ⓀK1557

tin
錫製品 すずせいひん tinware
錫婚式 すずこんしき tin wedding (anniversary)
錫石 すずいし cassiterite
酸化錫 さんかすず stannous oxide; stannic oxide

middle
中 央 心 核

中 ▷middle
チュウ ジュウ なか ⓀK2902

[original meaning] **middle, center, midway**
中間 ちゅうかん middle, midway
中心 ちゅうしん center, middle
中核 ちゅうかく core, nucleus; kernel
集中する しゅうちゅうする concentrate, focus;
    converge

央 ▷center
オウ ⓀK2944

[original meaning] **center, middle**
中央 ちゅうおう center
月央 げつおう middle of the month
震央 しんおう epicenter (of an earthquake)
中央線 ちゅうおうせん Chuo Line (central railway
    line in Tokyo)
道央 どうおう central Hokkaido

心 ▷heart
シン こころ -ごころ ⓀK0004

(central part) **heart, center, core**
中心 ちゅうしん center, middle
都心 としん heart [center] of a city
核心 かくしん core, heart
重心 じゅうしん center of gravity, centroid
遠心力 えんしんりょく centrifugal force
外心 がいしん circumcenter, outer center

核 ▷nucleus
カク ⓀK0836

(central part) **nucleus, core**
核仁 かくじん nucleus
核家族 かくかぞく nucleus family
中核 ちゅうかく core, nucleus; kernel

military
武 兵

武 ▷military
ブム ⓀK2764

ⓐ military, martial; military affairs, military might
ⓑ military [martial] arts, science of war, Bushido
a 武力 ぶりょく military power, armed might
  武術 ぶじゅつ military [martial] arts
b 武道 ぶどう martial arts
  文武 ぶんぶ literary and military arts

兵 ▷military
ヘイ ヒョウ ⓀK2207

military, military science
兵学 へいがく military science, strategy, tactics
兵法 ひょうほう(=へいほう) art of war, strategy

military officers and ranks
曹 尉 佐 将 督 帥

曹 ▷sergeant
ソウ ⓀK2394

sergeant, petty officer
曹長 そうちょう sergeant officer, sergeant major
軍曹 ぐんそう sergeant
海曹 かいそう petty officer (navy)
陸曹 りくそう noncommissioned officer

尉 ▷company officer
イ ⓀK1504

(military officer or rank such as captain or lieutenant)
company officer
尉官 いかん company officer
空軍大尉 くうぐんたいい air force captain
中尉 ちゅうい first lieutenant (U.S. Army)
少尉 しょうい second lieutenant

佐 ▷field officer
サ ⓀK0051

(military officer or rank below 将 しょう (general officer)
and above 尉 い (company officer) roughly equiv. to colonel or major (U.S. ranking)) **field officer**
佐官 さかん field officer
大佐 たいさ (army) colonel, (navy) captain

中佐 ちゅうさ (army) lieutenant colonel, (navy) commander
少佐 しょうさ (army) major, (navy) lieutenant commander

将 ▷**general officer**
ショウ   Ⓚ0415

general officer, general, admiral, commander; leader

将軍 しょうぐん commander, general
将校 しょうこう officer, commissioned officer
将兵 しょうへい officers and men
将官 しょうかん general, admiral
陸将 りくしょう lieutenant general, general officer
大将 たいしょう admiral, general; old chap
武将 ぶしょう commander, warlord

督 ▷**commander**
トク   Ⓚ2437

commander, governor-general, viceroy

総督 そうとく governor-general, viceroy
都督 ととく governor general
提督 ていとく admiral

帥 ▷**commander in chief**
スイ   Ⓚ1185

commander in chief, leader, general

元帥 げんすい marshal, general
将帥 しょうすい commander
総帥 そうすい commander in chief

mine
坑 鉱 礦 山

坑 ▷**pit**
コウ   Ⓚ0208

pit (of a mine), mine-pit, mine

坑口 こうこう pithead, minehead
坑外で こうがいで out of the pit
坑夫 こうふ miner
坑内 こうない mine-pit, shaft
坑底 こうてい mine-pit bottom
鉱坑 こうこう mine, shaft, pit
炭坑 たんこう coal-mine, coal pit

鉱 ▷**mine**
コウ   Ⓚ1525

ⓐ **mine**
ⓑ **suffix after names of mines**
ⓐ 鉱業 こうぎょう mining (industry)
炭鉱 たんこう coal mine

ⓑ 夕張鉱 ゆうばりこう Yubari Mine

礦 ▷**mine**
コウ

ⓐ **mine**
ⓑ **suffix after names of mines**
ⓐ 炭礦 たんこう coal mine
ⓑ 夕張礦 ゆうばりこう Yubari Mine

山 ▷**mine**
サン やま   Ⓚ2544

mine

鉱山 こうざん mine
閉山 へいざん closing a mine; closing of the climbing season

miraculous
妙 魔

妙 ▷**marvelous**
ミョウ   Ⓚ0210

(causing wonder) **marvelous, wonderful, miraculous**

妙薬 みょうやく miracle drug, golden remedy
絶妙な ぜつみような miraculous, exquisite, superb

魔 ▷**magic(al)**
マ   Ⓚ2747

(related to the powers of a demon) **magic(al), evil**

魔法 まほう magic, sorcery, witchcraft
魔法瓶 まほうびん thermos bottle
魔術 まじゅつ magic, sorcery, witchcraft
魔力 まりょく magical powers
魔女 まじょ witch, sorceress
魔笛 まてき magic flute; The Magic Flute (by Mozart)
魔手 ましゅ evil power

misfortune and disaster
災 難 禍 厄 凶

災 ▷**natural calamity**
サイ わざわ(い)   Ⓚ1888

[original meaning] **natural calamity, disaster, misfortune, serious trouble**

災難 さいなん calamity, disaster, accident, misfortune

災禍 さいか accident, natural calamity, disaster, misfortune
災害 さいがい calamity, disaster, accident
災厄 さいやく calamity, disaster, accident
火災 かさい fire, conflagration
天災 てんさい natural calamity [disaster]
人災 じんさい man-made calamity
戦災 せんさい war damage
被災地 ひさいち disaster stricken area

難 ▷disaster
ナン かた(い) −がた(い) むずか(しい) むつか(しい) Ⓚ1632

disaster, calamity, accident, misfortune

難民 なんみん refugee, displaced person
遭難する そうなんする meet with disaster
避難 ひなん refuge, shelter, evacuation
海難 かいなん disaster at sea, shipwreck
災難 さいなん calamity, disaster, accident, misfortune

禍 ▷calamity
カ Ⓚ0945

[original meaning] **calamity, misfortune, disaster, evil**

禍福 かふく fortune and misfortune
禍根 かこん root of evil
災禍 さいか accident, natural calamity, disaster, misfortune
黄禍 こうか Yellow Peril
水禍 すいか flood disaster; drowning
惨禍 さんか terrible disaster, crushing calamity

厄 ▷misfortune
ヤク Ⓚ2550

misfortune, trouble, evil, ill luck

厄除け やくよけ warding off evil fortune; talisman against evils
厄日 やくび unlucky day, critical day
厄年 やくどし climacteric [critical] age, unlucky year
厄介 やっかい trouble, annoyance
大厄 たいやく great misfortune [calamity]; grand climacteric
災厄 さいやく calamity, disaster, accident

凶 ▷bad luck
キョウ Ⓚ2557

ⓐ **bad luck, misfortune, calamity**
ⓑ **unlucky, bad, disastrous**

a 吉凶 きっきょう good or ill luck, fortune
b 凶事 きょうじ calamity, misfortune
凶報 きょうほう bad news
凶日 きょうじつ unlucky day
凶変(=兇変) きょうへん calamity, disaster; tragic accident

mistakes and mistaking
過 失 誤 謬 錯 違

過 ▷error
カ す(ぎる) −す(ぎ) す(ごす) あやま(つ) あやま(ち) Ⓚ2704

error, fault, mistake, slip

過失 かしつ error, fault, mistake; negligence
大過 たいか serious error, gross mistake
罪過 ざいか fault

失 ▷slip
シツ うしな(う) Ⓚ2947

ⓐ **slip (up), make a slip, make a mistake**
ⓑ **slip, oversight, mistake, error**
ⓒ *baseball* **error**

a 失言 しつげん slip of the tongue
失笑する しっしょうする burst out laughing
失策 しっさく blunder, slip, error
失敗 しっぱい failure, mistake
b 過失 かしつ error, fault, mistake; negligence
c 捕失 ほしつ catcher's error

誤 ▷mistake
ゴ あやま(る) Ⓚ1403

ⓐ **mistake, err, make a mistake**
ⓑ [also prefix] **mistaken, mis-, incorrect, wrong**
ⓒ **mistake, error**

a 誤解 ごかい misunderstanding, misconception
b 誤字 ごじ wrong character, misprint
誤報 ごほう misinformation, incorrect report
誤算 ごさん miscalculation; misjudgment
誤写 ごしゃ error in copying
誤投下 ごとうか accidental bombing
誤謬 ごびゅう mistake, error, fallacy
誤差 ごさ error, aberration
c 誤魔化す ごまかす deceive, cheat; evade; pretend
錯誤 さくご mistake, error
正誤 せいご correction of errors

謬 ▷mistake
ビュウ あやま(る)

mistake, make a mistake, err

謬説 びゅうせつ fallacy, mistaken opinion
謬見 びゅうけん wrong view, mistaken notion
謬伝 びゅうでん false report [rumor]
誤謬 ごびゅう mistake, error, fallacy

錯 ▷mistaken
サク   Ⓚ1555

mistaken, erroneous, wrong
錯誤 さくご mistake, error
錯覚 さっかく false perception, mistaken idea, (optical) illusion
錯乱 さくらん distraction, derangement, confusion

違 ▷mis-
イ ちが(う) ちが(い) -ちが(える)   Ⓚ2716

[verbal suffix] **mis-, make a mistake in performing an action**
言い違える いいちがえる mistake, make a slip
見違える みちがえる mistake, fail to recognize
薬を飲み違える くすりをのみちがえる take the wrong medicine

mistaking →MISTAKES AND MISTAKING

mix
混 淆 交 雑 錯

混 ▷mix
コン ま(じる) -ま(じり) ま(ざる) ま(ぜる) こ(む)   Ⓚ0475

(combine or cause to combine into an indistinguishable mass) **mix, blend, mingle**
混血 こんけつ mixed-blood, racial mixture
混合 こんごう mixing, mixture
混声合唱 こんせいがっしょう mixed chorus
混紡 こんぼう mixed spinning
混浴 こんよく mixed bathing

淆 ▷intermingle
コウ

[now usu. 交] [original meaning] **intermingle, mix, blend**
混淆する こんこうする mix up, jumble together

交 ▷intermingle
コウ まじ(わる) まじ(える) ま(じる) ま(ざる) ま(ぜる) -か(う) か(わす) Ⓚ1738

[formerly also 淆] **intermingle, mix, blend**
交織 こうしょく mixed weave
交錯 こうさく mixture, blending, complication
混交する こんこうする mix up, jumble together

雑 ▷mixed
ザツ ゾウ   Ⓚ1267

[original meaning] **mixed, blended**
雑種 ざっしゅ mixed breed, hybrid

雑居地 ざっきょち mixed residential quarter

錯 ▷mixed up
サク   Ⓚ1555

mixed up, intricate, confused, disordered, complicated
錯雑 さくざつ complication, intricacy
錯綜 さくそう complication, intricacy
交錯した こうさくした mingled, entangled, complicated, intricate

model
範 典 模 程 式 準 格

範 ▷model
ハン   Ⓚ2364

(something to be followed) **model, example, pattern, standard**
模範 もはん model, pattern, example
軌範 きはん standard, norm
師範 しはん teacher, master, coach
典範 てんぱん model, standard; law, code

典 ▷canon
テン   Ⓚ2283

(standard of authority or evaluation) **canon, model, standard, authority**
典範 てんぱん model, standard; law, code
典型 てんけい type, pattern, model, exemplar
典型的な てんけいてきな typical, representative
典拠 てんきょ authority

模 ▷pattern
モ ボ   Ⓚ0963

(something worthy of imitation) **pattern, model, norm, exemplar**
模範 もはん model, pattern, example
模型 もけい model, pattern, mold
模式標本 もしきひょうほん type specimen

程 ▷established form
テイ ほど   Ⓚ1100

established form or mode of behavior: **rule, regulation, standard procedure, pattern**
規程 きてい official regulations, inner rules
方程式 ほうていしき equation

式 ▷form
シキ   Ⓚ2623

form, prescribed regulation, model, law, standard
形式 けいしき form, model, formality

正式に せいしきに formally, regularly
略式の りゃくしきの informal, summary

準 ▷standard
ジュン   Ⓚ2486

standard, norm, criterion
準則 じゅんそく regulations, standard
水準 すいじゅん level, standard; water level
基準 きじゅん standard, criterion, basis
標準 ひょうじゅん standard, norm, criterion
平準 へいじゅん level; equality

格 ▷norm
カク コウ   Ⓚ0835

norm, standard, model, pattern, rule, regulation
格外の かくがいの nonstandard, extraordinary, special
格別な かくべつな particular, exceptional
格式 かくしき established form, formalities
規格 きかく standard, norm
本格 ほんかく fundamental rules, propriety
本格的な ほんかくてきな full-scale, full-fledged; standard
語格 ごかく rules of grammar, usage

modifier suffixes
然 乎 如 爾 的

然 ▷modifier forming suffix
ゼン ネン   Ⓚ2423

ⓐ suffix for forming modifiers (noun adjectives and adverbs); suffix attached to a one-character base to express a state of being or quality
ⓑ suffix after nouns to express likeness: **-like, smack of**

a 突然 とつぜん abruptly, suddenly, unexpectedly
公然の こうぜんの open, public
平然と へいぜんと calmly, quietly, with composure
純然たる じゅんぜんたる pure, sheer; absolute
憤然として ふんぜんとして indignantly, wrathfully, in a rage
全然 ぜんぜん wholly, totally, completely; (not) at all
断然 だんぜん resolutely, decisively
茫然(=呆然)とする ぼうぜんとする be struck dumb (with surprise), be stupefied
b 学者然としている がくしゃぜんとしている be quite like a scholar

乎 ▷modifier forming suffix
コ ヲ か   Ⓚ2939

[now also 固] **modifier forming suffix**
断乎たる だんこたる firm, conclusive, determined
確乎たる かっこたる firm, sure, resolute

醇乎たる じゅんこたる sheer, pure

如 ▷modifier suffix
ジョ ニョ ごと(し)   Ⓚ0183

suffix added to modifiers (noun adjectives or adverbs) to express a state
突如 とつじょ suddenly, unexpectedly
欠如 けつじょ lack, shortage
躍如たる やくじょたる vivid, graphic, lifelike

爾 ▷adjective suffix
ジ ニ なんじ   Ⓚ3001

suffix after adjectives
徒爾 とじ uselessness
莞爾として かんじとして with a smile

的 ▷adjectival suffix
テキ まと   Ⓚ1040

suffix for forming adjectives from nouns or word elements—used to express resemblance, relation or the like (similar to English *-tic* or *-al*)
劇的な げきてきな dramatic
歴史的 れきしてき historical
合理的な ごうりてきな rational, logical, reasonable
法的 ほうてき legal, legalistic
私的な してきな private, personal
規則的 きそくてき systematic, regular
知的 ちてき intellectual, mental
国際的な こくさいてきな international

moisten
潤 浸 漬

潤 ▷moisten
ジュン うるお(う) うるお(す)
うる(む)   Ⓚ0676

moisten, be moistened, ooze, be wet
潤滑油 じゅんかつゆ lubricant, lubricating oil
潤筆料 じゅんぴつりょう fee for writing or painting
肺浸潤 はいしんじゅん infiltration of the lungs

浸 ▷soak
シン ひた(す) ひた(る)   Ⓚ040

ⓐ [original meaning] **soak, immerse**
ⓑ [formerly also 滲] **permeate, infiltrate, penetrate; ooze, seep**
a 浸水 しんすい inundation, submergence
b 浸透 しんとう permeation, penetration
浸潤 しんじゅん permeation, infiltration
浸出 しんしゅつ percolation, exudation, effusion

漬 ▷immerse
つ(ける) つ(かる) -づ(け) ⓚ0636

immerse, steep, soak, dip

手を水に漬ける てをみずにつける immerse [dip] one's hand in water
衣服を良く漬けて置け いふくをよくつけておけ Give the clothes a thorough soak

monetary gifts
謝　礼

謝 ▷monetary gift of thanks
シャ あやま(る) ⓚ1465

monetary gift of thanks, remuneration, reward, fee

謝礼 しゃれい remuneration, reward; thanks
月謝 げっしゃ monthly fee
薄謝 はくしゃ small remuneration, small token of gratitude

礼 ▷monetary gift
レイ ライ ⓚ0724

monetary gift, remuneration, reward

謝礼 しゃれい remuneration, reward; thanks
返礼 へんれい return present; return call

money
金　銭　貨　幣　銀
財　資　玉　札

金 ▷money
キン コン かね かな- -がね ⓚ1771

money, cash, coin

金額 きんがく amount of money, sum
金融 きんゆう circulation of money, money market, finance
金利 きんり interest (on money); rate of interest
現金 げんきん cash
預金 よきん deposit, bank account
資金 しきん funds, capital
料金 りょうきん charge, rate, fee, fare
退職金 たいしょくきん retirement allowance [pay]

銭 ▷money
セン ぜに ⓚ1537

money, cash

金銭 きんせん money, cash
釣り銭 つりせん change

無銭の むせんの penniless, moneyless
守銭奴 しゅせんど miser, slave of money
賽銭 さいせん money offering

貨 ▷money (legal tender), coin
カ ⓚ2175

ⓐ [original meaning] (legal tender) **money, currency**
ⓑ coin

a 貨幣 かへい money, currency, coinage
外貨 がいか foreign currency [money]; foreign [imported] goods
通貨 つうか currency, current money
米貨 べいか American currency, U.S. dollar
b 硬貨 こうか coin, metallic currency
白銅貨 はくどうか nickel coin
鋳貨 ちゅうか coinage, mintage

幣 ▷currency
ヘイ ⓚ2507

currency, money, coins, legal tender

幣制 へいせい currency [monetary] system
貨幣 かへい money, currency, coinage
造幣 ぞうへい coinage, mintage
紙幣 しへい paper currency, bank note, bill

銀 ▷silver
ギン ⓚ1534

(medium of exchange) **silver, silver coin, money, wages**

銀行 ぎんこう bank
銀座 ぎんざ the Ginza; mint (during Edo period)
銀本位制 ぎんほんいせい silver standard
賃銀(=賃金) ちんぎん wages, pay
労銀 ろうぎん wages (for labor)

財 ▷finance
ザイ サイ ⓚ1326

finance, funds, revenue

財界 ざいかい business world, economic circles
財源 ざいげん revenue source, financial resources
財政 ざいせい public finance, financial affairs
財団法人 ざいだんほうじん juridical foundation, juridical person
財務 ざいむ financial affairs

資 ▷resources
シ ⓚ2351

[original meaning] **monetary resources, funds, capital, money**

資金 しきん funds, capital
資本 しほん funds, capital
資本主義 しほんしゅぎ capitalism
資本家 しほんか capitalist
資産 しさん property, assets, fortune

投資 とうし investment
融資 ゆうし financing, advance of funds, loan
増資 ぞうし increase of capital, capital increase
出資 しゅっし investment, financing
外資 がいし foreign capital
学資 がくし school expenses, education fund

玉 ▷coin suffix
ギョク たま -だま Ⓚ2919

coin suffix
十円玉 じゅうえんだま 10-yen coin
五セント玉 ごせんとだま nickel

札 ▷bill
サツ ふだ Ⓚ0723

[also suffix] **bill, paper money, bank note**
札入れ さついれ billfold, wallet
札束 さつたば bundle of (bank) notes, wad of bills
贋札 がんさつ(=にせさつ) counterfeit paper money, forged note
千円札 せんえんさつ 1000-yen bill

monkey
猿　　申

猿 ▷monkey
エン さる Ⓚ0612

[original meaning] **monkey, ape**
猿人 えんじん ape-man
類人猿 るいじんえん anthropoid, troglodyte
犬猿 けんえん dog and monkey
犬猿の仲である けんえんのなかである lead a cat and dog life; be at enmity

申 ▷the Monkey
シン もう(す) もう(し)- Ⓚ2942

ninth sign of the Oriental zodiac: **the Monkey**—(time) 3-5 p.m., (direction) WSW, (season) July (of the lunar calendar)
庚申 こうしん 57th of the sexagenary cycle

months →WEEKS AND MONTHS

moon
月　　陰

月 ▷moon
ゲツ ガツ つき Ⓚ2556

[original meaning] **moon**
月光 げっこう moonlight, moonshine

月面 げつめん lunar surface
月齢 げつれい moon's age
月食(=月蝕) げっしょく lunar eclipse
満月 まんげつ full moon

陰 ▷moon
イン かげ かげ(る) Ⓚ0494

moon
陰暦 いんれき lunar calendar
太陰 たいいん moon

moral goodness
徳　道　善　義

徳 ▷virtue
トク Ⓚ0623

ⓐ (moral excellence) **virtue, morality**
ⓑ (act of moral excellence) **virtue, virtuous deed**
a 徳行 とっこう virtuous deeds, goodness
　徳義 とくぎ morality, sincerity
　道徳 どうとく morality, morals
　悪徳 あくとく vice, corruption, immorality
　公徳 こうとく public morality
ab 美徳 びとく virtue, good deed

道 ▷the way of moral conduct
ドウ トウ みち Ⓚ2701

the way of moral conduct, moral principles, morality, right way of life (esp. according to Confucian precepts), truth
道徳 どうとく morality, morals
道理 どうり reason, right, justice, truth
道義 どうぎ morality, moral principles
正道 せいどう path of righteousness, right track
人道的な じんどうてきな humane, humanitarian

善 ▷good
ゼン よ(い) Ⓚ2030

good, goodness, virtue, moral excellence
善悪 ぜんあく good and evil
偽善 ぎぜん hypocrisy

義 ▷righteousness
ギ Ⓚ2052

righteousness, justice, right, morality
正義 せいぎ justice, righteousness
道義 どうぎ morality, moral principles
仁義 じんぎ humanity and justice; moral code; formal greeting among gamblers
情義 じょうぎ justice and humanity

moral principles
倫　道

倫 ▷**morals**
リン　　　　　　　　　　　　　Ⓚ0103

morals, ethics, moral rules, code of conduct
　倫理 りんり ethics, morals, code of conduct
　倫理学 りんりがく ethics, moral philosophy
　不倫な ふりんな immoral, illicit
　人倫 じんりん humanity, morality; human relations
　破倫 はりん immorality; incest

道 ▷**the way of moral conduct**
ドウ　トウ　みち　　　　　　　　Ⓚ2701

the way of moral conduct, moral principles, morality, right way of life (esp. according to Confucian precepts), truth
　道徳 どうとく morality, morals
　道理 どうり reason, right, justice, truth
　道義 どうぎ morality, moral principles
　正道 せいどう path of righteousness, right track
　人道的な じんどうてきな humane, humanitarian

morning and dawn
朝　暁　旦　曙　晨

朝 ▷**morning**
チョウ　あさ　　　　　　　　　Ⓚ1513

morning, forenoon, morn
　朝刊 ちょうかん morning edition [paper]
　朝食 ちょうしょく breakfast
　早朝 そうちょう early morning
　一朝一夕に いっちょういっせきに in one day, in a short time

暁 ▷**dawn**
ギョウ　あかつき　　　　　　　Ⓚ0892

[original meaning] **dawn, daybreak**
　暁天 ぎょうてん dawn
　暁星 ぎょうせい morning star, Venus
　今暁 こんぎょう at daybreak today

旦 ▷**daybreak**
タン　ダン　　　　　　　　　　Ⓚ2119

[original meaning] **daybreak, dawn, morn, morning**
　旦暮 たんぼ morn and eve, dawn and dusk
　旦夕 たんせき morning and evening, day and night

一旦 いったん once; for a while; [archaic] one morning, one day

曙 ▷**dawn**
ショ ジョ　あけぼの　　　　　　Ⓚ1002

dawn, daybreak
　曙光 しょこう first streak of daylight, dawn

晨 ▷**early morning**
シン　ジン　　　　　　　　　　Ⓚ2173

[rare] **early morning, dawn, daybreak**
　清晨 せいしん a refreshing morning

most
最　至　極

最 ▷**most**
サイ　もっと(も)　　　　　　　Ⓚ2181

[also prefix] **most, the most, -est, -most, ultra-, extreme**—used to indicate the superlative degree
　最高の さいこうの maximum, supreme, highest
　最少 さいしょう smallest, minimum, least
　最大の さいだいの biggest, largest, greatest
　最新の さいしんの newest, latest
　最中 さいちゅう in the middle [midst] of, during
　最終 さいしゅう last, the end; final
　最低の さいていの lowest
　最南の さいなんの southernmost
　最高級 さいこうきゅう highest grade, top class
　最強の さいきょうの strongest
　最上の さいじょうの best, the finest; highest
　最先端(=最尖端) さいせんたん leading edge; forefront
　最大限の さいだいげんの maximum, greatest

至 ▷**utmost**
シ　いた(る)　　　　　　　　　Ⓚ1869

utmost, most, extreme
　至急の しきゅうの urgent, pressing
　至難の しなんの most difficult
　至上 しじょう supremacy
　至極 しごく very, most, exceedingly, extremely
　至孝 しこう supreme filial piety

極 ▷**extreme**
キョク ゴク　きわ(める)　きわ(まる)
きわ(まり)　きわ(み)　　　　Ⓚ0900

[also suffix] (utmost or exceedingly great) **extreme, utmost, maximum, ultimate, highest, ultra-, hyper-**
　極端な きょくたんな extreme; radical
　極限 きょくげん utmost limits, limit

極楽 ごくらく *Buddhism* paradise

most recent
昨　去　先

昨 ▷**last**
　サク　　　　　　　　　　　　　Ⓚ0795

(most recent) **last (year, etc.)**
　昨年 さくねん last year
　昨春 さくしゅん last spring
　一昨昨日 いっさくさくじつ three days ago

去 ▷**last**
　キョ コ さ(る)　　　　　　　Ⓚ1850

last (year, etc.)
　去年 きょねん last year
　去月 きょげつ last month

先 ▷**last**
　セン さき ま(ず)　　　　　　Ⓚ2123

last (week, etc.)
　先月 せんげつ last month
　先週 せんしゅう last week
　先先週 せんせんしゅう week before last

motion
動　惰

動 ▷**motion**
　ドウ うご(く) うご(かす)　　Ⓚ1583

[also suffix] *phys* **motion, vibration, action**
　動静 どうせい movements, state of affairs, conditions
　波動 はどう wave motion, undulation
　反動 はんどう backlash, recoil, reaction
　上下動 じょうげどう vertical motion [shock]

惰 ▷**inertia**
　ダ　　　　　　　　　　　　　Ⓚ0531

inertia; force of habit
　惰性 だせい inertia, momentum; force of habit
　惰力 だりょく inertia, momentum; force of habit

motion picture
映　　画

映 ▷**motion picture**
　エイ うつ(る) うつ(す) は(える)
　-ば(え)　　　　　　　　　　Ⓚ079

abbrev. of 映画 えいが: **motion picture, movie, film**
　映倫 えいりん Motion Picture Code of Ethics Committee
　映配 えいはい film distributing company

画 ▷**film**
　ガ カク　　　　　　　　　　Ⓚ258

abbrev. of 映画 えいが: **film, movie, motion picture**
　洋画 ようが foreign film; Western painting
　邦画 ほうが Japanese film [movie]; Japanese painting

mountain parts
頂　峰　嶺　峠　崖　壁

頂 ▷**summit**
　チョウ いただ(く) いただき　Ⓚ012

(mountain top) **summit, peak**
　頂上 ちょうじょう summit, peak, top; climax
　登頂する とうちょうする climb to the summit

峰 ▷**peak**
　ホウ みね　　　　　　　　　Ⓚ037

[original meaning] (pointed summit of a mountain) **peak, summit, mountaintop**
　高峰 こうほう lofty peak, high mountain
　最高峰 さいこうほう highest peak; highest authority

嶺 ▷**ridge**
　レイ リョウ みね ね　　　　Ⓚ210

ridge, ridge of a mountain, summit, peak
　分水嶺 ぶんすいれい ridge, watershed
　海嶺 かいれい (submarine) ridge
　雪嶺 せつれい snow-capped peak
　峻嶺 しゅんれい steep peak, high rugged mountain

峠 ▷**mountain pass**
　とうげ　　　　　　　　　　Ⓚ031

ⓐ **mountain pass, ridge**
ⓑ **suffix after names of mountain passes**

a 峠を越える とうげをこえる cross a pass, pass over the peak

峠道 とうげみち road over a mountain pass

b 碓氷峠 うすいとうげ Usui Pass

崖 ▷cliff
ガイ がけ Ⓚ1988

cliff, bluff, precipice

懸崖 けんがい overhanging cliff

断崖絶壁 だんがいぜっぺき precipitous cliff, sheer precipice

壁 ▷wall-like structure
ヘキ かべ Ⓚ2515

any wall-like structure such as a cliff or precipice

絶壁 ぜっぺき precipice, cliff

岸壁 がんぺき quay (wall), wharf

胃壁 いへき walls of the stomach

北壁 ほくへき northern cliff

氷壁 ひょうへき ice ridge

城壁 じょうへき castle wall, rampart

火口壁 かこうへき crater wall

mountains
峰 岳 山

峰 ▷peak
ホウ みね Ⓚ0372

[also suffix] (mountain with pointed summit) **peak, high mountain**

峰頭 ほうとう [rare] summit of a peak

主峰 しゅほう main peak

連峰 れんぽう mountain range, series of mountain peaks

未踏峰 みとうほう unclimbed mountain

岳 ▷high mountain
ガク たけ Ⓚ2213

high mountain, mountain, peak

岳友会 がくゆうかい mountaineering club

山岳 さんがく mountains

山 ▷mountain
サン やま Ⓚ2544

ⓐ [original meaning] **mountain**
ⓑ **suffix after names of mountains**

a 山岳 さんがく mountains

山脈 さんみゃく mountain range

登山 とざん mountain climbing, mountaineering

火山 かざん volcano

b 富士山 ふじさん Mt. Fuji

須弥山 しゅみせん Mt. Sumeru (in Buddhism, said to be the highest mountain rising in the center of the world)

mourn and mourning
弔 悼 喪 忌

弔 ▷condole
チョウ とむら(う) Ⓚ2888

condole, offer one's condolences to a bereaved person, console, mourn

弔辞 ちょうじ message of condolence

弔電 ちょうでん telegram of condolence

弔問 ちょうもん condolence call

弔慰 ちょうい condolence, sympathy

悼 ▷mourn
トウ いた(む) Ⓚ0443

mourn, grieve, lament

悼辞 とうじ message of condolence

哀悼する あいとうする condole, mourn, grieve

追悼 ついとう mourning

喪 ▷mourning
ソウ も Ⓚ2459

[original meaning, now rare] **mourning**

喪家 そうか family in mourning

大喪 たいそう Imperial mourning

忌 ▷mourning
キ い(む) い(み) い(まわしい) Ⓚ1889

mourning, mourning period

忌中 きちゅう in mourning

忌引き きびき absence from work [school] due to mourning

忌服 きふく mourning

mourning →MOURN AND MOURNING

mouth parts
唇 歯 舌 牙

唇 ▷lip
シン くちびる Ⓚ2385

[original meaning] **lip, lips, labium, labia**

唇音 しんおん labial sound

陰唇 いんしん labium

口唇 こうしん lips, labia

歯 ▷tooth
シ は   Ⓚ2185

[original meaning] **tooth**
歯科 しか dentistry
歯石 しせき tartar (on teeth), dental calculus
抜歯 ばっし tooth extraction
永久歯 えいきゅうし permanent tooth
義歯 ぎし false tooth

舌 ▷tongue
ゼツ した   Ⓚ1871

[original meaning] **tongue**
舌端 ぜったん tip of the tongue; speech, way of talking
舌頭 ぜっとう tip of the tongue; speech, way of talking
舌音 ぜつおん lingual sound
舌癌 ぜつがん cancer of the tongue

牙 ▷fang
ガ ゲ きば   Ⓚ2891

fang, tusk
歯牙 しが teeth
毒牙 どくが poison fang
爪牙 そうが claws and tusks, devious design; right-hand man
象牙 ぞうげ ivory

move
動 運 滑 辷 移 転 遷 繰

動 ▷move
ドウ うご(く) うご(かす)   Ⓚ1583

[original meaning] **move, be in action, vibrate, pulsate**
動物 どうぶつ animal
動揺する どうようする shake, tremble; be disturbed, waver
運動 うんどう motion, movement; exercise; campaign
自動 じどう automatic operation; automatic
移動する いどうする move, shift, transfer
不動産 ふどうさん immovable property, real estate
機動性 きどうせい mobility, maneuverability

運 ▷move
ウン はこ(ぶ)   Ⓚ2707

[original meaning] **move, revolve**
運動 うんどう motion, movement; exercise; campaign

運動会 うんどうかい sports meeting, meet
運航 うんこう navigation; (airline or shipping) service
運行する うんこうする revolve, orbit; operate
運休 うんきゅう suspension of (bus) service

滑 ▷slide
カツ コツ すべ(る) なめ(らか)   Ⓚ060.

slide, glide, slip
滑走する かっそうする glide, volplane; slide
滑空機 かっくうき glider, sailplane
滑車 かっしゃ pulley, block, tackle

辷 ▷slip
すべ(る)

slip
辷らす すべらす let slip, slide, glide
地辷り じすべり landslide
口が辷る くちがすべる make a slip of the tongue

移 ▷shift
イ うつ(る) うつ(す)   Ⓚ108

ⓐ (change in position, time or state) **shift, move, change**
ⓑ **cause to shift, transfer, remove, move**
ⓐ 移行する いこうする shift [switch] over
移動する いどうする move, shift, transfer
移転 いてん transfer, removal; change of address
移植 いしょく transplanting
推移 すいい transition, change
ⓑ 移住 いじゅう migration, immigration; move
移籍 いせき transfer of one's name in the register
移民 いみん immigration, emigration; immigrant, emigrant

転 ▷remove
テン ころ(がる) ころ(げる) ころ(がす) ころ(ぶ)   Ⓚ134

remove, move, change, transfer
転居する てんきょする move, change one's residence
転職 てんしょく change of occupation
転転とする てんてんとする wander about; change hands; roll
移転する いてんする transfer, remove; move

遷 ▷transfer
セン   Ⓚ273

transfer, relocate, move
遷座 せんざ transfer of an object of worship
遷宮 せんぐう transfer of a shrine
遷都 せんと transfer of the capital

繰 ▷**shift onward**
くる Ⓚ1300

ⓐ **shift onward to the next stage, move up, carry over**
ⓑ **shift (a plan) to the next phase**

a 繰り上げる くりあげる advance, move up
　繰り込み理論 くりこみりろん renormalization theory
b 繰り入れ金 くりいれきん transfer balance
　繰り替える くりかえる exchange; appropriate (money to some other purpose)
　繰り延べる くりのべる postpone, put off
　繰り合わせる くりあわせる make time, arrange matters

move forward
進　突　這

進 ▷**advance**
シン すす(む) すす(める) Ⓚ2689

[original meaning] (move forward in position) **advance, go forward, proceed**

進行する しんこうする advance, make progress, go forward
進路 しんろ course, route
進出 しんしゅつ advance, march; debouchment
進入する しんにゅうする penetrate, go into, enter
前進する ぜんしんする advance, go ahead
行進する こうしんする march, parade
突進する とっしんする dash [rush] forward, push ahead
二進する にしんする advance to second (base)

突 ▷**dash**
トツ つ(く) Ⓚ1918

dash forward, thrust, charge

突進する とっしんする dash [rush] forward, push ahead
突貫する とっかんする charge at, make a dash at (the enemy's position)
突入する とつにゅうする dash into, thrust into, rush into
突撃する とつげきする charge at, make a dash at (the enemy's position)
突破する とっぱする break [smash] through; surmount; exceed

這 ▷**crawl**
シャ は(う) Ⓚ2775

crawl, creep

這い上がる はいあがる crawl up, creep up, climb up

這い這い はいはい crawling (of babies)
這い蹲る はいつくばる grovel, go down on one's hands and knees
横這い よこばい crawling sideways; remain at the same level
四つん這い よつんばい on all fours, on one's hands and feet

move through water
泳　游　渉　遡　漕

泳 ▷**swim**
エイ およ(ぐ) Ⓚ0289

[original meaning] **swim**

泳法 えいほう swimming style
水泳 すいえい swimming

游 ▷**swim**
ユウ およ(ぐ)

[now usu. 遊] [original meaning] **swim**

游泳 ゆうえい swimming
回游 かいゆう migration (of fish)
浮游する ふゆうする waft, float

渉 ▷**wade**
ショウ Ⓚ0482

[original meaning] **wade (across water), ford**

渉禽類 しょうきんるい wading birds
徒渉 としょう wading, fording

遡 ▷**go upstream**
ソ さかのぼ(る) Ⓚ2785

ⓐ [original meaning] **go upstream**
ⓑ **go back (to the past); retroact**

a 遡上 そじょう going upstream
　遡求 そきゅう (request for repayment) recourse
　遡河魚 そかぎょ anadromous fish
b 遡及する そきゅうする retroact

漕 ▷**row**
ソウ こ(ぐ) Ⓚ0638

ⓐ **row, scull, paddle**
ⓑ **pedal**

a 漕艇 そうてい rowing
　競漕 きょうそう regatta, boat race

multiply
乗　掛

乗 ▷**multiply**
ジョウ の(る) −の(り) の(せる)　　Ⓚ2992

multiply
乗法 じょうほう multiplication
相乗作用 そうじょうさよう synergism

掛 ▷**multiply**
か(ける) か(け) −が(け) か(かる)
−が(かる) か(かり) −が(かり)　　Ⓚ0449

multiply
掛け算 かけざん multiplication
八掛ける二 はちかけるに 2 times 8

musical elements
韻　律　拍　調　呂

韻 ▷**rhyme**
イン　　Ⓚ1609

[original meaning] **rhyme, rhyming**
韻律 いんりつ rhythm, meter, measure
押韻 おういん rhyme, rhyming
頭韻 とういん alliteration, head rhyme
脚韻 きゃくいん rhyme, end rhyme

律 ▷**rhythm**
リツ リチ　　Ⓚ0322

rhythm, tone, pitch
律動 りつどう rhythm, rhythmic movement
一律 いちりつ uniformity, equality
旋律 せんりつ melody
調律 ちょうりつ tuning
韻律 いんりつ rhythm, meter, measure

拍 ▷**beat**
ハク ヒョウ　　Ⓚ0269

ⓐ **beat, rhythm, time**
ⓑ **counter for beats or number of syllables in Japanese words**
ₐ 拍子 ひょうし time, beat, rhythm; chance, the moment
　手拍子 てびょうし beating time with the hand; careless move
　三拍子 さんびょうし simple triple time
ᵦ 三拍 さんぱく three beats, three syllables

調 ▷**tone**
チョウ しら(べる) しら(べ) ととの(う)
ととの(える)　　Ⓚ1417

ⓐ (characteristic quality, as of music, poetry or color) **tone, tune, key, note, pitch, rhythm, meter**
ⓑ (characteristic quality of speech) **tone, strain, note, accent**
ₐ 調子 ちょうし tone, tune; key, note; condition, state (of health); manner, way
　音調 おんちょう tune, tone, rhythm, melody, harmony
　短調 たんちょう minor key
　正調 せいちょう orthodox tune
　七五調で しちごちょうで in seven-and-five syllable meter
　色調 しきちょう tone (of color)
　強調 きょうちょう emphasis, stress
ᵦ 口調 くちょう tone, expression
　語調 ごちょう tone (of voice), note, accent
　声調 せいちょう tone of voice, style; tone (in Chinese phonetics)

呂 ▷**ancient musical note**
ロ　　Ⓚ1872

ancient musical note in traditional Chinese and Japanese music
呂律 ろれつ articulation
律呂 りつりょ Chinese system of musical sounds, standard tones

musical instrument
管　弦

管 ▷**wind instrument**
カン くだ　　Ⓚ2357

wind instrument, pipe
管弦 かんげん wind and string instruments
管楽器 かんがっき wind instruments
木管 もっかん woodwind (instrument); wood pipe

弦 ▷**string instrument**
ゲン つる　　Ⓚ0257

stringed instrument, the strings
弦楽 げんがく string music
弦歌 げんか singing and (string) music
管弦 かんげん wind and string instruments

musical instruments
琴箏鼓笛琵琶笙

琴 ▷koto
キン こと   ⓚ2422

[original meaning] **KOTO, (Japanese) zither**
　琴曲 きんきょく koto music
　弾琴 だんきん playing on the koto

箏 ▷koto
ソウ こと

[original meaning] **KOTO, (Japanese) zither**
　箏曲 そうきょく koto music

鼓 ▷drum
コ つづみ   ⓚ1589

drum
　鼓笛隊 こてきたい drum and fife band
　鼓手 こしゅ drummer
　鼓膜 こまく eardrum
　太鼓 たいこ (big) drum; professional jester; flatterer; big obi bow

笛 ▷flute
テキ ふえ   ⓚ2323

[original meaning] **flute, pipe, recorder**
　鼓笛隊 こてきたい drum and fife band
　牧笛 ぼくてき shepherd's pipe
　銀笛 ぎんてき flageolet
　魔笛 まてき magic flute; The Magic Flute (by Mozart)

琵 ▷lute
ビ   ⓚ2420

lute, Japanese lute
　琵琶 びわ biwa, Japanese lute
　琵琶湖 びわこ Lake Biwa
　琵琶行 びわこう Biwa Song

琶 ▷lute
ハ ワ   ⓚ2421

lute, Japanese lute
　琵琶 びわ biwa, Japanese lute
　琵琶湖 びわこ Lake Biwa
　琵琶行 びわこう Biwa Song

笙 ▷sho
ショウ ソウ セイ   ⓚ2322

sho: free-reed mouth organ used in Japanese court music

笙歌 しょうか (=せいか) singing and playing *sho*

music and songs
楽音節調曲歌謡唄

楽 ▷music
ガク ラク たの(しい) たの(しむ)   ⓚ2460

ⓐ [also suffix] **music, musical composition**
ⓑ **suffix after names of Japanese court music compositions**
　a 楽譜 がくふ (sheet of) music, musical score
　　楽器 がっき musical instrument
　　音楽 おんがく music
　　邦楽 ほうがく Japanese music
　b 越天楽 えてんらく Etenraku (name of a Japanese court music composition)

音 ▷sound of music
オン イン おと ね   ⓚ1783

ⓐ **sound of music, music, note, tune, melody**
ⓑ abbrev. of 音楽 おんがく: **music**
　a 音楽 おんがく music
　　音痴 おんち tone deafness
　　音符 おんぷ note; phonetic element of kanji
　　低音 ていおん low-pitched sound, bass
　　不協和音 ふきょうわおん discord, dissonance
　b 音大 おんだい music college
　　労音 ろうおん Workers' Music Council

節 ▷tune
セツ セチ ふし -ぶし   ⓚ2349

tune, air, melody
　節奏 せっそう rhythm
　曲節 きょくせつ tune, air

調 ▷melody
チョウ しら(べる) しら(べ) ととの(う) ととの(える)   ⓚ1417

melody, tune
　妙なる調べ たえなるしらべ sweet tune, enchanting melody
　六段の調べ ろくだんのしらべ Rokudan (name of a koto composition)

曲 ▷musical composition
キョク ま(がる) ま(げる)   ⓚ2956

[also suffix] **musical composition, (piece of) music, melody, tune, song**
　曲調 きょくちょう melody, tune
　曲節 きょくせつ tune, air

曲名 きょくめい title of a musical composition [song]
曲目 きょくもく number; program, selection (for a concert)
楽曲 がっきょく musical piece, composition, tune
作曲 さっきょく composition
編曲 へんきょく arrangement (of a melody)
名曲 めいきょく excellent [exquisite] piece of music, famous tune
新曲 しんきょく new musical composition, new tune [song]
舞曲 ぶきょく dance music, music and dancing
戯曲 ぎきょく drama, play
歌謡曲 かようきょく popular song
交響曲 こうきょうきょく symphony

歌 ▷song
カ うた うた(う)   Ⓚ1621

[also suffix] **song**

歌謡 かよう song, ballad
歌曲 かきょく song (in the classical style)
歌詞 かし words [lyrics] of a song
国歌 こっか national anthem
校歌 こうか school song, alma mater song
流行歌 りゅうこうか popular song

謡 ▷popular song
ヨウ うたい うた(う)   Ⓚ1445

popular song, ballad, folk song

俗謡 ぞくよう popular song, ballad
民謡 みんよう folk song [ballad]
歌謡曲 かようきょく popular song
童謡 どうよう children's song, nursery rhyme
里謡 りよう ballad, folk song

唄 ▷ditty
バイ うた うた(う)   Ⓚ0358

[usu. 歌] [also suffix] **ditty, song, ballad**—used esp. in reference to traditional Japanese songs

小唄 こうた ditty, ballad
子守唄 こもりうた lullaby
鼻唄 はなうた humming

mutual
相 互

相 ▷mutual
ソウ ショウ あい-   Ⓚ0808

mutual, reciprocal; mutually

相互の そうごの mutual, reciprocal
相談 そうだん consultation

相当する そうとうする correspond to, be proportionate; be suitable for, become
相違 そうい difference, disparity
相対的な そうたいてきな relative
相応な そうおうな suitable, fit; becoming; adequat
相殺 そうさい offset, cancellation
相関 そうかん mutual relationship, correlation
相似 そうじ similarity, resemblance
相思相愛 そうしそうあい mutual love

互 ▷reciprocal
ゴ たが(い)   Ⓚ289

[original meaning] **reciprocal, mutual, each other**

互恵 ごけい reciprocity, mutual benefits
互助 ごじょ mutual aid, cooperation
互角 ごかく equality; good match
互選 ごせん co-optation, mutual election
相互の そうごの mutual, reciprocal
交互に こうごに mutually, reciprocally, alternately

mythical animals
竜 辰 麒 麟 鵬 鳳 凰

竜 ▷dragon
リュウ たつ   Ⓚ180
see also →DRAGON

dragon

竜神 りゅうじん dragon god, dragon king
竜宮 りゅうぐう Palace of the Dragon King
竜虎 りゅうこ(=りょうこ) dragon and tiger; hero

辰 ▷the Dragon
シン たつ   Ⓚ258

fifth sign of the Oriental zodiac: **the Dragon**—(time) 7-9 a.m., (direction) ESE, (season) March (of the lunar calendar)

戊辰 ぼしん fifth of the sexagenary cycle

麒 ▷male Chinese unicorn
キ   Ⓚ166

male Chinese unicorn

麒麟 きりん giraffe; male and female Chinese unicorns
麒麟草 きりんそう orange stonecrop, *Sedum kamtschaticum*
麒麟児 きりんじ child prodigy, genius
麒麟血(麒麟竭) きりんけつ dragon's blood

麟 ▷female Chinese unicorn
リン   Ⓚ166

[original meaning] **female Chinese unicorn**

麒麟 きりん giraffe; male and female Chinese unicorns

鵬 ▷mythical huge bird
ホウ ボウ おおとり   Ⓚ1021

【ホウ ボウ】
[original meaning] **mythical huge bird, phoenix**
大鵬 たいほう mythical huge bird; sage

【おおとり】
[also 大鳥 or 鳳] **huge bird such as a mythical Chinese phoenix**

鳳 ▷male phoenix
ホウ ブウ おおとり   Ⓚ2601

male phoenix, mythical Chinese phoenix
鳳凰 ほうおう male and female Chinese phoenixes
白鳳時代 はくほうじだい name of an archaic Japanese era

凰 ▷female phoenix
オウ   Ⓚ2595

female phoenix, mythical Chinese phoenix
鳳凰 ほうおう male and female Chinese phoenixes
鳳凰座 ほうおうざ the Phoenix (constellation)

naked
裸　　素

裸 ▷naked
ラ はだか   Ⓚ1120

ⓐ [original meaning] (without clothing) **naked, nude, bare**
ⓑ (without covering) **naked, uncovered, bare**
a 裸婦 らふ nude woman
  裸体 らたい naked [nude] body, nudity
  全裸の ぜんらの stark naked, nude
b 裸出 らしゅつ exposure
  裸眼 らがん naked eye
  赤裸裸 せきらら nakedness, frankness

素 ▷bare
ソ ス   Ⓚ2171

bare, naked
素肌 すはだ bare skin
素手 すで bare hands
素足 すあし bare [naked] feet

---

name[1]
名 銘 姓 氏 称 題 号

名 ▷name
メイ ミョウ な   Ⓚ1857

[also suffix] **name, first name**
名簿 めいぼ register [list] of names
名刺 めいし calling [business] card
名称 めいしょう appellation, name, title
名字(=苗字) みょうじ surname, family name
氏名 しめい (full) name
署名 しょめい signature, autograph
指名 しめい nomination, designation
匿名の とくめいの anonymous, incognito, pseudonymous
題名 だいめい title
本名 ほんみょう one's real name
戒名 かいみょう posthumous Buddhist name
商品名 しょうひんめい trade [brand] name

銘 ▷name (inscribed by maker)
メイ   Ⓚ1536

name (inscribed by maker on finished product), appellation, signature
銘刀 めいとう sword inscribed by the sword smith
銘板 めいばん nameplate (of machines)
銘柄 めいがら brand name, brand, name
銘打つ めいうつ engrave an inscription; call [designate] itself
無銘の むめいの anonymous

姓 ▷surname
セイ ショウ   Ⓚ0251

ⓐ **surname, family name**
ⓑ **surname conferred by emperor in ancient times**
a 姓名 せいめい full name
  同姓 どうせい same surname
  旧姓 きゅうせい one's former name, née
  改姓する かいせいする change one's family name
  百姓 ひゃくしょう farmer, peasant
b 氏姓制度 しせいせいど former naming system

氏 ▷family name
シ うじ   Ⓚ2552

family name, surname
氏名 しめい (full) name
氏姓制度 しせいせいど former naming system

称 ▷appellation
ショウ   Ⓚ1075

appellation, name, title
称号 しょうごう title, degree
名称 めいしょう appellation, name, title
通称 つうしょう popular [common] name
俗称 ぞくしょう popular [common] name
愛称 あいしょう nickname, pet name
総称 そうしょう generic name, general term

題 ▷title
ダイ   Ⓚ2848

title, caption, heading, headline
題目 だいもく title, heading; theme; prayer of the
    Nichiren sect
題名 だいめい title
表題 ひょうだい title, heading, caption
改題 かいだい change of title

号 ▷designation
ゴウ   Ⓚ1847

ⓐ **designation, title, name, pen name, pseudonym**
ⓑ **suffix after names of ships, trains, aircraft, horses or dogs**
ₐ 称号 しょうごう title, degree
   雅号 がごう pen name, pseudonym
   屋号 やごう name of a store; stage title
   年号 ねんごう name of era, reign title
ᵦ クイーンメリー号 くいーんめりーごう S.S. *Queen Mary*
   ひかり号 ひかりごう *Hikari* (name of a bullet train)

name²
呼 言 称

呼 ▷call
コ よ(ぶ)   Ⓚ0246

(attach a name to) **call, name**
呼称する こしょうする call, name
称呼 しょうこ appellation, designation

言 ▷call
ゲン ゴン い(う) こと   Ⓚ1698

call, name; express (in a foreign language)
典子と言う人 のりこというひと person called Noriko
これを音素と言う これをおんそという To this is
    given the term "phoneme"

称 ▷name
ショウ   Ⓚ107?

name, call, designate, entitle
呼称する こしょうする call, name
誇称する こしょうする boast, exaggerate
自称する じしょうする profess oneself (to be some-
    one), call [style] oneself

name suffixes
郎 麿 彦 子

郎 ▷male name suffix
ロウ   Ⓚ118?

suffix for forming male names, usu. indicating order of birth
一郎 いちろう Ichiro (name of eldest son)
次郎 じろう Jiro (name of second son)
太郎 たろう Taro

麿 ▷classical male name suffix
まろ   Ⓚ274?

classical suffix for forming male names
坂上田村麿 さかのうえのたむらまろ Sakanoue
    Tamuramaro

彦 ▷male name element
ゲン ひこ   Ⓚ2808

ⓐ **element for forming male names**
ⓑ **[archaic] handsome man, prince**

子 ▷female name element
シス -こ -(っ)こ   Ⓚ2872

element for forming female names
恵子 けいこ Keiko
典子 のりこ Noriko

narrow
狭 窄

狭 ▷narrow
キョウ せま(い) せば(める)
せば(まる)   Ⓚ0355

ⓐ **[original meaning] narrow, constricted**
ⓑ **(of limited scope) narrow, limited, restricted**
ⓒ **narrow, contract**
ₐ 狭小な きょうしょうな narrow, cramped, small-sized
   狭窄 きょうさく stricture, stenosis
   広狭 こうきょう width and narrowness, width

b 狭量な きょうりょうな narrow-minded
狭義 きょうぎ narrow meaning
偏狭な へんきょうな narrow-minded, intolerant;
  parochial
c 狭心症 きょうしんしょう angina pectoris

 ▷**narrow**
サク すぼ(む) すぼ(める)
すぼ(まる) Ⓚ1966

❶ **narrow, contract**
❷ [original meaning] **narrow, constricted**
ab 狭窄 きょうさく stricture, stenosis

national

国　　内

 ▷**national**
コク くに Ⓚ2659

national, government-operated
国債 こくさい national bonds; national debt [loan]
国立 こくりつ national (park, etc.)
国鉄 こくてつ Japanese National Railways (defunct)
国道 こくどう national highway
国費 こくひ national expenditure
国営 こくえい government-managed; state-
  operated
国税 こくぜい national tax
国有の こくゆうの state-owned, nationalized
国力 こくりょく national power; national resources

内 ▷**internal**
ナイ ダイ うち Ⓚ2914

(pertaining to the affairs of a country) **internal, domestic**
内政 ないせい domestic administration, internal
  affairs
内戦 ないせん civil war
内紛 ないふん internal trouble [strife]; storm in a
  teacup
内務 ないむ internal [domestic] affairs
内需 ないじゅ domestic demand

natural

地　野　粗　原

 ▷**natural**
チ ジ Ⓚ0181

natural, in its natural [original] form, inherent
地力 じりき one's own strength

地声 じごえ natural voice
地髪 じがみ natural hair
地味な じみな plain, sober, unpretentious
地道な じみちな steady, straight, fair
素地 そじ inclination, makings; grounding, foundation
生地(=素地) きじ one's true color [character];
  (plain) cloth, texture; unglazed pottery

野 ▷**wild**
ヤ の Ⓚ1350

(growing or occurring in the field) **wild, undomesticated, savage**
野犬 やけん stray dog
野鳥 やちょう wild fowl, wild bird
野性 やせい wild nature, uncouthness
野獣 やじゅう wild animal, wild game

粗 ▷**crude**
ソ あら(い) あら- Ⓚ1214

(in the natural state) **crude, raw, unrefined, unprocessed**
粗製 そせい crude manufacture
粗鉱 そこう unprocessed ore
粗鋼 そこう crude steel

原 ▷**in the original state**
ゲン はら Ⓚ2593

in the original state, raw, crude
原料 げんりょう raw material
原油 げんゆ crude oil

nature and character

性　気　質　品　柄　格

 ▷**nature**
セイ ショウ Ⓚ0266

❶ [original meaning] **one's nature, inherent nature,
innate quality, character, temperament, disposition**
性格 せいかく character, personality
性質 せいしつ nature, temperament, character;
  (characteristic) property, quality
性悪な しょうわるな ill-natured
性向 せいこう inclination, disposition
性急な せいきゅうな impatient, quick-tempered;
  hasty
個性 こせい individuality
天性 てんせい nature, one's innate disposition

根性 こんじょう nature, spirit, temper; will power; guts

習性 しゅうせい habit, (one's) way

❷ **essential nature (of things), intrinsic quality, natural property, characteristic**

性能 せいのう performance, capacity, efficiency

属性 ぞくせい attribute, property

人間性 にんげんせい human nature, humanity

慢性の まんせいの chronic

気 ▷temperament
キ ケ   Ⓚ2751

[also suffix] **temperament, temper, disposition, one's nature, character**

気質 きしつ temperament, disposition

気性 きしょう disposition, nature, temper

気難しい きむずかしい moody, hard to please

気紛れ きまぐれ whim, caprice

強気の つよきの strong, firm, bullish

短気な たんきな short-tempered, hot-tempered

負けん気 まけんき unyielding [competitive] spirit

移り気 うつりぎ caprice, fickleness, frivolity

質 ▷quality
シツ シチ チ   Ⓚ2445

ⓐ [also suffix] (natural attribute) **quality, nature, character, property, temperament, disposition**

ⓑ (degree of excellence) **quality, grade**

a 本質 ほんしつ essence, reality

性質 せいしつ nature, temperament, character; (characteristic) property, quality

体質 たいしつ physical constitution

素質 そしつ character, nature, makings, constitution

実質 じっしつ substance, essence

特質 とくしつ characteristic, property, quality

神経質 しんけいしつ nervous temperament

b 品質 ひんしつ quality

悪質な あくしつな bad, malicious; malignant

音質 おんしつ sound [tone] quality

品 ▷grade of excellence
ヒン しな   Ⓚ1937

grade of excellence, quality, character

品質 ひんしつ quality

品性 ひんせい character

品位 ひんい dignity, grace, nobility; grade, quality

品格 ひんかく dignity, grace

柄 ▷character
ヘイ がら え   Ⓚ0799

[in compounds] [also suffix] **character, nature, quality, fineness, grade; social standing, status**

人柄 ひとがら character, personality

役柄 やくがら nature [quality] of one's office, one's position

作柄 さくがら harvest, crop; quality (of an artistic production)

事柄 ことがら matter, affair, circumstances

身柄 みがら one's person; social standing

間柄 あいだがら relation, terms

家柄 いえがら social standing of a family; lineage, descent; good family

身分柄 みぶんがら social standing, status

仕事柄 しごとがら character of work; because of [in connection with] one's work

格 ▷(good) character
カク コウ   Ⓚ083

(degree of excellence) (good) **character, personality; (high) quality, distinction, style**

格差 かくさ difference in quality [price]

格安な かくやすな inexpensive, reasonable in price

格調 かくちょう tone, strain, style

人格 じんかく character, personality

性格 せいかく character, personality

品格 ひんかく dignity, grace

風格の有る人物 ふうかくのあるじんぶつ man of distinctive character

厳格な げんかくな strict, stern, severe, rigorous

near

近 隣 傍 旁 沿

近 ▷near
キン ちか(い)   Ⓚ263

(close in space) **near, close, nearby, neighboring**

近視 きんし nearsightedness, shortsightedness

近郊 きんこう suburbs, outskirts

近所 きんじょ neighborhood

近隣 きんりん neighborhood

近県 きんけん neighboring prefectures

近距離 きんきょり short distance

付近 ふきん neighborhood, environs, vicinity

隣 ▷neighboring
リン とな(る) となり   Ⓚ0700

neighboring, adjoining, adjacent

隣国 りんこく neighboring country

隣家 りんか neighboring house

隣村 りんそん neighboring village

隣人 りんじん neighbor

近隣 きんりん neighborhood

傍 ▷beside
ボウ かたわ(ら) そば   Ⓚ0127

[sometimes also 旁] **beside, by, by the side, nearby; side**

傍観者 ぼうかんしゃ bystander, onlooker
傍系の ぼうけいの collateral, subsidiary, affiliated
傍受 ぼうじゅ interception, tapping
傍線 ぼうせん side line, underline
傍聴 ぼうちょう hearing; attendance
傍若無人な ぼうじゃくぶじんな overbearing, arrogant, audacious
路傍 ろぼう roadside, wayside
近傍 きんぼう neighborhood

旁 ▷beside
ボウ つくり かたがた

[now usu. 傍] **beside, side**

旁註(=傍注) ぼうちゅう side notes, gloss

沿 ▷along
エン そ(う) -ぞ(い)   Ⓚ0290

along, alongside

沿道 えんどう along the route
沿線の えんせんの along a railway line
沿海 えんかい coast, shore
沿岸 えんがん coast, shore

necessity →NEED AND NECESSITY

neck
首　　頸　　項

首 ▷neck
シュ くび   Ⓚ1956

neck

絞首刑 こうしゅけい death [execution] by hanging

頸 ▷neck
ケイ くび

[original meaning] **neck**

頸部 けいぶ neck (region)
頸椎 けいつい cervical vertebrae

項 ▷nape
コウ   Ⓚ0521

[original meaning, now rare] **nape**

項領 こうりょう neck, collar

need and necessity
要　必　須　需　入　用

要 ▷required
ヨウ かなめ い(る)   Ⓚ2290

[also prefix] **required, necessary, essential**

要注意 ようちゅうい attention [care] required
要確認 ようかくにん confirmation required

必 ▷must
ヒツ かなら(ず)   Ⓚ0006

must, required, compulsory, worthwhile

必読書 ひつどくしょ required reading
必見の物 ひっけんのもの something that deserves attention; a must
必修科目 ひっしゅうかもく required subject
必着 ひっちゃく (of mail) to be delivered (without fail)

須 ▷must
ス   Ⓚ0526

must, must have, absolutely necessary

須要な しゅような absolutely necessary
必須の ひっすの indispensable, essential

需 ▷demand
ジュ   Ⓚ2438

ⓐ **demand, needs, requirements**
ⓑ **need, require**

a 需給 じゅきゅう supply and demand
特需 とくじゅ emergency demand, special procurements
軍需品 ぐんじゅひん war supplies
実需 じつじゅ actual demand
民需 みんじゅ private demands, civilian requirements
外需 がいじゅ foreign demand
b 需要 じゅよう demand
必需品 ひつじゅひん necessaries, necessities

入 ▷necessary
ニュウ い(る) -い(り) い(れる) -い(れ) はい(る)   Ⓚ2859

necessary

入用 にゅうよう need, demand, necessity
入費 にゅうひ expense(s)

用 ▷needed for (a specific use)
ヨウ もち(いる)   Ⓚ2569

needed for (a specific use), required

用紙 ようし blank form, stationery
用地 ようち land, lot, site
用具 ようぐ tool, instrument, appliance; outfit
不用な ふような unnecessary, useless; disused, waste
入用 にゅうよう need, demand, necessity
学校用品 がっこうようひん school requisites [supplies]

needle

針　刺　茨

針 ▷needle
シン はり　　　　　　　　　　Ⓚ1488

ⓐ [original meaning] **needle**
ⓑ **needle-shaped object as the hand of clock or pointer of an instrument**
a 運針 うんしん handling of a needle
b 針葉樹 しんようじゅ conifer
　 長針 ちょうしん long [minute] hand
　 秒針 びょうしん second hand
　 指針 ししん compass needle; indicator, pointer; hand; guiding principle
　 磁針 じしん magnetic needle
　 検針 けんしん inspection of a meter
　 羅針盤 らしんばん compass
　 避雷針 ひらいしん lightning rod

刺 ▷prickle
シ さ(す) さ(さる) さ(し)　　Ⓚ1171

prickle, thorn, needle
刺状突起 しじょうとっき prickle (of plants)
有刺鉄線 ゆうしてっせん barbed wire

茨 ▷thorn
いばら　　　　　　　　　　　Ⓚ1952

(sharp process on a plant) **thorn, prickle**
茨の道 いばらのみち thorny path
茨の冠 いばらのかんむり crown of thorns

negative

負　陰

負 ▷negative
フ ま(ける) ま(かす) お(う)　Ⓚ1799

ⓐ math **negative**
ⓑ elec **negative**
a 負数 ふすう negative number
　 正負 せいふ positive and negative, plus and minus

b 負極 ふきょく cathode, negative pole; south magnetic pole

陰 ▷negative
イン かげ かげ(る)　　　　　Ⓚ049

negative
陰性 いんせい negative, dormant

net

網　羅

網 ▷net
モウ あみ　　　　　　　　　Ⓚ1255

ⓐ [original meaning] **net (for catching animals)**
ⓑ (reticulated fabric) **net, netting**
a 漁網 ぎょもう fishing net
　 鉄条網 てつじょうもう barbed wire entanglements
b 網状組織 もうじょうそしき network, reticulum
　 網膜 もうまく retina

羅 ▷bird net
ラ　　　　　　　　　　　　Ⓚ2278

[original meaning] **bird net, net**
雀羅 じゃくら sparrow net

new

新　鮮　生

新 ▷new
シン あたら(しい) あら(た) あら－ にい－
　　　　　　　　　　　　　Ⓚ1587

[also prefix] **new, novel, fresh**
新旧 しんきゅう old and new
新聞 しんぶん newspaper
新鮮な しんせんな fresh
新年 しんねん New Year
新製品 しんせいひん new products
新発明 しんはつめい new invention [discovery]
新世界 しんせかい new world, the New World
新設する しんせつする establish newly, create
新人 しんじん new talent, rookie; newcomer
新刊 しんかん new publication
新幹線 しんかんせん Shinkansen, Bullet Train
新学期 しんがっき new term
最新の さいしんの newest, latest

鮮 ▷**fresh**
セン あざ(やか)　　　　　Ⓚ1656

fresh
鮮魚 せんぎょ fresh fish
鮮度 せんど (degree of) freshness
新鮮な しんせんな fresh
生鮮な せいせんな fresh

生 ▷**raw**
セイ ショウ い(きる) い(かす) い(ける)
う(まれる) う(まれ) う(む) お(う) は(える)
は(やす) き なま な(る)　　　Ⓚ2933

raw, uncooked, crude
生乳 せいにゅう raw milk
生薬 しょうやく crude drug
生石灰 せいせっかい quicklime, unslaked lime

next
次　明　翌　来

次 ▷**next**
ジ シ つ(ぐ) つぎ　　　　　Ⓚ0039

[also prefix] **next, following, subsequent**
次回 じかい next time
次期 じき next term
次号 じごう next issue
次週 じしゅう next week
次年度 じねんど next (fiscal) year

明 ▷**next**
メイ
ミョウ あ(かり) あか(るい) あか(るむ)
あか(らむ) あき(らか) あ(ける) -あ(け)
あ(く) あ(くる) あ(かす)　　Ⓚ0756

[also prefix] **next, the coming (day or year)**
明日 みょうにち(=あした, あす) tomorrow
明年 みょうねん next year
明朝 みょうちょう tomorrow morning
明晩 みょうばん tomorrow night
明年度 みょうねんど next (fiscal) year
明後日 みょうごにち(=あさって) day after tomorrow

翌 ▷**the following**
ヨク　　　　　　　　　　　Ⓚ2325

the following, the next (month or year)
翌日 よくじつ the following [next] day
翌年 よくねん the next [following] year
翌春 よくしゅん next spring
翌翌日 よくよくじつ two days after
翌朝 よくあさ the following morning

来 ▷**the coming**
ライ く(る) きた(る) きた(す)　Ⓚ2975

the coming, the following, the next
来年 らいねん next year
来週 らいしゅう next week
来学期 らいがっき next school term

night →**EVENING AND NIGHT**

nine
九　　　玖

九 ▷**nine**
キュウ ク ここの ここの(つ)　Ⓚ2858

nine
九百 きゅうひゃく 900
九回 きゅうかい nine times
九星術 きゅうせいじゅつ astrology
九月 くがつ September
九人 きゅうにん nine people

玖 ▷**nine**
キュウ ク　　　　　　　　Ⓚ0744

nine — used in legal documents and checks
金玖萬参阡弐百円也 きんきゅうまんさんぜんにひ
ゃくえんなり the sum of ninety three thousand
two hundred yen

nitrogen
窒　　　硝

窒 ▷**nitrogen**
チツ　　　　　　　　　　　Ⓚ1980

nitrogen
窒素 ちっそ nitrogen
窒化物 ちっかぶつ nitride

硝 ▷**niter**
ショウ　　　　　　　　　　Ⓚ1097

niter, saltpeter, potassium nitrate
硝石 しょうせき saltpeter
硝酸 しょうさん nitric acid
硝薬 しょうやく gunpowder
硝煙 しょうえん gunpowder smoke
硝化 しょうか nitrification

nobility

爵　公　侯

爵 ▷rank of nobility
シャク　　　　　　　　Ⓚ2197

rank of nobility, peerage, court rank
爵位 しゃくい rank of nobility
伯爵 はくしゃく count, earl
男爵 だんしゃく baron
授爵 じゅしゃく ennoblement

公 ▷nobleman
コウ　おおやけ　　　　Ⓚ1715

nobleman, lord, prince
公子 こうし young nobleman
公家(=公卿) くげ court noble
公方 くぼう Imperial Court; shogun, tycoon

侯 ▷feudal lord
コウ　　　　　　　　　Ⓚ0079

ⓐ **feudal lord, daimyo**
ⓑ **honorific title after names of feudal lords [daimyos]**
a 諸侯 しょこう feudal lords
　王侯 おうこう princess, royalty, crowned heads
b 仙台侯 せんだいこう Lord of Sendai

noblemen

公　侯　伯　子　男

公 ▷duke
コウ　おおやけ　　　　Ⓚ1715

ⓐ **duke**
ⓑ **title after names of dukes**
a 公爵 こうしゃく duke, prince
b ヨーク公 よーくこう Duke of York

侯 ▷marquis
コウ　　　　　　　　　Ⓚ0079

ⓐ **marquis**
ⓑ **title after names of marquises**
a 侯爵 こうしゃく marquis
b 黒田侯 くろだこう Marquis Kuroda

伯 ▷count
ハク　　　　　　　　　Ⓚ0043

ⓐ **count, earl**
ⓑ **title after names of counts or earls**

a 伯爵 はくしゃく count, earl
b 前島伯 まえじまはく Count Maejima

子 ▷viscount
シ　ス　こ　-(っ)こ　　Ⓚ287

viscount
子爵 ししゃく viscount

男 ▷baron
ダン　ナン　おとこ　　Ⓚ219

ⓐ **baron**
ⓑ **title after names of barons**
a 男爵 だんしゃく baron
b 吉川男 よしかわだん Baron Yoshikawa

nominalizers

所　事　子　性

所 ▷particle of nominalization
ショ　ところ　どころ　Ⓚ075

particle of nominalization, function word for turning verbs into nouns
所以 ゆえん(=しょい) reason; way of doing
所有する しょゆうする have, own, possess
所属する しょぞくする belong to, be attached to
所得 しょとく income, earnings
所望 しょもう desire, wish
所信 しょしん one's belief, one's opinion
所在 しょざい whereabouts, position, situation
所轄 しょかつ jurisdiction

事 ▷nominalization word
ジ　ズ　こと　　　　　Ⓚ298

abstract thing or act—word used for the nominalization of verbs, adjectives or phrases
考える事 かんがえること what one thinks
. . .する事にしている …することにしている make a point of (doing), be in the habit of (doing)
永い事 ながいこと for a long time
. . .との事である …とのことである It is said that…/They say that…/I hear that…

子 ▷noun suffix
シ　ス　こ　-(っ)こ　　Ⓚ2872

suffix after nouns, esp. names of small objects:
ⓐ **various articles and fixtures, esp. furniture**
ⓑ **small entities such as particles, esp. nuclear particles**
ⓒ **various abstract concepts**
a 障子 しょうじ paper sliding-door, *shoji*
　椅子 いす chair

菓子 かし confectionery, cake, sweets
柚子 ゆず [also 柚] yuzu
帽子 ぼうし cap, hat
b 粒子 りゅうし particle, grain
原子 げんし atom
電子 でんし electron
遺伝子 いでんし gene
晶子 しょうし crystallite
c 骨子 こっし essence, gist
調子 ちょうし tone, tune; key, note; condition, state
   (of health); manner, way
様子 ようす situation, aspect, circumstances;
   appearance, looks; sign, indication
面子 めんつ face, honor

性 ▷-ity
セイ ショウ   Ⓚ0266

suffix indicating quality, state or degree: **-ity, -ness**

生産性 せいさんせい productivity
可能性 かのうせい possibility
安定性 あんていせい stability
アルカリ性 あるかりせい alkalinity
爆発性 ばくはつせい explosiveness

noon
午   昼

午 ▷noon
ゴ   Ⓚ1720

noon, noontime
午睡 ごすい nap, afternoon sleep
午前 ごぜん morning, forenoon
午後 ごご afternoon
正午 しょうご noon, noontime

昼 ▷midday
チュウ ひる   Ⓚ2668

midday, noon
昼食 ちゅうしょく lunch
白昼 はくちゅう daytime, broad daylight

North American countries
米   加

米 ▷America
ベイ マイ こめ   Ⓚ2958

America, United States; American
米国 べいこく U.S.A.
米軍 べいぐん American armed forces
米貨 べいか American currency, U.S. dollar
日米 にちべい Japan and U.S.

加 ▷Canada
カ くわ(える) くわ(わる)   Ⓚ0024

Canada
日加 にっか Japan and Canada

notebook
帳   帖   簿   籍

帳 ▷notebook
チョウ   Ⓚ0430

[formerly also 帖] [also suffix] **notebook, book, register, account book, album**
帳面 ちょうめん notebook, account book, register
帳簿 ちょうぼ account book, ledger, register
帳尻 ちょうじり balance of accounts
手帳 てちょう pocketbook, memo
日記帳 にっきちょう diary
通帳 つうちょう bankbook, passbook

帖 ▷notebook
ジョウ チョウ   Ⓚ0256

[now also 帳] **notebook, book, register**
画帖 がじょう picture album
手帖 てちょう pocketbook, memo

簿 ▷record book
ボ   Ⓚ2377

[also suffix] **record book, book(s), account book, register**
簿記 ぼき bookkeeping
帳簿 ちょうぼ account book, ledger, register
名簿 めいぼ register [list] of names
計算簿 けいさんぼ account book
登記簿 とうきぼ register

家計簿 かけいぼ housekeeping account book
通知簿 つうちぼ report card [book]

籍 ▷register
セキ   Ⓚ2381

register, family [domiciliary] register; record
戸籍 こせき family register
軍籍 ぐんせき army register
移籍 いせき transfer of one's name in the register
入籍 にゅうせき entry in the family register

nothing →EMPTINESS AND NOTHING

not moving
固 定 静 止

固 ▷firm
コ かた(める) かた(まる) かた(まり)
かた(い)   Ⓚ2658

[original meaning] (fixed in place) **firm, fixed, immovable, stable**
固定された こていされた fixed, stationary, permanent
固着する こちゃくする adhere to, stick fast

定 ▷fixed
テイ ジョウ さだ(める) さだ(まる)
さだ(か)   Ⓚ1916

(firmly in position) **fixed, stationary**
定着 ていちゃく fixing, fastening, fixation
定滑車 ていかっしゃ fixed pulley
固定する こていする fix, settle, be fixed
措定する そていする suppose, assume

静 ▷still
セイ ジョウ しず- しず(か) しず(まる)
しず(める)   Ⓚ1539

still, quiet, static, inactive
静止する せいしする stand still, come to a standstill
静脈 じょうみゃく vein
静座 せいざ sitting quietly, meditation

止 ▷still
シ と(まる) -ど(まり) と(める) -ど(め)
や(める) や(む)   Ⓚ2545

(motionless) **still, quiet**
止水 しすい still water
黙止する もくしする keep quiet; take no measures

nourish →RAISE AND NOURISH

number →QUANTITY AND NUMBER

numbers →KINDS OF NUMBERS

obey
守 遵 順 隷 従

守 ▷observe
シュ ス まも(る) まも(り) もり   Ⓚ186

observe, obey, keep, adhere, abide by
順守(=遵守)する じゅんしゅする observe, obey, follow, conform to
厳守 げんしゅ strict observance
保守 ほしゅ conservatism; maintenance

遵 ▷obey
ジュン   Ⓚ273

[also 順] [original meaning] **obey, observe, abide by, follow**
遵守する じゅんしゅする observe, obey, follow, conform to
遵法 じゅんぽう law observance
遵奉する じゅんぽうする observe, obey, follow

順 ▷obey
ジュン   Ⓚ0009

[also 遵] **obey, follow, submit to**
順守する じゅんしゅする observe, obey, follow, conform to
順法 じゅんぽう law observance
随順する ずいじゅんする obey meekly, faithfully follow (one's master)

隷 ▷be subordinate to
レイ   Ⓚ1563

[original meaning] **be subordinate [subject] to, be under, be attached to**
隷従 れいじゅう slavery, servitude; servile obedience
隷属 れいぞく subordination

従 ▷follow
ジュウ ショウ ジュ したが(う)
したが(える)   Ⓚ0376

(act in accordance with) **follow (a person's instructions), comply with, obey, observe, submit to**
従順な じゅうじゅんな submissive, obedient, docile
服従する ふくじゅうする obey, submit to
盲従する もうじゅうする follow blindly
屈従 くつじゅう servile submission, subservience
追従 ついしょう flattery, sycophancy

object
物　品　体

物 ▷thing
ブツ モツ もの　　　Ⓚ0777

[also suffix] (inanimate material entity) **thing, object, article**

物品 ぶっぴん goods, article, commodity
物体 ぶったい body, physical solid, object, substance
物的な ぶってきな material, physical
現物 げんぶつ (actual) thing; spot goods
見物 けんぶつ sightseeing, visit
実物 じつぶつ real thing, actual object, genuine article
風物 ふうぶつ natural objects [features], scenery; scenes and manners
荷物 にもつ baggage, load
書物 しょもつ book, volume
障害物 しょうがいぶつ obstacle, hurdle

品 ▷article
ヒン しな　　　Ⓚ1937

[original meaning] **article, thing**

品名 ひんめい name of article
作品 さくひん (piece of) work, performance, product
食品 しょくひん food, foodstuff
用品 ようひん article, supplies
薬品 やくひん medicine, drug; chemicals
貴重品 きちょうひん article of value

体 ▷body
タイ テイ からだ　　　Ⓚ0055

(physical object or mass) **body, object, substance**

体積 たいせき (cubic) volume, capacity
物体 ぶったい body, physical solid, object, substance
固体 こたい solid, solid matter
気体 きたい gas, vapor, gaseous body
天体 てんたい heavenly body
有機体 ゆうきたい organism, organic body
立体 りったい solid (body), cube

obliqueness and inclining
斜　　傾

斜 ▷oblique
シャ なな(め)　　　Ⓚ1351

[also prefix] [original meaning] **oblique, diagonal, slanting, inclined, sloping, leaning, tilting**

斜線 しゃせん oblique line, slanting line, slash mark
斜面 しゃめん slope, slanting surface
斜影 しゃえい slanting shadow
斜滑降 しゃかっこう traversing (in skiing)
斜投影 しゃとうえい oblique projection
傾斜 けいしゃ inclination, slant, tilt
ピサの斜塔 ぴさのしゃとう Leaning Tower of Pisa

傾 ▷incline
ケイ かたむ(く) かたむ(ける)
かし(げる)　　　Ⓚ0132

[original meaning] **incline, lean, tilt, slant**

傾斜する けいしゃする incline, slant, tilt
傾度 けいど inclination
傾角 けいかく (angle of) inclination

obstacle
障　　関

障 ▷hindrance
ショウ さわ(る)　　　Ⓚ0647

hindrance, obstruction, obstacle, barrier

障子 しょうじ paper sliding-door, *shoji*
故障 こしょう malfunction, breakdown; physical disorder; hindrance, obstacle, accident; objection, protest
支障 ししょう hindrance, obstacle, difficulty
万障 ばんしょう all hindrances, all obstacles
排障器 はいしょうき obstruction guard
罪障 ざいしょう sins

関 ▷barrier
カン せき -ぜき かか(わる)　　　Ⓚ2842

barrier, customs barrier, checkpoint

関税 かんぜい customs, custom duty
関門 かんもん barrier, gateway
関東 かんとう Kanto district
関西 かんさい Kansai district
税関 ぜいかん customhouse

難関 なんかん barrier, obstacle, difficulty
通関 つうかん customs clearance, entry

obstinate →FIRM AND OBSTINATE

obstruct and hinder

遮 塞 阻 沮 奄
妨 障 碍 害 梗

遮 ▷interrupt
シャ さえぎ(る)　　　　　Ⓚ2724

interrupt, block (off), intercept, obstruct
遮断する しゃだんする intercept, interrupt, block,
　blockade, isolate

塞 ▷stop up
サイ ソク ふさ(ぐ) ふさ(がる)　Ⓚ2033

[original meaning] **stop up, fill in**
塞栓 そくせん embolus
閉塞 へいそく blockade, stoppage
梗塞 こうそく stoppage; tightness; infarction

阻 ▷obstruct
ソ はば(む)　　　　　Ⓚ0308

[formerly also 沮] (prevent the progress or passage of)
obstruct, impede, hinder, check
阻害する そがいする obstruct, check, impede,
　hinder
阻止 そし obstruction, check, hindrance

沮 ▷obstruct
ソ はば(む)

(prevent the progress or passage of) **obstruct, impede,
hinder, check**
沮止 そし obstruction, check, hindrance
沮害 そがい obstruction, check, impediment,
　hindrance

奄 ▷obstruct (by covering)
エン　　　　　Ⓚ1903

obstruct (by covering), stop up
奄奄 えんえん gasping
気息奄奄 きそくえんえん gasping for breath, on the
　brink of death

妨 ▷hinder
ボウ さまた(げる)　　　　　Ⓚ0209

hinder, interfere with, disturb, obstruct, impede
妨害する ぼうがいする disturb, hinder, obstruct,
　hamper, impede, interfere

妨害放送 ぼうがいほうそう radio jamming

障 ▷hinder
ショウ さわ(る)　　　　　Ⓚ0647

[original meaning] **hinder, obstruct, block, screen**
障壁 しょうへき barrier, obstacle; [formerly also 牆壁]
　wall, fence
障壁 しょうへき [formerly also 牆壁] fence, wall;
　barrier
障害 しょうがい obstacle, hindrance; (physical)
　disorder

碍 ▷stand in the way
ガイ ゲ

[now also 害] **stand in the way, hinder, obstruct,
interfere with**
碍子 がいし insulator
妨碍する ぼうがいする disturb, hinder, obstruct,
　hamper, impede, interfere
障碍 しょうがい obstacle, hindrance; (physical)
　disorder
無碍 むげ free from obstacles

害 ▷stand in the way
ガイ　　　　　Ⓚ1962

[formerly also 碍] [original meaning] **stand in the way,
hinder, obstruct, interfere with**
障害 しょうがい obstacle, hindrance; (physical)
　disorder
妨害する ぼうがいする disturb, hinder, obstruct,
　hamper, impede, interfere
阻害する そがいする obstruct, check, impede,
　hinder

梗 ▷stop up
コウ キョウ　　　　　Ⓚ0871

stop up, close up, clog
梗塞 こうそく stoppage; tightness; infarction
脳梗塞 のうこうそく stroke, cerebral infarction

occasions

際 折 時 機 節

際 ▷occasion
サイ きわ -ぎわ　　　　　Ⓚ0646

occasion, time
実際の じっさいの true, real; actual; practical

折 ▷occasion
セツ お(る) おり お(れる)　　　　　Ⓚ0225

occasion, time, chance, opportunity

折折 おりおり sometimes, occasionally, once in a while

折悪しくして おりあしくして inopportunely, unseasonably

折りに触れて おりにふれて on opportunity, occasionally

時折 ときおり sometimes, occasionally

時 ▷timely occasion
ジ とき –どき   Ⓚ0830

(opportune moment) **timely occasion, right time, opportunity**

時機 じき opportunity, chance

時宜 じぎ right time [occasion], proper time

時節 じせつ season, times; occasion

機 ▷opportunity
キ はた   Ⓚ0989

opportunity, occasion, chance, time, crucial point

機会 きかい opportunity, occasion

機運 きうん opportunity, chance

時機 じき opportunity, chance

好機 こうき favorable opportunity, good chance

契機 けいき opportunity, chance; *philosophy* moment

危機 きき crisis, emergency

転機 てんき turning point

待機する たいきする wait for an opportunity, stand ready

投機 とうき speculation, venture

節 ▷time
セツ セチ ふし –ぶし   Ⓚ2349

(fixed time in the year) **season, time, occasion**

時節 じせつ season, times; occasion

当節 とうせつ these days

occupy
占 拠 領 専

占 ▷occupy
セン し(める) うらな(う)   Ⓚ1729

occupy, hold, seize, take (up)

占拠 せんきょ occupation, exclusive possession

占有する せんゆうする occupy, take possession of

占領地 せんりょうち occupied area

独占 どくせん exclusive possession, monopoly

拠 ▷occupy
キョ コ   Ⓚ0276

occupy, take possession of, hold one's ground

拠守 きょしゅ defense

占拠 せんきょ occupation, exclusive possession

割拠する かっきょする hold one's own ground

領 ▷take possession of
リョウ   Ⓚ1133

take possession of, occupy, have jurisdiction over

領有 りょうゆう possession

占領する せんりょうする capture, occupy, take possession of

横領する おうりょうする seize upon, embezzle, usurp

専 ▷take exclusive possession of
セン もっぱ(ら)   Ⓚ2297

take exclusive possession of, monopolize

専有 せんゆう exclusive possession, monopoly

offenses →CRIMES AND OFFENSES

offer
供 献 納 提 貢 奉 捧

供 ▷offer (to a person or god)
キョウ ク そな(える) とも –ども   Ⓚ0070

❶ (put at another's disposal) **offer, present, submit**

供覧 きょうらん display, show

提供する ていきょうする offer, tender; sponsor (a show)

試供品 しきょうひん sample, specimen

❷ [original meaning] **offer (sacrifices to a god), dedicate, sacrifice**

供物 くもつ offering

供養 くよう memorial service

供米 くまい rice offered to a god

供御 くご emperor's meal

人身御供 ひとみごくう human sacrifice, victim

献 ▷offer (esp. to a superior)
ケン コン   Ⓚ1588

offer (esp. to a superior), present, dedicate

献納する けんのうする offer, present, donate

献上する けんじょうする present (a gift to a superior)

献身 けんしん self-sacrifice, devotion

献呈 けんてい presentation

納 ▷offer (as to a god)
ノウ ナッ– ナ ナン トウ おさ(める) おさ(まる)   Ⓚ1195

offer (as to a god), dedicate, present

納采 のうさい presenting [exchanging] betrothal presents between royal families
奉納 ほうのう dedication (to a deity), offering
献納 けんのう offering, presentation, donation
結納 ゆいのう ceremonial exchange of betrothal gifts; betrothal present [gift]

提 ▷present
テイ チョウ さ(げる) Ⓚ0540

(bring before a person, as for consideration) **present, bring forward, offer, tender, propose**

提案 ていあん proposition, proposal, suggestion
提出する ていしゅつする present, submit, turn in
提供する ていきょうする offer, tender; sponsor (a show)
提言 ていげん proposal, suggestion
提示する ていじする present, exhibit
提訴する ていそする present a case to (the court), file an action
提議 ていぎ proposition, proposal, motion
前提 ぜんてい premise, presupposition

貢 ▷offer tribute
コウ ク みつ(ぐ) Ⓚ1970

offer tribute, pay tribute

入貢する にゅうこうする pay tribute
朝貢する ちょうこうする bring tribute

奉 ▷dedicate
ホウ ブ たてまつ(る) Ⓚ2215

[original meaning] **dedicate (esp. to a deity), offer, present, proffer**

奉納する ほうのうする dedicate (to a deity), offer
奉呈する ほうていする dedicate, present, offer (to a high personage)
奉献する ほうけんする offer (to a shrine)
奉加 ほうが donation
奉幣 ほうへい offering a wand with hemp and paper streamers to a Shinto god
奉灯 ほうとう dedicated lantern

捧 ▷offer respectfully
ホウ ささ(げる) ささ(ぐ) Ⓚ0447

[now also 奉 or 抱] [original meaning] **hold up in both hands**

捧持(=奉持)する ほうじする hold up, bear
捧腹絶倒(=抱腹絶倒)する ほうふくぜっとうする double up with laughter

offering

奠 幣 貢

奠 ▷offering
テン デン

[now replaced by 典] **offering**

香奠 こうでん obituary [condolence] gift, incense money

幣 ▷offering
ヘイ Ⓚ250

ⓐ offering of cloth or paper to the gods, esp. in Shinto rituals
ⓑ offering (to a ruler or guest), tribute, present

a 幣帛 へいはく Shinto offering of cloth (or paper)
御幣 ごへい pendant paper strips in a Shinto shrine, sacred staff with cut paper
奉幣 ほうへい offering a wand with hemp and paper streamers to a Shinto god
b 幣物 へいもつ(=へいぶつ) Shinto offerings; present to a guest
幣貢 へいこう tribute, offering

貢 ▷tribute
コウ ク みつ(ぐ) Ⓚ1970

[original meaning] **tribute**

貢租 こうそ tribute, annual tax
年貢 ねんぐ land tax

offer wine

酌 献 酬

酌 ▷pour wine
シャク く(む) Ⓚ1331

[original meaning] **pour [serve] wine or sake, fill a person's cup; drink wine**

酌婦 しゃくふ barmaid, waitress
晩酌 ばんしゃく evening drink
手酌 てじゃく self-service in sake drinking

献 ▷offer wine
ケン コン Ⓚ1588

offer wine to a guest

献酬 けんしゅう exchange of sake cups
献酌 けんしゃく offering a drink
献立 こんだて menu, preparations

酬 ▷reciprocate wineglasses
シュウ
Ⓚ1399

[original meaning] **reciprocate [exchange] wineglasses, offer wine in return**
献酬 けんしゅう exchange of sake cups

officials

官 吏 僚 司 役 事

官 ▷government official
カン
Ⓚ1912

[also suffix] **government official, officer**
長官 ちょうかん director, administrator, chief
警官 けいかん police officer, policeman
次官 じかん vice-minister, undersecretary
裁判官 さいばんかん judge
行政官 ぎょうせいかん executive [administrative] official

吏 ▷official
リ
Ⓚ2963

[also suffix] [original meaning] **official, officer**
吏人 りじん officials
吏員 りいん official
吏臭 りしゅう officialdom, red tape
官吏 かんり government official
公吏 こうり public official
税関吏 ぜいかんり customs officer

僚 ▷official
リョウ
Ⓚ0143

official
閣僚 かくりょう cabinet members
官僚 かんりょう government official(s); bureaucracy, officialdom
幕僚 ばくりょう staff, staff officer

司 ▷officiator
シ
Ⓚ2538

[also suffix] **officiator, officer, official, administrator**
上司 じょうし superior officer; superior
行司 ぎょうじ sumo umpire
保護司 ほごし probation officer

役 ▷executive
ヤク エキ
Ⓚ0217

executive, officer, public servant, official, director, person in charge
下役 したやく subordinate official

助役 じょやく assistant official; deputy mayor; deputy station-master
重役 じゅうやく director, executive
取締役 とりしまりやく director

事 ▷officer
ジ ズ こと
Ⓚ2986

officer, official, public officer [servant]
知事 ちじ (prefectural) governor
刑事 けいじ (police) detective
判事 はんじ judge
幹事 かんじ manager, secretary; organizer
領事 りょうじ consul, consular representative
理事 りじ director, trustee

offspring

子 仔 孤 嫡 息
男 惣 娘 女 姫

子 ▷child
シ ス こ -(っ)こ
Ⓚ2872

[original meaning] (offspring of man) **child, son, daughter, offspring**
子女 しじょ children, sons and daughters
子息 しそく son
子音 しいん(=しおん) consonant ("child sound")
母子 ぼし mother and child
養子 ようし foster [adopted] child

仔 ▷offspring
シ こ
Ⓚ0022

animal offspring
仔虫 しちゅう larva
胎仔 たいじ (nonhuman) embryo, fetus
同腹仔 どうふくし litter

孤 ▷orphan
コ
Ⓚ0317

[original meaning] **orphan**
孤児 こじ orphan

嫡 ▷legitimate child
チャク
Ⓚ0620

legitimate child, heir, successor
嫡子 ちゃくし legitimate child
廃嫡 はいちゃく disinheritance

息 ▷son
ソク いき Ⓚ2301

son, child
息女 そくじょ daughter
子息 しそく son

男 ▷son
ダン ナン おとこ Ⓚ2199

son—used esp. to indicate order of birth
一男二女 いちなんにじょ one son and two daughters
長男 ちょうなん eldest son
三男 さんなん third son

惣 ▷eldest son
ソウ Ⓚ2419

eldest son, eldest child—used esp. in names
惣領 そうりょう eldest son, eldest child

娘 ▷daughter
むすめ Ⓚ0367

daughter
一人娘 ひとりむすめ only daughter

女 ▷daughter
ジョ ニョ ニョウ おんな め Ⓚ2884

daughter—used esp. to indicate order of birth
長女 ちょうじょ eldest daughter
養女 ようじょ adopted daughter, stepdaughter
三女 さんじょ third daughter

姫 ▷daughter of noble birth
ひめ Ⓚ0368

ⓐ **daughter [young lady] of noble [gentle] birth, princess**
ⓑ [sometimes also 媛] **courtesy title after names of young ladies of noble birth**
ⓐ 姫君 ひめぎみ princess, highborn young lady
姫様 ひめさま daughter of a nobleman
姫宮 ひめみや princess
ⓑ 千姫 せんひめ Princess Sen
シンデレラ姫 しんでれらひめ Cinderella

offspring of siblings
甥　　　姪

甥 ▷nephew
セイ おい Ⓚ1089

nephew
令甥 れいせい [honorific] your nephew

姪 ▷niece
テツ めい Ⓚ031

niece, nephew
姪孫 てっそん grandniece, grandnephew
令姪 れいてつ your niece

# of long duration
長　永　久　恒

長 ▷long
チョウ なが(い) Ⓚ221

[also prefix] (of considerable duration) **long**
長期 ちょうき long period
長寿 ちょうじゅ long life, longevity
長時間 ちょうじかん long time

永 ▷eternal
エイ なが(い) Ⓚ169

eternal, everlasting, permanent, long, perpetual
永遠 えいえん eternity
永久 えいきゅう permanence, eternity
永住 えいじゅう permanent residence
永続する えいぞくする last long, remain permanently
永眠 えいみん eternal sleep, death
永寿 えいじゅ long life
永小作 えいこさく perpetual land lease

久 ▷of long duration
キュウ ク ひさ(しい) Ⓚ286

of long duration, longstanding, lasting for a long time
久遠 くおん eternity
永久の えいきゅうの permanent, eternal, lasting
恒久の こうきゅうの lasting, everlasting, permanent, eternal
耐久性 たいきゅうせい durability, persistence, lasting quality
悠久な ゆうきゅうな eternal, everlasting, permanent

恒 ▷permanent
コウ Ⓚ032

permanent, lasting
恒久 こうきゅう perpetuity, permanency

oils →FATS AND OILS

old

古 老 故 旧

古 ▷old (not new)
コ ふる(い) ふる- -ふる(す)　　Ⓚ1728

ⓐ [original meaning] (not new) **old**
ⓑ [also prefix] (of the remote past) **old, ancient, obsolete**
ⓒ **old times, ancient times**

a 古書 こしょ old book, rare book
　古風 こふう old style; old customs
　稽古 けいこ practice, rehearsal; learning
b 古典 こてん classics; old book
　古跡 こせき historic remains, ruins
　古代 こだい ancient times, antiquity, remote ages
　古語 こご obsolete word; old proverb
　古文書 こもんじょ ancient documents; paleography
　古今 ここん ancient and modern times
　古希 こき three score and ten, seventy years of age
　考古学 こうこがく archaeology
　復古 ふっこ revival (of the ancient regime), restoration
c 中古 ちゅうこ Middle Ages; secondhand [used] goods

老 ▷old (not young)
ロウ お(いる) ふ(ける)　　Ⓚ2754

[also prefix] (not young) **old, aged**

老人 ろうじん old person, old folks
老年 ろうねん old age
老齢 ろうれい old age
老木 ろうぼく old tree
老後 ろうご one's old age
老眼 ろうがん presbyopia, farsightedness due to old age
老政治家 ろうせいじか venerable statesman

故 ▷old (of the past)
コ ゆえ　　Ⓚ1056

(of the past) **old, of old, ancient**

故事 こじ tradition; historical fact, origin
故実 こじつ ancient customs
故老(=古老) ころう elder, old man; old-timer

旧 ▷old
キュウ　　Ⓚ0005

old, ancient, antique, old-fashioned, bygone

旧株 きゅうかぶ old stock
旧弊な きゅうへいな old-fashioned, conservative
旧式 きゅうしき old style, old type

新旧の しんきゅうの old and new
復旧する ふっきゅうする be restored, recover
懐旧 かいきゅう longing for the old days

old persons

老 爺 翁 婆 姥

老 ▷old person
ロウ お(いる) ふ(ける)　　Ⓚ2754

[original meaning] **old person**

老若 ろうにゃく(=ろうじゃく) the old and the young
敬老 けいろう respect for the aged
古老(=故老) ころう elder, old man; old-timer

爺 ▷old man
ヤ じじ じじい じい

old man

老爺 ろうや old man
好好爺 こうこうや good-natured old man

翁 ▷old man
オウ　　Ⓚ1809

old man, aged man, elder

老翁 ろうおう old man
村翁 そんおう village elder
白頭翁 はくとうおう white-haired old man; windflower

婆 ▷old woman
バ ばあ　　Ⓚ2407

old woman, old maid, old mother; woman

老婆 ろうば old woman
妖婆 ようば witch, hag
老婆心 ろうばしん grandmotherly solicitude
産婆 さんば midwife

姥 ▷old woman
ボ うば　　Ⓚ0314

old woman

姥捨て うばすて practice of abandoning old women
姥桜 うばざくら woman past her prime who is still attractive; cherry trees that blossom before putting forth leaves
姥貝 うばがい Sakhalin surf clam
山姥 やまんば(=やまうば) mountain witch

old times
昔　　往

昔 ▷former times
セキ シャク むかし　　Ⓚ2153

[original meaning] **former times, ancient times, past, antiquity**

昔時 せきじ former times, old times
昔日 せきじつ ancient times, former days, bygone days
昔年 せきねん antiquity, former years
今昔 こんじゃく past and present, yesterday and today

往 ▷bygone days
オウ　　Ⓚ0261

bygone days, ancient days

往時 おうじ bygone days
往古より おうこより from ancient times, from times immemorial
既往症 きおうしょう previous illness, medical history

omit
漏　脱　抜　欠

漏 ▷omit
ロウ も(る) も(れる) も(らす)　　Ⓚ0635

omit, leave out

遺漏 いろう omission, oversight, neglect
脱漏 だつろう omission
疎漏 そろう carelessness, inadvertence, oversight

脱 ▷leave out by mistake
ダツ ぬ(ぐ) ぬ(げる)　　Ⓚ0886

leave out by mistake, omit; be left out, be omitted

脱落する だつらくする be omitted; fall away [behind], drop out
脱漏 だつろう omission
逸脱 いつだつ deviation, departure from the norm

抜 ▷leave out
バツ ぬ(く) ぬ(き) ぬ(ける) ぬ(かす) ぬ(かる)　　Ⓚ0219

leave out, omit, skip

手を抜く てをぬく scamp [skimp] one's work, cut corners

欠 ▷missing
ケツ か(ける) か(く) か(かす)　　Ⓚ172

missing, omitted

欠字 けつじ omitted word, blank type

one
一　壱　片　隻　単　個

一 ▷one
イチ イツ ひと- ひと(つ)　　Ⓚ285

[also prefix] [original meaning] **one, unity, first**

一方 いっぽう one side, one hand; a party, the other party; in the meantime; only
一部 いちぶ part, portion, section; a copy (of a book)
一緒に いっしょに together; at the same time; in a lump
一番 いちばん first, first place; first verse; most, best; a game, a round, a bout; a number, a piece
一千 いっせん 1000
一体 いったい one body; a style, a form; (why, what) on earth, (what, why) in the world
一家 いっか family, household; one's family; style (of established reputation)
一応(=一往) いちおう once; in outline; tentatively; for the time being
一月 いちがつ January
一瞬 いっしゅん instant, moment
一生懸命(=一所懸命)に いっしょうけんめい(=いっしょけんめい)に for life, with all one's might
一大事 いちだいじ matter of great importance
一一 いちいち one by one; in detail
一層 いっそう more, even more, all the more
一度に いちどに at a time, all at once
一部分 いちぶぶん part, portion, section
一円 いちえん the entire region [district]; one yen
第一 だいいち the first, number one; the best; to begin with, above everything else
唯一の ゆいいつの the only, the sole

壱 ▷one (in legal documents)
イチ　　Ⓚ1879

one—used in legal documents and checks

金壱阡参百円也 きんいっせんさんびゃくえんなり one thousand three hundred yen

片 ▷one of two
ヘン かた-　　Ⓚ2910

one of two, one, single

片一方 かたいっぽう one side, the other one
片面 かためん one side, one face

片手 かたて one hand
片道 かたみち one way
片側 かたがわ one side

隻 ▷one of a pair
セキ ⓚ2403

ⓐ [original meaning] **one of a pair, esp. when the second member is absent**
ⓑ **one only, single, lone**
a 隻手 せきしゅ one arm, one hand
隻眼 せきがん one eye
b 隻影 せきえい a single shadow; a speck (of cloud)

単 ▷single
タン ⓚ1946

[also prefix] **single, one, lone, uni-, mono-**
単一な たんいつな single, simple, sole, individual
単車 たんしゃ motorcycle, motorbike
単独の たんどくの single, independent, sole, lone
単色 たんしょく single color, monochrome
単数 たんすう *gram* singular number
単眼 たんがん one eye, ocellus
単弁 たんべん univalve
単細胞 たんさいぼう single cell, one cell
単糖類 たんとうるい monosaccharide

個 ▷individual
コ カ ⓚ0100

[sometimes also 箇] [original meaning] **individual, single unit, single person or thing**
個々に ここに individually, separately
個有の こゆうの peculiar, inherent, characteristic
個室 こしつ private room, single room
個別的に こべつてきに individually, severally, singly
個人 こじん individual
個性 こせい individuality
個展 こてん personal exhibition
各個 かっこ one by one

one side
片　偏　頗

片 ▷one side
ヘン かた- ⓚ2910

one side, one part, one way
片言 かたこと imperfect speech, baby talk
片寄る かたよる concentrate on one side [place], go aside
片貿易 かたぼうえき one way [unbalanced] trade
片思い かたおもい unrequited [unreciprocated] love

片仮名 かたかな katakana

偏 ▷one-sided
ヘン かたよ(る) ⓚ0116

[original meaning] (occurring on one side) **one-sided, uneven, unbalanced**
偏頭痛 へんずつう headache on one side, migraine
偏在 へんざい uneven distribution
偏食 へんしょく unbalanced diet

頗 ▷one-sided
ハ すこぶ(る) ⓚ1121

one-sided, biased, partial, unfair, prejudiced
偏頗 へんぱ favoritism, discrimination

only
唯　一

唯 ▷only
ユイ イ ⓚ0419

[rarely also 惟] **only, sole, one and only**
唯一の ゆいいつの the only, the sole
唯一無二の ゆいいつむにの the one and only, unique
唯心論 ゆいしんろん idealism, spiritualism
唯美主義 ゆいびしゅぎ aestheticism
唯物主義 ゆいぶつしゅぎ materialism

一 ▷one and only
イチ イツ ひと- ひと(つ) ⓚ2850

one and only, sole, exclusive
一途に いちずに with all one's might; blindly
一意専心 いちいせんしん wholeheartedly, single-mindedly
一向(に) いっこう(に) (not) at all, (not) in the least
一心に いっしんに wholeheartedly, with one's whole heart

on the verge of
掛　将　際　臨

掛 ▷be on the verge of
か(ける) か(け) -が(け) -か(かる)
-が(かる) か(かり) -が(かり) ⓚ0449

be on the verge of
死に掛かる しにかかる be dying

将 ▷on the verge of
ショウ   Ⓚ0415

on the verge of, be about to happen
将来 しょうらい future; in the future

際 ▷on the verge of
サイ きわ -ぎわ   Ⓚ0646

on the verge of, on the point of
間際 まぎわ on the verge of, just before, on the
    point of
死に際に しにぎわに on the verge of death

臨 ▷on the point of
リン のぞ(む)   Ⓚ1470

on the point of, on the verge of, face to face with
臨時の りんじの temporary, provisional, special
臨終 りんじゅう hour of death, one's last moment
臨界点 りんかいてん critical point [temperature]
臨機応変 りんきおうへん adaptation to circum-
    stances

open
開　展　披

開 ▷open
カイ ひら(く) ひら(き) -びら(き)
ひら(ける) あ(く) あ(ける)   Ⓚ2835

[original meaning] **open, open up, become open,
unfold, expand**
開閉する かいへいする open and shut [close]; make
    and break (circuits)
開封する かいふうする open (a letter), unseal
開通 かいつう opening to [for] traffic
展開 てんかい unfolding, development, evolution;
    deployment
公開 こうかい opening to the public

展 ▷unfold
テン   Ⓚ2681

(open) **unfold, spread out, open (a letter)**
親展書 しんてんしょ confidential letter

披 ▷open and read
ヒ   Ⓚ0270

[original meaning] **open and read, unseal, unfold,
unroll**
披見する ひけんする open and read, peruse (a
    letter)
直披 ちょくひ(=じきひ) confidential letter

opinion
見　観　説　論

見 ▷view (personal opinion)
ケン み(る) み(える) み(せる)   Ⓚ2201

view, personal opinion
見解 けんかい opinion, view
見地 けんち standpoint, viewpoint
意見 いけん opinion, view; admonition
偏見 へんけん prejudice, biased view, narrow view

観 ▷view (conception)
カン   Ⓚ1659

[also suffix] **view, conception, outlook, theory**
観点 かんてん point of view
観念 かんねん idea, conception, notion
主観 しゅかん subjectivity; subject
先入観 せんにゅうかん preconception, bias, preju-
    dice
人生観 じんせいかん one's view [theory] of life,
    outlook on life
世界観 せかいかん world view, outlook on the
    world

説 ▷opinion
セツ ゼイ と(く)   Ⓚ1405

opinion, view
社説 しゃせつ editorial (article)
自説 じせつ one's own view
通説 つうせつ common opinion, popular view

論 ▷opinion
ロン   Ⓚ1424

opinion, view
世論 せろん(=よろん) public opinion
異論 いろん different [dissenting] opinion; objec-
    tion, dissent, protest
持論 じろん pet theory
時論 じろん current view, contemporary opinion;
    comments on current events
強硬論 きょうこうろん hard line

opposite
対　反　逆　倒

対 ▷opposite
タイ ツイ   Ⓚ0735

❶ **opposite, facing each other, opposed, opposing**

対談 たいだん talk, tête-à-tête, interview; personal negotiation
対話 たいわ dialogue, conversation
対岸 たいがん opposite bank [shore]
対座する たいざする sit opposite each other
対辺 たいへん opposite side
対局 たいきょく game of go [shogi]
❷ [also prefix] **counter-, opposite, contra-, anti-**
対策 たいさく countermeasure, counterplan
対案 たいあん counterproposal
対語 ついご(=たいご) antonym
対潜水艦の たいせんすいかんの antisubmarine

反 ▷**counter**
ハン ホン タン そ(る) そ(らす) Ⓚ2549

[also prefix] **counter, counter-, anti-, opposite, reverse, inverse**
反発する はんぱつする repulse, repel; rally; oppose
反論 はんろん counterargument, refutation
反撃 はんげき counterattack
反動 はんどう backlash, recoil, reaction
反戦 はんせん antiwar
反米 はんべい anti-America
反日 はんにち anti-Japanese
反落 はんらく reactionary fall (in stock prices)
反比例 はんぴれい inverse proportion
反政府 はんせいふ anti-government
反作用 はんさよう reaction

逆 ▷**reverse**
ギャク さか さか(さ) さか(らう) Ⓚ2662

[also prefix] **reverse, inverse, backward, contrary, counter**
逆転 ぎゃくてん reversal, turnabout, inversion; reverse rotation
逆流 ぎゃくりゅう countercurrent, adverse tide; regurgitation (of blood)
逆戻り ぎゃくもどり retrogression, reversal, going back
逆数 ぎゃくすう reciprocal number
逆説 ぎゃくせつ paradox
逆効果 ぎゃくこうか counter result, reverse effect
逆比例 ぎゃくひれい inverse proportion

倒 ▷**upside-down**

トウ たお(れる) -だお(れ) たお(す) Ⓚ0106

upside-down, inverted
倒立 とうりつ handstand
倒影 とうえい inverted image
倒錯 とうさく perversion, inversion

oppress →TORTURE AND OPPRESS

order
序 順 次 番 秩

序 ▷**order (sequence/arrangement)**
ジョ Ⓚ2639

ⓐ **order, precedence, sequence**
ⓑ **order(liness), methodical arrangement**
ⓒ [archaic] **order, arrange in order**
a 序列 じょれつ rank, grade, order
序次 じょじ order, sequence
順序 じゅんじょ order, sequence; system, procedure
b 秩序 ちつじょ order, discipline; method, system
花序 かじょ inflorescence
c 序歯 じょし [archaic] arranging seats by seniority

順 ▷**order (sequence)**
ジュン Ⓚ0009

[also suffix] **order, sequence, turn**
順番 じゅんばん order, turn
順序 じゅんじょ order, sequence; system, procedure
順位 じゅんい order, rank, precedence
順順に じゅんじゅんに by turns, in order
順路 じゅんろ suggested route (for visitors), way round
筆順 ひつじゅん stroke order (in writing Chinese characters)
道順 みちじゅん route, itinerary
手順 てじゅん procedure, program, process
先着順 せんちゃくじゅん order of arrival
年齢順に ねんれいじゅんに by priority of age
ＡＢＣ順に えーびーしーじゅんに in alphabetical order

次 ▷**order (sequence)**
ジ シ つ(ぐ) つぎ Ⓚ0039

order, sequence, arrangement
次第 しだい order; circumstances, reasons; as soon as
次第に しだいに gradually, by degrees
順次 じゅんじ order, turn; gradually
序次 じょじ order, sequence
席次 せきじ order of seats, seating precedence; class standing
目次 もくじ table of contents

番 ▷**numerical order**
バン Ⓚ2396

numerical order, order, ranking, place
番号 ばんごう number, serial number

番地 ばんち lot [house] number, address
番組 ばんぐみ (TV) program
番付 ばんづけ ranking list
番頭 ばんとう (head) clerk
番狂わせ ばんくるわせ upsetting of arrangements, upset, surprise
先番 せんばん one's turn to make the first move
本番 ほんばん acting for the audience, take, going on the air
順番 じゅんばん order, turn

秩 ▷order (methodical arrangement)
チツ   Ⓚ1073

order, methodical arrangement
秩序 ちつじょ order, discipline; method, system

ordinary
常 只 並 平 普 庸 凡 套

常 ▷normal
ジョウ つね とこ-   Ⓚ2247

normal, ordinary, usual, common, regular
常識 じょうしき common sense, common knowledge
常態 じょうたい normal state [condition]
非常 ひじょう emergency, calamity
異常な いじょうな abnormal, unusual, extraordinary
正常 せいじょう normality, normalcy
通常の つうじょうの common, ordinary, usual
平常の へいじょうの ordinary, normal, usual

只 ▷ordinary
シ ただ-   Ⓚ1849

ordinary, common, plain
只者 ただもの ordinary person, common mortal
只事ではない ただごとではない It is no common case

並 ▷ordinary
ヘイ なみ なら(べる) なら(ぶ)
なら(びに)   Ⓚ1936

[in compounds] ordinary, common, average
並製品 なみせいひん common article, article of average quality
並外れて なみはずれて extraordinary, uncommonly
月並な つきなみな conventional, commonplace; trite, hackneyed

平 ▷common
ヘイ ビョウ たい(ら) -だいら
ひら   Ⓚ292

common, ordinary, average
平日 へいじつ weekday
平凡な へいぼんな common, ordinary, commonplace, mediocre
平年 へいねん normal [average] year, common year
平常の へいじょうの ordinary, normal, usual

普 ▷common
フ   Ⓚ2028

common, ordinary
普通の ふつうの normal, regular, ordinary
普選 ふせん universal suffrage
普段(=不断)の ふだんの usual, ordinary, everyday, habitual

庸 ▷mediocre
ヨウ   Ⓚ2697

mediocre, commonplace, common, ordinary, banal, stupid
庸才 ようさい mediocre talent
庸愚 ようぐ mediocrity, imbecility
庸君 ようくん stupid ruler
凡庸な ぼんような commonplace, mediocre, banal
中庸 ちゅうよう the (golden) mean, the middle path

凡 ▷commonplace
ボン ハン   Ⓚ254

[also prefix] commonplace, mediocre, ordinary, common
凡庸な ぼんような commonplace, mediocre, banal
凡才 ぼんさい mediocrity, ordinary ability; (man of) mediocrity, man of no genius
凡夫 ぼんぷ(=ぼんぶ) ordinary man; *Buddhism* common mortal
凡人 ぼんじん (man of) mediocrity, ordinary person
凡俗 ぼんぞく mediocrity, commonplaceness; (man of) mediocrity, ordinary person
凡フライ ぼんふらい easy fly (in baseball)
凡試合 ぼんしあい dull game (of baseball)
平凡な へいぼんな common, ordinary, commonplace, mediocre
非凡な ひぼんな rare, unique, extraordinary

套 ▷trite
トウ   Ⓚ1959

trite, outdated, conventional
常套手段 じょうとうしゅだん old trick, usual practice
常套句 じょうとうく cliche, hackneyed expression
旧套 きゅうとう conventionalism, old style

organ
臓　器　官

臓 ▷**internal organ**
ゾウ ⓚ1022

[original meaning] **internal organ, viscus**
- 臓器 ぞうき internal organs, viscera
- 臓物 ぞうもつ entrails, giblets
- 内臓 ないぞう viscera, internal organs
- 心臓 しんぞう heart
- 肝臓 かんぞう liver
- 五臓 ごぞう the five viscera (liver, lungs, heart, kidneys and spleen)

器 ▷**organ**
キ うつわ ⓚ2368

[also suffix] **organ (of the body)**
- 器官 きかん (body) organ
- 臓器 ぞうき internal organs, viscera
- 呼吸器 こきゅうき respiratory organs
- 消化器 しょうかき digestive organs

官 ▷**organ**
カン ⓚ1912

organ (of the body)
- 官能 かんのう bodily function; fleshly sense, carnal desire
- 器官 きかん (body) organ
- 五官 ごかん the five organs (of sense)

organize
組　結　編

組 ▷**organize**
ソ く(む) くみ -ぐみ ⓚ1224

organize, form, arrange, unite
- 組織する そしきする organize, form, set up; constitute, construct
- 組成 そせい composition, formation, construction
- 組閣する そかくする form a cabinet, organize a ministry

結 ▷**form**
ケツ むす(ぶ) ゆ(う) ゆ(わえる) ⓚ1235

form (an organization), organize, set up
- 結成する けっせいする form, organize
- 結構 けっこう structure, construction; quite, well enough, fairly well; all right; no thank you

結社 けっしゃ association, society, fraternity
結団する けつだんする form into an organization

編 ▷**put together**
ヘン あ(む) -あ(み) ⓚ1270

(bring together and arrange) **put together, compile, organize, form, arrange**
- 編制する へんせいする organize, form
- 編曲 へんきょく arrangement (of a melody)
- 編入する へんにゅうする include, incorporate; admit
- 改編する かいへんする reorganize, remodel

organized bodies
会　協　団　体　組
労　連　講　院

会 ▷**society**
カイ エ あ(う) あ(わせる) ⓚ1741

ⓐ [also suffix] **society, association, club, circle, guild**
ⓑ suffix after names of societies or clubs
- *a* 会社 かいしゃ company, corporation, firm
- 会員 かいいん member
- 協会 きょうかい association, society
- 社会 しゃかい society, the world
- 同好会 どうこうかい association of like-minded persons; club
- *b* イエズス会 いえずすかい Society of Jesus

協 ▷**association**
キョウ ⓚ0074

[also suffix] **abbrev. of** 協会 きょうかい **or** 協同組合 きょうどうくみあい: **association, cooperative**
- 協会 きょうかい association, society
- 世界ボクシング協 せかいぼくしんぐきょう World Boxing Association
- 農協 のうきょう agricultural cooperative
- 生協 せいきょう cooperative association [society]
- 日米協 にちべいきょう Japan United States Cultural Exchange Association

団 ▷**body**
ダン トン ⓚ2628

(organized entity) **body, corporation, organization, association**
- 公団 こうだん public corporation
- 劇団 げきだん dramatic company, theatrical troupe
- 師団 しだん army division
- 社団 しゃだん corporation, association
- 財団 ざいだん foundation, consortium, endowment; syndicate

軍団 ぐんだん army corps, corps
経団連(=経済団体連合会) けいだんれん(=けいざいだんたいれんごうかい) Federation of Economic Organizations

体 ▷body
タイ テイ からだ　　　Ⓚ0055

(organized entity) **body, organization**

団体 だんたい group, party, body, corps; corporation, organization
自治体 じちたい self-governing body [community]
組織体 そしきたい body, organization

組 ▷union
ソ く(む) くみ -ぐみ　　　Ⓚ1224

abbrev. of 組合 くみあい **union**

日教組 にっきょうそ Japan Teachers Union
労組 ろうそ labor union
職組 しょくそ employees' union

労 ▷workers' union
ロウ　　　Ⓚ2205

abbrev. of 労働組合 ろうどうくみあい or 労働者 ろうどうしゃ **workers' union, labor union, labor, laborer**

労資 ろうし capital and labor
労相 ろうしょう Labor Minister
国労 こくろう National Railway Workers' Union

連 ▷federation
レン つら(なる) つら(ねる) つ(れる) -づ(れ)　　　Ⓚ2672

federation, union, alliance, league

ソ連 それん Soviet Union
国連 こくれん United Nations
全学連 ぜんがくれん All-Japan Federation of Student Self-Government Associations

講 ▷fraternity
コウ　　　Ⓚ1463

ⓐ **fraternity, religious association**
ⓑ **mutual financing association**

a 講社 こうしゃ religious association, fraternity
講中 こうじゅう religious association (of non-Christians); club
b 恵比須講 えびすこう fête in honor of *Ebisu*
頼母子講 たのもしこう mutual financing association

院 ▷institution
イン　　　Ⓚ0410

[also suffix] institution or organization, esp.:
ⓐ medical institution: **hospital, clinic, doctor's office**
ⓑ educational institution: **academy, institute, school**

a 院長 いんちょう hospital director; academy president
病院 びょういん hospital
医院 いいん clinic
入院する にゅういんする be hospitalized
退院 たいいん discharge from a hospital
養老院 ようろういん institution for the aged
b 院生 いんせい graduate student
学院 がくいん institute, academy
孤児院 こじいん orphanage
大学院 だいがくいん graduate school
美容院 びよういん beauty shop [parlor]

original
素　原　本　初

素 ▷primary
ソス　　　Ⓚ2171

ⓐ [also prefix] **primary, elemental, fundamental, original, primordial**
ⓑ math **prime**

a 素質 そしつ character, nature, makings, constitution
素因 そいん basic factor, predisposition
素粒子 そりゅうし elementary particle
b 素数 そすう prime (number)
素体 そたい prime field
素因数 そいんすう prime factor

原 ▷original
ゲン はら　　　Ⓚ2593

[also prefix] **original, primary, primitive**

原因 げんいん cause, origin
原則 げんそく principle, general rule
原作 げんさく original (work)
原子 げんし atom
原案 げんあん original bill [plan]
原始 げんし primitive; primeval
原始的な げんしてきな primitive, primeval
原色 げんしょく primary color
原告 げんこく plaintiff
原判決 げんはんけつ original decision [judgment]
原書 げんしょ the original (work)
原点 げんてん starting point, origin
原稿用紙 げんこうようし manuscript paper; writing pad

本 ▷original
ホン もと　　　Ⓚ2937

original, inherent, inborn

本質 ほんしつ essence, reality

本能 ほんのう instinct
本国 ほんごく one's native country, fatherland
本場 ほんば home, habitat, center

初 ▷first
ショ はじ(め) はじ(めて) はつ うい–
–そ(める) –ぞ(め) ⓚ1031
see also →**FIRST**

ⓐ first, initial, original
ⓑ [prefix] first

a 初回 しょかい first time; first inning
初日 しょにち first day, opening day
初版 しょはん first edition
初代 しょだい first generation, founder
初任給 しょにんきゅう initial salary
初志 しょし original aim [intention]
b 初対面 しょたいめん first meeting

other
他　余　別

他 ▷other
タ ほか ⓚ0023

[also prefix] **other, another**

他方 たほう other side [hand]
他意 たい other intention, secret purpose, ulterior motive
他人 たにん another person, other people; stranger
他国 たこく foreign countries, another province
他年 たねん some other year, some day
他府県 たふけん other prefectures
他者 たしゃ another person, other people
他面 ためん other side; while, whereas; on the other hand

余 ▷other
ヨ あま(る) あま(り) あま(す) ⓚ1757

other, another, additional

余所 よそ another place, strange parts
余罪 よざい other crimes [charges]
余儀無い よぎない unavoidable, inevitable
余録 よろく additional gain
余談 よだん digression

別 ▷another
ベツ わか(れる) ⓚ1032

[also prefix] **another, different, distinct**

別個の べっこの another, different; separate
別種 べっしゅ another kind, distinct species
別人 べつじん another [different] person
別名 べつめい alias, another name

別世界 べっせかい another world [planet]
別問題 べつもんだい another question [problem]

outside
外　表　面

外 ▷outside
ガイ ゲ そと ほか はず(す)
はず(れる) ⓚ0163

ⓐ (outer side) **outside, exterior; out, outer**
ⓑ [also suffix] (beyond the boundary) **outside, without, beyond**

a 外部の がいぶの outside, outer, external
外野 がいや outfield; outsiders
外角 がいかく outside corner; external angle
外見 がいけん outward appearance
外科 げか (department of) surgery
外出 がいしゅつ going out, outing
外食する がいしょくする eat out
外気 がいき open [fresh] air
外面 がいめん exterior, outside, surface
b 意外な いがいな unexpected, unforeseen, surprising
郊外 こうがい suburbs, outskirts
案外 あんがい contrary to one's expectations, unexpectedly
以外に いがいに except for, excluding
内外 ないがい inside and outside; approximately
海外 かいがい overseas, abroad
...の範囲外に …のはんいがいに beyond the scope of…
予想外の よそうがいの unexpected, unforeseen

表 ▷surface
ヒョウ おもて あらわ(す)
あらわ(れる) ⓚ2151

surface, face, exterior, outside

表面 ひょうめん surface, face, outside; appearance
表紙 ひょうし cover, binding
表皮 ひょうひ epidermis; bark, rind
表裏 ひょうり front and rear, both sides (of a thing or matter); duplicity
表記する ひょうきする write, express in writing; write on a surface
地表 ちひょう surface of the earth, ground surface
意表 いひょう limits of one's expectation

面 ▷face
メン おも おもて つら ⓚ1796

(outer surface) **face, surface, side**

地面 じめん surface, ground, land
月面 げつめん lunar surface

349

outside

overturn
覆 翻 反 顛 転 倒 轢

覆 ▷overturn
フク おお(う) くつがえ(す)
くつがえ(る)　　Ⓚ2376

overturn, upset, turn over
覆没する ふくぼつする capsize and sink
覆水盆に返らず ふくすいぼんにかえらず It is no use crying over spilt milk
転覆する てんぷくする overturn, turn over, upset; overthrow

翻 ▷turn over
ホン ひるがえ(る) ひるがえ(す)　　Ⓚ1676

turn over, reverse
翻倒する ほんとうする [rare] turn upside-down
翻意する ほんいする change one's mind
翻然と ほんぜんと suddenly

反 ▷turn over
ハン ホン タン そ(る) そ(らす)　　Ⓚ2549

[original meaning] **turn over, reverse**
反転する はんてんする turn around, reverse, roll over
反側する はんそくする turn over in bed

顛 ▷turn [roll] over
テン　　Ⓚ1635

[now usu. 転] [original meaning] **turn over, roll over, tumble down, fall**
顛倒する てんとうする tumble, fall down; invert, reverse; upset
顛落 てんらく fall, spill; degradation
顛覆する てんぷくする overturn, turn over, upset; overthrow
七顛八倒する しちてんばっとう(=しってんばっとう)する toss oneself about in great pain

転 ▷turn [roll] over
テン ころ(がる) ころ(げる) ころ(がす)
ころ(ぶ)　　Ⓚ1346

[formerly also 顛] **turn over, roll over, tumble down, fall over**
転倒する てんとうする tumble, fall down; invert, reverse; upset
転落 てんらくする fall off, tumble down
転覆する てんぷくする overturn, turn over, upset; overthrow

七転八倒する しちてんばっとう(しってんばっとう)する toss oneself about in great pain

倒 ▷topple
トウ たお(れる) −だお(れ)
たお(す)　　Ⓚ0106

cause to topple, overturn, overthrow, knock down
倒産 とうさん insolvency, bankruptcy; breech birth
倒閣する とうかくする overthrow the cabinet
倒幕 とうばく overthrowing the shogunate
打倒する だとうする overthrow, knock down, defeat

轢 ▷run over
レキ ひ(く)

[original meaning] **run over (with a vehicle), knock down**
轢死 れきし being killed by a train or automobile
轢断する れきだんする cut in two under train wheels

palace
宮 殿 閤

宮 ▷royal palace
キュウ グウ ク みや　　Ⓚ1964

ⓐ royal palace, imperial palace, magnificent dwelling
ⓑ suffix after names of palaces
a 宮殿 きゅうでん palace (of a royal person)
　王宮 おうきゅう King's palace, royal palace
　離宮 りきゅう detached palace, Imperial villa
　迷宮 めいきゅう labyrinth, maze; mystery
　竜宮 りゅうぐう Palace of the Dragon King
b エリゼ宮 えりぜきゅう Élysée

殿 ▷palace
デン テン との −どの　　Ⓚ1593

(residence of nobility) **palace, shrine, temple**
殿中で でんちゅうで in the palace
御殿 ごてん palace
宮殿 きゅうでん palace (of a royal person)
神殿 しんでん shrine, sanctuary

閤 ▷feudal palace
コウ　　Ⓚ2843

feudal palace
閤下 こうか [archaic] Your [His] Excellency
太閤 たいこう father of the imperial adviser; Toyotomi Hideyoshi

社会面 しゃかいめん local news page, city news
page
二面 にめん second page (of a newspaper)

parents
親　父　母

▷parent
シン　おや　した(しい)　した(しむ)　Ⓚ1599

parent
親権 しんけん parental authority
親子 しんし(=おやこ) parent and child
両親 りょうしん parents

父 ▷father
フ ちち　Ⓚ1714

(male parent) **father**
父母 ふぼ father and mother, parents
父兄 ふけい one's father and older brothers; guardians
父子 ふし father and child
祖父 そふ grandfather

母 ▷mother
ボ はは　Ⓚ2917

[original meaning] (female parent) **mother**
母子 ぼし mother and child
母乳 ぼにゅう mother's milk
母音 ぼいん vowel ("mother sound")
母細胞 ぼさいぼう mother cell
父母 ふぼ father and mother, parents
祖母 そぼ grandmother
聖母 せいぼ Holy Mother, Virgin Mary

part
分　部　局　片

▷part
ブン　フン　ブ　わ(ける)　わ(け)　わ(かれる)
わ(かる)　わ(かつ)　Ⓚ1713

ⓐ (segment of a whole) **part, division, section, piece**
ⓑ [also suffix] (equal portion of a whole) **part, fraction**
ⓒ (constituent element) **part, component**
ⓓ [also suffix] (allotted portion) **part, share, portion,
ration, helping**
ⓐ 分量 ぶんりょう quantity
部分 ぶぶん part, section, portion
半分 はんぶん half
積分 せきぶん integral calculus, integration

---

paper
紙　葉　丁　箋　頁　面

紙 ▷paper
シ かみ　Ⓚ1197

ⓐ [also suffix] [original meaning] **paper**
ⓑ **paper bearing writing**
ⓐ 紙幣 しへい paper currency, bank note, bill
白紙 はくし blank sheet, flyleaf; clean slate
用紙 ようし blank form, stationery
製紙 せいし paper manufacture
表紙 ひょうし cover, binding
包装紙 ほうそうし wrapping paper
ⓑ 紙面 しめん space (on a printed page)
紙上計画 しじょうけいかく paper plan

葉 ▷leaf
ヨウ は　Ⓚ2024

(sheet of paper) **leaf, sheet, page, paper**
薄葉 うすよう Japanese tissue
前葉 ぜんよう preceding page [leaf]

丁 ▷sheet
チョウ テイ　Ⓚ2851

**sheet or leaf, esp. of books bound in the Japanese
style**
丁数 ちょうすう number of pages; paging
丁付け ちょうづけ pagination, numbering
落丁 らくちょう missing page [leaf]

箋 ▷piece of paper
セン　Ⓚ2360

piece of paper, label
便箋 びんせん letter paper, stationery, writing
paper
付箋 ふせん tag, label, sticky note
用箋 ようせん stationery, writing paper
処方箋 しょほうせん prescription

頁 ▷page
ケツ ページ　Ⓚ1795

[also suffix] **page, leaf**
頁数 ページすう number of pages
頁付け ページづけ pagination
余白頁 よはくページ blank page

面 ▷page (of a newspaper)
メン おも おもて つら　Ⓚ1796

[also suffix] **page (of a newspaper)**
紙面 しめん space (on a printed page)

自分 じぶん self, oneself
b 三分の一 さんぶんのいち one third, a third part
c 分子 ぶんし molecule; numerator
成分 せいぶん ingredient, component, constituent
d 言い分 いいぶん one's say [claim]; objection, complaint
余分 よぶん excess, extra, surplus
取り分 とりぶん one's share, portion
四人分 よにんぶん four helpings [servings]
一年分 いちねんぶん a year's supply

部 ▷section
ブ @1498

[also suffix] **section, part, category, division, region**
部分 ぶぶん part, section, portion
部品 ぶひん parts, accessories
部門 ぶもん class, group, division, department, section; genus
部類 ぶるい class, category, division
一部 いちぶ part, portion, section; a copy (of a book)
北部 ほくぶ north, northern part
全部 ぜんぶ all, the whole; wholly, entirely
内部 ないぶ interior, inner parts
上部 じょうぶ upper part [section], top; surface
中央部 ちゅうおうぶ central part
心臓部 しんぞうぶ region of the heart
第三部 だいさんぶ Section 3

局 ▷limited part
キョク @2636

limited part, portion (of space), locality
局限する きょくげんする localize, limit, set limits to
局部 きょくぶ limited part, section; affected part
局所 きょくしょ (limited) part, section
局地的 きょくちてき local

片 ▷fragment
ヘン かた- @2910

[also suffix] **fragment, (flat thin) piece, slice, chip, flake**
片雲 へんうん scattered clouds
断片 だんぺん fragment, piece
破片 はへん fragment, broken piece, scrap
木片 もくへん block, chip [piece] of wood
一片 いっぺん piece, bit, fragment, scrap
雪片 せっぺん snowflake
紙片 しへん piece [scrap, bit] of paper
金属片 きんぞくへん piece of metal

part company
別　　離　　訣

別 ▷separate
ベツ わか(れる) @1032

[original meaning] (part company) **separate, part from, be separated**
別離 べつり separation, parting
別居 べっきょ separation, limited divorce
別辞 べつじ farewell address, parting words

離 ▷separate
リ はな(れる) はな(す) @1663

(part company) **separate, part from, be separated**
離別する りべつする part from, be separated from; divorce
会者定離 えしゃじょうり Those who meet must part

訣 ▷separate
ケツ @1336

separate, part, bid farewell
訣別 けつべつ separation, farewell
永訣 えいけつ last farewell

participate and join
参　　与　　加　　入

参 ▷participate
サン シン まい(る) @1778

participate, take part in, join in
参加する さんかする participate, join, take part in
参謀 さんぼう staff officer, the staff; adviser, counselor
参事 さんじ councilor, secretary
参議院 さんぎいん House of Councilors, Upper House
参戦 さんせん participation in a war
参与 さんよ participation (in public affairs); counselor, consultant

与 ▷take part in
ヨ あた(える) @2887

take part in, participate in, side with
与党 よとう party in power
与野党 よやとう both parties, parties in and out of power
与国 よこく ally

参与する さんよする participate in, take part in
関与する かんよする take part in, participate in, be concerned in

加 ▷join
カ くわ(える) くわ(わる)   Ⓚ0024

join, take part in, participate
加盟 かめい participation, affiliation
加入金 かにゅうきん admission fee
加担(=荷担) かたん assistance, support, participation
参加する さんかする participate, join, take part in

入 ▷enter
ニュウ い(る) -い(り) い(れる) -い(れ) はい(る)   Ⓚ2859

(become a member of) **enter, join, be admitted**
入学する にゅうがくする enter a school, matriculate
入門する にゅうもんする become a pupil of, enter a private school
入閣する にゅうかくする join the Cabinet, become a Cabinet member
入賞 にゅうしょう winning a prize
入選する にゅうせんする be accepted, be selected
加入する かにゅうする enter, join

particle
粒 子 核

粒 ▷grain
リュウ つぶ   Ⓚ1213

ⓐ (small particulate mass) **grain, granule**
ⓑ *phys* **grain, particle**
ⓒ **counter for grains**
a 粒子 りゅうし particle, grain
　粒状の りゅうじょうの granular
　顆粒 かりゅう granule
b 粒度 りゅうど particle size, grain size
　粒径 りゅうけい grain [particle] diameter
　粒界 りゅうかい grain boundary
　素粒子 そりゅうし elementary particle
c 米十粒 こめじゅうりゅう ten grains of rice

子 ▷particle suffix
シ ス こ -(つ)こ   Ⓚ2872

small entities such as particles, esp. nuclear particles
粒子 りゅうし particle, grain
原子 げんし atom
電子 でんし electron
遺伝子 いでんし gene

晶子 しょうし crystallite

核 ▷nucleus
カク   Ⓚ0836

ⓐ (central part of an atom) **nucleus**
ⓑ **nuclear, atomic**
a 核反応 かくはんのう nuclear reaction
　核融合 かくゆうごう nuclear fusion
　原子核 げんしかく atomic nucleus
b 核エネルギー かくえねるぎー nuclear energy
　核兵器 かくへいき nuclear weapons

parties and sects
党 閥 流 派 翼 系 門 宗

党 ▷party
トウ   Ⓚ2236

ⓐ (political group) **party, political party, faction**
ⓑ **suffix after names of political parties**
a 党員 とういん party member
　党首 とうしゅ party chief [leader]
　党大会 とうたいかい party convention
　党派 とうは party, faction, clique
　政党 せいとう political party
　野党 やとう opposition party
　粛党 しゅくとう purging disloyal elements from a party
b 共和党 きょうわとう Republican Party
　社会党 しゃかいとう Socialist Party

閥 ▷clique
バツ   Ⓚ2839

[also suffix] **clique, clan, power group**
派閥 はばつ clique, faction, coterie
財閥 ざいばつ financial clique [combine], *zaibatsu*
学閥 がくばつ academic clique, academic cliquism
軍閥 ぐんばつ military clique
藩閥 はんばつ clan favoritism, clanship
薩摩閥 さつまばつ Satsuma clan

流 ▷school
リュウ ル なが(れる) なが(れ) なが(す)   Ⓚ0400

[also suffix] **school, style, system**
流派 りゅうは school
流儀 りゅうぎ school, style, system, method
草月流 そうげつりゅう Sogetsu school of flower arrangement

派 ▷sect
ハ

ⓐ [also suffix] **sect, faction, party; school; clique, group**
ⓑ religious sect, denomination

- a 派閥 はばつ clique, faction, coterie
  - 一派 いっぱ sect, denomination; school; party
  - 党派 とうは party, faction, clique
  - 左派 さは left wing, left faction
  - 流派 りゅうは school
  - 学派 がくは school, sect
  - 古典派 こてんは the classical school
  - 田中派 たなかは Tanaka faction
- b 宗派 しゅうは religious sect, denomination
  - 真宗大谷派 しんしゅうおおたには Otani sect of Shinshu

翼 ▷wing
ヨク つばさ

Ⓚ2373

(political) **wing, faction**; (army) **wing, flank**

- 左翼 さよく left wing [flank]; left wing [faction]; left field
- 両翼 りょうよく both flanks; two wings

系 ▷faction
ケイ

Ⓚ1701

[suffix] **faction, clique, group**

- 左派系 さはけい left faction
- 田中系の政治家 たなかけいのせいじか politician of the Tanaka faction [clique]

門 ▷(religious) sect
モン かど

Ⓚ0789

(religious) **sect, branch, school**

- 門徒 もんと sectarian, follower, believer
- 破門 はもん excommunication, expulsion
- 宗門 しゅうもん religious sect
- 禅門 ぜんもん Zen sect
- 稲門 とうもん Waseda University

宗 ▷religious sect (esp. Buddhist)
シュウ ソウ

Ⓚ1915

ⓐ religious sect (esp. Buddhist), denomination
ⓑ suffix after names of religious sects

- a 宗派 しゅうは religious sect, denomination
  - 宗旨 しゅうし tenets of a religious sect; (religious) sect
- b 浄土宗 じょうどしゅう *Jodo* sect (of Buddhism)
  - 天台宗 てんだいしゅう *Tendai* sect (of Buddhism)

parts of boats and ships

舵 梶 櫓 櫂 舷 艙

舵 ▷steering device
ダ かじ

Ⓚ1226

ⓐ rudder
ⓑ helm, tiller, wheel

- a 方向舵 ほうこうだ rudder
  - 昇降舵 しょうこうだ *aeronautics* elevator
- b 舵手 だしゅ helmsman, coxswain
  - 操舵 そうだ steering

梶 ▷steering device
ビ かじ

Ⓚ0866

steering device:

ⓐ [usu. 舵] **rudder**
ⓑ [usu. 舵] **helm, tiller, wheel**
ⓒ oar
ⓓ shafts (of a rickshaw)

- a 梶木(=梶木鮪) かじき(=かじきまぐろ) marlin, sword-fish
- b 梶棒 かじぼう shafts (of a rickshaw or similar vehicle), thills

櫓 ▷scull
ロ やぐら

Ⓚ1018

scull

- 櫓櫂 ろかい sculls and paddles
- 櫓杭 ろぐい fulcrum peg (in a traditional oarlock)

櫂 ▷oar
トウ かい

Ⓚ1015

oar, paddle

- 櫂歌(=棹歌) とうか boat song, barcarole

舷 ▷gunwale
ゲン

Ⓚ1227

gunwale

- 舷窓 げんそう porthole
- 舷側 げんそく ship's side, broadside
- 舷梯 げんてい gangway (ladder)
- 右舷 うげん starboard
- 乾舷 かんげん freeboard (of a ship)
- 登舷礼 とうげんれい ceremonial assembling of a ship's crew on deck

艙 ▷ship's hold
ソウ

[now replaced by 倉] **ship's hold, cabin**
艙口 そうこう hatch, hatchway
船艙 せんそう hold (of a ship), hatch

parts of governments
閣　省

閣 ▷cabinet
カク　　　　　　　　　　　　Ⓚ2841

cabinet (of a government)
閣僚 かくりょう cabinet members
閣議 かくぎ cabinet conference
内閣 ないかく cabinet

省 ▷ministry
セイ ショウ かえり(みる) はぶ(く)　Ⓚ2164

[also suffix] **ministry, government department [office]**
省庁 しょうちょう Ministries and Agencies
省令 しょうれい Ministerial ordinance
同省 どうしょう the said Ministry
文部省 もんぶしょう Ministry of Education, Science and Culture
大蔵省 おおくらしょう Ministry of Finance

parts of periodicals
欄　面

欄 ▷column
ラン　　　　　　　　　　　　Ⓚ1023

column (as of a newspaper or periodical), section, page
本欄 ほんらん this column
広告欄 こうこくらん advertisement column
スポーツ欄 すぽーつらん sports section [page]

面 ▷page (of a newspaper)
メン おも おもて つら　　　Ⓚ1796

[also suffix] **page (of a newspaper)**
紙面 しめん space (on a printed page)
社会面 しゃかいめん local news page, city news page
二面 にめん second page (of a newspaper)

parts of plays
幕　場

幕 ▷act
マク バク　　　　　　　　　Ⓚ2044

ⓐ theater
ⓑ act, scene
ⓒ counter for acts
a 開幕 かいまく rising of the curtain; opening scene of a play
　序幕 じょまく opening act, curtain raiser
　終幕 しゅうまく end, close, curtainfall
b 第三幕 だいさんまく Act 3

場 ▷scene
ジョウ ば　　　　　　　　　Ⓚ0512

theater **scene**
場面 ばめん scene; situation
二幕三場 にまくさんば Act 2, Scene 3

parts of towns
区　街　町　丁　字

区 ▷ward
ク　　　　　　　　　　　　　Ⓚ2559

ⓐ (major subdivision of a city, esp. in Japan) **ward, municipal [urban] district, borough**
ⓑ suffix after names of wards or municipal districts
ⓒ counter for wards
a 区役所 くやくしょ ward office
　区長 くちょう ward headman, borough mayor
　区立の くりつの established by the ward
　区会 くかい ward assembly
b 新宿区 しんじゅくく Shinjuku Ward
　クイーンズ区 くいーんずく Queens Borough
c 東京二十三区 とうきょうにじゅうさんく the 23 wards of Tokyo

街 ▷city quarter
ガイ カイ まち　　　　　　　Ⓚ0528

ⓐ [also suffix] **city quarter(s), city center, busy street, shopping center, downtown**
ⓑ suffix after names of shopping centers and arcades
a 街路 がいろ street, road, avenue
　ビル街 びるがい street of big business buildings
　市街 しがい the streets, city, town
　スラム街 すらむがい slum quarters

繁華街 はんかがい business [shopping] quarters; amusement quarters
商店街 しょうてんがい shopping center
中国人街 ちゅうごくじんがい Chinatown
住宅街 じゅうたくがい residential quarter
歓楽街 かんらくがい amusement center [quarter]
b 銀天街 ぎんてんがい Gintengai Shopping Center

町 ▷town section (*cho*)
チョウ まち　　Ⓚ1028

ⓐ (subdivision in the Japanese addressing system) **town section, *cho***
ⓑ **suffix after names of town sections (*cho*)**
a 町会 ちょうかい town block association
b 一宮町 いちのみやちょう Ichinomiya-cho

丁 ▷town subsection (*chome*)
チョウ テイ　　Ⓚ2851

(minor subdivision in the Japanese addressing system) **town subsection, *chome*, subsection of a** 町 ちょう **(town section)**
二丁目 にちょうめ 2-chome
国府町三丁目 こくふちょうさんちょうめ 3-chome, Kokufu-cho

字 ▷village or town section
ジ あざ　　Ⓚ1860

village or town section in the Japanese addressing system
大字片山 おおあざかたやま name of a town section

parts of writing
章 段 節 款 条 項 目 箇

章 ▷chapter
ショウ　　Ⓚ1819

[also suffix] (division of text) **chapter**
章句 しょうく passage, chapter and verse
章節 しょうせつ chapter and verse
第一章 だいいっしょう Chapter 1

段 ▷passage
ダン　　Ⓚ1059

passage (of a text or music), paragraph
段落 だんらく end of paragraph; conclusion

節 ▷paragraph
セツ セチ ふし -ぶし　　Ⓚ2349

[also suffix] (subdivision, as of a text) **paragraph, passage, section, part**
章節 しょうせつ chapter and verse

第二節 だいにせつ Paragraph 2
小節 しょうせつ bar, measure

款 ▷article
カン　　Ⓚ151◆

ⓐ **article, item, subsection**
ⓑ **counter for articles or subsections**
a 定款 ていかん articles of association, company contract
約款 やっかん article, stipulation, provision, clause
条款 じょうかん article, stipulation, provision, clause
b 第二款 だいにかん Article 2

条 ▷article
ジョウ　　Ⓚ188◆

ⓐ **article, item, section, clause**
ⓑ (written regulations) **articles (of law), provision, stipulation, rule, law**
ⓒ **counter for articles or sections**
a 条項 じょうこう articles (and clauses), terms
条目 じょうもく article, stipulation
条件 じょうけん condition; item, proviso
箇条書きする かじょうがきする itemize
信条 しんじょう principle, creed, article of a religion◆
教条 きょうじょう tenet, dogma
b 条文 じょうぶん text (of a regulation), provision
条約 じょうやく treaty
条例 じょうれい regulations, rules, law
前条 ぜんじょう preceding article
c 憲法第九条 けんぽうだいきゅうじょう Article 9 of the constitution
百三条 ひゃくさんじょう 103 articles (of a constitution)

項 ▷clause
コウ　　Ⓚ052◆

[also suffix] **clause, subsection, item, paragraph**
項目 こうもく clause, item, provision
事項 じこう matters, facts; articles, items
別項 べっこう separate paragraph, another clause
要項 ようこう important points; gist
条項 じょうこう articles (and clauses), terms
第九条第二項 だいきゅうじょうだいにこう Section 9 Subsection 2

目 ▷item
モク ボク め ま-　　Ⓚ261◆

[also suffix] **item, subdivision, subitem, category**
項目 こうもく clause, item, provision
種目 しゅもく item; event (as a race)
細目 さいもく details, specified items
科目 かもく school subject; subdivision, items

箇 ▷item
カ   ⓚ2356

[sometimes also 個] **item, place**

箇条 かじょう items, articles
箇条書き かじょうがき itemization
不通箇所 ふつうかしょ tied-up places [spots]

pass

通 過 経 疏

通 ▷pass
ツウ ツ とお(る) とお(り)
-どお(り) とお(す) とお(し) -どお(し)
かよ(う)   ⓚ2678

ⓐ [original meaning] **pass (by), pass through**
ⓑ **pass current, pass for**

ⓐ 通過 つうか passing, passage
通行 つうこう passing, passage, transit, traffic
通路 つうろ passage, pathway, alley, aisle
開通する かいつうする be opened to [for] traffic
不通 ふつう impassability, interruption, stoppage, tie-up
ⓑ 通用する つうようする pass, circulate, pass [go] current, hold good
通貨 つうか currency, current money
流通 りゅうつう circulation of money or goods; flow of water; ventilation

過 ▷pass by
カ す(ぎる) -す(ぎ) す(ごす) あやま(つ)
あやま(ち)   ⓚ2704

[original meaning] **pass by, go past, pass through**

過程 かてい process, course
過渡期 かとき transitional period [stage]
通過する つうかする pass through, carry (a resolution)
経過 けいか progress, course, development; lapse, passage
一過性の いっかせいの temporary, transitory

経 ▷pass through
ケイ キョウ へ(る) た(つ)   ⓚ1218

(go through without stopping) **pass through, go through**

経由する けいゆする go via, pass through
神経 しんけい nerve; sensitivity; worry

疏 ▷let pass
ソ ショ   ⓚ1090

let pass, pass

意志の疏通 いしのそつう mutual understanding

pattern

模 文 柄 様 紋

模 ▷pattern (decorative design)
モ ボ   ⓚ0963

(decorative design) **pattern, design, figure**

模様 もよう pattern, design; appearance, circumstances
規模 きぼ scale, scope

文 ▷decorative pattern
ブン モン ふみ   ⓚ1708

[also suffix] [original meaning] **decorative pattern, figure, design**

文様 もんよう pattern, design
縄文 じょうもん straw-rope pattern
渦状文 かじょうもん spiral pattern

柄 ▷pattern (on cloth)
ヘイ がら え   ⓚ0799

[in compounds] **pattern (on cloth), design, figure**

柄物 がらもの patterned cloth
花柄 はながら flower pattern

様 ▷pattern
ヨウ さま   ⓚ0969

pattern, figure

模様 もよう pattern, design; appearance, circumstances
文様 もんよう pattern, design

紋 ▷figure
モン   ⓚ1194

[original meaning] **figure (on a surface), design, pattern, lines on a surface**

紋織り もんおり figured textiles
波紋 はもん ripple; stir, sensation
風紋 ふうもん wind-wrought pattern on the sands

pawn

質 当

質 ▷pawn
シツ シチ チ   ⓚ2445

(thing serving as security) **pawn, pledge**

質屋 しちや pawnshop
質草 しちぐさ article for pawning

質入れ しちいれ pawning

当 ▷pawn
トウ あ(たる) あ(たり) あ(てる)
あ(て)　　　　　　　　Ⓚ1865

pawn, mortgage
抵当 ていとう mortgage, security

払 ▷pay
フツ はら(う) –はら(い) –ばら(い) Ⓚ0171

(clear a debt) **pay, settle accounts**
払い はらい payment; account, bill
払い戻す はらいもどす pay back
払い込む はらいこむ pay in, pay up
勘定を払う かんじょうをはらう pay a bill, settle
　　one's account

納 ▷pay (to the authorities)
ノウ ナッ– ナ ナン トウ おさ(める)
おさ(まる)　　　　　　Ⓚ1195

pay to the authorities, make payment
納税 のうぜい tax payment
納入 のうにゅう payment; delivery
納付 のうふ payment; delivery
納期 のうき payment date; delivery date
滞納 たいのう nonpayment, delinquency (in
　　payment)
未納の みのうの unpaid, in arrears
分納 ぶんのう payment in installments; installment
　　delivery
返納する へんのうする return (to the authorities),
　　restore

済 ▷settle accounts
サイ す(む) –ず(み) す(まない) す(ます)
す(ませる)　　　　　　Ⓚ0478

settle accounts, pay back, clear
返済する へんさいする repay, reimburse
決済 けっさい settlement of accounts
弁済 べんさい repayment, payment, settlement
既済の きさいの paid up, already settled

支 ▷pay out
シ ささ(える)　　　　　Ⓚ1717

pay out, disburse, defray
支出 ししゅつ expenditure, disbursement, outgo
支払う しはらう pay

収支 しゅうし incomings and outgoings, earnings
　　and expenses

賦 ▷installment
フ　　　　　　　　　　Ⓚ1432

installment, payment by installment
賦払い ぶばらい installment system, easy payment
　　plan
月賦 げっぷ monthly installments
割賦 かっぷ(=わっぷ) payment by installments

償 ▷recompense
ショウ つぐな(う)　　　Ⓚ0155

(meet by payment) **recompense, pay**
償還 しょうかん repayment, refunding, reimburse-
　　ment
無償 むしょう gratuitous, free

給 ▷pay
キュウ　　　　　　　　Ⓚ123

[also suffix] **pay, salary, wages**
給料 きゅうりょう salary, pay, wages
給与 きゅうよ allowance, grant; pay, salary
給付する きゅうふする make a presentation, grant,
　　pay
月給 げっきゅう monthly pay [salary]
俸給 ほうきゅう salary, pay
時間給 じかんきゅう payment by the hour
固定給 こていきゅう regular pay, fixed salary
初任給 しょにんきゅう initial salary

賃 ▷wage
チン　　　　　　　　　Ⓚ2350

wage, wages, salary, pay
賃上げ ちんあげ wage increase
労賃 ろうちん wages, pay
工賃 こうちん wage, wages, pay
手間賃 てまちん wages [charge] for labor
最賃法 さいちんほう Minimum Wages Act

料 ▷fee
リョウ　　　　　　　　Ⓚ1187

(payment received for services) **fee, remuneration**
診察料 しんさつりょう consultation fee
給料 きゅうりょう salary, pay, wages

俸 ▷salary
ホウ   Ⓚ0096

salary, pay

俸給 ほうきゅう salary, pay
俸禄 ほうろく retainer's stipend, official pay [salary]
年俸 ねんぽう annual salary
減俸 げんぽう salary cut
五号俸 ごごうほう fifth grade salary
増俸 ぞうほう increase in salary, raise

禄 ▷retainer's stipend
ロク   Ⓚ0915

(ration of rice paid to samurai in feudal Japan) **retainer's stipend, official pay, fief**

禄高 ろくだか amount of one's fief [stipend]
俸禄 ほうろく retainer's stipend, official pay [salary]
微禄 びろく small stipend

収 ▷income
シュウ おさ(める) おさ(まる)   Ⓚ0016

income, receipts, revenue

収支 しゅうし incomings and outgoings, earnings and expenses
増収 ぞうしゅう increased income [revenue]; increased yield
月収 げっしゅう monthly income
税収 ぜいしゅう yield of taxes, tax revenues

peace
和   安   治

和 ▷peace
ワ オ やわ(らぐ) やわ(らげる) なご(む) なご(やか)   Ⓚ1044

peace

和平 わへい peace
和解する わかいする make peace, come to terms
平和 へいわ peace, harmony
講和 こうわ peace, reconciliation

安 ▷public peace
アン やす(い) やす やす(らか)   Ⓚ1859

public peace, order

治安 ちあん public peace and order
保安 ほあん preservation of public peace
公安 こうあん public peace

治 ▷public order
ジ チ おさ(める) おさ(まる) なお(る) なお(す)   Ⓚ0297

public order, peace

治安 ちあん public peace and order
治乱 ちらん war and peace
治平 ちへい peace and tranquility
退治 たいじ subjugation, subdual; extermination; crusade

peaceful →CALM AND PEACEFUL

penetrate
透   貫   破   滲

透 ▷pass through
トウ す(く) す(かす) す(ける)   Ⓚ2677

(move through something) **pass through, let through, permeate, penetrate**

透過 とうか penetration, transmission
透析 とうせき *chem* dialysis
透磁性 とうじせい magnetic permeability
浸透 しんとう permeation, penetration

貫 ▷penetrate
カン つらぬ(く)   Ⓚ2174

penetrate, pierce through, pass through

貫通する かんつうする penetrate, pierce, pass through
貫流する かんりゅうする flow through
貫入 かんにゅう penetration
縦貫する じゅうかんする run through, traverse
突貫 とっかん (bayonet) charge, rush

破 ▷break through
ハ やぶ(る) やぶ(れる)   Ⓚ1064

break through, penetrate

突破する とっぱする break [smash] through; surmount; exceed
看破する かんぱする see through, penetrate, read (another's thoughts)

滲 ▷permeate
シン し(みる) にじ(む)

[now usu. 浸] [original meaning] **permeate, infiltrate, penetrate; ooze, seep**

滲透する しんとうする permeate, penetrate
滲出 しんしゅつ percolation, exudation, effusion
滲炭鋼 しんたんこう cement steel

people →THE PEOPLE

     penetrate

people
民　族

民 ▷people
ミン たみ　　　　　　　Ⓚ2614

people, nation, race
民族 みんぞく race, people, nation
民衆 みんしゅう populace, the people, the masses
国民 こくみん people, nation; the people
選民 せんみん chosen people

族 ▷race
ゾク　　　　　　　　　　Ⓚ0863

race, clan, tribe
民族 みんぞく race, people, nation
部族 ぶぞく tribe
種族 しゅぞく race, tribe; family, genus; species
蛮族 ばんぞく savage tribe
アリアン族 ありあんぞく Aryan family
アイヌ族 あいぬぞく the Ainu race

perceive
覚　知　感　認

覚 ▷perceive
カク おぼ(える) さ(ます)' さ(める)　Ⓚ2258

perceive, sense, discern, feel, be conscious; realize, know, comprehend
覚悟 かくご readiness, preparedness; resignation; resolution
知覚 ちかく perception, sensation
自覚する じかくする be conscious of, realize

知 ▷know
チ し(る) し(らせる) し(れる)　Ⓚ1041

know, be aware of, understand; perceive, recognize
知識 ちしき knowledge
知覚 ちかく perception, sensation
周知の しゅうちの known to all, universally known
承知する しょうちする consent [agree] to; permit; forgive; know, understand
探知 たんち detection

感 ▷feel
カン　　　　　　　　　　Ⓚ2468

feel, perceive
感覚 かんかく sense, sensation, feeling
感知する かんちする perceive, become aware of

感応作用 かんのうさよう induction
共感する きょうかんする sympathize with, feel sympathy (for)
実感する じっかんする feel actually; realize, experience personally

認 ▷recognize
ニン みと(める)　　　　Ⓚ1404

[original meaning] (be aware of something perceived)
recognize, perceive, identify
認識 にんしき cognition, perception; understanding
誤認 ごにん mistake, misconception, misunderstanding
確認 かくにん confirmation, ascertainment

perforators
針　串　杭　釘

針 ▷needle
シン はり　　　　　　　Ⓚ1488
see also →NEEDLE

ⓐ [original meaning] **needle**
ⓑ **needle-shaped object as the hand of clock or pointer of an instrument**
a 運針 うんしん handling of a needle
b 針葉樹 しんようじゅ conifer
長針 ちょうしん long [minute] hand
秒針 びょうしん second hand
指針 ししん compass needle; indicator, pointer; hand; guiding principle
磁針 じしん magnetic needle
検針 けんしん inspection of a meter
羅針盤 らしんばん compass
避雷針 ひらいしん lightning rod

串 ▷skewer
くし　　　　　　　　　　Ⓚ2973

skewer, spit
串焼き くしやき grilling on a skewer; grilled skewered food
串刺し くしざし skewered
竹串 たけぐし bamboo skewer

杭 ▷stake
コウ くい　　　　　　　Ⓚ0763

stake, post, pile, picket
支持杭 しじこう bearing pile

釘 ▷**nail**
テイ くぎ   Ⓚ1489

nail
   釘頭 ていとう nailhead

performance
劇   演   芸

劇 ▷**drama**
ゲキ   Ⓚ1681

[also suffix] **drama, play, theatrical performance**
   劇場 げきじょう theater
   劇団 げきだん dramatic company, theatrical troupe
   劇映画 げきえいが film drama
   劇的な げきてきな dramatic
   演劇 えんげき drama, play
   歌劇 かげき opera
   喜劇 きげき comedy
   悲劇 ひげき tragedy, tragic drama
   時代劇 じだいげき period adventure drama, period
     film

演 ▷**performance**
エン   Ⓚ0630

performance, acting, enactment, play
   開演 かいえん raising the curtain, commencing a
     performance
   共演 きょうえん coacting, costarring
   公演 こうえん public performance
   初演 しょえん first performance, premier

芸 ▷**entertainment**
ゲイ   Ⓚ1892

[also suffix] **entertainment, performance, show
business, acting**
   芸能 げいのう public entertainment
   芸者 げいしゃ geisha girl
   芸名 げいめい stage name
   芸人 げいにん artiste, entertainer
   芸風 げいふう style (of one's performance)
   演芸 えんげい performance, entertainments
   名人芸 めいじんげい masterly performance, virtu-
     osity
   大道芸 だいどうげい street performing

performers
優   俳   伶   伎

優 ▷**actor**
ユウ やさ(しい) すぐ(れる)   Ⓚ0156

actor, actress, performer
   俳優 はいゆう actor, actress
   女優 じょゆう actress
   名優 めいゆう great actor
   声優 せいゆう radio actor; dialogue speaker (in
     dubbing)

俳 ▷**actor**
ハイ   Ⓚ0094

[original meaning] **actor**
   俳優 はいゆう actor, actress

伶 ▷**musician**
レイ   Ⓚ0050

[original meaning] **musician, court musician, performer of court music, minstrel; actor**
   伶人 れいじん minstrel, court musician
   伶官 れいかん court musician
   伶優 れいゆう actor

伎 ▷**performer**
キ ギ   Ⓚ0036

performer, actor
   伎楽 ぎがく ancient mask show
   歌舞伎 かぶき kabuki

periodicals
誌   紙   報

誌 ▷**magazine**
シ   Ⓚ1406

ⓐ [also suffix] **magazine, periodical**
ⓑ **suffix after names of magazines or periodicals**
 a 誌面 しめん page of a magazine
   誌上で しじょうで in a magazine
   雑誌 ざっし magazine, journal
   週刊誌 しゅうかんし weekly magazine
 b ニューズウィーク誌 にゅーずうぃーくし Newsweek

紙 ▷**newspaper**
シ かみ   Ⓚ1197

[also suffix] **newspaper, periodical, publication**

本紙 ほんし this newspaper
日刊紙 にっかんし daily newspaper
地方紙 ちほうし local newspaper

報 ▷bulletin
ホウ むく(いる) むく(う)　　Ⓚ1515

[also suffix] **bulletin, newspaper, magazine**
官報 かんぽう official gazette, official telegram
画報 がほう illustrated magazine
研究所報 けんきゅうしょほう research institute bulletin

periodicals →PARTS OF PERIODICALS

periphery
周　囲　郭　廓

周 ▷periphery
シュウ まわ(り)　　Ⓚ2585

periphery, circumference, perimeter
周囲 しゅうい circumference, periphery; surroundings
周辺 しゅうへん environs, outskirts; circumference
周回 しゅうかい circumference, girth, surroundings
円周 えんしゅう circumference
四周 ししゅう circumference, periphery

囲 ▷circumference
イ かこ(む) かこ(う) かこ(い)　　Ⓚ2643

circumference, surroundings
雰囲気 ふんいき atmosphere, mood
周囲 しゅうい circumference, periphery; surroundings
胸囲 きょうい chest measurement
外囲 がいい surroundings, periphery

郭 ▷outer enclosure
カク　　Ⓚ1499

[original meaning] **outer enclosure [walls], outline, contour**
外郭 がいかく outer block [enclosure]; outline, contour
城郭 じょうかく castle, fortress; castle walls, enclosure
輪郭 りんかく contour, outline, profile
胸郭 きょうかく thorax, chest

廓 ▷outer enclosure
カク くるわ

outer enclosure [walls], outline, contour
外廓 がいかく outer block [enclosure]; outline, contour

輪廓 りんかく contour, outline, profile
城廓 じょうかく castle, fortress; castle walls, enclosure

permit
許　免　准　允

許 ▷permit
キョ ゆる(す)　　Ⓚ133?

[original meaning] **permit, allow, approve, sanction**
許可 きょか permission, approval, authorization
許容する きょようする tolerate, allow, permit
許諾する きょだくする consent, approve, permit

免 ▷license
メン まぬか(れる) まぬが(れる)　　Ⓚ177?

license, permit, grant a request
免許 めんきょ license, permit
免状 めんじょう license, diploma

准 ▷grant permission
ジュン　　Ⓚ010?

grant permission, permit, sanction, authorize, allow
批准 ひじゅん ratification

允 ▷give consent
イン　　Ⓚ171?

give consent, comply, accede to, permit
允可 いんか compliance, permission, assent
允許 いんきょ compliance, permission, assent

person
人　者　方　氏

人 ▷human being
ジン ニン ひと -り -と　　Ⓚ285?

[also suffix] [original meaning] **human being, person, man; people, mankind**
人間 にんげん human being, man; people, mankind
人類 じんるい mankind, humankind
人工の じんこうの artificial
人為 じんい human work, artificiality
人造の じんぞうの artificial, man-made
人民 じんみん the people, populace, subjects
人生 じんせい human life, life
人気 にんき popularity; temperament of the people; business conditions
人名 じんめい personal name

人道主義 じんどうしゅぎ humanitarianism
夫人 ふじん wife, married lady, Mrs.
商人 しょうにん merchant, trader, tradesman
他人 たにん another person, other people; stranger
個人 こじん individual
現代人 げんだいじん modern person [people]

者 ▷person
シャ もの　　　　　　　　　Ⓚ2765

person
弱者 じゃくしゃ weak person, the weak
死者 ししゃ dead person, the deceased

方 ▷person (*honorific*)
ホウ かた -がた -なた　　　　Ⓚ1709

[honorific] **person, gentleman, lady**
方方 かたがた all gentlemen, all people
あの方 あのかた that gentleman [lady], he, she

氏 ▷person (*polite*)
シ うじ　　　　　　　　　　Ⓚ2552

[polite] **person**
某氏 ぼうし a certain person
同氏 どうし the said person, he
無名氏 むめいし anonymous person, a nobody

personal relations
縁 交 好 仲 誼 絆

縁 ▷relation
エン ふち　　　　　　　　　Ⓚ1269

relation (between persons), affinity, personal relations, connection, relationship
縁故 えんこ relation, connection; relative
腐れ縁 くされえん unhappy yet inseparable relation; fatal bonds
因縁 いんねん connection, affinity; pretext; origin
絶縁 ぜつえん breaking off relations; insulation, isolation
無縁の むえんの unrelated; without relatives, having no surviving relatives

交 ▷intercourse
コウ まじ(わる) まじ(える) ま(じる)
ま(ざる) ま(ぜる) -か(う) か(わす) Ⓚ1738

ⓐ intercourse, friendly relations, association, friendship
ⓑ have friendly relations with, associate
ⓐ 交際 こうさい association, friendship, intercourse
国交 こっこう diplomatic relations, national friendship

ⓑ 外交 がいこう diplomacy, foreign relations
断交 だんこう severing [breaking off] relations

好 ▷friendship
コウ この(む) す(く) よ(い) い(い) Ⓚ0184

friendship, friendly relations
好誼 こうぎ warm friendship
親好 しんこう friendship, good fellowship
友好的な ゆうこうてきな friendly, fraternal

仲 ▷personal relations
チュウ なか　　　　　　　　Ⓚ0028

personal relations, relationship, (familiar) terms, fellowship, friendship
仲が良い なかがよい be on good terms
仲良くする なかよくする become friendly with, make friends with
仲間 なかま company, fellow, comrade, associate
仲直り なかなおり reconciliation
恋仲 こいなか love relationship

誼 ▷friendship
ギ よしみ　　　　　　　　　Ⓚ1421

[also 宜 or 義] **friendship; favor, kindness**
友誼(=友宜) ゆうぎ friendship, fellowship
交誼(=交宜) こうぎ friendship, amity
好誼(=好宜) こうぎ warm friendship
高誼(=高宜) こうぎ your kindness [favor]
恩誼(=恩義) おんぎ obligation, debt of gratitude
情誼(=情宜, 情義)を尽くす じょうぎをつくす do (a person) a kindness

絆 ▷bonds
ハン きずな ほだ(す)　　　　Ⓚ1217

bonds, fetters, tether
脚絆 きゃはん gaiters, leggings
羈絆 きはん fetters, shackles, bonds

person in charge
係 方 員

係 ▷person in charge
ケイ かか(る) かかり -がかり
かか(わる)　　　　　　　　Ⓚ0078

【かかり】
person in charge, official in charge, clerk
係員 かかりいん clerk in charge
係長 かかりちょう chief clerk
係官 かかりかん official in charge

【-がかり】

[sometimes also 掛] [suffix] **person in charge, official in charge, clerk**

案内係 あんないがかり clerk at the information desk
会計係 かいけいがかり accountant, treasurer
受付係 うけつけがかり reception clerk

方 ▷**person in charge**
ホウ -かた -がた -なた ⓚ1709

[also suffix] **person in charge**

賄い方 まかないかた kitchen manager, chef
裏方 うらかた property man, sceneshifter
親方 おやかた boss, chief, master
土方 どかた construction laborer, navvy

員 ▷**member (of a staff)**
イン ⓚ1958

member of a staff [profession], personnel, person in charge

社員 しゃいん staff member, employee
職員 しょくいん staff, employee, personnel
全員 ぜんいん all members, entire staff
係員 かかりいん clerk in charge
検査員 けんさいん inspector
会社員 かいしゃいん company employee, office worker
公務員 こうむいん public service personnel, government worker
事務員 じむいん clerk, clerical staff
警備員 けいびいん guard

persons →COUNTERS FOR PERSONS

phenomenon
象 気 物

象 ▷**phenomenon**
ショウ ゾウ ⓚ1831

(outward manifestation of things) **phenomenon, outer appearance, material form; things, object**

現象 げんしょう phenomenon
気象 きしょう atmospheric phenomena, weather conditions
天象 てんしょう astronomical phenomena
万象 ばんしょう all things [manifestations] in the universe
対象 たいしょう object (of study), subject, target
抽象 ちゅうしょう abstraction

気 ▷**natural phenomenon**
キ ケ ⓚ2751

natural phenomenon

気象 きしょう atmospheric phenomena, weather conditions
気候 きこう climate, weather; season
天気 てんき weather, atmospheric conditions; fine weather

物 ▷**physical phenomena**
ブツ モツ もの ⓚ0777

physical phenomena, material world, reality

物理 ぶつり physics; natural law
物象 ぶっしょう material phenomena; science of inanimate nature
博物学 はくぶつがく natural history

phonetic [a]
亜 阿

亜 ▷**phonetic [a]**
ア ⓚ2966

used phonetically for _a_, esp. in the transliteration of foreign place names

亜米利加 あめりか America

阿 ▷**phonetic [a]**
ア お- おもね(る) ⓚ0305

used phonetically for _a_, esp. in the transliteration of names, foreign words or Sanskrit Buddhist terms

阿片 あへん opium
阿弥陀 あみだ _Amitābha_; lottery; wearing a hat on the back of the head
阿修羅 あしゅら _Asura_ (fighting demon)

phonetic [b]
毘 菩

毘 ▷**phonetic [bi]**
ヒ ビ ⓚ2217

used phonetically for _bi_, esp. in the transliteration of Sanskrit Buddhist terms

毘沙門天 びしゃもんてん _Vaiaśravaṇ_
毘廬遮那仏 びるしゃなぶつ _Vairocana-Buddha_
金毘羅 こんぴら guardian deity of seafaring
荼毘 だび cremation
大直毘神 おおなおびのかみ Great God of Restoration

菩 ▷phonetic [bo]
ボ   Ⓚ1992

used phonetically for *bo*, esp. in the transliteration of Sanskrit Buddhist terms

菩提 ぼだい *Bodhi*
菩提樹 ぼだいじゅ sacred fig, bo tree; linden, esp. *Tilia miqueliana*
菩提寺 ぼだいじ one's family temple
菩薩 ぼさつ *bodhisattva*
普賢菩薩 ふげんぼさつ *Samantabhadra* (a bodhisattva)

phonetic [d]
陀 達 提 胴

陀 ▷phonetic [da]
ダ   Ⓚ0306

used phonetically for *da*, esp. in the transliteration of Sanskrit Buddhist terms

陀羅尼 だらに *dhāraṇi*, mystic Buddhist incantation
御陀仏 おだぶつ dying; ruining oneself, falling through
阿弥陀 あみだ *Amitābha*; lottery; wearing a hat on the back of the head
仏陀 ぶっだ Buddha
曼陀羅(=曼荼羅) まんだら mandala
阿蘭陀(=和蘭、和蘭陀) おらんだ Holland, the Netherlands
加奈陀 かなだ Canada
頭陀袋 ずだぶくろ sack, carry-all bag

達 ▷phonetic [da]
タツ −たち   Ⓚ2706

used phonetically for *da* or similar sounds

達磨 だるま Bodhidharma; tumbler
曹達 そーだ soda

提 ▷phonetic [dai]
テイ チョウ さ(げる)   Ⓚ0540

used phonetically for *dai* in the transliteration of Sanskrit Buddhist terms

菩提 ぼだい *Bodhi*

胴 ▷phonetic [dō]
ドウ   Ⓚ0857

used phonetically for *dō*

胴欲 どうよく avarice, greed
胴元 どうもと bookmaker (in gambling)

phonetic [ha]
巴 波

巴 ▷phonetic [ha]
ハ ともえ   Ⓚ2894

used phonetically for *ha* or *pa*

巴旦杏 はたんきょう plum
巴里 ぱり Paris

波 ▷phonetic [ha]
ハ なみ   Ⓚ0292

used phonetically for *ha* and closely related sounds

波羅蜜 はらみつ *pāramitā*, entrance into Nirvana

phonetic [i]
伊 斐

伊 ▷phonetic [i]
イ   Ⓚ0033

used phonetically for *i*, esp. in proper names

伊太利 いたりー Italy
伊呂波 いろは *iroha*, the Japanese syllabary [alphabet]

斐 ▷phonetic [i]
ヒ イ   Ⓚ2417

used phonetically for *i*

甲斐(=詮)が有る かいがある fruitful, effective, worth, worthwhile

phonetic [k]/[g]
迦 珈 伽 瓦 祇

迦 ▷phonetic [ka]
カ   Ⓚ2767

used phonetically for *ka*, esp. in the transliteration of Sanskrit Buddhist terms

迦楼羅 かるら *Garuḍa*, man-bird deity in Hindu-Buddhist myth
釈迦 しゃか *Śākyamuni, Gautama*
宇迦御魂 うかのみたま god of foodstuffs, esp. of rice

珈 ▷phonetic [kō]
カ   (K)0817

used phonetically for *ka, kō* or *ko*, esp. in the sense of coffee

珈琲 こーひー coffee

伽 ▷phonetic [ga]
カ ガ キャ とぎ   (K)0049

used phonetically for *ga, ka, kya*, esp. in the transliteration of Sanskrit Buddhist terms

伽藍(=伽檻) がらん Buddhist temple, cathedral

瓦 ▷phonetic [ga]
ガ かわら   (K)2918

used phonetically for *ga*

瓦斯 がす gas

祇 ▷phonetic [gi]
ギ シ   (K)1049

used phonetically for *gi* in the transliteration of Sanskrit Buddhist terms

祇園 ぎおん name of an entertainment district in Kyoto; Jetavana (name of an ancient garden and monastery in India)

阿僧祇 あそうぎ 10^{56}, 10^{64}; *Buddhism* a number too great to count, *asaṃkhyeya*

phonetic [m]
弥 摩 昧 蜜 勿 牟

弥 ▷phonetic [mi]
ミ や   (K)0258

used phonetically for *mi*, esp. in the transliteration of Sanskrit Buddhist terms

弥勒 みろく Maitreya (a *bodhisattva*)

阿弥陀 あみだ Amitābha; lottery; wearing a hat on the back of the head

摩 ▷phonetic [ma]
マ   (K)2740

used phonetically for *ma* in the transliteration of Sanskrit Buddhist terms

摩利支天 まりしてん Marīci, god of war

護摩 ごま homa, Buddhist rite of cedar-stick burning

昧 ▷phonetic [mai]
マイ   (K)0794

used phonetically for *mai* in the transliteration of Sanskrit Buddhist terms

三昧 さんまい *Buddhism* spiritual concentration, *samādhi*; [suffix] absorption in, indulgence in, spree

贅沢三昧 ぜいたくざんまい indulging in every possible luxury

蜜 ▷phonetic [mitsu]
ミツ   (K)2060

used phonetically for *mitsu* in the transliteration of Sanskrit Buddhist terms

波羅蜜 はらみつ *pāramitā*, entrance into Nirvana

般若波羅蜜多 はんにゃはらみった *Buddhism* perfection of wisdom, *prajñāpāramitā*

勿 ▷phonetic [mot]
モチ モッ- ブツ なか(れ)   (K)2547

[sometimes also 物] used phonetically for *mot-*

勿体 もったい air of importance, superior airs

勿体無い もったいない wasteful; be more than one deserves

勿怪の幸い もっけのさいわい piece of good luck, windfall

牟 ▷phonetic [mu]
ム   (K)1745

used phonetically for *mu*, esp. in the transliteration of Sanskrit Buddhist terms

牟尼 むに *muni*, Indian ascetic [sage]; Buddha

釈迦牟尼 しゃかむに Śākyamuni, Buddha

phonetic [na]
那   奈

那 ▷phonetic [na]
ナ   (K)0748

used phonetically for *na*, esp. in the transliteration of Sanskrit Buddhist terms or names

旦那(=檀那) だんな master, husband, patron, protector; sir; [original meaning] donor

刹那 せつな moment, instant; *kṣaṇa* (1/75 of a second)

奈 ▷phonetic [na]
ナ   (K)190⁵

used phonetically for *na*, esp. in the transliteration of foreign words

奈落 ならく Hell; trap cellar

奈翁 なおう Napoleon

加奈陀 かなだ Canada

phonetic [r]

呂　路　羅

呂 ▷phonetic [ro]
ロ
Ⓚ1872

used phonetically for *ro*

風呂 ふろ bath
語呂 ごろ sound harmony
伊呂波 いろは *iroha*, the Japanese syllabary [alphabet]

路 ▷phonetic [ru]
ロ -じ
Ⓚ1394

used phonetically for *ru*, esp. in the transliteration of foreign names

路加 るか St. Luke

羅 ▷phonetic [ra]
ラ
Ⓚ2278

used phonetically for *ra* or similar sounds, esp. in the transliteration of proper names or Sanskrit Buddhist terms

羅紗 らしゃ woolen cloth
羅馬 ろーま Rome
天麩羅 てんぷら tempura, Japanese deep-fat fried food
阿羅漢 あらかん *Arhat*, Buddhist monk who has attained Nirvana
金毘羅 こんぴら guardian deity of seafaring

phonetic [s]/[sh]

沙　刹　遮　叉　世
須　修　西　相　薩

沙 ▷phonetic [sha]
サ すな
Ⓚ0236

used phonetically for *sha*, esp. in the transliteration of Sanskrit Buddhist terms

沙弥 しゃみ Buddhist novice, *śrāmaṇera*
沙門 しゃもん wandering Buddhist monk, *śramaṇa*
沙翁 さおう Shakespeare

刹 ▷phonetic [setsu]
サツ セツ
Ⓚ1167

used phonetically for *setsu* in the transliteration of Sanskrit Buddhist terms

刹那 せつな moment, instant; *kṣaṇa* (1/75 of a second)
刹那的 せつなてき ephemeral, transitory
羅刹 らせつ *rākṣasa*, evil spirit

遮 ▷phonetic [sha]
シャ さえぎ(る)
Ⓚ2724

used phonetically for *sha*, esp. in the transliteration of Sanskrit Buddhist terms

遮二無二 しゃにむに recklessly, madly
毘廬遮那仏 びるしゃなぶつ *Vairocana-Buddha*

叉 ▷phonetic [sha]
サ シャ また
Ⓚ2870

used phonetically for *sha*

夜叉 やしゃ *yakṣa*, demon

世 ▷phonetic [se]
セイ セ よ
Ⓚ2932

used phonetically for *se*

世帯 せたい household, home
仲見世通り なかみせどおり shopping street in the precincts of a shrine [temple]

須 ▷phonetic [shu]
ス
Ⓚ0526

used phonetically for *shu* or *su*, esp. in the transliteration of Sanskrit Buddhist terms

須弥壇 しゅみだん dais for a Buddhist image

修 ▷phonetic [shu]
シュウ シュ おさ(める) おさ(まる)
Ⓚ0105

used phonetically for *shu* in the transliteration of Sanskrit Buddhist terms

阿修羅 あしゅら *Asura* (fighting demon)

西 ▷phonetic [su]
セイ サイ にし
Ⓚ2951

used phonetically for *su*, esp. in the transliteration of foreign place names

仏蘭西 ふらんす France

相 ▷phonetic [sō]
ソウ ショウ あい-
Ⓚ0808

used phonetically for *sō*

相場 そうば market price; estimation

薩 ▷phonetic [satsu]
サツ
Ⓚ2104

used phonetically for *satsu* in the transliteration of Sanskrit Buddhist terms

菩薩 ぼさつ *bodhisattva*
弥勒菩薩 みろくぼさつ *Maitreya* (a bodhisattva)

金剛薩埵 こんごうさった Vajrasattva (a bodhisattva)

photograph
撮　　写

撮 ▷**photograph**
サツ と(る) –ど(り)　　Ⓚ0671

photograph, take a picture, film
撮影 さつえい photographing, shooting (of a movie)
撮像管 さつぞうかん image pick-up [camera] tube
特撮 とくさつ trick work

写 ▷**shoot**
シャ うつ(す) うつ(る)　　Ⓚ1726

shoot, photograph, take pictures
写植 しゃしょく phototypesetting
特写 とくしゃ exclusive shooting [photographing] (for a magazine)
接写 せっしゃ close-up photograph

picture
絵　　画　　図

絵 ▷**picture**
カイ エ　　Ⓚ1233

[sometimes also 画] [also prefix and suffix] [original meaning] **picture, painting, drawing, sketch, illustration**
絵画 かいが pictures, paintings, drawings
絵本 えほん picture book
絵描き えかき painter, artist
絵の具 えのぐ coloring materials, colors, oils, paint
絵葉書 えはがき picture postcard
絵日記 えにっき diary with illustrations
油絵 あぶらえ oil painting
浮世絵 うきよえ ukiyoe, color print of everyday life in old Japan

画 ▷**picture**
ガ カク　　Ⓚ2586

[also suffix] **picture, drawing, painting**
画廊 がろう picture gallery
画用紙 がようし drawing paper
絵画 かいが pictures, paintings, drawings
漫画 まんが cartoon, comic strip
名画 めいが famous picture, masterpiece; noted film
映画 えいが cinema, film, movie

日本画 にほんが picture in the Japanese style

図 ▷**drawing**
ズ ト はか(る)　　Ⓚ264◆

drawing, plan, diagram, figure, illustration, picture
図面 ずめん drawing, plan, map, sketch
図形 ずけい figure, diagram
図表 ずひょう chart, diagram
図鑑 ずかん picture [illustrated] book
図書 としょ books
図書室 としょしつ library
図示 ずし illustration, graphic(al) representation
設計図 せっけいず plan, blueprint

pigments
墨　　漆　　藍　　堊

墨 ▷**India ink**
ボク すみ　　Ⓚ240◆

India ink, Chinese ink, ink stick
墨汁 ぼくじゅう India ink, black writing fluid
水墨画 すいぼくが India ink drawing, painting in India ink

漆 ▷**lacquer**
シツ うるし　　Ⓚ063◆

[original meaning] (Japanese or Chinese) **lacquer, varnish, japan, urushi**
漆器 しっき lacquer ware
漆工 しっこう lacquer work, japanner

藍 ▷**indigo**
ラン あい　　Ⓚ210◆

indigo plant, indigo dye
出藍の誉れ しゅつらんのほまれ surpassing one's master

堊 ▷**whitewash**
アク ア

[now also 亜] **whitewash**
白堊 はくあ chalk; white wall

places and positions
所 処 場 地 席 位 点 座

所 ▷place
ショ ところ どころ   Ⓚ0752

ⓐ [sometimes also 処] (portion of space) **place, spot, point, part**
ⓑ [also suffix] **place for specific purpose, dwelling place, facilities, quarters**

a 場所 ばしょ place, spot, site; space, room
  箇所(=個所) かしょ place, spot, point; part
  住所 じゅうしょ one's dwelling, address
  近所 きんじょ neighborhood
  名所 めいしょ noted place, sights, scenic place
  一所懸命(=一生懸命)に いっしょけんめい(=いっしょうけんめい)に for life, with all one's might
  出所 しゅっしょ origin, source; release from prison
b 便所 べんじょ lavatory, bathroom
  停留所 ていりゅうじょ (bus) stop, station
  休憩所 きゅうけいじょ resting room [place], lounge

処 ▷place
ショ   Ⓚ2609

[usu. 所] **place, proper place, location**
  処処 しょしょ several places

場 ▷place (for specific activity)
ジョウ ば   Ⓚ0512

[also suffix] place or chamber for specific activity: **place, hall, room, house; plant**

  会場 かいじょう place of meeting, site
  式場 しきじょう hall of ceremony, stateroom
  工場 こうじょう(=こうば) factory, plant, workshop
  劇場 げきじょう theater
  入場 にゅうじょう entrance, admission
  出場する しゅつじょうする take part, participate
  試験場 しけんじょう examination hall [room]; laboratory

地 ▷place (particular location)
チ ジ   Ⓚ0181

[also suffix] (particular location) **place, grounds, position**

  地点 ちてん spot, point, place
  各地 かくち every place, various parts [areas] (of the country)
  基地 きち base
  団地 だんち (public) housing development
  現地 げんち actual place [locale]
  当地 とうち this place [locality], here
  番地 ばんち lot [house] number, address

  余地 よち room, space, margin
  墓地 ぼち graveyard, cemetery, burial grounds
  爆心地 ばくしんち center of explosion

席 ▷meeting place
セキ   Ⓚ2683

meeting place, hall; meeting

  席上で せきじょうで at the meeting; on the occasion
  出席 しゅっせき attendance, presence
  欠席 けっせき absence, nonattendance
  会席 かいせき meeting place
  宴席 えんせき banquet hall, dinner party

位 ▷position
イ くらい ぐらい   Ⓚ0045

[original meaning] **position, location, place; direction**

  位置 いち position, place
  機位 きい position of aircraft
  方位 ほうい direction, bearing
  転位 てんい transposition, displacement
  定位 ていい normal position; orientation

点 ▷point
テン   Ⓚ1793

[also suffix]
ⓐ (definite place) **point**
ⓑ (definite position) **point**

a 地点 ちてん spot, point, place
  焦点 しょうてん focus, focal point; (photographic) focus
  拠点 きょてん strongpoint, base
  終点 しゅうてん last stop, terminus
  出発点 しゅっぱつてん starting point
b 沸点 ふってん boiling point
  死点 してん dead point
  凝固点 ぎょうこてん freezing point

座 ▷place
ザ すわ(る)   Ⓚ2686

place, position

  座標 ざひょう coordinates
  即座に そくざに immediately, promptly, at once
  口座 こうざ (bank) account
  当座 とうざ the present, the time being; current account

places for landing or stopping

港 湊 津 駅 停

港 ▷port
コウ みなと   Ⓚ0552

ⓐ [also suffix] **port, harbor**
ⓑ suffix after names of ports or harbors

a 港湾 こうわん harbors
  港口 こうこう harbor entrance
  港内 こうない inside the harbor
  寄港 きこう calling at a port
  漁港 ぎょこう fishing port, fishery harbor
  空港 くうこう airport
  入港する にゅうこうする enter a port
  貿易港 ぼうえきこう trade port
b 神戸港 こうべこう Kobe Harbor

湊 ▷port
ソウ みなと   Ⓚ0557

[usu. 港] **port, harbor**

津 ▷harbor (*elegant*)
シン つ   Ⓚ0351

elegant **harbor, ferry**
  津津浦浦に つつうらうらに throughout the land, in
    every harbor and every bay
  津波 つなみ tsunami, tidal wave

駅 ▷station
エキ   Ⓚ1618

ⓐ [also prefix and suffix] **station, railway station, railroad depot**
ⓑ suffix after names of stations

a 駅前の えきまえの in front of the station
  駅長 えきちょう stationmaster
  駅員 えきいん station employee
  駅ビル えきびる station building
  駅弁 えきべん station lunch
  各駅 かくえき every station; local train
  貨物駅 かもつえき freight depot
b 神戸駅 こうべえき Kobe Station

停 ▷stopping place
テイ と(める) と(まる)   Ⓚ0121

abbrev. of 停留所 ていりゅうじょ: **stopping place, stop, station**
  バス停 ばすてい bus stop
  電停 でんてい tram stop

places of business

店 舗 屋 社

店 ▷shop (of any kind)
テン みせ   Ⓚ2657

ⓐ [also suffix] [original meaning] **shop, store; stall**
ⓑ [also suffix] (small) **business establishment, as a bank or restaurant**
ⓒ counter for shops or firms

a 店員 てんいん clerk
  店舗 てんぽ shop, store
  店頭 てんとう shop [store] front
  商店 しょうてん shop, store
  書店 しょてん bookstore
  売店 ばいてん booth, stand; store
  百貨店 ひゃっかてん department store
ab 支店 してん branch (office), branch (store)
  本店 ほんてん head [main] office [store]
b 店屋物 てんやもの dishes from a caterer
  代理店 だいりてん agency, agent
  特約店 とくやくてん special [sole] agency [agent]
  喫茶店 きっさてん coffee shop, tea house
c 五十店 ごじゅってん 50 shops [branch offices]

舗 ▷shop (esp. traditional)
ホ   Ⓚ1547

[also suffix] **shop, store**—said esp. of shops having a long tradition
  店舗 てんぽ shop, store
  老舗 ろうほ(=しにせ) old [long-established] shop
  名舗 めいほ famous store, quality shop
  本舗 ほんぽ head office, main shop
  薬舗 やくほ pharmacy, drugstore
  新聞舗 しんぶんほ newspaper distributor

屋 ▷small shop
オク や   Ⓚ2669

[also suffix] **small shop or place of business, store**
  屋台 やたい stall, stand; float, festival car
  店屋 みせや shop, store
  料理屋 りょうりや restaurant
  魚屋 さかなや fish shop; fish dealer
  花屋 はなや flower shop; florist
  本屋 ほんや bookstore; bookseller
  不動産屋 ふどうさんや real estate agent, Realtor

社 ▷company
シャ やしろ   Ⓚ0745

ⓐ [also suffix] **company, firm, corporation; office**
ⓑ counter for companies

a 社員 しゃいん staff member, employee

社長 しゃちょう president (of a company)
社団 しゃだん corporation, association
会社 かいしゃ company, corporation, firm
公社 こうしゃ public corporation
入社 にゅうしゃ entering [joining] a company
本社 ほんしゃ head office, this office; head shrine, this shrine
新聞社 しんぶんしゃ newspaper office
出版社 しゅっぱんしゃ publishing company
b 二十二社 にじゅうにしゃ 22 companies

places of worship
堂 塔 寺 刹 社 宮 院 教

堂 ▷temple building
ドウ   Ⓚ2246

ⓐ (building or hall for worship) **temple building, temple, shrine, church**
ⓑ **suffix after names of temple buildings**

a 堂塔 どうとう temple buildings, temple
堂宇 どうう edifice, temple, hall
b 聖堂 せいどう shrine [temple] of Confucius; sanctuary, church
本堂 ほんどう main temple, main building (of a temple)
金色堂 こんじきどう Konjikido (name of a temple building)

塔 ▷pagoda
トウ   Ⓚ0517

[also suffix] **pagoda**

卒塔婆 そとば(=そとうば) wooden grave tablet; stupa, dagoba
仏塔 ぶっとう pagoda, Buddhist pagoda
堂塔 どうとう temple buildings, temple

寺 ▷Buddhist temple
ジ てら   Ⓚ1853

ⓐ **Buddhist temple, temple**
ⓑ **suffix after names of Buddhist temples**
ⓒ **counter for Buddhist temples**

a 寺院 じいん temple
社寺 しゃじ shrines and temples
古寺 こじ old temple
b 国分寺 こくぶんじ state-established provincial temple
東大寺 とうだいじ Todaiji Temple
金閣寺 きんかくじ Temple of the Golden Pavilion
c 一箇寺 いっかじ one temple

刹 ▷temple
サツ セツ   Ⓚ1167

Buddhist temple

名刹 めいさつ famous temple
古刹 こさつ ancient temple
巨刹 きょさつ large temple
梵刹 ぼんさつ(=ぼんせつ) Buddhist temple

社 ▷Shinto shrine
シャ やしろ   Ⓚ0745

Shinto shrine

社殿 しゃでん Shinto shrine
神社 じんじゃ Shinto shrine
総社(=惣社) そうじゃ shrine enshrining several gods
寺社 じしゃ shrines and temples
出雲大社 いずもたいしゃ The Grand Shrine of Izumo

宮 ▷Shinto shrine
キュウ グウ ク みや   Ⓚ1964

ⓐ **Shinto shrine, imperial Shinto shrine**
ⓑ **suffix after names of Shinto shrines**

a 宮司 ぐうじ chief priest of a Shinto shrine
神宮 じんぐう Shinto shrine; Grand Shrine at Ise
遷宮 せんぐう transfer of a shrine
b 外宮 げくう Outer Shrine of Ise
東照宮 とうしょうぐう Toshogu Shrine

院 ▷monastery
イン   Ⓚ0410

religious institution: **monastery, (Buddhist) temple**

寺院 じいん temple
尼僧院 にそういん nunnery, convent
修道院 しゅうどういん monastery, convent

教 ▷church
キョウ おし(える) おそ(わる)   Ⓚ1356

church

教区 きょうく parish
教籍 きょうせき church membership

plain and simple
素 朴 単

素 ▷plain
ソ ス   Ⓚ2171

ⓐ [also prefix] (lacking ornament) **plain, simple, unpretentious, natural, unadorned, unrefined, raw, crude**
ⓑ (lacking distinction) **plain, ordinary, common**

a 素材 そざい material; subject matter
素描 そびょう (rough) sketch
素朴な そぼくな simple, naive, artless
素顔 すがお face without makeup
素直な すなおな docile, obedient; honest, frank
簡素な かんそな plain, simple
質素な しっそな simple, modest, frugal
b 素通りする すどおりする pass through without stopping, pass by
素泊まり すどまり staying overnight without board

朴 ▷simple (unadorned)
ボク Ⓚ0725

simple, unadorned, plain
朴訥 ぼくとつ rugged honesty
朴直な ぼくちょくな simple and honest, artless, naive
素朴な そぼくな simple, naive, artless
質朴な しつぼくな simple, plain, unsophisticated
敦朴(=敦樸)な とんぼくな [archaic] honest and simple

単 ▷simple (uncomplicated)
タン Ⓚ1946

simple, uncomplicated, plain
単純な たんじゅんな simple, uncomplicated, plain
単利 たんり simple interest
単調な たんちょうな monotonous, dull
簡単な かんたんな simple, easy, light

planning →PLANS AND PLANNING

plans and planning
計 画 案 企 図
謀 策 略 揆

計 ▷plan
ケイ はか(る) はか(らう) Ⓚ1309

ⓐ plan, design, devise, scheme
ⓑ plan, stratagem
a 計画 けいかく plan, project
設計 せっけい design, plan
b 計略 けいりゃく stratagem, plan, scheme
妙計 みょうけい ingenious trick, clever scheme
奸計 かんけい vicious plan, crafty design

画 ▷draw up a plan
ガ カク Ⓚ2586

[formerly also 劃]
ⓐ draw up a plan, plan, design
ⓑ plan

a 画策する かくさくする plan, scheme
b 計画 けいかく plan, project
企画 きかく plan, project
参画 さんかく participation in planning

案 ▷proposal
アン Ⓚ1960

[also suffix] proposal, plan, scheme
案件 あんけん matter, case, item
提案 ていあん proposition, proposal, suggestion
法案 ほうあん bill, legislative proposal
議案 ぎあん bill, measure
原案 げんあん original bill [plan]
試案 しあん tentative plan, draft
対案 たいあん counterproposal
立案する りつあんする make a plan, devise, draft
増税案 ぞうぜいあん tax increase proposal
具体案 ぐたいあん concrete proposal

企 ▷project
キ くわだ(てる) Ⓚction174

ⓐ (form a plan or intention for) project, draw up [organize] a project, lay plans, undertake a project
ⓑ project, plan, program
a 企図 きと plan, scheme, intention
企業 きぎょう undertaking, enterprise; business enterprise, company
企及する ききゅうする try to attain (something)
b 企画 きかく plan, project

図 ▷systematic plan
ズ ト はか(る) Ⓚ264

systematic plan, scheme, attempt
壮図 そうと grand scheme
企図する きとする plan, scheme, intend
雄図 ゆうと ambitious enterprise, grand project

謀 ▷scheme
ボウ ム はか(る) Ⓚ143

ⓐ scheme, plot, conspire, contrive
ⓑ scheme, plot, conspiracy, intrigue
a 謀殺 ぼうさつ premeditated murder
首謀者 しゅぼうしゃ ringleader, mastermind
b 謀略 ぼうりゃく stratagem, scheme, plot
謀反 むほん rebellion, revolt, treason
共謀 きょうぼう conspiracy, collusion
陰謀 いんぼう scheme, plot, conspiracy

策 ▷scheme
サク Ⓚ233

(clever plan of action) scheme, device, plan, stratagem
策謀 さくぼう artifice, stratagem
策士 さくし tactician; schemer, machinator

略 ▷**strategy**
リャク ⓚ1081

strategy, plan, tactics, scheme, stratagem
計略 けいりゃく stratagem, plan, scheme
戦略 せんりゃく strategy, stratagem
政略 せいりゃく political tactics [maneuver], politicking
策略 さくりゃく artifice, stratagem, scheme
謀略 ぼうりゃく stratagem, scheme, plot
党略 とうりゃく party politics [tactics]

揆 ▷**plot**
キ

plot, plan
一揆 いっき riot, uprising, revolt

lant →FARM AND PLANT

plants

菜 植 栽 茨 苔 蔓 桔

菜 ▷**vegetable**
サイ な ⓚ2004

vegetable, greens
菜食 さいしょく vegetable diet
菜食主義 さいしょくしゅぎ vegetarianism
菜園 さいえん vegetable garden
野菜 やさい vegetables, greens
白菜 はくさい Chinese cabbage, white rape
山菜 さんさい edible wild plant

植 ▷**plant**
ショク う(える) う(わる) ⓚ0903

plant, plants, vegetation
植物 しょくぶつ plant, vegetation
植物園 しょくぶつえん botanical garden
植生 しょくせい vegetation
動植物 どうしょくぶつ animals and plants

栽 ▷**garden plant**
サイ ⓚ2810

garden plant, potted plant
盆栽 ぼんさい bonsai (potted dwarf tree)
前栽 せんざい *elegant* trees and flowers in a garden; garden

茨 ▷**thorny shrub**
いばら ⓚ1952

thorny shrub, brier
茨棘 しきょく thorn

苔 ▷**moss**
タイ こけ ⓚ1935

ⓐ moss, liverwort, bryophyte
ⓑ lichen
a 苔類 たいるい liverworts, *Marchantiophyta*
蘚苔 せんたい moss, bryophyte
b 苔癬 たいせん (disease) lichen

蔓 ▷**vine**
マン つる かずら ⓚ2074

vine, creeper, runner, trailer, tendril
蔓生 まんせい (of vines) creeping, running, trailing, climbing

桔 ▷**plant name element**
キツ ケツ キ ⓚ0838

plant name element
桔梗 ききょう Chinese bellflower, balloon flower

plants →SUPPORTING PARTS OF PLANTS

plates →BOARDS AND PLATES

play

遊 戲 弄

遊 ▷**play**
ユウ ユ あそ(ぶ) あそ(ばす) ⓚ2709

ⓐ play, amuse oneself
ⓑ play around with (the opposite sex), flirt
a 遊戯 ゆうぎ game, pastime, amusement
遊興 ゆうきょう merrymaking, spree
遊園地 ゆうえんち amusement park
b 遊女 ゆうじょ harlot, prostitute
遊里 ゆうり licensed quarters, red-light district

戲 ▷**sport**
ギ たわむ(れる) ⓚ1654

ⓐ sport, frolic, play
ⓑ play with (a woman), dally, flirt
a 遊戯 ゆうぎ game, pastime, amusement
嬉戯する きぎする frisk, frolic
b 前戯 ぜんぎ foreplay

弄 ▷**toy with**
ロウ もてあそ(ぶ) ⓚ2129
【ロウ】

toy with, play with, fiddle with
玩弄する がんろうする make sport of, toy with, play with
翻弄する ほんろうする trifle with, make sport of, toss about (as of a boat)

play

【もてあそ(ぶ)】

ⓐ toy [fiddle] with (the hands)
ⓑ toy [trifle] with; do (with something) as one pleases

a 髪を弄ぶ かみをもてあそぶ fiddle with one's hair
b 人の気持ちを弄ぶ ひとのきもちをもてあそぶ toy with people's feelings

play music

奏　弾　吹

奏 ▷play music
ソウ かな(でる)　　　　Ⓚ2233

play music, perform (on a musical instrument)
演奏する えんそうする perform, play
吹奏楽 すいそうがく wind instrument music
重奏 じゅうそう duet
合奏 がっそう ensemble, concert
伴奏 ばんそう accompaniment
協奏曲 きょうそうきょく concerto

弾 ▷play on (stringed instruments)
ダン ひ(く) -ひ(き) はず(む) たま Ⓚ0524

[original meaning] play on (stringed instruments)
弾奏 だんそう playing on stringed instruments
連弾 れんだん four-handed performance (on the piano)

吹 ▷blow
スイ ふ(く)　　　　Ⓚ0204

blow on, play on a wind instrument
吹奏 すいそう playing wind instruments
鼓吹する こすいする inspire, inculcate, advocate

plays →PARTS OF PLAYS

pleasant →PLEASED AND PLEASANT

pleased and pleasant

楽 欣 爽 快 朗 愉
悦 嬉 喜 歓 驩

楽 ▷pleasurable
ガク ラク たの(しい) たの(しむ)　Ⓚ2460

pleasurable, pleasant, merry
楽園 らくえん paradise

欣 ▷joyful
キン ゴン　　　　Ⓚ075

[original meaning] joyful, glad, happy
欣悦 きんえつ gladness, joy
欣然と きんぜんと joyfully, gladly
欣喜雀躍する きんきじゃくやくする dance [jump] for joy
欣快 きんかい great pleasure

爽 ▷refreshing
ソウ さわ(やか)　　　　Ⓚ2998

refreshing, fresh
爽快な そうかいな refreshing, invigorating, exhilarating

快 ▷pleasant
カイ こころよ(い)　　　　Ⓚ021

[original meaning] pleasant, agreeable, comfortable, delightful, jolly
快感 かいかん agreeable sensation, comfort
快適な かいてきな comfortable, pleasant, agreeable
快楽 かいらく pleasure, enjoyment
快削鋼 かいさくこう free-cutting steel
愉快な ゆかいな pleasant, delightful, joyful
不快な ふかいな unpleasant, disagreeable

朗 ▷cheerful
ロウ ほが(らか)　　　　Ⓚ121

(marked by or conductive to cheer) cheerful, bright, cheery
朗報 ろうほう cheering [good] news
明朗な めいろうな cheerful, bright; clean (politics)

愉 ▷pleased
ユ　　　　Ⓚ0534

[original meaning] pleased, delighted, happy, cheerful, joyful
愉快な ゆかいな pleasant, delightful, joyful
愉悦 ゆえつ joy
愉色 ゆしょく pleased look, cheerful expression
愉楽 ゆらく pleasure, joy
不愉快な ふゆかいな unpleasant, disagreeable, cheerless

悦 ▷delighted
エツ　　　　Ⓚ0378

[original meaning] delighted, pleased, happy
悦楽 えつらく pleasure, joy
喜悦 きえつ delight, rapture, joy
満悦 まんえつ great joy, rapture
愉悦 ゆえつ joy
法悦 ほうえつ religious exultation; ecstasy

嬉 ▷glad
キ うれ(しい) Ⓚ0655

glad, pleased, happy, delighted; joyful, delightful
> 嬉しさ うれしさ joy, delight, gladness
> 嬉しそうな うれしそうな delightful, glad-looking

喜 ▷happy
キ よろこ(ぶ) よろこ(ばす) Ⓚ2008

ⓐ [original meaning] **be happy [glad], rejoice**
ⓑ joy, pleasure
> a 喜悦 きえつ delight, rapture, joy
> 喜色 きしょく glad countenance
> 歓喜する かんきする rejoice, be greatly delighted
> b 悲喜 ひき joy and sorrow
> 一喜一憂 いっきいちゆう alternation of joy and sorrow

歓 ▷joyous
カン Ⓚ1650

[original meaning] **be joyous, be happy, be merry, rejoice**
> 歓喜 かんき joy, delight
> 歓楽 かんらく pleasure, merriment
> 歓談 かんだん pleasant chat [talk]
> 歓迎 かんげい welcome
> 歓送 かんそう sending off
> 歓声 かんせい cheers, shout of joy

驩 ▷joyous
カン

be joyous, be happy, be merry, rejoice

pleasure
楽 娯 興 玩

楽 ▷pleasure
ガク ラク たの(しい) たの(しむ) Ⓚ2460

pleasure, joy
> 享楽 きょうらく enjoyment
> 快楽 かいらく pleasure, enjoyment
> 娯楽 ごらく amusement, pastime
> 行楽 こうらく excursion, outing, holidaymaking

娯 ▷enjoyment
ゴ Ⓚ0366

enjoyment, amusement, merriment, pleasure
> 娯楽 ごらく amusement, pastime
> 娯楽街 ごらくがい amusement quarter
> 娯楽室 ごらくしつ recreation room

興 ▷amusement
コウ キョウ おこ(る) おこ(す) Ⓚ2525

amusement, entertainment, fun, interest, desire to enjoy
> 興味 きょうみ interest
> 興行 こうぎょう public entertainment, show business
> 余興 よきょう entertainment, side show
> 遊興 ゆうきょう merrymaking, spree
> 感興 かんきょう interest, fun, inspiration
> 一興 いっきょう amusement, fun

玩 ▷take pleasure in
ガン もてあそ(ぶ) Ⓚ0778

(play with) **take pleasure in, toy with, trifle with**
> 玩弄する がんろうする make sport of, toy with, play with
> 玩具 がんぐ(=おもちゃ) toy, plaything
> 食玩(=食品玩具) しょくがん(=しょくひんがんぐ) small toy sold with food

plentiful
百 沃 万 多 豊
沢 穣 裕 饒 富

百 ▷numerous
ヒャク Ⓚ1746

numerous, various
> 百姓 ひゃくしょう farmer, peasant
> 百貨店 ひゃっかてん department store
> 百科事典 ひゃっかじてん encyclopedia
> 百計 ひゃっけい all means

沃 ▷fertile
ヨク Ⓚ0240

(of land or soil) **fertile, rich**
> 沃土 よくど fertile [rich] soil, fertile land
> 沃野 よくや fertile fields [plains]
> 肥沃な ひよくな fertile, productive

万 ▷myriad
マン バン Ⓚ2542

myriad, multitude, many
> 万緑 ばんりょく myriad green leaves
> 万歳 ばんざい Banzai!/Hurrah!/Long live…!
> 巨万 きょまん myriads, millions, vast fortune

多 ▷many
タ おお(い)   Ⓚ1858

ⓐ [original meaning] **many, much, numerous**
ⓑ [prefix] **many-, multi-, poly-**

- ⓐ 多角 たかく many-sided, versatile; polygonal
  多数 たすう large number, multitude
  多量 たりょう large quantity, great deal
  多面 ためん many sides, many phases
  多分 たぶん probably, perhaps, maybe
  多少 たしょう a little, somewhat
  多大の ただいの great, considerable, a great deal of; serious
  多湿 たしつ high humidity
- ⓑ 多目的 たもくてき multipurpose
  多神教 たしんきょう polytheism
  多音節 たおんせつ polysyllable

豊 ▷plentiful
ホウ ゆた(か)   Ⓚ2352

plentiful, abundant, ample, rich
豊富な ほうふな abundant, plentiful, rich
豊水 ほうすい abundance of water
豊潤な ほうじゅんな rich and prosperous, luxurious
豊麗な ほうれいな rich (design), beautiful, splendid
豊満な ほうまんな plump, corpulent

沢 ▷plentiful
タク さわ   Ⓚ0238

plentiful, abundant
沢山 たくさん large quantity, plenty, abundance
潤沢 じゅんたく abundance, plenty
贅沢 ぜいたく luxury, extravagance

穣 ▷yielding abundantly
ジョウ   Ⓚ1154

yielding abundantly, abundant (harvest), luxuriant, plentiful
豊穣 ほうじょう abundant crop, rich harvest

裕 ▷abundant
ユウ   Ⓚ1104

abundant, plentiful, ample
裕福な ゆうふくな rich, wealthy
余裕 よゆう surplus, margin, room; composure
富裕な ふゆうな wealthy, rich

饒 ▷abundant
ジョウ

[now also 冗] [original meaning] **abundant, plentiful, rich**
饒舌 じょうぜつ garrulity, loquacity
豊饒 ほうじょう fertility, fruitfulness

富 ▷rich
フ フウ フッ- と(む) とみ   Ⓚ2009

(abounding in) **rich, abundant, plentiful**
富鉱 ふこう rich ore
豊富な ほうふな abundant, plentiful, rich

plural suffixes
達 等 衆 共 方

達 ▷plural suffix
タツ -たち   Ⓚ2706

suffix, often polite, for forming the plural of pronouns, people or animals
私達 わたくしたち we
動物達 どうぶつたち animals

等 ▷plural suffix
トウ ひと(しい) -ら   Ⓚ2339

plural suffix with deprecatory overtones
奴等 やつら those guys, they

衆 ▷somewhat polite plural suffix
シュウ シュ   Ⓚ2342

somewhat polite plural suffix
旦那衆 だんなしゅう(=だんなしゅ) gentlemen, gents

共 ▷belittling plural suffix
キョウ とも とも(に) -ども   Ⓚ2122

belittling or humble plural suffix
私共 わたくしども we
大人共 おとなども adults
餓鬼共 がきども those damn kids

方 ▷polite plural suffix
ホウ かた -がた -なた   Ⓚ1709

polite plural suffix
お偉方 おえらがた dignitary, exalted personalities
奥方 おくがた wife of a nobleman
殿方 とのがた men, gentlemen
貴方方 あなたがた you (plural)
先生方 せんせいがた teachers; doctors

poetry
詩 歌 俳 句

詩 ▷poetry
シ   Ⓚ1384

[also suffix] [original meaning] **poetry, poem, verse**
- 詩人 しじん poet
- 詩情 しじょう poetic sentiment, poetical interest
- 詩集 ししゅう anthology of poems
- 詩的な してきな poetic
- 叙事詩 じょじし epic (poem), epic poetry

歌 ▷Japanese poetry
カ うた うた(う)   Ⓚ1621

Japanese poetry, waka, tanka, poem
- 詩歌 しいか(=しか) Chinese and Japanese poetry; poems
- 短歌 たんか tanka, Japanese verse
- 和歌 わか Japanese poem, tanka
- 連歌 れんが verse linking, poetic dialogue

俳 ▷haiku
ハイ   Ⓚ0094

haiku, 17-syllable poem
- 俳句 はいく haiku
- 俳人 はいじん haiku poet
- 俳壇 はいだん haiku world
- 俳諧(=誹諧) はいかい *haikai*, (humorous) haiku

句 ▷haiku
ク   Ⓚ2561

haiku, 17-syllable poem
- 句会 くかい gathering of haiku
- 句集 くしゅう collection of haiku poems
- 俳句 はいく haiku
- 発句 ほっく haiku, hokku

points of land
岬 崎 埼

岬 ▷cape
みさき   Ⓚ0255

[rare] **cape, promontory**
- 岬角 こうかく promontory; *anat* promontory

崎 ▷promontory
さき   Ⓚ0428

[archaic] **promontory, cape**
- 崎陽 きよう Nagasaki

埼 ▷promontory
さい さき   Ⓚ0422

ⓐ [now usu. 崎] **promontory, cape**
ⓑ **suffix after names of promontories or capes**
- ⓐ 犬吠埼 いぬぼうさき Cape Inubo

policy
策 是 綱

策 ▷policy
サク   Ⓚ2338

[also suffix] **policy**
- 政策 せいさく policy, political measures
- 方策 ほうさく plan, policy, scheme
- 国策 こくさく national policy
- 強硬策 きょうこうさく hard-line policy, drastic measures

是 ▷policy
ゼ   Ⓚ2157

policy, guideline
- 国是 こくぜ national policy
- 社是 しゃぜ company policy
- 店是 てんぜ shop policy

綱 ▷guiding principle
コウ つな   Ⓚ1253

guiding principle, discipline, morals
- 綱紀 こうき law and order, official discipline
- 政綱 せいこう political principle, policy

polish and rub
磨 擦 摩 摺 研 削 瑳

磨 ▷polish
マ みが(く)   Ⓚ2744

ⓐ [original meaning] **polish, grind**
ⓑ **wear down, rub away, abrade**
- ⓐ 磨滅 まめつ wear, defacement
  研磨する けんまする grind, polish; study hard, brush up
- ⓑ 消磨 しょうま abrasion, wearing out

擦 ▷rub
サツ す(る) す(れる) -ず(れ) Ⓚ0707

[original meaning] **rub**
擦過傷 さっかしょう abrasion, scratch
摩擦する まさつする rub, chafe
摩擦 まさつ friction; rubbing, chafing
塗擦剤 とさつざい liniment

摩 ▷rub against
マ Ⓚ2740

[also 磨] **rub against, rub, chafe, scrape, wear away**
摩擦 まさつ friction; rubbing, chafing
摩耗 まもう wear, abrasion
摩滅 まめつ wear, defacement
摩損 まそん wear and tear, friction loss, abrasion

摺 ▷rub against
ショウ す(る) Ⓚ0628

rub against
摺動 しょうどう(=しゅうどう) moving along a smooth
surface

研 ▷grind
ケン と(ぐ) Ⓚ1046

[original meaning] **grind, polish**
研磨する けんまする grind, polish; study hard,
brush up
研削 けんさく grinding
研米機 けんまいき rice polisher

削 ▷cut by chipping
サク けず(る) Ⓚ1316

**cut by chipping, whittle, cut metal (with a cutting
tool), machine**
切削 せっさく cutting, machining
研削 けんさく grinding
旋削 せんさく turning (on a lathe)

瑳 ▷polish
サ Ⓚ0973

polish, grind
切瑳(=切磋)する せっさする work [study] hard,
cultivate one's own character
切瑳琢磨 せっさたくま working hard together,
assiduity in friendly rivalry

貧 ▷poor
ヒン ビン まず(しい) Ⓚ1822

[original meaning] (lacking in wealth) **poor, destitute**
貧乏 びんぼう poverty, destitution
貧乏人 びんぼうにん poor person, the poor
貧困 ひんこん poverty, indigence, destitution; lack,
shortage
貧富 ひんぷ rich and poor
貧窮 ひんきゅう poverty
貧農 ひんのう needy peasant
素寒貧 すかんぴん dire poverty; pauper

乏 ▷poor
ボウ とぼ(しい) Ⓚ1691

(lacking in resources) **poor, destitute**
窮乏 きゅうぼう destitution, poverty
貧乏な びんぼうな poor, destitute
耐乏 たいぼう austerity, voluntary privation

窮 ▷destitute
キュウ きわ(める) きわ(まる) きわ(まり)
きわ(み) Ⓚ2078

destitute, poor
窮乏 きゅうぼう destitution, poverty
窮民 きゅうみん poor people, the poor
窮措大 きゅうそだい poor student [scholar]
困窮 こんきゅう destitution, poverty, distress
貧窮 ひんきゅう poverty

positions →PLACES AND POSITIONS

陽 ▷positive
ヨウ Ⓚ0572

ⓐ **positive**
ⓑ *elec* **positive, positive pole**
a 陽性 ようせい positivity
陽画 ようが positive photographic print
陽子 ようし proton
b 陽極 ようきょく positive pole, anode
陽電気 ようでんき positive electricity

正 ▷positive
セイ ショウ ただ(しい) ただ(す) まさ まさ(に)   Ⓚ2926

ⓐ *math* **positive**
ⓑ *elec* **positive**
a 正数 せいすう positive number
  正号 せいごう plus sign
  正比例 せいひれい direct proportion
b 正電気 せいでんき positive electricity

possess

有 蔵 持 属 享 具

有 ▷have
ユウ ウ あ(る)   Ⓚ2576

ⓐ [also prefix] **have, possess, own, retain**
ⓑ **having the characteristic [property] of**
a 有産階級 ゆうさんかいきゅう propertied [proprietary] classes, bourgeoisie
  有意義な ゆういぎな significant, useful, worthwhile
  有資格者 ゆうしかくしゃ eligible person, qualified person
  所有する しょゆうする have, own, possess
  保有 ほゆう possession, maintenance
b 有望な ゆうぼうな promising, hopeful
  有害な ゆうがいな harmful, pernicious, noxious
  有利な ゆうりな advantageous, favorable; profitable
  有名な ゆうめいな famous, noted, celebrated; notorious
  有効な ゆうこうな effective, valid
  有力な ゆうりょくな powerful, influential
  有限の ゆうげんの limited; finite
  有料の ゆうりょうの fee-charging, pay, toll

蔵 ▷own
ゾウ くら   Ⓚ2088

own, possess, keep (a collection of books)
  蔵書 ぞうしょ one's library, book collection
  蔵本 ぞうほん one's library
  所蔵 しょぞう possession

持 ▷hold
ジ も(つ) -も(ち) も(てる)   Ⓚ0333

hold in one's possession, possess, have
  持薬 じやく favorite medicine
  享持する きょうじする secure rights and profits
  住持 じゅうじ chief priest (of a temple)

属 ▷belong to
ゾク   Ⓚ2711

belong to, pertain to, be one of
  付属する ふぞくする be attached to, belong to
  所属する しょぞくする belong to, be attached to
  専属する せんぞくする belong exclusively to
  軍属 ぐんぞく army civilian employee

享 ▷enjoy
キョウ   Ⓚ1765

(benefit from something given) **enjoy, receive, be given, possess**
  享受する きょうじゅする enjoy, receive, be given
  享有する きょうゆうする enjoy, possess, participate in
  享楽 きょうらく enjoyment
  享年 きょうねん age at death

具 ▷possess
グ   Ⓚ2208

[original meaning] **possess, be possessed of, be endowed with**
  具備する ぐびする be endowed [equipped] with, possess
  具象する ぐしょうする embody, express concretely
  具体的な ぐたいてきな concrete, definite, specific
  具足 ぐそく completeness; armor, coat of mail

possessive particles

之 乃

之 ▷possessive particle
シ の これ   Ⓚ2886

possessive particle
  鳥之巣 とりのす bird's nest
  実業之日本社 じつぎょうのにほんしゃ Jitsugyo no Nihon Sha (name of a publisher)

乃 ▷possessive particle
ナイ ダイ の すなわ(ち)   Ⓚ2535

possessive particle
  日乃丸 ひのまる Rising Sun flag
  波乃花 なみのはな crest of a wave; salt

possible
可　能

可 ▷-able
カ　　　　　　　　　Ⓚ2562

[also prefix] -able, -ible, possible, can
可能な かのうな possible, potential, practical
可動の かどうの movable
可溶性 かようせい solubility
可視光線 かしこうせん visible ray
可処分の かしょぶんの disposable
可燃物 かねんぶつ combustibles, (in)flammable
　materials
不可解な ふかかいな incomprehensible, inexplica-
　ble, baffling

能 ▷possible
ノウ　　　　　　　Ⓚ1207

possible, can
可能性 かのうせい possibility
不能な ふのうな impossible; impotent

posthumous worlds
天　幽　獄

天 ▷Heaven
テン あめ あま-　　　　　Ⓚ2898

(abode of God and blessed souls) **Heaven, paradise**
天国 てんごく Kingdom of Heaven, Paradise
天使 てんし angel
昇天 しょうてん the Ascension; death

幽 ▷world of the dead
ユウ　　　　　　　Ⓚ2592

world of the dead, the other world, Hades
幽霊 ゆうれい ghost, apparition
幽冥 ゆうめい Hades, realm of the dead
幽界 ゆうかい Hades, realm of the dead
幽鬼 ゆうき departed soul, spirit of the dead

獄 ▷hell
ゴク　　　　　　　Ⓚ0644

hell
地獄 じごく hell; inferno
煉獄 れんごく purgatory

post station
駅　逓　宿

駅 ▷relay station
エキ　　　　　　　Ⓚ1618

[original meaning] relay station, post station, stage
宿駅 しゅくえき post town, relay station

逓 ▷relay
テイ　　　　　　　Ⓚ2675

(place where fresh horses are posted) **relay, post station**
駅逓 えきてい transportation from post to post;
　postal service in Meiji era

宿 ▷post station
シュク やど やど(る) やど(す)　Ⓚ1985

post station, relay station, stage, stopping place
宿場 しゅくば post station, relay station

posture
姿　態

姿 ▷posture
シ すがた　　　　　Ⓚ2291

posture, bearing, pose
姿勢 しせい posture, position, poise, attitude
姿態 したい figure, person; pose

態 ▷attitude
タイ　　　　　　　Ⓚ2478

[original meaning] attitude, posture
態度 たいど attitude, manner
態勢 たいせい attitude, preparedness, condition

potency
効　験　能　機

効 ▷effect
コウ き(く)　　　　　Ⓚ1164

effect, efficacy (esp. of drugs), virtue
効果 こうか effect, efficacy; result
効率 こうりつ efficiency
効能 こうのう effect, efficacy
即効 そっこう immediate effect

薬効 やっこう effect of a medicine
特効薬 とっこうやく specific medicine
効力 こうりょく effect, efficacy; effect (as of a law),
　　validity
有効な ゆうこうな effective, valid
無効 むこう invalidity, ineffectiveness

験 ▷efficacy
ケン　ゲン　　　　　　　　Ⓚ1628

efficacy (as of medicine), effectiveness
　効験 こうけん effect, efficacy, virtue

能 ▷action
ノウ　　　　　　　　　　　Ⓚ1207

action, function, effect, efficiency
　能率 のうりつ efficiency
　機能 きのう function, faculty
　性能 せいのう performance, capacity, efficiency
　効能 こうのう effect, efficacy

機 ▷function
キ　はた　　　　　　　　　Ⓚ0989

function (as of the mind), action
　機能 きのう function, faculty
　動機 どうき motive, incentive

powder
粉　　　　末

粉 ▷powder
フン　こ　こな　　　　　　Ⓚ1186

[original meaning] **powder, dust**
　粉末 ふんまつ powder
　粉乳 ふんにゅう powdered milk
　鉄粉 てっぷん iron powder
　精粉 せいふん fine powder

末 ▷powder
マツ　バツ　すえ　　　　　Ⓚ2940

ⓐ **powder**
ⓑ **suffix after names of powders**
　a 粉末 ふんまつ powder
　b 硼酸末 ほうさんまつ borax powder

power and authority
力　威　勢　権　覇

力 ▷power
リョク　リキ　ちから　　　Ⓚ2860

(power in general) **power to influence, strength,
influence, authority**
　権力 けんりょく power, authority, influence
　勢力 せいりょく influence, power, might; force (of a
　　typhoon)
　威力 いりょく power, might, authority, influence
　迫力 はくりょく power, force, punch, appeal
　有力者 ゆうりょくしゃ influential person, man of
　　importance
　金力 きんりょく power of money
　強力な きょうりょくな strong, powerful, mighty

威 ▷might
イ　　　　　　　　　　　　Ⓚ2993

**might, impressive strength, power, authority,
influence**
　威力 いりょく power, might, authority, influence
　威勢 いせい spirits, dash; power
　威張る いばる put on airs, be haughty; boast, brag
　権威 けんい authority, power
　示威 じい show of force
　猛威 もうい fierceness, fury, vehemence
　球威の有る投球 きゅういのあるとうきゅう baseball
　　powerful delivery
　神威 しんい might of Heaven

勢 ▷power (to influence)
セイ　いきお(い)　　　　　Ⓚ2487

(ability to influence) **power to influence, influence,
strength, authority**
　勢力 せいりょく influence, power, might; force (of a
　　typhoon)
　勢門 せいもん influential family
　権勢 けんせい power, influence, authority
　党勢 とうせい strength of a party
　優勢な ゆうせいな superior, leading, predominant
　豪勢な ごうせいな great, grand, magnificent
　虚勢 きょせい bluff, bluster, false show of power

権 ▷power (to control)
ケン　ゴン　　　　　　　　Ⓚ0977

**power to control, ability to exact obedience,
authority**
　権威 けんい authority, power
　権力 けんりょく power, authority, influence
　権勢 けんせい power, influence, authority

政権 せいけん political power, administrative power
実権 じっけん real power
制海権 せいかいけん command of the sea, naval supremacy

覇 ▷supremacy
ハ　㊀2379

supremacy, mastery, hegemony, domination, leadership
覇権 はけん supremacy, mastery, hegemony, supreme power
覇道 はどう military government [rule]
制覇する せいはする conquer, dominate, gain supremacy; win the championship

praise

賛 頌 謳 讃 美 褒
嘉 彰 称 賞 揚

賛 ▷praise
サン　㊀2446

[formerly also 讃] praise, laud, admire, commend
賛辞 さんじ eulogy, praise, compliment
賛美 さんび praise, admiration
賛嘆 さんたん praise, admiration
賞賛(=称賛)する しょうさんする laud, praise, admire, commend
絶賛 ぜっさん great admiration
礼賛 らいさん worship, adoration, glorification

頌 ▷eulogize
ショウ ジュ　㊀0956

eulogize, extol, praise highly
頌徳 しょうとく eulogy

謳 ▷extol
オウ うた(う)　

[original meaning] sing (a tune)
謳歌する おうかする glorify, eulogize, applaud

讃 ▷praise
サン たた(える)　㊀1485

[now usu. 賛] [original meaning] praise, laud, admire, commend
讃嘆 さんたん praise, admiration
讃辞 さんじ eulogy, praise, compliment
讃美歌 さんびか hymn, psalm
和讃 わさん Japanese translation of Buddhist hymns of praise

賞賛(=称賛)する しょうさんする praise, laud, admire

美 ▷regard as beautiful
ビ うつく(しい)　㊀195

regard as beautiful, praise, extol
賛美する さんびする praise, admire
嘆美する たんびする admire, adore, extol

褒 ▷commend
ホウ ほ(める)　㊀184

commend, praise, laud, award, give recognition to
褒章 ほうしょう medal of merit
褒美 ほうび reward, prize
褒賞 ほうしょう prize, reward
過褒 かほう overpraise, excessive compliment
毀誉褒貶 きよほうへん praise and censure, criticisms

嘉 ▷commend (esp. an inferior)
カ よみ(する)　㊀205

commend (esp. an inferior), praise, approve of, applaud
嘉納する かのうする accept with pleasure
嘉賞 かしょう commendation, approval

彰 ▷proclaim merits
ショウ　㊀164

[sometimes also 章] proclaim the merits of a person (to the public), make (a person's virtues) well known, give public recognition
彰徳する しょうとくする [rare] praise publicly, make another's virtues well known
顕彰する けんしょうする give recognition, exalt, honor
表彰する ひょうしょうする commend (officially), give public recognition

称 ▷acclaim
ショウ　㊀1075

acclaim, commend, praise, admire
称賛(=賞賛) しょうさん laudation, praise, admiration, commendation
称揚 しょうよう praise, admiration, exaltation

賞 ▷express admiration
ショウ　㊀2274

express admiration, praise, commend
賞賛(=称賛)する しょうさんする laud, praise, admire, commend
激賞 げきしょう high praise, unbounded admiration

揚 ▷exalt
ヨウ あ(げる) -あ(げ) あ(がる)　　Ⓚ0542

(raise to a higher level of dignity) **exalt, extol, praise, enhance, uplift**

　称揚する しょうようする praise, admire, exalt, extol
　発揚する はつようする exalt, raise, enhance
　高揚(=昂揚)する こうようする exalt, enhance, uplift; surge up

pray and worship
祈祷願拝祀崇斎呪

祈 ▷pray
キ いの(る)　　Ⓚ0779

[original meaning] **pray**

　祈祷 きとう prayer
　祈願する きがんする pray, implore
　祈念 きねん prayer

祷 ▷pray
トウ いの(る)　　Ⓚ0885

ⓐ [original meaning] **pray, wish for**
ⓑ **prayer**

a　祈祷 きとう prayer
　主祷文 しゅとうぶん The Lord's Prayer
b　黙祷 もくとう silent prayer
　祝祷 しゅくとう benediction, blessing (in Christianity)

願 ▷pray
ガン ねが(う)　　Ⓚ1637

pray, prayer

　願文 がんもん written petition read before a god
　祈願する きがんする pray, implore

拝 ▷worship
ハイ おが(む)　　Ⓚ0268

(render religious reverence to) **worship, pay reverence to, pay one's respects**

　拝殿 はいでん front shrine, hall of worship
　参拝する さんぱいする worship, pay reverence at, visit a shrine [temple]
　礼拝 れいはい(=らいはい) worship; church service

祀 ▷worship as god
シ まつ(る)

worship as god, deify

　祭祀 さいし religious service; festival

崇 ▷reverence
スウ　　Ⓚ1990

reverence, revere, worship, venerate, adore, esteem

　崇敬 すうけい reverence, admiration
　崇拝 すうはい worship, adoration
　崇高な すうこうな lofty, sublime, noble
　尊崇 そんすう reverence, veneration

斎 ▷observe religious abstinence
サイ　　Ⓚ1817

[rarely also 斉] **observe religious abstinence, abstain, purify oneself, fast**

　斎戒 さいかい religious purification
　潔斎 けっさい religious abstinence, purification

呪 ▷spell
ジュ のろ(う)　　Ⓚ0245

spell, incantation, curse, charm

　呪縛 じゅばく spell
　呪文 じゅもん spell, charm
　呪術 じゅじゅつ magic, sorcery; spell
　呪符 じゅふ amulet, charm
　呪詛 じゅそ curse, hex
　神呪 しんじゅ mystic spell, *dhāraṇī*

precept
戒　　訓

戒 ▷commandment
カイ いまし(める)　　Ⓚ2760

commandment, Buddhist commandment, *śīla*, precept

　戒律 かいりつ commandments, precepts
　十戒 じっかい the ten precepts of Buddhism
　破戒 はかい offense against the Buddhist commandments

訓 ▷precept
クン　　Ⓚ1322

precept, lesson, admonition, instruction, teachings

　家訓 かくん family precepts
　教訓 きょうくん lesson, precept, teachings
　処生訓 しょせいくん guiding motto for one's life

precious stones

玉 珂 璧 琥 珀 珠 瑛
瑠 璃 晶 玖 琉 琳

玉 ▷gem
ギョク たま -だま   Ⓚ2919

gem, jewel(ry), precious stone
- 玉石混淆(=玉石混交) ぎょくせきこんこう mixture of good and bad, jumble of wheat and tares
- 宝玉 ほうぎょく jewel, gem, precious stone
- 珠玉 しゅぎょく jewel, gem
- 硬玉 こうぎょく jadeite

珂 ▷white agate
カ   Ⓚ0816

[original meaning, now archaic] white agate, jewel

璧 ▷disk-shaped jewel
ヘキ   Ⓚ2519

disk-shaped jewel with a hole in the center
- 完璧な かんぺきな perfect, flawless

琥 ▷amber
コ   Ⓚ0912

amber
- 琥珀 こはく amber

珀 ▷amber
ハク   Ⓚ0815

amber
- 琥珀 こはく amber

珠 ▷pearl
シュ   Ⓚ0854

pearl
- 珠玉 しゅぎょく jewel, gem
- 真珠 しんじゅ pearl

瑛 ▷transparent gem
エイ   Ⓚ0910

[original meaning, now archaic] transparent gem, jewel
- 玉瑛 ぎょくえい transparent gem, crystal

瑠 ▷lapis lazuli
ル   Ⓚ0972

(kind of gemstone) lapis lazuli
- 瑠璃(=琉璃) るり lapis lazuli, lapis lazuli blue; [archaic] glass

璃 ▷glassy substance
リ   Ⓚ098◆

glassy substance, glass; crystal
- 瑠璃(=琉璃) るり lapis lazuli, lapis lazuli blue; [archaic] glass
- 玻璃 はり crystal; glass
- 浄瑠璃 じょうるり joruri, ballad drama; clear lapis lazuli

晶 ▷crystal
ショウ   Ⓚ218◆

(transparent mineral) crystal
- 水晶 すいしょう rock crystal

玖 ▷beautiful black jewel
キュウ ク   Ⓚ074◆

[original meaning, now archaic] beautiful black jewel

琉 ▷lapis lazuli
リュウ ル   Ⓚ0882

(kind of gemstone) lapis lazuli
- 琉璃(=瑠璃) るり lapis lazuli, lapis lazuli blue; [archaic] glass

琳 ▷beautiful gem
リン   Ⓚ0913

[rare] beautiful gem
- 琳瑯 りんろう beautiful gem
- 琳瑯たる りんろうたる like the tinkling sound of a jade

precipitation →KINDS OF PRECIPITATION

prepare

備 調

備 ▷provide
ビ そな(える) そな(わる)   Ⓚ0126

[original meaning] provide for [against], prepare for [against], get ready
- 備考 びこう explanatory note, remarks (for reference)
- 備蓄 びちく saving for [against] emergency, storing
- 準備する じゅんびする provide for [against], prepare for [against]

調 ▷prepare
チョウ しら(べる) しら(べ) ととの(う) ととの(える)   Ⓚ1417

prepare, make ready, make to order

調製 ちょうせい preparation, manufacture, execution (of an order)
調達 ちょうたつ supply, procurement; execution (of an order); raising (money)
調度 ちょうど personal effects, furnishings, supplies
新調する しんちょうする make (a new suit), have (new shoes) made

present

今　当　現

今 ▷present
コン キン いま　　　Ⓚ1712

present, now
今後 こんご after this, from now on
今日 こんにち today, these days
今昔 こんじゃく past and present, yesterday and today
今日は こんにちは Hello/Good morning [afternoon, day]
昨今 さっこん these days

当 ▷the present
トウ あ(たる) あ(たり) あ(てる) あ(て)　　　Ⓚ1865

(occurring presently) **the present, present, current**
当分 とうぶん for some time, for a while, for the present, temporarily
当面の とうめんの present, immediate; urgent, pressing

現 ▷actual
ゲン あらわ(れる) あらわ(す)　　　Ⓚ0879

[also prefix] (occurring at the present moment) **actual, present, current, existing, now**
現在 げんざい present time, now; present tense; actually
現代 げんだい present age, modern times, today
現行の げんこうの present, existing, current, actual
現職 げんしょく present post [office]; incumbent
現住所 げんじゅうしょ present address
現内閣 げんないかく present cabinet

preserve

留　保　持

留 ▷keep
リュウ ル と(める) -ど(め) と(まる) とど(まる)　　　Ⓚ2235

[original meaning] **keep in place, keep from moving, keep in position**
係留する けいりゅうする moor, anchor
慰留する いりゅうする dissuade from resigning

保 ▷preserve
ホ たも(つ)　　　Ⓚ0077

ⓐ (maintain unchanged) **preserve, maintain, keep, conserve, retain, hold**
ⓑ (maintain in good condition) **preserve, keep up, maintain**
ⓐ 保持する ほじする maintain, preserve, retain
保有する ほゆうする possess, maintain
留保する りゅうほする reserve, withhold, keep back
確保する かくほする secure, make sure of, ensure
ⓑ 保存する ほぞんする preserve, conserve, maintain, store, keep
保管する ほかんする take custody [charge] of, keep
保温 ほおん keeping warm, heat insulation
保安 ほあん preservation of public peace
保健 ほけん (preservation of) health, sanitation
保全 ほぜん integrity, preservation
保線 ほせん track maintenance

持 ▷uphold
ジ も(つ) -も(ち) も(てる)　　　Ⓚ0333

uphold, preserve, maintain, observe
持戒 じかい observance of the Buddhist commandments
矜持 きょうじ(=きんじ) pride, dignity

preserved foods

漬　干

漬 ▷pickles
つ(ける) つ(かる) -づ(け)　　　Ⓚ0636

pickles
千枚漬け せんまいづけ pickled sliced radishes
松前漬け まつまえづけ Matsumae pickles

干 ▷**dried food**
カン ほ(す) ほ(し)- -ぼ(し) ひ(る) Ⓚ2863

dried food
梅干し うめぼし pickled *ume*
白子干し しらすぼし dried young sardines

preserve food
漬 燻 薫

漬 ▷**pickle**
つ(ける) つ(かる) -づ(け) Ⓚ0636

pickle (vegetables), salt, preserve
漬け物 つけもの pickles, pickled vegetable
漬け菜 つけな pickled [salted] greens
菜を漬ける なをつける pickle greens
梅を塩に漬ける うめをしおにつける salt plums;
  preserve plums in salt

燻 ▷**smoke**
クン いぶ(す) いぶ(る) くす(ぶる)
くゆ(らす)

[now also 薫] [original meaning] **smoke, fumigate,
fume**
燻製 くんせい smoking (fish or meat)
燻蒸する くんじょうする fumigate, smoke

薫 ▷**smoke**
クン かお(る) Ⓚ2094

[formerly also 燻] **smoke, fumigate, fume**
薫香 くんこう incense; fragrance
薫製 くんせい smoking (fish or meat)

press →COMPEL AND PRESS

prevent
防 止

防 ▷**prevent**
ボウ ふせ(ぐ) Ⓚ0242

ⓐ **prevent, hold in check, keep away, shut out**
ⓑ **preventing, -proof, anti-**
a 防止する ぼうしする prevent, hold in check
  防除 ぼうじょ pest control, extermination
  防災 ぼうさい disaster prevention
  消防 しょうぼう fire fighting, prevention and
    extinction of fires
  予防 よぼう prevention, protection, precaution
b 防火 ぼうか fire prevention, fireproof

防音 ぼうおん soundproof
防水 ぼうすい waterproof
防虫剤 ぼうちゅうざい insecticide, vermicide
防腐剤 ぼうふざい antiseptic

止 ▷**stop**
シ と(まる) -ど(まり) と(める) -ど(め)
や(める) や(む) Ⓚ2545

**stop an action from occurring, check, deter, dis-
suade**
止音器 しおんき (piano) damper
抑止する よくしする deter, check, hold back
阻止する そしする obstruct, check, hinder
制止する せいしする control, check, stop (a person)
  from (doing)
禁止 きんし prohibition, forbiddance, ban
防止 ぼうし prevention, check
諫止する かんしする dissuade

price →FEE AND PRICE

principle
律 理

律 ▷**law**
リツ リチ Ⓚ0322

[suffix] **law (of nature), principle**
自然律 しぜんりつ natural law

理 ▷**basic principle**
リ Ⓚ0881

**basic principle(s) (as of a science), rationale of
things, law, theory, doctrine**
理論 りろん theory
原理 げんり principle, theory
真理 しんり truth
定理 ていり theorem, proposition
心理 しんり mental state, mentality; psychology
生理 せいり physiological functions, physiology;
  menstruation
地理 ちり geographical features, topography;
  geography
哲理 てつり philosophy (of something)

print and publish
刷印植刊版載掲幀

刷 ▷print
サツ す(る) -ず(り) Ⓚ1169

print, put in print
印刷 いんさつ printing
縮刷する しゅくさつする print in reduced size
増刷 ぞうさつ additional printing, reprinting

印 ▷print
イン しるし -じるし Ⓚ0733

print
印刷 いんさつ printing
印行する いんこうする print and publish
影印 えいいん phototype process, photoengraving

植 ▷typeset
ショク う(える) う(わる) Ⓚ0903

typeset, set in type
植字 しょくじ typesetting, composition
誤植 ごしょく typographical error, misprint
写植 しゃしょく phototypesetting

刊 ▷publish
カン Ⓚ0167

[also suffix] **publish**
刊行 かんこう publication
発刊 はっかん publication, issue
未刊の みかんの unpublished
既刊の きかんの already published
隔月刊 かくげつかん published bimonthly
創刊号 そうかんごう inaugural number, first issue

版 ▷publishing
ハン Ⓚ0775

publishing, printing
版行する はんこうする publish, print
版元 はんもと publisher
版権 はんけん copyright
出版 しゅっぱん publishing; publication
再版する さいはんする reprint

載 ▷put in print
サイ の(せる) の(る) Ⓚ2814

ⓐ put in print, publish, carry, put on record
ⓑ appear in print, be published
a 載録する さいろくする record
掲載 けいさい publication, insertion, printing
記載する きさいする record, state, mention

ab 連載 れんさい serialization, serial publication
転載する てんさいする reproduce, reprint
登載する とうさいする register, record

掲 ▷display in writing
ケイ かか(げる) Ⓚ0450

display in writing, mention, show
掲載する けいさいする publish, insert, print
前掲の ぜんけいの shown above, aforementioned

幀 ▷bookbinding
テイ

[now usu. 丁] **bookbinding**
装幀する そうていする bind (a book)

printing plate
版　梓

版 ▷printing plate
ハン Ⓚ0775

[sometimes also 板] [also suffix] **printing plate, printing block, wood block**
版木 はんぎ (printing) block, woodcut
版画 はんが woodcut print
活版 かっぱん printing, typography
凸版 とっぱん letterpress, relief printing
木版 もくはん wood block printing, wood engraving
原色版 げんしょくばん heliotype
謄写版 とうしゃばん mimeograph

梓 ▷printing block
シ あずさ Ⓚ0873

printing block, woodcut; wood printing
上梓 じょうし publishing

prison
獄　監

獄 ▷prison
ゴク Ⓚ0644

prison, jail
獄中記 ごくちゅうき diary written in prison
獄衣 ごくい prison uniform
獄死 ごくし death in prison
出獄 しゅつごく release from prison
牢獄 ろうごく prison, jail
脱獄 だつごく prison break, jailbreak

監 ▷**prison**
カン   Ⓚ2483

prison
監獄 かんごく prison, jail
監禁 かんきん imprisonment, confinement
監房 かんぼう cell, ward

prisoner
虜　囚

虜 ▷**captive**
リョ   Ⓚ2784

[original meaning] **captive, prisoner**
虜囚 りょしゅう captive, prisoner
捕虜 ほりょ prisoner of war, captive
俘虜 ふりょ prisoner, POW, captive

囚 ▷**prisoner**
シュウ   Ⓚ2618

[also suffix] **prisoner, convict, criminal**
囚人 しゅうじん prisoner, convict
囚衣 しゅうい prison uniform
女囚 じょしゅう female convict
虜囚 りょしゅう captive, prisoner
死刑囚 しけいしゅう criminal condemned to death
脱獄囚 だつごくしゅう jail-breaker, escaped prisoner

private →SECRET AND PRIVATE

prizes
賞　杯　章

賞 ▷**prize**
ショウ   Ⓚ2274

[also suffix] **prize, award, reward**
賞金 しょうきん prize, award, reward
賞状 しょうじょう certificate of merit
賞品 しょうひん prize, trophy
賞罰 しょうばつ reward and punishment
懸賞 けんしょう prize competition; prize, reward
受賞する じゅしょうする win a prize

杯 ▷**prize cup**
ハイ さかずき   Ⓚ0761

[also suffix] **prize cup, trophy**
賞杯 しょうはい prize cup, trophy
賜杯 しはい trophy given by the emperor [prince]

デ杯 ではい Davis Cup
優勝杯 ゆうしょうはい championship cup, trophy

章 ▷**decoration**
ショウ   Ⓚ1819

[also suffix] **decoration, medal, order**
勲章 くんしょう decoration, order, medal
褒章 ほうしょう medal of merit
瑞宝章 ずいほうしょう Order of the Sacred Treasure

products of combustion
灰　殻　炭　煤　煙

灰 ▷**ash**
カイ はい   Ⓚ2573

[original meaning] **ash, ashes**
灰燼 かいじん ashes, ashes and cinder
灰分 かいぶん ash content
重灰 じゅうかい dense ash

殻 ▷**cinders**
カク から がら   Ⓚ1354

cinders, ashes
燃え殻 もえがら cinders
石炭殻 せきたんがら coal cinders
吸い殻 すいがら cigarette butt

炭 ▷**charcoal**
タン すみ   Ⓚ1947

charcoal
木炭 もくたん charcoal
薪炭 しんたん firewood and charcoal
塗炭 とたん misery, distress

煤 ▷**soot**
バイ すす すす(ける)   Ⓚ0935

soot
煤煙 ばいえん soot and smoke
煤塵 ばいじん dust and soot, particulate matter

煙 ▷**smoke**
エン けむ(る) けむり けむ(い)   Ⓚ0936

smoke
煙突 えんとつ chimney, smokestack
煙幕 えんまく smoke screen

professionals →WORKERS AND PROFESSIONALS

profit
利 益 儲 得

利 ▷**profit**
リ き(く)　　　　　　Ⓚ1029

profit, gains, advantage, benefit
利益 りえき profit, gains; benefit
利害 りがい interests
利食い りぐい profit taking
利得 りとく profit, benefit, gain
営利 えいり profit, gain

益 ▷**profit**
エキ ヤク ま(す)　　　　Ⓚ1978

[also suffix] **profit, gain**
益金 えききん profit, gain
差益 さえき marginal profits
利益 りえき profit, gains; benefit
収益 しゅうえき profit, earnings, proceeds, returns
損益 そんえき profit and loss; advantage and disadvantage
売却益 ばいきゃくえき profit on sales

儲 ▷**profit**
チョ もう(ける) もう(かる)　Ⓚ0157

profit, make a profit, gain, earn
儲け もうけ profit, earnings
儲け話 もうけばなし get-rich-quick scheme, moneymaking scheme
儲け物 もうけもの good bargain, unexpected profit, windfall, godsend
金儲け かねもうけ making money
丸儲け まるもうけ clear profit
ぼろ儲け ぼろもうけ easy profit, easy money

得 ▷**gain**
トク え(る) う(る)　　　Ⓚ0435

(something earned) **gain, profit**
損得 そんとく advantage and disadvantage; loss and gain
利得 りとく profit, benefit, gain
両得 りょうとく double gain

profound
玄 幽 奥 深 滉

玄 ▷**profound**
ゲン　　　　　　　　Ⓚ1722

profound, abstruse, mystic, occult, mysterious, esoteric
玄妙な げんみょうな abstruse, occult, mysterious
玄関 げんかん entrance, (front) door
幽玄な ゆうげんな subtle and profound, quiet and beautiful, occult

幽 ▷**deep hidden**
ユウ　　　　　　　　Ⓚ2592

deep hidden, profound
幽玄な ゆうげんな subtle and profound, quiet and beautiful, occult
幽愁 ゆうしゅう deep contemplation

奥 ▷**inmost**
オウ おく　　　　　　Ⓚ2458

a **inmost, mysterious, deep, profound**
b **inmost part, innermost, mystery, inner depths**
a 奥義 おうぎ(=おくぎ) secret principles, secrets, hidden mysteries
胸奥 きょうおう one's heart of hearts, the depths of one's mind
b 深奥 しんおう esoteric doctrines, mysteries, depth
内奥 ないおう inner part, depths, recesses

深 ▷**deep**
シン ふか(い) −ぶか(い) ふか(まる)
ふか(める)　　　　　　Ⓚ0480

(difficult to fathom) **deep, profound, unfathomable, innermost**
深遠 しんえん profundity, depth
深奥 しんおう esoteric doctrines, mysteries, depth

滉 ▷**deep and vast**
コウ オウ　　　　　　Ⓚ0605

deep and vast like an expanse of water
滉漾 こうよう vastness, great depth

project
映　写

映 ▷**project**
エイ うつ(る) うつ(す) は(える)
-ば(え)　　　　　　　　　　Ⓚ0793

project (an image), screen (a film), show
映像 えいぞう (TV) picture, image; reflection
映写 えいしゃ projection
映画 えいが cinema, film, movie
上映する じょうえいする screen, show, project
放映する ほうえいする televise, telecast

写 ▷**project**
シャ うつ(す) うつ(る)　　　Ⓚ1726

project (an image), show (a film), screen
映写 えいしゃ projection
試写 ししゃ preview, private showing

projectiles and bombs
弾　丸　矢　槍　爆　雷

弾 ▷**projectile**
ダン ひ(く) -ひ(き) はず(む) たま Ⓚ0524

[also suffix] **projectile, bullet, shell, missile, (cannon) ball, bomb**
弾丸 だんがん shot, bullet, shell
弾薬 だんやく ammunition
弾頭 だんとう warhead
弾道弾 だんどうだん ballistic missile
爆弾 ばくだん bomb
砲弾 ほうだん cannonball, shell
銃弾 じゅうだん bullet, shot
散弾 さんだん shot
実弾 じつだん ball cartridge, live ammunition; money
不発弾 ふはつだん unexploded shell

丸 ▷**round projectile**
ガン まる まる(い) まる(める)　Ⓚ2883

round projectile, ball
砲丸 ほうがん cannonball
弾丸 だんがん shot, bullet, shell
銃丸 じゅうがん bullet

矢 ▷**arrow**
シ や　　　　　　　　　　　Ⓚ1733

[original meaning] **arrow**
弓矢 きゅうし(=ゆみや) bow and arrow
一矢を報いる いっしをむくいる return a blow, retaliate

槍 ▷**spear**
ソウ やり　　　　　　　　　Ⓚ0966

spear, lance
槍術 そうじゅつ spearmanship
槍騎兵 そうきへい lancer
聖槍 せいそう holy lance
竹槍 ちくそう bamboo spear

爆 ▷**bomb**
バク　　　　　　　　　　　Ⓚ1020

abbrev. of 爆弾 ばくだん: **bomb**
原爆 げんばく atomic bomb
水爆 すいばく hydrogen bomb

雷 ▷**explosive device**
ライ かみなり　　　　　　　Ⓚ2432

explosive device, mine, torpedo
雷撃 らいげき torpedo attack
機雷 きらい mine
地雷 じらい land mine
水雷 すいらい torpedo, mine

promise
約　締　協　契　盟　誓

約 ▷**promise**
ヤク　　　　　　　　　　　Ⓚ1177

ⓐ **promise, make an agreement, conclude a treaty**
ⓑ **promise, agreement, contract, treaty**
a 約束 やくそく promise, vow, pledge
契約 けいやく contract, agreement
予約 よやく reservation, preengagement; subscription
公約 こうやく public pledge [promise]
誓約 せいやく vow, pledge, oath, swearing
b 約款 やっかん article, stipulation, provision, clause
条約 じょうやく treaty
婚約 こんやく engagement, betrothal
解約 かいやく dissolution [cancellation] of a contract

締 ▷conclude (a treaty)
テイ し(まる) し(まり) し(める) -し(め)
-じ(め)　　　　　　　　　　　　Ⓚ1274

unite two nations by reaching an agreement: **conclude (a treaty), contract, form (an alliance)**

締結する ていけつする conclude, contract
締約 ていやく conclusion of a treaty
締盟 ていめい conclusion of a treaty of alliance

協 ▷reach an agreement
キョウ　　　　　　　　　　　Ⓚ0074

reach an agreement, agree upon, make an agreement

協議 きょうぎ conference, deliberation
協議会 きょうぎかい conference, council
協商 きょうしょう entente, agreement
協約 きょうやく pact, convention, agreement
協定 きょうてい agreement, pact
妥協 だきょう compromise, agreement, understanding

契 ▷make an agreement
ケイ ちぎ(る)　　　　　　　　Ⓚ2293

ⓐ **make an agreement, agree on, pledge, promise**
ⓑ **agreement, contract**

a 契約 けいやく contract, agreement
b 黙契 もっけい implicit agreement, tacit understanding

盟 ▷alliance
メイ　　　　　　　　　　　　Ⓚ2434

alliance, league, pledge, pact

盟約 めいやく pledge, pact, alliance, league
盟邦 めいほう ally, allied powers
盟友 めいゆう sworn friend
同盟 どうめい alliance, league, union
連盟 れんめい union, federation, league
加盟 かめい participation, affiliation

誓 ▷vow
セイ ちか(う)　　　　　　　　Ⓚ2401

[original meaning] **vow, swear, pledge, make [take] an oath**

誓約する せいやくする vow, pledge, make [take] an oath, swear
誓願 せいがん oath, vow, pledge
宣誓する せんせいする make [take] an oath, swear, vow

prospering and prosperity
隆 振 興 盛 昌 栄 繁 賑

隆 ▷prosper
リュウ　　　　　　　　　　　Ⓚ0498

prosper, rise to prosperity, flourish

隆隆たる りゅうりゅうたる prosperous, thriving; brawny
隆盛 りゅうせい prosperity
隆昌 りゅうしょう prosperity
隆運 りゅううん prosperity, good fortune
興隆 こうりゅう prosperity, rise

振 ▷rise
シン ふ(る) ぶ(る) ふ(り) -ぶ(り) ふ(るう)
ふ(れる)　　　　　　　　　　Ⓚ0388

rise, prosper, thrive

振興 しんこう promotion, furtherance, rousing
不振 ふしん dullness, depression, stagnation, slump

興 ▷rise to prosperity
コウ キョウ おこ(る) おこ(す)　Ⓚ2525

rise to prosperity, rise, prosper, flourish

興隆 こうりゅう prosperity, rise
興亡 こうぼう rise and fall, ups and downs
興起する こうきする rise, be in the ascendant; rouse, stir
新興の しんこうの rising, newly-established
勃興 ぼっこう sudden rise, sudden increase in power

盛 ▷prosperous
セイ ジョウ も(る) さか(る)
さか(ん)　　　　　　　　　　Ⓚ2332

prosperous, flourishing, successful, booming

盛衰 せいすい ups and downs, rise and fall, prosperity and decline
盛況 せいきょう prosperity, boom, success
繁盛(=繁昌)する はんじょうする prosper, flourish, thrive
隆盛 りゅうせい prosperity

昌 ▷prospering
ショウ　　　　　　　　　　　Ⓚ2140

prospering, flourishing, prosperous, glorious

繁昌(=繁盛) はんじょう prosperity

栄 ▷flourish
エイ さか(える) は(え) -ば(え)
は(える) Ⓚ2231

flourish, prosper, thrive, be prosperous
栄落 えいらく flourishing and declining
栄枯盛衰 えいこせいすい prosperity and decline,
　rise and fall
繁栄する はんえいする prosper, thrive, flourish

繁 ▷thrive
ハン Ⓚ2484

(enjoy prosperity) **thrive, prosper, flourish**
繁栄する はんえいする prosper, thrive, flourish
繁華 はんか prosperity, bustle
繁盛(=繁昌)する はんじょうする prosper, flourish,
　thrive

賑 ▷bustle
シン にぎ(わう) にぎ(わす)
にぎ(やか) Ⓚ1409

bustle, be lively, prosper, flourish, thrive
殷賑 いんしん prosperity, bustle

prosperity →PROSPERING AND PROSPERITY

protect
守 護 庇 衛 警
防 番 保 看

守 ▷protect (by watching over)
シュ ス まも(る) まも(り) もり Ⓚ1861

protect (from, against), defend, guard, watch over
守備 しゅび defense; fielding
守護 しゅご protection, guard, defense, safeguard
守衛 しゅえい guard, doorkeeper
守株 しゅしゅ stupidity, lack of innovation
留守 るす absence (from home); caretaking;
　defending when the lord is absent
攻守 こうしゅ offense and defense; batting and
　fielding
死守する ししゅする defend to the last, defend
　desperately

護 ▷protect (by safeguarding)
ゴ Ⓚ1481

[original meaning] **protect, safeguard, shield, defend**
護衛 ごえい guard, escort
護憲 ごけん safeguarding the constitution
護送 ごそう safeguard, convoy, escort
護身術 ごしんじゅつ art of self-defense

護符 ごふ charm, amulet
守護 しゅご protection, guard, defense, safeguard
保護する ほごする protect, safeguard, preserve,
　look after
援護 えんご support, protection; covering
弁護する べんごする defend, speak in defense of
　(another)
看護する かんごする nurse, attend on
擁護する ようごする protect, defend, support, safe
　guard

庇 ▷protect (by shielding)
ヒ かば(う) ひさし Ⓚ2638

protect, cover, shield
庇護 ひご patronage, protection
曲庇 きょくひ bending the truth [law] to protect
　someone

衛 ▷guard
エイ Ⓚ0686

guard, defend, escort, protect, preserve
衛生 えいせい hygiene, sanitation, preservation of
　health
衛生的 えいせいてき sanitary, hygienic
護衛 ごえい guard, escort
自衛 じえい self-defense, self-protection
防衛 ぼうえい defense, protection
紅衛兵 こうえいへい Red Guards
近衛兵 このえへい personal guard

警 ▷guard against
ケイ Ⓚ2512

guard against, protect, police, watch
警察 けいさつ police, police station
警官 けいかん police officer, policeman
警視庁 けいしちょう Metropolitan Police Office
警戒 けいかい caution, precaution, warning; watch,
　guard, vigilance
警備 けいび guard, defense
警手 けいしゅ guard, attendant

防 ▷defend
ボウ ふせ(ぐ) Ⓚ0242

ⓐ **defend, guard against, protect, resist**
ⓑ **defense**
a 防衛する ぼうえいする defend, protect, safeguard,
　shield
防備 ぼうび defense, defensive preparations
防御 ぼうぎょ defense, protection, safeguard
防戦 ぼうせん defensive battle
b 国防 こくぼう national defense

番 ▷watch
バン   Ⓚ2396

[also suffix] **watch, vigil, guard, lookout**
番人 ばんにん watchman, guard, caretaker
番犬 ばんけん watchdog
留守番 るすばん caretaking (during a person's absence); caretaker

保 ▷preserve
ホ たも(つ)   Ⓚ0077

ⓐ [original meaning] (maintain in safety) **preserve, protect, defend, shield, guard**
ⓑ **care for, look after**; [formerly 哺] **nurse, suckle**
a 保護する ほごする protect, safeguard, preserve, look after
保護者 ほごしゃ guardian; protector
保身 ほしん self-protection
b 保母 ほぼ nurse, kindergarten teacher
保育(=哺育) ほいく nurture, upbringing; lactation, nursing
保育園 ほいくえん day-care center

看 ▷care for
カン   Ⓚ2771

(keep a watchful eye on) **care for (the sick), watch, look after, nurse**
看病する かんびょうする nurse, care for
看護婦 かんごふ nurse
看守 かんしゅ jailer, prison guard

protective coverings
盾 楯 鎧 甲 縅 面 兜 幌

盾 ▷shield
ジュン たて   Ⓚ2590

[original meaning] **shield**
矛盾 むじゅん contradiction
矛盾する むじゅんする be contradictory, be at variance

楯 ▷shield
ジュン たて   Ⓚ0928

shield, escutcheon
楯鱗 じゅんりん placoid scale
防楯 ぼうじゅん gun shield, gun mantlet

鎧 ▷armor
ガイ よろい   Ⓚ1571

armor
鎧竜 がいりゅう ankylosaur
鎧球 がいきゅう American football

鎧袖一触 がいしゅういっしょく beating someone hands down

甲 ▷armor
コウ カン カ   Ⓚ2923

armor; helmet
甲鉄 こうてつ armor plate
甲冑 かっちゅう armor and helmet
装甲部隊 そうこうぶたい armored corps

縅 ▷braid of armor
おど(し)

[sometimes also 威し] **braid or thread of Japanese armor**
緋縅し鎧 ひおどしよろい scarlet-threaded suit of armor

面 ▷mask
メン おも おもて つら   Ⓚ1796

(protective covering for the face) **mask, face guard, protector, headgear**
面頬 めんぼう(=めんぽう) visor, face guard
防毒面 ぼうどくめん gas mask

兜 ▷helmet
ト トウ かぶと   Ⓚ2455

helmet (of armor), headpiece
兜虫 かぶとむし rhinoceros beetle, esp. Japanese rhinoceros beetle
兜蟹 かぶとがに horseshoe crab
鉄兜 てつかぶと steel helmet
鳥兜 とりかぶと aconite, wolfsbane, monkshood; hat used in *bugaku* dance

幌 ▷covering for vehicles
コウ ほろ   Ⓚ0586

covering for vehicles: **canopy, hood, top**
幌馬車 ほろばしゃ covered wagon, prairie schooner

prototype
型   儀

型 ▷type
ケイ かた -がた   Ⓚ2292

(pattern from which something is made) **type, mold, model**
原型 げんけい archetype, prototype, model
模型 もけい model, pattern, mold
紙型 しけい papier-mâché mold, paper mold
造型(=造形) ぞうけい molding, modeling

儀
▷**model**
ギ   Ⓚ0147

[suffix] (miniature representation) **model, globe**
地球儀 ちきゅうぎ globe (of the world)

protrude and protruding
突 凸 隆 起 出

突
▷**protruding**
トツ つ(く)   Ⓚ1918

protruding, projecting, sticking out
突角 とっかく convex angle
突出する とっしゅつする project, protrude, stick out, jut out
突起 とっき projection, protuberance
突端 とったん tip, point
突堤 とってい pier, breakwater

凸
▷**convex**
トツ でこ   Ⓚ2928

[original meaning] **convex, gibbous, protruding**
凸レンズ とつれんず convex lens
凸面 とつめん convex surface
凸角 とっかく convex angle
凸版 とっぱん letterpress, relief printing
凹凸 おうとつ unevenness, irregularities

隆
▷**protuberant**
リュウ   Ⓚ0498

protuberant, elevated, bulging
隆起 りゅうき protuberance, elevation

起
▷**rise**
キ お(きる) お(こる) お(こす)   Ⓚ2818

(project upward) **rise, protrude**
起伏 きふく ups and downs, undulations
突起する とっきする project, protrude
隆起 りゅうき protuberance, elevation

出
▷**stick out**
シュツ スイ で(る) -で だ(す)   Ⓚ2934

stick out, protrude, project
出っ張る でっぱる project, protrude
出っ歯 でっぱ projecting teeth
突き出る つきでる project, stick out, stand out

protruding →PROTRUDE AND PROTRUDING

pseudonym suffixes
亭 屋

亭
▷**pseudonym suffix**
テイ   Ⓚ1785

suffix for forming pseudonyms or stage names
二葉亭 ふたばてい Futabatei (name of a writer)
三遊亭円歌 さんゆうていえんか Enka Sanyutei (name of a comic story teller)

屋
▷**stage name suffix**
オク や   Ⓚ2669

[sometimes also 家] **suffix after stage family names**
音羽屋 おとわや Otowaya (stage name of a kabuki family)

psyche
心 霊 魂 魄 腹 衷
襟 胸 懐 神 気 精

心
▷**heart**
シン こころ -ごころ   Ⓚ0004

heart, mind, spirit, feelings, emotions, thoughts
心情 しんじょう one's heart, one's feelings
心身 しんしん mind and body
心理 しんり mental state, mentality; psychology
心配 しんぱい anxiety, concern, worry, uneasiness; good offices
心境 しんきょう frame of mind, mental attitude [state]
心中 しんちゅう heart, mind, true motives
心中 しんじゅう lovers' suicide, double suicide
関心 かんしん concern, interest
安心する あんしんする have one's heart at ease, feel easy, be relieved
熱心 ねっしん enthusiasm, zeal, fervor, earnestness
感心する かんしんする admire, be deeply impressed
初心 しょしん one's original intention [object]
良心 りょうしん conscience
決心する けっしんする make up one's mind, decide
苦心 くしん pains, efforts, hard work
以心伝心 いしんでんしん silent [tacit] understanding, empathy
孝心 こうしん filial devotion [affection]
好奇心 こうきしん curiosity

霊
▷**spirit (soul)**
レイ リョウ たま   Ⓚ2442

(incorporeal part of man) **spirit, soul**
  霊長類 れいちょうるい Primates
  霊的な れいてきな spiritual, incorporeal
  心霊 しんれい spirit
  全身全霊 ぜんしんぜんれい body and soul; one's
    best

魂
▷**soul, spirit**
コン たましい   Ⓚ0975

❶ [original meaning] **soul, spirit**
  魂魄 こんぱく soul, spirit, ghost
  霊魂 れいこん spirit, soul
  英魂 えいこん departed spirit
❷ **spirit, heart**
  魂胆 こんたん secret intention, ulterior motive
  闘魂 とうこん fighting spirit
  心魂 しんこん one's soul [heart]
  商魂 しょうこん commercial enthusiasm, salesman-
    ship

魄
▷**soul**
ハク

[now also 迫] **soul, spirit**
  気魄 きはく spirit, soul, vigor
  魂魄 こんぱく soul, spirit, ghost

腹
▷**heart**
フク はら   Ⓚ0949

heart, mind, intention
  腹案 ふくあん plan, scheme, idea
  腹心 ふくしん trusted friend, trusted retainer

衷
▷**inner heart**
チュウ   Ⓚ1802

inner heart, true heart, inner feelings; sincerity
  衷心 ちゅうしん inner heart, inmost feelings
  衷情 ちゅうじょう inmost feeling, true heart
  苦衷 くちゅう mental suffering, dilemma
  微衷 びちゅう one's innermost thoughts [feelings]

襟
▷**inner mind**
キン えり   Ⓚ1156

inner mind, heart, bosom, thoughts
  襟懐 きんかい inner thoughts, feelings
  胸襟 きょうきん bosom, heart

胸
▷**breast**
キョウ むね むな-   Ⓚ0858

(seat of emotions) **breast, (inmost) heart, mind,
feelings**

  胸裏 きょうり one's bosom, one's heart, one's feel-
    ings
  胸中 きょうちゅう mind, heart, one's feelings,
    thoughts
  度胸 どきょう courage, pluck, heart

懐
▷**bosom**
カイ ふところ なつ(かしい) なつ(かしむ)
なつ(く) なつ(ける)   Ⓚ0689

(thoughts cherished in one's heart) **bosom, heart,
feelings**
  本懐 ほんかい one's long-cherished desire [object]
  虚心担懐 きょしんたんかい frankness, candidness
  述懐 じゅっかい effusion of one's thoughts (and
    feelings), reminiscence

神
▷**mind**
シン ジン かみ かん- こう-   Ⓚ0821

mind, consciousness, spirit, soul
  神経 しんけい nerve; sensitivity; worry
  神髄(=真髄) しんずい essence, quintessence, soul
  精神 せいしん mind, soul, heart; intention, motive;
    the spirit (of something)
  失神する しっしんする lose consciousness, faint
  色神 しきしん color sense (ability of color discrimi-
    nation)

気
▷**spirit (consciousness)**
キ ケ   Ⓚ2751

spirit, mind, consciousness
  気付く きづく notice, become aware of, find out
  気の毒な きのどくな pitiable, miserable; regretta-
    ble, too bad
  気構え きがまえ readiness of mind, preparedness;
    expectation
  気絶 きぜつ fainting
  気違い きちがい insanity; insane person, lunatic
  正気 しょうき consciousness; sanity, reason
  狂気 きょうき insanity, madness

精
▷**spirit (mind)**
セイ ショウ   Ⓚ1248

(spiritual part of man) **spirit, mind, soul**
  精神 せいしん mind, soul, heart; intention, motive;
    the spirit (of something)
  精魂 せいこん spirit, soul; vitality

public
公　俗　巷

公 ▷public
コウ　おおやけ　　　Ⓚ1715

[original meaning] (relating to the public) **public, open**
公演 こうえん public performance
公園 こうえん park, public garden
公開 こうかい opening to the public
公害 こうがい environmental pollution
公表 こうひょう public [official] announcement, proclamation
公判 こうはん (public) trial [hearing]
公聴会 こうちょうかい public [open] hearing
公選 こうせん public election, election by popular vote
公募 こうぼ appeal for public subscription
公論 こうろん public opinion, consensus
公言する こうげんする declare in public; profess

俗 ▷popular
ゾク　　　Ⓚ0088

popular, folk, common
俗説 ぞくせつ common saying, popular version
俗称 ぞくしょう popular [common] name
俗習 ぞくしゅう popular custom, usage
俗語 ぞくご slang
通俗 つうぞく popularity, conventionality

巷 ▷the public
コウ　ちまた　　　Ⓚ2162

the public
巷間 こうかん around town, the public, the world
巷説 こうせつ gossip, talk of the town
巷談 こうだん rumor, gossip

public display
展　博

展 ▷exhibition
テン　　　Ⓚ2681

[also suffix] **abbrev. of** 展覧会 てんらんかい: **exhibition, exhibit**
個展 こてん personal exhibition
デザイン展 でざいんてん design exhibition
ダリ展 だりてん exhibition of Dali's paintings

博 ▷exposition
ハク　バク　　　Ⓚ0129

abbrev. of 博覧会 はくらんかい: **exposition, expo**
万博 ばんぱく world fair
宇宙博 うちゅうはく Space Expo

public offices
省　庁　府　公　署　局　所

省 ▷ministry
セイ　ショウ　かえり(みる)　はぶ(く)　Ⓚ2164

[also suffix] **ministry, government department [office]**
省庁 しょうちょう Ministries and Agencies
省令 しょうれい Ministerial ordinance
同省 どうしょう the said Ministry
文部省 もんぶしょう Ministry of Education, Science and Culture
大蔵省 おおくらしょう Ministry of Finance

庁 ▷government agency
チョウ　　　Ⓚ2612

[also suffix] [original meaning] **government agency, government [public] office**
庁舎 ちょうしゃ government building
官庁 かんちょう government office [agency]
都庁 とちょう Tokyo Metropolitan Government Office
県庁 けんちょう prefectural office
警視庁 けいしちょう Metropolitan Police Office
環境庁 かんきょうちょう Environment Agency

府 ▷government office
フ　　　Ⓚ2654

government office, seat of government
政府 せいふ government, administration
総理府 そうりふ Prime Minister's Office
国府 こくふ National Government (of China); provincial capital
幕府 ばくふ shogunate

公 ▷public office
コウ　おおやけ　　　Ⓚ1715

public office, government office
公邸 こうてい official residence
公文書 こうぶんしょ official document
公報 こうほう public [official] report [bulletin]
奉公 ほうこう public duty [service]; domestic service, apprenticeship

署 ▷public-service station
ショ   ⓀK2263

[also suffix] **public-service station or office, as a police station, fire station or tax office**

署長 しょちょう chief of police, office head
署員 しょいん member of an office, staff
警察署 けいさつしょ police station
消防署 しょうぼうしょ fire station
税務署 ぜいむしょ tax office
本署 ほんしょ chief police station, principal office
公署 こうしょ government office

局 ▷public service office
キョク   ⓀK2636

[also suffix] **public service office or station, as a post office, telegraph office, telephone exchange office or broadcasting station**

郵便局 ゆうびんきょく post office
電報局 でんぽうきょく telegraph office
放送局 ほうそうきょく radio broadcasting station
支局 しきょく branch office
テレビ局 てれびきょく TV station
電話局 でんわきょく telephone exchange office

所 ▷office
ショ ところ どころ   ⓀK0752

place for conducting specific activities: **office, bureau, organization, institution, institute, agency**

所長 しょちょう head, chief, manager
役所 やくしょ public [government] office
入所する にゅうしょする enter (an institute); be put in prison
事務所 じむしょ office, one's place of business
研究所 けんきゅうじょ(=けんきゅうしょ) research laboratory [institute]
裁判所 さいばんしょ court of justice, courthouse
保健所 ほけんじょ public health center

publish →PRINT AND PUBLISH

pull

引 曳 牽 惹 抽
抜 控 扣 寄

引 ▷draw
イン ひ(く) ひ(き) -び(き)
ひ(ける)   ⓀK0160

[original meaning] (pull toward one) **draw, pull, haul, tug**

引力 いんりょく gravitation
引航する いんこうする tug, tow

牽引する けんいんする pull, draw, haul
強引な ごういんな overbearing, coercive

曳 ▷draw
エイ ひ(く)   ⓀK2961

ⓐ draw, pull, haul, tug
ⓑ drag, trail

a 曳航 えいこう towing (of a ship)
  曳船 えいせん tugboat; towing
b 曳光弾 えいこうだん tracer bullet, star shell
  揺曳 ようえい flutter, linger

牽 ▷draw
ケン ひ(く)   ⓀK1816

draw, pull, haul, tug

牽引 けんいん hauling, towing, pulling
牽制する けんせいする check, restrain; divert, feint
牽連する けんれんする be connected
牽強 けんきょう distortion of facts
牽牛星 けんぎゅうせい Altair

惹 ▷draw attention
ジャク ひ(く)   ⓀK2015

draw (attention or sympathy), attract, catch
惹句 じゃっく catchphrase, slogan

抽 ▷draw out
チュウ   ⓀK0267

[original meaning] **draw out, extract**
抽出する ちゅうしゅつする extract, abstract, educe
抽選(=抽籤) ちゅうせん drawing of lots
抽象的 ちゅうしょうてき abstract

抜 ▷pull out
バツ ぬ(く) ぬ(き) ぬ(ける) ぬ(かす)
ぬ(かる)   ⓀK0219

[original meaning] **pull out, draw out, extract, remove**
抜歯 ばっし tooth extraction
抜糸 ばっし removal [extraction] of stitches
抜刀 ばっとう drawing a sword; drawn sword
抜本的な ばっぽんてきな radical, drastic
不抜の ふばつの indomitable, unswerving

控 ▷hold back
コウ ひか(える) ひか(え)   ⓀK0453

(keep in check) **hold back, keep**
馬を控える うまをひかえる hold back a horse

扣 ▷hold back
コウ ひか(える) ひか(え)

(keep in check) **hold back, keep**

寄 ▷draw near
キ よ(る) -よ(り) よ(せる)　　Ⓚ1983

draw (a thing) near, allow to approach; come near

寄せ付けない よせつけない keep off, keep away
車寄せ くるまよせ carriage porch
皺寄せ しわよせ shifting (the loss) to someone else
又寄せて頂きます またよせていただきます I shall
　call on you again
打ち寄せる うちよせる break upon, beat upon (the
　shore)
引き寄せる ひきよせる draw near, pull nearer
取り寄せる とりよせる order; get, obtain

punishment
刑　罰　懲　処

刑 ▷penalty
ケイ　　Ⓚ0734

[also suffix] **penalty, punishment, sentence**

刑罰 けいばつ penalty, punishment
刑期 けいき prison term
刑事 けいじ (police) detective
刑務所 けいむしょ prison
刑法 けいほう criminal law, penal code
処刑 しょけい execution, punishment
求刑する きゅうけいする demand a sentence (for
　the accused)
死刑 しけい capital punishment, death penalty
絞首刑 こうしゅけい death [execution] by hanging

罰 ▷punishment
バツ バチ　　Ⓚ2266

ⓐ **punishment, penalty**
ⓑ **divine punishment, Heaven's vengeance**
ⓒ [original meaning] **punish, penalize**

ⓐ 罰金 ばっきん fine, penalty
　罰則 ばっそく penal regulations, punitive provi-
　　sions
　罰点 ばってん black mark, X mark
　刑罰 けいばつ penalty, punishment
ⓑ 天罰 てんばつ divine punishment
ⓒ 懲罰 ちょうばつ discipline, punishment
　処罰 しょばつ punishment, penalty

懲 ▷chastise
チョウ こ(りる) こらす)
こ(らしめる)　　Ⓚ2526

[original meaning] **chastise, punish, discipline**

懲悪 ちょうあく chastisement, punishment
懲罰 ちょうばつ discipline, punishment
懲戒 ちょうかい official reprimand, discipline

懲役 ちょうえき penal servitude, imprisonment
　with hard labor

処 ▷deal with (lawbreakers)
ショ　　Ⓚ2609

deal with (lawbreakers), punish

処刑 しょけい execution, punishment
処罰 しょばつ punishment, penalty

purehearted
純　淳　清　潔　廉
敦　惇　直　侃

純 ▷pure
ジュン　　Ⓚ1192

purehearted, innocent, chaste

純潔な じゅんけつな purehearted, immaculate,
　innocent
純真な じゅんしんな naive, pure, genuine, sincere
純情 じゅんじょう pure heart; self-sacrificing devo-
　tion
純朴(=醇朴) じゅんぼく simplicity and honesty
清純な せいじゅんな pure (and innocent)

淳 ▷purehearted
ジュン　　Ⓚ0472

purehearted, simple, innocent

淳良な じゅんりょうな simple and kind, innocent
淳朴(=純朴) じゅんぼく simplicity and honesty

清 ▷clean
セイ ショウ きよ(い) きよ(まる)
きよ(める)　　Ⓚ0479

(free from moral taint) **clean, honest, pure, honorable**

清濁 せいだく purity and impurity; good and evil
清廉 せいれん integrity, honesty, uprightness
清貧 せいひん honest [honorable] poverty
清教徒 せいきょうと Puritan

潔 ▷immaculate
ケツ いさぎよ(い)　　Ⓚ0678

(free from moral blemish) **immaculate, pure, upright**

潔白な けっぱくな innocent, pure, upright
純潔な じゅんけつな purehearted, immaculate,
　innocent
貞潔 ていけつ chastity and purity

廉 ▷incorrupt
レン　　Ⓚ2720

incorrupt, honest and clean, upright, cleanhanded

廉直 れんちょく integrity, uprightness
廉潔な れんけつな honest, incorruptible
清廉な せいれんな incorruptible, honest, upright
破廉恥な はれんちな shameless, infamous, impudent

敦 ▷honest
トン   Ⓚ1511

[rare] **honest, staunch, sincere, simple**
  敦厚な とんこうな sincere and kindhearted, honest and simple
  敦朴(=敦樸)な とんぼくな [archaic] honest and simple

惇 ▷sincere
トン ジュン シュン   Ⓚ0444

[rare] **sincere, honest, solid**
  惇厚な とんこうな sincere and kindhearted, honest and simple
  惇朴(=惇樸)な とんぼくな simple and honest

直 ▷straightforward
チョク ジキ ジカ ただ(ちに) なお(す)
なお(る) なお(き) す(ぐ)   Ⓚ2539

straightforward, straight, upright, honest
  正直な しょうじきな honest, upright, frank
  実直な じっちょくな upright, honest, steady
  愚直な ぐちょくな honest to a fault, stupidly honest
  曲直 きょくちょく right and wrong
  司直 しちょく administration of justice; judicial authorities

侃 ▷forthright
カン   Ⓚ0069

forthright, straightforward, straight and bold
  侃侃諤諤の かんかんがくがくの outspoken (dispute), straightforward
  侃侃たる かんかんたる straight and bold (manner of speaking)

●urified →CLEAN AND PURIFIED

●urple colors →BLUE AND PURPLE COLORS

●ursue →FOLLOW AND PURSUE

push
押 突 圧 挨 按

押 ▷push
オウ お(す) お(し)- お(っ)-
お(さえる)   Ⓚ0278

[original meaning] **push or press downward**

押下する おうかする depress, press down (a computer key)

突 ▷thrust
トツ つ(く)   Ⓚ1918

ⓐ (strike forcibly with a pointed end) **thrust, push, give a push [thrust]**
ⓑ [sometimes also 撞く] **poke, strike (a bell)**
  a 突き つき thrust, push; lunge
  突き出す つきだす thrust out, push out; push out of a sumo ring
  突き当たる つきあたる hit against, run into; come to the end of (a street)
  突き当たり つきあたり end [bottom] of a street
  突っ込む つっこむ thrust in, ram into, stuff into; dash [run] into
  突っ掛ける つっかける slip on, slip into (slippers)
  b 鐘を突く かねをつく strike a bell

圧 ▷apply pressure
アツ   Ⓚ2563

[original meaning] **apply pressure, press down**
  圧力 あつりょく pressure
  圧縮する あっしゅくする compress, constrict
  圧搾する あっさくする press, compress
  圧砕 あっさい crushing

挨 ▷push
アイ   Ⓚ0383

push
  挨拶 あいさつ greeting, salutation; speech, address; reply, response
  挨拶状 あいさつじょう greeting card

按 ▷hold down
アン   Ⓚ0330

[original meaning] **hold down with the hand, press down with the hand, rub with the hand**
  按摩 あんま massage; massager, masseur, masseuse
  按腹 あんぷく ventral massage
  按手 あんしゅ ordination, laying on of hands

put
据 置 擱 掛 措

据 ▷install
す(える) す(わる)   Ⓚ0455

(set in position) **install, place in position, fix, mount, set up; set (a table); lay (a foundation)**
  据え付ける すえつける install, equip, fit

据え置き すえおき leaving (a thing) as it stands; deferred savings

据え膳 すえぜん meal set before one; women's advances

見据える みすえる fix one's eyes, look hard

置 ▷place
チ お(く) -お(き)　　　　Ⓚ2262

place, put, install, set

置換 ちかん substitution, replacement, displacement

倒置 とうち turning upside down; *gram* inversion

配置する はいちする arrange; post (troops)

布置 ふち arrangement, grouping

前置詞 ぜんちし preposition

安置する あんちする install, lay in state

対置する たいちする oppose (a thing) to (another)

装置 そうち equipment, device, installation

擱 ▷lay down
カク お(く)

lay down (one's pen)

擱筆する かくひつする stop writing

掛 ▷set
か(ける) か(け) -が(け) か(かる) -が(かる) か(かり) -が(かり)　　Ⓚ0449

ⓐ set, put on, put over, spread
ⓑ set against, put up against, fasten
ⓒ set on a scale, weigh
ⓓ (set on one's head or shoulders) wear, put on

a 掛け布団 かけぶとん covering quilt

薦を掛ける こもをかける spread a mat

b 掛け小屋 かけごや lean-to; temporary theater

薬缶を掛ける やかんをかける put a kettle on (the stove)

梯子を掛ける はしごをかける set a ladder up against

c 計りに掛ける はかりにかける weigh on a scale

d 眼鏡を掛ける めがねをかける wear glasses

ショールを掛ける しょーるをかける put a shawl on

措 ▷dispose
ソ　　　　Ⓚ0463

(put in the right position) dispose, place, arrange

措定する そていする suppose, assume

措辞 そじ phraseology, wording

措辞法 そじほう syntax

put in
入 挿 嵌 込

入 ▷put in
ニュウ い(る) -い(り) い(れる) -い(れ) はい(る)　　Ⓚ2859

put in, insert, enter, admit

入札 にゅうさつ tender, bidding

入手する にゅうしゅする obtain, get, come by, procure

入力 にゅうりょく input; power input

入金 にゅうきん receipt of money; money received

記入する きにゅうする enter, write in, record

注入 ちゅうにゅう pouring into, injection

輸入 ゆにゅう import, importation

導入 どうにゅう introduction

挿 ▷insert
ソウ さ(す)　　　　Ⓚ0390

[original meaning] **insert, put into, stick between**

挿入する そうにゅうする insert, put into

挿話 そうわ anecdote

挿画 そうが illustration (in a book)

挿花 そうか flower arrangement

嵌 ▷inlay
カン ガン は(める) は(まる)

[now also 眼] **inlay, set in**

嵌入する かんにゅうする set in, inlay, dovetail

嵌合 かんごう fitting together, fit

象嵌 ぞうがん inlaid work, inlaying

込 ▷cause to move inward
-こ(む) こ(み) こ(める)　　Ⓚ2608

cause to move inward, put in, bring in—used as a verbal suffix to indicate action directed inward

払い込む はらいこむ pay in, pay up

吸い込む すいこむ inhale, breathe in; suck in

持ち込む もちこむ carry [bring] in; propose, refer to; bring (a matter) to

put on →WEAR AND PUT ON

quantity and number

量 嵩 積 額 分 数 勢

量 ▷quantity
リョウ はか(る)　　　　　　Ⓚ2180

[also suffix] **quantity, amount, volume, capacity, magnitude; weight**

量産 りょうさん mass production
量感 りょうかん massiveness
量子論 りょうしろん quantum theory
数量 すうりょう quantity, volume
大量 たいりょう large quantity, great volume, mass
容量 ようりょう capacity, volume
重量 じゅうりょう weight
交通量 こうつうりょう traffic volume
消費量 しょうひりょう amount of consumption

嵩 ▷bulk
スウ かさ かさ(む)　　　　Ⓚ2035

bulk, volume, size, quantity

嵩に掛かって かさにかかって arrogantly, highhand-
　edly, overbearingly
嵩張る かさばる be bulky [voluminous], bulk large
年嵩の としかさの older, aged, elderly, senior
水嵩 みずかさ volume of water
値嵩株 ねがさかぶ high-priced stocks, blue-chip
　shares

積 ▷size
セキ つ(む) -づ(み) つ(もる)
つ(もり)　　　　　　　　　Ⓚ1142

size, volume, capacity, area

面積 めんせき area, square measure
体積 たいせき (cubic) volume, capacity
容積 ようせき capacity, volume, bulk

額 ▷amount
ガク ひたい　　　　　　　　Ⓚ1604

[also suffix] **amount (of money), sum, volume, quantity**

額面 がくめん face value; denomination
金額 きんがく amount of money, sum
多額 たがく large amount [sum]
総額 そうがく total amount, sum total
全額 ぜんがく sum total, total amount
月額 げつがく monthly amount [sum]
生産額 せいさんがく amount of production

分 ▷content
ブン フン ブ わ(ける) わ(け) わ(かれる)
わ(かる) わ(かつ)　　　　Ⓚ1713

[also suffix] **content, percentage; quantity, amount**

水分 すいぶん water, moisture, humidity
糖分 とうぶん sugar content
アルコール分 あるこーるぶん percentage of alcohol
栄養分 えいようぶん nutritious substance, nourish-
　ment
増加分 ぞうかぶん increment

数 ▷number
スウ ス かず かぞ(える)　Ⓚ1591

[also suffix] (amount) **number, quantity**

数量 すうりょう quantity, volume
総数 そうすう total (number)
多数の たすうの a number of, many
手数 てすう(=てかず) trouble, bother, pains
トン数 とんすう tonnage
人数 にんずう(=にんず) number of people
回数 かいすう frequency, number of times
生徒数 せいとすう number of pupils

勢 ▷strength
セイ いきお(い)　　　　　　Ⓚ2487

(numerical force) **strength, number (of soldiers or people), large numbers**

多勢 たぜい great numbers, superiority in number
大勢の おおぜいの great number of, multitude of

question

題 問 論 謎

題 ▷problem
ダイ　　　　　　　　　　　Ⓚ2848

problem, question

問題 もんだい problem, question, issue, matter
課題 かだい task, assignment; problem
難題 なんだい difficult problem [question]
出題する しゅつだいする set a problem
宿題 しゅくだい homework

問 ▷question (inquiry)
モン と(う) と(い) とん　Ⓚ2833

question, inquiry, problem

問題 もんだい problem, question, issue, matter
問答 もんどう questions and answers, catechism
難問 なんもん difficult problem [question]

論 ▷question (issue)
ロン   Ⓚ1424

[also suffix] **question, issue, problem**
> 論外な ろんがいな out of the question, beside the point
> 国防論 こくぼうろん the question of national defense
> 漢字制限論 かんじせいげんろん the question of limiting the use of Chinese characters

謎 ▷riddle
なぞ   Ⓚ1464

riddle, puzzle
> 謎謎 なぞなぞ riddle, puzzle
> 謎解き なぞとき solution of a riddle
> 謎掛け なぞかけ a word play in which a pun is played to connect two seemingly unrelated things or statements

quiet
静 閑 寂 幽 粛 黙

静 ▷quiet
セイ ジョウ しず- しず(か) しず(まる) しず(める)   Ⓚ1539

[original meaning] (free from noise) **quiet, still, silent**
> 静寂 せいじゃく silence, quietness, stillness
> 静聴する せいちょうする listen quietly

閑 ▷quiet
カン   Ⓚ2837

quiet, tranquil
> 閑静な かんせいな quiet, tranquil
> 閑寂な かんじゃくな quiet, tranquil
> 森閑とした しんかんとした quiet, still, silent as a graveyard

寂 ▷quiet
ジャク セキ さび さび(しい) さび(れる)   Ⓚ1982

[original meaning] **quiet, still, serene**
> 静寂 せいじゃく silence, quietness, stillness
> 閑寂 かんじゃく quietness, tranquility

幽 ▷quiet and secluded
ユウ   Ⓚ2592

quiet and secluded, deep and remote
> 幽棲(=幽栖)する ゆうせいする live a quiet life in seclusion away from the masses
> 幽谷 ゆうこく deep ravine, secluded valley
> 幽寂な ゆうじゃくな quiet, sequestered

粛 ▷still
シュク   Ⓚ2990

still, hushed, quiet
> 粛粛と しゅくしゅくと in solemn silence
> 静粛 せいしゅく silence, stillness

黙 ▷silent
モク だま(る)   Ⓚ2494

silent, taciturn
> 黙秘する もくひする keep silent, keep secret
> 黙祷 もくとう silent prayer
> 黙読する もくどくする read silently
> 沈黙 ちんもく silence, reticence, taciturnity
> 寡黙な かもくな silent, taciturn, reticent

quote
引 挙

引 ▷quote
イン ひ(く) ひ(き) -び(き) ひ(ける)   Ⓚ0160

quote, cite, refer to
> 引用 いんよう quotation, citation
> 引照 いんしょう reference
> 引喩 いんゆ allusion
> 索引 さくいん index

挙 ▷cite
キョ あ(げる) あ(がる)   Ⓚ2169

cite, give (an example), mention
> 挙証 きょしょう presentation of proof
> 列挙する れっきょする enumerate, list
> 枚挙する まいきょする list, enumerate

rabbit
兎 卯

兎 ▷rabbit
ト うさぎ   Ⓚ2981

[original meaning] **rabbit, hare**
> 家兎 かと tame rabbit
> 野兎病 やとびょう tularemia
> 脱兎の如く だっとのごとく with lightning speed ("like a fleeing rabbit")
> 二兎を追う者は一兎をも得ず にとをおうものはいっとをもえず If you run after two hares, you will catch neither

卯 ▷**the Hare**
ボウ う ⓚ0177

fourth sign of the Oriental zodiac: **the Hare**—(time) 5-7 a.m., (direction) east, (season) February (of the lunar calendar)

卯月 ぼうげつ second month of the lunar calendar

ailway →KINDS OF RAILWAY

raise
揚 掲 挙 上 起 擡 立 拾

揚 ▷**raise high**
ヨウ あ(げる) -あ(げ) あ(がる) ⓚ0542

(cause to rise high) **raise high, lift, hoist, elevate, fly; rise, fly**

揚力 ようりょく lift, lifting power
揚抗比 ようこうひ lift-drag ratio
揚炭機 ようたんき coal hoist
掲揚する けいようする hoist, put up, fly (a flag)
飛揚 ひよう flying, flight

掲 ▷**put up**
ケイ かか(げる) ⓚ0450

put up, display, hoist, raise

掲揚する けいようする hoist, put up, fly (a flag)
掲示する けいじする put up a notice [bulletin]

挙 ▷**raise**
キョ あ(げる) あ(がる) ⓚ2169

[original meaning] **raise (one's hand), hold up, lift**

挙手 きょしゅ raising [holding up] one's hand; salute

上 ▷**raise**
ジョウ ショウ うえ うわ- かみ あ(げる)
あ(がる) あ(がり) のぼ(る) のぼ(り)
のぼ(せる) のぼ(す) ⓚ2876

【ジョウ ショウ】
(cause to move upward) **raise**

上棟式 じょうとうしき ceremony of raising the ridgepole

【あ(げる)】
(cause to move upward) **raise, elevate, lift up**

顔を上げる かおをあげる raise one's face
引き上げる ひきあげる draw [pull] up; promote; increase
棚上げする たなあげする shelve (up), pigeonhole

起 ▷**raise up**
キ お(きる) お(こる) お(こす) ⓚ2818

raise up, lift

起重機 きじゅうき crane, derrick

擡 ▷**raise (one's head)**
タイ もた(げる)

[now also 台] [original meaning] **raise (one's head), lift**

擡頭する たいとうする raise one's head; come to the fore

立 ▷**stand**
リツ リュウ た(つ) た(ち)- た(てる)
た(て)- -だ(て) -だ(てる) ⓚ1723

stand, make stand, erect, raise, set

立て掛ける たてかける lean against, set against
旗を立てる はたをたてる hoist a flag
候補者を立てる こうほしゃをたてる put up a candidate

拾 ▷**pick up**
シュウ ジュウ ひろ(う) ⓚ0339

pick up, gather; find; (acquire something hard to get) **get hold of, gain; pick out, select**

拾い上げる ひろいあげる pick up; pick out
拾い集める ひろいあつめる gather
拾い出す ひろいだす pick out, select
拾い物 ひろいもの thing picked up [found]; bargain
拾い読みする ひろいよみする read here and there, skim through
石を拾う いしをひろう pick up a stone
命拾い いのちびろい narrow escape (from death), close shave

raise and nourish
育 飼 養 滋 哺 牧

育 ▷**raise**
イク そだ(つ) そだ(ち) そだ(てる)
はぐく(む) ⓚ1764

(care for the growth of children, animals or plants) **raise, bring up, rear, breed, cultivate**

育成する いくせいする bring up, rear
育児 いくじ infant rearing, nursing of children
育種 いくしゅ plant breeding
保育 ほいく nurture, upbringing; lactation, nursing
養育 よういく fostering, bringing up, education
飼育する しいくする raise animals, breed, rear

飼 ▷raise animals
シ か(う)   ®1529

[original meaning] **raise animals, rear, breed, keep**
飼育する しいくする raise animals, breed, rear
飼養 しよう breeding, raising
飼料 しりょう fodder

養 ▷foster
ヨウ やしな(う)   ®2089

ⓐ foster, bring up, raise to maturity, rear, support, care for
ⓑ (affording parental care) **foster (parent), adopted**
ⓒ breed, raise (animals or plants), keep

a 養育する よういくする foster, bring up, educate
  養護 ようご protective care
  扶養 ふよう support, maintenance
b 養子 ようし foster [adopted] child
  養父 ようふ foster father
c 養殖 ようしょく culture, cultivation, raising
  養鶏 ようけい chicken raising
  養毛剤 ようもうざい hair tonic
  培養する ばいようする cultivate, culture, incubate

滋 ▷nourish
ジ   ®0549

nourish, moisten
滋養 じよう nourishment, nutrition
滋雨 じう beneficial rain

哺 ▷nurse
ホ   ®0359

[now also 保] **nurse, suckle**
哺乳類 ほにゅうるい Mammalia
哺乳瓶 ほにゅうびん baby bottle
哺育(=保育)する ほいくする nurture, bring up; suckle, nurse
反哺 はんぽ caring for one's parents in return

牧 ▷pasture
ボク まき   ®0776

[original meaning] (put cattle to pasture) **pasture, tend cattle, herd, shepherd, raise cattle**
牧畜 ぼくちく livestock farming, cattle breeding
牧歌的な ぼっかてきな pastoral, idyllic
牧童 ぼくどう cowboy; shepherd
牧人 ぼくじん shepherd, herdsman
牧羊 ぼくよう sheep farming
放牧する ほうぼくする pasture, put to grass, graze
遊牧 ゆうぼく nomadism

raise the temperature
暖 煖 温 熱

暖 ▷warm (the air)
ダン ノン あたた(か) あたた(かい)
あたた(まる) あたた(める)   ®092

【ダン ノン】
[formerly also 煖] **warm (the surrounding air), warm up, heat**
暖房 だんぼう heating
暖炉 だんろ fireplace, stove
暖気 だんき warmth, warm weather
暖簾 のれん shop curtain, *noren*; credit, reputation

【あたた(める)】
(warm up the surrounding air) **warm, warm up, heat**
部屋を暖める へやをあたためる heat the room

煖 ▷warm (the air)
ダン

[now replaced by 暖] [original meaning] **warm, warm up, heat**
煖房 だんぼう heating
煖炉 だんろ fireplace, stove
煖気 だんき warmth, warm weather

温 ▷warm (a thing)
オン あたた(か) あたた(かい)
あたた(まる) あたた(める)   ®055

(raise the temperature of a thing) **warm, heat**
コーヒーを温める こーひーをあたためる warm up coffee

熱 ▷heat
ネツ あつ(い)   ®249

heat, make hot
過熱する かねつする overheat, superheat

range
程 範 域 圏 野 界 場

程 ▷extent
テイ ほど   ®110

(range of distance) **extent, distance, range, mileage, journey**
射程 しゃてい shooting range

旅程 りょてい distance to be covered; plan of one's trip
航程 こうてい run (of a ship), sail; flight
マイル程 まいるてい mileage
音程 おんてい (musical) interval, distance (between tones)

範 ▷range
ハン Ⓚ2364

range, limits, scope, sphere
範囲 はんい range, scope
範疇 はんちゅう category

域 ▷area
イキ Ⓚ0421

(scope of something) **area, range**
聖域 せいいき holy [sacred] precincts, sanctuary
領域 りょういき territory, domain, sphere, province; *math* domain
音域 おんいき compass, (singing) range
職域 しょくいき range of one's work [occupation]
暴風域 ぼうふういき storm area

圏 ▷sphere
ケン Ⓚ2714

❶ (spherical domain of action) **sphere, realm, circle, domain, zone, radius, range**
対流圏 たいりゅうけん troposphere
生物圏 せいぶつけん biosphere
暴風圏 ぼうふうけん storm zone
通信圏外 つうしんけんがい out of the range of communication
ポンド圏 ぽんどけん sterling zone
北極圏 ほっきょくけん arctic zone; Arctic Circle
❷ (domain of influence) **sphere, circle, domain**
影響圏 えいきょうけん sphere of influence
共産圏 きょうさんけん the Communist bloc

野 ▷field
ヤ の Ⓚ1350

(sphere of action) **field, range, area**
分野 ぶんや field, sphere, area
視野 しや field of vision; one's mental horizon
照射野 しょうしゃや irradiation field (of x rays)

界 ▷field (*phys*)
カイ Ⓚ2220

phys **field**
界磁極 かいじきょく field pole
視界 しかい field of vision, visibility
電界 でんかい electric field

場 ▷field (*phys, psychol*)
ジョウ ば Ⓚ0512

phys, psychol **field**
磁場 じば magnetic field
力の場 ちからのば field of force

ranks →MILITARY OFFICERS AND RANKS

rare
珍　希　稀

珍 ▷rare
チン めずら(しい) Ⓚ0814

[original meaning] (of infrequent occurrence or unusual excellence) **rare, infrequent, precious**
珍味 ちんみ food of delicate flavor, delicacy
珍品 ちんぴん rare article, curio
珍客 ちんきゃく unexpected (but welcome) visitor

希 ▷rare
キ まれ Ⓚ1763

[also 稀] (not frequent) **rare, uncommon, unusual, scarce**
希書 きしょ rare book
希元素 きげんそ rare element
希少な きしょうな scarce, rare
希有な けう(=きゆう)な rare, unusual, uncommon
古希 こき three score and ten, seventy years of age

稀 ▷rare
キ ケ まれ Ⓚ1099

【キ ケ】
[also 希] (not frequent) **rare, uncommon, unusual, scarce**
稀代の きたい(=きだい)の uncommon, rare
稀有な けう(=きゆう)な rare, unusual, uncommon
稀少な きしょうな scarce, rare
古稀 こき three score and ten, seventy years of age
【まれ】
[sometimes also 希な] **rare, uncommon, scarce, unique**

rare and sparse
薄　希　疎　粗　稀

薄 ▷thin
ハク うす(い) うす- うす(める) うす(まる) うす(らぐ) うす(ら)- うす(れる) Ⓚ2093

(not dense) **thin, weak, watery**

髪が薄い かみがうすい have thin hair

希 ▷rare
キ まれ   ⓚ1763

[formerly also 稀]
ⓐ (thin in density) **rare, rarefied, dilute, thin**
ⓑ [also prefix] *chem* **dilute**
a 希薄な きはくな dilute, thin, rare, sparse
 希釈 きしゃく dilution
b 希硫酸 きりゅうさん dilute sulfuric acid

疎 ▷sparse
ソ うと(い) うと(む)   ⓚ1091

sparse, thin, scattered, sporadic
 疎開 そかい dispersal, evacuation
 疎密 そみつ sparseness and luxuriant growth
 疎林 そりん sparse woods
 過疎 かそ depopulation
 空疎な くうそな empty, unsubstantial

粗 ▷coarse
ソ あら(い) あら-   ⓚ1214

(not fine) **coarse, rough, rugged**
 粗密 そみつ roughness and fineness
 粗大な そだいな coarse, rough, unpolished
 粗布 そふ coarse cloth
 精粗 せいそ fineness or coarseness; minuteness or
  roughness

稀 ▷rare
キ ケ まれ   ⓚ1099

[now usu. 希]
ⓐ [original meaning] (thin in density) **rare, rarefied,**
 dilute, thin
ⓑ [also prefix] *chem* **dilute**
a 稀薄な きはくな dilute, thin, rare, sparse
 稀釈 きしゃく dilution
b 稀硫酸 きりゅうさん dilute sulfuric acid

rash
滅 妄 盲 暴 荒 濫 乱

滅 ▷unreasonable
メツ ほろ(びる) ほろ(ぶ)
ほろ(ぼす)   ⓚ0606

unreasonable, excessive, reckless, extreme
 滅法 めっぽう extraordinarily, unreasonably
 滅多な めったな reckless, careless
 滅茶苦茶(=目茶苦茶)な めちゃくちゃな confused,
  incoherent; absurd, unreasonable

滅茶滅茶(=目茶目茶) めちゃめちゃ mess, wreck,
 ruin, shambles

妄 ▷rash
モウ ボウ   ⓚ173◻

[also 盲] [original meaning] **rash, reckless, wild, outra-**
geous, thoughtless, indiscriminate
 妄言 ぼうげん(=もうげん) rash remark, thoughtless
  words
 妄想 もうそう wild idea [fancy], paranoiac delusion
 妄信 もうしん blind belief, credulity
 妄評 ぼうひょう(=もうひょう) unjust [unfair] criticism
 軽挙妄動する けいきょもうどうする act rashly

盲 ▷blind
モウ   ⓚ176◻

[also 妄] (not based on reason) **blind, reckless, aimless**
 盲従 もうじゅう blind obedience
 盲動 もうどう acting blindly
 盲信 もうしん blind belief
 盲想 もうそう wild idea [fancy], paranoiac delusion
 盲爆 もうばく blind [unscrupulous] bombing

暴 ▷unrestrained
ボウ バク あば(く) あば(れる)   ⓚ219◻

unrestrained, inordinate, wild, excessive, irrational
 暴飲 ぼういん heavy drinking
 暴利 ぼうり excessive profits, usury

荒 ▷wild
コウ あら(い) あら- あ(れる) あ(らす)
-あ(らし)   ⓚ195◻

(unrestrained by reason) **wild, absurd, ridiculous**
 荒唐無稽な こうとうむけいな absurd, nonsensical
 破天荒の はてんこうの record-breaking, unprecedented

濫 ▷excessive
ラン   ⓚ071◻

[also 乱] **excessive, indiscriminate, extravagant,**
inordinate, haphazard, reckless
 濫造 らんぞう excessive production, careless
  manufacture
 濫伐 らんばつ indiscriminate deforestation, overcutting of forests
 濫費 らんぴ extravagance, money wasting
 濫用する らんようする abuse, use to excess
 紙幣の濫発 しへいのらんぱつ excessive [reckless]
  issue of bank notes

乱 ▷excessive
ラン みだ(れる) みだ(る) みだ(す) ⓚ1161

[also 濫] **excessive, indiscriminate, extravagant,**
inordinate, haphazard, reckless

乱読 らんどく indiscriminate reading
乱用 らんよう abuse, misuse, misappropriation
乱造 らんぞう excessive production, careless manufacture
乱開発 らんかいはつ indiscriminate development

rate
率　割　比　歩

 ▷**rate**
ソツ　リツ　ひき(いる)　　　　Ⓚ1820

[also suffix] **rate, proportion; index, coefficient; modulus**

比率 ひりつ ratio, percentage
効率 こうりつ efficiency
百分率 ひゃくぶんりつ percentage
能率 のうりつ efficiency
伸び率 のびりつ growth rate; coefficient of extension
利率 りりつ interest rate, interest
打率 だりつ batting average
確率 かくりつ probability
保険料率 ほけんりょうりつ premium rate
弾性率 だんせいりつ modulus of elasticity

割 ▷**rate**
カツ　わ(る)　わり　わ(れる)　さ(く)　Ⓚ1611

rate, proportion, ratio

割に わりに comparatively, rather
割引く わりびく give a discount, make a reduction
割引 わりびき discount, reduction
割合 わりあい rate, proportion, ratio; comparatively
割合に わりあいに relatively; a little, rather
一日百円の割で いちにちひゃくえんのわりで at the rate of 100 yen a day

比 ▷**ratio**
ヒ　くら(べる)　　　　Ⓚ0014

[also suffix] **ratio**

比例 ひれい proportion, ratio
比率 ひりつ ratio, percentage
正比 せいひ direct ratio
容積比 ようせきひ volume ratio

歩 ▷**percentage**
ホ　ブ　フ　ある(く)　あゆ(む)　Ⓚ2141

percentage, rate

歩合 ぶあい rate, percentage; commission
歩留まり ぶどまり yield, yield rate

rear
後　背　裏　尻　尾

後 ▷**after-**
ゴ　コウ　のち　うし(ろ)　あと　おく(れる)　　　　Ⓚ0321

[also prefix] (behind in space) **after-, rear, back, hind**

後部 こうぶ back part, rear
後援 こうえん support, backing
後退する こうたいする retreat, recede
後甲板 こうかんぱん afterdeck
後頭部 こうとうぶ back (part) of the head
後方 こうほう back, rear
前後 ぜんご before and after; order, sequence
背後 はいご back, rear
落後(=落伍)する らくごする straggle, drop out of line, fall out of the ranks

背 ▷**back**
ハイ　せ　せい　そむ(く)　そむ(ける)　Ⓚ2230

(backside) **back, reverse side, rear**

背面 はいめん rear, back, reverse
背景 はいけい background; (stage) scenery, setting, scene; backing
腹背 ふくはい back and front; opposition in the heart

裏 ▷**rear**
リ　うら　　　　Ⓚ1836

rear, back, reverse, other side

裏面 りめん back, reverse, other side, inside; background
表裏 ひょうり front and rear, both sides (of a thing or matter); duplicity
庫裏 くり temple's kitchen; priest's living quarters

尻 ▷**tail end**
しり　　　　Ⓚ2610

tail end, end, back part, rear

尻取り しりとり capping (verses)
尻切れ蜻蛉 しりきれとんぼ unfinished ending
尻上がり しりあがり rising intonation; head over heels; rising market
尻込みする しりごみする flinch, shrink back
尻窄み しりつぼみ tapering, weak ending
尻目に懸ける しりめにかける look askance (contemptuously)
台尻 だいじり butt end (of a gun)
縄尻 なわじり end of a rope
どん尻 どんじり tail end; tailender

言葉尻を捉える ことばじりをとらえる cavil at a person's words

尾 ▷tail
ビ お ⓚ2635

(rear part) **tail, rear**

尾部 びぶ tail, tail section
尾翼 びよく tail, tail plane
尾灯 びとう taillight
尾行 びこう following, shadowing
船尾 せんび stern, poop

reason
理　訳

理 ▷reason
リ ⓚ0881

reason, what is right and proper

理想 りそう ideal
理由 りゆう reason, cause, ground
理念 りねん concept, idea
道理 どうり reason, right, justice, truth
合理的な ごうりてきな rational, logical, reasonable
無理な むりな unreasonable, unjustifiable; impossible; forced; excessive; irrational (equation)

訳 ▷sense
ヤク わけ ⓚ1340

(good) **sense, reason**

訳の分かった人 わけのわかったひと sensible man
訳知り わけしり person who knows the world; possessing an understanding about love affairs

reason →CAUSE AND REASON

reasoning
理　筋　脈

理 ▷reason
リ ⓚ0881

(rational thought) **reason, logic, line of thought**

理性 りせい reason, reasoning power
理屈 りくつ reason, logic; argument; pretext; theory
理不尽な りふじんな unreasonable, unjust, absurd
論理 ろんり logic
条理 じょうり reason, logic

筋 ▷thread
キン すじ ⓚ2337

thread, coherence, reason, logic

筋合い すじあい reason
筋道 すじみち reason, thread (of an argument), coherence; systematic method, due formality
筋の通った すじのとおった logical, rational, coherent
本筋 ほんすじ right course (of action); main thread
大筋 おおすじ outline

脈 ▷vein
ミャク ⓚ0860

(distinctive thread) **vein, thread, line**

脈絡 みゃくらく logical connection, chain of reasoning
文脈 ぶんみゃく context
乱脈 らんみゃく disorder, confusion, chaos
人脈 じんみゃく line of connections
金脈 きんみゃく (questionable) financial connections; vein of gold

rebellions →WARFARE AND REBELLIONS

receive
受　享　領　収　納
貰　戴　頂　拝

受 ▷receive
ジュ う(ける) -う(け) う(かる) ⓚ2146

[original meaning] **receive, accept, take, get**

受信 じゅしん reception (of radio waves); receipt of a message
受講 じゅこう attending lectures
受領 じゅりょう receipt
受注する じゅちゅうする receive an order
受納する じゅのうする accept, receive
受賞する じゅしょうする win a prize
受諾する じゅだくする receive, accept
受験する じゅけんする take an examination
受動的な じゅどうてきな passive
受話器 じゅわき (telephone) receiver
感受性 かんじゅせい sensibility

享 ▷enjoy
キョウ ⓚ1765

(benefit from something given) **enjoy, receive, be given, possess**

享受する きょうじゅする enjoy, receive, be given
享有する きょうゆうする enjoy, possess, participate in

享楽 きょうらく enjoyment
享年 きょうねん age at death

領 ▷receive
リョウ   Ⓚ1133

receive

領収書 りょうしゅうしょ receipt, voucher
受領 じゅりょう receipt
拝領する はいりょうする receive (from a superior),
    be bestowed

収 ▷take in
シュウ おさ(める) おさ(まる)   Ⓚ0016

(take possession of, esp. in payment) **take in, receive,
accept**

収入 しゅうにゅう income, earnings, receipts
収益 しゅうえき profit, earnings, proceeds, returns
収賄 しゅうわい acceptance of a bribe, corruption
収得する しゅうとくする take possession of
領収 りょうしゅう receipt

納 ▷accept
ノウ ナッ– ナ ナン トウ おさ(める)
おさ(まる)   Ⓚ1195

accept, receive, enjoy

納涼 のうりょう enjoying the evening cool
納受する のうじゅする accept, receive
受納 じゅのう acceptance, receipt
出納 すいとう receipts and expenses, incomings
    and outgoings
御笑納下さい ごしょうのうください Please accept
    this small present

貰 ▷get
セイ もら(う)   Ⓚ2259

get, be given, receive, accept, take

貰い手 もらいて receiver, recipient
貰い物 もらいもの (received) present, gift
貰い泣き もらいなき crying in sympathy
物貰い ものもらい beggar; sty (on the eyelid)

戴 ▷receive humbly
タイ いただ(く)   Ⓚ2815

receive humbly, accept with thanks

頂戴する ちょうだいする [humble] receive, accept,
    take; eat, drink

頂 ▷receive humbly
チョウ いただ(く) いただき   Ⓚ0125

receive humbly, accept with thanks

頂戴する ちょうだいする [humble] receive, accept,
    take; eat, drink

拝 ▷have the honor to receive
ハイ おが(む)   Ⓚ0268

have the honor to receive

拝命 はいめい receiving an official appointment
拝領する はいりょうする receive (from a superior),
    be bestowed

recent
近   新

近 ▷recent
キン ちか(い)   Ⓚ2634

(close in time) **recent, near, modern**

近況 きんきょう recent condition [situation]
近影 きんえい one's recent photograph
近年 きんねん recent years, late years
近世 きんせい modern ages
近代 きんだい modern [recent] times
近代的な きんだいてきな modern
近日 きんじつ soon, shortly, one of these days
最近の さいきんの late, recent

新 ▷new
シン あたら(しい) あら(た) あら–
にい–   Ⓚ1587

(close in time) **new, recent; newly**

新興の しんこうの rising, newly-established
新入生 しんにゅうせい new student [pupil], fresh-
    man
新米 しんまい new rice; new hand, novice

receptacles →VESSELS AND RECEPTACLES

recite
吟   誦   唱   読   詠

吟 ▷recite
ギン   Ⓚ0203

recite (a poem), chant, intone

吟詠 ぎんえい reciting [chanting] a poem; poem
吟唱(=吟誦)する ぎんしょうする recite, chant
詩吟 しぎん reciting Chinese poems

誦 ▷recite
ショウ ジュ ズ

[now also 唱, rarely also 頌] **recite, read aloud, chant,
intone**

誦経 ずきょう reciting [chanting] a sutra

暗誦する あんしょうする recite from memory
吟誦 ぎんしょう reciting (poetry), chanting
愛誦する あいしょうする love to recite (a poem), read with pleasure
読誦する どくじゅする read aloud, recite, intone

唱 ▷chant
ショウ とな(える)   Ⓚ0418

[formerly also 誦] **chant, recite, intone**
唱和する しょうわする chant [cheer] in chorus
吟唱する ぎんしょうする recite, chant
暗唱する あんしょうする recite from memory
詠唱する えいしょうする chant
三唱 さんしょう cheering (banzai) three times

読 ▷read
ドク トク トウ よ(む) -よ(み)   Ⓚ1401

read (aloud), recite, chant
朗読 ろうどく reading aloud
音読する おんどくする read aloud

詠 ▷recite poetry
エイ よ(む)   Ⓚ1360

[original meaning] **recite poetry, chant, sing**
詠唱 えいしょう chanting; aria
吟詠 ぎんえい reciting [chanting] a poem; poem
朗詠 ろうえい reciting, chanting

reclaim
拓　墾　開

拓 ▷open up
タク   Ⓚ0282

open up (farmland or new frontiers), clear land, reclaim, develop
拓殖 たくしょく colonization, exploitation
開拓 かいたく reclamation, opening up, clearing; exploitation
干拓 かんたく land reclamation by drainage

墾 ▷reclaim
コン   Ⓚ2516

[original meaning] **reclaim (wasteland), open up new land for farming, clear land, cultivate**
墾田 こんでん new rice field
開墾 かいこん clearing, reclamation
未墾の みこんの uncultivated, wild

開 ▷open
カイ ひら(く) ひら(き) -びら(き)
ひら(ける) あ(く) あ(ける)   Ⓚ283

open up land, develop, clear (land), reclaim
開発する かいはつする develop, open out; enlighten
開拓 かいたく reclamation, opening up, clearing; exploitation
新開地 しんかいち newly opened land

recommend
薦　推

薦 ▷recommend
セン すす(める)   Ⓚ209

recommend (a person to a post or a product)
薦挙 せんきょ recommendation
推薦する すいせんする recommend, nominate
自薦 じせん self-recommendation

推 ▷recommend
スイ お(す)   Ⓚ046

recommend, propose, nominate
推薦する すいせんする recommend, nominate
推挙する すいきょする recommend, nominate

records
記　録　譜　誌　史　伝

記 ▷written account
キ しる(す)   Ⓚ132

[also suffix] **written account, record, description**
日記 にっき diary
手記 しゅき note, memorandum; memoirs
伝記 でんき biography
旅行記 りょこうき travel record, travel book
古事記 こじき Kojiki (Ancient Chronicles)

録 ▷record
ロク   Ⓚ155

[also suffix] **record, records; proceedings, annals**
目録 もくろく catalog
付録 ふろく appendix, supplement
会議録 かいぎろく minutes, proceedings
語録 ごろく analects, sayings

譜 ▷systematic record
フ   Ⓚ1476

[also suffix] systematic record, as:

ⓐ record, chronology, chart
ⓑ record of shogi, chess or go
ⓒ family record, genealogy

a 年譜 ねんぷ chronological record
b 棋譜 きふ record of a game of shogi [go]
c 譜代 ふだい successive generations; hereditary Tokugawa daimyo
  系譜 けいふ genealogy, family tree
  家譜 かふ genealogy, pedigree
  皇統譜 こうとうふ Imperial family record

誌 ▷records
シ   Ⓚ1406

[also suffix] records, document

日誌 にっし diary
植物誌 しょくぶつし flora
地誌 ちし topography, geographical description

史 ▷history
シ   Ⓚ2946
see also →HISTORY

[also suffix] history, chronicles; history book

史料 しりょう historical materials [records]
史書 ししょ history book
史跡 しせき historic spot [remains]
史学者 しがくしゃ historian
史上に例を見ない しじょうにれいをみない be unparalleled in history
歴史 れきし history
青史 せいし history, history book
世界史 せかいし world history
日本史 にほんし Japanese history

伝 ▷biography
デン つた(わる) つた(える) つた(う) -づた(い)   Ⓚ0029

[also suffix] biography

伝記 でんき biography
列伝 れつでん series of biographies
ナポレオン伝 なぽれおんでん life of Napoleon

recover →CURE AND RECOVER

---

red colors
赤 紅 緋 朱 丹 茜

赤 ▷red
セキ シャク あか あか(い) あか(らむ) あか(らめる)   Ⓚ1876

red, crimson, scarlet

赤銅 しゃくどう gold-copper alloy
赤外線 せきがいせん infrared rays
赤痢 せきり dysentery
赤十字 せきじゅうじ Red Cross
赤面する せきめんする blush [turn red] (with shame), feel ashamed
赤色 せきしょく red; Communism
赤化する せっか(=せきか)する turn red; go Communist

紅 ▷crimson
コウ ク べに くれない   Ⓚ1174

crimson, deep red, red

紅白 こうはく red and white
紅海 こうかい Red Sea
紅葉 こうよう(=もみじ) red leaves, crimson foliage, autumn tints
紅旗 こうき Red Flag
紅茶 こうちゃ black tea
紅衛兵 こうえいへい Red Guards
深紅色 しんこうしょく deep crimson, scarlet
深紅 しんく crimson

緋 ▷scarlet
ヒ あけ   Ⓚ1250

scarlet

緋縅し ひおどし scarlet-threaded suit of armor
緋鯉 ひごい red carp, golden carp

朱 ▷vermilion
シュ   Ⓚ2960

vermilion, red

朱顔 しゅがん flushed face
朱色 しゅいろ vermilion, Chinese red
朱肉 しゅにく red ink pad
朱書する しゅしょする write in red
丹朱 たんしゅ vermilion, red; cinnabar

丹 ▷cinnabar
タン   Ⓚ2897

cinnabar red, vermilion, red

丹朱 たんしゅ vermilion, red; cinnabar
丹青 たんせい red and blue; painting

丹花 たんか red flower
牡丹 ぼたん peony, *Paeonia suffruticosa*

茜 ▷madder
セン あかね　　　　　　　　Ⓚ1951

madder red, crimson
茜色 あかねいろ madder, crimson
茜差す空 あかねさすそら glowing sky

reduce the temperature
凍　　冷

凍 ▷freeze
トウ こお(る) こご(える)　　Ⓚ0111

(turn solid because of cold) **freeze, congeal**
凍結 とうけつ freezing
冷凍 れいとう freezing, cold storage
不凍港 ふとうこう ice-free port

冷 ▷cool
レイ つめ(たい) ひ(える) ひ(や)
ひ(ややか) ひ(やす) ひ(やかす) さ(める)
さ(ます)　　　　　　　　　　Ⓚ0061

[original meaning] **cool, chill, refrigerate**
冷房 れいぼう air conditioning
冷凍 れいとう freezing, cold storage
冷却 れいきゃく cooling, refrigeration
冷蔵 れいぞう cold storage
冷蔵庫 れいぞうこ refrigerator
水冷 すいれい water cooling

refine
錬　　精　　留

錬 ▷refine (crude metals)
レン　　　　　　　　　　　　Ⓚ1553

[formerly also 煉] [original meaning] **refine (crude metals), smelt; work metals, temper**
錬金術 れんきんじゅつ alchemy
錬鉄 れんてつ wrought iron
錬鋼 れんこう wrought steel
精錬 せいれん refining, smelting; tempering
製錬 せいれん smelting
鍛錬する たんれんする temper, forge; train, discipline

精 ▷refine (crude materials)
セイ ショウ　　　　　　　　Ⓚ124

refine (crude materials), polish
精錬 せいれん refining, smelting; tempering
精製 せいせい refining; careful manufacture

留 ▷distill
リュウ ル と(める) –ど(め) と(まる)
とど(まる)　　　　　　　　Ⓚ223

[formerly 溜] **distill**
蒸留 じょうりゅう distillation
分留 ぶんりゅう fraction, fractional distillation
乾留 かんりゅう dry distillation

reflect →SHINE AND REFLECT

reform
改　革　更　新

改 ▷reform
カイ あらた(める) あらた(まる)　Ⓚ021

reform, renew, rectify, correct, revise, amend
改善する かいぜんする improve, ameliorate
改新 かいしん renovation, reformation
改革 かいかく reform, reformation
改正 かいせい revision, amendment
改築 かいちく remodeling, rebuilding

革 ▷reform
カク かわ　　　　　　　　　Ⓚ216

ⓐ **reform, transform, change**
ⓑ abbrev. of 改革 かいかく: **reform, reformation**
ⓐ 革新 かくしん innovation, reform, renovation
革命 かくめい revolution
改革 かいかく reform, reformation
変革 へんかく change, reform, revolution
沿革 えんかく history, annals
ⓑ 保革 ほかく conservatives and reformists
行革(=行政改革) ぎょうかく(=ぎょうせいかいかく) administrative reform

更 ▷renew
コウ さら さら(に) ふ(ける)
ふ(かす)　　　　　　　　　Ⓚ296

renew, replace, change, alter
更新する こうしんする renew, renovate, innovate
更改 こうかい renewal, renovation
更正 こうせい correction, revision, rectification
更生 こうせい rebirth, rehabilitation; recycling
更衣する こういする change one's clothes
変更する へんこうする alter, change, modify, shift

新 ▷make new
シン あたら(しい) あら(た) あら−
にい− Ⓚ1587

make new, renew, renovate
一新する いっしんする renovate, change completely; be renovated
革新 かくしん innovation, reform, renovation
更新する こうしんする renew, renovate, innovate
維新 いしん renovation, restoration; Imperial Restoration of 1868

refuse and reject
拒 断 否 却

拒 ▷refuse
キョ こば(む) Ⓚ0275

refuse, reject, deny
拒絶する きょぜつする refuse, reject, deny
拒否する きょひする deny, reject
拒止 きょし refusal
峻拒 しゅんきょ flat refusal, stern rejection

断 ▷refuse
ダン た(つ) ことわ(る) Ⓚ1355

refuse, reject, decline; give notice beforehand, call attention to; obtain consent, ask for permission
断り ことわり refusal, declining; prohibition; notice, warning; permission; excuse, apology
断る迄も無く ことわるまでもなく needless to say
断らずに ことわらずに without permission
申し出を断る もうしでをことわる turn down an offer

否 ▷say no
ヒ いな Ⓚ2130

say no, negate, deny
否定する ひていする deny, negate
否決 ひけつ rejection, voting down, negation
否認 ひにん denial, negation
拒否 きょひ denial, rejection

却 ▷reject
キャク Ⓚ1034

reject, turn down, decline
却下する きゃっかする reject, dismiss, turn down
棄却する ききゃくする turn down, reject, renounce

regret
惜 恨 憾 悔

惜 ▷regret
セキ お(しい) お(しむ) Ⓚ0442

regret, lament
惜別 せきべつ parting regrets
惜敗 せきはい regrettable defeat
哀惜 あいせき lamentation, grief

恨 ▷regret
コン うら(む) うら(めしい) Ⓚ0328

regret
恨事 こんじ regrettable matter
悔恨 かいこん regret, repentance
痛恨 つうこん deep regret, great sorrow

憾 ▷strongly regret
カン Ⓚ0690

[original meaning] **strongly regret, be sorry for, be dissatisfied**
遺憾な いかんな regrettable

悔 ▷repent
カイ く(いる) く(やむ) くや(しい) Ⓚ0324

repent, regret, be sorry
悔悛 かいしゅん repentance, penitence
悔恨 かいこん regret, repentance
悔悟 かいご repentance, remorse
後悔する こうかいする be sorry, regret, repent

regular
正 本

正 ▷regular
セイ ショウ ただ(しい) ただ(す) まさ
まさ(に) Ⓚ2926

[also prefix] **regular, full, normal, proper, formal, orthodox; legitimate, legal**
正規の せいきの regular, formal, legitimate
正式の せいしきの formal, regular
正統の せいとうの legitimate, orthodox, traditional
正常な せいじょうな normal, regular
正座する せいざする sit upright [straight]
正気 しょうき consciousness; sanity, reason
正妻 せいさい lawful [legal] wife
正会員 せいかいいん regular member

正教授 せいきょうじゅ full professor

本 ▷regular
ホン もと   Ⓚ2937

[also prefix] **regular, proper, formal, legal, full-fledged**

本格 ほんかく fundamental rules, propriety
本番 ほんばん acting for the audience, take, going on the air
本会議 ほんかいぎ plenary session, regular session

reject →REFUSE AND REJECT

relate
関 係 絡 渉 連 聯

関 ▷concern
カン せき -ぜき かか(わる)   Ⓚ2842

concern (oneself), be concerned (with), relate, involve, be connected with

関係 かんけい relation, relationship, connection
関連 かんれん connection, relation, association
関心 かんしん concern, interest
関与する かんよする take part in, participate in, be concerned in
関知する かんちする be concerned (with), have a concern (in)
相関 そうかん mutual relationship, correlation

係 ▷connect
ケイ かか(る) かかり -がかり
かか(わる)   Ⓚ0078

(have a relationship with) **connect, be connected with, relate to, interrelate**

係累 けいるい family ties, dependents
係争 けいそう dispute, contention; lawsuit
係属 けいぞく pendency (of a legal case); relationship
関係 かんけい relation, relationship, connection
連係 れんけい connection, linking, contact

絡 ▷interlink
ラク から(む) から(まる)
から(める)   Ⓚ1238

interlink, link, connect, join

連絡 れんらく connection, contact; communication
脈絡 みゃくらく logical connection, chain of reasoning
短絡 たんらく short circuit

渉 ▷have relations with
ショウ   Ⓚ0482

have relations [connections] with, relate, interrelate

渉外 しょうがい public relations
交渉 こうしょう negotiation, bargaining, discussion
干渉 かんしょう interference, intervention

連 ▷link
レン つら(なる) つら(ねる) つ(れる)
-づ(れ)   Ⓚ2672

(connect as if by linking) **link, connect, join, unite**

連絡 れんらく connection, contact; communication
連立 れんりつ alliance, coalition
連係 れんけい connection, linking, contact
連帯 れんたい solidarity
連合 れんごう combination, union, alliance; association
連盟 れんめい union, federation, league
関連 かんれん connection, relation, association

聯 ▷link
レン

[now replaced by 連]
ⓐ (join together) **link, join**
ⓑ (connect as if by linking) **link, connect, join, unite**

a 聯立 れんりつ alliance, coalition
聯句 れんく linked verse
聯珠 れんじゅ gobang
b 聯絡 れんらく connection, contact; communication
聯想 れんそう association (of ideas)
聯合 れんごう combination, union, alliance; association
聯邦 れんぽう federation, confederation, union
聯盟 れんめい union, federation, league
聯隊 れんたい regiment
関聯 かんれん connection, relation, association

related by marriage
義 継

義 ▷-in-law
ギ   Ⓚ2052

-in-law; step-, foster

義父 ぎふ father-in-law; foster father, stepfather
義兄 ぎけい brother-in-law
義母 ぎぼ mother-in-law

継 ▷step-
ケイ つ(ぐ)   Ⓚ1242

step-; second (wife or husband)

継母 けいぼ stepmother
継夫 けいふ second husband

elations →FAMILY AND RELATIONS

release
放　　釈

放 ▷let go
ホウ　はな(す)　-(っ)ぱな(し)　はな(つ)
はな(れる)　ほう(る)　　　　Ⓚ0754

(set free) **let go, release, free**

放流する ほうりゅうする discharge; stock (a river)
　　with (fish)
放牧 ほうぼく pasturage, grazing
放課後 ほうかご after school
解放する かいほうする release, set free
釈放する しゃくほうする release, liberate,
　　discharge, acquit

釈 ▷release
シャク　　　　　　　Ⓚ1349

release, free

釈放 しゃくほう release, liberation, discharge,
　　acquittal
保釈する ほしゃくする bail, let (a prisoner) out on
　　bail

religion
教　　宗　　道

教 ▷religion
キョウ　おし(える)　おそ(わる)　　　Ⓚ1356

ⓐ **religion, religious teachings, religious sect**
ⓑ **suffix after names of religions**

a 教会 きょうかい church
　教祖 きょうそ founder of a religion, head of a sect
　宗教 しゅうきょう religion, faith, creed
　殉教 じゅんきょう martyrdom
　布教する ふきょうする propagate (a religion)
b 仏教 ぶっきょう Buddhism
　キリスト教 きりすときょう Christianity
　ユダヤ教 ゆだやきょう Judaism
　イスラム教 いすらむきょう Islam

宗 ▷religion
シュウ ソウ　　　　　　Ⓚ1915

religion

宗教 しゅうきょう religion, faith, creed

改宗 かいしゅう conversion; proselytism

道 ▷the Way
ドウ トウ みち　　　　　　Ⓚ2701

the Way, Tao, Do—a basic concept in Oriental religion
and philosophy:
ⓐ Taoism **unitary first principle of existence, Taoism**
ⓑ Confucianism **ultimate principle of cosmic reason**
ⓒ Buddhism **the way of the Buddha, the teachings
　of Buddha**
ⓓ other religions **the way, religious teachings**
　神道 しんとう Shinto, the Way of the Gods
　伝道 でんどう gospel preaching, missionary work,
　　evangelism
a 道教 どうきょう Taoism
　道家 どうか Taoist scholar
b 道学 どうがく Confucian philosophy; Taoism
c 道具 どうぐ tool, utensil, implement; furniture;
　　theatrical appurtenances; tool, means; ingredi-
　　ent
　道心 どうしん faith (in Buddha), piety; bonze, priest;
　　sense of morality
　入道する にゅうどうする become a bonze,
　　renounce the world
d 神道 しんとう Shinto, the Way of the Gods
　伝道 でんどう gospel preaching, missionary work,
　　evangelism

religions and sects
仏　法　禅　儒　道

仏 ▷Buddhism
ブツ フツ ほとけ　　　　　Ⓚ0010

Buddhism

仏教 ぶっきょう Buddhism
念仏 ねんぶつ Buddhist invocation, prayer to
　Amitabha

法 ▷Buddha's teachings
ホウ ハッ- ホッ-　　　　　Ⓚ0295

**Buddha's teachings, Buddha's doctrine, dharma,
Buddhism; religious tenets**

法王 ほうおう pope
法主 ほっす(=ほうしゅ, ほっしゅ) high priest (of a
　Buddhist sect)
仏法 ぶっぽう Buddhism
説法 せっぽう (Buddhist) sermon, preaching,
　moralizing

禅 ▷Zen
ゼン　　　　　　　Ⓚ0947

ⓐ **Zen Buddhism, Chan**
ⓑ **Zen meditation, dhyana**

a 禅宗 ぜんしゅう Zen sect
禅僧 ぜんそう Zen priest [monk]
禅寺 ぜんでら Zen temple
b 禅定 ぜんじょう Samadhi, meditative concentration
座禅 ざぜん Zen meditation

儒 ▷Confucianism
ジュ　Ⓚ0153

Confucianism
儒教 じゅきょう Confucianism
儒仏 じゅぶつ Confucianism and Buddhism

道 ▷Taoism
ドウ トウ みち　Ⓚ2701

Taoism unitary first principle of existence, Taoism
道教 どうきょう Taoism
道家 どうか Taoist scholar

religious persons
聖　仙

聖 ▷saint
セイ　Ⓚ2464

ⓐ saint
ⓑ title before names of saints: **St.**
a 聖賢 せいけん saints and sages
b 聖ペテロ せいぺてろ St. Peter
聖路加病院 せいろかびょういん St. Luke Hospital

仙 ▷immortal mountain fairy
セン　Ⓚ0020

ⓐ transcendent immortal fairy living in the mountains and capable of performing miracles, Taoist immortal, supernatural being
ⓑ hermit, recluse
a 仙人 せんにん immortal mountain fairy; hermit, unworldly person
仙術 せんじゅつ fairy magic
仙境 せんきょう fairyland, enchanted land
神仙 しんせん supernatural being
b 酒仙 しゅせん hermit who enjoys drinking; son of Bacchus

rely on
頼　依

頼 ▷rely on
ライ たの(む) たの(もしい) たよ(る)　Ⓚ145

rely on, depend on, trust
信頼する しんらいする rely on, have confidence, trust in
無頼漢 ぶらいかん villain, scoundrel

依 ▷depend on
イ エ　Ⓚ006

depend on, rely on
依存する いぞん(=いそん)する depend on, rely on
依嘱する いしょくする entrust with
依頼する いらいする request, make a request; entrust, commission; rely on, depend on
帰依 きえ faith, devotion; conversion

remain
残　余　留　滞

残 ▷remain
ザン のこ(る) のこ(す)　Ⓚ085

remain, linger, stay
残余 ざんよ remainder, residue, remnant
残高 ざんだか balance, remainder
残額 ざんがく balance (of an account)
残業 ざんぎょう overtime
残飯 ざんぱん leftover food [rice]
残雪 ざんせつ lingering snow
残念 ざんねん regret, disappointment, chagrin

余 ▷remaining
ヨ あま(る) あま(り) あま(す)　Ⓚ175

remaining, lingering, secondary
余地 よち room, space, margin
余暇 よか leisure, spare time
余生 よせい one's remaining years
余波 よは secondary effect, aftereffect
余韻 よいん lingering tone, resonance, reverberation; aftertaste, impregnated elegance
刑余の人 けいよのひと ex-convict

留 ▷stay
リュウ ル と(める) -ど(め) と(まる)
とど(まる)　　　Ⓚ2235

(remain in a given condition) **stay, remain, continue**
留任する りゅうにんする remain [stay] in office
留年する りゅうねんする stay more than two years
　in the same class
残留する ざんりゅうする stay behind
停留所 ていりゅうじょ (bus) stop, station

滞 ▷stay
タイ とどこお(る)　　　Ⓚ0609
see also →STAY

(remain in a given place) **stay, remain, sojourn**
滞在 たいざい stay, sojourn
滞留 たいりゅう sojourn, stay
滞米 たいべい staying in America
滞欧 たいおう staying in Europe
滞空 たいくう staying [remaining] in the air

remember
憶 覚 記 追 顧 偲

憶 ▷remember
オク　　　Ⓚ0691

remember, recall, recollect
記憶 きおく memory, recollection
追憶 ついおく recollection, retrospection

覚 ▷commit to memory
カク おぼ(える) さ(ます) さ(める)　Ⓚ2258

commit to memory, remember, memorize
覚え おぼえ recollection, memory; learning; favor;
　feeling
覚え書き おぼえがき memorandum, memo, note
見覚え みおぼえ recognition, remembrance
物覚え ものおぼえ memory

記 ▷commit to memory
キ しる(す)　　　Ⓚ1321

commit to memory, memorize, remember, bear in mind
記憶 きおく memory, recollection
記念日 きねんび memorial day, anniversary
暗記 あんき learning by heart, memorizing
銘記する めいきする bear in mind, remember;
　inscribe, engrave
強記 きょうき good memory

追 ▷reminisce
ツイ お(う)　　　Ⓚ2667

reminisce, recollect, recall the past
追想 ついそう recollection, reminiscence

顧 ▷look back
コ かえり(みる)　　　Ⓚ1677

look back upon (the past), retrospect
後顧 こうこ looking back, worry
回顧する かいこする look back on, retrospect

偲 ▷recollect
サイ シ しの(ぶ)　　　Ⓚ0118

recall, recollect, remember, reminisce
故人を偲ぶ こじんをしのぶ think of the dead
昔を偲ばせる品 むかしをしのばせるしな things
　reminiscent of bygone days

repair
直 修 繕

直 ▷fix
チョク ジキ ジカ ただ(ちに) なお(す)
なお(る) なお(き) す(ぐ)　　　Ⓚ2539

fix, repair, mend, set right
直し物 なおしもの mending, thing to be mended
パンクを直す ぱんくをなおす fix a flat tire

修 ▷repair
シュウ シュ おさ(める) おさ(まる)　Ⓚ0105

repair, mend, rectify
修正 しゅうせい amendment, revision, correction;
　retouch
修理 しゅうり repair, mending
修復 しゅうふく restoration
修繕する しゅうぜんする mend, repair
改修する かいしゅうする repair, improve
補修 ほしゅう repair, mending

繕 ▷mend
ゼン つくろ(う)　　　Ⓚ1296

[original meaning] (fix and/or make whole) **mend, repair**
修繕する しゅうぜんする mend, repair
営繕 えいぜん building and repairs, maintenance

repeating and repetition
再 又 復 重 畳
改 換 直 返

再 ▷**another time**
サイ サ ふたた(び)　　　Ⓚ2950

[also prefix] **another time, re-, again, a second time, another**

再度 さいど another time, a second time
再開 さいかい reopening, resumption
再来 さいらい return, second coming; Second Advent
再現する さいげんする reenact, reproduce
再三 さいさん again and again, repeatedly
再興 さいこう revival, restoration
再生 さいせい reclamation; regeneration, resuscitation; playback
再訂版 さいていばん second revised edition
再婚 さいこん remarriage, second marriage
再検討 さいけんとう reexamination, restudying

又 ▷**again**
また また(の)-　　　Ⓚ2853

[formerly also 復] **again, once more [again], repeatedly**

又会う日迄 またあうひまで till we meet again
又しても またしても once again

復 ▷**repeat**
フク　　　Ⓚ0527

repeat, redo

復習 ふくしゅう review
復誦(=復唱) ふくしょう recital, repetition, rehearsal
復刻する ふっこくする [sometimes also 覆刻する] republish, reissue
復文 ふくぶん retranslation (into the original language); reply letter
反復 はんぷく [sometimes also 反覆] repetition, reiteration

重 ▷**duplicate**
ジュウ チョウ え おも(い) おも(り)
かさ(ねる) かさ(なる)　　　Ⓚ2991

duplicate, repeat, redo

重重 じゅうじゅう repeatedly; extremely, very much
重複 ちょうふく(=じゅうふく) duplication, overlapping; repetition

畳 ▷**reduplicate**
ジョウ たた(む) たた(み)-　　　Ⓚ2249

reduplicate (a word), repeat, reiterate

畳成語 じょうせいご reiterative
畳語 じょうご syllable repetition to indicate plurals (as 人人 ひとびと)
畳韻 じょういん repeated [recurring] rhymes (in Chinese poetry)

改 ▷**redo**
カイ あらた(める) あらた(まる)　　　Ⓚ0216

redo, renew

改選 かいせん reelection
改葬 かいそう reburial

換 ▷**redo**
カン -か(える) か(わる)　　　Ⓚ0537

[verbal suffix] **redo, renew, change**

書き換える かきかえる rewrite, renew (a bill), transfer
作り換える つくりかえる remake, reconstruct
乗り換える のりかえる change (trains), transfer

直 ▷**repetition suffix**
チョク ジキ ジカ ただ(ちに) -なお(す)
なお(る) なお(き) す(ぐ)　　　Ⓚ2539

verbal suffix indicating repetition: **do over again**

やり直す やりなおす do over again
書き直す かきなおす rewrite
思い直す おもいなおす reconsider, think better of
焼き直し やきなおし rebaking; adaptation (from)
やり直し やりなおし doing over again, redoing

返 ▷**do over**
ヘン -かえ(す) かえ(る)　　　Ⓚ2633

do over, redo, re-

繰り返す くりかえす repeat, do over again
読み返す よみかえす reread, read again

repetition →REPEATING AND REPETITION

replace →CHANGE AND REPLACE

reproductive cells
卵　　　精

卵 ▷**ovum**
ラン たまご　　　Ⓚ075

ovum

卵子 らんし ovum, ovule, egg
卵巣 らんそう ovary

排卵 はいらん ovulation

精 ▷sperm
セイ ショウ　　　　　　　　Ⓚ1248

(essential substance of life) **sperm, semen**
精子 せいし sperm
精液 せいえき semen, sperm
受精 じゅせい fertilization, impregnation; pollination
夢精 むせい nocturnal emission, wet dream

reptiles and amphibians
亀　蛇　竜　蛙　黽

亀 ▷turtle
キ かめ　　　　　　　　　　Ⓚ1826

[original meaning] **turtle, tortoise**
亀甲 きっこう carapace of a turtle, tortoiseshell
亀卜 きぼく divination by tortoiseshells

蛇 ▷snake
ジャ ダ へび　　　　　　　Ⓚ1230
see also →SNAKE

[original meaning] **snake, serpent**
蛇蝎 だかつ snake and scorpion, viper
蛇行する だこうする meander, zigzag
蛇足 だそく superfluity, redundancy
蛇の目 じゃのめ umbrella with a snake's eye pattern; double circle pattern
大蛇 だいじゃ big snake, serpent

竜 ▷dragon
リュウ たつ　　　　　　　Ⓚ1805
see also →DRAGON

dragon
竜神 りゅうじん dragon god, dragon king
竜宮 りゅうぐう Palace of the Dragon King
竜虎 りゅうこ(=りょうこ) dragon and tiger; hero

蛙 ▷frog
ア ワ かえる かわず

[original meaning] **frog, toad**
蛙鳴蝉噪 あめいせんそう annoying noise, loud buzz; fruitless argument
蛙声 あせい croak of a frog [toad]
蛙黽 あぼう [archaic] tree frog [toad]

黽 ▷frog
ボウ ビン ベン

[original meaning] **frog, toad**
蛙黽 あぼう [archaic] tree frog [toad]

repute
声　誉　名　望

声 ▷reputation
セイ ショウ こえ こわ-　　Ⓚ1880

reputation
声価 せいか reputation, fame
名声 めいせい fame, reputation

誉 ▷honor
ヨ ほま(れ)　　　　　　　Ⓚ2193

honor, good reputation, fame, glory
名誉 めいよ honor, glory; dignity
栄誉 えいよ honor, glory, distinction
声誉 せいよ fame, reputation, honor and distinction, credit

名 ▷name
メイ ミョウ な　　　　　　Ⓚ1857

(reputation, esp. good reputation) **name, fame, reputation**
名誉 めいよ honor, glory; dignity
名声 めいせい fame, reputation
有名な ゆうめいな famous, noted, celebrated; notorious
著名 ちょめい prominence, eminence, distinction
汚名 おめい bad name, ill fame, disgrace
功名 こうみょう great exploit; distinction, fame

望 ▷popularity
ボウ モウ のぞ(む)　　　　Ⓚ2390

popularity, reputation
信望 しんぼう prestige, popularity
人望 じんぼう popularity, popular favor
声望 せいぼう popularity, reputation

request
請　訴　頼　嘱　要　願　求　乞

請 ▷request
セイ シン こ(う) う(ける)　Ⓚ1426

[original meaning] **request, ask, beg, solicit**

請求 せいきゅう demand, request, claim
請願 せいがん petition
請訓 せいくん request for instructions
申請 しんせい application, petition, request
要請する ようせいする request, demand
懇請する こんせいする request earnestly, solicit, entreat
普請 ふしん building, construction

訴 ▷appeal to
ソ うった(える)　⑥1367

(try to deal with one's grievances by asking for sympathy)
appeal to, entreat, implore
哀訴 あいそ entreaty, complaint
愁訴する しゅうそする entreat, implore, appeal

頼 ▷ask
ライ たの(む) たの(もしい)
たよ(る)　⑥1458

ask, request
頼信紙 らいしんし telegraph (application) blank
依頼する いらいする request, make a request; entrust, commission; rely on, depend on

嘱 ▷charge with
ショク　⑥0650

[original meaning] **charge (a person) with (a job), ask someone to do something; entrust**
嘱託する しょくたくする entrust with
委嘱する いしょくする charge, commission [entrust] with

要 ▷require
ヨウ かなめ い(る)　⑥2290

require, demand, request
要求 ようきゅう requirement, demand, request
要請 ようせい request, demand
要望 ようぼう demand, request
強要 きょうよう coercion, extortion
必要な ひつような needed, necessary
需要 じゅよう demand
所要の しょようの required, needed

願 ▷ask a favor
ガン ねが(う)　⑥1637

ask a favor, petition, apply for, request, beg
願書 がんしょ written application
出願 しゅつがん application
志願する しがんする volunteer, apply for
請願 せいがん petition
懇願する こんがんする beg earnestly, implore, entreat
依願退職 いがんたいしょく retirement at one's own request

求 ▷seek
キュウ もと(める)　⑥297

(ask for) **seek, request, demand**
求婚 きゅうこん proposal of marriage
求刑する きゅうけいする demand a sentence (for the accused)
要求する ようきゅうする require, demand, request
請求 せいきゅう demand, request, claim

乞 ▷beg
コツ コ こ(う)　⑥170

ⓐ [original meaning] **beg**
ⓑ [in compounds] **solicit, pray for**
ⓐ 乞食 こじき beggar
乞丐 こつがい(=きっかい) begging; beggar
乞士 こっし bhikkhu, fully ordained Buddhist monk

rescue
救　　済

救 ▷save
キュウ すく(う)　⑥135

[original meaning] **save, rescue, deliver, help**
救済する きゅうさいする relieve, help, save, deliver
救命 きゅうめい lifesaving
救出 きゅうしゅつ rescue, relief, deliverance
救世主 きゅうせいしゅ the Savior, the Messiah
救援 きゅうえん relief, rescue, help
救助 きゅうじょ rescue, relief
救難 きゅうなん rescue, salvage
救急車 きゅうきゅうしゃ ambulance

済 ▷relieve
サイ す(む) –ず(み) す(まない) す(ます)
す(ませる)　⑥047

relieve, aid, save, redeem
済民 さいみん relieving the sufferings of the people
済度 さいど Buddhism salvation
経済 けいざい economy, economics
救済する きゅうさいする relieve, help, save, deliver
共済 きょうさい mutual aid

resemble
似　　類

似 ▷resemble
ジ に(る)　⑥004

[original meaning] **resemble, be similar**

類似する るいじする resemble, be alike, be similar
酷似 こくじ close resemblance
相似 そうじ similarity, resemblance
近似する きんじする approximate to, resemble closely
疑似コレラ ぎじこれら suspected case of cholera, para-cholera

類 ▷be similar
ルイ たぐ(い) Ⓚ1606

be similar, resemble, be alike
類似 るいじ resemblance, similarity

reside
住 居 棲 栖 生 植

住 ▷live
ジュウ す(む) す(まう) -ず(まい) Ⓚ0047

live, reside, dwell, inhabit
住民 じゅうみん residents, dwellers
住居 じゅうきょ house, dwelling, residence
住所 じゅうしょ one's dwelling, address
住職 じゅうしょく Buddhist priest, chief priest
在住する ざいじゅうする live, reside, dwell
居住する きょじゅうする live, dwell, reside
移住する いじゅうする migrate, immigrate; move

居 ▷reside
キョ い(る) -い お(る) Ⓚ2653

reside, live, dwell
居住する きょじゅうする live, dwell, reside
居留地 きょりゅうち settlement, concession
同居する どうきょする live together
別居 べっきょ separation, limited divorce
群居する ぐんきょする live gregariously

棲 ▷inhabit (said of animals), live
セイ す(む) Ⓚ0902

ⓐ [now usu. 生] (of animals) **inhabit, live**
ⓑ (of people) **live, dwell, reside**
ⓐ 棲息する せいそくする inhabit, live
水棲の すいせいの aquatic, living in the water
両棲類 りょうせいるい Amphibia, amphibian
ⓑ 同棲する どうせいする live together, cohabit with
隠棲 いんせい secluded life
幽棲する ゆうせいする live a quiet life in seclusion away from the masses

栖 ▷inhabit (said of animals), live
セイ す す(む) すみか Ⓚ0844

ⓐ [now replaced by 生] (of animals) **inhabit, live**

ⓑ (of people) **live, dwell, reside**
ⓐ 栖息する せいそくする inhabit, live
ⓑ 隠栖 いんせい secluded life
幽栖する ゆうせいする live a quiet life in seclusion away from the masses

生 ▷inhabit
セイ ショウ い(きる) い(かす) い(ける) う(まれる) う(まれ) う(む) お(う) は(える) は(やす) き なま な(る) Ⓚ2933

[formerly 棲 or 栖] (of animals) (occupy a habitat) **inhabit, live**
生息する せいそくする inhabit, live
水生の すいせいの aquatic, living in the water
両生類 りょうせいるい Amphibia, amphibian

植 ▷colonize
ショク う(える) う(わる) Ⓚ0903

[sometimes also 殖] **colonize, settle**
植民地 しょくみんち colony, settlement
入植 にゅうしょく settlement, immigration

resign
辞 退

辞 ▷resign
ジ や(める) Ⓚ1245

resign, retire, quit
辞職 じしょく resignation
辞表 じひょう (letter of) resignation
辞意 じい intention to resign

退 ▷retire
タイ しりぞ(く) しりぞ(ける) Ⓚ2665

(retreat from public life) **retire, resign, leave**
退職 たいしょく retirement, resignation
引退する いんたいする retire, go into retirement
隠退 いんたい retirement, seclusion from the world

resist
抗 抵 耐 対 反 逆 撥 叛

抗 ▷resist
コウ Ⓚ0224

[original meaning] **resist, defy, oppose**
抗争 こうそう dispute, resistance
抗議 こうぎ protest, remonstrance, objection
反抗 はんこう resistance, opposition, defiance

抵抗する ていこうする resist, oppose, defy
対抗する たいこうする oppose, antagonize, rival; counteract
不可抗力 ふかこうりょく act of god, irresistible force

抵 ▷resist
テイ   Ⓚ0284

resist, withstand, oppose, stand up to
抵抗する ていこうする resist, oppose, defy

耐 ▷withstand
タイ た(える)   Ⓚ1178

a (resist physical forces) **withstand, resist**
b [also prefix] **-proof, -resistant, -resisting**
ab 耐火 たいか fireproof
耐震 たいしん earthquake-proof
耐熱 たいねつ heat-resisting
耐水 たいすい waterproof
耐アルカリ性 たいあるかりせい alkali resistance

対 ▷oppose
タイ ツイ   Ⓚ0735

oppose, confront (each other), counter
対立 たいりつ opposition, antagonism
対抗 たいこう opposition, antagonism, rivalry; counteraction
対決 たいけつ confrontation, showdown
対戦 たいせん waging war; competition
反対する はんたいする oppose, object (to)
敵対 てきたい hostility, antagonism

反 ▷counter
ハン ホン タン そ(る) そ(らす)   Ⓚ2549

counter, oppose, go against
反対する はんたいする oppose, object (to)
反抗 はんこう resistance, opposition, defiance
反目 はんもく antagonism, hostility, feud
反則 はんそく violation of rules, infringement, foul
反感 はんかん ill feeling, antipathy

逆 ▷rebel
ギャク さか さか(さ) さか(らう)   Ⓚ2662

rebel, defy, disobey
逆徒 ぎゃくと rebel, traitor
反逆する はんぎゃくする revolt [rebel] against, rise in mutiny

撥 ▷repel
ハツ バチ は(ねる)

[now usu. 発] [original meaning] **repel, repulse, rebound**
撥水 はっすい water repellency

反撥 はんぱつ repulsion, repelling; rally (of the market); opposition

叛 ▷rebel
ハン ホン そむ(く)

[now replaced by 反 はん,] [original meaning] **rebel, revolt**
叛乱 はんらん rebellion, revolt
叛逆 はんぎゃく revolt, rebellion, mutiny
叛旗 はんき flag [standard] of revolt
叛徒 はんと rebels, insurgents
謀叛 むほん rebellion, revolt, treason

resolutely

敢   断   決

敢 ▷boldly
カン あ(えて) あ(えず)   Ⓚ1522

boldly, daringly, bravely, fearlessly, resolutely
敢闘する かんとうする fight bravely
敢然(と) かんぜん(と) boldly, bravely

断 ▷resolutely
ダン た(つ) ことわ(る)   Ⓚ1355

resolutely, decisively, absolutely
断固たる だんこたる firm, conclusive, determined
断行する だんこうする carry out resolutely
断然 だんぜん resolutely, decisively

決 ▷decisively
ケツ き(める) -ぎ(め) き(まる)   Ⓚ0233

decisively, resolutely
決行 けっこう decisive action
決然たる けつぜんたる decisive, resolute, determined

respect

敬   尊   畏   欽   仰
崇   尚   重   拝   慕

敬 ▷respect
ケイ うやま(う)   Ⓚ1517

respect, revere, honor
敬意 けいい respect, regard, honor
敬称 けいしょう honorific title, term of respect
敬老 けいろう respect for the aged
敬語 けいご honorific language, polite speech

敬遠する けいえんする keep at a respectful
   distance; avoid
敬具 けいぐ Yours truly [respectfully]
敬服する けいふくする have great admiration for
敬愛 けいあい respect and affection, veneration
尊敬する そんけいする respect, esteem, honor,
   revere
失敬な しっけいな disrespectful, rude, impolite
愛敬 あいきょう (personal) charm, winsomeness,
   courtesy

尊 ▷honor
ソン たっと(い) とうと(い) たっと(ぶ)
とうと(ぶ)   Ⓚ2029

honor, respect, venerate, esteem
尊重する そんちょうする respect, esteem, value
尊敬する そんけいする respect, esteem, honor,
   revere
自尊心 じそんしん (spirit of) self-respect, pride

畏 ▷respect
イ おそ(れる)   Ⓚ2218

respect, revere
畏友 いゆう one's respected friend
畏敬 いけい awe and respect, reverence

欽 ▷revere
キン   Ⓚ1508

revere, respect, adore, admire
欽慕 きんぼ admiration, adoration, reverence

仰 ▷look up to
ギョウ コウ あお(ぐ) おお(せ)   Ⓚ0032

look up to, respect, revere
仰望する ぎょうぼうする look up to, revere
信仰する しんこうする believe in, have faith

崇 ▷reverence
スウ   Ⓚ1990

**reverence, revere, worship, venerate, adore,
esteem**
崇敬 すうけい reverence, admiration
崇拝 すうはい worship, adoration
崇高な すうこうな lofty, sublime, noble
尊崇 そんすう reverence, veneration

尚 ▷value highly
ショウ なお   Ⓚ1919

value highly, esteem, be enthusiastically devoted
尚古 しょうこ worship of ancient things
尚武 しょうぶ militarism, warlike spirit
好尚 こうしょう taste, fancy, fashion

重 ▷set value on
ジュウ チョウ え おも(い) おも(り)
かさ(ねる) かさ(なる)   Ⓚ2991

set value on, value, attach importance to, esteem
重商主義 じゅうしょうしゅぎ mercantilism
尊重する そんちょうする respect, esteem, value
偏重する へんちょうする attach too much importance, overemphasize
珍重する ちんちょうする value highly, treasure

拝 ▷worship
ハイ おが(む)   Ⓚ0268

(feel an adoring reverence for) **worship, adore**
拝金 はいきん money worship, worship of
   mammon
拝外的な はいがいてきな pro-foreign, xenophilous
崇拝 すうはい worship, adoration

慕 ▷adore
ボ した(う)   Ⓚ2069

adore, love deeply, be attached to
敬慕する けいぼする adore, love and respect,
   admire
恋慕 れんぼ love, attachment

respectful
恭   謹   奉   拝

恭 ▷respectful
キョウ うやうや(しい)   Ⓚ2172

[original meaning] **respectful, reverent**
恭敬 きょうけい respect, reverence
恭順 きょうじゅん obedience, submission
恭賀 きょうが respectful congratulations
恭謙 きょうけん modesty, humility
恭検 きょうけん humility, respect

謹 ▷respectfully
キン つつし(む)   Ⓚ1462

respectfully, with respect, reverently; respectful
謹賀新年 きんがしんねん Happy New Year
謹呈する きんていする present, make a present
謹厳な きんげんな stern, grave, solemn
謹告する きんこくする inform with respect,
   announce respectfully
謹啓 きんけい Dear Sirs, Gentlemen
謹書 きんしょ written respectfully

奉 ▷**reverentially**
ホウ ブ たてまつ(る)   Ⓚ2215

❶ **reverentially, respectfully, humbly**—honorific term expressing respect toward the person addressed, esp. the emperor of Japan
❷ **serve reverentially, serve under (a master)**
  a 奉読する ほうどくする read reverentially
   奉還 ほうかん restoration to the emperor
   奉答 ほうとう reply to the Throne
   奉賀 ほうが respectful congratulation
  b 奉仕する ほうしする attend, serve
   奉公 ほうこう public duty [service]; domestic service, apprenticeship
   奉職する ほうしょくする be in the service of

拝 ▷**humbly**
ハイ おが(む)   Ⓚ0268

humbly, respectfully, reverentially—honorific term expressing humility in reference to an action of the speaker
  拝見する はいけんする have the honor of seeing, see, look at, inspect
  拝借する はいしゃくする borrow
  拝聴する はいちょうする listen attentively [respectfully]
  拝受する はいじゅする receive [accept] (humbly)

responsibility
務 任 責 分

務 ▷**duty**
ム つと(める) つと(まる)   Ⓚ1085

(moral or legal obligations) **duty, responsibility, obligation**
  義務 ぎむ duty, obligation
  責務 せきむ responsibility and obligation, responsibility to do one's duty
  債務 さいむ debt, obligation, liabilities

任 ▷**duty**
ニン まか(せる) まか(す)   Ⓚ0038

duty, responsibility
  任務 にんむ duty, part, function; mission
  責任 せきにん responsibility, liability
  重任 じゅうにん heavy responsibility, important duty; reappointment

責 ▷**responsibility**
セキ せ(める)   Ⓚ2176

responsibility, liability
  責任 せきにん responsibility, liability

責務 せきむ responsibility and obligation, responsibility to do one's duty
重責 じゅうせき heavy responsibility, important duty
職責 しょくせき responsibilities pertaining to one's work
引責する いんせきする take responsibility upon oneself

分 ▷**one's part**
ブン フン ブ わ(ける) わ(け) わ(かれる) わ(かる) わ(かつ)   Ⓚ171.

(one's share in something) **one's part, one's duty**
  本分 ほんぶん one's duty, one's part
  職分 しょくぶん duty, vocation
  名分 めいぶん justification, just cause

rest
休 息 憩 歇

休 ▷**rest**
キュウ やす(む) やす(まる) やす(める)   Ⓚ003

[original meaning] **rest, repose, relax**
  休憩 きゅうけい rest, repose
  休息 きゅうそく rest, repose
  休養 きゅうよう rest, recuperation, relaxation
  休止 きゅうし pause, standstill, dormancy; rest
  休日 きゅうじつ holiday, day off
  休暇 きゅうか holiday, vacation
  休業 きゅうぎょう suspension of business
  休火山 きゅうかざん dormant volcano
  本日休診 ほんじつきゅうしん Office Closed Today (sign at doctor's office)

息 ▷**rest**
ソク いき   Ⓚ2301

rest, repose
  休息 きゅうそく rest, repose
  安息日 あんそくび Sabbath

憩 ▷**take a rest**
ケイ いこ(い) いこ(う)   Ⓚ2510

take a rest, repose, relax, rest
  憩室 けいしつ diverticulum
  休憩する きゅうけいする rest, repose
  小憩 しょうけい short rest, brief recess

歇 ▷**take a rest**
ケツ

[now replaced by 欠] [original meaning] **take a rest**

restaurant suffixes
亭　閣　園　苑

亭 ▷quality restaurant suffix
テイ　　　　　　　　　　Ⓚ1785

suffix after names of quality restaurants

夕月亭 ゆうづきてい The Yuzukitei (name of a Japanese restaurant)

閣 ▷high-class restaurant suffix
カク　　　　　　　　　　Ⓚ2841

suffix after names of magnificent buildings such as high-class restaurants

山水閣 さんすいかく Sansuikaku (restaurant's name)

園 ▷restaurant suffix
エン　その　　　　　　　Ⓚ2722

[sometimes also 苑] suffix after names of business establishments such as restaurants and tea shops, esp. where there are gardens

永谷園 ながたにえん Nagatanien (name of a food company)

苑 ▷restaurant suffix
エン　オン　その　　　　Ⓚ1926

[usu. 園] suffix after names of business establishments such as restaurants and tea shops, esp. where there are gardens

珈琲苑 こーひーえん name of a coffee shop

restore →RETURN AND RESTORE

---

restrain
制　禁　限　抑　束
縛　控　扣　渋

制 ▷control (restrain)
セイ　　　　　　　　　　Ⓚ1170

(hold in restraint) **control, restrain, restrict, suppress, inhibit**

制止する せいしする control, check, stop (a person) from (doing)

制限 せいげん restriction, limit

制御する せいぎょする control, govern, suppress

抑制する よくせいする control, suppress, inhibit

禁 ▷prohibit
キン　　　　　　　　　　Ⓚ2435

prohibit, forbid, ban

禁止する きんしする prohibit, forbid, ban

禁煙 きんえん NO SMOKING; giving up smoking

禁句 きんく tabooed word

厳禁する げんきんする prohibit strictly, taboo

発禁 はっきん prohibition of sale, suppression (of a book)

限 ▷limit
ゲン　かぎ(る)　かぎ(り)　Ⓚ0357

[original meaning] **limit, set a limit, restrict**

限定する げんていする limit, restrict, define

制限する せいげんする restrict, limit

局限する きょくげんする localize, limit, set limits to

時限爆弾 じげんばくだん time bomb

抑 ▷suppress
ヨク　おさ(える)　　　　Ⓚ0229

(hold down) **suppress, repress, restrain**

抑制する よくせいする control, suppress, inhibit

抑止する よくしする deter, check, hold back

抑留 よくりゅう detainment, detention, internment, arrest

束 ▷tie up
ソク　たば　たば(ねる)　つか　Ⓚ2978

(restrict the freedom of) **tie (a person) up, restrain, bind**

束縛する そくばくする restrain, restrict, bind, fetter

約束する やくそくする promise, vow, pledge

拘束 こうそく restriction, restraint, binding

結束する けっそくする band together, unite

縛 ▷bind
バク　しば(る)　　　　　Ⓚ1282

(restrain as if with bonds) **bind, restrict, restrain**

束縛する そくばくする restrain, restrict, bind, fetter

呪縛 じゅばく spell

自縄自縛に陥る じじょうじばくにおちいる be caught in one's own trap

控 ▷hold back
コウ　ひか(える)　ひか(え)　Ⓚ0453

ⓐ (refrain from) **hold back (from), restrain oneself, refrain**

ⓑ **be moderate, be sparing**

a 差し控える さしひかえる be moderate in; withhold, desist from, refrain from

手控える てびかえる hang [hold] back, hold off, refrain

食べ物を控える たべものをひかえる be temperate in eating

b 控え目な ひかえめな modest, temperate, reserved

扣 ▷hold back
コウ ひか(える) ひか(え)

a (refrain from) **hold back (from), restrain oneself, refrain**
b **be moderate, be sparing**

渋 ▷hang [hold] back
ジュウ しぶ しぶ(い) しぶ(る)　　Ⓚ0471

hang [hold] back, hesitate, be reluctant
渋渋 しぶしぶ reluctantly, grudgingly
言い渋る いいしぶる be reluctant [unwilling] to say
答えを渋る こたえをしぶる hesitate to answer, be reluctant to answer

return
帰 還 回 廻 戻 復

帰 ▷return
キ かえ(る) かえ(す)　　Ⓚ0113

return, come back, go back, take one's leave
帰着する きちゃくする return, come back; arrive at, result in
帰還する きかんする return, come home, be repatriated
帰国する きこくする return to one's country
帰京 ききょう returning to Tokyo
帰路 きろ homeward journey, return circuit
帰宅する きたくする come [return] home
復帰する ふっきする return, be restored, revert

還 ▷return
カン　　Ⓚ2743

[original meaning] **return, come back, come round**
還流 かんりゅう return current; convection
帰還する きかんする return, come home, be repatriated
償還 しょうかん repayment, refunding, reimbursement
生還する せいかんする return alive; *baseball* reach the home plate

回 ▷turn back
カイ エ まわ(る) -まわ(り) まわ(す)
まわ(し)-　　Ⓚ2630

turn back, return, come round
回復 かいふく [formerly also 恢復] recovery, restoration; rehabilitation
回帰 かいき revolution, recurrence, regression

回忌 かいき death anniversary
回向 えこう Buddhist memorial service
輪回 りんね *Buddhism* transmigration of souls, *saṃsāra*

廻 ▷turn back
カイ エ まわ(る) まわ(す)　　Ⓚ2660

turn back, return, come back
廻向 えこう Buddhist memorial service
輪廻 りんね *Buddhism* transmigration of souls, *saṃsāra*

戻 ▷return
レイ もど(す) もど(る)　　Ⓚ1699

return, come [go] back; turn back; return to, revert to, unwind itself
戻り もどり return; reaction, recovery
戻り道 もどりみち the way back
立ち戻る たちもどる return, come back

復 ▷return to
フク　　Ⓚ0527

[original meaning] **return to (a place), go back**
復帰する ふっきする return, be restored, revert
復路 ふくろ return trip
往復 おうふく going and returning; round trip

return and restore
返 戻 還 復 蘇 甦

返 ▷return
ヘン かえ(す) かえ(る)　　Ⓚ2633

return, give back, send back, repay
返還 へんかん return, restoration, repayment
返上する へんじょうする return, send back
返戻する へんれいする return, give back
返品 へんぴん returning goods; returned goods, article sent back
返送する へんそうする send back, return
返却 へんきゃく return
返金 へんきん repayment
返報 へんぽう requital, retaliation, revenge

戻 ▷return
レイ もど(す) もど(る)　　Ⓚ1699

【レイ】
return, give back
返戻する へんれいする return, give back
【もど(す)】
return, give back, send back; throw up, vomit
戻し もどし returning, giving back

払い戻し はらいもどし refund, repayment
取り戻す とりもどす take back, regain, restore
買い戻し かいもどし redemption, repurchase

還 ▷return
カン   Ⓚ2743

return, give back, restore
還付する かんぷする return, restore, refund
還元 かんげん restoration; reduction, deoxidization
返還 へんかん return, restoration, repayment
送還 そうかん sending back, repatriation
奪還 だっかん recapture, recovery

復 ▷return to
フク   Ⓚ0527

return to (a previous state or position), be restored, revert, reinstate
復活 ふっかつ revival, rebirth, resurrection
復旧 ふっきゅう restoration, recovery
復職 ふくしょく reinstatement, resumption of office
復元 ふくげん restoration to original state
回復 かいふく [formerly also 恢復] recovery, restoration; rehabilitation

蘇 ▷revive
ソ ス よみがえ(る)   Ⓚ2115

[sometimes also 甦] **revive, come back to life**
蘇生 そせい revival, resuscitation
蘇鉄 そてつ king sago palm, *Cycas revoluta*
屠蘇 とそ spiced sake

甦 ▷revive
ソ コウ よみがえ(る)

[now usu. 更 or 蘇] [original meaning] **revive, come back to life**
甦生する そせい(=こうせい)する revive, resuscitate

reveal
発 露 曝 晒 暴 披 顕 現

発 ▷reveal
ハツ ホツ た(つ)   Ⓚ2222

reveal, open up, disclose, make public, announce
発表する はっぴょうする announce, make public, publish
発見 はっけん discovery, revelation, detection
発掘する はっくつする dig, excavate
発揮する はっきする display, exhibit, demonstrate
発露 はつろ expression, manifestation
摘発する てきはつする expose, lay bare, disclose

露 ▷expose
ロ ロウ つゆ   Ⓚ2454

expose, bare to view, disclose
露出 ろしゅつ exposure, disclosure; (photographic) exposure
露呈 ろてい exposure, disclosure
露顕(=露見) ろけん discovery, detection, exposure

曝 ▷expose
バク さら(す) さら(ける)   Ⓚ1017

[original meaning] **expose to the sun**
曝書 ばくしょ airing of books

晒 ▷expose
サイ さら(す)   Ⓚ0831

[also 曝す] **expose (to view, to the elements)**
晒し者 さらしもの pilloried criminal exposed to public view; someone subjected to public scorn [humiliation]
恥晒し はじさらし disgrace, shame
野晒し のざらし weather-beaten

暴 ▷disclose
ボウ バク あば(く) あば(れる)   Ⓚ2194

[formerly also 曝] **disclose, divulge, expose**
暴露 ばくろ exposure, disclosure

披 ▷open out
ヒ   Ⓚ0270

open out (one's heart), reveal
披講 ひこう introduction of poems at a poetry party
披露する ひろうする announce, introduce; [original meaning, now archaic] open one's heart
披瀝する ひれきする express (one's opinion), reveal (one's thoughts)
お披露目(=お広め) おひろめ début

顕 ▷manifest
ケン   Ⓚ1605

[original meaning] (show plainly) **manifest, reveal, expose**
顕微鏡 けんびきょう microscope

現 ▷cause to appear
ゲン あらわ(れる) あらわ(す)   Ⓚ0879

cause to appear, show, reveal
現像 げんぞう developing (a film)
再現する さいげんする reenact, reproduce
顕現 けんげん manifestation

revise

訂　閲　校

訂 ▷revise
テイ　　　　　　　　　Ⓚ1310

revise, correct, edit
訂正する ていせいする correct, amend, revise
改訂する かいていする revise, edit
校訂する こうていする revise

閲 ▷review
エツ　　　　　　　　　Ⓚ2845

review manuscripts, read carefully, look over, revise, edit
閲覧する えつらんする read, pursue
検閲 けんえつ censorship; inspection, review
校閲 こうえつ revision, reviewing, editing

校 ▷collate
コウ　　　　　　　　　Ⓚ0840

collate, proofread, check, examine, revise
校合する きょうごう(=こうごう)する collate, examine and compare
校正 こうせい proofreading
校訂 こうてい revision
校正刷り こうせいずり galley proofs
校閲 こうえつ revision, reviewing, editing
校了 こうりょう final proof

rice

米　飯　稲　籾　餅　粥

米 ▷rice
ベイ　マイ　こめ　　　　Ⓚ2958

[also suffix] rice
米穀 べいこく rice
米価 べいか price of rice
米作 べいさく rice crop
米飯 べいはん cooked rice
玄米 げんまい unpolished rice
精米 せいまい rice polishing; polished [white] rice
外米 がいまい foreign [imported] rice
配給米 はいきゅうまい rationed rice
新潟米 にいがたまい Niigata rice

飯 ▷cooked rice
ハン　めし　　　　　　Ⓚ150

cooked rice, boiled rice
御飯 ごはん boiled rice; meal
炊飯器 すいはんき rice cooker
赤飯 せきはん cooked rice and red beans

稲 ▷rice plant
トウ　いね　いな–　　　Ⓚ1129

rice plant, rice
水稲 すいとう paddy-rice plant, aquatic rice
陸稲 りくとう(=おかぼ) rice grown in a dry field
晩稲 ばんとう late growing rice

籾 ▷unhulled rice
もみ　　　　　　　　　Ⓚ1172

unhulled rice
籾摺り もみすり rice hulling
種籾 たねもみ seed rice

餅 ▷rice cake
ヘイ　もち　　　　　　Ⓚ1596

rice cake; food made from cereal dough
餅餤 へいだん Heian-period confection made of boiled duck [goose] eggs and vegetables wrapped in rice cake and cut in squares
煎餅 せんべい rice cracker, wafer
血餅 けっぺい (blood) clot
画餅に帰す がべいにきす come to naught, fall through

粥 ▷rice gruel
シュク　かゆ　　　　　Ⓚ0525

rice gruel
粥腫 しゅくしゅ atheroma

rich

富　豪

富 ▷rich
フ　フウ　フッ–　と(む)　とみ　　Ⓚ2009

[original meaning] rich, wealthy, affluent
富裕 ふゆう wealth, richness

豪 ▷wealthy
ゴウ　　　　　　　　　Ⓚ1838

wealthy
豪農 ごうのう wealthy farmer
豪族 ごうぞく wealthy and powerful family [clan]
豪商 ごうしょう wealthy merchant

right

正　是　尤　端

正 ▷right
セイ ショウ ただ(しい) ただ(す) まさ まさ(に)　　Ⓚ2926

(not mistaken) **right, correct, proper**

正解 せいかい right answer, correct solution
正味の しょうみの net, full, clear
適正な てきせいな proper, appropriate, reasonable, right

是 ▷right
ゼ　　Ⓚ2157

right

是非 ぜひ right and/or wrong; by all means, at any cost
是非とも ぜひとも at any cost, by some means or other
是是非非主義 ぜぜひひしゅぎ fair and unbiased policy, principle of being fair and just
是認 ぜにん approval

尤 ▷right
ユウ もっと(も)　　Ⓚ2604

right, reasonable, natural

尤度 ゆうど plausibility, likelihood

端 ▷correct
タン はし は はた -ばた　　Ⓚ1131

[original meaning] **correct, proper, upright**

端正な たんせいな correct, just, proper
端然と たんぜんと properly
端座(=端坐)する たんざする sit upright [properly]
端麗な たんれいな graceful, elegant, handsome

rise in rank

陞　昇　進

陞 ▷ascend to a higher rank
ショウ

[now replaced by 昇] **ascend to a higher rank, rise in rank, be promoted**

陞叙 しょうじょ promotion, advancement
陞進する しょうしんする be promoted, rise in rank
陞任 しょうにん promotion, advancement

昇 ▷ascend to a higher rank
ショウ のぼ(る)　　Ⓚ2139

[formerly also 陞] **ascend to a higher rank, rise in rank, be promoted**

昇順 しょうじゅん ascending order
昇格する しょうかくする be promoted [raised] to a higher status
昇進する しょうしんする be promoted, rise in rank
昇給 しょうきゅう salary raise
昇叙 しょうじょ promotion, advancement

進 ▷advance in rank
シン すす(む) すす(める)　　Ⓚ2689

(move forward in rank) **advance in rank, become promoted**

進学 しんがく entering a school of higher grade
進級 しんきゅう promotion (to a higher grade)
昇進 しょうしん promotion, advancement

risk

冒　賭　懸

冒 ▷risk
ボウ おか(す)　　Ⓚ2155

risk, brave, defy

冒険 ぼうけん adventure, risk
冒涜する ぼうとくする desecrate, profane

賭 ▷wager
ト か(ける)　　Ⓚ1451

wager, bet money

賭博 とばく gambling
賭場 とば gambling den

懸 ▷stake
ケン ケ か(ける) か(かる)　　Ⓚ2532

stake, risk

一生懸命(=一所懸命)に いっしょうけんめい(=いっしょけんめい)に for life, with all one's might

rivers and streams

川　河　江　渓　流

川 ▷river
セン かわ　　Ⓚ0001

[original meaning] **river**

河川 かせん rivers
山川 さんせん mountains and rivers

河 ▷river
カ かわ   Ⓚ0298

[original meaning] **river, large river**

河川 かせん rivers
河流 かりゅう stream
河口 かこう river mouth, estuary
河岸 かし riverside; fish market
運河 うんが canal
銀河 ぎんが Milky Way; galaxy
暴虎馮河 ぼうこひょうが foolhardy courage

江 ▷large river
コウ え   Ⓚ0195

ⓐ [original meaning] **large river**
ⓑ **suffix after names of large rivers**

ₐ 江上 こうじょう bank of a large river
江山 こうざん [rare] rivers and mountains
江湖 こうこ general public, the world ("rivers and lakes")
ᵦ 揚子江 ようすこう Yangtze River

渓 ▷mountain stream
ケイ   Ⓚ0474

[original meaning] **mountain stream, valley stream**

渓流 けいりゅう mountain stream
渓声 けいせい sound of a valley stream

流 ▷stream
リュウ ル なが(れる) なが(れ)
なが(す)   Ⓚ0400

(body of running water) **stream, river**

本流 ほんりゅう main course (of a river), main stream
分流 ぶんりゅう distributary, river branch

rob →STEAL AND ROB

rock and stone
石   岩   巌

石 ▷stone
セキ シャク コク いし   Ⓚ2564

[also suffix] [original meaning] **stone, rock**

石像 せきぞう stone statue
石炭 せきたん coal
石鹸 せっけん soap
石油 せきゆ petroleum, oil
岩石 がんせき rock
宝石 ほうせき gem, jewel
磁石 じしゃく magnet; compass
大理石 だいりせき marble

岩 ▷rock
ガン いわ   Ⓚ192

[sometimes also 巌] [also suffix] [original meaning] **rock**

岩石 がんせき rock
岩層 がんそう rock formation
岩床 がんしょう bedrock
岩礁 がんしょう reef
岩塩 がんえん rock salt
火山岩 かざんがん volcanic rock, lava
花崗岩 かこうがん granite

巌 ▷crag
ガン いわお いわ   Ⓚ211

[usu. 岩] [original meaning] **crag, (massive) rock**

巌頭 がんとう top of a massive rock
巌窟 がんくつ cave, rocky cavern
奇巌 きがん massive rock of unusual shape

roof
屋   宇

屋 ▷roof
オク や   Ⓚ266

[original meaning] **roof**

屋上 おくじょう housetop, roof

宇 ▷roof
ウ   Ⓚ186

[original meaning] **roof, eaves**

八紘一宇 はっこういちう the whole world under one roof

roof parts
軒   庇   棟   瓦

軒 ▷eaves
ケン のき   Ⓚ1328

eaves, canopy

軒灯 けんとう eaves lantern, door light

庇 ▷eaves
ヒ かば(う) ひさし   Ⓚ263

[original meaning] **eaves**

雪庇 せっぴ (=ゆきびさし) overhanging snow

棟 ▷ridge
トウ むね むな‐   Ⓚ0904

[original meaning] **ridge, edge of a roof**
　上棟式 じょうとうしき ceremony of raising the ridgepole

瓦 ▷roof tile
ガ かわら   Ⓚ2918

[original meaning] **tile, roof tile**
　瓦礫 がれき tiles and pebbles; trash
　煉瓦 れんが brick

rooms
室　間　房　斎　堂

室 ▷room
シツ むろ   Ⓚ1943

[also suffix] [original meaning] **room, chamber, compartment**
　室内 しつない indoors
　教室 きょうしつ classroom, class
　個室 こしつ private room, single room
　寝室 しんしつ bedroom
　和室 わしつ Japanese style room
　一等室 いっとうしつ first-class compartment
　更衣室 こういしつ changing room

間 ▷room
カン ケン あいだ ま   Ⓚ2836

room, chamber
　居間 いま living [sitting] room
　茶の間 ちゃのま living room
　応接間 おうせつま drawing room, guest room
　孔雀の間 くじゃくのま the Peacock Room

房 ▷chamber
ボウ ふさ   Ⓚ1702

ⓐ [original meaning] **chamber, (small) room, cell**
ⓑ **chamber for sleeping, bedroom**
ⓒ **enclosed space resembling a chamber**
a　暖房 だんぼう heating
　冷房 れいぼう air conditioning
　監房 かんぼう cell, ward
　官房 かんぼう secretariat
　書房 しょぼう bookstore, publishing company
　文房具 ぶんぼうぐ stationery, writing materials
b　房事 ぼうじ sex, lovemaking
　女房 にょうぼう wife; court lady
c　心房 しんぼう atrium, chamber of the heart
　子房 しぼう ovary (of plants)

斎 ▷study
サイ   Ⓚ1817

ⓐ **study, room for study**
ⓑ **suffix after names of studies**
a　書斎 しょさい study, library

堂 ▷hall
ドウ   Ⓚ2246

ⓐ (large room for public gatherings) **hall, meeting place**
ⓑ [original meaning] **large reception room**
a　講堂 こうどう lecture hall, auditorium
　食堂 しょくどう dining hall [room]; restaurant
　音楽堂 おんがくどう concert hall
b　殿堂 でんどう hall, palace, shrine; sanctuary

ropes and lines
綱　絃　縄　緒　組
索　鎖　線　紐　弦

綱 ▷rope (esp. of fiber)
コウ つな   Ⓚ1253

rope (esp. of fiber), line, cord, cable; sumo grand championship
　綱渡り つなわたり tightrope walking [walker]
　綱引き つなひき tug of war; forward puller (of a rickshaw)
　綱を張る つなをはる be a grand champion
　手綱 たづな bridle, reins
　頼みの綱 たのみのつな last ray of hope
　横綱 よこづな (grand) champion sumo wrestler

絃 ▷string
ゲン   Ⓚ1216

string or chord of a musical instrument
　絃楽器 げんがっき stringed instruments

縄 ▷rope (esp. of straw)
ジョウ なわ   Ⓚ1271

[original meaning] **rope, straw rope, cord, spun yarn**
　縄文 じょうもん straw-rope pattern
　捕縄 ほじょう rope for binding criminals
　自縄自縛に陥る じじょうじばくにおちいる be caught in one's own trap

緒 ▷cord
ショ チョ お   Ⓚ1260

cord, strap, thong; string
　緒締め おじめ string-fastener
　臍の緒 へそのお umbilical cord

鼻緒 はなお clog thong, strap

組 ▷braid
ソ く(む) くみ -ぐみ ⓚ1224

[original meaning] **braid, plait**
編組機械 へんそきかい knitting machinery

索 ▷cable
サク ⓚ2168

[original meaning] **cable, thick rope, cord**
索条 さくじょう cable, rope
索道 さくどう cableway, ropeway
鋼索 こうさく cable, steel wire rope
鉄索 てっさく cable, cableway
軸索 じくさく axon, axis cylinder

鎖 ▷chain
サ くさり ⓚ1573

[original meaning] **chain**
鎖状 さじょう chainlike
測鎖 そくさ measuring chain
側鎖 そくさ *chem* side chain

線 ▷line
セン ⓚ1273

elec **line, wire, cable**
無線 むせん radio, wireless
電線 でんせん electric wire
内線 ないせん telephone extension; inner line
回線 かいせん circuit
電話線 でんわせん telephone line

紐 ▷string
チュウ ひも ⓚ1190

[original meaning] **string**
紐帯 ちゅうたい cords and belts; bond, ties; important social ties [foundations]

弦 ▷string
ゲン つる ⓚ0257

string or chord of a musical instrument
弦楽器 げんがっき stringed instruments
調弦 ちょうげん tuning

round
丸　　　円

丸 ▷round
ガン まる まる(い) まる(める) ⓚ2883

ⓐ (shaped like a ball) **round, spherical**

ⓑ [also 円い] (shaped like a circle) **round, circular**
ⓐ 丸み まるみ roundness
背が丸い せがまるい round-backed
ⓑ 丸くなって まるくなって in a circle [ring]

円 ▷circular
エン まる(い) まる ⓚ2555

[also prefix] **circular, round**
円卓 えんたく round table
円盤 えんばん disk; flying saucer
円軌道 えんきどう circular orbit

routes →WAYS AND ROUTES

rub →POLISH AND RUB

ruins
墟　　　虚

墟 ▷ruins
キョ

[now also 虚] [original meaning] **ruins**
廃墟 はいきょ ruins, remains

虚 ▷ruins
キョ コ ⓚ2778

[also 墟] **ruins**
廃虚 はいきょ ruins, remains

rulers
君 王 帝 天 皇 尭 舜

君 ▷ruler
クン きみ -ぎみ ⓚ2762

[original meaning] **ruler, sovereign, monarch, king; lord**
君主 くんしゅ monarch, sovereign
君臨する くんりんする reign, rule over, dominate
暴君 ぼうくん tyrant, despot
主君 しゅくん one's lord, one's master
名君 めいくん wise ruler, enlightened monarch, benevolent lord

王 ▷king
オウ ⓚ2895

king, monarch, ruler, emperor
王様 おうさま king
王国 おうこく kingdom, monarchy
王座 おうざ throne

王子 おうじ prince
王女 おうじょ royal princess, princess
国王 こくおう king, monarch
女王 じょおう(=じょうおう) queen; belle, mistress
帝王 ていおう monarch, emperor

帝 ▷emperor

テイ   Ⓚ1786

ⓐ emperor, empress
ⓑ imperial

a 帝王 ていおう monarch, emperor
皇帝 こうてい emperor
女帝 じょてい empress, queen
露帝 ろてい Czar, Russian emperor
b 帝国 ていこく empire, imperial
帝政 ていせい imperial government
帝劇 ていげき The Imperial Theatre

天 ▷Heaven's messenger on earth
テン あめ あま−   Ⓚ2898

ⓐ Heaven's messenger on earth, the emperor
ⓑ imperial

a 天皇 てんのう emperor of Japan
天子 てんし son of Heaven, emperor
天顔 てんがん emperor's countenance
b 天覧 てんらん imperial inspection

皇 ▷emperor
コウ オウ   Ⓚ2223

emperor, sovereign

皇帝 こうてい emperor
皇后 こうごう empress, queen
皇妃 こうひ empress, queen
皇太子 こうたいし crown prince
天皇 てんのう emperor of Japan

尭 ▷Yao
ギョウ   Ⓚ1776

name of a legendary sage monarch in ancient China: **Yao**

尭舜 ぎょうしゅん Yao and Shun (two of the most celebrated monarchs in ancient China)

舜 ▷Shun
シュン   Ⓚ2192

name of a legendary sage monarch in ancient China: **Shun**

尭舜 ぎょうしゅん Yao and Shun (two of the most celebrated monarchs in ancient China)

rules →LAWS AND RULES

走 ▷run
ソウ はし(る)   Ⓚ1877

ⓐ [original meaning] **run, dash, rush**
ⓑ [suffix] **run, dash**

a 走者 そうしゃ runner
御馳走 ごちそう feast, treat
御馳走様 ごちそうさま Thank you (for the meal)/I've enjoyed the meal
奔走する ほんそうする bustle about, exert oneself for, devote oneself to
競走 きょうそう race, sprint
独走 どくそう running alone; easy victory, walkover
b 五十メートル走 ごじゅうめーとるそう 50 meter dash

奔 ▷rush
ホン   Ⓚ1904

[original meaning] **rush, rush about, run fast, gallop, hurry**

奔走する ほんそうする bustle about, exert oneself for, devote oneself to
奔流 ほんりゅう torrent, rapids
奔騰 ほんとう price jump, boom
奔馬 ほんば galloping horse
狂奔する きょうほんする rush around, run madly about, run wild; make frantic efforts, be very busy (in)
東奔西走する とうほんせいそうする be on the run, bustle about, bestir oneself

馳 ▷run quickly
チ は(せる)   Ⓚ1615

[original meaning] **run quickly; gallop**

御馳走 ごちそう feast, treat
御馳走様 ごちそうさま Thank you (for the meal)/I've enjoyed the meal
背馳 はいち inconsistency, contradiction

駆 ▷gallop
ク か(ける) か(る)   Ⓚ1619

gallop, run quickly

疾駆する しっくする ride fast, drive a horse fast
長駆 ちょうく long march, expedition to a distant region
先駆者 せんくしゃ pioneer, forerunner
前駆する ぜんくする ride in advance, lead the way

running water
流 潮 汐 瀬 滝 洪 渦

渦動 かどう vortex
渦紋 かもん whirlpool design
渦線 かせん spiral line
渦中 かちゅう maelstrom, vortex, whirlpool

流 ▷current
リュウ ル なが(れる) なが(れ)
なが(す)　　　　　　　Ⓚ0400

(water or air flow) **current, stream, flow**
海流 かいりゅう ocean current
気流 きりゅう air [atmospheric] current, air stream
暖流 だんりゅう warm current
上流 じょうりゅう upper stream (of a river); upper class
潮流 ちょうりゅう tide, current; tendency, trend
急流 きゅうりゅう rapid stream, swift current; swift-running river; rapids

潮 ▷tide
チョウ しお　　　　　　Ⓚ0675

[original meaning] **tide, current**
潮汐 ちょうせき ebb and flow, tide
干潮 かんちょう ebb tide
満潮 まんちょう high tide, high water

汐 ▷tide
セキ しお　　　　　　　Ⓚ0197

tide, ebb tide
潮汐 ちょうせき ebb and flow, tide

瀬 ▷rapids
せ　　　　　　　　　　Ⓚ0717

rapids, torrent, swift current
瀬を下る せをくだる descend the rapids

滝 ▷waterfall
たき　　　　　　　　　Ⓚ0607

waterfall, falls, cascade
滝壺 たきつぼ pool below a waterfall
滝川 たきがわ rapids
雄滝(=男滝) おだき the greater waterfall (of the two)

洪 ▷flood
コウ　　　　　　　　　Ⓚ0346

[original meaning] **flood, inundation**
洪水 こうずい flood, inundation
洪積世 こうせきせい diluvial epoch

渦 ▷whirlpool
カ うず　　　　　　　　Ⓚ0550

[original meaning] **whirlpool, eddy**

sacrifice
犠　　　牲

犠 ▷sacrifice
ギ　　　　　　　　　　Ⓚ101●

🅐 sacrifice
🅑 *baseball* sacrifice
a 犠牲 ぎせい sacrifice
b 犠打 ぎだ sacrifice, sacrifice batting
　 犠飛 ぎひ sacrifice fly

牲 ▷sacrifice
セイ　　　　　　　　　Ⓚ081●

sacrifice
犠牲 ぎせい sacrifice

sad and depressed
悲 悄 哀 愁 鬱
陰 沈 寂 淋 惨

悲 ▷sad
ヒ かな(しい) かな(しむ)　　Ⓚ241●

🅐 sad, sorrowful, pathetic
🅑 sorrow, grief
a 悲痛な ひつうな sad, grievous
　 悲惨な ひさんな miserable, wretched, tragic, pitiable
　 悲壮な ひそうな pathetic, tragic
　 悲劇 ひげき tragedy, tragic drama
　 悲鳴 ひめい shriek, scream
　 悲観する ひかんする be pessimistic, lose heart
　 悲観的な ひかんてきな pessimistic
b 悲喜 ひき joy and sorrow

悄 ▷become dispirited
ショウ

[now usu. 消] **become dispirited, become disheartened; be worried**
悄然たる しょうぜんたる dejected, dispirited
悄悄と しょうしょうと dejectedly, dispiritedly

哀 ▷sorrowful
アイ あわ(れ) あわ(れむ)
かな(しい)　　　　Ⓚ1781

sorrowful, sad, pathetic
哀感 あいかん pathos
哀愁 あいしゅう sadness, sorrow, pensiveness
哀話 あいわ sad story, tragic tale
哀切な あいせつな pathetic, plaintive
悲哀 ひあい sorrow, sadness

愁 ▷melancholy
シュウ うれ(える) うれ(い)　　Ⓚ2463

ⓐ melancholy, sad, gloomy, worried
ⓑ melancholy, sadness, grief, sorrow, loneliness
a 愁眉 しゅうび worried look, melancholy air
　憂愁 ゆうしゅう melancholy, gloom, grief
b 哀愁 あいしゅう sadness, sorrow, pensiveness
　郷愁 きょうしゅう homesickness, nostalgia
　旅愁 りょしゅう loneliness on a journey

鬱 ▷gloom

ウツ　　　　Ⓚ2528

gloom, depression, melancholy
鬱陶しい うっとうしい gloomy, depressing; dull,
　　cloudy
憂鬱 ゆううつ melancholy, gloom
陰鬱 いんうつ gloominess, melancholy
抑鬱 よくうつ depression, dejection
躁鬱病 そううつびょう manic-depressive psychosis
抗鬱剤 こううつざい antidepressant

陰 ▷gloomy
イン かげ かげ(る)　　Ⓚ0494

gloomy, melancholy, dejected
陰気 いんき gloominess, cheerlessness
陰鬱 いんうつ gloominess, melancholy
陰惨 いんさん sadness and gloom

沈 ▷depressed

チン しず(む) しず(める)　　Ⓚ0231

(sink into depression) **depressed, melancholy**
沈鬱な ちんうつな melancholy, gloomy

寂 ▷lonesome
ジャク セキ さび さび(しい)
さび(れる)　　Ⓚ1982

lonesome, lonely, desolate, deserted
寂寥たる せきりょうたる lonely, desolate
寂然たる せきぜんたる(=じゃくねんたる) lonely, deso-
　late

淋 ▷lonesome
リン さび(しい) さみ(しい)　　Ⓚ0476

lonesome, lonely, desolate, deserted
淋しがる さびしがる feel lonely, miss someone
物淋しい ものさびしい lonesome, desolate, dreary
心淋しい うらさびしい lonely, forlorn, melancholy

惨 ▷miserable
サン ザン みじ(め)　　Ⓚ0441

**miserable, wretched, pitiable, tragic; terrible, horri-
ble, disastrous**
惨事 さんじ disaster, tragic incident, catastrophe
惨状 さんじょう pitiful situation
惨禍 さんか terrible disaster, crushing calamity
惨劇 さんげき tragedy, tragic event
惨憺たる さんたんたる pitiable, wretched, misera-
　ble, terrible, horrible
惨敗 ざんぱい miserable defeat
悲惨な ひさんな miserable, wretched, tragic, piti-
　able
凄惨な せいさんな ghastly, gruesome, lurid

same and uniform
等 平 均 斉 同 一

等 ▷equal
トウ ひと(しい) −ら　　Ⓚ2339

[also prefix] [original meaning] **equal, same, alike**
等号 とうごう equal sign [mark]
等分する とうぶんする divide equally
等価 とうか equivalence, equal value; parity
平等 びょうどう equality, impartiality
均等 きんとう equality, uniformity
二等辺三角形 にとうへんさんかっけい equilateral
　[isosceles] triangle

平 ▷equal
ヘイ ビョウ たい(ら) −だいら
ひら　　Ⓚ2921

equal, impartial, fair
平均 へいきん average, (arithmetical) mean; equilib-
　rium, balance
平行 へいこう parallelism, parallel; going side by
　side; occurring together
平等 びょうどう equality, impartiality
公平 こうへい impartiality, fairness

均 ▷even
キン　　Ⓚ0207

**even, uniform, equal, same, symmetrical, well-
balanced**

均一な きんいつな uniform, equal, even
均等の きんとうの equal, uniform
均質 きんしつ homogeneity
均分 きんぶん equal division
均勢 きんせい balance [equilibrium] of power, uniformity

斉 ▷uniform
セイ   Ⓚ1768

uniform, equal, even, symmetrical
斉一 せいいつ uniformity, good order
均斉(=均整) きんせい symmetry
整斉の せいせいの symmetrical
不斉地用タイヤ ふせいちようたいや off-the-road tire

同 ▷same
ドウ おな(じ)   Ⓚ2578

same, similar, equal
同一 どういつ sameness, identity
同様の どうようの similar
同好 どうこう similar tastes
同盟 どうめい alliance, league, union
同胞 どうほう brothers; brethren, fellow countrymen
同窓会 どうそうかい alumni association
同意 どうい consent, approval
同音の どうおんの of the same sound, homophonous
同音語 どうおんご homophone, homonym
同等 どうとう equality
同期 どうき same period
同上 どうじょう as above, ditto
同性の どうせいの of the same sex
同列 どうれつ same rank

一 ▷same
イチ イツ ひと- ひと(つ)   Ⓚ2850

(one and the) **same, identical**
一致 いっち accord, agreement
一律 いちりつ uniformity, equality
均一 きんいつ uniformity, equality, evenness

sand
砂   沙

砂 ▷sand (fine)
サ シャ すな   Ⓚ1047

sand (of fine constitution)
砂漠 さばく desert
砂丘 さきゅう sand dune, sand hill

砂岩 さがん sandstone
砂州(=砂洲) さす sandbar, sandbank
土砂 どしゃ earth and sand

沙 ▷sand (granular)
サ すな   Ⓚ023◀

[original meaning] **sand (of granular constitution), tiny gravel or pebbles**
沙丘 さきゅう sand dune, sand hill

savage
蛮   夷   蕃

蛮 ▷barbarian
バン   Ⓚ182▸

[formerly also 蕃] **barbarian, savage, uncivilized tribe**
蛮人 ばんじん savage, barbarian; aboriginal
蛮語 ばんご language of the barbarians
蛮族 ばんぞく savage tribe
野蛮な やばんな savage, barbarous, uncivilized
南蛮 なんばん southern barbarians, Europeans from the South (from 16th to 18th centuries); meat cooked with onions; red pepper

夷 ▷barbarian
イ えびす   Ⓚ2962

ⓐ **barbarian, savage**
ⓑ **foreigner**
a 夷狄 いてき barbarians, aliens
夷人 いじん barbarian, savage
征夷大将軍 せいいたいしょうぐん Commander in Chief of the Expeditionary Force Against the Barbarians
b 攘夷 じょうい expulsion of foreigners

蕃 ▷barbarian
バン ハン   Ⓚ2082

ⓐ [now also 蛮] **barbarian, savage**
ⓑ **barbarian, aboriginal; foreign**
a 蕃夷 ばんい savages, barbarians
蕃族 ばんぞく savage tribe
蕃人 ばんじん savage, barbarian; aborigine
b 蕃社 ばんしゃ aborigines' village
蕃椒 ばんしょう [rare] Guinea pepper

say →SPEAK AND SAY

schools

校 学 院 塾 大
高 中 小 園

校 ▷school
コウ   Ⓚ0840

a [also suffix] **school**
b **counter for schools**

- a 校長 こうちょう principal, schoolmaster, rector
  校舎 こうしゃ school building
  校内 こうない school grounds
  校友 こうゆう schoolmate, alumnus
  校則 こうそく school regulations
  学校 がっこう school, college
  母校 ぼこう one's alma mater, one's old school
  登校 とうこう attending school
  高校 こうこう senior high school
  予備校 よびこう preparatory school
- b 二十五校 にじゅうごこう 25 schools

学 ▷educational institution
ガク まな(ぶ)   Ⓚ2211

[original meaning] **educational institution, school, university, academy**

- 学園 がくえん educational institution, school
  学校 がっこう school, college
  学院 がくいん institute, academy
  学長 がくちょう college president, rector; dean
  学年 がくねん school year, grade
  小学校 しょうがっこう elementary [primary] school
  中学 ちゅうがく junior high school
  大学 だいがく university, college
  私学 しがく private [nongovernmental] school [college, university]
  通学する つうがくする attend [go to] school
  入学する にゅうがくする enter a school, matriculate

院 ▷institution
イン   Ⓚ0410

educational institution: **academy, institute, school**

- 院生 いんせい graduate student
  学院 がくいん institute, academy
  孤児院 こじいん orphanage
  大学院 だいがくいん graduate school
  美容院 びよういん beauty shop [parlor]

塾 ▷private school
ジュク   Ⓚ2490

[also suffix] **private school, school run outside normal school hours, cram school**

塾長 じゅくちょう principal of a private school
塾生 じゅくせい private school student
入塾 にゅうじゅく entering a private school
英語塾 えいごじゅく private school for the study of English

大 ▷university
ダイ タイ おお- おお(きい)
おお(いに)   Ⓚ2882

a abbrev. of 大学 だいがく: **university, college**
b **suffix after names of universities**

- a 大卒 だいそつ university graduate
  女子大生 じょしだいせい female university student
  短大 たんだい junior college
- b オックスフォード大 おっくすふぉーどだい Oxford University
  東大 とうだい Tokyo University

高 ▷high school
コウ たか(い) たか -だか たか(まる)
たか(める)   Ⓚ1803

a abbrev. of 高等学校 こうとうがっこう: **high school**
b **suffix after names of high schools**

- a 高卒 こうそつ high school graduate
- b 城北高 じょうほくこう Johoku High School

中 ▷junior high school
チュウ ジュウ なか   Ⓚ2902

a abbrev. of 中学校 ちゅうがっこう: **junior high school, middle school**
b **suffix after names of junior high schools**

- a 中二 ちゅうに second year of junior high
  中卒 ちゅうそつ junior high graduate
- b 武蔵中 むさしちゅう Musashi Junior High School

小 ▷elementary school
ショウ ちい(さい) こ- お-   Ⓚ0002

a abbrev. of 小学校 しょうがっこう: **elementary school, grade school**
b **suffix after names of elementary schools**

- a 小一 しょういち first-year student of an elementary school
  同小 どうしょう the above-mentioned elementary school
- b 佃小 つくだしょう Tsukuda Elementary School

園 ▷kindergarten
エン その   Ⓚ2722

a abbrev. of 幼稚園 ようちえん: **kindergarten**
b **counter for kindergartens**

- a 園児 えんじ kindergarten child
  入園 にゅうえん entering kindergarten
- b 四百園 よんひゃくえん 400 kindergartens

sea

海 洋 沖 灘

海 ▷sea
カイ うみ   Ⓚ0344

ⓐ sea, ocean
ⓑ (large landlocked body of water) sea, large lake
ⓒ suffix after names of seas

ⓐ 海洋 かいよう ocean, sea
　海外 かいがい overseas, abroad
　海水浴 かいすいよく sea bathing
　海岸 かいがん seashore, (sea) coast, beach
　海産物 かいさんぶつ marine products
　海軍 かいぐん navy
　海面 かいめん surface of the sea
　海里 かいり [also 浬] nautical mile
　航海 こうかい voyage, ocean navigation
　南海 なんかい southern sea; South Seas
ⓑ カスピ海 かすぴかい Caspian Sea
　日本海 にほんかい Japan Sea

洋 ▷ocean
ヨウ   Ⓚ0353

ⓐ ocean, sea
ⓑ suffix after names of oceans

ⓐ 洋上 ようじょう in the ocean, on the sea
　海洋 かいよう ocean, sea
　大洋 たいよう ocean
ⓑ 太平洋 たいへいよう Pacific Ocean
　インド洋 いんどよう Indian Ocean

沖 ▷offing
チュウ おき   Ⓚ0232

[also suffix] offing, offshore, open sea
　沖合い おきあい offing, offshore
　沖釣り おきづり offshore fishing
　二キロ沖 にきろおき two kilometers offshore

灘 ▷open sea
タン なだ   Ⓚ0722

open sea; rough sea

seals

印 判 璽

印 ▷seal
イン しるし -じるし   Ⓚ0733

[also suffix] seal, stamp; seal impression

印鑑 いんかん personal seal
印税 いんぜい royalty (on a book)
印紙 いんし (revenue) stamp
調印 ちょういん signing, sealing; signature
消印 けしいん postmark, (postal) cancellation mark
封印 ふういん (stamped) seal
押印する おういんする seal, affix a seal
刻印 こくいん carved seal, stamp
ゴム印 ごむいん rubber stamp
偽造印 ぎぞういん forged seal

判 ▷personal seal
ハン バン   Ⓚ1038

personal seal, seal, stamp, chop; seal impression
　判子 はんこ handstamp, seal; seal impression
　盲判 めくらばん undeliberated endorsement
　血判 けっぱん seal of blood

璽 ▷Imperial seal
ジ   Ⓚ2527

ⓐ Imperial seal
ⓑ [original meaning] seal

ⓐ 御璽 ぎょじ Imperial seal
ⓑ 国璽 こくじ seal of state

seasonings

糖 塩 酢 醋 油 醬 噌 蜜

糖 ▷sugar
トウ   Ⓚ1281

(sweet substance derived from sugar cane or beets) sugar
　砂糖 さとう sugar
　グラニュー糖 ぐらにゅーとう granulated sugar
　精糖 せいとう refined sugar, sugar refining
　製糖業 せいとうぎょう sugar manufacturing industry

塩 ▷salt
エン しお   Ⓚ0578

[original meaning] salt
　塩分 えんぶん salt, salinity
　塩水 えんすい salt water
　食塩 しょくえん table salt
　天然塩 てんねんえん natural salt

酢 ▷vinegar
サク す   Ⓚ1373

[formerly also 醋] [original meaning] vinegar
　酢酸 さくさん acetic acid

醋 ▷vinegar
サク す

[now replaced by 酢] [original meaning] **vinegar**
醋酸 さくさん acetic acid

油 ▷oil
ユ あぶら Ⓚ0303

oil, animal oil, vegetable oil
油脂 ゆし fats and oils
油断 ゆだん negligence, carelessness, inattentiveness
醬油 しょうゆ soy sauce
サラダ油 さらだゆ(=さらだあぶら) salad oil
オリーブ油 おりーぶゆ olive oil

醬 ▷fermented sauce
ショウ ジャン ひしお Ⓚ2503

fermented sauce [paste]; kind of miso
醬油 しょうゆ soy sauce
魚醬 ぎょしょう fish sauce
豆板醬 とうばんじゃん chili bean paste
XO醬 えっくすおーじゃん XO sauce

噌 ▷miso
ソ ソウ Ⓚ0651

miso, **bean paste**
味噌 みそ *miso*, bean paste; flattery
蟹味噌 かにみそ crab guts
手前味噌 てまえみそ singing one's own praises
脳味噌 のうみそ brain, brains

蜜 ▷honey
ミツ Ⓚ2060

honey, nectar, syrup, molasses
蜜蜂 みつばち honeybee, hive bee
蜜月 みつげつ honeymoon
蜜蠟 みつろう beeswax
蜂蜜 はちみつ honey
花蜜 かみつ nectar
黒蜜 くろみつ brown sugar syrup
糖蜜 とうみつ molasses, syrup

seat
席　座　椅　鞍

席 ▷seat
セキ Ⓚ2683

[also suffix] **seat, one's place**
席次 せきじ order of seats, seating precedence; class standing

座席 ざせき seat
議席 ぎせき seat (in an assembly house)
即席の そくせきの impromptu, offhand
打席 だせき batter's box; one's turn at bat
主席 しゅせき top seat; the Chairman
指定席 していせき reserved seat
一般席 いっぱんせき general admission seat

座 ▷seat
ザ すわ(る) Ⓚ2686

[formerly also 坐]
ⓐ [original meaning] (place for sitting) **seat**
ⓑ (part on which one sits) **seat, bottom**
a 座席 ざせき seat
座右の書 ざゆうのしょ one's desk-side book
座敷 ざしき drawing room, parlor; Japanese-style room
座布団 ざぶとん (floor) cushion
王座 おうざ throne
上座 かみざ(=じょうざ) top seat, seat of honor
b 便座 べんざ toilet seat

椅 ▷chair
イ Ⓚ0896

chair
椅子 いす chair
車椅子 くるまいす wheelchair
長椅子 ながいす couch, bench

鞍 ▷saddle
アン くら Ⓚ1595

saddle
鞍馬 あんば pommel horse, side horse; saddled horse
鞍上 あんじょう on top of a saddle
鞍部 あんぶ col, saddle between mountains

second
乙　次　後　中

乙 ▷second
オツ おと- Ⓚ2849

the second, B; second class, grade B; the latter
乙種 おつしゅ second grade
甲乙 こうおつ first and second, former and latter

次 ▷second
ジ シ つ(ぐ) つぎ Ⓚ0039

second
次男 じなん second son
次女 じじょ second daughter

次位 じい second rank, second place

後 ▷after (latter)
ゴ コウ のち うし(ろ) あと
おく(れる)　　　Ⓚ0321

(subsequent in order) **after, latter, second**
後者 こうしゃ the latter
後半 こうはん latter half, second half
後期 こうき latter period
後場 ごば afternoon session [market]
後半生 こうはんせい latter half of one's life
後手 ごて moving second (in a board game); rear
guard
最後の さいごの last, final

中 ▷middle
チュウ ジュウ なか　　　Ⓚ2902

second in a series of three: **middle, second**
中編 ちゅうへん second part [volume]; medium-
length story
中旬 ちゅうじゅん middle [second] ten days of a
month
中元 ちゅうげん midyear gift; July 15th (lunar calendar)

second person pronouns
君 汝 爾 貴 卿

君 ▷you (*familiar*)
クン きみ -ぎみ　　　Ⓚ2762

you, old boy—familiar second person pronoun used in
addressing friends, peers or inferiors
君達 きみたち you (plural)
君の きみの your

汝 ▷thou
ジョ なんじ　　　Ⓚ0193

thou, you
爾汝 じじょ addressing someone familiarly in the
second person or without using a title

爾 ▷thou
ジ ニ なんじ　　　Ⓚ3001

thou, you
爾汝 じじょ addressing someone familiarly in the
second person or without using a title

貴 ▷you (*honorific*)
キ たっと(い) とうと(い) たっと(ぶ)
とうと(ぶ)　　　Ⓚ2260

[honorific] **you**
貴下 きか you
貴殿 きでん you
貴様 きさま [belittling] **you**; [original meaning] **sir,
madam**

卿 ▷you (*archaic, honorific*)
キョウ ケイ　　　Ⓚ0570

you

secret and private
秘 密 暗 私 内 隠

秘 ▷secret
ヒ ひ(める)　　　Ⓚ1074

ⓐ [original meaning] (without the knowledge of others)
secret, private, clandestine, hidden
ⓑ (something kept secret) **secret, secrecy**
a 秘密 ひみつ secret, mystery; privacy
秘術 ひじゅつ secret (art); the best of one's skill
秘訣 ひけつ secret, key
秘伝 ひでん secret, mystery
秘宝 ひほう (hidden) treasure
秘書 ひしょ secretary; treasured book
黙秘する もくひする keep silent, keep secret
b 極秘 ごくひ strict secrecy, top secret
部外秘の ぶがいひの restricted

密 ▷secret
ミツ　　　Ⓚ1984

[also suffix] **secret, private, clandestine, illegal,
stealthy**
密使 みっし secret messenger
密告 みっこく secret information
密輸 みつゆ smuggling, contraband trade
密売 みつばい smuggling
密入国 みつにゅうこく illegal entry [immigration]
秘密 ひみつ secret, mystery; privacy
内密の ないみつの secret, confidential, private

暗 ▷in the dark
アン くら(い)　　　Ⓚ0921

in the dark, hidden, secret
暗殺 あんさつ assassination
暗号 あんごう code, password
暗礁 あんしょう sunken rock, unknown reef; deadlock
暗黙の あんもくの tacit

暗示 あんじ hint, suggestion

 ▷**private**
シ わたくし わたし　　　Ⓚ1030

ⓐ [also suffix] [original meaning] (pertaining to a particular person) **private, personal**
ⓑ (intimate) **private, clandestine, secret, confidential**

a 私的な してきな private, personal
　私学 しがく private [nongovernmental] school [college, university]
　私鉄 してつ nongovernmental [private] railroad line
　私物 しぶつ private property
　私立の しりつ(=わたくしりつ)の private, nongovernmental
　私書箱 ししょばこ post office box (P.O.B.)
　私生活 しせいかつ one's private life
　私費 しひ private expense
　公私 こうし public and private
b 私語 しご secret talk, whispering

 ▷**not public**
ナイ ダイ うち　　　Ⓚ2914

not public, private, secret, unofficial, informal
　内内の ないないの private, informal; secret, confidential
　内定 ないてい informal decision
　内申 ないしん unofficial report
　内規 ないき private rules [regulations], bylaws
　内報 ないほう secret report [information]
　内密の ないみつの secret, confidential, private

 ▷**hidden from view**
イン かく(す) かく(し)- かく(れる)　Ⓚ0645

hidden from view, concealed, secret
　隠語 いんご secret language, jargon
　隠密 おんみつ secrecy, privacy; detective, spy
　隠花植物 いんかしょくぶつ cryptogamic plant

ects →RELIGIONS AND SECTS

ects →PARTIES AND SECTS

securities
株　　　債

株 ▷**stock**
かぶ　　　Ⓚ0846

[also suffix] **stock, stocks, shares**
　株を買う かぶをかう buy stock
　株式 かぶしき stocks, shares
　株価 かぶか price of stocks

株券 かぶけん share [stock] certificate
株主 かぶぬし stockholder
株式会社 かぶしきがいしゃ joint stock corporation
新株 しんかぶ new stock
優先株 ゆうせんかぶ preference shares

債 ▷**bond**
サイ　　　Ⓚ0135

[also suffix] **bond, debenture, loan**
　債券 さいけん bond, debenture
　社債 しゃさい debenture, corporation bond
　国債 こくさい national bonds; national debt [loan]
　起債 きさい flotation of a loan, issue of bonds
　公債 こうさい public bond; public loan

see and look
見 看 察 窺 瞥 目 観
覧 眺 望 仰 顧 視

見 ▷**see**
ケン み(る) み(える) み(せる)　Ⓚ2201

[original meaning] **see, look at, observe**
　見物 けんぶつ sightseeing, visit
　見学 けんがく tour [field trip] for study and observation
　見聞する けんぶんする experience, observe
　拝見する はいけんする have the honor of seeing, see, look at, inspect
　一見 いっけん a look, a glance; apparently
　外見 がいけん outward appearance

看 ▷**watch**
カン　　　Ⓚ2771

[original meaning] (look carefully) **watch, look, see, observe**
　看板 かんばん signboard, sign
　看破する かんぱする see through, penetrate, read (another's thoughts)
　看取する かんしゅする perceive, detect; see through

察 ▷**inspect**
サツ　　　Ⓚ2062

(examine carefully) **inspect, observe, scrutinize, examine**
　観察 かんさつ observation, supervision
　洞察する どうさつする see through, penetrate

窺 ▷watch furtively
キ うかが(う) Ⓚ2092

watch furtively, peek, spy on
窺知する きちする perceive, understand

瞥 ▷glance at
ベツ Ⓚ2511

glance at, look at
瞥見する べっけんする glance at, take a brief look
一瞥 いちべつ a glance, a look

目 ▷look
モク ボク め ま- Ⓚ2619

(perform an action with the eyes) **look, eye, gaze, glance, keep an eye on**
目撃する もくげきする observe, witness, see
目測 もくそく eye measurement
目礼する もくれいする nod, greet
目送する もくそうする follow with one's eyes, gaze after
注目 ちゅうもく attention, notice
一目瞭然の いちもくりょうぜんの quite obvious, as clear as day

観 ▷view
カン Ⓚ1659

[original meaning] **view, behold, look; observe, inspect**
観光 かんこう sightseeing
観客 かんきゃく audience, spectators
観劇 かんげき theatergoing
観察 かんさつ observation, supervision
観賞 かんしょう admiration, enjoyment
傍観する ぼうかんする look on, sit as a spectator
楽観 らっかん optimism, hopeful view

覧 ▷look over
ラン Ⓚ2485

ⓐ [original meaning] **look over (a wide area), look at, glance at, view, see**
ⓑ (make an overall inspection of) **look over, inspect, read**

a 御覧 ごらん [honorific] look, see; try
一覧 いちらん a look, a glance, a reading; summary, synopsis
一覧する いちらんする look, glance through, inspect
観覧車 かんらんしゃ Ferris wheel
b 展覧する てんらんする exhibit, show
博覧会 はくらんかい exhibition, fair, exposition
閲覧室 えつらんしつ reading room
便覧 べんらん(=びんらん) handbook, manual
要覧 ようらん survey, outline, handbook

眺 ▷look out over
チョウ なが(める) Ⓚ108

[original meaning] **look out over, look far and wide, look afar, gaze**
眺望 ちょうぼう view, prospect, outlook

望 ▷look afar
ボウ モウ のぞ(む) Ⓚ239

look afar, gaze into the distance, command a view of
望見する ぼうけんする watch from afar
望郷 ぼうきょう homesickness, nostalgia
望遠鏡 ぼうえんきょう telescope
展望する てんぼうする have a view of
眺望 ちょうぼう view, prospect, outlook

仰 ▷look up
ギョウ コウ あお(ぐ) おお(せ) Ⓚ003

[original meaning] **look up, face upward**
仰視する ぎょうしする look up
仰角 ぎょうかく angle of elevation
仰臥 ぎょうが lying face up
仰天する ぎょうてんする be astounded

顧 ▷look back
コ かえり(みる) Ⓚ167

[original meaning] **look back, turn around**
顧問 こもん adviser, consultant
一顧もしない いっこもしない take no notice of, not give a damn
右顧左眄する うこさべんする look to the right and left, hesitate

視 ▷regard
シ み(る) Ⓚ088

ⓐ [original meaning] (look at attentively) **regard, look at, gaze**
ⓑ **inspect, watch over**

a 視聴者 しちょうしゃ viewer, audience
視界 しかい field of vision, visibility
視野 しや field of vision; one's mental horizon
視力 しりょく eyesight
視覚 しかく sense of sight
視点 してん viewpoint, point of view
凝視する ぎょうしする stare, gaze at
注視する ちゅうしする gaze steadily at, observe (a person) closely
b 視察 しさつ inspection, observation
監視する かんしする watch, keep under observation, exercise surveillance
巡視 じゅんし inspection tour
警視庁 けいしちょう Metropolitan Police Office

seek
探 索 捜 求 猟

探 ▷search
タン さぐ(る) さが(す)　　　Ⓚ0466

search, look for
探索 たんさく search, quest; inquiry, investigation
探鉱 たんこう prospecting
探照灯 たんしょうとう searchlight

索 ▷search for
サク　　　Ⓚ2168

search for (a word in a dictionary), look up, retrieve, locate
索引 さくいん index
捜索する そうさくする search for, investigate
探索する たんさくする search for; inquire into, investigate
模索(=摸索)する もさくする grope for
検索する けんさくする look up (a word in a dictionary), search for, refer to
思索する しさくする think, speculate

捜 ▷look for
ソウ さが(す)　　　Ⓚ0389

[original meaning] **look for, search**
捜査 そうさ criminal investigation, search
捜索 そうさく search, investigation
博捜 はくそう searching far and wide

求 ▷seek
キュウ もと(める)　　　Ⓚ2974

(go in search of) **seek (for), search, pursue; wish for, desire**
求人 きゅうじん job offer
求職 きゅうしょく seeking employment
求道 きゅうどう(=ぐどう) seeking for truth; seeking for enlightenment
探求する たんきゅうする investigate, search (for), pursue
追求 ついきゅう pursuit
欣求浄土 ごんぐじょうど seeking rebirth in the Pure Land
欲求 よっきゅう want(s), desire, wish

猟 ▷hunt for
リョウ　　　Ⓚ0491

hunt for, search for, seek
猟奇 りょうき bizarrerie hunting
猟色 りょうしょく lewdness, debauchery

渉猟 しょうりょう searching far and wide (for); extensive reading

sell and trade
売 卸 販 商 貿 易

売 ▷sell
バイ う(る) う(れる)　　　Ⓚ1878

ⓐ [original meaning] **sell**
ⓑ **sale**
a 売買 ばいばい buying and selling, trade
売店 ばいてん booth, stand; store
売却 ばいきゃく sale
売春 ばいしゅん prostitution
商売 しょうばい trade, business, commerce
販売 はんばい sale, selling, marketing
発売する はつばいする sell, put on the market
b 即売 そくばい sale on the spot, spot sale
特売 とくばい special sale, bargain sale

卸 ▷wholesale
おろ(す) おろし　　　Ⓚ1315

wholesale, sell wholesale
小売りに卸す こうりにおろす sell wholesale to a retailer

販 ▷engage in sales
ハン　　　Ⓚ1343

ⓐ **engage in sales, deal in, sell, trade, market**
ⓑ abbrev. of 販売 はんばい: **sales**
a 販売する はんばいする engage in sales, sell, market
販路 はんろ market, outlet
市販 しはん marketing
再販 さいはん resale
b 信販 しんぱん sales on credit
自販 じはん automobile sales

商 ▷trade
ショウ あきな(う)　　　Ⓚ1818

trade, trade in, deal in
商品 しょうひん goods, commodities
商店 しょうてん shop, store
商業 しょうぎょう commerce, trade, business
商社 しょうしゃ company, firm
商売 しょうばい trade, business, commerce
商法 しょうほう trade, business, commerce; commercial law
商人 しょうにん merchant, trader, tradesman
商船 しょうせん merchant ship, trading vessel
商標 しょうひょう trademark

貿 ▷**trade**
ボウ   Ⓚ2255

[original meaning] **trade, buy and sell, exchange**
- 貿易 ぼうえき trade, commerce
- 貿易会社 ぼうえきがいしゃ trading firm
- 貿易風 ぼうえきふう trade wind
- 貿易品 ぼうえきひん articles of commerce
- 貿易業 ぼうえきぎょう trading business

易 ▷**exchange**
エキ イ やさ(しい) やす(い)   Ⓚ2135

exchange, trade
- 貿易 ぼうえき trade, commerce
- 交易 こうえき trade, commerce

send
送 投 回 遣 派

送 ▷**send**
ソウ おく(る)   Ⓚ2664

ⓐ [original meaning] **send, dispatch, deliver, mail**
ⓑ transmit
- *a* 送金 そうきん remittance
  - 送付 そうふ sending, remittance
  - 送検する そうけんする commit for trial, send to the prosecutors office
  - 送料 そうりょう postage, carriage
  - 郵送する ゆうそうする mail, send by mail
  - 輸送 ゆそう transport, conveyance
  - 発送する はっそうする send out, dispatch, ship
- *b* 送電 そうでん electrical transmission
  - 送信 そうしん transmission (of a message)
  - 放送 ほうそう broadcasting

投 ▷**send in**
トウ な(げる) -な(げ)   Ⓚ0228

send in [to], submit, deliver
- 投書 とうしょ contribution, letter (from a reader)
- 投稿 とうこう contribution (to a magazine)
- 投票する とうひょうする vote, cast a ballot
- 投資 とうし investment
- 投入する とうにゅうする invest; throw into

回 ▷**send round**
カイ エ まわ(る) -まわ(り) まわ(す)
まわ(し)-   Ⓚ2630

[formerly 廻] **send round, forward, transport**
- 回送 かいそう forwarding
- 回漕業 かいそうぎょう shipping business
- 回船 かいせん lighter, cargo vessel

遣 ▷**dispatch**
ケン つか(う) -つか(い) -づか(い)
つか(わす)   Ⓚ2717

dispatch, send
- 遣外の けんがいの dispatched abroad
- 遣唐使 けんとうし Japanese envoy to Tang China
- 遣米 けんべい sending to America
- 派遣する はけんする dispatch, send
- 分遣 ぶんけん detachment, detail
- 先遣する せんけんする send ahead [in advance]

派 ▷**dispatch**
ハ   Ⓚ0341

dispatch, send
- 派出する はしゅつする send out, dispatch
- 派米する はべいする dispatch to the U.S.
- 派遣する はけんする dispatch, send
- 派兵 はへい dispatch of troops
- 特派員 とくはいん special correspondent; delegate

sense
感 覚 勘

感 ▷**sense**
カン   Ⓚ2468

(faculty of perception) **sense**
- 五感 ごかん the five senses
- 第六感 だいろっかん the sixth sense, intuition
- 敏感な びんかんな sensitive

覚 ▷**sense**
カク おぼ(える) さ(ます) さ(める) Ⓚ2258

sense, sensation
- 感覚 かんかく sense, sensation, feeling
- 視覚 しかく sense of sight
- 痛覚 つうかく sense of pain

勘 ▷**intuitive perception**
カン   Ⓚ1582

intuitive perception: **sense, perception; horse sense, intuition, sixth sense**
- 勘違い かんちがい wrong guess [impression]
- 勘付く かんづく sense (a danger)
- 山勘で やまかんで by guesswork

sentence and sentence parts
句　文　節

句 ▷phrase
ク　　　　　　　　　　　　Ⓚ2561

gram (sentence subdivision) **phrase, clause**
　句読点 くとうてん punctuation marks
　句法 くほう phraseology, diction
　名詞句 めいしく noun phrase

文 ▷sentence
ブン モン ふみ　　　　　　　Ⓚ1708

[also suffix]
ⓐ sentence
ⓑ *computer science* **statement**
a 文脈 ぶんみゃく context
　文化的 ぶんかてき cultural
　単文 たんぶん simple sentence
　疑問文 ぎもんぶん interrogative sentence
b 条件文 じょうけんぶん conditional statement

節 ▷clause
セツ セチ ふし ーぶし　　　　Ⓚ2349

[also suffix] (subdivision of a sentence) **clause**
　主節 しゅせつ principal clause
　従属節 じゅうぞくせつ subordinate clause

sentence parts →SENTENCE AND SENTENCE PARTS

separate
割 分 解 析 別 離 隔

割 ▷divide
カツ わ(る) わり わ(れる) さ(く)　Ⓚ1611

(separate into parts) **divide (up), split; cede**
　割賦 かっぷ(=わっぷ) payment by installments
　割拠する かっきょする hold one's own ground
　割愛する かつあいする part with (something), give up; omit (reluctantly)
　割譲 かつじょう cession of territory
　分割する ぶんかつする divide up, partition, split

分 ▷divide
ブン フン ブ わ(ける) わ(け) わ(かれる) わ(かる) わ(かつ)　Ⓚ1713

ⓐ [original meaning] **divide into parts, part, separate, sever**
ⓑ (become separated into parts) **divide, be divided, come apart**
ⓒ (group according to kind) **divide, separate, sort, classify**
a 分割する ぶんかつする divide up, partition, split
　分譲 ぶんじょう sale (of land) in lots, lotting-out
　分析 ぶんせき analysis
　分離 ぶんり separation, split
　分担 ぶんたん partial charge, allotment
　分解 ぶんかい disintegration, disassembly; analysis, decomposition
　分数 ぶんすう fraction
　処分する しょぶんする dispose of, deal [do] with; punish
　区分する くぶんする divide, section, subdivide
b 分野 ぶんや field, sphere, area
　分裂する ぶんれつする be divided, split, break up, be disrupted
　分科会 ぶんかかい sectional subcommittee
　分散 ぶんさん dispersion, breakup, divergence; variance
　分立 ぶんりつ separation, segregation
　分泌 ぶんぴつ(=ぶんぴ) secretion
　分布 ぶんぷ distribution
c 分類する ぶんるいする classify, divide into classes
　分別する ぶんべつする classify, distinguish; divide, separate

解 ▷take apart
カイ ゲ と(く) と(かす) と(ける)　Ⓚ1375

[original meaning] (break into component parts) **take apart, resolve, dissolve, separate, dissect**
　解体 かいたい dismantling (a machine), scrapping; dissolution, disorganization; dissection
　解剖 かいぼう dissection, autopsy; analysis
　解像力 かいぞうりょく resolving power (of a lens)
　解析 かいせき analysis, analytical research
　分解する ぶんかいする take apart [to pieces]; analyze, decompose; be decomposed, break down
　瓦解 がかい collapse, breakup, downfall
　電解 でんかい electrolysis

析 ▷analyze
セキ　　　　　　　　　　　Ⓚ0766

ⓐ (separate an abstract entity into parts) **analyze, dissect**
ⓑ (separate a material entity into parts) **analyze, separate, dissect, divide**
a 分析 ぶんせき analysis

解析 かいせき analysis, analytical research

b 析出 せきしゅつ *chem* separating, eduction

開析台地 かいせきだいち dissected plateau

透析 とうせき *chem* dialysis

別 ▷separate
ベツ わか(れる) Ⓚ1032

(divide by differences) **separate (into groups), sort, classify, distinguish**

差別 さべつ discrimination

個別的に こべつてきに individually, severally, singly

区別する くべつする distinguish; classify, divide

分別する ぶんべつする classify, distinguish; divide, separate

分別 ふんべつ discretion, prudence, judgment, good sense

判別する はんべつする distinguish, discriminate

類別 るいべつ classification

戸別 こべつ each house

大別する たいべつする divide into major classes

離 ▷separate
リ はな(れる) はな(す) Ⓚ1663

(be or become disconnected) **separate (from), be separated, be detached, disjoin, scatter**

離散する りさんする scatter, disperse, be broken up

分離する ぶんりする separate, split; be separated

電離 でんり electrolytic dissociation, ionization

剝離 はくり exfoliation, peeling off

支離滅裂な しりめつれつな incoherent, inconsistent, disconnected

隔離 かくり isolation, segregation

隔 ▷partition
カク へだ(てる) へだ(たる) Ⓚ0615

[original meaning] **partition, screen, interpose; separate, set apart**

隔壁 かくへき partition, bulkhead; septum

隔膜 かくまく partition; diaphragm

隔離する かくりする isolate, segregate

横隔膜 おうかくまく diaphragm; midriff

servants
僕 奴 隷 臣 従 供

僕 ▷manservant
ボク Ⓚ0142

[original meaning] **manservant, servant, menial**

忠僕 ちゅうぼく faithful servant

従僕 じゅうぼく servant, attendant

家僕 かぼく manservant, house boy

下僕 げぼく servant, your humble servant

公僕 こうぼく public servant

奴 ▷slave
ド やつ Ⓚ0164

slave, serf, manservant, menial

奴隷 どれい slave, servant

農奴 のうど serf

黒奴 こくど black slave

隷 ▷underling
レイ Ⓚ1563

(lowly person in servitude) **underling, subordinate, servant, lackey**

隷下 れいか followers, subordinates

奴隷 どれい slave, servant

臣 ▷retainer
シン ジン Ⓚ2642

retainer, subject, vassal

臣下 しんか retainer, subject, vassal

臣民 しんみん subjects

家臣 かしん retainer, vassal

君臣 くんしん sovereign and subject, lord and vassal

忠臣 ちゅうしん loyal retainer, loyal subject

大臣 だいじん minister (of state)

従 ▷follower
ジュウ ショウ ジュ したが(う) したが(える) Ⓚ0376

follower, attendant, servant, vassal

従者 じゅうしゃ follower, attendant, squire

従僕 じゅうぼく servant, attendant

主従 しゅじゅう(=しゅうじゅう) master and servant, lord and vassal

侍従 じじゅう chamberlain

供 ▷attendant
キョウ ク そな(える) とも -ども Ⓚ0070

attendant, retinue

供回り ともまわり train of attendants, retinue

お供する おともする go with, accompany, follow

set forth →LEAVE AND SET FORTH

土着の どちゃくの native, indigenous, aboriginal
b 決着 けっちゃく conclusion, decision
落着 らくちゃく settlement, conclusion
c 着着と ちゃくちゃくと steadily, step by step
着実な ちゃくじつな steady, solid, sound
横着な おうちゃくな impudent, brazen; idle, lazy
沈着 ちんちゃく composure, self-possession

set in motion
動　駆　掛

動
▷**move**
ドウ うご(く) うご(かす)　　　Ⓚ1583

(set in motion, esp. machines) **move, drive, operate**
動力 どうりょく power
駆動 くどう drive (of a machine)
始動 しどう starting (machines)
原動力 げんどうりょく motive force
伝動 でんどう transmission, drive, gearing
電動の でんどうの electric powered

駆
▷**drive**
ク か(ける) か(る)　　　Ⓚ1619

drive (a machine), set in motion, handle
駆動 くどう drive (of a machine)
駆使する くしする use freely, have good command of

掛
▷**set going**
か(ける) か(け) −が(け) か(かる)
−が(かる) か(かり) −が(かり)　　　Ⓚ0449

set going, set in motion, turn on, start, operate;
phone
火を掛ける ひをかける set fire
レコードを掛ける れこーどをかける play a record
仕掛け しかけ device, mechanism
電話を掛ける でんわをかける make a phone call,
telephone

settle
着　帰　落

着
▷**settle (down)**
チャク ジャク き(る) −ぎ き(せる) −き(せ)
つ(く) つ(ける)　　　Ⓚ2826

ⓐ (come to rest in one place) **settle (down), settle
[seat] oneself, become situated, settle down (in
a place)**
ⓑ (reach a decision) **settle, come to a settlement**
ⓒ **settle down, become calm [composed], become
steady**
a 着席する ちゃくせきする take one's seat
着座 ちゃくざ taking a seat
着氷 ちゃくひょう icing (on a plane); ice formed by
icing
着床 ちゃくしょう implantation

帰
▷**settle in place**
キ かえ(る) かえ(す)　　　Ⓚ0113

ⓐ **settle in place, conclude**
ⓑ **settle in one place, be brought together, unite**
a 帰結 きけつ conclusion, end, result
帰一する きいつする be united into one
帰納法 きのうほう inductive method

落
▷**be concluded**
ラク お(ちる) お(ち) お(とす)　　　Ⓚ2019

be concluded, be settled, be completed
落着する らくちゃくする be settled, come to a
conclusion
落成 らくせい completion
一段落 いちだんらく pause; (figuratively) end of
chapter

sew →WEAVE AND SEW

sex
性　情　春　色　淫

性
▷**sex**
セイ ショウ　　　Ⓚ0266

(sexual intercourse) **sex, sexuality, sexual desire**
性欲 せいよく sexual desire, lust
性的 せいてき sexual
性行為 せいこうい sexual act, intercourse
性教育 せいきょういく sex education

情
▷**(illicit) love**
ジョウ セイ なさ(け)　　　Ⓚ0439

(illicit) **love, love affair, lovemaking, sexual desire**
情死 じょうし double love suicide
情事 じょうじ love affair, romance
情交 じょうこう sexual intercourse, illicit intercourse

春
▷**love**
シュン はる　　　Ⓚ2232

love, sex, sexual desire, eros
春情 しゅんじょう sexual passion
春画 しゅんが pornography, obscene picture
売春 ばいしゅん prostitution

思春期 ししゅんき puberty, adolescence

色 ▷lust
ショク シキ いろ　　　　　　Ⓚ1748

lust, sensual pleasure, sexual passion, love
色情 しきじょう lust
色欲 しきよく lust, carnal desire, sexual passion
色魔 しきま woman hunter, sex fiend
女色 じょしょく woman's charms, lust
好色家 こうしょくか lecher, Don Juan
酒色 しゅしょく wine and women, sensual pleasures

淫 ▷lewd
イン みだ(ら)　　　　　　Ⓚ0470

lewd, vulgar, lascivious
淫乱 いんらん lewdness, lasciviousness
淫行 いんこう obscene [lewd] behavior
淫蕩 いんとう lewdness; sexual abandon
催淫剤 さいいんざい aphrodisiac

shadow
影　翳　陰　蔭

影 ▷shadow
エイ かげ　　　　　　Ⓚ1671

[formerly also 翳] [original meaning] (partial darkness)
shadow, silhouette
影響 えいきょう influence, effect
暗影 あんえい shadow, gloom
陰影 いんえい shadow

翳 ▷shadow
エイ かげ(る) かす(む) かざ(す)

[now replaced by 影] **shadow, shade**
暗翳 あんえい shadow, gloom
陰翳 いんえい shadow

陰 ▷shade
イン かげ かげ(る)　　　　　　Ⓚ0494

shade
陰影 いんえい shadow
緑陰 りょくいん shade of trees
樹陰 じゅいん [rare] shade of a tree

蔭 ▷shade
イン かげ　　　　　　Ⓚ2073

[now usu. 陰] [original meaning] **shade**
樹蔭 じゅいん [rare] shade of a tree
緑蔭 りょくいん shade of trees

shake
振　震　揺

振 ▷swing
シン ふ(る) ぶ(る) ふ(り) -ぶ(り) ふ(るう)
ふ(れる)　　　　　　Ⓚ0388

[original meaning] **swing, oscillate, vibrate**
振動 しんどう vibration
振幅 しんぷく amplitude (of vibration)

震 ▷quake
シン ふる(う) ふる(える)　　　　　　Ⓚ2443

quake, shake, vibrate
震動 しんどう shock, tremor, vibration
地震 じしん earthquake

揺 ▷shake
ヨウ ゆ(れる) ゆ(る) ゆ(らぐ) ゆ(るぐ)
ゆ(する) ゆ(さぶる) ゆ(すぶる)　　　　　　Ⓚ0543

[original meaning] **shake, sway, rock**
揺動 ようどう titubation; shaking, swinging
揺籃 ようらん cradle
動揺 どうよう shaking, trembling; restlessness, uneasiness, disquiet

sharp
鋭　先　尖

鋭 ▷sharp
エイ するど(い)　　　　　　Ⓚ1544

ⓐ [original meaning] (having an acute point) **sharp, pointed**
ⓑ (having an acute edge) **sharp, acute**
ａ 鋭鋒 えいほう brunt (of an attack); incisive reasoning
　先鋭(=尖鋭)な せんえいな radical; acute, sharp
ｂ 鋭利な えいりな sharp, keen; acute, sharp, clever
　鋭角 えいかく acute angle

先 ▷pointed
セン さき ま(ず)　　　　　　Ⓚ2123

pointed, acute
先鋭な せんえいな radical; acute, sharp

尖 ▷pointed
セン とが(る) とんが(る)　　　　　　Ⓚ1864

[original meaning] **pointed, acute**

尖塔 せんとう pinnacle, spire
尖頭 せんとう pointed end, cusp
尖鋭な せんえいな radical; acute, sharp

sheep
羊　　未

羊 ▷sheep
ヨウ ひつじ　　Ⓚ1870

[original meaning] **sheep, ram, ewe**
羊肉 ようにく mutton
羊毛 ようもう wool
羊頭狗肉 ようとうくにく using a better name to sell inferior goods, crying wine and selling vinegar
羊羹 ようかん sweet jelly of beans
牧羊 ぼくよう sheep farming

未 ▷the Ram
ミ いま(だ) ま(だ)　　Ⓚ2941

eighth sign of the Oriental zodiac: **the Ram**—(time) 1-3 p.m., (direction) SSW, (season) June (of the lunar calendar)
癸未 きび 20th of the sexagenary cycle

shells
殻　甲　貝　螺　瑚

殻 ▷shell (of any kind)
カク から がら　　Ⓚ1354

shell (of any kind), crust
殻頂 かくちょう umbo, apex of a shell
甲殻類 こうかくるい Crustacea
地殻 ちかく crust (of the earth)
卵殻 らんかく eggshell

甲 ▷shell (of animals)
コウ カン カ　　Ⓚ2923

shell (of animals); carapace, tortoise carapace
甲殻 こうかく carapace, shell, crust
甲羅 こうら shell, carapace
甲骨文 こうこつぶん ancient inscriptions of Chinese characters on oracle bones and carapaces
甲虫 こうちゅう beetle
甲板 かんぱん(=こうはん) deck
亀甲 きっこう carapace of a turtle, tortoiseshell

貝 ▷seashell
バイ かい　　Ⓚ2200

【バイ】
seashell, shell
貝独楽 ばいごま shell top

【かい】
seashell, shell
貝殻 かいがら shell
貝細工 かいざいく shellwork

螺 ▷spiral-shelled gastropod
ラ つぶ にし　　Ⓚ1293

spiral-shelled gastropod, conch, snail
螺鈿 らでん mother-of-pearl
法螺 ほら conch; boasting, bragging, big talk

瑚 ▷coral
ゴ コ　　Ⓚ0941

coral
珊瑚 さんご coral

shine and reflect
輝 光 照 映 耀 燿 閃 煌

輝 ▷shine brilliantly
キ かがや(く)　　Ⓚ1280

shine brilliantly, glitter, sparkle, radiate
輝線 きせん bright line
輝石 きせき pyroxene, augite
輝度 きど brightness
輝輝 きき brilliance
光輝有る こうきある shining, brilliant, glorious, splendid

光 ▷shine
コウ ひか(る) ひかり　　Ⓚ2121

[original meaning] **shine, glow, glitter**
光照 こうしょう shining
光輝有る こうきある shining, brilliant, glorious, splendid

照 ▷illuminate
ショウ て(る) て(らす) て(れる)　　Ⓚ2461

[original meaning] **illuminate, shine, reflect**
照明 しょうめい illumination, lighting
照射 しょうしゃ irradiation
照度 しょうど intensity of illumination
日照権 にっしょうけん right to sunshine

映 ▷**reflect**
エイ　うつ(る)　うつ(す)　は(える)
-ば(え)　　　　　　　　　Ⓚ0793

reflect, mirror, shine
映射する えいしゃする [rare] reflect, shine
反映 はんえい reflection

耀 ▷**shine brilliantly**
ヨウ　かがや(く)　　　　Ⓚ1301

[original meaning] **shine brilliantly**
眩耀する げんようする shine dazzlingly

燿 ▷**shine**
ヨウ　シャク　　　　　Ⓚ1016

[original meaning, now rare] **shine, illuminate**
燿燿 ようよう shining brightly

閃 ▷**flash**
セン　ひらめ(く)　ひらめ(かす)　Ⓚ2830

flash, flicker, glitter
閃光 せんこう flash, glint
閃緑岩 せんりょくがん diorite
一閃 いっせん a flash (of light)
角閃石 かくせんせき amphibole

煌 ▷**glitter**
コウ　きら(めく)　　　Ⓚ0938

[original meaning] **glitter, twinkle, sparkle, glisten, gleam**
煌煌と こうこうと brilliantly, dazzlingly, brightly

ships →BOATS AND SHIPS

ships →PARTS OF BOATS AND SHIPS

shoals
瀬　州　礁

瀬 ▷**shallows**
せ　　　　　　　　　Ⓚ0717

shallows, shoal
瀬戸 せと strait, channel
瀬戸物 せともの pottery, china
浅瀬 あさせ shoal, shallows
早瀬 はやせ rapids, swift current

州 ▷**sandbar**
シュウ　す　　　　　Ⓚ0040

[formerly also 洲] **sandbar, shallows, shoal**
三角州 さんかくす delta
砂州 さす sandbar, sandbank

座州する ざすする strand, run aground

礁 ▷**reef**
ショウ　　　　　　　Ⓚ1148

[original meaning] **reef, sunken rock**
岩礁 がんしょう reef
珊瑚礁 さんごしょう coral reef
座礁(=坐礁)する ざしょうする run aground, be stranded
環礁 かんしょう atoll
暗礁 あんしょう sunken rock, unknown reef; deadlock

shoot
射　撃　発

射 ▷**shoot**
シャ　い(る)　さ(す)　　Ⓚ1327

ⓐ shoot, fire
ⓑ [original meaning] **shoot an arrow**
a 射撃 しゃげき shooting, gunshot, firing
射的 しゃてき target practice, shooting
射程 しゃてい shooting range
射殺する しゃさつする shoot to death
発射する はっしゃする discharge, shoot, launch
高射砲 こうしゃほう antiaircraft gun, high-angle gun

撃 ▷**fire**
ゲキ　う(つ)　　　　　Ⓚ2492

fire, shoot, discharge
撃墜する げきついする shoot down
撃沈する げきちんする attack and sink a ship
射撃する しゃげきする shoot, fire at
銃撃 じゅうげき shooting, gunning (down)

発 ▷**discharge**
ハツ　ホツ　た(つ)　　Ⓚ2222

[original meaning] (emit a projectile) **discharge, fire, shoot**
発射する はっしゃする discharge, shoot, launch
発砲 はっぽう firing, discharge of a gun
連発 れんぱつ running fire, volley
暴発 ぼうはつ spontaneous discharge, accidental gun discharge

shores and watersides
畔 辺 浜 岸 浦 渚 磯 汀

畔 ▷waterside
ハン ⓚ1060

waterside, water's edge, bank, shore
- 湖畔 こはん lake shore, lakeside
- 河畔 かはん riverside, banks of a river
- 池畔 ちはん edge of a pond
- 橋畔 きょうはん approach to a bridge
- 吉野川畔 よしのがわはん the banks of Yoshino River

辺 ▷-side
ヘン あた(り) –べ ⓚ2607

(space next to a body of water) **-side, waterside, bank**
- 海辺 うみべ seaside, beach, seashore
- 川辺 かわべ riverside, edge of a river
- 岸辺に きしべに ashore, on the shore

浜 ▷beach
ヒン はま ⓚ0394

beach, seashore, coast
- 海浜 かいひん seashore, seaside, beach

岸 ▷shore
ガン きし ⓚ1920

[original meaning] **shore, bank, coast, beach**
- 岸壁 がんぺき quay (wall), wharf
- 沿岸 えんがん coast, shore
- 海岸 かいがん seashore, (sea) coast, beach
- 左岸 さがん left bank (of a river)
- 対岸 たいがん opposite bank [shore]

浦 ▷seaside
ホ うら ⓚ0395

elegant **seaside, seashore**
- 浦風 うらかぜ sea breeze
- 浦人 うらびと seaside dweller
- 浦里 うらざと village by the sea
- 津津浦浦に つつうらうらに throughout the land, in every harbor and every bay

渚 ▷strand
ショ なぎさ ⓚ0481

[archaic] **strand, beach, waterside, shore**
- 渚畔 しょはん waterside, shore

磯 ▷rocky beach
キ いそ ⓚ1147

rocky beach, beach, seashore
- 磯辺 いそべ rocky beach, beach
- 磯巾着 いそぎんちゃく sea anemone, seaflower
- 磯釣り いそづり fishing from rocks near the shore
- 磯伝いに いそづたいに along the beach
- 荒磯 あらいそ reefy coast, windswept and wave-beaten shore

汀 ▷strand
テイ チョウ みぎわ なぎさ ⓚ0174

【テイ チョウ】
strand, beach, waterside, shore
- 汀線 ていせん shoreline, coastline
- 汀洲 ていしゅう sandbar, islet in a stream; shoreline

【みぎわ なぎさ】
❶ **strand, beach, waterside, shore**
- 汀に寄せる細波 みぎわによせるさざなみ ripples beating upon the seashore

❷ [usu. 渚] **strand, beach, waterside, shore**
- 汀伝い なぎさづたい along the shore

short and shortened
短 簡 略

短 ▷short
タン みじか(い) ⓚ1093

[also prefix] [original meaning] (not long) **short**
- 短波 たんぱ shortwave
- 短気 たんき short [hot] temper
- 短歌 たんか tanka, Japanese verse

簡 ▷simplified
カン ⓚ2374

simplified, brief, concise
- 簡明な かんめいな terse, concise
- 簡略 かんりゃく simplicity, brevity, conciseness; informality
- 簡潔な かんけつな brief, concise
- 簡裁 かんさい summary court

略 ▷abridged
リャク ⓚ1081

abridged, brief, concise
- 略語 りゃくご abbreviation
- 略字 りゃくじ simplified character; abbreviation
- 略文 りゃくぶん abridged sentence
- 略歴 りゃくれき brief personal history
- 簡略な かんりゃくな simple, brief, concise; informal

short time periods
頃 瞬 秒 分 時 暫

頃 ▷**moment**
ころ ごろ　　　　　　　　Ⓚ0124

[archaic] **moment, instant, short time**
頃刻 けいこく short moment

瞬 ▷**instant**
シュン またた(く)　　　　Ⓚ1151

instant, moment; in the twinkling of an eye
瞬間 しゅんかん instant, moment, second
瞬時 しゅんじ instant, moment; minute
一瞬 いっしゅん instant, moment

秒 ▷**second**
ビョウ　　　　　　　　　Ⓚ1052

(unit of time) **second**
秒速 びょうそく speed per second
秒針 びょうしん second hand
秒時計 びょうどけい stop watch
秒読み びょうよみ counting the seconds; count-
down

分 ▷**minute**
ブン フン ブ わ(ける) わ(け) わ(かれる)
わ(かる) わ(かつ)　　　　Ⓚ1713

(unit of time) **minute**
分速 ふんそく speed per minute
毎分 まいふん every minute

時 ▷**hour**
ジ とき –どき　　　　　　Ⓚ0830

hour
時速 じそく speed per hour
時給 じきゅう payment by the hour
一時間 いちじかん one hour

暫 ▷**short while**
ザン しばら(く)　　　　　Ⓚ2493

[original meaning] **short while, a while**
暫時 ざんじ short while, a moment

show
示 見 呈

示 ▷**show**
ジ シ しめ(す)　　　　　Ⓚ1694

(cause to be seen) **show, display, present**
示圧計 しあつけい pressure gauge
展示 てんじ display, exhibition
表示する ひょうじする indicate, show, express,
manifest
標示する ひょうじする post up, declare, demonstrate
掲示 けいじ notice, bulletin
提示する ていじする present, exhibit
告示 こくじ notification, bulletin

見 ▷**show**
ケン み(る) み(える) み(せる)　Ⓚ2201

**show, let see, disclose, exhibit; make (a thing) look
like, give an air of, pretend; make (a person) experience [understand];** [following the TE-form of verbs] **be
determined to**
見せ物 みせもの show, exhibition
見せびらかす みせびらかす show off, display
見せ掛ける みせかける make (a thing) look like,
pretend
見せしめ みせしめ lesson, warning
古く見せる ふるくみせる impart an ancient appearance
彼を負かして見せる かれをまかしてみせる I'll win
him over

呈 ▷**present**
テイ　　　　　　　　　　Ⓚ1874

(offer to view) **present, show, display, exhibit**
呈示する ていじする exhibit, present
呈色 ていしき color, coloring
露呈 ろてい exposure, disclosure

shrink →CONTRACT AND SHRINK

shrubs
藤 蔦 萩 茉 莉 芭

藤 ▷**wisteria**
トウ ふじ　　　　　　　　Ⓚ2109

wisteria
葛藤 かっとう complication, troubles, discord

蔦 ▷**Japanese ivy**
チョウ つた ⓚ2071

Japanese [Boston] ivy, ivy
　蔦蘿 つたかずら ivy and vine, creepers
　蔦紅葉 つたもみじ scarlet-tinged ivy; maple
　木蔦 きづた ivy, *Hedera rhombea*

萩 ▷*hagi*
シュウ はぎ ⓚ2020

hagi, **Japanese bush clover**, *Lespedeza bicolor*
　萩属 はぎぞく *Lespedeza*

茉 ▷**jasmine**
マツ ⓚ1933

jasmine, white jasmine
　茉莉 まつり jasmine, *Jasminum sambac*
　茉莉花 まつりか jasmine, *Jasminum sambac*

莉 ▷**jasmine**
リ ⓚ1975

jasmine, white jasmine
　茉莉 まつり jasmine, *Jasminum sambac*
　茉莉花 まつりか jasmine, *Jasminum sambac*

芭 ▷**Japanese fiber banana**
バ ⓚ1890

Japanese fiber banana
　芭蕉 ばしょう Japanese banana plant, *Musa basjoo*;
　　plantain
　水芭蕉 みずばしょう Asian skunk cabbage, *Lysichiton camtschatcense*

siblings
妹　姉　兄　弟

妹 ▷**younger sister**
マイ いもうと ⓚ0250

[original meaning] **younger sister**
　姉妹 しまい(=きょうだい) sisters
　義妹 ぎまい sister-in-law
　弟妹 ていまい younger brothers and sisters
　実妹 じつまい one's true (younger) sister
　令妹 れいまい your younger sister

姉 ▷**older sister**
シ あね ⓚ0253

older sister
　姉妹 しまい(=きょうだい) sisters
　実姉 じっし one's true (older) sister
　義姉 ぎし older sister-in-law

令姉 れいし your older sister
同母姉 どうぼし uterine sisters, sisters of the same
　mother

兄 ▷**older brother**
ケイ キョウ あに ⓚ1848

older brother
　兄弟 きょうだい(=けいてい) brother
　長兄 ちょうけい eldest brother
　実兄 じっけい one's own older brother
　義兄 ぎけい brother-in-law
　父兄 ふけい one's father and older brothers; guardians

弟 ▷**younger brother**
テイ ダイ デ おとうと ⓚ1759

younger brother
　弟妹 ていまい younger brothers and sisters
　兄弟 きょうだい(=けいてい) brother
　義弟 ぎてい brother-in-law
　愚弟 ぐてい my foolish younger brother

siblings of parents
叔　伯

叔 ▷**younger sibling of parent**
シュク ⓚ1168

younger sibling of one's parent, uncle, aunt
　叔父 しゅくふ(=おじ) uncle (younger than one's
　　parent)
　叔母 しゅくぼ(=おば) aunt (younger than one's
　　parent)

伯 ▷**older sibling of parent**
ハク ⓚ0043

older sibling of one's parent, uncle, aunt
　伯父 はくふ(=おじ) uncle (older than one's parent)
　伯母 はくぼ(=おば) aunt (older than one's parent)

side
側　脇　方　辺　面　傍　横

側 ▷**side**
ソク がわ かわ ⓚ0120

ⓐ (one of two or more opposing parts) **side, part**
ⓑ (lateral surface) **side, flank**
　a 右側 うそく(=みぎがわ) right side
　b 側聞(=仄聞)する そくぶんする learn by hearsay

側面 そくめん side, flank
側壁 そくへき side wall
船側 せんそく side of a ship

脇 ▷side
キョウ わき Ⓚ0859

side, flank
脇侍(=脇士、夾侍、挟侍) きょうじ flanking atten-
　dants to principal image of Buddha in a temple
脇息 きょうそく (portable) armrest

方 ▷side
ホウ かた -がた -なた Ⓚ1709

ⓐ (one part of) **side, one side**
ⓑ (one of concerned persons) **side, party, part**
ⓐ 一方 いっぽう one side, one hand; a party, the other
　party; in the meantime; only
片方 かたほう one side, the other side
両方 りょうほう both
他方 たほう other side [hand]
ⓑ 双方 そうほう both sides [parties]
当方 とうほう I, we, our part
先方 せんぽう the other party, they; one's destina-
　tion

辺 ▷-side
ヘン あた(り) -べ Ⓚ2607

(space next to something, as a body of water) **-side**
水辺 すいへん waterside, shore

面 ▷side
メン おも おもて つら Ⓚ1796

side, quarter, direction
側面 そくめん side, flank
両面 りょうめん both sides
方面 ほうめん direction, district; field, sphere
一面 いちめん one side; on the other hand; whole
　surface
反面 はんめん the other side
全面的 ぜんめんてき all-out, overall, general

傍 ▷beside
ボウ かたわ(ら) そば Ⓚ0127

[sometimes also 旁] **beside, by, by the side, nearby;
side**
傍観者 ぼうかんしゃ bystander, onlooker
傍系の ぼうけいの collateral, subsidiary, affiliated
傍受 ぼうじゅ interception, tapping
傍線 ぼうせん side line, underline
傍聴 ぼうちょう hearing; attendance
傍若無人な ぼうじゃくぶじんな overbearing, arro-
　gant, audacious
路傍 ろぼう roadside, wayside
近傍 きんぼう neighborhood

横 ▷sideways
オウ よこ Ⓚ0979

**sideways, horizontal, across, crosswise, transverse,
lateral, latitudinal**
横転する おうてんする roll, fall down sidelong;
　barrel roll
横断する おうだんする cross, traverse
横断歩道 おうだんほどう pedestrian crossing;
　crosswalk
横隔膜 おうかくまく diaphragm; midriff
縦横に じゅうおうに vertically and horizontally, in
　all directions; freely

sigh →CRY AND SIGH

signal
号　　報

号 ▷signal
ゴウ Ⓚ1847

signal
号砲 ごうほう signal gun
信号 しんごう signal; traffic light

報 ▷signal
ホウ むく(いる) むく(う) Ⓚ1515

signal, warning
時報 じほう time signal; review
警報 けいほう warning signal, alarm
大雨注意報 おおあめちゅういほう storm warning

signs →MARKS AND SIGNS

signs
候　徴　症　気　兆

候 ▷indication
コウ そうろう Ⓚ0101

indication, sign, symptom; condition
兆候(=徴候) ちょうこう symptom, sign; omen
症候 しょうこう symptom

徴 ▷symptom
チョウ Ⓚ0622

(evidence of a fact or event) **symptom, sign, indication,
omen**
徴候 ちょうこう symptom, sign; omen
徴証 ちょうしょう token, sign
象徴 しょうちょう symbol

症 ▷symptom (of a disease)
ショウ   Ⓚ2794

[original meaning] **symptom, nature of a disease, syndrome**
> 症状 しょうじょう symptom
> 症候 しょうこう symptom
> 後遺症 こういしょう sequela, aftereffect (of a disease)
> ダウン症 だうんしょう Down's syndrome

気 ▷sign
キ ケ   Ⓚ2751

[also suffix] **sign, indication, symptom, trace, air**
> 気配 けはい sign, indication
> 気品 きひん dignity, grace, nobility
> 気取る きどる make an affected pose, assume airs
> 気高い けだかい noble, lofty, high-minded
> 人気が無い ひとけがない no sign of life
> 色気 いろけ sex appeal, sensuality; fancifulness; inclination, interest; shade of color
> 飾り気 かざりけ affectation, love of display
> 得意気に とくいげに with an air of expertise
> 惜し気に おしげに grudgingly

兆 ▷omen
チョウ きざ(す) きざ(し)   Ⓚ0199

omen, sign, indication, symptom; foreboding
> 兆候(=徴候) ちょうこう symptom, sign; omen
> 前兆 ぜんちょう omen, sign
> 吉兆 きっちょう good omen, lucky sign

similar

類　様　如　通　云

類 ▷similar
ルイ たぐ(い)   Ⓚ1606

similar, resembling, synonymous
> 類書 るいしょ books of the same kind, similar books
> 類型 るいけい similar type, prototype, pattern
> 類語 るいご synonym, correlated word

様 ▷like
ヨウ さま   Ⓚ0969

[suffix] **like, such as**
> 歯ブラシ様の物 はぶらしようのもの something resembling a toothbrush

如 ▷as
ジョ ニョ ごと(し)   Ⓚ0183

as, like, as if, such as
> 如上の じょじょうの above-mentioned
> 如実に にょじつに truly, realistically
> 如是 にょぜ thus, so, like this
> 如来 にょらい Buddha
> 不如意の ふにょいの contrary to one's wishes, hard up, pressed for money

通 ▷as
ツウ ツ とお(る) とお(り)
-どお(り) とお(す) とお(し) -どお(し)
かよ(う)   Ⓚ2678

[also suffix] **as, according to, in accordance with**
> 型通り かたどおり formally, in due form
> 注文通り ちゅうもんどおり as ordered

云 ▷such
ウン い(う)   Ⓚ1692

such, so
> 云云 うんぬん so and so, such and such, and so forth, et cetera
> 云云する うんぬんする say something or other, comment, criticize
> 云爾 うんじ(=しかいう) [archaic] such as

simple →PLAIN AND SIMPLE

sing

唱　　歌

唱 ▷sing
ショウ とな(える)   Ⓚ0418

[original meaning] **sing, chant**
> 合唱 がっしょう chorus
> 独唱する どくしょうする sing solo

歌 ▷sing
カ うた うた(う)   Ⓚ1621

[original meaning] **sing**
> 歌手 かしゅ singer
> 歌劇 かげき opera
> 歌舞伎 かぶき kabuki

sink

没　沈　潜　溺

没 ▷sink
ボツ　　　　　　　　　　　　　Ⓚ0230

[original meaning] **sink into the water, submerge; sink below the horizon**
- 水没する すいぼつする sink, submerge
- 沈没する ちんぼつする sink, go to the bottom
- 日没 にちぼつ sunset

沈 ▷sink
チン　しず(む)　しず(める)　　　Ⓚ0231

- ⓐ **sink, submerge, go down**
- ⓑ [original meaning] **(cause to) sink, submerge**
- ⓐ 沈没する ちんぼつする sink, go to the bottom
- 沈下 ちんか subsidence, sinking
- 沈澱 ちんでん precipitation, settlement
- 沈滞 ちんたい stagnation, dullness
- 浮沈 ふちん rise and fall, ebb and flow; ups and downs
- ⓑ 撃沈する げきちんする attack and sink a ship

潜 ▷submerge
セン　ひそ(む)　もぐ(る)　　　Ⓚ0680

[original meaning] **submerge, dive**
- 潜水 せんすい diving
- 潜水艦 せんすいかん submarine
- 潜航 せんこう submarine voyage, underwater navigation

溺 ▷drown
デキ　おぼ(れる)　　　　　　Ⓚ0599

[original meaning] **drown**
- 溺死 できし death by drowning
- 溺水 できすい drowning

sit

座　坐　居

座 ▷sit
ザ　すわ(る)　　　　　　　　Ⓚ2686

sit, take a seat, sit down
- 座臥 ざが sitting and lying down
- 座禅 ざぜん Zen meditation
- 座礁する ざしょうする run aground, be stranded
- 正座する せいざする sit upright [straight]

坐 ▷sit
ザ　すわ(る)　　　　　　　　Ⓚ2970

[original meaning] **sit, take a seat, sit down**
- 坐像 ざぞう sedentary statue [image]
- 坐禅 ざぜん Zen meditation
- 坐礁する ざしょうする run aground, be stranded
- 正坐する せいざする sit upright [straight]
- 行住坐臥 ぎょうじゅうざが the four cardinal behaviors (walking, stopping [standing], sitting and lying); daily life

居 ▷sit
キョ　い(る)　-い　お(る)　　　Ⓚ2653

[original meaning] **sit**
- 起居 ききょ one's daily life

situations →STATES AND SITUATIONS

six

六　　　陸

六 ▷six
ロク　む　む(つ)　むっ(つ)　むい　　Ⓚ1710

six, sixth
- 六百 ろっぴゃく 600
- 六時 ろくじ six o'clock
- 六月 ろくがつ June
- 六角 ろっかく hexagon
- 六法 ろっぽう the six codes (of law), statute book
- 六書 りくしょ the six classes of Chinese characters; Hexateuch
- 第六感 だいろっかん the sixth sense, intuition

陸 ▷six (in legal documents)
リク　　　　　　　　　　　　Ⓚ0496

six—used in legal documents and checks
- 陸萬円也 ろくまんえんなり sum of 60,000 yen

size

寸　　　大

寸 ▷measurement
スン　　　　　　　　　　　　Ⓚ2541

measurement, measure, dimensions, length, size
- 寸法 すんぽう measurements, size; plan
- 原寸 げんすん full [actual] size
- 採寸 さいすん taking measurements

大 ▷**size**
ダイ タイ おお- おお(きい)
おお(いに)　　　　　　　　Ⓚ2882

[suffix] **size**
卵大の たまごだいの egg-sized
20cm×20cm大 にじゅっせんちかけるにじゅっせんちだい 20 cm by 20 cm in size

skill

力　能　技　倆　腕　才

力 ▷**power**
リョク リキ ちから　　　　　Ⓚ2860

[also suffix] (ability to do or act) **power, ability, faculty**
能力 のうりょく ability, capacity, faculty
実力 じつりょく real ability [power], capability, competence
理解力 りかいりょく comprehensive faculty, power to understand
戦力 せんりょく war potentials, fighting power
学力 がくりょく scholarship, scholastic ability
魅力 みりょく charm, glamour, appeal
効力 こうりょく effect, efficacy; effect (as of a law), validity
弾力 だんりょく elasticity, spring
極力 きょくりょく to the utmost, to the best of one's power

能 ▷**ability**
ノウ　　　　　　　　　　　Ⓚ1207

ability, capability
能力 のうりょく ability, capacity, faculty
技能 ぎのう skill, ability, capacity
芸能 げいのう public entertainment
才能 さいのう talent, ability
万能 ばんのう omnipotence
有能な ゆうのうな able, competent
知能 ちのう intelligence, mental capacity
本能 ほんのう instinct

技 ▷**skill**
ギ わざ　　　　　　　　　　Ⓚ0221

[sometimes also 伎] [original meaning] **skill, ability, craft, art**
技術 ぎじゅつ technique, art, skill; technology
技能 ぎのう skill, ability, capacity
技師 ぎし engineer, technician
技量 ぎりょう skill, ability, capacity
技巧 ぎこう art, craftsmanship, technical skill; trick
競技 きょうぎ match, contest, game; sporting event
演技 えんぎ acting, performance

特技 とくぎ one's special ability [talent], one's special skill [art]
実技 じつぎ practical technique [skill]

倆 ▷**skill**
リョウ

[now usu. 量] **skill**
技倆(=伎倆) ぎりょう skill, ability, capacity

腕 ▷**skill**
ワン うで　　　　　　　　　Ⓚ0919

skill, ability
手腕 しゅわん ability, skill
才腕 さいわん ability, skill
敏腕 びんわん ability, capability

才 ▷**talent**
サイ　　　　　　　　　　　Ⓚ2880

talent, natural ability, gift, genius
才能 さいのう talent, ability
才気 さいき talent
才知 さいち wit and intelligence
英才 えいさい [formerly also 穎才] talent, genius; gifted person, talented person
詩才 しさい poetic genius
商才 しょうさい business ability [talent]

skillful

巧　　　能

巧 ▷**skillful**
コウ たく(み)　　　　　　　Ⓚ0166

skillful, ingenious, clever
巧妙な こうみょうな skillful, ingenious, clever
巧拙 こうせつ skill, dexterity, workmanship
巧者 こうしゃ skillful [ingenious] person
巧言 こうげん flattery
技巧 ぎこう art, craftsmanship, technical skill; trick
精巧な せいこうな elaborate, exquisite, ingenious
俐巧(=利口)な りこうな clever, bright, sharp, shrewd

能 ▷**able**
ノウ　　　　　　　　　　　Ⓚ1207

able, skilled, skillful
能筆 のうひつ skillful penmanship
能弁 のうべん eloquence, oratory
能吏 のうり able official

skin →KINDS OF SKIN

sky

空 昊 穹 天 宙

空 ▷sky
クウ そら あ(く) あ(き) あ(ける) から むな(しい)　　　Ⓚ1913

ⓐ **sky, heavens, the air, space**
ⓑ (space where aircraft operate) **air, airspace**
ⓐ 空中で くうちゅうで in the air [sky]
空間 くうかん space, room
天空 てんくう sky, air, firmament, heavens
虚空 こくう empty space, sky
ⓑ 東京上空 とうきょうじょうくう the skies of Tokyo
航空 こうくう aviation, aerial navigation
制空権 せいくうけん command of the air

昊 ▷sky
コウ　　　Ⓚ2137

sky
昊天 こうてん summer sky; wide sky, the heavens
蒼昊 そうこう [rare] blue sky

穹 ▷sky
キュウ　　　Ⓚ1914

sky
蒼穹 そうきゅう blue sky

天 ▷heaven
テン あめ あま-　　　Ⓚ2898

heaven(s), sky, celestial sphere
天地 てんち heaven and earth; top and bottom
天空 てんくう sky, air, firmament, heavens
天体 てんたい heavenly body
天文学 てんもんがく astronomy
天下 てんか the whole country [empire], the world
天衣無縫 てんいむほう perfect beauty with no trace of artifice
衝天 しょうてん high spirits

宙 ▷midair
チュウ　　　Ⓚ1907

(point above the ground) **midair, air, space**
宙乗り ちゅうのり aerial stunts
宙吊り ちゅうづり hanging in midair
宙返り ちゅうがえり somersault

sleep

眠 睡 寝

眠 ▷sleep
ミン ねむ(る) ねむ(い)　　　Ⓚ106

[original meaning] **sleep**
睡眠 すいみん sleep, slumber
催眠術 さいみんじゅつ hypnotism, mesmerism
不眠 ふみん sleeplessness, insomnia
冬眠 とうみん hibernation ("winter sleep")
安眠 あんみん quiet sleep, peaceful slumber
永眠 えいみん eternal sleep, death

睡 ▷sleep
スイ　　　Ⓚ110

ⓐ [original meaning] **sleep, doze**
ⓑ **sleep, nap**
ⓐ 睡眠 すいみん sleep, slumber
睡魔 すいま sleepiness, drowsiness
睡蓮 すいれん water lily
熟睡 じゅくすい sound sleep
昏睡状態 こんすいじょうたい comatose state
ⓐⓑ 仮睡 かすい nap, doze
午睡 ごすい nap, afternoon sleep
一睡もしなかった いっすいもしなかった had a sleepless night

寝 ▷go to sleep
シン ね(る) ね(かす) ね(かせる)　　　Ⓚ203

[original meaning]
ⓐ **go to sleep [bed], sleep**
ⓑ **going to bed, sleeping, sleep**
ⓐ 寝台 しんだい bed, sleeping berth
寝室 しんしつ bedroom
寝具 しんぐ bedclothes, bedding
不寝番 ふしんばん night watch
ⓑ 寝食 しんしょく eating and sleeping
就寝する しゅうしんする go to bed

slips →LABELS AND SLIPS

slow

徐 遅 緩 慢

徐 ▷slowly
ジョ　　　Ⓚ037

slowly, gently, quietly
徐徐に じょじょに slowly, gradually

徐行する じょこうする go slowly
緩徐楽章 かんじょがくしょう adagio

遅 ▷**slow**
チ おく(れる) おく(らす) おそ(い)　Ⓚ2700

[original meaning] (not fast) **slow, tardy**
　遅遅たる ちちたる slow, lagging, tardy
　遅脈 ちみゃく slow pulse

緩 ▷**slack**
カン ゆる(い) ゆる(やか) ゆる(む)
ゆる(める)　Ⓚ1272

(not fast or lively) **slack, slow, sluggish**
　緩慢な かんまんな slack, slow-moving, dull, inactive
　緩球 かんきゅう slow ball
　緩行 かんこう going slowly
　緩急 かんきゅう fast and slow motion, high and low speed; emergency
　緩下剤 かんげざい laxative

慢 ▷**sluggish**
マン　Ⓚ0625

(slow to act) **sluggish, slow, dragging**
　慢性の まんせいの chronic
　緩慢な かんまんな slack, slow-moving, dull, inactive

small and tiny

小 豆 微 細 寸

小 ▷**small**
ショウ ちい(さい) こ- お-　Ⓚ0002

[also prefix] [original meaning] (less in size, extent or quantity) **small, little, minor, short, tiny, miniature, minute**
　小国 しょうこく small nation, lesser power
　小説 しょうせつ novel, story, fiction
　小史 しょうし short history
　小額 しょうがく small denomination
　小アジア しょうあじあ Asia Minor
　小規模 しょうきぼ small-scale
　小東京 しょうとうきょう miniature Tokyo, epitome of Tokyo
　小数 しょうすう decimal (fraction)
　大小 だいしょう large and small; size; long and short swords
　縮小する しゅくしょうする reduce, curtail, cut down
　中小企業 ちゅうしょうきぎょう small-to-medium-sized enterprises
　最小 さいしょう the smallest, minimum

豆 ▷**miniature**
トウ ズ まめ-　Ⓚ1700

[prefix] **miniature, midget, mini-, small**
　豆電球 まめでんきゅう miniature light bulb
　豆台風 まめたいふう small typhoon

微 ▷**slight**
ビ かす(か)　Ⓚ0587

(of very small size) **slight, minute, small, tiny, microscopic, fine**
　微細な びさいな minute, fine; detailed, minute; delicate, subtle
　微生物 びせいぶつ microorganism
　微粒子 びりゅうし (minute) particle, corpuscle
　微調整 びちょうせい minute adjustment; fine tuning
　顕微鏡 けんびきょう microscope

細 ▷**minute**
サイ ほそ(い) ほそ(る) こま(か)
こま(かい)　Ⓚ1220

(very small) **minute, fine, small, microscopic**
　細胞 さいぼう cell
　細菌 さいきん bacteria, germ, microbe
　細分する さいぶんする subdivide, fractionate
　微細な びさいな minute, fine; detailed, minute; delicate, subtle

寸 ▷**a bit of**
スン　Ⓚ2541

(of small size) **a bit of, very little, small**
　寸劇 すんげき skit, short play
　寸描 すんびょう thumbnail [brief] sketch
　寸断する すんだんする cut into pieces [shreds]

small numbers

一 十 廿 二 三 四
五 六 七 八 九

一 ▷**one**
イチ イツ ひと- ひと(つ)　Ⓚ2850
see also →ONE

[also prefix] [original meaning] **one, unity, first**
　一方 いっぽう one side, one hand; a party, the other party; in the meantime; only
　一部 いちぶ part, portion, section; a copy (of a book)
　一緒に いっしょに together; at the same time; in a lump

一番 いちばん first, first place; first verse; most, best; a game, a round, a bout; a number, a piece
一千 いっせん 1000
一体 いったい one body; a style, a form; (why, what) on earth, (what, why) in the world
一家 いっか family, household; one's family; style (of established reputation)
一応(=一往) いちおう once; in outline; tentatively; for the time being
一月 いちがつ January
一瞬 いっしゅん instant, moment
一生懸命(=一所懸命)に いっしょうけんめい(=いっしょけんめい)に for life, with all one's might
一大事 いちだいじ matter of great importance
一一 いちいち one by one; in detail
一層 いっそう more, even more, all the more
一度に いちどに at a time, all at once
一部分 いちぶぶん part, portion, section
一円 いちえん the entire region [district]; one yen
第一 だいいち the first, number one; the best; to begin with, above everything else
唯一の ゆいいつの the only, the sole

十 ▷ten
ジュウ ジッ- ジュッ- とお と Ⓚ2855
see also →TEN

ten, tenth
十時 じゅうじ ten o'clock
七十 しちじゅう 70
第十 だいじゅう tenth
二十 にじゅう [sometimes also 廿] 20

廿 ▷twenty
ジュウ ニュウ にじゅう Ⓚ2900

[usu. 二十] **twenty**
廿五日 にじゅうごにち 25 days; 25th of the month

一 ▷two
ニ ふた ふた(つ) Ⓚ1688
see also →TWO

[original meaning] **two, second**
二百 にひゃく 200
二月 にがつ February
二次 にじ second, secondary
二塁 にるい second base
二階 にかい second floor; upstairs

三 ▷three
サン み み(つ) みっ(つ) Ⓚ1689
see also →THREE

[original meaning] **three, third**
三千 さんぜん 3000
三角 さんかく triangle
三角形 さんかくけい triangle

三人称 さんにんしょう *gram* third person
三塁 さんるい third base
三分する さんぶんする trisect
三脚 さんきゃく tripod
三流の さんりゅうの third-rate
七五三 しちごさん the lucky numbers; gala day for children of three, five and seven
第三 だいさん third

四 ▷four
シ よ よ(つ) よっ(つ) よん Ⓚ262
four
四角 しかく square, quadrilateral
四月 しがつ April
四球 しきゅう base on balls
四季 しき the four seasons
四角い しかくい square, four-sided
十四 じゅうし 14

五 ▷five
ゴ いつ いつ(つ) Ⓚ289
see also →FIVE

[original meaning] **five, fifth**
五百 ごひゃく 500
五十音 ごじゅうおん Japanese syllabary
五感 ごかん the five senses
五指 ごし the five fingers
五分 ごぶ half, 50 percent
五分五分 ごぶごぶ evenly matched; tie
五輪旗 ごりんき five-ringed Olympic flag
五目飯 ごもくめし Japanese pilaf
五月 ごがつ May
五階 ごかい fifth floor

六 ▷six
ロク む む(つ) むっ(つ) むい Ⓚ171
see also →SIX

six, sixth
六百 ろっぴゃく 600
六時 ろくじ six o'clock
六月 ろくがつ June
六角 ろっかく hexagon
六法 ろっぽう the six codes (of law), statute book
六書 りくしょ the six classes of Chinese characters; Hexateuch
第六感 だいろっかん the sixth sense, intuition

七 ▷seven
シチ なな なな(つ) なの Ⓚ285
seven, seventh
七曜表 しちようひょう calendar
七月 しちがつ July
十七日 じゅうしちにち 17 days; 17th of the month

八 ▷eight
ハチ や や(つ) やっ(つ) よう　　Ⓚ2536

eight, eighth
八十 はちじゅう 80
八面 はちめん eight faces
八苦 はっく the eight sufferings (of Buddhism)
尺八 しゃくはち bamboo flute

九 ▷nine
キュウ ク ここの ここの(つ)　　Ⓚ2858
see also →NINE

nine
九百 きゅうひゃく 900
九回 きゅうかい nine times
九星術 きゅうせいじゅつ astrology
九月 くがつ September
九人 きゅうにん nine people

small water masses
滴　雫　泡　沫

滴 ▷drop
テキ しずく したた(る)　　Ⓚ0640

[original meaning] (liquid globule) **drop**
水滴 すいてき water drop
雨滴 うてき raindrops

雫 ▷drop
ダ しずく　　Ⓚ2405

(liquid globule) **drop**
露の雫 つゆのしずく dewdrop

泡 ▷bubble
ホウ あわ　　Ⓚ0296

[original meaning] **bubble, foam**
泡沫 ほうまつ bubble, foam, froth
泡沫会社 ほうまつがいしゃ bubble company, fly-by-night concern
発泡 はっぽう foaming, effervescence
気泡 きほう air bubble, bubble
水泡 すいほう bubble, foam

沫 ▷bubble
マツ あわ　　Ⓚ0301

bubble, foam
泡沫 ほうまつ bubble, foam, froth
泡沫会社 ほうまつがいしゃ bubble company, fly-by-night concern

smell and fragrance
気匂臭香馨芳薫郁

気 ▷smell
キ ケ　　Ⓚ2751

smell, odor
香気 こうき fragrance, perfume, scent
臭気 しゅうき offensive [odious] smell, bad [foul] odor, stench

匂 ▷smell
にお(う) にお(い) にお(わせる) にお(わす)　　Ⓚ2548

ⓐ **smell, scent, fragrance, aroma**
ⓑ **flavor, touch (of something agreeable)**
a 匂い袋 においぶくろ sachet
b 文学的な匂い ぶんがくてきなにおい literary flavor

臭 ▷bad smell
シュウ くさ(い) にお(う) にお(い)　　Ⓚ2289

ⓐ **bad smell, stink**
ⓑ [also suffix] **smell, odor**
ⓒ **smelly, stinking**
a 臭味 しゅうみ bad smell, offensive odor; a smack of
　体臭 たいしゅう body smell
　悪臭 あくしゅう offensive [foul] odor, stench
　防臭 ぼうしゅう deodorization
　異臭 いしゅう offensive smell, stink
b 臭覚 しゅうかく sense of smell
　刺激臭 しげきしゅう irritating smell [odor], irritant odor
c 臭気 しゅうき offensive [odious] smell, bad [foul] odor, stench

香 ▷sweet smell
コウ キョウ か かお(り) かお(る)　　Ⓚ2225

ⓐ [original meaning] **sweet smell, pleasant odor, perfume, fragrance, aroma, scent**
ⓑ **sweet-smelling, fragrant**
a 香ばしい こうばしい nice-smelling, fragrant
　芳香 ほうこう perfume, fragrance, aroma
b 香水 こうすい perfume
　香気 こうき fragrance, perfume, scent
　香油 こうゆ pomade, balm, perfumed oil
　新香 しんこう pickles

馨 ▷perfume
ケイ キョウ　　Ⓚ2505

[original meaning, now archaic] **perfume, fragrance, aroma**

馨香 けいこう(=けいきょう) perfume, fragrance, aroma; honor, fame

芳 ▷fragrant
ホウ かんば(しい)　　　Ⓚ1893

fragrant, aromatic, balmy
芳香 ほうこう perfume, fragrance, aroma
芳気 ほうき fragrant scent
芳草 ほうそう fragrant herb
芳潤な ほうじゅんな aromatic, rich

薫 ▷balmy
クン かお(る)　　　Ⓚ2094

ⓐ [original meaning] **balmy, sweet-smelling, fragrant**
ⓑ **fragrance, sweet smell**
a 薫風 くんぷう balmy breeze
　薫煙 くんえん fragrant smoke
b 余薫 よくん lingering fragrance

郁 ▷aromatic
イク　　　Ⓚ1183

aromatic, rich in aroma, fragrant, sweet-smelling
馥郁たる ふくいくたる sweet-smelling, fragrant

smooth
流　暢　滑

流 ▷flowing
リュウ ル なが(れる) なが(れ)
なが(す)　　　Ⓚ0400

flowing, fluent
流暢に りゅうちょうに fluently, flowingly, smoothly
流麗な りゅうれいな fluent, flowing

暢 ▷fluent
チョウ　　　Ⓚ1134

fluent(ly), smooth(ly), free(ly), with ease
暢達 ちょうたつ fluency, facileness
流暢な りゅうちょうな fluent, flowing, smooth

滑 ▷smooth
カツ コツ すべ(る) なめ(らか)　　　Ⓚ0603

smooth
滑脱 かつだつ adaptation to circumstances
滑剤 かつざい lubricant
円滑な えんかつな smooth, harmonious
潤滑 じゅんかつ lubrication

snake
蛇　巳

蛇 ▷snake
ジャ ダ へび　　　Ⓚ123◖

[original meaning] **snake, serpent**
蛇蝎 だかつ snake and scorpion, viper
蛇行する だこうする meander, zigzag
蛇足 だそく superfluity, redundancy
蛇の目 じゃのめ umbrella with a snake's eye pattern; double circle pattern
大蛇 だいじゃ big snake, serpent

巳 ▷the Serpent
シ み　　　Ⓚ287

sixth sign of the Oriental zodiac: **the Serpent**—(time) 9-1 a.m., (direction) SSE, (season) April (of the lunar calendar)
上巳 じょうし March 3rd of the lunar calendar (one of the five annual festivals)

social gatherings
宴　饗　会

宴 ▷banquet
エン　　　Ⓚ196◖

[also suffix] **banquet, feast, dinner party, dinner; entertainment**
宴会 えんかい dinner party, banquet, feast
宴席 えんせき banquet hall, dinner party
招宴 しょうえん invitation to a party; party
披露宴 ひろうえん wedding reception
歓迎宴 かんげいえん welcome party
饗宴 きょうえん banquet, feast, dinner

饗 ▷banquet
キョウ　　　Ⓚ252◖

[now also 供] [original meaning] **banquet, treat, provide dinner for, entertain**
饗応 きょうおう treat, feast, banquet
饗宴 きょうえん banquet, feast, dinner

会 ▷party
カイ エ あ(う) あ(わせる)　　　Ⓚ1741

[also suffix] **party**
忘年会 ぼうねんかい year-end party ("forget the year party")
晩餐会 ばんさんかい dinner party

society

社 世 公

社 ▷society
シャ やしろ   Ⓚ0745

society, community, the public, the world
- 社会 しゃかい society, the world
- 社会人 しゃかいじん (full-fledged) member of society
- 社会科学 しゃかいかがく social sciences
- 社交 しゃこう social intercourse, society
- 社交的な しゃこうてきな sociable, friendly

世 ▷world
セイ セ よ   Ⓚ2932

(human society) **world, society, community, public**
- 世間 せけん world, society; the public, people
- 世論 せろん(=よろん) public opinion
- 出世 しゅっせ success in life; promotion

公 ▷public
コウ おおやけ   Ⓚ1715

the public, society, community
- 公共 こうきょう public society, community
- 公会堂 こうかいどう town [public] hall
- 公衆 こうしゅう the public

soft

柔 軟 塑

柔 ▷soft (supple and yielding)
ジュウ ニュウ やわ(らか)
やわ(らかい)   Ⓚ1797

[original meaning] (supple and yielding) **soft, tender, pliant**
- 柔毛 じゅうもう soft hair
- 柔軟な じゅうなんな soft, pliable, flexible

軟 ▷soft (not hard)
ナン やわ(らか) やわ(らかい)   Ⓚ1345

[original meaning] (not hard) **soft**
- 軟化 なんか softening; weakening (of the market)
- 軟骨 なんこつ cartilage
- 柔軟な じゅうなんな soft, pliable, flexible
- 硬軟 こうなん hardness

塑 ▷plastic
ソ   Ⓚ2475

phys **plastic**
- 塑性変形 そせいへんけい plastic deformation
- 塑弾性 そだんせい plasto-elasticity
- 可塑材 かそざい plastic material

soil →LAND AND SOIL

soldiers and warriors

兵 卒 士 武 侍

兵 ▷soldier
ヘイ ヒョウ   Ⓚ2207

- **ⓐ** [also suffix] **soldier, private, rank and file**
- **ⓑ** [suffix] (rank of) **private**
- a 兵士 へいし soldier
- 兵卒 へいそつ private, common soldier
- 兵隊 へいたい soldier; troops
- 兵舎 へいしゃ barracks
- カナダ兵 かなだへい Canadian soldier
- 騎兵 きへい cavalry soldier, cavalry
- b 上等兵 じょうとうへい private first class

卒 ▷private
ソツ   Ⓚ1769

[original meaning] **private, common soldier; pawn (in Chinese chess)**
- 兵卒 へいそつ private, common soldier

士 ▷military man
シ   Ⓚ2877

- **ⓐ** **military man, warrior, soldier, knight; officer**
- **ⓑ** warrior class of feudal Japan: **samurai, retainer**
- **ⓒ** **private (military rank of Japanese Self-Defense Forces)**
- a 士官 しかん officer
- 士気 しき fighting spirit
- 兵士 へいし soldier
- 騎士 きし knight
- 武士 ぶし samurai, warrior
- b 士族 しぞく descendant of samurai
- 士分 しぶん status of samurai
- 士農工商 しのうこうしょう warriors, farmers, artisans and tradesmen (the four classes of Tokugawa Japan)
- 四十七士 しじゅうしちし Forty-Seven Loyal Retainers
- c 一等陸士 いっとうりくし private first class

武 ▷warrior
ブム   Ⓚ2764

warrior, samurai; military man, officer

武士 ぶし samurai, warrior
武者 むしゃ warrior, soldier
武官 ぶかん military officer

侍 ▷samurai
ジ さむらい   Ⓚ0066

[also suffix] **samurai, warrior; man of resolution and ability**

若侍 わかざむらい young samurai
犬侍 いぬざむらい shameless [depraved] samurai
田舎侍 いなかざむらい country samurai

solidify and coagulate
固 凝 結 凍

固 ▷solidify
コ かた(める) かた(まる) かた(まり) かた(い)   Ⓚ2658

solidify, harden

固化 こか solidification
凝固 ぎょうこ solidification, coagulation, congelation

凝 ▷congeal
ギョウ こ(る) こ(らす)   Ⓚ0154

congeal, coagulate, solidify

凝結する ぎょうけつする congeal, coagulate, solidify
凝固する ぎょうこする solidify, coagulate, congeal
凝着 ぎょうちゃく adhesion
凝血 ぎょうけつ blood clot
凝脂 ぎょうし solidified oil
凝乳 ぎょうにゅう curd, curdled milk
凝縮 ぎょうしゅく condensation

結 ▷form into a mass
ケツ むす(ぶ) ゆ(う) ゆ(わえる)   Ⓚ1235

form into a mass, congeal, coagulate

結晶 けっしょう crystallization, crystal; grain; fruit(s)
結核 けっかく tuberculosis
結集 けっしゅう concentration, regimentation
凍結 とうけつ freezing
凝結する ぎょうけつする congeal, coagulate, solidify

凍 ▷freeze
トウ こお(る) こご(える)   Ⓚ011

(turn solid because of cold) **freeze, congeal**

凍結 とうけつ freezing
冷凍 れいとう freezing, cold storage
不凍港 ふとうこう ice-free port

some
幾 何 数 或

幾 ▷some
キ いく- いく(つ) いく(ら)   Ⓚ299

(being of indefinite number or quantity) **some, several**

幾夜も いくよも for several nights
幾分 いくぶん partially, somewhat, in a way
幾千と云う人 いくせんというひと thousands of people

何 ▷several
カ なに- なん-   Ⓚ004

several, some, odd

何十 なんじゅう several tens
何百 なんびゃく several hundred, hundreds
何千 なんぜん several thousand, thousands
何時間 なんじかん several hours

数 ▷several
スウ ス かず かぞ(える)   Ⓚ159

[prefix] (a small number, esp. between three and five) **several**

数回 すうかい several times
数年間 すうねんかん several years
十数頁 じゅうすうページ ten odd pages

或 ▷a certain
ワク あ(る) ある(いは)   Ⓚ276
see also →A CERTAIN

a certain, some

或る日 あるひ a certain day, one day
或る程度 あるていど a certain extent, some extent
或る種 あるしゅ certain, some kind, some sort
或る人 あるひと someone
と或る とある a certain

songs →MUSIC AND SONGS

sorrow

哀　　憂

哀
▷**sorrow**
アイ　あわ(れ)　あわ(れむ)
かな(しい)
Ⓚ1781

sorrow, grief, sadness, pathos
哀歓 あいかん joys and sorrows
喜怒哀楽 きどあいらく joy and anger; emotion

憂
▷**grief**
ユウ　うれ(える)　うれ(い)　う(い)
う(き)
Ⓚ1842

grief, sorrow
憂鬱 ゆううつ melancholy, gloom
憂愁 ゆうしゅう melancholy, gloom, grief

ound →KINDS OF SOUND

sour substances

酢　　酸

酢
▷**vinegar**
サク　す
Ⓚ1373

[formerly also 醋] [original meaning] **vinegar**
酢酸 さくさん acetic acid

酸
▷**acid**
サン　す(い)
Ⓚ1415

[also suffix] **acid, acidity**
酸性 さんせい acidity
酸基 さんき acid radical
硫酸 りゅうさん sulfuric acid
塩酸 えんさん hydrochloric acid
胃酸 いさん stomach acid
乳酸 にゅうさん lactic acid
アミノ酸 あみのさん amino acid

pace →UNIVERSE AND SPACE

pacecraft →AIRCRAFT AND SPACECRAFT

parse →RARE AND SPARSE

speak and say

言 語 談 喋 諷 謂 云
曰 話 口 申 述 陳 弁

言
▷**say**
ゲン　ゴン　い(う)　こと
Ⓚ1698

[original meaning] **say, speak, talk**
言明 げんめい declaration, announcement
言及する げんきゅうする refer to, mention, touch upon
発言する はつげんする speak, utter
宣言 せんげん declaration, proclamation
予言する よげんする predict, forecast
断言する だんげんする assert, declare
提言 ていげん proposal, suggestion
過言 かごん saying too much, exaggeration
他言する たごんする tell to others, divulge

語
▷**tell**
ゴ　かた(る)　かた(らう)
Ⓚ1402

ⓐ (express in words) **tell, talk, speak**
ⓑ **tell (a story), narrate, relate**
a 真実を語る しんじつをかたる speak the truth
b 語り手 かたりて narrator, storyteller
語り伝える かたりつたえる pass on (a story or tradition)
語り合う かたりあう talk together, have a chat with
語り かたり narrative
語り草(=語り種) かたりぐさ story, topic
物語 ものがたり story, tale, legend

談
▷**talk**
ダン
Ⓚ1419

[original meaning] **talk, converse, speak, confer, discuss**
談合 だんごう consultation, negotiation
談話 だんわ talk, conversation
会談 かいだん conversation, talk, conference
相談する そうだんする consult, talk over, confer
対談する たいだんする talk with, converse; negotiate in person with

喋
▷**talk**
チョウ　しゃべ(る)
Ⓚ0502

talk, chat, chatter
喋喋喃喃 ちょうちょうなんなん billing and cooing

諷
▷**insinuate**
フウ

[now usu. 風] **insinuate, hint, satirize**

諷刺 ふうし satire, sarcasm
諷喩 ふうゆ hint, insinuation, allegory

謂 ▷refer to
イ い(う) いわ(れ) Ⓚ1441

[usu. 言う] **refer to, call**—used chiefly in certain set expressions

謂わば いわば as it were, so to call it
これを音素と謂う これをおんそという To this is given the term "phoneme"
ここで船とは宇宙船を謂う ここでふねとはうちゅうせんをいう By "ship" here is meant a spaceship

云 ▷say
ウン い(う) Ⓚ1692

say, speak

云為 うんい words and deeds, sayings and doings

曰 ▷say that
エツ いわ(く) のたま(わく)

literary **say that…**

曰く言い難し いわくいいがたし It is hard to say

話 ▷speak
ワ はな(す) はなし Ⓚ1388

[original meaning] **speak, talk, converse**

話者 わしゃ speaker, narrator
会話 かいわ conversation
対話 たいわ dialogue, conversation
電話 でんわ telephone; phone call
談話 だんわ talk, conversation

口 ▷give mouth to
コウ ク くち Ⓚ2865

give mouth to, mouth, speak, talk

口論 こうろん argument
口語 こうご colloquial language
口外する こうがいする tell, divulge
口実 こうじつ excuse, pretext, pretense
口調 くちょう tone, expression
口説く くどく persuade; seduce
口述 こうじゅつ oral statement, dictation

申 ▷speak humbly
シン もう(す) もう(し)- Ⓚ2942
see also →SPEAK HUMBLY

speak humbly, say, tell, speak of, talk about

主人もそう申しております しゅじんもそうもうしております My husband also says so

述 ▷state
ジュツ の(べる) Ⓚ2648

state orally, expound, mention, declare

述懐 じゅっかい effusion of one's thoughts (and feelings), reminiscence
述語 じゅつご predicate
供述 きょうじゅつ testimony, statement; confession
口述する こうじゅつする state orally, dictate
陳述 ちんじゅつ statement, declaration
叙述 じょじゅつ description, depiction
詳述 しょうじゅつ (detailed) expatiation, full account
前述の通り ぜんじゅつのとおり as stated [mentioned] above

陳 ▷set forth
チン Ⓚ049?

set forth, state, explain, declare

陳情 ちんじょう petition, appeal
陳述する ちんじゅつする state, set forth, declare, expound
陳謝 ちんしゃ apology
開陳する かいちんする state, express (one's opinion)

弁 ▷speak eloquently
ベン Ⓚ173?

speak eloquently, orate, talk

弁士 べんし speaker, talker; film interpreter
雄弁 ゆうべん eloquence, fluency
熱弁 ねつべん fervent speech, passionate eloquence
能弁家 のうべんか eloquent speaker, orator
答弁する とうべんする reply, answer; defend oneself

speak humbly
申　　啓

申 ▷speak humbly
シン もう(す) もう(し)- Ⓚ2942

speak humbly, say, tell, speak of, talk about

主人もそう申しております しゅじんもそうもうしております My husband also says so

啓 ▷address respectfully
ケイ Ⓚ240?

address respectfully—used esp. in polite salutations

啓上する けいじょうする speak respectfully
拝啓 はいけい Dear Sir, Dear Madam
謹啓 きんけい Dear Sirs, Gentlemen

独特 どくとく peculiarity, uniqueness

speak in public
講　演

 ▷lecture
コウ ⒦1463

lecture, speak in public
　講演 こうえん lecture
　講師 こうし speaker, lecturer
　講堂 こうどう lecture hall, auditorium
　講座 こうざ lectureship, (professor's) chair; course of study
　講壇 こうだん lecture platform
　講読する こうどくする read and explain

演 ▷make a speech
エン ⒦0630

ⓐ **make a speech, lecture, expound**
ⓑ **speech, lecture**
ⓐ 演説 えんぜつ (public) speech, address, oration
　講演 こうえん lecture
ⓑ 演題 えんだい subject of a speech, speech title

special
特　別　殊　専

特 ▷special (distinct)
トク ⒦0852

(distinct among others) **special, peculiar, unique, exclusive**
　特別の とくべつの special, particular; extraordinary
　特色 とくしょく characteristic
　特徴 とくちょう distinctive feature, characteristic
　特価 とっか special price, bargain price
　特集 とくしゅう special edition
　特許 とっきょ patent; special permission; concession
　特権 とっけん privilege, exclusive right
　特使 とくし special envoy [messenger]
　特定の とくていの specific, particular
　特殊な とくしゅな special, unique
　特急 とっきゅう super-express
　特大 とくだい extra large, oversize
　特有の とくゆうの characteristic (of); special, peculiar
　特異な とくいな peculiar, unique
　特産 とくさん special product, specialty
　特訓 とっくん special [intensive] training, crash course

別 ▷special (distinct)
ベツ わか(れる) ⒦1032

(distinct among others) **special, particular**
　別段の べつだんの particular, special
　別格 べっかく extra status
　特別の とくべつの special, particular; extraordinary
　格別な かくべつな particular, exceptional

殊 ▷special (exceptional)
シュ こと ⒦0850

(exceptional) **special, distinguished, unusual, above others**
　殊勲 しゅくん meritorious deeds, distinguished service
　殊勝な しゅしょうな laudable, praiseworthy
　殊遇 しゅぐう special favor
　特殊な とくしゅな special, unique

専 ▷exclusive
セン もっぱ(ら) ⒦2297

[original meaning] **exclusive, special, specialized**
　専用 せんよう exclusive use, private use
　専攻する せんこうする major in, specialize in
　専門 せんもん specialty, profession
　専念 せんねん close attention, concentration
　専売 せんばい monopoly

speech
言　談　舌　口

 ▷speech
ゲン ゴン い(う) こと ⒦1698

speech, words, saying
　言語 げんご language, speech, words
　言論 げんろん speech, discussion
　言語道断な ごんごどうだんな inexcusable, outrageous, absurd
　証言 しょうげん testimony, verbal evidence
　格言 かくげん maxim, proverb
　方言 ほうげん dialect
　狂言 きょうげん noh farce, comic interlude in a noh drama; kabuki play; sham, put-up job
　無言 むごん silence, muteness

談 ▷talk
ダン ⒦1419

[also suffix] **talk, conversation**
　懇談 こんだん familiar talk [chat]
　座談会 ざだんかい round-table talk, symposium

冗談 じょうだん joke
政談 せいだん political talk
車中談 しゃちゅうだん informal talk given (as by a
    politician) aboard a train

舌 ▷tongue
ゼツ した   Ⓚ1871

(manner of speech) **tongue, speech, language, words**
舌戦 ぜっせん war of words
舌鋒 ぜっぽう (sharp) tongue
弁舌 べんぜつ speech
毒舌 どくぜつ wicked tongue, abusive language,
    blistering remarks
饒舌 じょうぜつ garrulity, loquacity
筆舌に尽くし難い ひつぜつにつくしがたい be
    beyond description

口 ▷mouth
コウ ク くち   Ⓚ2865

(expression in words) **mouth, speech**
悪口 あっこう(=わるくち) slander, abuse, foul
    language
異口同音に いくどうおんに with one voice, unani-
    mously
利口(=悧巧)な りこうな clever, bright, sharp,
    shrewd

spherical object
玉 球 丸 鞠 毬

玉 ▷spherical object
ギョク たま -だま   Ⓚ2919

various spherical objects, as:
ⓐ **ball, globe; lump of noodles; egg; lens**
ⓑ *slang* **testicles**
a 玉突き たまつき billiards; serial collisions (of cars)
玉子 たまご [also 卵] egg
目玉 めだま eyeball; loss leader (of merchandise)
鉄砲玉(=鉄砲弾) てっぽうだま gunshot, bullet; lost
    [truant] messenger; bull's-eye
b 金玉 きんたま testicles, balls

球 ▷ball
キュウ たま   Ⓚ0880

[original meaning] (spherical body) **ball, globe, sphere**
球体 きゅうたい sphere, globe
球形 きゅうけい globular shape
球根 きゅうこん bulb
地球 ちきゅう the Earth
眼球 がんきゅう eyeball

丸 ▷round body
ガン まる まる(い) まる(める)   Ⓚ288

round body, pellet, ball
丸薬 がんやく pill
一丸となって いちがんとなって in a body [lump]

鞠 ▷ball
キク キュウ クウ まり   Ⓚ160

【キク キュウ クウ】
[rare] **ball**
蹴鞠 しゅうきく ancient football game
【まり】
[also 毬] **ball**
鞠靴 まりぐつ ancient football shoes
鞠突き まりつき ball-bouncing game
蹴鞠 けまり ancient football game

毬 ▷ball
キュウ グ まり いが   Ⓚ277

【キュウ グ】
❶ **ball**
打毬 だきゅう ancient Japanese polo
❷ **ball-shaped object**
毬果 きゅうか cone (of a plant)
【まり】
[also 鞠] **ball**
毬歌 まりうた (children's) handball song

spoons
斗 杓 匕

斗 ▷dipper
ト   Ⓚ255

[original meaning] **dipper, ladle**
漏斗 ろうと funnel ("dipper for leaking")

杓 ▷dipper
シャク

[rarely also 勺] **dipper, ladle, spoon**
杓子 しゃくし dipper, (wooden) ladle
柄杓 ひしゃく ladle, dipper, scoop
茶杓 ちゃしゃく tea scoop

匕 ▷spoon
ヒ

[original meaning, now archaic] **spoon**
匕箸 ひちょ spoon and chopsticks

sports fields
場　庭　野

場 ▷ground(s)
ジョウ ば　　　　　　　　　　　Ⓚ0512

[also suffix] place or open area for conducting activities
such as sports: **ground(s), field, arena, course**
　球場 きゅうじょう baseball ground, ball park
　戦場 せんじょう battlefield, front
　運動場 うんどうじょう(うんどうば) playground,
　　sports field
　ゴルフ場 ごるふじょう golf links, golf course
　競輪場 けいりんじょう cycle racing track [course]

庭 ▷court
テイ にわ　　　　　　　　　　　Ⓚ2684

(sports) **court, tennis court**
　庭球 ていきゅう tennis

野 ▷baseball field
ヤ の　　　　　　　　　　　　　Ⓚ1350

baseball field
　野球 やきゅう baseball
　内野 ないや infield
　外野 がいや outfield; outsiders

spread
散　布　敷　舗　塗　抹　撒

散 ▷scatter
サン ち(る) ち(らす) ち(らかす)
ち(らかる) ち(らばる)　　　　　Ⓚ1518

scatter, disperse, break up
　散乱 さんらん dispersion, scattering
　散発的な さんぱつてきな sporadic
　解散 かいさん breakup, dispersion; dissolution
　拡散 かくさん scattering, diffusion
　分散 ぶんさん dispersion, breakup, divergence;
　　variance
　四散する しさんする scatter (in all directions)
　一目散に いちもくさんに at full [top] speed

布 ▷spread
フ ぬの　　　　　　　　　　　　Ⓚ2566

[also 敷] **spread, lay out, apply**
　塗布する とふする apply (an ointment)
　散布する さんぷ(=さっぷ)する scatter, sprinkle, spray

敷 ▷lay
フ し(く) -し(き)　　　　　　　Ⓚ1653

(spread over a surface) **lay, spread, lay under**
　敷き詰める しきつめる spread all over
　敷物 しきもの carpet, rug
　敷布 しきふ sheet
　敷布団 しきぶとん (Japanese style) mattress
　布団を敷く ふとんをしく make a bed

舗 ▷pave
ホ　　　　　　　　　　　　　　Ⓚ1547

pave, lay
　舗装 ほそう paving
　舗道 ほどう pavement, paved street

塗 ▷apply on a surface
ト ぬ(る) ぬ(り)　　　　　　　Ⓚ2473

[original meaning] **apply on a surface, lay on, spread
on, coat, paint**
　塗装 とそう painting, coating
　塗料 とりょう paint
　塗布する とふする apply (an ointment)
　塗工 とこう painter

抹 ▷wipe over
マツ　　　　　　　　　　　　　Ⓚ0277

(spread over) **wipe over [on], coat with, paint over**
　塗抹する とまつする coat with, paint over
　一抹 いちまつ a touch of, a tinge of

撒 ▷scatter
サン サツ ま(く)　　　　　　　Ⓚ0670

[now replaced by 散] [original meaning] **scatter, sprinkle, disperse**
　撒水 さんすい(=さっすい) water sprinkling
　撒布する さんぷ(=さっぷ)する scatter, sprinkle, spray

spring back
弾　　反

弾 ▷spring back
ダン ひ(く) -ひ(き) はず(む) たま Ⓚ0524

spring back (to the original shape), resile
　弾性 だんせい elasticity, resilience
　弾力性 だんりょくせい elasticity, resilience; flexibili-
　　ty, adaptability
　弾機 だんき(=ばね) spring

反
▷**return in original direction**
ハン ホン タン そ(る) そ(らす) Ⓚ2549

return in the original direction, reflect, be reflected; react

反応 はんのう reaction, response
反響 はんきょう echo, reverberation; response, repercussions
反射 はんしゃ reflection
反射的 はんしゃてき reflective, reflexive
反省 はんせい reflection, introspection

sprout and bloom
萌　咲

萌
▷**germinate**
ホウ ボウ も(える) きざ(す) Ⓚ1995

germinate, sprout, bud

萌芽 ほうが germination, beginning; sprout

咲
▷**bloom**
さ(く) -ざき Ⓚ0310

bloom, blossom, flower; effloresce

咲き渡る さきわたる bloom over a wide area
早咲き はやざき early blooming, early flowering
狂い咲く くるいざく bloom out of season
文化が花と咲く ぶんかがはなとさく Fine arts effloresce

spy
偵　探

偵
▷**spy**
テイ Ⓚ0122

spy, detect, scout, investigate

偵察 ていさつ scouting, reconnaissance
偵知 ていち [rare] spying, investigating
内偵する ないていする make secret inquiries, scout

探
▷**spy on**
タン さぐ(る) さが(す) Ⓚ0466

spy on, trace, detect

探偵 たんてい detective work; detective, sleuth
探知 たんち detection

square
方　角

方
▷**square**
ホウ かた -がた -なた Ⓚ170

(equal-sided rectangle) **square**

方円 ほうえん squares and circles
方眼紙 ほうがんし graph paper
正方形 せいほうけい square

角
▷**square**
カク かど つの Ⓚ176

[also prefix and suffix] **square, squared**

角瓶 かくびん square [shoulder] bottle
角材 かくざい squared timber
角行灯 かくあんどん square paper lantern
五センチ角 ごせんちかく 5 cm sq.

squeeze
搾　絞　圧

搾
▷**squeeze**
サク しぼ(る) Ⓚ059

[original meaning] **squeeze, extract, press**

搾乳 さくにゅう milking
搾油 さくゆ oil expression [extraction]
圧搾する あっさくする press, compress

絞
▷**wring**
コウ しぼ(る) し(める) し(まる) Ⓚ123

wring, wring out

絞り しぼり iris diaphragm; white spots on a dyed ground, tie-dyed fabrics; variegation, spots (in flowers)
お絞り おしぼり wet towel, steamed towel
雑巾を絞る ぞうきんをしぼる wring a floorcloth

圧
▷**apply pressure**
アツ Ⓚ2563

[original meaning] **apply pressure, press down**

圧力 あつりょく pressure
圧縮する あっしゅくする compress, constrict
圧搾する あっさくする press, compress
圧砕 あっさい crushing

stab
刺　　突

刺 ▷stab
シ さ(す) さ(さる) さ(し)　　Ⓚ1171

[original meaning] **stab, pierce, prick, thrust**
　刺傷 ししょう stab, pierced wound
　刺繍 ししゅう embroidery
　刺殺する しさつする stab to death

突 ▷thrust
トツ つ(く)　　Ⓚ1918

(penetrate with a pointed end) **thrust, pierce, stab, prick**
　突き刺す つきさす stab, pierce, thrust
　突き殺す つきころす stab to death
　突き抜く つきぬく pierce through
　突き抜ける つきぬける go [push, thrust] through, penetrate
　突き破る つきやぶる break [smash] through, pierce
　楯突く たてつく oppose, defy; rebel

stagnate
滞　淀　澱　渋　吃

滞 ▷stagnate
タイ とどこお(る)　　Ⓚ0609

[original meaning] **stagnate, be at [in] a standstill, be blocked up, be retarded, congest**
　滞貨 たいか freight congestion; accumulation of stocks
　停滞 ていたい stagnation, accumulation; arrearage
　渋滞 じゅうたい delay, retardation, stagnation
　沈滞 ちんたい stagnation, dullness
　遅滞 ちたい delay, retardation

淀 ▷stagnate
デン よど(む) よど　　Ⓚ0467

stagnate, be stagnant
　淀み よどみ pool (in river), backwater, stagnation; sedimentation, sediment, deposit; faltering, hesitation, pause
　淀んだ空気 よどんだくうき stale air

澱 ▷settle
デン おり よど(む) よど

settle, precipitate
　澱粉 でんぷん starch

　沈澱 ちんでん precipitation, settlement

渋 ▷not go smoothly
ジュウ しぶ しぶ(い) しぶ(る)　　Ⓚ0471

[original meaning] **not go smoothly, make poor progress**
　渋滞 じゅうたい delay, retardation, stagnation
　苦渋 くじゅう distress, affliction

吃 ▷stammer
キツ ども(る)

[original meaning] **stammer, stutter**
　吃音 きつおん stammering

stagnating water
淵　淀　澱

淵 ▷deep water
エン ふち　　Ⓚ0547

deep water [pool], depths, abyss
　淵源 えんげん origin
　海淵 かいえん ocean depths, deep
　深淵 しんえん abyss, depths

淀 ▷pool
デン よど(む) よど　　Ⓚ0467

[also 澱] **pool, backwater, stagnation**

澱 ▷pool
デン おり よど(む) よど

[also 淀] **pool, backwater, stagnation**

standpoint
地　　立

地 ▷one's ground
チ ジ　　Ⓚ0181

one's ground, one's stand, one's place, one's position
　地位 ちい position, status, post, social standing
　地歩 ちほ one's stand, foothold, position
　見地 けんち standpoint, viewpoint
　窮地 きゅうち predicament, difficult situation, dilemma
　実地 じっち actuality, reality; practice
　境地 きょうち state, stage; field, ground

立 ▷standpoint
リツ リュウ た(つ) た(ち)- た(てる)
た(て)- -だ(て) -だ(てる)　Ⓚ1723

standpoint, stand, position

対立 たいりつ opposition, antagonism
中立 ちゅうりつ neutrality; neutralization
孤立する こりつする be isolated, stand alone

stands →TABLES AND STANDS

stars
星　　　座

星 ▷star
セイ ショウ ほし -ぼし　Ⓚ2156

ⓐ [also suffix] **star**
ⓑ suffix after names of stars
a 星座 せいざ constellation
恒星 こうせい fixed star
超巨星 ちょうきょせい supergiant star
一等星 いっとうせい first magnitude star
b 北極星 ほっきょくせい Polaris
織女星 しょくじょせい Vega

座 ▷constellation
ザ すわ(る)　Ⓚ2686

ⓐ constellation
ⓑ suffix after names of constellations
a 星座 せいざ constellation
b 大熊座 おおくまざ the Big Bear

states and situations
態　調　様　相　状　況
景　勢　境　局　情　訳

態 ▷state
タイ　Ⓚ2478

[also suffix] **state, condition, situation; form, appearance**

状態 じょうたい state, condition, appearance, situation, aspect
生態 せいたい ecology; mode of life
実態 じったい actual conditions, state
重態(=重体) じゅうたい serious condition, critical state
事態 じたい situation, state of affairs
形態(=形体) けいたい shape, form, structure, morphology

姿態 したい figure, person; pose

調 ▷tone
チョウ しら(べる) しら(べ) ととの(う)
ととの(える)　Ⓚ141?

(general quality or well-balanced condition) **tone, condition, state (of health)**

好調 こうちょう favorable [good] condition
順調に じゅんちょうに favorably, smoothly
基調 きちょう keynote, underlying tone, basis
歩調 ほちょう pace, step, cadence
単調な たんちょうな monotonous, dull
体調 たいちょう health condition

様 ▷mode
ヨウ さま　Ⓚ0969

(manner of being) **mode, state, aspect, appearance**

様相 ようそう aspect, phase, condition
様子 ようす situation, aspect, circumstances; appearance, looks; sign, indication
様態 ようたい mode
異様な いような strange, odd, singular

相 ▷phase
ソウ ショウ あい-　Ⓚ0808

(outer appearance or state, esp. as indication of characteristic essence) **phase, looks, appearance, aspect, state condition**

様相 ようそう aspect, phase, condition
時代相 じだいそう phases of the times
貧相な ひんそうな poor-looking
寝相 ねぞう one's sleeping posture
色相 しきそう color phase
世相 せそう phases [aspect] of life, social conditions
真相 しんそう truth, facts, real situation
諸相 しょそう various aspects, various phases
実相 じっそう real state of affairs

状 ▷condition
ジョウ　Ⓚ0244

(actual) **condition, state, situation, circumstances**

状態 じょうたい state, condition, appearance, situation, aspect
状況 じょうきょう state of affairs, conditions, circumstances
現状 げんじょう present condition
商状 しょうじょう market condition
症状 しょうじょう symptom
病状 びょうじょう condition of a disease [patient]
罪状 ざいじょう offense, charges

況 ▷conditions
キョウ   Ⓚ0299

conditions, condition, situation, state of affairs

状況 じょうきょう state of affairs, conditions, circumstances
戦況 せんきょう war situation, progress of a battle
近況 きんきょう recent condition [situation]
実況 じっきょう actual conditions
概況 がいきょう general condition [situation], outlook
好況 こうきょう brisk market, prosperity
市況 しきょう market conditions, tone of the market
不況 ふきょう depression, slump, recession
盛況 せいきょう prosperity, boom, success

景 ▷business conditions
ケイ   Ⓚ2179

business conditions, market situation, conditions, circumstances

景気 けいき things, times; business conditions
景況 けいきょう situation, outlook
不景気 ふけいき business depression, slump, dull market

勢 ▷course of events
セイ いきお(い)   Ⓚ2487

course of events, state of affairs, situation, condition, circumstances

形勢 けいせい situation, state of affairs; prospects
情勢 じょうせい state of things, situation
態勢 たいせい attitude, preparedness, condition
国勢 こくせい state [condition] of a country

境 ▷situation
キョウ ケイ さかい   Ⓚ0618

situation, condition(s), state

境遇 きょうぐう one's lot, circumstances, situation in life
境地 きょうち state, stage; field, ground
環境 かんきょう environment, surroundings, circumstances
心境 しんきょう frame of mind, mental attitude [state]
逆境 ぎゃっきょう adversity, adverse [unfavorable] circumstances
進境 しんきょう progress, improvement

局 ▷current situation
キョク   Ⓚ2636

current situation, state of affairs

局面 きょくめん situation, aspect of an affair; position (in a chess game)
時局 じきょく situation, circumstances

戦局 せんきょく state of the war, war situation
難局 なんきょく difficult [delicate] situation, deadlock
政局 せいきょく political situation

情 ▷actual conditions
ジョウ セイ なさ(け)   Ⓚ0439

actual conditions, actual facts, real circumstances

情勢 じょうせい state of things, situation
情報 じょうほう information, intelligence, report, news
情況 じょうきょう conditions, circumstances
事情 じじょう circumstances, conditions, situation
実情 じつじょう actual circumstances, real state of affairs

訳 ▷circumstances
ヤク わけ   Ⓚ1340

circumstances, matter, case

訳を説明する わけをせつめいする explain the circumstances
どう云う訳だ どういうわけだ What's the matter?
内訳 うちわけ items (of an account), details, breakdown

stay

滞 頓 留 逗 駐
屯 在 泊 宿 寓

滞 ▷stay
タイ とどこお(る)   Ⓚ0609

(remain in a given place) **stay, remain, sojourn**

滞在 たいざい stay, sojourn
滞留 たいりゅう sojourn, stay
滞米 たいべい staying in America
滞欧 たいおう staying in Europe
滞空 たいくう staying [remaining] in the air

頓 ▷stay in place
トン   Ⓚ0957

ⓐ sudden
ⓑ at once [one time]

a 頓智(=頓知) とんち (quick or ready) wit
頓死 とんし sudden death
頓悟 とんご *Buddhism* sudden enlightenment
素っ頓狂 すっとんきょう harum-scarum, hysteric

b 頓服 とんぷく dose of medicine

留 ▷stay
リュウ ル と(める) –ど(め) と(まる)
とど(まる) Ⓚ2235

(remain in a given place) **stay, sojourn, reside**
留学生 りゅうがくせい student studying abroad
留守 るす absence (from home); caretaking; defending when the lord is absent
駐留する ちゅうりゅうする be stationed at, stay
逗留する とうりゅうする stay, sojourn
在留邦人 ざいりゅうほうじん Japanese residents

逗 ▷stay
トウ Ⓚ2777

(remain in a given place) **stay, sojourn, reside**
逗留 とうりゅう staying, sojourn

駐 ▷stationed
チュウ Ⓚ1622

[also prefix] **stationed (at, in), resident in**
駐留する ちゅうりゅうする be stationed at, stay
駐在 ちゅうざい residence, stay
駐屯する ちゅうとんする be stationed, occupy
駐日大使 ちゅうにちたいし ambassador to Japan
駐英 ちゅうえい stationed in England
駐独 ちゅうどく stationed in Germany

屯 ▷station troops
トン Ⓚ2908

station troops, encamp, post
駐屯する ちゅうとんする be stationed, occupy

在 ▷reside temporarily
ザイ あ(る) Ⓚ2577

ⓐ reside [live] temporarily, stay
ⓑ [prefix] resident in
ⓐ 在日の ざいにちの (staying) in Japan
在外の ざいがいの overseas
在住する ざいじゅうする live, reside, dwell
在米中 ざいべいちゅう while resident in America
在留する ざいりゅうする reside, stay, be resident
駐在 ちゅうざい residence, stay
滞在 たいざい stay, sojourn
ⓑ 在ベルリン邦人 ざいべるりんほうじん Japanese (resident) in Berlin

泊 ▷stay overnight
ハク と(まる) と(める) Ⓚ0293

stay overnight, lodge, stay at
宿泊 しゅくはく lodging
外泊 がいはく staying out overnight
民泊 みんぱく private residence temporarily taking lodgers

宿 ▷lodge
シュク やど やど(る) やど(す) Ⓚ198⁵

[original meaning] **lodge, board, stay overnight**
宿泊する しゅくはくする lodge, stay
宿直 しゅくちょく night duty, night watch
寄宿 きしゅく lodging, boarding
合宿する がっしゅくする lodge together, stay in a camp for training
下宿 げしゅく lodging, boarding house

寓 ▷stay temporarily
グウ Ⓚ2010

stay [reside] temporarily
寄寓 きぐう lodging with; temporary residence

steal and rob
盗 窃 取 奪 略 掠 鹵

盗 ▷steal
トウ ぬす(む) Ⓚ2327

steal, burglarize
盗品 とうひん stolen article [goods]
盗癖 とうへき kleptomania
盗難 とうなん robbery, burglary, theft
窃盗 せっとう theft, larceny

窃 ▷steal
セツ Ⓚ1942

steal, pilfer
窃盗 せっとう theft, larceny
窃取 せっしゅ theft, larceny
剽窃する ひょうせつする plagiarize

取 ▷take
シュ と(る) と(り) –ど(り) Ⓚ1162

take away from, steal
詐取 さしゅ fraud, swindle
搾取 さくしゅ exploitation, sweating, squeezing

奪 ▷rob
ダツ うば(う) Ⓚ2058

rob, take by force, seize, deprive
奪還 だっかん recapture, recovery
奪取 だっしゅ capture, seizure
略奪 りゃくだつ pillage, plunder, looting
強奪する ごうだつする rob, seize, plunder; hijack
争奪 そうだつ scramble, contest, struggle
剥奪する はくだつする deprive, divest

略 ▷plunder
リャク   Ⓚ1081

[formerly also 掠] **plunder, pillage**
  略奪 りゃくだつ pillage, plunder, looting
  略取 りゃくしゅ capture, occupation, plunder
  侵略する しんりゃくする invade, aggress (against)
  攻略 こうりゃく capture, conquest; invasion

掠 ▷plunder
リャク かす(める) かす(れる)
かす(る)   Ⓚ0458

[now replaced by 略] **plunder, pillage, rob**
  掠奪 りゃくだつ pillage, plunder, looting
  侵掠する しんりゃくする invade, aggress (against)
  劫掠 ごうりゃく extortion
  奪掠 だつりゃく pillage, plunder, looting

鹵 ▷plunder
ロ

plunder, rob, capture
  鹵獲する ろかくする capture, seize, plunder

teel →IRON AND STEEL

steep
険 嶮 岨 急 峻

険 ▷steep
ケン けわ(しい)   Ⓚ0495

[formerly also 嶮]
ⓐ steep, precipitous
ⓑ [original meaning] **steep [inaccessible] place, steep pass, stronghold**
  ⓐ 険路 けんろ steep pass
  険阻(=嶮岨) けんそ steepness, precipice
  峻険な しゅんけんな steep, precipitous
  ⓑ 天険 てんけん natural stronghold

嶮 ▷steep
ケン けわ(しい)

ⓐ [original meaning] **steep, precipitous**
ⓑ steep [inaccessible] place, steep pass, stronghold
  ⓐ 嶮岨 けんそ steepness, precipice
  峻嶮な しゅんけんな steep, precipitous
  ⓑ 天嶮 てんけん natural stronghold

岨 ▷steep
ソ

[now replaced by 阻] **steep**
  嶮岨(=険阻)な けんそな steep (mountain pass),
  precipitous

急 ▷steep
キュウ いそ(ぐ) いそ(ぎ)   Ⓚ1800

[also prefix] (sharply inclined) **steep**
  急坂 きゅうはん steep hill [slope]
  急傾斜 きゅうけいしゃ steep slope [incline]

峻 ▷high and steep
シュン   Ⓚ0373

(esp. of mountains) **high and steep, rising sharply, precipitous, towering, lofty**
  峻険な しゅんけんな steep, precipitous
  峻嶺 しゅんれい steep peak, high rugged mountain
  急峻な きゅうしゅんな steep, sharp

step on
踏 蹈 藉

踏 ▷tread
トウ ふ(む) ふ(まえる)   Ⓚ1435

[original meaning] **tread (on), step on, stamp, trample**
  踏破する とうはする crush underfoot; travel on
    foot
  未踏の みとうの untrodden, unexplored
  舞踏(=舞蹈) ぶとう dancing

蹈 ▷step on
トウ

[original meaning] **step on, tread**
  舞蹈(=舞踏) ぶとう dancing

藉 ▷trample on
シャ セキ

trample on, step on
  狼藉 ろうぜき disorder; violence

steps
段 階 陛 梯

段 ▷step
ダン   Ⓚ1059

ⓐ step, stair, rung
ⓑ counter for steps
  ⓐ 段丘 だんきゅう terrace, bench (in geography)
  階段 かいだん steps, flight of stairs
  石段 いしだん stone steps
  ⓑ 百段 ひゃくだん 100 steps

階 ▷stairs
カイ   Ⓚ0569

stairs, flight of stairs, steps, staircase
階段 かいだん steps, flight of stairs
階下 かいか lower floor, downstairs
階梯 かいてい step, ladder; stepping-stone; guide

陛 ▷imperial palace steps
ヘイ   Ⓚ0409

[original meaning] **imperial palace steps, steps leading to the imperial palace hall**
陛下 へいか His [Her, Your] Majesty; [original meaning] at the palace steps
陛衛 へいえい [archaic] Imperial guard
天皇陛下 てんのうへいか His Majesty the Emperor, His Imperial Majesty

梯 ▷ladder
テイ はし はしご   Ⓚ0875

[original meaning] **ladder, stairs, bridge**
梯形 ていけい trapezoid
階梯 かいてい step, ladder; stepping-stone; guide
雲梯 うんてい monkey bars; scaling ladder used in ancient China
舷梯 げんてい gangway (ladder)

stick
着 貼 付 附

着 ▷stick
チャク ジャク き(る) -ぎ き(せる) -き(せ) つ(く) つ(ける)   Ⓚ2826

stick, adhere, become attached
付着 ふちゃく adhesion, agglutination; cohesion
密着 みっちゃく close adhesion
吸着 きゅうちゃく adsorption
接着 せっちゃく adhesion, gluing
癒着 ゆちゃく adhesion, conglutination; connection, collusion
粘着する ねんちゃくする stick to, be glued to, adhere to

貼 ▷stick
チョウ テン は(る) -ばり   Ⓚ1369

[original meaning] **stick, paste; apply to**
貼付する ちょうふ(=てんぷ)する stick, paste, append

付 ▷attach itself to
フ つ(ける) -づ(ける) つ(け) -づ(け) つ(く) -づ(く) つ(き) -づ(き)   Ⓚ001

[original meaning] **attach itself to, stick to, adhere to**
付着する ふちゃくする adhere [cling] to, agglutinate; cohere

附 ▷attach itself to
フ   Ⓚ030

attach itself to, stick to, adhere to
附着する ふちゃくする adhere [cling] to, agglutinate; cohere

still
未 尚

未 ▷not yet
ミ いま(だ) ま(だ)   Ⓚ294*

[also prefix] **not yet, un- (as in *unpublished*)**
未満 みまん less than
未来 みらい future
未練 みれん lingering affection, reluctance to give up
未完成 みかんせい incompletion
未知の みちの unknown
未刊の みかんの unpublished
未定の みていの undecided, pending
未払いの みはらいの unpaid
未婚の みこんの unmarried
未成年の みせいねんの minor, underage
未開の みかいの primitive, uncivilized; savage
未然に みぜんに before it happens, beforehand, previously
前代未聞の ぜんだいみもんの unheard-of, unprecedented

尚 ▷still
ショウ なお   Ⓚ1919

still, yet
尚早の しょうそうの premature

stone →ROCK AND STONE

stone →KINDS OF STONE

stop

止 停 駐

▷**stop**
シ と(まる) –ど(まり) と(める) –ど(め)
や(める) や(む)
Ⓚ2545

(cease moving) **stop, come to a standstill, halt; stop over**

止宿 ししゅく lodging
停止する ていしする stop, stand still; suspend, put to an end
静止する せいしする stand still, come to a standstill

▷**halt**
テイ と(める) と(まる)
Ⓚ0121

(make a temporary stop) **halt, pause, stop**

停留する ていりゅうする halt, stop
停止 ていし stop, halt; suspension
停車 ていしゃ stoppage (of a vehicle)

駐
▷**park**
チュウ
Ⓚ1622

park

駐車場 ちゅうしゃじょう parking area
駐輪場 ちゅうりんじょう bicycle parking lot
駐停車する ちゅうていしゃする park or stop a vehicle

stoppers

栓 弁

▷**stopper**
セン
Ⓚ0845

❶ [original meaning] **stopper, plug, cork, peg; door bolt**

栓抜き せんぬき bottle opener, corkscrew
コルク栓 こるくせん cork
脳血栓 のうけっせん cerebral thrombosis

❷ [also suffix] **stopcock, tap, faucet, spigot**

水栓 すいせん water tap, faucet
消火栓 しょうかせん fire hydrant, fireplug

弁
▷**valve**
ベン
Ⓚ1730

(machine part) **valve**

安全弁 あんぜんべん safety valve
排気弁 はいきべん exhaust valve

store

蔵 蓄 貯 納

蔵
▷**store**
ゾウ くら
Ⓚ2088

store, put away, lay by

貯蔵 ちょぞう storage, preservation
収蔵 しゅうぞう garnering, storage
死蔵する しぞうする hoard (up), keep (something) idle
秘蔵 ひぞう treasuring
冷蔵庫 れいぞうこ refrigerator
内蔵する ないぞうする have (a thing) within, have (something) built in

蓄
▷**store up**
チク たくわ(える)
Ⓚ2038

store up, accumulate, amass, lay aside

蓄積 ちくせき accumulation, stockpiling
蓄電池 ちくでんち storage battery, accumulator
蓄音機 ちくおんき phonograph, gramophone
蓄財 ちくざい accumulation of wealth
貯蓄する ちょちくする save (money), lay aside
備蓄 びちく saving for [against] emergency, storing
含蓄 がんちく implication, significance, suggestiveness

貯
▷**lay up**
チョ
Ⓚ1368

[original meaning] **lay up (money or supplies), lay by, save, store up, lay in, stock**

貯金 ちょきん savings, deposit
貯蓄 ちょちく savings
貯蔵する ちょぞうする store, preserve, set aside
貯水池 ちょすいち reservoir
貯炭 ちょたん storing coal; stored coal
預貯金 よちょきん deposits and savings, bank account
郵貯(=郵便貯金) ゆうちょ(=ゆうびんちょきん) postal [post-office] savings [deposit]

▷**put away**
ノウ ナッ– ナ ナン トウ おさ(める)
おさ(まる)
Ⓚ1195

[original meaning] **put away, put in, store, put in place, consign**

納棺 のうかん placing in the coffin
納屋 なや outhouse, shed, barn
納戸 なんど back room, closet
納豆 なっとう fermented soybeans
収納 しゅうのう storing; harvesting; receipt

格納する かくのうする house

storehouse
倉 蔵 庫

倉 ▷storehouse
ソウ くら   Ⓚ1807

storehouse, warehouse, granary
倉庫 そうこ warehouse, storehouse
穀倉 こくそう granary, grain elevator
弾倉 だんそう magazine (of a rifle)

蔵 ▷storehouse
ゾウ くら   Ⓚ2088

storehouse, storing place, treasury
土蔵 どぞう storehouse, godown
宝蔵 ほうぞう treasury
経蔵 きょうぞう scripture house

庫 ▷storage chamber
コク   Ⓚ2682

[also suffix] [original meaning] **storage chamber, esp.
a large structure for storing vehicles; storehouse,
warehouse**
倉庫 そうこ warehouse, storehouse
金庫 きんこ strong box, cashbox
車庫 しゃこ car shed, garage
艇庫 ていこ boathouse
宝庫 ほうこ treasure house, treasury
文庫 ぶんこ library; collection of literary works; box
     for stationery
在庫 ざいこ stock, stockpile
国庫 こっこ (National) Treasury
公庫 こうこ municipal [state] treasury
格納庫 かくのうこ hangar, airplane shed

stories
話 談 語 説 噂

話 ▷story
ワ はな(す) はなし   Ⓚ1388

story, tale, fable
神話 しんわ myth, mythology
童話 どうわ nursery tale, fairy tale
民話 みんわ folk tale, folk story
実話 じつわ true story
挿話 そうわ anecdote

談 ▷account
ダン   Ⓚ141

account, story, tale
怪談 かいだん ghost story
講談 こうだん storytelling, narration; historical
     narrative
冒険談 ぼうけんだん account of an adventure;
     adventure story

語 ▷tale
ゴ かた(る) かた(らう)   Ⓚ140

tale, story, narrative, legend
落語 らくご *rakugo*, Japanese-style comic story

説 ▷narrative
セツ ゼイ と(く)   Ⓚ140

narrative, story
説話 せつわ narrative, tale
小説 しょうせつ novel, story, fiction
伝説 でんせつ legend, folk tale

噂 ▷rumor
ソン うわさ   Ⓚ065

rumor, hearsay, gossip
噂話 うわさばなし gossip
噂通り うわさどおり as rumored
噂をすれば影 うわさをすればかげ Speak of the
     devil
根も葉も無い噂 ねもはもないうわさ groundless
     rumor
人の噂も七十五日 ひとのうわさもしちじゅうごにち A
     wonder lasts but nine days

straight
直 棒

直 ▷straight
チョク ジキ ジカ ただ(ちに) なお(す)
なお(る) なお(き) す(ぐ)   Ⓚ253

[original meaning] (unbent) **straight**
直線 ちょくせん straight line
直球 ちょっきゅう straight ball [pitch]
直進する ちょくしんする go straight on
直滑降 ちょっかっこう straight descent, schuss
直径 ちょっけい diameter
直視する ちょくしする look in the face, look straight
     at
硬直 こうちょく stiffness, rigidity

棒 ▷straight
ボウ   Ⓚ0894

in a straight line, straight
- 棒立ち ぼうだち standing erect
- 棒読み ぼうよみ reading without expression; reading a Chinese classical text without translating it into Japanese
- 棒暗記 ぼうあんき memorization word by word

streams →RIVERS AND STREAMS

strict

厳 酷 辣 峻

厳 ▷strict
ゲン ゴン おごそ(か) きび(しい)   Ⓚ2804

[original meaning] **strict, severe, stern, rigorous, harsh**
- 厳格な げんかくな strict, stern, severe, rigorous
- 厳密な げんみつな strict, precise, rigid, exact
- 厳正 げんせい exactness, strictness, rigor
- 厳重な げんじゅうな strict, severe, close; secure, firm, strong
- 厳守 げんしゅ strict observance
- 厳罰 げんばつ severe punishment
- 厳選 げんせん careful selection
- 戒厳令 かいげんれい martial law

酷 ▷severe
コク   Ⓚ1414

severe, harsh, cruel, brutal, merciless
- 酷刑 こっけい severe punishment
- 酷評 こくひょう severe criticism
- 酷薄(=刻薄)な こくはくな cruel, inhumane
- 酷使する こくしする drive (a person) hard, abuse, sweat (one's workers), overwork
- 残酷な ざんこくな cruel, ruthless, atrocious
- 苛酷(=過酷)な かこくな severe, harsh, cruel

辣 ▷severe
ラツ   Ⓚ1412

(strict) **severe, exacting, harsh**
- 辣腕 らつわん shrewdness, acumen, tact
- 辛辣な しんらつな bitter, pungent, acrid, poignant, severe

峻 ▷stern
シュン   Ⓚ0373

stern, strict, severe, uncompromising
- 峻厳な しゅんげんな strict, stern, rigorous, severe
- 峻拒する しゅんきょする refuse flatly, reject sternly

- 峻別 しゅんべつ sharp distinction, strict discrimination
- 峻下剤 しゅんげざい drastic aperient

strike

打 撲 殴 蹴 撃 挌
撞 撥 当 叩 拍 搏

打 ▷strike
ダ う(つ) うち-   Ⓚ0170

[also prefix] [original meaning] **strike, hit, beat**
- 打撃 だげき blow, strike; batting, hitting
- 打撲 だぼく blow, stroke
- 打診 だしん sounding, tapping; percussion
- 打電 だでん sending a telegram
- 打楽器 だがっき percussion instrument, traps
- 殴打する おうだする give a blow, beat, strike

撲 ▷deal a blow
ボク   Ⓚ0666

[original meaning] **deal [give] a blow, beat, strike forcefully, strike a blow**
- 撲殺 ぼくさつ clubbing to death
- 撲滅 ぼくめつ eradication, destruction
- 打撲 だぼく blow, stroke

殴 ▷beat (strike a person)
オウ なぐ(る)   Ⓚ0788

[original meaning] (strike a person) **beat (up), hit, strike, thrash**
- 殴打 おうだ blow, beating
- 殴殺する おうさつする beat to death

蹴 ▷kick
シュウ け(る) け-   Ⓚ1479

kick
- 蹴球 しゅうきゅう soccer
- 一蹴する いっしゅうする kick; defeat easily; reject [turn down] flatly

撃 ▷strike
ゲキ う(つ)   Ⓚ2492

[original meaning] **strike, beat**
- 打撃 だげき blow, strike; batting, hitting
- 直撃 ちょくげき direct hit
- 衝撃 しょうげき impact, shock, impulse
- 目撃者 もくげきしゃ eyewitness
- 電撃 でんげき electric shock; lightning attack, blitz

搰 ▷strike (a person)
カク

[now replaced by 挌] [original meaning] **strike, hit, fight**
搰闘する かくとうする grapple, fight hand to hand

撞 ▷strike (a ball or bell)
ドウ シュ つ(く)　　　Ⓚ0668

strike, thrust, hit
撞球 どうきゅう billiards
撞着 どうちゃく contradiction
撞木 しゅもく wooden bell hammer

撥 ▷strike (knock down)
ハツ バチ は(ねる)

strike, knock down
車に撥ねられる くるまにはねられる be struck by a
car

当 ▷hit
トウ あ(たる) あ(たり) あ(てる)
あ(て)　　　Ⓚ1865

hit, strike; touch
当て逃げ あてにげ hit-and-run accident (causing
property damage)
鞘当て さやあて rivalry ("touching of sheaths")

叩 ▷knock
コウ たた(く) はた(く)

knock, rap, beat, strike, hit
叩扉する こうひする knock on a door; visit someone
叩解 こうかい beating (of pulp fibers)
叩音 こうおん rap, rapping sound
打叩 だこう tapping

拍 ▷beat (strike repeatedly)
ハク ヒョウ　　　Ⓚ0269

[also 搏] [original meaning] (strike repeatedly or rhythmi-
cally) **beat, clap (one's hands), throb**
拍手 はくしゅ applause, clapping
拍車 はくしゃ spur, rowel spur
拍動 はくどう pulsation, pulsebeat
脈拍 みゃくはく pulse, pulsation

搏 ▷beat (throb)
ハク

[now also 拍] [original meaning] **beat, clap, throb**
搏動 はくどう pulsation, pulsebeat
脈搏 みゃくはく pulse, pulsation

---

strong
強 壮 丈 健 逞 康 旺 濻

強 ▷strong
キョウ ゴウ つよ(い) つよ(まる)
つよ(める) し(いる)　　　Ⓚ043□

(having great strength) **strong, powerful; robust**
強力な きょうりょくな strong, powerful, mighty
強者 きょうしゃ strong man
強大な きょうだいな mighty, powerful, strong
強敵 きょうてき powerful enemy [rival]
強国 きょうこく powerful country
強力(=剛力) ごうりき Herculean strength; mountain carrier [guide]
屈強な くっきょうな strong, sturdy, robust

壮 ▷vigorous
ソウ　　　Ⓚ0198

vigorous, robust, strong, able-bodied, energetic
壮健な そうけんな vigorous, healthy, robust
強壮な きょうそうな robust, strong, vigorous

丈 ▷stout
ジョウ たけ　　　Ⓚ2885

stout, robust, strong, tough
丈夫な じょうぶな healthy, strong, robust; stout,
solid
気丈な きじょうな stouthearted, courageous
頑丈な がんじょうな solid, firm; strong

健 ▷robust (healthy)
ケン すこ(やか)　　　Ⓚ011□

(strong and in good health) **robust, healthy, sound,
strong**
健康な けんこうな healthy, sound, well
健保(=健康保険) けんぽ(=けんこうほけん) health
insurance
健在だ けんざいだ be well, be in good health
健全 けんぜん health, soundness
健脚の けんきゃくの strong in walking
強健な きょうけんな robust, healthy, strong
保健 ほけん (preservation of) health, sanitation
穏健な おんけんな moderate, temperate, sound
剛健な ごうけんな strong and sturdy, virile; manly

逞 ▷robust (sturdy)
テイ たくま(しい)　　　Ⓚ2776

(sturdy) **robust, brawny, strapping**
逞しい体付き たくましいからだつき sturdy build

康 ▷healthy
コウ   Ⓚ2693

see also →HEALTHY

healthy, robust
> 健康 けんこう health
> 健康な けんこうな healthy, sound, well

旺 ▷energetic
オウ さか(ん)   Ⓚ0757

【オウ】
energetic, vigorous; flourishing
> 旺盛な おうせいな vigorous, in a flourishing condition

【さか(ん)】
[also 盛んな] **vigorous, energetic, lively**
> 精力が旺んだ せいりょくがさかんだ be full of energy [vigor]

潑 ▷lively
ハツ

[now also 発] **lively, energetic**
> 潑剌たる はつらつたる lively, sprightly, vivid
> 活潑な かっぱつな lively, active

---

strongholds
城 塁 塞 砦 堡

城 ▷castle
ジョウ しろ き   Ⓚ0312

ⓐ (fortified building) **castle, fort, fortress, citadel, stronghold**
ⓑ (fortified stately residence) **castle, palace**
ⓒ **suffix after names of castles**

a 城塞(=城砦) じょうさい fortress, stronghold, citadel
> 城壁 じょうへき castle wall, rampart
> 城下町 じょうかまち castle town, fief capital
> 城郭 じょうかく castle, fortress; castle walls, enclosure
> 籠城 ろうじょう confinement, keeping inside; holding a castle, sustaining a siege
> 牙城 がじょう stronghold, inner citadel
> 落城 らくじょう fall of a castle
> 築城 ちくじょう castle construction
b 城主 じょうしゅ lord of a castle
> 王城 おうじょう Imperial castle, royal palace
c 大阪城 おおさかじょう Osaka Castle

塁 ▷small fort
ルイ   Ⓚ2250

[original meaning] (small military fortification consisting of raised earthwork) **small fort, rampart, parapet, fortress, redoubt**
> 塁壁 るいへき rampart
> 敵塁 てきるい enemy fortress, enemy position
> 堅塁 けんるい strong fort(ress)
> 堡塁 ほうるい(=ほるい) fort, fortress, stronghold
> 土塁 どるい earthwork, fieldwork

塞 ▷fort
サイ ソク ふさ(ぐ) ふさ(がる)   Ⓚ2033

[sometimes also 砦] **fort, fortress, stronghold**
> 城塞(=城砦) じょうさい fortress, stronghold, citadel
> 要塞 ようさい fortress, stronghold
> 人間万事塞翁が馬 じんかんばんじさいおうがうま Inscrutable are the ways of heaven

砦 ▷fort
サイ とりで   Ⓚ2328

[usu. 塞] **fort, fortress, stronghold**
> 城砦(=城塞) じょうさい fortress, stronghold, citadel
> 山砦 さんさい mountain stronghold

堡 ▷fort
ホ ホウ

[now also 保] **fort**
> 堡塁 ほうるい(=ほるい) fort, fortress, stronghold
> 堡礁 ほしょう barrier reef
> 海堡 かいほう coast battery; breakwater
> 橋頭堡 きょうとうほ bridgehead, beachhead

---

structure
構 造

構 ▷structure
コウ かま(える) かま(う)   Ⓚ0962

structure, framework, construction, fabrication
> 機構 きこう mechanism, structure; system, organization; frame, framework
> 結構 けっこう structure, construction; quite, well enough, fairly well; all right; no thank you
> 虚構 きょこう fabrication, fiction

造 ▷make
ゾウ つく(る) つく(り) -づく(り)   Ⓚ2679

make, structure, construction

造りの頑丈な家 つくりのがんじょうないえ house of solid structure

students and followers
生 卒 学 門 弟 徒

生 ▷student
セイ ショウ い(きる) い(かす) い(ける)
う(まれる) う(まれ) う(む) お(う) は(える)
は(やす) き なま な(る)　　　Ⓚ2933

[also suffix] **student, pupil; scholar**
生徒 せいと pupil, student
学生 がくせい student
高校生 こうこうせい high school student
同級生 どうきゅうせい classmate
門下生 もんかせい disciple, pupil
教生 きょうせい student teacher
先生 せんせい teacher; doctor
儒生 じゅせい Confucianist, student of Confucianism

卒 ▷graduate student
ソツ　　　Ⓚ1769

[also suffix] **graduate student, graduate**
学卒 がくそつ (university or school) graduate
中卒 ちゅうそつ junior high graduate
東大卒 とうだいそつ graduate from Tokyo University

学 ▷scholar
ガク まな(ぶ)　　　Ⓚ2211

scholar, student
学究 がっきゅう scholar, student
学生 がくせい student
学者 がくしゃ scholar, learned man
学割 がくわり student discount
学界 がっかい academic circles [world]
先学 せんがく scholars of the past, senior scholar
宿学 しゅくがく renowned scholar
後学 こうがく junior scholar; future reference
篤学 とくがく love of learning, devotion to one's studies

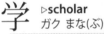
門 ▷pupil
モン かど　　　Ⓚ0789

(persons under same teacher) **pupil, disciple**
門下生 もんかせい disciple, pupil
門弟 もんてい pupil, disciple

入門する にゅうもんする become a pupil of, enter a private school
同門 どうもん fellow pupil

弟 ▷disciple
テイ ダイ デ おとうと　　　Ⓚ1759

(someone who follows a master) **disciple, pupil, apprentice**
弟子 でし disciple, pupil, apprentice
弟子入りする でしいりする become a disciple [pupil, apprentice]
徒弟 とてい apprentice
門弟 もんてい pupil, disciple
師弟 してい master and pupil

徒 ▷follower
ト　　　Ⓚ0377

[also suffix] (adherent) **follower, believer, disciple, pupil**
信徒 しんと believer, devotee; the faithful
十二使徒 じゅうにしと the Twelve Apostles
学徒 がくと student, follower
生徒 せいと pupil, student
仏教徒 ぶっきょうと Buddhist

study →LEARN AND STUDY

style →WAY AND STYLE

styles of Chinese characters
楷 行 草

楷 ▷square style
カイ　　　Ⓚ0929

square style of Chinese characters, *kaisho*
楷書 かいしょ square style of Chinese characters

行 ▷*gyosho*
コウ ギョウ アン い(く) ゆ(く) -ゆ(き)
-い(き) おこな(う)　　　Ⓚ0187

***gyosho*, semicursive style of Chinese characters**
行書 ぎょうしょ semicursive style of Chinese characters
行体 ぎょうたい semicursive characters

草 ▷*sosho*
ソウ くさ -ぐさ　　　Ⓚ1953

***sosho*, cursive style of Chinese characters**
草書 そうしょ *sosho*, cursive writing

submit and surrender

服 伏 屈 降

服 ▷submit
フク   Ⓚ0782

ⓐ [also 伏] submit to, yield to, surrender; obey, observe
ⓑ cause to submit

a 服罪 ふくざい submitting to a sentence
服従 ふくじゅう obedience, submission
屈服する くっぷくする bend in submission, submit to, surrender, yield to
承服 しょうふく consent, acceptance
感服 かんぷく admiration, wonder
不服 ふふく dissatisfaction, discontent; disagreement; objection; complaint
b 征服 せいふく conquest, subjugation
克服する こくふくする conquer, overcome, subjugate

伏 ▷submit
フク ふ(せる) ふ(す)   Ⓚ0030

[also 服] submit to, yield to

屈伏 くっぷく submission, surrender
降伏 こうふく surrender, submission
折伏 しゃくぶく preaching down

屈 ▷bend in submission
クツ   Ⓚ2652

bend in submission, bow, submit to, yield

屈伏(=屈服)する くっぷくする bend in submission, submit to, surrender, yield to
屈従 くつじゅう servile submission, subservience
屈辱 くつじょく humiliation, disgrace, insult
不屈の ふくつの indomitable, unyielding
卑屈な ひくつな mean, mean-spirited; servile

降 ▷surrender
コウ お(りる) お(ろす) ふ(る) ふ(り)   Ⓚ0414

surrender, submit to

降参する こうさんする surrender, submit, yield
降伏(=降服) こうふく surrender, submission

subordinate

副 次 従 亜 準 半 准 助

副 ▷secondary
フク   Ⓚ1581

secondary, sub-, subordinate, vice-, deputy, assistant

副作用 ふくさよう secondary effect, reaction
副次的な ふくじてきな secondary
副大統領 ふくだいとうりょう vice-president
副総理 ふくそうり deputy prime minister
正副 せいふく principal and vice [assistant]; original and copy

次 ▷secondary
ジ シ つ(ぐ) つぎ   Ⓚ0039

secondary, sub-, vice, deputy, assistant

次類 じるい subgenus
次官 じかん vice-minister, undersecretary
次長 じちょう assistant director
次席 じせき next in rank, associate
副次的な ふくじてきな secondary

従 ▷subordinate
ジュウ ショウ ジュ したが(う) したが(える)   Ⓚ0376

[also prefix] subordinate, second grade, secondary

従属する じゅうぞくする be subordinate, depend
従的な じゅうてきな subordinate, secondary
従節 じゅうせつ subordinate clause
従三位 じゅさんみ second grade of the third rank of honor
従因 じゅういん secondary cause

亜 ▷sub-
ア   Ⓚ2966

sub-, subordinate

亜熱帯 あねったい subtropics
亜科 あか suborder
亜麻 あま flax
亜鉛 あえん zinc

準 ▷quasi-
ジュン   Ⓚ2486

[also prefix] quasi-, semi-, associate

準急 じゅんきゅう local express, semi-express (train)
準星 じゅんせい quasar
準決勝 じゅんけっしょう semifinal
準会員 じゅんかいいん associate member

subordinate

半 ▷semi-
ハン なか(ば)   Ⓚ2936

[also prefix] (not fully) **semi-, quasi-, partly**
半製品 はんせいひん semimanufactured goods
半導体 はんどうたい semiconductor
半永久的 はんえいきゅうてき semipermanent

准 ▷junior
ジュン   Ⓚ0108

[also prefix] (of secondary rank) **junior, assistant**
准教員 じゅんきょういん junior [assistant] teacher
准尉 じゅんい warrant officer
准看護婦 じゅんかんごふ junior nurse

助 ▷assistant
ジョ たす(ける) たす(かる) すけ   Ⓚ1037

[also prefix] **assistant, auxiliary**
助詞 じょし *gram* postpositional particle
助役 じょやく assistant official; deputy mayor;
  deputy station-master
助教授 じょきょうじゅ assistant [associate] professor
助監督 じょかんとく assistant director [manager]
助動詞 じょどうし auxiliary verb

substitute
代   摂

代 ▷substitute
ダイ タイ か(わる) か(わり) -が(わり)
か(える) よ しろ   Ⓚ0018

[original meaning] **substitute, replace, represent, act
for another, alternate**
代用する だいようする substitute, use for another
代行する だいこうする act for another, execute
  (business) for another
代表する だいひょうする represent, stand for; typify
代理人 だいりにん representative, deputy, proxy
代議 だいぎ popular representation
代議士 だいぎし member of the Diet [House of
  Representatives]
代打 だいだ pinch-hitting; pinch hitter
代替エネルギー だいたいえねるぎー alternative
  [substitute] energy
代謝(=新陳代謝) たいしゃ(=しんちんたいしゃ)
  metabolism; renewal, regeneration
代名詞 だいめいし pronoun
交代する こうたいする relieve (a person), take turns,
  alternate

摂 ▷act as regent
セツ   Ⓚ059

**act as regent, represent, act as deputy; carry on in
addition to**
摂政 せっしょう regency; regent
摂関家 せっかんけ line of regents
兼摂する けんせつする hold an additional post

subtract
減   引   控   扣

減 ▷subtract
ゲン へ(る) へ(らす)   Ⓚ054█

math **subtract**
減法 げんぽう subtraction
加減 かげん addition and subtraction; degree,
  extent; adjustment

引 ▷subtract
イン ひ(く) ひ(き) -び(き)
ひ(ける)   Ⓚ016█

subtract, deduct, deduce; allow discount
引き算 ひきざん subtraction
三引く二は一 さんひくにはいち Three minus two
  equals one
割引 わりびき discount, reduction

控 ▷hold back
コウ ひか(える) ひか(え)   Ⓚ0453

[formerly 扣] **hold back part of something, deduct,
subtract**
控除 こうじょ (tax) deduction, subtraction

扣 ▷hold back
コウ ひか(える) ひか(え)

[now replaced by 控] **hold back part of something,
deduct, subtract**
扣除 こうじょ (tax) deduction, subtraction

succeed
継   承   嗣

継 ▷succeed
ケイ つ(ぐ)   Ⓚ1242

(come after and take the place of) **succeed (to), accede,
inherit**
継承する けいしょうする succeed to, accede to,
  inherit

継嗣 けいし successor, heir, heiress
継投 けいとう relieving the (starting) pitcher
後継 こうけい succession; successor, inheritor, heir

承 ▷succeed to
ショウ うけたまわ(る) ㉕0007

succeed to, take over, inherit; receive
承継 しょうけい succession
承前 しょうぜん continued (from the previous text)
継承する けいしょうする succeed to, accede to, inherit
伝承 でんしょう tradition, legend

嗣 ▷inherit
シ ㉕1532

inherit, succeed
継嗣 けいし successor, heir, heiress

sudden
急 激 暴 俄 頓 勃 突

急 ▷sudden
キュウ いそ(ぐ) いそ(ぎ) ㉕1800

[also prefix] sudden, unexpected
急激な きゅうげきな sudden, abrupt
急増 きゅうぞう sudden [rapid] increase
急落 きゅうらく sudden drop [fall], steep decline
急変 きゅうへん sudden change [turn]; accident
急死 きゅうし sudden death
急病 きゅうびょう sudden (attack of) illness
急カーブ きゅうかーぶ sharp curve [turn]
急停車 きゅうていしゃ sudden stop

激 ▷sudden
ゲキ はげ(しい) ㉕0696

sudden, rapid
激変(=劇変) げきへん sudden change, upheaval
激増 げきぞう sudden [rapid] increase
激動する げきどうする shake violently; be thrown into turmoil
急激な きゅうげきな sudden, abrupt

暴 ▷sudden
ボウ バク あば(く) あば(れる) ㉕2194

sudden, abrupt
暴落 ぼうらく slump, crash, heavy decline (in prices)
暴発 ぼうはつ spontaneous discharge, accidental gun discharge
暴騰 ぼうとう sudden (price) rise

俄 ▷sudden
ガ にわか ㉕0076

sudden, abrupt
俄然 がぜん suddenly, all of a sudden, abruptly

頓 ▷sudden
トン ㉕0957

ⓐ sudden
ⓑ at once [one time]
ⓐ 頓智(=頓知) とんち (quick or ready) wit
頓死 とんし sudden death
頓悟 とんご Buddhism sudden enlightenment
素っ頓狂 すっとんきょう harum-scarum, hysteric
ⓑ 頓服 とんぷく dose of medicine

勃 ▷suddenly
ボツ ㉕1317

suddenly, abruptly
勃発 ぼっぱつ outbreak, sudden occurrence
勃然として ぼつぜんとして suddenly, with sudden force; in a fit of anger
勃興 ぼっこう sudden rise, sudden increase in power
勃起 ぼっき (male) erection

突 ▷abruptly
トツ つ(く) ㉕1918

abruptly, suddenly, unexpectedly
突然 とつぜん abruptly, suddenly, unexpectedly
突如 とつじょ suddenly, unexpectedly
突風 とっぷう squall, sudden gust
突飛な とっぴな wild, extravagant, extraordinary
唐突に とうとつに abruptly

sue
訴 訟 告 控

訴 ▷sue
ソ うった(える) ㉕1367

sue, litigate, take legal action
訴訟 そしょう lawsuit, litigation
訴願 そがん appeal, petition
訴状 そじょう written complaint
起訴 きそ prosecution, indictment, litigation
告訴 こくそ legal action, complaint, accusation
公訴 こうそ arraignment, prosecution
敗訴 はいそ losing a suit [case]

訟 ▷litigate
ショウ   Ⓚ1339

litigate, bring a case to court, sue
訟務部 しょうむぶ Litigation Department (of the Ministry of Justice)
訴訟 そしょう lawsuit, litigation

告 ▷accuse of
コク つ(げる)   Ⓚ2134

accuse of (an offense), sue, accuse, appeal to the law
告訴する こくそする sue, complain, accuse
告発 こくはつ prosecution, indictment, accusation
上告 じょうこく final appeal
被告 ひこく defendant, the accused
宣告 せんこく sentence, verdict, pronouncement
誣告 ぶこく false accusation

控 ▷accuse in court
コウ ひか(える) ひか(え)   Ⓚ0453

accuse in court, charge, sue
控訴 こうそ (intermediate) appeal

suffering →TROUBLE AND SUFFERING

suffice
足   満

足 ▷suffice
ソク あし た(りる) た(る) た(す) Ⓚ1873

suffice, be enough, be adequate
満足 まんぞく satisfaction, contentment
不足 ふそく insufficiency, shortage, deficit; want; dissatisfaction
自足 じそく self-sufficiency

満 ▷satisfied
マン み(ちる) み(つ) み(たす) Ⓚ0553

satisfied
満足 まんぞく satisfaction, contentment
満喫する まんきつする have enough, enjoy fully
不満 ふまん dissatisfaction, discontent
円満な えんまんな perfect, harmonious, well-rounded

suitable
適   当   宜   便

適 ▷suitable
テキ   Ⓚ272◆

suitable, fit, proper, appropriate, right
適当な てきとうな suitable, fit; irresponsible
適正な てきせいな proper, appropriate, reasonable; right
適切な てきせつな appropriate, adequate, proper
適時の てきじの timely, opportune
適宜 てきぎ suitableness, appropriateness; suitably
適量 てきりょう proper quantity
適者 てきしゃ suitable person
適度 てきど moderate, proper
適齢期 てきれいき marriageable age
最適な さいてきな optimum

当 ▷proper
トウ あ(たる) あ(たり) あ(てる) あ(て)   Ⓚ186⑤

proper, appropriate, fitting, applicable
当然 とうぜん naturally, as a matter of course
当否 とうひ right or wrong, justice; propriety
正当な せいとうな just, right, due; legal
適当な てきとうな suitable, fit; irresponsible
妥当な だとうな proper, appropriate
該当する がいとうする come under, be applicable to
不当な ふとうな unfair, unreasonable, unjust
本当の ほんとうの true, real, genuine

宜 ▷right
ギ よろ(しい) よろ(しく)   Ⓚ190⑨

right, just right, appropriate, suitable, opportune, good
機宜 きぎ opportunity, occasion
便宜 べんぎ convenience, facility
適宜 てきぎ suitableness, appropriateness; suitably
時宜 じぎ right time [occasion], proper time

便 ▷convenient
ベン ビン たよ(り)   Ⓚ0075

[original meaning] **convenient, expedient, handy**
便利な べんりな convenient, handy, useful
便宜 べんぎ convenience, facility
便覧 べんらん(=びんらん) handbook, manual
便法 べんぽう convenient method, shortcut, expedient
不便な ふべんな inconvenient
方便 ほうべん expedient, instrument

sun

日　陽　旭

日 ▷sun
ニチ ジツ ひ -び -か　　Ⓚ2606

[original meaning] **sun, sunlight**

日光 にっこう sunshine, sunlight
日没 にちぼつ sunset
日食 にっしょく solar eclipse
日月 じつげつ sun and moon; time, days, years
落日 らくじつ setting sun

陽 ▷sun
ヨウ　　Ⓚ0572

sun, sunlight

陽光 ようこう sunshine, sunlight, sun
陽暦 ようれき solar calendar
太陽 たいよう sun
落陽 らくよう setting sun
春陽 しゅんよう spring sunshine

旭 ▷rising sun
キョク あさひ　　Ⓚ2571

[original meaning] **rising sun, morning sun**

旭日 きょくじつ rising sun
旭日章 きょくじつしょう Order of the Rising Sun
旭光 きょっこう rays of the morning [rising] sun

superior →EXCELLENT AND SUPERIOR

supernatural and evil beings

鬼　魔　怪　霊　精

鬼 ▷devil
キ おに　　Ⓚ2313

ⓐ (harmful evil spirit) **devil, demon**
ⓑ (imaginary evil monster with horns) **devil, ogre**

a 鬼神 きしん terrible god; departed spirit, ghost
鬼畜 きちく devil
鬼気迫る ききせまる ghastly, bloodcurdling
鬼女 きじょ demoness, witch
悪鬼 あっき devil, demon, evil spirit, goblin
疑心暗鬼 ぎしんあんき suspicion and fear
b 鬼面 きめん mask of a devil, startling appearance

魔 ▷demon
マ　　Ⓚ2747

demon, devil, evil spirit

魔神 まじん evil spirit, devil
魔物 まもの goblin, apparition
悪魔 あくま devil, demon, satan
病魔 びょうま demon of ill health; disease
邪魔 じゃま hindrance, obstruction, impediment

怪 ▷monster
カイ ケ あや(しい) あや(しむ)　　Ⓚ0264

monster, ghost, goblin, demon

怪獣 かいじゅう monster; beast
怪物 かいぶつ monster; ghost, goblin, bogey; mysterious figure
怪談 かいだん ghost story
妖怪 ようかい ghost, apparition, phantom, goblin

霊 ▷spirit
レイ リョウ たま　　Ⓚ2442

ⓐ **departed spirit, ghost**
ⓑ [also suffix] (supernatural being) **spirit, ghost**

a 霊園 れいえん cemetery park
霊前に れいぜんに before the spirit of the departed
霊魂 れいこん spirit, soul
慰霊祭 いれいさい memorial service
幽霊 ゆうれい ghost, apparition
亡霊 ぼうれい departed spirit, ghost
英霊 えいれい spirit of the war dead
精霊 しょうりょう spirit of a dead person
b 神霊 しんれい divine spirit
悪霊 あくりょう evil spirit
聖霊 せいれい Holy Ghost, Holy Spirit
守護霊 しゅごれい guardian spirit

精 ▷spirit
セイ ショウ　　Ⓚ1248

(supernatural being) **spirit, sprite, fairy**

精霊 せいれい spirit of a dead person; spirit, sprite
妖精 ようせい fairy, elf, sprite

supervise →DIRECT AND SUPERVISE

supplement

補　足　給　充

補 ▷supplement
ホ おぎな(う)　　Ⓚ1103

supplement, make up for, compensate; replenish, supply

補足 ほそく supplement, replenishment

補遺 ほい supplement
補償する ほしょうする compensate, indemnify
補充する ほじゅうする supplement, replenish, recruit
補給 ほきゅう supply, replenishment
補欠 ほけつ filling a vacancy; substitute, alternate
補正する ほせいする revise, correct

足 ▷supplement
ソク あし た(りる) た(る) た(す)　Ⓚ1873

supplement
補足 ほそく supplement, replenishment
充足 じゅうそく sufficiency

給 ▷supply
キュウ　Ⓚ1237

[original meaning] (make up for a deficiency) **supply, supplement**
補給 ほきゅう supply, replenishment
自給 じきゅう self-supply, self-support

充 ▷fill up (a vacancy)
ジュウ あ(てる)　Ⓚ1737

fill up (a vacancy), make up for (a deficiency)
充員 じゅういん reserves
補充する ほじゅうする supplement, replenish, recruit

supply
供　給　納

供 ▷supply
キョウ ク そな(える) とも -ども　Ⓚ0070

supply, deliver, furnish
供給する きょうきゅうする supply, furnish, provide
供与する きょうよする offer, present, submit
供出 きょうしゅつ delivery of allotment to the government
供米 きょうまい delivery of rice to the government; rice delivered to the government

給 ▷supply
キュウ　Ⓚ1237

(provide with something requisite) **supply, provide**
給水 きゅうすい water supply
給油 きゅうゆ supply of oil
給食 きゅうしょく (provision of) meals
支給 しきゅう provision, supply; allowance, grant; payment
配給 はいきゅう distribution, supply; rationing
供給する きょうきゅうする supply, furnish, provide

納 ▷deliver goods to a customer
ノウ ナッ- ナ ナン トウ おさ(める) おさ(まる)　Ⓚ119

deliver goods to a customer, supply goods
納品 のうひん delivery of goods; delivered goods

support
支　擁　扶　賛

支 ▷support
シ ささ(える)　Ⓚ171

(provide with aid) **support, maintain**
支持 じじ support, maintenance, backing
支援 しえん support, backing, aid

擁 ▷support
ヨウ　Ⓚ069

support, protect
擁立する ようりつする give backing to, support, help (to the throne)
擁護する ようごする protect, defend, support, safeguard

扶 ▷lend support to
フ　Ⓚ022

lend support to, support, hold up, sustain
扶養する ふようする support, maintain
扶助する ふじょする support, sustain
扶育 ふいく bringing up (children)

賛 ▷back up
サン　Ⓚ244

back up, give support, assist, help
賛助 さんじょ backing, support, approval
協賛 きょうさん support, cooperation
翼賛 よくさん support, countenance, assistance

supporting parts of plants
根　株　幹　茎

根 ▷root
コン ね　Ⓚ0841

[original meaning] **root (of a plant)**
根菜 こんさい root crops
毛根 もうこん root of a hair

大根 だいこん Japanese radish
球根 きゅうこん bulb

株 ▷**stump**
シュ かぶ   ⓚ0846

【シュ】
[original meaning] **stump, stub**
  守株 しゅしゅ stupidity, lack of innovation

【かぶ】
stump, stub
  切り株 きりかぶ stump

幹 ▷**trunk**
カン みき   ⓚ1531

[original meaning] **tree trunk**
  樹幹 じゅかん trunk, shaft
  根幹 こんかん basis, root; keynote; [original meaning] root and trunk
  躯幹 くかん body, trunk, physique

茎 ▷**stem**
ケイ くき   ⓚ1931

[also suffix] [original meaning] **stem, stalk**
  茎葉 けいよう stems and leaves
  球茎 きゅうけい corn, bulb
  地下茎 ちかけい subterranean shoot, rootstock

supporting structures
柱 礎 桁 梁

柱 ▷**pillar**
チュウ はしら   ⓚ0797

ⓐ [original meaning] **pillar, post, column, pole**
ⓑ **something shaped like a pillar**
ⓒ *mining* **pillar, post**
a 石柱 せきちゅう stone pillar
  円柱 えんちゅう column, shaft, cylinder
  電柱 でんちゅう telegraph [telephone, electric] pole
  門柱 もんちゅう gate post, pier
b 氷柱 ひょうちゅう icicle; block [square pillar] of ice
c 炭柱 たんちゅう coal pillar
  鉱柱 こうちゅう pillar, rib
  残柱 ざんちゅう pillar

礎 ▷**foundation stone**
ソ いしずえ   ⓚ1152

foundation stone, cornerstone, foundation
  礎石 そせき foundation stone, cornerstone

礎材 そざい foundation materials
柱礎 ちゅうそ plinth
定礎 ていそ laying of a foundation stone

桁 ▷**beam**
けた   ⓚ0839

beam, girder, spar

梁 ▷**beam**
リョウ はり やな   ⓚ2391

ⓐ **beam, crossbeam, girder**
ⓑ **something resembling a beam or girder**
a 棟梁 とうりょう chief support, pillar (of a nation), chief, leader, foreman
  臥梁 がりょう perimeter beam
b 鼻梁 びりょう bridge of the nose
  脊梁 せきりょう backbone, spine

suppress →CONQUER AND SUPPRESS

surrender →SUBMIT AND SURRENDER

surround
囲 環 包

囲 ▷**enclose**
イ かこ(む) かこ(う) かこ(い)   ⓚ2643

【イ】
[original meaning] **enclose, encircle, surround**
  囲碁 いご (the game of) go
  包囲する ほういする surround, encircle, envelop
  範囲 はんい range, scope

【かこ(む)】
enclose, encircle, surround; enclose with a fence, fence in; besiege
  囲み かこみ enclosure; siege
  取り囲む とりかこむ enclose, encircle

環 ▷**surround**
カン   ⓚ1011

surround, encircle; around
  環境 かんきょう environment, surroundings, circumstances
  環海 かんかい surrounding seas
  循環 じゅんかん circulation, rotation; cycle

包 ▷**encompass**
ホウ つつ(む)   ⓚ2560

[original meaning] (surround with) **encompass, surround, encircle**
  包括的 ほうかつてき inclusive, comprehensive
  包囲する ほういする surround, encircle, envelop

swell and swelling
脹　腫　瘍　爛

脹 ▷swell
チョウ は(れる) ふく(らむ) ふく(れる)　⒦0916

swell, expand, bulge
膨脹(=膨張) ぼうちょう expansion, swelling; growth, increase
腫脹 しゅちょう swelling, puffiness

腫 ▷swelling
シュ は(れる) は(らす)　⒦0951

[also suffix] **swelling; tumor, neoplasm**
腫脹 しゅちょう swelling, puffiness
腫瘍 しゅよう tumor, neoplasm, growth
腫瘤 しゅりゅう lump, mass, tumor
筋腫 きんしゅ myoma
肉腫 にくしゅ sarcoma
浮腫 ふしゅ(=むくみ) swelling, edema
リンパ腫 りんぱしゅ lymphoma

瘍 ▷swelling
ヨウ　⒦2801

swelling, boil, malignant growth [tumor]
潰瘍 かいよう ulcer
腫瘍 しゅよう tumor, neoplasm, growth
腫瘍学 しゅようがく oncology
膿瘍 のうよう abscess, boil

爛 ▷break out in sores
ラン ただ(れる)

break out in sores, be inflamed, be ulcerated
糜爛 びらん sore, inflammation, ulceration

swelling →SWELL AND SWELLING

swine
豚　豕　猪　亥

豚 ▷pig
トン ぶた　⒦0889

[original meaning] **pig, hog, swine**
豚舎 とんしゃ pigsty, pigpen
養豚 ようとん swine keeping

豕 ▷swine
シ いのこ

[original meaning] **swine, pig, hog, boar**
魯魚亥豕 ろぎょがいし miswriting a word

猪 ▷wild boar
チョ いのしし い　⒦048

[original meaning] **wild boar, boar**
野猪 やちょ wild boar

亥 ▷the Boar
ガイ い　⒦173

twelfth sign of the Oriental zodiac: **the Boar**—(time) 9-11 p.m., (direction) NNW, (season) October (of the lunar calendar)
亥月 がいげつ October (of the lunar calendar)

system
系　制　統　網

系 ▷system
ケイ　⒦170

[also suffix] (group of interrelated elements) **system, interrelated group**
系統 けいとう system; geological formation; lineage, ancestry
系列 けいれつ order, succession; series
体系 たいけい system, organization

制 ▷system
セイ　⒦117⑥

ⓐ (organizational form) **system, organization, institution**
ⓑ [suffix] **system**
a 制度 せいど system, organization, institution
体制 たいせい system, structure, organization
市制 しせい city organization
税制 ぜいせい tax system
b 天皇制 てんのうせい emperor system of Japan
六・三制 ろくさんせい the 6-3 school year system

統 ▷interconnected system
トウ す(べる)　⒦1239

interconnected system, lineage
系統 けいとう system; geological formation; lineage, ancestry
血統 けっとう lineage, blood, bloodline
正統派 せいとうは orthodox school
伝統 でんとう tradition, convention

網 ▷network
モウ あみ   Ⓚ1255

[suffix] **network**

通信網 つうしんもう communications network
鉄道網 てつどうもう railway network
放送網 ほうそうもう broadcasting network

tables and stands
卓　机　几　台

卓 ▷table
タク   Ⓚ1777

table, desk

卓球 たっきゅう table tennis, ping-pong
卓上電話 たくじょうでんわ desk phone
食卓 しょくたく dining table
円卓 えんたく round table
電卓 でんたく pocket calculator

机 ▷desk
キ つくえ   Ⓚ0726

desk, table

机上 きじょう top of desk; academic, theoretical
机辺 きへん around the desk [table]
机下(=几下) きか under the desk

几 ▷desk
キ

[original meaning] **desk, small table**

几案 きあん [rare] desk
几下(=机下) きか under the desk
几帳 きちょう screen
几帳面な きちょうめんな exact, precise, punctual
浄几(=浄机) じょうき clean [tidy] writing desk
床几(=床机) しょうぎ campstool, folding stool

台 ▷stand
ダイ タイ   Ⓚ1731

[also suffix]
ⓐ (structure for placing on) **stand, pedestal, rack, table, support, mount**
ⓑ (elevated structure) **stand, platform**

a 台座 だいざ pedestal, base, stand
燭台 しょくだい candlestick, candlestand
楽譜台 がくふだい music stand
鏡台 きょうだい dressing table
荷台 にだい carrier, bed (of a truck)
寝台 しんだい bed, sleeping berth
流し台 ながしだい sink, washstand

実験台 じっけんだい testing bench; subject of an experiment
b 閲兵台 えっぺいだい reviewing stand
証人台 しょうにんだい witness stand
滑り台 すべりだい (playground) slide; launching platform

take
把　握　捉　執　摑　捕　取　持

把 ▷grip
ハ ワ   Ⓚ0222

[original meaning] **grip, grasp, seize, hold**

把握する はあくする grip, grasp; understand, grasp
把持する はじする grasp, hold, grip

握 ▷grasp
アク にぎ(る)   Ⓚ0535

grasp, seize, clasp, hold

握力 あくりょく grasping power
握手 あくしゅ handshake, handshaking
一握 いちあく a handful (of sand)

捉 ▷grasp
ソク とら(える)   Ⓚ0391

(take hold as if with the hand) **grasp (an idea), seize (an opportunity)**

把捉する はそくする grasp (a meaning, etc.)

執 ▷seize
シツ シュウ と(る)   Ⓚ1501

seize [hold] an object (such as a pen) and perform an action with

執筆 しっぴつ writing
執刀する しっとうする perform an operation

摑 ▷grasp
カク つか(む) つか(まえる)
つか(まる)   Ⓚ0627

grasp, grip, clutch, catch, seize

摑み取り つかみどり taking (as much as one can hold) by the hand
摑み掛かる つかみかかる grab at
摑み所 つかみどころ hold, grip; point
鷲摑み わしづかみ grabbing hold
溺れる者は藁をも摑む おぼれるものはわらをもつかむ A drowning man will catch at a straw

捕 ▷catch
ホ と(らえる) と(らわれる) と(る)
つか(まえる) つか(まる)　　　Ⓚ0387

catch, seize, grasp

捕獲する ほかくする catch (fish); capture (a ship),
　　seize
捕捉する ほそくする catch, seize, capture; appre-
　　hend; understand
捕球 ほきゅう a catch (in baseball)
捕手 ほしゅ catcher
逮捕 たいほ arrest, capture

取 ▷take
シュ と(る) と(り) -ど(り)　　　Ⓚ1162

【シュ】

[original meaning] (grasp with the hands) **take, pick,
gather**

採取 さいしゅ picking, collecting, harvesting
摘取する てきしゅする pick, pluck up

【と(る)】

take, take hold of, seize

取れる とれる can be held; come off, fall off; be
　　removed; be produced; be understood; be
　　interpreted
取り柄 とりえ merit, worth, recommendable
　　feature
取り上げる とりあげる take [pick] up; take away,
　　confiscate; deliver a baby; accept, listen to;
　　adopt (a proposal)
取り分け とりわけ especially, above all
塵取り ちりとり dustpan
遣り取り やりとり giving and taking, exchanges
手に取る てにとる take in one's hand
色取る いろどる [also 彩る] color, paint, dye; make
　　up

持 ▷hold
ジ も(つ) -も(ち) も(てる)　　　Ⓚ0333
see also →HOLD

[original meaning] **hold, grasp, have; have with one**

持参する じさんする bring [take] with one, carry
把持 はじ grasp, hold, grip
棒持する ほうじする hold up, bear, present
支持する しじする support, maintain, back up
所持する しょじする have (money) about one;
　　possess

奪 ▷rob
ダツ うば(う)　　　Ⓚ2058

rob, take by force, seize, deprive

奪還 だっかん recapture, recovery
奪取 だっしゅ capture, seizure
略奪 りゃくだつ pillage, plunder, looting
強奪する ごうだつする rob, seize, plunder; hijack
争奪 そうだつ scramble, contest, struggle
剝奪する はくだつする deprive, divest

拐 ▷kidnap
カイ　　　Ⓚ0272

kidnap, abduct

拐取する かいしゅする abduct (legal term)
誘拐 ゆうかい kidnapping, abduction

収 ▷take possession by force
シュウ おさ(める) おさ(まる)　　　Ⓚ0016

take possession by force, confiscate, seize

収用 しゅうよう expropriation
押収する おうしゅうする seize, confiscate
没収 ぼっしゅう confiscation, seizure, forfeiture
接収 せっしゅう requisition, takeover, seizure

take from water
撈　掬　汲

撈 ▷dredge
ロウ

[now usu. 捞] [original meaning] **dredge up, drag for,
fish for**

漁撈 ぎょろう fishing, fishery
海底撈月 かいていろうげつ totally useless effort
　　(like dredging for the reflected moon from the
　　bottom of the sea)

掬 ▷scoop up
キク すく(う)　　　Ⓚ0452

scoop up

一掬 いっきく scooping water in the hands; small
　　amount

汲 ▷draw water
キュウ く(む) Ⓚ0235

[original meaning] **draw (water), scoop up, ladle, pump**

汲水 きゅうすい drawing [pumping] up water

take in
収 摂 喫 吸

収 ▷take in
シュウ おさ(める) おさ(まる) Ⓚ0016

take in, gather in, absorb

収容する しゅうようする accommodate, receive (guests)
収納 しゅうのう storing; harvesting; receipt
収穫 しゅうかく harvest; harvesting
収着 しゅうちゃく sorption
吸収 きゅうしゅう absorption, assimilation; merger
買収 ばいしゅう buying up, purchasing; bribing
回収する かいしゅうする collect, recover; withdraw

摂 ▷take in
セツ Ⓚ0595

take in, ingest, absorb, assimilate

摂取する せっしゅする take (in), ingest, absorb
摂動 せつどう (gravitational) perturbation
包摂する ほうせつする connote, subsume
カロリーの摂取量 かろりーのせっしゅりょう caloric intake

喫 ▷ingest
キツ Ⓚ0505
see also →INGEST

(introduce into one's body) **ingest, eat, drink, inhale, swallow**

喫飯 きっぱん [rare] eating, taking a meal
喫茶店 きっさてん coffee shop, tea house
喫煙 きつえん smoking
満喫する まんきつする have enough, enjoy fully

吸 ▷suck
キュウ す(う) Ⓚ0179

[original meaning] **suck, suck in, absorb**

吸収 きゅうしゅう absorption, assimilation; merger
吸着 きゅうちゃく adsorption
吸引する きゅういんする suck (in), absorb, aspirate; attract
吸塵 きゅうじん dust vacuuming
吸血鬼 きゅうけつき vampire
吸盤 きゅうばん sucker, sucking disk

take precautions
戒 警

戒 ▷take caution
カイ いまし(める) Ⓚ2760

[original meaning] **take caution (against), guard against, be careful**

戒厳令 かいげんれい martial law
戒心 かいしん caution, precaution, care
戒慎する かいしんする be cautious, be discreet
警戒 けいかい caution, precaution, warning; watch, guard, vigilance

警 ▷guard against
ケイ Ⓚ2512

guard against, protect, police, watch

警察 けいさつ police, police station
警官 けいかん police officer, policeman
警視庁 けいしちょう Metropolitan Police Office
警戒 けいかい caution, precaution, warning; watch, guard, vigilance
警備 けいび guard, defense
警手 けいしゅ guard, attendant

talented persons →WISE AND TALENTED PERSONS

tall buildings
閣 楼 塔 台

閣 ▷tall magnificent building
カク Ⓚ2841

tall magnificent building, tower, pavilion, stately mansion, palace

閣下 かっか Your [His] Excellency
楼閣 ろうかく multistoried building
天守閣 てんしゅかく castle-tower; dungeon, keep
仏閣 ぶっかく Buddhist temple
銀閣寺 ぎんかくじ Ginkaku Temple

楼 ▷tall building
ロウ Ⓚ0931

[original meaning] **tall building, tower, storied building; watchtower, lookout**

楼閣 ろうかく multistoried building
鐘楼 しょうろう bell tower, belfry
望楼 ぼうろう watchtower, observation tower, lookout
五層楼 ごそうろう five-storied building [tower]
高楼 こうろう lofty [high] building; skyscraper

tall buildings

登楼する とうろうする go into a tall building; visit a brothel
摩天楼 まてんろう skyscraper

塔 ▷tower
トウ ⓚ0517

[also suffix] **tower**
鉄塔 てっとう steel tower; pylon
テレビ塔 てれびとう television tower
管制塔 かんせいとう control tower
エッフェル塔 えっふぇるとう Eiffel Tower

台 ▷observatory
ダイ タイ ⓚ1731

[also suffix] [original meaning] (elevated structure commanding a wide view) **observatory, lookout, tower, tall building**
天文台 てんもんだい astronomical observatory
気象台 きしょうだい meteorological observatory
灯台 とうだい lighthouse; oil-lamp stand
露台 ろだい balcony
見張り台 みはりだい lookout

target
的 標 狙 目

的 ▷target
テキ まと ⓚ1040

target, mark, bull's eye
標的 ひょうてき target, mark
射的 しゃてき target practice, shooting
目的 もくてき object, purpose

標 ▷mark
ヒョウ ⓚ0976

(something aimed at) **mark, target, standard**
標的 ひょうてき target, mark
標準 ひょうじゅん standard, norm, criterion
目標 もくひょう mark, target, goal, object

狙 ▷aim
ソ ねら(う) ⓚ0304

aim, take aim, target
狙撃 そげき shooting, sniping

目 ▷aim
モク ボク め ま- ⓚ2619

aim, object, objective
目標 もくひょう mark, target, goal, object
目的 もくてき object, purpose

目的地 もくてきち destination, goal

taste
味 嘗 舐

味 ▷taste (savor)
ミ あじ あじ(わう) ⓚ0247

taste, savor, appreciate, enjoy
味読する みどくする appreciate a book
吟味 ぎんみ close examination, scrutiny

嘗 ▷taste (have a taste)
ショウ ジョウ な(める) な(めずる) かつ(て) ⓚ2268

taste, have a taste
塩を嘗める しおをなめる taste the salt

舐 ▷taste (have a taste)
シ な(める) な(めずる)

taste, have a taste
塩を舐める しおをなめる taste the salt

tastes
甘 苦 辛 辣 酸 渋 鹹

甘 ▷sweet
カン あま(い) あま(える) あま(やかす) ⓚ2930

(of sugary taste) **sweet**
甘味料 かんみりょう sweetener
甘薯 かんしょ sweet potato
甘露 かんろ nectar, honeydew
甘蔗 かんしょ sugar cane
甘酸 かんさん sweet and bitter; pain and pleasure

苦 ▷bitter
ク くる(しい) -ぐる(しい) くる(しむ) くる(しめる) にが(い) にが(る) ⓚ1932

[original meaning] **bitter**
苦味 くみ bitter taste
苦土 くど magnesia
苦情 くじょう complaint, grievance
苦杯 くはい bitter ordeal

辛 ▷pungent
シン から(い) ⓚ1755

pungent, hot, spicy

辛辣な しんらつな bitter, pungent, acrid, poignant, severe
香辛料 こうしんりょう spices, seasoning

辣 ▷pungent
ラツ　　　　　　　Ⓚ1412

pungent, hot, spicy
辣韮(=薤、辣韭) らっきょう Japanese shallot, *Allium chinense*
辣油 らーゆ Chinese red chili oil

酸 ▷sour
サン す(い)　　　　Ⓚ1415

sour, acid, tart
酸味 さんみ sourness

渋 ▷astringent
ジュウ しぶ しぶ(い) しぶ(る)　Ⓚ0471

astringent, puckery, rough—said esp. of the taste of unripe persimmons
渋柿 しぶがき puckery persimmon
渋い酒 しぶいさけ rough wine

鹹 ▷salty
カン から(い)

[original meaning] **salty, briny, saline**
鹹水湖 かんすいこ saltwater lake
鹹味 かんみ saltiness

tax
税　租　貢　賦

税 ▷tax
ゼイ　　　　　　　Ⓚ1101

[also suffix] **tax, duty**
税金 ぜいきん tax, duty; rates
税関 ぜいかん customhouse
租税 そぜい taxes, taxation
課税 かぜい taxation
脱税 だつぜい tax evasion
減税 げんぜい reduction of taxes, tax cut
納税 のうぜい tax payment
所得税 しょとくぜい income tax
間接税 かんせつぜい indirect tax

租 ▷land tax
ソ　　　　　　　　Ⓚ1076

land tax, crop tax, taxes
租税 そぜい taxes, taxation

租庸調 そようちょう taxes in kind or service (former tax system), corvée
田租 でんそ rice field tax
地租 ちそ land tax
免租 めんそ tax exemption
貢租 こうそ tribute, annual tax

貢 ▷tribute
コウ ク みつ(ぐ)　　Ⓚ1970

[original meaning] **tribute**
貢租 こうそ tribute, annual tax
年貢 ねんぐ land tax

賦 ▷levy
フ　　　　　　　　Ⓚ1432

levy, levying, tax; exacted service
賦課する ふかする levy, impose, assess
賦役 ふえき slave labor, corvée, levy of labor

teach
教　啓　諄　授　育　練
訓　誨　諭　導　迪

教 ▷teach
キョウ おし(える) おそ(わる)　Ⓚ1356

[original meaning] **teach, instruct, educate**
教育 きょういく education, teaching
教授する きょうじゅする teach, instruct, give lessons
教師 きょうし teacher, instructor
教員 きょういん teacher, teaching staff
教室 きょうしつ classroom, class
教養 きょうよう culture, education, cultivation
教科 きょうか school subject; course of study, curriculum
教材 きょうざい teaching materials [aids]
教訓 きょうくん lesson, precept, teachings
文教 ぶんきょう education, culture

啓 ▷enlighten
ケイ　　　　　　　Ⓚ2408

ⓐ enlighten, edify, awaken, educate
ⓑ reveal
a 啓蒙 けいもう enlightenment, instruction
啓発する けいはつする enlighten, develop, edify
b 啓示 けいじ revelation
天啓 てんけい divine revelation

諄 ▷teach with care
ジュン シュン くど(い)   Ⓚ1422

teach with care
　諄諄たる じゅんじゅんたる teaching with care

授 ▷teach
ジュ さず(ける) さず(かる)   Ⓚ0448

teach, instruct, initiate
　授業 じゅぎょう teaching, instruction; lesson
　教授 きょうじゅ teaching; professor
　伝授 でんじゅ instruction, initiation
　口授 こうじゅ oral instruction

育 ▷educate
イク そだ(つ) そだ(ち) そだ(てる)
はぐく(む)   Ⓚ1764

educate, teach, train
　育英 いくえい education of the gifted or promising
　教育 きょういく education, teaching
　体育 たいいく physical training [education]

練 ▷train
レン ね(る) ね(り)-   Ⓚ1256

(make proficient) **train, drill**
　訓練 くんれん training, drill
　教練 きょうれん military drill

訓 ▷instruct
クン   Ⓚ1322

instruct, teach, admonish
　訓練 くんれん training, drill
　訓辞 くんじ admonitory speech
　訓戒 くんかい admonition, warning
　訓導 くんどう old word for licensed elementary
　　school teacher; instruction

誨 ▷instruct
カイ

[now replaced by 戒] [original meaning] **instruct, teach**
　教誨 きょうかい exhortation, preaching

諭 ▷admonish
ユ さと(す)   Ⓚ1446

**admonish, give guidance, instruct, advise, per-
suade**
　諭旨 ゆし official suggestion or instruction (to a
　　subordinate)
　教諭 きょうゆ teacher, instructor
　説諭 せつゆ admonition, reproof
　訓諭 くんゆ [rare] admonition, caution, warning

導 ▷guide
ドウ みちび(く)   Ⓚ2509

(give guidance to) **guide, teach, instruct, direct**
　指導する しどうする guide, lead, instruct
　教導する きょうどうする instruct, teach, train

迪 ▷edify
テキ   Ⓚ2649

[rare] **edify, enlighten, guide, teach**
　啓迪する けいてきする edify, enlighten, guide
　訓迪 くんてき guide, teach; master

temporary
仮　　暫

仮 ▷temporary
カ ケ かり   Ⓚ0034

temporary, provisional, transient
　仮設の かせつの provisional, temporary; hypothet-
　　ic
　仮眠 かみん nap, doze
　仮定 かてい assumption, supposition
　仮説 かせつ hypothesis
　仮称 かしょう temporary name
　仮寓 かぐう temporary residence
　仮死 かし suspended animation, apparent death
　仮性近視 かせいきんし false nearsightedness,
　　pseudomyopia

暫 ▷for the time being
ザン しばら(く)   Ⓚ2493

for the time being, temporary, provisional
　暫定の ざんていの provisional, tentative
　暫定案 ざんていあん provisional plan

temporary quarters
舎　寮　宿　館　亭　寓

舎 ▷temporary quarters
シャ   Ⓚ1774

temporary quarters, dormitory, lodging house, inn
　舎監 しゃかん dormitory inspector [superinten-
　　dent]
　兵舎 へいしゃ barracks
　宿舎 しゅくしゃ lodgings, quarters
　客舎 きゃくしゃ hotel, inn
　寄宿舎 きしゅくしゃ dormitory, boarding house;
　　hostel

寮 ▷dormitory
リョウ   Ⓚ2079

lodging accommodations or similar facilities for use by students, company employees or members of an organization:

ⓐ student dormitory, hostel
ⓑ [also suffix] company dormitory, lodging house, villa
ⓒ suffix after names of dormitories

a 寮長 りょうちょう dormitory leader
   寮母 りょうぼ matron of a dormitory
   寮歌 りょうか dormitory song
   寮生 りょうせい boarder
   学寮 がくりょう dormitory, hostel; seminary
b 工員寮 こういんりょう dormitory for factory workers
   独身寮 どくしんりょう company dormitory for unmarried employees
c 若葉寮 わかばりょう Wakaba Dormitory

宿 ▷lodging
シュク やど やど(る) やど(す)   Ⓚ1985

lodging, inn, hotel, lodging house
   宿舎 しゅくしゃ lodgings, quarters
   宿所 しゅくしょ address, lodgings
   宿営 しゅくえい billeting, camp
   宿題 しゅくだい homework
   民宿 みんしゅく tourist home

館 ▷inn
カン やかた   Ⓚ1562

ⓐ [original meaning] inn, lodge
ⓑ suffix after names of inns, hotels, restaurants or movie theaters

a 旅館 りょかん Japanese inn
b 風月館 ふうげつかん The Fugetsukan Inn

亭 ▷inn
テイ   Ⓚ1785

ⓐ inn, hostelry
ⓑ suffix after names of inns

a 亭主 ていしゅ husband; master, host
   旅亭 りょてい inn, hotel
b 石亭 せきてい The Sekitei (name of an inn)

寓 ▷temporary abode
グウ   Ⓚ2010

temporary abode
   仮寓 かぐう temporary residence

---

ten

十   拾

十 ▷ten
ジュウ ジッ– ジュッ– とお と   Ⓚ2855

ten, tenth
   十時 じゅうじ ten o'clock
   七十 しちじゅう 70
   第十 だいじゅう tenth
   二十 にじゅう [sometimes also 廿] 20

拾 ▷ten (in legal documents)
シュウ ジュウ ひろ(う)   Ⓚ0339

ten—used in legal documents and checks
   金拾万円 きんじゅうまんえん 100,000 yen

---

tendency

向 性 勢 傾 潮 流

向 ▷tendency
コウ む(く) む(き) む(ける) –む(け) む(かう) む(こう)   Ⓚ2627

[formerly also 嚮] **tendency, inclination, turn**
   傾向 けいこう tendency, trend; disposition
   意向 いこう intention, inclination
   動向 どうこう trend, tendency, movement
   性向 せいこう inclination, disposition
   趣向 しゅこう idea, contrivance, plan

性 ▷nature
セイ ショウ   Ⓚ0266

[suffix] **nature, propensity towards, habit**
   肥満性 ひまんしょう tendency to be obese
   苦労性 くろうしょう worry habit, pessimistic nature

勢 ▷trend
セイ いきお(い)   Ⓚ2487

trend of events, drift, tendency
   勝勢である しょうせいである stand a good chance of winning the game
   大勢 たいせい general trend [tendency]
   時勢 じせい trend of the times, spirit of the age
   運勢 うんせい one's star, fortune, luck

傾 ▷**inclination**
ケイ かたむ(く) かたむ(ける)
かし(げる)　　　　　　　Ⓚ0132

(trend toward) **inclination, tendency**

潮 ▷**tide**
チョウ しお　　　　　　Ⓚ0675

(stream of events) **tide, tendency, trend, drift**
風潮 ふうちょう tide, trend, tendency
思潮 しちょう trend of thought

流 ▷**current**
リュウ ル なが(れる) なが(れ)
なが(す)　　　　　　　Ⓚ0400

(general tendency) **current, drift, trend**
時流 じりゅう fashion [current] of the times, general drift of affairs
主流 しゅりゅう main current, mainstream
底流 ていりゅう bottom current, undercurrent

tender feelings for others
仁　慈　情　悲　哀　憐

仁 ▷**benevolence**
ジン ニ　　　　　　　　Ⓚ0011

benevolence, the perfect virtue, humaneness, compassion, kindness, love, mercy (a basic Confucian precept)
仁愛 じんあい benevolence, charity
仁術 じんじゅつ benevolent act
仁義礼智信 じんぎれいちしん the five Confucian virtues (benevolence, justice, courtesy, wisdom and sincerity)
仁徳 じんとく benevolence, goodness
仁義 じんぎ humanity and justice; moral code; formal greeting among gamblers

慈 ▷**compassion**
ジ いつく(しむ)　　　　Ⓚ2053

Buddhism **compassion, active benevolence, universal love, loving kindness**
慈悲 じひ mercy, compassion
慈善 じぜん charity
慈雨 じう beneficial [welcome] rain

情 ▷**sympathy**
ジョウ セイ なさ(け)　　Ⓚ0439

sympathy, compassion, kindness
同情 どうじょう sympathy, compassion

人情 にんじょう human feelings, humanity, sympathy

悲 ▷**mercy**
ヒ かな(しい) かな(しむ)　Ⓚ2416

Buddhism **mercy, compassion**
慈悲 じひ mercy, compassion
大慈大悲 だいじだいひ great mercy and compassion

哀 ▷**pity**
アイ あわ(れ) あわ(れむ)
かな(しい)　　　　　　Ⓚ1781

pity, sympathy
哀憐 あいれん pity, compassion

憐 ▷**pity**
レン あわ(れ) あわ(れむ)　Ⓚ0692

pity, sympathize, feel compassion
憐憫(=憐愍) れんびん compassion, mercy
憐情 れんじょう pity, compassion
哀憐 あいれん pity, compassion
愛憐 あいれん tenderness, affection, sympathy
可憐な かれんな cute, sweet, pretty; tiny

terms of assent
然　　　諾

然 ▷**so**
ゼン ネン　　　　　　　Ⓚ2423

ⓐ so, be definitely so, be as it is
ⓑ just so, just as you say, yes
a 天然の てんねんの natural
自然 しぜん nature
偶然 ぐうぜん chance, accident, coincidence
当然 とうぜん naturally, as a matter of course
依然 いぜん still, as yet
b 然諾する ぜんだくする consent, say yes

諾 ▷**yes**
ダク　　　　　　　　　Ⓚ1418

yes, aye
諾否 だくひ definitive answer, yes or no
諾諾 だくだく yes, yes

terms of negation

不 非 無 没 欠
否 未 莫 勿

不 ▷not (negation)
フブ   Ⓚ2890

[also prefix] **not, un-, in-, non-, dis**—-element of negation usu. placed before nouns or noun adjectives

不足 ふそく insufficiency, shortage, deficit; want; dissatisfaction
不安 ふあん uneasiness, anxiety
不動の ふどうの immobile
不況 ふきょう depression, slump, recession
不運 ふうん misfortune, bad luck
不満 ふまん dissatisfaction, discontent
不思議 ふしぎ mystery, wonder
不尽 ふじん Yours sincerely
不気味な ぶきみな uncanny, weird, ghastly
不器用な ぶきような clumsy, unskillful
不用心 ぶようじん insecurity; carelessness
不平 ふへい discontent, dissatisfaction, complaint
不利 ふり disadvantage
不意に ふいに suddenly, unexpectedly
不時着する ふじちゃくする make an emergency landing; ditch
不順な ふじゅんな unseasonable; irregular
不純な ふじゅんな impure; mixed
不燃物 ふねんぶつ incombustibles
不備 ふび defect, imperfection
不法 ふほう unlawfulness, illegality, wrong
不本意に ふほんいに reluctantly, unwillingly
不慮の ふりょの unexpected, unforeseen; accidental
不親切な ふしんせつな unkind, unfriendly; inattentive
不安定 ふあんてい instability
不可能な ふかのうな impossible
不完全 ふかんぜん imperfection, incompleteness
不機嫌 ふきげん bad mood, displeasure
不規則な ふきそくな irregular
不合格 ふごうかく failure, disqualification
不公平な ふこうへいな unfair, unjust
不自然な ふしぜんな unnatural, artificial
不自由 ふじゆう inconvenience; disability; poverty
不十分 ふじゅうぶん insufficiency, lack
不確かな ふたしかな unreliable, uncertain
不注意 ふちゅうい carelessness, inattention
不得意 ふとくい one's weak point
不必要な ふひつような unnecessary; superfluous
不平等な ふびょうどうな unequal, unfair
不可 ふか F, fail(ure); improper; inadvisable

不合理な ふごうりな irrational, unreasonable
不始末 ふしまつ mismanagement, irregularity
不条理 ふじょうり absurdity
不相応な ふそうおうな unsuited, unbecoming
不都合 ふつごう inconvenience; misconduct
不透明な ふとうめいな opaque
不慣れな ふなれな inexperienced, unfamiliar
不変な ふへんな unchanging, invariable; eternal
不利益 ふりえき disadvantage

非 ▷is not (contrariety)
ヒ   Ⓚ0790

[also prefix] **is not, not, non-, un-, in**—-element of contrariety usu. placed before nouns

非常 ひじょう emergency, calamity
非常に ひじょうに very, extremely, greatly
非鉄金属 ひてつきんぞく nonferrous metals
非番 ひばん off duty
非情の ひじょうの coldhearted; inanimate
非礼 ひれい impoliteness
非売品 ひばいひん articles not for sale
非公式の ひこうしきの informal, unofficial
非金属 ひきんぞく nonmetal
非科学的な ひかがくてきな unscientific
非常識 ひじょうしき lack of common sense

無 ▷without (nonexistence)
ムブ な(い)   Ⓚ1832

[also prefix] **without, -less, non-, un-, in-, no**—element indicating nonexistence or lack

無給で むきゅうで without pay [salary]
無用の むようの useless; unnecessary; forbidden
無限の むげんの infinite, endless, unfathomable
無断で むだんで without permission; without notice [warning]
無料 むりょう no charge, free
無理な むりな unreasonable, unjustifiable; impossible; forced; excessive; irrational (equation)
無理やりに むりやりに by force, against one's will
無死 むし *baseball* with no outs
無礼 ぶれい discourtesy, rudeness
無能 むのう inefficiency, incompetence
無毒の むどくの nonpoisonous
無休で むきゅうで without leave [holiday]
無関係の むかんけいの irrelevant, unrelated
無責任 むせきにん irresponsibility
無事故 むじこ no accident, no trouble
無職の むしょくの without occupation, unemployed
無期限の むきげんの indefinite
無条件の むじょうけんの unconditional, unqualified
無意識に むいしきに unconsciously, without thinking
無人の むじんの uninhabited; unmanned

無神経な むしんけいな insensitive, inconsiderate
無造作に むぞうさに easily; casually
無恥 むち shamelessness, impudence
無名の むめいの nameless, obscure
無闇に むやみに rashly, thoughtlessly; excessively; needlessly
無意味な むいみな meaningless; absurd
無害な むがいな harmless
無関心 むかんしん apathy, indifference
無制限の むせいげんの unlimited, free, unrestricted
無生物 むせいぶつ inanimate object
無知 むち ignorance
無用心 ぶようじん insecurity, carelessness
無色の むしょくの colorless; neutral
無力 むりょく powerlessness, helplessness, impotence
無数の むすうの countless, innumerable
無論 むろん of course, no doubt, naturally
無益な むえきな useless; futile
無法な むほうな lawless, unlawful; unreasonable; outrageous
無形の むけいの immaterial, incorporeal; invisible; abstract
無実の むじつの innocent; false, untrue; groundless
無情な むじょうな heartless, coldhearted
無性に むしょうに very much, extremely
無心 むしん innocence; request
無風の むふうの calm, windless
無機物 むきぶつ inorganic substance
無欲な むよくな unselfish; disinterested

没 ▷lacking in
ボツ   Ⓚ0230

[prefix] **lacking in, not, un-**
没常識 ぼつじょうしき lack of common sense
没個性 ぼつこせい lack of individuality

欠 ▷lack
ケツ か(ける) か(く) か(かす)   Ⓚ1721

lack, be short of, be deficient
欠乏 けつぼう lack, shortage, scarcity
欠如 けつじょ lack, shortage
欠員 けついん vacant position
不可欠な ふかけつな indispensable

否 ▷or not
ヒ いな   Ⓚ2130

ⓐ **or not**—used as the second element of a compound to negate the meaning of the first
ⓑ **no, nay**
ａ 良否 りょうひ good or bad, quality
当否 とうひ right or wrong, justice; propriety
賛否 さんぴ approval or disapproval; yes or no

未 ▷not yet
ミ いま(だ) ま(だ)   Ⓚ2941

[also prefix] **not yet, un- (as in unpublished)**
未満 みまん less than
未来 みらい future
未練 みれん lingering affection, reluctance to give up
未完成 みかんせい incompletion
未知の みちの unknown
未刊の みかんの unpublished
未定の みていの undecided, pending
未払いの みはらいの unpaid
未婚の みこんの unmarried
未成年の みせいねんの minor, underage
未開の みかいの primitive, uncivilized; savage
未然に みぜんに before it happens, beforehand, previously
前代未聞の ぜんだいみもんの unheard-of, unprecedented

莫 ▷not
バク ボ なか(れ)   Ⓚ1971

not, never, no
莫大な ばくだいな vast, immense, enormous
莫逆 ばくぎゃく(=ばくげき) very close relations ("never opposing")

勿 ▷do not
モチ モッ- ブツ なか(れ)   Ⓚ2547

do not, not, never
勿論 もちろん of course, no doubt, naturally

territorial divisions
州 県 府 道 都 省 郡

州 ▷state
シュウ す   Ⓚ0040

ⓐ **state (as of the U.S. or Brazil), province (of Canada)**
ⓑ **suffix after names of states**
ａ 州政府 しゅうせいふ state government
州立大学 しゅうりつだいがく state-run college
州都 しゅうと state capital
ｂ テキサス州 てきさすしゅう State of Texas
リオ・デ・ジャネイロ州 りおでじゃねいろしゅう State of Rio de Janeiro

県 ▷prefecture
ケン   Ⓚ2294

ⓐ [also prefix and suffix] (largest administrative subdivision of Japan) **prefecture**

b suffix after names of prefectures

a 県庁 けんちょう prefectural office
県警 けんけい prefectural police
県税 けんぜい prefectural tax
県立の けんりつの prefectural
県立病院 けんりつびょういん prefectural hospital
県民 けんみん citizens of a prefecture
県知事 けんちじ prefectural governor
府県 ふけん prefectures
隣接県 りんせつけん neighboring prefecture
b 香川県 かがわけん Kagawa Prefecture

府 ▷**urban prefecture**
フ Ⓚ2654

urban [metropolitan] prefecture (limited to Kyoto and Osaka prefectures)
府庁 ふちょう urban prefectural office
府警 ふけい prefectural police
府税 ふぜい urban prefectural tax
府立の ふりつの prefectural
京都府 きょうとふ Kyoto Prefecture

道 ▷**District of Hokkaido**
ドウ トウ みち Ⓚ2701

[also prefix] **District of Hokkaido (northern island of Japan)**
道民 どうみん people of Hokkaido
道議会 どうぎかい Hokkaido Prefectural Assembly
北海道 ほっかいどう Hokkaido
都道府県 とどうふけん urban and rural prefectures

都 ▷**Metropolis of Tokyo**
ト ツ みやこ Ⓚ1505

ⓐ Metropolis of Tokyo, Tokyo
ⓑ (of the Metropolis of Tokyo) **Metropolitan, Tokyo**
a 都立の とりつの metropolitan, under control of the Tokyo Metropolitan government
都内で とないで in Tokyo Metropolis
都営 とえい run by the metropolitan government
東都 とうと Tokyo Metropolis
b 都庁 とちょう Tokyo Metropolitan Government Office
都電 とでん Metropolitan Electric Railway
都議選 とぎせん Tokyo Assembly elections

省 ▷**province in China**
セイ ショウ かえり(みる) はぶ(く) Ⓚ2164

[suffix] **province in China**
山東省 さんとうしょう Shandong Province

郡 ▷**county**
グン Ⓚ1333

ⓐ county (of a Japanese prefecture or U.S. state), **district, subprefecture**

---

b suffix after names of counties

a 郡部 ぐんぶ counties; rural districts
郡長 ぐんちょう head county official, district headman
郡制 ぐんせい county system
郡県 ぐんけん counties and prefectures
b 名西郡 みょうざいぐん Myozai District

thanking and gratitude
謝 礼 恩

謝 ▷**thank**
シャ あやま(る) Ⓚ1465

thank, be grateful
謝恩 しゃおん expression of gratitude
感謝 かんしゃ gratitude, thanks

礼 ▷**thanks**
レイ ライ Ⓚ0724

thanks, gratitude, appreciation
礼状 れいじょう letter of thanks
礼金 れいきん reward, fee, honorarium

恩 ▷**debt of gratitude**
オン Ⓚ2311

debt of gratitude, gratitude, obligation, indebtedness
恩義 おんぎ obligation, debt of gratitude
恩師 おんし one's respected teacher, one's former teacher
恩給 おんきゅう pension
恩知らず おんしらず ingratitude, ingrate
謝恩 しゃおん expression of gratitude
忘恩 ぼうおん ingratitude

that →THIS AND THAT

the country
郊 里 鄙 郷 辺

郊 ▷**suburb**
コウ Ⓚ1181

[original meaning] **suburb, outskirts, country**
郊外 こうがい suburbs, outskirts
郊野 こうや suburban fields
近郊 きんこう suburbs, outskirts
断郊競争 だんこうきょうそう cross-country race

西郊 せいこう [rare] western suburb

里 ▷countryside
リ さと Ⓚ2968

countryside, country, rural district
郷里 きょうり one's old home, native place

鄙 ▷the country
ヒ ひな ひな(びる)

[original meaning] the country, countryside, out-of-the-way place
都鄙 とひ town and country
辺鄙な へんぴな out-of-the-way, unfrequented, remote

郷 ▷the country
キョウ ゴウ Ⓚ0501

the country, countryside, rural district
郷士 ごうし country samurai
在郷者 ざいごうしゃ countryman, rustic

辺 ▷borderland
ヘン あた(り) -べ Ⓚ2607

borderland, frontier, remote region, outer regions, deep rural areas
辺地 へんち remote place
辺境 へんきょう frontier (district), remote region, border(land)
辺鄙な へんぴな out-of-the-way, unfrequented, remote

theory
論　　　説

論 ▷theory (systematic knowledge)
ロン Ⓚ1424

(systematically organized knowledge) theory, doctrine, system of thought
進化論 しんかろん theory of evolution
音韻論 おんいんろん phonology

説 ▷theory (proposed explanation)
セツ ゼイ と(く) Ⓚ1405

[also suffix] (proposed explanation) theory, doctrine
学説 がくせつ theory
仮説 かせつ hypothesis
新説 しんせつ new theory [doctrine]; new opinion
地動説 ちどうせつ heliocentric [Copernican] theory
原子説 げんしせつ atomic theory

the people
民　衆　庶　公

民 ▷people
ミン たみ Ⓚ2614

the people, populace, folk, civilians, citizens, inhabitants
民主 みんしゅ democracy
民主主義 みんしゅしゅぎ democracy
民謡 みんよう folk song [ballad]
民間 みんかん private citizens, civilians
民営 みんえい private management
民法 みんぽう civil law [code]
人民 じんみん the people, populace, subjects
住民 じゅうみん residents, dwellers
庶民 しょみん common people, the masses
県民 けんみん citizens of a prefecture
農漁民 のうぎょみん the fishing and agrarian populace

衆 ▷the multitude(s)
シュウ シュ Ⓚ2342

the multitude(s), populace, the masses, the public
民衆 みんしゅう populace, the people, the masses
大衆 たいしゅう the masses, populace
公衆 こうしゅう the public

庶 ▷the masses
ショ Ⓚ2696

the masses, common people, populace
庶民 しょみん common people, the masses
衆庶 しゅうしょ common people, the masses

公 ▷public
コウ おおやけ Ⓚ1715

the public, society, community
公共 こうきょう public society, community
公会堂 こうかいどう town [public] hall
公衆 こうしゅう the public

thick
厚　　太

厚 ▷thick (great in depth)
コウ あつ(い) Ⓚ2588

(great in depth) thick, deep
厚薄 こうはく (relative) thickness

太 ▷**thick (great in diameter)**
タイ タ ふと(い) ふと(る)　　Ⓚ1846

【タイ タ】
(great in diameter) **thick**
　丸太 まるた log

【ふと(い)】
(of great diameter or width) **thick, big; fat; broad, wide**
　太さ ふとさ thickness; depth (of voice)
　太糸 ふといと thick thread, low count yarn
　太字 ふとじ thick character, bold-faced type
　太い線 ふといせん thick line
　太っちょ ふとっちょ fat person
　太い腕 ふというで big arm
　太い鉛筆 ふといえんぴつ broad pencil

thieves

盗　泥　賊

盗 ▷**thief**
トウ ぬす(む)　　Ⓚ2327

thief, burglar, robber
　盗賊 とうぞく thief, robber, bandit
　怪盗 かいとう mysterious thief
　群盗 ぐんとう group [gang] of robbers
　夜盗 やとう night thief

泥 ▷**petty thief**
デイ どろ　　Ⓚ0288

[in compounds] [also suffix] **petty thief, sneak thief, pilferer**
　泥縄 どろなわ expediency coming too late (like making a rope after finding the thief)
　こそ泥 こそどろ sneak, pilferer
　自動車泥 じどうしゃどろ auto [car] thief

賊 ▷**bandit**
ゾク　　Ⓚ1391

bandit, robber, pirate, thief
　賊徒 ぞくと bandit, robber; rebels, traitors
　盗賊 とうぞく thief, robber, bandit
　海賊 かいぞく pirate
　山賊 さんぞく bandit, mountain robber
　匪賊 ひぞく bandit

thin

薄　細　繊　痩

薄 ▷**thin**
ハク うす(い) うす- うす(める) うす(まる)
うす(らぐ) うす(ら)- うす(れる)　　Ⓚ2093

(not thick) **thin, flimsy**
　薄片 はくへん thin leaf; slice
　薄氷 はくひょう thin ice; danger
　厚薄 こうはく (relative) thickness

細 ▷**slender**
サイ ほそ(い) ほそ(る) こま(か)
こま(かい)　　Ⓚ1220

[also prefix] [original meaning] **slender, fine, thin, narrow**
　細流 さいりゅう streamlet, brooklet, rivulet
　細腰 さいよう slender hips
　細動脈 さいどうみゃく arteriole
　毛細血管 もうさいけっかん capillary vessel
　繊細な せんさいな delicate, fine, subtle

繊 ▷**fine**
セン　　Ⓚ1289

fine, slender
　繊細な せんさいな delicate, fine, subtle
　繊毛 せんもう cilia, fine hair
　繊切り(=千切り) せんぎり long thin strips (of a vegetable)

痩 ▷**get thin**
ソウ や(せる)　　Ⓚ2797

get thin, slim [thin] down, lose weight
　痩身 そうしん slimming; slim [lean] figure

think and consider

思　惟　省　稽　考　存
案　想　慮　勘　銓　量

思 ▷**think**
シ おも(う)　　Ⓚ2221

【シ】
[original meaning] **think, consider, regard, believe, feel**
　思考 しこう thinking, thought, consideration
　思惟 しい thinking, speculation

思案する しあんする think, consider, reflect
思索する しさくする think, speculate
思慮 しりょ consideration, thought, discretion
思想 しそう thought, conception, idea
意思 いし intention, purpose
不思議な ふしぎな strange, mysterious, wonderful

【おも(う)】
think, consider; regard
思い おもい thought, idea; feelings; desire, wish; heart
思い付く おもいつく think of, hit upon
思い付き おもいつき idea, plan
思い上がる おもいあがる get conceited, get stuck-up
思い込む おもいこむ be under the impression that, be convinced that

惟 ▷meditate
イ ユイ おも(んみる) これ　Ⓚ0438

meditate, ponder, think
思惟 しい thinking, speculation

省 ▷introspect
セイ ショウ かえり(みる) はぶ(く)　Ⓚ2164

(examine oneself critically) introspect, reflect upon oneself
反省 はんせい reflection, introspection
三省する さんせいする reflect upon oneself (three times a day), examine oneself over and over again
自省 じせい self-examination [reflection], introspection

稽 ▷think
ケイ　Ⓚ1137

think about, consider, contemplate
稽古 けいこ practice, rehearsal; learning
荒唐無稽 こうとうむけい absurdity, nonsense

考 ▷think
コウ かんが(える) かんが(え)　Ⓚ2753

think, give thought to, consider, reflect
考慮 こうりょ consideration, deliberation, careful thought
考察する こうさつする consider, contemplate, study
考案 こうあん idea, plan; project
思考 しこう thinking, thought, consideration
一考 いっこう consideration, thought

存 ▷hold an opinion
ソン ゾン　Ⓚ2575

hold an opinion, believe, think

存外 ぞんがい contrary to one's expectations; beyond expectation
存分に ぞんぶんに to one's heart's content, freely
所存 しょぞん one's opinion [view], intention
異存 いぞん objection

案 ▷think out
アン　Ⓚ1960

think out, devise
案出する あんしゅつする think out, contrive, devise, invent
思案 しあん thought, consideration, reflection
考案 こうあん idea, plan; project

想 ▷conceive
ソウ ソ　Ⓚ2462

conceive, think of, think, contemplate, imagine
想像 そうぞう imagination
想定 そうてい hypothesis, supposition, assumption
予想 よそう prospect, expectation, conjecture
感想 かんそう thoughts, impressions
連想 れんそう association (of ideas)

慮 ▷consider
リョ　Ⓚ2789

[original meaning] consider, think over, deliberate
考慮する こうりょする consider, deliberate, give thought to
浅慮 せんりょ indiscretion, imprudence, thoughtlessness
思慮 しりょ consideration, thought, discretion
深慮 しんりょ thoughtfulness, prudence

勘 ▷take into consideration
カン　Ⓚ1582

take into consideration, give consideration to, think about
勘考 かんこう consideration, deliberation
勘案する かんあんする take into consideration, give consideration (to)
勘弁する かんべんする pardon, forgive; tolerate

銓 ▷weigh
セン

[now replaced by 選] [original meaning] weigh, evaluate
銓衡(=選考)する せんこうする select, screen

量 ▷weigh
リョウ はか(る)　Ⓚ2180

weigh, consider, estimate, assess
量刑 りょうけい assessment of a case
推量する すいりょうする guess, conjecture, infer
裁量 さいりょう discretion

third person pronouns

彼　氏　奴

彼 ▷third person pronoun (*neutral*)
ヒ かれ かの　　　　　Ⓚ0259

【ヒ】
third person pronoun, the other party, he, she
彼我 ひが he [she] and I, they and we, both sides

【かれ】
he; boyfriend, lover
彼等 かれら they
彼氏 かれし he; lover, beau

氏 ▷third person pronoun (*polite*)
シ うじ　　　　　Ⓚ2552

[polite] third person pronoun, he; family name
氏の意見 しのいけん his opinion

奴 ▷third person pronoun (*slang*)
ド やつ　　　　　Ⓚ0164

third person pronoun

thirst →HUNGER AND THIRST

this and that

本　爾　其　彼　今　当
該　同　之　是　此　斯

本 ▷this
ホン もと　　　　　Ⓚ2937

[also prefix] this, the same, the present, in question
本日 ほんじつ today
本年 ほんねん this year
本書 ほんしょ this book
本紙 ほんし this newspaper
本人 ほんにん the person himself, the said person
本年度 ほんねんど the current fiscal year

爾 ▷that
ジ ニ なんじ　　　　　Ⓚ3001

that
爾来 じらい from that time on, ever since
爾後 じご from this [that] time onward, henceforth, thereafter

其 ▷that
キ そ(れ) そ(の)　　　　　Ⓚ2285

[sometimes also 夫れ] *pronoun* that, it
其れ其れ それぞれ respectively, each
其れから それから and then, after that
其れでも それでも nevertheless, even so
其れなりに それなりに in its own way
其れと無く それとなく indirectly, obliquely

彼 ▷that
ヒ かれ かの　　　　　Ⓚ0259

that, the other
彼岸 ひがん equinoctial week; the other shore

今 ▷this (week, etc.)
コン キン いま　　　　　Ⓚ1712

[also prefix] this (week, etc.), the present (term)
今回 こんかい this time; lately
今月 こんげつ this month
今週 こんしゅう this week
今期 こんき present term

当 ▷the present
トウ あ(たる) あ(たり) あ(てる)
あ(て)　　　　　Ⓚ1865

[also prefix] the present, this, that, the said, the very
当局 とうきょく the authorities concerned
当時 とうじ at that time, in those days; at the present time
当事者 とうじしゃ the person [party] concerned
当人 とうにん the one concerned, the said person
当店 とうてん this shop, we
当駅 とうえき this station
当該 とうがい the said, the concerned
当日 とうじつ the appointed day, that day
当社 とうしゃ this firm; this shrine
当営業所 とうえいぎょうしょ our [the present] business office

該 ▷the said
ガイ　　　　　Ⓚ1377

[also prefix] the said, the one in question, that
該案 がいあん the said proposal
該問題 がいもんだい the said problem, the matter in question

同 ▷the same
ドウ おな(じ)　　　　　Ⓚ2578

(the one previously mentioned) the same (as above), the said, the aforementioned
同日 どうじつ the same day, the said day
同氏 どうし the said person, he
同国 どうこく the same country, the said country

同委員会 どういいんかい the same committee

之 ▷this
シ の これ   Ⓚ2886

[also 是] *pronoun* **this**
之は何ですか これはなんですか What is this?

是 ▷this
ゼ これ   Ⓚ2157

[also 之] *pronoun* **this**

此 ▷this
シ こ(れ) こ(の)   Ⓚ0728

demonstrative **this**
此岸 しがん this world [life]

斯 ▷this
シ か(く) か(かる) こ(の) こ(う)   Ⓚ1521

ⓐ *demonstrative* **this**
ⓑ *pronoun* **this**
a 斯文 しぶん this field of study; Confucian studies
斯界 しかい this world [circle, field]

thought
念 考 意 想

念 ▷thoughts
ネン   Ⓚ1773

thoughts, inner thoughts, mind, idea, conception
念頭に置く ねんとうにおく give thought to, bear in
mind
観念 かんねん idea, conception, notion
概念 がいねん general idea, concept
残念 ざんねん regret, disappointment, chagrin
信念 しんねん belief, faith
懸念する けねんする be anxious, feel concern, fear
断念する だんねんする give up (an idea), abandon,
relinquish
専念する せんねんする give undivided attention to,
concentrate (on), devote oneself to
邪念 じゃねん vicious mind, evil thoughts

考 ▷thought
コウ かんが(える) かんが(え)   Ⓚ2753

**thought, thinking, consideration, reflection,
deliberation; thought, view, opinion; idea, fancy,
imagination; intention, resolution**
考えを伝える かんがえをつたえる convey one's
thoughts

意 ▷mind
イ   Ⓚ183◄

mind, heart, thoughts, feelings; opinion
意識 いしき consciousness, awareness
意見 いけん opinion, view; admonition
意気 いき heart, mind, (high) spirits
意外な いがいな unexpected, unforeseen, surprising
意地 いじ nature, disposition; will power, backbone
意地悪 いじわる nastiness; ill-natured person
注意 ちゅうい attention, care, advice
用意する よういする prepare, ready oneself, make
arrangements
好意 こうい goodwill, favor, kindness
誠意 せいい sincerity, good faith
合意 ごうい mutual agreement [consent]

想 ▷conception
ソウ ソ   Ⓚ2462

conception, idea, thought, image, concept
思想 しそう thought, conception, idea
構想 こうそう conception, idea; plot, plan
理想 りそう ideal
幻想 げんそう fantasy, illusion
愛想 あいそ(=あいそう) civility, hospitality
発想 はっそう conception; *music* expression

threads and fibers
糸 緯 経 繊 維 綸 緝

糸 ▷thread
シ いと   Ⓚ186◄

[original meaning] **thread, yarn, filament**
綿糸 めんし cotton yarn [thread]
絹糸 けんし(=きぬいと) silk thread
抜糸 ばっし removal [extraction] of stitches
一糸も纏わずに いっしもまとわずに without a
stitch of clothing on, stark-naked

緯 ▷woof
イ   Ⓚ1285

[original meaning] **woof, weft**
経緯 けいい warp and woof; circumstances, details

経 ▷warp
ケイ キョウ へ(る) た(つ)   Ⓚ1218

[original meaning] **warp**
整経機 せいけいき warping machine

繊 ▷fiber
セン   Ⓚ1289

[original meaning] **fiber, filament**
  繊維 せんい fiber, textile
  繊条 せんじょう filament
  化繊 かせん synthetic fiber
  合繊 ごうせん synthetic fiber

維 ▷fiber
イ   Ⓚ1251

fiber
  繊維 せんい fiber, textile
  線維束 せんいそく fascicle

綸 ▷thread
リン カン ケン   Ⓚ1257

[original meaning] **thread, thick thread, cord**
  綸子(=綾子) りんず figured satin
  経綸する けいりんする govern, administer (state affairs)

緬 ▷fine thread
メン

fine thread
  緬羊(=綿羊) めんよう sheep
  縮緬 ちりめん crepe, silk crepe

threaten

脅 劫 威 嚇 喝

脅 ▷threaten
キョウ おびや(かす) おど(す)
おど(かす)   Ⓚ1811

threaten (with force), intimidate, menace, coerce
  脅迫する きょうはくする threaten, intimidate, menace
  脅威 きょうい threat, menace
  脅迫状 きょうはくじょう intimidating letter

劫 ▷threaten
コウ ゴウ おびや(かす)   Ⓚ1033

Buddhism **kalpa, aeon**
  永劫 えいごう eternity
  億劫 おっくう(=おっこう) bothersome, a hassle

威 ▷threaten by force
イ   Ⓚ2993

threaten by force, dominate by power
  威圧 いあつ coercion, high-handedness
  威嚇する いかくする intimidate, threaten, menace

  脅威 きょうい threat, menace

嚇 ▷intimidate
カク   Ⓚ0702

intimidate, frighten, threaten, scare
  威嚇する いかくする intimidate, threaten, menace
  恐嚇(=脅嚇) きょうかく [rare] intimidation, threat

喝 ▷shout threats at
カツ   Ⓚ0417

shout threats at someone, intimidate, threaten
  恐喝する きょうかつする threaten, menace
  恫喝 どうかつ threat, intimidation

three

三 参 鼎

三 ▷three
サン み み(つ) みっ(つ)   Ⓚ1689

[original meaning] **three, third**
  三千 さんぜん 3000
  三角 さんかく triangle
  三角形 さんかくけい triangle
  三人称 さんにんしょう *gram* third person
  三塁 さんるい third base
  三分する さんぶんする trisect
  三脚 さんきゃく tripod
  三流の さんりゅうの third-rate
  七五三 しちごさん the lucky numbers; gala day for children of three, five and seven
  第三 だいさん third

参 ▷three (in legal documents)
サン シン まい(る)   Ⓚ1778

three—used in legal documents and checks
  金参千円也 きんさんぜんえんなり 3000 yen

鼎 ▷triangular
テイ かなえ   Ⓚ3000

(involving three parts or things) **triangular, three-party**
  鼎立 ていりつ triangular [three-party] confrontation
  鼎談 ていだん three-man talk, tricornered conversation
  鼎坐する ていざする sit in a triangle

喉頭 こうとう larynx
咽喉 いんこう throat
耳鼻咽喉科 じびいんこうか department of otolar-
yngology

three-dimensional shapes

錐 筒 角 球

錐 ▷cone
スイ きり
Ⓚ1558

cone or conelike object (such as a pyramid)
錐体 すいたい cone, pyramid
円錐 えんすい cone
三角錐 さんかくすい triangular pyramid

筒 ▷cylinder
トウ つつ
Ⓚ2341

[also suffix] [original meaning] **tube, cylinder, pipe**
円筒 えんとう cylinder
発煙筒 はつえんとう smoke ball [bomb]

角 ▷cube
カク かど つの
Ⓚ1761

cube, block
角砂糖 かくざとう cube sugar

球 ▷sphere
キュウ たま
Ⓚ0880

[original meaning] (spherical body) **ball, globe, sphere**
球体 きゅうたい sphere, globe
球形 きゅうけい globular shape
球根 きゅうこん bulb
地球 ちきゅう the Earth
眼球 がんきゅう eyeball

throat

咽 喉

咽 ▷throat
イン
Ⓚ0309

ⓐ throat
ⓑ swallow

a 咽頭 いんとう pharynx; pharyngeal
耳鼻咽喉 じびいんこう nose, ear and throat
b 咽下 えんか(=えんげ) (act of) swallowing, degluti-
tion

喉 ▷throat
コウ のど
Ⓚ0506

throat

throughout

通 徹 終 中

通 ▷through
ツウ ツ とお(る) とお(り)
-どお(り) とお(す) とお(し) -どお(し)
かよ(う)
Ⓚ2678

through, from beginning to end
通算 つうさん sum total, aggregate
通読する つうどくする read through
通巻 つうかん consecutive number of volumes
通夜 つや vigil, deathwatch

徹 ▷all through
テツ
Ⓚ0659

all through, throughout
徹夜 てつや all night vigil [sitting]
徹宵 てっしょう all night long, throughout the night

終 ▷from beginning to end
シュウ お(わる) お(える)
Ⓚ1223

from beginning to end, all through, all
終日 しゅうじつ all [throughout] the day
終身 しゅうしん all through life
終夜 しゅうや all night

中 ▷throughout
チュウ ジュウ なか
Ⓚ2902

(during the entire time) **throughout (the night), all through**
一年中 いちねんじゅう throughout the year, always
一日中 いちにちじゅう all day long

throw

投 抛 放

投 ▷throw
トウ な(げる) -な(げ)
Ⓚ0228

[original meaning] **throw, cast, throw down**
投下 とうか throwing down, dropping, airdrop;
investment
投棄する とうきする abandon, give up, throw away
投石 とうせき throwing stones

投擲する とうてきする throw

拋 ▷toss
ホウ なげう(つ) ほう(る)

[original meaning] toss, throw, let fly
拋物線 ほうぶつせん parabola

放 ▷toss
ホウ はな(す) -(つ)ぱな(し) はな(つ)
はな(れる) ほう(る)　　　Ⓚ0754

toss, throw, let fly
放物線 ほうぶつせん parabola

tiger
虎　　寅

虎 ▷tiger
コ とら　　　Ⓚ2766

[original meaning] tiger
虎穴 こけつ tiger's den; dangerous place
虎口 ここう tiger's den; dangerous place
虎視眈眈 こしたんたん on the alert, eye covetously
竜虎の争い りゅうこのあらそい well matched
　　contest ("serpent and tiger fight")
暴虎馮河 ぼうこひょうが foolhardy courage

寅 ▷the Tiger
イン とら　　　Ⓚ1981

third sign of the Oriental zodiac: the Tiger—(time)
3-5 a.m., (direction) ENE, (season) January (of the lunar
calendar)

tighten
締　　緊　　張

締 ▷tighten
テイ し(まる) し(まり) し(める) -し(め)
-じ(め)　　　Ⓚ1274

tighten, tauten
ベルトを締める べるとをしめる tighten one's belt

緊 ▷tighten
キン　　　Ⓚ2471

[original meaning] tighten, make tight [tense], become tight [tense]
緊縛する きんばくする bind tightly
緊張する きんちょうする become tense, be strained,
　　be keyed up

緊縮 きんしゅく contraction, shrinkage; strict economy

張 ▷strain
チョウ は(る) -は(り) -ば(り)　　　Ⓚ0431

[original meaning] strain, stretch, be tense, tighten
張力 ちょうりょく tension, tensile strength
緊張 きんちょう tension, strain

time and time counters
回　　度　　遍　　返

回 ▷time
カイ エ まわ(る) -まわ(り) まわ(す)
まわ(し)-　　　Ⓚ2630

Ⓐ [also suffix] time; round, game; inning
Ⓑ counter for number of times, rounds or innings
a 回数 かいすう frequency, number of times
　回数券 かいすうけん book of tickets
　今回 こんかい this time; lately
　最終回 さいしゅうかい last time; last inning
b 百回 ひゃっかい 100 times
　八回裏 はちかいうら second half of the eighth
　　inning

度 ▷time
ド トタク たび　　　Ⓚ2670

Ⓐ time, occasion
Ⓑ counter for number of times
a 度数 どすう number of times
　今度 こんど this time; next time, another time;
　　recently
　何度 なんど how many degrees; how many times
　毎度 まいど every [each] time, always
b 二度 にど two times [degrees]

遍 ▷counter for number of times
ヘン　　　Ⓚ2703

[sometimes also 返] counter for number of times
　五遍 ごへん five times
　何遍 なんべん how many times
　何遍も なんべんも several [many] times, very often

返 ▷counter for number of times
ヘン かえ(す) かえ(る)　　　Ⓚ2633

[usu. 遍] counter for number of times
　二返 にへん two times

time counters →TIME AND TIME COUNTERS

time periods

時 季 候 頃 暇 般
刻 間 隙 期 節

時 ▷time
ジ とき -どき   Ⓚ0830

ⓐ [original meaning] (continuous duration) **time, duration, interval**
ⓑ (specific time) **the time, o'clock, hour**
ⓒ [suffix] **time, at the time of, when**

a 時間 じかん time, period; hour
時刻 じこく time; hour
時効 じこう prescription, limitation (of action)
同時の どうじの simultaneous
臨時の りんじの temporary, provisional, special
一時 いちじ for a time, temporarily; once; one o'clock
b 時限 じげん time limit, closing time; period, hour
八時 はちじ eight o'clock
何時ですか なんじですか What time is it?
日時 にちじ date, time
c 昼食時 ちゅうしょくじ lunch time
出願時 しゅつがんじ (at the) time of application

季 ▷season (quarter)
キ   Ⓚ2210

ⓐ (division of the year) **season, quarter**
ⓑ (period of time) **season**

a 季節 きせつ season
季候 きこう season
季刊 きかん quarterly publication
夏季 かき summer, summer season
四季 しき the four seasons
b ボーナス季 ぼうなすき bonus season
年季 ねんき one's term of service
雨季(=雨期) うき rainy season

候 ▷season (time of year)
コウ そうろう   Ⓚ0101

season, time of year
候鳥 こうちょう migratory bird
時候 じこう season, time of the year

頃 ▷time
ころ ごろ   Ⓚ0124

time, approximate time
この頃 このごろ now, these days; lately
もう彼が帰る頃だ もうかれがかえるころだ It's about time for him to come home

暇 ▷free time
カ ひま   Ⓚ0923

free time, spare time, leisure
余暇 よか leisure, spare time
寸暇 すんか moment's leisure
休暇 きゅうか holiday, vacation

般 ▷period of time
ハン   Ⓚ120.

period of time
先般 せんぱん the other day, some time ago
今般 こんぱん now, recently
過般 かはん some time ago, recently

刻 ▷point of time
コク きざ(む) きざ(み)   Ⓚ1166

ⓐ **point of time, time, moment, hour**
ⓑ (period of time) **time, interval**
ⓒ **two-hour period in former system of measuring time**

a 刻限 こくげん time, appointed time
刻一刻 こくいっこく moment by moment, hour by hour
時刻 じこく time; hour
遅刻 ちこく tardiness, lateness
定刻 ていこく regular [appointed] time
即刻 そっこく immediately, instantly
b 夕刻 ゆうこく evening
c 上刻 じょうこく first third of a two-hour period

間 ▷interval
カン ケン あいだ ま   Ⓚ2836

(time between) **interval, duration of time, period**
時間 じかん time, period; hour
夜間に やかんに at night
期間 きかん term, period
週間 しゅうかん week

隙 ▷gap
ゲキ すき   Ⓚ0614

[original meaning] **gap, interval, opening, space**
間隙 かんげき gap, interval
空隙 くうげき opening, crevice, gap, void
填隙 てんげき caulking

期 ▷term
キ ゴ   Ⓚ1520

[also suffix] **term, school term, period, season, quarter; stage, phase; session**
期間 きかん term, period
期末試験 きまつしけん term-end examination
学期 がっき school term
時期 じき time, season

第一期計画 だいいっきけいかく first phase of a plan
初期 しょき early days, early stage, beginning; early, initial
上半期 かみはんき first half of the (fiscal) year
定期 ていき fixed term; fixed deposit; commuter's pass; regular, periodic

節 ▷**season**
セツ セチ ふし -ぶし   Ⓚ2349

season [division] of the year, season, turning of the seasons
節分 せつぶん eve of the beginning of spring, close of winter
節季 せっき end of year, year end
季節 きせつ season

ny →SMALL AND TINY

tire
疲 労 倦 厭

疲 ▷**tired**
ヒ つか(れる) -づか(れ)   Ⓚ2792

[original meaning] **tired, fatigued**
疲労 ひろう fatigue
疲弊 ひへい exhaustion; impoverishment

労 ▷**fatigue**
ロウ   Ⓚ2205

fatigue, become fatigued
疲労 ひろう fatigue
心労 しんろう cares, worries, anxiety

倦 ▷**tire of**
ケン あぐ(ねる) う(む) あ(きる)   Ⓚ0099

【ケン】
tire of, be weary of
倦厭する けんえんする weary of
【あぐ(ねる)】
[also suffix] **tire of, weary of, be at a loss**
思い倦ねる おもいあぐねる think something over and over, rack one's brains
攻め倦ねる せめあぐねる be unable to mount a successful offensive

厭 ▷**tire of**
エン オン いや あ(きる) いと(う)

tire of, weary of, lose interest in
厭世観 えんせいかん pessimism
厭戦 えんせん war-weariness
倦厭する けんえんする weary of

titles of address
氏 兄 君 嬢 様 殿 師 公

氏 ▷**courtesy title**
シ うじ   Ⓚ2552

courtesy title after family names: **Mr., Mister**
田中氏 たなかし Mr. Tanaka

兄 ▷**familiar title (seniors)**
ケイ キョウ あに   Ⓚ1848

familiar title used in addressing seniors or close friends
山田兄 やまだけい Mr. Yamada

君 ▷**familiar title (peers)**
クン きみ -ぎみ   Ⓚ2762

familiar title used in addressing peers, friends or inferiors (usu. restricted to men)
山田君 やまだくん Mr. Yamada
太郎君 たろうくん Taro

嬢 ▷**Miss**
ジョウ   Ⓚ0685

title after names of unmarried young ladies: **Miss**
良子嬢 よしこじょう Miss Yoshiko

様 ▷**formal title**
ヨウ さま   Ⓚ0969

formal title: **Mr., Miss, Mrs., Ms., Esq.**
山本様 やまもとさま Mr. Yamamoto
貴様 きさま [belittling] you; [original meaning] sir, madam

殿 ▷**formal honorific title**
デン テン との -どの   Ⓚ1593

【デン テン】
[also suffix] **formal honorific title**
殿下 でんか His Imperial Highness
貴殿 きでん you
保善院殿 ほぜんいんでん His Lordship Hozen of Blessed Memory
【-どの】
formal honorific title: **Esquire, Esq., Mister**
山田太郎殿 やまだたろうどの Taro Yamada, Esq.
議長殿 ぎちょうどの Mr. Chairman

師 ▷**honorific title (clergymen)**
シ   Ⓚ1211

honorific title, esp. after names of clergymen or traditional artists

ホメイニ師 ほめいにし the Ayatollah Khomeini
宝井馬琴師 たからいばきんし Master Bakin Takarai

公 ▷honorific title (noblemen)
コウ おおやけ   Ⓚ1715

honorific title after names of noblemen
徳川公 とくがわこう Prince Tokugawa

today →YESTERDAY AND TODAY

today →YESTERDAY AND TODAY

together
共 同 併 並 兼 倶

共 ▷joint
キョウ とも とも(に) −ども   Ⓚ2122

[original meaning] **joint, united, together, co-**
共同の きょうどうの joint; common, concerted,
    united; public
共通の きょうつうの common
共通語 きょうつうご common language; lingua
    franca
共和国 きょうわこく republic
共和制 きょうわせい republicanism
共催 きょうさい joint auspices, cosponsorship
共感 きょうかん sympathy
共演 きょうえん coacting, costarring
共産党 きょうさんとう Communist Party
共存 きょうぞん coexistence
共闘 きょうとう joint struggle, common [united]
    front
共著 きょうちょ joint authorship, coauthorship
共有の きょうゆうの common, joint
共用する きょうようする share, use in common
公共の こうきょうの public, common

同 ▷together
ドウ おな(じ)   Ⓚ2578

together, in common
同居する どうきょする live together
同情 どうじょう sympathy, compassion
同封する どうふうする enclose (in a letter)
同棲 どうせい cohabitation, living together
共同する きょうどうする work together, cooperate
一同 いちどう all (of us), all persons concerned

併 ▷together
ヘイ あわ(せる)   Ⓚ0064

[also 並] **together, collectively, simultaneously, side
by side**
併用する へいようする use together [jointly]
併発 へいはつ concurrence
併記する へいきする line up together (in writing)

併呑 へいどん annexation, merger
併殺 へいさつ double play

並 ▷side by side
ヘイ なみ なら(べる) なら(ぶ)
なら(びに)   Ⓚ193

[also 併] [original meaning] **side by side, in line,
together**
並行(=平行) へいこう going side by side; occurring
    together
並置 へいち juxtaposition, placing side by side
並用する へいようする use together [jointly]

兼 ▷concurrently
ケン か(ねる)   Ⓚ197

(serving two functions) **concurrently, simultaneously,
together**
兼用 けんよう combined use; serving two purposes
兼備する けんびする combine (one thing with
    another)
兼行 けんこう doing simultaneously

倶 ▷together
グ ク とも(に)   Ⓚ009

[original meaning] **together**
倶発 ぐはつ concurrence (of offenses)
不倶戴天の敵 ふぐたいてんのてき bitter enemy

tolerant
寛 甘

寛 ▷lenient
カン   Ⓚ203

**lenient, tolerant, largehearted, generous, magnani-
mous, broad-minded**
寛大な かんだいな generous, magnanimous,
    lenient
寛容な かんような tolerant, liberal, generous
寛厳 かんげん lenity and severity
寛闊な かんかつな generous, largehearted
寛厚 かんこう kindness and largeheartedness

甘 ▷indulgent
カン あま(い) あま(える)
あま(やかす)   Ⓚ293

indulgent, lenient, generous
甘んじる あまんじる be resigned to (one's fate), be
    contented [satisfied] with (one's lot)
子供に甘い こどもにあまい be indulgent to (one's)
    children

tools →MACHINES AND TOOLS

tools →MACHINES AND TOOLS

tops

上 頂 頭

上 ▷upper part
ジョウ ショウ うえ うわ- かみ あ(げる)
あ(がる) あ(がり) のぼ(る) のぼ(り)
のぼ(せる) のぼ(す)   Ⓚ2876

【ジョウ ショウ】
upper part, top; up, above
- 上下 じょうげ upper and lower parts [sides], high and low; going up and down, rise and fall; first and second volumes
- 頂上 ちょうじょう summit, peak, top; climax
- 屋上 おくじょう housetop, roof

【うえ】
upside, upper part, top, summit; the surface
- 上下 うえした up and down, above and below
- 上を向く うえをむく look upward

頂 ▷summit
チョウ いただ(く) いただき   Ⓚ0125

(highest part) **summit, top, peak, apex, vertex**
- 頂点 ちょうてん apex, peak
- 絶頂 ぜっちょう summit, peak, climax
- 有頂天 うちょうてん exaltation, ecstasy
- 山頂 さんちょう summit

頭 ▷head
トウ ズ ト あたま かしら -がしら Ⓚ1450

(upper end) **head, top**
- 喉頭 こうとう larynx
- 弾頭 だんとう warhead
- 先頭 せんとう forefront, head, top
- 毛頭 もうとう (not) in the least, (not) a bit

torture and oppress

拷 責 虐 迫

拷 ▷torture
ゴウ   Ⓚ0332

torture, flog, beat
- 拷問 ごうもん torture; rack; third degree
- 拷問台 ごうもんだい rack, instrument of torture
- 拷器 ごうき [archaic] instruments of torture

責 ▷torture
セキ せ(める)   Ⓚ2176

torture, persecute
- 責め道具 せめどうぐ instruments of torture
- 責め立てる せめたてる torture severely; urge
- 水責め みずぜめ water torture

虐 ▷treat cruelly
ギャク しいた(げる)   Ⓚ2769

[original meaning] **treat cruelly, oppress, tyrannize**
- 虐政 ぎゃくせい oppressive [tyrannical] government
- 虐殺 ぎゃくさつ massacre, butchery, genocide

迫 ▷oppress
ハク せま(る)   Ⓚ2647

(cause distress) **oppress, press hard, persecute**
- 迫害 はくがい persecution, oppression
- 窮迫 きゅうはく straitened circumstances, distress
- 逼迫する ひっぱくする be tight, get stringent

total

総 計 和

総 ▷total
ソウ   Ⓚ1261

[also prefix] **total, whole, combined, full, complete, gross**
- 総額 そうがく total amount, sum total
- 総数 そうすう total (number)
- 総点 そうてん sum total of one's marks
- 総体 そうたい the whole, all; on the whole, generally
- 総掛かり そうがかり combined efforts
- 総二階 そうにかい full two-story house
- 総予算 そうよさん complete budget
- 総量 そうりょう gross weight [volume]

計 ▷total
ケイ はか(る) はか(らう)   Ⓚ1309

total, sum total
- 合計 ごうけい sum total, total
- 総計 そうけい total, total amount
- 小計 しょうけい subtotal

和 ▷sum
ワ オ やわ(らぐ) やわ(らげる) なご(む)
なご(やか)   Ⓚ1044

sum, total
- 総和 そうわ sum total, lump sum
- 代数的和 だいすうてきわ algebraic sum

touch

触 接 撫 当

触 ▷touch
ショク ふ(れる) さわ(る)   Ⓚ1376

ⓐ touch, contact
ⓑ perceive by touching, feel

ⓐ 接触 せっしょく contact, touch
一触即発 いっしょくそくはつ touch-and-go situation, hair-trigger crisis
感触 かんしょく (sense of) touch, feeling
ⓑ 触角 しょっかく feeler, antenna
触覚 しょっかく sense of touch
触媒 しょくばい catalyst, catalyzer

接 ▷contact
セツ つ(ぐ)   Ⓚ0460

contact, touch, come in contact with
接触 せっしょく contact, touch
接種 せっしゅ vaccination, inoculation
接点 せってん point of contact, contact
接線(=切線) せっせん tangent
接吻 せっぷん kiss
隣接 りんせつ contiguity, adjacency

撫 ▷stroke
ブ な(でる)   Ⓚ0667

stroke, caress, fondle, rub, pat
撫育する ぶいくする raise with love and care
愛撫する あいぶする caress, fondle, pet

当 ▷apply
トウ あ(たる) あ(たり) あ(てる)
あ(て)   Ⓚ1865

apply (to), put (to), lay, place
当て嵌まる あてはまる be applicable, come under (a category), fulfill (criteria)
当て嵌める あてはめる apply, fit, adapt
手当て てあて provision; medical care, treatment
手当てあて allowance, compensation, benefits
双眼鏡に目を当てる そうがんきょうにめをあてる put binoculars to one's eyes
座布団を当てる ざぶとんをあてる sit on a cushion

towns →PARTS OF TOWNS

towns →CITIES AND TOWNS

towns →VILLAGES AND TOWNS

trace

軌 跡

軌 ▷track
キ   Ⓚ131

ⓐ (wheel) track, rut, path
ⓑ railway track

ⓐ 軌跡 きせき locus; tracks
軌道 きどう track, railway; planetary orbit; beaten track
ⓑ 軌条 きじょう rails

跡 ▷trace
セキ あと   Ⓚ139

(mark left by something) trace(s), track, mark, footprint, trail
足跡 そくせき footprint, footmark; the course of one's life, one's achievements
追跡 ついせき pursuit, chase, follow-up
軌跡 きせき locus; tracks
航跡 こうせき wake, track; flight path, vapor trail
人跡 じんせき human traces
筆跡 ひっせき handwriting, holograph

trade →SELL AND TRADE

transfer

譲 渡 付 附

譲 ▷cede
ジョウ ゆず(る)   Ⓚ148?

cede, transfer, assign, give up, yield
譲渡 じょうと transfer, conveyance
譲与 じょうよ transfer
譲位 じょうい abdication
委譲 いじょう transfer, assignment

渡 ▷hand over
ト わた(る) わた(す)   Ⓚ0560

hand over, transfer, turn over
譲渡する じょうとする transfer, hand over

付 ▷deliver
フ つ(ける) -づ(ける) つ(け) -づ(け)
つ(く) -づ(く) つ(き) -づ(き)   Ⓚ001?

deliver, hand over, grant
付与する ふよする give, grant, allow, bestow
寄付する きふする contribute, donate

交付 こうふ delivery, grant, transfer, service
給付する きゅうふする make a presentation, grant, pay
送付する そうふする send, remit
配付する はいふする distribute, deal out

付 ▷deliver
フ   Ⓚ0307

deliver, hand over, grant
交附する こうふする deliver, grant, hand (a ticket) to (a person)
寄附する きふする contribute, donate

translate

訳 翻

訳 ▷translate
ヤク わけ   Ⓚ1340

[original meaning] **translate, interpret, render**
訳者 やくしゃ translator
通訳 つうやく interpreting; interpreter
翻訳 ほんやく translation, rendering

翻 ▷render
ホン ひるがえ(る) ひるがえ(す)   Ⓚ1676

render (written texts) in another form, translate, adapt, transcribe
翻訳する ほんやくする translate, render
翻字 ほんじ transliteration
翻案 ほんあん adaptation

transmit and deliver

伝 逓 届 達

伝 ▷transmit
デン つた(わる) つた(える) つた(う) -づた(い)   Ⓚ0029

ⓐ (convey from one person or place to another) **transmit, convey, pass on, communicate, initiate**
ⓑ (pass down by inheritance) **transmit, hand down**

ⓐ 伝達する でんたつする transmit, convey, communicate; propagate
伝染 でんせん contagion, infection, communication (of a disease)
伝言 でんごん verbal message, word
伝授する でんじゅする instruct, initiate
中国伝来の ちゅうごくでんらいの imported [transmitted] from China
直伝 じきでん direct initiation

ⓑ 伝統 でんとう tradition, convention
伝説 でんせつ legend, folk tale
伝承する でんしょうする hand down, tell from generation to generation
以心伝心 いしんでんしん silent [tacit] understanding, empathy
遺伝 いでん hereditary transmission

逓 ▷relay
テイ   Ⓚ2675

(transmit by stages) **relay, forward**
逓伝する ていでんする relay (a message)
逓信 ていしん communications
逓送 ていそう forwarding

届 ▷deliver
とど(ける) -とど(け) とど(く)   Ⓚ2651

deliver (a letter or goods), send, forward
届け先 とどけさき destination, address
送り届ける おくりとどける send to, deliver; escort (a person) home
付け届け つけとどけ present, tip; bribe

達 ▷deliver
タツ -たち   Ⓚ2706

deliver, convey
達意 たつい intelligibility, perspicuity
配達 はいたつ delivery
速達 そくたつ special delivery, express mail
伝達 でんたつ transmission, conveyance, communication; propagation
送達 そうたつ conveyance, delivery, dispatch

travel by vehicle

乗 走 航 騎

乗 ▷ride
ジョウ の(る) -の(り) の(せる)   Ⓚ2992

ride, ride in, travel
乗用車 じょうようしゃ passenger car, automobile
乗客 じょうきゃく passenger, fare
乗務員 じょうむいん trainman, crewman
乗馬する じょうばする ride a horse; mount a horse
同乗する どうじょうする ride together
試乗 しじょう trial ride
警乗する けいじょうする police (a train)
便乗する びんじょうする take advantage of an opportunity; go on board

走 ▷**travel by vehicle**
ソウ はし(る) ⓚ1877

travel by vehicle or craft, drive, sail
走行 そうこう traveling, driving
暴走 ぼうそう reckless driving; running wild
滑走路 かっそうろ runway
帆走 はんそう sailing by boat

航 ▷**navigate**
コウ ⓚ1204

(travel over water) **navigate, sail, cruise**
航行 こうこう navigation, cruise
航法 こうほう navigation
航海 こうかい voyage, ocean navigation
航路 こうろ sea route, course
潜航 せんこう submarine voyage, underwater navigation
運航 うんこう navigation; (airline or shipping) service
難航 なんこう hard passage, rough going

騎 ▷**ride on horseback**
キ ⓚ1629

[original meaning] **ride on horseback**
騎馬 きば horse riding
騎手 きしゅ rider, horseman, jockey
騎乗の きじょうの mounted, on horseback
騎兵 きへい cavalry soldier, cavalry
騎士 きし knight

treat and welcome
遇 待 扱 款 接 迎

遇 ▷**treat**
グウ ⓚ2702

treat, entertain, receive, deal with
待遇する たいぐうする treat, receive, entertain
処遇する しょぐうする treat, deal with
冷遇 れいぐう cold treatment, frigid reception
知遇 ちぐう favor, warm friendship
優遇する ゆうぐうする treat favorably, receive warmly

待 ▷**treat**
タイ ま(つ) -ま(ち) ⓚ0323

treat, entertain, receive
待遇する たいぐうする treat, receive, entertain
接待する せったいする receive (guests), welcome; offer, serve, entertain
招待 しょうたい invitation

優待する ゆうたいする treat kindly, receive hospitably, give special consideration
歓待する かんたいする give a cordial [warm] reception, entertain

扱 ▷**handle**
あつか(う) あつか(い) ⓚ018

(treat a person in a particular way) **handle, receive, entertain**
人を公平に扱う ひとをこうへいにあつかう deal justly with a person

款 ▷**treat cordially**
カン ⓚ151

[usu. 歓] **treat cordially, have friendly relations with**
款待 かんたい cordial [warm] reception
交款 こうかん exchange of cordialities

接 ▷**receive**
セツ つ(ぐ) ⓚ046

receive (guests), welcome, meet
接待する せったいする receive (guests), welcome; offer, serve, entertain
面接 めんせつ interview
応接 おうせつ reception

迎 ▷**welcome**
ゲイ むか(える) ⓚ263

welcome, greet, receive
迎賓 げいひん welcoming guests
歓迎する かんげいする welcome
送迎する そうげいする welcome and send off

tree
木　樹

木 ▷**tree**
ボク モク き こ- ⓚ290

[also suffix] [original meaning] **tree**
木石 ぼくせき trees and stones, inanimate objects
樹木 じゅもく tree; trees and shrubs
草木 そうもく trees and plants, vegetation
大木 たいぼく gigantic tree
香木 こうぼく fragrant wood; aromatic tree

樹 ▷**standing tree**
ジュ ⓚ098

[also suffix] [original meaning] **standing tree, tree**
樹木 じゅもく tree; trees and shrubs
樹脂 じゅし resin
樹氷 じゅひょう trees covered with ice

植樹 しょくじゅ tree planting
街路樹 がいろじゅ roadside trees

trees

桜 桐 桂 梓 桑 漆 樺 椛
梧 檀 椿 柳 柊 椋 柾 槻
楢 樫 柏 榎 梶 柘 楊 桧
梛 榊 楓 松 杉 槙 楠 樟

桜 ▷cherry
オウ さくら   Ⓚ0842

cherry tree, (Japanese) flowering cherry, *sakura*
桜花 おうか cherry blossoms
桜桃 おうとう cherry

桐 ▷paulownia
トウ ドウ きり   Ⓚ0847

paulownia
桐油 とうゆ tung oil, (Chinese) wood oil
梧桐 ごとう Chinese parasol (tree), phoenix tree,
Firmiana platanifolia

桂 ▷aromatic tree, katsura tree
ケイ かつら   Ⓚ0837

【ケイ】
general term for aromatic trees, esp. cinnamon or cassia
桂冠 けいかん crown of laurel
肉桂 にっけい cinnamon tree
月桂樹 げっけいじゅ laurel
カシア桂皮 かしあけいひ cassia
【かつら】
katsura tree, katsura
桂男 かつらおとこ man in the moon

梓 ▷catalpa
シ あずさ   Ⓚ0873

[archaic] **catalpa, catalpa tree, Japanese catalpa tree**
梓宮 しきゅう emperor's coffin (so called because it was made of catalpa wood)

桑 ▷mulberry
ソウ くわ   Ⓚ1814

mulberry; mulberry tree
桑園 そうえん mulberry farm [plantation]
桑田 そうでん mulberry plantation

漆 ▷Japanese lacquer tree
シツ うるし   Ⓚ0637

Japanese lacquer [varnish] tree
漆かぶれ うるしかぶれ lacquer poisoning

樺 ▷birch
カ ゲ かば   Ⓚ0961

【カ ゲ】
[original meaning, now archaic] **birch**
【かば】
birch
白樺 しらかば white birch, Betula tauschii

椛 ▷birch
かば   Ⓚ0869

birch

梧 ▷Chinese parasol tree
ゴ ギョ   Ⓚ0867

[rare] **Chinese parasol tree, phoenix tree**
梧桐 ごとう Chinese parasol (tree), phoenix tree,
Firmiana platanifolia

檀 ▷spindle tree
ダン タン まゆみ   Ⓚ1003

❶ **spindle tree, *Euonymus Sieboldiana***
檀紙 だんし spindle-tree paper
❷ **sandalwood**
白檀 びゃくだん sandalwood, *Santalum album*

椿 ▷camellia
チン チュン つばき   Ⓚ0925

【チン チュン】
[original meaning, now archaic] **fragrant cedar, *Cedrela chinensis***
香椿 ちゃんちん *Cedrela chinensis*
【つばき】
camellia
椿油 つばきあぶら camellia oil

柳 ▷willow
リュウ やなぎ   Ⓚ0803

[original meaning] **willow**
蒲柳 ほりゅう purple willow; infirmity, delicate constitution
花柳 かりゅう geisha girls, courtesans; red-light district
花柳界 かりゅうかい red-light district

柊 ▷holly
シュウ シュ ひいらぎ   Ⓚ0807

holly, *Osumanthus ilicifolius*

椋 ▷*Aphananthe aspera*
リョウ むく Ⓚ0901

【リョウ】
Aphananthe aspera
椋木 りょうぼく *Aphananthe aspera*

【むく】
Aphananthe aspera
椋の木 むくのき *Aphananthe aspera*

柾 ▷spindle tree
キュウ まさ まさき Ⓚ0802

[also 正木] spindle tree

槻 ▷Zelkova
キ つき Ⓚ0978

tsuki: Zelkova *serrata var. tsuki*; old name for *keyaki* (Zelkova)

楢 ▷oak
ユウ なら Ⓚ0934

oak, esp. konara oak
小楢 こなら konara oak, *Quercus serrata*
水楢 みずなら mizunara oak, *Quercus mongolica* var. *grosseserrata*

樫 ▷evergreen oak
かし Ⓚ0988

evergreen oak
樫粉 かしこ(=かしご) oak flour, acorn flour
白樫 しらかし Chinese evergreen oak, bamboo-leaf oak

柏 ▷cypress, Japanese emperor oak
ハク ヒャク かしわ Ⓚ0798

【ハク ヒャク】
cypress, tree of the cypress family
柏槙 びゃくしん juniper
松柏 しょうはく pine and cypress, evergreen; dutiful

【かしわ】
Japanese emperor oak, daimyo oak
柏木 かしわぎ Japanese emperor oak tree
柏餅 かしわもち rice cakes wrapped in oak leaves
赤芽柏 あかめがしわ Japanese mallotus, *Mallotus japonicus*

榎 ▷hackberry
カ えのき え Ⓚ0960

Chinese hackberry
榎茸 えのきたけ enokitake, enoki mushroom

梶 ▷paper mulberry
ビ かじ Ⓚ086

paper mulberry
梶の木 かじのき paper mulberry

柘 ▷Japanese boxwood
シャ つげ Ⓚ080

[usu. 柘植 or 黄楊] Japanese boxwood

楊 ▷willow
ヨウ Ⓚ093

willow
爪楊枝(=爪楊子) つまようじ toothpick; [rare] willow-made toothbrush

桧 ▷Japanese cypress
カイ ひのき ひ Ⓚ083

[also 桧木] Japanese cypress, *hinoki*
桧林 ひのきばやし Japanese cypress forest

梛 ▷*Nageia nagi*
ナ なぎ Ⓚ087

Nageia nagi
梛筏 なぎいかだ butcher's broom, *Ruscus aculeatus*

榊 ▷sacred shinto tree
さかき Ⓚ096

ⓐ *Cleyera japonica*
ⓑ evergreen tree planted or used at a shrine

楓 ▷maple
フウ かえで Ⓚ0927

maple, maple tree
楓林 ふうりん maple grove
観楓会 かんぷうかい maple-leaf viewing

松 ▷pine
ショウ まつ Ⓚ0769

pine
松竹梅 しょうちくばい pine-bamboo-plum; congratulatory tree decorations
松根油 しょうこんゆ pine oil
青松 せいしょう green pine

杉 ▷cryptomeria
すぎ Ⓚ0737

[archaic] cryptomeria, Japanese [Japan] cedar, sugi
老杉 ろうさん old cryptomeria

槙 ▷podocarpus
テン シン まき Ⓚ0967

podocarpus; cedar, white cedar

犬槙 いぬまき podocarpus, *Podocarpus macrophyllus*

楠 ▷**camphor tree**
ナン くす くすのき   Ⓚ0930

[sometimes also 樟] **camphor tree**
  楠の木 くすのき camphor tree

樟 ▷**camphor tree**
ショウ くす くすのき   Ⓚ0980

camphor tree
  樟脳 しょうのう camphor

---

trouble and suffering

困 苛 窮 悶 悩
苦 痛 辛 煩 難

困 ▷**be in trouble**
コン こま(る)   Ⓚ2644

[original meaning] **be in trouble, be hard-pressed, be distressed, suffer**
  困難 こんなん difficulty, trouble, distress, hardship
  困惑 こんわく embarrassment, perplexity, confusion
  困窮 こんきゅう destitution, poverty, distress
  困苦 こんく hardships, privation
  貧困 ひんこん poverty, indigence, destitution; lack, shortage

苛 ▷**torment**
カ いじ(める)   Ⓚ1929

torment, tease, persecute
  苛め いじめ bullying, teasing
  苛められっ子 いじめられっこ bullied child

窮 ▷**be in extremity**
キュウ きわ(める) きわ(まる) きわ(まり)
きわ(み)   Ⓚ2078

be in extremity, come to an extreme, be in distress
  窮地 きゅうち predicament, difficult situation, dilemma
  窮状 きゅうじょう distress, wretched condition
  窮余の策 きゅうよのさく desperate measure
  窮迫 きゅうはく straitened circumstances, distress
  窮屈な きゅうくつな cramped, confined; formal; poor

悶 ▷**be in agony**
モン もだ(える)

[original meaning] **be in agony, worry, fret**
  悶着 もんちゃく trouble(s), difficulty, dispute
  悶悶とする もんもんとする worry endlessly, suffer mental agony
  悶絶する もんぜつする faint in agony
  苦悶 くもん agony, anguish
  煩悶 はんもん anguish, worry
  遣悶する けんもんする drive away melancholy

悩 ▷**suffer**
ノウ なや(む) なや(ます)   Ⓚ0380

ⓐ [original meaning] **suffer, be distressed**
ⓑ **cause suffering, afflict**
ⓒ **suffering, distress, pain, trouble, affliction**
  a 悩乱 のうらん worry, anguish
  懊悩 おうのう agony, anguish, trouble
  b 悩殺する のうさつする fascinate, enchant
  c 苦悩 くのう suffering, distress, anguish
  煩悩 ぼんのう worldly desires, carnal desires

苦 ▷**suffering**
ク くる(しい) -ぐる(しい) くる(しむ)
くる(しめる) にが(い) にが(る)   Ⓚ1932

ⓐ **suffering, hardship, pain, distress**
ⓑ (characterized by suffering) **hard, painful, distressing**
ⓒ **hardship, trouble, difficulty**
  a 苦痛 くつう pain, agony, anguish
  苦悶 くもん agony, anguish
  苦悩 くのう suffering, distress, anguish
  苦難 くなん suffering, hardship
  苦渋 くじゅう distress, affliction
  b 苦境 くきょう distressing circumstances, straits
  苦界 くがい bitter [hard] world; life of prostitution
  苦労 くろう difficulties, trouble, hardships, labor
  c 苦楽 くらく pleasure and pain, joys and sorrows
  辛苦 しんく hardships, trials; labor, trouble
  貧苦 ひんく hardship of poverty

痛 ▷**pain**
ツウ いた(い) いた(む) いた(ましい)
いた(める)   Ⓚ2799

ⓐ [also suffix] [original meaning] (physical suffering) **pain, ache**
ⓑ (mental suffering) **pain, agony, grief, sadness**
  a 痛覚 つうかく sense of pain
  苦痛 くつう pain, agony, anguish
  頭痛 ずつう headache
  鎮痛剤 ちんつうざい anodyne, painkiller
  神経痛 しんけいつう neuralgia
  筋肉痛 きんにくつう muscular pain
  b 痛痒 つうよう interest, concern; pain and tickling
  心痛 しんつう mental agony, heartache

悲痛な ひつうな sad, grievous
沈痛な ちんつうな grave, serious, sad

辛 ▷hard
シン から(い) Ⓚ1755

(difficult to bear) **hard, trying, bitter, painful, toilsome**

辛苦 しんく hardships, trials; labor, trouble
辛酸 しんさん hardships, privations
辛抱 しんぼう patience, endurance, forbearance
辛労 しんろう toil, trouble

煩 ▷vexed
ハン ボン わずら(う) わずら(わす) Ⓚ0937

[original meaning] **vexed, annoyed, irritated, troubled, worried**

煩悶 はんもん anguish, worry
煩悩 ぼんのう worldly desires, carnal desires

難 ▷difficult
ナン かた(い) –がた(い) むずか(しい)
むつか(しい) Ⓚ1632

ⓐ [also prefix] **difficult, hard, troublesome**
ⓑ [also suffix] **difficulty, trouble, hardship, distress**

ⓐ 難航 なんこう hard passage, rough going
難問 なんもん difficult problem [question]
難解な なんかいな difficult, hard to understand
難易 なんい (relative) difficulty, hardness (or ease)
難事業 なんじぎょう difficult undertaking [project],
　uphill task
難儀 なんぎ hardship, trouble
至難の しなんの most difficult
困難 こんなん difficulty, trouble, distress, hardship
万難 ばんなん thousand and one difficulties, innumerable difficulties
ⓑ 難無く なんなく easily, without difficulty
生活難 せいかつなん living difficulties, economic
　distress
就職難 しゅうしょくなん difficulty of finding
　employment, job shortage

true
真 洵 実 本 正 現

真 ▷true
シン ま Ⓚ1813

ⓐ [also prefix] **true, real, actual, genuine**
ⓑ **truth, reality, genuineness**

ⓐ 真価 しんか true value
真意 しんい true meaning [signification]; real intention
真剣 しんけん real sword; seriousness

真相 しんそう truth, facts, real situation
真犯人 しんはんにん the real criminal
ⓑ 真実 しんじつ truth, reality
真偽 しんぎ truth or falsehood; authenticity
写真 しゃしん photograph

洵 ▷truly
ジュン Ⓚ034.

[archaic] **truly, really, utterly**

洵美 じゅんび truly beautiful, exquisite

実 ▷real
ジツ み みの(る) Ⓚ191.

ⓐ [also prefix] **real, actual, true**
ⓑ **reality, fact, truth**

ⓐ 実施する じっしする carry out, enforce, execute
実現する じつげんする realize, materialize
実験 じっけん experiment
実力 じつりょく real ability [power], capability,
　competence
実績 じっせき (actual) result, positive achievement
実費 じっぴ actual expenses, cost price
実名 じつめい one's real name
実社会 じっしゃかい actual world
実際 じっさい truth, reality; actual state; practice
ⓑ 事実 じじつ fact, reality; as a matter of fact
現実 げんじつ actuality, reality
確実な かくじつな certain, sure, reliable; sound,
　solid
真実 しんじつ truth, reality

本 ▷real
ホン もと Ⓚ2937

real, true, genuine

本体 ほんたい substance, thing itself; object of
　worship; main part
本当の ほんとうの true, real, genuine
本当に ほんとうに really, truly, indeed
本物 ほんもの real thing [stuff], genuine article;
　expert performance
本名 ほんみょう one's real name
本心 ほんしん one's true mind, one's real intention;
　one's conscience

正 ▷genuine
セイ ショウ ただ(しい) ただ(す) まさ
まさ(に) Ⓚ2926

genuine, authentic, pure

正真正銘の しょうしんしょうめいの true, genuine,
　authentic
正史 せいし authentic history
正体 しょうたい one's natural [true] shape;
　consciousness

現 ▷actual
ゲン あらわ(れる) あらわ(す) Ⓚ0879

(existing in fact) **actual, real**
現実 げんじつ actuality, reality
現状 げんじょう present condition
現地 げんち actual place [locale]
現役 げんえき active service
現場 げんば actual spot; job site, building site

trunk parts
胸 腹 胴 腰 背
肩 股 脇 腋

胸 ▷chest
キョウ むね むな-
see also →CHEST
Ⓚ0858

[original meaning] **chest, breast, thorax**
胸囲 きょうい chest measurement
胸部 きょうぶ breast, chest
胸骨 きょうこつ breastbone
胸郭 きょうかく thorax, chest
気胸 ききょう pneumothorax

腹 ▷belly
フク はら Ⓚ0949

[original meaning] **belly, abdomen, stomach, bowels**
腹部 ふくぶ abdomen, belly
腹痛 ふくつう stomachache, abdominal pain
満腹 まんぷく full belly, satiety
切腹 せっぷく harakiri, suicide by disembowelment
空腹 くうふく empty stomach, hunger

胴 ▷trunk
ドウ Ⓚ0857

[original meaning] **trunk (of the body), torso, abdomen**
胴体 どうたい trunk, body, torso, hull
胴巻き どうまき bellyband
胴衣 どうい jacket, vest
胴上げ どうあげ tossing (a person in triumph)

腰 ▷waist
ヨウ こし Ⓚ0952

[original meaning] **waist, hips, loin, pelvic region**
腰部 ようぶ waist, hips
腰間 ようかん hips
腰痛 ようつう lumbago, pain in the hips
腰囲 ようい hip measurement
細腰 さいよう slender hips

背 ▷back
ハイ せ せい そむ(く) そむ(ける) Ⓚ2230

back (of the body)
背部 はいぶ back
背泳 はいえい backstroke
背後 はいご back, rear

肩 ▷shoulder
ケン かた Ⓚ1703

[original meaning] **shoulder**
肩甲骨 けんこうこつ shoulder blade, scapula
肩章 けんしょう shoulder strap
双肩 そうけん both shoulders
比肩する ひけんする equal, rank with, compare
  favorably
強肩 きょうけん baseball strong arm

股 ▷crotch
コ また もも Ⓚ0785

[original meaning] **crotch (of the human body), inner thigh**
股関節 こかんせつ coxa
股間 こかん crotch
股肱 ここう one's right-hand man, one's trusted
  henchman
四股 しこ stamping on the sumo ring

脇 ▷armpit
キョウ わき Ⓚ0859

[original meaning] **armpit**

腋 ▷armpit
エキ わき

armpit
腋窩腺 えきかせん axillary gland
腋芽 えきが(=わきめ) axillary bud

try
試 験

試 ▷try
シ こころ(みる) ため(す) Ⓚ1385

ⓐ [original meaning] (attempt to do) **try, attempt**
ⓑ (test the quality of) **try, test, sample**
a 試案 しあん tentative plan, draft
  試作 しさく trial manufacture
  試算する しさんする make a trial calculation
  試写 ししゃ preview, private showing
  試行錯誤 しこうさくご trial and error
b 試食 ししょく sampling (of food)

試験 しけん test, examination
試練 しれん trial, test, probation
試運転 しうんてん test run

験 ▷test
ケン ゲン Ⓚ1628

[original meaning] **test, try, attempt, examine, verify**
験算(=検算) けんざん verification of accounts, checking figures
試験する しけんする test, examine
実験 じっけん experiment
体験する たいけんする experience, go through, (actually) feel
受験する じゅけんする take an examination

tubular passages
管 筒 道 脈 樋

管 ▷pipe
カン くだ Ⓚ2357

[also suffix]
ⓐ (tubular conveyance) **pipe, tube, duct**
ⓑ anat **(tubular part or organ) tube, pipe, duct**
a 管状の かんじょうの tubular
鋼管 こうかん steel pipe [tubing]
配管 はいかん piping
真空管 しんくうかん vacuum tube
試験管 しけんかん test tube
b 血管 けっかん blood vessel
気管 きかん trachea, windpipe

筒 ▷tube
トウ つつ Ⓚ2341

ⓐ [also suffix] [original meaning] **tube, cylinder, pipe**
ⓑ **tube-shaped encasement**
a 円筒 えんとう cylinder
発煙筒 はつえんとう smoke ball [bomb]
b 水筒 すいとう canteen
封筒 ふうとう envelope

道 ▷passage
ドウ トウ みち Ⓚ2701

passage, duct
地下道 ちかどう underpass, underground passage
水道 すいどう water service [supply]; channel
気道 きどう air passage
食道 しょくどう esophagus
外耳道 がいじどう external auditory meatus

脈 ▷vein
ミャク Ⓚ0860

[original meaning] (any blood vessel) **vein, artery, blood vessel**
脈管 みゃっかん blood vessel; duct
動脈 どうみゃく artery
静脈 じょうみゃく vein

樋 ▷water pipe
トウ とい ひ Ⓚ0982

water [rainwater] pipe, gutter, (eaves) trough, downspout
雨樋 あまどい rainwater pipe, rain gutter, eaves trough
竪樋(=縦樋) たてどい downspout
鎖樋 くさりとい rain chain

turn
旋 転 回 廻 巡 循 幹 捻

旋 ▷gyrate
セン Ⓚ0862

gyrate, whirl, revolve, spiral, go around
旋回 せんかい revolution, rotation, circling, swiveling
旋転 せんてん gyration, whirling, revolution, rotation
旋盤 せんばん lathe
旋削 せんさく turning (on a lathe)
旋風 せんぷう whirlwind
旋律 せんりつ melody
螺旋 らせん spiral, helix; screw

転 ▷turn
テン ころ(がる) ころ(げる) ころ(がす) ころ(ぶ) Ⓚ1346

[original meaning] **turn, revolve, rotate**
回転する かいてんする revolve, rotate, turn
自転 じてん rotation (of the earth)
運転する うんてんする operate, drive, run

回 ▷turn round
カイ エ まわ(る) -まわ(り) まわ(す) まわ(し)- Ⓚ2630

[formerly 廻]
ⓐ [original meaning] **turn round, revolve, rotate, circulate**
ⓑ **go round, make the rounds; circulate, make a circular tour**
a 回転する かいてんする revolve, rotate, turn
転回 てんかい turning over; revolution, rotation

旋回 せんかい revolution, rotation, circling, swiveling
b 回診 かいしん make a round of visits (to one's patients)
回路 かいろ (electric) circuit
回覧する かいらんする circulate, send round
巡回する じゅんかいする go round, make the rounds, patrol
徘回(=徘徊)する はいかいする loiter, wander about

廻 ▷turn round
 カイ エ まわ(る) まわ(す) Ⓚ2660

[now usu. 回]
ⓐ turn round, revolve, rotate, circulate
ⓑ go round, make the rounds; circulate, make a circular tour
a 廻転する かいてんする revolve, rotate, turn
旋廻 せんかい revolution, rotation, circling, swiveling
b 廻覧する かいらんする circulate, send round
廻状 かいじょう circular (letter)
廻文 かいぶん palindrome; circular
廻廊 かいろう corridor, gallery

巡 ▷make the rounds
ジュン めぐ(る) めぐ(り) Ⓚ2622

make the rounds, patrol, make a round of inspection, go round
巡査 じゅんさ police, patrolman
巡視 じゅんし inspection tour
巡回 じゅんかい round, patrol
巡洋艦 じゅんようかん cruiser
巡察する じゅんさつする make a round of inspection, patrol
巡航 じゅんこう cruise, cruising
一巡する いちじゅんする make a round

循 ▷circulate
 ジュン Ⓚ0530

circulate, go round
循環 じゅんかん circulation, rotation; cycle

斡 ▷revolve
アツ Ⓚ1542

revolve, go around
斡旋 あっせん good offices, services; mediation

捻 ▷twist
 ネン Ⓚ0457

twist, wrench, screw
捻挫 ねんざ sprain
捻転 ねんてん twisting, torsion
捻出する ねんしゅつする manage to raise (funds), squeeze out (money, time), work out (a solution)

---

twigs →BRANCHES AND TWIGS

twine →WIND AND TWINE

two
二 弐 双 対 偶 両

二 ▷two
ニ ふた ふた(つ) Ⓚ1688

[original meaning] **two, second**
二百 にひゃく 200
二月 にがつ February
二次 にじ second, secondary
二塁 にるい second base
二階 にかい second floor; upstairs

弐 ▷two (in legal documents)
 ニ Ⓚ2752

[original meaning] **two**—used in legal documents and checks
金弐阡円 きんにせんえん the sum of two thousand yen

双 ▷set of two
ソウ ふた Ⓚ0013

ⓐ [original meaning] **set of two** (identical things such as hands), **pair, both, two**
ⓑ counter for pairs
a 双肩 そうけん both shoulders
双生児 そうせいじ twins
双方 そうほう both sides [parties]
b 双眼鏡 そうがんきょう binoculars
一双 いっそう a pair

対 ▷pair
 タイ ツイ Ⓚ0735

ⓐ (two things of the same kind) **pair, couple, set**
ⓑ counter for pairs
a 対遇 たいぐう pair; antithesis
対句 ついく couplet, antithesis
b 一対 いっつい a pair

偶 ▷couple
グウ Ⓚ0115

couple, pair
偶力 ぐうりょく couple (of forces)
対偶 たいぐう contrapositive; spouse, companion

両 ▷both
 リョウ Ⓚ2949

[also prefix] **both, two**

two

両方 りょうほう both
両側 りょうがわ both sides
両院 りょういん both Houses
両手 りょうて both hands
両用 りょうよう dual use
両親 りょうしん parents
両雄 りょうゆう two great men
両性的 りょうせいてき bisexual
両義 りょうぎ double meaning, two meanings

types →KINDS AND TYPES

uncultivated expanses of land
野　原　漠

野 ▷field
ヤ の　　　　　　　　　　Ⓚ1350

[original meaning] (uncultivated) **field, open country, wilderness**

野外 やがい field, fields, open air
平野 へいや plain(s), open field
原野 げんや vast plain, wilderness, field
荒野 こうや wilderness, the wilds, wasteland

原 ▷plain
ゲン はら　　　　　　　　　Ⓚ2593

[also suffix] **plain, field, plateau**

原野 げんや vast plain, wilderness, field
高原 こうげん plateau, tableland, heights
草原 そうげん grassland, prairie, savannah, pampas, steppe
平原 へいげん plain, prairie
氷原 ひょうげん ice field
火口原 かこうげん crater basin

漠 ▷desert
バク　　　　　　　　　　Ⓚ0598

desert

漠北 ばくほく north of the Gobi Desert, Outer Mongolia
砂漠 さばく desert

understand →KNOW AND UNDERSTAND

undertake
負　担

負 ▷bear
フ ま(ける) ま(かす) お(う)　　Ⓚ179

ⓐ bear (responsibility), take upon oneself, sustain
ⓑ bear a debt, owe

ⓐ 負担 ふたん burden, charge, responsibility
負託する ふたくする charge (someone) with responsibility
負傷する ふしょうする be injured [wounded], get hurt
ⓑ 負債 ふさい debt, liabilities

担 ▷undertake
タン かつ(ぐ) にな(う)　　Ⓚ028

undertake (a task), take (a job) upon oneself

担当する たんとうする undertake, be in charge of
担保 たんぽ security, mortgage
担任する たんにんする be in charge of, take (a class under one's charge
負担 ふたん burden, charge, responsibility
分担 ぶんたん partial charge, allotment

undomesticated mammals
虎 猿 鯨 犀 狼 狐 羚 鼠
獅 豹 熊 象 麒 麟 猪 鹿

虎 ▷tiger
コ とら
see also →TIGER　　　　Ⓚ2766

[original meaning] **tiger**

虎穴 こけつ tiger's den; dangerous place
虎口 ここう tiger's den; dangerous place
虎視眈眈 こしたんたん on the alert, eye covetously
竜虎の争い りゅうこのあらそい well matched contest ("serpent and tiger fight")
暴虎馮河 ぼうこひょうが foolhardy courage

猿 ▷monkey
エン さる
see also →MONKEY　　　　Ⓚ0612

[original meaning] **monkey, ape**

猿人 えんじん ape-man
類人猿 るいじんえん anthropoid, troglodyte

犬猿 けんえん dog and monkey
犬猿の仲である けんえんのなかである lead a cat and dog life; be at enmity

鯨 ▷whale
ゲイ くじら　　　　　　　　Ⓚ1661

[original meaning] whale

鯨肉 げいにく whale meat
鯨油 げいゆ whale oil
鯨骨 げいこつ whale bone
巨鯨 きょげい huge whale
捕鯨 ほげい whaling

犀 ▷rhinoceros
サイ セイ　　　　　　　　Ⓚ2710

rhinoceros

犀角 さいかく rhinoceros horn
黒犀 くろさい black rhinoceros
一角犀 いっかくさい great one-horned rhinoceros
金木犀 きんもくせい orange osmanthus, *Osmanthus fragrans* var. *aurantiacus*

狼 ▷wolf
ロウ おおかみ　　　　　　Ⓚ0407

[original meaning] wolf

狼藉 ろうぜき disorder; violence
狼瘡 ろうそう lupus, esp. lupus vulgaris
餓狼 がろう hungry wolf
虎狼 ころう tigers and wolves; greedy brute
天狼星 てんろうせい Sirius
周章狼狽する しゅうしょうろうばいする be disconcerted, be confused

狐 ▷fox
コ きつね

[original meaning] fox

狐狸 こり foxes and raccoon dogs; trickster, deceiver
白狐 びゃっこ spiritual white fox; Arctic fox

羚 ▷serow
レイ　　　　　　　　　　Ⓚ1225

[original meaning] serow

羚羊 れいよう antelope

鼠 ▷rat
ソ ねずみ ねず

[original meaning] rat, mouse

鼠蹊部 そけいぶ inguinal region
窮鼠 きゅうそ cornered mouse
殺鼠剤 さっそざい rat poison

獅 ▷lion
シ　　　　　　　　　　　Ⓚ0613

lion

獅子 しし lion; left-hand guardian dog at a Shinto shrine
獅子座 ししざ Leo, the Lion (constellation)
獅子舞 ししまい lion dance

豹 ▷leopard
ヒョウ　　　　　　　　　Ⓚ1325

[original meaning] leopard, panther

豹柄 ひょうがら leopard print, leopard pattern
豹変 ひょうへん sudden drastic change (in behavior)
黒豹 くろひょう black panther
アメリカ豹 あめりかひょう jaguar
全豹 ぜんぴょう whole picture, entirety

熊 ▷bear
くま　　　　　　　　　　Ⓚ2479

[rare] bear

熊掌 ゆうしょう bear's paw (as a rare Chinese delicacy)

象 ▷elephant
ショウ ゾウ　　　　　　　Ⓚ1831

[original meaning] elephant

象さん ぞうさん elephant
象牙 ぞうげ ivory
巨象 きょぞう gigantic elephant
アフリカ象 あふりかぞう African elephant

麒 ▷male Chinese unicorn
キ　　　　　　　　　　　Ⓚ1662

male Chinese unicorn

麒麟 きりん giraffe; male and female Chinese unicorns
麒麟草 きりんそう orange stonecrop, *Sedum kamtschaticum*
麒麟児 きりんじ child prodigy, genius
麒麟血(麒麟竭) きりんけつ dragon's blood

麟 ▷female Chinese unicorn
リン　　　　　　　　　　Ⓚ1669

[original meaning] female Chinese unicorn

麒麟 きりん giraffe; male and female Chinese unicorns

猪 ▷wild boar
チョ いのしし い　　　　Ⓚ0489

[original meaning] wild boar, boar

野猪 やちょ wild boar

　　　　　　　　undomesticated mammals

鹿 ▷deer
ロク しか か   Ⓚ2695

deer, stag, hind
鹿皮 しかがわ deerskin

ungual
爪　蹄

爪 ▷nail
ソウ つめ つま   Ⓚ2605

[original meaning] **nail, claw, talon, hoof**
爪牙 そうが claws and tusks, devious design; right-hand man
距爪 きょそう cockspur
有爪動物 ゆうそうどうぶつ velvet worms, *Onychophora*

蹄 ▷hoof
テイ ひづめ   Ⓚ1452

[original meaning] **hoof**
蹄鉄 ていてつ horseshoe
蹄叉 ていさ fourchette
装蹄 そうてい shoeing a horse, horseshoeing
馬蹄 ばてい horse's hooves
口蹄疫 こうていえき foot-and-mouth disease
偶蹄類 ぐうているい artiodactyls

uniform →SAME AND UNIFORM

unimportant
細　微　小　末

細 ▷minute
サイ ほそ(い) ほそ(る) こま(か)
こま(かい)   Ⓚ1220

(beneath notice) **minute, minor, trifling, insignificant**
細事 さいじ minor details
細君 さいくん wife
零細な れいさいな small, trifling, petty
些細な ささいな trifling, slight, insignificant

微 ▷slight
ビ かす(か)   Ⓚ0587

(of little importance or influence) **slight, insignificant, beneath notice, mean, humble**
微賤 びせん low rank, humble station
軽微な けいびな slight, little, insignificant

小 ▷small
ショウ ちい(さい) こ- お-   Ⓚ000?

(less in importance) **small, minor, petty**
小前提 しょうぜんてい minor premise
小事 しょうじ trifle
小委 しょうい subcommittee
小学校 しょうがっこう elementary [primary] school
小学生 しょうがくせい schoolchild, schoolboy, schoolgirl
過小評価する かしょうひょうかする underestimate, underrate

末 ▷last in importance
マツ バツ すえ   Ⓚ294?

last in importance, trivial, insignificant
末節 まっせつ minor details, nonessentials
粗末な そまつな coarse, crude, inferior, humble
本末 ほんまつ root and branch, means and end

units of learning
課　科　講

課 ▷lesson
カ   Ⓚ1423

ⓐ **lesson, task**
ⓑ **counter for lessons**
a 課程 かてい course, curriculum
課目(=科目) かもく school subject, course, curriculum
学課 がっか lesson, school work
日課 にっか daily lesson, daily task
放課後 ほうかご after school
b 二課勉強する にかべんきょうする study two lessons

科 ▷course
カ   Ⓚ1053

[also suffix] **course (of study), department (of a university or hospital)**
内科 ないか (department of) internal medicine
外科 げか (department of) surgery
歯科 しか dentistry
本科 ほんか regular course [department]
文科 ぶんか literary department
小児科 しょうにか (department of) pediatrics

講 ▷lecture
コウ   Ⓚ1463

lecture
開講する かいこうする begin a series of one's lectures

豪宕な ごうとうな bold and unconstrained, magnanimous

universe and space
宇　宙

宇 ▷**universe**
ウ
Ⓚ1863

universe, infinite space, world
　宇宙 うちゅう universe, cosmos; (outer) space
　宇内 うだい the whole universe, the whole world

宙 ▷**space**
チュウ
Ⓚ1907

(expanse of the universe) **space, outer space, heavens**
　宇宙 うちゅう universe, cosmos; (outer) space
　航宙 こうちゅう space flight

unrefined →VULGAR AND UNREFINED

unrestrained
漫　散　宕

漫 ▷**rambling**
マン
Ⓚ0633

rambling, random, discursive, desultory, aimless, unrestrained, casual
　漫遊する まんゆうする make a leisurely tour
　漫文 まんぶん random notes
　漫然たる まんぜんたる rambling, random, desulto-ry
　漫歩する まんぽする ramble, saunter
　散漫な さんまんな desultory, vagrant, vague
　放漫 ほうまん laxity, looseness, indiscretion
　冗漫な じょうまんな diffuse, verbose, prolix

散 ▷**unrestrained**
サン　ち(る)　ち(らす)　ち(らかす)
ち(らかる)　ち(らばる)
Ⓚ1518

ⓐ **unrestrained, free, carefree, relaxed, loose**
ⓑ **random, haphazard**
a　散歩 さんぽ walk, (leisurely) stroll
　散文 さんぶん prose
　閑散 かんさん leisure, inactivity
b　散散に さんざんに severely, terribly, unsparingly
　散漫な さんまんな desultory, vagrant, vague

宕 ▷**unconstrained**
トウ
Ⓚ1917

unconstrained, self-willed, carefree

urge
勧　催　促　誘　励　侑

勧 ▷**urge**
カン　すす(める)
Ⓚ1645

[original meaning] (persuade to act) **urge, persuade, advise**
　勧告 かんこく advice, counsel, recommendation
　勧誘する かんゆうする induce, invite, canvass, persuade

催 ▷**press for**
サイ　もよお(す)
Ⓚ0136

press for, urge, hasten
　催促する さいそくする press for, urge, demand
　催告 さいこく notification, demand

促 ▷**hasten**
ソク　うなが(す)
Ⓚ0087

(cause to act with haste) **hasten, urge, hurry, press (for)**
　促進する そくしんする promote, spur on, facilitate
　促成 そくせい growth promotion
　催促する さいそくする press for, urge, demand
　督促状 とくそくじょう demand note, dunning letter [note]

誘 ▷**induce**
ユウ　さそ(う)
Ⓚ1407

(move by persuasion) **induce, lure, tempt, entice, seduce; lead, guide**
　誘致する ゆうちする lure, entice, invite; bring about, cause
　誘惑 ゆうわく temptation, seduction
　誘引する ゆういんする entice, induce, attract
　誘導する ゆうどうする induce, incite; guide, lead
　誘拐 ゆうかい kidnapping, abduction
　誘蛾灯 ゆうがとう luring lamp
　誘殺する ゆうさつする seduce and kill
　勧誘する かんゆうする induce, invite, canvass, persuade

励 ▷**encourage**
レイ　はげ(む)　はげ(ます)
Ⓚ1035

(impart confidence or spirit) **encourage, cheer up, inspire**
　奨励 しょうれい encouragement, promotion, stim-ulation, incitement
　激励する げきれいする encourage, urge, cheer up

督励 とくれい urging (one's subordinates)

侑 ▷urge to eat
ユウ ⓚ0073

[archaic] **urge someone to eat or drink, assist with a meal**

侑觴 ゆうしょう urging one to drink more good wine during a banquet

侑食 ゆうしょく dining with a superior, assisting at dinner

urgent

急　緊　迫

急 ▷urgent
キュウ いそ(ぐ) いそ(ぎ) ⓚ1800

urgent, imminent, pressing

急務 きゅうむ urgent business, pressing need

急迫 きゅうはく urgency, imminence

急用 きゅうよう urgent business

緊急な きんきゅうな urgent, pressing, emergent

早急な さっきゅう(=そうきゅう)な urgent, pressing

至急に しきゅうに urgently, with all haste, at once

緊 ▷exigent
キン ⓚ2471

exigent, urgent, pressing, imminent

緊急な きんきゅうな urgent, pressing, emergent

緊要な きんような important, momentous; exigent, urgent

緊迫した きんぱくした tense, strained

緊切な きんせつな urgent, pressing

喫緊事 きっきんじ urgent [pressing] matter

迫 ▷pressing
ハク せま(る) ⓚ2647

pressing, urgent, imminent, impending, close

急迫した きゅうはくした pressing, urgent, imminent

緊迫する きんぱくする become tense, grow strained

use

使　用

使 ▷use
シ つか(う) つか(い) -づか(い) ⓚ0072

use, make use of, employ

使用する しようする use, employ, apply

使用人 しようにん employee; servant

使途 しと how money is spent

使役 しえき employment, service; *gram* causative

行使する こうしする use, employ, exercise

駆使する くしする use freely, have good command of

用 ▷employ
ヨウ もち(いる) ⓚ2569

employ, use, make use of, utilize, apply

用意する よういする prepare, ready oneself, make arrangements

用語 ようご terminology; diction, wording; vocabulary

用途 ようと use, service, application

用法 ようほう usage, directions for use, use

用心 ようじん care; caution

用心深い ようじんぶかい careful; cautious; watchful

利用する りようする utilize, make use of, avail oneself of

使用する しようする use, employ, apply

採用 さいよう adoption, acceptance; employment, appointment

適用 てきよう application

運用する うんようする make use of; invest in; apply to

vain

空　虚　徒

空 ▷empty
クウ そら あ(く) あ(き) あ(ける) から むな(しい) ⓚ1913

(insubstantial) **empty, void, vain, idle, futile, meaningless**

空虚 くうきょ emptiness, voidness; inanity

空想 くうそう fancy, fantasy; imagination

空論 くうろん abstract [impractical] theory

空費 くうひ waste

虚 ▷without substance
キョ コ ⓚ2778

without substance, in name only, empty, vain, inane, hollow, void

虚栄 きょえい vanity, vainglory

虚栄心 きょえいしん vanity

虚勢 きょせい bluff, bluster, false show of power

虚飾 きょしょく ostentation, affectation, show

虚礼 きょれい empty [useless] formalities

徒 ▷vain
ト ⓚ0377

vain, futile, wasted, worthless
徒労 とろう vain effort, lost labor
徒食 としょく idle life

---

valley

谷　渓　峡

谷 ▷valley
コク たに ⓚ1758

[original meaning] **valley, gorge, ravine**
渓谷 けいこく ravine, valley, canyon
峡谷 きょうこく gorge, ravine, canyon, valley
幽谷 ゆうこく deep ravine, secluded valley

渓 ▷ravine
ケイ ⓚ0474

[also suffix] **ravine, valley**
渓谷 けいこく ravine, valley, canyon
渓間 けいかん ravine
雪渓 せっけい snowy valley [ravine]
耶馬渓 やばけい Yabakei Valley

峡 ▷gorge
キョウ ⓚ0318

ⓐ **gorge, ravine, glen**
ⓑ **suffix after names of gorges or valleys**
a 峡谷 きょうこく gorge, ravine, canyon, valley
　峡間 きょうかん between the mountains; ravine
　山峡 さんきょう(=やまかい) gorge, ravine, glen
b 黒部峡 くろべきょう Kurobe Canyon

---

value
値　　価

値 ▷value
チ ね あたい ⓚ0091

ⓐ **value, worth, merit**
ⓑ [also suffix] *math* **value**
a 価値 かち value, merit
　数値 すうち numerical value
b 絶対値 ぜったいち absolute value
　平均値 へいきんち mean value

価 ▷value
カ あたい ⓚ0067

[also suffix] **value, worth, merit**
価値 かち value, merit
評価する ひょうかする evaluate, appraise
声価 せいか reputation, fame
栄養価 えいようか nutritive value

---

vapor →GAS AND VAPOR

---

vaporize
蒸　　留

蒸 ▷evaporate
ジョウ む(す) む(れる) む(らす) ⓚ2043

evaporate
蒸発 じょうはつ evaporation, volatilization; mysterious disappearance
蒸散 じょうさん transpiration
蒸留 じょうりゅう distillation
蒸気 じょうき steam, vapor

留 ▷distill
リュウ ル と(める) –ど(め) と(まる) とど(まる) ⓚ2235

[formerly 溜] **distill**
蒸留 じょうりゅう distillation
分留 ぶんりゅう fraction, fractional distillation
乾留 かんりゅう dry distillation

---

various
諸　庶　雑

諸 ▷various
ショ ⓚ1427

[also prefix] **various, all kinds of; many, all**
諸説 しょせつ various views [theories]
諸島 しょとう archipelago
諸派 しょは minor parties
諸君 しょくん Ladies and Gentlemen, my friends, you
諸国 しょこく various [all] countries
諸般の しょはんの various, several, all, every
諸問題 しょもんだい various [all] questions [problems]
諸行無常 しょぎょうむじょう All things flow and nothing is permanent (a Buddhist concept)

庶 ▷**manifold**
ショ Ⓚ2696

manifold, many, numerous, various, general
庶務 しょむ general affairs
庶事(=諸事) しょじ various matters
庶政(=諸政) しょせい all phases of government

雑 ▷**miscellaneous**
ザツ ゾウ Ⓚ1267

[also prefix] **miscellaneous, various, sundry, motley**
雑多 ざった miscellaneous, various
雑誌 ざっし magazine, journal
雑用 ざつよう miscellaneous business
雑費 ざっぴ miscellaneous expenses
雑貨 ざっか sundries, general cargo; miscellaneous
　　goods
雑文家 ざつぶんか miscellaneous writer, miscella-
　　nist
雑木 ぞうき miscellaneous trees
雑歌 ぞうか miscellaneous poems
雑所得 ざっしょとく miscellaneous [sundry]
　　incomes
雑談 ざつだん chat, idle talk
雑煮 ぞうに rice cakes boiled with vegetables

vegetables

菜　蕪　芋　豆　蕗
茄　芹　瓜　瓢　芥

菜 ▷**greens**
サイ な Ⓚ2004

greens, vegetables; rape
菜っ葉 なっぱ greens
菜種 なたね rapeseed, coleseed
青菜 あおな greens

蕪 ▷**turnip**
ブ かぶ かぶら Ⓚ2083

【かぶ】
[also 蕪菁] **turnip**
赤蕪 あかかぶ red turnip

【かぶら】
[also 蕪菁] **same as** 蕪 かぶ
蕪菜 かぶらな turnip

芋 ▷**potato**
いも Ⓚ1868

potato; sweet potato; tuber
芋蔓 いもづる sweet potato vine

芋虫 いもむし green caterpillar
ジャガ芋 じゃがいも potato, white potato
里芋 さといも taro
薩摩芋 さつまいも sweet potato
焼き芋 やきいも baked sweet potato

豆 ▷**bean**
トウ ズ まめ Ⓚ1700

ⓐ **bean, pea**
ⓑ **soybean**
ⓐ 豆腐 とうふ tofu (Japanese bean curd)
　　大豆 だいず soybean
ⓑ 豆乳 とうにゅう soybean milk
　　納豆 なっとう fermented soybeans

蕗 ▷**butterbur**
ロ ル ふき Ⓚ2090

butterbur

茄 ▷**eggplant**
カ ケ Ⓚ1930

eggplant
蕃茄 ばんか tomato

芹 ▷**Japanese parsley**
キン ゴン せり Ⓚ1896

Japanese parsley, *Oenanthe stolonifera*, dropwort
オランダ芹 おらんだぜり parsley

瓜 ▷**gourd**
カ うり Ⓚ2626

gourd, melon
瓜科 うりか gourd family, *Cucurbitaceae*
瓜二つ うりふたつ as alike as two peas
瓜実顔 うりざねがお oval face
瓜坊 うりぼう wild boar piglet
苦瓜 にがうり bitter melon
真桑瓜 まくわうり Oriental melon, *Cucumis melo*
　　var. *makuwa*

瓢 ▷**bottle gourd**
ヒョウ ひさご ふくべ Ⓚ1657

[original meaning] **bottle gourd, calabash**
瓢簞 ひょうたん bottle gourd, calabash
干瓢(=乾瓢) かんぴょう strips of dried gourd
青瓢簞 あおびょうたん green [unripe] calabash;
　　weakling

芥 ▷**mustard**
カイ ケ あくた ごみ Ⓚ1895

mustard, rape
芥子(=罌粟) けし poppy

vehicle

車 輌 乗 輪 駕 輿 台

車 ▷vehicle
シャ くるま ⓚ2976

[also suffix] any wheeled vehicle:
- ⓐ [original meaning] **vehicle, cart, wagon**
- ⓑ **motor vehicle, car, automobile**
- ⓒ **railway car, train**
- ⓓ **suffix for wheeled vehicles, -cycle**

- *a* 馬車 ばしゃ horse-drawn carriage, coach, wagon
  唇歯輔車 しんしほしゃ mutual dependence
  人力車 じんりきしゃ rickshaw, man-pulled cart
- *ab* 戦車 せんしゃ tank; chariot
- *b* 車道 しゃどう road, roadway
  単車 たんしゃ motorcycle, motorbike
  自動車 じどうしゃ automobile
  駐車 ちゅうしゃ parking
  救急車 きゅうきゅうしゃ ambulance
- *bc* 車両 しゃりょう vehicle, car; rolling stock
  車内 しゃない inside a vehicle (as a car or train)
  下車する げしゃする alight, get off
  停車 ていしゃ stoppage (of a vehicle)
- *c* 電車 でんしゃ train, electric train, trolley
  列車 れっしゃ (railway) train
  客車 きゃくしゃ passenger car
  機関車 きかんしゃ locomotive
- *d* 三輪車 さんりんしゃ tricycle, three-wheeler

輌 ▷vehicle
リョウ

vehicle, railway car
車輌 しゃりょう vehicle, car; rolling stock

乗 ▷vehicle
ジョウ の(る) -の(り) の(せる) ⓚ2992

- ⓐ **vehicle**
- ⓑ *literary* **counter for vehicles**

- *a* 下乗する げじょうする alight from a vehicle; get off a horse
- *b* 万乗 ばんじょう ten thousand chariots; throne, sovereignty

輪 ▷wheeled vehicle
リン わ ⓚ1436

wheeled vehicle, cycle, bicycle, automobile
輪業 りんぎょう bicycle industry
輪禍 りんか automobile accident, traffic accident
輪タク りんたく pedicab, trishaw
競輪 けいりん bicycle race
駐輪場 ちゅうりんじょう bicycle parking lot

駕 ▷carriage
ガ ⓚ2273

carriage, litter, vehicle
駕輿 がよ palanquin, litter, *kago*
来駕 らいが [honorific] coming, attendance, presence (of a person)
鳳駕 ほうが imperial carriage

輿 ▷palanquin
ヨ こし ⓚ2529

[original meaning] **palanquin, litter**
輿丁 よてい palanquin bearer
駕輿 がよ palanquin, litter, *kago*
鸞輿 らんよ imperial palanquin

台 ▷counter for vehicles
ダイ タイ ⓚ1731

counter for vehicles (as automobiles or bicycles)
台数 だいすう number of vehicles [machines]
自動車十台 じどうしゃじゅうだい ten cars

vertical

縦 竪 垂 立 直

縦 ▷vertical
ジュウ たて ⓚ1286

vertical, lengthwise, perpendicular, longitudinal
縦断 じゅうだん cutting vertically
縦横に じゅうおうに vertically and horizontally, in all directions; freely
縦貫する じゅうかんする run through, traverse
縦走 じゅうそう running lengthwise; mountain range traversing
縦線 じゅうせん vertical line, bar (in music)

竪 ▷vertical
ジュ たて- ⓚ2470

[now usu. 縦-] **vertical, upright**
竪琴 たてごと harp
竪縞 たてじま vertical stripes
竪穴 たてあな pit
竪樋 たてどい downspout

垂 ▷perpendicular
スイ た(れる) た(らす) た(れ) ⓚ2985

perpendicular, vertical
垂直の すいちょくの vertical, perpendicular
垂線 すいせん perpendicular line

vertical

立 ▷standing
リツ リュウ た(つ) た(ち)- た(てる)
た(て)- −だ(て) −だ(てる)　Ⓚ1723

ⓐ standing
ⓑ [formerly also 竪] vertical, upright
a 立て看板 たてかんばん standing signboard
b 立て型ピアノ たてがたぴあの upright piano

直 ▷straight
チョク ジキ ジカ ただ(ちに) なお(す)
なお(る) なお(き) す(ぐ)　Ⓚ2539

(upright) straight, vertical, perpendicular, right
直立する ちょくりつする stand erect [upright], rise
　　perpendicularly
直角 ちょっかく right angle
直円柱 ちょくえんちゅう right cylinder
垂直の すいちょくの vertical, perpendicular

vessels and receptacles

盤 鍋 釜 鼎 臼 碓 托 皿
盆 膳 杯 鉢 椀 碗 丼

盤 ▷dish
バン　Ⓚ2481

ⓐ dish, plate, tray, platter
ⓑ [original meaning] basin, pan, tub, bowl
a 杯盤 はいばん glasses and plates
　銀盤 ぎんばん silver plate; surface of ice, skating
　　rink
b 水盤 すいばん basin; flower bowl
　銅盤 どうばん bronze bowl
　骨盤 こつばん pelvis

鍋 ▷pot
なべ　Ⓚ1564

[also suffix] pot, pan
鍋蓋 なべぶた pot lid; nabebuta, "lid" radical (⼍)
鍋焼き なべやき scalloped; scalloped noodles
土鍋 どなべ earthen pot
大鍋 おおなべ cauldron
片手鍋 かたてなべ single-handled pot
シチュー鍋 しちゅーなべ stew pot [pan], skillet

釜 ▷iron pot
フ かま　Ⓚ1808

[original meaning] iron pot, kettle, cauldron
釜中 ふちゅう inside of a pot

鼎 ▷tripod cauldron
テイ かなえ　Ⓚ300●

[original meaning] tripod cauldron
鼎足 ていそく legs of a tripod cauldron; three-
　legged (vessel)

臼 ▷mortar
キュウ うす　Ⓚ295●

[original meaning] mortar; hand mill
臼砲 きゅうほう (trench) mortar

碓 ▷mortar
タイ うす　Ⓚ110●

[usu. 臼] mortar; trip-hammer mill
碓氷峠 うすいとうげ Usui Pass

托 ▷receptacle
タク　Ⓚ019●

ⓐ receptacle [base] for holding an object
ⓑ place [hold] in the hand
a 托子 たくし(=たくす) teacup saucer
　茶托 ちゃたく teacup saucer
　花托 かたく (of plants) receptacle, torus
b 托鉢 たくはつ religious mendicancy, begging
　bonze

皿 ▷plate
さら　Ⓚ2916

[also suffix] [original meaning] (shallow container for holding food) plate, dish
皿洗い さらあらい dishwashing; dishwasher
皿回し さらまわし dish-spinning
スープ皿 すーぷざら soup plate
受け皿 うけざら saucer
蒸発皿 じょうはつざら evaporating dish
製氷皿 せいひょうざら ice-making pan

盆 ▷tray
ボン　Ⓚ1788

ⓐ tray, dish
ⓑ [original meaning] basin, pot
a 茶盆 ちゃぼん tea tray
　菓子盆 かしぼん cake tray [dish]
b 盆景 ぼんけい tray landscape, miniature garden
　盆栽 ぼんさい bonsai (potted dwarf tree)
　盆地 ぼんち basin, valley

膳 ▷legged tray
ゼン　Ⓚ1000

legged tray, low table
お膳立て おぜんだて setting the table; preparation
配膳 はいぜん setting the table; serving a meal
食膳 しょくぜん dining tray, food on a tray

会席膳 かいせきぜん elaborate legless dinner tray; legless tray for formal dinners

杯 ▷cup
ハイ さかずき   Ⓚ0761

ⓐ [original meaning] **wine cup, cup, glass, goblet**
ⓑ counter for cupfuls, glassfuls, bowlfuls or spoonfuls

a 杯盤 はいばん glasses and plates
金杯 きんぱい gold cup [goblet]
苦杯 くはい bitter ordeal
祝杯 しゅくはい a toast
乾杯 かんぱい a toast

b 一杯 いっぱい a cup (as of tea), a glass (as of beer)
茶二杯 ちゃにはい two cups of tea
砂糖三杯 さとうさんばい three spoons of sugar

鉢 ▷bowl
ハチ ハツ   Ⓚ1524

bowl, pot, basin

鉢物 はちもの food served in bowls; bonsai
菓子鉢 かしばち bowl for confectioneries
鉄鉢 てっぱち mendicant priest's begging bowl
托鉢 たくはつ religious mendicancy, begging bonze
衣鉢 いはつ(=えはつ) mysteries (of Buddhism or an art)

椀 ▷wooden bowl
ワン   Ⓚ0906

wooden bowl, bowl

椀盛 わんもり dish consisting of cooked food served in a bowl with clear soup
椀子蕎麦 わんこそば style of serving *soba* in which small portions are continuously added to the bowl until the eater is full
汁椀 しるわん soup bowl

碗 ▷ceramic bowl
ワン   Ⓚ1110

ceramic bowl, bowl

茶碗 ちゃわん teacup; rice bowl
茶碗蒸し ちゃわんむし savory egg custard
夫婦茶碗 めおとぢゃわん pair of matching teacups

丼 ▷large bowl
どんぶり どん   Ⓚ2945

large bowl

丼飯 どんぶりめし rice in a large bowl
ラーメン丼 らーめんどんぶり Chinese noodle bowl

view
景 風 光 観

景 ▷scene
ケイ   Ⓚ2179

scene, scenery, view, -scape

景勝 けいしょう picturesque scenery
背景 はいけい background; (stage) scenery, setting, scene; backing
夜景 やけい night view [scene]
風景 ふうけい scenery, landscape, view
光景 こうけい spectacle, sight, scene
絶景 ぜっけい superb view, picturesque scenery
情景 じょうけい scene, sight; nature and sentiment
海景 かいけい seascape
全景 ぜんけい complete view
雲景 うんけい cloudscape

風 ▷(beautiful) scenery
フウ フ かぜ かざ-   Ⓚ2591

(beautiful) scenery

風景 ふうけい scenery, landscape, view
風物 ふうぶつ natural objects [features], scenery; scenes and manners
風光 ふうこう (beautiful) scenery, natural beauty
風土記 ふどき topography

光 ▷scenery
コウ ひか(る) ひかり   Ⓚ2121

scenery, sight

光景 こうけい spectacle, sight, scene
風光 ふうこう (beautiful) scenery, natural beauty
観光 かんこう sightseeing

観 ▷view
カン   Ⓚ1659

view, spectacle, sight

景観 けいかん scene, spectacle, view, sight
美観 びかん fine view, beautiful sight
壮観 そうかん grand sight, magnificent view

villages and towns
町 村 里 郷 庄 邑

町 ▷town
チョウ まち   Ⓚ1028

ⓐ town, city
ⓑ (unit of local administration) **town**

c suffix after names of towns

a 町人 ちょうにん tradesman (in Edo period), townsman, townsfolk

町家 ちょうか town house; tradesman's house

町長 ちょうちょう town headman [manager]

町名 ちょうめい town name

b 町立の ちょうりつの established by the town

市町村 しちょうそん cities, towns and villages; municipalities

c 小山町 おやまちょう town of Oyama

村 ▷**village**
ソン むら   Ⓚ0738

ⓐ [also suffix] [original meaning] **village, hamlet; rural district**

ⓑ (unit of local administration) **village**

ⓒ counter for villages

a 村落 そんらく village, hamlet

農村 のうそん farm village, agricultural community

漁村 ぎょそん fishing village

無医村 むいそん doctorless village

一宮村 いちのみやそん Ichinomiya Village

b 村長 そんちょう village mayor

市町村 しちょうそん cities, towns and villages; municipalities

c 六か村 ろっかそん six villages

里 ▷**hamlet**
リ さと   Ⓚ2968

hamlet, village

里人 りじん villagers, countryfolk

遊里 ゆうり licensed quarters, red-light district

郷 ▷**hometown**
キョウ ゴウ   Ⓚ0501

hometown, homeland, native place, birthplace

郷里 きょうり one's old home, native place

郷土 きょうど one's birthplace

郷愁 きょうしゅう homesickness, nostalgia

故郷 こきょう hometown, birthplace

愛郷心 あいきょうしん love of one's hometown

同郷人 どうきょうじん person from the same province [town, village]

帰郷する ききょうする go [come] home

庄 ▷**feudal village**
ショウ ソウ   Ⓚ2625

feudal farm village, hamlet or district in Edo period that used to be a manor until the end of Muromachi period

庄屋 しょうや village headman

邑 ▷**village**
ユウ   Ⓚ187

village, town; fief

邑落 ゆうらく [archaic] hamlet

都邑 とゆう city, town

---

violate

违 破 犯 反 悖 背

違 ▷**violate**
イ ちが(う) ちが(い) ちが(える)   Ⓚ271⓪

violate, break, disobey

違反(=違犯) いはん violation (of the law), infringement; breach

違法 いほう illegality, unlawfulness

違憲 いけん unconstitutionality, violation of the constitution

違約 いやく breach of promise

破 ▷**break**
ハ やぶ(る) やぶ(れる)   Ⓚ1064

(act contrary to) **break (as a promise), breach, violate**

破棄 はき breaking (a treaty), annulment

破談 はだん cancellation, breaking off

破約 はやく breach of contract

犯 ▷**offend against**
ハン おか(す)   Ⓚ0175

offend against, violate, infringe

犯則 はんそく transgression, violation (of the law)

侵犯 しんぱん invasion; violation

違犯(=違反) いはん violation (of the law), infringement; breach

不犯 ふぼん strict observance of the Buddhist commandment that all priests should be celibate

反 ▷**act contrary to**
ハン ホン タン そ(る) そ(らす)   Ⓚ2549

act contrary to (the rule), act against, violate, infringe

違反(=違犯)する いはんする violate (the law), infringe; act contrary to

背反する はいはんする revolt, rebel; go against, violate

悖 ▷**go against**
ハイ もと(る)

[now replaced by 背] **go against, be contrary to**

悖徳 はいとく immorality, corruption, lapse from virtue

背 ▷go against
ハイ せ せい そむ(く) そむ(ける) Ⓚ2230

[formerly also 悖] (turn one's back on) **go against, disobey, rebel, betray**

背反 はいはん revolt, rebellion; going against, violation
背信 はいしん breach of faith [trust], betrayal
背徳 はいとく immorality, corruption, lapse from virtue

violent
暴　猛　荒

暴 ▷violent
ボウ バク あば(く) あば(れる)　Ⓚ2194

(acting with destructive force) **violent, rough, wild, cruel, harsh, tyrannical**

暴力 ぼうりょく violence, force
暴行 ぼうこう act of violence, assault
暴走 ぼうそう reckless driving; running wild
暴言 ぼうげん offensive [abusive] language
暴君 ぼうくん tyrant, despot
暴風 ぼうふう storm, violent wind
暴風雨 ぼうふうう tempest, rainstorm
乱暴 らんぼう violence, roughness; rape
横暴な おうぼうな arbitrary, tyrannical, despotic

猛 ▷fierce
モウ　Ⓚ0490

[original meaning] (having a ferocious nature) **fierce, violent, savage, ferocious**

猛犬 もうけん fierce [ferocious] dog
猛獣 もうじゅう fierce [savage] animal [beast]
獰猛な どうもうな fierce, ferocious

荒 ▷wild
コウ あら(い) あら- あ(れる) あ(らす) -あ(らし)　Ⓚ1950

(of behavior) **wild, rough, rude, savage**

荒荒しい あらあらしい wild, violent; rough, rude, gruff
荒っぽい あらっぽい rough, wild, rude
手荒な てあらな violent, rough

virtuous
正　義　善　良　鯁

正 ▷right
セイ ショウ ただ(しい) ただ(す) まさ まさ(に)　Ⓚ2926

(morally correct) **right, righteous, just, upright**

正邪 せいじゃ right and wrong
正義 せいぎ justice, righteousness
正当な せいとうな just, right, due; legal
正論 せいろん sound argument
正直な しょうじきな honest, upright, frank
公正な こうせいな just, fair, impartial
不正 ふせい injustice, wrong, illegality

義 ▷righteous
ギ　Ⓚ2052

righteous, just, upright

義人 ぎじん righteous man
義憤 ぎふん righteous indignation

善 ▷good
ゼン よ(い)　Ⓚ2030

(morally excellent) **good, virtuous**

善人 ぜんにん good people
善行 ぜんこう good deed, benevolence

良 ▷good
リョウ よ(い) い(い)　Ⓚ2980

(having good character or moral excellence) **good, good-natured, virtuous**

良心 りょうしん conscience
良識 りょうしき good sense
善良な ぜんりょうな good, virtuous

鯁 ▷upright
コウ

[now replaced by 硬] **upright, firm, staunch, unyielding**

鯁骨の こうこつの firm, uncompromising
鯁骨漢 こうこつかん man of firm character

visit

訪 参 詣 寄 伺

訪 ▷**visit**
ホウ おとず(れる) たず(ねる)　　Ⓚ1335

ⓐ visit, call on
ⓑ visit, call
a 訪問 ほうもん visit
訪日 ほうにち visiting Japan, visit to Japan
訪米 ほうべい visit to the United States
訪客 ほうきゃく visitor
来訪する らいほうする visit, call
b 歴訪 れきほう round of calls

参 ▷**visit a holy place**
サン シン まい(る)　　Ⓚ1778

visit a holy place (as a temple, shrine or the Imperial
Palace), make a pilgrimage; visit (a superior) in
order to pay one's respects
参拝 さんぱい worship, visit to a shrine [temple]
参詣 さんけい visit to a temple [shrine], worship,
pilgrimage
参上する さんじょうする go to see, call on, pay one's
respects
参内 さんだい attendance at the Imperial Court
墓参 ぼさん visit to a grave
日参 にっさん daily visit (of worship); frequent visit

詣 ▷**visit a holy place**
ケイ もう(でる)　　Ⓚ1379

visit a holy place (as a temple, shrine or the Imperial
Palace), make a pilgrimage
参詣 さんけい visit to a temple [shrine], worship,
pilgrimage

寄 ▷**call at**
キ よ(る) -よ(り) よ(せる)　　Ⓚ1983

call at, call on, make a short visit
寄港する きこうする call at a port
寄航する きこうする call at a(n) (air)port

伺 ▷**call on**
シ うかが(う)　　Ⓚ0053

call on (a superior), pay a visit
伺候する しこうする pay one's respects, make a
courtesy call; wait upon (a nobleman)

visitor

客 賓

客 ▷**visitor**
キャク カク　　Ⓚ1939

ⓐ [original meaning] **visitor, caller, guest**
ⓑ (someone or something in a visiting capacity) **guest,
associate**
a 客人 きゃくじん caller, visitor, company
客室 きゃくしつ guest room, stateroom
客間 きゃくま drawing room
来客 らいきゃく visitor, guest
珍客 ちんきゃく unexpected (but welcome) visitor
b 客員 きゃくいん guest [associate] member
客演 きゃくえん guest appearance
客土 きゃくど earth brought from another place to
mix with the soil

賓 ▷**guest**
ヒン　　Ⓚ2077

[original meaning] **guest, visitor**
賓客 ひんきゃく(=ひんかく) guest, guest of honor
国賓 こくひん state guest
来賓 らいひん guest, visitor
迎賓館 げいひんかん guest house [palace]

vivid

明 鮮

明 ▷**bright**
メイ
ミョウ あ(かり) あか(るい) あか(るむ)
あか(らむ) あき(らか) あ(ける) -あ(け)
あ(く) あ(くる) あ(かす)　　Ⓚ0756

(of colors) **bright, light**
明色 めいしょく bright [light] color
明度 めいど lightness, value of color

鮮 ▷**vivid**
セン あざ(やか)　　Ⓚ1656

(of colors) **vivid, brightly-colored**
鮮紅 せんこう scarlet, bright red

vote and election
票　選

票 ▷**vote**
ヒョウ　　　　　　　　Ⓚ2326

[also suffix] **vote, ballot**
- 票田 ひょうでん favorable voting constituency
- 投票 とうひょう vote, ballot
- 白票 はくひょう blank ballot
- 得票 とくひょう number of votes obtained
- 開票 かいひょう official counting of votes
- 賛否同票 さんぴどうひょう tie vote

選 ▷**election**
セン えら(ぶ)　　　　Ⓚ2734

[also suffix] **election**
- 当選 とうせん election to office; winning (a lottery)
- 公選 こうせん public election, election by popular vote
- 再選 さいせん reelection
- 市長選 しちょうせん mayoral election

vulgar and unrefined
俗　卑　賤　鄙　俚
里　粗　野　蛮

俗 ▷**vulgar**
ゾク　　　　　　　　　Ⓚ0088

vulgar, low
- 俗っぽい ぞくっぽい common, vulgar
- 俗悪 ぞくあく vulgarity, inelegance
- 低俗な ていぞくな vulgar

卑 ▷**mean**
ヒ いや(しい) いや(しむ)
いや(しめる)　　　　Ⓚ2295

[formerly also 鄙] (lacking in elevating human qualities) **mean, vulgar, despicable**
- 卑屈な ひくつな mean, mean-spirited; servile
- 卑劣な ひれつな mean, base, cowardly
- 卑怯 ひきょう cowardice, meanness, unfairness
- 卑語 ひご vulgarism, vulgar word
- 野卑 やひ vulgarity, meanness

賤 ▷**mean**
セン いや(しい) いや(しむ) いや(しめる)
しず

(low in social status) **mean, lowly, humble, inferior in position**
- 賤民 せんみん lowly people, outcasts
- 貴賤 きせん high and low, all ranks
- 下賤の げせんの of low birth, vulgar
- 卑賤 ひせん lowly position, humble condition

鄙 ▷**mean**
ヒ ひな ひな(びる)

[now replaced by 卑] (lacking in elevating human qualities) **mean, vulgar, despicable**
- 鄙劣な ひれつな mean, base, cowardly
- 鄙猥な ひわいな indecent, obscene
- 野鄙な やひな vulgar, base, mean

俚 ▷**rural**
リ

[now also 里] [original meaning] **rural, rustic, vulgar**
- 俚謡 りよう ballad, folk song
- 俚言 りげん dialect; slang
- 俚諺 りげん traditional [folk] saying, proverb
- 俚耳 りじ public ears

里 ▷**rural**
リ さと　　　　　　　　Ⓚ2968

[formerly also 俚] (of the countryside) **rural, rustic, vulgar**
- 里謡 りよう ballad, folk song
- 里言 りげん dialect

粗 ▷**coarse**
ソ あら(い) あら-　　　Ⓚ1214

(of unrefined manner) **coarse, crude, rude, rough, harsh**
- 粗雑な そざつな coarse, rough, crude
- 粗暴な そぼうな wild, rude

野 ▷**rustic**
ヤ の　　　　　　　　　Ⓚ1350

rustic, unrefined, coarse, vulgar, savage
- 野蛮な やばんな savage, barbarous, uncivilized
- 野趣 やしゅ charms of the countryside, rural beauty
- 野暮な やぼな unrefined, rustic, boorish
- 粗野な そやな rustic, rude, vulgar

蛮 ▷**barbaric**
バン　　　　　　　　　Ⓚ1827

barbaric, barbarous, coarse, wild
- 蛮声 ばんせい rough voice

蛮カラ ばんから rough and uncouth vigor
蛮勇 ばんゆう brute courage, reckless valor

wait

待　控

待 ▷wait
タイ ま(つ) -ま(ち)　　　Ⓚ0323

wait
待機する たいきする wait for an opportunity, stand ready
待避する たいひする take shelter; shunt

控 ▷be in waiting
コウ ひか(える) ひか(え)　　　Ⓚ0453

be in waiting, wait
別の間に控える べつのまにひかえる wait in another room

walk

歩　徒　脚　足　踏

歩 ▷walk
ホ ブ フ ある(く) あゆ(む)　　　Ⓚ2141

[original meaning] **walk, go on foot**
歩行する ほこうする walk
歩行者 ほこうしゃ pedestrian
歩行者天国 ほこうしゃてんごく pedestrians' "paradise" (an area of streets temporarily closed to vehicular traffic)
歩道 ほどう sidewalk, footpath
歩兵 ほへい foot soldier, infantry
散歩する さんぽする go for a walk [stroll]
徒歩 とほ walking, going on foot

徒 ▷go on foot
ト　　　Ⓚ0377

[original meaning] **go on foot, walk, run**
徒歩 とほ walking, going on foot
徒競走 ときょうそう foot race

脚 ▷move on foot
キャク キャ あし　　　Ⓚ0887

move on foot, walk, run
行脚 あんぎゃ pilgrimage; walking tour; tour
飛脚 ひきゃく express messenger; postman (in former times)

足 ▷travel on foot
ソク あし た(りる) た(る) た(す)　　　Ⓚ1873

travel on foot, walk, run
足労 そくろう trouble of going somewhere
遠足 えんそく excursion, hike, long walk
発足 ほっそく(=はっそく) starting, inauguration
長足の進歩 ちょうそくのしんぽ rapid progress [strides]

踏 ▷tread
トウ ふ(む) ふ(まえる)　　　Ⓚ1435

[original meaning] **tread (on), step on, stamp, trample**
踏破する とうはする crush underfoot; travel on foot
未踏の みとうの untrodden, unexplored
舞踏(=舞踊) ぶとう dancing

walls →FENCES AND WALLS

wander

浪　遊　漂　流　彽　徊

浪 ▷wander
ロウ　　　Ⓚ0398

wander, roam, ramble, drift about
浪浪 ろうろう wandering
浪人 ろうにん lordless samurai, *ronin*; unsuccessful examinee; jobless person
放浪する ほうろうする wander about, roam
浮浪者 ふろうしゃ vagabond, loafer, hobo
流浪する るろうする wander [roam] about from place to place

遊 ▷move about freely
ユウ ユ あそ(ぶ) あそ(ばす)　　　Ⓚ2709

move about freely, wander, roam
遊星 ゆうせい wandering star, planet
遊牧 ゆうぼく nomadism
遊離する ゆうりする isolate, separate

漂 ▷drift about
ヒョウ ただよ(う)　　　Ⓚ0632

drift about, roam, wander
漂泊 ひょうはく roaming, drifting about, wandering
漂浪 ひょうろう [rare] wandering
漂然(=飄然)と ひょうぜんと aimlessly, unexpectedly

流 ▷**drift**
リュウ ル なが(れる) なが(れ)
なが(す)
Ⓚ0400

drift, wander
流民 るみん(=りゅうみん) roaming [wandering]
  people, displaced persons
流浪 るろう vagrancy
流離する りゅうりする wander alone in a strange
  country

低 ▷**wander about**
テイ

[now replaced by 低] **wander about, linger**
低徊(=低回)する ていかいする linger, loiter, wander
低徊趣味(=低回趣味) ていかいしゅみ dilettantism

徊 ▷**move to and fro**
カイ

[now also 回] [original meaning] **move to and fro, walk around**
徘徊する はいかいする loiter, wander about
低徊(=低回)する ていかいする linger, loiter, wander

war →FIGHT AND WAR

warfare and rebellions
戦 軍 役 陣 乱 変 闘

戦 ▷**war**
セン いくさ たたか(う)
Ⓚ1590

[also suffix] **war, battle, combat, warfare**
戦前 せんぜん prewar period, period before Second
  World War
戦後 せんご postwar period, period after Second
  World War
戦線 せんせん (war) front, battle line
作戦 さくせん tactics, strategy; (military) operations,
  maneuvers
敗戦 はいせん lost battle, defeat
挑戦 ちょうせん challenge, defiance
空中戦 くうちゅうせん air battle, dogfight
生物戦 せいぶつせん biological warfare

軍 ▷**war**
グン
Ⓚ1789

war, battle
軍陣 ぐんじん camp, battlefield
軍船 ぐんせん warship
軍歌 ぐんか war song

軍記 ぐんき war chronicle

役 ▷**war**
ヤク エキ
Ⓚ0217

war, battle, expedition
戦役 せんえき war, battle

陣 ▷**battle**
ジン
Ⓚ0411

battle, war
陣没 じんぼつ death in battle
先陣 せんじん advance guard, vanguard

乱 ▷**rebellion**
ラン みだ(れる) みだ(る) みだ(す) Ⓚ1161

rebellion, civil war, war, riot, revolt
反乱 はんらん rebellion, revolt

変 ▷**uprising**
ヘン か(わる) か(わり) か(える)
Ⓚ1782

uprising, upheaval, disturbance
事変 じへん incident, upheaval; accident
政変 せいへん coup d'état

闘 ▷**fight**
トウ たたか(う)
Ⓚ2847

fight, fighting, struggle

warm seasons
春 夏 暑

春 ▷**spring**
シュン はる
Ⓚ2232

[original meaning] **spring**
春季 しゅんき spring
春闘 しゅんとう spring labor offensive
春分 しゅんぶん vernal equinox
春眠 しゅんみん morning sleep in spring
春夏秋冬 しゅんかしゅうとう four seasons, all (the)
  year round
立春 りっしゅん first day of spring
来春 らいしゅん next spring
今春 こんしゅん this spring

夏 ▷**summer**
カ ゲ なつ
Ⓚ1815

summer
夏季 かき summer, summer season
夏期 かき summer, summertime
夏至 げし summer solstice

春夏秋冬 しゅんかしゅうとう four seasons, all (the) year round
初夏 しょか early summer
盛夏 せいか midsummer

暑 ▷**summer heat**
ショ あつ(い)　　　Ⓚ2182

[original meaning] **summer heat, hot weather, hottest day of summer, summer**
暑気 しょき hot weather
暑中 しょちゅう midsummer
暑中見舞 しょちゅうみまい best wishes for the hot season
暑熱 しょねつ heat of summer
避暑 ひしょ summering
炎暑 えんしょ scorching heat of summer
残暑 ざんしょ lingering summer
猛暑 もうしょ fierce heat
酷暑 こくしょ severe heat
大暑 たいしょ Japanese midsummer day

warn
警　戒　誡　諭　告

警 ▷**warn**
ケイ　　　Ⓚ2512

[original meaning] **warn, admonish**
警告 けいこく warning, admonition
警報 けいほう warning signal, alarm
警鐘 けいしょう alarm bell, warning

戒 ▷**caution**
カイ いまし(める)　　　Ⓚ2760

[formerly also 誡] **caution against, admonish, warn, give warning**
戒告 かいこく caution, warning, reprimand
訓戒する くんかいする admonish, warn
自戒する じかいする admonish oneself

誡 ▷**caution against**
カイ いまし(める)

caution against, admonish, warn, give warning
誡告 かいこく caution, warning, reprimand
訓誡する くんかいする admonish, warn

諭 ▷**admonish**
ユ さと(す)　　　Ⓚ1446

admonish, give guidance, instruct, advise, persuade
諭旨 ゆし official suggestion or instruction (to a subordinate)

教諭 きょうゆ teacher, instructor
説諭 せつゆ admonition, reproof
訓諭 くんゆ [rare] admonition, caution, warning

告 ▷**advise**
コク つ(げる)　　　Ⓚ2134

advise, instruct, warn, admonish
忠告 ちゅうこく advice; counsel, warning; admonition
警告 けいこく warning, admonition
勧告 かんこく advice, counsel, recommendation

warriors →SOLDIERS AND WARRIORS

wash →CLEAN AND WASH

waste
屑　芥　塵

屑 ▷**waste**
セツ くず　　　Ⓚ2680

waste, rubbish, trash, scraps, junk, dust
砕屑物 さいせつぶつ clastic material

芥 ▷**trash**
カイ ケ あくた ごみ　　　Ⓚ1895

trash, garbage, rubbish, litter; dirt, dust
雑芥 ざっかい miscellaneous trash
厨芥 ちゅうかい kitchen waste

塵 ▷**dust**
ジン ちり ごみ

[also suffix] **dust; trash, garbage, rubbish, litter**
塵肺 じんぱい pneumoconiosis
塵埃 じんあい dust, dirt; this drab world, worldly squalor
粉塵 ふんじん dust
砂塵 さじん cloud of sand
吸塵 きゅうじん dust vacuuming
宇宙塵 うちゅうじん cosmic dust
微塵 みじん particle, atom; pieces, fragments; [in negative constructions] the slightest bit
後塵を拝する こうじんをはいする play second fiddle (to), be outdone (by)

water →KINDS OF WATER

watersides →SHORES AND WATERSIDES

water sources
源　泉　井

源
▷**source**
ゲン みなもと ⓚ0600

[original meaning] (place where water originates) **source (of a river), fountainhead**
源流 げんりゅう source (of a stream)
水源 すいげん source [head] (of a stream), fountain-head

泉
▷**spring**
セン いずみ ⓚ2224

(source or issue of water) **spring, fountain**
泉水 せんすい fountain, garden pond
温泉 おんせん hot spring
冷泉 れいせん cold water spring

井
▷**well**
セイ ショウ い ⓚ2905

[original meaning] **well**
油井 ゆせい oil well
鑿井 さくせい well drilling
ガス井 がすせい gas well

waves
波　浪　漣

波
▷**wave**
ハ なみ ⓚ0292

ⓐ [also suffix] [original meaning] **wave**
ⓑ *phys* **wave**
a 波浪 はろう waves, billows
波紋 はもん ripple; stir, sensation
波止場 はとば wharf, quay
波瀾(=波乱) はらん disturbance, troubles; fluctuation
風波 ふうは wind and waves, rough seas, storm
b 波動 はどう wave motion, undulation
波長 はちょう wavelength
電磁波 でんじは electromagnetic waves
電波 でんぱ electromagnetic waves, radio waves
短波 たんぱ shortwave
音波 おんぱ sound waves
光波 こうは light waves

浪
▷**billow**
ロウ ⓚ0398

billow, large wave, wave
波浪 はろう waves, billows
風浪 ふうろう wind and waves, heavy seas

漣
▷**ripples**
レン さざなみ ⓚ0634

[original meaning] **ripples, wavelets**
漣音 れんおん mordent

way and style
風　様　方　途　法　流　式　調

風
▷**manner**
フウ フ かぜ かざ- ⓚ2591

[also suffix] (characteristic style) **manner, style, school**
整風 せいふう rectification
洋風 ようふう Western [foreign] style
歌風 かふう style of poetry
日本風 にほんふう Japanese style
鷗外風に おうがいふうに in [after] the manner of Ogai

様
▷**mode**
ヨウ さま ⓚ0969

ⓐ (manner of doing) **mode, method, way, manner, style**
ⓑ [verbal suffix] **way of doing**
a 様式 ようしき mode, manner; style, order
今様の いまようの modern, up to date
各人各様 かくじんかくよう So many men, so many ways
唐様 からよう Chinese style [design]
同様に どうように similarly
b 泳ぎ様 およぎよう way of swimming
仕様が無い しょうがない have no choice; it is no use; cannot bear

方
▷**way**
ホウ -かた -がた -なた ⓚ1709

【ホウ】
way of doing, method, means, procedure
方法 ほうほう method, way; system; scheme, means; process, procedure; plan
方針 ほうしん course, policy, plan
方策 ほうさく plan, policy, scheme
方式 ほうしき formula, mode; method
方程式 ほうていしき equation
【-かた】
way of doing, manner, style, method; how to (do)

仕方 しかた way, method, means
話し方 はなしかた one's way of speaking
教え方 おしえかた method of teaching
綴り方 つづりかた composition; spelling
出方 でかた one's attitude, move; theater attendant, usher
やり方 やりかた way of doing, method, procedure; step, measure

途 ▷way
ト   Ⓚ2676

(method of doing) **way, means**

方途 ほうと means, way, measure
用途 ようと use, service, application
金の使途 かねのしと how money is used

法 ▷method
ホウ ハッ‐ ホッ‐   Ⓚ0295

[also suffix] **method, way, manner, system, process, technique**

方法 ほうほう method, way; system; scheme, means; process, procedure; plan
手法 しゅほう technique, mechanism, style
療法 りょうほう method of treatment, cure, remedy
製法 せいほう method of manufacture, process of preparation, recipe
生活法 せいかつほう way of life, art of living
教授法 きょうじゅほう method of teaching
銅アンモニア法 どうあんもにあほう cuprous ammoniacal process

流 ▷style
リュウ ル なが(れる) なが(れ) なが(す)   Ⓚ0400

[also suffix] **style, way, mode, manner, form, fashion**

自己流 じこりゅう one's own style, one's way of doing things
三島流の みしまりゅうの in the style of Mishima

式 ▷style
シキ   Ⓚ2623

[also suffix]
ⓐ **style, type, form, sort, manner**
ⓑ (way of doing) **style, method, system, way**

a 様式 ようしき mode, manner; style, order
旧式 きゅうしき old style, old type
株式 かぶしき stocks, shares
ドリス式 どりすしき Doric style (architecture)
和式 わしき Japanese style
b 方式 ほうしき formula, mode; method
電動式 でんどうしき electric, electrically operated
ヘボン式ローマ字 へぼんしきろーまじ Hepburn romanization system

山本式 やまもとしき Yamamoto's way (of doing things)

調 ▷tone
チョウ しら(べる) しら(べ) ととの(う) ととの(える)   Ⓚ1417

[suffix] (characteristic style or general trend) **tone, style, form, manner, atmosphere**

軍国調 ぐんこくちょう wartime atmosphere
文語調 ぶんごちょう flavor of literary style
である調 であるちょう de aru style

ways and routes

道 径 軌 線 澪 途 路
筋 通 街 辻 岐 巷

道 ▷way (path)
ドウ トウ みち   Ⓚ2701

[original meaning] **way, path, road, track**

道路 どうろ road, street, way
道程 どうてい distance, journey, itinerary; process
鉄道 てつどう railway
街道 かいどう thoroughfare, highway
軌道 きどう track, railway; planetary orbit; beaten track
歩道 ほどう sidewalk, footpath

径 ▷path
ケイ   Ⓚ0260

[original meaning] (narrow) **path, footpath, shortcut**

径路 けいろ path; process
捷径 しょうけい path, lane
山径 さんけい mountain path
小径 しょうけい path, lane

軌 ▷track
キ   Ⓚ1312

ⓐ (wheel) **track, rut, path**
ⓑ **railway track**

a 軌跡 きせき locus; tracks
軌道 きどう track, railway; planetary orbit; beaten track
b 軌条 きじょう rails

線 ▷line
セン   Ⓚ1273

(public transportation route) **line, track, route**

線路 せんろ (railway) line, track
路線 ろせん route, way, line
沿線の えんせんの along a railway line

脱線 だっせん derailment; deviation, aberration
東海道線 とうかいどうせん Tokaido Line
二番線 にばんせん Track No. 2

澪 ▷waterway
レイ リョウ みお   Ⓚ0698

【レイ リョウ】
waterway, water route, channel, fairway
澪標 れいひょう *elegant* channel mark

【みお】
waterway, water route, channel, fairway for small boats
澪標 みおつくし channel mark
澪を引く みおをひく leave a wake behind

途 ▷way (route)
ト   Ⓚ2676

[original meaning] way, route, course, road, path
途中で とちゅうで on the way
途上で とじょうで on the way
中途で ちゅうとで halfway, in the middle
発展途上国 はってんとじょうこく developing countries
前途 ぜんと one's future, prospects; distance yet to cover
帰途 きと one's way home, return trip

路 ▷road
ロ -じ   Ⓚ1394

[also suffix] road, route, way
路上 ろじょう on the road, road
路面 ろめん road surface
路線 ろせん route, way, line
路地 ろじ alley, lane
道路 どうろ road, street, way
空路 くうろ air route, airway
線路 せんろ (railway) line, track
通路 つうろ passage, pathway, alley, aisle
悪路 あくろ bad road
滑走路 かっそうろ runway

筋 ▷wayside
キン すじ   Ⓚ2337

[in compounds] wayside, roadside, route, way
道筋 みちすじ route, course, way
東海道筋の町 とうかいどうすじのまち towns on the Tokaido
川筋 かわすじ course of a river; land along a river

通 ▷street
ツウ ツ とお(る) とお(り) -どお(り) とお(す) とお(し) -どお(し) かよ(う)   Ⓚ2678

【とお(り)】
street, avenue, road
大通り おおどおり main street

【-どお(り)】
suffix after names of streets [avenues]
青山通り あおやまどおり Aoyama Street

街 ▷city street
ガイ カイ まち   Ⓚ0528

[original meaning] city street, thoroughfare, crossroads
街道 かいどう thoroughfare, highway
街頭 がいとう street
街灯 がいとう street lamp

辻 ▷crossroads
つじ   Ⓚ2750

ⓐ [original meaning] crossroads, crossing, intersection
ⓑ street, roadside, street corner
ₐ 四つ辻 よつつじ crossroads, intersection
♭ 辻占 つじうら slip of paper with a fortune-telling message
辻辻に つじつじに at every crossing, at every street corner
辻君 つじぎみ streetwalker, nightwalker
辻説法 つじせっぽう street preaching
辻店 つじみせ street stall

岐 ▷forked road
キ ギ   Ⓚ0214

[original meaning] forked road, branch road
岐路 きろ forked road, crossroad

巷 ▷the streets
コウ ちまた   Ⓚ2162

the streets, the town
陋巷 ろうこう narrow, dirty backstreet
柳巷花街 りゅうこうかがい [archaic] red-light district

weak

弱　柔　脆　癈

弱 ▷**weak**
ジャク よわ(い) よわ(る) よわ(まる)
よわ(める)　　　　Ⓚ1080

[also prefix] [original meaning] (lacking strength) **weak, feeble**
　弱点 じゃくてん weak point
　弱肉強食 じゃくにくきょうしょく law of the jungle
　　(the strong prey on the weak)
　虚弱な きょじゃくな weak, feeble, sickly

柔 ▷**soft**
ジュウ ニュウ やわ(らか)
やわ(らかい)　　　　Ⓚ1797

(weakly) **soft, weak-looking, frail**
　柔弱な にゅうじゃくな weak, effeminate
　優柔不断の ゆうじゅうふだんの indecisive, vacillat-
　　ing

脆 ▷**fragile**
ゼイ もろ(い)

fragile, brittle, flimsy, weak
　脆弱な ぜいじゃくな fragile, frail, weak
　脆弱性 ぜいじゃくせい vulnerability, fragility
　脆性 ぜいせい brittleness, fragility

癈 ▷**disabled**
ハイ

[now also 廃] [original meaning] **disabled, crippled**
　癈疾 はいしつ disablement
　癈人 はいじん invalid, crippled person
　癈兵 はいへい disabled soldier, crippled soldier

weaken

衰　弱

衰 ▷**decline**
スイ おとろ(える)　　　　Ⓚ1806

decline, fall into decay, degenerate, weaken, emaciate
　衰退 すいたい decline, decay, degeneration
　衰弱する すいじゃくする weaken, lose vigor
　減衰する げんすいする damp, be attenuated
　老衰 ろうすい senility
　盛衰 せいすい ups and downs, rise and fall, pros-
　　perity and decline

弱 ▷**weaken**
ジャク よわ(い) よわ(る) よわ(まる)
よわ(める)　　　　Ⓚ1080

weaken
　衰弱する すいじゃくする weaken, lose vigor

wealth

財　産　富　宝

財 ▷**wealth**
ザイ サイ　　　　Ⓚ1326

wealth, fortune, money; property, assets, goods, commodities
　財貨 ざいか wealth, money and property; goods
　財産 ざいさん property, fortune, wealth
　財布 さいふ purse, wallet
　私財 しざい private funds, private property
　蓄財 ちくざい accumulation of wealth
　資財 しざい property, fortune, assets

産 ▷**property**
サン う(む) う(まれる) うぶ-　　　Ⓚ2812

property, fortune, wealth
　財産 ざいさん property, fortune, wealth
　資産 しさん property, assets, fortune
　倒産 とうさん insolvency, bankruptcy; breech birth
　破産 はさん bankruptcy
　共産主義 きょうさんしゅぎ Communism
　不動産 ふどうさん immovable property, real estate

富 ▷**riches**
フ フウ フッ- と(む) とみ　　　Ⓚ2009

riches, wealth
　富豪 ふごう wealthy man, millionaire
　富農 ふのう rich farmer
　富力 ふりょく wealth, riches
　富貴な ふうきな(=ふっきな) wealthy and noble

宝 ▷**treasure**
ホウ たから　　　　Ⓚ1910

ⓐ **treasure, treasured object**
ⓑ (something very valuable) **treasure, heirloom**
　ａ 宝庫 ほうこ treasure house, treasury
　　宝石 ほうせき gem, jewel
　　財宝 ざいほう treasure, valuables; riches, wealth
　　重宝 じゅうほう(=ちょうほう) priceless treasure
　ｂ 宝典 ほうてん thesaurus, treasury of words;
　　　precious book
　　国宝 こくほう national treasure
　　家宝 かほう family treasure, heirloom

weapons for shooting
銃 砲 火 弓

銃 ▷gun (portable firearm)
ジュウ   Ⓚ1535

(portable firearm) **gun, rifle, firearm**
銃声 じゅうせい sound of gunfire
銃撃 じゅうげき shooting, gunning (down)
銃砲 じゅうほう firearm
拳銃 けんじゅう pistol, handgun
猟銃 りょうじゅう hunting gun
短銃 たんじゅう pistol
ライフル銃 らいふるじゅう rifle
機関銃 きかんじゅう machine gun

砲 ▷heavy gun
ホウ   Ⓚ1065

[rarely also 炮]
ⓐ [also suffix] **heavy gun, gun, artillery, ordnance**
ⓑ cannon
a 砲火 ほうか gunfire
砲声 ほうせい sound of firing, roar of cannon
砲術 ほうじゅつ gunnery, artillery
祝砲 しゅくほう feu de joie, artillery [gun] salute
鉄砲 てっぽう gun, firearm
銃砲 じゅうほう firearm
重砲 じゅうほう heavy gun
発砲する はっぽうする fire, discharge (a gun)
対戦車砲 たいせんしゃほう antitank gun
b 砲丸 ほうがん cannonball
大砲 たいほう gun, cannon, artillery

火 ▷firearms
カ ひ -び ほ-   Ⓚ2911

firearms
火器 かき firearms
地雷火 じらいか (land) mine

弓 ▷bow
キュウ ゆみ   Ⓚ2869

[original meaning] **bow**
弓道 きゅうどう archery
弓状の きゅうじょうの bow-shaped, arched
弓術 きゅうじゅつ archery
洋弓 ようきゅう Western archery

wear and put on
着 装 帯 穿 纏 履 被

着 ▷put on
チャク ジャク き(る) -ぎ き(せる) -き(せ)
つ(く) つ(ける)   Ⓚ2826

put on (clothes), don, dress, wear
着用する ちゃくようする wear, have on
着衣 ちゃくい one's clothes [clothing]
着帽 ちゃくぼう putting on one's hat

装 ▷dress
ソウ ショウ よそお(う)   Ⓚ2344

dress, put on clothes
正装する せいそうする dress up

帯 ▷wear (esp. at the belt)
タイ お(びる) おび   Ⓚ2237

wear (esp. at [on] the belt), bear, carry on one's person, be armed with
帯刀 たいとう wearing a sword
帯剣する たいけんする wear a sword, be armed with a sword
携帯する けいたいする carry, bring with one, equip oneself with

穿 ▷put on
セン は(く) うが(つ) ほじく(る)
ほじ(る)   Ⓚ1941

put on (trousers or socks), wear (a skirt)
下穿き したばき undershorts, underpants
スカートを穿く すかーとをはく put on a skirt

纏 ▷put on
テン まと(める) まと(う) まと(まる)
まつ(わる)   Ⓚ1302

[now also 天] **put on, be wrapped in**
半纏 はんてん short coat, workman's livery coat

履 ▷put on footwear
リ は(く)   Ⓚ2736

put on footwear, wear (shoes)
履物 はきもの footwear, footgear; clogs, sandals
履き違える はきちがえる put on another's shoes; be mistaken

被 ▷put on headgear
ヒ かぶ(る) こうむ(る)　　　Ⓚ1077

**put on headgear, wear; pour (as water) on oneself,
be covered with; take upon oneself;** *photography* **be
fogged**
　猫被り ねこかぶり hypocrisy, false modesty; hypo-
　　crite, wolf in a lamb's skin
　引っ被る ひっかぶる pull (a thing) over one's head
　泥を被る どろをかぶる be covered with mud; take
　　another's fault upon oneself

weather
候　天　晴

候 ▷seasonal weather
コウ そうろう　　　Ⓚ0101

seasonal weather, climate, weather
　天候 てんこう weather
　気候 きこう climate, weather; season
　測候所 そっこうじょ weather station

天 ▷weather
テン あめ あま−　　　Ⓚ2898

(state of the) weather, look of the sky
　天気 てんき weather, atmospheric conditions; fine
　　weather
　天気予報 てんきよほう weather forecast
　天候 てんこう weather
　晴天 せいてん fine [fair] weather, cloudless sky
　雨天 うてん rainy weather, rainy day

晴 ▷fine weather
セイ は(れる) は(れ) −ば(れ)
は(らす)　　　Ⓚ0893

[original meaning] **fine weather, fair weather, clear
[cloudless] sky, bright sky**
　晴天 せいてん fine [fair] weather, cloudless sky
　晴雨計 せいうけい barometer
　晴耕雨読 せいこううどく working in the field in fine
　　weather and reading at home in rainy weather
　晴曇 せいどん fine and cloudy weather

weave and sew
織 紡 績 縫 編 辮 組 繡

織 ▷weave
ショク シキ お(る) お(り)　　　Ⓚ1295

[original meaning] **weave**

　織工 しょっこう weaver
　織機 しょっき loom
　織女星 しょくじょせい Vega
　紡織 ぼうしょく spinning and weaving
　染織 せんしょく dyeing and weaving
　製織 せいしょく weaving

紡 ▷spin
ボウ つむ(ぐ)　　　Ⓚ1189

[original meaning] **spin, make yarn**
　紡糸 ぼうし spinning; spun cotton [wool]
　紡績 ぼうせき spinning
　紡織 ぼうしょく spinning and weaving
　紡錘 ぼうすい spindle
　紡毛 ぼうもう carded wool
　混紡 こんぼう mixed spinning
　綿紡 めんぼう cotton spinning

績 ▷spin
セキ　　　Ⓚ1288

[original meaning] **spin thread, make yarn**
　紡績 ぼうせき spinning

縫 ▷sew
ホウ ぬ(う)　　　Ⓚ1284

[original meaning] **sew, stitch**
　縫合する ほうごうする suture, stitch (a wound)
　縫工 ほうこう seamstress, tailor
　裁縫 さいほう sewing, needlework, dressmaking
　天衣無縫 てんいむほう perfect beauty with no
　　trace of artifice

編 ▷knit
ヘン あ(む) −あ(み)　　　Ⓚ1270

[original meaning] **knit**
　編組機械 へんそきかい knitting machinery

辮 ▷plait
ベン

[now usu. 弁] **plait, braid**
　辮髪 べんぱつ pigtail, queue

組 ▷braid
ソ く(む) くみ −ぐみ　　　Ⓚ1224

to braid

繡 ▷embroider
シュウ　　　Ⓚ1299

embroider; embroidery
　繡花 しゅうか flower-pattern embroidery
　刺繡 ししゅう embroidery
　錦繡 きんしゅう brocades and embroidered
　　textiles; beautiful textile, beautiful clothes

weeks and months
週　旬　月

週 ▷**week**
シュウ　　　　　　　　　　　Ⓚ2690

week, weekly
週間 しゅうかん week
週刊 しゅうかん weekly publication, weekly
今週 こんしゅう this week
二週間 にしゅうかん two weeks

旬 ▷**ten-day period**
ジュン　シュン　　　　　　　　Ⓚ2572

[original meaning] **ten-day period**
旬日 じゅんじつ ten-day period
旬刊 じゅんかん published every ten days
旬報 じゅんぽう ten-day report
上旬 じょうじゅん first ten days of a month
中旬 ちゅうじゅん middle [second] ten days of a
　month

月 ▷**month**
ゲツ　ガツ　つき　　　　　　　Ⓚ2556

a month
b suffix after names of the months
c monthly
a 月日 がっぴ date
月末 げつまつ end of the month
今月 こんげつ this month
来月 らいげつ next month
二箇月 にかげつ two months
正月 しょうがつ New Year, New Year's day; January
生年月日 せいねんがっぴ date of birth
b 二月 にがつ February
c 月賦 げっぷ monthly installments
月給 げっきゅう monthly pay [salary]
月刊の げっかんの published monthly

weight
錘　鎮　碇

錘 ▷**weight**
スイ　つむ　おもり　　　　　　Ⓚ1559

[original meaning] **weight, counterweight, plumb**
鉛錘 えんすい plumb
平衡錘 へいこうすい counterpoise, counterweight

鎮 ▷**weight**
チン　しず(める)　しず(まる)　　Ⓚ1570

[original meaning] **weight (for pressing down)**
文鎮 ぶんちん paperweight

碇 ▷**anchor**
テイ　いかり

[now usu. 碇] **anchor**
碇泊する ていはくする anchor, moor
碇置 ていち anchorage

weight units
匁　斤　貫　噸　屯

匁 ▷**momme (3.75 g)**
もんめ　　　　　　　　　　　Ⓚ2913

momme: **unit of weight equiv. to 3.75 g or 1/1000 of
a kan (貫), now used esp. for weighing pearls**
一匁 いちもんめ 1 momme

斤 ▷**catty (600 g)**
キン　　　　　　　　　　　　Ⓚ2551

**catty, kin: unit of weight equiv. to 600 g or 160
momme (匁)**
斤目 きんめ weight (in catties)
斤量 きんりょう weight
パン三斤 ぱんさんぎん three catties of bread

貫 ▷**kan (3.75 kg)**
カン　つらぬ(く)　　　　　　Ⓚ2174

**unit of weight equiv. to 3.75 kg or 1000 momme
(匁)**
尺貫法 しゃっかんほう Japanese system of weights
　and measures
八貫目 はっかんめ 8 kan

噸 ▷**ton**
トン

[original meaning] **ton, tonnage**
十六噸 じゅうろくとん 16 tons
英噸 えいとん British [long] ton

屯 ▷**ton**
トン　　　　　　　　　　　　Ⓚ2908

[also 噸]
a ton, tonnage
b shipping ton
a 五屯 ごとん 5 tons
英屯 えいとん British [long] ton

welcome →TREAT AND WELCOME

west
洋　西

洋 ▷**Western**
ヨウ　Ⓚ0353

ⓐ [also prefix] **Western, European, foreign**
ⓑ **the West, the Occident**
- ⓐ 洋風 ようふう Western [foreign] style
  洋画 ようが foreign film; Western painting
  洋服 ようふく (Western) clothes
  洋品 ようひん haberdashery
  洋裁 ようさい foreign-style dressmaking
  洋酒 ようしゅ foreign wine [liquors]
  洋式 ようしき Western style
  洋室 ようしつ Western-style room
  洋間 ようま Western-style room
  洋食 ようしょく Western cooking, European dish
  洋書 ようしょ foreign [Western] book
- ⓑ 西洋 せいよう the West, the Occident

西 ▷**the West**
セイ　サイ　にし　Ⓚ2951

the West, the Occident; Western
　西欧 せいおう West Europe, the Occident
　西暦 せいれき Christian Era, A.D.
　泰西 たいせい the Occident

wet
湿　潤　濡

湿 ▷**damp**
シツ　しめ(る)　しめ(す)　Ⓚ0555

[original meaning] **damp, moist, wet, humid**
　湿地 しっち damp ground, swamp
　湿布 しっぷ wet compress
　湿気 しっけ(=しっき) moisture, dampness, humidity
　湿電池 しつでんち wet cell

潤 ▷**moist**
ジュン　うるお(う)　うるお(す)
うる(む)　Ⓚ0676

moist, wet
　湿潤な しつじゅんな moist, damp, wet

濡 ▷**get wet**
ジュ　ぬ(れる)　ぬ(らす)　Ⓚ0709

get wet, get moist, get damp

濡れ縁 ぬれえん open veranda
濡れ衣 ぬれぎぬ false charge, unfounded suspicion
濡れ手で粟 ぬれてであわ easy profit ("Grabbing
　millet with wet hands")
びしょ濡れ びしょぬれ dripping wet, drenched
　[soaked] to the skin, wet through
泣き濡れる なきぬれる be tear-stained
露に濡れた つゆにぬれた dewy, wet with dew

white colors
白　皓　銀

白 ▷**white**
ハク　ビャク　しろ　しら-　しろ(い)　Ⓚ292

[also prefix] **white**
　白人 はくじん white man, Caucasian
　白鳥 はくちょう swan
　白書 はくしょ white paper [book]
　白色 はくしょく white
　白墨 はくぼく chalk
　白衣 はくい(=びゃくえ) white robe [dress]; white coat
　白蓮 びゃくれん white lotus
　白血球 はっけっきゅう leucocyte
　白線 はくせん white line; warning line (on station
　platform)

皓 ▷**bright white**
コウ　Ⓚ109

[original meaning] **bright white, sparkling white,
beautifully white, pure white**
　皓月 こうげつ [archaic] bright white moon
　皓礬 こうばん white vitriol, zinc sulfate heptahy-
　drate
　明眸皓歯 めいぼうこうし starry eyes and beautiful
　white teeth (said of beautiful women)

銀 ▷**silver**
ギン　Ⓚ153

(of silvery color) **silver**
　銀色 ぎんいろ silver color, silveriness
　銀婚式 ぎんこんしき silver wedding
　銀河 ぎんが Milky Way; galaxy
　銀髪 ぎんぱつ silver hair
　銀紙 ぎんがみ aluminum [tin] foil, silver paper

wide and extensive
広 紘 博 恢 浩
洸 滉 曠 闊

広 ▷**wide**
コウ ひろ(い) ひろ(まる) ひろ(める)
ひろ(がる) ひろ(げる)　　　　Ⓚ2613

ⓐ [original meaning] (extending over a large area) **wide, broad, vast, extensive, large, spacious**
ⓑ [also prefix] (having great scope) **wide, wide-ranging**

- a 広大な こうだいな vast, extensive, grand
  広域 こういき wide area
  広野 こうや [formerly also 曠野] vast plain, prairie
- b 広角 こうかく wide angle
  広義 こうぎ broad sense, broader application
  広範囲 こうはんい wide scope, vast range

紘 ▷**wide-ranging**
コウ　　　　Ⓚ1193

wide-ranging, throughout the breadth and length of the land, vast, spacious
八紘 はっこう eight directions; the whole world
八紘一宇 はっこういちう the whole world under one roof

博 ▷**extensive**
ハク バク　　　　Ⓚ0129

extensive (knowledge), wide (learning), well-informed, learned
博士 はくし doctor, Ph.D.
博物学 はくぶつがく natural history
博物館 はくぶつかん museum
博覧 はくらん extensive reading, wide knowledge
博覧会 はくらんかい exhibition, fair, exposition
博愛主義 はくあいしゅぎ philanthropy, humanity
博識 はくしき extensive knowledge
博学 はくがく extensive learning, erudition, wide knowledge
該博な がいはくな extensive (knowledge), profound (learning)

恢 ▷**extensive**
カイ　　　　Ⓚ0325

[original meaning] **extensive, great, vast**
天網恢恢疎にして漏らさず てんもうかいかいそにしてもらさず Heaven's net has large meshes, but nothing escapes

浩 ▷**vast**
コウ　　　　Ⓚ0396

vast (like an expanse of water), extensive, immense, great
浩然たる こうぜんたる vast; magnanimous

洸 ▷**vast (expanse of water)**
コウ　　　　Ⓚ0347

vast and deep like an expanse of water
洸洋 こうよう great expanse of water; unfathomable, incoherent

滉 ▷**deep and vast**
コウ オウ　　　　Ⓚ0605

deep and vast like an expanse of water
滉漾 こうよう vastness, great depth

曠 ▷**spacious**
コウ

[now usu. 広] [original meaning] **spacious, vast, open**
曠野 こうや vast plain, prairie
曠然とした こうぜんとした spacious, wide open

闊 ▷**broad**
カツ

[original meaning] **broad, wide**
闊葉樹 かつようじゅ broadleaf tree
闊歩する かっぽする stride, swagger

widespread
普 遍 通 公

普 ▷**widespread**
フ　　　　Ⓚ2028

widespread, general, universal, common
普及 ふきゅう diffusion, spread, propagation
普遍 ふへん universality, generality
普遍的な ふへんてきな universal, omnipresent, ubiquitous
普請 ふしん building, construction

遍 ▷**all over**
ヘン　　　　Ⓚ2703

all over, everywhere, universal, ubiquitous, widespread
遍在 へんざい omnipresence, ubiquity
遍歴 へんれき travels, pilgrimage
遍路 へんろ pilgrim
普遍的な ふへんてきな universal, omnipresent, ubiquitous

満遍無く(=万遍無く) まんべんなく evenly, equally; without exception; all over

▷common

通 ツウ ツ とお(る) とお(り) -どお(り) とお(す) とお(し) -どお(し) かよ(う) 　　　　Ⓚ2678

common, general, universal, popular
通常の つうじょうの common, ordinary, usual
通称 つうしょう popular [common] name
通念 つうねん common idea, generally accepted idea
通説 つうせつ common opinion, popular view
通俗的 つうぞくてき popular, common
普通の ふつうの normal, regular, ordinary
共通の きょうつうの common

▷common (math)

公 コウ おおやけ 　　　　Ⓚ1715

[also prefix] math **common, general**
公式 こうしき formula; formality
公算 こうさん probability
公約数 こうやくすう common divisor
公倍数 こうばいすう common multiple

width
幅 員 径

▷width

幅 フク はば 　　　　Ⓚ0523

[sometimes also 巾] **width, breadth, range**
幅員 ふくいん width [extent] of roads or ships
増幅 ぞうふく amplification
振幅 しんぷく amplitude (of vibration)
全幅 ぜんぷく overall width, extreme breadth (of a ship), wing span

▷girth

員 イン 　　　　Ⓚ1958

girth
幅員 ふくいん width [extent] of roads or ships

▷diameter

径 ケイ 　　　　Ⓚ0260

diameter
直径 ちょっけい diameter
半径 はんけい radius, semidiameter
口径 こうけい caliber, bore; diameter

will and intention
志 意 図 気 念 趣 欲

▷ambition

志 シ こころざ(す) こころざし 　　　　Ⓚ1881

❶ **ambition, aim, intention, purpose, aspiration, desire, wishes**
志願する しがんする volunteer, apply for
立志 りっし fixing one's aim in life
大志 たいし lofty ambition, aspiration
初志 しょし original aim [intention]
有志の ゆうしの voluntary, interested
❷ **will, mind, purpose, determination**
闘志 とうし fighting spirit, will to fight
意志 いし will, volition
同志 どうし like-minded person, comrade
遺志 いし wishes of a deceased person

▷mind

意 イ 　　　　Ⓚ1834

mind (to do something), intention, will, inclination, desire
意向 いこう intention, inclination
意志 いし will, volition
意欲 いよく volition, will, desire
意図 いと intention, aim
決意する けついする make up one's mind, resolve, determine
得意 とくい one's forte; pride; customer
善意 ぜんい good intention; favorable sense
任意の にんいの optional, voluntary, discretionary; arbitrary

▷intention

図 ズ ト はか(る) 　　　　Ⓚ2645

intention
意図 いと intention, aim
合図 あいず signal, sign

▷mind to do something

気 キ ケ 　　　　Ⓚ2751

mind to do something, intention, will
気儘な きままな willful, selfish
気乗りしない きのりしない halfhearted, indisposed
気楽な きらくな easygoing; comfortable, easy, carefree
買い気 かいき bullish [buying] sentiment [feeling]
やる気 やるき mind to do something, determination to do
眠気 ねむけ sleepiness
吐き気 はきけ nausea

何気無い なにげない casually, unconcernedly

念 ▷thought of doing something
ネン   Ⓚ1773

thought of doing something, intention, desire, wish

念願 ねんがん one's heart's desire, one's heartiest wish

執念 しゅうねん tenacity of purpose, vindictiveness, spite

一念 いちねん wholehearted wish, determined soul

趣 ▷purpose
シュ おもむき   Ⓚ2827

purpose, aim, motive, object, meaning, purport

趣旨 しゅし purpose, aim; purport, meaning

趣意 しゅい purpose, motive, aim; purport, meaning, point

趣向 しゅこう idea, contrivance, plan

意趣 いしゅ spite, grudge, enmity; [original meaning] purpose, meaning

欲 ▷desire
ヨク ほっ(する) ほ(しい)   Ⓚ1341

[formerly also 慾] [original meaning] **desire, craving; avarice, greed**

欲情 よくじょう sexual desire, craving, passion

欲深 よくふか(=よくぶか) greed, avarice; miser, greedy person

欲深い よくぶかい greed, avaricious

欲張り よくばり greed; greedy

食欲 しょくよく appetite (for food)

物欲 ぶつよく worldly desires

性欲 せいよく sexual desire, lust

意欲 いよく volition, will, desire

知識欲 ちしきよく intellectual thirst

win

勝 克 剋 征 破 凱

勝 ▷win
ショウ か(つ) -が(ち) まさ(る)   Ⓚ0918

Ⓐ win, defeat
Ⓑ win, victory
Ⓒ counter for wins (in sports)

a 勝者 しょうしゃ winner

全勝する ぜんしょうする win all the games, make a clean sweep

優勝 ゆうしょう victory, championship

b 勝利 しょうり victory, triumph, win

勝敗 しょうはい victory or defeat

勝負 しょうぶ victory or defeat; match, game

決勝戦 けっしょうせん final round match, finals

大勝 たいしょう great [sweeping] victory

連勝 れんしょう straight victories

c 二勝三敗 にしょうさんぱい two wins and three defeats

克 ▷overcome
コク   Ⓚ1760

[formerly also 剋] **overcome, conquer, win**

克服 こくふく conquest, subjugation

克復 こくふく restoration

克己 こっき self-denial, self-control

超克する ちょうこくする overcome, conquer, surmount, get over

相克する そうこくする struggle with each other, conflict

下克上 げこくじょう the lower dominating the upper

剋 ▷overcome
コク

[now usu. 克] [original meaning] **overcome, conquer, win**

下剋上 げこくじょう the lower dominating the upper

相剋する そうこくする struggle with each other, conflict

征 ▷conquer
セイ   Ⓚ0262

conquer, subjugate (the enemy), attack, assault, invade

征服 せいふく conquest, subjugation

征伐 せいばつ subjugation, conquest

征討 せいとう subjugation, conquest

破 ▷break
ハ やぶ(る) やぶ(れる)   Ⓚ1064

break the enemy, defeat

撃破する げきはする defeat, rout; destroy

論破する ろんぱする refute, defeat in argument

連破する れんぱする defeat one's enemy in succession

凱 ▷triumph
ガイ カイ   Ⓚ1612

triumph, victory

凱旋する がいせんする return from a victorious campaign

凱旋門 がいせんもん arch of triumph

凱歌 がいか triumphal song

wind
風 嵐 颱 台 凪 颯

風 ▷**wind**
フウ フ かぜ かざ- Ⓚ2591

[also suffix] **wind, breeze**
風速 ふうそく wind velocity
風波 ふうは wind and waves, rough seas, storm
風力 ふうりょく force of the wind; wind power
台風(=颱風) たいふう typhoon
強風 きょうふう strong [high] wind
扇風機 せんぷうき electric fan
季節風 きせつふう seasonal wind, periodic wind

嵐 ▷**storm**
ラン あらし Ⓚ2012

storm, tempest
春嵐 しゅんらん spring storm

颱 ▷**typhoon**
タイ

[now replaced by 台] **typhoon**
颱風 たいふう typhoon

台 ▷**typhoon**
ダイ タイ Ⓚ1731

[formerly 颱] **typhoon**
台風 たいふう typhoon

凪 ▷**calm**
な(ぐ) なぎ Ⓚ2579

【な(ぐ)】
(of the wind) **become calm, calm down, abate, drop**
風が凪ぐ かぜがなぐ The wind drops
【なぎ】
(of the wind) **calm, lull**
夕凪 ゆうなぎ evening calm

颯 ▷**sound of gusting wind**
サツ ソウ Ⓚ1130

[archaic] **sound of gusting winds; gust of wind**
颯然たる さつぜんたる (of a gust of wind) blowing suddenly

wind and twine
巻 捲 繰 絡 纏

巻 ▷**roll up**
カン ま(く) まき Ⓚ2298

[original meaning] **roll up, roll, scroll**
巻子本 かんしほん scroll, roll, rolled book
巻雲(=絹雲) けんうん cirrus cloud

捲 ▷**roll up**
ケン ま(く) まく(る) まくし- めく(る) Ⓚ0451

roll up, wind, coil, whirl
捲土重来 けんどちょうらい making another attempt with redoubled efforts
席捲(=席巻) せっけん sweeping conquest, sweeping over

繰 ▷**reel**
くる Ⓚ1300

ⓐ reel (silk off a cocoon); gin (cotton); spin
ⓑ reel in, reel up, wind, roll out
a 繰り綿 くりわた ginned cotton
繰り取る くりとる reel off
b 繰り出す くりだす draw out; call out (troops), sally forth
手繰る たぐる pull in hand over hand, draw in, reel in; retrace
掻い繰る かいぐる haul in hand over hand
雨戸を繰る あまどをくる roll open the shutters

絡 ▷**entwine**
ラク から(む) から(まる) から(める) Ⓚ1238

[original meaning] **entwine, twine, intertwine**
籠絡する ろうらくする inveigle, ensnare, entice
交絡 こうらく *statistics* confounding, interrelationship

纏 ▷**wind around**
テン まと(める) まと(う) まと(まる) まつ(わる) Ⓚ1302

[original meaning] **wind around, bind, tangle**
纏足 てんそく foot-binding
纏綿 てんめん entanglement, involvement

知情意 ちじょうい intellect, emotion and volition

wings

翼　羽　葉

翼 ▷**wing (of birds or aircraft)**
ヨク　つばさ　　　　　　　　　　Ⓚ2373

ⓐ [original meaning] **wing of a bird, wings**
ⓑ [also suffix] **wing of an aircraft, airfoil**

 a　翼状 よくじょう wing shape
　　羽翼 うよく wings; assistance
b　主翼 しゅよく wing (of an aircraft)
　　水平翼 すいへいよく horizontal plane
　　補助翼 ほじょよく aileron

羽 ▷**wing (of birds or insects)**
ウ　は　わ　はね　　　　　　　Ⓚ0200

wing (of birds or insects), ala
　　羽翼 うよく wings; assistance
　　羽化 うか emergence (of insects)

葉 ▷**plane**
ヨウ　は　　　　　　　　　　　Ⓚ2024

plane (of an aircraft)
　　単葉飛行機 たんようひこうき monoplane
　　複葉機 ふくようき biplane

wisdom

識　知　智　慧　哲

識 ▷**knowledge**
シキ　　　　　　　　　　　　　Ⓚ1477

(acquired) **knowledge, sense, wisdom, learning**
　　識見 しきけん knowledge, judgment, discernment
　　知識 ちしき knowledge
　　常識 じょうしき common sense, common knowl-
　　　edge
　　良識 りょうしき good sense
　　有識者 ゆうしきしゃ learned [informed, intellectu-
　　　al] people, the wise
　　学識 がくしき learning, scholarship

知 ▷**knowledge**
チ　し(る)　し(らせる)　し(れる)　　Ⓚ1041

[formerly also 智] **knowledge, wisdom, intelligence,
intellect**
　　知恵 ちえ wisdom, intelligence, sagacity
　　知能 ちのう intelligence, mental capacity
　　知性 ちせい intellect, intelligence
　　知覚知 ちかくち knowledge by acquaintance

智 ▷**wisdom**
チ　　　　　　　　　　　　　　Ⓚ2425

wisdom, intelligence
　　智能 ちのう intelligence, mental capacity
　　智慧(=知恵) ちえ wisdom, intelligence, sagacity
　　智識 ちしき wisdom; Buddhist priest of renown
　　智謀 ちぼう resources, artifice
　　無智 むち ignorance, stupidity

慧 ▷**prajna (transcendental wisdom)**
ケイ　エ　　　　　　　　　　　Ⓚ2447

Buddhism **prajna, transcendental wisdom**—often
used in the names of Buddhist priests
　　慧遠 えおん Hui-Yuan (Chinese priest of the Jin
　　　Dynasty)

哲 ▷**philosophy**
テツ　　　　　　　　　　　　　Ⓚ2386

philosophy
　　哲学 てつがく philosophy
　　哲理 てつり philosophy (of something)
　　中哲 ちゅうてつ Chinese philosophy
　　印哲 いんてつ Indian philosophy

wise →INTELLIGENT AND WISE

wise and talented persons

哲　賢　博　秀　俊　才　通

哲 ▷**sage**
テツ　　　　　　　　　　　　　Ⓚ2386

sage, philosopher, wise man
　　哲人 てつじん philosopher, sage
　　西哲 せいてつ Western philosopher
　　先哲 せんてつ ancient sage [wise man]
　　十哲 じってつ ten sages

賢 ▷**wise man**
ケン　かしこ(い)　　　　　　　Ⓚ2472

wise man, sage
　　賢哲 けんてつ sage, wise man

博 ▷**doctor**
ハク　バク　　　　　　　　　　Ⓚ0129

abbrev. of 博士 はくし: **doctor, Ph.D.**
　　医博 いはく doctor of medicine, M.D.
　　文博 ぶんはく doctor of literature

秀 ▷genius
シュウ ひい(でる) ⓚ2202

genius, prodigy
- 秀才 しゅうさい (person of) genius
- 俊秀 しゅんしゅう genius, prodigy
- 閨秀 けいしゅう accomplished lady

俊 ▷brilliant person
シュン ⓚ0086

[original meaning] **brilliant [talented] person, genius**
- 俊秀 しゅんしゅう genius, prodigy
- 俊才 しゅんさい genius, person of exceptional talent
- 俊英 しゅんえい talent, genius; gifted person

才 ▷person of talent
サイ ⓚ2880

person of talent, man of ability, capable person
- 俊才 しゅんさい genius, person of exceptional talent
- 天才 てんさい (person of) genius
- 秀才 しゅうさい (person of) genius

通 ▷well-informed person
ツウ ツ とお(る) とお(り)
-どお(り) とお(す) とお(し) -どお(し)
かよ(う) ⓚ2678

[also suffix] **well-informed person, authority, expert**
- 食通 しょくつう gourmet
- 消息通 しょうそくつう well-informed person, insider

wish and desire

願 憧 憬 貪 望 希
懐 慕 渇 欲 慾 求

願 ▷wish
ガン ねが(う) ⓚ1637

ⓐ wish, desire, hope for
ⓑ one's wish, one's desire

- a 願望 がんぼう wish, desire, aspiration
  念願する ねんがんする desire, wish (for), pray (for)
- b 宿願 しゅくがん long-cherished desire
  悲願 ひがん one's pathetic wish; vows resulting from the compassion of the Buddhas

憧 ▷yearn after
ショウ ドウ あこが(れる) ⓚ0664

yearn after
- 憧憬する しょうけい(=どうけい)する yearn after

憬 ▷yearn after
ケイ ⓚ066

yearn after
- 憧憬する しょうけい(=どうけい)する yearn after

貪 ▷covet
ドン むさぼ(る) ⓚ182

covet, lust insatiably for, be greedy for; devour
- 貪欲 どんよく greed, avarice
- 貪婪 どんらん(=とんらん、たんらん) covetousness, greed
- 貪食 どんしょく voracity, ravenousness
- 貪愛 とんあい(=どんあい) insatiable lust; *Buddhism* attachment, craving
- 貪汚 たんお filthy greed

望 ▷hope
ボウ モウ のぞ(む) ⓚ239◯

hope, expect, wish, aspire to, desire
- 望外の ぼうがいの unexpected, unanticipated
- 希望する きぼうする hope, wish, aspire to
- 要望 ようぼう demand, request
- 絶望 ぜつぼう despair, hopelessness
- 失望する しつぼうする be disappointed, lose hope
- 欲望 よくぼう desire, craving
- 志望する しぼうする desire, wish, aspire to
- 待望の たいぼうの hoped-for, long-awaited
- 有望な ゆうぼうな promising, hopeful
- 本望 ほんもう one's long cherished desire; satisfaction
- 大望 たいもう(=たいぼう) ambition, aspiration
- 懇望する こんもうする entreat, solicit, beg earnestly

希 ▷aspire
キ まれ ⓚ176

aspire, hope, desire, long for
- 希望 きぼう hope, wish, aspiration
- 希求する ききゅうする aspire to, seek, demand

懐 ▷long for
カイ ふところ なつ(かしい) なつ(かしむ)
なつ(く) なつ(ける) ⓚ068◯

long for, miss, yearn, be attached to, be filled with nostalgia
- 懐旧 かいきゅう longing for the old days
- 懐古 かいこ yearning for the old days
- 懐郷 かいきょう nostalgia, homesickness
- 追懐 ついかい recollection, reminiscence

慕 ▷yearn for
ボ した(う)　　Ⓚ2069

yearn for, long for
慕情 ぼじょう longing; love, affection
思慕する しぼする love dearly, yearn for
追慕する ついぼする cherish one's memory, yearn after, sigh for

渇 ▷thirst for
カツ かわ(く)　　Ⓚ0473

thirst for, long for, crave
渇望する かつぼうする thirst for, long for, crave
渇仰 かつごう adoration

欲 ▷desire
ヨク ほっ(する) ほ(しい)　　Ⓚ1341

desire, wish, want, crave for
欲念 よくねん desire, wish; passion
欲求 よっきゅう want(s), desire, wish
欲望 よくぼう desire, craving
貪欲 どんよく greed, avarice

慾 ▷desire
ヨク

[now replaced by 欲] [also suffix] [original meaning]
desire, craving; avarice, greed
性慾 せいよく sexual desire, lust
愛慾 あいよく love and lust, sexual passion
物慾 ぶつよく worldly desires
無慾 むよく freedom from avarice
色慾 しきよく sexual appetite
食慾 しょくよく appetite (for food)
名誉慾 めいよよく love of fame

求 ▷seek

キュウ もと(める)　　Ⓚ2974
see also →SEEK

(go in search of) **seek (for), search, pursue; wish for, desire**
求人 きゅうじん job offer
求職 きゅうしょく seeking employment
求道 きゅうどう(=ぐどう) seeking for truth; seeking for enlightenment
探求する たんきゅうする investigate, search (for), pursue
追求 ついきゅう pursuit
欣求浄土 ごんぐじょうど seeking rebirth in the Pure Land
欲求 よっきゅう want(s), desire, wish

---

wives
妻 奥 内 室 嫡 婦 嫁 寡

妻 ▷wife
サイ つま　　Ⓚ2214

[original meaning] **wife**
妻子 さいし one's wife and children, one's family
夫妻 ふさい husband and wife, Mr. and Mrs., married couple
恐妻家 きょうさいか henpecked husband, man bossed by his wife
正妻 せいさい lawful [legal] wife

奥 ▷wife
オウ おく　　Ⓚ2458

(from the idea that the wife of a nobleman lives in the inner chambers) **wife**
奥さん おくさん married lady, Mrs.; your wife
奥様 おくさま married lady, Mrs.; your wife
奥方 おくがた wife of a nobleman

内 ▷wife
ナイ ダイ うち　　Ⓚ2914

(person inside the house) **wife**
内助 ないじょ wife's help
内儀 ないぎ other's wife
家内 かない family, household; wife

室 ▷wife (esp. of persons of rank)
シツ むろ　　Ⓚ1943

wife, esp. of persons of rank or noblemen
正室 せいしつ legal wife
後室 こうしつ widow

嫡 ▷legitimate wife
チャク　　Ⓚ0620

[original meaning] **legitimate wife, legal wife**
嫡男 ちゃくなん heir, eldest son; legitimate son
嫡出 ちゃくしゅつ legitimacy (of birth)
嫡妻 ちゃくさい legitimate wife
嫡室 ちゃくしつ legitimate wife

婦 ▷married woman
フ　　Ⓚ0426

[original meaning] **married woman, wife, housewife**
主婦 しゅふ housewife
夫婦 ふうふ husband and wife, married couple
新婦 しんぷ bride

嫁 ▷**bride**
カ よめ とつ(ぐ)　　　　　　Ⓚ0582

bride
惣嫁(=総嫁) そうか streetwalker (in the Edo period)

寡 ▷**widow**
カ　　　　　　Ⓚ2059

widow, widower, widowed spouse; widowed
寡婦 かふ(=やもめ) widow
寡居 かきょ widowhood

wives of rulers
后　妃　室

后 ▷**empress**
コウ　　　　　　Ⓚ2574

(wife of an emperor) **empress, queen**
后妃 こうひ queen consort, empress, queen
皇后 こうごう empress, queen
皇太后 こうたいこう empress dowager, queen mother

妃 ▷**princess**
ヒ　　　　　　Ⓚ0182

(wife of a member of the Imperial or Royal family) **princess, queen, empress; consort (as of an emperor)**
妃殿下 ひでんか Her Imperial Highness
王妃 おうひ queen, empress
后妃 こうひ queen consort, empress, queen
親王妃 しんのうひ Imperial princess

室 ▷**wife (esp. of persons of rank)**
シツ むろ　　　　　　Ⓚ1943

wife, esp. of persons of rank or noblemen
正室 せいしつ legal wife
後室 こうしつ widow

woman
女　婦　婆　嬢　娘　雌　牝　媛

女 ▷**woman**
ジョ ニョ ニョウ おんな め　　　　　　Ⓚ2884

[also prefix and suffix]
ⓐ [original meaning] **woman, female**
ⓑ **girl, maiden**
a 女性 じょせい woman, female; feminine gender
　女性的 じょせいてき feminine, womanly

女子 じょし woman, girl
女優 じょゆう actress
女王 じょおう(=じょうおう) queen; belle, mistress
女人 にょにん woman
女房 にょうぼう wife; court lady
女中 じょちゅう maidservant, maid
彼女 かのじょ she; one's sweetheart
男女 だんじょ men and women, both sexes
修道女 しゅうどうじょ nun, sister
b 女生徒 じょせいと schoolgirl, girl student
少女 しょうじょ girl
処女 しょじょ virgin, maiden
織女星 しょくじょせい Vega

婦 ▷**adult woman**
フ　　　　　　Ⓚ0426

adult woman, woman, lady
婦人 ふじん woman, lady, female
婦警 ふけい policewoman
婦女 ふじょ woman, the fair sex
裸婦 らふ nude woman

婆 ▷**old woman**
バ ばあ　　　　　　Ⓚ2407

old woman, old maid, old mother; woman
老婆 ろうば old woman
妖婆 ようば witch, hag
老婆心 ろうばしん grandmotherly solicitude
産婆 さんば midwife

嬢 ▷**young lady**
ジョウ　　　　　　Ⓚ0685

unmarried young lady, girl, mademoiselle
令嬢 れいじょう daughter; young lady
老嬢 ろうじょう spinster

娘 ▷**girl**
むすめ　　　　　　Ⓚ0367

[also suffix] **girl, maiden**
娘心 むすめごころ girlish innocence
小娘 こむすめ young girl, lass
箱入り娘 はこいりむすめ innocent [naive] girl of a good family
花売り娘 はなうりむすめ flower girl

雌 ▷**female**
シ め- めす　　　　　　Ⓚ0971

[original meaning] (of plants or animals) **female**
雌雄 しゆう male and female; victory or defeat
雌蕊 しずい pistil

牝 ▷**female**
ヒン めす め- めん

[original meaning] (of animals) **female**
　牝馬 ひんば mare

媛 ▷**damsel**
エン ひめ　　　　　　Ⓚ0519

beautiful young lady
　才媛 さいえん talented girl, accomplished woman,
　　girl with scholastic ability

wood →KINDS OF WOOD

words and expressions

語 辞 詞 句 諺 喩

語 ▷**word**
ゴ かた(る) かた(らう)　　Ⓚ1402

[also suffix] **word, term, phrase**
　語意 ごい meaning of a word
　語句 ごく words and phrases
　語彙 ごい vocabulary
　単語 たんご word
　用語 ようご terminology; diction, wording; vocabu-
　　lary
　主語 しゅご subject (word)
　流行語 りゅうこうご word [phrase] in fashion, word
　　[phrase] on everybody's lips

辞 ▷**word**
ジ や(める)　　　　　Ⓚ1245

ⓐ **word, term, phrase, expression, sentence**
ⓑ *gram* **function word, particle**
ⓐ 辞典 じてん dictionary
　辞書 じしょ dictionary
　世辞 せじ compliment
　式辞 しきじ address
　措辞 そじ phraseology, wording
ⓑ 接辞 せつじ affix

詞 ▷**words**
シ　　　　　　　　　Ⓚ1363

ⓐ **words, wording, lyrics, expressions**
ⓑ [also suffix] **part of speech**
ⓐ 歌詞 かし words [lyrics] of a song
　祝詞 しゅくし congratulations
　賞詞(=頌詞) しょうし (words of) praise, eulogy
　誓詞 せいし oath, pledge
　作詞 さくし writing lyrics

ⓑ 品詞 ひんし part of speech
　動詞 どうし verb
　名詞 めいし noun
　定冠詞 ていかんし definite article
　前置詞 ぜんちし preposition

句 ▷**phrase**
ク　　　　　　　　　Ⓚ2561

phrase, expression, set phrase
　語句 ごく words and phrases
　文句 もんく phrase, expression; complaint
　慣用句 かんようく idiom, common phrase

諺 ▷**proverb**
ゲン ことわざ　　　　Ⓚ1440

proverb, maxim, saying
　諺文 げんぶん(=おんもん, うんむん) old name for
　　Hangul
　俗諺 ぞくげん popular saying, proverb
　俚諺 りげん traditional [folk] saying, proverb

喩 ▷**metaphor**
ユ たと(える)　　　　Ⓚ0508

metaphor, simile, allegory
　比喩(=譬喩) ひゆ simile, metaphor, allegory
　直喩 ちょくゆ simile
　暗喩 あんゆ metaphor
　諷喩(=風喩) ふうゆ hint, insinuation, allegory
　引喩 いんゆ allusion

work

働 稼 労 勤 仕

働 ▷**work**
ドウ はたら(く)　　　Ⓚ0130

[original meaning] **work, labor, serve**
　労働 ろうどう (manual) labor, toil
　稼働(=稼動) かどう working, work; operation (of a
　　machine)
　実働時間 じつどうじかん actual working hours
　重労働 じゅうろうどう heavy labor

稼 ▷**work (for a living)**
カ かせ(ぐ)　　　　　Ⓚ1136

work, work for a living, earn
　稼働(=稼動) かどう working, work; operation (of a
　　machine)
　稼業 かぎょう trade, business; work; occupation

労 ▷labor
ロウ   Ⓚ2205

(work hard) **labor, toil, do manual work**

労働 ろうどう (manual) labor, toil
労働者 ろうどうしゃ laborer, worker
労務 ろうむ labor, work, service
労力 ろうりょく trouble, labors, efforts

勤 ▷serve (in an office)
キン ゴン つと(める) –づと(め)
つと(まる)   Ⓚ1613

serve (in an office), hold a job, be in the service of

勤め つとめ service, employment, duties; Buddhistic service, sutra chanting; prostitute service
勤め先 つとめさき (one's place of) employment
勤め上げる つとめあげる serve out one's time, perform one's service

仕 ▷serve
シ ジ つか(える)   Ⓚ0021

serve (under), take service under, enter the government service

仕官 しかん entering the government service; find service with (a lord)
奉仕 ほうし attendance, service
出仕する しゅっしする enter the service of; attend (one's office)

work and employment
務 任 役 勤 業 職 労

務 ▷duty
ム つと(める) つと(まる)   Ⓚ1085

(task required by one's occupation) **duty, task, office, function**

任務 にんむ duty, part, function; mission
勤務 きんむ duty, service, work
職務 しょくむ duty, duties, function
業務 ぎょうむ business, affairs, work, service

任 ▷office
ニン まか(せる) まか(す)   Ⓚ0038

office, duties, official post

任期 にんき one's term of office
就任 しゅうにん assumption of office, inauguration
辞任 じにん resignation
留任 りゅうにん remaining in office
赴任する ふにんする proceed to a new post

解任 かいにん release from office, dismissal, discharge

役 ▷service (esp. public)
ヤク エキ   Ⓚ0217

❶ **service, public service, duty, official post, office**

役所 やくしょ public [government] office
役場 やくば public office
役柄 やくがら nature [quality] of one's office, one's position
役目 やくめ duty, function; role
役員 やくいん officer, leader, director
役人 やくにん government official

❷ **unpaid service, exacted labor, work, corvée**

役務 えきむ labor, service
役牛 えきぎゅう work cattle

勤 ▷service (employment)
キン ゴン つと(める) –づと(め)
つと(まる)   Ⓚ1613

(employment in general) **service, duty, work, employment**

勤続 きんぞく continuous service, continuance in service
通勤する つうきんする commute, go to one's office
転勤する てんきんする be transferred (to another office)
欠勤 けっきん absence (from work)
夜勤 やきん night duty

業 ▷work
ギョウ ゴウ わざ   Ⓚ2265

(work as a means of livelihood) **work, occupation, business, employment, trade, profession**

職業 しょくぎょう occupation, vocation, profession
失業する しつぎょうする be out of work, lose one's job
生業 せいぎょう occupation, calling
生業 せいぎょう (=なりわい) livelihood; calling, occupation
従業員 じゅうぎょういん employee, workers

職 ▷employment
ショク   Ⓚ1297

[also suffix]

ⓐ **employment, occupation, work, job**
ⓑ abbrev. of 職業 しょくぎょう or 職務 しょくむ: **employment, duty**
ⓒ **post, office**

a 職業 しょくぎょう occupation, vocation, profession
職務 しょくむ duty, duties, function
職場 しょくば place of work, workshop
職種 しょくしゅ type of occupation, occupational category
職員 しょくいん staff, employee, personnel

職歴 しょくれき one's professional [work] experience, one's business career
就職 しゅうしょく finding employment
退職 たいしょく retirement, resignation
無職の むしょくの without occupation, unemployed
内職 ないしょく side job
専門職 せんもんしょく profession, professional job
b 職安 しょくあん Public Employment Security Office
c 公職 こうしょく public office
現職 げんしょく present post [office]; incumbent
管理職 かんりしょく administrative [managerial] position
汚職 おしょく (official) corruption, bribery

労 ▷labor
ロウ Ⓚ2205

(hard work) **labor, toil, work, trouble, pains**
勤労 きんろう labor, work, service
苦労 くろう difficulties, trouble, hardships, labor

workers and professionals

家 婦 嬢 夫 匠 工 客
士 師 者 人 員 屋 手

家 ▷professional
カ ケ いえ や うち Ⓚ1963

[also suffix]
Ⓐ **professional, member of a profession**
Ⓑ **performer of an action or person associated with something**
a 作家 さっか writer, novelist, author
画家 がか artist, painter
政治家 せいじか politician
専門家 せんもんか specialist, expert
b 勉強家 べんきょうか diligent student, studious person
財産家 ざいさんか person of wealth
儒家 じゅか Confucian, Confucianist
道家 どうか Taoist scholar

婦 ▷woman worker
フ Ⓚ0426

[also suffix] **woman worker, working [career] woman**
娼婦 しょうふ prostitute, harlot
看護婦 かんごふ nurse
掃除婦 そうじふ charwoman, cleaning woman

嬢 ▷(unmarried) female worker
ジョウ Ⓚ0685

[also suffix] (unmarried) **female worker**
交換嬢 こうかんじょう telephone operator
案内嬢 あんないじょう usherette

夫 ▷man laborer
フ フウ ブ おっと Ⓚ2909

[also suffix] **man laborer, male worker**
農夫 のうふ peasant, plowman
人夫 にんぷ coolie, porter, laborer
煙突掃除夫 えんとつそうじふ chimney sweeper [cleaner]

匠 ▷craftsman
ショウ Ⓚ2581

(skilled workman) **craftsman, artisan, workman**
工匠 こうしょう artisan, mechanic
名匠 めいしょう skilled craftsman

工 ▷workman
コウ ク Ⓚ2866

[also suffix] **workman, worker, artisan, craftsman, mechanic**
工人 こうじん workman, craftsman
職工 しょっこう workman, mechanic, (factory) hand
大工 だいく carpenter
石工 いしく(=せっこう) stonemason, mason
印刷工 いんさつこう printer
熟練工 じゅくれんこう skilled workman, master mechanic

客 ▷skilled person
キャク カク Ⓚ1939

skilled person, -er, -ian
剣客 けんきゃく swordsman, fencer
侠客 きょうかく chivalrous person, self-styled humanitarian
刺客 しかく assassin

士 ▷profession suffix
シ Ⓚ2877

suffix for members of a profession, esp. a licensed profession
弁護士 べんごし lawyer, attorney
力士 りきし sumo wrestler
棋士 きし professional go [shogi] player

師 ▷profession suffix
シ Ⓚ1211

[also suffix] **member of a profession or performer of an action**
医師 いし doctor, physician, surgeon

技師 ぎし engineer, technician
牧師 ぼくし pastor, minister, priest
絵師 えし painter, artist
美容師 びようし beauty artist
ペテン師 ぺてんし swindler, finagler

者 ▷person who
シャ もの   Ⓚ2765

[also suffix] **person [one]** who performs an action or holds an occupation: **-er (as in** *reader***)**

読者 どくしゃ reader, subscriber
学者 がくしゃ scholar, learned man
記者 きしゃ journalist, reporter; editor
著者 ちょしゃ author, writer
医者 いしゃ doctor
打者 だしゃ batter, hitter
賛成者 さんせいしゃ approver, supporter
被爆者 ひばくしゃ victim of atomic air raid
科学者 かがくしゃ scientist

人 ▷person of certain category
ジン ニン ひと –り –と   Ⓚ2857

person of certain category, as the performer of an action or holder of an occupation: **-er (as in** *manager***)**

見物人 けんぶつにん spectator, sightseer
料理人 りょうりにん cook
支配人 しはいにん manager, executive
芸能人 げいのうじん performing artist

員 ▷member (of a staff)
イン   Ⓚ1958

member of a staff [profession], personnel, person in charge

社員 しゃいん staff member, employee
職員 しょくいん staff, employee, personnel
全員 ぜんいん all members, entire staff
係員 かかりいん clerk in charge
検査員 けんさいん inspector
会社員 かいしゃいん company employee, office worker
公務員 こうむいん public service personnel, government worker
事務員 じむいん clerk, clerical staff
警備員 けいびいん guard

屋 ▷colloquial occupation suffix
オク や   Ⓚ2669

colloquial occupation suffix—sometimes indicates slight contempt or humility

事務屋 じむや clerk, office worker
何でも屋 なんでもや jack-of-all-trades

手 ▷occupation suffix
シュ ズ て た–   Ⓚ290?

ⓐ [also suffix] holder of an occupation or performer of an action: **-er (as in** *singer***)**
ⓑ **skilled person**
a 歌手 かしゅ singer
騎手 きしゅ rider, horseman, jockey
選手 せんしゅ representative athlete [player]
投手 とうしゅ pitcher
助手 じょしゅ assistant, helper
運転手 うんてんしゅ driver
b 名手 めいしゅ master, expert

work metals
錬 煉 鍛 鋳 焼 冶

錬 ▷refine (crude metals)
レン   Ⓚ155?

[formerly also 煉] [original meaning] **refine (crude metals), smelt; work metals, temper**
錬金術 れんきんじゅつ alchemy
錬鉄 れんてつ wrought iron
錬鋼 れんこう wrought steel
精錬 せいれん refining, smelting; tempering
製錬 せいれん smelting
鍛錬する たんれんする temper, forge; train, discipline

煉 ▷refine (crude metals)
レン ね(る)   Ⓚ0939

[now also 錬] [original meaning] **refine (crude metals), smelt; work metals, temper**
煉丹術 れんたんじゅつ art of making elixirs, alchemy
精煉する せいれんする refine (metals), smelt (copper); temper

鍛 ▷forge
タン きた(える)   Ⓚ156?

[original meaning] **forge, work metal, temper**
鍛練(=鍛錬)する たんれんする temper, forge; train, discipline
鍛造 たんぞう forging
鍛接 たんせつ forge welding
鍛鋼 たんこう forged steel
鍛工 たんこう metalworker
鍛鉄 たんてつ tempering iron, wrought iron
鍛冶 たんや(=かじ) forging; smith

鋳 ▷**cast**
チュウ い(る)   Ⓚ1543

[original meaning] **cast, mint, coin**
- 鋳鉄 ちゅうてつ iron casting
- 鋳造 ちゅうぞう casting, minting, coining
- 鋳金 ちゅうきん casting
- 鋳鋼 ちゅうこう cast steel
- 改鋳 かいちゅう recoinage, recasting

焼 ▷**annealing**
ショウ や(く) や(き) や(ける)   Ⓚ0909

annealing
- 焼き戻し やきもどし tempering
- 焼き入れ やきいれ quenching, hardening
- 焼きを入れる やきをいれる harden, temper; discipline; torture

冶 ▷**work metals**
ヤ   Ⓚ0062

work metals: **smelt forge, cast**
- 冶金 やきん metallurgy
- 鍛冶する たんやする forge

world
世 　 界

世 ▷**world**
セイ せ よ   Ⓚ2932

(physical world) **world, universe**
- 世界 せかい world, universe
- 創世記 そうせいき Genesis

界 ▷**world**
カイ   Ⓚ2220

ⓐ (physical world) **world**
ⓑ [also suffix] (sphere or realm) **world, kingdom, realm**
- a 世界 せかい world, universe
- 他界する たかいする die, pass away
- 外界 がいかい external world
- b 界隈 かいわい neighborhood, vicinity
- 自然界 しぜんかい realm of nature
- 動物界 どうぶつかい animal kingdom

worldly
世 　 俗

世 ▷**worldly**
セイ せ よ   Ⓚ2932

worldly, earthly, public, popular
- 世事 せじ worldly affairs
- 世話 せわ help, aid, good offices; care; everyday affairs
- 世評 せひょう public opinion; reputation
- 世俗の せぞくの common, worldly

俗 ▷**worldly**
ゾク   Ⓚ0088

worldly, mundane; worldliness
- 俗事 ぞくじ worldly affairs
- 俗人 ぞくじん layman, man of the world
- 俗情 ぞくじょう worldly-mindedness, worldliness
- 俗世間 ぞくせけん the workaday world
- 脱俗 だつぞく unworldliness
- 世俗の せぞくの common, worldly

worry
憂 配 構 虞

憂 ▷**be anxious**
ユウ うれ(える) うれ(い) う(い) う(き)   Ⓚ1842

ⓐ be [feel] anxious, fear, worry, be concerned
ⓑ anxiety, fears, apprehension
- a 憂慮 ゆうりょ anxiety, concern, worry
- 憂国 ゆうこく patriotism, concern for one's country
- b 一喜一憂 いっきいちゆう alternation of joy and sorrow
- 杞憂 きゆう imaginary fears

配 ▷**concern oneself**
ハイ くば(る)   Ⓚ1330

concern oneself with (a person's welfare), **be concerned about**
- 配慮 はいりょ consideration, care, concern
- 心配 しんぱい anxiety, concern, worry, uneasiness; good offices
- 高配 こうはい your trouble, your good offices
- 手配 てはい arrangement, preparation; search instruction (by police)

構 ▷mind
コウ かま(える) かま(う)　　Ⓚ0962

mind, care about, be concerned about
構わない かまわない do not care [mind], be indifferent (to)
人が何と言おうと構わない ひとがなんといおうとかまわない I don't care what people say about me

虞 ▷fears (of undesirable event)
おそれ　　Ⓚ2783

[also 恐れ] **fears (of undesirable event), danger, risk, signs, adverse chance, possibility**
失敗の虞 しっぱいのおそれ risk of failure
雨の虞が有る あめのおそれがある There is some fear of rain
感染の虞を無くす かんせんのおそれをなくす preclude the possibility of infection

worship →PRAY AND WORSHIP

wrap →COVER AND WRAP

write
書 筆 写 記 紀
控 録 登 註

書 ▷write
ショ か(く) -が(き)　　Ⓚ2314

write
書写 しょしゃ transcription, copying, handwriting
書記 しょき clerk, secretary
清書する せいしょする write out fair, make a fair [clean] copy
代書する だいしょする write for another

筆 ▷write
ヒツ ふで　　Ⓚ2335

write
筆者 ひっしゃ writer
筆記する ひっきする take notes of, write down
筆記試験 ひっきしけん written examination
筆記用具 ひっきようぐ writing materials, pens and pencils
執筆 しっぴつ writing
特筆する とくひつする mention specially

写 ▷copy
シャ うつ(す) うつ(る)　　Ⓚ1726

(reproduce an original, esp. by writing) **copy, make a copy, transcribe, reproduce, imitate**

写経 しゃきょう copying of a sutra, copied sutra
写生 しゃせい sketching [drawing] from nature; portrayal
写本 しゃほん manuscript, written copy
謄写 とうしゃ copy, reproduction, mimeograph
複写 ふくしゃ copy, duplication
書写 しょしゃ transcription, copying, handwriting
模写(=摸写) もしゃ copying, tracing, reproduction

記 ▷write down
キ しる(す)　　Ⓚ132

[original meaning] **write down, record, put down in writing**
記録 きろく record, document, chronicle; (new) record
記者 きしゃ journalist, reporter; editor
記事 きじ news, article; account
記入 きにゅう entry, record
記名する きめいする sign one's name, register
明記する めいきする write clearly, specify
登記 とうき registration, registry
下記の かきの following, undermentioned
表記する ひょうきする write, express in writing; write on a surface
標記する ひょうきする mark; write a title

紀 ▷record in writing
キ　　Ⓚ117

record [put down] in writing, record systematically, chronicle
紀要 きよう bulletin, proceedings
紀行 きこう travelogue

控 ▷note down
コウ ひか(える) ひか(え)　　Ⓚ0453

note down, write down, take notes
電話番号を控える でんわばんごうをひかえる jot down a phone number

録 ▷record
ロク　　Ⓚ155

ⓐ [original meaning] **record, write down, register**
ⓑ **record on tape**
ⓐ 記録する きろくする record, register, write down; set a record
収録する しゅうろくする collect, record, write down
登録 とうろく registration
ⓑ 録音 ろくおん sound recording
録音テープ ろくおんてーぷ tape (for recording)
録画 ろくが videotaping

登 ▷register
トウ ト のぼ(る)　　Ⓚ225

register, enter, record

登録 とうろく registration
登記 とうき registration, registry
登載 とうさい registration, record

註 ▷annotate
チュウ   Ⓚ1359

ⓐ annotate, explain with notes
ⓑ annotation, explanatory notes, comment

a 註釈 ちゅうしゃく annotation, note, comment
註解 ちゅうかい annotation, explanatory notes
註記 ちゅうき annotation, commentary
評註 ひょうちゅう commentary, notes and
     comments
脚註 きゃくちゅう footnote
b 標註 ひょうちゅう marginal notations

writing
文　筆　書　銘

文 ▷writings
ブン モン ふみ   Ⓚ1708

ⓐ [also suffix] **writings, composition, text, document**
ⓑ **written or spoken language**

a 文章 ぶんしょう writing, composition, essay; prose
文書 ぶんしょ(=もんじょ) document, letter, note
文献 ぶんけん literature, documentary records
文体 ぶんたい (literary) style
文房具 ぶんぼうぐ stationery, writing materials
論文 ろんぶん thesis, paper, treatise, dissertation
作文 さくぶん composition, essay; writing
原文 げんぶん text, original text
全文 ぜんぶん whole text
不文律 ふぶんりつ unwritten law [rule]
注文 ちゅうもん order, ordering; request
判決文 はんけつぶん judgment paper
起請文 きしょうもん written pledge
b 文法 ぶんぽう grammar
文句 もんく phrase, expression; complaint
和文 わぶん Japanese text

筆 ▷writing
ヒツ ふで   Ⓚ2335

ⓐ **writing, literary profession**
ⓑ **art of writing, calligraphy, penmanship**
ⓒ (something written) **writings, handwriting, writing,
composition**

a 文筆業 ぶんぴつぎょう literary profession, writing
b 筆力 ひつりょく power of the pen; ability to write
筆才 ひっさい literary talent
筆法 ひっぽう style of penmanship
筆跡 ひっせき handwriting, holograph
c 自筆 じひつ one's own handwriting

随筆 ずいひつ essay; stray notes

書 ▷writing(s)
ショ か(く) -が(き)   Ⓚ2314

❶ **writing, art of writing, calligraphy, penmanship**
書法 しょほう penmanship, calligraphy
書道 しょどう calligraphy, penmanship
書家 しょか calligrapher
❷ [also suffix] **writings, document, papers, certificate**
書類 しょるい documents, papers
書面 しょめん letter, document
文書 ぶんしょ(=もんじょ) document, letter, note
秘書 ひしょ secretary; treasured book
証明書 しょうめいしょ certificate, diploma

銘 ▷inscription
メイ   Ⓚ1536

[original meaning] (name or words inscribed on metal or
stone) **inscription, epitaph** (usu. written in classical
Chinese)
銘文 めいぶん inscription
碑銘 ひめい inscription, epitaph
墓碑銘 ぼひめい epitaph, inscription on a tomb-
     stone

writing →PARTS OF WRITING

writing strips
簡　竹

簡 ▷bamboo writing strips
カン   Ⓚ2374

[original meaning] **bamboo strips used for writing in
ancient China**
簡札 かんさつ wooden tag
竹簡 ちくかん bamboo writing strip

竹 ▷bamboo writing tablets
チク たけ   Ⓚ0201

**bamboo writing tablets used for recording history
in ancient China**
竹簡 ちくかん bamboo writing strip
竹帛 ちくはく history

written communications
状 文 翰 書 信 電 牒

状 ▷letter
ジョウ   Ⓚ0244

letter, note, card
- 書状 しょじょう letter, note
- 賞状 しょうじょう certificate of merit
- 招待状 しょうたいじょう letter of invitation
- 年賀状 ねんがじょう New Year's card
- 公開状 こうかいじょう open letter

文 ▷letter
ブン モン ふみ   Ⓚ1708

letter, note
- 文通 ぶんつう correspondence, exchange of letters
- 文面 ぶんめん contents of a letter

翰 ▷letter
カン

[now also 簡] **letter, note**
- 書翰 しょかん letter, correspondence
- 手翰 しゅかん letter
- 宸翰 しんかん imperial letter

書 ▷letter
ショ か(く) -が(き)   Ⓚ2314

(written message) **letter, note, message**
- 書簡 しょかん letter, correspondence
- 書状 しょじょう letter, note
- 投書 とうしょ contribution, letter (from a reader)
- 遺書 いしょ testamentary letter, will
- 私書箱 ししょばこ post office box (P.O.B.)
- 親展書 しんてんしょ confidential letter
- 一般教書 いっぱんきょうしょ State of the Union message

信 ▷written communication
シン   Ⓚ0084

written communication or message, letter, telegram
- 返信 へんしん reply, answer
- 短信 たんしん brief note [letter], brief message
- 私信 ししん private note [letter]
- 電信 でんしん telegraph, telegram

電 ▷telegram
デン   Ⓚ243

abbrev. of 電報 でんぽう: [also suffix] **telegram**
- 外電 がいでん foreign telegram, cablegram
- 打電する だでんする send a telegram, telegraph
- ロイター電 ろいたーでん Reuters dispatch

牒 ▷official notice
チョウ   Ⓚ094

official notice
- 通牒 つうちょう notification, circular
- 最後通牒 さいごつうちょう ultimatum

wrongdoing and evil
罪 非 邪 悪 弊

罪 ▷sin
ザイ つみ   Ⓚ226

sin
- 罪悪 ざいあく crime, sin, vice
- 罪業 ざいごう sin, iniquity
- 罪障 ざいしょう sins
- 原罪 げんざい original sin

非 ▷wrong(doing)
ヒ   Ⓚ079

wrong, wrongdoing, mistake
- 是非 ぜひ right and/or wrong; by all means, at any cost
- 前非 ぜんぴ one's past folly [sin]

邪 ▷wrong
ジャ   Ⓚ103

wrong, evil
- 無邪気 むじゃき innocence, simplicity
- 正邪の区別 せいじゃのくべつ discrimination between right and wrong

悪 ▷evil (something bad)
アク オ わる(い) わる- あ(し)   Ⓚ239

[also suffix] (something bad) **evil, badness, vice**
- 善悪 ぜんあく good and evil
- 諸悪 しょあく various evils
- 社会悪 しゃかいあく social ills
- 必要悪 ひつようあく necessary evil

弊 ▷evil(s) (something undesirable)
ヘイ   Ⓚ2508

(something undesirable) **evil(s), abuse**
- 弊害 へいがい evil, abuse, vice
- 悪弊 あくへい evil, vice, abuse
- 語弊 ごへい defects in expression, improper word
- 党弊 とうへい party evils

yang →YIN AND YANG

year

年   歳

年 ▷year
ネン とし   Ⓚ1752

ⓐ [also suffix] (period of revolution around the sun) **year, solar year**
ⓑ [also suffix] (period from January 1 to December 31 or equiv.) **year, calendar year**
ⓒ yearly, annual
ⓓ counter for years
ⓔ suffix indicating the chronological order of years in a given era

a
- 年年 ねんねん year by year, annually
- 太陽年 たいようねん solar year
- 火星年 かせいねん Martian year

b
- 年度 ねんど year, fiscal year; school year; term
- 年間 ねんかん period of one year
- 年月 ねんげつ years (and months), time
- 年月日 ねんがっぴ date
- 毎年 まいねん every year
- 去年 きょねん last year
- 新年 しんねん New Year
- 一昨年 いっさくねん(=おととし) the year before last

c
- 年金 ねんきん annuity, pension
- 年産 ねんさん yearly output, annual production
- 年収 ねんしゅう annual income

d
- 五十年 ごじゅうねん 50 years

e
- 千九百五十八年 せんきゅうひゃくごじゅうはちねん 1958
- 昭和六十年 しょうわろくじゅうねん sixtieth year of the Showa era (1985)

歳 ▷year
サイ セイ とし   Ⓚ2190

year
- 歳末 さいまつ year end
- 歳費 さいひ annual expenditure
- 歳月 さいげつ time
- 歳入 さいにゅう revenue, annual income
- 歳暮 せいぼ end of the year; year-end present

yellow colors
黄   金

黄 ▷yellow
コウ オウ き こ-   Ⓚ2177

[original meaning] **yellow**
- 黄色 こうしょく(=おうしょく) yellow
- 黄海 こうかい the Yellow Sea
- 黄金 おうごん gold; money
- 黄鉄鉱 おうてっこう iron pyrite, fool's gold
- 黄熱病 おうねつびょう yellow fever
- 卵黄 らんおう yolk
- 硫黄 いおう sulfur

金 ▷golden
キン コン かね かな- -がね   Ⓚ1771

golden, yellow
- 金色 きんいろ(=こんじき) golden color
- 金髪 きんぱつ blonde, golden hair

yesterday and today
今   昨

今 ▷today
コン キン いま   Ⓚ1712

today, today's
- 今夜 こんや tonight, this evening

昨 ▷yesterday
サク   Ⓚ0795

[also prefix] **yesterday, yesterday's**
- 昨日 さくじつ yesterday
- 昨晩 さくばん last night, last evening
- 昨夜 さくや last night
- 昨紙 さくし yesterday's paper
- 昨五月二日 さくごがつふつか yesterday, May 2
- 昨今 さっこん these days

yin and yang
陰　　陽

陰 ▷**yin**
イン　かげ　かげ(る)　　　Ⓚ0494

yin: **the female and passive principle in Chinese du-alistic philosophy representing negative concepts such as femininity, moon, darkness, earth, etc.**

　陰陽 いんよう yin and yang, positive and negative, active and passive

陽 ▷**yang**
ヨウ　　　Ⓚ0572

yang: **the masculine and active principle in Chinese dualistic philosophy representing positive concepts such as masculinity, sun, light, heaven, etc.**

　陰陽 いんよう yin and yang, positive and negative, active and passive

young
若　弱　少　青　幼　稚

若 ▷**young**
ジャク　ニャク　わか(い)　わか-　も(しくは)　も(し)　　　Ⓚ1928

[also 弱] **young**
　若年 じゃくねん youth, early age
　若輩 じゃくはい young people; greenhorn
　老若男女 ろうじゃくだんじょ(=ろうにゃくなんにょ) people of all ages and both sexes

弱 ▷**young**
ジャク　よわ(い)　よわ(る)　よわ(まる)　よわ(める)　　　Ⓚ1080

[also 若] **young**
　弱年 じゃくねん youth, early age
　弱冠 じゃっかん 20 years old; youth

少 ▷**young**
ショウ　すく(ない)　すこ(し)　　　Ⓚ2915

young
　少年 しょうねん boy
　少女 しょうじょ girl
　年少の ねんしょうの young, juvenile

青 ▷**youthful**
セイ　ショウ　チン　あお　あお(い)　　　Ⓚ215

youthful, young
　青春 せいしゅん bloom of youth
　青年 せいねん youth, young man
　青少年 せいしょうねん youth, young people

幼 ▷**very young**
ヨウ　おさな(い)　　　Ⓚ016

ⓐ very young, infant
ⓑ infantile, immature
a 幼児 ようじ young child, infant
　幼女 ようじょ baby girl
　幼時 ようじ childhood, infancy
　幼年 ようねん infancy, childhood
b 幼稚な ようちな childish, infantile, crude
　幼稚園 ようちえん kindergarten

稚 ▷**childish**
チ　　　Ⓚ111

childish, infantile, immature; very young
　稚気 ちき childishness
　稚拙な ちせつな childish, unskillful
　稚児 ちご infant, child
　幼稚な ようちな childish, infantile, crude
　幼稚園 ようちえん kindergarten

zero
零　　◯

零 ▷**zero**
レイ　　　Ⓚ243

zero, naught
　零度 れいど zero, freezing point
　零下 れいか below zero, sub-zero
　零時 れいじ twelve o'clock
　零敗 れいはい whitewash, being shut out
　零点 れいてん zero, no marks

 ▷**zero**
レイ　まる　ぜろ

zero (the numeral)
　電話二三◯の九四一一 でんわにさんれいのきゅうよんいちいち Phone 230-9411
　九◯字 きゅうじゅうじ 90 characters

ON-KUN INDEX
音 訓 索 引

The **On-Kun Index** lists the characters alphabetically by their *on* (Chinese-derived) and *kun* (native Japanese) readings. It offers a quick way to look up a **synonym group** from the reading of one of the characters it contains.

1. **Scope** This index lists all the readings given for each entry character (the **kanji synonym**). Readings identical in form (は¹, は²) or readings differing only in *okurigana* (ゆ(き), ゆき) appear only once.
2. **Format** *On* readings are given in katakana and *kun* readings are given in hiragana. *Okurigana* endings are not shown in parentheses. The tiny numerals to the left of the character column indicate the total stroke-count if a reading block has more than ten items. The text on the right lists the **group headwords** (separated by a middle dot) the character appears in.
3. **Order of entries** The characters are listed in *a-i-u-e-o* order of their readings. They appear in the following order: (1) *on* readings precede *kun* readings (アク, あく), (2) characters having the same reading are listed in increasing order of their total stroke-counts, and (3) characters with the same stroke count are further ordered by their radical numbers.

──────── あ ────────

ア	亜 continents · phonetic [a] · subordinate	
	阿 continents · phonetic [a]	
	堊 pigments	
	蛙 reptiles and amphibians	
あ	吾 first person pronouns	
アイ	哀 sad and depressed · sorrow · tender feelings for others	
	娃 beautiful	
	挨 push	
	愛 love · love and like	
	曖 dark	
あい	合 capacity units · combine · fit	
	相 appearance · high officials · mutual · phonetic [s]/[sh] · states and situations	
	藍 blue and purple colors · pigments	
あいだ	間 between · distance and interval · during · length units · rooms · time periods	
あう	会 assembly · ceremonies and festivities · legislature · meet · organized bodies · social gatherings	
	合 capacity units · combine · fit	
	逢 meet	
	遭 meet	
あえず	敢 brave · resolutely	
あえて	敢 brave · resolutely	
あお	青 blue and purple colors · green colors · young	

	襖 clothing · doors	
あおい	青 blue and purple colors · green colors · young	
	葵 flowering plants	
	蒼 blue and purple colors	
あおぐ	仰 respect · see and look	
	煽 incite	
あおる	煽 incite	
あか	赤 Communism · red colors	
あかい	赤 Communism · red colors	
あかす	明 bright · clear · evident · explain · intelligent and wise · later Chinese dynasties · light · next · vivid	
	飽 full	
あかつき	暁 morning and dawn	
あかね	茜 red colors	
あからむ	赤 Communism · red colors	
	明 bright · clear · evident · explain · intelligent and wise · later Chinese dynasties · light · next · vivid	
あからめる	赤 Communism · red colors	
あかり	明 bright · clear · evident · explain · intelligent and wise · later Chinese dynasties · light · next · vivid	
あがり	上 ascend · aspect · end · excellent and superior · give · high² · high-ranking · raise · tops	
あがる	上 ascend · aspect · end · excellent and superior · give · high² · high-ranking · raise · tops	

	挙	acts · appoint · behavior · hold an event · quote · raise	あご	顎	front parts of head
	揚	cook · cooked dishes · elated · praise · raise	あこがれる	憧	wish and desire
あかるい	明	bright · clear · evident · explain · intelligent and wise · later Chinese dynasties · light · next · vivid	あさ	麻	become stupefied · fabrics · fiber-producing plants
				朝	governments · Korea · long time periods · morning and dawn
あかるむ	明	bright · clear · evident · explain · intelligent and wise · later Chinese dynasties · light · next · vivid	あざ	字	characters · parts of towns
			あさい	浅	less in degree · light-colored
あき	空	aircraft and spacecraft · emptiness and nothing · gas and vapor · sky · vain	あざける	嘲	disdain
			あさひ	旭	sun
	秋	cold seasons	あざむく	欺	deceive
あきなう	商	earlier Chinese dynasties · industry and business · merchant · sell and trade	あざやか	鮮	Asian countries · evident · Korea · new · vivid
あきらか	明	bright · clear · evident · explain · intelligent and wise · later Chinese dynasties · light · next · vivid	あし	芦	kinds of grasses
				足	add · footwear · leg · suffice · supplement · walk
あきらめる	諦	discard and abandon		悪	bad · evil · hate and dislike · wrongdoing and evil
あきる	倦	tire			
	飽	full		脚	leg · limbs · walk
	厭	hate and dislike · tire		葦	kinds of grasses
あきれる	呆	foolish	あじ	味	essential content · flavor and elegance · taste
アク	堊	pigments	あじわう	味	essential content · flavor and elegance · taste
	悪	bad · evil · hate and dislike · wrongdoing and evil	あずかる	預	commit
	握	take	あずける	預	commit
	渥	kind	あずさ	梓	printing plate · trees
あく	明	bright · clear · evident · explain · intelligent and wise · later Chinese dynasties · light · next · vivid	あせ	汗	bodily secretions · excreta
			あせる	焦	burn · impatient
	空	aircraft and spacecraft · emptiness and nothing · gas and vapor · sky · vain		褪	discolor
			あそばす	遊	journey · play · wander
	開	begin · open · reclaim	あそぶ	遊	journey · play · wander
	飽	full	あだ	仇	enemy
あくた	芥	vegetables · waste	あたい	価	fee and price · value
あぐねる	倦	tire		値	fee and price · value
あくる	明	bright · clear · evident · explain · intelligent and wise · later Chinese dynasties · light · next · vivid	あたえる	与	give · participate and join
			あたかも	恰	exact
			あだする	仇	enemy
あけ	明	bright · clear · evident · explain · intelligent and wise · later Chinese dynasties · light · next · vivid	あたたか	温	hot · kind · raise the temperature
				暖	hot · raise the temperature
	緋	red colors	あたたかい	温	hot · kind · raise the temperature
あげ	揚	cook · cooked dishes · elated · praise · raise		暖	hot · raise the temperature
			あたたまる	温	hot · kind · raise the temperature
あけぼの	曙	morning and dawn		暖	hot · raise the temperature
あける	明	bright · clear · evident · explain · intelligent and wise · later Chinese dynasties · light · next · vivid	あたためる	温	hot · kind · raise the temperature
				暖	hot · raise the temperature
	空	aircraft and spacecraft · emptiness and nothing · gas and vapor · sky · vain	あたま	頭	counters for animals · head · leaders · tops
			あたらしい	新	calendars · new · recent · reform
	開	begin · open · reclaim	あたり	辺	approximately · areas and localities · edges and boundaries · lines and line segments · shores and watersides · side · the country
あげる	上	ascend · aspect · end · excellent and superior · give · high² · high-ranking · raise · tops			
				当	allot · collide · correspond to · pawn · present · strike · suitable · this and that · touch
	挙	acts · appoint · behavior · hold an event · quote · raise	あたる	当	allot · collide · correspond to · pawn · present · strike · suitable · this and that · touch
	揚	cook · cooked dishes · elated · praise · raise	アツ	圧	compel and press · energy and force · push · squeeze

	斡 turn		あや	綾 fabrics	
あつい	厚 kind · thick		あやうい	危 danger	
	暑 heat · hot · warm seasons		あやしい	妖 abnormal	
	熱 diseases and disease symptoms · eager · heat · hot · mania and maniacs · raise the temperature			怪 abnormal · doubt · supernatural and evil beings	
あつかい	扱 deal with · handle · treat and welcome		あやしむ	怪 abnormal · doubt · supernatural and evil beings	
あつかう	扱 deal with · handle · treat and welcome		あやつる	操 chastity · fidelity · handle	
あつまる	集 assembly · collection · compile · gather		あやぶむ	危 danger	
あつめる	集 assembly · collection · compile · gather		あやまち	過 elapse · exceeding and excess · mistakes and mistaking · pass	
あて	当 allot · collide · correspond to · pawn · present · strike · suitable · this and that · touch		あやまつ	過 elapse · exceeding and excess · mistakes and mistaking · pass	
	宛 indicate		あやまる	誤 mistakes and mistaking	
あてる	充 allot · fill · supplement			謝 apologize · monetary gifts · thanking and gratitude	
	当 allot · collide · correspond to · pawn · present · strike · suitable · this and that · touch			謬 mistakes and mistaking	
	宛 indicate		あゆ	鮎 fishes	
あと	後 after · be late and delay · future · rear · second		あゆむ	歩 area units · rate · walk	
	痕 marks and signs		あら	荒 barren · extreme in power · rash · violent	
	跡 marks and signs · trace			粗 bad · natural · rare and sparse · vulgar and unrefined	
	蹟 marks and signs			新 calendars · new · recent · reform	
あな	穴 holes and cavities		あらい	荒 barren · extreme in power · rash · violent	
あなどる	侮 disdain · disgrace			粗 bad · natural · rare and sparse · vulgar and unrefined	
あに	兄 siblings · titles of address		あらう	洗 clean and wash	
あね	姉 siblings		あらし	荒 barren · extreme in power · rash · violent	
あばく	暴 rash · reveal · sudden · violent			嵐 wind	
あばら	肋 bone		あらす	荒 barren · extreme in power · rash · violent	
あばれる	暴 rash · reveal · sudden · violent		あらそう	争 argue and discuss · compete	
あびせる	浴 baths · clean and wash		あらた	新 calendars · new · recent · reform	
あびる	浴 baths · clean and wash		あらたか	灼 burn	
あぶない	危 danger		あらたまる	改 change and replace · correct · reform · repeating and repetition	
あぶら	油 fats and oils · kinds of fuel · seasonings		あらためる	改 change and replace · correct · reform · repeating and repetition	
	脂 fats and oils		あらわす	表 diagram · express · outside	
	膏 fats and oils			現 appear · present · reveal · true	
あふれる	溢 flow and drip			著 books · compile · compose · conspicuous	
あま	天 god · posthumous worlds · rulers · sky · weather		あらわれる	表 diagram · express · outside	
	尼 clergymen			現 appear · present · reveal · true	
	雨 kinds of precipitation		ある	在 exist and be · stay	
あまい	甘 tastes · tolerant			有 exist and be · possess	
あまえる	甘 tastes · tolerant			或 a certain · some	
あます	余 after · exceeding and excess · first person pronouns · other · remain		あるいは	或 a certain · some	
あまやかす	甘 tastes · tolerant		あるく	歩 area units · rate · walk	
あまり	余 after · exceeding and excess · first person pronouns · other · remain		あるじ	主 god · husband · leaders · main	
あまる	余 after · exceeding and excess · first person pronouns · other · remain		あれる	荒 barren · extreme in power · rash · violent	
あみ	網 net · system		あわ	泡 small water masses	
	編 books · compile · organize · weave and sew			沫 small water masses	
あむ	編 books · compile · organize · weave and sew			粟 cereals	
あめ	天 god · posthumous worlds · rulers · sky · weather		あわい	淡 light-colored	
	雨 kinds of precipitation		あわす	合 capacity units · combine · fit	
	飴 confectionery		あわせる	会 assembly · ceremonies and festivities · legislature · meet · organized bodies · social gatherings	
				合 capacity units · combine · fit	
				併 combine · together	
				遭 meet	

ON-KUN INDEX

あわただしい	慌	busy
あわてる	慌	busy
あわれ	哀	sad and depressed · sorrow · tender feelings for others
	憐	tender feelings for others
あわれむ	哀	sad and depressed · sorrow · tender feelings for others
	憐	tender feelings for others
アン	安	calm and peaceful · comfortable · easy · inexpensive · peace
	行	acts · bank · behavior · direction indicators · do and act · execute · go and come · journey · linear arrangements · styles of Chinese characters
	杏	fruits and fruit trees
	按	push
	晏	late
	案	manuscript · plans and planning · think and consider
	庵	houses
	暗	dark · dark-colored · foolish · secret and private
	鞍	seat
	闇	dark · foolish
あんず	杏	fruits and fruit trees

い

イ	³己	discontinue
	⁵以	direction indicators
	⁶伊	European countries · phonetic [i]
	夷	savage
	衣	clothing
	⁷位	approximately · class · places and positions
	医	cure and recover
	囲	fences and walls · periphery · surround
	⁸依	rely on
	委	commit
	易	change and replace · divine · easy · sell and trade
	⁹威	dignified · power and authority · threaten
	為	benefit · cause and reason · do and act
	畏	fear · respect
	胃	internal organs
	¹⁰倭	Japan
	韋	kinds of skin
	¹¹唯	only
	尉	military officers and ranks
	惟	think and consider
	異	abnormal · differing and difference · foreign
	移	move
	萎	decay · die
	¹²偉	great
	斐	beautiful · phonetic [i]
	椅	seat
	¹³彙	collection
	意	meaning · thought · will and intention
	葦	kinds of grasses

	違	differing and difference · mistakes and mistaking · violate
	¹⁴維	threads and fibers
	¹⁵慰	console
	遺	forget · leave
	¹⁶緯	latitude and longitude · threads and fibers
	謂	speak and say
い	井	water sources
	亥	swine
	居	exist and be · houses · reside · sit
	猪	swine · undomesticated mammals
いい	好	good · love and like · personal relations
	良	good · virtuous
いう	云	similar · speak and say
	言	name² · speak and say · speech
	謂	speak and say
いえ	家	family and relations · houses · workers and professionals
いえる	癒	cure and recover
いおり	庵	houses
いが	毬	spherical object
いかす	生	animal · create · give birth · grow · healthy · life · live · new · reside · students and followers
	活	active · live
いかり	碇	weight
いかる	怒	anger
イキ	域	areas and localities · range
いき	行	acts · bank · behavior · direction indicators · do and act · execute · go and come · journey · linear arrangements · styles of Chinese characters
	息	breathe and blow · offspring · rest
	粋	clean and purified · elegant · essential part
いきおい	勢	armed forces · energy and force · power and authority · quantity and number · states and situations · tendency
いきどおる	憤	anger
いきる	生	animal · create · give birth · grow · healthy · life · live · new · reside · students and followers
	活	active · live
イク	育	grow · raise and nourish · teach
	郁	smell and fragrance
いく	行	acts · bank · behavior · direction indicators · do and act · execute · go and come · journey · linear arrangements · styles of Chinese characters
	逝	die
	幾	how many · some
いくさ	戦	compete · fight and war · game · warfare and rebellions
いくつ	幾	how many · some
いくら	幾	how many · some
いけ	池	lakes and marshes
いける	生	animal · create · give birth · grow · healthy · life · live · new · reside · students and followers
いこい	憩	rest

いこう	憩 rest		いびつ	歪 bend
いさぎよい	潔 clean and purified · purehearted		いぶす	燻 preserve food
いささか	些 few		いぶる	燻 preserve food
いさむ	勇 brave · courage		いま	今 present · this and that · yesterday and today
いし	石 capacity units · rock and stone		いましめる	戒 precept · take precautions · warn
いしずえ	礎 basis · bottoms and bases · supporting structures			誡 warn
いじめる	苛 trouble and suffering		いまだ	未 sheep · still · terms of negation
いずみ	泉 baths · water sources		いまわしい	忌 avoid and abstain · date · hate and dislike · mourn and mourning
いそ	磯 shores and watersides		いみ	忌 avoid and abstain · date · hate and dislike · mourn and mourning
いそがしい	忙 busy			
いそぎ	急 fast · hurry · steep · sudden · urgent		いむ	忌 avoid and abstain · date · hate and dislike · mourn and mourning
いそぐ	急 fast · hurry · steep · sudden · urgent			
いた	板 boards and plates		いも	芋 vegetables
いたい	痛 extreme in degree · trouble and suffering		いもうと	妹 siblings
いだく	抱 embrace · hold in the mind		いや	嫌 hate and dislike
いたす	致 cause · do and act			厭 hate and dislike · tire
いただき	頂 mountain parts · receive · tops		いやしい	卑 lowly · vulgar and unrefined
いただく	頂 mountain parts · receive · tops			賤 vulgar and unrefined
	戴 receive		いやしむ	卑 lowly · vulgar and unrefined
いたましい	痛 extreme in degree · trouble and suffering			賤 vulgar and unrefined
いたむ	悼 grieve · mourn and mourning		いやしめる	卑 lowly · vulgar and unrefined
	痛 extreme in degree · trouble and suffering			賤 vulgar and unrefined
	傷 grieve · harm and damage · injury		いやす	癒 cure and recover
いためる	痛 extreme in degree · trouble and suffering		いり	入 enter · need and necessity · participate and join · put in
	傷 grieve · harm and damage · injury			
いたる	至 arrive · direction indicators · most		いる	入 enter · need and necessity · participate and join · put in
イチ	一 a certain · all · one · only · same and uniform · small numbers			居 exist and be · houses · reside · sit
	壱 one			要 abridge · essential part · important · need and necessity · request
いち	市 cities and towns · market			
いちご	苺 fruits and fruit trees			射 emit · shoot
いちじるしい	著 books · compile · compose · conspicuous			煎 cook
イツ	一 a certain · all · one · only · same and uniform · small numbers			鋳 form and carve · work metals
			いれ	入 enter · need and necessity · participate and join · put in
	佚 losing and loss			
	逸 deviate · excellent and superior · losing and loss		いれる	入 enter · need and necessity · participate and join · put in
	溢 flow and drip			
いつ	五 five · small numbers		いろ	色 appearance · color¹ · expression · kinds and types · sex
いつくしむ	慈 kind · tender feelings for others			
いつつ	五 five · small numbers		いろどる	彩 color¹ · color²
いつわる	偽 deceive · false · falsehood		いわ	岩 rock and stone
いと	糸 threads and fibers			磐 bottoms and bases
いとう	厭 hate and dislike · tire			巌 rock and stone
いとしい	愛 love · love and like		いわう	祝 celebrating and congratulating
いとなむ	営 camps · direct and supervise		いわお	巌 rock and stone
いどむ	挑 incite		いわく	曰 speak and say
いな	否 refuse and reject · terms of negation		いわし	鰯 fishes
	稲 rice		いわれ	謂 speak and say
いぬ	犬 dog · domesticated mammals		イン	⁴允 permit
	戌 dog			引 lead and escort · pull · quote · subtract
	狗 dog			⁶印 Asian countries · mark · marks and signs · print and publish · seals
いね	稲 rice			
いのこ	豕 swine			因 cause and reason
いのしし	猪 swine · undomesticated mammals			⁹咽 throat
いのち	命 command · fate and fortune · life			姻 family and relations · marrying and marriage
いのる	祈 pray and worship			
	祷 pray and worship			胤 descendant
いばら	茨 needle · plants			音 kinds of sound · music and songs

	[10] 員	kinds of numbers • person in charge • width • workers and professionals
	院	legislature • organized bodies • places of worship • schools
	[11] 寅	tiger
	淫	sex
	陰	dark • genitals • moon • negative • sad and depressed • shadow • yin and yang
	[12] 飲	ingest
	[14] 蔭	shadow
	隠	hide • secret and private
	[19] 韻	kinds of sound • musical elements

う

ウ	[5] 右	left and right
	[6] 宇	buildings • roof • universe and space
	有	exist and be • possess
	羽	counters for animals • hair • wings
	[7] 佑	help
	迂	distant
	[8] 雨	kinds of precipitation
	[9] 宥	forgive
	胡	China
	祐	help
	[10] 烏	birds
う	卯	rabbit
	鵜	birds
うい	初	beginnings • first • original
	憂	sorrow • worry
うえ	上	ascend • aspect • end • excellent and superior • give • high[2] • high-ranking • raise • tops
うえる	飢	hunger and thirst
	植	farm and plant • plants • print and publish • reside
うお	魚	fish
うかがう	伺	inquire • visit
	窺	see and look
うがつ	穿	dig • wear and put on
うかぶ	浮	float
うかべる	浮	float
うかる	受	be subjected to • receive
うかれる	浮	float
うき	憂	sorrow • worry
うく	浮	float
うけ	受	be subjected to • receive
うけたまわる	承	agree and approve • succeed
うける	受	be subjected to • receive
	請	request
うごかす	動	active • behavior • feel deeply • incite • motion • move • set in motion
うごく	動	active • behavior • feel deeply • incite • motion • move • set in motion
うさぎ	兎	domesticated mammals • rabbit
うし	丑	cattle
	牛	cattle • domesticated mammals
うじ	氏	family and relations • name[1] • person • third person pronouns • titles of address
うしとら	艮	cardinal points

うしなう	失	losing and loss • mistakes and mistaking
うしろ	後	after • be late and delay • future • rear • second
うす	臼	vessels and receptacles
	碓	vessels and receptacles
	薄	few • less in degree • light-colored • rare and sparse • thin
うず	渦	running water
うすい	薄	few • less in degree • light-colored • rare and sparse • thin
うすまる	薄	few • less in degree • light-colored • rare and sparse • thin
うすめる	薄	few • less in degree • light-colored • rare and sparse • thin
うすら	薄	few • less in degree • light-colored • rare and sparse • thin
うすらぐ	薄	few • less in degree • light-colored • rare and sparse • thin
うすれる	薄	few • less in degree • light-colored • rare and sparse • thin
うそ	嘘	falsehood
うた	唄	music and songs
	歌	music and songs • poetry • sing
うたい	謡	music and songs
うたう	唄	music and songs
	歌	music and songs • poetry • sing
	謡	music and songs
	謳	praise
うたがう	疑	doubt
うち	内	during • inside • national • secret and private • wives
	打	strike
	家	family and relations • houses • workers and professionals
ウツ	鬱	sad and depressed
うつ	打	strike
	討	conquer and suppress • investigate and examine
	撃	attack • shoot • strike
うつくしい	美	beautiful • good • praise
うつす	写	copy • describe • photograph • project • write
	映	motion picture • project • shine and reflect
	移	move
うったえる	訴	request • sue
うつる	写	copy • describe • photograph • project • write
	映	motion picture • project • shine and reflect
	移	move
うつわ	器	containers • machines and tools • organ
うで	腕	hand and arm • limbs • skill
うとい	疎	estrange • rare and sparse
うとむ	疎	estrange • rare and sparse
うながす	促	hurry • urge
うね	畝	area units • hills
うば	姥	old persons
うばう	奪	steal and rob • take forcibly
うぶ	産	give birth • industry and business • make • merchandise • wealth
うま	馬	domesticated mammals • horse

うまや	厩 buildings	
うまる	埋 bury	
うまれ	生 animal · create · give birth · grow · healthy · life · live · new · reside · students and followers	

エ	会 assembly · ceremonies and festivities · legislature · meet · organized bodies · social gatherings
	回 return · send · time and time counters · turn
	依 rely on
	廻 return · turn
	恵 donate · favor
	彗 constellation
	絵 picture
	慧 intelligent and wise · wisdom

うまれる 生 animal · create · give birth · grow · healthy · life · live · new · reside · students and followers
産 give birth · industry and business · make · merchandise · wealth
うみ 海 sea
うむ 生 animal · create · give birth · grow · healthy · life · live · new · reside · students and followers
倦 tire
産 give birth · industry and business · make · merchandise · wealth
うめ 梅 flowering plants · fruits and fruit trees
うめる 埋 bury
うもれる 埋 bury
うやうやしい 恭 respectful
うやまう 敬 respect
うら 浦 inlets and bays · shores and watersides
裏 inside · rear
うらない 卜 divine
うらなう 卜 divine
占 divine · occupy
うらむ 恨 hate and dislike · regret
うらめしい 恨 hate and dislike · regret
うらやましい 羨 jealous and envious
うらやむ 羨 jealous and envious
うり 瓜 vegetables
うる 売 sell and trade
得 get · know and understand · profit
うるおう 潤 moisten · wet
うるおす 潤 moisten · wet
うるし 漆 black colors · pigments · trees
うるむ 潤 moisten · wet
うるわしい 麗 beautiful
うれい 愁 sad and depressed
憂 sorrow · worry
うれえる 愁 sad and depressed
憂 sorrow · worry
うれしい 嬉 pleased and pleasant
うれる 売 sell and trade
熟 attain proficiency · mature
うろこ 鱗 kinds of skin
うわ 上 ascend · aspect · end · excellent and superior · give · high[2] · high-ranking · raise · tops
うわさ 噂 stories
うわる 植 farm and plant · plants · print and publish · reside
ウン 云 similar · speak and say
耘 eliminate
運 carry · fate and fortune · handle · move
雲 kinds of atmospheric vapor

え 江 inlets and bays · rivers and streams
柄 aspect · handles · nature and character · pattern
重 accumulate · compound · extreme in degree · -fold · important · repeating and repetition · respect
榎 trees
餌 food
エイ [5]永 of long duration
[6]曳 pull
[8]泳 move through water
英 European countries · excellent and superior
[9]映 motion picture · project · shine and reflect
栄 great respect · prospering and prosperity
[11]彗 constellation
[12]営 camps · direct and supervise
瑛 precious stones
詠 recite
[15]影 image · shadow
鋭 intelligent and wise · sharp
[16]叡 intelligent and wise
穎 excellent and superior · inflorescences
衛 guard · protect
[17]翳 shadow
えがく 描 describe · draw
エキ 亦 additionally
役 benefit · employ · officials · warfare and rebellions · work and employment
易 change and replace · divine · easy · sell and trade
疫 disease
益 benefit · profit
液 liquid
腋 trunk parts
駅 places for landing or stopping · post station
えさ 餌 food
えだ 枝 branches and twigs
エツ 曰 speak and say
悦 pleased and pleasant
越 Asian countries · cross · exceeding and excess · excel

ON-KUN INDEX

	謁	meet
	閲	investigate and examine • revise
えのき	榎	trees
えび	蝦	crustaceans
えびす	夷	savage
えむ	笑	laugh
えらい	偉	great
えらぶ	撰	choose • compile
	選	choose • collection • vote and election
えり	衿	garment parts
	襟	garment parts • psyche
える	得	get • know and understand • profit
	獲	get • hunt and fish
エン	[4]円	circle • Japanese money denominations • round
	[8]奄	obstruct and hinder
	宛	indicate
	延	be late and delay • expand
	沿	near
	炎	diseases and disease symptoms • fire • hot
	苑	gardens • restaurant suffixes
	[9]怨	hate and dislike
	[10]宴	social gatherings
	晏	late
	[11]掩	cover and wrap
	[12]堰	embankment
	媛	woman
	援	help
	淵	kinds of water • stagnating water
	焔	fire
	[13]園	cultivated fields • gardens • restaurant suffixes • schools
	塩	lighter elements • seasonings
	煙	products of combustion
	猿	monkey • undomesticated mammals
	遠	distant • estrange
	鉛	metals
	[14]厭	hate and dislike • tire
	演	performance • speak in public
	鳶	birds
	[15]縁	edges and boundaries • family and relations • fate and fortune • marrying and marriage • personal relations
	[16]燕	birds
	[19]艶	beautiful • love • luster

お

オ	汚	dirty[1] • dirty[2] • disgrace
	和	familiar and friendly • Japan • peace • total
	烏	birds
	悪	bad • evil • hate and dislike • wrongdoing and evil
お	小	humble prefixes • schools • small and tiny • unimportant
	尾	body projections • ends • rear
	牡	man
	阿	continents • phonetic [a]

	御	honorific prefixes
	雄	brave • great • great persons • man
	緒	beginnings • ropes and lines
おい	笈	containers
	甥	offspring of siblings
おいる	老	Asian countries • honorific suffixes • old • old persons
オウ	[4]王	leaders • rulers
	[5]凹	bowed • holes and cavities
	央	middle
	[7]応	answer
	[8]往	go and come • old times
	押	compel and press • force to move • mark • push
	旺	strong
	欧	continents
	殴	strike
	[9]皇	rulers
	[10]桜	flowering plants • trees
	翁	honorific suffixes • man • old persons
	[11]凰	birds • mythical animals
	黄	yellow colors
	[12]奥	inner • inside • profound • wives
	[13]滉	profound • wide and extensive
	[15]横	acting arbitrarily • side
	[16]鴨	birds
	[18]襖	clothing • doors
	謳	praise
	[22]鷗	birds
	[24]鷹	birds
おう	生	animal • create • give birth • grow • healthy • life • live • new • reside • students and followers
	負	bear • lose • negative • undertake
	追	additional • add to • drive out • follow and pursue • remember
おうぎ	扇	incite
おえる	終	end • ends • last • throughout
おお	大	approximately • big and huge • extreme in degree • great • schools • size
おおい	多	plentiful
おおいに	大	approximately • big and huge • extreme in degree • great • schools • size
おおう	掩	cover and wrap
	蓋	cover and wrap
	覆	cover and wrap • overturn
おおかみ	狼	undomesticated mammals
おおきい	大	approximately • big and huge • extreme in degree • great • schools • size
おおせ	仰	respect • see and look
おおとり	鳳	birds • mythical animals
	鴻	birds
	鵬	birds • mythical animals
おおやけ	公	impartial • nobility • noblemen • public • public offices • society • the people • titles of address • widespread
おか	丘	hills
	岡	hills

おびる	帯	areas and localities • wear and put on
おぼえる	覚	awake • perceive • remember • sense
おぼれる	溺	sink
おも	主	god • husband • leaders • main
	面	aspect • face • front • front parts of head • outside • paper • parts of periodicals • protective coverings • side
おもい	重	accumulate • compound • extreme in degree • -fold • important • repeating and repetition • respect
おもう	思	think and consider
おもて	表	diagram • express • outside
	面	aspect • face • front • front parts of head • outside • paper • parts of periodicals • protective coverings • side
おもねる	阿	continents • phonetic [a]
おもむき	趣	flavor and elegance • meaning • will and intention
おもむく	赴	go and come
おもり	重	accumulate • compound • extreme in degree • -fold • important • repeating and repetition • respect
	錘	long slender objects • weight
おもんみる	惟	think and consider
おや	親	familiar and friendly • family and relations • main • parents
およぐ	泳	move through water
	游	move through water
および	及	additionally • arrive • extend over • make widely known
およぶ	及	additionally • arrive • extend over • make widely known
およぼす	及	additionally • arrive • extend over • make widely known
おり	折	bend • break • fold • occasions
	澱	stagnate • stagnating water
	織	fabrics • weave and sew
おりる	下	bad • bottoms and bases • descend and fall • diseases and disease symptoms • get off • give • low • lower • lowly
	降	descend and fall • get off • submit and surrender
おる	折	bend • break • fold • occasions
	居	exist and be • houses • reside • sit
	織	fabrics • weave and sew
おれ	俺	first person pronouns
おれる	折	bend • break • fold • occasions
おろか	愚	foolish • humble prefixes
おろし	卸	sell and trade
おろす	下	bad • bottoms and bases • descend and fall • diseases and disease symptoms • get off • give • low • lower • lowly
	卸	sell and trade
	降	descend and fall • get off • submit and surrender
おわる	畢	ends
	終	end • ends • last • throughout
オン	苑	gardens • restaurant suffixes
	怨	hate and dislike
	音	kinds of sound • music and songs

	恩	favor • thanking and gratitude
	温	hot • kind • raise the temperature
	遠	distant • estrange
	厭	hate and dislike • tire
	穏	calm and peaceful • gentle
おん	牡	man
	御	honorific prefixes
おんな	女	offspring • woman

か

カ	下	bad • bottoms and bases • descend and fall • diseases and disease symptoms • get off • give • low • lower • lowly
	4化	change and replace • disguise
	戈	cutting weapons
	火	days of the week • fire • weapons for shooting
	5加	add • add to • increase • North American countries • participate and join
	可	agree and approve • possible
	甲	first • protective coverings • shells
	禾	cereal
	6仮	false • temporary
	瓜	vegetables
	7伽	phonetic [k]/[g]
	何	how many • interrogatives • some
	花	flower
	8価	fee and price • value
	佳	beautiful • good
	果	execute • extreme • fruit
	河	rivers and streams
	加	vegetables
	苛	cruel • trouble and suffering
	9架	equip and install • flat supports
	珂	precious stones
	珈	drinks • phonetic [k]/[g]
	科	branch of study • units of learning
	迦	phonetic [k]/[g]
	10倭	Japan
	個	general counters • one
	夏	earlier Chinese dynasties • warm seasons
	家	family and relations • houses • workers and professionals
	華	Asian countries • beautiful • China • flower
	荷	bear • burden
	11菓	confectionery
	袈	clothing
	貨	burden • merchandise • money
	12渦	running water
	過	elapse • exceeding and excess • mistakes and mistaking • pass
	13嘩	loud
	嫁	in-laws • marrying and marriage • wives
	暇	holiday • leisure • time periods
	禍	misfortune and disaster
	靴	footwear
	14嘉	good fortune • praise
	寡	few • wives
	榎	trees

ON-KUN INDEX

かさなる	重	accumulate · compound · extreme in degree · -fold · important · repeating and repetition · respect
かさねる	重	accumulate · compound · extreme in degree · -fold · important · repeating and repetition · respect
かさむ	嵩	quantity and number
かざり	飾	decorate
かざる	飾	decorate
かし	貸	lend and borrow
	樫	trees
かじ	梶	parts of boats and ships · trees
	舵	parts of boats and ships
かしげる	傾	concentrate on · inclining toward · obliqueness and inclining · tendency
かしこい	賢	intelligent and wise · wise and talented persons
かしましい	喧	loud
かしら	頭	counters for animals · head · leaders · tops
がしら	頭	counters for animals · head · leaders · tops
かしわ	柏	trees
かす	貸	lend and borrow
かず	数	calculate and count · kinds of numbers · quantity and number · some
かすか	微	few · less in degree · small and tiny · unimportant
かすみ	霞	kinds of atmospheric vapor
かすむ	翳	shadow
	霞	kinds of atmospheric vapor
かすめる	掠	steal and rob
かずら	蔓	plants
かする	掠	steal and rob
かすれる	掠	steal and rob
かぜ	風	appearance · custom · disease · flavor and elegance · view · way and style · wind
かせぐ	稼	work
かぞえる	数	calculate and count · kinds of numbers · quantity and number · some
かた	方	approximately · areas and localities · direction · mathematical power · person · person in charge · plural suffixes · side · square · way and style
	片	one · one side · part
	形	form
	肩	trunk parts
	型	example · kinds and types · prototype
	潟	lakes and marshes
がた	方	approximately · areas and localities · direction · mathematical power · person · person in charge · plural suffixes · side · square · way and style
	形	form
	型	example · kinds and types · prototype
	潟	lakes and marshes
かたい	固	firm and obstinate · hard · not moving · solidify and coagulate
	堅	firm and obstinate · hard
	硬	firm and obstinate · hard

	難	blame and accuse · faults and flaws · misfortune and disaster · trouble and suffering
がたい	堅	firm and obstinate · hard
	難	blame and accuse · faults and flaws · misfortune and disaster · trouble and suffering
かたがた	旁	characters · near
かたき	仇	enemy
	敵	enemy
かたち	形	form
かたな	刀	cutting instruments · cutting weapons
かたまり	固	firm and obstinate · hard · not moving · solidify and coagulate
	塊	bodies
かたまる	固	firm and obstinate · hard · not moving · solidify and coagulate
かたむく	傾	concentrate on · inclining toward · obliqueness and inclining · tendency
かたむける	傾	concentrate on · inclining toward · obliqueness and inclining · tendency
かためる	固	firm and obstinate · hard · not moving · solidify and coagulate
かたよる	偏	inclining toward · one side
かたらう	語	language · speak and say · stories · words and expressions
かたる	語	language · speak and say · stories · words and expressions
	騙	deceive
かたわら	傍	additionally · near · side
がち	勝	excel · win
カッ	合	capacity units · combine · fit
	恰	exact
カツ	括	combine
	活	active · live
11	喝	give out a call · threaten
	渇	dry · hunger and thirst · wish and desire
12	割	break · cut · divide · rate · separate
	筈	certain
	葛	flowering plants
13	滑	move · smooth
	褐	brown colors
17	轄	direct and supervise
	闊	wide and extensive
かつ	且	additionally
	勝	excel · win
ガッ	合	capacity units · combine · fit
ガツ	月	days of the week · moon · weeks and months
かつぐ	担	bear · undertake
かつて	嘗	former · taste
かつら	桂	trees
かて	糧	food
かど	角	angle and angular measure · body projections · corners · square · three-dimensional shapes
	門	branch of study · doors · family and relations · parties and sects · students and followers

ON-KUN INDEX

かな	金	days of the week · metal · metals · money · yellow colors
	哉	classical particles
かなう	叶	accomplish
かなえ	鼎	three · vessels and receptacles
かなえる	叶	accomplish
かなしい	哀	sad and depressed · sorrow · tender feelings for others
	悲	grieve · sad and depressed · tender feelings for others
かなしむ	悲	grieve · sad and depressed · tender feelings for others
かなでる	奏	play music
かなめ	要	abridge · essential part · important · need and necessity · request
かならず	必	certain · need and necessity
かに	蟹	crustaceans
かね	金	days of the week · metal · metals · money · yellow colors
	矩	laws and rules
	鐘	bells
がね	金	days of the week · metal · metals · money · yellow colors
かねる	兼	additionally · together
かの	彼	third person pronouns · this and that
かのえ	庚	calendar signs
かば	椛	trees
	蒲	kinds of grasses
	樺	trees
かばう	庇	protect · roof parts
かばん	鞄	bags · containers
かび	黴	fungus
かびる	黴	fungus
かぶ	株	securities · supporting parts of plants
	蕪	vegetables
かぶと	兜	headgear · protective coverings
かぶら	蕪	vegetables
かぶる	被	wear and put on
かべ	壁	fences and walls · mountain parts
かま	釜	vessels and receptacles
	蒲	kinds of grasses
	窯	ceramics ware · heating devices
	鎌	cutting instruments
がま	蒲	kinds of grasses
かまう	構	make · structure · worry
かまえる	構	make · structure · worry
かます	噛	bite
かませる	噛	bite
かまびすしい	喧	loud
かみ	上	ascend · aspect · end · excellent and superior · give · high² · high-ranking · raise · tops
	神	god · holy · Kansai cities · psyche
	紙	paper · periodicals
	髪	hair
かみなり	雷	atmospheric discharges · projectiles and bombs
かむ	噛	bite
かめ	亀	reptiles and amphibians
かも	鴨	birds

かもす	醸	brew and ferment
かもめ	鴎	birds
かや	茅	kinds of grasses
	萱	kinds of grasses
かゆ	粥	rice
かよう	通	counters for flat things · go and come · inform and communicate · know and understand · pass · similar · throughout · ways and routes · widespread · wise and talented persons
から	空	aircraft and spacecraft · emptiness and nothing · gas and vapor · sky · vain
	唐	China · later Chinese dynasties
	殻	products of combustion · shells
がら	柄	aspect · handles · nature and character · pattern
	殻	products of combustion · shells
からい	辛	almost · tastes · trouble and suffering
	鹹	tastes
からす	枯	decay · die
	烏	birds
	涸	dry
からだ	体	appearance · bodies · body · essential content · form · object · organized bodies
からまる	絡	relate · wind and twine
からむ	絡	relate · wind and twine
からめる	絡	relate · wind and twine
かり	仮	false · temporary
	狩	hunt and fish
	雁	birds
がり	狩	hunt and fish
かりがね	雁	birds
かりる	借	lend and borrow
かる	刈	cut · harvest
	狩	hunt and fish
	駆	drive out · force to move · run · set in motion
かるい	軽	disdain · easy · less in degree
かれ	彼	third person pronouns · this and that
かれる	枯	decay · die
	涸	dry
かろやか	軽	disdain · easy · less in degree
かわ	川	rivers and streams
	皮	kinds of skin
	河	rivers and streams
	革	kinds of skin · reform
	側	side
がわ	側	side
かわかす	乾	dry
かわく	乾	dry
	渇	dry · hunger and thirst · wish and desire
かわす	交	alternate · change and replace · intercross · mix · personal relations
かわず	蛙	reptiles and amphibians
かわら	瓦	phonetic [k]/[g] · roof parts
かわり	代	change and replace · fee and price · generation · long time periods · substitute
	変	abnormal · change and replace · incident · warfare and rebellions

がわり	代	change and replace · fee and price · generation · long time periods · substitute
かわる	代	change and replace · fee and price · generation · long time periods · substitute
	変	abnormal · change and replace · incident · warfare and rebellions
	換	change and replace · repeating and repetition
	替	change and replace
カン	³干	dry · preserved foods
	⁵刊	editions · print and publish
	甘	tastes · tolerant
	甲	first · protective coverings · shells
	⁶汗	bodily secretions · excreta
	缶	containers · heating devices
	⁷完	all · end
	旱	dry
	肝	internal organs
	⁸侃	purehearted
	函	containers
	官	governments · officials · organ
	⁹冠	headgear
	巻	books · counters for books · wind and twine
	柑	fruits and fruit trees
	看	protect · see and look
	竿	counters for flat things · counters for long objects · long slender objects
	¹⁰栞	marks and signs
	莞	laugh
	陥	collapse · faults and flaws
	¹¹乾	dry
	勘	investigate and examine · sense · think and consider
	患	disease
	菅	kinds of grasses
	貫	penetrate · weight units
	¹²喚	call and invite · give out a call
	堪	bear and endure
	寒	cold · cold seasons
	嵌	put in
	換	change and replace · repeating and repetition
	敢	brave · resolutely
	棺	containers
	款	parts of writing · treat and welcome
	萱	kinds of grasses
	閑	leisure · leisurely · quiet
	間	between · distance and interval · during · length units · rooms · time periods
	¹³勧	advance · urge
	寛	tolerant
	幹	essential part · supporting parts of plants
	感	detect · feel deeply · feeling · perceive · sense
	漢	characters · China · Chinese · earlier Chinese dynasties · fellow
	¹⁴慣	custom
	管	direct and supervise · musical instrument · tubular passages
	綸	threads and fibers
	関	joint · obstacle · relate
	¹⁵歓	pleased and pleasant
	監	direct and supervise · prison
	緩	loosen · slow
	¹⁶憾	regret
	翰	written communications
	還	return · return and restore
	館	buildings · mansions · temporary quarters
	¹⁷環	circular objects · surround
	¹⁸簡	easy · short and shortened · writing strips
	観	opinion · see and look · view
	韓	Korea
	²⁰鹹	tastes
	²¹艦	boats and ships
	²³鑑	books · judge
	²⁷驩	pleased and pleasant
かん	神	god · holy · Kansai cities · psyche
ガン	³丸	all · circle · medicines · projectiles and bombs · round · spherical object
	⁴元	beginnings · element · former · later Chinese dynasties
	⁷含	contain and include
	⁸岸	shores and watersides
	岩	rock and stone
	玩	love and like · pleasure
	¹⁰莞	laugh
	¹¹眼	discernment · eye
	¹²嵌	put in
	雁	birds
	¹³頑	firm and obstinate
	¹⁷癌	diseases and disease symptoms
	¹⁸顔	expression · front parts of head
	¹⁹願	pray and worship · request · wish and desire
	²⁰巌	rock and stone
かんがえ	考	learn and study · think and consider · thought
かんがえる	考	learn and study · think and consider · thought
かんがみる	鑑	books · judge
かんばしい	芳	smell and fragrance
かんむり	冠	headgear

き

キ	²几	tables and stands
	³己	first person pronouns
	⁶企	plans and planning
	伎	performers
	危	danger
	机	tables and stands
	気	atmosphere · attention · breathe and blow · energy and force · feeling · gas and vapor · life energy · nature and character · phenomenon · psyche · signs · smell and fragrance · will and intention
	⁷岐	diverge · furcation · ways and routes

	吉 good fortune	
	迄 direction indicators	
	桔 plants	
	喫 ingest · take in	
	詰 blame and accuse · fill · inquire	
	橘 fruits and fruit trees	
きっさき	鋒 energy and force · extremity	
きつね	狐 undomesticated mammals	
きぬ	絹 fabrics	
きぬた	砧 instruments for beating or pounding	
きね	杵 instruments for beating or pounding	
きのこ	茸 fungus	
きば	牙 mouth parts	
きび	黍 cereals	
きびしい	厳 dignified · extreme in degree · strict	
きまる	決 decide · judge · resolutely	
きみ	君 rulers · second person pronouns · titles of address	
ぎみ	君 rulers · second person pronouns · titles of address	
ぎめ	決 decide · judge · resolutely	
きめる	決 decide · judge · resolutely	
きも	肝 internal organs	
キャ	伽 phonetic [k]/[g]	
	脚 leg · limbs · walk	
キャク	却 eliminate · refuse and reject	
	客 visitor · workers and professionals	
	脚 leg · limbs · walk	
ギャク	虐 cruel · torture and oppress	
	逆 opposite · resist	
きゃん	俠 brave	
キュウ	² 九 nine · small numbers	
	³ 及 additionally · arrive · extend over · make widely known	
	久 of long duration	
	弓 weapons for shooting	
	⁴ 仇 enemy	
	⁵ 丘 hills	
	旧 calendars · former · old	
	⁶ 休 discontinue · holiday · rest	
	吸 breathe and blow · take in	
	朽 decay	
	臼 vessels and receptacles	
	⁷ 求 request · seek · wish and desire	
	汲 take from water	
	灸 medicines	
	玖 nine · precious stones	
	究 investigate and examine · learn and study	
	⁸ 泣 cry and sigh	
	穹 sky	
	⁹ 急 fast · hurry · steep · sudden · urgent	
	柩 trees	
	級 class · class in school	
	糾 investigate and examine	
	¹⁰ 宮 governments · palace · places of worship	
	笈 containers	
	赳 brave	
	¹¹ 救 rescue	
	毬 spherical object	

	球 bodies · spherical object · three-dimensional shapes	
	¹² 給 pay and earnings · supplement · supply	
	¹³ 嗅 detect	
	鳩 birds	
	¹⁴ 厩 buildings	
	¹⁵ 窮 extreme · poor · trouble and suffering	
	¹⁷ 鞠 spherical object	
ギュウ	牛 cattle · domesticated mammals	
キョ	⁵ 巨 big and huge	
	去 die · elapse · eliminate · leave and set forth · most recent	
	⁸ 居 exist and be · houses · reside · sit	
	拠 basis · occupy	
	拒 refuse and reject	
	¹⁰ 挙 acts · appoint · behavior · hold an event · quote · raise	
	¹¹ 虚 emptiness and nothing · false · ruins · vain	
	許 forgive · permit	
	¹² 距 distance and interval	
	¹⁵ 嘘 falsehood	
	墟 ruins	
	¹⁶ 鋸 cutting instruments	
	²⁰ 醵 donate	
ギョ	梧 trees	
	魚 fish	
	御 honorific prefixes	
	馭 handle	
	漁 hunt and fish	
	禦 avoid and abstain	
きよい	清 clean and purified · clean and wash · clear · later Chinese dynasties · purehearted	
キョウ	⁴ 凶 crimes and offenses · cruel · evil · misfortune and disaster	
	⁵ 兄 siblings · titles of address	
	叶 accomplish	
	⁶ 兇 evil	
	共 Communism · plural suffixes · together	
	匡 correct	
	叫 give out a call	
	⁷ 亨 make progress	
	杏 fruits and fruit trees	
	狂 extreme in power · mania and maniacs	
	⁸ 享 possess · receive	
	京 cities and towns · Kansai cities · Kanto region · large numbers	
	供 offer · servants · supply	
	協 cooperate · organized bodies · promise	
	怯 fear	
	況 states and situations	
	⁹ 俠 brave	
	勁 hard	
	峡 inlets and bays · valley	
	挟 contain and include	
	狭 narrow	
	香 smell and fragrance	
	¹⁰ 恭 respectful	
	恐 fear	
	脅 threaten	
	脇 side · trunk parts	

胸 chest · psyche · trunk parts
11 強 compel and press · extreme in degree · hard · strong
教 places of worship · religion · teach
梗 close · obstruct and hinder
経 books · direct and supervise · elapse · latitude and longitude · pass · threads and fibers
郷 the country · villages and towns
12 卿 high officials · second person pronouns
喬 high¹
14 兢 fear
境 edges and boundaries · states and situations
15 蕎 cereals
鋏 cutting instruments
鞏 hard
16 橋 bridges
興 advance · pleasure · prospering and prosperity
頬 front parts of head
17 矯 correct
19 嚮 go and come
疆 edges and boundaries
鏡 machines and tools
20 競 compete
響 kinds of sound · make sound or noise
馨 smell and fragrance
22 饗 social gatherings

ギョウ 叶 accomplish
仰 respect · see and look
行 acts · bank · behavior · direction indicators · do and act · execute · go and come · journey · linear arrangements · styles of Chinese characters
形 form
尭 rulers
暁 morning and dawn
業 acts · fate and fortune · industry and business · learning and knowledge · work and employment
凝 solidify and coagulate
驍 brave

キョク 旭 sun
曲 bend · music and songs
局 board games · divisions of organizations · ends · part · public offices · states and situations
極 extreme · extreme in degree · most

ギョク 玉 money · precious stones · spherical object
きよまる 清 clean and purified · clean and wash · clear · later Chinese dynasties · purehearted
きよめる 清 clean and purified · clean and wash · clear · later Chinese dynasties · purehearted
きらい 嫌 hate and dislike
きらう 嫌 hate and dislike
きらめく 煌 shine and reflect
きり 切 cut · eager · extreme in degree
桐 trees

錐 cutting instruments · three-dimensional shapes
霧 kinds of atmospheric vapor
ぎり 切 cut · eager · extreme in degree
きる 切 cut · eager · extreme in degree
伐 conquer and suppress · cut
剪 cut
斬 cut
着 adhere to · arrive · clothing · settle · stick · wear and put on
截 cut
きれ 切 cut · eager · extreme in degree
ぎれ 切 cut · eager · extreme in degree
きれる 切 cut · eager · extreme in degree
きわ 際 between · edges and boundaries · occasions · on the verge of
ぎわ 際 between · edges and boundaries · occasions · on the verge of
きわまり 極 extreme · extreme in degree · most
窮 extreme · poor · trouble and suffering
きわまる 極 extreme · extreme in degree · most
窮 extreme · poor · trouble and suffering
きわみ 極 extreme · extreme in degree · most
窮 extreme · poor · trouble and suffering
きわめる 究 investigate and examine · learn and study
極 extreme · extreme in degree · most
窮 extreme · poor · trouble and suffering

キン 3 巾 fabric
4 今 present · this and that · yesterday and today
斤 weight units
7 均 same and uniform
芹 vegetables
近 approach · familiar and friendly · near · recent
8 京 cities and towns · Kansai cities · Kanto region · large numbers
欣 pleased and pleasant
金 days of the week · metal · metals · money · yellow colors
9 衿 garment parts
11 菌 fungus
菫 flowering plants
12 勤 exert oneself · work · work and employment
欽 respect
琴 musical instruments
筋 counters for long objects · flesh · line · reasoning · ways and routes
13 僅 few
禁 avoid and abstain · imprison and confine · restrain
禽 bird
15 緊 tighten · urgent
16 錦 fabrics
17 謹 careful · respectful
18 襟 garment parts · psyche

ギン 吟 recite
銀 bank · metals · money · white colors

━━━━ く ━━━━

ク	²九 nine · small numbers	
	³久 of long duration	
	口 doors · face orifices · holes and cavities · speak and say · speech	
	工 industry and business · make · workers and professionals	
	⁴区 areas and localities · parts of towns	
	⁵功 accomplishment	
	句 poetry · sentence and sentence parts · words and expressions	
	⁷玖 nine · precious stones	
	⁸供 offer · servants · supply	
	狗 dog	
	苦 tastes · trouble and suffering	
	⁹紅 cosmetics · red colors	
	¹⁰倶 together	
	宮 governments · palace · places of worship	
	庫 storehouse	
	矩 laws and rules	
	貢 offer · offering · tax	
	¹⁴駆 drive out · force to move · run · set in motion	
グ	弘 make widely known	
	具 machines and tools · possess	
	倶 together	
	惧 fear	
	毬 spherical object	
	愚 foolish · humble prefixes	
	鴻 birds	
くい	杭 perforators	
くいる	悔 regret	
クウ	空 aircraft and spacecraft · emptiness and nothing · gas and vapor · sky · vain	
	腔 holes and cavities	
	鞠 spherical object	
くう	食 food · ingest	
	喰 ingest	
グウ	宮 governments · palace · places of worship	
	偶 images · two	
	寓 express · stay · temporary quarters	
	遇 meet · treat and welcome	
	隅 corners	
くき	茎 supporting parts of plants	
くぎ	釘 perforators	
くさ	草 kinds of grasses · manuscript · styles of Chinese characters	
ぐさ	草 kinds of grasses · manuscript · styles of Chinese characters	
くさい	臭 lighter elements · smell and fragrance	
くさむら	叢 crowd · kinds of grasses	
くさらす	腐 decay	
くさり	鎖 close · ropes and lines	
くさる	腐 decay	
くされ	腐 decay	
くされる	腐 decay	

くし	串 perforators	
	櫛 comb	
くじ	籤 fate and fortune	
くしけずる	梳 comb	
くじら	鯨 undomesticated mammals	
くしろ	釧 circular objects	
くす	楠 trees	
	樟 trees	
くず	屑 waste	
	葛 flowering plants	
くずす	崩 break · collapse	
くすのき	楠 trees	
	樟 trees	
くすぶる	燻 preserve food	
くすり	薬 medicines	
くずれ	崩 break · collapse	
くずれる	崩 break · collapse	
くせ	癖 custom	
くせに	癖 custom	
くだ	管 direct and supervise · musical instrument · tubular passages	
くだく	砕 break · break into small pieces	
	摧 break	
くだける	砕 break · break into small pieces	
	摧 break	
くださる	下 bad · bottoms and bases · descend and fall · diseases and disease symptoms · get off · give · low · lower · lowly	
くだす	下 bad · bottoms and bases · descend and fall · diseases and disease symptoms · get off · give · low · lower · lowly	
くだり	下 bad · bottoms and bases · descend and fall · diseases and disease symptoms · get off · give · low · lower · lowly	
くだる	下 bad · bottoms and bases · descend and fall · diseases and disease symptoms · get off · give · low · lower · lowly	
くち	口 doors · face orifices · holes and cavities · speak and say · speech	
くちすすぐ	漱 clean and wash	
くちびる	唇 mouth parts	
くちる	朽 decay	
クツ	屈 bend · submit and surrender	
	掘 dig	
	窟 holes and cavities	
くつ	沓 footwear	
	靴 footwear	
くつがえす	覆 cover and wrap · overturn	
くつがえる	覆 cover and wrap · overturn	
くどい	諄 teach	
くに	国 country · feudal territorial divisions · Japan · national	
くばる	配 distribute · interest and dividend · worry	
くび	首 front · head · leaders · main · neck	
	頸 neck	
くびき	軛 long slender objects	
くぼ	窪 holes and cavities	
くぼまる	窪 holes and cavities	

くぼむ	窪	holes and cavities
くま	隈	corners
	熊	undomesticated mammals
くみ	組	class in school · groups · make · organize · organized bodies · ropes and lines · weave and sew
ぐみ	組	class in school · groups · make · organize · organized bodies · ropes and lines · weave and sew
くむ	汲	take from water
	酌	offer wine
	組	class in school · groups · make · organize · organized bodies · ropes and lines · weave and sew
くも	雲	kinds of atmospheric vapor
ぐも	雲	kinds of atmospheric vapor
くやしい	悔	regret
くやむ	悔	regret
くゆらす	燻	preserve food
くら	倉	storehouse
	蔵	possess · store · storehouse
	鞍	seat
くらい	位	approximately · class · places and positions
	昏	dark
	暗	dark · dark-colored · foolish · secret and private
ぐらい	位	approximately · class · places and positions
くらう	食	food · ingest
	喰	ingest
くらす	暮	evening and night · live
くらべる	比	arrange · Asian countries · compare · rate
くらます	晦	dark · days
くり	栗	fruits and fruit trees
くりや	厨	kitchen
くる	来	direction indicators · future · go and come · next
	繰	move · wind and twine
くるう	狂	extreme in power · mania and maniacs
くるおしい	狂	extreme in power · mania and maniacs
くるしい	苦	tastes · trouble and suffering
ぐるしい	苦	tastes · trouble and suffering
くるしむ	苦	tastes · trouble and suffering
くるしめる	苦	tastes · trouble and suffering
くるま	車	circular objects · kinds of railway · vehicle
くるわ	廓	periphery
くるわす	狂	extreme in power · mania and maniacs
くるわせる	狂	extreme in power · mania and maniacs
くれない	紅	cosmetics · red colors
くれる	呉	give
	暮	evening and night · live
くろ	黒	black colors · dark
くろい	黒	black colors · dark
くわ	桑	trees
	鍬	cutting instruments
くわえる	加	add · add to · increase · North American countries · participate and join
くわしい	詳	detailed
くわだてる	企	plans and planning

くわわる	加	add · add to · increase · North American countries · participate and join
クン	君	rulers · second person pronouns · titles of address
	訓	instruct · precept · teach
	勲	accomplishment
	薫	preserve food · smell and fragrance
	燻	preserve food
グン	軍	armed forces · groups · warfare and rebellions
	郡	territorial divisions
	群	crowd · groups

け

ケ	[4]化	change and replace · disguise
	[6]仮	false · temporary
	圭	corners
	気	atmosphere · attention · breathe and blow · energy and force · feeling · gas and vapor · life energy · nature and character · phenomenon · psyche · signs · smell and fragrance · will and intention
	[7]芥	vegetables · waste
	[8]怪	abnormal · doubt · supernatural and evil beings
	茄	vegetables
	[10]家	family and relations · houses · workers and professionals
	華	Asian countries · beautiful · China · flower
	[11]袈	clothing
	[12]稀	rare · rare and sparse
	[20]懸	hang · risk
け	毛	fabrics · hair
	蹴	strike
ゲ	下	bad · bottoms and bases · descend and fall · diseases and disease symptoms · get off · give · low · lower · lowly
	牙	mouth parts
	外	come off · deviate · eliminate · foreign · outside
	夏	earlier Chinese dynasties · warm seasons
	碍	obstruct and hinder
	解	answer · dismiss · disperse · explain · know and understand · liquefy · separate
	欅	trees
ケイ	[5]兄	siblings · titles of address
	[6]刑	punishment
	圭	corners
	[7]形	form
	系	lineage · parties and sects · system
	[8]京	cities and towns · Kansai cities · Kanto region · large numbers
	径	lines and line segments · ways and routes · width
	茎	supporting parts of plants
	[9]係	join · person in charge · relate
	勁	hard
	型	example · kinds and types · prototype
	奎	constellation

契 promise
計 calculate and count • measuring devices • plans and planning • total
10 恵 donate • favor
桂 trees
11 啓 speak humbly • teach
掲 display • print and publish • raise
渓 rivers and streams • valley
経 books • direct and supervise • elapse • latitude and longitude • pass • threads and fibers
蛍 bright • insects
12 卿 high officials • second person pronouns
敬 respect
景 states and situations • view
軽 disdain • easy • less in degree
13 傾 concentrate on • inclining toward • obliqueness and inclining • tendency
携 cooperate • hold
継 continue • related by marriage • succeed
詣 visit
14 境 edges and boundaries • states and situations
15 慶 celebrating and congratulating
慧 intelligent and wise • wisdom
憬 wish and desire
稽 think and consider
16 憩 rest
頸 neck
19 繋 join
警 guard • protect • take precautions • warn
鶏 birds
20 競 compete
馨 smell and fragrance

ゲイ 芸 art • performance
迎 treat and welcome
鯨 undomesticated mammals

けがす 汚 dirty¹ • dirty² • disgrace
けがらわしい 汚 dirty¹ • dirty² • disgrace
けがれる 汚 dirty¹ • dirty² • disgrace
ゲキ 戟 cutting weapons
隙 distance and interval • time periods
劇 performance
撃 attack • shoot • strike
激 extreme in degree • extreme in power • incite • sudden
けす 消 consume • destroy • disappear • extinguish
けずる 削 cut • decrease • dig • eliminate • polish and rub
梳 comb
けた 桁 kinds of numbers • supporting structures
ケツ ⁴ 欠 faults and flaws • omit • terms of negation
⁵ 穴 holes and cavities
⁶ 血 lineage
⁷ 決 decide • judge • resolutely
⁹ 頁 counters for flat things • paper
¹⁰ 桔 plants
¹¹ 訣 part company

12 結 combine • end • join • organize • solidify and coagulate
13 傑 conspicuous • excellent and superior • great persons
歇 rest
15 潔 clean and purified • purehearted
蕨 kinds of grasses
19 蹶 jump

ゲツ 月 days of the week • moon • weeks and months
けむい 煙 products of combustion
けむり 煙 products of combustion
けむる 煙 products of combustion
けもの 獣 animal
ける 蹴 strike
けわしい 険 danger • steep
嶮 steep

ケン ⁴ 犬 dog • domesticated mammals
⁶ 件 affair • general counters
⁷ 見 meet • opinion • see and look • show
⁸ 券 certificates • labels and slips
肩 trunk parts
⁹ 建 build
県 territorial divisions
研 learn and study • polish and rub
¹⁰ 倦 tire
倹 economizing and economy
兼 additionally • together
剣 cutting weapons
拳 hand and arm
軒 counters for houses • houses • roof parts
¹¹ 健 healthy • strong
捲 wind and twine
牽 pull
菅 kinds of grasses
険 danger • steep
¹² 喧 loud
圏 areas and localities • circle • range
堅 firm and obstinate • hard
検 detect • examination • investigate and examine
硯 kinds of stone
絢 beautiful
萱 kinds of grasses
間 between • distance and interval • during • length units • rooms • time periods
¹³ 嫌 hate and dislike
献 donate • offer • offer wine
絹 fabrics
遣 send
¹⁴ 縑 threads and fibers
¹⁵ 権 power and authority
¹⁶ 嶮 steep
憲 laws and rules
賢 intelligent and wise • wise and talented persons
¹⁷ 謙 humble
鍵 locks and keys
¹⁸ 繭 insect

顕 appear · conspicuous · evident · reveal
験 investigate and examine · potency · try
20 懸 hang · risk

ゲン

4 元 beginnings · element · former · later Chinese dynasties
幻 charm · illusory mental images
5 玄 profound
7 言 name² · speak and say · speech
8 弦 lines and line segments · musical instrument · ropes and lines
9 彦 name suffixes
限 extreme · restrain
10 原 natural · original · uncultivated expanses of land
11 現 appear · present · reveal · true
眼 discernment · eye
絃 ropes and lines
舷 parts of boats and ships
12 減 decrease · subtract
13 嫌 hate and dislike
源 beginnings · water sources
16 諺 words and expressions
17 厳 dignified · extreme in degree · strict
18 験 investigate and examine · potency · try
22 儼 dignified

こ

コ

3 乞 request
己 first person pronouns
4 戸 counters for houses · doors · houses
5 乎 modifier suffixes
去 die · elapse · eliminate · leave and set forth · most recent
古 old
8 呼 breathe and blow · call and invite · give out a call · name²
固 firm and obstinate · hard · not moving · solidify and coagulate
姑 in-laws
拠 basis · occupy
股 furcation · trunk parts
虎 tiger · undomesticated mammals
9 孤 alone · offspring
弧 lines and line segments
故 cause and reason · dead · former · incident · old
胡 China
枯 decay · die
狐 undomesticated mammals
10 個 general counters · one
庫 storehouse
11 涸 dry
虚 emptiness and nothing · false · ruins · vain
袴 clothing
12 壺 containers
湖 lakes and marshes
琥 precious stones
雇 employ
13 瑚 shells

誇 boasting and arrogance
跨 extend over
鼓 musical instruments
16 錮 imprison and confine
21 顧 remember · see and look

こ

子 child · Confucius and Confucianists · gentleman · interest and dividend · name suffixes · noblemen · nominalizers · offspring · particle
小 humble prefixes · schools · small and tiny · unimportant
木 days of the week · kinds of wood · tree
仔 offspring
粉 cereal · cosmetics · decorate · powder
黄 yellow colors

ゴ

4 五 five · small numbers
互 mutual
午 horse · noon
6 伍 five · groups · linear arrangements
7 冴 clear
呉 China · give
吾 first person pronouns
9 後 after · be late and delay · future · rear · second
胡 China
10 娯 pleasure
悟 awake · know and understand
11 梧 trees
12 御 honorific prefixes
期 expect · long time periods · time periods
13 瑚 shells
碁 board games
14 誤 mistakes and mistaking
語 language · speak and say · stories · words and expressions
16 醐 dairy products
17 檎 fruits and fruit trees
20 護 protect

こい

恋 love · love and like
濃 dark-colored · dense
鯉 fishes

こいしい

恋 love · love and like

コウ

3 口 doors · face orifices · holes and cavities · speak and say · speech
工 industry and business · make · workers and professionals
4 亢 elated
公 impartial · nobility · noblemen · public · public offices · society · the people · titles of address · widespread
勾 bend · catch a criminal
孔 Confucius and Confucianists · holes and cavities
5 功 accomplishment
叩 strike
巧 skillful
広 expand · make widely known · wide and extensive
弘 make widely known
甲 first · protective coverings · shells

こう

ゴウ

	¹¹強	compel and press • extreme in degree • hard • strong
	郷	the country • villages and towns
	¹³傲	boasting and arrogance
	業	acts • fate and fortune • industry and business • learning and knowledge • work and employment
	¹⁴豪	brave • continents • great • great persons • rich
	¹⁷壕	holes and cavities
	濠	holes and cavities
	¹⁸嚙	bite
	²¹轟	make sound or noise
こうむる	被	be subjected to • cover and wrap • wear and put on
	蒙	Asian countries • foolish
こえ	声	kinds of sound • repute
	肥	fatten
ごえ	越	Asian countries • cross • exceeding and excess • excel
こえる	肥	fatten
	越	Asian countries • cross • exceeding and excess • excel
	超	exceeding and excess • excel • extreme in degree
こおり	氷	kinds of frozen water • kinds of water
こおる	凍	reduce the temperature • solidify and coagulate
こがす	焦	burn • impatient
こがれる	焦	burn • impatient
コク	石	capacity units • rock and stone
	克	win
	告	inform and communicate • sue • warn
	谷	valley
	刻	form and carve • time periods
	国	country • feudal territorial divisions • Japan • national
	剋	win
	黒	black colors • dark
	穀	cereal
	酷	cruel • extreme in degree • strict
こぐ	漕	move through water
ゴク	極	extreme • extreme in degree • most
	獄	posthumous worlds • prison
こけ	苔	plants
こげる	焦	burn • impatient
こごえる	凍	reduce the temperature • solidify and coagulate
ここの	九	nine • small numbers
ここのつ	九	nine • small numbers
こころ	心	central parts • feeling • internal organs • middle • psyche
ごころ	心	central parts • feeling • internal organs • middle • psyche
こころざし	志	will and intention
こころざす	志	will and intention
こころみる	試	examination • try
こころよい	快	cure and recover • excellent and superior • fast • pleased and pleasant
こし	腰	trunk parts

	輿	vehicle
ごし	越	Asian countries • cross • exceeding and excess • excel
こす	越	Asian countries • cross • exceeding and excess • excel
	超	exceeding and excess • excel • extreme in degree
こずえ	梢	branches and twigs • extremity
こたえ	答	answer
こたえる	応	answer
	答	answer
コツ	乞	request
	忽	immediate
	骨	bone
	惚	love and like
	滑	move • smooth
こと	言	name² • speak and say • speech
	事	abstract thing • affair • affairs • incident • nominalizers • officials
	殊	special
	異	abnormal • differing and difference • foreign
	琴	musical instruments
	箏	musical instruments
ことごとく	悉	all
ごとし	如	modifier suffixes • similar
ことなる	異	abnormal • differing and difference • foreign
ごとに	毎	all
ことぶき	寿	age • celebrating and congratulating • life
ことわざ	諺	words and expressions
ことわる	断	cut • decide • discontinue • refuse and reject • resolutely
こな	粉	cereal • cosmetics • decorate • powder
この	此	this and that
	斯	this and that
このむ	好	good • love and like • personal relations
こばむ	拒	refuse and reject
こび	媚	charm
こびる	媚	charm
こぶし	拳	hand and arm
こぼす	溢	flow and drip
こぼれる	溢	flow and drip
こま	駒	horse
こまか	細	detailed • small and tiny • thin • unimportant
こまかい	細	detailed • small and tiny • thin • unimportant
こまる	困	trouble and suffering
こみ	込	enter • put in
ごみ	芥	vegetables • waste
	塵	waste
こむ	込	enter • put in
	混	disordered • mix
こめ	米	cereals • continents • length units • North American countries • rice
こめる	込	enter • put in
こもる	籠	containers
こやし	肥	fatten
こやす	肥	fatten

こよみ 暦 calendars
こらしめる 懲 punishment
こらす 凝 solidify and coagulate
懲 punishment
こり 梱 join
こりる 懲 punishment
こる 凝 solidify and coagulate
これ 之 possessive particles · this and that
此 this and that
是 this and that
惟 think and consider
ころ 頃 approximately · short time periods · time periods
ごろ 頃 approximately · short time periods · time periods
ころがす 転 change and replace · move · overturn · turn
ころがる 転 change and replace · move · overturn · turn
ころげる 転 change and replace · move · overturn · turn
ごろし 殺 kill
ころす 殺 kill
ころぶ 転 change and replace · move · overturn · turn
ころも 衣 clothing
こわ 声 kinds of sound · repute
こわい 怖 fear
こわがる 怖 fear
こわす 毀 break
壊 break
こわれる 壊 break
コン ⁴今 present · this and that · yesterday and today
⁶艮 cardinal points
⁷困 trouble and suffering
⁸昆 insect
昏 dark
金 days of the week · metal · metals · money · yellow colors
⁹建 build
恨 hate and dislike · regret
¹⁰根 basis · beginnings · supporting parts of plants
¹¹婚 marrying and marriage
梱 join
混 disordered · mix
痕 marks and signs
紺 blue and purple colors
菫 flowering plants
¹²渾 all
¹³献 donate · offer · offer wine
¹⁴魂 psyche
¹⁶墾 reclaim
¹⁷懇 eager · familiar and friendly · kind
ゴン 艮 cardinal points
芹 vegetables
言 name² · speak and say · speech
欣 pleased and pleasant

勤 exert oneself · work · work and employment
権 power and authority
厳 dignified · extreme in degree · strict

━━━━━ さ ━━━━━

サ ³叉 furcation · phonetic [s]/[sh]
⁵左 Communism · left and right
⁶再 repeating and repetition
⁷佐 help · military officers and ranks
作 compose · create · do and act · farm and plant · make
沙 phonetic [s]/[sh] · sand
⁸些 few
⁹査 investigate and examine
砂 sand
茶 brown colors · drinks
¹⁰唆 incite
差 differing and difference · intercross
紗 fabrics
¹²詐 deceive
¹³嵯 bowed
蓑 clothing
裟 clothing
¹⁴瑳 polish and rub
¹⁸鎖 close · ropes and lines
さ 早 fast
ザ 坐 sit
座 flat supports · places and positions · seat · sit · stars
挫 break
嵯 bowed
サイ ³才 age · skill · wise and talented persons
⁴切 cut · eager · extreme in degree
⁶再 repeating and repetition
西 cardinal points · European countries · phonetic [s]/[sh] · west
⁷災 misfortune and disaster
⁸妻 wives
采 gather
⁹哉 classical particles
砕 break · break into small pieces
¹⁰宰 direct and supervise · high officials
晒 discolor · reveal
栽 farm and plant · plants
柴 kinds of wood
殺 kill
財 money · wealth
¹¹偲 remember
彩 color¹ · color²
採 choose · gather · harvest
済 end · help · pay · rescue
砦 strongholds
祭 ceremonies and festivities
細 detailed · small and tiny · thin · unimportant
菜 plants · vegetables
斎 ceremonies and festivities · pray and worship · rooms

ON-KUN INDEX

ヂツ	雑	disordered · mix · various
と	里	length units · the country · villages and towns · vulgar and unrefined
さとい	聡	intelligent and wise
さとす	諭	teach · warn
さとる	悟	awake · know and understand
さばく	裁	court · cut · judge
さび	寂	quiet · sad and depressed
	錆	decay
さびしい	寂	quiet · sad and depressed
	淋	diseases and disease symptoms · sad and depressed
さびる	錆	decay
さびれる	寂	quiet · sad and depressed
さま	様	kinds and types · pattern · similar · states and situations · titles of address · way and style
さます	冷	cold · reduce the temperature
	覚	awake · perceive · remember · sense
さまたげる	妨	obstruct and hinder
さみしい	淋	diseases and disease symptoms · sad and depressed
さむい	寒	cold · cold seasons
さむらい	侍	accompany · soldiers and warriors
さめ	雨	kinds of precipitation
	鮫	fishes
さめる	冷	cold · reduce the temperature
	覚	awake · perceive · remember · sense
さや	鞘	containers
さら	皿	vessels and receptacles
	更	additionally · change and replace · reform
さらける	曝	reveal
さらす	晒	discolor · reveal
	曝	reveal
さらに	更	additionally · change and replace · reform
さる	去	die · elapse · eliminate · leave and set forth · most recent
	猿	monkey · undomesticated mammals
さわ	沢	lakes and marshes · luster · plentiful
さわぐ	騒	loud · make sound or noise
さわやか	爽	pleased and pleasant
さわる	触	touch
	障	obstacle · obstruct and hinder
サン	3 三	small numbers · three
	山	mine · mountains
	8 参	compare · go and come · participate and join · three · visit
	10 桟	bridges · long slender objects
	蚕	insects
	11 惨	cruel · sad and depressed
	産	give birth · industry and business · make · merchandise · wealth
	12 喰	ingest
	散	disperse · spread · unrestrained
	14 算	calculate and count
	酸	lighter elements · sour substances · tastes
	15 撰	choose · compile
	撒	spread
	賛	agree and approve · praise · support
	17 燦	bright
	20 纂	compile

	22 讃	praise
ザン	残	cruel · leave · remain
	惨	cruel · sad and depressed
	斬	cut
	暫	short time periods · temporary

— し —

シ	3 之	possessive particles · this and that
	士	gentleman · soldiers and warriors · workers and professionals
	子	child · Confucius and Confucianists · gentleman · interest and dividend · name suffixes · noblemen · nominalizers · offspring · particle
	尸	body
	巳	snake
	4 支	bear · branch · China · pay · support
	止	discontinue · not moving · prevent · stop
	氏	family and relations · name[1] · person · third person pronouns · titles of address
	5 仕	do and act · work
	仔	offspring
	史	history · records
	只	ordinary
	司	direct and supervise · officials
	四	small numbers
	市	cities and towns · market
	矢	projectiles and bombs
	示	indicate · show
	6 弛	loosen
	旨	essential part · meaning
	次	kinds of numbers · next · order · second · subordinate
	此	this and that
	死	die
	糸	threads and fibers
	自	direction indicators · first person pronouns
	至	arrive · direction indicators · most
	7 伺	inquire · visit
	孜	exert oneself
	志	will and intention
	私	first person pronouns · secret and private
	豕	swine
	8 使	agents · employ · use
	刺	kill · needle · stab
	姉	siblings
	始	begin · beginnings
	枝	branches and twigs
	祀	pray and worship
	祉	happiness
	肢	limbs
	9 姿	appearance · form · posture
	屍	body
	思	think and consider
	指	hand and arm · indicate · instruct
	施	donate · execute
	柿	fruits and fruit trees
	祇	god · phonetic [k]/[g]

ON-KUN INDEX

シュ		醬 seasonings
	4 手	hand and arm · handles · means · workers and professionals
	5 主	god · husband · leaders · main
	6 守	guard · obey · protect
	朱	red colors
	8 取	get · steal and rob · take
	9 柊	trees
	狩	hunt and fish
	首	front · head · leaders · main · neck
	10 修	cultivate · phonetic [s]/[sh] · repair
	株	supporting parts of plants
	殊	special
	珠	precious stones
	酒	drinks
	12 衆	crowd · plural suffixes · the people
	13 腫	swell and swelling
	14 種	early states of plant life · kinds and types
	15 撞	strike
	諏	argue and discuss
	趣	flavor and elegance · meaning · will and intention
	22 鬚	hair
ジュ	7 寿	age · celebrating and congratulating · life
	8 受	be subjected to · receive
	呪	pray and worship
	10 従	accompany · follow and pursue · obey · servants · subordinate
	11 授	give · teach
	12 就	begin
	13 頌	praise
	14 竪	vertical
	聚	gather
	誦	recite
	需	need and necessity
	16 儒	religions and sects
	樹	tree
	17 濡	wet
	18 雛	bird
	23 鷲	birds
シュウ	4 収	gather · get · pay and earnings · receive · take forcibly · take in
	5 囚	prisoner
	6 州	elevations in water · shoals · territorial divisions
	舟	boats and ships
	7 秀	excellent and superior · wise and talented persons
	8 周	earlier Chinese dynasties · periphery
	宗	parties and sects · religion
	9 拾	get · raise · ten
	柊	trees
	洲	elevations in water
	祝	celebrating and congratulating
	秋	cold seasons
	臭	lighter elements · smell and fragrance
	10 修	cultivate · phonetic [s]/[sh] · repair
	袖	garment parts
	11 執	adhere to · execute · take
	終	end · ends · last · throughout

	羞	disgrace
	習	custom · learn and study
	脩	meat
	週	weeks and months
	12 就	begin
	萩	flowering plants · shrubs
	葺	cover and wrap
	衆	crowd · plural suffixes · the people
	集	assembly · collection · compile · gather
	13 愁	sad and depressed
	蒐	gather
	酬	compensate · offer wine
	14 聚	gather
	16 輯	compile
	17 鍬	cutting instruments
	19 繡	weave and sew
	蹴	strike
	22 襲	attack
	23 鷲	birds
ジュウ	2 十	small numbers · ten
	4 中	between · China · Chinese · during · inside · middle · schools · second · throughout
	廿	small numbers
	5 汁	drinks · liquid
	6 充	allot · fill · supplement
	7 住	houses · reside
	9 拾	get · raise · ten
	柔	gentle · soft · weak
	重	accumulate · compound · extreme in degree · -fold · important · repeating and repetition · respect
	10 従	accompany · follow and pursue · obey · servants · subordinate
	11 渋	restrain · stagnate · tastes
	14 銃	weapons for shooting
	16 獣	animal
	縦	vertical
しゅうと	姑	in-laws
しゅうとめ	姑	in-laws
シュク	叔	siblings of parents
	祝	celebrating and congratulating
	宿	post station · stay · temporary quarters
	淑	elegant
	粛	clean and wash · dignified · quiet
	粥	rice
	縮	contract and shrink · decrease
ジュク	塾	schools
	熟	attain proficiency · mature
シュツ	出	appear · attend · begin · emit · go and come · leave and set forth · protrude and protruding
ジュッ	十	small numbers · ten
ジュツ	戌	dog
	述	speak and say
	術	art
シュン	6 旬	weeks and months
	9 俊	intelligent and wise · wise and talented persons
	春	sex · warm seasons
	10 峻	high[1] · steep · strict

渉 cross • move through water • relate
章 insignia • parts of writing • prizes
笙 musical instruments
紹 mediating and mediators
菖 flowering plants
訟 sue
12 勝 excel • win
掌 direct and supervise • hand and arm
晶 precious stones
湘 Kanto region
焦 burn • impatient
焼 burn • cook • cooked dishes • work metals
硝 nitrogen
粧 decorate
翔 fly
装 clothing • decorate • disguise • equip and install • wear and put on
証 certificates
詔 imperial decree
象 imitate • phenomenon • undomesticated mammals
13 傷 grieve • harm and damage • injury
剿 destroy
奬 advance
照 compare • light • shine and reflect
詳 detailed
頌 praise
14 嘗 former • taste
彰 praise
摺 polish and rub
精 bodily secretions • careful • clean and purified • detailed • essential part • exert oneself • life energy • psyche • refine • reproductive cells • supernatural and evil beings
蔣 cereals
裳 clothing
誦 recite
障 obstacle • obstruct and hinder
15 憧 wish and desire
樟 trees
蕉 fruits and fruit trees
衝 collide
賞 praise • prizes
銷 consume
16 鞘 containers
17 償 compensate • pay
牆 fences and walls
礁 elevations in water • shoals
篠 bamboo
18 醬 seasonings
20 鐘 bells

ジョウ 3 丈 height • length units • strong
上 ascend • aspect • end • excellent and superior • give • high[2] • high-ranking • raise • tops
4 冗 exceeding and excess
6 丞 assistant
成 accomplish • grow • make • mature
7 条 line • parts of writing

杖 long slender objects
状 certificates • form • states and situations • written communications
8 定 constant • decide • not moving
帖 notebook
9 乗 get on • mathematical power • multiply • travel by vehicle • vehicle
城 strongholds
浄 clean and purified • clean and wash
茸 fungus
10 晟 bright
11 剰 exceeding and excess
常 constant • ordinary
情 feeling • love • sex • states and situations • tender feelings for others
捷 fast
盛 accumulate • prospering and prosperity
12 場 market • parts of plays • places and positions • range • sports fields
畳 fold • mats • repeating and repetition
13 蒸 cook • vaporize
14 嘗 former • taste
濯 clean and wash
静 calm and peaceful • not moving • quiet
15 縄 ropes and lines
鄭 courteous
16 壤 land and soil
嬢 titles of address • woman • workers and professionals
錠 locks and keys • medicines
18 穰 plentiful
20 譲 compromise • transfer
醸 brew and ferment
21 饒 plentiful

ショク 6 色 appearance • color[1] • expression • kinds and types • sex
9 拭 clean and wash
食 food • ingest
11 埴 land and soil
12 植 farm and plant • plants • print and publish • reside
殖 give birth • increase
13 触 touch
飾 decorate
15 嘱 commit • request
蝕 decrease
17 燭 light
18 織 fabrics • weave and sew
職 work and employment

ジョク 辱 disgrace

しら 白 emptiness and nothing • European countries • white colors

しらせる 知 inform and communicate • know and understand • learning and knowledge • perceive • wisdom

しらべ 調 cooperate • investigate and examine • make • musical elements • music and songs • prepare • states and situations • way and style

す

ON-KUN INDEX

	[13] 跡	marks and signs • trace
	[14] 碩	great
	[16] 積	accumulate • load • quantity and number
	[17] 績	accomplishment • weave and sew
	藉	step on
	[18] 蹟	marks and signs
	[20] 籍	books • notebook
せき	堰	embankment
	関	joint • obstacle • relate
ぜき	関	joint • obstacle • relate
せく	堰	embankment
セチ	節	economizing and economy • fidelity • joint•labels•and•slips•music•and•songs•occasions•parts•of writing•sentence•and•sentence•parts•time•periods
セツ	[4] 切	cut • eager • extreme in degree
	[7] 折	bend • break • fold • occasions
	[8] 刹	phonetic [s]/[sh] • places of worship
	拙	humble prefixes
	[9] 窃	steal and rob
	[10] 屑	waste
	殺	kill
	[11] 接	approach • join • touch • treat and welcome
	設	build • equip and install • found
	雪	kinds of frozen water • kinds of precipitation
	[13] 摂	substitute • take in
	節	economizing and economy • fidelity • joint • labels and slips • music and songs • occasions • parts of writing • sentence and sentence parts • time periods
	[14] 截	cut
	説	advocate • explain • opinion • stories • theory
ゼツ	舌	mouth parts • speech
	絶	come to an end • discontinue • end • excellent and superior
ぜに	銭	fee and price • Japanese money denominations • money
せばまる	狭	narrow
せばめる	狭	narrow
せまい	狭	narrow
せまる	迫	approach • compel and press • torture and oppress • urgent
せみ	蝉	insects
せめる	攻	attack • learn and study
	責	blame and accuse • responsibility • torture and oppress
せり	芹	vegetables
せる	競	compete
ぜろ	○	zero
セン	[3] 千	large numbers
	川	rivers and streams
	[5] 仙	religious persons
	占	divine • occupy
	[6] 先	before • extremity • former • in front • most recent • sharp
	尖	extremity • sharp
	[9] 宣	imperial decree • inform and communicate

	専	acting arbitrarily • occupy • special
	染	color[2] • dirty[1]
	洗	clean and wash
	浅	less in degree • light-colored
	泉	baths • water sources
	穿	dig • wear and put on
	茜	red colors
	[10] 扇	incite
	栓	stoppers
	閃	shine and reflect
	[11] 剪	cut
	旋	turn
	船	aircraft and spacecraft • boats and ships
	釧	circular objects
	[12] 揃	arrange • fit
	[13] 戦	compete • fight and war • game • warfare and rebellions
	煎	cook
	羨	jealous and envious
	詮	explain
	践	execute
	[14] 煽	incite
	箋	paper
	銑	iron and steel
	銓	think and consider
	銭	fee and price • Japanese money denominations • money
	[15] 撰	choose • compile
	潜	boats and ships • hide • sink
	線	line • lines and line segments • ropes and lines • ways and routes
	賤	vulgar and unrefined
	遷	change and replace • move
	選	choose • collection • vote and election
	[16] 擅	acting arbitrarily
	薦	mats • recommend
	[17] 繊	thin • threads and fibers
	鮮	Asian countries • evident • Korea • new • vivid
	[18] 蟬	insects
	[23] 籤	fate and fortune
ゼン	全	all
	前	before • former • front • in front
	善	good • moral goodness • virtuous
	然	conditional conjunctions • modifier suffixes • terms of assent
	禅	religions and sects
	漸	in succession
	膳	food • vessels and receptacles
	繕	repair

そ

ソ	[8] 岨	steep
	沮	obstruct and hinder
	狙	target
	阻	obstruct and hinder
	[10] 租	tax
	素	basis • element • naked • original • plain and simple

¹¹措 deal with · put
梳 comb
粗 bad · natural · rare and sparse · vulgar and unrefined
組 class in school · groups · make · organize · organized bodies · ropes and lines · weave and sew
¹²甦 return and restore
疏 pass
疎 estrange · rare and sparse
訴 request · sue
¹³塑 form and carve · soft
想 think and consider · thought
楚 clean and purified
鼠 undomesticated mammals
¹⁴遡 move through water
¹⁵噌 seasonings
¹⁸礎 basis · bottoms and bases · supporting structures
¹⁹蘇 return and restore
曽 family and relations · former
沿 near

ゾ
ぞい
ソウ

⁴双 two
爪 ungual
⁶争 argue and discuss · compete
壮 brave · great · strong
庄 villages and towns
早 fast
⁷宋 later Chinese dynasties
走 escape · run · travel by vehicle
⁸宗 parties and sects · religion
⁹奏 play music
相 appearance · high officials · mutual · phonetic [s]/[sh] · states and situations
草 kinds of grasses · manuscript · styles of Chinese characters
荘 dignified · feudal territorial divisions · mansions
送 send
¹⁰倉 storehouse
挿 put in
捜 seek
桑 trees
¹¹掃 clean and wash
曹 military officers and ranks
曽 family and relations · former
爽 pleased and pleasant
笙 musical instruments
¹²創 begin · create · injury
喪 losing and loss · mourn and mourning
惣 general · offspring
湊 gather · places for landing or stopping
痩 thin
葬 bury
装 clothing · decorate · disguise · equip and install · wear and put on
¹³僧 clergymen
剿 destroy
想 think and consider · thought
蒼 blue and purple colors

¹⁴層 class · floor
槍 projectiles and bombs
漕 move through water
漱 clean and wash
箏 musical instruments
綜 combine
総 all · combine · general · high-ranking · total
聡 intelligent and wise
遭 meet
颯 wind
¹⁵噌 seasonings
槽 containers
踪 marks and signs
¹⁶操 chastity · fidelity · handle
艙 parts of boats and ships
¹⁷燥 dry · impatient
簇 crowd
霜 kinds of precipitation
¹⁸叢 crowd · kinds of grasses
贈 give
騒 loud · make sound or noise
²⁰躁 impatient

そう
沿 near
添 accompany · add to

ゾウ
造 build · make · structure
象 imitate · phenomenon · undomesticated mammals
像 image · images
増 increase
憎 hate and dislike
雑 disordered · mix · various
蔵 possess · store · storehouse
贈 give
臓 organ

そうろう
候 signs · time periods · weather

そえる
添 accompany · add to

ソク
⁴仄 less in degree
⁷即 fast · immediate
束 bundles and clusters · join · restrain
足 add · footwear · leg · suffice · supplement · walk
⁹促 hurry · urge
則 laws and rules
¹⁰息 breathe and blow · offspring · rest
捉 take
速 fast
¹¹側 side
¹²測 conjecture · measure
¹³塞 close · obstruct and hinder · strongholds
¹⁴熄 extinguish
¹⁷燭 light

ゾク
俗 custom · public · vulgar and unrefined · worldly
族 family and relations · groups · people
属 kinds and types · possess
粟 cereals
続 continue
賊 thieves
簇 crowd

そこ	底	basis · bottoms and bases
そこなう	損	fail · harm and damage · losing and loss
そこねる	損	fail · harm and damage · losing and loss
そしる	誹	disgrace
	譏	disgrace
そそぐ	注	concentrate on · explain · explanatory remarks · flow and drip
そそのかす	唆	incite
そだち	育	grow · raise and nourish · teach
そだつ	育	grow · raise and nourish · teach
そだてる	育	grow · raise and nourish · teach
ソツ	卒	soldiers and warriors · students and followers
	率	lead and escort · rate
そで	袖	garment parts
そと	外	come off · deviate · eliminate · foreign · outside
そなえる	供	offer · servants · supply
	備	equip and install · prepare
そなわる	備	equip and install · prepare
その	其	this and that
	苑	gardens · restaurant suffixes
	園	cultivated fields · gardens · restaurant suffixes · schools
そば	傍	additionally · near · side
そまる	染	color² · dirty¹
そむく	叛	resist
	背	height · rear · trunk parts · violate
そむける	背	height · rear · trunk parts · violate
ぞめ	初	beginnings · first · original
	染	color² · dirty¹
そめる	初	beginnings · first · original
	染	color² · dirty¹
そら	空	aircraft and spacecraft · emptiness and nothing · gas and vapor · sky · vain
そらす	反	area units · length units · opposite · overturn · resist · spring back · violate
そる	反	area units · length units · opposite · overturn · resist · spring back · violate
それ	其	this and that
そろい	揃	arrange · fit
ぞろい	揃	arrange · fit
そろう	揃	arrange · fit
そろえる	揃	arrange · fit
ソン	存	exist and be · think and consider
	村	villages and towns
	孫	descendant
	尊	honorific prefixes · respect
	巽	cardinal points
	損	fail · harm and damage · losing and loss
	遜	humble
	噂	stories
	樽	containers
	鱒	fishes
ゾン	存	exist and be · think and consider

た

タ	太	big and huge · fatten · high-ranking · thick

		他	other
		多	plentiful
		汰	choose
		詫	apologize
		駄	bad · footwear
た		手	hand and arm · handles · means · workers and professionals
		田	cultivated fields
ダ		打	strike
	⁷	妥	compromise
	⁸	陀	phonetic [d]
	¹¹	唾	bodily secretions
		舵	parts of boats and ships
		蛇	reptiles and amphibians · snake
		霏	small water masses
	¹²	堕	degenerate
		惰	lazy · motion
	¹³	楕	circle
	¹⁴	駄	bad · footwear
タイ	³	大	approximately · big and huge · extreme in degree · great · schools · size
	⁴	太	big and huge · fatten · high-ranking · thick
	⁵	代	change and replace · fee and price · generation · long time periods · substitute
		台	China · flat supports · hills · tables and stands · tall buildings · vehicle · wind
	⁷	体	appearance · bodies · body · essential content · form · object · organized bodies
		対	compare · face · opposite · resist · two
	⁸	苔	plants
	⁹	待	expect · treat and welcome · wait
		怠	lazy
		殆	almost · danger
		耐	bear and endure · resist
		胎	early states of animal life · genitals
		退	drive out · leave and set forth · resign
	¹⁰	帯	areas and localities · wear and put on
		泰	Asian countries · calm and peaceful
	¹¹	堆	accumulate
		袋	bags · containers
		逮	catch a criminal
	¹²	替	change and replace
		貸	lend and borrow
		隊	armed forces · groups
	¹³	滞	be late and delay · remain · stagnate · stay
		碓	vessels and receptacles
	¹⁴	態	posture · states and situations
		颱	wind
	¹⁵	褪	discolor
	¹⁶	頽	degenerate
		黛	cosmetics
	¹⁷	戴	receive
		擡	raise
		鯛	fishes
たい	²	乃	possessive particles
ダイ	³	大	approximately · big and huge · extreme in degree · great · schools · size

⁴内 during · inside · national · secret and private · wives

⁵代 change and replace · fee and price · generation · long time periods · substitute

台 China · flat supports · hills · tables and stands · tall buildings · vehicle · wind

⁷弟 siblings · students and followers

¹⁰悌 fidelity

¹¹第 kinds of numbers

¹⁶醍 dairy products

黛 cosmetics

¹⁸題 name¹ · question

だいだい 橙 fruits and fruit trees

たいら 平 calm and peaceful · flat · impartial · mathematical power · ordinary · same and uniform

だいら 平 calm and peaceful · flat · impartial · mathematical power · ordinary · same and uniform

たえる 耐 bear and endure · resist
堪 bear and endure
絶 come to an end · discontinue · end · excellent and superior

たおす 倒 descend and fall · opposite · overturn
斃 die

だおれ 倒 descend and fall · opposite · overturn

たおれる 倒 descend and fall · opposite · overturn
斃 die

たか 高 elated · expensive · extreme in degree · height · high¹ · high² · high-ranking · loud · schools
鷹 birds

だか 高 elated · expensive · extreme in degree · height · high¹ · high² · high-ranking · loud · schools

たかい 高 elated · expensive · extreme in degree · height · high¹ · high² · high-ranking · loud · schools

たがい 互 mutual

たかまる 高 elated · expensive · extreme in degree · height · high¹ · high² · high-ranking · loud · schools

たかめる 高 elated · expensive · extreme in degree · height · high¹ · high² · high-ranking · loud · schools

たがやす 耕 farm and plant

たから 宝 wealth

たき 滝 running water

だき 炊 cook

たきぎ 薪 kinds of fuel · kinds of wood

タク ⁶宅 houses
託 commit · vessels and receptacles
⁷択 choose
沢 lakes and marshes · luster · plentiful
⁸卓 conspicuous · excellent and superior · tables and stands
拓 copy · reclaim

⁹度 angle and angular measure · degree · time and time counters

¹⁰啄 bite · ingest
託 commit

¹¹琢 cultivate

¹⁷濯 clean and wash

たく 炊 cook
焚 burn

ダク 諾 agree and approve · terms of assent
濁 dirty²

だく 抱 embrace · hold in the mind

たぐい 類 kinds and types · resemble · similar

たくましい 逞 acting arbitrarily · strong

たくみ 巧 skillful

たくわえる 蓄 store

たけ 丈 height · length units · strong
竹 bamboo · writing strips
岳 mountains
茸 fungus

たしか 確 certain · exact · firm and obstinate

たしかめる 確 certain · exact · firm and obstinate

たす 足 add · footwear · leg · suffice · supplement · walk

だす 出 appear · attend · begin · emit · go and come · leave and set forth · protrude and protruding

たすかる 助 help · subordinate

たすける 助 help · subordinate

たずさえる 携 cooperate · hold

たずさわる 携 cooperate · hold

たずねる 訊 inquire
訪 visit
尋 inquire · length units

ただ 只 ordinary
湛 fill
讃 praise

たたかう 戦 compete · fight and war · game · warfare and rebellions
闘 compete · fight and war · warfare and rebellions

たたく 叩 strike

ただし 但 conditional conjunctions

ただしい 正 correct · exact · main · positive · regular · right · true · virtuous

ただす 正 correct · exact · main · positive · regular · right · true · virtuous

ただちに 直 correct · immediate · purehearted · repair · repeating and repetition · straight · vertical

たたみ 畳 fold · mats · repeating and repetition

たたむ 畳 fold · mats · repeating and repetition

ただよう 漂 float · wander

ただれる 爛 mature · swell and swelling

たち 立 assume upright position · capacity units · found · raise · standpoint · vertical
達 accomplish · arrive · attain proficiency · inform and communicate · phonetic [d] · plural suffixes · transmit and deliver

ON-KUN INDEX

たちばな	橘	fruits and fruit trees
たちまち	忽	immediate
タツ	達	accomplish · arrive · attain proficiency · inform and communicate · phonetic [d] · plural suffixes · transmit and deliver
たつ	立	assume upright position · capacity units · found · raise · standpoint · vertical
	辰	dragon · mythical animals
	建	build
	発	begin · create · emit · explode · grow · leave and set forth · reveal · shoot
	竜	dragon · mythical animals · reptiles and amphibians
	断	cut · decide · discontinue · refuse and reject · resolutely
	経	books · direct and supervise · elapse · latitude and longitude · pass · threads and fibers
	絶	come to an end · discontinue · end · excellent and superior
	裁	court · cut · judge
ダツ	捺	mark
	脱	come off · eliminate · escape · omit
	奪	steal and rob · take forcibly
たっとい	尊	honorific prefixes · respect
	貴	expensive · high-ranking · honorific prefixes · second person pronouns
たっとぶ	尊	honorific prefixes · respect
	貴	expensive · high-ranking · honorific prefixes · second person pronouns
たつみ	巽	cardinal points
たて	立	assume upright position · capacity units · found · raise · standpoint · vertical
	建	build
	盾	protective coverings
	楯	protective coverings
	竪	vertical
	縦	vertical
だて	立	assume upright position · capacity units · found · raise · standpoint · vertical
	建	build
たてまつる	奉	offer · respectful
たてる	立	assume upright position · capacity units · found · raise · standpoint · vertical
	建	build
だてる	立	assume upright position · capacity units · found · raise · standpoint · vertical
たとえる	例	constant · custom · example
	喩	words and expressions
	譬	compare
たどる	辿	follow and pursue
たな	棚	flat supports
だな	棚	flat supports
たに	谷	valley
たね	胤	descendant
	種	early states of plant life · kinds and types
たのしい	楽	comfortable · music and songs · pleased and pleasant · pleasure
たのしむ	楽	comfortable · music and songs · pleased and pleasant · pleasure
たのむ	頼	rely on · request
たのもしい	頼	rely on · request
たば	束	bundles and clusters · join · restrain
たばねる	束	bundles and clusters · join · restrain
たび	度	angle and angular measure · degree · time and time counters
	旅	journey
たべる	食	food · ingest
たま	玉	money · precious stones · spherical object
	球	bodies · spherical object · three-dimensional shapes
	弾	blame and accuse · play music · projectiles and bombs · spring back
	霊	holy · psyche · supernatural and evil beings
だま	玉	money · precious stones · spherical object
たまご	卵	early states of animal life · reproductive cells
たましい	魂	psyche
だます	騙	deceive
たまる	堪	bear and endure
	溜	accumulate
だまる	黙	quiet
たまわる	賜	give
たみ	民	people · the people
ため	為	benefit · cause and reason · do and act
	溜	accumulate
ためす	試	examination · try
ためる	溜	accumulate
	矯	correct
たもつ	保	preserve · protect
たやす	絶	come to an end · discontinue · end · excellent and superior
たゆむ	弛	loosen
たより	便	excreta · mail · suitable
たよる	頼	rely on · request
たらす	垂	hang · vertical
たりる	足	add · footwear · leg · suffice · supplement · walk
たる	足	add · footwear · leg · suffice · supplement · walk
	樽	containers
たるむ	弛	loosen
たれ	垂	hang · vertical
だれ	誰	interrogatives
たれる	垂	hang · vertical
たわむれる	戯	comic · play
たわら	俵	bags
タン	[4]丹	red colors
	反	area units · length units · opposite · overturn · resist · spring back · violate
	[5]旦	days · morning and dawn
	[8]坦	flat
	担	bear · undertake
	[9]単	element · one · plain and simple
	炭	kinds of fuel · lighter elements · products of combustion
	胆	courage · internal organs
	[10]耽	acting arbitrarily
	[11]探	investigate and examine · seek · spy

淡 light-colored
12 堪 bear and endure
湛 fill
短 faults and flaws · short and shortened
13 嘆 cry and sigh · feel deeply · grieve
14 端 beginnings · edges and boundaries · extremity · right
綻 degenerate
15 歎 cry and sigh
誕 give birth
16 壇 circles · flat supports
17 檀 trees
鍛 cultivate · work metals
18 簞 containers
22 灘 sea

ダン

5 旦 days · morning and dawn
6 団 groups · organized bodies
7 男 man · noblemen · offspring
9 段 class · means · parts of writing · steps
11 断 cut · decide · discontinue · refuse and reject · resolutely
12 弾 blame and accuse · play music · projectiles and bombs · spring back
13 暖 hot · raise the temperature
煖 raise the temperature
15 談 speak and say · speech · stories
16 壇 circles · flat supports
17 檀 trees

ち

チ

6 地 areas and localities · fabric · land and soil · natural · places and positions · standpoint
池 lakes and marshes
8 治 cure and recover · govern · government · peace
知 inform and communicate · know and understand · learning and knowledge · perceive · wisdom
10 値 fee and price · value
恥 disgrace · genitals
致 cause · do and act
12 智 intelligent and wise · wisdom
遅 be late and delay · late · slow
13 痴 foolish · mania and maniacs
稚 young
置 deal with · found · imprison and confine · put
馳 run
15 質 inquire · matter · nature and character · pawn
16 緻 detailed
薙 cut

ち
千 large numbers
血 lineage
乳 bodily secretions · chest · dairy products · drinks

ちいさい
小 humble prefixes · schools · small and tiny · unimportant

ちかい
近 approach · familiar and friendly · near · recent

ちがい
違 differing and difference · mistakes and mistaking · violate

ちかう
誓 promise

ちがう
違 differing and difference · mistakes and mistaking · violate

ちがえる
違 differing and difference · mistakes and mistaking · violate

ちがや
茅 kinds of grasses

ちから
力 energy and force · power and authority · skill

ちぎる
契 promise

チク
竹 bamboo · writing strips
畜 animal
逐 drive out · in succession
蓄 store
築 build

ちち
父 clergymen · parents
乳 bodily secretions · chest · dairy products · drinks

ちぢまる
縮 contract and shrink · decrease

ちぢむ
縮 contract and shrink · decrease

ちぢめる
縮 contract and shrink · decrease

ちぢらす
縮 contract and shrink · decrease

ちぢれる
縮 contract and shrink · decrease

チツ
秩 order
窒 kill · lighter elements · nitrogen

ちまた
巷 public · ways and routes

チャ
茶 brown colors · drinks

チャク
着 adhere to · arrive · clothing · settle · stick · wear and put on
嫡 inheritors · offspring · wives

チュウ
4 丑 cattle
中 between · China · Chinese · during · inside · middle · schools · second · throughout
6 仲 between · mediating and mediators · personal relations
虫 insect
7 沖 sea
肘 hand and arm
8 宙 sky · universe and space
忠 fidelity
抽 pull
注 concentrate on · explain · explanatory remarks · flow and drip
9 昼 days · noon
柱 supporting structures
10 紐 ropes and lines
衷 psyche
酎 drinks
11 紬 fabrics
12 厨 kitchen
註 write
15 鋳 form and carve · work metals
駐 stay · stop

チュン
椿 trees

チョ
猪 swine · undomesticated mammals
著 books · compile · compose · conspicuous
貯 store

	緒	beginnings · ropes and lines	ちらばる	散 disperse · spread · unrestrained
	儲	profit	ちり	塵 waste
チョウ	²丁	counters for flat things · courteous · general counters · paper · parts of towns	ちる	散 disperse · spread · unrestrained
			チン	沈 sad and depressed · sink
	⁴弔	console · mourn and mourning		青 blue and purple colors · green colors · young
	⁵庁	public offices		
	汀	shores and watersides		珍 abnormal · rare
	⁶兆	large numbers · signs		朕 first person pronouns
	吊	hang		砧 instruments for beating or pounding
	⁷町	area units · cities and towns · length units · parts of towns · villages and towns		陳 arrange · display · speak and say
				椿 trees
	⁸帖	notebook		賃 fee and price · pay and earnings
	長	grow · leaders · of long duration		鎮 conquer and suppress · weight
	⁹挑	incite		

━━━ つ ━━━

重	accumulate · compound · extreme in degree · -fold · important · repeating and repetition · respect	
ツ	通	counters for flat things · go and come · inform and communicate · know and understand · pass · similar · throughout · ways and routes · widespread · wise and talented persons

	¹⁰挺	counters for long objects		
	¹¹帳	curtain · notebook		都 all · cities and towns · Kanto region · territorial divisions
	張	expand · tighten		
	彫	form and carve	つ	津 places for landing or stopping
	眺	see and look	ツイ	対 compare · face · opposite · resist · two
	釣	hang · hunt and fish		追 additional · add to · drive out · follow and pursue · remember
	頂	mountain parts · receive · tops		
	鳥	bird		椎 bone · fruits and fruit trees
	¹²喋	speak and say		槌 instruments for beating or pounding
	提	hold · offer · phonetic [d]		墜 descend and fall
	朝	governments · Korea · long time periods · morning and dawn	ついえる	費 consume · fee and price
			ついたち	朔 days
	脹	expand · swell and swelling	ついに	遂 accomplish · execute
	貼	stick	ついばむ	啄 bite · ingest
	超	exceeding and excess · excel · extreme in degree	ついやす	費 consume · fee and price
			ツウ	通 counters for flat things · go and come · inform and communicate · know and understand · pass · similar · throughout · ways and routes · widespread · wise and talented persons
	¹³牒	written communications		
	腸	internal organs		
	跳	jump		
	¹⁴徴	enlist · impose · signs		
	暢	smooth		痛 extreme in degree · trouble and suffering
	肇	begin	つえ	杖 long slender objects
	蔦	shrubs	つか	束 bundles and clusters · join · restrain
	¹⁵嘲	disdain		塚 graves · hills
	澄	clear	づか	塚 graves · hills
	潮	running water · tendency	つかい	使 agents · employ · use
	蝶	insects		遣 send
	調	cooperate · investigate and examine · make · musical elements · music and songs · prepare · states and situations · way and style	づかい	使 agents · employ · use
				遣 send
			つかう	使 agents · employ · use
				遣 send
	¹⁷聴	hear	つかえる	仕 do and act · work
	¹⁸懲	punishment	つかす	尽 come to an end · consume · exert oneself
	¹⁹寵	love		
	鯛	fishes	つかまえる	捕 catch a criminal · take
チョク	直	correct · immediate · purehearted · repair · repeating and repetition · straight · vertical		摑 take
			つかまる	捕 catch a criminal · take
				摑 take
	勅	imperial decree	つかむ	摑 take
	捗	make progress	つかる	漬 moisten · preserved foods · preserve food
ちらかす	散	disperse · spread · unrestrained		
ちらかる	散	disperse · spread · unrestrained	づかれ	疲 tire
ちらす	散	disperse · spread · unrestrained		

つかれる	疲 tire	
つかわす	遣 send	
つき	月 days of the week • moon • weeks and months	
	付 add to • stick • transfer	
	槻 trees	
つぎ	次 kinds of numbers • next • order • second • subordinate	
づき	付 add to • stick • transfer	
つきる	尽 come to an end • consume • exert oneself	
つく	付 add to • stick • transfer	
	突 collide • move forward • protrude and protruding • push • stab • sudden	
	就 begin	
	着 adhere to • arrive • clothing • settle • stick • wear and put on	
	撞 strike	
つぐ	次 kinds of numbers • next • order • second • subordinate	
	接 approach • join • touch • treat and welcome	
	継 continue • related by marriage • succeed	
づく	付 add to • stick • transfer	
つくえ	机 tables and stands	
づくし	尽 come to an end • consume • exert oneself	
つくす	尽 come to an end • consume • exert oneself	
つくだ	佃 cultivated fields	
つぐなう	償 compensate • pay	
つくり	作 compose • create • do and act • farm and plant • make	
	旁 characters • near	
	造 build • make • structure	
づくり	作 compose • create • do and act • farm and plant • make	
	造 build • make • structure	
つくる	作 compose • create • do and act • farm and plant • make	
	造 build • make • structure	
	創 begin • create • injury	
つくろう	繕 repair	
つけ	付 add to • stick • transfer	
つげ	柘 trees	
づけ	付 add to • stick • transfer	
	漬 moisten • preserved foods • preserve food	
つける	付 add to • stick • transfer	
	就 begin	
	着 adhere to • arrive • clothing • settle • stick • wear and put on	
	漬 moisten • preserved foods • preserve food	
つげる	告 inform and communicate • sue • warn	
づける	付 add to • stick • transfer	
っこ	子 child • Confucius and Confucianists • gentleman • interest and dividend • name suffixes • noblemen • nominalizers • offspring • particle	
つごもり	晦 dark • days	
つじ	辻 ways and routes	
つた	蔦 shrubs	
づたい	伝 history • make widely known • records • transmit and deliver	

つたう	伝 history • make widely known • records • transmit and deliver	
つたえる	伝 history • make widely known • records • transmit and deliver	
つたない	拙 humble prefixes	
つたわる	伝 history • make widely known • records • transmit and deliver	
つち	土 country • days of the week • land and soil	
	槌 instruments for beating or pounding	
つちかう	培 farm and plant	
つちのえ	戊 calendar signs	
つつ	筒 three-dimensional shapes • tubular passages	
つづく	続 continue	
つづける	続 continue	
つつしむ	慎 careful	
	謹 careful • respectful	
つつみ	堤 embankment	
つづみ	鼓 musical instruments	
つつむ	包 bags • contain and include • cover and wrap • surround	
つづる	綴 create • join	
つどう	集 assembly • collection • compile • gather	
つとまる	務 affairs • responsibility • work and employment	
	勤 exert oneself • work • work and employment	
づとめ	勤 exert oneself • work • work and employment	
つとめる	努 exert oneself	
	務 affairs • responsibility • work and employment	
	勤 exert oneself • work • work and employment	
つな	綱 essential part • policy • ropes and lines	
つながる	繋 join	
つなぐ	繋 join	
つなげる	繋 join	
つね	常 constant • ordinary	
つの	角 angle and angular measure • body projections • corners • square • three-dimensional shapes	
つのる	募 enlist	
つば	唾 bodily secretions	
つばき	唾 bodily secretions	
	椿 trees	
つばさ	翼 parties and sects • wings	
っぱなし	放 emit • let do • release • throw	
つばめ	燕 birds	
つぶ	粒 particle	
	螺 shells	
つぶす	潰 break	
つぶれる	潰 break	
つぼ	坪 area units	
	壺 containers	
つぼみ	蕾 early states of plant life	
つぼむ	蕾 early states of plant life	
つま	爪 ungual	
	妻 wives	
つまる	詰 blame and accuse • fill • inquire	

つみ	罪	crimes and offenses • wrongdoing and evil
づみ	積	accumulate • load • quantity and number
つむ	剪	cut
	詰	blame and accuse • fill • inquire
	摘	choose • harvest
	積	accumulate • load • quantity and number
	錘	long slender objects • weight
つむぎ	紬	fabrics
つむぐ	紡	weave and sew
つめ	爪	ungual
	詰	blame and accuse • fill • inquire
づめ	詰	blame and accuse • fill • inquire
つめたい	冷	cold • reduce the temperature
つめる	詰	blame and accuse • fill • inquire
つもり	積	accumulate • load • quantity and number
つもる	積	accumulate • load • quantity and number
つや	艶	beautiful • love • luster
つゆ	露	European countries • kinds of precipitation • reveal
つよい	強	compel and press • extreme in degree • hard • strong
つよまる	強	compel and press • extreme in degree • hard • strong
つよめる	強	compel and press • extreme in degree • hard • strong
つら	面	aspect • face • front • front parts of head • outside • paper • parts of periodicals • protective coverings • side
つらなる	連	continue • groups • in succession • join • lead and escort • organized bodies • relate
つらぬく	貫	penetrate • weight units
つらねる	連	continue • groups • in succession • join • lead and escort • organized bodies • relate
つり	吊	hang
	釣	hang • hunt and fish
つる	吊	hang
	弦	lines and line segments • musical instrument • ropes and lines
	釣	hang • hunt and fish
	蔓	plants
	鶴	birds
	攣	contract and shrink
つるぎ	剣	cutting weapons
つるす	吊	hang
づれ	連	continue • groups • in succession • join • lead and escort • organized bodies • relate
つれる	連	continue • groups • in succession • join • lead and escort • organized bodies • relate

て

て	手	hand and arm • handles • means • workers and professionals
デ	弟	siblings • students and followers
で	出	appear • attend • begin • emit • go and come • leave and set forth • protrude and protruding
テイ	² 丁	counters for flat things • courteous • general counters • paper • parts of towns

	⁵ 叮	courteous
	汀	shores and watersides
	⁷ 低	inexpensive • less in degree • low • lower • lowly
	体	appearance • bodies • body • essential content • form • object • organized bodies
	呈	give • show
	廷	court • governments
	弟	siblings • students and followers
	⁸ 定	constant • decide • not moving
	底	basis • bottoms and bases
	低	wander
	抵	resist
	邸	houses • mansions
	⁹ 亭	pseudonym suffixes • restaurant suffixes • temporary quarters
	帝	god • rulers
	柢	bottoms and bases
	牴	collide
	訂	correct • editions • revise
	貞	chastity
	¹⁰ 庭	gardens • sports fields
	悌	fidelity
	挺	counters for long objects
	逓	in succession • post station • transmit and deliver
	釘	perforators
	¹¹ 停	discontinue • places for landing or stopping • stop
	偵	agents • spy
	梯	steps
	逞	acting arbitrarily • strong
	¹² 堤	embankment
	幀	print and publish
	提	hold • offer • phonetic [d]
	程	approximately • degree • distance and interval • model • range
	觝	collide
	¹³ 碇	weight
	禎	good fortune
	艇	boats and ships
	鼎	three • vessels and receptacles
	¹⁴ 綴	create • join
	¹⁵ 締	promise • tighten
	鄭	courteous
	¹⁶ 薙	cut
	諦	discard and abandon
	蹄	ungual
	¹⁸ 鵜	birds
ディ	泥	land and soil • thieves
	祢	graves
テキ	的	modifier suffixes • target
	迪	teach
	荻	kinds of grasses
	笛	musical instruments
	摘	choose • harvest
	滌	clean and wash
	滴	flow and drip • small water masses
	適	fit • suitable
	敵	enemy

擢 choose · excel

デキ 溺 sink

濯 clean and wash

でこ 凸 bowed · protrude and protruding

テツ 迭 alternate · change and replace

姪 offspring of siblings

哲 intelligent and wise · wisdom · wise and talented persons

鉄 iron and steel · kinds of railway · metals

綴 create · join

徹 accomplish · throughout

撤 eliminate · leave and set forth

てら 寺 places of worship

てらす 照 compare · light · shine and reflect

てる 照 compare · light · shine and reflect

でる 出 appear · attend · begin · emit · go and come · leave and set forth · protrude and protruding

てれる 照 compare · light · shine and reflect

テン ⁴天 god · posthumous worlds · rulers · sky · weather

⁷迢 follow and pursue

⁸典 books · ceremonies and festivities · laws and rules · model

店 places of business

⁹点 general counters · places and positions

¹⁰展 display · grow · open · public display

¹¹添 accompany · add to

転 change and replace · move · overturn · turn

¹²奠 offering

貼 stick

¹³填 fill · fit

殿 buildings · palace · titles of address

¹⁴槙 trees

¹⁹顛 overturn

²¹纏 combine · wear and put on · wind and twine

デン 田 cultivated fields

伝 history · make widely known · records · transmit and deliver

佃 cultivated fields

淀 stagnate · stagnating water

奠 offering

殿 buildings · palace · titles of address

電 atmospheric discharges · electricity and magnetism · kinds of railway · written communications

澱 stagnate · stagnating water

鮎 fishes

と

ト ³土 country · days of the week · land and soil

⁴斗 capacity units · spoons

⁶吐 discharge from mouth · emit

⁷兎 domesticated mammals · rabbit

図 diagram · picture · plans and planning · will and intention

杜 forest

⁸妬 jealous and envious

⁹度 angle and angular measure · degree · time and time counters

¹⁰徒 fellow · students and followers · vain · walk

途 way and style · ways and routes

¹¹兜 headgear · protective coverings

都 all · cities and towns · Kanto region · territorial divisions

¹²堵 fences and walls

渡 cross · transfer

登 ascend · attend · write

¹³塗 spread

¹⁶賭 risk

と 頭 counters for animals · head · leaders · tops

人 counters for persons · person · workers and professionals

十 small numbers · ten

戸 counters for houses · doors · houses

ド 砥 kinds of stone

土 country · days of the week · land and soil

奴 fellow · servants · third person pronouns

努 exert oneself

度 angle and angular measure · degree · time and time counters

怒 anger

とい 問 inquire · question

樋 tubular passages

トウ ²刀 cutting instruments · cutting weapons

⁵冬 cold seasons

⁶当 allot · collide · correspond to · pawn · present · strike · suitable · this and that · touch

灯 light

⁷投 send · throw

杜 forest

豆 cereals · small and tiny · vegetables

⁸到 arrive

宕 unrestrained

東 cardinal points · Kanto region

沓 footwear

⁹逃 avoid and abstain · escape

¹⁰倒 descend and fall · opposite · overturn

党 groups · parties and sects

凍 reduce the temperature · solidify and coagulate

唐 China · later Chinese dynasties

套 ordinary

島 elevations in water

桃 fruits and fruit trees

桐 trees

納 offer · pay · receive · store · supply

討 conquer and suppress · investigate and examine

透 clear · penetrate

¹¹兜 headgear · protective coverings

悼 grieve · mourn and mourning

桶 containers

盗 steal and rob · thieves

祷 pray and worship

	逗 stay		とお	十 small numbers · ten
	陶 ceramics ware		とおい	遠 distant · estrange
	12 塔 places of worship · tall buildings		とおし	通 counters for flat things · go and come · inform and communicate · know and understand · pass · similar · throughout · ways and routes · widespread · wise and talented persons
	搭 get on · load			
	棟 buildings · counters for houses · roof parts			
	湯 baths · kinds of water			
	痘 diseases and disease symptoms			
	登 ascend · attend · write		どおし	通 counters for flat things · go and come · inform and communicate · know and understand · pass · similar · throughout · ways and routes · widespread · wise and talented persons
	等 class · plural suffixes · same and uniform			
	筒 three-dimensional shapes · tubular passages			
	答 answer			
	統 combine · govern · system		とおす	通 counters for flat things · go and come · inform and communicate · know and understand · pass · similar · throughout · ways and routes · widespread · wise and talented persons
	董 machines and tools			
	道 art · moral goodness · moral principles · religion · religions and sects · territorial divisions · tubular passages · ways and routes			
			とおり	通 counters for flat things · go and come · inform and communicate · know and understand · pass · similar · throughout · ways and routes · widespread · wise and talented persons
	14 稲 rice			
	読 recite			
	15 樋 tubular passages			
	踏 step on · walk			
	16 橙 fruits and fruit trees		どおり	通 counters for flat things · go and come · inform and communicate · know and understand · pass · similar · throughout · ways and routes · widespread · wise and talented persons
	糖 seasonings			
	頭 counters for animals · head · leaders · tops			
	17 謄 copy			
	蹈 step on			
	18 櫂 parts of boats and ships		とおる	通 counters for flat things · go and come · inform and communicate · know and understand · pass · similar · throughout · ways and routes · widespread · wise and talented persons
	藤 flowering plants · shrubs			
	闘 compete · fight and war · warfare and rebellions			
	20 騰 ascend			
とう	問 inquire · question		とかす	梳 comb
ドウ	6 同 same and uniform · this and that · together			溶 liquefy
				解 answer · dismiss · disperse · explain · know and understand · liquefy · separate
	9 洞 holes and cavities			
	10 桐 trees			熔 liquefy
	胴 phonetic [d] · trunk parts			鎔 liquefy
	11 動 active · behavior · feel deeply · incite · motion · move · set in motion		とがる	尖 extremity · sharp
			とき	時 long time periods · occasions · short time periods · time periods
	堂 buildings · places of worship · rooms			
	萄 fruits and fruit trees		とぎ	伽 phonetic [k]/[g]
	12 童 child		どき	時 long time periods · occasions · short time periods · time periods
	道 art · moral goodness · moral principles · religion · religions and sects · territorial divisions · tubular passages · ways and routes		トク	匿 hide
				啄 bite · ingest
				特 special
	13 働 work			得 get · know and understand · profit
	14 銅 metals			督 direct and supervise · military officers and ranks
	15 導 lead and escort · teach			
	憧 wish and desire			徳 favor · moral goodness
	撞 strike			読 recite
	17 瞳 eye			篤 eager · kind
とうげ	峠 mountain parts		とく	梳 comb
とうとい	尊 honorific prefixes · respect			溶 liquefy
	貴 expensive · high-ranking · honorific prefixes · second person pronouns			解 answer · dismiss · disperse · explain · know and understand · liquefy · separate
とうとぶ	尊 honorific prefixes · respect			説 advocate · explain · opinion · stories · theory
	貴 expensive · high-ranking · honorific prefixes · second person pronouns		とぐ	研 learn and study · polish and rub

	砥 kinds of stone	
ドク	独 acting arbitrarily · alone · European countries	
	読 recite	
とける	溶 liquefy	
	解 answer · dismiss · disperse · explain · know and understand · liquefy · separate	
	熔 liquefy	
	鎔 liquefy	
とげる	遂 accomplish · execute	
とこ	床 bottoms and bases · flat supports	
	常 constant · ordinary	
ところ	所 nominalizers · places and positions · public offices	
どころ	所 nominalizers · places and positions · public offices	
とざす	閉 close · end	
とし	年 age · year	
	歳 age · year	
とじる	閉 close · end	
	綴 create · join	
とち	栃 fruits and fruit trees	
トツ	凸 bowed · protrude and protruding	
	突 collide · move forward · protrude and protruding · push · stab · sudden	
とつぐ	嫁 in-laws · marrying and marriage · wives	
とどく	届 arrive · inform and communicate · transmit and deliver	
とどけ	届 arrive · inform and communicate · transmit and deliver	
とどける	届 arrive · inform and communicate · transmit and deliver	
とどこおる	滞 be late and delay · remain · stagnate · stay	
ととのう	調 cooperate · investigate and examine · make · musical elements · music and songs · prepare · states and situations · way and style	
	整 arrange	
ととのえる	調 cooperate · investigate and examine · make · musical elements · music and songs · prepare · states and situations · way and style	
	整 arrange	
とどまる	留 imprison and confine · preserve · refine · remain · stay · vaporize	
とどろく	轟 make sound or noise	
となえる	唱 advocate · recite · sing	
となり	隣 near	
となる	隣 near	
との	殿 buildings · palace · titles of address	
どの	殿 buildings · palace · titles of address	
とばす	飛 fly	
とび	跳 jump	
	鳶 birds	
とびら	扉 doors	
とぶ	飛 fly	
	翔 fly	
	跳 jump	
とぼしい	乏 few · poor	
どまり	止 discontinue · not moving · prevent · stop	

とまる	止 discontinue · not moving · prevent · stop	
	泊 stay	
	留 imprison and confine · preserve · refine · remain · stay · vaporize	
	停 discontinue · places for landing or stopping · stop	
とみ	富 plentiful · rich · wealth	
とむ	富 plentiful · rich · wealth	
とむらう	弔 console · mourn and mourning	
どめ	止 discontinue · not moving · prevent · stop	
	留 imprison and confine · preserve · refine · remain · stay · vaporize	
とめる	止 discontinue · not moving · prevent · stop	
	泊 stay	
	留 imprison and confine · preserve · refine · remain · stay · vaporize	
	停 discontinue · places for landing or stopping · stop	
とも	友 friends and associates	
	共 Communism · plural suffixes · together	
	供 offer · servants · supply	
	朋 friends and associates	
ども	共 Communism · plural suffixes · together	
	供 offer · servants · supply	
ともえ	巴 phonetic [ha]	
ともしび	燭 light	
ともなう	伴 accompany	
ともに	共 Communism · plural suffixes · together	
	倶 together	
どもる	吃 stagnate	
とら	虎 tiger · undomesticated mammals	
	寅 tiger	
とらえる	捉 take	
	捕 catch a criminal · take	
とらわれる	捕 catch a criminal · take	
とり	酉 birds	
	取 get · steal and rob · take	
	鳥 bird	
	禽 bird	
どり	取 get · steal and rob · take	
	撮 photograph	
とりで	砦 strongholds	
とる	取 get · steal and rob · take	
	捕 catch a criminal · take	
	執 adhere to · execute · take	
	採 choose · gather · harvest	
	撮 photograph	
どろ	泥 land and soil · thieves	
トン	屯 stay · weight units	
	団 groups · organized bodies	
	沌 disordered	
	惇 purehearted	
	豚 domesticated mammals · swine	
	敦 purehearted	
	遁 escape	
	頓 stay · sudden	
	褪 discolor	
	噸 weight units	
とん	問 inquire · question	
ドン	呑 ingest	

	貪	wish and desire
	鈍	foolish · light-colored
どん	丼	vessels and receptacles
とんがる	尖	extremity · sharp
とんび	鳶	birds
どんぶり	丼	vessels and receptacles

━━━━━━ な ━━━━━━

ナ	那	interrogatives · phonetic [na]
	奈	interrogatives · phonetic [na]
	南	cardinal points
	納	offer · pay · receive · store · supply
	捺	mark
	梛	trees
な	名	counters for persons · excellent and superior · name[1] · repute
	菜	plants · vegetables
ナイ	乃	possessive particles
	内	during · inside · national · secret and private · wives
ない	亡	dead · destroy · die · escape
	無	emptiness and nothing · terms of negation
なえ	苗	early states of plant life
なえる	萎	decay · die
なお	尚	additionally · respect · still
なおき	直	correct · immediate · purehearted · repair · repeating and repetition · straight · vertical
なおす	治	cure and recover · govern · government · peace
	直	correct · immediate · purehearted · repair · repeating and repetition · straight · vertical
なおる	治	cure and recover · govern · government · peace
	直	correct · immediate · purehearted · repair · repeating and repetition · straight · vertical
なか	中	between · China · Chinese · during · inside · middle · schools · second · throughout
	仲	between · mediating and mediators · personal relations
ながい	永	of long duration
	長	grow · leaders · of long duration
ながす	流	class · electricity and magnetism · flow and drip · make widely known · parties and sects · rivers and streams · running water · smooth · tendency · wander · way and style
なかば	半	subordinate
ながめる	眺	see and look
なかれ	勿	phonetic [m] · terms of negation
	莫	terms of negation
ながれ	流	class · electricity and magnetism · flow and drip · make widely known · parties and sects · rivers and streams · running water · smooth · tendency · wander · way and style

ながれる	流	class · electricity and magnetism · flow and drip · make widely known · parties and sects · rivers and streams · running water · smooth · tendency · wander · way and style
なき	亡	dead · destroy · die · escape
なぎ	凪	wind
	梛	trees
なぎさ	汀	shores and watersides
	渚	shores and watersides
なく	泣	cry and sigh
	鳴	give out a call · make sound or noise
なぐ	凪	wind
	薙	cut
なぐさむ	慰	console
なぐさめる	慰	console
なぐる	殴	strike
なげ	投	send · throw
なげうつ	抛	throw
なげかわしい	嘆	cry and sigh · feel deeply · grieve
なげく	嘆	cry and sigh · feel deeply · grieve
	歎	cry and sigh
なげる	投	send · throw
なごむ	和	familiar and friendly · Japan · peace · total
なごやか	和	familiar and friendly · Japan · peace · total
なさけ	情	feeling · love · sex · states and situations · tender feelings for others
なし	梨	fruits and fruit trees
なす	成	accomplish · grow · make · mature
	為	benefit · cause and reason · do and act
なぞ	謎	question
なた	方	approximately · areas and localities · direction · mathematical power · person · person in charge · plural suffixes · side · square · way and style
なだ	灘	sea
なだめる	宥	forgive
ナチ	捺	mark
ナツ	納	offer · pay · receive · store · supply
ナツ	捺	mark
なつ	夏	earlier Chinese dynasties · warm seasons
なつかしい	懐	garment parts · hold in the mind · psyche · wish and desire
なつかしむ	懐	garment parts · hold in the mind · psyche · wish and desire
なつく	懐	garment parts · hold in the mind · psyche · wish and desire
なつける	懐	garment parts · hold in the mind · psyche · wish and desire
なでる	撫	touch
なな	七	small numbers
ななつ	七	small numbers
ななめ	斜	obliqueness and inclining
なに	何	how many · interrogatives · some
なの	七	small numbers
なべ	鍋	vessels and receptacles
なま	生	animal · create · give birth · grow · healthy · life · live · new · reside · students and followers
なまける	怠	lazy

なまり	鉛 metals	におわせる	匂 smell and fragrance
なみ	並 additionally · arrange · ordinary · together	にがい	苦 tastes · trouble and suffering
	波 phonetic [ha] · waves	にがす	逃 avoid and abstain · escape
なみだ	涙 bodily secretions	にがる	苦 tastes · trouble and suffering
なめずる	舐 taste	にぎやか	賑 prospering and prosperity
	嘗 former · taste	にぎる	握 take
なめらか	滑 move · smooth	にぎわう	賑 prospering and prosperity
なめる	舐 taste	にぎわす	賑 prospering and prosperity
	嘗 former · taste	ニク	肉 body · flesh · meat
なやます	悩 trouble and suffering	にくい	憎 hate and dislike
なやむ	悩 trouble and suffering	にくしみ	憎 hate and dislike
なら	楢 trees	にくむ	憎 hate and dislike
ならい	習 custom · learn and study	にくらしい	憎 hate and dislike
ならう	倣 imitate	にげる	逃 avoid and abstain · escape
	習 custom · learn and study	にごす	濁 dirty[2]
ならす	慣 custom	にごる	濁 dirty[2]
	鳴 give out a call · make sound or noise	にし	西 cardinal points · European countries · phonetic [s]/[sh] · west
ならびに	並 additionally · arrange · ordinary · together		
ならぶ	並 additionally · arrange · ordinary · together		螺 shells
ならべる	並 additionally · arrange · ordinary · together	にじ	虹 light
なり	也 classical particles · exist and be	にしき	錦 fabrics
なる	生 animal · create · give birth · grow · healthy · life · live · new · reside · students and followers	にじむ	滲 penetrate
		にじゅう	廿 small numbers
		にせ	偽 deceive · false · falsehood
	成 accomplish · grow · make · mature	ニチ	日 Asian countries · date · days · days of the week · Japan · sun
	鳴 give out a call · make sound or noise		
なれる	慣 custom	になう	担 bear · undertake
なわ	苗 early states of plant life	にぶ	鈍 foolish · light-colored
	縄 ropes and lines	にぶい	鈍 foolish · light-colored
ナン	男 man · noblemen · offspring	にぶる	鈍 foolish · light-colored
	南 cardinal points	ニャク	若 young
	納 offer · pay · receive · store · supply	にやす	煮 cook · cooked dishes
	軟 soft	ニュウ	入 enter · need and necessity · participate and join · put in
	楠 trees		
	難 blame and accuse · faults and flaws · misfortune and disaster · trouble and suffering		廿 small numbers
			乳 bodily secretions · chest · dairy products · drinks
なん	何 how many · interrogatives · some		
なんじ	汝 second person pronouns		柔 gentle · soft · weak
	爾 modifier suffixes · second person pronouns · this and that	ニョ	女 offspring · woman
			如 modifier suffixes · similar
		ニョウ	女 offspring · woman

に

ニ	二 small numbers · two		尿 excreta
	仁 central parts · tender feelings for others	にる	似 resemble
	尼 clergymen		煮 cook · cooked dishes
	弐 two	にわ	庭 gardens · sports fields
	児 child	にわか	俄 sudden
	爾 modifier suffixes · second person pronouns · this and that	にわとり	鶏 birds
		ニン	人 counters for persons · person · workers and professionals
に	荷 bear · burden		
	煮 cook · cooked dishes		任 appoint · commit · responsibility · work and employment
にい	新 calendars · new · recent · reform		
にえる	煮 cook · cooked dishes		妊 conceive
におい	匂 smell and fragrance		忍 bear and endure · hide
	臭 lighter elements · smell and fragrance		認 agree and approve · perceive
におう	匂 smell and fragrance		

ぬ

におう	匂 smell and fragrance	ぬう	縫 weave and sew
	臭 lighter elements · smell and fragrance	ぬかす	抜 choose · excel · omit · pull
におわす	匂 smell and fragrance	ぬかる	抜 choose · excel · omit · pull

ぬき	抜	choose • excel • omit • pull
ぬきんでる	擢	choose • excel
ぬく	抜	choose • excel • omit • pull
ぬぐ	脱	come off • eliminate • escape • omit
ぬぐう	拭	clean and wash
ぬける	抜	choose • excel • omit • pull
ぬげる	脱	come off • eliminate • escape • omit
ぬし	主	god • husband • leaders • main
ぬすむ	盗	steal and rob • thieves
ぬの	布	fabric • make widely known • spread
ぬま	沼	lakes and marshes
ぬらす	濡	wet
ぬり	塗	spread
ぬる	塗	spread
ぬれる	濡	wet

ね

ネ	祢	graves
ね	音	kinds of sound • music and songs
	値	fee and price • value
	根	basis • beginnings • supporting parts of plants
	嶺	mountain parts
ネイ	寧	calm and peaceful • courteous
	嚀	courteous
ねがう	願	pray and worship • request • wish and desire
ねかす	寝	lie down • sleep
ねかせる	寝	lie down • sleep
ねこ	猫	domesticated mammals
ねず	鼠	undomesticated mammals
ねずみ	鼠	undomesticated mammals
ねたましい	妬	jealous and envious
ねたむ	妬	jealous and envious
ネツ	熱	diseases and disease symptoms • eager • heat • hot • mania and maniacs • raise the temperature
ねむい	眠	sleep
ねむる	眠	sleep
ねらう	狙	target
ねり	練	cultivate • teach
ねる	寝	lie down • sleep
	煉	work metals
	練	cultivate • teach
ネン	年	age • year
	念	attention • thought • will and intention
	捻	turn
	然	conditional conjunctions • modifier suffixes • terms of assent
	稔	mature
	燃	burn
	鮎	fishes
ねんごろ	懇	eager • familiar and friendly • kind

の

の	乃	possessive particles
	之	possessive particles • this and that
	野	natural • range • sports fields • uncultivated expanses of land • vulgar and unrefined
ノウ	悩	trouble and suffering
	納	offer • pay • receive • store • supply
	能	possible • potency • skill • skillful
	脳	head
	農	farm and plant
	濃	dark-colored • dense
のがす	逃	avoid and abstain • escape
のがれる	逃	avoid and abstain • escape
	遁	escape
のき	軒	counters for houses • houses • roof parts
のこ	鋸	cutting instruments
のこぎり	鋸	cutting instruments
のこす	残	cruel • leave • remain
のこる	残	cruel • leave • remain
のせる	乗	get on • mathematical power • multiply • travel by vehicle • vehicle
	載	load • print and publish
のぞく	除	divide • eliminate
のぞむ	望	repute • see and look • wish and desire
	臨	attend • exist and be • on the verge of
のたまわく	曰	speak and say
のち	後	after • be late and delay • future • rear • second
のっと	浬	length units
のど	喉	throat
ののしる	罵	disgrace
のばす	伸	expand • grow
	延	be late and delay • expand
のびやか	伸	expand • grow
のびる	伸	expand • grow
	延	be late and delay • expand
のべ	延	be late and delay • expand
のべる	伸	expand • grow
	延	be late and delay • expand
	述	speak and say
のぼす	上	ascend • aspect • end • excellent and superior • give • high² • high-ranking • raise • tops
のぼせる	上	ascend • aspect • end • excellent and superior • give • high² • high-ranking • raise • tops
のぼり	上	ascend • aspect • end • excellent and superior • give • high² • high-ranking • raise • tops
のぼる	上	ascend • aspect • end • excellent and superior • give • high² • high-ranking • raise • tops
	昇	ascend • rise in rank
	登	ascend • attend • write
のみ	飲	ingest
	鑿	cutting instruments • dig
のむ	呑	ingest
	飲	ingest
のり	乗	get on • mathematical power • multiply • travel by vehicle • vehicle

	暴	rash • reveal • sudden • violent
	縛	join • restrain
	曝	reveal
	爆	attack • explode • projectiles and bombs
はぐくむ	育	grow • raise and nourish • teach
はげしい	激	extreme in degree • extreme in power • incite • sudden
はげます	励	exert oneself • urge
はげむ	励	exert oneself • urge
はげる	剥	come off • eliminate
ばける	化	change and replace • disguise
はこ	函	containers
	箱	containers
はこぶ	運	carry • fate and fortune • handle • move
はさまる	挟	contain and include
はさみ	鋏	cutting instruments
はさむ	挟	contain and include
	鋏	cutting instruments
はし	梯	steps
	端	beginnings • edges and boundaries • extremity • right
	箸	long slender objects
	橋	bridges
はじ	恥	disgrace • genitals
はしご	梯	steps
はしばみ	榛	fruits and fruit trees
はじまる	始	begin • beginnings
はじめ	初	beginnings • first • original
はじめて	初	beginnings • first • original
	甫	almost
はじめる	始	begin • beginnings
はしら	柱	supporting structures
はじらう	恥	disgrace • genitals
はしる	走	escape • run • travel by vehicle
はじる	恥	disgrace • genitals
はす	蓮	flowering plants
はず	筈	certain
はずかしい	恥	disgrace • genitals
はずかしめる	辱	disgrace
はずす	外	come off • deviate • eliminate • foreign • outside
はずむ	弾	blame and accuse • play music • projectiles and bombs • spring back
はずれる	外	come off • deviate • eliminate • foreign • outside
はせる	馳	run
はた	畑	cultivated fields
	畠	cultivated fields
	秦	earlier Chinese dynasties
	旗	flag
	端	beginnings • edges and boundaries • extremity • right
	幡	flag
	機	aircraft and spacecraft • machines and tools • occasions • potency
はだ	肌	kinds of skin
ばた	端	beginnings • edges and boundaries • extremity • right
はだか	裸	naked
はたく	叩	strike

はたけ	畑	cultivated fields
	畠	cultivated fields
ばたけ	畑	cultivated fields
	畠	cultivated fields
はたす	果	execute • extreme • fruit
はたらく	働	work
ハチ	八	small numbers
	鉢	vessels and receptacles
はち	蜂	insects
バチ	罰	punishment
	撥	resist • strike
はちす	蓮	flowering plants
ハツ	法	laws and rules • religions and sects • way and style
ハツ	発	begin • create • emit • explode • grow • leave and set forth • reveal • shoot
	鉢	vessels and receptacles
	髪	hair
	撥	resist • strike
	潑	strong
	醗	brew and ferment
はつ	初	beginnings • first • original
バツ	末	descendant • ends • extremity • last • powder • unimportant
	伐	conquer and suppress • cut
	抜	choose • excel • omit • pull
	罰	punishment
	閥	parties and sects
はて	果	execute • extreme • fruit
はてる	果	execute • extreme • fruit
はと	鳩	birds
はな	花	flower
	華	Asian countries • beautiful • China • flower
	鼻	face orifices
はなし	話	speak and say • stories
はなす	放	emit • let do • release • throw
	話	speak and say • stories
	離	distant • estrange • leave and set forth • part company • separate
はなつ	放	emit • let do • release • throw
はなはだ	甚	extreme in degree
はなはだしい	甚	extreme in degree
はなれる	放	emit • let do • release • throw
	離	distant • estrange • leave and set forth • part company • separate
はに	埴	land and soil
はね	羽	counters for animals • hair • wings
はねる	跳	jump
	撥	resist • strike
はは	母	parents
はば	巾	fabric
	幅	width
はばむ	沮	obstruct and hinder
	阻	obstruct and hinder
はぶく	省	economizing and economy • eliminate • parts of governments • public offices • territorial divisions • think and consider
はま	浜	Kanto region • shores and watersides
はまる	嵌	put in
	填	fit

はめる	嵌	put in
はや	早	fast
	速	fast
はやい	早	fast
	速	fast
はやし	林	forest
はやす	生	animal · create · give birth · grow · healthy · life · live · new · reside · students and followers
はやぶさ	隼	birds
はやまる	早	fast
	速	fast
はやめる	早	fast
	速	fast
はら	原	natural · original · uncultivated expanses of land
	腹	psyche · trunk parts
ばら	肋	bone
はらい	払	clean and wash · drive out · eliminate · pay
ばらい	払	clean and wash · drive out · eliminate · pay
はらう	払	clean and wash · drive out · eliminate · pay
はらす	晴	weather
	腫	swell and swelling
はり	針	needle · perforators
	張	expand · tighten
	梁	supporting structures
	榛	fruits and fruit trees
	鍼	medicines
ばり	張	expand · tighten
	貼	stick
はる	春	sex · warm seasons
	張	expand · tighten
	貼	stick
はるか	遥	distant
はれ	晴	weather
ばれ	晴	weather
はれる	晴	weather
	脹	expand · swell and swelling
	腫	swell and swelling
ハン	³凡	ordinary
	⁴反	area units · length units · opposite · overturn · resist · spring back · violate
	⁵半	subordinate
	氾	expand
	犯	crimes and offenses · violate
	⁶汎	general
	⁷伴	accompany
	判	judge · seals
	坂	hills
	阪	hills · Kansai cities
	⁸板	boards and plates
	版	editions · print and publish · printing plate
	⁹叛	resist
	¹⁰班	groups
	畔	shores and watersides
	般	kinds and types · time periods

	¹¹絆	personal relations
	販	sell and trade
	¹²飯	food · rice
	¹³搬	carry
	煩	complex · trouble and suffering
	頒	distribute
	¹⁵幡	flag
	範	model · range
	蕃	savage
	¹⁶繁	busy · complex · flourish · prospering and prosperity
	¹⁸藩	feudal territorial divisions
はん	榛	fruits and fruit trees
バン	³万	all · large numbers · plentiful
	⁷伴	accompany
	判	judge · seals
	⁸板	boards and plates
	¹⁰挽	cut
	¹²晩	evening and night · late
	番	kinds of numbers · order · protect
	蛮	savage · vulgar and unrefined
	鈑	metal
	¹⁵幡	flag
	播	farm and plant
	盤	boards and plates · bottoms and bases · circular objects · vessels and receptacles
	磐	bottoms and bases
	蕃	savage

ひ

ヒ	²匕	spoons
	⁴比	arrange · Asian countries · compare · rate
	⁵皮	kinds of skin
	⁶妃	wives of rulers
	⁷否	refuse and reject · terms of negation
	庇	protect · roof parts
	批	blame and accuse · comment upon
	⁸彼	third person pronouns · this and that
	披	open · reveal
	泌	flow and drip
	肥	fatten
	非	terms of negation · wrongdoing and evil
	⁹卑	lowly · vulgar and unrefined
	毘	phonetic [b]
	飛	fly
	¹⁰疲	tire
	秘	secret and private
	被	be subjected to · cover and wrap · wear and put on
	¹²悲	grieve · sad and depressed · tender feelings for others
	扉	doors
	斐	beautiful · phonetic [i]
	費	consume · fee and price
	¹⁴緋	red colors
	蜚	fly
	鄙	the country · vulgar and unrefined
	¹⁵罷	dismiss
	誹	disgrace

	7 兵	armed forces · military · soldiers and warriors
	8 拍	musical elements · strike
	表	diagram · express · outside
	10 俵	bags
	秤	measuring devices
	豹	undomesticated mammals
	11 彪	beautiful
	票	labels and slips · vote and election
	12 評	comment upon · explanatory remarks · judge
	14 漂	float · wander
	15 標	indicate · marks and signs · target
	17 瓢	vegetables
ビョウ	平	calm and peaceful · flat · impartial · mathematical power·ordinary·same and uniform
	苗	early states of plant life
	秒	short time periods
	病	disease
	描	describe · draw
	猫	domesticated mammals
	廟	graves
ひよこ	雛	bird
ひら	平	calm and peaceful · flat · impartial · mathematical power · ordinary · same and uniform
ひらき	開	begin · open · reclaim
びらき	開	begin · open · reclaim
ひらく	開	begin · open · reclaim
ひらける	開	begin · open · reclaim
ひらめかす	閃	shine and reflect
ひらめく	閃	shine and reflect
ひる	干	dry · preserved foods
	昼	days · noon
ひるがえす	翻	overturn · translate
ひるがえる	翻	overturn · translate
ひるむ	怯	fear
ひろい	広	expand · make widely known · wide and extensive
ひろう	拾	get · raise · ten
ひろがる	広	expand · make widely known · wide and extensive
ひろげる	広	expand · make widely known · wide and extensive
ひろまる	広	expand · make widely known · wide and extensive
	弘	make widely known
ひろめる	広	expand · make widely known · wide and extensive
	弘	make widely known
ヒン	牝	woman
	品	flavor and elegance · kinds and types · merchandise · nature and character · object
	浜	Kanto region · shores and watersides
	彬	elegant
	貧	poor
	稟	inform and communicate
	賓	visitor
	瀕	almost

ビン	便	excreta · mail · suitable
	敏	fast · intelligent and wise
	秤	measuring devices
	瓶	containers
	貧	poor
	黽	reptiles and amphibians

ふ

フ	4 不	terms of negation
	夫	husband · man · workers and professionals
	父	clergymen · parents
	5 付	add to · stick · transfer
	布	fabric · make widely known · spread
	6 缶	containers
	7 扶	support
	甫	almost
	芙	flowering plants
	8 府	public offices · territorial divisions
	怖	fear
	斧	cutting instruments
	歩	area units · rate · walk
	阜	hills
	附	add to · stick · transfer
	9 訃	information
	負	bear · lose · negative · undertake
	赴	go and come
	風	appearance · custom · disease · flavor and elegance · view · way and style · wind
	10 浮	float
	釜	vessels and receptacles
	11 婦	wives · woman · workers and professionals
	符	labels and slips · marks and signs
	12 富	plentiful · rich · wealth
	普	ordinary · widespread
	13 蒲	kinds of grasses
	14 腐	decay
	輔	help
	15 敷	equip and install · mats · spread
	膚	kinds of skin
	賦	pay · tax
	19 譜	records
ブ	4 不	terms of negation
	分	branch · degree · discriminate · distribute · diverge · know and understand · part · quantity and number · responsibility · separate · short time periods
	夫	husband · man · workers and professionals
	8 侮	disdain · disgrace
	奉	offer · respectful
	歩	area units · rate · walk
	武	military · soldiers and warriors
	11 部	counters for books · divisions of organizations · part
	12 無	emptiness and nothing · terms of negation
	葡	European countries · fruits and fruit trees

	撫[15] touch		ふじ	藤 flowering plants • shrubs
	舞 dance		ぶし	節 economizing and economy • fidelity •
	蕪 vegetables			joint • labels and slips • music and songs •
フウ	夫 husband • man • workers and			occasions • parts of writing • sentence and
	professionals			sentence parts • time periods
	封 close • feudal territorial divisions		ふす	伏 hide • lie down • submit and surrender
	風 appearance • custom • disease • flavor and			臥 disease • lie down
	elegance • view • way and style • wind		ふすま	襖 clothing • doors
	富 plentiful • rich • wealth		ふせぐ	防 embankment • prevent • protect
	楓 trees			禦 avoid and abstain
	諷 speak and say		ふせる	伏 hide • lie down • submit and surrender
ブウ	鳳 birds • mythical animals			臥 disease • lie down
ふえ	笛 musical instruments		ふた	二 small numbers • two
ふえる	殖 give birth • increase			双 two
	増 increase			蓋 cover and wrap
ふかい	深 dark-colored • extreme in degree • inner •		ふだ	札 labels and slips • money
	profound		ぶた	豚 domesticated mammals • swine
ぶかい	深 dark-colored • extreme in degree • inner •		ふたたび	再 repeating and repetition
	profound		ふたつ	二 small numbers • two
ふかす	更 additionally • change and replace • reform		ふち	淵 kinds of water • stagnating water
ふかまる	深 dark-colored • extreme in degree • inner •			縁 edges and boundaries • family and
	profound			relations • fate and fortune • marrying and
ふかめる	深 dark-colored • extreme in degree • inner •			marriage • personal relations
	profound		フッ	富 plentiful • rich • wealth
ふき	蕗 vegetables		フツ	仏 Buddha • European countries • images •
ぶき	葺 cover and wrap			religions and sects
フク	伏 hide • lie down • submit and surrender			払 clean and wash • drive out • eliminate •
	服 clothing • ingest • submit and surrender			pay
	副 additional • subordinate			沸 cook
	幅 width		ブツ	仏 Buddha • European countries • images •
	復 repeating and repetition • return • return			religions and sects
	and restore			勿 phonetic [m] • terms of negation
	福 good fortune • happiness			物 abstract thing • animal • fellow • matter •
	腹 psyche • trunk parts			merchandise • object • phenomenon
	複 compound • copy		ふで	筆 compose • write • writing
	覆 cover and wrap • overturn		ふとい	太 big and huge • fatten • high-ranking •
ふく	吹 breathe and blow • discharge from mouth			thick
	• play music		ふところ	懐 garment parts • hold in the mind • psyche
	拭 clean and wash			• wish and desire
	葺 cover and wrap		ふとる	太 big and huge • fatten • high-ranking •
	噴 emit			thick
ふくべ	瓢 vegetables		ふな	舟 boats and ships
ふくむ	含 contain and include			船 aircraft and spacecraft • boats and ships
ふくめる	含 contain and include		ふね	舟 boats and ships
ふくらむ	脹 expand • swell and swelling			船 aircraft and spacecraft • boats and ships
	膨 expand		ぶね	舟 boats and ships
ふくれる	脹 expand • swell and swelling			船 aircraft and spacecraft • boats and ships
	膨 expand		ふまえる	踏 step on • walk
ふくろ	袋 bags • containers		ふみ	文 characters • Japanese money
ふける	老 Asian countries • honorific suffixes • old •			denominations • learning and knowledge
	old persons			• pattern • sentence and sentence parts •
	更 additionally • change and replace • reform			writing • written communications
	耽 acting arbitrarily		ふむ	踏 step on • walk
ふさ	房 bundles and clusters • rooms		ふもと	麓 bottoms and bases
ふさがる	塞 close • obstruct and hinder • strongholds		ふやす	殖 give birth • increase
ふさぐ	塞 close • obstruct and hinder • strongholds			増 increase
ふし	節 economizing and economy • fidelity •		ふゆ	冬 cold seasons
	joint • labels and slips • music and songs •		ふり	振 incite • prospering and prosperity • shake
	occasions • parts of writing • sentence and			降 descend and fall • get off • submit and
	sentence parts • time periods			surrender

ぶり	振 incite · prospering and prosperity · shake	
ふる	古 old	
	振 incite · prospering and prosperity · shake	
	降 descend and fall · get off · submit and surrender	
ぶる	振 incite · prospering and prosperity · shake	
ふるい	古 old	
ふるう	振 incite · prospering and prosperity · shake	
	震 shake	
	奮 elated · incite	
ふるえる	震 shake	
ふるす	古 old	
ふれる	振 incite · prospering and prosperity · shake	
	触 touch	
フン	分 branch · degree · discriminate · distribute · diverge · know and understand · part · quantity and number · responsibility · separate · short time periods	
	吻 front parts of head	
	粉 cereal · cosmetics · decorate · powder	
	紛 disordered	
	焚 burn	
	雰 atmosphere	
	噴 emit	
	墳 graves	
	憤 anger	
	奮 elated · incite	
ブン	分 branch · degree · discriminate · distribute · diverge · know and understand · part · quantity and number · responsibility · separate · short time periods	
	文 characters · Japanese money denominations · learning and knowledge · pattern · sentence and sentence parts · writing · written communications	
	聞 hear · inquire	

へ

べ	辺 approximately · areas and localities · edges and boundaries · lines and line segments · shores and watersides · side · the country	
ヘイ	平 calm and peaceful · flat · impartial · mathematical power · ordinary · same and uniform	
	7 兵 armed forces · military · soldiers and warriors	
	8 並 additionally · arrange · ordinary · together	
	併 combine · together	
	9 柄 aspect · handles · nature and character · pattern	
	10 病 disease	
	陛 steps	
	11 閉 close · end	
	12 塀 fences and walls	
	15 幣 money · offering	
	弊 bad · custom · humble prefixes · wrongdoing and evil	
	蔽 cover and wrap · hide	
	餅 rice	

	18 斃 die	
ベイ	米 cereals · continents · length units · North American countries · rice	
	吠 give out a call	
ページ	頁 counters for flat things · paper	
ヘキ	碧 blue and purple colors	
	壁 fences and walls · mountain parts	
	璧 precious stones	
	癖 custom	
へだたる	隔 distant · separate	
へだてる	隔 distant · separate	
ベツ	別 other · part company · separate · special	
	蔑 disdain	
	瞥 see and look	
べに	紅 cosmetics · red colors	
へび	蛇 reptiles and amphibians · snake	
へらす	減 decrease · subtract	
へる	経 books · direct and supervise · elapse · latitude and longitude · pass · threads and fibers	
	減 decrease · subtract	
ヘン	片 one · one side · part	
	辺 approximately · areas and localities · edges and boundaries · lines and line segments · shores and watersides · side · the country	
	返 answer · repeating and repetition · return and restore · time and time counters	
	変 abnormal · change and replace · incident · warfare and rebellions	
	扁 flat	
	偏 inclining toward · one side	
	遍 time and time counters · widespread	
	篇 books	
	編 books · compile · organize · weave and sew	
	騙 deceive	
ベン	弁 argue and discuss · discriminate · language · speak and say · stoppers	
	便 excreta · mail · suitable	
	勉 exert oneself	
	娩 give birth	
	黽 reptiles and amphibians	
	辦 deal with	
	辮 hair · weave and sew	

ほ

ホ	7 甫 almost	
	8 歩 area units · rate · walk	
	9 保 preserve · protect	
	10 哺 raise and nourish	
	圃 cultivated fields	
	捕 catch a criminal · take	
	浦 inlets and bays · shores and watersides	
	12 堡 strongholds	
	葡 European countries · fruits and fruit trees	
	補 additional · appoint · assistant · help · supplement	
	13 蒲 kinds of grasses	

ON-KUN INDEX

	墨 pigments	
	撲 strike	
ぼける	呆 foolish	
	惚 love and like	
ほこ	戈 cutting weapons	
	矛 cutting weapons	
	戟 cutting weapons	
	鉾 cutting weapons	
	鋒 energy and force · extremity	
ぼこ	凹 bowed · holes and cavities	
ほこさき	鋒 energy and force · extremity	
ほこる	誇 boasting and arrogance	
ほころびる	綻 degenerate	
ほころぶ	綻 degenerate	
ほし	干 dry · preserved foods	
	星 stars	
ぼし	干 dry · preserved foods	
	星 stars	
ほしい	欲 will and intention · wish and desire	
ほしいまま	擅 acting arbitrarily	
ほじくる	穿 dig · wear and put on	
ほじる	穿 dig · wear and put on	
ほす	干 dry · preserved foods	
ほそい	細 detailed · small and tiny · thin · unimportant	
ほそる	細 detailed · small and tiny · thin · unimportant	
ほだす	絆 personal relations	
ほたる	蛍 bright · insects	
ホツ	法 laws and rules · religions and sects · way and style	
ホツ	発 begin · create · emit · explode · grow · leave and set forth · reveal · shoot	
ボツ	坊 child · clergymen · fellow	
ボツ	没 collapse · die · disappear · sink · terms of negation	
	歿 die	
	勃 sudden	
ほっする	欲 will and intention · wish and desire	
ほど	程 approximately · degree · distance and interval · model · range	
ほとけ	仏 Buddha · European countries · images · religions and sects	
ほどこす	施 donate · execute	
ほとんど	殆 almost · danger	
ほね	骨 bone	
ほの	仄 less in degree	
ほのお	炎 diseases and disease symptoms · fire · hot	
	焔 fire	
ほのか	仄 less in degree	
ほのめかす	仄 less in degree	
ほのめく	仄 less in degree	
ほほ	頬 front parts of head	
ほまれ	誉 great respect · repute	
ほめる	褒 praise	
ほら	洞 holes and cavities	
ほり	堀 holes and cavities	
	掘 dig	
	壕 holes and cavities	
	濠 holes and cavities	

ぼり	彫 form and carve	
ほる	彫 form and carve	
	掘 dig	
ほれる	惚 love and like	
ほろ	幌 protective coverings	
ほろびる	滅 destroy · extinguish · rash	
ほろぶ	滅 destroy · extinguish · rash	
ほろぼす	滅 destroy · extinguish · rash	
ホン	反 area units · length units · opposite · overturn · resist · spring back · violate	
	本 basis · beginnings · books · counters for long objects · main · original · regular · this and that · true	
	奔 run	
	叛 resist	
	翻 overturn · translate	
ボン	凡 ordinary	
	盆 vessels and receptacles	
	煩 complex · trouble and suffering	

ま

マ	麻 become stupefied · fabrics · fiber-producing plants	
	摩 phonetic [m] · polish and rub	
	磨 cultivate · polish and rub	
	魔 mania and maniacs · miraculous · supernatural and evil beings	
ま	目 eye · face orifices · kinds of numbers · parts of writing · see and look · target	
	真 exact · true	
	間 between · distance and interval · during · length units · rooms · time periods	
マー	麻 become stupefied · fabrics · fiber-producing plants	
マイ	毎 all	
	米 cereals · continents · length units · North American countries · rice	
	妹 siblings	
	枚 counters for flat things	
	昧 dark · phonetic [m]	
	埋 bury	
まい	舞 dance	
まいる	参 compare · go and come · participate and join · three · visit	
	哩 length units	
まう	舞 dance	
まえ	前 before · former · front · in front	
まかす	任 appoint · commit · responsibility · work and employment	
	負 bear · lose · negative · undertake	
まかせる	任 appoint · commit · responsibility · work and employment	
まかなう	賄 give	
まがる	曲 bend · music and songs	
まき	牧 cultivated fields · raise and nourish	
	巻 books · counters for books · wind and twine	
	槙 trees	
まぎらす	紛 disordered	

ON-KUN INDEX

まぎらわしい	紛 disordered			街 parts of towns • ways and routes
まぎらわす	紛 disordered		マツ	末 descendant • ends • extremity • last • powder • unimportant
まぎれ	紛 disordered			
まぎれる	紛 disordered			抹 break into small pieces • eliminate • spread
マク	幕 curtain • governments • parts of plays			
まく	巻 books • counters for books • wind and twine			沫 small water masses
				茉 shrubs
	捲 wind and twine		まつ	松 trees
	蒔 farm and plant			待 expect • treat and welcome • wait
	撒 spread		まったく	全 all
	播 farm and plant		まつり	祭 ceremonies and festivities
まくし	捲 wind and twine		まつりごと	政 government
まくる	捲 wind and twine		まつる	祀 pray and worship
まける	負 bear • lose • negative • undertake			祭 ceremonies and festivities
まげる	曲 bend • music and songs		まつわる	纏 combine • wear and put on • wind and twine
まご	孫 descendant			
まこと	誠 fidelity		まで	迄 direction indicators
まさ	正 correct • exact • main • positive • regular • right • true • virtuous		まと	的 modifier suffixes • target
			まとう	纏 combine • wear and put on • wind and twine
	柾 trees			
まさき	柾 trees		まどう	惑 bewildered • deceive
まさに	正 correct • exact • main • positive • regular • right • true • virtuous		まとまる	纏 combine • wear and put on • wind and twine
まさる	勝 excel • win		まとめる	纏 combine • wear and put on • wind and twine
まざる	交 alternate • change and replace • intercross • mix • personal relations			
			まなこ	眼 discernment • eye
	混 disordered • mix		まなぶ	学 branch of study • learn and study • learning and knowledge • schools • students and followers
まし	増 increase			
まじえる	交 alternate • change and replace • intercross • mix • personal relations			
			まぬかれる	免 certificates • dismiss • forgive • permit
まじり	混 disordered • mix		まぬがれる	免 certificates • dismiss • forgive • permit
まじる	交 alternate • change and replace • intercross • mix • personal relations		まねく	招 call and invite
			まぼろし	幻 charm • illusory mental images
	混 disordered • mix		まめ	豆 cereals • small and tiny • vegetables
まじわる	交 alternate • change and replace • intercross • mix • personal relations		まもり	守 guard • obey • protect
			まもる	守 guard • obey • protect
ます	升 capacity units		まゆ	眉 hair
	枡 measuring devices			繭 insect
	益 benefit • profit		まゆずみ	黛 cosmetics
	増 increase		まゆみ	檀 trees
	鱒 fishes		まよう	迷 bewildered
まず	先 before • extremity • former • in front • most recent • sharp		まり	毬 spherical object
				鞠 spherical object
まずしい	貧 poor		まる	○ zero
まぜる	交 alternate • change and replace • intercross • mix • personal relations			丸 all • circle • medicines • projectiles and bombs • round • spherical object
	混 disordered • mix			円 circle • Japanese money denominations • round
また	又 additionally • repeating and repetition			
	叉 furcation • phonetic [s]/[sh]		まるい	丸 all • circle • medicines • projectiles and bombs • round • spherical object
	亦 additionally			
	股 furcation • trunk parts			円 circle • Japanese money denominations • round
	俣 furcation			
まだ	未 sheep • still • terms of negation		まるめる	丸 all • circle • medicines • projectiles and bombs • round • spherical object
またがる	跨 extend over			
またぐ	跨 extend over		まれ	希 European countries • rare • rare and sparse • wish and desire
またたく	瞬 short time periods			
またの	又 additionally • repeating and repetition			稀 rare • rare and sparse
まち	町 area units • cities and towns • length units • parts of towns • villages and towns		まろ	麿 first person pronouns • name suffixes
			まわし	回 return • send • time and time counters • turn
	待 expect • treat and welcome • wait			

まわす	回	return · send · time and time counters · turn
	廻	return · turn
まわり	回	return · send · time and time counters · turn
	周	earlier Chinese dynasties · periphery
まわる	回	return · send · time and time counters · turn
	廻	return · turn
マン	万	all · large numbers · plentiful
	満	all · fill · full · suffice
	慢	boasting and arrogance · lazy · slow
	漫	comic · unrestrained
	蔓	plants
	幡	flag

━━━━ み ━━━━

ミ	未	sheep · still · terms of negation
	味	essential content · flavor and elegance · taste
	弥	phonetic [m]
	眉	hair
	魅	charm
み	三	small numbers · three
	巳	snake
	身	body · class · first person pronouns · meat
	実	essential content · fidelity · fruit · mature · true
みえる	見	meet · opinion · see and look · show
みお	澪	ways and routes
みがく	磨	cultivate · polish and rub
みき	幹	essential part · supporting parts of plants
みぎ	右	left and right
みぎわ	汀	shores and watersides
みことのり	詔	imperial decree
みさお	操	chastity · fidelity · handle
みさき	岬	points of land
みささぎ	陵	graves · hills
みじかい	短	faults and flaws · short and shortened
みじめ	惨	cruel · sad and depressed
みず	水	days of the week · kinds of water · lighter elements · liquid
	瑞	good fortune
みずうみ	湖	lakes and marshes
みずから	自	direction indicators · first person pronouns
みずのえ	壬	calendar signs
みせ	店	places of business
みせる	見	meet · opinion · see and look · show
みぞ	溝	holes and cavities
みたす	満	all · fill · full · suffice
みだす	乱	disordered · rash · warfare and rebellions
みだら	淫	sex
みだる	乱	disordered · rash · warfare and rebellions
みだれる	乱	disordered · rash · warfare and rebellions
みち	道	art · moral goodness · moral principles · religion · religions and sects · territorial divisions · tubular passages · ways and routes

みちびく	導	lead and escort · teach
みちる	満	all · fill · full · suffice
ミツ	密	dense · detailed · familiar and friendly · secret and private
	蜜	phonetic [m] · seasonings
みつ	三	small numbers · three
	満	all · fill · full · suffice
みつぐ	貢	offer · offering · tax
みっつ	三	small numbers · three
みとめる	認	agree and approve · perceive
みどり	緑	green colors
	翠	green colors
みな	皆	all
みなと	湊	gather · places for landing or stopping
	港	places for landing or stopping
みなみ	南	cardinal points
みなもと	源	beginnings · water sources
みね	峰	mountain parts · mountains
	嶺	mountain parts
みの	蓑	clothing
みのる	実	essential content · fidelity · fruit · mature · true
	稔	mature
みみ	耳	face orifices
みや	宮	governments · palace · places of worship
ミャク	脈	line · reasoning · tubular passages
みやこ	都	all · cities and towns · Kanto region · territorial divisions
ミョウ	名	counters for persons · excellent and superior · name[1] · repute
	妙	abnormal · beautiful · excellent and superior · miraculous
	命	command · fate and fortune · life
	明	bright · clear · evident · explain · intelligent and wise · later Chinese dynasties · light · next · vivid
	苗	early states of plant life
	茅	kinds of grasses
	冥	dark
みる	見	meet · opinion · see and look · show
	視	judge · see and look
	診	investigate and examine
ミン	民	people · the people
	眠	sleep
みんな	皆	all

━━━━ む ━━━━

ム	矛	cutting weapons
	牟	phonetic [m]
	武	military · soldiers and warriors
	務	affairs · responsibility · work and employment
	無	emptiness and nothing · terms of negation
	夢	illusory mental images
	謀	plans and planning
	霧	kinds of atmospheric vapor
む	六	six · small numbers
むい	六	six · small numbers

ON-KUN INDEX

むかう	向	direction • direction indicators • face • go and come • tendency
むかえる	迎	treat and welcome
むかし	昔	old times
むき	向	direction • direction indicators • face • go and come • tendency
むぎ	麦	cereals
むく	向	direction • direction indicators • face • go and come • tendency
	椋	trees
むくいる	報	compensate • inform and communicate • information • periodicals • signal
むくう	報	compensate • inform and communicate • information • periodicals • signal
むけ	向	direction • direction indicators • face • go and come • tendency
むける	向	direction • direction indicators • face • go and come • tendency
むこ	婿	in-laws
むこう	向	direction • direction indicators • face • go and come • tendency
むさぼる	貪	wish and desire
むし	虫	insect
むしばむ	蝕	decrease
むす	蒸	cook • vaporize
むずかしい	難	blame and accuse • faults and flaws • misfortune and disaster • trouble and suffering
むすぶ	結	combine • end • join • organize • solidify and coagulate
むすめ	娘	offspring • woman
むつ	六	six • small numbers
むつかしい	難	blame and accuse • faults and flaws • misfortune and disaster • trouble and suffering
むっつ	六	six • small numbers
むつまじい	睦	familiar and friendly
むつむ	睦	familiar and friendly
むな	胸	chest • psyche • trunk parts
	棟	buildings • counters for houses • roof parts
むなしい	空	aircraft and spacecraft • emptiness and nothing • gas and vapor • sky • vain
むね	旨	essential part • meaning
	胸	chest • psyche • trunk parts
	棟	buildings • counters for houses • roof parts
むら	村	villages and towns
	群	crowd • groups
	叢	crowd • kinds of grasses
むらがる	群	crowd • groups
	叢	crowd • kinds of grasses
むらさき	紫	blue and purple colors
むらす	蒸	cook • vaporize
むれ	群	crowd • groups
むれる	群	crowd • groups
	蒸	cook • vaporize
むろ	室	rooms • wives • wives of rulers

め

め	女	offspring • woman
	目	eye • face orifices • kinds of numbers • parts of writing • see and look • target
	牝	woman
	芽	early states of plant life
	眼	discernment • eye
	雌	woman
メイ	名	counters for persons • excellent and superior • name[1] • repute
	命	command • fate and fortune • life
	明	bright • clear • evident • explain • intelligent and wise • later Chinese dynasties • light • next • vivid
	迷	bewildered
	冥	dark
	盟	promise
	銘	name[1] • writing
	鳴	give out a call • make sound or noise
めい	姪	offspring of siblings
めぐむ	恵	donate • favor
めぐり	巡	journey • turn
めくる	捲	wind and twine
めぐる	巡	journey • turn
めし	飯	food • rice
めす	召	call and invite
	牝	woman
	雌	woman
めずらしい	珍	abnormal • rare
メツ	滅	destroy • extinguish • rash
メン	免	certificates • dismiss • forgive • permit
	面	aspect • face • front • front parts of head • outside • paper • parts of periodicals • protective coverings • side
	棉	fabrics
	綿	fabrics • fiber-producing plants
	緬	Asian countries • threads and fibers
めん	牝	woman

も

モ	茂	flourish
	摸	imitate
	模	imitate • model • pattern
も	喪	losing and loss • mourn and mourning
	裳	clothing
モウ	[3] 亡	dead • destroy • die • escape
	[4] 毛	fabrics • hair
	[6] 妄	rash
	[8] 孟	Confucius and Confucianists
	盲	rash
	[10] 耗	consume • decrease
	[11] 望	repute • see and look • wish and desire
	猛	extreme in power • violent
	[13] 摸	imitate
	蒙	Asian countries • foolish
	[14] 網	net • system
もうかる	儲	profit
もうける	設	build • equip and install • found
	儲	profit
もうし	申	inform and communicate • monkey • speak and say • speak humbly

もうす	申	inform and communicate • monkey • speak and say • speak humbly
もうでる	詣	visit
もえる	萌	sprout and bloom
	燃	burn
モク	木	days of the week • kinds of wood • tree
	目	eye • face orifices • kinds of numbers • parts of writing • see and look • target
	黙	quiet
もぐる	潜	boats and ships • hide • sink
もし	若	young
もしくは	若	young
もす	燃	burn
もだえる	悶	trouble and suffering
もたげる	擡	raise
モチ	勿	phonetic [m] • terms of negation
もち	持	continue • hold • hold in the mind • possess • preserve • take
	餅	rice
もちいる	用	affairs • benefit • employ • need and necessity • use
モッ	勿	phonetic [m] • terms of negation
モツ	物	abstract thing • animal • fellow • matter • merchandise • object • phenomenon
もつ	持	continue • hold • hold in the mind • possess • preserve • take
もって	以	direction indicators
もっとも	尤	excellent and superior • right
	最	most
もっぱら	専	acting arbitrarily • occupy • special
もてあそぶ	弄	play
	玩	love and like • pleasure
もてる	持	continue • hold • hold in the mind • possess • preserve • take
もと	下	bad • bottoms and bases • descend and fall • diseases and disease symptoms • get off • give • low • lower • lowly
	元	beginnings • element • former • later Chinese dynasties
	本	basis • beginnings • books • counters for long objects • main • original • regular • this and that • true
	基	basis • bottoms and bases
もとい	基	basis • bottoms and bases
もどす	戻	return • return and restore
もとめる	求	request • seek • wish and desire
もとる	悖	violate
もどる	戻	return • return and restore
もの	物	abstract thing • animal • fellow • matter • merchandise • object • phenomenon
	者	person • workers and professionals
もみ	籾	rice
もも	股	furcation • trunk parts
	桃	fruits and fruit trees
もやす	燃	burn
もよおす	催	hold an event • urge
もらう	貰	receive
もらす	漏	flow and drip • omit
もり	守	guard • obey • protect
	杜	forest

	森	forest
もる	盛	accumulate • prospering and prosperity
	漏	flow and drip • omit
もれる	漏	flow and drip • omit
もろい	脆	weak
モン	文	characters • Japanese money denominations • learning and knowledge • pattern • sentence and sentence parts • writing • written communications
	門	branch of study • doors • family and relations • parties and sects • students and followers
	紋	insignia • marks and signs • pattern
	問	inquire • question
	悶	trouble and suffering
	聞	hear • inquire
もんめ	匁	weight units

や

ヤ	也	classical particles • exist and be
	冶	work metals
	夜	evening and night
	耶	classical particles
	野	natural • range • sports fields • uncultivated expanses of land • vulgar and unrefined
	椰	fruits and fruit trees
	爺	man • old persons
や	八	small numbers
	也	classical particles • exist and be
	矢	projectiles and bombs
	弥	phonetic [m]
	哉	classical particles
	屋	fellow • houses • merchant • places of business • pseudonym suffixes • roof • workers and professionals
	耶	classical particles
	家	family and relations • houses • workers and professionals
やいと	灸	medicines
やかた	館	buildings • mansions • temporary quarters
やかましい	喧	loud
やき	焼	burn • cook • cooked dishes • work metals
ヤク	厄	misfortune and disaster
	役	benefit • employ • officials • warfare and rebellions • work and employment
	疫	disease
	約	abridge • approximately • contract and shrink • promise
	益	benefit • profit
	訳	cause and reason • meaning • reason • states and situations • translate
	軛	long slender objects
	薬	medicines
	躍	jump
やく	灼	burn
	焼	burn • cook • cooked dishes • work metals
やぐら	櫓	parts of boats and ships
やける	焼	burn • cook • cooked dishes • work metals

やさしい	易	change and replace · divine · easy · sell and trade
	優	elegant · excellent and superior · gentle · kind · performers
やしなう	養	cultivate · raise and nourish
やしろ	社	places of business · places of worship · society
やす	安	calm and peaceful · comfortable · easy · inexpensive · peace
やすい	安	calm and peaceful · comfortable · easy · inexpensive · peace
	易	change and replace · divine · easy · sell and trade
やすまる	休	discontinue · holiday · rest
やすむ	休	discontinue · holiday · rest
やすめる	休	discontinue · holiday · rest
やすらか	安	calm and peaceful · comfortable · easy · inexpensive · peace
やせる	痩	thin
やつ	八	small numbers
	奴	fellow · servants · third person pronouns
やっつ	八	small numbers
やど	宿	post station · stay · temporary quarters
やとう	雇	employ
	傭	employ
やどす	宿	post station · stay · temporary quarters
やどる	宿	post station · stay · temporary quarters
やな	梁	supporting structures
やなぎ	柳	trees
やぶる	破	accomplish · break · degenerate · penetrate · violate · win
やぶれる	破	accomplish · break · degenerate · penetrate · violate · win
	敗	fail · lose
やま	山	mine · mountains
やまい	病	disease
やまと	倭	Japan
やみ	病	disease
	闇	dark · foolish
やむ	已	discontinue
	止	discontinue · not moving · prevent · stop
	病	disease
やめる	已	discontinue
	止	discontinue · not moving · prevent · stop
	辞	resign · words and expressions
やり	槍	projectiles and bombs
やわらか	柔	gentle · soft · weak
	軟	soft
やわらかい	柔	gentle · soft · weak
	軟	soft
やわらぐ	和	familiar and friendly · Japan · peace · total
やわらげる	和	familiar and friendly · Japan · peace · total

ゆ

ユ	由	cause and reason
	油	fats and oils · kinds of fuel · seasonings
	柚	fruits and fruit trees
	喩	words and expressions
	愉	pleased and pleasant

	遊	journey · play · wander
	諭	teach · warn
	輸	carry
	癒	cure and recover
ゆ	湯	baths · kinds of water
ユイ	由	cause and reason
	唯	only
	惟	think and consider
	遺	forget · leave
ユウ	⁴友	friends and associates
	尤	excellent and superior · right
	⁵右	left and right
	由	cause and reason
	⁶有	exist and be · possess
	⁷佑	help
	邑	villages and towns
	酉	birds
	⁸侑	urge
	⁹勇	brave · courage
	宥	forgive
	幽	inner · posthumous worlds · profound · quiet
	柚	fruits and fruit trees
	祐	help
	¹¹悠	distant · leisurely
	郵	mail
	¹²游	move through water
	湧	emit
	猶	be late and delay
	裕	plentiful
	遊	journey · play · wander
	雄	brave · great · great persons · man
	¹³楢	trees
	¹⁴誘	cause · urge
	¹⁵憂	sorrow · worry
	¹⁶融	lend and borrow · liquefy
	¹⁷優	elegant · excellent and superior · gentle · kind · performers
ゆう	夕	evening and night
	結	combine · end · join · organize · solidify and coagulate
ゆえ	故	cause and reason · dead · former · incident · old
ゆか	床	bottoms and bases · flat supports
ゆがむ	歪	bend
ゆがめる	歪	bend
ゆき	行	acts · bank · behavior · direction indicators · do and act · execute · go and come · journey · linear arrangements · styles of Chinese characters
	雪	kinds of frozen water · kinds of precipitation
ゆく	行	acts · bank · behavior · direction indicators · do and act · execute · go and come · journey · linear arrangements · styles of Chinese characters
	逝	die
ゆさぶる	揺	shake
ゆず	柚	fruits and fruit trees
ゆすぶる	揺	shake

ゆする	揺	shake
ゆずる	譲	compromise · transfer
ゆたか	豊	plentiful
ゆだねる	委	commit
ゆび	指	hand and arm · indicate · instruct
ゆみ	弓	weapons for shooting
ゆめ	夢	illusory mental images
ゆらぐ	揺	shake
ゆる	揺	shake
ゆるい	緩	loosen · slow
ゆるがせ	忽	immediate
ゆるぐ	揺	shake
ゆるす	許	forgive · permit
ゆるむ	弛	loosen
	緩	loosen · slow
ゆるめる	弛	loosen
	緩	loosen · slow
ゆるやか	緩	loosen · slow
ゆれる	揺	shake
ゆわえる	結	combine · end · join · organize · solidify and coagulate

よ

ヨ	与	give · participate and join
	予	before · first person pronouns
	余	after · exceeding and excess · first person pronouns · other · remain
	誉	great respect · repute
	預	commit
	輿	vehicle
よ	世	generation · long time periods · phonetic [s]/[sh] · society · world · worldly
	代	change and replace · fee and price · generation · long time periods · substitute
	四	small numbers
	夜	evening and night
よい	好	good · love and like · personal relations
	良	good · virtuous
	宵	evening and night
	酔	become stupefied
	善	good · moral goodness · virtuous
ヨウ	5 幼	child · young
	用	affairs · benefit · employ · need and necessity · use
	6 羊	domesticated mammals · sheep
	7 妖	abnormal
	9 洋	sea · west
	要	abridge · essential part · important · need and necessity · request
	10 容	agree and approve · appearance · contain and include
	11 庸	ordinary
	12 揚	cook · cooked dishes · elated · praise · raise
	揺	shake
	葉	counters for flat things · paper · wings
	遥	distant
	陽	positive · sun · yin and yang

	13 傭	employ
	楊	trees
	溶	liquefy
	瑶	beautiful
	腰	trunk parts
	蓉	flowering plants
	14 様	kinds and types · pattern · similar · states and situations · titles of address · way and style
	熔	liquefy
	瘍	swell and swelling
	踊	dance
	15 窯	ceramics ware · heating devices
	養	cultivate · raise and nourish
	16 擁	embrace · support
	謡	music and songs
	18 曜	days
	燿	shine and reflect
	鎔	liquefy
	20 耀	shine and reflect
	24 鷹	birds
よう	八	small numbers
	酔	become stupefied
ヨク	弋	hunt and fish
	抑	restrain
	沃	plentiful
	浴	baths · clean and wash
	欲	will and intention · wish and desire
	翌	next
	慾	wish and desire
	翼	parties and sects · wings
よこ	横	acting arbitrarily · side
よごす	汚	dirty¹ · dirty² · disgrace
よごれる	汚	dirty¹ · dirty² · disgrace
よし	由	cause and reason
	芦	kinds of grasses
	葦	kinds of grasses
よしみ	誼	personal relations
よせる	寄	approach · donate · pull · visit
よそおう	装	clothing · decorate · disguise · equip and install · wear and put on
よつ	四	small numbers
よっつ	四	small numbers
よど	淀	stagnate · stagnating water
	澱	stagnate · stagnating water
よどむ	淀	stagnate · stagnating water
	澱	stagnate · stagnating water
よぶ	呼	breathe and blow · call and invite · give out a call · name²
よみ	読	recite
よみがえる	甦	return and restore
	蘇	return and restore
よみする	嘉	good fortune · praise
よむ	詠	recite
	読	recite
よめ	嫁	in-laws · marrying and marriage · wives
よもぎ	蓬	flowering plants
より	寄	approach · donate · pull · visit
よる	因	cause and reason
	夜	evening and night

ON-KUN INDEX

ら

り

虜 prisoner
慮 think and consider

ョウ
² 了 end · know and understand
⁶ 両 Japanese money denominations · kinds of railway · two
⁷ 良 good · virtuous
⁹ 亮 evident
¹⁰ 倆 art · skill
凌 excel
料 fee and price · matter · pay and earnings
¹¹ 崚 high²
梁 supporting structures
涼 cold
猟 hunt and fish · seek
菱 fruits and fruit trees
陵 graves · hills
¹² 椋 trees
量 measure · quantity and number · think and consider
¹³ 稜 hills
¹⁴ 僚 friends and associates · officials
寥 barren
漁 hunt and fish
綾 fabrics
領 areas and localities · feudal territorial divisions · leaders · occupy · receive
¹⁵ 寮 temporary quarters
諒 know and understand
輛 kinds of railway · vehicle
遼 distant
霊 holy · psyche · supernatural and evil beings
¹⁶ 澪 ways and routes
燎 burn
¹⁷ 嶺 mountain parts
療 cure and recover
瞭 evident
¹⁸ 糧 food

ョク
力 energy and force · power and authority · skill
緑 green colors

ン
⁸ 林 forest
⁹ 厘 Japanese money denominations
¹⁰ 倫 moral principles
¹¹ 淋 diseases and disease symptoms · sad and depressed
¹² 琳 precious stones
¹³ 稟 inform and communicate
鈴 bells
¹⁴ 綸 threads and fibers
¹⁵ 凛 brave · cold
輪 alternate · circular objects · vehicle
¹⁶ 隣 near
¹⁸ 臨 attend · exist and be · on the verge of
²⁴ 鱗 kinds of skin
麟 mythical animals · undomesticated mammals

る

ル
流 class · electricity and magnetism · flow and drip · make widely known · parties and sects · rivers and streams · running water · smooth · tendency · wander · way and style
留 imprison and confine · preserve · refine · remain · stay · vaporize
琉 precious stones
瑠 blue and purple colors · precious stones
蕗 vegetables

ルイ
涙 bodily secretions
累 accumulate
塁 strongholds
類 kinds and types · resemble · similar

れ

レイ
¹ ○ zero
⁵ 令 age · command · honorific prefixes · laws and rules
礼 bow · ceremonies and festivities · etiquette · monetary gifts · thanking and gratitude
⁷ 伶 performers
冷 cold · reduce the temperature
励 exert oneself · urge
戻 return · return and restore
⁸ 例 constant · custom · example
怜 intelligent and wise
⁹ 玲 kinds of sound
¹¹ 羚 undomesticated mammals
¹³ 鈴 bells
零 zero
¹⁵ 霊 holy · psyche · supernatural and evil beings
黎 black colors
¹⁶ 澪 ways and routes
隷 obey · servants
¹⁷ 嶺 mountain parts
齢 age
¹⁹ 麗 beautiful

レキ
暦 calendars
歴 elapse · history · in succession
瀝 flow and drip
轢 overturn

レツ
列 arrange · linear arrangements
劣 bad
烈 extreme in power
裂 break

レン
⁸ 怜 intelligent and wise
¹⁰ 恋 love · love and like
連 continue · groups · in succession · join · lead and escort · organized bodies · relate
¹³ 廉 inexpensive · purehearted

煉 work metals
蓮 flowering plants
14 漣 waves
練 cultivate · teach
16 憐 tender feelings for others
錬 cultivate · refine · work metals
17 聯 relate
19 簾 curtain
23 攣 contract and shrink

ろ

ロ
7 呂 musical elements · phonetic [r]
芦 kinds of grasses
8 炉 heating devices
11 鹵 steal and rob
13 賂 give
路 phonetic [r] · ways and routes
15 魯 foolish
16 蕗 vegetables
19 櫓 parts of boats and ships
21 露 European countries · kinds of precipitation · reveal
24 鷺 birds

ロウ
6 老 Asian countries · honorific suffixes · old · old persons
7 労 organized bodies · tire · work · work and employment
弄 play
9 郎 man · name suffixes
10 朗 clear · loud · pleased and pleasant
浪 wander · waves
狼 undomesticated mammals
13 楼 tall buildings
稜 hills
14 漏 flow and drip · omit
15 撈 take from water
18 糧 food
21 蠟 fats and oils
露 European countries · kinds of precipitation · reveal
22 籠 containers

ロク
六 six · small numbers
肋 bone
鹿 undomesticated mammals
禄 pay and earnings
緑 green colors
録 records · write
麓 bottoms and bases

ロン
論 argue and discuss · opinion · question · theory

わ

ワ
把 handles · take
和 familiar and friendly · Japan · peace · total
杷 fruits and fruit trees
倭 Japan
琶 musical instruments
蛙 reptiles and amphibians

話 speak and say · stories
窪 holes and cavities
わ 羽 counters for animals · hair · wings
我 first person pronouns
輪 alternate · circular objects · vehicle
ワイ 歪 bend
隈 corners
賄 give
わか 若 young
わが 吾 first person pronouns
我 first person pronouns
わかい 若 young
わかす 沸 cook
わかつ 分 branch · degree · discriminate · distribute · diverge · know and understand · part · quantity and number · responsibility · separate · short time periods
わかる 分 branch · degree · discriminate · distribute · diverge · know and understand · part · quantity and number · responsibility · separate · short time periods
わかれる 分 branch · degree · discriminate · distribute · diverge · know and understand · part · quantity and number · responsibility · separate · short time periods
別 other · part company · separate · special
わき 脇 side · trunk parts
腋 trunk parts
ワク 或 a certain · some
惑 bewildered · deceive
わく 枠 frames
沸 cook
湧 emit
わけ 分 branch · degree · discriminate · distribute · diverge · know and understand · part · quantity and number · responsibility · separate · short time periods
訳 cause and reason · meaning · reason · states and situations · translate
わける 分 branch · degree · discriminate · distribute · diverge · know and understand · part · quantity and number · responsibility · separate · short time periods
わざ 技 art · game · skill
業 acts · fate and fortune · industry and business · learning and knowledge · work and employment
わざわい 災 misfortune and disaster
わし 鷲 birds
わずか 僅 few
わずらう 患 disease
煩 complex · trouble and suffering
わずらわす 煩 complex · trouble and suffering
わすれる 忘 forget
わた 棉 fabrics
綿 fabrics · fiber-producing plants
わたくし 私 first person pronouns · secret and private
わたし 私 first person pronouns · secret and private
わたす 渡 cross · transfer
わたる 亘 extend over

	渡 cross・transfer		われ	吾 first person pronouns
わびる	詫 apologize			我 first person pronouns
わら	藁 kinds of grasses		われる	割 break・cut・divide・rate・separate
わらう	笑 laugh		ワン	椀 vessels and receptacles
わらび	蕨 kinds of grasses			湾 inlets and bays
わらべ	童 child			腕 hand and arm・limbs・skill
わり	割 break・cut・divide・rate・separate			碗 vessels and receptacles
わる	悪 bad・evil・hate and dislike・wrongdoing and evil			彎 bend
	割 break・cut・divide・rate・separate			

──────── を ────────

わるい	悪 bad・evil・hate and dislike・wrongdoing and evil	
	ヲ	乎 modifier suffixes

635 ON-KUN INDEX

GROUP INDEX
類 義 漢 字 系 列 索 引

The **Group Index** is an alphabetical list of keywords for quickly finding the **synonym groups** from their **group headwords, synonym keywords,** or their derivatives. For example, if you look up the word "advance" you find the following group headwords: **advance • make progress • move forward,** separated by a middle dot. This means that the characters that have the synonym keyword **advance** can be found under these three synonym groups.

——— A ———

a bit	few
a bit of	few • small and tiny
a certain	a certain • some
a little	few
abandon	discard and abandon
abhor	hate and dislike
ability	skill
-able	possible
able	skillful
abnormal	abnormal
abolish	discontinue
about	approximately
abridged	short and shortened
abruptly	sudden
abstain	avoid and abstain
abstain from	avoid and abstain
abstract thing	
	abstract thing
abundant	plentiful
abuse	disgrace
accept	receive
accessory	additional
acclaim	praise
accompaniment for drinks	
	food
accompany	accompany
accompany a superior	
	accompany
accomplish	accomplish • execute
account	stories
accumulate	accumulate
accuse	blame and accuse
accuse in court	
	sue
accuse of	sue
achieve	accomplish
achievements	
	accomplishment
acid	sour substances
acquire	get

act	acts • do and act • execute • parts of plays
act arbitrarily	
	acting arbitrarily
act as regent	substitute
act contrary to	
	violate
act of kindness	
	favor
action	potency
active	active
actor	performers
actual	present • true
actual conditions	
	states and situations
acupuncture	medicines
add	add • add to
add to	add to • increase
additional	additional
address	indicate
address respectfully	
	speak humbly
adhere to	adhere to
adjectival suffix	
	modifier suffixes
adjective suffix	
	modifier suffixes
admonish	teach • warn
adore	love and like • respect
adult woman	woman
advance	advance • make progress • move forward
advance in rank	
	rise in rank
advantage	benefit
advise	warn
advocate	advocate
affair	affair • incident
affairs	affairs
affected by disease	
	disease
affection	love

affectionate	kind
affix a seal	mark
Africa	continents
after	after • second
after-	rear
afteryears	future
again	repeating and repetition
age	age • long time periods
age suffix	age
agile	fast
agree to	agree and approve
ahead	before • in front
aid	help
aide	assistant
aim	target
air	appearance • gas and vapor
aircraft	aircraft and spacecraft
alcoholic drink	
	drinks
alight	get off
all	all
all in one	all
all over	widespread
all through	throughout
alliance	promise
allot	allot
almost	almost
alone	alone
along	near
already	former
also	additionally
alternate	alternate • change and replace
amber	precious stones
ambition	will and intention
America	continents • North American countries
amnesty	forgive
amount	quantity and number
amphibians	reptiles and amphibians

barrel	containers	bear	bear · bear and	bewildered	bewildered
barrier	obstacle		endure · undertake	bewitch	charm
base	basis · bottoms and		· undomesticated	bifurcation	furcation
	bases		mammals	big	big and huge · extreme
baseball field		bear fruit	mature		in degree · great
	sports fields	bear on shoulder		bill	money
bases	bottoms and bases		bear	billow	waves
basic principle		beard	hair	bind	join · restrain
	principle	beast	animal	bind up	join
basis	basis	beat	musical elements ·	biography	history · records
basket	containers		strike	birch	trees
bath	baths	beautiful	beautiful · good	bird	bird
bathe	clean and wash	beautiful black jewel		bird net	net
battle	warfare and rebellions		precious stones	bite	bite
bay	inlets and bays	beautiful coloring		bitter	tastes
bays	inlets and bays		color[1]	bitter orange	fruits and fruit trees
be	exist and be	beautiful gem		bitter(ly)	extreme in degree
be afraid	fear		precious stones	black	black colors · dark
be anxious	worry	beautiful scenery		black kite	birds
be bent	bend		view	blade	cutting instruments
be born	give birth	because	cause and reason	blame	blame and accuse
be concluded		become dispirited		blazing	bright
	settle		grieve · sad and	bleach	discolor
be defeated	lose		depressed	blessedness	happiness
be equivalent		become intoxicated		blind	rash
	correspond to		become stupefied	block	buildings
be exhausted		become numb		block for beating cloth	
	come to an end		become stupefied		instruments for beating
be frightened		become pregnant			or pounding
	fear		conceive	blood	lineage
be fulfilled	accomplish	become skilled		bloom	sprout and bloom
be full of	fill		attain proficiency	blow	breathe and blow ·
be granted an audience		bed	bottoms and bases ·		discharge from mouth ·
	meet		flat supports		play music
be impatient	impatient	bedrock	bottoms and bases	blue	blue and purple colors
be in agony	trouble and suffering	bee	insects	board	boards and plates · get
be in extremity		before	before · in front		on
	trouble and suffering	beg	request	board game	board games
be in fear	fear	begin	begin	boast	boasting and arrogance
be in trouble	trouble and suffering	begin to do	begin	boat	boats and ships
be in waiting	wait	beginning	beginnings	boats	parts of boats and ships
be late	be late and delay	behavior	behavior	body	bodies · body · groups
be moved	feel deeply	Belgium	European countries		· object · organized
be on the verge of		belittling plural suffix			bodies
	on the verge of		plural suffixes	body cavity	holes and cavities
be overawed	fear	bell	bells	boil	cook
be present	exist and be	belly	trunk parts	boiled food	cooked dishes
be present at	attend · exist and be	belong to	possess	boisterous	loud
be sick in bed		belt	areas and localities	bold	brave
	disease	bend	bend	bold and unrestrained	
be similar	resemble	bend in submission			brave
be subjected to			submit and surrender	boldly	resolutely
	be subjected to	benefit	benefit	bomb	attack · projectiles and
be subordinate to		benevolence	tender feelings for		bombs
	obey		others	bombs	projectiles and bombs
beach	shores and watersides	beside	near · side	bond	securities
beam	supporting structures	besides	additionally	bonds	personal relations
bean	cereals · vegetables	between	between	bone	bone

come close to	approach
come off	come off
come out	appear
come to	arrive
come to an end	come to an end · end
come to terms	compromise
come together	gather
comet	constellation
comfortable	comfortable
comic	comic
coming generations	future
command	command
commander	military officers and ranks
commander in chief	military officers and ranks
commandment	precept
commend	praise
comment	comment upon · explanatory remarks
commit	commit
commit to memory	remember
commodity	merchandise
common	ordinary · widespread
common reed	kinds of grasses
common-interest group	groups
commonplace	ordinary
communicate	inform and communicate
Communism	Communism
companion	friends and associates
company	places of business
company officer	military officers and ranks
compare	compare
compare to	compare
compassion	tender feelings for others
compensate	compensate
compete	compete
compile	compile
complete	all · end
complete(ly)	all
completion suffix	end
complicated	complex
compose	compose · create

compound	compound
comprehend	know and understand
compute	calculate and count
comrade	friends and associates
concave	bowed
concavity	holes and cavities
conceal	hide
concede	compromise
conceive	conceive · think and consider
concentrate	concentrate on
conception	thought
concern	relate
concern oneself	worry
conclude	end · promise
concurrently	additionally · together
condition	states and situations
conditions	states and situations
condole	console · mourn and mourning
conduct	behavior
cone	three-dimensional shapes
confectionery	confectionery
confer	give
confine	imprison and confine
Confucianism	religions and sects
Confucianists	confucius and confucianists
Confucius	Confucius and Confucianists
confused	disordered
congeal	solidify and coagulate
congratulate	celebrating and congratulating
congratulating	celebrating and congratulating
congratulations	celebrating and congratulating
conjecture	conjecture
connect	join · relate
connection	joint
conquer	conquer and suppress · win
consent	agree and approve
consider	think and consider
considering the character of	aspect
console	console
conspicuous	conspicuous
constancy	fidelity
constant	constant
constellation	stars
constitution	laws and rules

construct	build · make
consult	argue and discuss · inquire
contact	touch
contain	contain and include
contaminate	dirty[1]
contend	argue and discuss · compete
content	quantity and number
contents	essential content
contest	compete
continue	continue
contract	abridge · contract and shrink
contribute	donate
contribute money	donate
control	direct and supervise · restrain
control movement skillfully	handle
convenient	suitable
convex	bowed · protrude and protruding
cook	cook
cook by fire	cook
cooked rice	rice
cool	cold · reduce the temperature
cooperate	cooperate
copper	metals
copy	copy · write
copy after	imitate
copy by rubbing	copy
coral	shells
cord	ropes and lines
cordial	kind
core	central parts
cormorant	birds
corner	corners
corpse	body
correct	correct · right
correspond to	correspond to
cotton	fabrics · fiber-producing plants
cotton rose	flowering plants
count	calculate and count · noblemen
counter	opposite · resist
counter for animals	counters for animals
counter for articles	general counters
counter for birds	counters for animals
counter for books	counters for books

debt	lend and borrow	descendant	descendant	dish	vessels and receptacles
debt of gratitude		describe	describe	disk	circular objects
	thanking and gratitude	desert	uncultivated expanses	disk-shaped jewel	
decay	decay		of land		precious stones
decease	die	designation	name[1]	dislike	hate and dislike
deceased	dead	desire	will and intention · wish	dismiss	dismiss
deceive	deceive		and desire	disordered	disordered
decide	decide · judge	desk	tables and stands	dispatch	send
decisively	resolutely	desolate	barren	display	display
decline	degenerate · weaken	despise	disdain	display in writing	
decoct	cook	destitute	poor		print and publish
decorate	decorate	destroy	destroy	dispose	put
decoration	prizes	detailed	detailed	dispose of	deal with
decorative halberd		detect	detect	dissect	cut
	cutting weapons	develop	grow	disseminate	make widely known
decorative pattern		deviate	deviate	dissolve	disperse · liquefy
	pattern	devil	supernatural and evil	distance	distance and interval
decrease	decrease		beings	distant	distant · estrange
dedicate	offer	devote oneself to		distill	refine · vaporize
deed	acts		concentrate on	distinguish	discriminate
deep	dark-colored · extreme	devoted	eager	distinguished	
	in degree · inner ·	dew	kinds of precipitation		excellent and superior
	profound	dialect	language	distort	bend
deep and vast		diameter	lines and line segments	distribute	distribute
	profound · wide and		· width	distribute widely	
	extensive	diarrhea	diseases and disease		distribute
deep blue	blue and purple colors		symptoms	district	areas and localities
deep hidden	profound	die	die	District of Hokkaido	
deep water	kinds of water ·	die a martyr	die		territorial divisions
	stagnating water	differ	differing and difference	ditch	holes and cavities
deer	undomesticated	difference	differing and difference	ditty	music and songs
	mammals	different	differing and difference	diverge	diverge
defect	faults and flaws	difficult	trouble and suffering	divide	distribute · divide ·
defend	protect	dig	dig		separate
defile	disgrace	digit	kinds of numbers	dividend	interest and dividend
defraud	deceive	dignified	dignified	divination	divine
degenerate	degenerate	dike	embankment	divine	divine · holy
degree	angle and angular	dim-witted	foolish	divine help	help
	measure · degree	dipper	spoons	do	do and act
deign to give	give	direct	instruct	do as one pleases	
delay	be late and delay	direction	direction		acting arbitrarily
delighted	pleased and pleasant	direction word		do humbly	do and act
deliver	transfer · transmit and		direction indicators	do not	terms of negation
	deliver	dirty	dirty[1] · dirty[2]	do over	repeating and
deliver goods to a customer		disabled	weak		repetition
	supply	disagreeable	hate and dislike	doctor	wise and talented
demand	need and necessity	disappear	disappear		persons
demon	supernatural and evil	disaster	misfortune and disaster	dog	dog · domesticated
	beings	discard	discard and abandon		mammals
depart this life		discharge	dismiss · emit · explode	donate	donate
	die		· shoot	door	doors
department	divisions of	disciple	students and followers	dormitory	temporary quarters
	organizations	discipline	laws and rules	double	compound · increase
depend on	rely on	disclose	reveal	doubt	doubt
depict	describe · draw	discriminate	discriminate	draft	manuscript
deplore	grieve	discuss	argue and discuss	dragon	dragon · mythical
deportment	behavior	disease	disease		animals · reptiles and
deposit	commit	disease symptoms			amphibians
depressed	sad and depressed		diseases and disease	drama	performance
descend	descend and fall		symptoms	drapery	curtain

draw	draw • pull	early evening		employ	employ • use	
draw attention			evening and night	employment	work and employment	
	pull	early morning		empress	wives of rulers	
draw near	approach • pull		morning and dawn	empty	emptiness and nothing	
draw out	pull	earnest	eager		• vain	
draw up a plan		earnings	pay and earnings	enclose	surround	
	plans and planning	earthenware jar		enclosure	fences and walls	
draw water	take from water		containers	encompass	contain and include •	
drawing	diagram • picture	earthly god	god		surround	
dream	illusory mental images	east	cardinal points	encounter	meet	
dredge	take from water	easy	comfortable • easy	encourage	advance • urge	
dress	clothing • decorate •	eat	ingest	end	end • ends • extreme •	
	wear and put on	eaves	roof parts		extremity	
dress up	disguise	economize	economizing and	endeavor	exert oneself	
dried food	preserved foods		economy	endure	bear and endure	
dried meat	meat	economy	economizing and	enemy	enemy	
drift	float • wander		economy	energetic	strong	
drift about	wander	edge	edges and boundaries	energy	energy and force	
drill	cutting instruments •	edify	teach	engage in sales		
	dig	edit	compile		sell and trade	
drink	ingest	edition	editions	England	European countries	
drip	flow and drip	educate	teach	engrave	form and carve	
drive	force to move • set in	educational institution		enjoy	possess • receive	
	motion		schools	enjoyment	pleasure	
drive away	drive out	effect	execute • potency	enlarge	expand	
drive out	drive out	efficacy	potency	enlighten	teach	
drop	flow and drip • small	egg	early states of animal	enter	enter • participate and	
	water masses		life		join	
drop down	descend and fall	eggplant	vegetables	entertainment		
drought	dry	eight	small numbers		performance	
drown	sink	elbow	hand and arm	entire	all	
drug	medicines	eldest son	offspring	entrance	doors	
drum	musical instruments	election	vote and election	entrust	commit	
dry	dry	electric current		entwine	wind and twine	
dry up	dry		electricity and	envious	jealous and envious	
duck	birds		magnetism	envoy	agents	
duke	noblemen	electric railway		epidemic	disease	
dull	foolish • light-colored		kinds of railway	equal	impartial • same and	
duplicate	compound • copy	electricity	electricity and		uniform	
	• repeating and		magnetism	era	long time periods	
	repetition	elegance	flavor and elegance	erode	decrease	
dusk	evening and night	elegant	elegant	error	mistakes and mistaking	
dust	waste	element	basis • element	escape	avoid and abstain •	
duty	responsibility • work	elementary school			escape	
	and employment		schools	escape from	escape	
dwarf bamboo		elephant	undomesticated	escort	lead and escort	
	bamboo		mammals	essence	essential part	
dwelling house		eliminate	eliminate	essential points		
	houses	ellipse	circle		essential part	
dye	color[2]	elucidate	explain	establish	found	
dynamic	active	embankment		established form		
dynastic period			embankment		model	
	long time periods	emblem	marks and signs	established practice		
		embosom	hold in the mind		custom	
		embrace	embrace	estrange	estrange	
▬▬▬ E ▬▬▬		embroider	weave and sew	eternal	of long duration	
		eminent	great	etiquette	etiquette	
each	all	emit	emit	eulogize	praise	
eager	eager	emotion	feeling	Europe	continents	
eagle	birds	emperor	rulers	evaluate	judge	
ear	face orifices					

evaporate	vaporize	explain	explain	false	false
even	same and uniform	explode	explode	falsehood	falsehood
evening	evening and night	explosive device		falsify	deceive
evergreen oak			projectiles and bombs	familiar	familiar and friendly
	trees	expose	reveal	familiar title	titles of address
every	all	expose crimes		family	family and relations
evil	evil · wrongdoing and		blame and accuse	family name	name[1]
	evil	exposition	public display	fan	incite
evil beings	supernatural and evil	expound	explain	fang	mouth parts
	beings	express	express	far	distant
evil practice	custom	express admiration		far-off	distant
evil(s)	wrongdoing and evil		praise	faraway	distant
exalt	praise	expressions	words and expressions	farm	farm and plant
exalted	elated	exquisite	beautiful	farming	farm and plant
examination	examination	extend	expand	fast	fast
examine	investigate and	extend over	extend over	fat	fats and oils
	examine	extensive	wide and extensive	fate	fate and fortune
examine a patient		extent	degree · distance and	Father	clergymen
	investigate and		interval · range	father	parents
	examine	exterminate	destroy	father's mausoleum	
examine carefully		extinguish	destroy · extinguish		graves
	investigate and	extol	praise	fathom	length units
	examine	extreme	extreme · extreme in	fatigue	tire
example	example		degree · most	fatten	fatten
excavate	dig	extremely	extreme in degree	fault	faults and flaws
exceed	exceeding and excess	extremity	extreme	favor	favor
exceedingly	extreme in degree	eye	discernment · eye · face	favorable	good
excel	excel		orifices	fawn upon	charm
excellent	excellent and superior	eyebrow	hair	fear	fear
exceptional	excellent and superior	eyebrow ink	cosmetics	fearful	fear
excerpt	abridge			fears	worry
excess	exceeding and excess			feather	hair
excessive	exceeding and excess ·	**F**		federation	organized bodies
	rash			fee	fee and price · pay and
exchange	change and replace ·	fabric	fabric		earnings
	sell and trade	face	expression · face · front	feel	perceive
excite	incite		· front parts of head ·	feel deeply	feel deeply
exclamatory particle			outside	feel sad	grieve
	classical particles	face powder	cosmetics	feel timid	fear
exclude	drive out · eliminate	faction	parties and sects	felicitation	celebrating and
exclusive	special	fade	discolor		congratulating
excreta	excreta	fail	fail	fellow	fellow · friends and
execute	execute	fail to	fail		associates
executive	officials	faint	less in degree	fellows	fellow
exempt	forgive	faith	fidelity	female	woman
exercise control		faithfulness	fidelity	female Chinese unicorn	
	direct and supervise	fake	false		mythical animals
exercise jurisdiction over		falcon	birds		· undomesticated
	direct and supervise	fall	collapse · decrease ·		mammals
exert	exert oneself		degenerate · descend	female name element	
exhaust	consume		and fall		name suffixes
exhibition	public display	fall behind	be late and delay	female phoenix	
exigent	urgent	fall down dead			birds · mythical animals
exist	exist and be		die	female worker	
expand	expand · grow	fall ill	disease		workers and
expect	expect	fall in	collapse		professionals
expel	drive out	fall in love	love and like	fence	fences and walls
expend	consume	fall into arrears		ferment	brew and ferment
expense	fee and price		be late and delay		
		fall through	fail		

fermented sauce	seasonings	**firm**	firm and obstinate · hard · not moving	**footprints**	marks and signs
fertile	plentiful	**first**	first · original	**footwear**	footwear
festival	ceremonies and festivities	**first day**	days	**for**	direction indicators
festivities	ceremonies and festivities	**first day of the lunar month**	days	**for an interval of**	during
fetus	early states of animal life	**first-rate**	excellent and superior	**for the time being**	temporary
feudal domain	feudal territorial divisions	**fish**	fish · hunt and fish	**force**	compel and press · energy and force
feudal lord	nobility	**fist**	hand and arm	**forces**	armed forces
feudal palace	palace	**fit**	fit	**forehead**	front parts of head
feudal village	villages and towns	**fit out**	equip and install	**foreign**	foreign
fever	diseases and disease symptoms · mania and maniacs	**five**	five · small numbers	**forest**	forest
		fix	decide · repair	**forge**	work metals
		fixed	constant · not moving	**forget**	forget
few	few	**fixed number**	kinds of numbers	**forgive**	forgive
fiber	threads and fibers			**forgive with compassion**	forgive
fibers	threads and fibers	**flag**	flag		
fidelity	fidelity	**flame**	fire	**fork**	furcation
fief	feudal territorial divisions	**flash**	shine and reflect	**forked road**	furcation · ways and routes
field	branch of study · cultivated fields · range · uncultivated expanses of land	**flat**	flat	**form**	appearance · form · make · model · organize
		flat things	counters for flat things		
		flavor	flavor and elegance	**form a cluster**	crowd
		flaws	faults and flaws	**form into a mass**	solidify and coagulate
field officer	military officers and ranks	**flee**	escape	**formal ceremony**	ceremonies and festivities
fierce	extreme in power · violent	**fleet steed**	horse		
		flesh	body · flesh · meat	**formal divided skirt**	clothing
fifth calendar sign	calendar signs	**float**	float	**formal honorific title**	titles of address
fight	compete · fight and war · warfare and rebellions	**flood**	running water	**formal title**	titles of address
		floor	floor	**former**	former
		florid	beautiful	**former times**	old times
figure	appearance · form · images · pattern	**flour**	cereal	**fort**	strongholds
		flourish	prospering and prosperity	**forthright**	purehearted
filial piety	fidelity			**fortune**	fate and fortune · good fortune · happiness
fill	fill	**flow**	flow and drip		
fill up	supplement	**flower**	flower	**foster**	cultivate · raise and nourish
film	motion picture	**flowing**	smooth		
finance	lend and borrow · money	**fluent**	smooth	**found**	found
		fluid	liquid	**foundation**	basis
find fault with	blame and accuse	**fluorescent**	bright	**foundation stone**	bottoms and bases · supporting structures
fine	beautiful · good · thin	**flurried**	busy		
fine thread	threads and fibers	**flute**	musical instruments	**four**	small numbers
fine weather	weather	**fly**	fly	**fox**	undomesticated mammals
finger	hand and arm	**foe**	enemy		
finish	end	**fog**	kinds of atmospheric vapor	**foxtail millet**	cereals
fire	fire · shoot			**fragile**	weak
firearms	weapons for shooting	**-fold**	-fold	**fragment**	part
firefly	insects	**fold**	fold	**fragrance**	smell and fragrance
firewood	kinds of fuel · kinds of wood	**fold up**	fold	**fragrant**	smell and fragrance
		follow	accompany · follow and pursue · obey	**frame**	frames
		follower	servants · students and followers	**framework**	frames
		followers	students and followers	**France**	European countries
		food	food		
		food provisions	food		
		foolish	foolish		
		foot	leg		
		foot of mountain	bottoms and bases		

H

honorific title	titles of address
hoof	ungual
hope	wish and desire
horn	body projections
horse	domesticated mammals • horse
horse stable	buildings
hot	eager • hot
hot bath	baths
hot spring	baths
hot water	kinds of water
hour	short time periods
House	legislature
house	houses
household	houses
houses	counters for houses
housing	houses
how many	how many
however	conditional conjunctions
hug	embrace • hold in the mind
huge	big and huge
human being	person
humble	humble
humbly	humble • respectful
humiliate	disgrace
hundred	large numbers
hundred million	large numbers
hunt	hunt and fish
hunt for	seek
hunting	hunt and fish
hurry	hurry
husband	husband
hydrogen	lighter elements

—— I ——

I	first person pronouns
ice	kinds of frozen water • kinds of water
idle	leisurely
ignorance	foolish
illicit love	sex
illness	disease
illuminate	shine and reflect
image	image • images
imitate	imitate
imitation	false
immaculate	clean and purified • purehearted
immediate	fast • immediate
immerse	moisten
immortal mountain fairy	religious persons
impartial	impartial
impeach	blame and accuse

Imperial Court	governments
imperial decree	imperial decree
imperial edict	imperial decree
imperial garden	gardens
imperial mausoleum	graves
imperial palace steps	steps
imperial proclamation	imperial decree
Imperial seal	seals
imperial we	first person pronouns
implement	execute • machines and tools
imply	express
important	important
impose	impose
imprint	mark
imprison	imprison and confine
in	during • inside
in advance	before
in an instant	immediate
in substance	approximately
in succession	continue • in succession
in the dark	secret and private
in the original state	natural
-in-law	related by marriage
incident	incident
inclination	tendency
incline	obliqueness and inclining
incline toward	inclining toward
inclining	obliqueness and inclining
include	contain and include
income	pay and earnings
incompleteness	faults and flaws
incorrupt	purehearted
increase	increase
India	Asian countries
India ink	pigments
indication	signs
indignation	anger
indigo	blue and purple colors • pigments
individual	one
induce	cause • urge
indulge in	acting arbitrarily
indulgent	tolerant
industry	industry and business
inertia	motion
inexpensive	inexpensive
infatuated	mania and maniacs

infectious disease	disease
infer	conjecture
inferior	bad
inflammation	diseases and disease symptoms
inform	inform and communicate
information	information
ingest	ingest • take in
inhabit	reside
inherit	succeed
initiate	begin
inkstone	kinds of stone
inlay	put in
inlet	inlets and bays
inmost	profound
inn	temporary quarters
inner	inner
inner heart	psyche
inner mind	psyche
inner part	inside
inquire	inquire
inquire into	investigate and examine
inscription	writing
insect	insect
insert	put in
inside	inside
insinuate	speak and say
inspect	investigate and examine • see and look
install	equip and install • put
installment	pay
instant	short time periods
instigate	incite
institution	organized bodies • schools
instruct	instruct • teach
instrument	machines and tools
insult	disgrace
integrate	combine
intelligent	intelligent and wise
intense	extreme in degree
intention	will and intention
inter-	between
interchange	alternate • change and replace
interconnected system	system
intercourse	personal relations
intercross	intercross
interest	interest and dividend
interlink	relate
intermediary	mediating and mediators
intermediate	between • mediating and mediators
intermingle	mix

leap · jump
learn · learn and study
learning · learning and knowledge
leather · kinds of skin
leave · leave • leave and set forth
leave behind · forget • leave
leave of absence · holiday
leave out · eliminate • omit
leave out by mistake · omit
leave to · commit
lecture · speak in public • units of learning
left · left and right
leg · leg • limbs
legged tray · vessels and receptacles
legislative body · legislature
legitimate child · inheritors • offspring
legitimate wife · wives
leisure · leisure
leisurely · leisurely
lend · lend and borrow
lend support to · support
lenient · tolerant
leopard · undomesticated mammals
lesson · units of learning
let do · let do
let go · let do • release
let know · inform and communicate
let pass · pass
let slip · losing and loss
letter · characters • written communications
level · flat
levy · enlist • impose • tax
lewd · sex
license · certificates • permit
lie · falsehood
lie down · lie down
lie in concealment · hide
life · animal • life
life span · age
light · easy • less in degree • light • light-colored
light brown · brown colors
lightning · atmospheric discharges
like · love and like • similar
limb · limbs
limit · extreme • restrain
limited part · part

limpid · clear
line · line • linear arrangements • lines and line segments • ropes and lines • ways and routes
line segments · lines and line segments
line up · arrange
lineage · lineage
lines · ropes and lines
lineup · groups
link · join • relate
lion · undomesticated mammals
lip · mouth parts
liquid · liquid
listen · hear
liter · capacity units
literary work · books
litigate · sue
little · few
live · live • reside
lively · strong
liver · internal organs
livestock · animal
living thing · animal
load · burden • load
load on board · load
localities · areas and localities
locality · areas and localities
lock · locks and keys
lock up · close
lodge · stay
lodging · temporary quarters
lofty · high^2
lonesome · sad and depressed
long · of long duration
long flag · flag
long for · wish and desire
long objects · counters for long objects
longevity · life
longitude · latitude and longitude
look · see and look
look afar · see and look
look back · remember • see and look
look for · seek
look into · investigate and examine
look out over · see and look
look over · see and look
look up · see and look
look up to · respect
loquat · fruits and fruit trees
Lord · god
lose · lose • losing and loss
loss · losing and loss

lost · losing and loss
lot · fate and fortune
lotus · flowering plants
loud · loud
love · love • love and like • sex
low · less in degree • low • lowly
low-priced · inexpensive
lower · low • lower
lower part · bottoms and bases
loyalty · fidelity
lucid · evident
lucky · good fortune
luminous · bright
lump · bodies
lump together · combine
lung · internal organs
lurk · hide
lust · sex
luster · luster
lute · musical instruments

M

machine · machines and tools
madder · red colors
magazine · periodicals
magic(al) · miraculous
magnetism · electricity and magnetism
magnificent · beautiful • great
mahjong · board games
mail · mail
main · main
make · make • structure
make a speech · speak in public
make an agreement · promise
make clear · explain
make diligent efforts · exert oneself
make efforts · exert oneself
make light of · disdain
make new · reform
make peace · compromise
make progress · make progress
make the rounds · turn
make uniform · fit
male · man
male adult · man
male Chinese unicorn · mythical animals • undomesticated mammals

male name element		**meal**	food	**mild**	gentle	
	name suffixes	**mean**	lowly · vulgar and	**mile**	length units	
male name suffix			unrefined	**military**	military	
	name suffixes	**meaning**	meaning	**military man**	soldiers and warriors	
male phoenix		**means**	means	**milk**	bodily secretions · dairy	
	birds · mythical animals	**measure**	means · measure ·		products · drinks	
mallow	flowering plants		measuring devices	**mind**	psyche · thought · will	
man	man	**measurement**			and intention · worry	
man laborer	workers and		size	**mind to do something**		
	professionals	**measuring instrument**			will and intention	
man of learning and virtue			machines and tools	**mine**	mine	
	gentleman	**meat**	meat	**Ming Dynasty**		
manage	direct and supervise	**mechanical contrivance**			later Chinese dynasties	
mandarin	fruits and fruit trees		machines and tools	**miniature**	small and tiny	
maniac	mania and maniacs	**mediate**	mediating and	**minister**	high officials	
maniacs	mania and maniacs		mediators	**ministry**	parts of governments ·	
manifest	appear · conspicuous ·	**mediators**	mediating and		public offices	
	evident · reveal		mediators	**minute**	detailed · short time	
manifold	various	**mediocre**	ordinary		periods · small and tiny	
manipulate	handle	**meditate**	think and consider		· unimportant	
manner	way and style	**meet**	meet	**miraculous**	holy	
manners	custom	**meet with**	meet	**mis-**	mistakes and mistaking	
manor	feudal territorial	**meeting**	assembly	**miscellaneous**		
	divisions	**meeting place**			various	
manservant	servants		places and positions	**miscellaneous counter**		
manufacture	make	**melancholy**	sad and depressed		general counters	
manufacturing industry		**melodious tone**		**miserable**	sad and depressed	
	industry and business		kinds of sound	**misfortune**	misfortune and disaster	
manuscript	manuscript	**melody**	music and songs	**mislead**	deceive	
many	plentiful	**melt**	liquefy	**miso**	seasonings	
maple	trees	**member**	person in charge	**Miss**	titles of address	
mark	indicate · marks and		· workers and	**miss**	deviate	
	signs · target		professionals	**missing**	omit	
mark off	mark	**membranous sac**		**mist**	kinds of atmospheric	
market	market		bags		vapor	
marquis	noblemen	**Mencius**	Confucius and	**mistake**	mistakes and mistaking	
marriage	marrying and marriage		Confucianists	**mistaken**	mistakes and mistaking	
marriage relation		**mend**	repair	**mistaking**	mistakes and mistaking	
	marrying and marriage	**merchant**	merchant	**mix**	mix	
married woman		**mercy**	tender feelings for	**mixed**	mix	
	wives		others	**mixed up**	disordered · mix	
marrow	bone	**merit**	accomplishment	**moat**	holes and cavities	
marry	marrying and marriage	**meritorious service**		**mode**	states and situations ·	
marsh	lakes and marshes		accomplishment		way and style	
marshes	lakes and marshes	**message**	information	**model**	form and carve · imitate	
marvelous	excellent and superior ·	**metal**	metal		· model · prototype	
	miraculous	**metaphor**	words and expressions	**Modern Chinese**		
mask	protective coverings	**meter**	length units ·		Chinese	
master	leaders		measuring devices	**modifier forming suffix**		
master of the house		**method**	way and style		modifier suffixes	
	husband	**meticulous**	careful · detailed	**modifier suffix**		
match	game	**metropolis**	cities and towns		modifier suffixes	
material	matter	**Metropolis of Tokyo**		**moist**	wet	
material resources			Kanto region · territorial	**moisten**	moisten	
	matter		divisions	**mold**	fungus	
materials	matter	**midair**	sky	**moment**	short time periods	
matter	affair · matter	**midday**	noon	**momme**	weight units	
mature	mature	**middle**	between · middle ·	**mon**	Japanese money	
mausoleum	graves		second		denominations	
meager	few	**might**	power and authority	**monastery**	places of worship	

obstinate	firm and obstinate	omen	signs	**outer enclosure**	
obstruct	obstruct and hinder	omit	abridge • omit		periphery
obtain	get	**on the point of**		outer limits	edges and boundaries
occasion	occasions		on the verge of		extreme
occupation suffix		**on the verge of**		outset	beginnings
	workers and		almost • on the verge of	outside	outside
	professionals	one	a certain • one • small	outstanding	conspicuous • excellent
occupy	occupy		numbers		and superior
ocean	sea	**one and only**	only	**outstanding person**	
oceangoing ship		**one by one**	in succession		great persons
	boats and ships	**one of a pair**	one	overall	general
of graceful beauty		**one of two**	one	overcome	win
	beautiful	**one side**	one side	overflow	flow and drip
of highest rank		**one's ground**	standpoint	overgarment	clothing
	high-ranking	**one's part**	responsibility	overripe	mature
of long duration		**one's person**	first person pronouns	oversee	direct and supervise
	of long duration	**one-sided**	inclining toward • one	overturn	overturn
of low grade	bad		side	ovum	reproductive cells
of low rank	lowly	oneself	first person pronouns	own	possess
of marvelous beauty		only	only	oxygen	lighter elements
	beautiful	**opaque sliding door**			
of upper grade			doors		
	excellent and superior	open	begin • open • reclaim		
offend against		**open and read**		**P**	
	violate		open		
offense	crimes and offenses	**open hole**	holes and cavities	pacify	conquer and suppress
offenses	crimes and offenses	**open out**	reveal	pack	join
offer	offer	**open sea**	sea	page	paper • parts of
offer respectfully		**open up**	reclaim		periodicals
	offer	opinion	opinion	pagoda	places of worship
offer tribute	offer	opportunity	occasions	pain	trouble and suffering
offer wine	offer wine	oppose	compare • resist	pair	two
offering	offering	opposite	opposite	palace	buildings • palace
office	public offices • work	oppress	torture and oppress	palanquin	vehicle
	and employment	**optical instrument**		pale	light-colored
officer	officials		machines and tools	**pale blue**	blue and purple colors
official	officials	**or not**	terms of negation	palm	hand and arm
official document		**…or thereabouts**		paper	paper
	certificates		approximately	**paper mulberry**	
official notice		orchid	flowering plants		trees
	written	order	command • order	paragraph	parts of writing
	communications	**ordinal number prefix**		pardon	forgive
officiate	direct and supervise		kinds of numbers	parent	main • parents
officiator	officials	**ordinal number suffix**		park	stop
offing	sea		kinds of numbers	part	part
offspring	offspring	ordinance	laws and rules	participate	participate and join
oil	fats and oils • kinds of	ordinary	ordinary	**particle of nominalization**	
	fuel • seasonings	ore	metal		nominalizers
oils	fats and oils	organ	organ	**particle suffix**	
old	former • old	organize	organize		particle
old calendar	calendars	origin	beginnings	partition	separate
old man	man • old persons	original	original	party	armed forces • groups
old person	old persons	originate	begin		• parties and sects •
old tool	machines and tools	orphan	offspring		social gatherings
old woman	old persons • woman	Osaka	Kansai cities	pass	elapse • pass
older brother		other	other	**pass away**	die • elapse
	siblings	**ought to**	certain	**pass by**	elapse • pass
older sibling of parent		**our humble**	humble prefixes	**pass through**	pass • penetrate
	siblings of parents	outdo	excel	passage	parts of writing •
older sister	siblings				tubular passages
				pasture	cultivated fields • raise
					and nourish

path	ways and routes	persons	counters for persons	plant name element	
pathological condition		petty thief	thieves		plants
	disease	phantom	illusory mental images	plantain	fruits and fruit trees
pattern	model · pattern	phase	appearance · states and	plants	supporting parts of
pattern after	imitate		situations		plants
paulownia	trees	phenomenon		plastic	soft
pave	spread		phenomenon	plate	boards and plates ·
pawn	pawn	Philippines	Asian countries		vessels and receptacles
pay	pay · pay and earnings	philosophy	wisdom	plates	boards and plates
pay out	pay	photograph	photograph	platform	flat supports
peace	peace	phrase	sentence and sentence	play	play
peaceful	calm and peaceful		parts · words and	play music	play music
peach	fruits and fruit trees		expressions	play on	play music
peak	mountain parts ·	physical phenomena		plays	parts of plays
	mountains		phenomenon	pleasant	pleased and pleasant
pear	fruits and fruit trees	physical power		pleased	pleased and pleasant
pearl	precious stones		energy and force	pleasurable	pleased and pleasant
peck	bite · ingest	pick	choose · harvest	pleasure	pleasure
peel off	come off · eliminate	pick out	choose	Pleiades	constellation
penalty	punishment	pick up	get · raise	plentiful	plentiful
penetrate	penetrate	pickle	preserve food	plot	plans and planning
people	people · the people	pickles	preserved foods	pluck	courage
People's Republic of China		picture	picture	plum	fruits and fruit trees
	China	picture frame		plunder	steal and rob
perceive	perceive		frames	plural suffix	plural suffixes
percentage	rate	piece of paper		podocarpus	trees
perform by stealth			paper	poetry	poetry
	hide	piece of writing		point	extremity · indicate ·
performance	performance		books		places and positions
performer	performers	pig	domesticated	point of a blade	
perfume	smell and fragrance		mammals · swine		extremity
period	long time periods	pig iron	iron and steel	point of time	time periods
period of time		pigeon	birds	pointed	sharp
	time periods	pile up	accumulate	pole	long slender objects
periodicals	parts of periodicals	piled high	accumulate	policy	policy
periphery	periphery	pill	medicines	polish	cultivate · polish and
perish	destroy	pill suffix	medicines		rub
permanent	of long duration	pillar	supporting structures	polite plural suffix	
permeate	penetrate	pine	trees		plural suffixes
permit	permit	pipe	tubular passages	political administration	
perpendicular		pit	holes and cavities ·		government
	vertical		mine	pond	lakes and marshes
perplexed	bewildered	pitch-black	black colors	pongee	fabrics
persimmon	fruits and fruit trees	pity	tender feelings for	pool	stagnating water
person	person		others	poor	poor
person in charge		pivot	essential part	popular	public
	person in charge	place	areas and localities ·	popular custom	
person of certain category			places and positions ·		custom
	workers and		put	popular song	
	professionals	place in custody			music and songs
person of talent			imprison and confine	popularity	repute
	wise and talented	plain	plain and simple ·	porcelain	ceramics ware
	persons		uncultivated expanses	port	places for landing or
person who	workers and		of land		stopping
	professionals	plait	hair · weave and sew	portray	describe
personal history		plan	plans and planning	Portugal	European countries
	history	plane	wings	position	places and positions
personal relations		plank bridge	bridges	positions	places and positions
	personal relations	planning	plans and planning	positive	positive
personal seal	seals	plant	farm and plant · plants	possess	possess

possessive particle	possessive particles	
possible	possible	
post	mail	
post station	post station	
posterity	descendant	
postpone	be late and delay	
posture	posture	
pot	vessels and receptacles	
potato	vegetables	
pottery	ceramics ware	
pour	flow and drip	
pour wine	offer wine	
powder	powder	
power	energy and force · mathematical power · power and authority · skill	
power of discrimination	discernment	
practical art	art	
praise	praise	
prajna	wisdom	
pray	pray and worship	
preach	advocate	
precept	precept	
precious	expensive	
precipitation	kinds of precipitation	
prefecture	territorial divisions	
preparation	medicines	
prepare	make · prepare	
present	give · offer · present · show	
present a gift	give	
present to a superior	give	
preserve	preserve · protect	
preside	direct and supervise	
press	approach · compel and press	
press for	urge	
press into service	employ	
pressing	urgent	
pressure	compel and press · energy and force	
prevent	prevent	
previous	former	
previously	former	
price	fee and price	
prickle	needle	
primary	original	
primeval chaos	disordered	
princess	wives of rulers	
print	marks and signs · print and publish	

printing	editions	
printing block	printing plate	
printing plate	printing plate	
prison	prison	
prisoner	prisoner	
private	secret and private · soldiers and warriors	
private parts	genitals	
private school	schools	
prize	prizes	
prize cup	prizes	
probe	investigate and examine	
problem	question	
proboscis	front parts of head	
proceed to	go and come	
proclaim	inform and communicate	
proclaim merits	praise	
produce	create · make	
product	merchandise	
profession suffix	workers and professionals	
professional	workers and professionals	
professionals	workers and professionals	
profit	profit	
profound	profound	
profoundly wise	intelligent and wise	
progeny	descendant	
progressively	in succession	
prohibit	restrain	
project	plans and planning · project	
projectile	projectiles and bombs	
prominent	conspicuous · excellent and superior	
promise	promise	
promontory	points of land	
propel	force to move	
proper	suitable	
property	wealth	
propitious omen	good fortune	
proposal	plans and planning	
proso millet	cereals	
prosper	prospering and prosperity	

prospering	prospering and prosperity	
prosperity	prospering and prosperity	
prosperous	prospering and prosperity	
prostrate	lie down	
protect	protect	
protruding	protrude and protruding	
protuberant	protrude and protruding	
proverb	words and expressions	
provide	equip and install · prepare	
provided that	conditional conjunctions	
province	feudal territorial divisions	
province in China	territorial divisions	
provoke	incite	
prudent	careful	
prune	cut	
pseudonym suffix	pseudonym suffixes	
public	public · society · the people	
public building	buildings	
public office	public offices	
public order	peace	
public peace	peace	
public service office	public offices	
public-service station	public offices	
publication	editions	
publish	print and publish	
publishing	print and publish	
pull out	pull	
pulverize	break into small pieces	
pungent	tastes	
punishment	punishment	
pupil	eye · students and followers	
purchase	buy	
pure	clean and purified · purehearted	
purehearted	purehearted	
purge	clean and wash	
purified	clean and purified	
purple	blue and purple colors	
purple colors	blue and purple colors	
purport	essential part · meaning	

purpose	meaning · will and intention
pursue	follow and pursue
push	compel and press · force to move · push
put away	store
put in	put in
put in order	arrange
put in print	print and publish
put on	wear and put on
put on footwear	wear and put on
put on headgear	wear and put on
put one's heart into	exert oneself
put out	emit
put together	combine · organize
put up	display · raise

Q

Qin Dynasty	earlier Chinese dynasties
Qing Dynasty	later Chinese dynasties
quake	shake
quality	nature and character
quality restaurant suffix	restaurant suffixes
quantity	quantity and number
quasi-	subordinate
quell	conquer and suppress
query	inquire
question	inquire · question
question closely	inquire
quick	fast
quiet	calm and peaceful · quiet
quiet and secluded	inner · quiet
quote	quote

R

rabbit	domesticated mammals · rabbit
race	people
rack	flat supports
radiant	bright
radiate	emit
raging	extreme in power
rags	clothing
raid	attack
railing	fences and walls
railway	kinds of railway
railway car	kinds of railway
rain	kinds of precipitation
rainbow	light

raise	enlist · raise · raise and nourish
raise animals	raise and nourish
raise crops	farm and plant
raise high	raise
raise up	raise
rambling	unrestrained
range	range
rank	arrange · class · linear arrangements
rank of nobility	nobility
ranks	groups · military officers and ranks
rapid	fast
rapids	running water
rare	rare · rare and sparse
rash	rash
rat	undomesticated mammals
rate	rate
ratio	rate
ravine	valley
raw	new
reach	arrive
reach an agreement	promise
reach to	arrive · extend over · make widely known
read	recite
real	true
reap	harvest
rear	rear
reason	cause and reason · reason · reasoning
rebel	resist
rebellion	warfare and rebellions
rebellions	warfare and rebellions
receive	receive · treat and welcome
receive humbly	receive
recent	recent
receptacle	vessels and receptacles
receptacles	vessels and receptacles
recess	corners
reciprocal	mutual
reciprocate	compensate
reciprocate wineglasses	offer wine
recite	recite
recite poetry	recite
reclaim	reclaim
recognize	agree and approve · perceive
recollect	remember
recommend	recommend
recompense	compensate · pay
record	records · write
record book	notebook

record in writing	write
records	records
recover	cure and recover
rectify	correct
Red	Communism
red	red colors
redo	repeating and repetition
redundant	exceeding and excess
reduplicate	repeating and repetition
reed	kinds of grasses
reef	elevations in water · shoals
reel	wind and twine
refer	compare
refer to	speak and say
reference volume	books
refine	cultivate · refine · work metals
refined	clean and purified · elegant
refined and gentle	elegant
refinement	flavor and elegance
reflect	shine and reflect
reform	correct · reform
refreshing	pleased and pleasant
refuse	refuse and reject
regard	judge · see and look
regard as beautiful	praise
register	notebook · write
regret	regret
regular	constant · regular
regulation	laws and rules
reject	refuse and reject
relation	family and relations · personal relations
relations	family and relations
relative by marriage	family and relations
relative degree	degree
relatives	family and relations
relay	post station · transmit and deliver
relay station	post station
release	release
release from office	dismiss
relieve	help · rescue
religion	religion
religious classic	books
religious ritual	ceremonies and festivities

Spain	European countries	stab to death	kill	stem	supporting parts of plants
sparrow	birds	staff	long slender objects	step	means · steps
sparse	rare and sparse	stage name suffix		step on	step on
speak	speak and say		pseudonym suffixes	step-	related by marriage
speak eloquently		stagnate	stagnate	stern	strict
	speak and say	stairs	steps	stick	stick
speak humbly		stake	perforators · risk	stick out	protrude and protruding
	speak and say · speak humbly	stammer	stagnate	stick to	adhere to
spear	projectiles and bombs	stand	assume upright position · flat supports · raise · tables and stands	stiff	firm and obstinate
special	special			still	additionally · not moving · quiet · still
specialize	learn and study	stand in the way			
speculate	conjecture		obstruct and hinder	stock	securities
speech	speech	stand out	excel	stomach	internal organs
spell	pray and worship	standard	model	stone	kinds of stone · rock and stone
spend	consume	standard work			
sperm	bodily secretions · reproductive cells		books	stop	discontinue · prevent · stop
		standing	vertical		
spew	discharge from mouth · emit	standing tree		stop up	close · obstruct and hinder
			tree		
sphere	areas and localities · range · three-dimensional shapes	standpoint	standpoint	stopper	stoppers
		stands	tables and stands	stopping place	
		star	stars		places for landing or stopping
spherical object		start	begin · beginnings · create · leave and set forth	storage chamber	
	spherical object				storehouse
spike	inflorescences			store	store
spin	weave and sew	start doing	begin	store up	store
spindle	long slender objects	starve	hunger and thirst	storehouse	storehouse
spindle tree	trees	starved	hunger and thirst	storm	wind
spine	bone	state	country · speak and say · states and situations · territorial divisions	story	floor · stories
spiral-shelled gastropod				stout	strong
	shells			straddle	extend over
spirit	life energy · psyche · supernatural and evil beings	state minister		straight	straight · vertical
			high officials	straight away	
		stately mansion			immediate
spirits	feeling		mansions	straight line	line
splendid	excellent and superior	stately residence		straightforward	
split	break		houses · mansions		purehearted
spoon	spoons	station	places for landing or stopping	strain	tighten
sport	play			strand	shores and watersides
sportive	comic	station troops		strange	abnormal
spout	emit		stay	strangle	kill
sprain	break	stationed	stay	strategy	plans and planning
spread	expand · make widely known · spread	stature	height	stratum	class
		status	class	straw	kinds of grasses
spread out	arrange · expand	stay	remain · stay	straw mat	mats
spring	warm seasons · water sources	stay in place	stay	straw raincoat	
		stay overnight			clothing
spring back	spring back		stay	straw sack	bags
spring to one's feet		stay temporarily		strawberry	fruits and fruit trees
	jump		stay	stream	rivers and streams
spy	agents · spy	steal	steal and rob	streams	rivers and streams
spy on	spy	steam	cook · gas and vapor · kinds of water	street	ways and routes
squad	groups			strength	quantity and number
square	mathematical power · square	steam boiler	heating devices	stretch	expand
		steel	iron and steel	strict	strict
square style	styles of Chinese characters	steep	steep	strike	attack · strike
squeeze	squeeze	steering device		string	ropes and lines
stab	stab		parts of boats and ships		

string instrument

string instrument	
	musical instrument
strip	line
stripe	line
stroke	touch
strong	extreme in degree • hard • strong
strongly regret	
	regret
structure	structure
stubborn	firm and obstinate
student	students and followers
studies	learning and knowledge
study	investigate and examine • learn and study • rooms
study exhaustively	
	investigate and examine • learn and study
stuff	fill
stump	supporting parts of plants
stupid	foolish
style	way and style
sub-	subordinate
subject of study	
	branch of study
subjected to	be subjected to
submarine	boats and ships
submerge	sink
submit	submit and surrender
subordinate	subordinate
substance	essential content • matter
substitute	change and replace • substitute
subtract	subtract
suburb	the country
succeed	continue • succeed
succeed to	succeed
successive	in succession
such	similar
suck	take in
sudden	sudden
suddenly	sudden
sue	sue
suffer	trouble and suffering
suffering	trouble and suffering
suffice	suffice
sugar	seasonings
suit	fit
suitable	suitable
sulfur	lighter elements
sum	add • total
summarize	abridge
summary	essential part
summer	warm seasons
summer heat	heat • warm seasons

summit	mountain parts • tops
summon	call and invite
sun	length units • sun
Sunday	days of the week
sunlight	light
sunny	bright
super-	extreme in degree
superior	excellent and superior
supervise	direct and supervise
supplement	supplement
supplementary	
	additional
supply	supplement • supply
support	bear • support
suppress	conquer and suppress • restrain
suppress by armed force	
	conquer and suppress
supremacy	power and authority
surface	outside
surname	name[1]
surpass	exceeding and excess • excel
surplus	exceeding and excess
surrender	submit and surrender
surround	surround
suspect	doubt
suspend	discontinue • hang
suspended	hang
swallow	birds • ingest
sweat	bodily secretions • excreta
sweep	clean and wash
sweet	tastes
sweet smell	smell and fragrance
swell	expand • swell and swelling
swelling	swell and swelling
swift	fast
swim	move through water
swindle	deceive
swine	swine
swing	shake
sword	cutting weapons
symbol	marks and signs
sympathy	tender feelings for others
symptom	signs
system	system
systematic plan	
	plans and planning
systematic record	
	records

─────── **T** ───────

table	diagram • tables and stands
tag	labels and slips
tai	fishes

tail	body projections • rear
tail end	rear
Taiwan	China
take	get • ingest • steal and rob • take
take a rest	rest
take along	lead and escort
take apart	separate
take away	eliminate
take caution	take precautions
take charge of	
	direct and supervise
take exclusive possession of	
	occupy
take in	get • receive • take in
take into consideration	
	think and consider
take off	eliminate
take part in	participate and join
take pleasure in	
	pleasure
take possession by force	
	take forcibly
take possession of	
	occupy
take proper steps	
	deal with
take turns	alternate
tale	stories
talent	skill
talented	excellent and superior
talented persons	
	wise and talented persons
talk	speak and say • speech
tall	high[1]
tall building	tall buildings
tall magnificent building	
	buildings • tall buildings
tally	labels and slips
tan	area units • length units
Tang Dynasty	
	later Chinese dynasties
tank	containers
tanned leather	
	kinds of skin
Taoism	religions and sects
target	target
taste	flavor and elegance • taste
tatami	mats
tax	tax
tea	drinks
teach	teach
teach with care	
	teach
team	groups
tear	bodily secretions
telegram	written communications

tell	speak and say	the Supreme Being		tiger	tiger · undomesticated mammals
tell apart	discriminate		god		
temperament		the Tiger	tiger	tighten	tighten
	nature and character	the Way	religion	till	farm and plant
temple	places of worship	the way of an art		timber	kinds of wood
temple building			art	time	long time periods · occasions · time and time counters · time periods
	places of worship	the way of moral conduct			
temporary	temporary		moral goodness · moral principles		
temporary abode					
	temporary quarters	the West	west	time counters	
temporary quarters		theory	theory		time and time counters
	temporary quarters	thereabouts	approximately	timely occasion	
ten	small numbers · ten	thick	dense · thick		occasions
ten quadrillion		thick woods	forest	times	-fold
	large numbers	thief	thieves	tin	metals
ten thousand		thin	less in degree · rare and sparse · thin	tinkling of jades	
	large numbers				kinds of sound
ten-day period		thing	abstract thing · object	tiny	small and tiny
	weeks and months	things to do	affairs	tip	extremity
tendency	tendency	think	think and consider	tip of a twig	branches and twigs
term	time periods	think out	think and consider	tire of	tire
territory	areas and localities	third person pronoun		tired	tire
test	investigate and examine · try		third person pronouns	title	name[1]
		thirst	hunger and thirst	to	capacity units · direction indicators
Thailand	Asian countries	thirst for	wish and desire		
thank	thanking and gratitude	this	this and that	to the...of	direction indicators
thanks	thanking and gratitude	thorn	needle	today	yesterday and today
that	this and that	thorny shrub	plants	together	together
thatch	cover and wrap	thoroughly	all	token	labels and slips
thatch grass	kinds of grasses	thou	second person pronouns	Tokyo	Kanto region
the Boar	swine			tolerate	agree and approve
the coming	next	thought	thought	ton	weight units
the country	the country	thought of doing something		tone	musical elements · states and situations · way and style
the Dog	dog		will and intention		
the Dragon	dragon · mythical animals	thoughts	thought		
		thousand	large numbers	tongue	mouth parts · speech
the following		thread	reasoning · threads and fibers	tools	machines and tools
	next			tooth	mouth parts
the Hare	rabbit	threadlike structure		topple	descend and fall · overturn
the Horse	horse		line		
the late	dead	threaten	threaten	torment	trouble and suffering
the Left	Communism	threaten by force		torture	torture and oppress
the masses	the people		threaten	toss	throw
the Master	Confucius and Confucianists	three	small numbers · three	total	all · total
		thrive	flourish · prospering and prosperity	touch	touch
the military	armed forces			tough	firm and obstinate · hard
the Monkey	monkey	throat	throat		
the multitude(s)		through	throughout	tough guy	fellow
	the people	throughout	throughout	tour	journey
the Netherlands		throw	throw	tour around	journey
	European countries	thrust	push · stab	tower	tall buildings
the Ox	cattle	thumb	hand and arm	town	cities and towns · villages and towns
the present	present · this and that	thunder	atmospheric discharges		
the public	public	Thursday	days of the week	town section	parts of towns
the Ram	sheep	ticket	labels and slips	town subsection	
the said	this and that	tide	running water · tendency		parts of towns
the same	this and that			towns	cities and towns · parts of towns · villages and towns
the Serpent	snake	tie	combine · join		
the streets	ways and routes	tie up	join · restrain		

toy with	play
trace	marks and signs • trace
track	trace • ways and routes
trade	industry and business • sell and trade
train	cultivate • teach
trample on	step on
tranquil	calm and peaceful
transcribe	copy
transfer	move
translate	translate
transmit	transmit and deliver
transparent	clear
transparent gem	
	precious stones
transport	carry
trash	waste
travel	journey
travel by vehicle	
	travel by vehicle
travel on foot	
	walk
tray	vessels and receptacles
tread	step on • walk
treasure	wealth
treat	cure and recover • treat and welcome
treat cordially	
	treat and welcome
treat cruelly	torture and oppress
tree	tree
tremble with fear	
	fear
tremendous	extreme in degree
trench	holes and cavities
trend	tendency
triangular	three
tribute	offering • tax
trick	deceive
trillion	large numbers
trip	journey
tripod cauldron	
	vessels and receptacles
trite	ordinary
triumph	win
trout	fishes
true	true
truly	true
trunk	essential part • supporting parts of plants • trunk parts
try	judge • try
tsubo	area units
tube	tubular passages
Tuesday	days of the week
tuft	bundles and clusters
tumulus	graves
tune	music and songs
turbid	dirty²
turn	turn

turn back	return
turn into	change and replace
turn over	overturn
turn round	turn
turn toward	face
turnip	vegetables
turtle	reptiles and amphibians
twenty	small numbers
twigs	branches and twigs
twill	fabrics
twine	wind and twine
twist	turn
two	small numbers • two
type	example • kinds and types • prototype
types	kinds and types
typeset	print and publish
typhoon	wind

U

ume blossom	
	flowering plants
uncanny	fear
unconstrained	
	unrestrained
undergo transition	
	change and replace
underlay	mats
underling	servants
understand	know and understand
undertake	undertake
undiluted wine	
	drinks
unexpected event	
	incident
unfold	grow • open
unhulled rice	rice
uniform	same and uniform
union	organized bodies
unit	element
unite	combine
universe	universe and space
university	schools
unmarried female worker	
	workers and professionals
unravel	degenerate
unreasonable	
	rash
unrefined	vulgar and unrefined
unrestrained	rash • unrestrained
unusual	abnormal
up to	direction indicators
uphold	preserve
upper	high-ranking • high²
upper part	tops
upright	virtuous
uprising	warfare and rebellions

upside-down	
	opposite
urban prefecture	
	territorial divisions
urge	urge
urge to eat	urge
urgent	urgent
urine	excreta
use	use
use all one's strength	
	exert oneself
use up	consume
use(ful)	benefit
utmost	most

V

vain	vain
valiant	brave
valley	valley
value	value
value highly	respect
valve	stoppers
vapor	gas and vapor
variety	kinds and types
various	all • various
vast	big and huge • wide and extensive
vegetable	plants
vegetable garden	
	cultivated fields
vehement	extreme in power
vehicle	vehicle
vein	line • reasoning • tubular passages
verge	edges and boundaries
vermilion	red colors
vertical	vertical
very young	young
vessel	containers
vexatious	complex
vexed	trouble and suffering
vicinity	areas and localities
Vietnam	Asian countries
view	opinion • see and look • view
vigorous	strong
villa	mansions
village	villages and towns
village or town section	
	parts of towns
vine	plants
vinegar	seasonings • sour substances
violate	violate
violent	extreme in power • violent
violet	flowering plants
virtue	moral goodness
viscount	noblemen

worldly	worldly
worship	pray and worship • respect
worship as god	pray and worship
wound	harm and damage • injury
woven fabric	fabrics
wrap	cover and wrap
wrapper	bags
wring	squeeze
write	compose • write
write down	write
writing	parts of writing • writing
writings	writing
writing(s)	writing
written account	records
written communication	written communications
wrong	wrongdoing and evil
wrong(doing)	wrongdoing and evil

——— X ———

| Xia Dynasty | earlier Chinese dynasties |

——— Y ———

yang	yin and yang
Yao	rulers
year	year
yearn after	wish and desire
yearn for	wish and desire
years	age
yellow	yellow colors
yen	Japanese money denominations
yes	terms of assent
yesterday	yesterday and today
yielding abundantly	plentiful
yin	yin and yang
yoke	long slender objects
Yokohama	Kanto region
you	second person pronouns

young	young
young child	child
young lady	woman
young man	man
younger brother	siblings
younger sibling of parent	siblings of parents
younger sister	siblings
your honorable	honorific prefixes
youthful	young
Yuan Dynasty	later Chinese dynasties
yuzu	fruits and fruit trees

——— Z ———

Zelkova	trees
Zen	religions and sects
zero	zero
Zhou Dynasty	earlier Chinese dynasties